AFTER ALEXANDER

ADAPA MONOGRAPHS

Series Editors: Alison Betts and Barbara Helwing
Executive Editor: Stephen Bourke

The Adapa Monographs series focuses on the archaeology of the ancient Near East and adjacent regions from North Africa to Central Asia. Archaeology in these regions is a vibrant and active field of research, further stimulated by issues relating to the loss of cultural heritage to war and other factors. The series is peer-reviewed and published in association with the Near Eastern Archaeology Foundation at the University of Sydney.

The ebb and flow of the Ghūrid empire
David C. Thomas

Game drives of the Aralo-Caspian region
Vadim N. Yagodin, edited by W. Paul van Pelt and Alison Betts

The gazelle's dream: game drives of the Old and New Worlds
Edited by Alison Betts and W. Paul van Pelt

A land in between: the Orontes valley in the early urban age
Edited by Melissa A. Kennedy

After Alexander: the Hellenistic and Early Roman periods at Pella in Jordan
John Tidmarsh

PELLA IN JORDAN: MONOGRAPHS

Smith, R.
1973   *Pella of the Decapolis Vol 1. The 1967 Season of The College of Wooster Expedition to Pella* (Wooster, College of Wooster).

McNicoll, A., Smith, R. & Hennessy B.
1982   *Pella in Jordan 1* (Canberra, Australian National Gallery).

Smith, R. & Day, L.
1989   *Pella of the Decapolis Vol 2. The Civic Complex Excavations* (Wooster, College of Wooster).

McNicoll, A., Edwards, P., Hanbury-Tenison, J., Hennessy, J., Potts, T., Smith, R., Walmsley, A. & Watson, P.
1992   *Pella in Jordan 2* (Sydney, Mediterranean Archaeology Supplement 2).

Richards, F.
1992   *Scarab Seals from a Middle to Late Bronze Age Tomb at Pella in Jordan* (Fribourg, Orbis Biblicus et Orientalis 117).

Knapp, A.
1993   *Society and Polity at Bronze Age Pella* (Sheffield, Sheffield Academic Press).

Sheedy, K., Carson, R. & Walmsley, A.
2001   *Pella in Jordan 1979-1990: The Coins* (Sydney, Near Eastern Archaeology Foundation).

Edwards, P.
2013   *Wadi Hammeh 27: An Early Natufian Settlement at Pella in Jordan* (Leiden, Brill).

AFTER ALEXANDER

The Hellenistic and Early Roman periods at Pella in Jordan

John Tidmarsh

Pella in Jordan 3: The final publications of the Sydney–Wooster excavations at Pella in Jordan

SYDNEY UNIVERSITY PRESS

In memory of

J. Basil Hennessy and Anthony McNicoll

First published by Sydney University Press
© John Tidmarsh 2024
© Sydney University Press 2024

Sydney University Press
Gadigal Country
Fisher Library F03
University of Sydney NSW 2006
Australia
sup.info@sydney.edu.au
sydneyuniversitypress.com.au

A catalogue record for this
book is available from the
National Library of Australia

 ISBN 9781743329634 paperback
ISBN 9781743329658 epub
ISBN 9781743329641 pdf

Cover image: Pella during the first season (1979) of the University of Sydney excavations. Courtesy of Jon Hosking.
Cover design: Naomi van Groll

CONTENTS

Contents

LIST OF FIGURES

LIST OF PLATES

LIST OF TABLES

ABBREVIATIONS IN TEXT

CN   inventory number

RN   registration number

H   height

L   length

D   diameter

P   Preserved (for example, PL: preserved length; PH: preserved height, etc.)

est   estimated (for example, D (est): estimated diameter)

Type   In many of the tables, as well as in some of the footnotes, the various pottery forms have been allocated a "type" (also noted in the catalogue). This is for the sake of brevity in the text, especially for the footnotes, rather than to launch yet another ceramic typology. The correlation of pottery forms and types in both fine and plain wares is seen in the tables (for example, Tables 2.4, 2.15)

ESA   Eastern Sigillata A

BSP   Black-slipped predecessor

SAH   Stamped amphora handle

ACKNOWLEDGEMENTS

Over the forty years I have worked at Pella, there have been many people I would like to thank (unfortunately too many to name) and this certainly includes the members of the core staff (excavators, surveyors, photographers, illustrators, conservators and other specialists), numerous volunteers from Australia and elsewhere, and, just as importantly, those men and women from Tabaqat Fahl, Masharia and other local villages who have worked alongside us in the field or in the dighouse. In particular, for the encouragement and support they have given me both during my time at Pella and in seeing this volume through to completion, I would like to thank Stephen Bourke (current Director of the Pella Project), Maree Browne (for the inordinate amount of time she spent gathering and scanning images), the late Jon Hosking, the late Graeme Clarke, Kate da Costa, Sandra Gordon (for many fruitful discussions), Bob Miller (for his high-quality images), Leah McKenzie (for her valuable early work on Hellenistic Pella), Ted Nixon, Margaret O'Hea, Kathirine Sentas (for her swift reproductions of profiles), Pamela Watson, Karyn Wesselingh, Holly Winter, Bernadette Drabsch and, especially, Bob Stone. Also, my fellow co-director at Jebel Khalid in Syria, Heather Jackson, who is always an inexhaustible source of knowledge about Hellenistic Levantine ceramics. As well, I would like to acknowledge the anonymous reviewers of this work whose sage advice and comments have done so much to improve my manuscript and Sydney University Press (in particular Naomi van Groll, Nathan Grice and Susan Brazel). Sincere thanks also to those members of the Department of Antiquities of Jordan, who have worked alongside us during each excavation year, and to Dr Fadi Bala'awi, the current director-general of the Department of Antiquities of Jordan, as well as to those directors-general who preceded him.

Finally, I would like to dedicate this volume to my family, Jill, Will and Edwina, without whose extraordinary patience and support I would have not completed this work.

PREFACE

In many ways, students of the history of the southern Levant in antiquity have been well served (Figure 0.1). This state of affairs is largely because the land is central to three of the world's great religions – Judaism, Christianity and Islam – and as such has always been the focus of intense scholarship. Its central position, lying as it does within the Fertile Crescent and yet bordering the eastern Mediterranean, left it open to a great number of cultural cross-influences that had much to do with the final form of Judaeo-Christianity. But for this, neither the Bible nor, indeed, the Qur'an would exist in their present forms and the same applies to the sphere of Biblical Studies that has done so much to expand our knowledge of those peoples, towns and events mentioned in the Old and New Testaments as well as in other ancient texts.

For the Hellenistic and Early Roman periods,[1] the works of modern scholars of the calibre of Schürer, Tcherikover, Bickerman and Hengel (to name but a few), although primarily concerned with the interaction between Jews and Greeks, provide invaluable material for the last three centuries BC and first centuries AD in Palestine.[2] In many areas the contribution of these historians, along with, of course, the first-century AD Jewish diplomat, soldier and historian Flavius Josephus (Chapman and Rodgers 2016), has been greatly enhanced by that of archaeology, despite the fact that until recently Hellenistic archaeology in particular was a relatively neglected field. Numerous Palestinian sites including 'Akko-Ptolemais, Ashdod, Gezer, Jerusalem, Marisa, Qumran, Samaria, Sepphoris, Shechem, Tel Anafa and Tel Dor have yielded impressive quantities of Hellenistic and/or Early Roman material, although not always from well-defined stratigraphic contexts. Although much of this material awaits careful analysis and publication, enough has been studied to allow us to form a fairly comprehensive view of what life was like in Palestine under the Ptolemies, Seleucids, Hasmoneans and Romans.[3]

East of the Jordan River the picture was, until recently, somewhat different (Adams [ed.] 2008; Geraty and Herr 1986: 3–72; Moorey 1991: 167–70). Relatively neglected under Ottoman rule and for many centuries largely populated by nomadic Bedouin, Transjordan did not have the same appeal or ease of access for scholars and Biblical archaeologists of the nineteenth and early twentieth centuries as Cisjordan; in many ways this was fortunate for, while delaying the onset of serious large-scale excavations, it meant that Transjordanian archaeology was spared the worst excesses of the pre-Kenyon/Wheeler era that have so bedevilled archaeological research in many other parts of the ancient world.

Archaeological exploration east of the Jordan River began in earnest during the period between

---

1   For the chronology of the Persian, Hellenistic and Early Roman periods I have followed that used by the University of Sydney Pella Project. Thus Persian (539–332 BC); Hellenistic (332–63 BC); Early Roman (63 BC–135 AD). However, it should be noted that the chronology of the Early Roman and, indeed, the Roman periods in Jordan, is far from settled (Freeman 2008: 413).

2   Amongst many works by these scholars, Schürer 1973–87; Tcherikover 1959; Bickerman 1988; Hengel 1974. Palestine is used in this work to denote the territory covered by the state of modern Israel, the West Bank and Gaza Strip. See Jacobson (1999) for the use of the term "Palestine" in antiquity.

3   See, for example, Berlin 1997b; Magness 2011, 2013, 2021; Stern 1993–2008.

the two world wars (Adams 2008: 2–3; Geraty and Herr 1986: 6) and has continued apace following the formation of the modern state of Jordan in 1948. As an example of this explosion in archaeological research, some fifty permits have been granted to foreign excavation teams in most years since at least the 1990s (for example, Green et al. 2018), not to mention the numerous planned and rescue digs carried out by the Department of Antiquities of Jordan and university departments, most notably those from the universities of Jordan and Yarmouk. These investigations have cast much light on the history of Transjordan up until the present day (Adams [ed.] 2008; Harding 1967; Homès-Fredericq and Hennessy 1989). This light, however, has been shed unevenly, with the result that while much is known about the Prehistoric, Bronze and Iron ages, as well as later periods such as Late Roman, Byzantine and Islamic, less has been published from the Persian, Hellenistic and Early Roman eras, leaving us in a relative state of ignorance about the Persian and Hellenistic periods in particular.[4] After forty years of fieldwork conducted by both the College of Wooster, Ohio, and the University of Sydney, an impressive quantity of Hellenistic and Early Roman material has been recovered from Pella (modern Tabaqat Fahl) in the north Jordan Valley. Some of this material, from both the Wooster and Sydney excavations, has already been published in *Pella of the Decapolis 1*, *Pella of the Decapolis 2*, *Pella in Jordan 1*, *Pella in Jordan 2*, as well as in the *Annual of the Department of Antiquities of Jordan*, the *Bulletin of the American Schools of Oriental Research*, and other academic and more popular journals.[5] Undoubtedly, continued work at Pella will unearth further important finds from these periods necessitating a re-evaluation and modification of some of the views and theories put forward in this volume; in the meantime, this work includes a summary of both the College of Wooster and University of Sydney

excavations between 1979 and 2019 along with the Hellenistic and Early Roman pottery recovered as a result.[6] A further volume, planned to follow, aims to bring together the remaining material recovered during these years, making it readily accessible to those scholars working in the Hellenistic and Early Roman periods in the Levant and beyond.[7]

Although I have been involved with the Pella excavations from the first University of Sydney excavation season in 1979 – at that time as an undergraduate student – it was only as a result of Anthony McNicoll's tragic death in December 1985 that I became a co-director of the project and undertook to study and publish the Hellenistic and Early Roman material. This volume is presented as part of this undertaking.

John Tidmarsh
March 2024

---

4   As demonstrated by the chapters on the Persian and the Hellenistic periods east of the Jordan River (Bienkowski; Schmid) in Adams (2008), in many ways the successor to MacDonald et al. (eds) 2001: *The Archaeology of Jordan*. See also Millar (1987) for an overall view of the problems in understanding the Hellenistic period "anywhere west of the Euphrates and south of the Amanus Mountains".

5   For the results of the earlier seasons, see Tidmarsh (1989).

6   Only the published Hellenistic and Early Roman pottery from the Wooster College excavations will be dealt with here as the author has not had the opportunity to examine the unpublished pottery.

7   The necessity to publish the results obtained so far has been greatly emphasised by the disruption experienced throughout the world as a result of the COVID-19 pandemic. Along with the profoundly tragic consequences with which we are all familiar, the pandemic has clearly demonstrated how "routine" archaeological work can be unexpectedly curtailed.

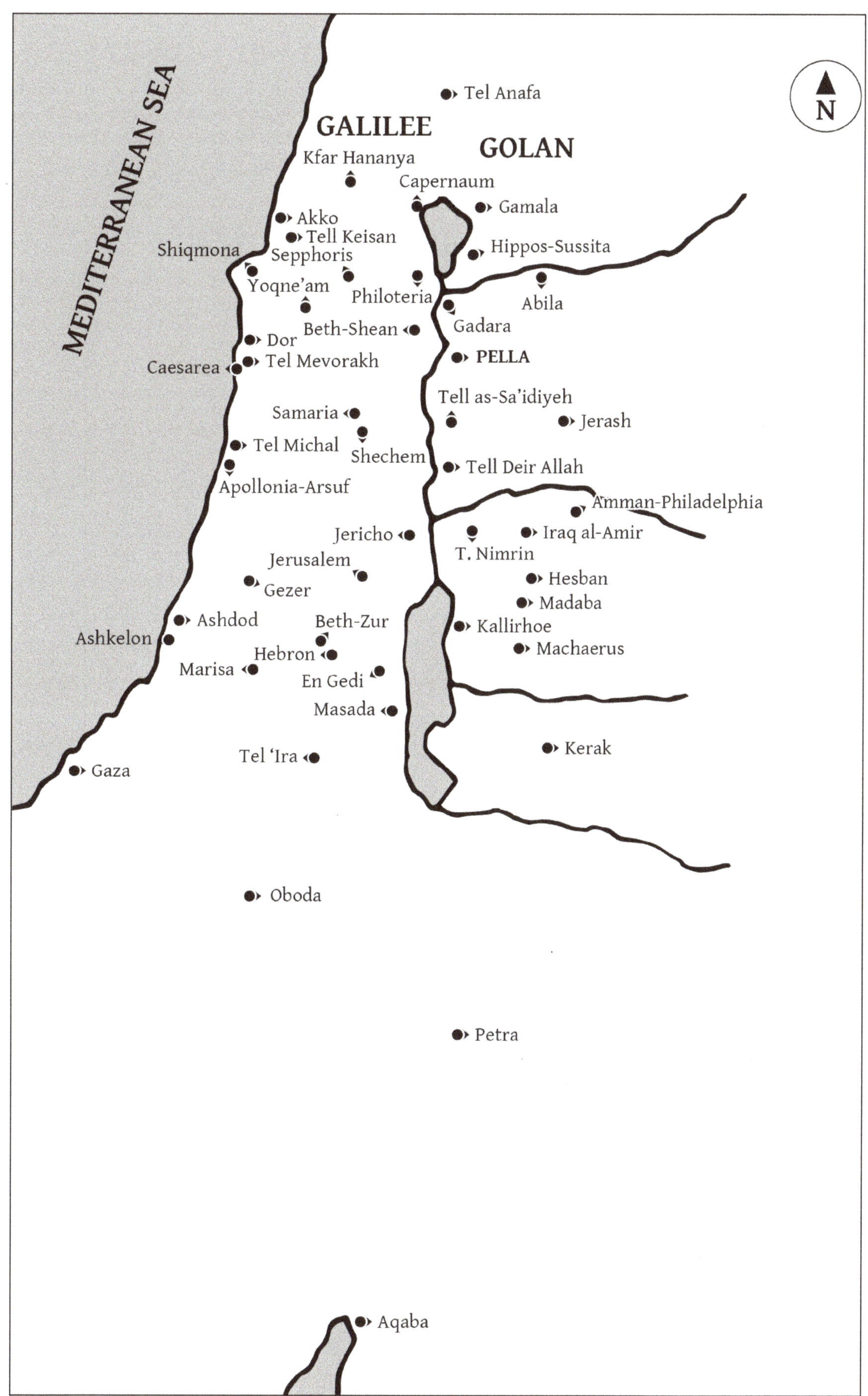

Figure 0.1. The southern Levant, showing main sites mentioned in the text.

Part 1

THE EXCAVATIONS

INTRODUCTION

Ancient Pella, modern Tabaqat Fahl (Plate 1), lies on the lower foothills of the East Jordan Valley, some 28 kilometres south of Lake Tiberias and approximately 5 kilometres east of the Jordan River (coordinates 32°27′N, 35°37′E). Its perennial spring (Plate 2) and position close to two of the major trade routes of the Levant – the north–south route from Damascus to Arabia and the east–west route from the Jordanian plateau to the coast of Palestine via the Jezreel Valley – have made it a site of great antiquity with evidence of human activity in the region dating back to Lower Palaeolithic times (McNicoll et al. 1982: 17–34).[1] Its mention in numerous texts and historical documents from the early second millennium onwards emphasises its continuing importance in the region (Knapp 1993: 39–51; Smith 1973: 23–82).

While Pella had been visited by the English travellers Charles Leonard Irby and James Mangles in the early nineteenth century (Irby and Mangles 1823: 92–3), identified by Edward Robinson during his visit to the site in 1852 (Robinson 1856: 320–4), and its remains extensively surveyed by the German scholar Gottlieb Schumacher in 1887 (Schumacher 1888), the first archaeological soundings were not carried out until 1958 by the American Schools of Oriental Research under R.W. Funk and H.N. Richardson. These soundings were confined to limited excavations in two squares on the main mound and only a brief summary of the results was published (Funk and Richardson 1958).[2]

The first major archaeological excavations at the site were commenced in the spring of 1967 by the College of Wooster under the direction of Robert Smith, who published his results in *Pella of the Decapolis 1* (1973). Unfortunately the excavation program was curtailed in its first season by the outbreak of the Arab–Israeli war in June, and work was not resumed until 1979 as a joint project between Wooster and the University of Sydney under the direction of Smith, the late J. Basil Hennessy and the late Anthony McNicoll.[3] In 1985 the College of Wooster ceased its involvement with the site, the excavations continuing under the auspices of the University of Sydney, at first under the overall direction of Basil Hennessy and, subsequently, of Stephen Bourke.

Besides the excavation reports in the *Annual of the Department of Antiquities of Jordan*, *Bulletin of the American Schools of Oriental Research* and numerous more specialised articles, the results so far have appeared in detail in *Archaeology of Jordan II.2* (Homès-Fredericq and Hennessy 1989), the College of Wooster publications *Pella of the Decapolis 1* (Smith 1973), *Pella of the Decapolis 2* (Smith and L.P. Day 1989), the University of Sydney's *Pella in Jordan 1* (McNicoll et al. 1982) and *Pella in Jordan 2* (McNicoll et al. 1992). More recently, the coins from the excavations of 1979–90 have been published

---

1   Since 1999, a Jordanian–German project has diverted the water from the spring, via a pumping station on site, to supply irrigated areas in the Jordan Valley (Margane et al. 2010).

2   For a full discussion of the early exploration of Pella by Western travellers and archaeologists, see Smith 1973: 10–14.

3   See Smith 1973: 20–2, for a vivid account of the problems faced by the expedition, which was in the field at the outbreak of the 1967 war.

(Sheedy et al. 2001), as have the results of excavations at the Natufian site of Wadi al-Hammeh, a westward-flowing tributary of the Jordan River located some 2 kilometres to the north of the *tell* (Edwards 1992, 2007, 2013; McNicoll et al. 1982: 17–27). Numerous Palaeolithic, Kebaran and Natufian artefacts have also been unearthed from scattered sites on the interfluvial ridge and terrace sections adjacent to the wadi and close to the shores of the ancestral Lake Lisan (Macumber 1992).

Excavations at Pella itself have demonstrated that the main mound (Khirbet Fahl) was settled by at least Pre-Pottery Neolithic times (Bourke 1997: 96–7, 2008, 2015/16) with relatively few gaps – most notably the Late Iron IIB/C (c. 730–540 BC) and Persian (539–332 BC) periods – in its occupation sequence until modern times when, in 1967, the small village of Tabaqat Fahl was moved from the *tell* to a more westerly position. Work on Tell Husn – the largely natural hill immediately to the south of the Wadi Jirm al-Moz separating it from the main mound – has indicated intermittent occupation since the Chalcolithic period (Bourke 2014; Bourke et al. 1999; Watson and Tidmarsh 1996).

Hellenistic (332–63 BC) architectural remains and artefacts have now been unearthed from many of the plots on the main mound (Figure 1.1) in Areas III, IV, VIII, XXIII, XXVIII, XXXII; in the Wadi Jirm al-Moz (Area IX) and on Tell Husn (Areas XI, XXXIV). Furthermore, two fortresses from this period have been located on nearby Jebel Sartaba (Area XIII) and Jebel Hammeh (Area XXX). The fort on Sartaba has been planned and investigated by limited soundings by the College of Wooster inside the structure (McNicoll et al. 1982: 65–7) while the defensive wall on Jebel Hammeh has been partially traced by a University of Sydney team but no excavations undertaken (McNicoll et al. 1992: 103–5).

Whereas Hellenistic artefacts have been recovered from numerous plots on the main mound and elsewhere, Early Roman (63 BC–135 AD) material, represented chiefly by "Roman" forms of Eastern Sigillata A (ESA), is found only in small quantities and in disturbed deposits on the main mound in plots IIIP, IIIQ and IVL (Table 1.1). The structure(s) associated with this latter material were, however, completely obliterated by later Byzantine and early Islamic (mainly Ummayad) overbuilding. Thus, architectural evidence for the Early Roman period is essentially restricted to the Civic Complex in the Wadi Jirm al-Moz (Area IX), Tell Husn (Areas XI and XXXIV) and the tombs of Areas VI and VII. From Area VI to the south-west of Husn, an unplundered tomb (Tomb 54) dating to the late first or early second century AD was cleared in 1983 (McNicoll et al. 1992: 124–33). Much of the organic material from this tomb – including cedar beams, pine planking and a pair of leather soles – was well preserved with many intact glass vessels also recovered. The tomb contained little in the way of pottery, although worth noting was the presence of a wheelmade knife-pared ("Herodian") lamp (McNicoll et al. 1992: pl. 87.4) and three fragments of a "Galilean" bowl of Kfar Hananya Form 1B (Adan-Bayewitz 1993: 91–7).[4] A further tomb (Tomb 40) from the same area of late first century BC or early first century AD was also explored (McNicoll et al. 1982: 87–8). Five other tombs of Early Roman date (first to second centuries AD), of which at least four had been robbed, were unearthed by the Wooster team in the South Cemetery (Area VII) in 1979 (McNicoll et al. 1980: 75–6).[5]

---

4   With the exception of Areas VIII, IX and XIII (College of Wooster), the other areas from which Hellenistic and Early Roman material has been recovered were excavated by University of Sydney teams. The results of the College of Wooster excavations in these three areas are dealt with briefly in this volume for the sake of completion, but for a fuller description (although much remains unpublished) see the relevant sections in Smith (1973), Smith and Day (1989) and McNicoll et al. (1982, 1992), as well as the excavation reports in *Annual of the Department of Antiquities of Jordan*, and *Bulletin of the American Schools of Oriental Research*.

5   I am grateful to Sandra Gordon (pers. com.) for further information regarding the Early Roman tombs from Areas VI and VII. For the later reuse of an Early Roman sarcophagus in the West Church complex (Area I), see Smith 1973: 143–9.

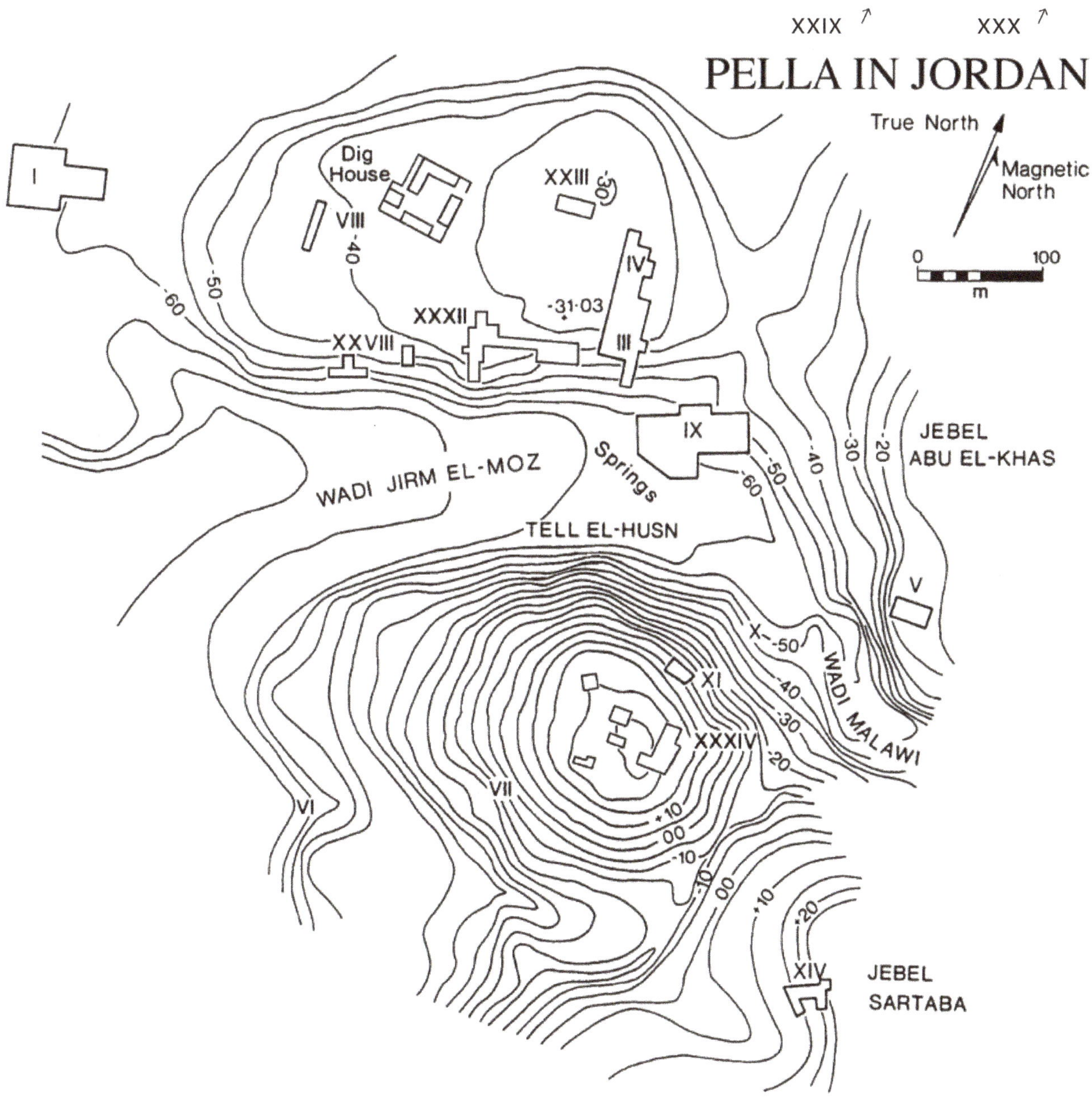

Figure 1.1. Pella. Excavation areas.

THE RECORDING TECHNIQUES USED AT PELLA: AN OUTLINE OF TERMINOLOGY AND ABBREVIATIONS

For a full outline see McNicoll (1992: xvi–xvii). The terms relevant to this volume are outlined here.

Provenance/field terminology

Area

The first part of identification. Shown by Roman numerals and allotted to zones within the Pella district excavated by the Joint Expedition. Thus, for example, Area VIII (College of Wooster) signifies that plots in this area were excavated by the College of Wooster whereas Area XXIII (University of Sydney) signifies that plots in this area were excavated by the University of Sydney.

Plot

The second part of identification. An alphabetical letter (A, seq.) is given to each trench termed a Plot, excavated within an Area.

Locus

The third part of identification. During the course of the excavation each plot is divided into loci defined by baulks established by the excavator or by archaeological remains (for example, walls) or by a combination of the two.

Level
The final part of identification. Levels are the stratified deposits resulting from human or natural activity. Thus XXIIIA 3.6 = Area XXIII, Plot A, Locus 3, Level 6.

Feature (F)
A term used to refer to any fixed archaeological object (for example, a pit, oven, bench) planned and recorded individually. Thus, F36 may be an oven recorded as Feature 36.

Walls
Numbered sequentially in each plot.

House terminology

Inventory Number (CN)
Each ceramic (or the uncommon chalkstone) specimen, when inducted into the pottery series, was originally allocated an inventory number (CN).

Registration Number (RN)
Each museum or study object allocated to Jordan, Australia or the USA by the Department of Antiquities of Jordan is given a registration number. More recently, these objects have all been allocated to Jordan.

Table 1.1. Pella: Summary of Hellenistic and Early Roman occupation sequence. College of Wooster and University of Sydney excavations.

OCCUPATION	STRATUM	DATE	REMAINS	DATABLE MATERIAL
Alexander/ *Diadochi* 334–301 BC	Hellenistic 1	334–301 BC	None	Stray lamp CN 7129 (Tell Husn, Hellenistic 1 or 2A) Feline sculpture? (north-west of main mound)
Ptolemaic 301–c. 200 BC	Hellenistic 2A	301–c. 220 BC	None	Lamp CN 7129 (Hellenistic 1 or 2A)
	Hellenistic 2B	c. 220–c. 200 BC	XXXIVF (Tell Husn) Rubbish fill (?)	Lamps CN 7143, 7390 Coin RN 16036 (?)
	Hellenistic 2B	c. 220–c. 200 BC	XXXIVB (Tell Husn) "Antiochus Destruction" level (c. 217 BC? 200 BC?)	Stamped Rhodian amphora handles (SAHs): CN 7655, 7656, 7657, 7658, 7678 Coin: RN 090279 Lamp: CN 7674
Seleucid c. 200–63 BC	Hellenistic 3A	c. 200–c. 140 BC	XXVIIIB (Main mound) Dwelling	Mould-made bowls Lamp CN 7391
	Hellenistic 3A	c. 200–c. 140 BC	XXXIIY (Main mound) Wash	SAH CN 7868
	Hellenistic 3B	c.140–c. 100 (?) BC	XXIII A–D (Main mound) Earlier walls	Lamp: CN 7392 Coins: Sheedy et al. (2001) no. 1.015; RN 110982, 111554 Eastern Sigillata A (ESA)
	Hellenistic 3B/3C (Tell Husn)	c. 140–c. 80/79 BC	XXXIVB, XXXIVG (Tell Husn) Earlier walls	ESA

OCCUPATION	STRATUM	DATE	REMAINS	DATABLE MATERIAL
	Hellenistic 3C	c. 100 (?)–c. 80/79 BC	III, IV, XXIII A–D VIII (Wooster) (Main mound) Latest walls, Jannaeus Destruction Level	Coins: Sheedy et al. (2001) no. 1.019, 1.020, 1.023, 2.002, 2.006, 2.007; RN 110973, 110668, 110889 ESA "Galilean" cooking pot
	Hellenistic 3D	c. 80/79–63 BC		No firmly dated material
Early Roman 63 BC–c. 135 AD	Early Roman 1	63 BC–late first century (c. 100) AD	XIA/B, XXXIVB, XXXIVG XXXIVT (Tell Husn) Fortification wall (XIA/B, XXXIVT) Domestic walls (XXXIVB, XXXIVG) Paved stylobate (XXXIVB) VIII, IX (Wooster) (VIII: Main mound; IX: Wadi Jirm al-Moz)	ESA Hayes Forms: 4B, 9, 12, 22B, 24, 28, 33, 34, 37A, 44, 47, 48, 111 Long-collared and ridged neck jars (Types 6B, 7A, 7B)[6] "Galilean" cooking pot (Type 7) "Herodian" lamps Chalkstone vessels Coins: Sheedy et al. (2001) no. 2.014, 2.018; RN 16040.
	Early Roman 2	Late first century (c. 100–c. 135 AD)	IIIP, IIIQ, IVL (Main mound) XIA/B, XXXIVT (Tell Husn) No architectural remains in Areas III, IV; Fortification wall in XIA/B, XXXIVT	ESA Hayes Forms: 54, 57, 59, 60, 111(?) Coins: Sheedy et al. (2001) no. 3.002

---

6   See under "Abbreviations in text", for the explanation of "type".

THE EXCAVATIONS

THE MAIN MOUND (KHIRBET FAHL)

Areas III, IV (University of Sydney)

The south-eastern sector of the main mound seems to have undergone extensive re-terracing during the second century BC. The remains of a small Hellenistic dwelling built on one of these terraces (in plot IIIB/C) were unearthed (McNicoll et al. 1982: 68–71) but, as it was necessary to preserve the overlying Byzantine and Ummayad remains, only partially excavated (Plate 3). The tentative plan (Figure 1.2) shows the building to be rectangular and entered via a doorway (F1) with three well-cut ashlar threshold blocks of limestone on its south-west. Its walls consisted of rubble, bound with mud mortar in their lower courses, with plastered mudbrick above. Originally the interior had been divided into two rooms (room 1 = locus 1; room 2 = locus 2) by the east–west wall 3 but, in its latest phase, the addition of a north–south cross-wall (wall 5) partially divided the southern room 2 into two further chambers (room 3 = locus 3; room 4 = locus 5) whose internal floors consisted of at least six layers of tamped earth or thin white plaster. The northern (inner) room 1 (locus 1) was paved with hard yellow unbaked clay tiles (40 × 40 cm and 40 × 20 cm), one of which was pierced by a post-hole. Within the destruction level, described below, were the charred remains of burnt beams and a thin fibrous matting, no doubt forming part of the mud roof.[7] Outside the entrance, to the west, was a series of thick, coarse white and yellow plaster layers on a bedding of soil and pebbles; these layers had been cut by several shallow plaster-lined pits and represent the remains of a courtyard (locus 4). The relatively small dimensions of the building, its humble construction and the simple ceramic corpus of lamps, small bowls and cooking vessels found on the occupation surfaces suggest that it was a small residence.[8]

A thick black deposit of burnt mudbrick, carbonised beams, and scorched earth inside and around the dwelling (Figure 1.3) showed that it had been destroyed by fire, almost certainly as a result of the sack of the city by Alexander Jannaeus in (or soon after) c. 80/79 BC (Josephus *Ant. Jud.* XIII. 15.2–4).[9] The latest coins found within the deposit – a bronze of Antiochus XII Dionysus (87/6–83/2 BC) and a *prutah* of Alexander Jannaeus (104–76 BC) – are consistent with this date.[10] The destruction had resulted in the presence of two pottery groups from within and around the structure – one coming from the latest occupation/destruction level itself (levels 1.1–5, 2.1–9, 3.1–3, 4.1–2, 9.1, 14.1–6, 15.2–3) and the other from the earlier fill, or pre-construction (Mixed Context) phase, found under the house (1.6–11, 1.13–25, 5.1, 6.1). This latter mixed deposit, although clearly formed at one time, contained pottery and other artefacts – including a silver tetradrachm of

---

7 Radiocarbon (C-14) dating of one of these beams was unhelpful (McNicoll et al. 1992: 106, fn1).

8 Ceramic corpus (see also McNicoll et al. 1982: pl. 129): fishplate **PW 9**; uncatalogued plate Type 2 CN 0207; bowls Types 2–4 **PW 116**, **PW 140–4**; jars Type 4A **PW 334**, Type 5A **PW 392–3**; cooking pot Type 1 **PW 499**; moulded grey lamps RN 20055, RN 20103.

9 The likely cause, date and extent of the destruction level encountered at the end of the Hellenistic period on the main mound but not on Tell Husn is discussed in more detail in later sections of this work.

10 Sheedy et al. 2001: no. 1.020 (Antiochus XII Dionysus), no. 2.002 (Alexander Jannaeus).

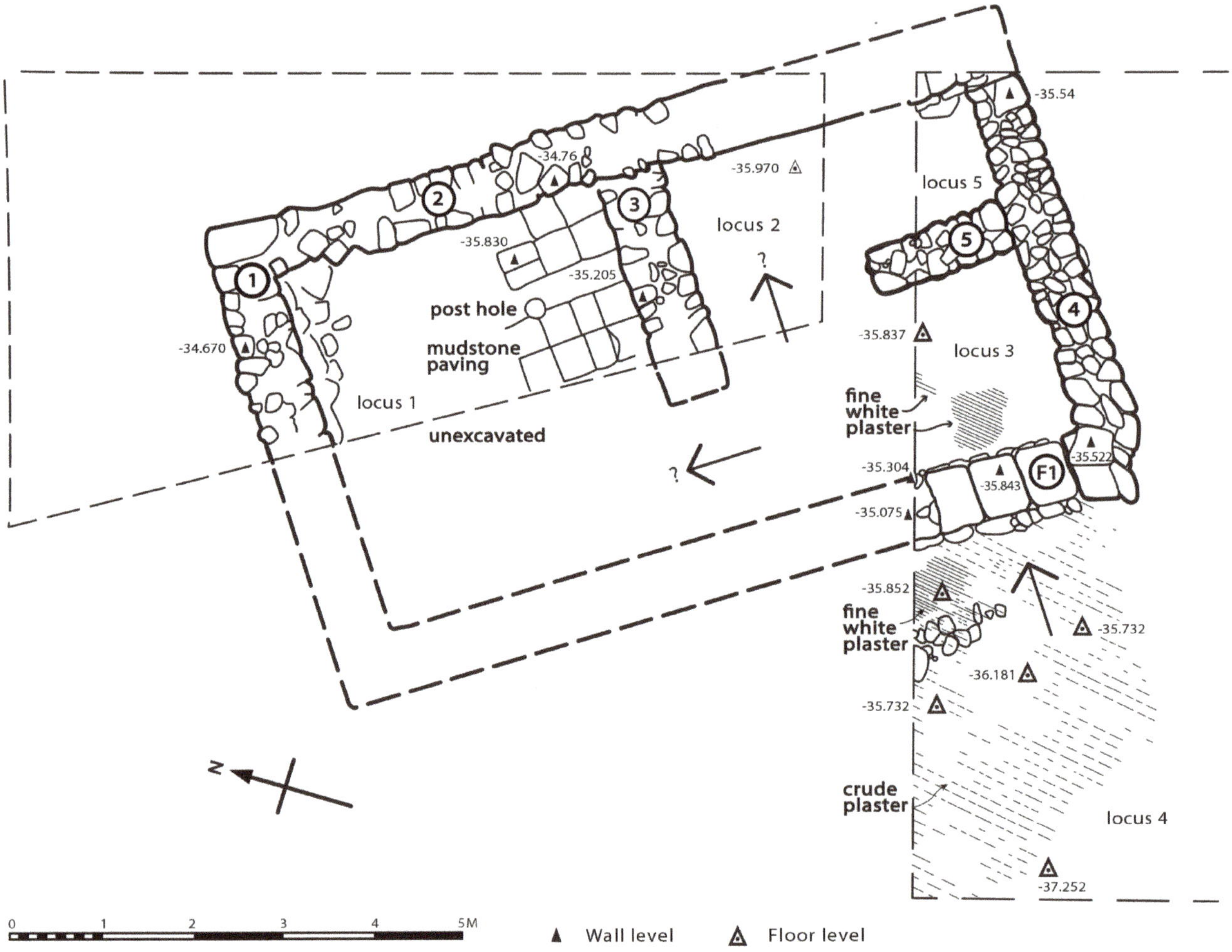

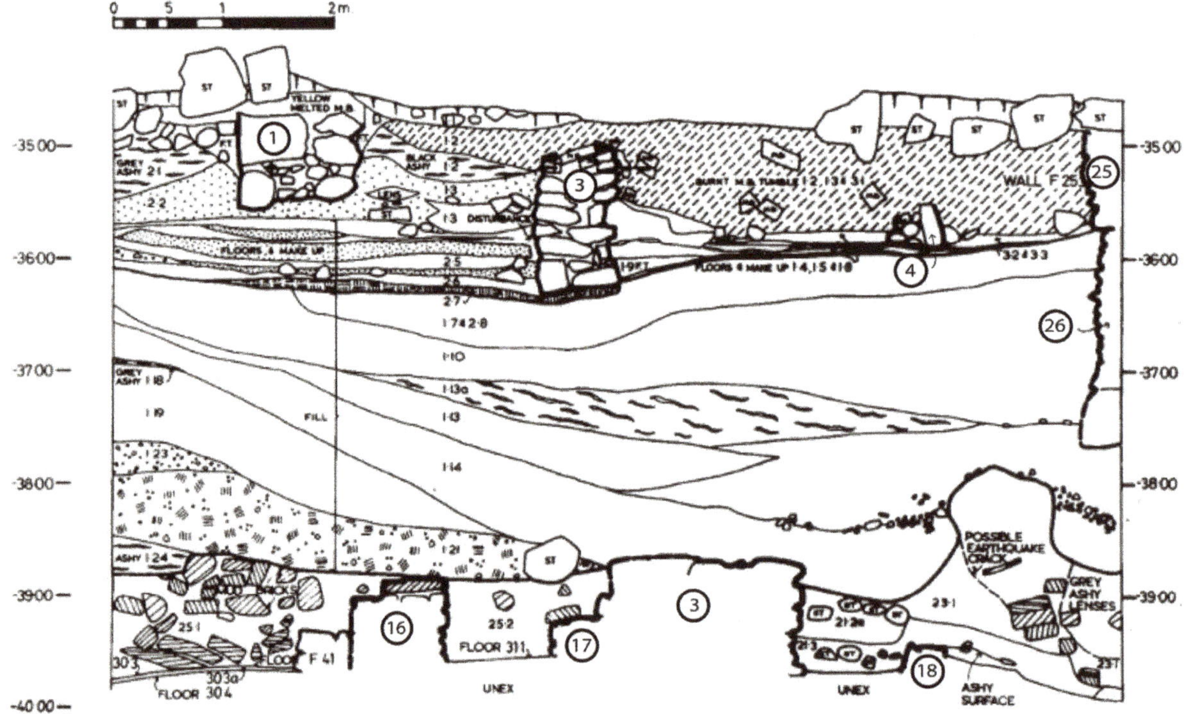

Figure 1.2. Plot IIIB/C. Plan.

Figure 1.3. Plot IIIB/C. North section.

Ptolemy II Philadelphus (285–246 BC), a bronze of Antiochus III (223–187 BC), a city coin of 'Akko-Ptolemais (175–164 BC) and two third-century BC stamped Rhodian amphora handles – spanning more than one millennium (McNicoll and Hennessy 1980: 16).[11] The presence of several body fragments of ESA within the fill suggests that it was laid down no earlier than the second half of the second century BC.[12]

The very scanty remains of more Hellenistic structures have come to light in Area IV, plots IVD and IVE, as well as in Area III, plots IIIP and IIIQ, further to the south (McNicoll et al. 1992: 109–11). Once again, preservation of the overlying Byzantine and Ummayad buildings restricted the area of the Hellenistic occupation that could be uncovered, although, with the exception of wall foundations, much of the architecture from this period had already been destroyed (totally in plots IVG–IVU) by later Roman and Byzantine rebuilding.

When considered together, the structures in plots IIIP, IIIQ, IVD, IVE (Figure 1.4) represent further evidence of the widespread Late Hellenistic housing covering much of the mound from at least the mid-second century BC or slightly earlier. The architecture is similar to that seen in the small dwelling from plot IIIB/C described above with the walls constructed of rubble, mud mortar and plastered mudbrick. Where preserved, the interior floors were of tamped earth or thin plaster with the courtyard surfaces of much thicker plaster on a base of small stones. The fragmentary remains of several clay ovens (F1, F2, F3) were uncovered within these courtyards.[13]

In plot IVE (above an Iron Age destruction level throughout the complete plot), room 1 (loci 13, 16) was defined. It was bounded by the north–south walls 19 and 26 (a continuation from IIIP) as well as the two east–west walls 20 and 27. Small patches of thin white plaster flooring (16.3) survived in the corners of the room but had been worn away (or,

later, dug away) in the centre. Above the worn section of this floor another surface of solid yellow plaster (13.6) had been laid down. Other rooms to the south (room 2: loci 17, 23) and east (room 3: locus 15) of this central room were partially revealed though their full extent was concealed in the baulks on either side of the plot. Several small patches of red and green plaster – applied in two layers – still adhered to the walls in room 1; fragments of similar plaster from the deposits within rooms 2 and 3 suggest a widespread use of this medium, also employed in Area XXIII. Associated with each of these three rooms were the occupation surfaces that, with the exception of the plaster flooring 13.6 and 16.3, were of tamped earth. While it is likely that the associated surfaces in IVE locus 19 (19.10) and IIIP locus 25 (25.10–11) were the remnants of lanes or alleyways, the restricted access to the Hellenistic levels in these plots makes any attempt at discerning an overall plan futile.

Whereas only scanty construction and wall foundation deposits remained in IIIP and IIIQ, a well-stratified destruction deposit partially survived in IVD both to the east of wall 12 and to its west, south of wall 11 of which only two courses remained (Figure 1.5). The deposit consisted of a thick layer of burnt mudbrick collapse and ash overlying an occupation surface of tamped earth to the east of wall 12 (locus 13) and a series of yellow-white plaster floors supported by small rounded stones – undoubtedly a courtyard – to the west of the wall (loci 10, 12). On the courtyard's occupation surface (12.1) were the remains of a mudbrick oven (F1) with, in the east baulk, the well-preserved wall of a further oven (F2) dug into the plaster floors of locus 12. From the destruction level was recovered a large quantity of charred pottery as well as several coins of Hellenistic date of which the latest (Sheedy et al: 2001, no. 1.023) was most likely minted during the reign of Antiochus XII Dionysus. So, like the destructions in IIIB/C,

---

11 Stamped amphora handles (SAHs): RN 20338: (a) EPICHARMOS, eponym belonging to Period 1b, c. 260–247, (b) MOKLEUS, possibly the fabricant [POTA]MOKLES; RN 20310: PAU/SANIA, eponym belonging to Period IIa (c. 234–220). Sheedy et al. 2001: no. 1.001 (Ptolemy II); no. 1.006 (Antiochus III); no. 1.037 ('Akko-Ptolemais). For the revised dating of stamped Rhodian amphora handles see Finkielsztejn 2001. My thanks to the late Graeme Clarke for his reading of the stamped amphora handles.

12 For the initial mid-second century (or slightly later) appearance of ESA in the southern Levant see Berlin et al. 2014; Hayes 1985a: 12; 1991a: 32; Slane 1997: 274.

13 See Ebeling and Rogel (2015) for the frequent misidentification of clay ovens found in archaeological excavations as *tawabin* (sing. *tabun*). Therefore, these terms will not be used here.

After Alexander

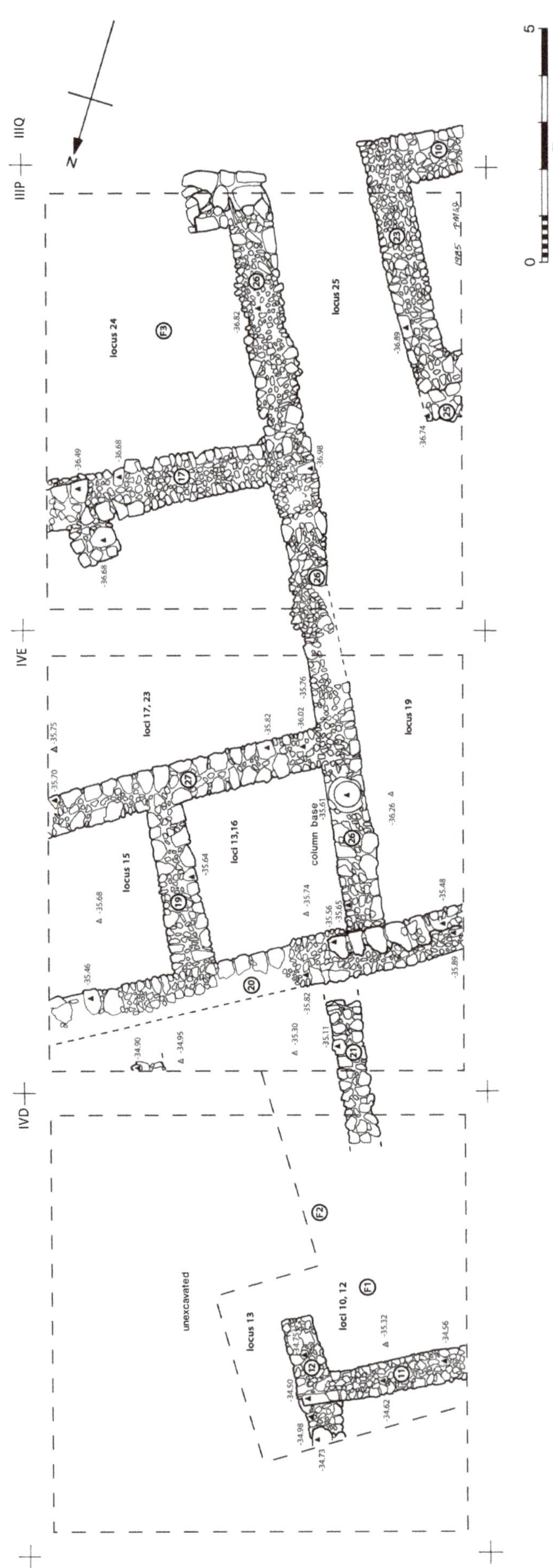

Figure 1.4. Plots IIIP, IIIQ, IVD, IVE. Plan.

16

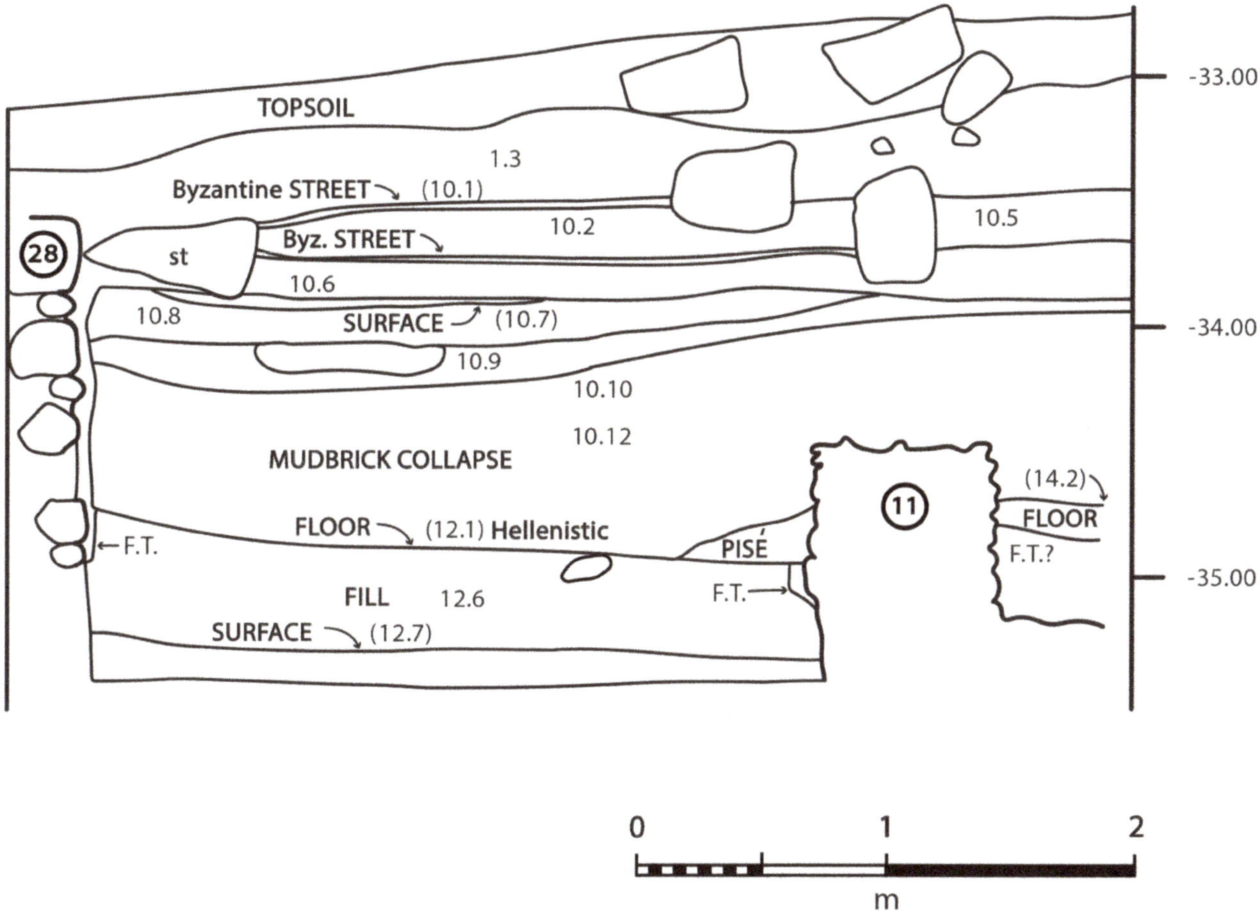

Figure 1.5. Plot IVD. Sounding, west section.

the destruction should be attributed to the sack of Alexander Jannaeus.[14]

Area VIII (College of Wooster)

The excavations carried out in the West Cut on the main mound (Area VIII) by the College of Wooster (McNicoll et al. 1982: 72–5) uncovered thick Hellenistic deposits averaging about 2 metres in depth and representing two architectural phases of domestic architecture (Smith 1981: 315–18; Smith et al. 1980: 33–5; Smith et al. 1981: 12–17; Smith et al. 1982: 61–4, fig. 17), both dating to the second half of the second century through the first quarter of the first century (c. 150–c. 80 BC) as shown by the ceramic and numismatic material. Such a chronological range is consistent with the findings of the University of Sydney team in Plots XXIIIA, XXIIIB and XXIIID. As in Areas III and IV, there was ample evidence of widespread destruction and burning at the end of

the Hellenistic phase with the latest coin from within these destruction deposits minted during the reign of Alexander Jannaeus.

Above the Jannaeus Destruction level the excavators claimed to have isolated a thin Early Roman level greatly disturbed by later building. Apart from a small, non-specific selection of potsherds displayed in McNicoll and colleagues (1982: pl. 22), no further information on the important ceramic assemblage from this level has been published.

Area XXIII (University of Sydney)

Much of the Hellenistic material recovered from the main mound comes from Area XXIII, the site of an impressive apparent domestic structure or "villa". The excavated area was centred on the first ("Square I") of two soundings carried out on the main mound in 1958 by Funk and Richardson. Although the soundings were never fully published, the preliminary report

---

14 Sheedy et al. 2001: nos 1.007, 1.023, 1.033, 1.043, 1.047, 1.048, 1.049. The attribution of no. 1.023 to Demetrius II Nicator, second reign (129–126/5 BC) is less likely.

Table 1.2. Area III and IV stratified deposits.

PLOT	NATURE OF DEPOSIT	DEPOSIT
IIIB/C (main mound)	**Hellenistic 3C** c. 100 (?)–c. 80/79 BC Latest use: Occupation surfaces (a) internal surfaces (b) external (courtyard) surfaces Destruction	 1.4–5 4.1–2 1.1–3, 2.1–9, 3.1–3, 9.1, 14.1–6, 15.2–3
IIIP (main mound)	**Hellenistic 3B** c. 140–c.1 00 (?) BC Pre-Jannaeus Destruction: Wall 17 Wall 19 Occupation Laneway surface	 Foundation trench = 24.6 Foundation trench = 24.5 24.2–4 25.10–11
IIIQ	**Hellenistic 3B** c. 140–c. 100 (?) BC Pre-Jannaeus Destruction: Wall 10	 Foundation trench = 11.35
IVD	**Hellenistic 3C** c. 100 (?)–c. 80/79 BC Latest use: Occupation surfaces (a) tamped earth (b) plaster surfaces Destruction	 12.1, 13.14, 13.17–18, 14.2 10.10, 10.12, 10.14, 11.1, 13.10, 13.13, 14.1
IVE	**Hellenistic 3B** c. 140–c. 100 (?) BC Pre-Jannaeus Destruction: Wall 19 Wall 26 Wall 27	 Foundation trench = 15.5, 16.8 Foundation trench = 16.9, 17.13 Foundation trench = 15.9, 17.10, 17.12
	Hellenistic 3C c. 100 (?)–c. 80/79 BC Latest use: Occupation surfaces (a) tamped clay (b) plaster surface Laneway surface	 13.11, 15.3–4, 15.6, 16.2, 17.6–7 13.6, 16.3 19.10

(Funk and Richardson 1958: 82–96), not accompanied by plans or sections of the Hellenistic levels, stated that Square I provided evidence of "Medieval and Early Arab occupation" in its upper layers as well as Byzantine, Late Hellenistic and Early Iron Age material below.

Within the Hellenistic stratum, Funk and Richardson uncovered the corner of a "room". Its walls in their preserved courses were of stone, reinforced with ashlar masonry at various points, and had at least in part been covered with painted plaster. The presence of a "fine stone floor", however, suggests the possibility that the "room" may well have been a paved courtyard. From the courtyard/room were recovered "quantities of pottery and objects including fine red-gloss ware (Hellenistic Pergamene[15]), several nearly whole

---

15 Hellenistic Pergamene is the earlier (and inaccurate) term for the ware we now know as Eastern Sigillata A (Hayes 1997: 54, 2008: 3–4, 13; Kenrick 1985: 223; Kenyon in Crowfoot et al. 1957: 281–3).

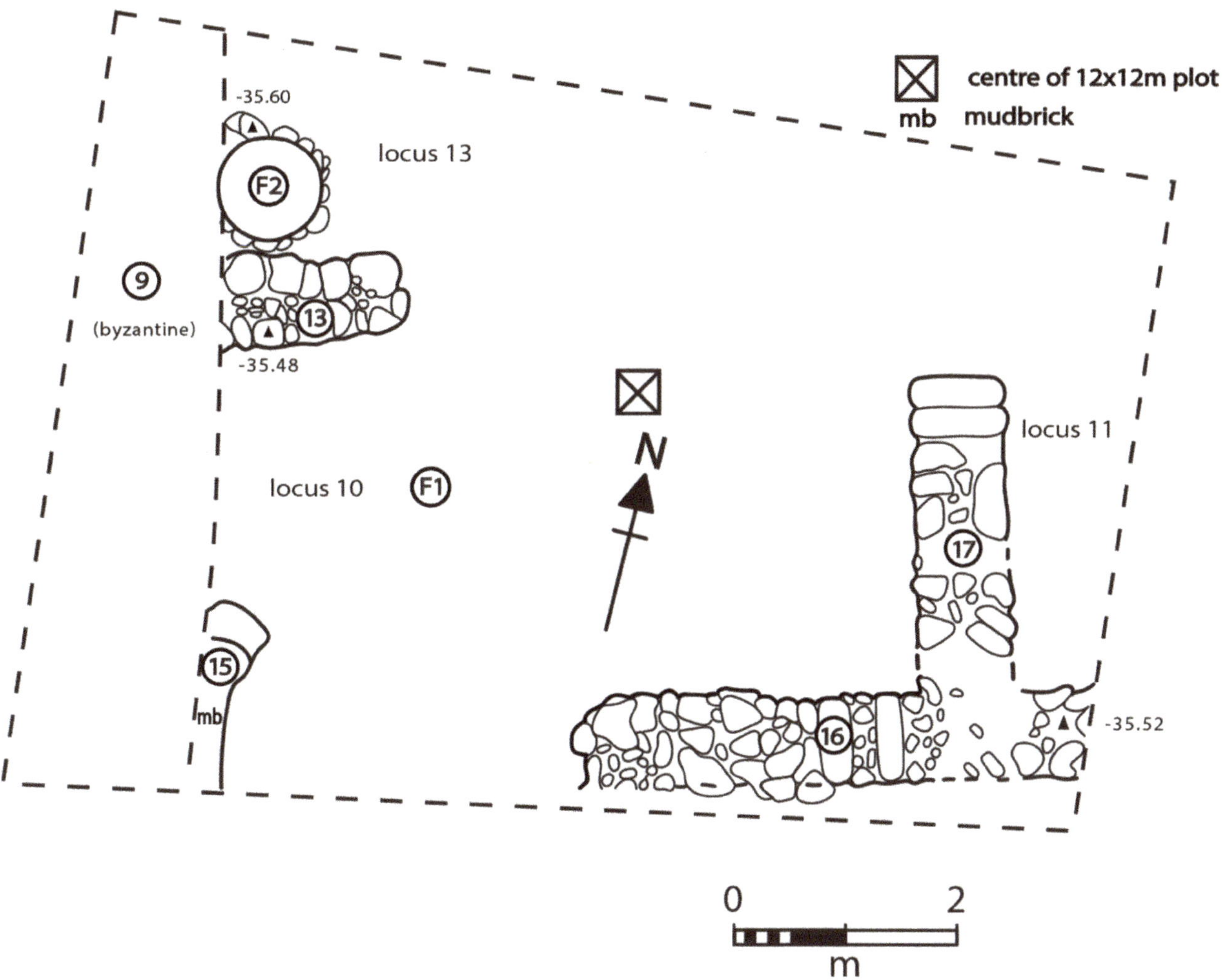

Figure 1.6. Plot XXIIIA. Funk and Richardson trench, Hellenistic levels. Plan.

storage jars, an incised two-handled pot, nineteen loom weights, and several shattered cooking pots". A thick layer of burnt debris, including "the charcoal remains of timbers which had once supported the roof; in places traceable for a metre or more" showed that the structure had been destroyed by fire.

The Funk and Richardson sounding has formed the central part of Area XXIII and has been re-excavated as plot XXIIIA (Figure 1.6). Although at first there were problems in delineating the full extent of the sondage, with no plan having been produced by the excavators, these hurdles were overcome and

abundant material from uncontaminated Hellenistic deposits around its periphery has been recovered (McNicoll et al. 1992: 107–9; Tidmarsh 1990: 72).

As Funk and Richardson had found in 1958, the Hellenistic levels in XXIIIA were sealed by a thick layer of burning/collapse made up of burnt beams, iron nails, charcoal, plaster fragments (painted and undecorated) and burnt mudbrick. From this destruction level was recovered a large quantity of pottery, including stamped Rhodian amphora handles, bronze coins and a tanged bronze arrowhead (RN 60350: Figure 1.7).[16] The amphora handles cover

---

16 Arrowheads of similar form "are common in Hellenistic assemblages in the region" with one such example published from the early first century BC Hasmonean fortress at Horvat Tefen (Sabar 2022).

Figure 1.7. Plot XXIIIA. Jannaeus Destruction level. Arrowhead RN 60350.

the last three-quarters of the second century[17] whereas coins such as one from the reign of Antiochus XII Dionysus and two *prutoth* of Alexander Jannaeus point to a date early in the first century BC for this destruction that must be the work of Jannaeus.[18]

Sealed by this destruction level, and to the east and west of the Funk and Richardson sounding, were areas combining domestic use with storage, manufacture and food processing. Walls 13, 16 and 17 were of stone rubble bound with mud mortar, although it is likely that their upper courses were of mudbrick or *pisé*; wall 15 seems to have been entirely of mudbrick. As noted previously by Funk and Richardson (1958: 89) and by Smith in Area VIII (1973: 72, pl. 9), worked

ashlar blocks were used as "headers" at various points within the walls.

In locus 13 the fine clay oven F2 was found, largely complete, adjacent to the north face of wall 13 (Figure 1.8), while from the destruction level in locus 11 (11.1–2) was unearthed a group of least six smashed plain ware fishplates that had clearly been stored together (Figure 1.9). In locus 10 was revealed a further clay oven (F1), well preserved (Figure 1.10). In this latter locus, from the plaster floor 10.8 directly underneath the destruction level (Figure 1.11), were recovered more than sixty unbaked clay loom weights of largely pyramidal form (Figure 1.12), along with three stamped amphora handles (Rhodian and

---

17 CN 5459 (McNicoll et al. 1992: pls 76.1; 80.d–f): (a) IASON 2nd, fabricant, (b) ANDRIAS, eponym belonging to period Va (c. 137–133); CN 7146a: ARISTAKOS eponym dated c. 137/6–c. 135/4; CN 7121: DAMOKLES, fabricant active in Periods IV–V (c. 160–108); CN 7094: EPIGONOS 2nd, fabricant active during Period IV (c. 160–146); CN 7093: HIPPOKRATES fabricant active from Periods IIIb–Vb (c. 198–140); CN 7856: (a and b), combination of eponym ANDRON[E]IKOS and fabricant TIMOXENOS, belonging to Period Vb (c. 132–1 BC).

18 Sheedy et al. 2001: no. 1.019 (Antiochus XII Dionysus); nos 2.006, 2.007 (Alexander Jannaeus).

                              [text continues on page 23]

Figure 1.8. Plot XXIIIA. Locus 13. Oven F2. To west.

Figure 1.9. Plot XXIIIA. Locus 11. Fishplate smash.

Figure 1.10. Plot XXIIIA. Locus 10. Oven F1. To north.

Figure 1.11. Plot XXIIIA. Plaster floor 10.8 and east face of mudbrick wall 15. To south-west.

Figure 1.12. Plot XXIIIA. Loom weights from floor 10.8.

Knidian).[19] From the Jannaeus Destruction level, in locus 11 in particular but also from other loci, came numerous fragments of painted and moulded plaster – including one larger preserved segment (RN 70087) – which had most likely fallen from an upper level (Plate 4; Figure 1.13).[20] It is worth noting that Funk and Richardson (1958: 89–90) also recovered many loom weights and a large quantity of painted plaster from the same destruction level. In locus 22 (the remains of an external courtyard), a bronze drapery fragment was revealed on the cobblestone floor (22.10–11) sealed by the destruction level (22.2–9) (Plate 5; Figure 1.14).

In the northern sector of the plot (loci 100–113) an exploratory sondage uncovered a series of four more-or-less parallel walls (Figures 1.15–17) whose orientation and method of construction were similar to walls 13, 16 and 17, discussed above. The latest phase in this probe was clearly related to the Jannaeus Destruction with a thick layer of burnt mudbrick and ash sealing the latest occupation levels. From these destruction and occupation levels was recovered a bronze finger (Figures 1.18–19) – perhaps from the same bronze figure as the aforementioned drapery – as well as an iron spear butt with broken spike (Figure 1.20), iron spearhead and very fragmentary sword blade.[21]

Earlier well-stratified levels (Hellenistic 3B) were present in loci 108 and 109, both of which were small courtyards. Locus 109 (courtyard 1) was bounded on its western side by the rubble stone wall 8 and to the east by wall 4 (Figures 1.21–22). Its earliest surface (109.4) was of tamped earth upon which rested a crude hearth (F2) constructed of small stones and surrounded by appreciable quantities of ash and animal bone (Figure 1.23).[22] Both the surface and hearth had at a later stage been covered by at least two floors of thick white plaster (109.1–2) resting on stone packing (109.3) and also resting on the upper courses of wall 8 that now functioned as stone packing similar to 109.3.[23] Above 109.1 was a thin occupation surface (100.6) lying directly below the Jannaeus Destruction (Figure 1.24).

Locus 108 (courtyard 2) had as its latest surface the remains of a rough stone floor resting on a layer of thin white plaster (108.1), bounded on its eastern side by wall 1, abutting the eastern section of wall 7 to its west (Figure 1.25). The stone wall 6, also associated with this phase, is separated from wall 7 by a doorway, with the clay oven (F9) over which wall 6 was constructed earlier still to be fully revealed (Figure 1.26). Below the plaster floor 108.1 and resting on a subsurface fill (108.4–6) was a further plaster floor (108.3), above which was the occupation deposit 108.2. Very little pottery was found in this locus although from 108.2 was recovered a bronze coin of Antiochus VIII Grypus (126/5–96 BC).[24]

Further to the east loci 103, 104 and 105, each constituting small rooms (rooms 3, 2, 1), were only partially excavated (Figure 1.27). The floors in all three were of tamped earth (103.4, 104.3, 105.3), at least in their final phase, with thin occupation levels above

---

19 CN 6996 (McNicoll et al. 1992: pl. 80c): Knidian. (a) ARISTANDROS fabricant, (b) EUPHRAGORAS eponym belonging to Period IVb (c. 150); CN 6998 (McNicoll et al. 1992: pl. 80.b): Rhodian. DAMOKLES 2nd, eponym whose date falls within Period IIIc (c. 176/4); CN 6566 (McNicoll et al. 1992: pl. 76.2): Rhodian. No stamp survives; on upper side of handle close to neck, an 8-rayed star.

20 The design on the larger preserved segment consisted of an orthostat zone of black panels in relief below a simple band of "Lesbian leaf". Above were bands of relief panels in orange and yellow ochre below a further band of white panels outlined in red. "Technically the plaster is relatively fine white plaster with medium sand in moderate quantity … it is unlikely that this example was produced after 40 BC … and far more likely 125–69 BC." I thank Robert L. Gordon Jr. (pers. com.), who examined the fragments at Pella, for these and other valuable comments on the decorative plaster along with his reconstruction of the painted fragments. For a similar decorative scheme in the Late Hellenistic Stuccoed Building at Tel Anafa, see Kidd and Gordon 2018: fig. 2.

21 Bronze finger RN 110388; iron arrowhead RN 110615; iron spearhead RN 110452; iron sword blade RN 110451. The objects of metal will be published in a later volume.

22 From 109.4: bowls **FW 75, FW 112, FW 203, FW 275, PW 67–9, PW 102, PW 118**; jar Type 3 **PW 291**; unguentarium **PW 681**; cooking pot Type 1 **PW 496**. The animal bones recovered from plot XXIII are mainly cattle, pigs or sheep/goat in approximately equal proportions. I thank Karyn Wesselingh (pers. com.) for this information. She will be publishing the Hellenistic and Early Roman animal bones from Pella in a subsequent volume.

23 From 109.1–3: cup **FW 135**; bowl **PW 120**; jars Type 4B **PW 373**, Type 5A **PW 387**.

24 Sheedy et al. 2001: no. 1.015.

     [text continues on page 26]

Figure 1.13. Plot XXIIIA. Painted plaster fragments from Jannaeus Destruction level in locus 11.

Figure 1.14. Plot XXIIIA. Cobblestone surface 22.10–11. East at top of image. The stairs are modern (for ease of access).

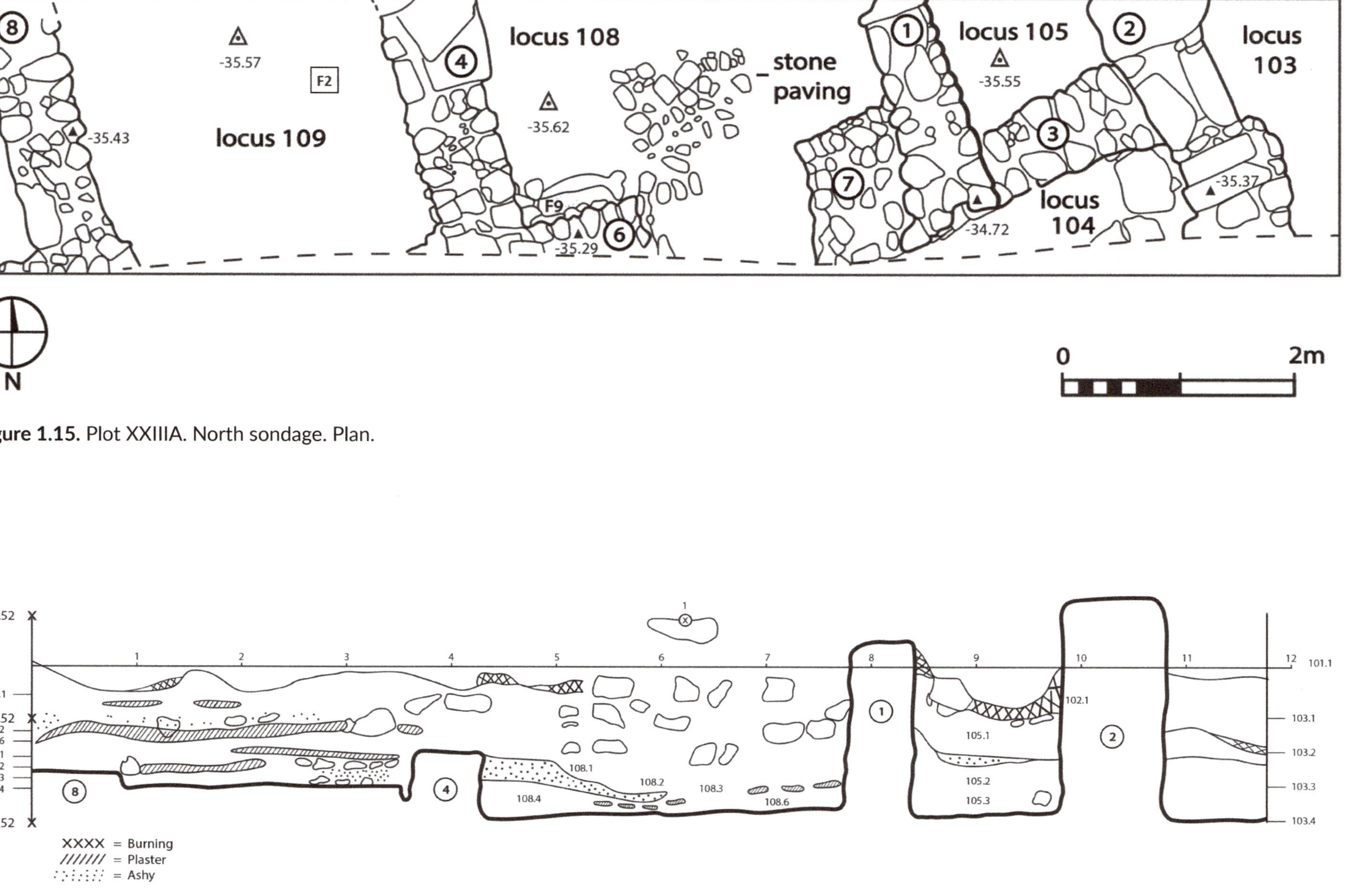

Figure 1.15. Plot XXIIIA. North sondage. Plan.

Figure 1.16. Plot XXIIIA. North sondage. North section.

Figure 1.17. Plot XXIIIA. North sondage. To west.

(103.3, 104.2, 105.2).[25] Room 3 (locus 103) would appear to have been associated with the preparation of food, as large quantities of ash, animal bones and burnt potsherds were recovered from the floor.

In the south-west corner of XXIIIA, a further 5 × 2 m sondage – plot XXIIIB – was opened. Its upper levels (1.1–5) were clearly part of the same Alexander Jannaeus Destruction level encountered in plots XXIIIA and XXIIID (discussed below) and in areas III, IV and VIII (Figure 1.28). Below locus 1 the trench was divided into locus 2 (interior room) and locus 3 (external courtyard) respectively by the rubble and mud-mortar wall 2 (Figure 1.29) running north–south and associated with surfaces 2.5 and 3.7. This wall had been constructed directly above, and on the same line as, an earlier (Iron Age) wall that consisted of rubble masonry supporting upper courses of mudbrick or adobe.

Locus 2 consisted of a series of occupation deposits between 5 and 10 centimetres thick, interspersed with patchy plaster floors (2.5, 2.7, 2.13) and a tamped-earth surface (2.2). At least some of these deposits consisted of degenerate mudbrick while the ashy consistency of 2.12 was associated with the badly decomposed remains of one or more clay ovens on floor 2.13 in the south-east corner of the trench. No significant architectural features were uncovered in the locus. Noteworthy, however, is the lamp (CN 7392) from 2.3; although not an Attic import, it has its closest parallels amongst those of Howland Types 29 A and B from the Athenian Agora (Howland 1958: 94–7) and those of Scheibler's Forms FSL 1 and 2 from Athenian Kerameikos (Scheibler 1976: 50–2).[26] These lamps were made in Athens during much of the third century (Rotroff 1997b: 500) with local copies continuing to be produced throughout the second century and possibly into the first century BC (Rosenthal-Heginbottom 1995: 236–7, Type 10).

Locus 3, to the east of wall 2, also consisted of narrow fills or soft ashy deposits and degenerate

---

25 From occupation levels 103.3, 104.2, 105.2: bowl **FW 103**; jars Type 3 **PW 296**, **PW 298**; jar Type 4A **PW 353**.

26 An Athenian lamp of this Type (CN 7391) was recovered from Plot XXVIIIB and a further non-Attic example (CN 7596) from plot XXXIVB (below).

[text continues on page 33]

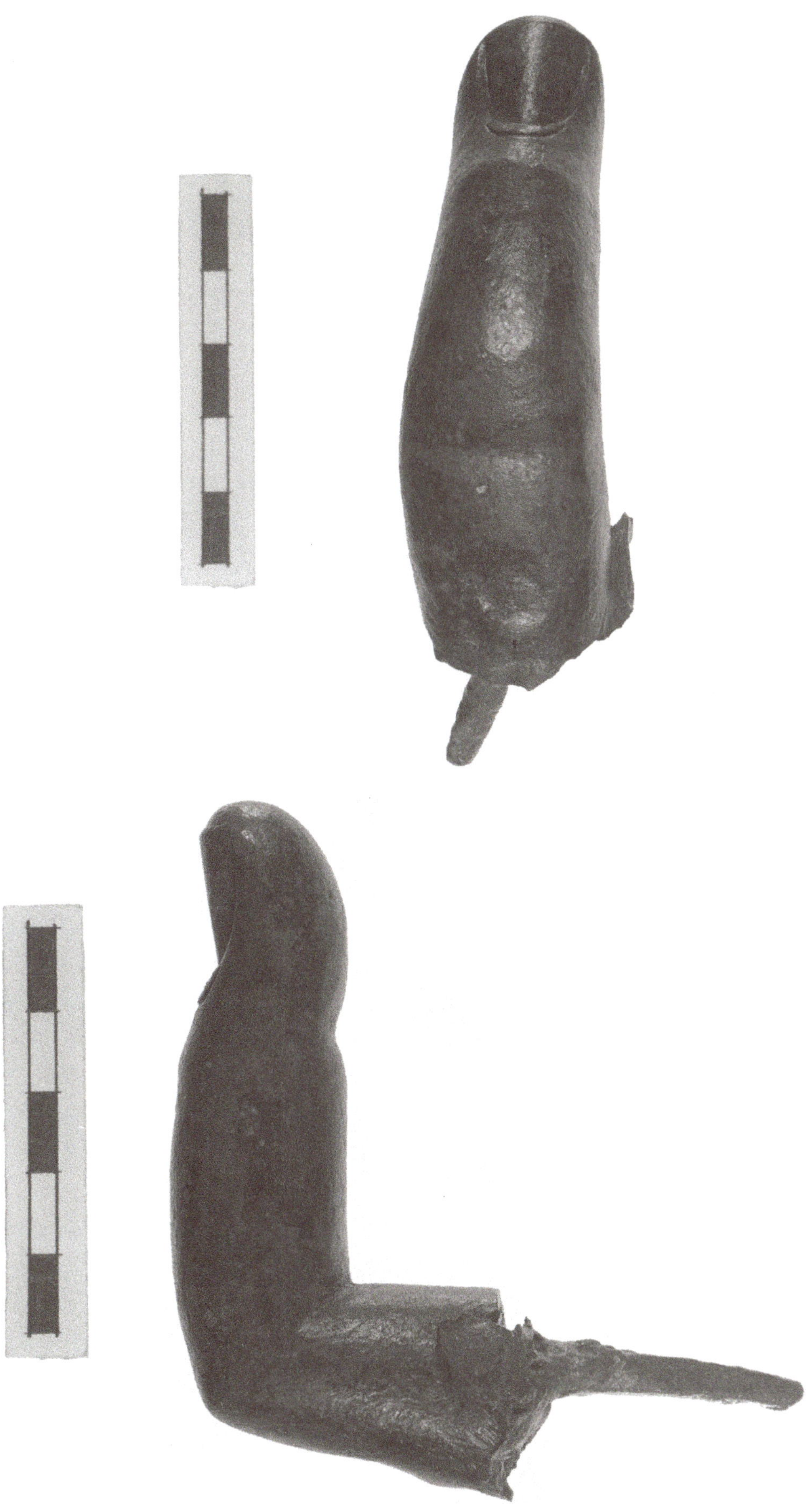

Figures 1.18–19. Plot XXIIIA. Bronze fragment (finger) from Jannaeus Destruction level.

Figure 1.20. Plot XXIIIA. Spear butt RN 110615 from Jannaeus Destruction level.

Figure 1.21. Plot XXIIIA. Locus 109. Walls 8 (west) and 4. South at top of image.

Figure 1.22. Plot XXIIIA. Locus 109. Wall 4. To east.

Figure 1.23. Plot XXIIIA. Locus 109. Crude hearth F2, south of scale. To north.

Figure 1.24. Plot XXIIIA. Locus 109. Thin occupation surface 100.6. East at top of image.

Figure 1.25. Plot XXIIIA. Locus 108. Wall 1 and wall 7. To east.

Figure 1.26. Plot XXIIIA. Locus 108. Wall 6 above oven F9. To south.

Figure 1.27. Plot XXIIIA. Loci 103, 104, 105. Mamluk-era pit (*upper left*). To south.

Figure 1.28. Plot XXIIIB. Pyramidal loom weight from Jannaeus Destruction level (1.4).

Figure 1.29. Plot XXIIIB. Wall 2 with bench F3 to its east. To north.

Figure 1.30. Plot XXIIIB. Bench F3 resting on plaster floor 3.7. To south.

mudbrick sealed by a plaster floor 3.7 – which proved continuous with the plaster floor 2.5 in locus 2 – and occupation surfaces 3.9, 3.14–16. A well-constructed clay oven, F4, was uncovered next to wall 2. It lay partially within the south baulk and was associated with occupation surface 3.15. Also abutting wall 2 on its north-east aspect was a low rubble bench (F3) resting on the plaster floor surface 3.7 (Figure 1.30). These loci immediately overlay Late Iron Age (eighth century BC) deposits.

Directly to the west of XXIIIA, a further plot – XXIIID – was opened to explore more of the Hellenistic structure partially revealed in XXIIIA and XXIIIB (Figures 1.31–33). As with these latter two plots, the Hellenistic levels were immediately below Late Roman, Byzantine and Ummayad strata.

As expected, the Hellenistic levels were sealed by the same thick Jannaeus Destruction level encountered in XXIIIA and XXIIIB. This was most marked in the southern sector of the trench where the thick ash layer and burnt mudbrick contained blackened pottery, charcoal and, in loci 70, 71 and 82, the well-preserved remains of a series of roof timbers (Figure 1.34). This last find recalls "the charcoal remains of timbers which had once supported the roof; in places traceable for a metre or more" uncovered by Funk and Richardson (1958: 90) in their 1958 sounding. Stamped Rhodian amphora handles, including those of the upper half of an amphora (CN 7758) and an almost complete example (CN 7794),[27] along with the latest coins recovered from the destruction, were once again consistent with this being the work of Alexander Jannaeus. From 19.5 was recovered a bronze of Antiochus XII Dionysus, RN 110973, and from 19.3 a further bronze coin RN 110668, attributed by our numismatist Ted Nixon to the same ruler. From 20.6 a worn bronze coin RN 110889 of Alexander Jannaeus of Type 5

---

27 CN 7824: HIPPOKRATES, fabricant active from Periods IIIb–Vb (c. 198–140); CN 7836: ARISTRATOS (uncertain reading), eponym belonging to Period Vb (c. 114); CN 7759: KALLON, fabricant active during Period V (second half of second century); CN 7758: TIMO 2nd, fabricant active in Periods IV–V (c. 160–108); CN 7794: (a) HESTIEIOS, eponym dated to Period Vc (c. 114), (b) D[IONY]SIOS 2nd, fabricant.

          [text continues on page 37]

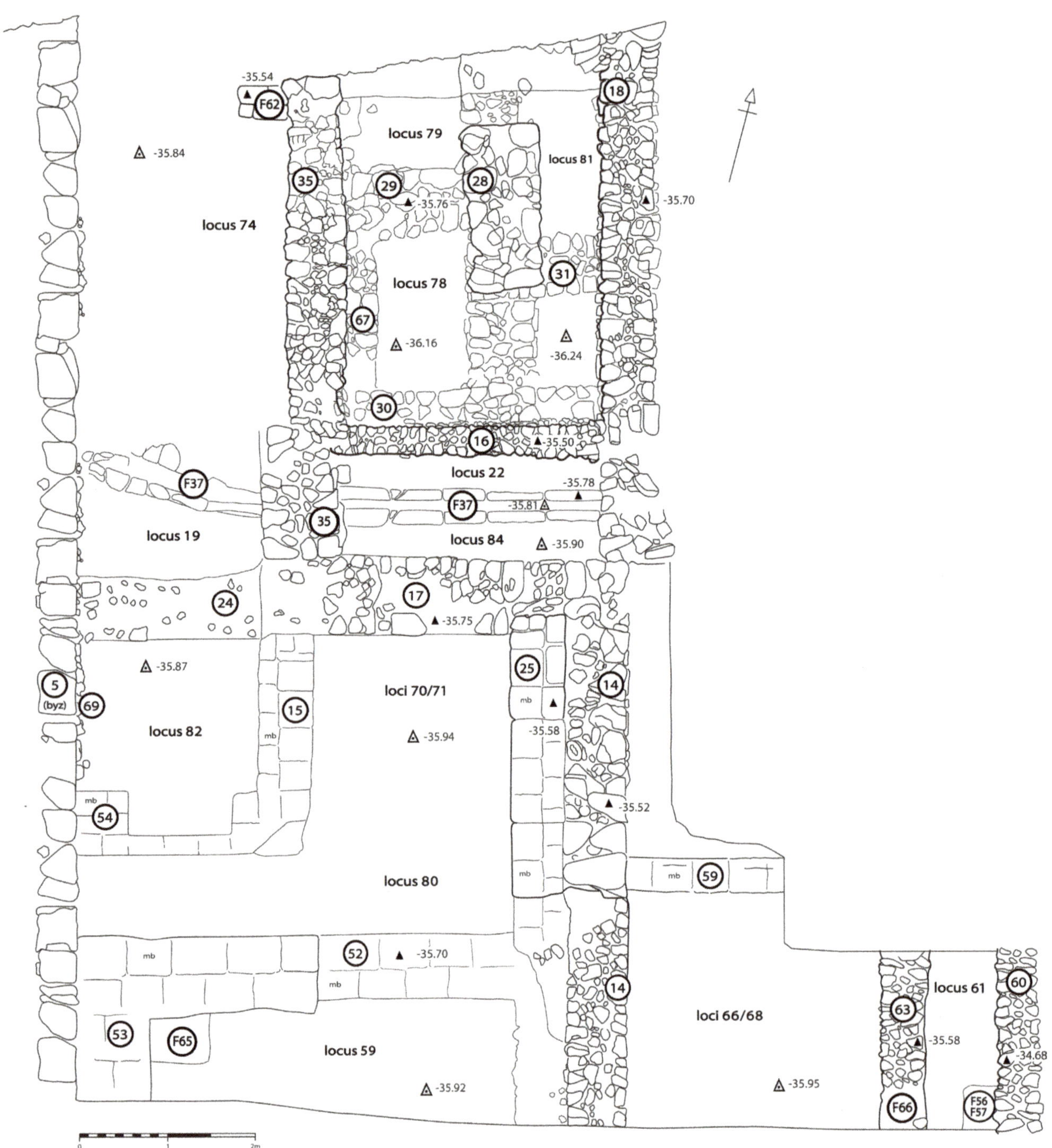

Figure 1.31. Plot XXIIID. Plan.

Figure 1.32. Plot XXIIID. Hellenistic levels. To north.

Figure 1.33. Plot XXIIID. Hellenistic levels. To south.

Figure 1.34. Plot XXIIID. Jannaeus Destruction level with burnt roof timbers (*top left*), south of drain F37.

Figure 1.35. Plot XXIIID. Hellenistic levels. Loci 70/71 and 82 (west of wall 15, *foreground*). To north.

(Meshorer 2001: Group L, subgroups L1–L6: that is, "Year 25" = 80/79 BC. See Meshorer 1982: 79–81, 2001: 39–40; Shachar 2004).[28] From the destruction level were also recovered numerous loom weights (both spherical and pyramidal) (Plate 6)[29], fragments of a stamped Coan amphora, a bronze spear tip, bronze tanged arrowhead (Plate 7), the flexed upper limb of a marble statuette (Plate 8), a seven-spouted star-shaped clay lamp (Plate 9) and fragment of a "box-shaped" clay lamp (Plate 10).[30] The seven-spouted star-shaped lamp CN 7863 and another very similar lamp P20311 recovered from a Hellenistic 3C context in plot IIIB/C (McNicoll and Hennessy 1980: 17–18, pl. XVII.4) appear to be the only examples of this type so far recorded from Transjordan.[31]

In the southern sector of the trench, four Hellenistic walls – each running north–south and forming at least two spacious rooms (locus 82 and loci 70/71) – were revealed (Figure 1.35). In the west baulk, underlying the impressive Byzantine wall 5, wall 69 (Figure 1.36) was barely visible. Further east, the mudbrick wall 15, on its rough stone footing and originally plastered on its eastern face, extended north–south before turning west to become wall 54 and abut wall 69 (Figure 1.37). On the top of wall 15 were two square post-holes into which, as shown by the base of a truss still within the most southerly of these holes (Figure 1.38), had been inserted vertical wooden trusses supporting the wooden ceiling (or upper floor?) whose burnt beams were uncovered in the destruction level. To the east of wall 15 was the further mudbrick wall 25, resting on a stone socle and with small traces of plaster still on its western face; this wall was constructed immediately to the west of the stone wall 14 (Figure 1.39). On the top of

wall 25 were two niches, plastered on their interior surfaces, that probably functioned as receptacles as suggested by the shattered Rhodian amphora (CN 7794) recovered from just below one of the niches (Plate 11). It is likely that wall 25 was constructed after wall 14, which is bonded to the east–west wall 17, while further west wall 24 continues on the same line as wall 17.

Further to the south, and separated by a narrow corridor (locus 80) from locus 82 and loci 70/71 was what appears to be a further spacious room (locus 59) bounded by the mudbrick wall 52 running east–west and joined by the partially revealed north–south mudbrick wall 53 before it enters the western baulk (Figure 1.40). Only the northern sector of the room has been cleared as its southern part lies within the south baulk as does a further shattered Rhodian amphora which currently remains in situ (Plate 12). Within the room was a well-constructed stone-lined storage bin F65 (Figure 1.41).

In the south-east corner of the plot, south of wall 59, the Jannaeus Destruction level (68.1–4) remained very thick, containing a large quantity of ash and animal bones and resting on the occupation surface 68.5. Below 68.5 a possible earlier phase (yet to be explored, so undated) was suggested by the upper courses of the north–south wall 63 with a doorway (F66) in its southern section blocked with a combination of rubble and mudbrick (Figures 1.42–43). In locus 61, within a thick-walled mudbrick bin F56 (Figure 1.44) and resting on a tamped earth floor (61.2) covered by heavy levels of ash seemingly separate from the higher destruction level, was a well-preserved clay kiln F57 (Plate 13; Figure 1.45). Numerous iron nails and bolts, as well as possible

---

28 My great thanks to Ted Nixon and also to Donald Ariel, previously Head Curator of the Coin Department at the Israel Antiquities Authority, for his very generous and learned assistance with this coin. See Sheedy et al. 2001: 77, nos 2.014, 2.015 for similar coins from Tell Husn.

29 For Hellenistic loom weights from Jebel Khalid in Syria, see Crewe 2002.

30 CN 7768: Coan amphora with stamp of NIKARCHOS (retrograde); RN 150409: bronze spear tip; RN 170001: bronze tanged arrowhead; RN 170398: marble statuette upper limb; CN 7863: seven-spouted lamp; CN 7861: "box-shaped" lamp. For CN 7863 compare lamps L167, 168 from Tel Anafa (Dobbins 2012: 150, fig. 5, pl. 9); lamp from Samaria (Crowfoot et al. 1957: 371, fig. 87.9); lamp Types 16A (compare CN 7861) and 16B (compare CN 7863) from Tel Dor (Rosenthal-Heginbottom 1995: 240–1, figs 5.18.7, 5.19.2). See Rosenthal-Heginbottom 2009, 2020/2021 for further discussion of the "box-shaped" and seven-spouted star-shaped lamps. The date range – from the second half of the second century to the beginning of the first century BC – is consistent with the context of CN 7863.

31 I thank Renate Rosenthal-Heginbottom (pers. com.) for her kind information about these lamps. See also Rosenthal-Heginbottom 2020/2021.

traces of iron slag, were recovered from the floor adjacent to the kiln, causing the excavator to raise the possibility of minor iron recycling (Plate 14). Wall 60, to its east, is certainly post-Hellenistic, although its date of construction is still to be ascertained.

Although not as thick, the Jannaeus Destruction level also extended to the north of the trench. Immediately below the destruction level, from which was recovered a bronze coin of Alexander Jannaeus, RN 110890 (mid–late 80s BC), were uncovered two limestone steps (F62) to the west of wall 35 (Figure 1.46) denoting a change of level between the north and south sectors of the "villa". To the east of wall 35 were the remains of a cobbled floor, 11.4–6 (Plate 15) – probably an exterior courtyard whose northern half had been dug away by a Late Roman pit – on the surface of which was unearthed the almost complete ESA plate **FW 204** (Plate 16). The southern boundary of the courtyard floor was the east–west wall 16, to the north of which was a layer of stone and clay packing (11.7, 11.9) immediately above decayed mudbrick (11.11–13) from which was recovered a bronze coin of Antiochus VII/Demetrius II, RN 110982 (138–125 BC). Below the decayed mudbrick was a further packing layer of large stones (11.18).[32] On its eastern side the courtyard was bounded by wall 18 bonded with wall 16.

The removal of this stone packing revealed the presence of an earlier Hellenistic phase (Figure 1.47) as shown by the thin tamped earth surface 24.1–3 continuing under wall 18. From this surface was recovered a worn bronze coin RN 111554 of Antiochus VII/Demetrius II (138–125 BC) with an uncatalogued ESA bowl (Hayes Form 22) also consistent with a date in the later second half of the second century BC for this occupation level.[33] Further to the west, beneath the cobbled floor 11.4–6, wall 28 runs parallel to the later wall 18 and is of similar construction with its southern end abutting the stone east–west wall 30. To the west of wall 28, further earlier Hellenistic levels were exposed, although the limited exposure meant that no diagnostic pottery was recovered from the tamped earth floors 35.1 and 36.1. Below this earlier Hellenistic phase, on both sides of wall 28, Iron Age

levels were associated with two further cross-walls 29 and 31, and the north–south wall 67.

South of wall 16 and to the north of the early wall 17, the poorly preserved remains of another cobbled floor (22.1) were covered by the destruction level and lay above the earlier Hellenistic phase. The east–west plaster-lined stone drain, F37 (Figures 1.34, 1.48–49), had seemingly gone out of use and was sealed beneath the floor, running across the trench and beneath the later phase wall 35 before disappearing into the western baulk. To the east, F37 continued into the eastern baulk, passing under two large ashlar blocks fallen from a later Islamic structure but yet to be removed.

In summary, XXIIID would appear to be part of the extensive Hellenistic "villa", also investigated in XXIIIA and XXIIIB, whose rooms were – at least in the latest phase – centred around a paved courtyard, the "fine stone floor" of Funk and Richardson. Below the latest (Jannaeus Destruction, Hellenistic 3C) phase were the remains of earlier Hellenistic walls, also seen in Plots XXIIIA and XXIIIB, as well as the east–west drain (F37) that was later covered over. The finds (which include ESA sherds throughout the phase) from this earlier, Pre-Jannaeus Destruction (Hellenistic 3B) phase would suggest a date in the second half of the second century BC.

Area XXVIII (University of Sydney)

Area XXVIII is situated in the south-west sector of the main mound. Below the Byzantine levels of plot XXVIIIB, substantial stratified Hellenistic deposits were encountered in loci 10, 11 and 13 (Figures 1.50–51). The structure associated with these deposits, only partially revealed, would seem to be part of a substantial domestic residence that had undergone alterations in its latest phase.

Locus 10 was bounded on its north and east sides by the foundation courses of the Byzantine walls 10 and 4. The rubble walls 13 (partially dismantled) and 11, part of the Hellenistic structure, formed the southern and western boundaries respectively of the locus. Within the locus (part of an interior room) lay an undisturbed series of tamped earth floors with

---

32 Pottery from levels 11.6–7, 11.9, 11.11–12 and 11.18 includes ESA Hayes Form 3 **FW 190**, uncatalogued ESA Hayes Form 22; uncatalogued jar Types 4A, 5A; uncatalogued plain ware Type 1 fishplates and plain ware Type 1 plates.

33 Also fishplate **FW 15**; cup **FW 136**; krater Type 1 **PW 159**; jars Type 4A **PW 332**, Type 4B **PW 370**; cooking pot Type 3 **PW 528**. Also uncatalogued pottery: Type 1 plate (black-gloss); ESA Hayes Form 22; Type 2 bowl (plain ware); Type 1 cooking pots.

Table 1.3. Area XXIII stratified deposits.

PLOT	NATURE OF DEPOSIT	DEPOSIT
XXIIIA (main mound)	**Hellenistic 3B** c. 140–c. 100 (?) BC Pre-Jannaeus Destruction: Occupation deposit Occupation surfaces (a) tamped earth (b) stone packing (c) plaster Sub-surface fill	108.2 109.4 109.3 108.3, 109.1–2 108.4–6
XXIIIA (main mound)	**Hellenistic 3C** c. 100 (?)– c. 80/79 BC Latest use: Occupation surfaces (a) tamped earth (b) plaster (c) cobblestone Jannaeus Destruction	100.6, 103.3–4, 104.2–3, 105.2–3 10.8, 11.3, 13.3, 100.2, 108.1 22.10–11 10.5, 10.7, 10.11, 11.1–2, 19.23, 20.4 22.2–9, 71.2, 71.4–5, 72.5, 72.9, 74.2, 75.2, 77.2, 78.1, 83.4–5, 84.1–2, 84.4, 85.1–3, 87.2–4, 100.1–5, 101.1–2, 102.1, 103.1–2, 104.1, 105.1, 106.1, 107.1
XXIIIB (main mound)	**Hellenistic 3B** c. 140–c. 100 (?) BC Pre-Jannaeus Destruction: Occupation deposits Occupation surfaces (a) tamped earth (b) plaster	2.1–4, 2.6, 2.8–12, 2.14 3.1–2, 3.6, 3.10–3 2.2, 3.9, 3.14–6 2.5, 2.7, 2.13, 3.7
XXIIIB (main mound)	**Hellenistic 3C** c. 100 (?)–c. 80/79 BC Jannaeus Destruction	1.1–5
XXIIID (main mound)	**Hellenistic 3B** c. 140–c. 100 (?) BC Pre-Jannaeus Destruction: Sub-floor packing Occupation surfaces tamped earth	11.7, 11.9, 11.11–3, 11.16, 11.18, 23.1, 32.2, 33.1 24.1–3, 35.1, 36.1
XXIIID (main mound)	**Hellenistic 3C** c.100 (?)–c.80/79 BC Latest use: Occupation surfaces (a) tamped earth (b) cobbled	61.2, 68.5, 69.1, 70.2, 71.2, 74.3, 83.2, 22.1, 11.4–6
XXIIID (main mound)	**Hellenistic 3C** c. 100 (?)–c. 80/79 BC Jannaeus Destruction	11.10, 16.3, 17.1, 18.1–9, 19.1–6, 20.1–10, 21.1, 29.15–25, 30.1–2, 31.1–3, 32.1, 43.1–2, 44.1–2, 45.2–4, 59.3, 62.2, 63.2–3, 67.1, 68.1–4, 74.2, 75.1, 76.1, 77.2, 80.1, 82.1–2, 83.1

occupation levels (10.1–4, 10.6, 10.9–10) and subfloor fills (10.5, 10.7). Walls 11 and 13 were constructed directly on the floor 10.4/10.9. From the floor 10.6 was recovered the Athenian lamp (CN 7391, Figure 1.52) belonging to Howland's Type 29B (Scheibler's Form FSL 2) produced in that city during the second and third quarters of the third century BC (Howland 1958: 96–7; Rotroff 1997b: 500; Scheibler 1976: 51–2, 191).[34] Locus 5, to the south of wall 13, was also part of the structure although its floor and occupation levels had been cleared by later construction.

To the west of locus 10, and separated from it by wall 11, lay locus 11 bounded to the north and west by the Byzantine walls 10 and 9. Its southern sector had been destroyed by later Byzantine construction. Very few Hellenistic deposits were recovered from this locus with the exception of a levelling fill (11.1–4) below a very degenerate tamped earth floor (11.5).

Below the Hellenistic walls 11 and 13 was a further Hellenistic phase – the courtyard locus 13 – now bounded by the Byzantine walls 10 (north), 4 (east) and 9 (west) with its southern extent limited by a later erosion gully. The upper levels of this locus (13.1–10) consisted of a thick layer of mudbrick used as a fill to support the later Hellenistic structures mentioned above. Below was a thin grey occupation level (13.11–13) containing abundant ash, animal bones and a fragmentary clay oven F1 (Figure 1.53) above the floor itself (13.14–15), with levels 13.16–17 representing earthen packing below the floor.

It is noteworthy that, of all those trenches sunk on the main mound reaching in situ Hellenistic levels, only XXVIIIB has revealed no trace of those thick destruction levels associated with the sack of Alexander Jannaeus. The recovery of lamp CN 7391, along with the presence of mould-made bowls **FW 297, 300–1** but absence of any ESA fragments, shows that the structure had gone out of use well before the Jannaeus sack.[35]

Area XXXII (University of Sydney)

Area XXXII is on the crest of the southern slope of the main mound, just to the west of Area III. Of note here is plot XXXIIY, commenced in 2001 to investigate further the impressive Bronze Age temple first revealed in 1995 (Bourke 2005, 2014). From deposits 1.2, 1.6, 2.1–2, 2.5 and 4.3 were recovered Hellenistic ceramic fragments of black-gloss bowls, fishplates and other fine wares of high quality along with a number of table amphorae, jars and other plain wares.

Table 1.4. Area XXVIII stratified deposits.

PLOT	NATURE OF DEPOSIT	DEPOSIT
XXVIIIB (main mound)	**Hellenistic 3A** c. 200–c. 140 BC Pre-Jannaeus Destruction: Occupation surfaces	
	tamped earth	10.2, 10.4, 10.6, 10.9, 11.5, 13.14–5
	Occupation levels	10.1, 10.3, 10.10, 13.11–3
	Sub-floor fill/packing	10.5, 10.7, 11.1–4, 13.16–7
	Mudbrick collapse	13.1–10

Table 1.5. Area XXXII stratified deposits.

PLOT	NATURE OF DEPOSIT	DEPOSIT
XXXIIY (main mound)	**Hellenistic 3A** c. 200–c. 140 BC Pre-Jannaeus Destruction: Wash or clearance deposit	1.2, 1.6, 2.1–2, 2.5, 4.3

---

34 As noted, non-Attic examples of this type were recovered from plots XXIIIB and XXXIVB.

35 For the earliest mould-made bowls c. 200 BC see Rotroff 2005, 2006a. For the beginnings of ESA production and its possible arrival in the southern Levant some ten to twenty years later, see Berlin 2006: 13–14; Berlin et al. 2014.

[text continues on page 50]

Figure 1.36. Plot XXIIID. Wall 69 (supporting base of scale) beneath Byzantine wall 5. To west.

Figure 1.37. Plot XXIIID. Western sector, south of drain F37. Top of wall 52 and walls 15, 54 (*foreground*). To north.

Figure 1.38. Plot XXIIID. Wall 15 with remains of burnt wooden truss (*bottom*).

Figure 1.39. Plot XXIIID. Eastern sector, south of drain F37. Walls 25 (mudbrick), 14 (stone) and east–west wall 17 (rubble). To north.

Figure 1.40. Plot XXIIID. Southern sector. Walls 52 and 53 with storage bin F65 in the south-west corner. Walls 15 and 54 further north. Wall 14 (*foreground*, beneath scale). To west.

Figure 1.41. Plot XXIIID. Storage bin F65 (to east of scale), south of wall 52.

Figure 1.42. Plot XXIIID. South-east sector, locus 68. Wall 63 with doorway F66 (*foreground*) and later Roman wall 60 (*background*).

Figure 1.43. Plot XXIIID. Southern sector. Walls 52, 54 and loci 80 and 59 (*foreground*). To east.

Figure 1.44. Plot XXIIID. South-east sector. Mudbrick bin F56.

Figure 1.45. Plot XXIIID. South-east sector. Kiln F57 at central top of image.

Figure 1.46. Plot XXIIID. Limestone steps (F62), west of wall 35.

Figure 1.47. Plot XXIIID. Earlier Hellenistic phase (walls 28, 30) and pre-Hellenistic phases (walls 29, 31, 67) below cobbled courtyard 11.4–6. Later Hellenistic wall 18 supporting scale.

Figure 1.48. Plot XXIIID. Plaster-lined stone drain F37 between walls 16 and 17, passing underneath wall 35. To west.

Figure 1.49. Plot XXIIID. Plaster-lined stone drain F37. To east.

Figure 1.50. Plot XXVIIIB. Byzantine walls 10 (*immediate foreground*), 4 (upper left corner). Locus 10 (*foreground*, with scale) separated by north–south wall 11 from locus 11 to west. Locus 5 to the south of wall 13 and locus 10. To south.

Figure 1.51. Plot XXVIIIB. Partially revealed locus 13 (supporting scale) with fragmentary oven F1 (*foreground*) before removal of walls 11 and 13. To south-east.

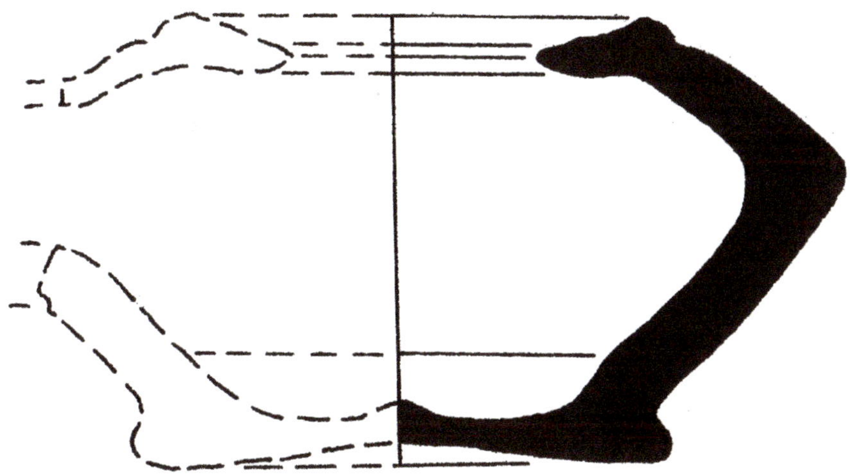

Figure 1.52. Plot XXVIIIB. Athenian lamp CN 7391. H.03.

Figure 1.53. Plot XXVIIIB. Courtyard locus 13 with oven F1. To west.

Although not associated with any architectural remains, these deposits lay within a discrete and easily identifiable yellow layer, most likely originating from unexcavated areas further to the north (now underlying a later Muslim cemetery left undisturbed) either as a wash level or as a result of later, deliberate clearance.

The later of the two stamped Rhodian amphora handles (CN 7867, CN 7868), along with the absence of ESA commonly encountered in later Hellenistic levels at Pella, points to a date for the deposit early in the second half of the second century BC.[36]

THE WADI JIRM AL-MOZ
Area IX (College of Wooster)

Soundings in the Civic Complex (Area IX) undertaken by the Wooster expedition have found traces of architectural remains associated with Hellenistic pottery seemingly contemporary with that from the Late Hellenistic stratum in Area VIII (Smith and Day 1989: 2–3, 97).[37] The architectural remains comprise only small sections of walls, modest in size and construction, differing in their orientation from the subsequent major Roman and Byzantine wall alignments; currently the function of these Hellenistic structures remains unknown. The presence of the later Roman-Byzantine-Ummayad remains, as well as the previously high watertable and large amount of residual silt in the wadi, has made further exposure of these early walls very challenging (Smith and McNicoll 1992: 120).

From soundings 8 and 9 was recovered a small assemblage of Early Roman pottery (Smith and Day 1989: 97–100, pls 43–5), many of whose forms find close parallels with those from the Early Roman levels discussed below.[38]

TELL HUSN
Area XI (University of Sydney)

Limited investigations on the upper north-east slope of Tell Husn (Plate 17) in plot XIA/B (Hennessy et al. 1983: 348; McNicoll et al. 1986: 175) have uncovered short lengths of two walls (walls 1 and 2) forming an approximate right angle. Both were between 1.2 m and 1.5 m in thickness and constructed of rubble bound by mud mortar except for the external (north) face of the east–west wall 1 that consisted of well-cut ashlar isodomic blocks with occasional headers on a rubble base and bound by lime mortar (Figure 1.54). In contrast to its outer face, the inner face of wall 1 was of much rougher masonry set in a clay mortar, and so would have been largely concealed by the steep slope of Husn rising to the south. On the south (upslope) side of wall 1 a small section of a further wall (wall 2) was uncovered running into the southern baulk and, abutting on its east, part of a thick wall or, more likely, the lower section of a platform (F1) which may have supported a further storey. In view of its position high on the north-east slope of the *tell* it is certainly possible that the structure formed part of a projecting tower.

The only floor isolated (2.2) consisted of tamped earth over a packing of small stones, with the floor eroded away in its northern section due to the steep slope of Husn. In a shallow pit were recovered the complete jar **PW 465** and amphoriskos **PW 236** (Figure 1.55), both of Early Roman date, as well as a coin of Augustus minted at Ephesus (Carson 2001, CN 3.001). Further material also belonging within the late first century BC and first century AD – including fragments of knife-pared ("Herodian") lamps CN 3003 (Figure 1.56), CN 6606–6608, CN 6841, and chalkstone vessels CN 2668, CN 2987 (Figure 1.57) – was recovered from occupation debris (1.1–4; 2.1, 2.3; 4.3–6; 20.4, 20.6–7) along with a small number (four in all) of second century AD forms of ESA (**FW 241–2, FW 244–5**) from the undisturbed

---

36 Amphora handle CN 7867: (a) combined eponym-fabricant stamp of the eponym SIM[ULINOS] active in Period IIb (c. 220–210), (b) fabricant EPIGO[NOS] first active over the period c. 230–205; CN 7868: ALEXIADAS eponym belonging to Period Va (c. 145–c. 133).

37 Only a small sample of the Hellenistic pottery from the Wooster excavations in Areas VIII and IX has been published so far (McNicoll et al. 1982: pls 130–2; Smith and Day 1989: 97).

38 No reliable stratigraphy was obtained from these deep soundings in the Civic Complex (Area IX).

occupation level 20.5 and unstratified levels.[39] All these strata were sealed by Byzantine wash layers.

The exact nature of these walls, as well as a short stretch of wall (wall 7; Figure 1.58), revealed in a small sondage (XXXIVT) on the south of the *tell* (Watson and Tidmarsh 1996: 311–13), is yet to be clarified although it is likely that the walls formed part of the fortifications of Tell Husn at the very end of the Hellenistic period and during much of the subsequent Early Roman phase (Early Roman 1–2). The recovery of a "year 25" *prutah* of Alexander Jannaeus, similar to that found in the destruction level of XXIIID (above), from the foundation trench (1.5) of wall 1, along with jar Types 6B (**PW 434**, long-collared rim; prominent lower edge) and 7B (**PW 479**, neck ridge; overhanging lip) is consistent with a strengthening of Husn's defences not long after the Jannaeus conquest.[40]

Area XXXIV (University of Sydney)

Extensive excavations on the summit of Tell Husn have revealed the impressive remains of a Late Byzantine cavalry barracks as well as a number of Byzantine domestic complexes (Watson and Tidmarsh 1996). In some areas the Byzantine levels overlaid substantial Early and Middle Bronze Age architecture and deposits (Bourke 2015/2016; Bourke et al. 1999) while in other areas they were immediately above Early Roman and Hellenistic structures. Material

from these latter periods was recovered from plots XXXIVB, F and G.

In contrast to the situation encountered on the main mound in Areas III, IV, VIII and XXIII, none of the Hellenistic strata on Tell Husn demonstrates signs of a Jannaeus Destruction level whereas there exists evidence for third century BC occupation, demonstrated by stamped Rhodian amphora handles, coins and lamps. Plot XXXIVB lies in the south-west quadrant of Husn. The first two seasons of excavation saw the removal of the Byzantine levels (essentially loci 1–4) with the plot more or less divided in half by the Byzantine north–south wall 1 (Figure 1.59). Of interest here is the late fourth or early third century BC Attic lamp CN 7129 (Figure 1.60) of Howland Type 25 A or B Prime (Howland 1958: 67–82; Rotroff 1997b: 494–7) recovered out of context from within these levels.

Area XXXIVB (West)

To the west of the Byzantine wall 1 (possibly supported by the lower courses of an earlier but as yet undated wall) and lying directly underneath Byzantine deposits, the latest phase consists of the partially uncovered remains of two more-or-less contemporary dwellings separated by a narrow lane (locus 5) – running north–south and then turning to the west – bounded by walls (6, 9, 12, 13, 14) of unworked fieldstones bonded with mud mortar

Table 1.6. Tell Husn. Area XI stratified deposits.

PLOT	NATURE OF DEPOSIT	DEPOSIT
XIA/B	**Early Roman 1** 63 BC–late first century AD	
	Occupation surface	
	(a) tamped earth/stone packing	2.2
	Occupation debris	1.1–4, 2.1, 2.3, 4.3–6, 20.4, 20.6–7
	Wall 1	Foundation trench = 1.5
	Early Roman 2 Late first century–c. 135 AD	
	Occupation	20.5

---

39 From 20.5: ESA Hayes Forms 59 **FW 244**, 60B **FW 245**; juglet Type 4 **PW 222**; Type 7A jars **PW 446**, **PW 452**, **PW 454**; Type 1 cooking pot **PW 518**. From Mixed Contexts: ESA Hayes Form 54 **FW 241–2**.

40 Sheedy et al. 2001: no. 2.014. It is likely that this strengthening took place shortly after Pompey's incorporation of Coele-Syria into the Roman Empire, during the governorship of Aulus Gabinius (Josephus, *Ant. Jud.* XIV.74–6, 87–8; *BJ* I.155–7). See Hillard 1992: 42–5 for the rebuilding program of Gabinius in 57–54 BC.

(Figures 1.61–63). Strata 5.10–48 represent the use levels (heavily disturbed by Byzantine construction) associated with the laneway which, from the mixed pottery assemblage recovered from those levels, functioned as such from the later second century BC through to Early Roman (first century AD) times.[41]

Locus 12, bounded by walls 12 and 13, constitutes part of a room (room 1), with the tamped earth floor 12.2, belonging to a dwelling to the north-west of the lane. Very little pottery was recovered from this locus but **PW 617**, a fragment of a cooking pot Type 8 (thickened lip) from the foundation trench (12.3) of wall 13 indicates an Early Roman date for at least the latest phase of the room.

A second dwelling of at least two rooms (rooms 2, 3 = loci 6, 7) lay to the east of the lane (locus 5). Locus 6, to the south of the east–west wall 10, represented the larger room 2 with its associated tamped earth surface 6.27 while room 3 (locus 7) to the north was only partially revealed. The pottery from room 2 is consistent with an Early Roman date as was that from the tamped earth floor (7.17) of room 3.[42] Locus 10, to the south of wall 6, remains to be investigated with the upper course of a curving stone-lined drain (F25), possibly belonging to the earlier phase mentioned below and passing under the aforementioned wall 6, now visible (Figure 1.64).

Below this structure, a sounding within the area bounded by the later walls 9 and 10 revealed an earlier phase (Figure 1.65). The orientation of walls 18, 19, 20, 21 – associated with this phase – was on a different alignment from that of the later-phase walls though their construction (of unworked fieldstones) was similar. The southern parts of three probable rooms (rooms 1, 2, 3 = loci 15, 16, 17) were revealed with locus 13, a probable laneway, further to the south. Walls 18 and 21 formed the corner of locus 15 which lay largely within the south and west baulks.

Table 1.7. Tell Husn. Area XXXIV stratified deposits (XXXIVB west).

NATURE OF DEPOSIT	DEPOSIT
Early Roman 1 (later phase) 63 BC–late first century AD	
Occupation surfaces	
tamped earth	6.27, 7.17, 12.2
Wall 9	Foundation trench = 6.42
Wall 12	Foundation trench = 6.48
Wall 13	Foundation trench = 12.3
Hellenistic 3B/3C c. 140–c. 80/79 BC	
Floors	13.11, 15.1–2, 16.2
Occupation deposits	13.7, 13.9, 17.1, 18.3
Wall 20/21 rubble packing	16.4
Pits	18.5, 18.7–11
Wall 20	Foundation trench = 13.5–6, 17.2
Wall 18	Foundation trench = 18.1–2

41 From 5.10–48: mould-made bowl fragments, for example, **FW 281–2**, **FW 286**; uncatalogued ESA forms (Hayes Forms 4B, 22A); jar Type 4C **PW 381**; jug Type 5 **PW 209**; cooking pots Types 1, 3–5, for example, **PW 502**, **PW 508**, **PW 546**, **PW 575**; knife-pared "Herodian" lamp (CN 7340); uncatalogued jars (Types 4–6); uncatalogued grey ware lamp fragments. From 5.10 also a Hasmonean coin of uncertain attribution but probably of Alexander Jannaeus (Sheedy et al. 2001: 79, no. 2.018).

42 From 6.27: uncatalogued jars Type 5; Type 6B jars **PW 416–8**; cooking pots Type 1 **PW 503**, Type 2 **PW 520**, **PW 576** and uncatalogued cooking pots Type 5; cooking pot Type 8 **PW 618**; casserole Type 2 **PW 638**. From the wall 9 foundation trench 6.48: jug Type 5 **PW 203**; casserole Type 1 **PW 627**. From 7.17: jar Type 7A **PW 441**; casserole Type 1 **PW 628**. Also from 6.48, a bronze *prutah* of Alexander Jannaeus RN 16040.

Originally, room 2 (locus 16) had been entered by a doorway in its south-east corner before this was filled in by the addition of rubble packing (16.4) and buttressing (F4) to the south face of wall 20 to bring it into the same alignment as wall 21. At much the same time, wall 19 was built against the north face of wall 20; most of this former wall was, however, removed during later Byzantine building activity. Within this room was a series of poorly preserved plaster floors (16.2) from which two jars of Type 7B (neck ridge; overhanging lip: **PW 463** and a further uncatalogued example), as well as the ointment pot **PW 694** were unearthed. No diagnostic pottery was recovered from room 1 with the occupation debris (17.1) in room 3 including uncatalogued fragments of a Hellenistic grey ware lamp, a Type 1 cookpot rim and three plain ware Type 7 ("echinus") bowls. To the south of walls 20 and 21 in room 4, traces of a thin plaster floor (13.11) were uncovered. Immediately above 13.11 the occupation debris (13.7, 13.9) consisted of uncatalogued fragments of black-gloss out-turned rim bowls (Type 1), mould-made bowls, ESA body sherds, cooking pots with simple rims (Type 1) and jars with short-collared rims (Type 4A). This admittedly meagre ceramic assemblage, with its ESA but, with the exception of **PW 463**, lacking late forms of jars and cooking pots seen in the later phase above, suggests that this earlier dwelling was in use from the later second century BC until at least the time of the Jannaeus conquest (Hellenistic 3B/3C).

Area XXXIVB (East)

To the east and south of the Byzantine walls 1 and 31, XXXIVB was further divided by the north–south wall 33 whose upper courses appear to have been reinforced in Byzantine times (Figure 1.66). Once below the disturbed strata on both sides of this latter wall, a thin Early Roman stratum (Figure 1.67) lay above a more substantial Hellenistic deposit. To the west of wall 33 the Early Roman levels (25.4–7)

were associated with the upper courses (latest phase) of wall 30 to the south, consistent with the Type 5 (bevelled rim) cooking pot **PW 584** and fragment of a Type 6A (long-collared rim; uniform thickness) jar and a knife-pared ("Herodian") lamp nozzle (both uncatalogued) from within this phase.[43] No further walls of this probable simple dwelling were revealed in the northern or western sectors of the plot. The paved stylobate (Plate 18) partly above and to the south of walls 30 and 35, which were utilised to support it, clearly belongs to the period of Byzantine construction although the column base resting on the stylobate, not in situ, is certainly earlier.[44]

Directly below the Early Roman phase west of wall 33 were the Hellenistic levels. A thin, fine ashy layer (28.1–2, 29.1–4) was contained within walls 30 (earlier phase), 32 and 36, representing part of the courtyard of a simple dwelling.[45] Level 29.5 was a tamped earth surface, embedded in which were cooking-pot fragments **PW 501** (Type 1, simple rim) and **PW 540** (Type 3, ledge rim).

Below the surface 29.5 were further Hellenistic levels (29.9–10; 30.1–10) contained within the aforementioned walls, as well as wall 38 lying underneath wall 33 and clearly visible from its east. The foundation trench was defined for wall 36 (29.6) from which was retrieved lamp CN 7596 (Figure 1.68) – a non-Attic version of the Athenian lamp Howland 29A (Scheibler Form FSL 1) produced in that city during the third century (Rotroff 1997b: 500, with Howland's and Scheibler's dates) but copied elsewhere well into the second century BC and perhaps later (Rosenthal-Heginbottom 1995: 236–7)[46] – and jar **PW 306** (Type 4A, short neck; short-collared square rim). Further foundation trenches (Figure 1.69) were defined for wall 32 (29.7), and the earlier phase of wall 30 (29.8).[47]

No further surface was isolated but the fragmentary lowest course of a short remaining segment of the plastered rough mudbrick wall 39

---

43 From 25.6: jars Type 6B **PW 412**, Type 7A **PW 440**.

44 Compare, for example, the Ionic bases from the Herodian peristyle at Machaerus (Vörös 2013: 295–318).

45 From 28.2: saucers **FW 52**, **PW 91–2**; Rhodian amphora rim fragments **PW 240**, **PW 243**; jars Type 3 **PW 303**, Type 4B **PW 367**; pithos **PW 487**. From 29.1–4: saucer **PW 93**; jars Type 2B **PW 269**, Type 4A **PW 305**, Type 4B **PW 364**; transport amphora **PW 253**; cooking pot Type 1 (uncatalogued).

46 As noted, an Attic lamp of Howland Type 29 (CN 7391) was recovered from plot XXVIIIB; a non-Attic lamp (CN 7392) of similar Type was recovered from plot XXIIIB.

47 From 29.7: jars Type 4B **PW 369**, Type 4A (uncatalogued). From 29.8: jar Type 4B **PW 366** and a further non-catalogued Type 4B jar fragment.

[text continues on page 60]

Figure 1.54. Plot XIA/B. North face of wall 1. To south.

Figure 1.55. Plot XIA/B. Jar **PW 465** and amphoriskos **PW 236** in situ.

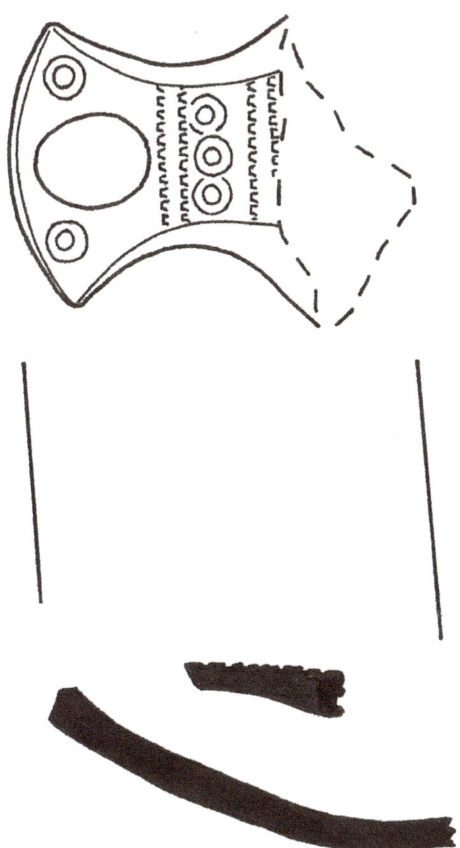

Figure 1.56. Plot XIA/B. "Herodian" lamp CN 3003. PL.04.

Figure 1.57. Plot XIA/B. Chalkstone *qalal* CN 2987. PH.15. (For the *qalal* (sometimes *kalal*) see Geva 2010b: 167, pls. 5.7–5.9; Magen 1994: 249–52.)

Figure 1.58. Plot XXXIVT. Wall 7 (with scale). To north-east.

Figure 1.59. Plot XXXIVB (west). Byzantine wall 1 (*rear*). Walls 6, 9, 10 (*foreground*). To east.

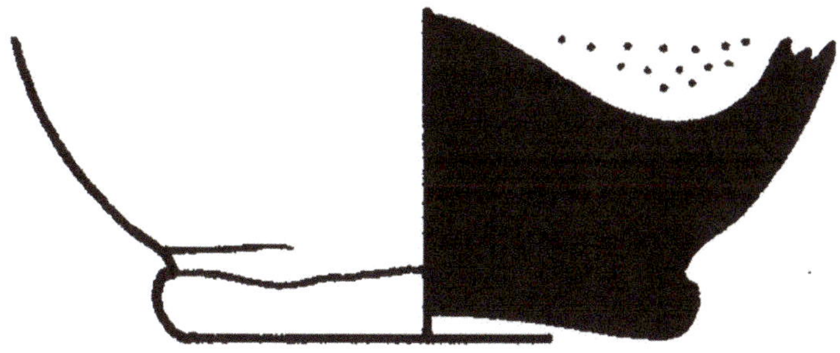

Figure 1.60. Plot XXXIVB (west). Athenian lamp CN 7129. PH.02.

Figure 1.61. Plot XXXIVB (west). Laneway (locus 5) with wall 12 (*foreground*) and walls 6, 9 and 10. To east.

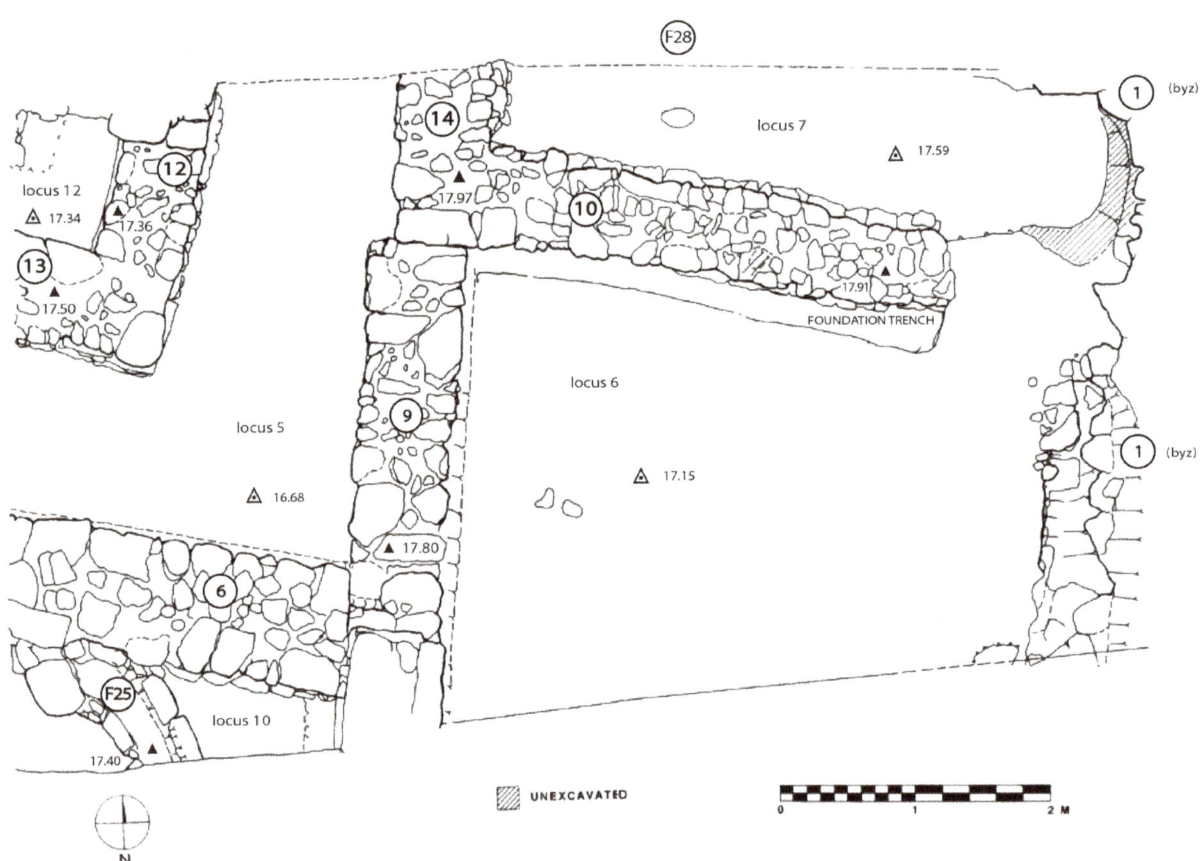

Figure 1.62. Plot XXXIVB (west). Early Roman phase. Plan.

Figure 1.63. Plot XXXIVB (west). Drain F25 passing into south baulk. To south.

Figure 1.64. Plot XXXIVB (west). Drain F25 passing under wall 6. To north.

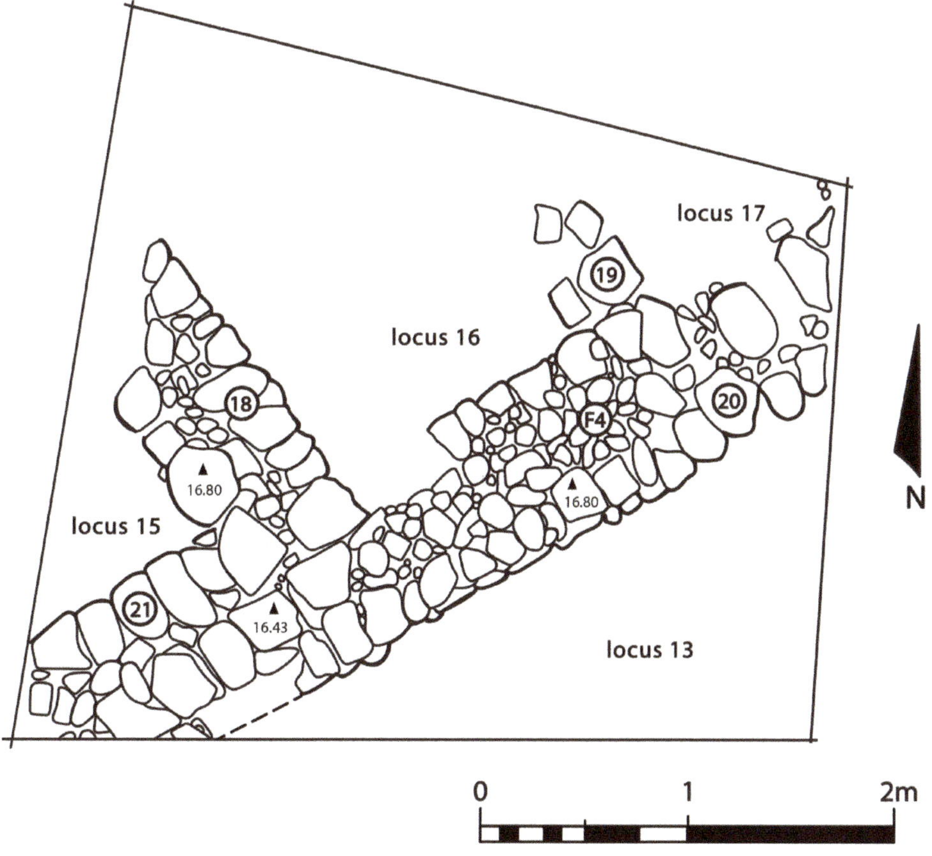

Figure 1.65. Plot XXXIVB (west). Hellenistic IIIB/C phase. Plan.

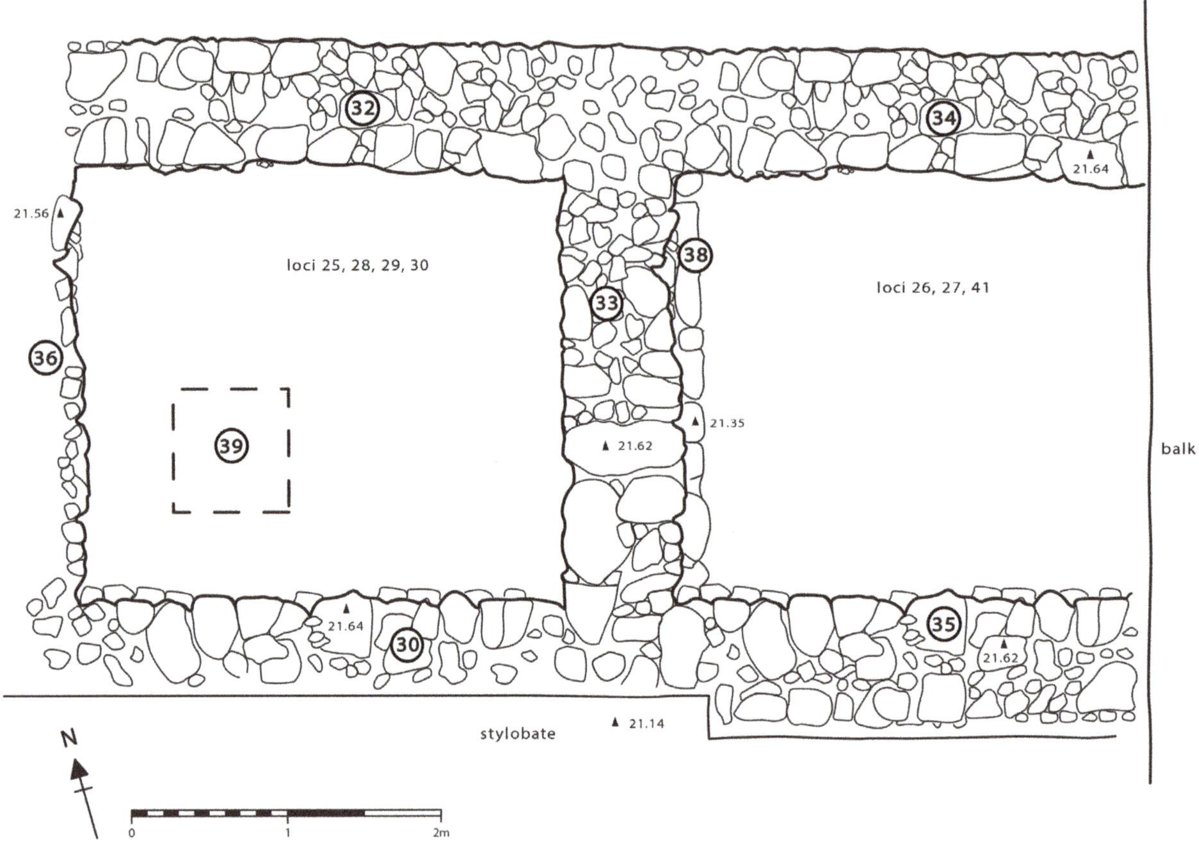

Figure 1.66. Plot XXXIVB (east). Plan.

(Figure 1.70) was clearly related to these levels, as demonstrated by a small number of jar and bowl fragments embedded within the wall and recovered on its removal (as 30.5). Underneath these Hellenistic levels was a thin mixed stratum containing scanty Early Bronze Age and Hellenistic sherds; this, in turn, lay directly on bedrock (Figure 1.71). The abundance of Type 4A (short neck; short-collared square rim) and 4B jars (short neck; short-collared triangular rim), along with the presence of ESA body sherds, suggests a date for these levels in the second half of the second century and early years of the first century BC (Hellenistic 3B/3C).

To the east of wall 33, the Early Roman levels (26.1–2, 27.1–7) consisted of occupation debris lying directly above 27.7: the remains of a thin, and almost completely destroyed, plaster floor (Figure 1.72) that was associated with wall 38 to the west, to the north with the east–west wall 34 and, to the south, with wall 35. These walls were constructed from well-worked fieldstones, with only their lower courses still in situ. No foundation trench was isolated although the walls did not continue into the Hellenistic levels. The ceramic assemblage from these Early Roman levels was typical,[48] comprising mainly cooking pot Types 4–5, 8, cooking bowl Types 1–3 and jar with ridged neck Types 6B, 7A, 7B along with ESA Hayes Forms 24, 28 and 47, and knife-pared ("Herodian") lamps (Plate 19).[49]

Below the floor 27.7 was a series of fill levels (27.8–15) whose latest pottery, though mixed with Hellenistic and occasional Early Bronze Age

---

48 Cooking pots: Type 4 with concave rim; Type 5 with bevelled rim; Type 8 with thickened lip. Cooking bowls: Type 1 with narrow ledge rim; Type 2 with angled broad rim; Type 3 ("Galilean" bowl). Jars: Type 6B with long-collared rim, prominent lower edge; Type 7 with ridged neck (7A: simple lip; 7B: overhanging lip). ESA Hayes Forms 24 (mould-made bowl), 28 (small plate with grooved everted wall), 47 (cup with moulded rim).

49 From 26.1–2, 27.1–7: ESA Hayes Forms 24, 28, 47 (**FW 229, FW 232, FW 239**); jar Types 6B, 7A, 7B (**PW 411, PW 438–9, PW 462**); cooking pot Types 4–5, 8 (for example, **PW 563–7, PW 578, PW 612**); cooking bowl (pan) Types 1–3 (for example, **PW 647, PW 652, PW 655**); knife-pared ("Herodian") lamps (CN 7563, 7592, 7605).

     [text continues on page 64]

Figure 1.67. Plot XXXIVB (east). Early Roman stratum east of wall 33. To west.

Figure 1.68. Plot XXXIVB (east). Hellenistic lamp CN 7596. H.03.

Figure 1.69. Plot XXXIVB (east). Foundation trenches for walls 32 (north) and 30 (south).

Figure 1.70. Plot XXXIVB (east). Fragmentary wall 39 (supporting scale). North at top of image.

Figure 1.71. Plot XXXIVB (east). West of wall 33. After removal of Hellenistic levels.

Figure 1.72. Plot XXXIVB (east). East of wall 33. Early Roman levels (occupation debris). To south.

Table 1.8. Tell Husn. Area XXXIV stratified deposits (XXXIVB east).

NATURE OF DEPOSIT	DEPOSIT
Early Roman 1 63 BC–late first century AD	
Occupation levels	25.4–7, 26.1–2, 27.1–6
Plaster floor	27.7
Hellenistic 2B c. 220–c. 200 BC	
"Antiochus Destruction" level	27.16–30, 41.2
Hellenistic 3B/3C c. 140–c. 80/79 BC	
(West of Wall 33) Occupation levels	28.1–2, 29.1–4
(West of Wall 33) Tamped earth floor	29.5
(West of Wall 33) Subsurface levels	29.9–10, 30.1–4, 30.6–10
(West of Wall 33) Wall 39	30.5
(West of Wall 33) Wall 36	Foundation trench = 29.6
(West of Wall 33) Wall 32	Foundation trench = 29.7
(West of Wall 33) Wall 30 (earlier phase)	Foundation trench = 29.8

fragments, was essentially of similar date to that of the Early Roman levels 26.1–2, 27.1–7. From 27.10 also came the residual stamped Rhodian amphora handle CN 7621 from Finkielsztejn's period IIA (c. 234–220 BC).[50]

Directly underneath these fill levels was a thick destruction deposit (27.16–25, 41.2) of ash, charcoal and burnt mudbrick (Plate 20) from which was recovered a large quantity of plain ware along with numerous clay spherical loom weights (Plate 21).[51] More useful for dating this destruction level, provisionally labelled "Antiochus Destruction level" (Hellenistic 2B), were the four stamped Rhodian amphora handles (CN 7655–7658) and the bronze coin RN 090279 of Ptolemy IV (221–204 BC) or Ptolemy V (204–180 BC) with the former being more likely (Plates 22–23). The amphora handles (Plates 24–25) all belong to Finkielsztejn's period II and can be dated to the years c. 240–200 BC.[52] Noteworthy was the large iron blade RN 071273, heavily corroded but largely intact, from 27.19 (Plates 26–27). While spreading over much of the trench east of wall 33 and filling an Early Bronze Age pit (F21) partially revealed in the northern baulk, the destruction deposit was not associated with any meaningful architectural feature and, in fact, was definitely laid down before the Early Roman and Hellenistic walls discussed above were constructed (Figure 1.73). Rather, the destruction debris seemed to have washed down from higher ground to the north-east; unfortunately, a further limited sounding in this direction failed to locate its origin. Beneath the thick destruction layer, but still part of it, was a finer ashy layer (27.26–30). From the small quantity of pottery from this layer came the Attic black-gloss plate fragment **FW 31**, the Attic lamp fragment of Howland Type 25A or 25B (CN 7674) and the stamped Rhodian handle (CN 7678) belonging to Finkielsztejn's Period IIb.[53]

Plot XXXIVF lies on the north side of the summit and was commenced in 1989 when the Byzantine stratum was explored and partially removed. It was reopened in 1993 (Tidmarsh 1996: 308–11) in order to investigate the abundance of Hellenistic pottery previously found in locus 6 (Watson 1993: 208).

---

50 CN 7621: KREON 1st, fabricant active during Periods Ic–IIa (c. 234–220).

51 From 27.16–30, 41.2: unguentarium **PW 673**; uncatalogued pottery jar Types 2B, 4B; cooking pot Types 3–4; black-gloss bowls Types 1–2. For Hellenistic loom weights at Jebel Khalid in Syria see Crewe 2002.

52 CN 7655: PASION, fabricant active in Period IIc (last decade of third century); CN 7656: XENOTIMOS, fabricant active in Period IIa (c. 234–220); CN 7657: DAMONIKOS, fabricant active in Periods Ic–II (c. 244–200); CN 7658: ARCHELAS, fabricant dated to Period IIa (c. 234–200).

53 Attic lamp CN 7674 c. 350–275 (see Rotroff 1997b: 494–6 who gives similar dates to Howland and Scheibler); Rhodian amphora handle CN 7678: DISKOS 1st, fabricant active in Period IIb (c. 219–c. 210).

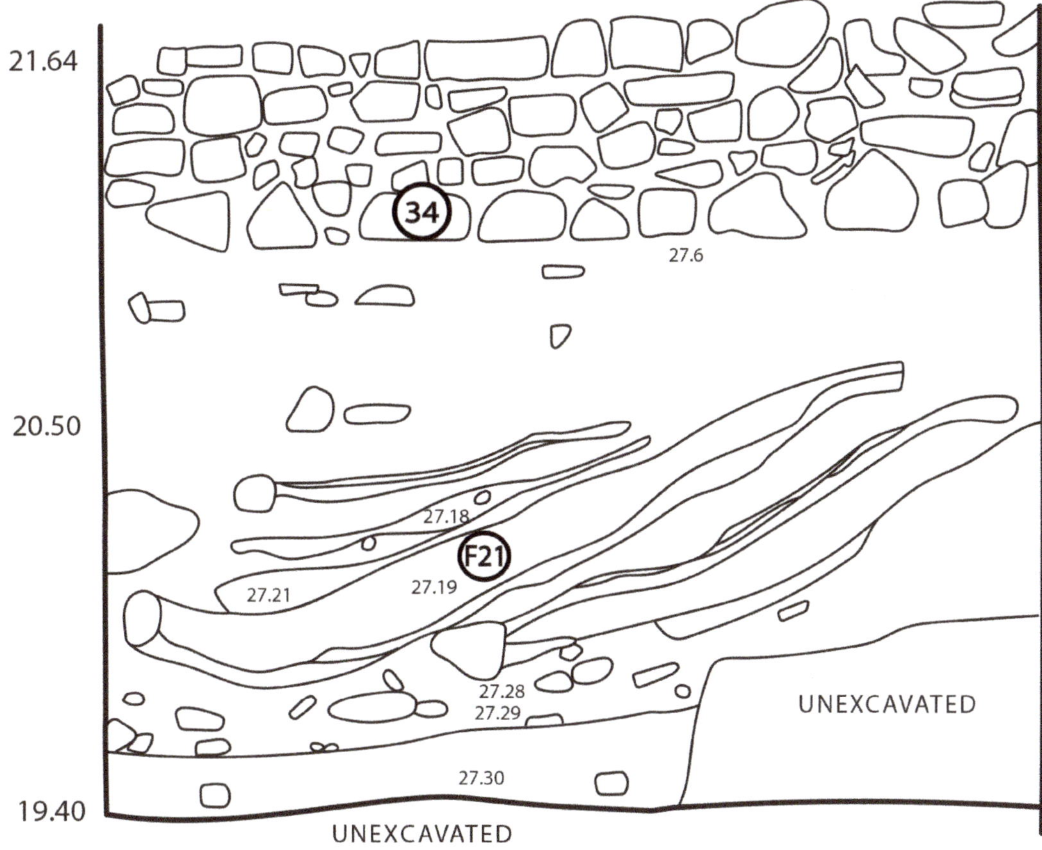

Figure 1.73. Plot XXXIVB east. North section. Below 27.30 bedrock was reached.

Figure 1.74. Plot XXXIVF. Third-century BC pottery fill or rubbish deposit.

Table 1.9. Tell Husn. Area XXXIV stratified deposits (XXXIVF).

NATURE OF DEPOSIT	DEPOSIT
Hellenistic 2B c. 220–c. 200 BC	
Rubbish deposit	6.1–5

Further levels from the same locus in 1993 contained an impressive number of Rhodian amphora body sherds (but no stamped handles) and large storage jar fragments (Types 2–3).

The pottery from locus 6 (6.1–5) was not associated with any architectural features, and so should probably be considered as part of a rubbish deposit (Figure 1.74). From within the deposit was recovered a very worn Ptolemaic bronze (RN 16036); although the poor state of the coin prevents its accurate identification, it was from a Phoenician or Palestinian mint. The extreme paucity of second-century Ptolemaic coins in Coele-Syria, subsequent to the battle of Panium in 198 BC (Bagnall 1976: 180–2; Duyrat 2016: 349–66; Rappaport 1984: 31; Sheedy 2001: 15–25), makes a third-century date more likely. Furthermore, two lamp fragments – CN 7143 and CN 7390 – from the same deposit should date to the late fourth or third centuries BC as they were clearly modelled on Athenian lamps of Howland Type 25, commonly imitated during this timespan (Rosenthal-Heginbottom 2015a: 622).

When all the evidence is considered, the rubbish deposit should date as a whole to the later third century BC – possibly at much the same time as the "Antiochus Destruction" level (Hellenistic 2B) in Plot XXXIVB or, more likely in view of the absence (admittedly from a small sample) of Type 4 jars with their early collared rims seen in the XXXIVB destruction level, slightly earlier within the second half of the third century. It is likely that this deposit was detritus from the garrison that must have existed on Tell Husn during the period of Ptolemaic (third century) control (see below).

Directly below this rubbish deposit, impressive Early Bronze Age remains were revealed and no further Hellenistic material was recovered.

Plot XXXIVG was first opened in 1989 when part of the Byzantine fortress complex was investigated (Watson 1993). Further excavations (Tidmarsh 1996:

305–8) revealed a complex of rooms of uniform orientation that, while seriously disturbed by the later Byzantine construction (loci 1–4) cutting deeply into the *tell*, represented part of a dwelling occupied during both the Early Roman and Hellenistic periods (Figures 1.75–76).

The complex comprised two distinct Early Roman phases with the uppermost (Figure 1.77) represented by loci 7, 8, 12, 13 (Figure 1.78). The area (locus 7) to the south of wall 8 and to the west of wall 7 must have been a further open-cooking space as the remains of three ovens of stone and clay (F28, F29, F32) and a fireplace (F30) indicate, as well as the jar and cooking-pot fragments of similar types to those seen in locus 6. The well-built mudbrick and stone oven F28 was built directly upon the tamped degenerate mudbrick surface 7.12, with the stone-lined oven F29 cut into this level. The only other undisturbed surfaces associated with this phase were in locus 8 (8.11–12) and a further courtyard (12.1, 12.3, 13.2) resting on a compacted layer of degenerate mudbrick and small stones (12.2, 13.3–6, 13.9) used to smooth the surface of the bedrock lying just underneath. The scanty latest pottery on both the surfaces was of Early Roman date, while within the packing there was a mixture of Early Roman and Hellenistic sherds.[54] In Byzantine times wall 8, resting on a broader footing course and separating the loci, was dismantled in its eastern half during the construction of wall 10. To the west, wall 12 abutted wall 8 and ran approximately north–south. Both these walls rested partially on a broader stone footing that had been built up to the level of the bedrock surface to support them; they appeared contemporary as the foundation trench of both cut into bedrock and both were of similar construction. On both the north face of wall 8 and the east face of wall 12 small traces of white plaster still remained in situ.

Wall 13 (running into the south baulk) consists on its northern face of small to large unworked fieldstones arranged in courses with a door (F19) blocked by rubble

---

54 From 8.11–2, 12.1: cooking pots Type 5 (uncatalogued), Type 8 **PW 613**. Uncatalogued pottery from 8.14–6, 12.2, 13.2–6: fishplate bases (plain wares); bowl Types 1, 5, 7 (black-gloss and plain wares); jar Types 4, 7; cooking pot Type 5.

Table 1.10. Tell Husn. Area XXXIV stratified deposits (XXXIVG).

NATURE OF DEPOSIT	DEPOSIT
Early Roman I (later phase)	
63 BC–late first century AD	
Surface	6.1, 6.4, 9.5–6, 11.1, 11.5
Subsurface packing	6.2–3, 6.7–11, 11.2–4, F14, F16/21
Early Roman 1 (earlier phase)	
63 BC–late first century AD	
Surface	7.12, 8.11–2, 12.1, 12.3, 13.2

fill during this later phase. Wall 14, with its impressive dimensions and well-cut masonry (Figure 1.79), was constructed over the earlier wall 5 (which served as a base) and functioned as a retaining wall for the Early Roman cobbled courtyard floor (F14) to its south (Figure 1.80).

The lower Early Roman phase is seen in loci 6, 9 and 11 (Figures 1.81–82). Locus 6, with the traces of a very fragmentary hearth F12 (Figure 1.83) surrounded by ash and numerous animal bones, comprised a cooking complex (courtyard) bounded by walls 4, 5 and 6, and associated with the plaster surface 6.1 and 6.4 (F11) and subsurface packing 6.2–6.3 and 6.7–6.11, the southern half of which had been largely destroyed by later Byzantine construction.[55] From this locus were recovered the uncatalogued nozzle of a wheelmade knife-pared ("Herodian") lamp, a cooking pot Type 5 (**PW 587**, bevelled rim), and multiple fragments of Type 6B (long-collared rim; prominent lower edge) and 7A (neck ridge; simple lip) jars, both uncatalogued and catalogued.[56]

To the west of locus 6, and contemporary with it, was a further living space, locus 9, whose plaster/rubble surface (9.5–6) – of a greater thickness than that seen in locus 6 and from which came the neckless Type 1B jar **PW 262** – and the scanty remains of a further hearth (F9) also suggested an open courtyard. Locus 9 was bounded on its west side by wall 11 (essentially parallel to walls 6 and 4) and to the north by wall 15 (largely dismantled), separated from wall 11 by a narrow doorway (F10).

Locus 11 (Figure 1.84), to the east of wall 4 and only partially cleared, was also part of this earlier phase with the plaster surfaces 11.1 and 11.5 and subsurface packing 11.2–4 contemporary with levels mentioned above.[57] The occupation surfaces lay almost directly on bedrock that had been levelled with the subsurface packing.

JEBEL SARTABA
Area XIII (College of Wooster)

Jebel Sartaba lies within the Transjordanian hill country at a distance of 2.2 kilometres east-south-east of Pella (Plate 28; Figure 1.85). Being some 350 metres higher in elevation than Pella itself, it has a commanding view over the ancient city and Tell Husn to the west as well as the Jordan Valley to the south, west and north. To the north, the Hellenistic fortress on Jebel Hammeh is also clearly visible from Sartaba. To the east, the view is restricted to the Jordanian hills, although the routes along the Wadi Malawi are clearly seen (Kouky 1992: 200). To the south-east, the medieval Arab fortress of Ajlun (Qalat al-Rabadh) can just be made out on the skyline.

Lying on the plateau summit of Sartaba are the impressive remains of a fortress (Plates 29–31; Figures 1.86–90), some 70 metres square, planned and sounded by Smith in 1981 (McNicoll et al. 1982: 64–7). The stone-built fortress with its eight towers, one at each corner and one midway along each wall, is approximately square in plan and so its trace differs markedly from the fortress on Jebel Hammeh

---

55   A preliminary examination of the animal bones by Karyn Wesselingh (pers. com.) suggests that ovicaprid and pig bones are the most prevalent.
56   From locus 6: jars Type 6B **PW 420–4**, Type 7A **PW 442**.
57   From 11.1: casserole Type 1 **PW 629**; jar Type 7A (uncatalogued). From 11.4: Type 3 jar **PW 299**; krater Type 1 **PW 162**; bowl Type 2 **PW 134**.

(Figure 1.93). Furthermore, it is set well back from the brow of the hill, lying almost at the centre of Sartaba's broad summit. At a small distance to the south-east lies a small stone tower, yet to be investigated (Plate 32).

The unfinished state of the walls (Plates 30–31; Figure 1.89), crudely constructed from roughly-hewn stone blocks, and the absence of any interior structures, apart from two interconnecting cisterns roughly dug into the rock (Figure 1.90), indicate that the fortress was never completed, with the pottery recovered from clearing the walls and from the limited soundings undertaken within the complex almost exclusively made up of plain wares comprising Type 1 (simple rim) cooking pots and jars – the latter consisting mainly of Types 4–6 along with two examples (McNicoll et al. 1982: pl. 127, 1, 12) of Type 7.[58] Currently it is premature to arrive at any firm conclusions as to the role of the fortress although it may well have been intended to serve as an observation post over the Jordan Valley, while, at the same time, together with an ashlar tower and major defensive walls nearby (Watson and O'Hea 1996: 67), performing a defensive function against incursions from the east. Whether it was a late Seleucid (or, more likely, Hasmonean) construction is uncertain, with the small published ceramic corpus (McNicoll et al. 1982: pl. 127) consistent with that seen in Jannaeus Destruction levels (Hellenistic 3C) on the main mound.[59]

JEBEL HAMMEH (TELL AL-HUSAIN)
Area XXX (University of Sydney)

Traces of a further fortress, on Jebel Hammeh, 2 kilometres to the north-east of Pella and overlooking the Wadi al-Hammeh with its Natufian remains (Area XX) to the west (Edwards 2013), have been partially planned but not excavated (McNicoll 1992: 103–5).[60] Positioned on the summit of the jebel, the fortress was in a prime position to regulate access via the Wadi al-Hammeh from the Jordan Valley to the plateau further east, while commanding wide views over the Jordan Valley (Plate 33; Figure 1.91) with Tell Husn, Khirbet Fahl and the summit of Jebel Sartaba also easily visible. In contrast to the fortress on Sartaba, the trace of the Hammeh fort follows the contours of the hilltop in a fashion somewhat reminiscent of the Hellenistic *Geländemauer* (though on a much smaller scale) commonly employed by Greek-trained or Greek-influenced architects during the fourth and third centuries BC in response to the great advances in siege warfare during those years (McNicoll 1997: 4; Winter 1971: 110–14).

Of its wall and five remaining towers, only one or two courses survive (Plate 34; Figures 1.92–93) although, as opposed to the Sartaba fort, the stones are well cut with drafted margins and quarry-faced bosses. No ancient structures can be discerned within the walls although they may lie beneath the ruins of a modern farmhouse. A fortlet (73) on the same ridge line almost one kilometre to the east, surveyed by Watson and O'Hea but as yet not investigated, may be associated with the fortress along with a small tower or outpost (59A) further to the south (Watson and O'Hea 1996: 67). Surface sherding makes it clear that the Jebel Hammeh fort was built at some time during the Hellenistic period though the lack, as yet, of a detailed study of the ceramic evidence prevents further refinement of these dates. Noteworthy also are the eight stone ballista balls picked up from the surface in the western sector of the fortress (Plate 35; Figure 1.94).

---

58 Jars: Type 4 with short neck (4A: short-collared square rim; 4B: short-collared triangular rim; 4C: short-collared rim, prominent edge); Type 5 with tall neck (5A: short-collared, square rim; 5B: short-collared triangular rim); Type 6 with long-collared rim (6A: uniform thickness; 6B: prominent lower edge); Type 7 with neck ridge (7A: simple lip; 7B: overhanging lip).

59 Sabar (2022) has correctly pointed out the similarity between the ceramic corpus of the Hasmonean fortress at Horvat Tefen (in the Western Galilee overlooking 'Akko-Ptolemais), which he attributes to Alexander Jannaeus, and the small published assemblage (essentially cooking pots and storage jars) from Jebel Sartaba. Both coins and stamped amphora handles point to a date in the early first century BC (c. 80s to 70s) for Horvat Tefen, whereas similar evidence (possibly due to its unfinished state) is lacking at Jebel Sartaba.

60 My sincere thanks to Brita Jansen of the German Archaeological Institute for her information and images as to the current state of the fort on Jebel Hammeh following her recent visit there, and for supplying me with a summary of her doctoral thesis on the Hellenistic fortifications at Gadara/Umm Qais.

Figure 1.75. Plot XXXIVG. Early Roman levels. Byzantine walls 10 and 3 to north and east respectively. To east.

Figure 1.76. Plot XXXIVG. To west.

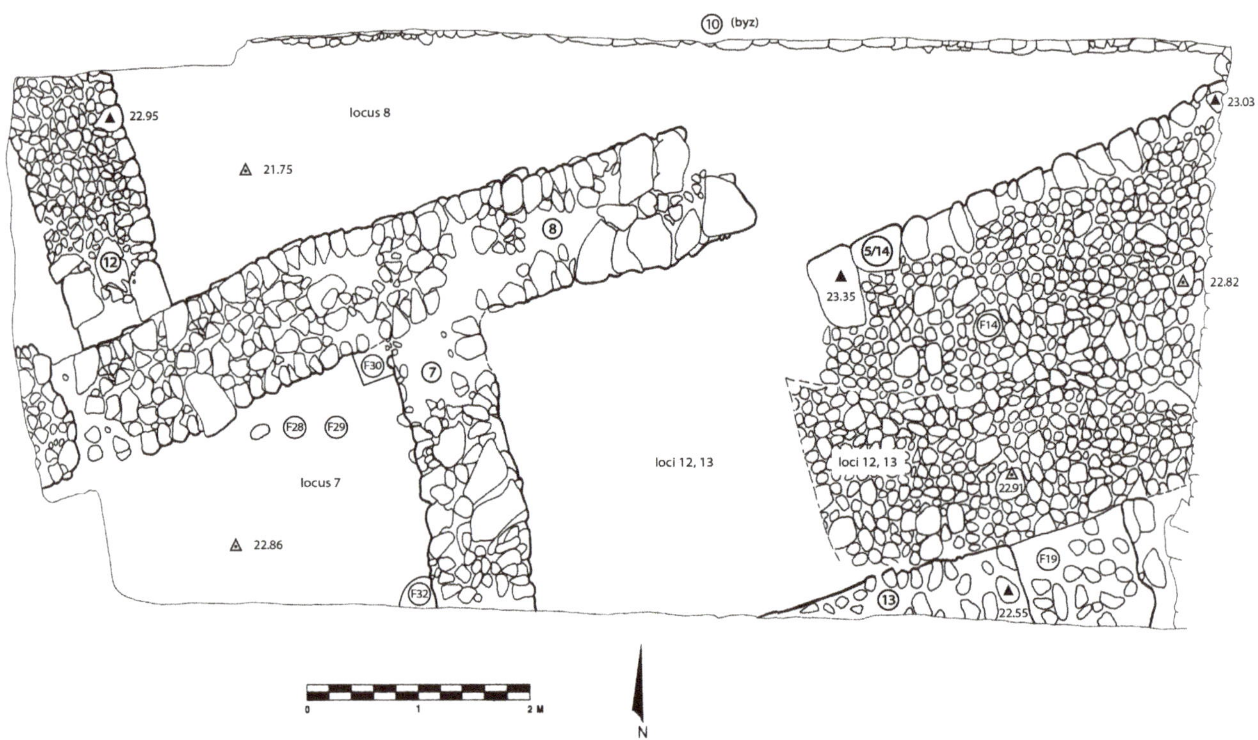

Figure 1.77. Plot XXXIVG. Early Roman phase (upper). Plan.

Figure 1.78. Plot XXXIVG. Upper Early Roman phase (loci 7, 8, 12, 13). Note stone levelling courses under walls 8, 12. To south-west.

Figure 1.79. Plot XXXIVG. Wall 14. To east.

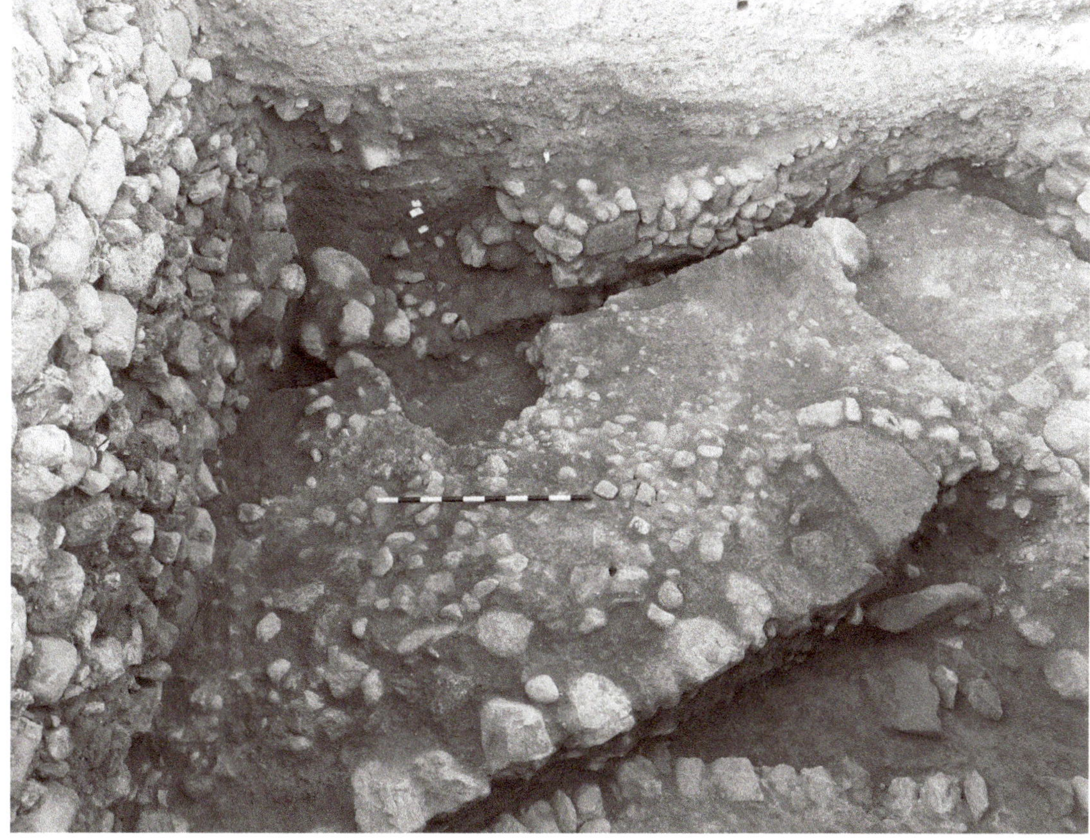

Figure 1.80. Plot XXXIVG. Cobbled courtyard floor F14. To south.

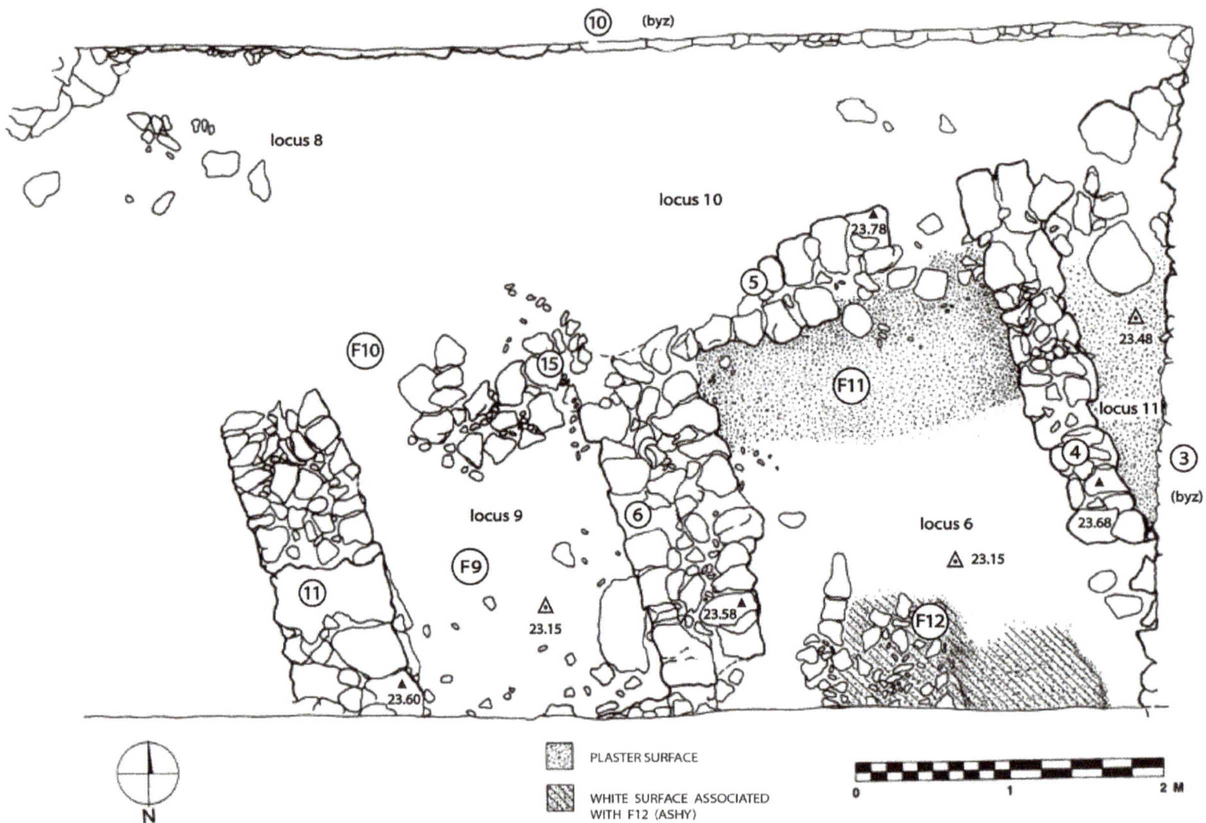

Figure 1.81. Plot XXXIVG. Early Roman phase (lower). Plan.

Figure 1.82. Plot XXXIVG. Lower Early Roman loci 6 and 9. The later (upper) Early Roman walls 7 and 8 also seen. To south.

Figure 1.83. Plot XXXIVG. Locus 6. Fragmentary hearth F12. To south.

Figure 1.84. Plot XXXIVG. Loci 6 and 11 (further east). To south.

Figure 1.85. Jebel Sartaba (Area XIII). View from main mound to south-east.

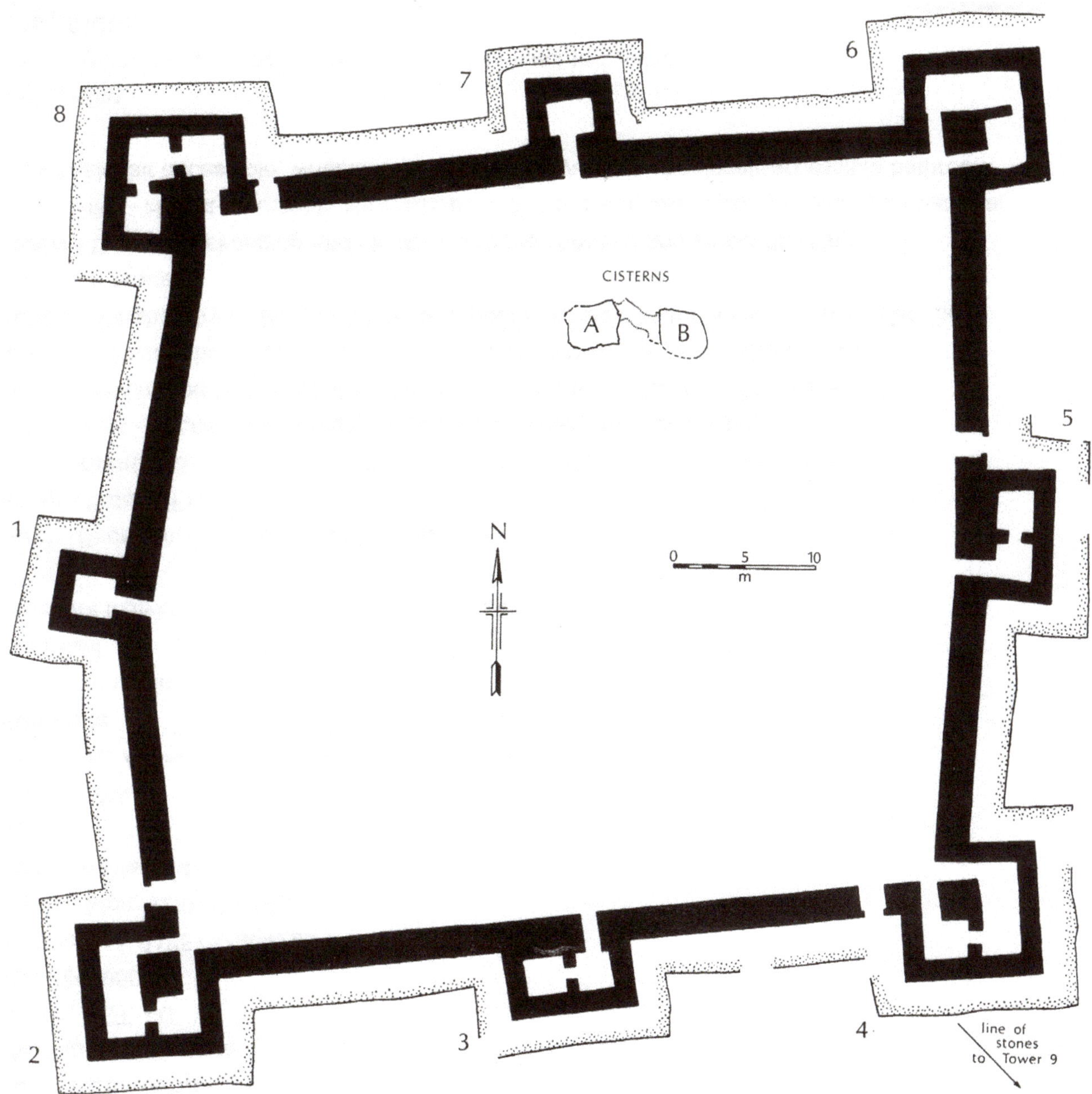

Figure 1.86. Area XIII. Jebel Sartaba fort. Plan.

Figure 1.87. Jebel Sartaba (Area XIII). Aerial view of fortress.

Figure 1.88. Jebel Sartaba (Area XIII). North-west corner of fortress. Jordan valley in the background.

Figure 1.89. Jebel Sartaba (Area XIII). Unfinished walls of fortress.

Figure 1.90. Jebel Sartaba (Area XIII). Fortress. One of the two interconnecting cisterns.

Figure 1.91. Jebel Hammeh, Area XXX (the most distant hill) from the south-west.

Figure 1.92. Jebel Hammeh (Area XXX). Remaining lowest courses of fortress wall.

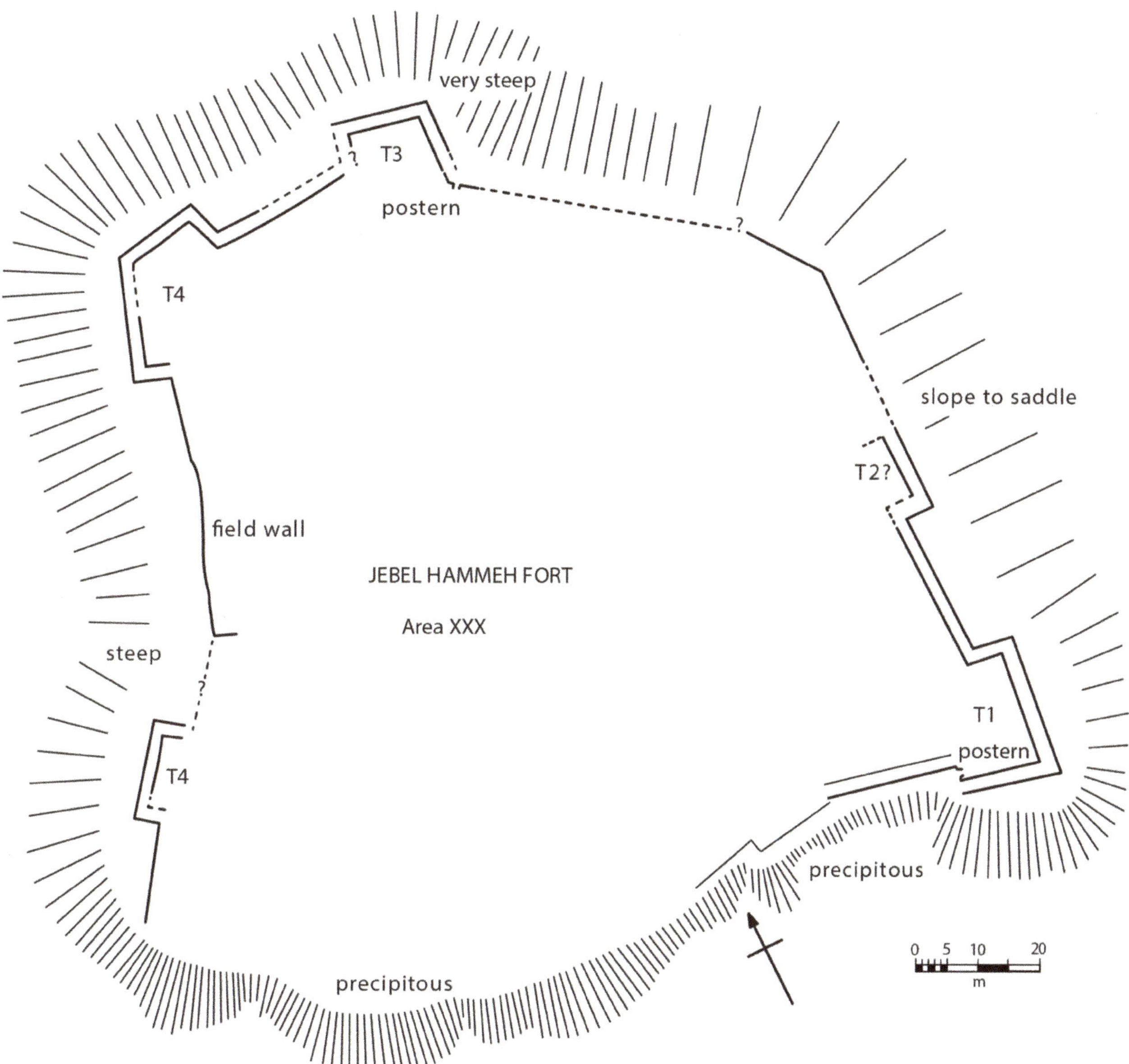

Figure 1.93. Area XXX. Jebel Hammeh fort. Trace of walls.

Figure 1.94. Jebel Hammeh (Area XXX). Ballista balls.

THE PLATES

Plate 1. Pella excavations. Tell Husn (*left*), separated by the Wadi Jirm al-Moz from the main mound (Khirbet Fahl, *right*). The village of Tabaqat Fahl with the Jordan Valley (*background*). To west.

Plate 2. Pella during the first season (1979) of the University of Sydney excavations. Note the perennial spring (before the installation of a pumping station) in the Wadi Jirm al-Moz. To west.

Plate 3. Byzantine and Ummayad remains on the main mound. To north-east.

Plate 4. Plot XXIIIA. Painted plaster fragment from Jannaeus Destruction level in locus 11.

Plate 5. Plot XXIIIA. Jannaeus Destruction level. Bronze drapery fragment from 22.10–11.

Plate 6. Plot XXIIID. Loom weights from Jannaeus Destruction level.

Plate 7. Plot XXIIID. Arrowhead RN 170001 from Jannaeus Destruction level.

Plate 8. Plot XXIIID. Statuette arm RN 170398 from Jannaeus Destruction level.

Plate 9. Plot XXIIID. Seven-spouted clay lamp CN 7863 from Jannaeus Destruction level.

Plate 10. Plot XXIIID. Fragment of box lamp CN 7861 from Jannaeus Destruction level.

Plate 11. Plot XXIIID. Shattered Rhodian amphora CN 7794 fallen from plastered niche in wall 25. To east.

Plate 12. Plot XXIIID. Shattered and burnt Rhodian amphora within south baulk.

Plate 13. Plot XXIIID. South-east sector. Kiln F57.

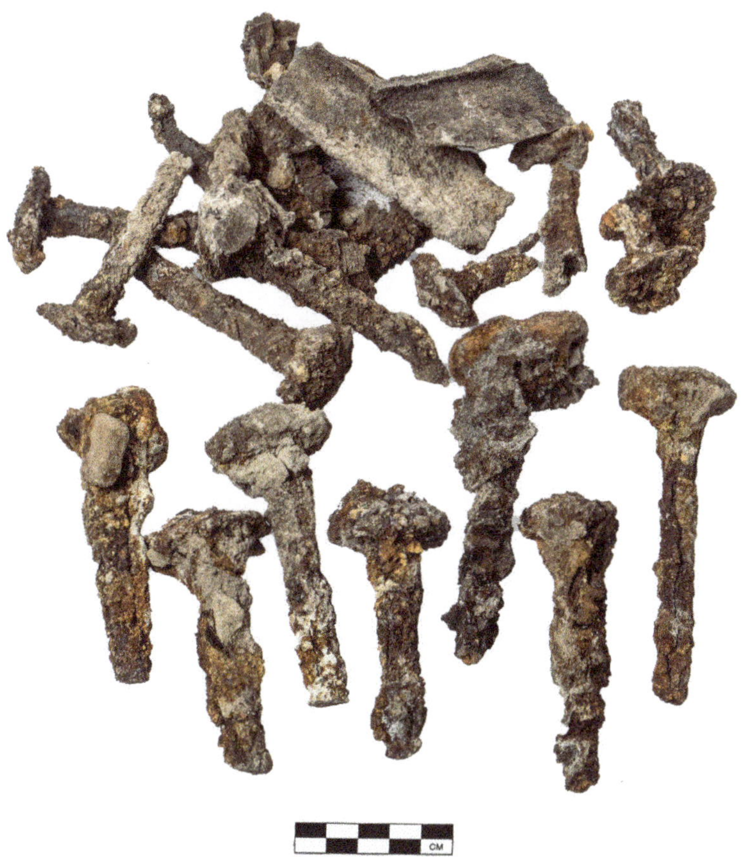

Plate 14. Plot XXIIID. Iron nails from locus 61.

Plate 15. Plot XXIIID. Cobbled courtyard 11.4–6 with ESA plate FW 204 on its surface. Wall 16 to the south, below the courtyard. To north.

Plate 16. Plot XXIIID. FW 204 in situ.

Plate 17. Plot XIA/B on north-east slope of Tell Husn. View from main mound to south.

Plate 18. Plot XXXIVB (east). Byzantine stylobate and earlier column base (not in situ) to the south of wall 30. North–south wall 33 (*foreground*). To south.

Plate 19. Plot XXXIVB (east). Knife-pared "Herodian" lamp CN 7592 from 27.4.

Plate 20. Plot XXXIVB (east). "Antiochus Destruction" level on bedrock.

Plate 21. Plot XXXIVB (east). Loom weights within "Antiochus Destruction" level.

Plate 22. Plot XXXIVB (east). Bronze Ptolemaic coin RN 090279.

Plate 23. Plot XXXIVB (east). Bronze Ptolemaic coin RN 090279.

Plate 24. Plot XXXIVB (east). Rhodian amphora handle CN 7657, fabricant DAMONIKOS.

Plate 25. Plot XXXIVB (east). Rhodian amphora handle CN 7655, fabricant PASION.

Plate 26. Plot XXXIVB (east). Iron blade RN 071273 in situ.

Plate 27. Plot XXXIVB (east). Iron blade RN 071273 after conservation.

Plate 28. Tell Husn (Area XXXIV, *foreground*). Jebel Sartaba (Area XIII, *behind*). View from main mound to south-east.

Plate 29. Jebel Sartaba (Area XIII). Interior of fortress.

Plate 30. Jebel Sartaba (Area XIII). Unfinished walls of fortress.

Plate 31. Jebel Sartaba (Area XIII). Unfinished walls of fortress. Ben Churcher (Project Field Director) in foreground.

Plate 32. Jebel Sartaba (Area XIII). Interior of tower to south-east.

Plate 33. View to west over Jordan Valley from Jebel Hammeh (Area XXX).

Plate 34. Jebel Hammeh (Area XXX). Remaining lowest courses of fortress wall.

Plate 35. Jebel Hammeh (Area XXX). Ballista balls.

Plate 36. FW 57. CN 7540. XXXIIY 4.3. Hellenistic 3A.

Plate 37. FW 71. CN 0416. IIIB/C 1.19. Mixed Context.

Plate 38. FW 96. CN 6711. IIIP 25.11. Hellenistic 3B.

Plate 39. FW 102. CN 4327. IVD 10.12. Hellenistic 3C.

Plate 40. FW 119. CN 7829. XXIIID 67.1/68.1. Hellenistic 3C.

Plate 41. FW 122. CN 7529. XXXIIY 2.1. Hellenistic 3A.

Plate 42. FW 136. CN 7810. XXIIID 24.3. Hellenistic 3B.

Plate 43. FW 158. CN 0116. IIIB/C 5.1. Mixed Context.

Plate 44. FW 165. CN 7827. XXIIID 64.2. Mixed Context.

Plate 45. FW 166. CN 3276. XIV J 1.2, 2.2. Mixed Context.

Plate 46. FW 170. CN 7845. XXXIIY 1.2. Hellenistic 3A.

Plate 47. FW 173. CN 0216. IIIB/C 2.8. Hellenistic 3C.

Plate 48. FW 182. CN 7860. XXXIIY 1.3. Hellenistic 3A.

Plate 49. FW 183. CN 7833. XXIIID 59.3. Hellenistic 3C.

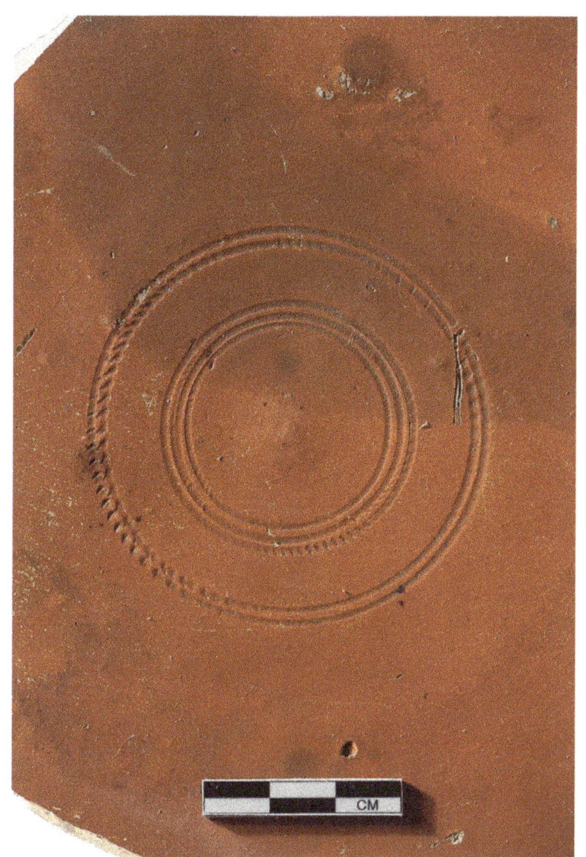

Plate 50. FW 200. CN 7728. XXIIIA. 71.2. Hellenistic 3C.

Plate 51. FW 204. CN 7779. XXIIID 11.5. Hellenistic 3C.

Plate 52. FW 210. CN 7823. XXIIID 31.3. Hellenistic 3C.

Plate 53. FW 229. CN 7617. XXXIVB 27.7. Early Roman 1.

Plate 54. FW 258. CN 3870. IIIQ 11.2. Mixed Context.

Plate 55. FW 277. CN 6708. IIIP 25.20. Mixed Context.

Plate 56. FW 282. CN 7147. XXXIVB 5.37. Mixed Context.

Plate 57. PW 29. CN 7834. XXIIID 63.2. Hellenistic 3C.

Plate 58. PW 29. CN 7834. XXIIID 63.2. Hellenistic 3C.

Plate 59. PW 78. CN 7047. XXIIIA 105.1. Hellenistic 3C.

Plate 60. PW 236. CN 2670. XIA/B 2.2. Early Roman 1.

Plate 61. PW 465. CN 2865. XIA/B 2.2. Early Roman 1.

Plate 62. PW 675. CN 7778. XXIIID 11.18. Hellenistic 3B.

Part 2
THE CATALOGUE

INTRODUCTION

Relatively little archaeological material belonging to the Hellenistic and Early Roman periods and recovered from excavations east of the Jordan River has been published in detail.[1] This lack of published data is particularly striking in the area of ceramic studies which, while not an end in itself, along with numismatics and stamped Aegean transport amphorae, still remains the foundation for chronology as well as providing vital information on trade, cultural relations, social status and other important aspects of daily life.

Small Hellenistic and/or Early Roman assemblages have been published from Jerash and Tell es-Sa'idiyeh, with larger corpora from Amman/Philadelphia, Gadara/Umm Qais, Hesban, Kallirhoe, Machaerus, 'Iraq al-Amir and Pella itself.[2] Of these, only 'Iraq al-Amir, Hesban, Kallirhoe and Machaerus can boast published assemblages to rival those from Palestinian sites such as 'Akko-Ptolemais, Ashdod, Ashkelon, Gezer, Jaffa, Jerusalem, Samaria, Tel Anafa and Tel Dor – all frequently cited in this work for parallels with the Pella material – along with the more limited reports from numerous other sites.[3] In the case of Machaerus, the ceramic timespan is relatively restricted, limited as it is to the first centuries BC and AD, with the published Early Roman assemblage from Kallirhoe strictly Herodian (end of first century BC–c. 70 AD). On the other hand, Gerber's publication of the "Classical" pottery from Hesban includes a large corpus of Hellenistic and Early Roman ceramics, although, as she points out, "the ceramic assemblages . . . were not well stratified" and "based purely on typological criteria and on comparisons with published pottery from other sites in Palestine/Israel and Jordan" (Gerber 2012: 175). A similar situation ("Almost all sherds come from mixed pottery assemblage") is seen in the Hellenistic to Byzantine assemblage from Gadara/Umm Qais (Kenkel 2020: 15) and the majority of published Hellenistic and Roman ceramics from Jerash (Brizzi 2022; Lichtenberger and Raja 2020: 2). Moreover, although Paul Lapp's chronology of the strata from the Village site (Field 1) at 'Iraq al-Amir (Zimmerman 2020a) has been followed here as regards parallel forms, Zimmerman (2020b: 39, Table 2.1, 79–80) has raised significant doubts as to the accuracy of the chronology of Stratum IIIb and Stratum IV.

And so, of the Hellenistic and Early Roman pottery published from the Jordanian sites mentioned above, only a relatively small quantity has been

---

1   For a brief overview of Hellenistic and Early Roman ceramics in Jordan see Abushmais 2022; Parker 2022.

2   Jerash (for example, Braemer 1989; Kehrberg 2004a, 2004b; Rasson-Seigne and Seigne 2020a, 2020b); Tell as-Sa'idiyeh (Pritchard 1985); Amman/Philadelphia (Hadidi 1970; Koutsoukou and Najjar 1997; Zayadine 1977–78); Gadara/Umm Qais (Kenkel 2012, 2020; Kenrick 2000); Hesban (Gerber 2012); Kallirhoe (Clamer 1997); Machaerus (Corbo and Loffreda 1981; Loffreda 1980, 1996); 'Iraq al-Amir (Zimmerman 2020b, with smaller assemblages presented by N.L. Lapp 1979, 1983); Pella (McNicoll et al. 1982; McNicoll et al. 1992; Smith and Day 1989).

3   For example, 'Akko-Ptolemais (Berlin and Stone 2016; Regev 2009/10;); Ashdod (Dothan 1971: 142–4; Dothan and Freedman 1967: 21–3); Ashkelon (Birney 2022; Johnson 2008); Gezer (Gitin 1990); Jaffa (Tsuf 2018); Jerusalem (e.g. Berlin 2005a; Geva 2003, 2010a; Geva and Rosenthal-Heginbottom 2003; Hayes 1985b; Tchekhanovets 2013; Tushingham 1985); Samaria (Crowfoot et al. 1957; Hennessy 1970; Zayadine 1966); Tel Anafa (Berlin 1997a; Slane 1997); Tel Dor (Guz-Zilberstein 1995; Rosenthal-Heginbottom 1995).

recovered from deposits that are sealed and can be independently dated by coins, imported pottery types – such as Eastern Sigillata A whose dates have been, in general, well worked out (Hayes 1985a, 2008: 13–30) – or by stamped Aegean transport amphora handles (Finkielsztejn 2001).[4] As a result, the dating of most ceramic assemblages rests largely on stylistic comparison with those recovered from sites west of the Jordan River, providing some difficulties; for not only is disparate regional distribution of pottery forms as apparent in the Hellenistic and Early Roman eras as in other periods, most pottery of this period from Palestine has itself, until recently, been dated by comparative analysis rather than on firm stratigraphical grounds (Gitin 1990: 111, 1996: 91–2).[5]

The ceramic corpus presented here, presenting scholars with a large assemblage from a Decapolis city in northern Jordan, comprises pottery recovered by the University of Sydney excavations in well-stratified Hellenistic (later third, second, and earlier first centuries BC) and Early Roman (later first century BC, first and earlier second centuries AD) levels and deposits sealed by surfaces, architectural features or significant destruction levels.[6] For the Hellenistic and Early Roman pottery recovered by the College of Wooster expeditions see the relevant sections in Smith (1973), Smith and Day (1989), McNicoll and colleagues (1982) and McNicoll and colleagues (1992), as well as the excavation reports in the *Annual of the Department of Antiquities of Jordan* and *Bulletin of American Schools of Oriental Research*.

While the ceramic assemblage is largely from stratified deposits, pottery from unstratified levels ("Mixed Contexts") is also included, helping to provide a more accurate picture of the occurrence and frequency of various ceramic types (Tables 3.12–3.14). This applies particularly to the fine wares where, for example, the large number of mould-made bowls (not strictly a "ware" but for convenience included at the end of the fine wares) from mixed contexts gives a truer picture of the frequency of this class of bowl at Pella as well as its range of decorative motifs; to a lesser degree, the same applies to the West Slope ware from Pella. Furthermore, if ESA from unstratified contexts had not been included, the quantity and range of forms would have seemed much more restricted, while our one example of Italian Sigillata **FW 259** was also not stratified as were two (**FW 185–6**) of our four examples of thin-walled ware. It is also worth remembering that the impressive white ground lagynos **FW 166** was a stray find.

The corpus has been separated into the standard categories of fine wares and plain wares. A separation into these categories proves useful as certain classes of fine ware – in particular Athenian black-gloss ware and Eastern Sigillata A – can provide useful information as to dating the particular context in which they were found. The same applies to ceramic lamps and stamped Rhodian amphora handles, which, while dealt with *in toto* in a separate future study, have been referred to in this volume when relevant. Increasingly, the origin of a number of these fine wares can be confidently identified, providing further information as regards the intricate web of relationships and interconnections that existed amongst the vast number of peoples who made up the Hellenistic world.

In the Levant, as elsewhere, much less time has been devoted to comprehensive studies of the so-called "plain wares". Being generally found closer to their source of production than the fine wares (Rasson-Seigne and Seigne 2020b: 123), jars, jugs, cooking pots and other plain ware vessels can often give a useful insight into intra-regional trade relations

---

4   For the use and misuse of coins as archaeological evidence see Rotroff (1997a) and Walker (1997). For the revised dating of stamped Rhodian amphora handles, see Finkielsztejn 2001.

5   On regional variation and chronology as well as overall typology see now the important chapters by Andrea Berlin (2015) and Renate Rosenthal-Heginbottom (2015b). Also, very useful from this point of view, but dealing with ceramics within a much wider date range, is the Levantine Ceramic Project n.d.

6   From the Hellenistic, Early Roman and Mixed Context levels some 35,000 Hellenistic sherds were recovered. With the exception of the first three seasons (when non-diagnostic sherds were discarded prior to recording), all diagnostic fragments – including rims, bases, handles and representative samples of the various wares – were retained with non-diagnostic sherds recorded (but not weighed) and then discarded. See Orton and Hughes (2013: 203–18) and Byrd and Owens (1997) for the methodology involved in the quantification of ceramic assemblages. The methodology and problems associated with compiling such a ceramic corpus are also well discussed by Gitin (1996).

and connections. Furthermore, plain wares generally make up the great bulk of pottery recovered from a site and so can also be useful in terms of dating once their chronological and typological development has been worked out. It should always be remembered, however, that those forms associated with simple domestic functions tend to change more slowly than do the less utilitarian forms seen amongst the fine wares.

It is important to note that the pottery in this study comes from the settlement site itself rather than from tombs: the Hellenistic cemetery still awaits discovery while very few tombs of Early Roman date have been opened. As a result, we have few examples of intact vessels, with the typology presented here relying heavily on diagnostic rim forms.

NOTES FOR THE CATALOGUE AND TABLES

All measurements are given in metres.

The catalogue entry for each example consists of two numbers: the first is the catalogue number preceded by either **FW** (fine ware) or **PW** (plain ware), with the second the inventory number (CN). Following these numbers is the findspot consisting of area and plot (for example, XXVIIIB = Area XXVIII, plot B) and the locus and level (for example, 13.7 = locus 13, level 7).

Where appropriate, parallels for each example are given at the end of the catalogue entry. Some of these parallels come from well-dated deposits, strata or phases at various sites and this is noted with the parallel. Thus, for example: 'Akko-Ptolemais (Berlin and Stone 2016: fig. 9.23.1, second half of 1st c. BC = second half of first century BC).

In the relevant tables, the numbers not in brackets indicate catalogued examples and those enclosed by brackets represent examples that have been examined and classified but not entered into the catalogue in this volume.

As already noted, some of the various pottery forms (especially in the plain wares) have been allocated a "type" for the sake of brevity in the footnotes and tables (particularly those dealing with the excavations discussed above) rather than for the aim of launching yet another ceramic typology.

Finally, it should be noted that while the line drawings accompanying each example are not strictly to scale, the actual dimensions of each fragment are included in the catalogue entry alongside the drawing.

THE FINE WARES

Table 2.1. Distribution of pottery catalogued under "fine wares" by areas.

WARE	TOTAL	AREAS III, IV MAIN MOUND	AREA XXIII MAIN MOUND	AREA XXVIII MAIN MOUND	AREA XXXII MAIN MOUND	AREA XI TELL HUSN	AREA XXXIV TELL HUSN
Black-gloss	143	56	16	45	7	4	15
Moulded grey ware	21	6	13	1	0	0	1
White-ground lagynos	1 (Area XIV)	0	0	0	0	0	0
West Slope	17	8	2	2	5	0	0
Thin-walled ware	4	0	1	0	0	2	1
ESA	71	32	14	0	0	12	13
Italian Sigillata	1	0	0	0	0	0	1
Mould-made bowls	46	14	5	15	1	1	10
Green-glazed	1	0	0	1	0	0	0

Table 2.2. Distribution of pottery catalogued under "fine wares" by Hellenistic phases.

	2B c. 220– c. 200 BC	3A c. 200– c. 140 BC	3B c. 140– c. 100 (?) BC	3C c. 100 (?)– c. 80/79 BC	3B/3C c. 140– c. 80/79 BC	ER 63 BC– c. 135 AD	MIXED
Black-gloss	5	47	14	27	2	6	42
Moulded grey ware	0	1 (4)	0	14 (5)	0	0	6
White-ground lagynos	0	0	0	0	0	0	1
West Slope	0	6	1	2	0	0	8
Thin-walled	0	0	0	0	0	2	2
ESA	0	0	1	19 (15)	0	12 (1)	39
Italian Sigillata	0	0	0	0	0	0	1
Mould-made	0	14	1	6	0	2 (residual)	23
Green-glazed	0	1	0	0	0	0	(2)

BLACK-GLOSS WARE

Within the corpus of fine wares, consisting of both the diagnostic sherds presented here and the large number of retained body sherds, black-gloss wares are the most numerous throughout the Seleucid (Hellenistic 3A–3C) levels. Five black-gloss wares (Wares 1–4, Campana B) can be recognised, with Wares 1–3 being more abundant than the other two. There is also a smaller number of black-gloss vessels whose disparate fabrics have not been included within the above wares.

As also seen amongst the plain wares, a number of the ceramic types within the black-gloss wares (in particular the ovoid and spouted bowl as well as the skyphos/kantharos) are only represented by one or several examples, making any discussion as to their chronological distribution at Pella essentially meaningless.

Ware 1 (Attic)

Generally, the Attic ware is recognised by its well-levigated clay, often with fine mica, that usually fires pink (5YR 7/4; 7.5YR 7/4), light reddish-brown (5YR 6/4), or reddish-yellow (5YR 6/6). Slight variations outside this range also occur (Rotroff 1982: 14).[7] The gloss is usually black and of good quality but may also be thin, dull and misfired (Bailey 1975: 31; Sparkes and Talcott 1970: 2). Nearly all of the few Attic imports were recovered from Pre-Jannaeus Destruction levels (Hellenistic 2B, 3A–3B) with a small number from the Jannaeus Destruction (Hellenistic 3C) horizons; none was found in Early Roman contexts. This is consistent with the progressive decline in Athenian ceramic imports beginning in the late third century seen in most Hellenistic sites in Asia Minor and the Levant (Hannestad 1983: 85, 1990: 179; Rosenthal-Heginbottom 2014: 383).

---

7   Rotroff (1997b: 10) also describes a second ware, paler and with poorly adering black gloss, seen occasionally on third- and early second-century BC vases. She suggests it was a short-lived experiment that proved unsuccessful due to problems with gloss adherence.

Table 2.3. Frequency of catalogued black-gloss wares by Hellenistic phases.

WARE	2B c. 220– c. 200 BC	3A c. 200– c. 140 BC	3B c. 140– c. 100 (?) BC	3C c. 100 (?)– c. 80/79 BC	3B/3C c. 140– c. 80/79 BC	ER 63 BC– c. 135 AD
Ware 1 (Attic)	1	2	0	1	0	1 (residual)
Ware 2 (BSP)	1	27	8	12	1	1 (residual)
Ware 3 (BSP)	1	9	2	6	0	2
Ware 4	1	0	1	0	1	0
Campana B	0	0	0	2	0	0
Miscellaneous	1	9	3	6	0	2

As well as amongst the black-gloss vessels, Ware 1 is encountered on the West Slope amphora **FW 180** (Mixed Context) and two mould-made ("Megarian") bowls, **FW 265** and **FW 278**, both in Hellenistic 3A strata.

Ware 2 (BSP)

This is the commonest ware amongst both the black-gloss ceramics from Pella and the mould-made bowls. The clay is very carefully levigated and of pink to a light reddish-yellow colour (5YR 7/4–7/8, 7.5YR 7/4–7/8); mica is absent. Gloss is generally well applied and of high quality, albeit often a rich brown or deep red rather than lustrous black; deliberate red-black or red-brown firing is common (for example, **FW 102**, **FW 122**) though also seen in Athenian specimens (**FW 71**). The same ware is encountered in several West Slope ware fragments (for example, **FW 167**, **FW 176**, **FW 178**) and a number of mould-made bowls (for example, **FW 260–1**, **FW 266**). The technical expertise with which this ware was prepared, together with its frequency on northern Syrian sites such as Jebel Khalid, suggests that it emanated from a Seleucid centre of some importance, with recent geochemical analysis (neutron activation analysis) on sherds of this ware (= "Fabric 2" at Jebel Khalid) along with Ware 3 (= "Fabric 3" at Jebel Khalid) from Jebel Khalid, Pella and Antioch pointing to Antioch itself or its environs as a possible source (Garnett 2011; Tidmarsh 2011: 283–4).[8] Vessels of this ware (along with Ware 3) were most commonly encountered in the Pre-Jannaeus Destruction phases although smaller numbers were seen in both Jannaeus Destruction and (residual) Early Roman levels.

Ware 3 (BSP)

Like the previous ware, the clay of Ware 3 is well levigated and lacking in mica or other inclusions. The clay fires somewhat lighter (10YR 7/3–7/6) than that of Ware 2 although the gloss is similar. Wares 2 and 3 are seen at Pella in a number of forms common to both these wares and to Eastern Sigillata A (ESA) whilst also appearing in both "Ivy Platter" plates (Table 2.7) and mould-made bowls (Table 2.11).

It is reasonable to equate Wares 2 and 3 with the "black-slipped predecessor" (BSP) of ESA first identified at Tel Anafa and discussed by Slane (1997: 269–74). With a seemingly short lifespan of some fifty years (c. 175–c. 125 BC), the black-slipped predecessor, as with ESA, which is of identical mineralogical characteristics, is generally believed to have originated from Antioch or the north Syrian coast. The difference in firing colour of Wares 2 and 3 would be more likely explained by a variation in firing temperatures in kilns within

---

8   Twenty-two samples (black-gloss wares typical of Antioch fabrics, along with Attic black-gloss and Eastern Sigillata A) from the 1930s excavations at Antioch-on-the-Orontes were recovered by Heather Jackson from the Museum of Art, Princeton University, and submitted as part of the neutron activation analysis (NAA) study.

a single locality (but in separate workshops employing somewhat different firing techniques) rather than by variable clay sources.[9]

There remain questions as regards the origins, chronology and distribution patterns of BSP, along with its relationship to ESA (Berlin et al. 2014: 318–20). As at Kedesh, and elsewhere in the southern Levant, ESA arrived later than it did in the north (Table 2.9) with Wares 2 and 3 (BSP) at Pella seemingly "filling the gap" and then continuing in use into the early first century BC (Tables 2.3, 2.7, 2.12). At least one explanation for this (though as yet not demonstrated) would be the continuing output of BSP from a workshop (or workshops) further south – perhaps in "one of the large, wealthy central or southern Phoenician cities such as Berytus, Sidon, or Tyre" (Berlin et al. 2014: 318–20).

Ware 4

Although the fired clay is sometimes similar in appearance to that of Athenian pottery, it is generally darker (5YR 5/6–10YR 6/4), less refined and completely lacking in mica. The gloss is of quite good quality and generally of matt black appearance. It is found mainly in Pre-Jannaeus Destruction horizons. Its place of origin is unclear.

Italian black-gloss wares

Perhaps surprisingly, no examples of the Italian black-gloss Campana A ware, recognised by its somewhat granular reddish-brown clay (5YR 6/3–7.5YR 6/4) and shiny metallic grey-black gloss, have as yet been recovered from Pella. Produced in the region of Ischia and the Bay of Naples (Morel 2014), the ware is spread widely in significant numbers throughout the western Mediterranean and North Africa where, for example, it is the "principal imported black-glazed ware found in the Hellenistic levels" (Kenrick 1985: 8–29). It also has a wide distribution in the eastern Mediterranean as well as the Black Sea – especially during the mid to late second century BC – although not in large quantities at any site (Élaigne 2012: 33–39; Handberg et al. 2013; Lund 2015: 188; Morel 2014).

There are two definite specimens of Campana B ware (**FW 42–3**) in the Pella corpus. The ware is poorly represented in the eastern Mediterranean as its beige or buff-pink clay (5YR 7/3–7.5YR 7/4) and greyish-black gloss can often lead to it being unrecognised or incorrectly identified (Kenrick 1985: 43–4; Lamboglia 1952: 140; Lund 2015: 188; Morel 1986: 469–77; Slane 1997: 317–18). At first regarded as a product of Etruria, it is now clear that a ware (or wares) similar to Campana B was (were) produced in at least three regions of Italy (Roth 2013: 88–9; Stone 2014: 164).[10]

BLACK-GLOSS WARE: PLATES AND BOWLS

Bowls and plates are the shapes most commonly seen in Hellenistic deposits throughout the eastern Mediterranean. With fragments, the distinction is often arbitrary but, in general, the plate is a more open and shallow form.

Fishplates (FW 1–30)

Fishplates – both in black-gloss and plain wares – are common, although, as at other sites, often only the wall and rim are preserved. The majority of black-gloss fishplates were recovered from the main mound in Pre-Jannaeus Destruction (Hellenistic 3A–3B) contexts with smaller numbers from the Jannaeus Destruction (Hellenistic 3C) levels showing that they were still being produced by at least some workshops during the

---

9   See Slane et al. in Levantine Ceramics Project: n.d. Ware/Ware Families: black-slipped predecessor (BSP). Also Élaigne (2012: 122–8) for the similarity in wares of BSP, ESA and a group of mould-made bowls from Hama.

10   Hence the recently suggested term "Cerchia della Campana B" (Roth 2013: 88) or the earlier "Campaniennes B-oïdes" (Morel 1986: 469).

Table 2.4. Frequency of black-gloss shapes by phases.

FORM	2B c. 220– c. 200 BC	3A c. 200– c. 140 BC	3B c. 140– c. 100 (?) BC	3C c. 100 (?)– c. 80/79 BC	3B/3C c. 140–c. 80/79 BC	ER 63 BC– c. 135 AD	MIXED
Fishplates	1	12	4	4	0	3 (residual)	6
Plates Type 1: simple thickened rim	1	0	0	1	0	0	2
Plates Type 2: undercut thickened rim	0	0	0	0	0	0	1
Plates Type 3: grooved thickened rim	0	3	1	0	0	0	2
Plates with upright rim	0	0	0	3	0	0	0
Saucers	1	1	2	2	1	1	4
Bowls Type 1: out-turned rim	0	11 (18)	1	3	1	2 (residual)	7
Bowls Type 2: in-turned rim	1(4)	15 (22)	2	7	0	0 (2)	4
Bowls Type 3: ovoid; plain/grooved rim	1	0	2	0	0	0	4
Bowls Type 4: ovoid; decorated rim	0	0	0	1	0	0	1
Spouted bowl	0	0	0	0	0	1 (residual?)	0
Applied relief bowl	0	0	0	1	0	0	0
Bowls: uncertain shape	0	3	0	0	0	0	2
Krater Type 1: horizontal rim	0	0	0	0	0	0	1
Krater Type 2: everted rim	0	2	0	0	0	0	1
Skyphoi/kantharoi	0	0	0	2	0	1 (residual)	1
Cups: band rim, pinched handles	0	0	2 (1)	3 (3)	0	0	5
Cups: "Palestinian form"	0	1	0	0	0	0	1

Table 2.5. Frequency of black-gloss shapes by wares.

TYPE	WARE 1	WARE 2	WARE 3	WARE 4	CAMPANA	MISCELLANEOUS
Fishplates	3	17	2	2	0	5 + 1 (green-glazed)
Plates Type 1: simple thickened rim	1	2	1	0	0	0
Plates Type 2: undercut thickened rim	0	1	0	0	0	1
Plates Type 3: grooved thickened rim	0	4	1	0	0	1
Plates with upright rim	0	0	1	0	2	0
Saucers	0	4	2	1	0	5
Bowls Type 1: out-turned rim	1 + 2 (?)	12	4	0	0	4
Bowls Type 2: in-turned rim	0	17	5	2	0	5
Bowls Type 3: ovoid; plain/ grooved rim	0	1	3	0	0	3
Bowls Type 4: ovoid; decorated rim	0	1	1	0	0	0
Spouted bowl	0	1	0	0	0	0
Applied relief bowl	0	0	0	0	0	1
Bowls: uncertain shape	1	3	1	0	0	0
Krater Type 1: horizontal rim	0	0	0	0	0	1
Krater Type 2: everted rim	0	0	0	0	0	3
Skyphoi/kantharoi	1	2	0	0	0	1
Cups: narrow band rim, pinched handles	0	7	3	0	0	0
Cups: "Palestinian form"	0	0	0	0	0	2
Total	**6 + 2 (?)**	**72**	**24**	**5**	**2**	**32 + 1 (green-glazed)**

earlier first century BC. In the Jannaeus Destruction levels especially, the high proportion of plain ware fishplates in Coarse Light Brown fabric points to a continuing strong local demand for the form. **FW 6**, **FW 8** and the base **FW 29** are the only certain examples of imported Athenian (Ware 1) fishplates at Pella with by far the greatest number of black-gloss fishplates being of Ware 2.

While only **FW 6** has the sharply down-turned rim and thick wall seen in the late fourth- and early third-century examples from Athens (Rotroff 1983: fig. 53), there is a tendency for those fishplates with the more acutely angled rims (for example, **FW 1–3**) to come from earlier, second-century levels with those with more drooping rims seen in the Jannaeus Destruction levels. **FW 5–7** are from Early Roman strata on Tell Husn and clearly residual. The absence of a base on most of the black-gloss examples makes it impossible to ascertain whether the interior central depression would have been surrounded by a ridge, seen in many of the plain ware fishplates, and suggested to be "typical of the second century BCE" (Guz-Zilberstein 1995: 291). Among Athenian black-gloss fishplates, this feature is seen in some examples produced after the mid-third century BC (Rotroff 1997b: 148); at Pella it occurs in both Pre-Jannaeus Destruction (**FW 28**) and Jannaeus Destruction (**FW 21**) contexts.

Fishplate **FW 30**, along with two very small uncatalogued body sherds from closed vessels (in Mixed Contexts: both very pale brown clay 10YR 8/3, greenish-grey glaze 6/1), are our only examples of "Parthian" glazed ware (Debevoise 1934; Haerinck 1983; Jackson 2011b; Oates and Oates 1958; Toll 1943) – a ware that is rare in the southern Levant (Berlin 1997a: 169–71; Rosenthal-Heginbottom 2015b: 685) notwithstanding the incursion of the Parthians as far south as Jerusalem and Marisa in 40 BC (Josephus *Ant. Jud.* XIV.330–373, *BJ* I.248–273).[11]

FW 1. CN 7446.
XXVIIIB 13.7. Hellenistic 3A.
Part of wall, rim. PH 0.02; D rim (est.) 0.19. Yellowish-red clay 5YR 5/8. Grey core.
Thin dull black gloss on interior; dull red gloss on exterior. Flaring upper wall separated on interior by shallow groove from down-turned rim.
Parallels: 'Akko-Ptolemais (Dothan 1976: fig. 30.1); Hippos-Sussita (Osband and Eisenberg 2018: pl. 2.2.17); Jerusalem (Hayes 1985b: fig. 46.6); Samaria (Crowfoot et al. 1957: fig. 54.2 upper profile).

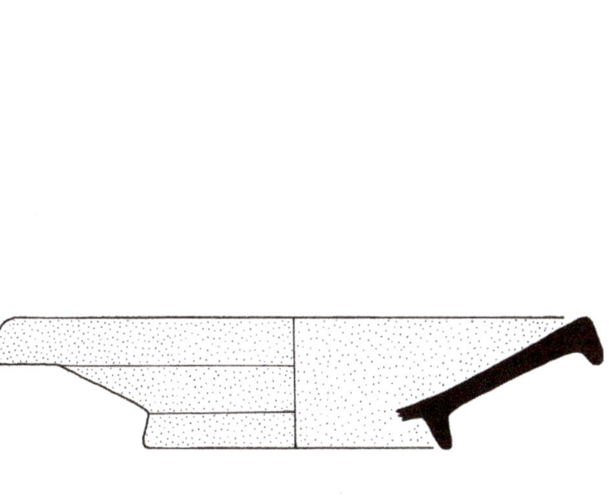

FW 2. CN 7781.
XXIIID 11.16. Hellenistic 3B.
Fragment of rim, wall, base. H 0.04; PL 0.13; D rim (est.) 0.22; D base (est.) 0.10. Reddish-yellow clay 7.5YR 7/6. Ware 2.
Good black gloss on interior, exterior. Ring base. Flaring wall. Rim overhanging exterior.

---

11   See also Schmid (1997: 419) for relations between Nabateans and Parthians during the latter half of the first century BC. Not surprisingly, therefore, a small number of Parthian sherds has turned up at Petra (Horsfield and Horsfield 1941: no. 264b; Schneider 1996: 138, 142, nos 579–591). Fragments of three Parthian amphorae were also recovered in 1978 from a tomb near Rajib about 8 kilometres south-east of Amman (Sauer 1979).

FW 3. CN 7142.

XXXIVF 6.1. Hellenistic 2B.

Part of rim, wall, base. H 0.04; PL 0.11; D rim (est.) 0.11. Yellowish-red clay 5YR 5/6. Occasional coarse white inclusions. Ware 4.

Thick dark brown gloss on interior, exterior. Ring base. Central depression. Slightly curving wall; sharply angled rim.

Parallels: Samaria (Crowfoot et al. 1957: fig. 54.4); Tel Dor (Guz-Zilberstein 1995: fig. 6.3:7, 275–225 BC).

FW 4. CN 0228.

IIIB/C 1.7. Mixed Context.

Part of wall, rim. PH 0.02; D rim (est.) 0.26.

Irregularly fired clay. Reddish-yellow 7.5YR 7/6 to light yellowish-brown 10YR 6/4. Occasional mica. Ware 2.

Worn thin black gloss on interior, exterior. Straight flaring wall; markedly down-turned rim.

Parallel: Jerusalem (Geva 2003: pl. 5.10.39).

FW 5. CN 7170.

XXXIVG 6.10. Early Roman (residual).

Part of wall, rim. PH 0.02; PL 0.04; D rim (est.) 0.21. Red clay 2.5YR 6/8.

Black gloss on interior, exterior. Flaring wall. Almost vertical down-turned rim.

Parallels: Jaffa (Tsuf 2018: fig. 9.47.794); Tel Mevorakh (Rosenthal 1978: fig. 3.14).

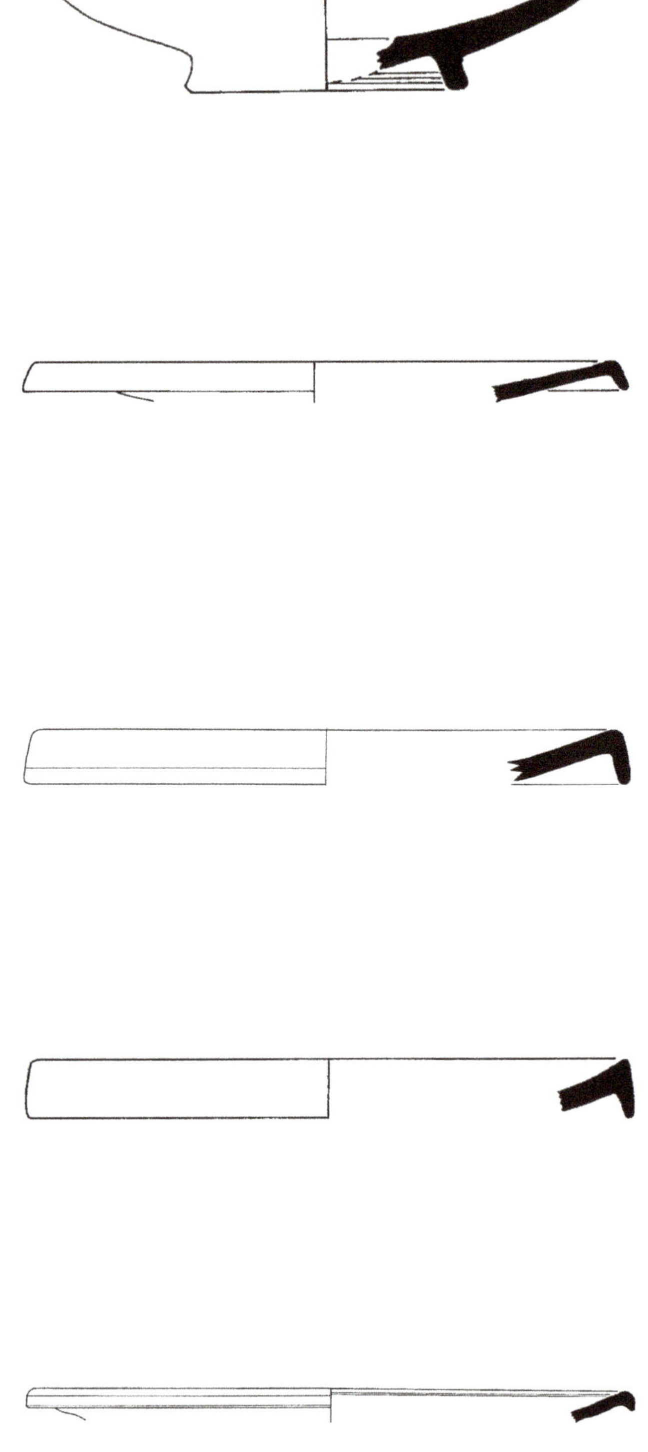

FW 6. CN 3002.

XIA/B 2.1/2. Early Roman (residual).

Part of wall, rim. PH 0.025; D rim (est.) 0.21. Red clay 2.5YR 6/6. Ware 1.

Shiny black gloss on interior, exterior. Vertical down-turned rim.

Parallel: Scythopolis/Beth-Shean (Johnson 2006: fig. 15.1.9).

FW 7. CN 2954.

XIA/B 1.5. Early Roman (residual).

Part of wall, rim. PH 0.03; D rim (est.) 0.37. Very pale brown clay 10YR 7/3. Ware 3.

Thin black gloss on exterior; red gloss interior. Flaring straight upper wall; down-turned rim.

Parallel: Amman/Philadelphia (Zayadine 1977–78: fig. 14.141).

FW 8. CN 7696.

XXXIVB 54.5. Mixed Context.

Two joining fragments forming part of wall, rim. PH (a) 0.01; (b) 0.02. PL (a) 0.04; (b) 0.05; D rim (est.) 0.40. Red clay 2.5YR 6/8. Ware 1.

Lustrous black gloss on exterior, interior. Flaring wall separated on interior by scraped groove from drooping rim.

FW 9. CN 7319.

XXVIIIB 13.2. Hellenistic 3A.

Part of wall, rim. PH 0.035; D rim (est.) 0.19. Reddish-yellow clay 7.5YR 7/6. Well levigated. Ware 2.

Good red gloss on interior, exterior. Flaring upper wall; drooping rim.

Parallels: Ashdod (Dothan 1971: fig. 8.10, first half of second c. BC–2nd half of 2nd c. BC; Dothan and Freedman 1967: fig. 2.2, first half of 2nd c. BC–second half of 2nd c. BC); Tel Anafa (Slane 1997: pl.1. FW 6, 98–75 BC, contaminated).

FW 10. CN 7183.

XXVIIIB 13.2. Hellenistic 3A.

Part of rim, wall, base. PH 0.04; D rim (est.) 0.19. Reddish-yellow clay 7.5YR 7/6. Ware 2.

Red gloss on interior, exterior. Tall ring base. Flaring wall; drooping rim.

Parallels: Samaria (Crowfoot et al. 1957: fig. 54.6); Southern Ghors and Northeast 'Araba Survey (MacDonald 1992: pl. 21.3 upper profile).

FW 11. CN 7485.

XXVIIIB 13.16. Hellenistic 3A.

Part of wall, rim. PH 0.02; D rim (est.) 0.26. Reddish-yellow clay 7.5YR 7/6. Well levigated. Ware 2.

Black gloss on interior, exterior. Flaring upper wall; drooping rim.

Parallels: Ashdod (Dothan 1971: fig. 10.2, first half of 2nd c. BC–second half of 2nd c. BC); Southern Ghors and Northeast 'Araba Survey (MacDonald 1992: pl. 21.4).

FW 12. CN 7188.

XXVIIIB 13.7. Hellenistic 3A.

Part of wall, rim. PH 0.02; D rim (est.) 0.24. Reddish-yellow clay 7.5YR 7/6. Ware 2.

Black gloss on interior, exterior. Fairly straight flaring wall; drooping rim.

Parallels: Gadara/Umm Qais (Kenrick 2000: fig. 10.224); Gezer (Gitin 1990: pl. 43.1, mid-1st c. BC); Tel Michal (Fischer 1989: fig. 13.2.16, 2nd c. BC).

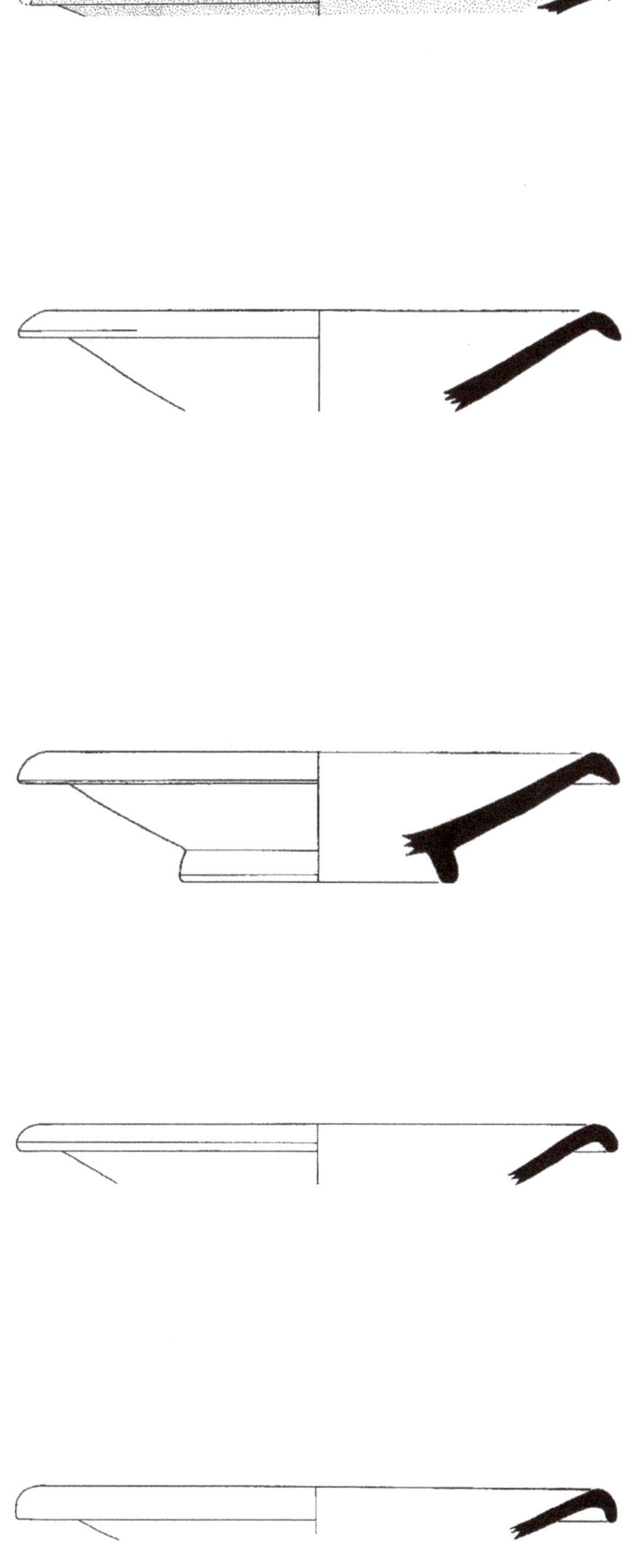

FW 13. CN 7454.
XXVIIIB 13.9. Hellenistic 3A.
Part of wall, rim. PH 0.04; D rim (est.) 0.26. Pale yellow clay 2.5YR 8/3. Well levigated.
Thick black gloss on interior, exterior. Shallow; drooping rim.

FW 14. CN 7440.
XXVIIIB 13.4. Hellenistic 3A.
Part of wall, rim. PH 0.025; D rim (est.) 0.29. Reddish-yellow clay 7.5YR 7/6. Well levigated. Ware 2.
Dull black gloss on interior, exterior. Flaring upper wall. Markedly down-turned rim.
Parallels: Gezer (Gitin 1990: pl. 40.7 profile, late 2nd c. BC); Scythopolis/Beth-Shean (Johnson 2006: fig. 15.1.8).

FW 15. CN 7791.
XXIIID 24.1. Hellenistic 3B.
Fragment of wall, rim. PH 0.04; PL 0.08; D rim (est.) 0.22. Yellowish-red clay 5YR 4/6. Ware 2.
Lustrous black gloss on interior, exterior. In-turned body. Broad slightly convex rim overhanging exterior.

FW 16. CN 7199.
XXVIIIB 13.13. Hellenistic 3A.
Part of wall, rim. PH 0.03; D rim (est.) 0.22. Reddish-yellow clay 7.5YR 7/6. Ware 2.
Dark brown gloss on interior, exterior. Flaring upper wall. Prominent convex down-sloping rim.
Parallel: Hesban (Gerber 2012: 218, 221, fig. 3.11.9).

FW 17. CN 7470. (Figure shows largest fragment)
XXVIIIB 13.10. Hellenistic 3A.
Multiple non-joining fragments of rim, wall, base. (a) PH 0.03; (b) PH 0.025; D rim (est.) 0.21. Reddish-yellow clay 7.5YR 7/6. Well levigated. Ware 2.
Good thick dark red gloss on interior, exterior. Ring base. Central interior depression surrounded by groove. Flaring upper wall; down-turned rim.

FW 18. CN 7373.
XXXIVF 3.2. Mixed Context.
Part of wall, rim. PL 0.09; D rim (est.) 0.19. Reddish-yellow clay 7.5YR 6/6. Ware 2.
Black gloss, fired red in patches, over interior, exterior. Almost vertical down-turned rim. Thick wall.
Parallels: Jebel Khalid in Syria (Tidmarsh 2016: fig. 9.2); Machaerus (Corbo and Loffreda 1981: fig. 35.18).

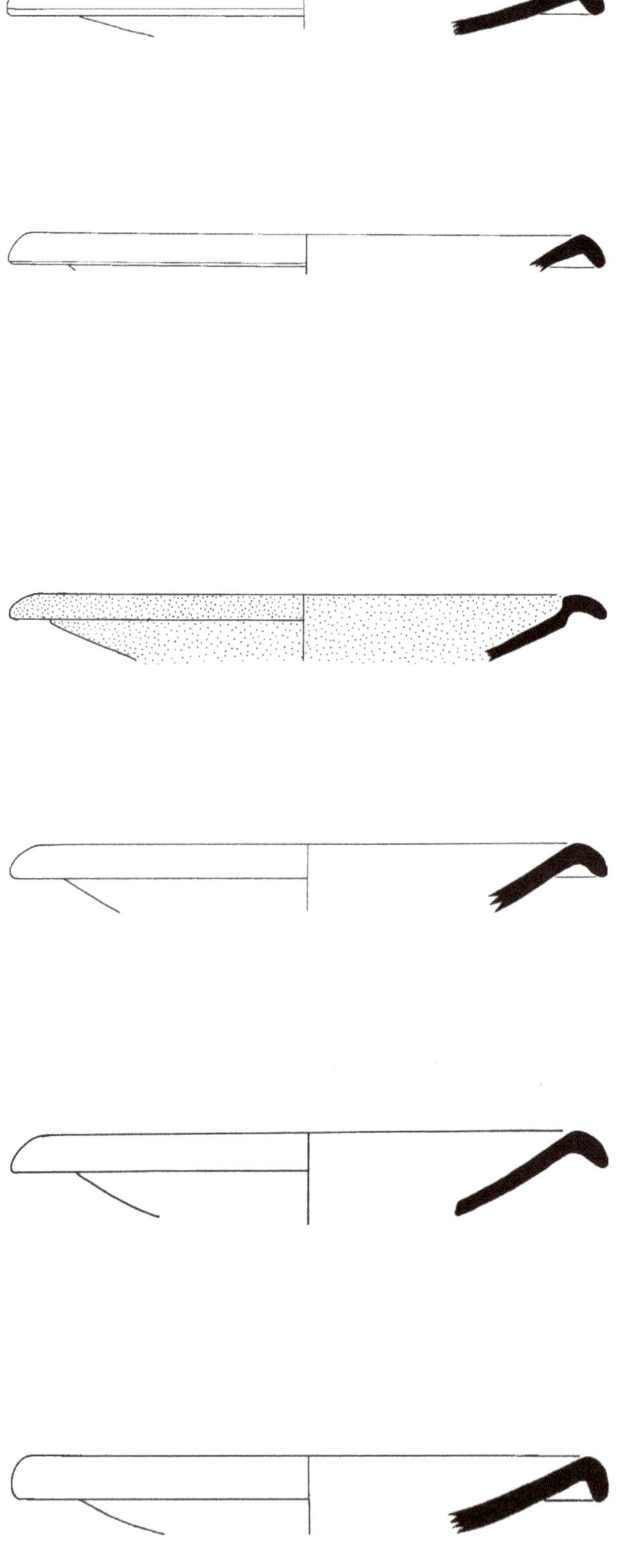

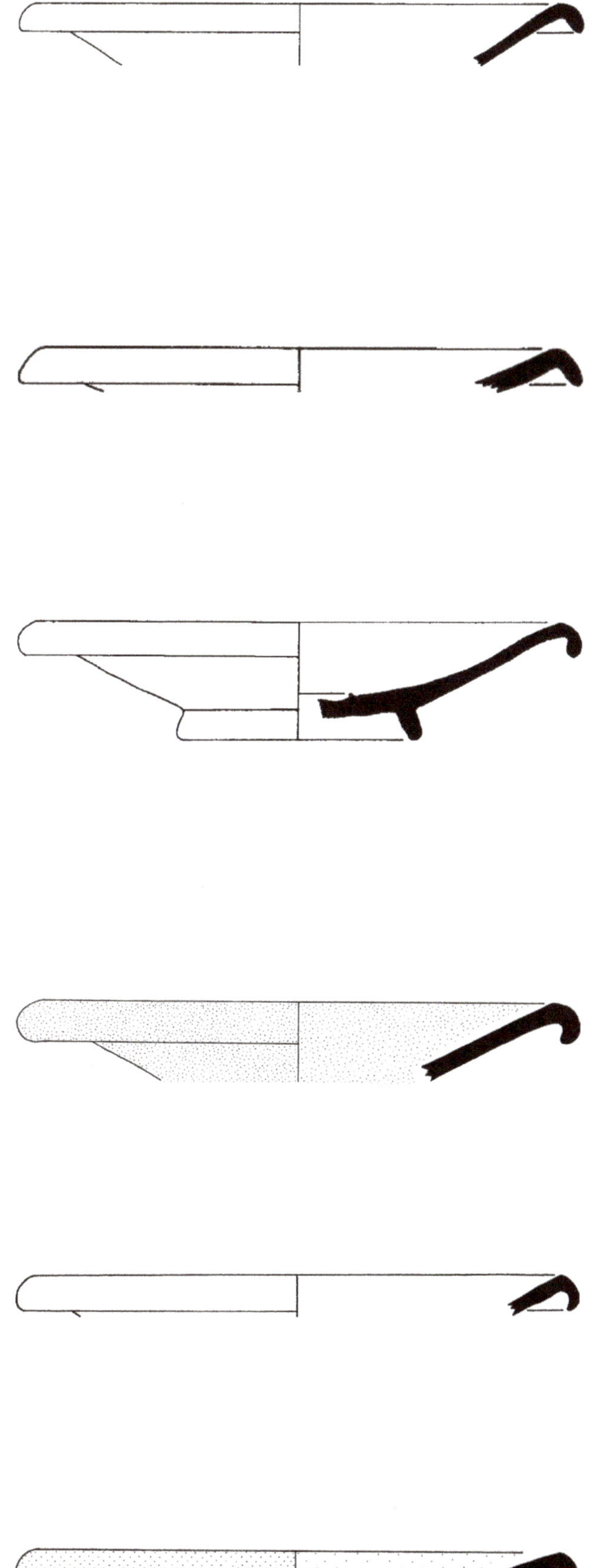

FW 19. CN 6647.
IIIP 25.10. Hellenistic 3B.
Part of wall, rim. PH 0.03; PL 0.075; D rim (est.) 0.25.
Reddish-yellow clay 7.5YR 7/6. Ware 2.
Thick black gloss on interior, exterior. Straight flaring
upper wall; drooping rim.
Parallels: Ashdod (Dothan 1971: fig. 8.2, first half
of 2nd c. BC–second half of 2nd c. BC); Tel Zahara
(Bar-Nathan and Gärtner 2013: fig. 3.15.129).

FW 20. CN 6561.
IIIP 24.5. Hellenistic 3B.
Part of wall, rim. PH 0.015; PL 0.05; D rim (est.)
0.15. Light yellowish-brown clay 10YR 6/4. Ware 4.
Black gloss on interior, exterior. Flaring upper wall;
down-turned rim.
Parallel: Gadara/Umm Qais (Kerner 1997: fig. 12.3).

FW 21. CN 3928.
IVD 10.12. Hellenistic 3C.
Part of rim, wall, base. H 0.055; PL 0.14; D rim
(est.) 0.23. Reddish-yellow clay 7.5YR 7/6. Very well
levigated. Ware 2.
Good black gloss interior, exterior. Tall ring base.
Ridged central depression. Drooping rim.
Parallels: Apollonia (Fischer and Tal 1999a: fig.
5.12.3); Samaria (Crowfoot et al. 1957: fig. 54.5); Tel
Anafa (Slane 1997: pl. 1. FW 1, 125–? BC).

FW 22. CN 3929.
IVD 10.12. Hellenistic 3C.
Part of wall, rim. PH 0.01; D rim (est.) 0.22. Light
reddish-brown clay 5YR 6/4. Ware 2.
Black gloss on interior, exterior. Flaring upper wall;
drooping rim.
Parallel: Hesban (Gerber 2012: 218, 221, fig. 3.11.16).

FW 23. CN 6814.
IVD 13.10. Hellenistic 3C.
Part of wall, rim. PH 0.015; D rim (est.) 0.21. Light
reddish-brown clay 5YR 6/4. Grey core.
Thin black gloss, fired red in patches, on interior,
exterior. Drooping out-turned rim.
Parallel: Samaria (Crowfoot et al. 1957: fig. 54.5).

FW 24. CN 7019.
XXIIIA 100.2. Hellenistic 3C.
Part of wall, rim. PH 0.015; D rim (est.) 0.21. Reddish-
yellow clay 7.5YR 7/6. Ware 2.
Dull black-brown gloss on rim and exterior. Red-
orange gloss on interior. Drooping out-turned rim.

FW 25. CN 6589.
IVE 14.22. Mixed Context.
Part of wall, rim. PH 0.035; PL 0.10; D rim (est.) 0.23.
Reddish-yellow clay 7.5YR 6/6. Ware 2.
Worn brown-black gloss on interior, exterior. Flaring
wall; down-turned rim.
Parallels: Ashdod (Dothan 1971: fig. 8.9, first half of
2nd c. BC–second half of 2nd c. BC); Jerusalem (Geva
2003: pl. 5.3.31).

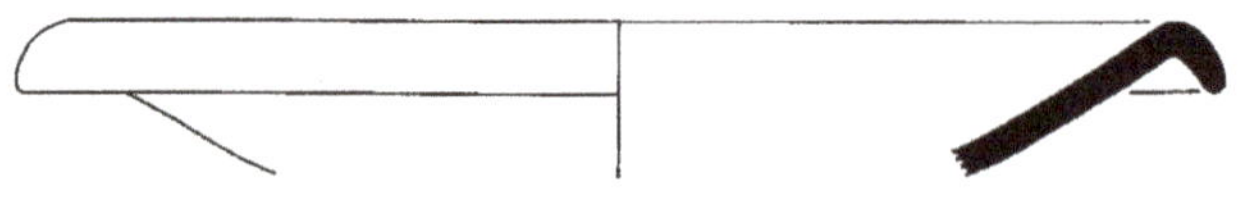

FW 26. CN 6731.
IIIF 1.28. Mixed Context.
Part of rim, wall, base. PH 0.03; D rim (est.) 0.20.
Light yellowish-brown clay 10YR 6/4. Thick grey
core. Ware 3.
Worn black gloss on interior, exterior of rim. Ring
base. Slightly in-turned wall; horizontal convex rim.

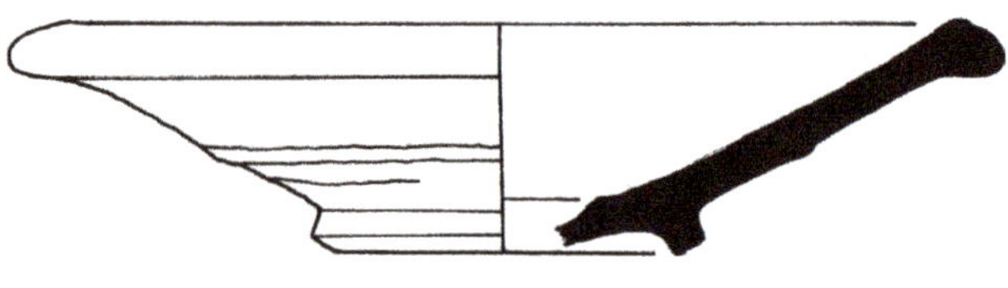

FW 27. CN 7493.
XXVIIIB 13.17. Hellenistic 3A.
Part of wall, base. PH 0.025; PL 0.15. Reddish-yellow
clay 5YR 6/6. Ware 2.
Red gloss on resting surface within ring base; black
gloss on exterior wall. Red gloss on lower interior wall,
well demarcated from black gloss on upper interior.
Ring base. Central interior depression surrounded
by groove.

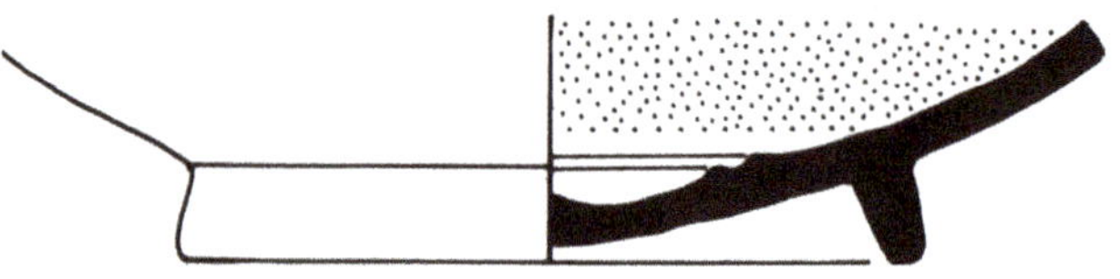

FW 28. CN 7401.
XXVIIIB 10.5. Hellenistic 3A.
Part of wall, base. PH 0.02; D base (est.) 0.03. Red
clay 2.5YR 5/6.
Traces of poor dull black gloss on interior. Raised
disc base. Ridged central depression.

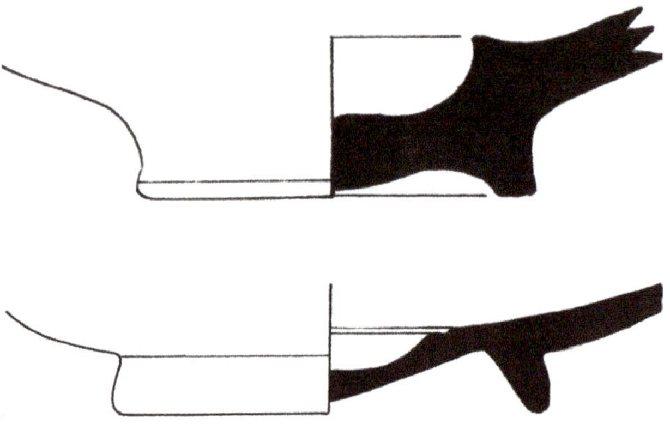

FW 29. CN 0572.
IIIB/C 1.23. Mixed Context.
Part of wall, base. PH 0.03; PL 0.10. Reddish-yellow
clay 7.5YR 6/8. Ware 1.
Thick black gloss on interior, exterior. Tall ring base.
Flaring lower wall. Deep interior depression separated
from wall by groove.

FW 30. CN 7201.
XXVIIIB 13.13. Hellenistic 3A.
Part of wall, rim. PH 0.03; D rim (est.) 0.32. Green-
glazed ware. Light brown clay 7.5YR 6/4.
Green glaze on interior, exterior. Upper wall separated
by faint groove from straight, down-sloping rim.
Parallel: Jebel Khalid in Syria (Jackson 2011b:
GG 13, fig. 138.1, c. 280–150 BC).

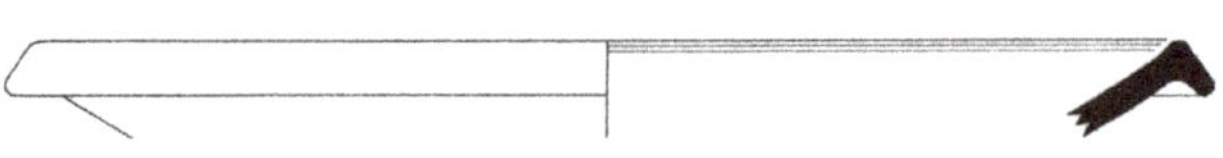

Plates: thickened rim (FW 31–41)

The plate with thickened or "rolled" rim occurs frequently in black-gloss and plain wares at Hellenistic sites, both in mainland Greece itself and in the eastern Mediterranean. The form originated in Athens in the early fourth century where it remained the most popular plate in use during the Hellenistic period (Rotroff 1997b: 142–5). As Rotroff (Rotroff 1997b: 143) points out, "Attic examples are also frequently found as imports elsewhere, mostly in the early Hellenistic period", consistent with the findspot of the Athenian plate **FW 31**. At Pella, however, plates of this form, with its three sub-types (simple thickened rim; undercut thickened rim; grooved thickened rim), are uncommon amongst the black-gloss wares but seen in larger numbers (in particular those plates with undercut thickened rim) amongst the plain wares. With the exception of **FW 31** and **FW 36**, all the black-gloss examples are of Wares 2 and 3.

Although missing its upper wall and rim, **FW 31** should belong within this group. Its lower profile and interior decoration of stamped palmettes within rouletting is close to examples of the second half of the third century from the Athenian Agora (Rotroff 1997b: fig. 47.664, fig. 48.667), consistent with the Hellenistic 2B context from which **FW 31** was recovered.

The plates with grooved thickened rims (**FW 36–41**) are seen in Hellenistic 3A–3B deposits (main mound) at Pella, consistent with their findspots at ʿAkko-Ptolemais (Berlin and Stone 2016: fig. 9.20.3) and Tel Dor (Guz-Zilberstein 1995: fig. 6.3:15).

Simple thickened rim (Type 1)

FW 31. CN 7673.
XXXIVB 27.26. Hellenistic 2B.
Part of base, floor, non-joining small rim fragment.
PL 0.11; D base (est.) 0.11. Reddish-yellow clay
5YR 6/8. Ware 1.
Lustrous black gloss over interior, exterior. Ring base. Flaring lower wall; simple thick rim. Impressed palmette within band of rouletting.
Parallel: Beirut (Élaigne 2007: fig. 1.800-21, first half of 3rd c. BC).

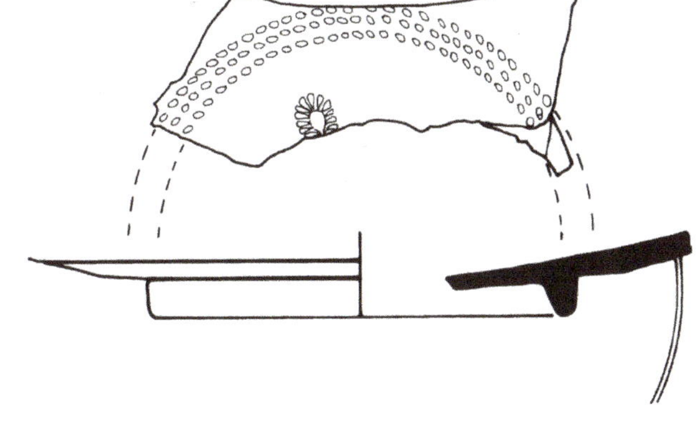

FW 32. CN 6880.
IIIB/C 1.21. Mixed Context.
Part of wall, rim. PH 0.025; PL 0.04; D rim (est.) 0.19.
Yellowish-red clay 5YR 5/6. Ware 2.
Metallic black gloss on interior, exterior. Flaring wall; convex thickened rim.
Parallel: ʿAkko-Ptolemais (Berlin and Stone 2016: fig. 9.4.9, 3rd c. BC).

FW 33. CN 3927.
IVD 10.12. Hellenistic 3C.
Upper wall and rim preserved (two non-joining fragments). PH 0.01; (a) PL 0.055; (b) PL 0.055; D rim (est.) 0.19. Reddish-yellow clay 7.5YR 7/6. Ware 3.
Metallic, slightly dull black gloss on interior, exterior. Shallow. Faint interior groove between upper wall and thickened rim.
Parallel: ʿAkko-Ptolemais (Berlin and Stone 2016: fig. 9.10.10, late 3rd–mid-2nd centuries BC).

FW 34. CN 7481.
XXVIIIB 13.18. Mixed Context.
Part of wall, rim. PH 0.01; D rim (est.) 0.15. Pink clay
7.5YR 7/3. Ware 2.
Patchy thin dull red gloss on interior, exterior. Straight
upper wall. Thickened convex rim.
Parallels: ʿAkko-Ptolemais (Berlin and Stone 2016: fig.
9.12.6, mid–late 2nd c. BC); Ashdod (Dothan 1971:
fig. 15.2).

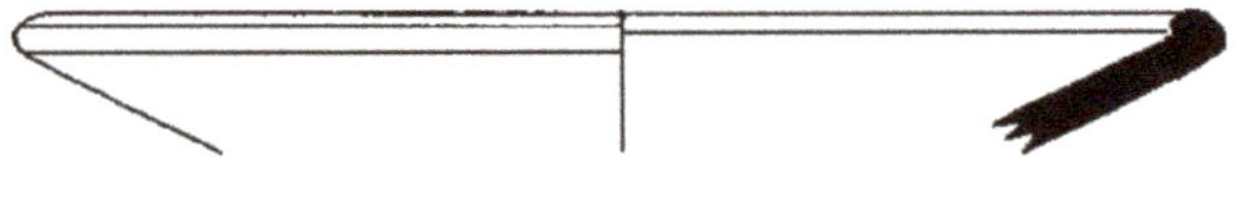

Undercut thickened rim (Type 2)

FW 35. CN 7642.
XXXIVB 150.4. Mixed Context.
Part of rim, wall. PL 0.08; D rim (est.) 0.20. Reddish-
yellow clay 7.5YR 6/6. Ware 2.
Thin patchy black slip over interior, outer exterior.
Thickened undercut rim.
Parallels: ʿAkko-Ptolemais (Berlin and Stone 2016: fig.
9.4.10, 3rd c. BC); Ashkelon (Birney 2022: fig. 14.76).

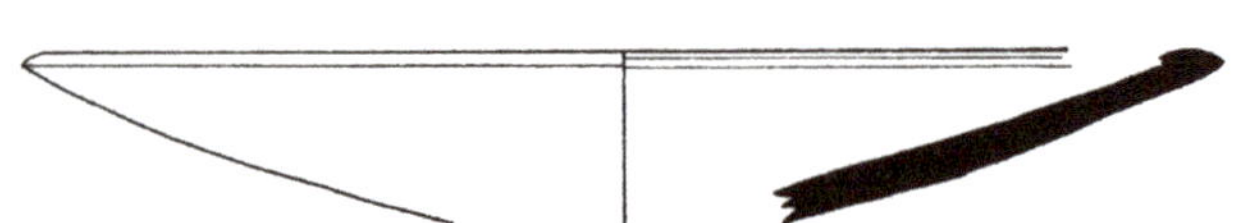

Grooved thickened rim (Type 3)

FW 36. CN 7229.
XXVIIIB 10.5. Hellenistic 3A.
Part of wall, rim. PH 0.015; D rim (est.) 0.15. Light
brown clay 7.5YR 6/4.
Patchy dull red gloss on interior, exterior. Wall separated
by deep groove from thickened indistinct rim.
Parallel: Samaria (Crowfoot et al. 1957: fig. 43.9,
c. 150–108 BC).

FW 37. CN 7203.
XXVIIIB 13.14. Hellenistic 3A.
Part of wall, rim. PH 0.015; D rim (est.) 0.15. Pink
clay 5YR 7/4. Ware 2.
Dull red gloss on interior, exterior. Wall separated
by deep groove from thickened rim.
Parallel: Tel Dor (Guz-Zilberstein 1995: fig. 6.4:4,
300–275 BC).

FW 38. CN 6649.
IIIP 25.10. Hellenistic 3B.
Part of wall, rim. PH 0.01; PL 0.04; D rim (est.) 0.17.
Reddish-yellow clay 7.5YR 8/6. Ware 2.
Dull metallic black gloss on interior, exterior. Flaring
upper wall. Ridged and grooved thickened rim.
Parallel: Tel Dor (Guz-Zilberstein 1995: fig. 6.3:15,
275–150 BC).

FW 39. CN 7848.
XXXIIY 1.2. Hellenistic 3A.
Part of wall, rim. PH 0.015; PL 0.055; D rim (est.) 0.19. Reddish-yellow clay 5YR 7/6. Ware 2. Red gloss on interior, exterior. Flaring wall separated by deep groove from thickened rim.

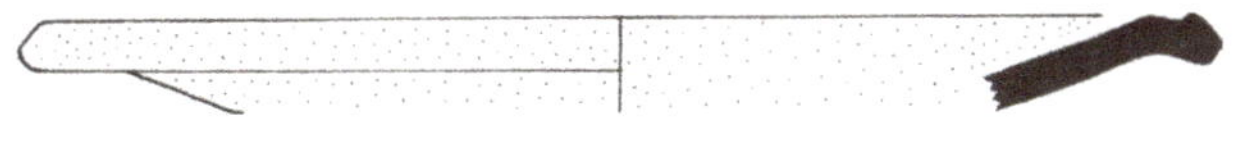

FW 40. CN 7719.
IIIP 25.16. Mixed Context.
Part of wall, rim. PH 0.01; PL 0.045; D rim (est.) 0.26. Very pale brown clay 10YR 8/4. Ware 3. Dull red-brown gloss on interior, exterior. Horizontal offset rim with two broad grooves.

FW 41. CN 6727.
IIIP 25.20. Mixed Context.
Part of wall, rim. PH 0.01; D rim (est.) 0.18. Reddish-yellow clay 5YR 7/6. Occasional small inclusions. Ware 2. Red gloss on interior, exterior. Shallow. Flaring wall separated by deep groove from thickened rim.
Parallel: 'Akko-Ptolemais (Berlin and Stone 2016: fig. 9.20.3, mid–late 2nd c. BC).

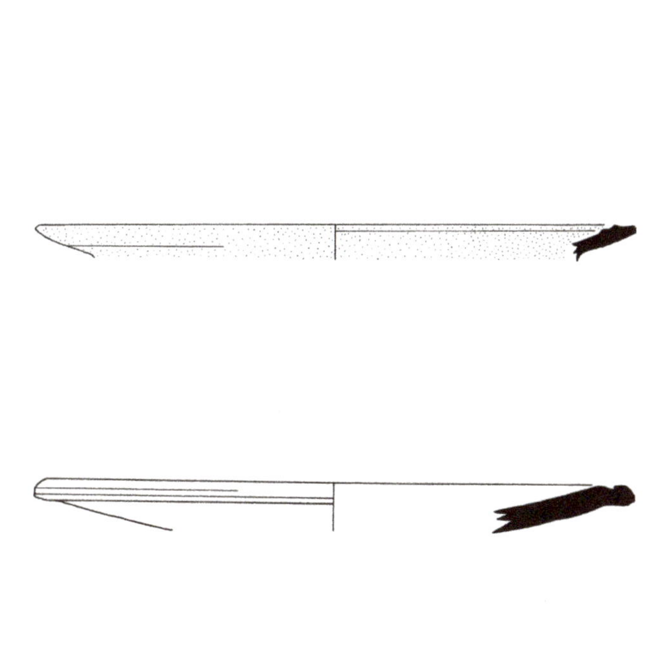

Plates: upright rim (FW 42–44)

While common in ESA (Hayes Forms 2–4; Tel Anafa Type 13), the form, with its slightly sloping floor and short upright rim, is otherwise rare in the eastern Mediterranean. It is, however, more popular amongst the Campana wares of Italian origin. The pale clay and lustrous grey-black gloss of **FW 42–3** point to a source within the so-called "Campana B" wares. Its fabric and variable red-brown gloss do not exclude the possibility that **FW 44** is also of the same ware but, of our Ware 3, is more likely a specimen of Slane's "black-slipped predecessor" Tel Anafa Type 3 (Slane 1997: 277).[12]

Less common in the eastern Mediterranean than Campana A,[13] Campana B ceramics have been identified at Athens, Corinth, Delos and in the Levant at Tel Anafa and Jebel Khalid in Syria;[14] at all these sites plates of the same form – Morel form (*espèce*) 2250 – as the Pella examples have been recovered. The form is dated to the second century BC;[15] at Pella it occurs on the main mound in early first century BC (Hellenistic 3C) levels.

---

12 Slane (1997: 437) makes the point that Campana B "is scarcely distinguishable from the black-slipped predecessor of ESA".

13 Handberg et al. 2013; Lund 2004: 4–7. See also Vogeikoff (1993) who argues that Italian black-gloss wares are more common than generally believed (but not recognised as such) in eastern Mediterranean contexts.

14 See Lund 2004: 6. Also Lund 2004: fig. 7 (Delos); Morel 1986: 469–77; Romano 1994: 74–7, nos 33–36 (Corinth); Rotroff 1997b: 406–7, fig. 98, 1638–1641 (Athens); Slane 1997: 347 pl. 28, FW 465 (Tel Anafa); Tidmarsh 2011: 292 (Jebel Khalid).

15 Morel 1981: 152–5 pls. 39–41; 1986: 473–4.

FW 42. CN 3926.
IVD 10.12. Hellenistic 3C.
Multiple joining and non-joining fragments forming part of wall, rim. PH 0.05; D rim (est.) 0.36. Pink clay. 7.5YR 7/4. Campana B.
Lustrous grey-black gloss of high quality on interior, exterior. Large shallow plate with upright rim.

FW 43. CN 3930.
IVD 10.12. Hellenistic 3C.
Most of wall, rim preserved (multiple fragments). PH 0.03; PL (largest fragment) 0.15; D rim (est.) 0.34. Reddish-yellow clay 7.5YR 6/6. Campana B.
Lustrous grey-black gloss interior, exterior. Shallow. Upright rim.
Morel series ("*série*") 2252 (essentially of 2nd c. BC date). Parallel: Beirut (Élaigne 2007: fig. 14.386-161, second half of 2nd and first half of 1st c. BC).

FW 44. CN 7089.
XXIIIA 100.1. Hellenistic 3C.
Part of wall, rim. PH 0.05; PL 0.10; D rim (est.) 0.27. Very pale brown clay 10YR 8/3. Ware 3.
Red gloss interior. Brown gloss exterior. Deep; flaring upper wall. Vertical simple rim.
Parallels: Ashkelon (Birney 2022: close to fig. 14.93); Tel Anafa (Slane 1997: pl. 2. FW15 = black-slipped predecessor Type 3b, late 1st c. BC–early 1st c. AD).

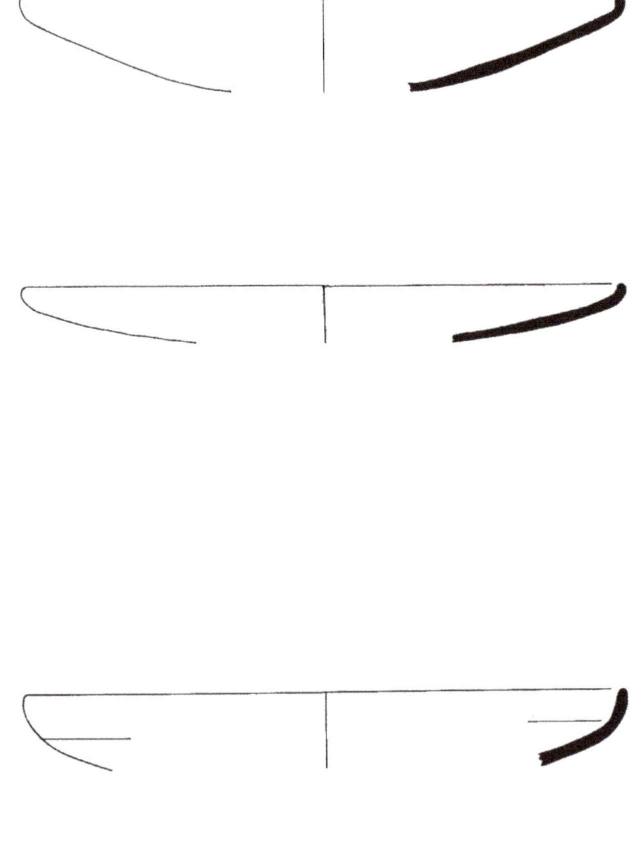

Saucers (FW 45–56)

Most fine ware examples of this form have been found at Pella in second-century and early first-century BC contexts although **FW 45** (from the XXXIVF rubbish deposit on Tell Husn) demonstrates that black-gloss examples first appeared in the previous century. The plain ware form is still encountered in an Early Roman deposit on Husn.

Bowls of this form (in both black-gloss and plain wares) are seen at numerous sites including Samaria, Tel Dor and Tel Michal. Bowls of somewhat similar shape, although smaller and deeper, occur within the Tel Anafa assemblage, first appearing in Hellenistic 1B (second-century BC) levels.[16]

---

16 Crowfoot et al. 1957: figs 37.11–13; 55 (Samaria); Guz-Zilberstein 1995: 293, fig. 6.4: 10–17 Type BL 5b (Tel Dor); Fischer 1989: fig. 13.1.8 (Tel Michal); Berlin 1997a: pl. 16. PW 141–4 (Tel Anafa). Despite the lack of an interior depression, the Samaria examples (Crowfoot et al. 1957: fig. 37) are termed "fishplates" whereas the distinction is made in fig. 55.

FW 45. CN 7145.
XXXIVF 6.2. Hellenistic 2B.
Part of base, wall, rim. H 0.03; PL 0.08; D rim
(est.) 0.13. Yellowish-brown clay 10YR 5/4. Coarse
white inclusions.
Dull black gloss on interior, exterior. Central depression.
Ring base. Curving wall; gently angled rim.
Parallels: ʿAkko-Ptolemais (Berlin and Stone 2016:
fig. 9.4.6, 3rd c. BC); Kedesh (Levantine Ceramics
Project: n.d. K09P196, 3rd c. BC).

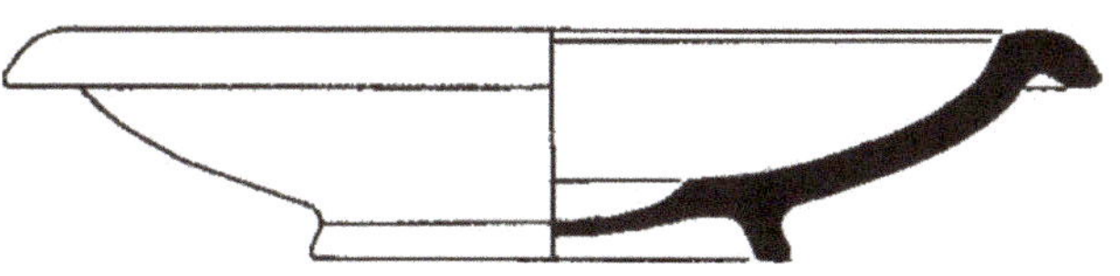

FW 46. CN 0174.
IIIB/C 1.10. Mixed Context.
Part of base, wall, rim, giving complete profile.
H 0.025; PL 0.06; D rim (est.) 0.13. Red clay 2.5YR 6/6.
Dull black gloss on interior, exterior. Thick ring base.
In-curving wall; slightly down-turned rim.
Parallel: Samaria (Zayadine 1966: pl. XXX.65).

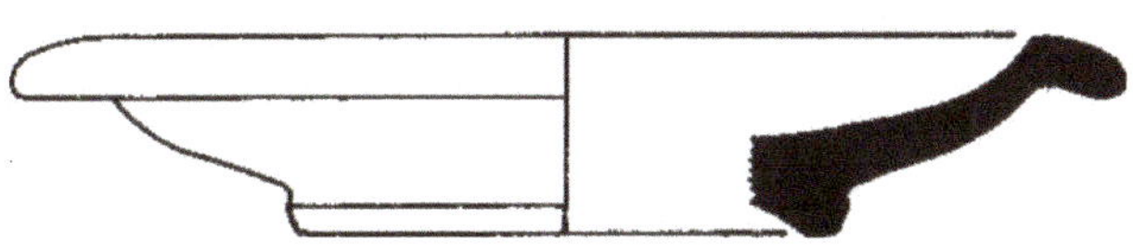

FW 47. CN 0229.
IIIB/C 1.7. Mixed Context.
Part of base, wall, rim, giving complete profile.
H 0.03; PL 0.04; D rim (est.) 0.15. Brown clay 7.5YR 5/4.
Dull black gloss on interior, exterior. Ring base.
Almost vertical upper wall. Broad horizontal out-
turned rim.
Parallels: Ashkelon (Birney 2022: fig. 14.71); Samaria
(Crowfoot et al. 1957: fig. 37.11; Hennessy 1970: fig.
10.25; Zayadine 1966: pl. XXIX.59); Scythopolis/
Beth-Shean (Johnson 2006: fig. 15.1.7); Shechem
(N.L. Lapp 1985: fig. 3.4); Tel Dor (Guz-Zilberstein
1995: fig. 6.4:14, 250–200 BC).

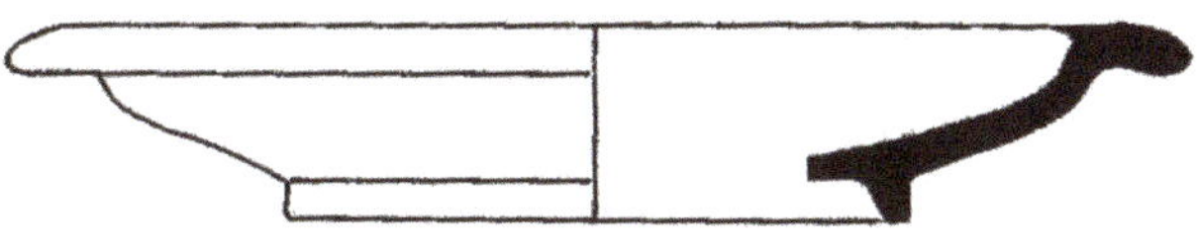

FW 48. CN 7211.
XXVIIIB 13.17. Hellenistic 3A.
Part of wall, rim. PH 0.02; D rim (est.) 0.15. Yellowish-
brown clay 10YR 5/4. Ware 3.
Dull black gloss on interior, exterior. Gently in-curving
wall. Broad horizontal rim.
Parallels: Gadara/Umm Qais (Kerner 1997: fig. 12.4);
Gezer (Gitin 1990: pl. 38.11, mid-2nd c. BC); Samaria
(Zayadine 1966: pl. XXX.65).

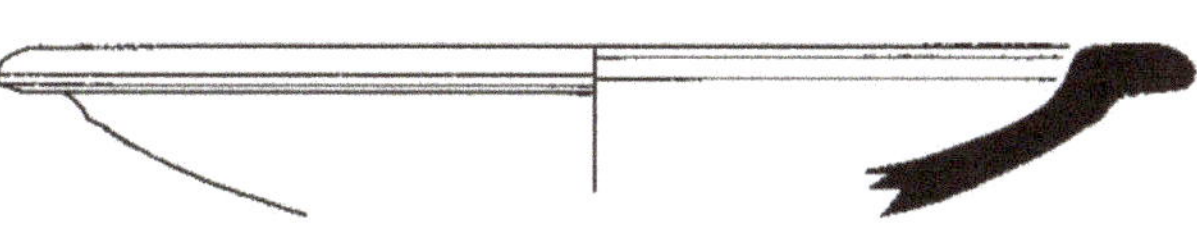

FW 49. CN 6764.
IIIB/C 1.10. Mixed Context.
Part of wall, rim. PH 0.02; PL 0.05; D rim (est.) 0.13.
Reddish-yellow clay 7.5YR 6/6. Ware 2.
Black gloss on interior, exterior. In-curving wall;
out-turned rim.
Parallel: Samaria (Zayadine 1966: pl. XXX.68).

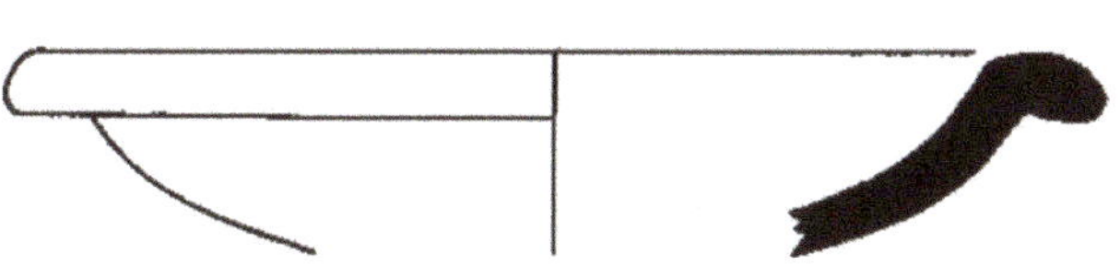

FW 50. CN 6628.
IIIP 24.5. Hellenistic 3B.
Part of wall, rim. PH 0.022; PL 0.065; D rim
(est.) 0.18. Light yellowish-brown clay 10YR 6/4.
Worn black gloss on interior, exterior. Broad rim
overhanging exterior.

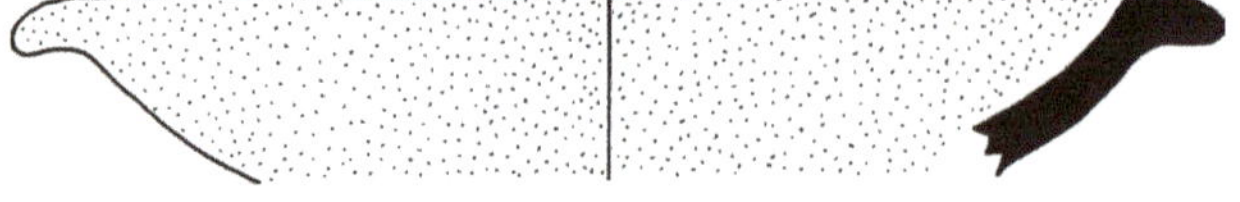

FW 51. CN 7065.
XXIIIA 108.4. Hellenistic 3B.
Part of base, wall, rim. H 0.035; PL 0.105; D rim
(est.) 0.13. Reddish-yellow clay 5YR 6/6. Ware 2.
Dull brown gloss fired red in patches on interior,
exterior. Ring base. In-curving wall; out-turned rim.
Parallels: Samaria (Crowfoot et al. 1957: fig. 43.6);
Tel Yoqne'am (Ben-Tor and Rosenthal 1978: fig. 9.1).

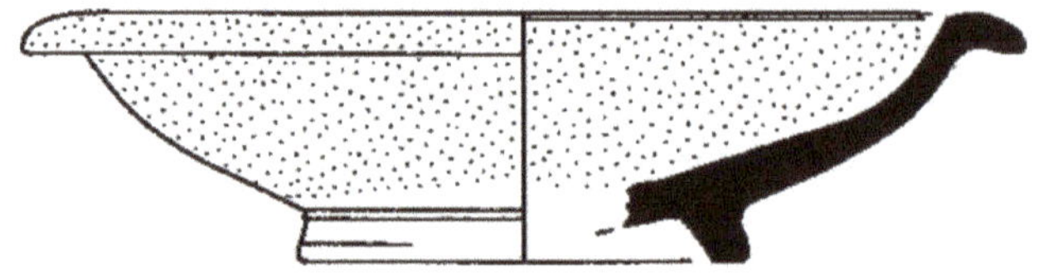

FW 52. CN 7580.
XXXIVB 28.2. Hellenistic 3B/3C.
Part of rim, wall. PL 0.04; D rim (est.) 0.16. Yellowish-
brown clay 10YR 5/4. Ware 4.
Matt black gloss over interior, exterior. Shallow.
Almost horizontal rim.

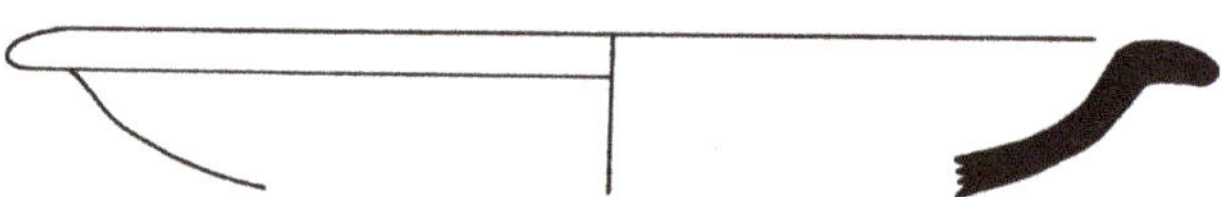

FW 53. CN 6680.
IVD 12.1. Hellenistic 3C.
Part of wall, rim. PH 0.03; PL 0.06; D rim (est.) 0.14.
Reddish-yellow clay 7.5YR 6/6. Ware 2.
Lustrous metallic black gloss on interior, exterior.
Parallels: Samaria (Crowfoot et al. 1957: fig. 55.2); Tel
Keisan (Briend 1980: pl. 13.12a, first half of 2nd c. BC).

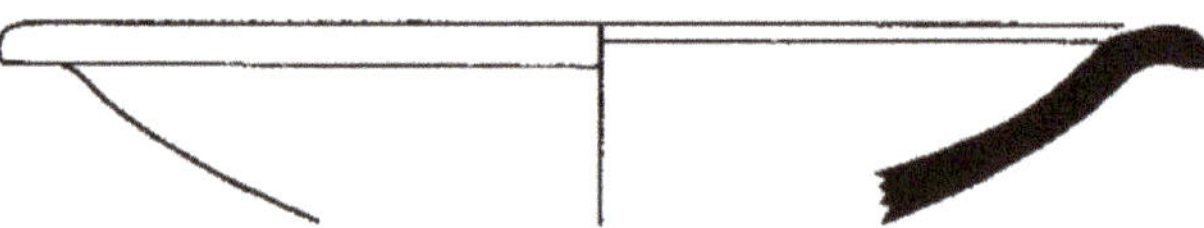

FW 54. CN 4316.
IVD 10.10. Hellenistic 3C.
Upper wall, rim preserved. PH 0.025; D rim
(est.) 0.15. Pale yellow clay 2.5Y 7/4. Small inclusions.
Worn black-brown gloss on interior, exterior.

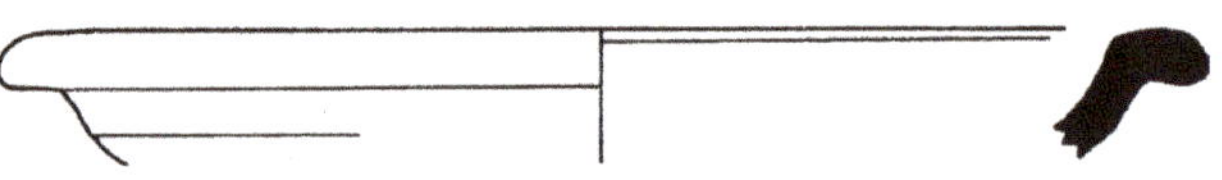

FW 55. CN 7356.
XXXIVB 6.27. Early Roman (residual).
Part of wall, rim. PL 0.05; PH 0.03; D rim (est.) 0.17.
Very pale brown clay 10YR 7/4. Ware 3.
Worn patchy red gloss on interior, exterior. Flaring
wall. Broad horizontal rim.

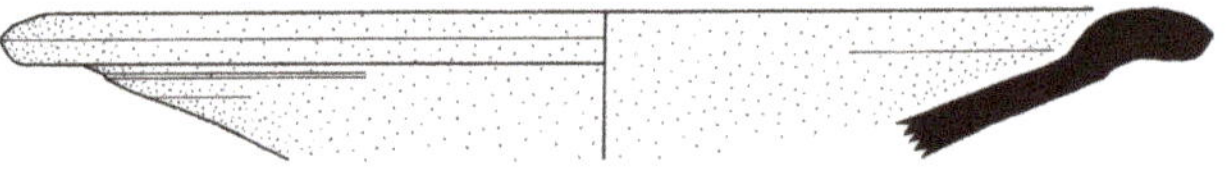

FW 56. CN 0970.
IIIB/C 5.7. Mixed Context.
Part of wall, rim. PH 0.025; PL 0.08; D rim (est.) 0.13.
Reddish-yellow clay 5YR 7/8. Ware 2.
Worn dull gloss on interior, exterior. Broad down-
sloping rim.
Parallel: 'Akko-Ptolemais (Berlin and Stone 2016: fig.
9.4.8, 3rd c. BC).

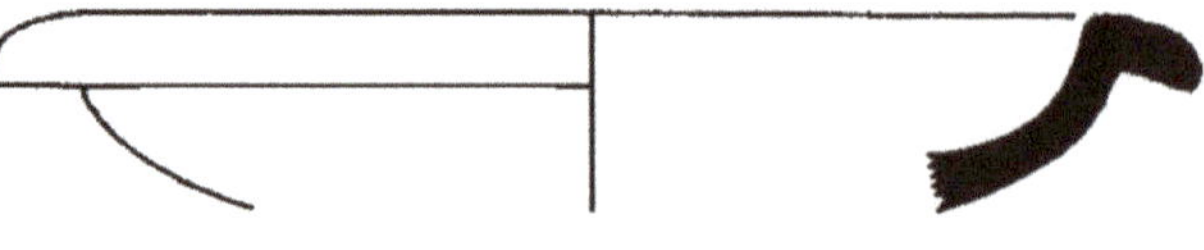

Bowls (FW 57–124)

Out-turned rim (Type 1)

Examples of this type (**FW 57–79**) are seen in larger numbers from deposits of the second and early first centuries BC (Hellenistic 3A–3C) in both black-gloss and plain wares. Generally, the wall flares gently outwards although more angular examples, such as **FW 70**, are also seen. By the later first century BC the type seems to have lost favour.

Black-gloss examples are common from Samaria in deposits spanning all of the second century BC, whilst at Tel Dor bowls of this shape (Type BL 7) appear in large numbers in the late fourth century and remain popular until the end of the second century BC; at both these sites (but not Pella) the profile becomes more angular with time.[17] At Pella the great majority of black-gloss specimens were recovered from deposits of the second century BC with only **FW 77–9** from Jannaeus Destruction levels. With the exception of **FW 60** (Tell Husn), all are from the main mound.

Despite its interior stamped decoration, rare on Athenian examples (Rotroff 1997b: 158), **FW 71** would seem to be Attic as, possibly, are the fragments **FW 62** and **FW 64**.

FW 57 (Ware 2) with its crisp form, rich brown and black gloss and well-drawn palmettes, is a splendid example of how vessels of high quality are not restricted to Athenian workshops but, especially during the earlier Hellenistic years, were produced in Levantine centres as well (in this case probably Antioch or its environs).

FW 57. CN 7540. (Plate 36)
XXXIIY 4.3. Hellenistic 3A.
Two joining fragments forming part of base, wall, rim.
H 0.055; PL 0.19; D rim (est.) 0.23. Reddish-yellow clay 7.5YR 7/6. Ware 2.
Brown gloss on floor inside and outside of rouletting. Black gloss on upper interior, exterior. Well drawn palmettes inside rouletting. Tall ring base. Sloping floor. Markedly flaring wall. Narrow out-turned rim.
Parallels: 'Akko-Ptolemais (Berlin and Stone 2016: fig. 9.15.5 profile, mid–late 2nd c. BC); Kedesh (Levantine Ceramics Project: n.d. K08P172, 2nd c. BC); Marisa (Rosenthal-Heginbottom 2019: fig. 3.2.7).

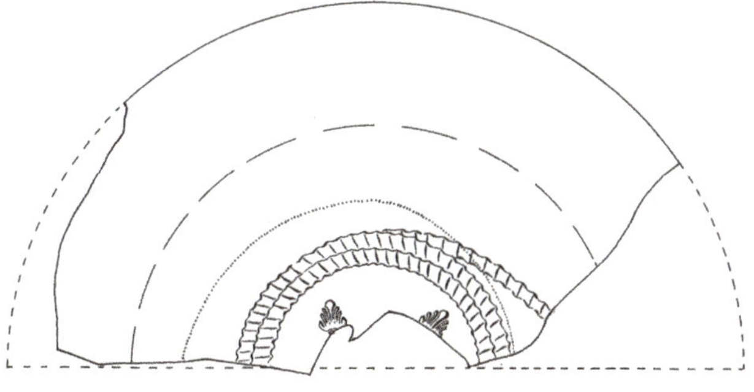

FW 58. CN 7847.
XXXIIY 1.2. Hellenistic 3A.
Part of wall, rim. D rim (est.) 0.18; PH.03. Reddish-yellow clay 7.5YR 7/6. Ware 2.
Good black gloss on interior, exterior.

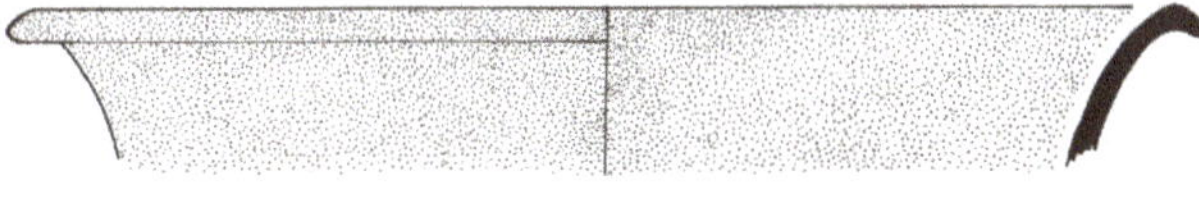

---

17 Crowfoot et al. 1957: figs 37.14–16; 43.4–6; 48 (Samaria); Guz-Zilberstein 1995: 290–1 (Tel Dor).

FW 59. CN 7487.
XXVIIIB 13.16. Hellenistic 3A.
Part of wall, rim. PH 0.045; D rim (est.) 0.14. Reddish-
yellow clay 7.5YR 7/6. Ware 2.
Black-brown gloss on interior, exterior. Flaring,
straight upper wall. Broad slightly down-turned rim.

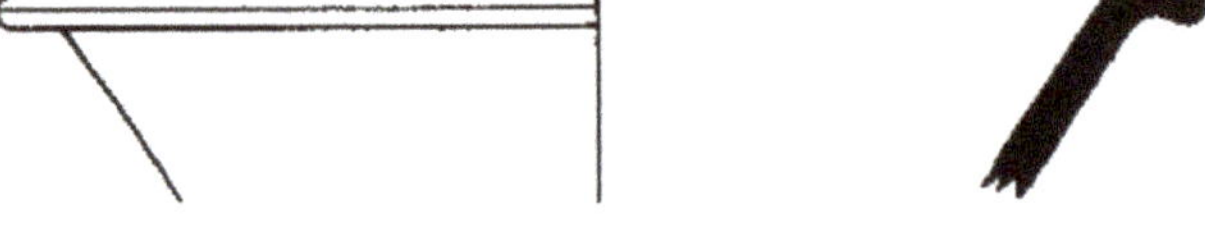

FW 60. CN 7652.
XXXIVB 27.20. Hellenistic 3B/3C.
Part of wall, rim. PL 0.055; D rim (est.) 0.14. Reddish-
yellow clay 5YR 6/8. Ware 2.
Red gloss on interior, exterior. Narrow rim.
Parallel: 'Akko-Ptolemais (Berlin and Stone 2016: fig.
9.1.1, 3rd c. BC).

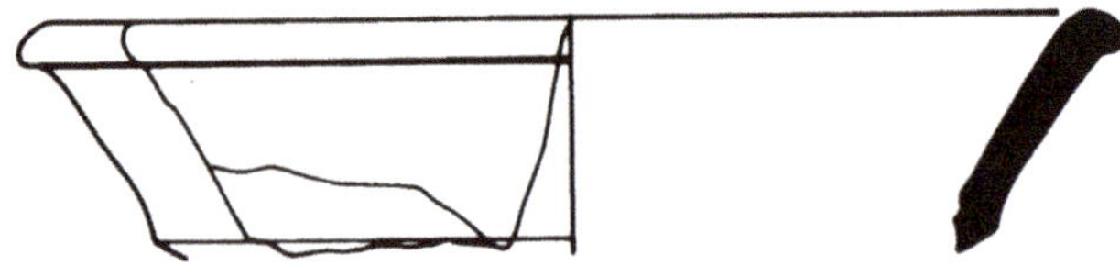

FW 61. CN 7498.
XXVIIIB 13.17. Hellenistic 3A.
Part of wall, rim. PH 0.03; D rim (est.) 0.14. Yellow
clay 10YR 7/6. Ware 3.
Dull black gloss on interior, exterior.

FW 62. CN 7486.
XXVIIIB 13.16. Hellenistic 3A.
Part of wall, rim. PH.03; D rim (est.) 0.18. Reddish-
yellow clay 7.5YR 7/6. Ware 1?
Dull black gloss on interior, exterior.

FW 63. CN 7499.
XXVIIIB 13.17. Hellenistic 3A.
Part of wall, rim. PH.03; D rim (est.) 0.14. Very pale
brown clay 10YR 7/3. Ware 3.
Lustrous black gloss on interior, exterior. Slightly
everted upper wall; out-turned horizontal rim.
Parallel: Samaria (Zayadine 1966: pl. XXIX.41).

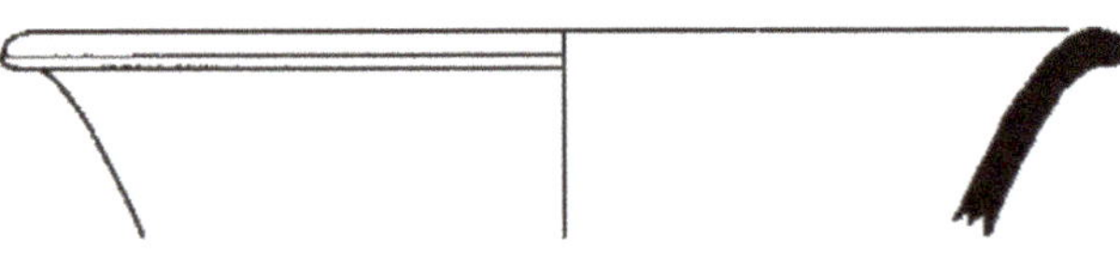

FW 64. CN 7192.
XXVIIIB 13.8. Hellenistic 3A.
Part of wall, rim. PH 0.03; D rim (est.) 0.19. Reddish-
yellow clay 7.5YR 7/6. Ware 1?
Black gloss on interior, exterior.
Parallels: 'Akko-Ptolemais (Berlin and Stone 2016:
fig. 9.6.10, 3rd c. BC); Tel Yoqne'am (Avissar 1996:
fig. X.1.5).

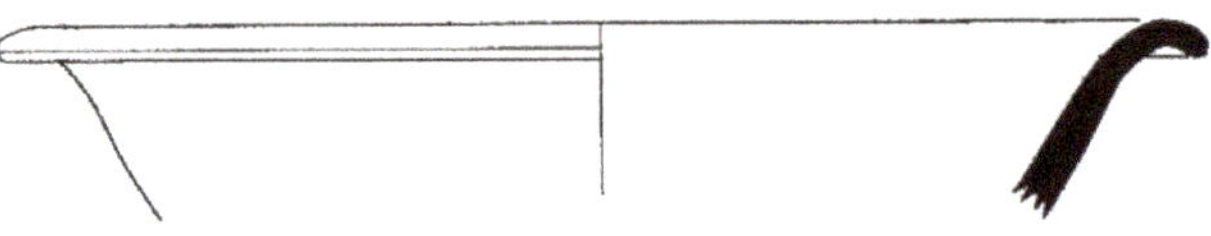

FW 65. CN 7209.
XXVIIIB 13.17. Hellenistic 3A.
Part of wall, rim. PH 0.035; D rim (est.) 0.18. Reddish-yellow clay 7.5YR 7/6. Ware 2.
Dull black-brown gloss on interior, exterior. Flaring straight upper wall. Horizontal out-turned rim.
Parallels: 'Akko-Ptolemais (Berlin and Stone 2016: fig. 9.4.3, 3rd c. BC); Ashdod (Dothan 1971: fig. 14.11); Gadara/Umm Qais (Kerner 1997: fig. 12.2); Marisa (Kloner and Hess 1985: fig. 2.12); Samaria (Zayadine 1966: pl. XXVIII. 33); Tel Dor (Guz-Zilberstein 1995: fig. 6.2:14, 250–200 BC).

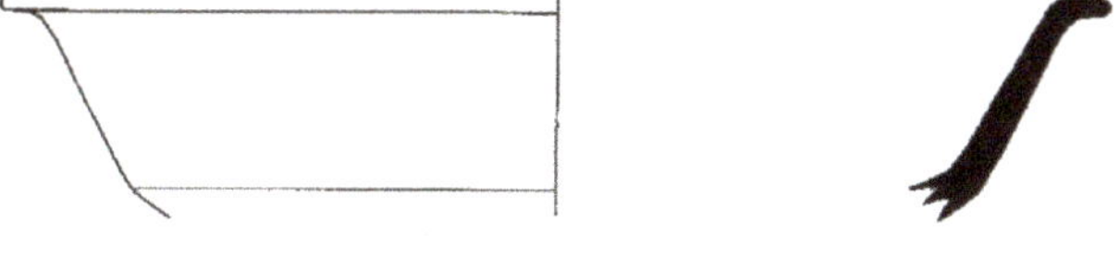

FW 66. CN 7210.
XXVIIIB 13.17. Hellenistic 3A.
Part of wall, rim. PH 0.035; D rim (est.) 0.15. Pink clay 7.5YR 7/4. Ware 2.
Good dull brown gloss. Flaring wall; out-turned convex rim.

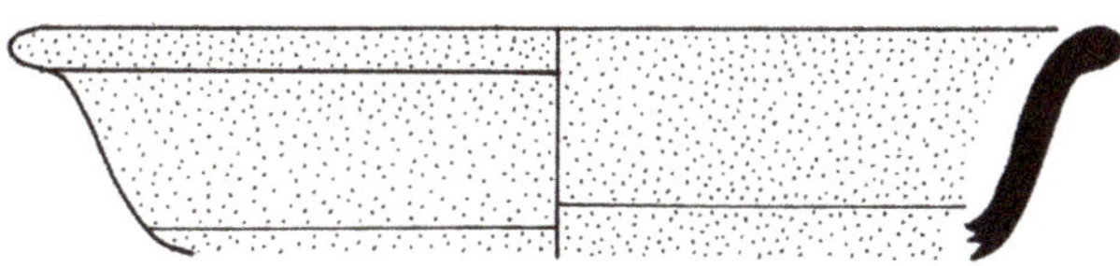

FW 67. CN 7232.
XXVIIIB 10.10. Hellenistic 3A.
Part of wall, rim. PH 0.03; D rim (est.) 0.12. Yellowish-red clay 5YR 5/6. Ware 2.
Dull black gloss on interior, exterior. Relatively shallow. Thickened indistinct out-turned rim.

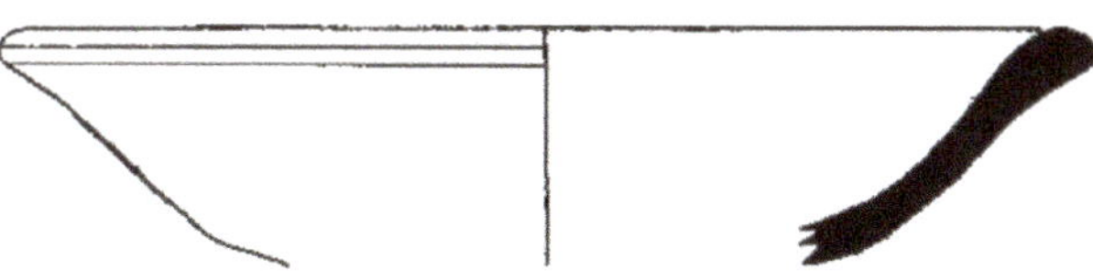

FW 68. CN 0325.
IIIB/C 1.14. Mixed Context.
Part of wall, rim. PH 0.04; PL 0.07; D rim (est.) 0.19. Red clay 2.5YR 6/6.
Mottled brown-red gloss on interior, exterior.
Parallels: Amman/Philadelphia (Koutsoukou and Najjar 1997: 105, no. 119); Tel Dor (Guz-Zilberstein 1995: fig. 6.47:4, 250–200 BC).

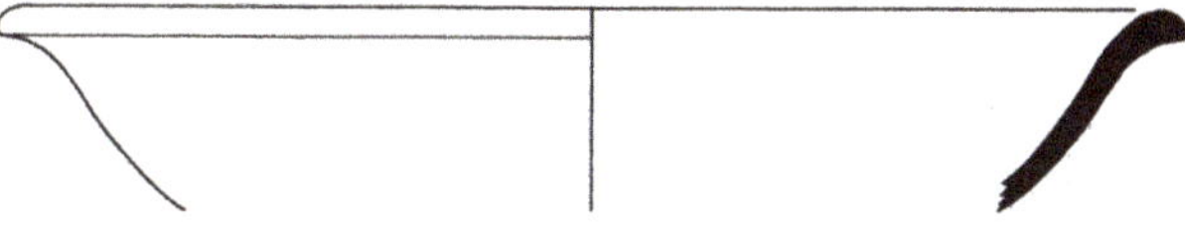

FW 69. CN 0336.
IIIB/C 1.14. Mixed Context.
Part of wall, rim. PH 0.025; PL 0.055; D rim (est.) 0.12. Brown clay 7.5YR 5/4. Fine white inclusions.
Dull brown gloss on interior; red gloss on upper exterior, reserved lower exterior.

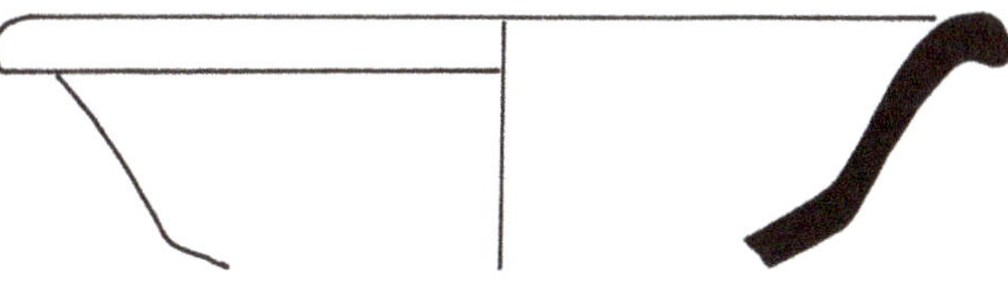

FW 70. CN 0447.
IIIB/C 1.17. Mixed Context.
Part of base, wall, rim, giving whole profile. H0.04; PL 0.06; D rim (est.) 0.125. Brown clay 7.5YR 5/3. Ware 2.
Dull red gloss on interior, exterior. Ring base. Sharply carinated wall, everted in upper section. Indistinct out-turned rim.
Parallel: Samaria (Zayadine 1966: pl. XXVIII.34).

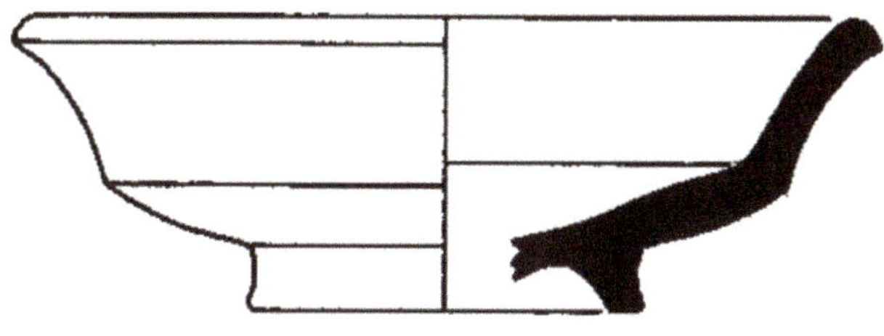

FW 71. CN 0416. (Plate 37)
IIIB/C 1.19. Mixed Context.
Multiple joining fragments giving complete profile.
H 0.065; D rim (est.) 0.19. Reddish-yellow clay 7.5YR
6/6. Ware 1.
Black gloss on exterior, upper interior; red gloss
on lower interior. Two bands of rouletting and five
impressed palmettes on lower interior. Tall ring base.
Gently flaring wall; narrow out-turned rim.
Parallels: Beirut (Élaigne 2007: fig. 1.800–20, first half
of 3rd c. BC); Samaria (Crowfoot et al. 1957: fig. 48.5).

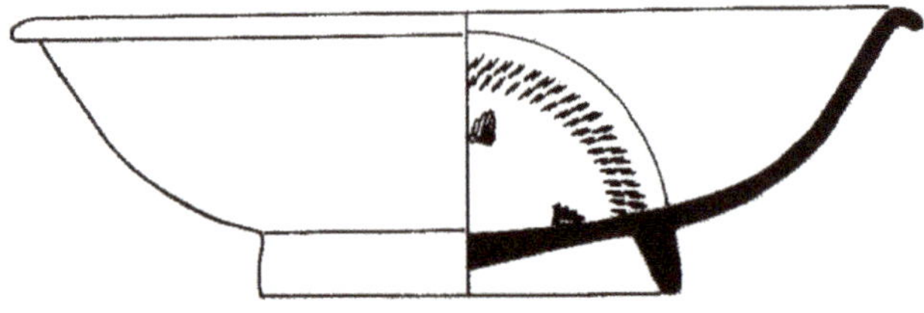

FW 72. CN 6763.
IIIB/C 1.14. Mixed Context.
Part of wall, rim. PH 0.035; PL 0.07; D rim (est.) 0.19.
Light red clay 10R 6/6.
Dull metallic gloss on interior, exterior.
Parallel: Samaria (Hennessy 1970: fig. 9.21).

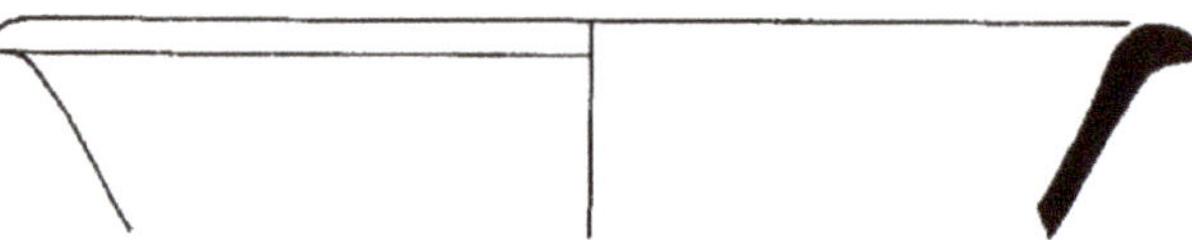

FW 73. CN 7469.
XXVIIIB 13.10. Hellenistic 3A.
Part of wall, rim. PH 0.04; D rim (est.) 0.15. Very
pale brown clay 10YR 7/4. Ware 3.
Dull black-brown gloss on interior, exterior. Carinated
wall; almost vertical upper section. Slightly drooping rim.

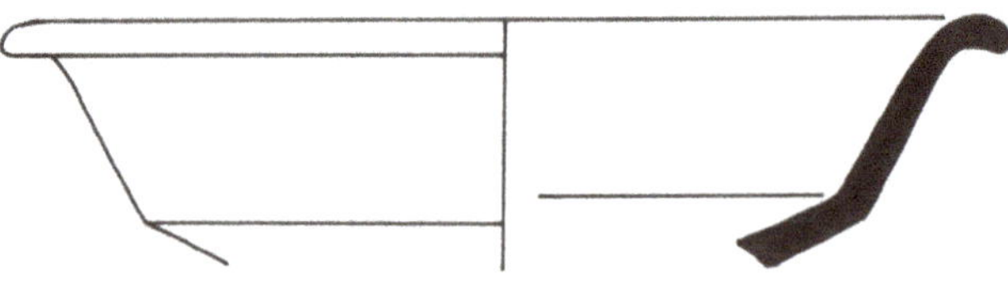

FW 74. CN 0344.
IIIB/C 1.14. Mixed Context.
Part of wall, rim. PH 0.035; D rim (est.) 0.13. Brown
clay 7.5YR 5/4. Ware 2.
Dull black-brown gloss on interior, exterior. Flaring
upper wall; indistinct rim.

FW 75. CN 7078.
XXIIIA 109.4. Hellenistic 3B.
Part of wall, rim. PH 0.025; D rim (est.) 0.10. Reddish-
yellow clay 5YR 6/8. Ware 2.
Mottled black-brown gloss on interior, exterior.
Everted upper wall; indistinct rim.

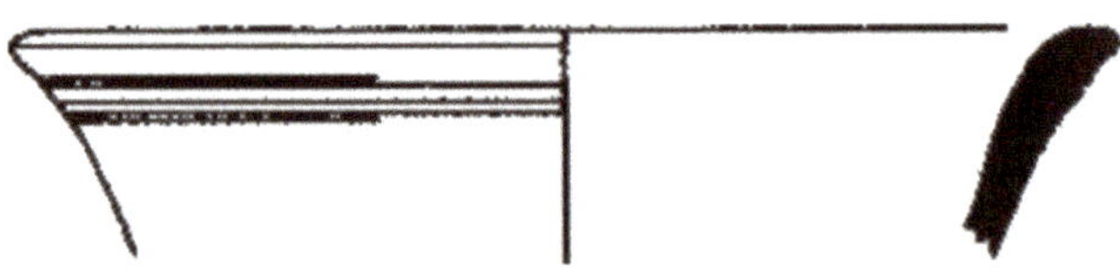

FW 76. CN 0244.
IIIB/C 1.10. Mixed Context.
Part of wall, rim. PH 0.03; D rim (est.) 0.15. Strong
brown clay 7.5YR 5/6. Ware 2.
Brown gloss on interior, exterior. Flaring upper wall;
indistinct rim.

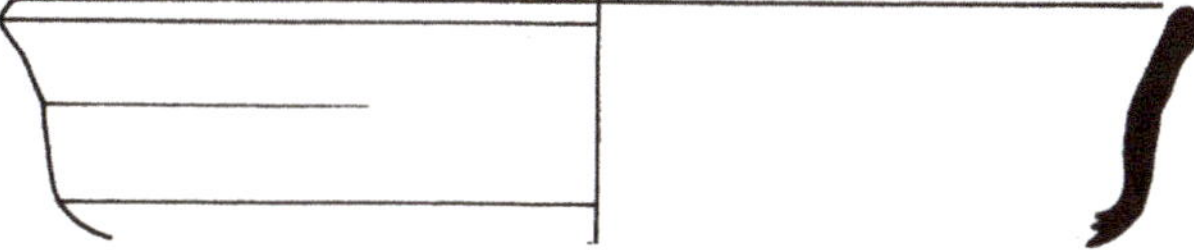

FW 77. CN 0905.
IIIB/C 15.2. Hellenistic 3C.
Part of wall, rim. PH 0.02; D rim (est.) 0.14. Dark
brown clay 7.5YR 3/2.
Thin black gloss on interior, exterior.

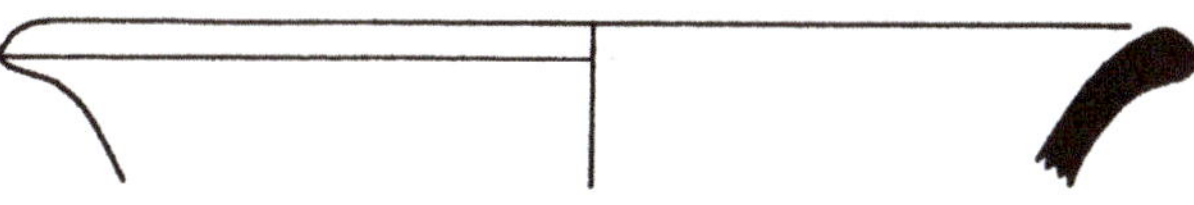

FW 78. CN 4311.
IVD 10.10. Hellenistic 3C.
Part of wall, rim. PH 0.025; PL 0.06; D rim (est.) 0.15.
Pink clay 7.5YR 7/4. Ware 2.
Thin dull brown-black gloss. Very worn.
Parallel: Machaerus (Corbo and Loffreda 1981:
fig. 35.19).

FW 79. CN 6681.
IVD 12.1. Hellenistic 3C.
Part of wall, rim. PH 0.035; PL 0.065; D rim
(est.) 0.15. Light brown clay 7.5YR 6/4. Ware 3.
Lustrous metallic gloss on interior; thin dull black
gloss on exterior. Flaring upper wall; narrow out-
turned rim.
Parallels: ʿAkko-Ptolemais (Dothan 1976: fig. 30.7);
Gadara/Umm Qais (Kerner 1997: fig. 12.2); Tel Dor
(Guz-Zilberstein 1995: fig. 6.2:10, 275–125 BC); Tel
Yoqneʿam (Ben-Tor et al. 1983: fig. 7.6).

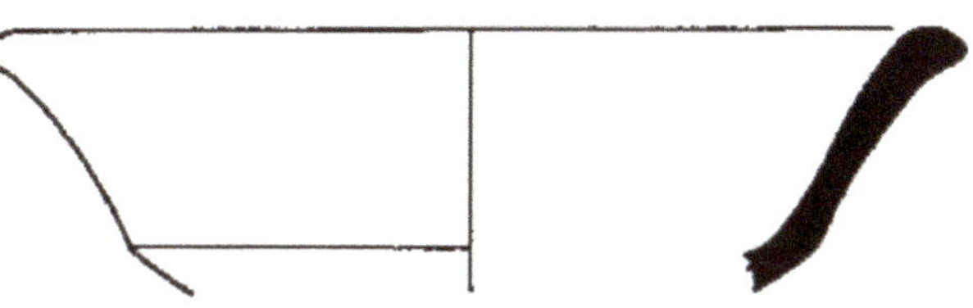

In-turned rim (Type 2)

FW 80–108 are small deep bowls making up the largest bowl type at Pella. They appear in all Hellenistic phases
in both fine and plain wares with the fine ware examples largely replaced by plain ware bowls in Hellenistic
3C levels. In some examples, the wall is gently in-curving whilst in others it is straighter; at Pella there appears
to be no chronological significance in this variation and so the two forms have been included within the
one type. Most of our fine ware examples consist solely of wall and rim with only **FW 80–1, FW 102** and
FW 107–8 retaining a complete profile.

Bowls with in-turned rim ("echinus bowls") exist at virtually all Hellenistic sites in the eastern
Mediterranean, appearing as early as the mid-fourth century and remaining popular until the end of the
second century BC (Guz-Zilberstein 1995: 289).

Although it may have originated in Athens during the fifth century BC (Sparkes and Talcott 1970: 131–2),
the shape only became popular in Hellenistic times. During the third and second centuries, its distribution
was widespread throughout the Mediterranean world, appearing in a number of wares including black-gloss,
ESA and numerous local versions.

In Athens there is a tendency for the shape to lose its "subtlety of line" during the second century
(Thompson 1934: 437) and a similar progression can be followed at Tarsus (F.F. Jones 1950: 157) and Samaria

(Crowfoot et al. 1957: 225) but not at Tel Dor (Guz-Zilberstein 1995: 290) or Pella. The shape is common at Gezer (Gitin 1990: Types 193–195) where it appears around the beginning of the second century and finishes around the mid-first century BC. In contrast to Pella, the later examples of Type 195 adopt an increased angularity of rim although Gitin detected no other typological development (Gitin 1990: 246).

FW 80. CN 7197.
XXVIIIB 13.11. Hellenistic 3A.
Two joining fragments giving complete profile. H 0.54; D rim (est.) 0.105. Pink clay 7.5YR 7/4. Ware 2. Black gloss on interior, exterior. Ring base. Fairly straight wall curving inwards in upper section.
Parallels: 'Akko-Ptolemais (Berlin and Stone 2016: fig. 9.17.2, mid–late 2nd c. BC); Amman/Philadelphia (Greene and 'Amr 1992: fig. 4.8); Ashkelon (Birney 2022: fig. 14.47); Beirut (Élaigne 2007: fig. 14.361–239, second half of 2nd and first half of 1st c. BC); Samaria (Hennessy 1970: fig. 10.19).

FW 81. CN 7204.
XXVIIIB 13.16. Hellenistic 3A.
Part of base, wall, rim. H 0.045; D rim (est.) 0.105. Reddish-yellow clay 7.5YR 7/6. Ware 2.
Patchy red gloss on interior, exterior. Ring base. Fairly straight wall; in-turned rim.
Parallels: Amman/Philadelphia (Zayadine 1977–78: fig. 13.407); Ashkelon (Birney 2022: fig. 14.44); Gadara/Umm Qais (Kenrick 2000: fig. 5.36); Jerusalem (Geva 2003: pl. 5.5.3); Sha'ar ha-Amakim (Mlynarczyk 2000: pl. 117.11); Tel Dor (Guz-Zilberstein 1995: fig. 6.47.8, 250–200 BC).

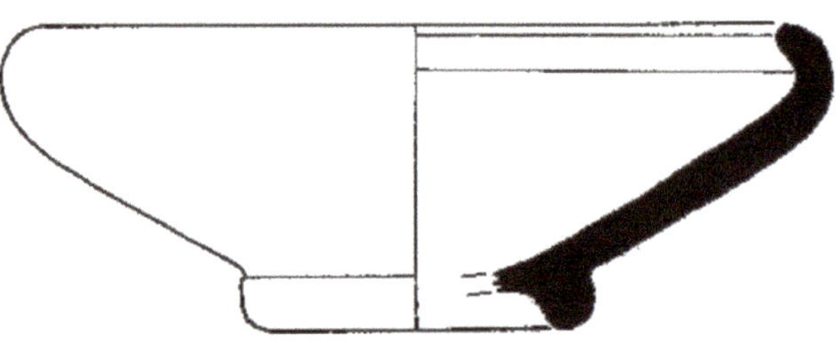

FW 82. CN 7500.
XXVIIIB 13.17. Hellenistic 3A.
Part of wall, rim. PH 0.025; D rim (est.) 0.135. Reddish-yellow 7.5YR 7/6. Occasional coarse white inclusions.
Thin red gloss on interior, exterior.

FW 83. CN 7215.
XXVIIIB 13.17. Hellenistic 3A.
Two joining fragments of upper wall, rim. PH 0.03; D rim (est.) 0.105. Very pale brown clay 10YR 7/4. Ware 3.
Thin dull black gloss, fired brown in patches, on interior, exterior.
Parallel: Tel Keisan (Briend 1980: pl. 13.1d, late 4th–mid-2nd c. BC).

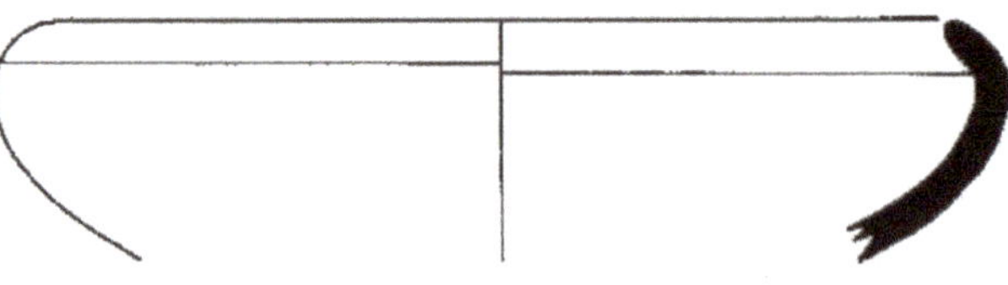

FW 84. CN 7404.
XXVIIIB 10.6. Hellenistic 3A.
Part of wall, rim. PH 0.03; D rim (est.) 0.14. Reddish-yellow clay 7.5YR 7/6. Thick grey core. Occasional coarse white inclusions.
Dull thin patchy red gloss on interior, exterior.
Parallel: Kedesh (Levantine Ceramics Project: n.d. K99P131, early–mid-2nd c. BC).

FW 85. CN 7479.
XXVIIIB 13.14. Hellenistic 3A.
Part of wall, rim. PH 0.035; D rim (est.) 0.11. Yellow clay 10YR 7/6. Ware 3.
Good black gloss on upper exterior; brown gloss on interior and lower exterior.
Parallels: Amman/Philadelphia (Zayadine 1977–78: fig. 13.343); Tel 'Ira (Fischer and Tal 1999b: fig. 6.127.1).

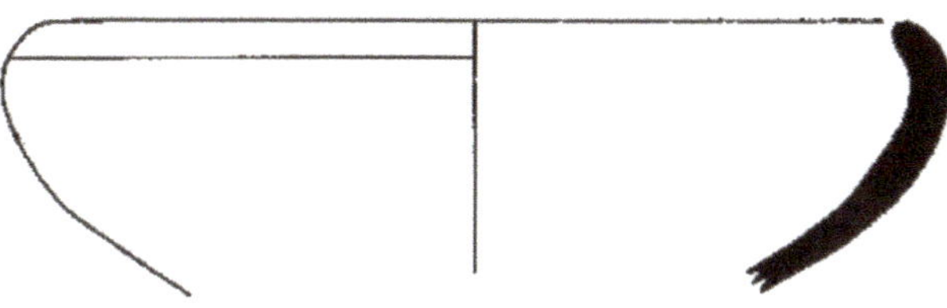

FW 86. CN 7309.
XXVIIIB 10.4. Hellenistic 3A.
Two joining fragments of wall, rim. PH.04; D rim (est.) 0.14. Pink clay 7.5YR 7/4. Ware 2.
Thin red gloss on interior; patchy black-brown gloss on upper exterior; thin red gloss on lower exterior. Straight flaring upper wall; sharply in-turned rim.
Parallel: Tel Dor (Guz-Zilberstein 1995: fig. 6.1:27, 275–150 BC).

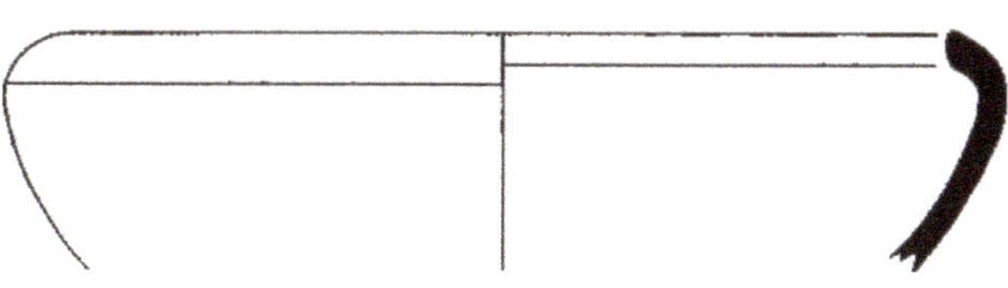

FW 87. CN 7313.
XXVIIIB 10.10. Hellenistic 3A.
Part of wall, rim. PH 0.05; D rim (est.) 0.15. Reddish-yellow clay 7.5YR 7/6. Ware 2.
Red gloss on interior; black gloss on upper exterior and rim. Red gloss on lower exterior.
Parallel: Tel Anafa (Slane 1997: pl. 32. FW 525, 198–? BC).

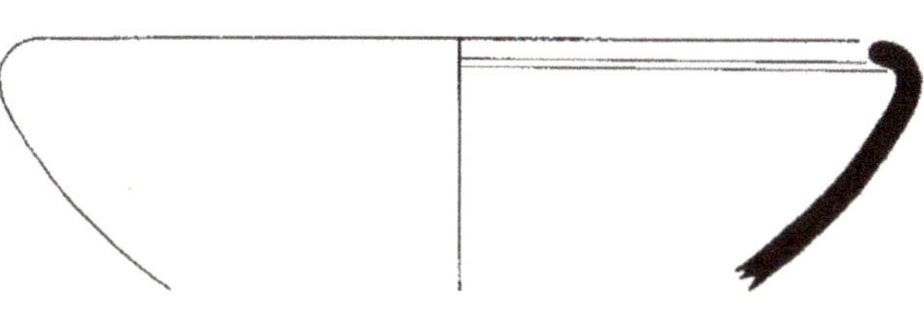

FW 88. CN 7441.
XXVIIIB 13.4. Hellenistic 3A.
Part of wall, rim. PH 0.025; D rim (est.) 0.10. Very pale brown clay 10YR 7/4. Ware 3.
Lustrous red-brown gloss on interior, exterior. Markedly in-turned rim.

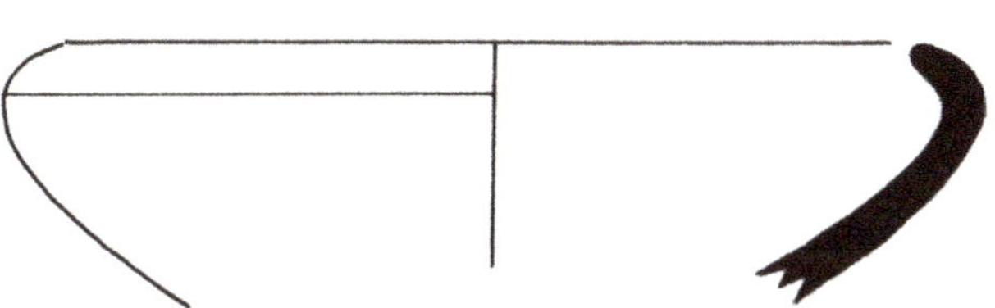

FW 89. CN 7496.

XXVIIIB 13.17. Hellenistic 3A.

Part of wall, rim. PH 0.045; D rim (est.) 0.15. Reddish-yellow clay 7.5YR 6/6. Well levigated. Ware 2.

Black gloss on upper exterior; dark red gloss on lower exterior, interior.

Parallels: Gadara/Umm Qais (Kenrick 2000: fig. 11.225); Samaria (Zayadine 1966: pl. XXIX.47); Tel Dor (Guz-Zilberstein 1995: fig. 6.48: 22, 275–250 BC).

FW 90. CN 7217.

XXVIIIB 13.18. Mixed Context.

Two joining fragments of wall, rim. PH 0.055; D rim (est.) 0.165. Pink clay 5YR 7/4. Ware 4.

Dark brown-red gloss on interior. Brown-black gloss on exterior. Upper wall curves inwards to indistinct rim. Two rows of rouletting on interior.

Parallel: Tell es-Sa'idiyeh (Pritchard 1985: fig. 19.12).

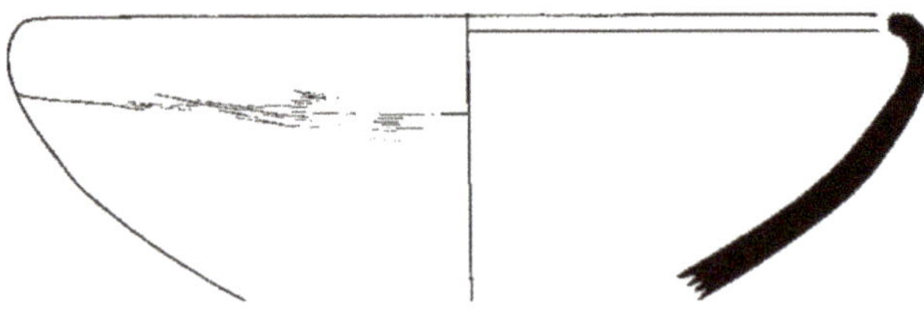

FW 91. CN 7214.

XXVIIIB 13.17. Hellenistic 3A.

Part of wall, rim. PH 0.04; D rim (est.) 0.15. Pink clay 7.5YR 7/4. Ware 2.

Dull black gloss on interior, exterior.

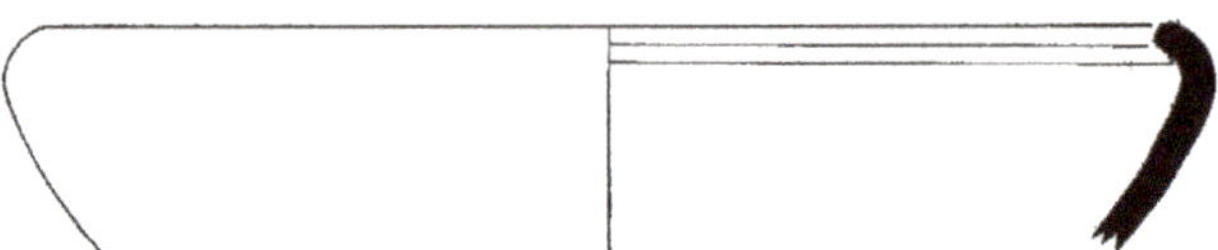

FW 92. CN 7449.

XXVIIIB 13.8. Hellenistic 3A.

Part of wall, rim. PH 0.045; D rim (est.) 0.12. Reddish-yellow clay 7.5YR 7/6. Ware 2.

Brown gloss on interior, upper exterior. Well-demarcated zone of red gloss on lower exterior.

Parallels: 'Akko-Ptolemais (Berlin and Stone 2016: fig. 9.4.4, 3rd c. BC); Gezer (Gitin 1990: pl. 33.14, late 3rd–early 2nd c. BC); Tel Keisan (Briend 1980: pl. 13.1b, first half of 2nd c. BC).

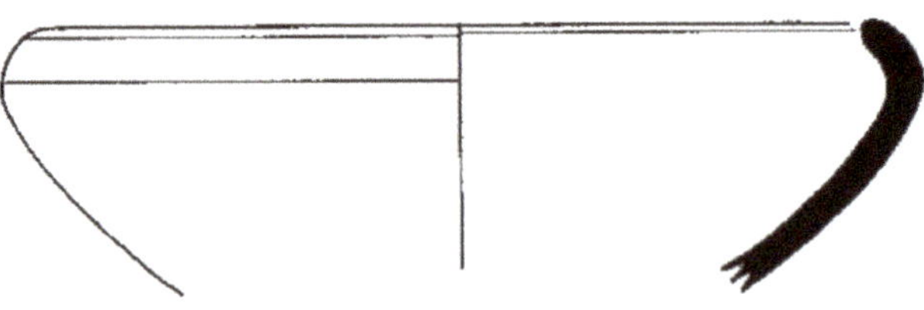

FW 93. CN 7497.

XXVIIIB 13.17. Hellenistic 3A.

Part of wall, rim. PH 0.03; D rim (est.) 0.15. Reddish-yellow clay 7.5YR 7/6. Ware 2.

Black gloss on interior, exterior.

Parallels: 'Akko-Ptolemais (Berlin and Stone 2016: fig. 9.12.1, mid–late 2nd c. BC); Tell es-Sa'idiyeh (Pritchard 1985: fig. 19.11 profile).

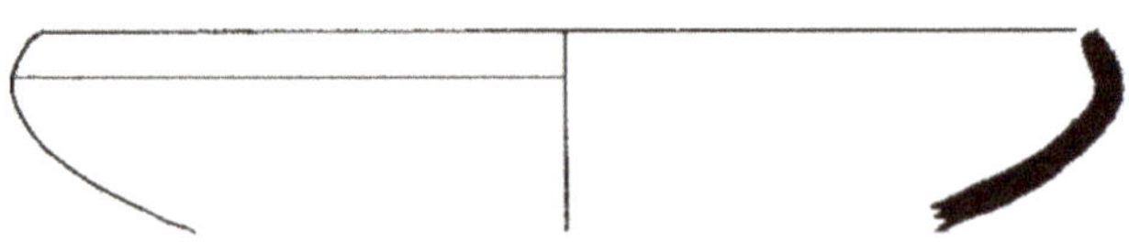

FW 94. CN 7484.
XXVIIIB 13.16. Hellenistic 3A.
Part of wall, rim. PH 0.025; D rim (est.) 0.13. Yellow clay 10YR 7/6. Ware 3.
Black-brown gloss on interior, exterior.
Parallel: 'Akko-Ptolemais (Berlin and Stone 2016: fig. 9.4.5, 3rd c. BC).

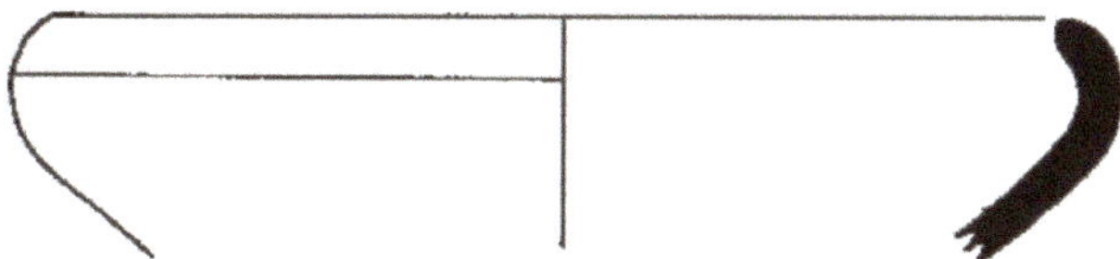

FW 95. CN 7290.
XXIIIB 1.4. Hellenistic 3C.
Part of wall, rim. PH 0.05; D rim (est.) 0.10. Dark grey clay 2.5YR 4.1.
Black gloss on interior, exterior.
Parallel: 'Akko-Ptolemais (Berlin and Stone 2016: fig. 9.10.13, late 3rd–mid-2nd c. BC).

FW 96. CN 6711. (Plate 38)
IIIP 25.11. Hellenistic 3B.
Part of wall, rim. PH 0.03; D rim (est.) 0.12. Reddish-yellow clay 7.5YR 6/6. Ware 2.
Rich dark brown gloss on interior, lower exterior. Well-demarcated band of black gloss on upper exterior.

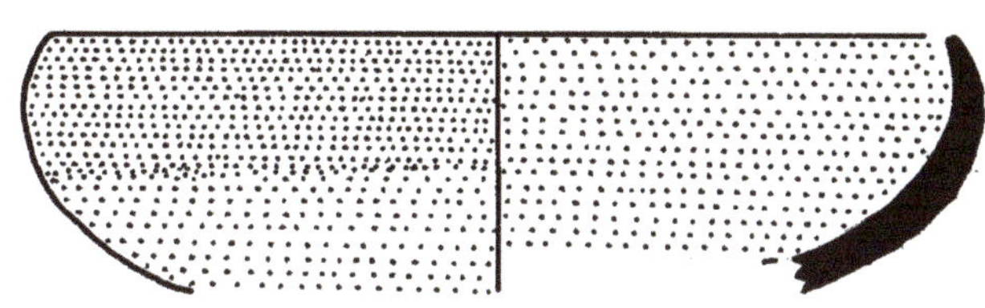

FW 97. CN 7034.
XXIIIA 100.6. Hellenistic 3C.
Part of wall, rim. PH 0.03; PL 0.04; D rim (est.) 0.12. Reddish brown clay 5YR 5/4.
Dull black brown gloss on interior, exterior. In-turned slightly thickened rim.
Parallel: Tell Nimrin (Dornemann 1990: fig. 2.24).

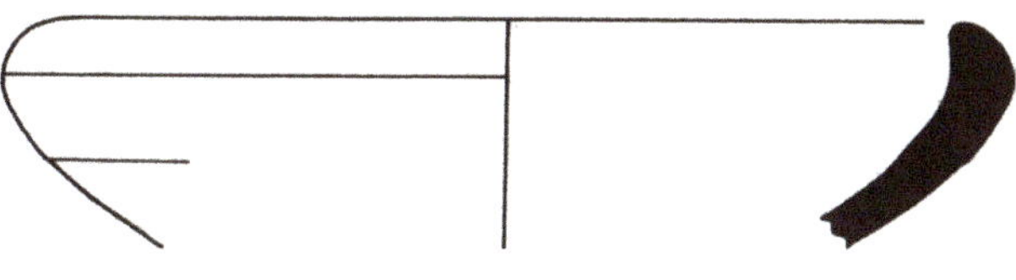

FW 98. CN 6626.
IIIP 24.2. Hellenistic 3B.
Part of wall, rim. PH 0.02; D rim (est.) 0.15. Very pale brown clay 10YR 7/4. Ware 3.
Lustrous thick brown gloss on interior, lower exterior. Well-demarcated band of black-brown gloss on upper exterior.
Parallels: 'Akko-Ptolemais (Berlin and Stone 2016: fig. 9.17.1, mid–late 2nd c. BC); Amman/Philadelphia (Koutsoukou and Najjar 1997: 105, no. 110).

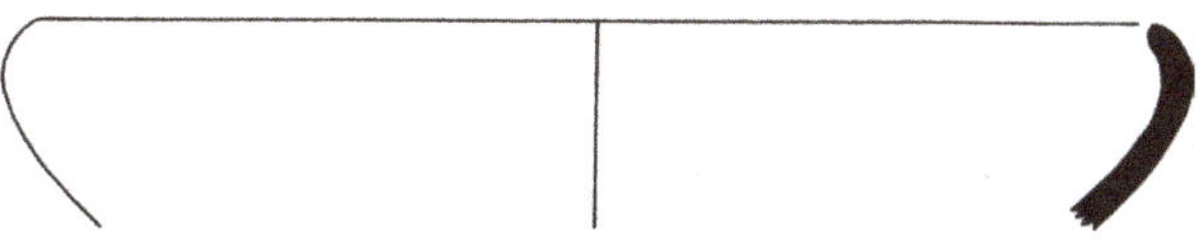

FW 99. CN 7482.
XXVIIIB 13.18. Mixed Context.
Part of wall, rim. PH 0.04; D rim (est.) 0.15. Reddish-yellow clay 7.5YR 7/6. Ware 4.
Black gloss on upper exterior, sharply set off from dark red gloss on lower exterior. Dull red-black gloss on interior.
Parallel: Jerusalem (Geva 2003: pl. 5.3.28).

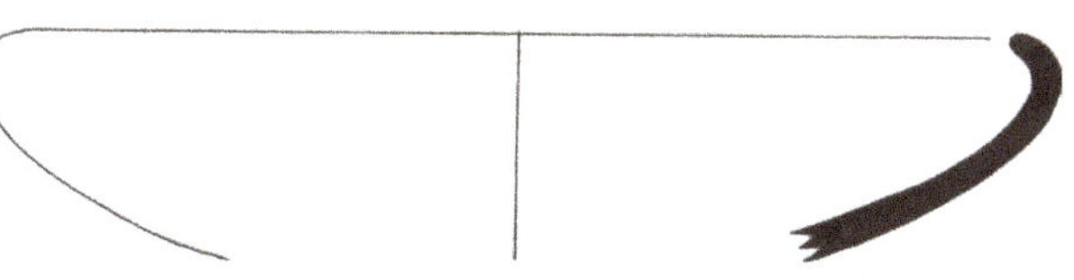

FW 100. CN 7144.
XXXIVF 6.2. Hellenistic 2B.
Part of wall, rim. PH 0.045; PL 0.13; D rim (est.)
0.135. Pink clay 7.5YR 7/4. Ware 2.
Good black gloss on exterior; red gloss on interior.
Parallels: ʿAkko-Ptolemais (Berlin and Stone 2016: fig.
9.12.2, mid–late 2nd c. BC); Jerash (Braemer 1986:
fig. 15.5); Tel Dor (Guz-Zilberstein 1995: fig. 6.1: 27,
275–150 BC).

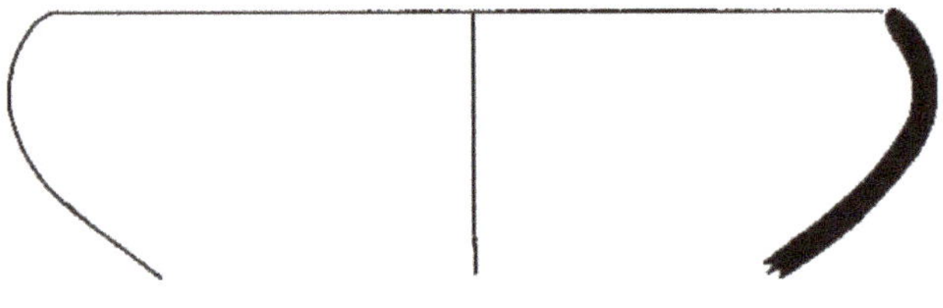

FW 101. CN 7445.
XXVIIIB 13.7. Hellenistic 3A.
Part of wall, rim. PH 0.03; D rim (est.) 0.13. Yellow
clay 10YR 7/6. Ware 2.
Black-brown gloss on interior, exterior.
Parallels: ʿAkko-Ptolemais (Berlin and Stone 2016:
fig. 9.10.14, late 3rd–mid-2nd c. BC); Gadara/Umm
Qais (Kerner 1997: fig. 12.1).

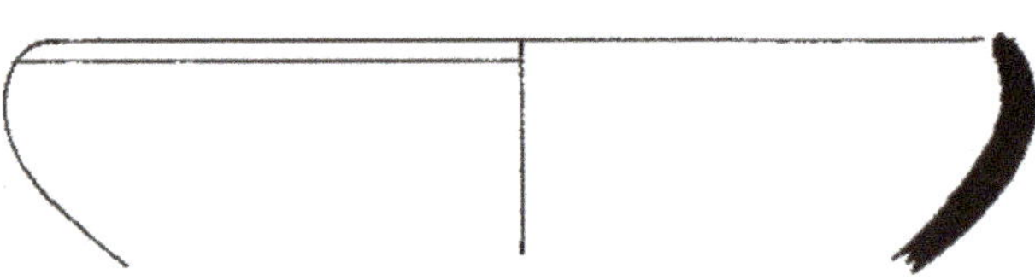

FW 102. CN 4327. (Plate 39)
IVD 10.12. Hellenistic 3C.
Part of base, wall, rim (seven non-joining fragments).
Base fragment: PH 0.04; PL 0.06; D base (est.) 0.09;
Rim fragment: PL 0.055; D rim (est.) 0.18. Reddish-
yellow clay 5YR 7/6. Ware 2.
Mottled red and black gloss on interior. Band of
lustrous black gloss on exterior upper wall; red gloss
on exterior lower wall. Ring base. Faint rouletting
on interior.
Parallel: ʿAkko-Ptolemais (Berlin and Stone 2016: fig.
9.15.6, mid–late 2nd c. BC).

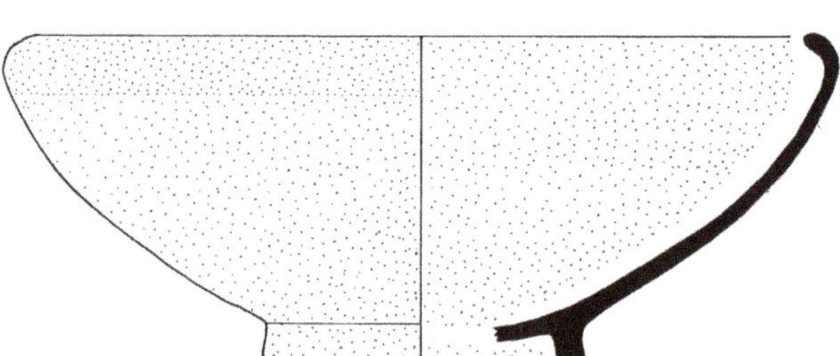

FW 103. CN 7057.
XXIIIA 103.3. Hellenistic 3C.
Part of wall, rim. PH 0.025; PL 0.035; D rim (est.)
0.12. Reddish-yellow clay 7.5YR 6/6. Ware 2.
Thin black-brown gloss on interior, exterior.
Parallels: Amman/Philadelphia (Hadidi 1970:
pl. III.3); Gezer (Gitin 1990: pl. 35.1, mid-2nd c. BC).

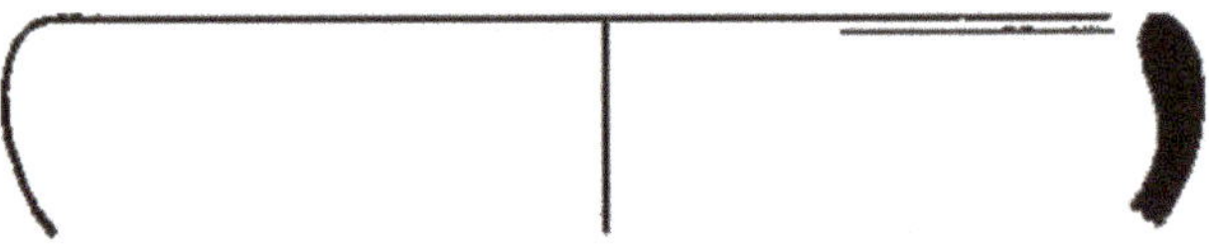

FW 104. CN 6916.
XXIIIA 10.7. Hellenistic 3C.
Part of wall, rim. PH 0.03; PL 0.075; D rim (est.) 0.13.
Reddish-yellow clay 7.5YR 6/6. Ware 2.
Patchy red-brown gloss on interior, exterior.
Parallels: Amman/Philadelphia (Hadidi 1970: pl. III.4);
Ashdod (Dothan 1971: figs 8.12, first half of 2nd c. BC–
second half of 2nd c. BC); Gezer (Gitin 1990: pl. 33.14,
late 3rd–early 2nd c. BC); Samaria (Hennessy 1970: fig.
9.17); Tel Anafa (Slane 1997: pl. 3. FW 18, 125–? BC).

FW 105. CN 6847.
IIIB/C 3.2. Hellenistic 3C.
Part of wall, rim. PH 0.03; PL 0.055; D rim (est.) 0.12.
Reddish-yellow clay 5YR 6/6. Ware 2.
Dull red gloss on interior, exterior.

FW 106. CN 0064.
IIIB/C 1.2. Hellenistic 3C.
Part of wall, rim. PH 0.035; D rim (est. 0.13. Light
reddish-brown clay 5YR 6/4. Ware 2.
Lustrous brown gloss on exterior; mottled on interior.
Wall curves evenly to ill-defined rim.

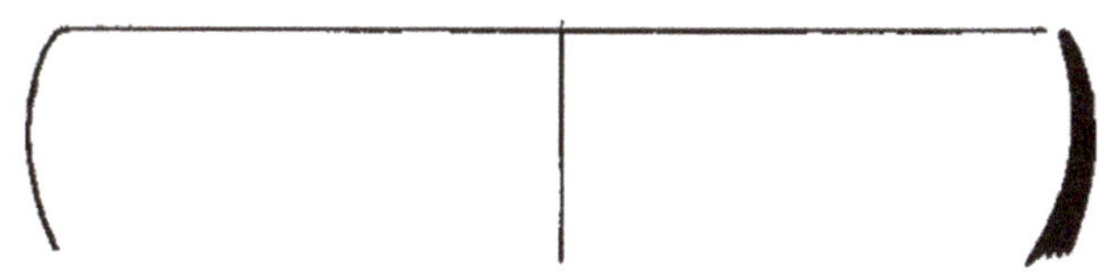

FW 107. CN 2520.
IVJ 19.3. Mixed Context.
Part of base, wall, rim. H 0.04; PL 0.05; D rim (est.)
0.13. Reddish-yellow clay 7.5YR 6/6. Ware 2.
Patchy red-brown gloss on interior, exterior. Ring
base. Flaring straight wall; in-turned rim.
Parallels: Amman/Philadelphia (Koutsoukou
and Najjar 1997: 105, no. 109; Zayadine 1977–78:
fig. 13.407); Ashdod (Dothan and Freedman 1967:
fig. 5.3, second half of 2nd c. BC–mid-1st c. BC).

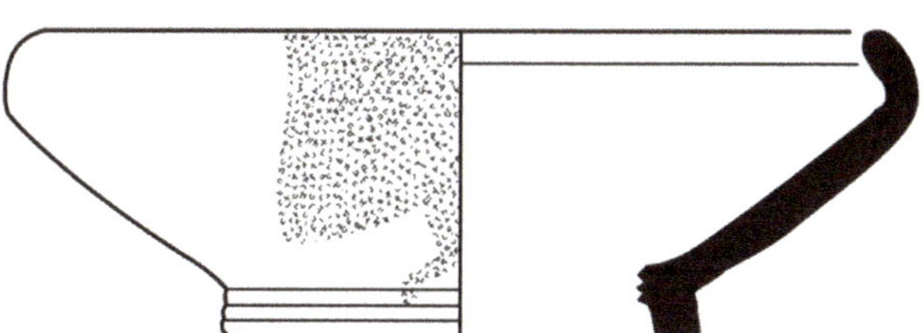

FW 108. CN 7835.
XXXIVB 6.36. Mixed Context.
Part of base, wall, rim. H 0.045; PL 0075; D rim (est.)
0.13; D base (est.) 0.06. Reddish-yellow clay 5YR 6/6.
Black gloss on interior, exterior. Ring base; flaring
wall. In-turned rim.
Parallel: ʿAkko-Ptolemais (Berlin and Stone 2016: fig.
9.6.7, 3rd c. BC).

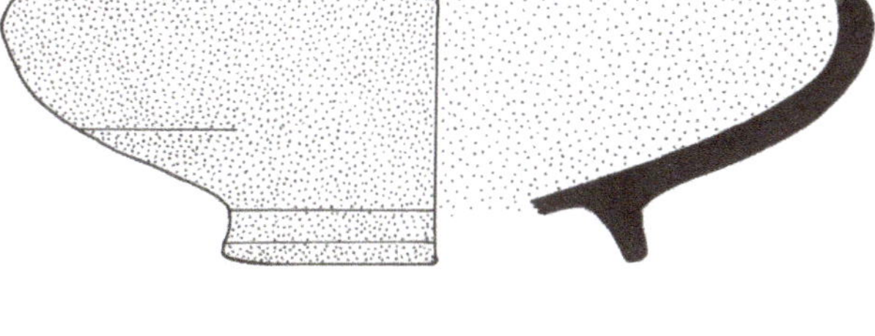

Ovoid, plain/grooved rim (Type 3)

The ovoid bowl with plain or decorated rim seems largely a creation of the Hellenistic era, appearing *de novo* at Athens and elsewhere early in the Hellenistic period and owing its ultimate inspiration to Alexandrian workshops (Rotroff 1997b: 109–13).

Possibly inspired by similar forms in cut glass or precious metal, black-gloss bowls with a simple rim (**FW 109**) or with one or more horizontal grooves on the upper interior or exterior (**FW 110–5**) are found in small numbers in mainland Greece.[18] More common in ESA (Hayes Form 17), the black-gloss form is infrequently seen in the Levant although examples have been recovered from Antioch, Jebel Khalid and, further to the south, Gadara/Umm Qais, 'Akko-Ptolemais, Ashdod, Marisa, Samaria and Tel Dor.[19] At this last site they occur in third- and second-century BC levels, consistent with the Hellenistic 2B and 3B strata from Pella. Similar vessels occur in quite large numbers, but in a "céramique gris-noir", at Aï Khanoum.[20]

FW 109. CN 6770.
IIIA 9.5. Mixed Context.
Part of wall, rim. PH 0.035; PL 0.035; D rim (est.)
0.14. Pinkish white clay 7.5YR 8/2. Ware 3.
Dull dark red gloss on interior, exterior. Plain rim.
Parallels: Ashdod (Dothan 1971: figs 14.13; 16.11);
Beirut (Élaigne 2007: fig. 14.403–45, end 2nd c.
BC); Gadara/Umm Qais (Kenrick 2000: fig. 7.114);
Marisa (Kloner and Hess 1985: fig. 2.14); Tel Dor
(Guz-Zilberstein 1995: fig. 6.41:7, 125 BC–105 AD).

FW 110. CN 6586.
IIIP 25.10. Hellenistic 3B.
Part of wall, rim. PH 0.025; D rim (est.) 0.21. Greyish-
brown clay 10YR 5/2.
Thick black gloss on interior, exterior. Single groove
on interior below rim.

FW 111. CN 6749.
IVD 14.6. Mixed Context.
Two non-joining fragments forming part of wall, rim
(a) PH 0.03; PL 0.06; (b) PH 0.058; PL 0.05; D rim
(est.) 0.18. Light yellowish-brown clay 10YR 6/4.
Dull black gloss on interior, exterior. Single groove
on interior below rim.

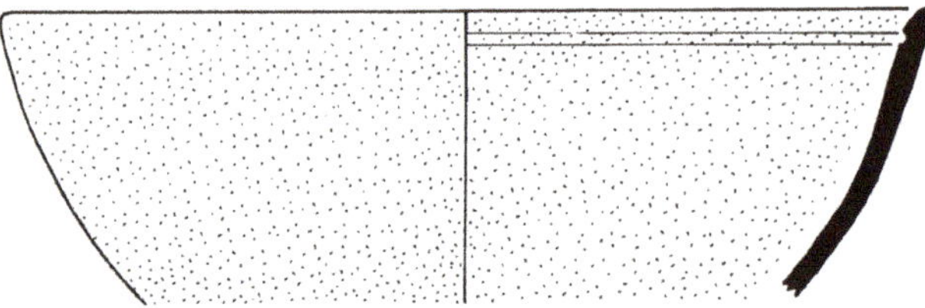

18 For example, Athens (Rotroff 1997b: fig. 20. 328–31).
19 Waagé 1948: 12, pl. II, Form 55 (Antioch); Tidmarsh 2011: 306–7, FW 124–5 (Jebel Khalid in Syria); Kenrick 2000: fig. 7.114 (Gadara/Umm Qais); Berlin and Stone 2016: fig. 9.6.3 ('Akko-Ptolemais); Dothan 1971: figs 14.13; 16.11 (Ashdod); Kloner and Hess 1985: fig. 2.14 (Marisa); Crowfoot et al. 1957: fig. 53:1 (Samaria); Guz-Zilberstein 1995: figs 6.41:7, 8; 6.52:7; 6.54:28 (Tel Dor).
20 Gardin 1973: 130, fig. 11, Forms d1, d2.

FW 112. CN 7085.
XXIIIA 109.4. Hellenistic 3B.
Part of wall, rim (three joining fragments). PH 0.045;
PL 0.135; D rim (est.) 0.21. Light brown clay 7.5YR
6/4. Slightly micaceous.
Lustrous black gloss on exterior, brown-black on
interior. Grooves on interior, exterior below rim.
Parallels: Kedesh (Levantine Ceramics Project: n.d.
K08P114, 200–140 BC); Samaria (Crowfoot et al. 1957:
fig. 53.1); Tel Dor (Guz-Zilberstein 1995: figs 6.52:7,
275–150 BC; 6.54:28, 275–175 BC).

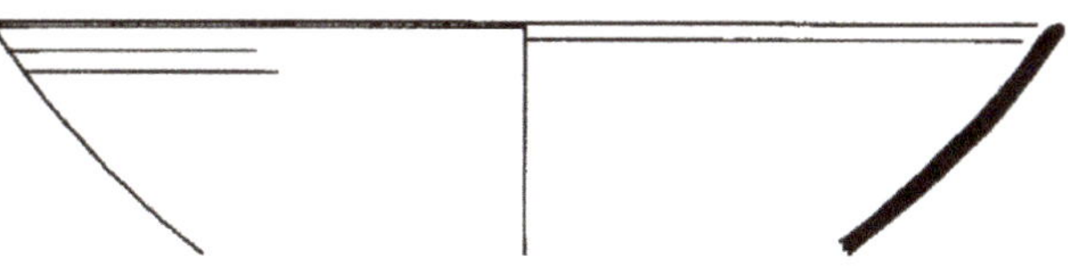

FW 113. CN 7709.
XXXIVA 8.9. Mixed Context.
Part of wall, rim. PH 0.03; PL 0.025; D rim (est.) 0.16.
Very pale brown clay 10YR 8/4. Ware 3.
Good black gloss on interior, exterior. Grooves and
ridges on interior, exterior below rim.

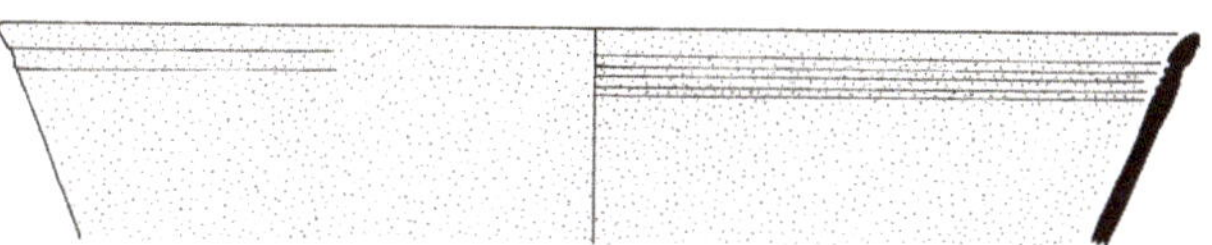

FW 114. CN 7388.
XXXIVF 6.5. Hellenistic 2B.
Part of wall, rim. PH 0.055; PL 0.09; D (est.) 0.17.
Light brown clay 7.5YR 6/4. Ware 3.
Patchy thin brown-black gloss on interior, exterior.
Broad groove on interior below rim.

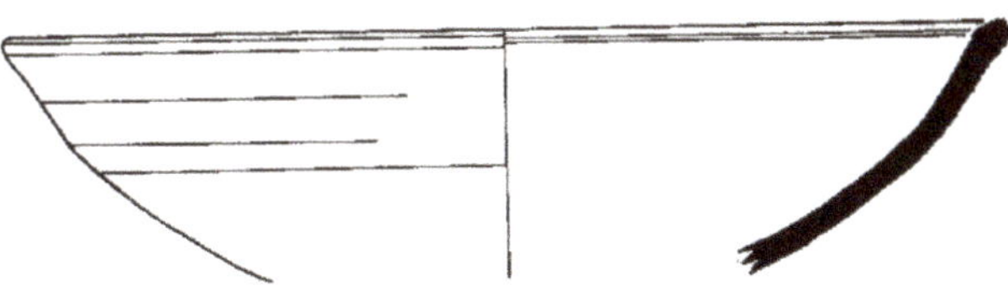

FW 115. CN 7282.
XXXIVG 2.3. Mixed Context.
Part of wall, rim. PH 0.03; D rim (est.) 0.135. Pink
clay 7.5YR 7/4. Ware 2.
Dull black-brown gloss on interior, exterior. Grooves
and ridges on interior below thickened rim.

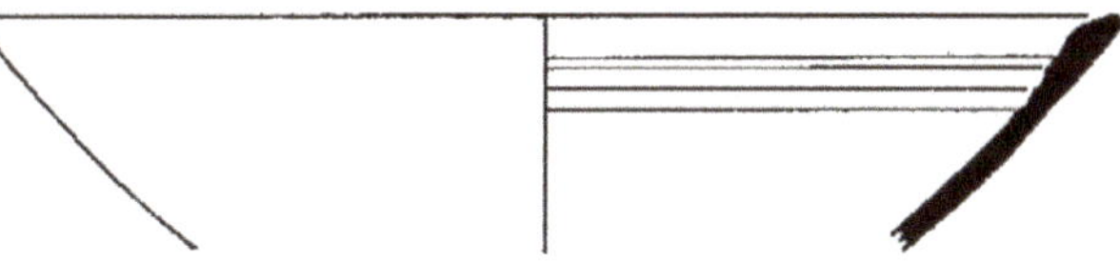

Ovoid, decorated rim (Type 4)

More elaborate interior decoration – generally multiple grooves and prominent ridges often in combination
with a horizontal row of beading – seems less common in Greece itself and appears largely confined to the
eastern Mediterranean where it is seen at Ashdod, Samaria, Tel Anafa, Tel Dor, Tel Yoqne'am and further to
the north at Dura-Europos, Jebel Khalid and Tarsus.[21] East of the Jordan River examples are rare, although
a single example has been published from Gadara/Umm Qais (Kenrick 2000: 250, fig. 7.118).

While generally in second-century BC contexts at these sites, black-gloss bowls with grooves and horizontal
beading are seen in Hellenistic 2B (c. 100 BC) and Roman 1A (late first century BC/early first century AD)
deposits at Tel Anafa. The shape is also well recognised in ESA with the black-gloss examples from Tel Anafa
and 'Akko-Ptolemais being included within the "black-slipped predecessors" (BSP) of ESA (Regev 2009/10:
168–9; Slane 1997: 269–74), consistent with the wares of **FW 116–7.**

---

21 Dothan 1971: figs 16.14, 99.2 (Ashdod); Crowfoot et al. 1957: fig. 53:5; Hennessy 1970: fig. 9:6 (red slip)
    (Samaria); Slane 1997: 279–80 FW 30–1 (Tel Anafa); Guz-Zilberstein 1995: figs 6.41:9; 6.43:9 (Tel Dor); Avissar
    1996: fig. X.1.23 (Tel Yoqne'am); Cox 1949: 5, no. 25 (Dura-Europos); Tidmarsh 2011: 307–8, FW 126–34; 2016:
    225–6, FW 649–51(Jebel Khalid in Syria); F.F. Jones 1950: 219, fig. 125.114 (Tarsus).

FW 116. CN 4312.
IVD10.10. Hellenistic 3C.
Most of wall, rim preserved. PH 0.055; PL 0.065;
D rim (est.) 0.135. Very pale brown clay 10YR 7/4.
Ware 3.
Thin black lustrous gloss on exterior and interior.
Moulded interior rim with two grooves, raised ridge,
and a row of globules.
Parallels: 'Akko-Ptolemais (Berlin and Stone 2016: fig.
9.23.4, second half of 1st c. BC; Regev 2009/10: fig.
38.250); Ashdod (Dothan 1971: figs 16.14; 99.2, first
half of 2nd c. BC–mid-1st c. BC); Gadara/Umm Qais
(Kenrick 2000: fig. 7.118); Hippos-Sussita (Osband
and Eisenberg 2018: pl. 2.3.4, 2nd c. BC); Samaria
(Hennessy 1970: fig. 9.6; Crowfoot et al. 1957: fig.
53.5); Tel Anafa (Slane 1997: pl. 3. FW 31, late 1st c.
BC–early 1st c. AD); Tel Dor (Guz-Zilberstein 1995:
figs 6.41:9; 6.43:9); Tel Yoqne'am (Ben-Tor et al. 1979:
7.5).

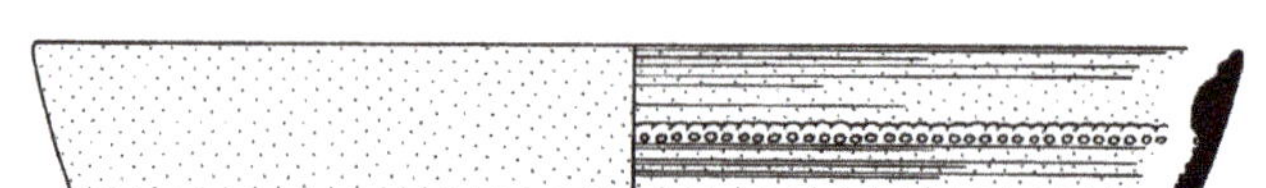

FW 117. CN 7114.
XXIIIA 72.7. Mixed Context.
Part of wall, rim. PH 0.03; D rim (est.) 0.21. Reddish-
yellow clay 7.5YR 6/6. Ware 2.
Good black gloss on interior, exterior. Interior
moulding of horizontal ridges and globules.

Spouted bowl

The black-gloss spouted bowl **FW 118** was recovered – possibly out of context – from an Early Roman deposit
on Tell Husn and is the only example of the type at Pella. Spouted bowls (or lekanai) are uncommon in the
Hellenistic and Early Roman repertoire, although they occur in Athens as early as the fourth century (Sparkes
and Talcott 1970: 58, fig. 2. 88) and also, with a spout in the form of a lion's head, in Athenian Hellenistic
deposits (Thompson 1934: 371, fig. 56. D13; 398, fig. 86. E57). There appear to have been no published
examples in black-gloss from the Levant, including Antioch – in the environs of which this example seems
to have been produced – although plain ware examples are known from Sha'ar ha-Amakim and Tel Dor.[22]

FW 118. CN 3072.
XIA/B 1.5. Early Roman 1 (residual?).
Part of rim, spout. PH 0.025; D rim (est.) 0.23.
Reddish-yellow clay 5YR 7/6. Ware 2.
Pink gloss 7.5YR 8/3. In-turned upper wall;
overhanging rim. Horizontal spout to exterior.
Parallels: Tel Dor (close to Guz-Zilberstein 1995:
fig. 6.64: 6, 300–275 BC, no gloss); Tel Keisan (close
to Briend 1980: pl. 17.14, no gloss).

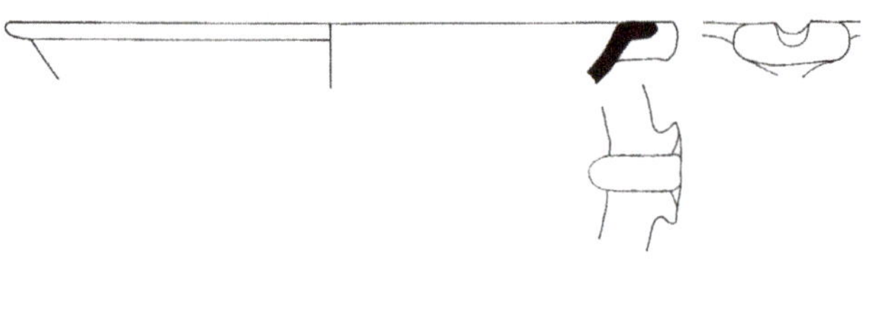

22   Mlynarczyk 2000: pl. 120a.7 (Sha'ar ha-Amakim); Guz-Zilberstein 1995: fig. 6.10.5, 9, 11 (Tel Dor).

Applied relief bowl

Though not as common as mould-made relief bowls, ceramic bowls, along with a wide variety of other shapes (including amphorae, jugs and oinochoe) with applied relief decoration (moulded separately and then applied to the surface), were common in the Hellenistic world (Evridiki 2002; Rotroff 2003).[23] It is likely that, as with the ceramic mould-made bowls, this class of vessel originally gained its inspiration from similarly embellished vessels, especially those in silver or bronze (Rotroff 1982: 6–10; Stone 2014: 91–2; Treister 2012: 76–7).

FW 119, from the Jannaeus Destruction level (Hellenistic 3C) on the main mound, would have originally have rested on three applied shell feet, two of which survive. This class of bowl had a wide circulation in Hellenistic and Roman times with examples found from Sicily in the west through to Greece and Asia Minor and as far east as the Persian Gulf.[24]

FW 119. CN 7829. (No line drawing) (Plate 40)
XXIIID 67.1/68.1. Hellenistic 3C.
Five fragments (two joining) of base, lower wall. PH (two joining fragments) 0.045; PL (two joining fragments) 0.075; D rim (est.) 0.11. Light red clay 10R 6/8.
Shiny black-brown gloss on exterior; thin dull gloss on interior. Two applied shells preserved as feet overlapping two concentric grooves on base. Two horizontal grooves on exterior below simple rim.
Parallels: New Halos (Reinders 1988: 255, figs 114, 115, no. 33.01); Seleucia-on-the-Tigris/Tell Umar (Salles 1990: 320, fig. 7.d, Parthian).

Uncertain shape

FW 120. CN 7495.
XXVIIIB 13.17. Hellenistic 3A.
Part of base and wall. PH 0.045; PL 0.15. Reddish-yellow clay 7.5YR 7/6. Ware 2.
Thick black-brown gloss (fired red in patches) on interior, exterior. Tall ring base; marked carination of wall. Two rows of rouletting in interior.

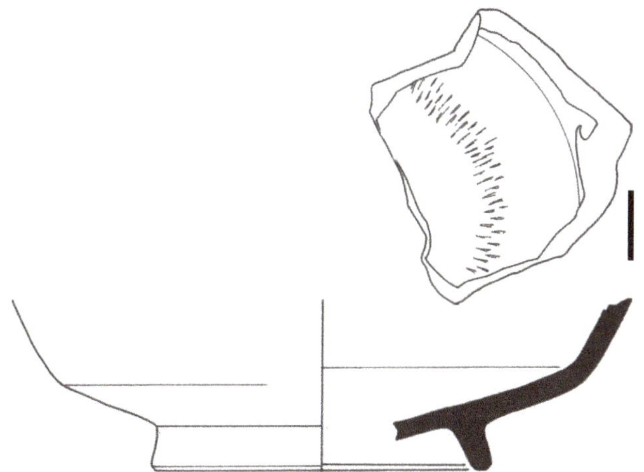

---

23 For example, West Slope fragment **FW 180**. See also Rotroff (1982: 55, pl. 11.65) for an Attic moulded bowl fragment with preserved foot. Also Stone (2014: pl. 140. 60–256) for a mould of a shell foot for a tripod bowl.
24 For example, Stone 2014: 91–2, 314, pls 4.24, 24B, 73.24, 24B; Malfitana and Giuseppe Cacciaguerra 2015: 256–60 (Sicily); Reinders 1988: 255 (Greece); Hayes 1991a: pl. IV.12 (Cyprus); Evridiki 2002 (Asia Minor); Salles 1990: 320–4 (Mesopotamia, Persian Gulf).

FW 121. CN 7494.
XXVIIIB 13.17. Hellenistic 3A.
Part of base, wall. PH 0.03; PL 0.13. Reddish-yellow clay 5YR 6/6. Ware 2.
Good thick brown gloss on interior, exterior; fired red in patches. Ring base. Flaring lower wall. One crude stamped palmette and part of another within single row of rouletting in interior.

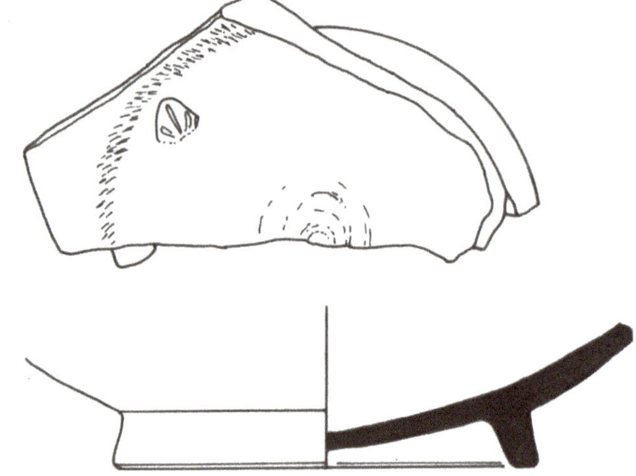

FW 122. CN 7529. (Plate 41)
XXXIIY 2.1. Hellenistic 3A.
Part of base, wall. PH 0.04; PL 0.15; D base 0.11. Reddish-yellow clay 7.5YR 7/6. Ware 3.
Rich brown gloss within rouletting; black gloss on outer interior, exterior. Brown gloss on exterior within ring base. Tall ring base. Flaring lower wall. Three preserved stamped palmettes enclosed within double row of rouletting on interior floor.

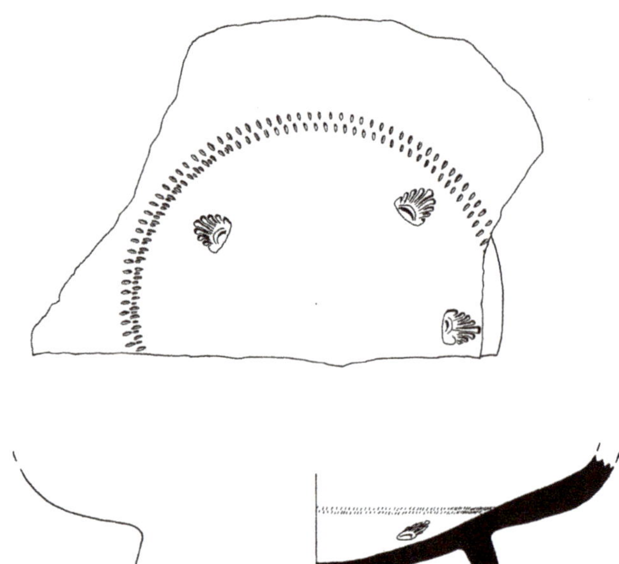

FW 123. CN 6668.
IIIP 25.19. Mixed Context.
Part of base, wall. PH 0.05; PL 0.14; D base (est.) 0.06. Reddish-yellow clay 5YR 6/6. Ware 2.
Low ring base. In-turned wall. Band of rouletting with palmette on interior.

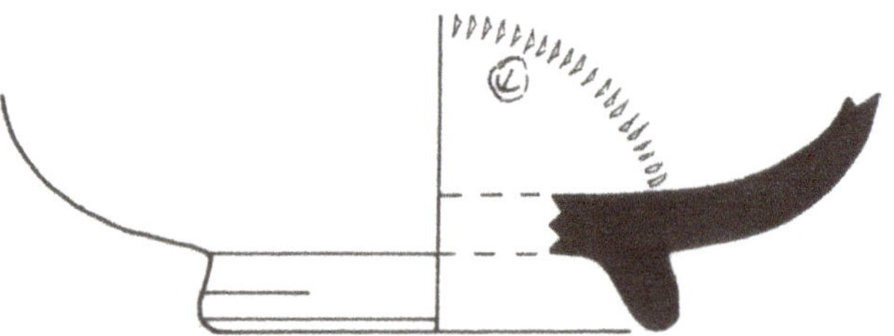

FW 124. CN 6565a.
IIIP 22.7. Mixed Context.
Part of base, lower wall. PH 0.055; D base 0.075. Reddish-yellow clay 7.5YR 7/6. Ware 1.
Lustrous black gloss on interior, exterior. Tall ring base separated by scraped groove from wall. Two rows of rouletting between grooves; two palmettes preserved.

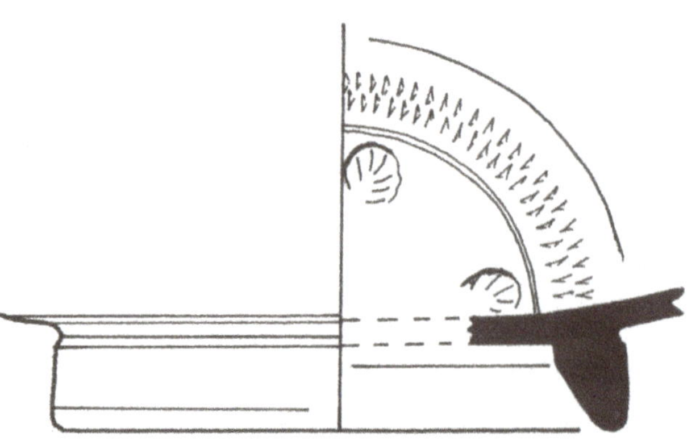

BLACK-GLOSS WARE: MIXING VESSELS

Kraters (FW 125–128)

Large open kraters, or deep bowls, resembling domestic lekanai with their ring base and out-turned rim but partially or totally covered with a black gloss, are known in Athens from the early sixth century BC. They remain popular during the fifth and fourth centuries (Sparkes and Talcott 1970: 56–7) and by Hellenistic times have become probably "the commonest large black-gloss bowl in the Hellenistic repertoire" (Rotroff 1997b: 167), employed in food preparation or for the mixing of wine with water.[25]

Deep black-gloss kraters are much less popular in the Levant with none published from Antioch, Gezer or Tel Anafa. Three examples are found at Tel Dor (Guz-Zilberstein 1995: 296, fig. 6.12:7) with the only stratified specimen coming from a locus dated to 200–175 (150) BC; a further eight examples have been recovered from Jebel Khalid in Syria where they have been found in both Phase A (c. 280–150 BC) and Phase B (c. 150–70 BC) levels.[26] Black-gloss kraters are also uncommon at Pella (from second century BC and Mixed Context levels on the main mound) where the rim profile is either horizontal (**FW 125**) or everted (**FW 126–8**). A wider range of krater forms is encountered amongst the plain wares.

Horizontal rim (Type 1)

FW 125. CN 7236.
XXVIIIB 5.8. Mixed Context.
Part of wall, rim. PH 0.04; D rim (est.) 0.24. Reddish-yellow clay 5YR 6/6.
Worn dull red gloss on interior, exterior. Rounded upper wall.
Parallels: Scythopolis/Beth-Shean (Johnson 2006: fig. 15.1.16); Sha'ar ha-Amakim (Mlynarczyk 2000: pl. 118.2); Tel Dor (Guz-Zilberstein 1995: 6.12:1, 250–125 BC).

Everted rim (Type 2)

FW 126. CN 7184.
XXVIIIB 13.2. Hellenistic 3A.
Part of rim, wall. PH 0.07; D rim (est.) 0.30. Reddish-yellow clay 7.5YR 6/6.
Red-black gloss on interior, exterior. Slightly concave upper wall.

FW 127. CN 7528.
XXXIIY 2.1. Hellenistic 3A.
Part of rim, wall. PH 0.06; PL 0.015; D rim (est.) 0.26. Light yellowish-brown clay 10YR 6/4.
Good black gloss over interior, exterior. Flaring wall.

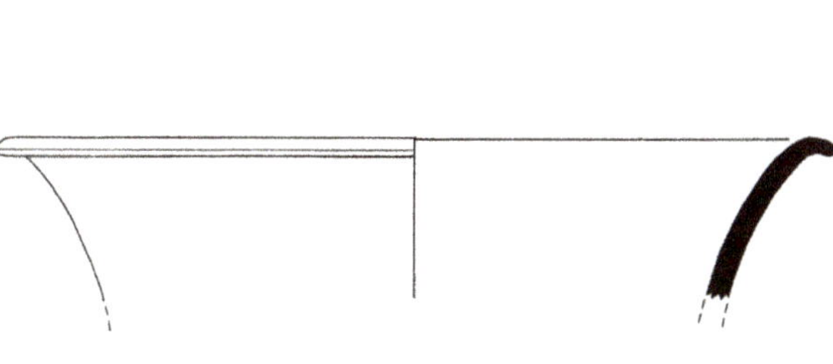

25 The shape is generally termed "deep bowl" when used for food preparation and "krater" when used for mixing wine. Here the general term "krater" will be used.
26 Tidmarsh 2011: 301, fig. 105. **FW 93–100.**

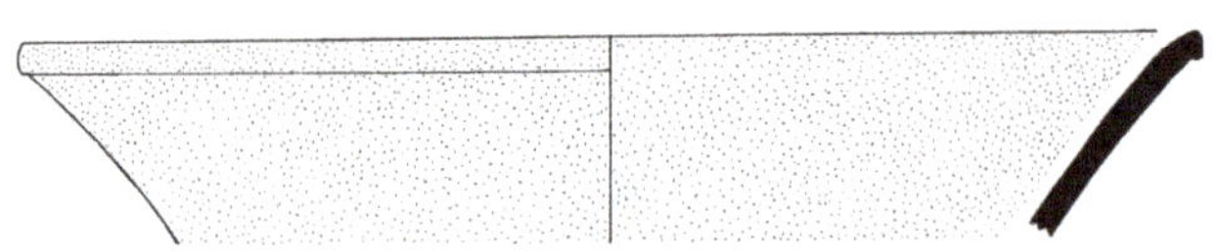

FW 128. CN 6895.
IIIQ 11.22. Mixed Context.
Part of wall, rim. PH 0.06; PL 0.07; D rim (est.) 0.27.
Reddish brown clay 5YR 5/4.
Thick black gloss on interior, exterior. Flaring wall;
narrow rim.
Parallel: Jebel Khalid in Syria (Tidmarsh 2011:
fig. 105. FW 100, c. 280–150 BC).

BLACK-GLOSS WARE: DRINKING VESSELS

In Hellenistic Athens, skyphoi and kantharoi are the most popular form of drinking vessel throughout the late fourth and third centuries (Rotroff 1997b: Appendix I, graphs 3–4); in the second and first centuries they are largely replaced by the mould-made ("Megarian") bowl and a variety of cups. This is consistent with the situation at Pella where the majority of Hellenistic ceramic drinking vessels recovered so far, from second- and first-century BC levels, comprise fine ware (black-gloss, ESA, mould-made) or plain ware bowls as well as small cups with narrow rims and pinched handles. The Greek-influenced skyphoi or kantharoi are rare although still seen in West Slope ware.

Skyphoi and kantharoi (FW 129–132)

Only four black- or red-gloss skyphos or kantharos fragments have been recovered along with a further plain ware example (**PW 150**). The black-gloss skyphos **FW 129** (Hellenistic 3C) and the spur handle **FW 131** (Mixed Context) are both of Ware 2; the red-gloss kantharos fragment **FW 130** was recovered (out of context) from an Early Roman horizon on Husn. **FW 132** is an Athenian skyphos base with its presence in a Jannaeus Destruction context (Hellenistic 3C) suggesting it may have been a residual fragment or heirloom piece.

Skyphoi were recovered from all the Hellenistic levels at Tarsus (F.F. Jones 1950: 157–60); at Tel Dor they are numerous although confined largely to third- and second-century levels (Guz-Zilberstein 1995: 294). At Ashdod a vertical-handled skyphos (Dothan 1971: 47, fig. 10.4) was recovered from a late second-century BC context. Skyphoi and kantharoi seem rare east of the Jordan River although a possible fluted kantharos fragment ("H Slip B": of local manufacture?) was reported from Gadara/Umm Qais (Kenrick 2000: 252, fig. 7.136) and a black-gloss/West Slope ware (?) kantharos handle from Tell Zira'a (Kenkel 2020: 17–18, 118–19, pl. 1.1:Sgk1).

FW 129. CN 6958.
IVD 10.12. Hellenistic 3C.
Part of wall, rim. PH 0.03; PL 0.07; D rim (est.) 0.135.
Pink clay 5YR 7/4. Ware 2.
Thin red glaze on interior; dull black glaze on exterior.
Hemispherical; slightly out-turned narrow rim.
Parallels: Amman/Philadelphia (Zayadine 1977–78:
fig. 13.143); Marisa (Kloner and Hess 1985: fig. 2.10);
Tel Dor (close to Guz-Zilberstein 1995: fig. 6.6:1,
275–175 BC).

FW 130. CN 2647.
XIA/B 1.1/2. Early Roman 1 (residual).
Part of wall, rim. PH 0.07; D rim (est.) 0.13. Very
pale brown clay 10YR 7/4.
Dull red glaze on interior, exterior. Thickened rim.
Upper part of spur handle preserved.

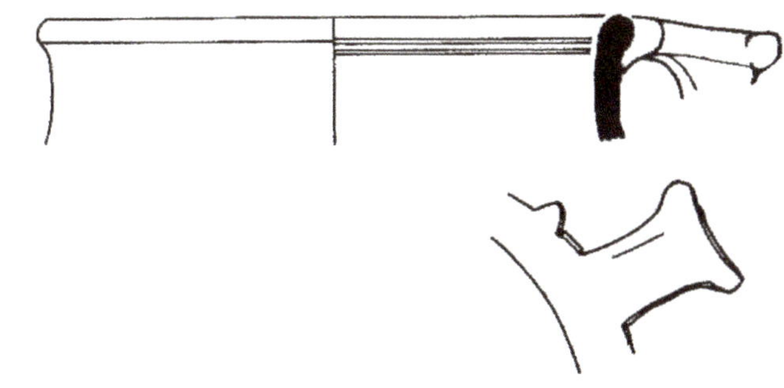

FW 131. CN 7775.
XXXIIM 8.1. Mixed Context.
Handle fragment PH 0.02; PL 0.03. Reddish-yellow
clay 7.5YR 6/6. Ware 2.
Mottled black-brown gloss. Spur handle.
Parallel: Scythopolis/Beth-Shean (Johnson 2006:
fig. 15.1.14).

FW 132. CN 7715.
IIIB/C 14.2. Hellenistic 3C.
Part of base, lower wall. PH 0.04; D base 0.03. Light
red clay 2.5YR 6/6. Ware 1.
Lustrous black gloss on interior, exterior. Torus base
separated from upper member by scraped groove.
Narrow stem. Flaring lower wall.
Parallel: Athens (Rotroff 1997b: fig. 12.161, base
profile).

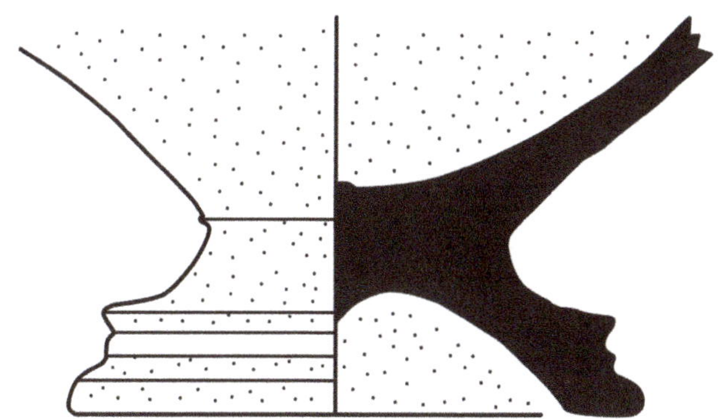

Cups (FW 133–144)

Small; narrow band rim; horizontal pinched handles

Cups of this form are relatively widespread throughout the Hellenistic east Mediterranean, although never
appearing in large numbers. They occur at many Levantine sites – commonly within a second-century
context (Guz-Zilberstein 1995: 294; Rotroff 1997b: 118, n.160).[27] A small number of cups of similar shape,
considered by Rotroff (1997b: 117–18) as imitations of the Palestinian type, has been recovered from the
Athenian Agora; though most were within second-century BC contexts, one was recovered from debris laid
down as a result of the sack of the city by L. Cornelius Sulla (87/86 BC).[28]

Of the fine ware examples of these forms (**FW 133–42**), all were recovered from the main mound. **FW
135–6** and one non-catalogued specimen come from second century (Hellenistic 3B) deposits; **FW 137–8**,
FW 140 and a further three examples (non-catalogued) were recovered from the Jannaeus Destruction levels
(Hellenistic 3C) of plot XXIIIA. The remainder are from unstratified contexts. Thus, as also seen at Athens,
the shape continued in use during the early first century BC. None preserves its base although a ring base is

---

27 Three bowls from Tel Dor were recovered from late fourth-/early third-century BC horizons (Guz-Zilberstein
    1995: 294).
28 For Sulla's sack of Athens see Appian, *Mithradates*, 28–41; Plutarch, *Sulla*, 12–14; Hoff 1997; Parigi 2019;
    Rogers 2021. As well, for the formation of the Sullan debris and the problems with its chronology, Rotroff
    1997b: 34–6; 1997c.

certain. As is usually the case elsewhere, most are covered with a black or red-brown gloss on the exterior and red gloss on the interior that may often be quite thickly applied.

FW 133. CN 7712.
IIIB/C. 1.14. Mixed Context.
Part of wall, rim. PH 0.05; PL 0.04; D rim (est.) 0.175.
Reddish-yellow clay 7.5YR 7/6. Ware 2.
Thick black gloss on exterior; red gloss on interior.
Convex wall. Narrow everted thickened rim.
Parallel: ʿAkko-Ptolemais (Berlin and Stone 2016: fig. 9.21.7, first half of 1st c. BC).

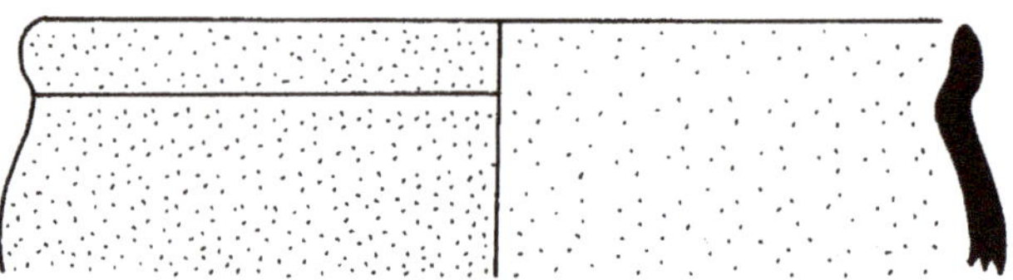

FW 134. CN 6879.
IIIB/C 1.14. Mixed Context.
Part of wall, rim, handle. PH 0.03; PL 0.035; D rim (est.) 0.15. Reddish-yellow clay 5YR 6/6. Ware 2.
Lustrous red gloss on interior; matt brown gloss on exterior.
Parallels: Apollonia (Fischer and Tal 1996: fig. 9.14); Gezer (Gitin 1990: pl. 38.9, mid-2nd c. BC); Marisa (Levine 2003: fig. 6.1.3); Samaria (Crowfoot et al. 1957: fig. 57.2); Scythopolis/Beth-Shean (Johnson 2006: fig. 15.1.19); Shaʿar ha-Amakim (Mlynarczyk 2000: pl. 118.4); Tel Dor (Guz-Zilberstein 1995: fig. 6.47:10, 250–200 BC).

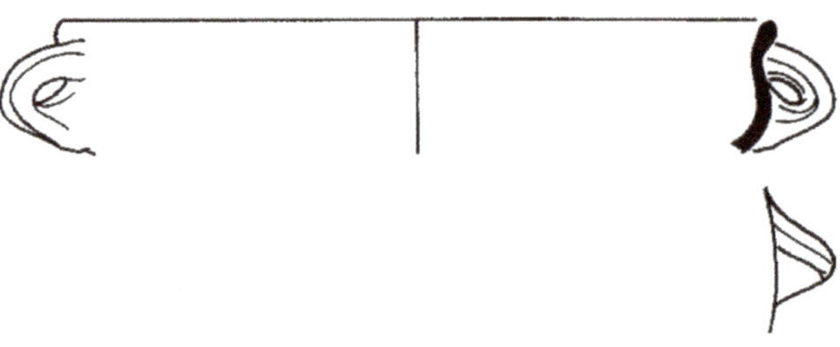

FW 135. CN 7070.
XXIIIA 109.3. Hellenistic 3B.
Part of wall, rim. PH 0.03; PL 0.04; D rim (est.) 0.15.
Light brown clay 7.5YR 6/4. Ware 3.
Worn gloss: red on interior, dark brown on exterior.
Parallels: Ashdod (Dothan 1971: figs 16.1 upper profile, 78.17); Gezer (Gitin 1990: pl. 42.7, early 1st c, BC); Kedesh (Levantine Ceramics Project: n.d. K99P077, 200–140 BC); Samaria (Crowfoot et al. 1957: fig. 39.5, c. 150–100 BC); Tel Anafa (Slane 1997: pl. 4. FW 39, early 1st c. AD).

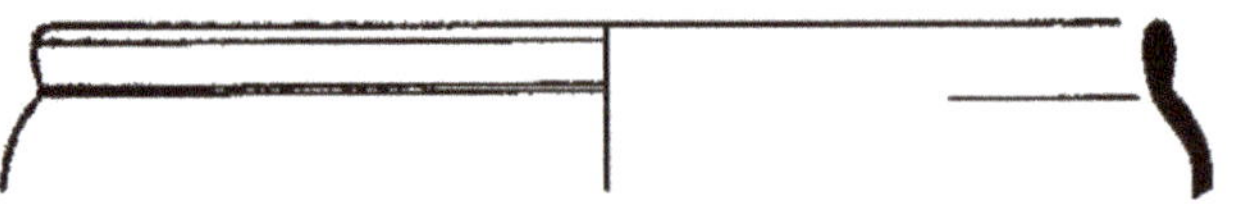

FW 136. CN 7810. (Plate 42)
XXIIID 24.3. Hellenistic 3B.
Part of wall, rim, handle. PH 0.04; PL 0.055 D rim (est.) 0.19. Reddish-yellow clay 5YR 6/6. Ware 2.
Rich brown gloss on interior, lower exterior. Lustrous black gloss on upper exterior.
Parallel: Tel Zahara (Bar-Nathan and Gärtner 2013: fig. 3.16.142).

FW 137. CN 7753.
XXIIID 20.1. Hellenistic 3C.
Part of wall, rim. PH 0.03; PL 0.05; D rim (est.) 0.15.
Very pale brown clay 10YR 7/6. Ware 3.
Black gloss on exterior; red gloss on interior.

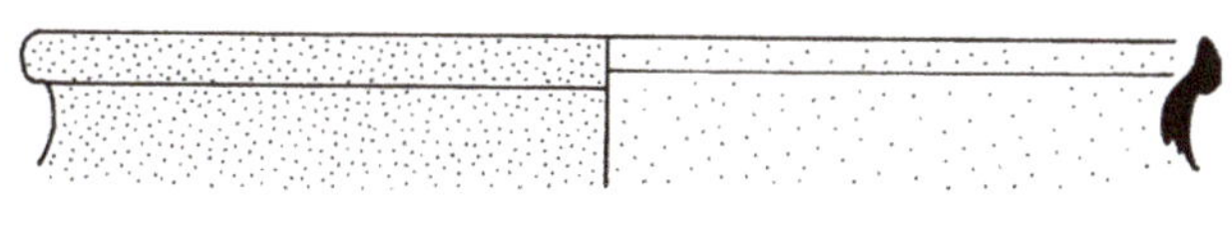

FW 138. CN 0235.
IIIB/C 2.8. Hellenistic 3C.
Part of wall, rim, handle. PH 0.06; PL 0.03; D rim
(est.) 0.14. Very pale brown clay 10YR 7/6. Ware 3.
Red gloss on interior, exterior.
Parallels: ʿAkko-Ptolemais (Berlin and Stone 2016:
fig. 9.12.15, mid–late 2nd c. BC); Gadara/Umm Qais
(Kenrick 2000: fig. 8.137).

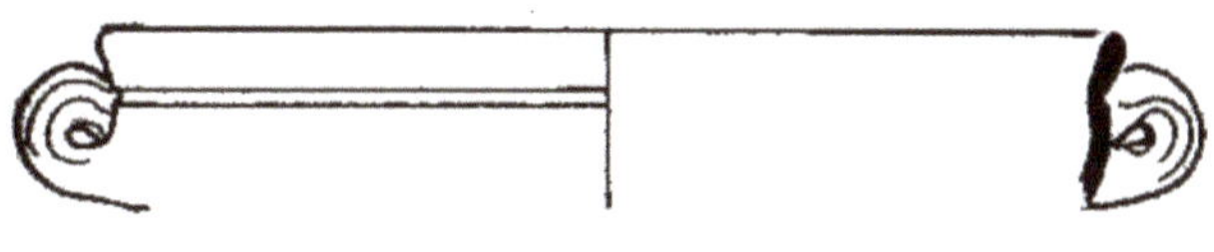

FW 139. CN 6878.
IIIB/C 1.25. Mixed Context.
Part of wall, rim. PH 0.035; PL 0.04; D rim (est.) 0.165.
Reddish-yellow clay 7.5YR 6/6. Ware 2.
Reddish brown gloss on exterior; red gloss in interior.
Parallels: Ashdod (Dothan 1971: fig. 78.17, first half
of 2nd c. BC–c. 70 AD); Ashkelon (Birney 2022: fig.
14.18); Scythopolis/Beth-Shean (Johnson 2006: fig.
15.1.18); Tel Yoqneʿam (Avissar 1996: fig.X.1.7); Tel
Zahara (Bar-Nathan and Gärtner 2013: fig. 3.16.141).

FW 140. CN 0234.
IIIB/C 2.8. Hellenistic 3C.
Part of wall, rim, handle. PH 0.035; PL 0.04; D rim
(est.) 0.14. Reddish-yellow clay 7.5YR 6/6. Ware 2.
Lustrous black gloss on exterior; red gloss in interior.
Parallels: Ashdod (Dothan 1971: fig. 78.18, first half
of 2nd c. BC–mid-1st c. BC); Samaria (Crowfoot et
al. 1957: fig. 57.1); Scythopolis/Beth-Shean (Johnson
2006: fig. 15.1.18); Tel Dor (Guz-Zilberstein 1995: fig.
6.7:7, 125 BC–105 AD).

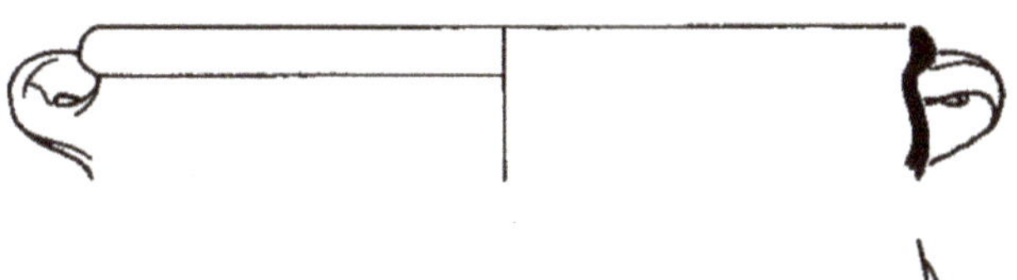

FW 141. CN 6700.
IIIP 24.14. Mixed Context.
Part of wall, rim. PH 0.03; PL 0.05; D rim (est.) 0.14.
Reddish-yellow clay 7.5YR 7/6. Ware 2.
Red gloss: dull on exterior, lustrous on interior.
Convex upper wall narrowing to slightly everted rim.
Parallel: Hippos-Sussita (Osband and Eisenberg 2018:
pl. 1.11, 2nd c. BC).

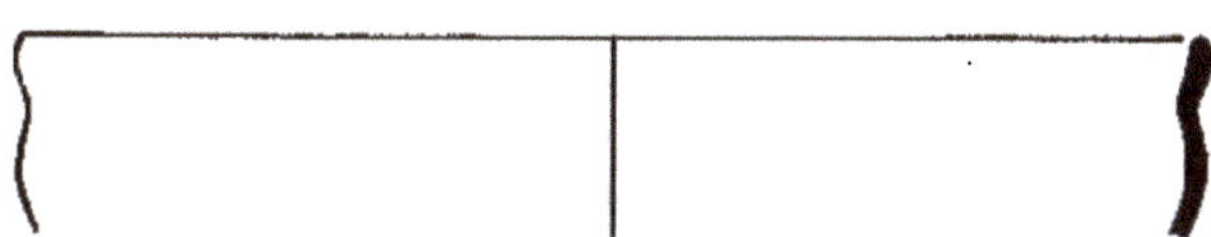

FW 142. CN 6834.
IIIP 24.15. Mixed Context.
Part of wall, rim, handle. PH 0.03; PL 0.04; D rim
(est.) 0.18. Reddish-yellow clay 7.5YR 7/6. Ware 2.
Red gloss on interior; thick brown gloss on exterior.

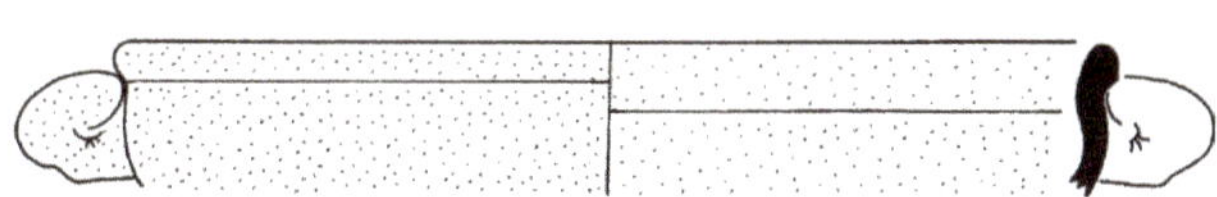

"Palestinian form"

FW 143–4 recall those two-handled cups of "Palestinian" form seen in small numbers in Athens and other Greek sites but "particularly common in Hellenistic levels in the Levant, chiefly in Palestine" where they seem to have been produced from the third through to the first centuries BC (Rotroff 1997b: 117–18 with references). The findspots (on the main mound) of both Pella examples are consistent with this chronology. Interestingly, the form entered the Knidian repertory around the mid-second century with the rounded shoulder quickly replaced by the more typical Knidian carination (Kögler 2014: 159).

FW 143. CN 7535.
XXXIIY 2.5. Hellenistic 3A.
Six non-joining fragments forming part of wall, rim.
D rim (est.) 0.17. Light yellowish-brown clay 10YR 6/4.
Black gloss over interior, exterior. Upright rim set off from convex body. Root of handle preserved on body.
Parallel: Athens (profile close to Rotroff 1997b: fig. 22.394 from Sullan debris, c. 86 BC).

FW 144. CN 0385.
IIIB/C. 1.14. Mixed Context.
Part of wall, rim. PH 0.04; PL 0.065; D rim (est.) 0.17.
Light yellowish-brown clay 10YR 6/4.
Thick reddish-brown gloss on interior, exterior.
Convex wall. Narrow everted rim; bevelled lip.

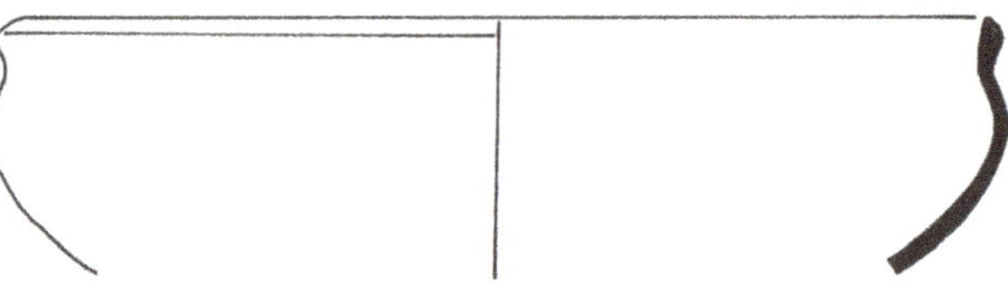

MOULDED GREY WARES

The ware is similar to that of the grey ware moulded lamps encountered in later Hellenistic levels throughout the east Aegean and southern Levant and whose centres of manufacture remains largely unknown (Howland 1958: 143–4; Koutsoukou 1997: 120–1; Rosenthal and Sivan 1978: 12–13; Rosenthal-Heginbottom 2015b: 686).[29] While wheelmade grey ware vessels are encountered in the eastern Mediterranean and even further east (Cox 1949: 6, 16–18; Gardin 1973: 127–8; Kenrick 1985: 58–64; Lyonnet 2012: 155; Thompson 1934: 471; Tidmarsh 2011: 310–24), moulded vessels in this ware, other than lamps, are rare.

In the Levant so far, as ascertained from published examples, more of these moulded grey ware vessels have been recovered from northern Jordan – in particular Pella and Jerash (Rasson-Seigne and Seigne 2020b: 122–3, figs 12–19) – than from elsewhere. Moulded grey ware juglets are also seen at 'Akko–Ptolemais, Samaria and Scythopolis/Beth-Shean as well as Tel Yoqne'am, and, possibly, Straton's Tower/Caesarea. One juglet and a "jar" (probably also a juglet) of similar shape and ware (but different decorative pattern) were recovered from Tell es-Sa'idiyeh Stratum II that Pritchard broadly dates to between 395 and 170 BC. One definite moulded grey ware bowl fragment comes from the Armenian Garden excavations in Jerusalem.[30] Moulded grey ware vessels (in very small numbers) have also been reported from Tell Zira'a and Gadara/Umm

---

29 Jerash appears to have been one such production centre for Hellenistic grey ware moulded lamps (Rasson-Seigne and Seigne 2020b).

30 Regev 2009/10: 140, fig. 17.107, 108 (Akko–Ptolemais); Reisner et al. 1924: fig. 186; Hennessy 1970: fig. 9.8, pl. XIIA (Samaria); Johnson 2006: 528–9, fig. 15.2.32 (Scythopolis/Beth-Shean); Avissar 1996: fig. X.7.23 (Tel Yoqne'am); Rosenthal-Heginbottom 2016b: 156–7, no. 97 (Straton's Tower/Caesarea); Pritchard 1985: fig 19:19, 20 (Tell es-Sa'idiyeh); Hayes 1985b: fig. 47.3 (Jerusalem).

Table 2.6. Frequency of moulded grey ware by shapes, areas, phases.

		JUGLETS	BOTTLES
Area	III, IV (main mound)	6	0
	XXIII (main mound)	10	3
	XXVIII (main mound)	1	0
	XXXIV (Tell Husn)	1	0
Phase	Hellenistic 3A (c. 200–c. 140 BC)	1	0
	Hellenistic 3C (c. 100 (?)–c. 80/79 BC)	12	2
	Mixed Context	5	1

Qais – where it is known at this latter site as Hellenistic Slip H ware – as well as in a late second-century/early first-century BC context at Hippos-Sussita.[31]

At Pella, like Jerash, the repertoire of shapes is largely confined to juglets and bottles with a very fine fluted bowl recovered by the Wooster team from a late first- to third-century AD Roman tomb in the South Cemetery (Smith et al. 1980: 38, pl. XXXVIII). Examination of both the juglets and bottles shows that the two halves were made in a two-piece mould before being pressed together and fired in a reducing kiln. With the exception of **FW 148–9**, each of the vessels recovered so far was made in a different mould although often with similar decorative features (for example, **FW 153**). Given the grey slip, the ribbing, ovolo and other elaborate moulded linear surface decoration (for example, vertical, oblique, horizontal, herringbone) as well as details such as the small bosses projecting from the base of **FW 146** and **FW 158**, it is likely that this ware owes its inspiration mainly to the techniques of the silverworker rather than to those of the potter.[32]

At Pella most of the moulded grey ware vessels have been recovered from Jannaeus Destruction levels (Hellenistic 3C) on the main mound, in particular from Areas III, IV and, especially, from the "villa" in XXIII. Only **FW 145** is from an earlier context (Hellenistic 3A) with **FW 158–62** and **FW 165** from mixed contexts. Thus, the evidence from Pella suggests that these vessels were being produced throughout much (or all) of the second century and into at least the early first century BC – certainly consistent with the evidence from Hippos-Sussita (Mlynarczyk 2011: pl. 245.51) – although at Jerash they are still recovered from first century AD levels, which could explain the presence of the aforementioned fluted bowl in the South Cemetery Roman tomb.

The appearance of the ware in a Hellenistic 3A level at Pella and Stratum II at Tell es-Sa'idiyeh would suggest a starting date in the early second century BC at the latest, although there is no doubt that Pritchard's chronology for Stratum II (c. 395–170 BC) is too high. It is worth noting that lamps of similar ware were already in production by the beginning of the second century BC or earlier (Howland 1958: 143).

A workshop on the southern coast of Asia Minor has been suggested by Regev (2009/10: 140); however, moulded grey ware appears restricted to the southern Levant, suggesting a manufacturing centre (or centres?) somewhere within this region – probably east of the Jordan River at Jerash (although the actual workshop has not been located) or, perhaps less likely, Pella itself.

---

31 Kenkel 2020: 43, 140–1, pl. 1.12Tg6 (Tell Zira'a); Braemer 1987: 527; Rasson-Seigne and Seigne 2020b: 122–3 (Jerash); Kerner 1997: 300; Kenrick 2000: 238 (Gadara/Umm Qais); Mlynarczyk 2011: 580, 585–6, pl. 245.51, 52 (Hippos-Sussita).

32 For the ceramic imitation of silverwork see, for example, Vickers and Gill 1994: chapter 5, especially 123–9. See also the applied relief bowl **FW 119**.

Juglets (FW 145–162)

FW 145. CN 7466.
XXVIIIB 13.9. Hellenistic 3A.
Part of wall, shoulder. PH 0.06; PL 0.06. Light bluish-grey clay 5PB 7/1. Bluish-grey slip.
Shoulder set off from almost vertical wall. Moulded vertical ridge-and-groove pattern on wall.

FW 146. CN 3487.
IVD 10.10. Hellenistic 3C.
Missing handle. H 0.105; D rim 0.04. Light grey clay 10YR 7/1. Grey-black slip.
Flat resting surface. Globular lower body curving inwards to slightly concave neck. Thickened rim. Roots of band handle from rim to shoulder preserved. Ovolo decoration in relief on under-surface and lower body. Parallels: Jerash (Rasson-Seigne and Seigne 2020b: 127, fig. 12); Tell Zira'a (Kenkel 2020: 43, 140–1, pl. 1.12:Tg6); Tel Yoqne'am (Avissar 1996: fig. X.7.23 lower profile). Similar to **FW 150**, **FW 152**, **FW 153**.

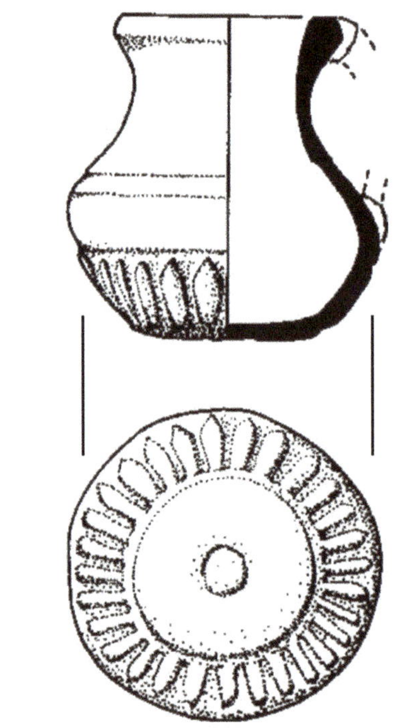

FW 147. CN 6676.
IVD 11.1. Hellenistic 3C.
Part of wall, rim. PH 0.09; D rim (est.) 0.07. Light grey clay 10YR 7/1 to grey clay 10YR 6/1. Dark grey slip.
Tall concave neck with thickened in-turning rim. Moulded ovolo band on shoulder.

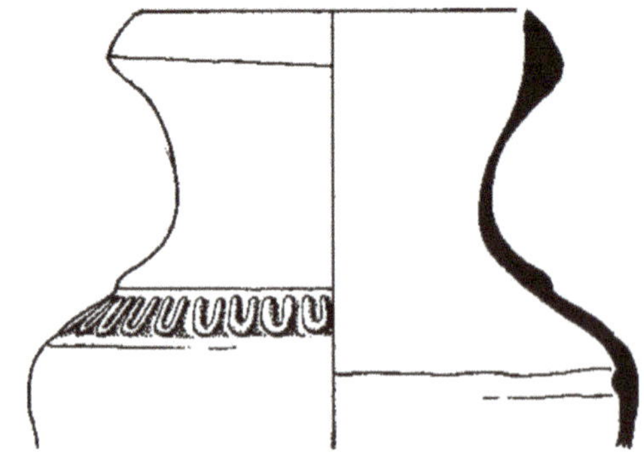

FW 148. CN 3492. (No line drawing)
IVD 10.10. Hellenistic 3C.
Complete. H 0.12; D (rim) 0.045. Light grey clay 10YR
7/1; small black inclusions. Dark grey slip.
Low raised base. Globular body curving inwards to
slightly thickened rim. Grooved strap handle from
rim to shoulder. Moulded linear decoration on body.
Parallel: From the same mould as **FW 149**.

FW 149. CN 7012.
XXIIIA 74.2. Hellenistic 3C.
Missing part of neck. H 0.12; D rim (est.) 0.06. Light
grey clay 10YR 7/1. Dark grey slip.
Low raised base. Globular body; everted neck with
slightly thickened rim. Grooved strap handle from
rim to body. Moulded linear decoration on body.
Parallel: From the same mould as **FW 148**.

FW 150. CN 4397.
XXIIIA 10.7. Hellenistic 3C.
Complete. H 0.12; D rim 0.04. Light grey clay 10YR
7/1. Dark grey slip.
Flat resting surface. Carinated body; slightly concave
neck. Upright rim. Moulded linear decoration on
under-surface and lower body. Band handle from
rim to body.
Parallels: Jerash (Rasson-Seigne and Seigne 2020b:
127, fig. 12). Similar to **FW 146**, **FW 152**, **FW 153**.

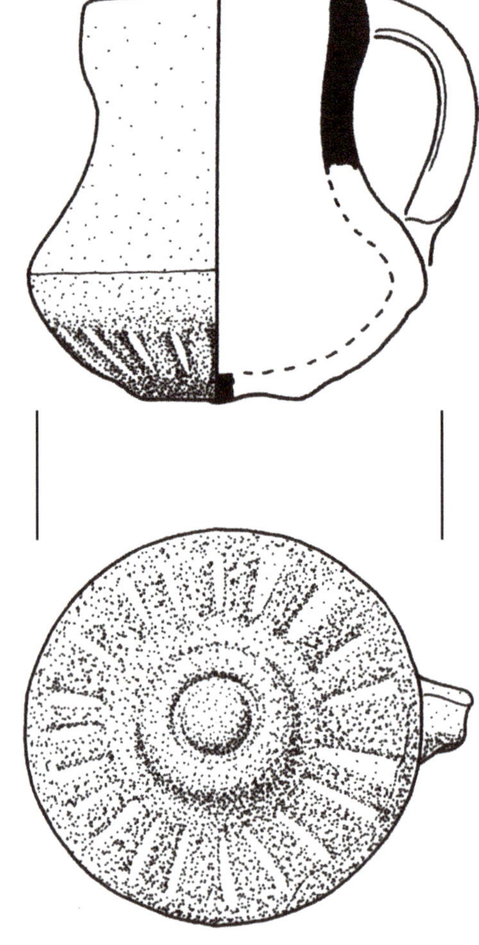

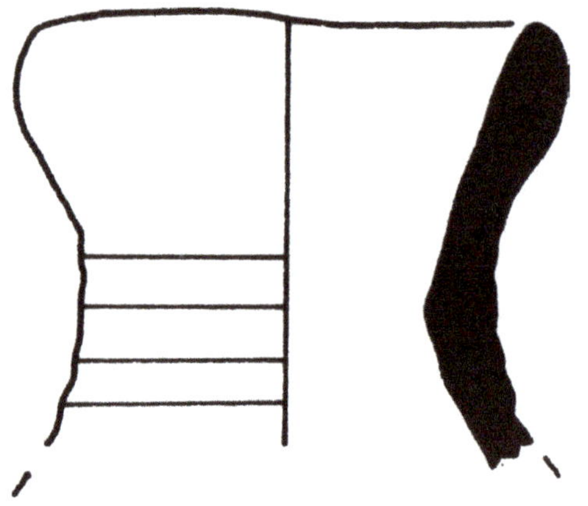

FW 151. CN 6963.
XXIIIA 10.7. Hellenistic 3C.
Rim, part of neck. PH 0.05; PL 0.05; D rim 0.04.
Light grey clay 10YR 7/1 to grey clay 10YR 5/1. Dark
grey slip.
Everted, slightly thickened rim. Horizontal grooves
on neck.

FW 152. CN 4396.

Complete. H 0.11; D rim 0.03. Grey clay 10YR 6/1. Dark grey slip.

Flat resting surface. Carinated body. Concave neck; slightly thickened rim. Moulded linear decoration on body. Band handle from rim to body.

Parallels: Jerash (Rasson-Seigne and Seigne 2020b: 127, fig. 12). Similar to **FW 146**, **FW 150**, **FW 153**.

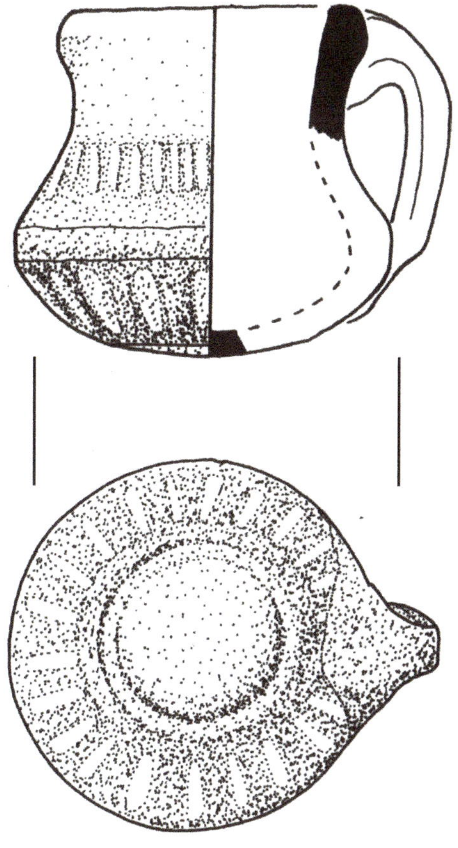

FW 153. CN 7799.

XXIIID 31.2. Hellenistic 3C.

Missing small part of wall. H 0.10; D rim 0.06. Grey clay 2.5Y 6/1. Dark grey slip.

Carinated wall. Concave neck; wide mouth. Worn impressed decoration on lower wall. Strap handle from lip to carination.

Parallels: Jerash (Rasson-Seigne and Seigne 2020b: 127, fig. 12). Similar to **FW 146**, **FW 150**, **FW 152**.

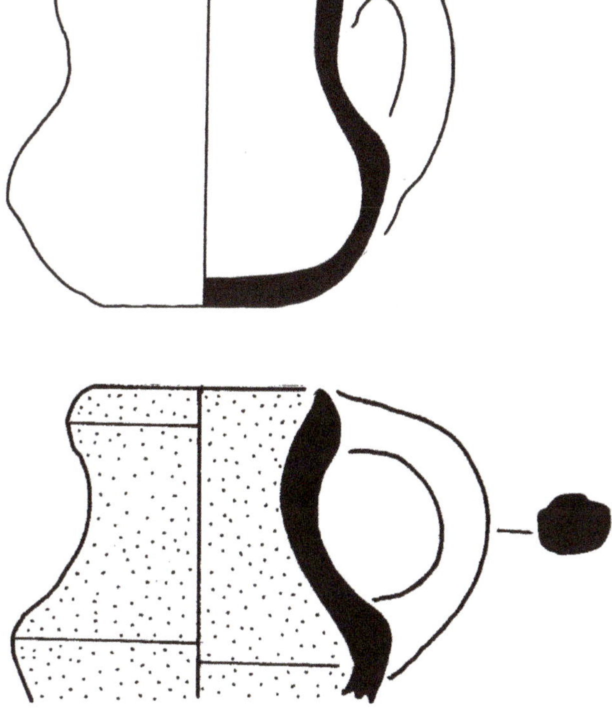

FW 154. CN 7763.

XXIIID 20.4. Hellenistic 3C.

Part of rim, neck, handle. PH 0.07; PL 0.04; D rim (est.) 0.05. Grey clay 7.5YR 5/1. Dark grey slip.

Concave neck; slightly in-turned pointed rim. Narrow ring handle from lip to shoulder.

FW 155. CN 7772.
XXIIIA 22.10. Hellenistic 3C.
Part of shoulder, wall. PH 0.065; PL 0.06. Light grey
clay 2.5Y 7.1. Grey slip.
Carinated body. Deep vertical grooving on shoulder
and upper body.

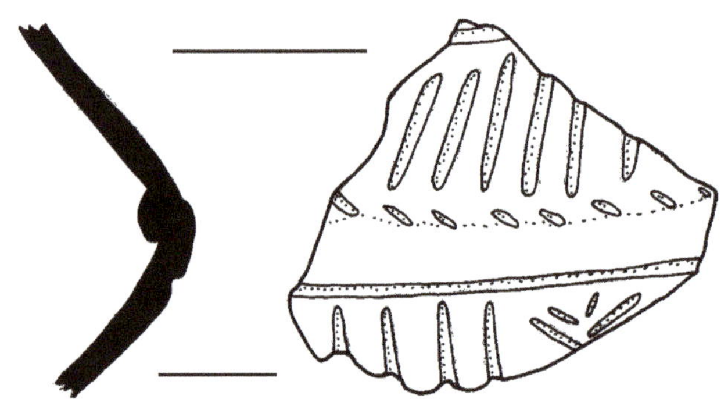

FW 156. CN 7013.
XXIIIA 74.2. Hellenistic 3C.
Base, lower wall. PH 0.02; D base 0.07. Light grey
clay 10YR 7/1. Dark grey slip.
Three broad low applied feet. Two concentric grooves
in centre of under-surface. Herringbone in vertical
columns on exterior.

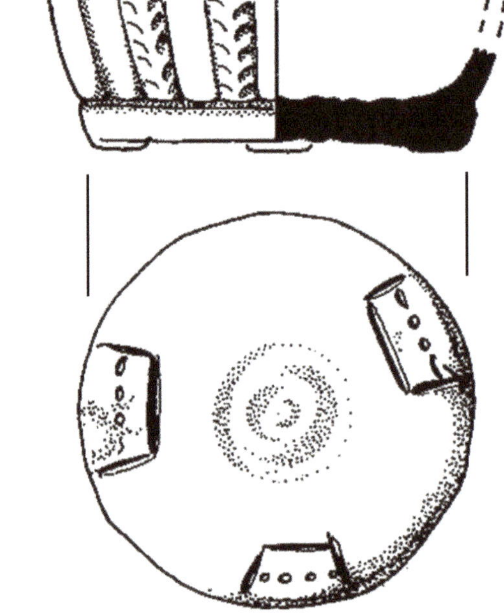

FW 157. CN 7773.
XXIIIA 71.2. Hellenistic 3C.
Part of neck, shoulder. PH 0.06; PL 0.055. Light grey
clay 2.5Y 7/1. Grey slip.
Deep vertical grooving on shoulder.

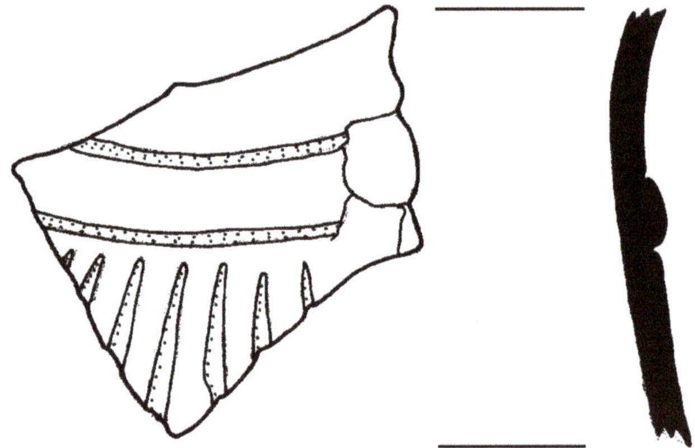

FW 158. CN 0116. (Plate 43)
IIIB/C 5.1. Mixed Context.
Missing part of shoulder. H 0.11; D rim 0.08. Grey clay 10YR 5/1. Dark grey slip.
Three broad low applied feet embellished by horizontal and vertical grooves. Schematic impressed rosette on under-surface within two low ridges; two bands of inverse ovolo above and below shoulder. Carinated wall; tall concave neck; angular rim. Strap handle from rim to shoulder.

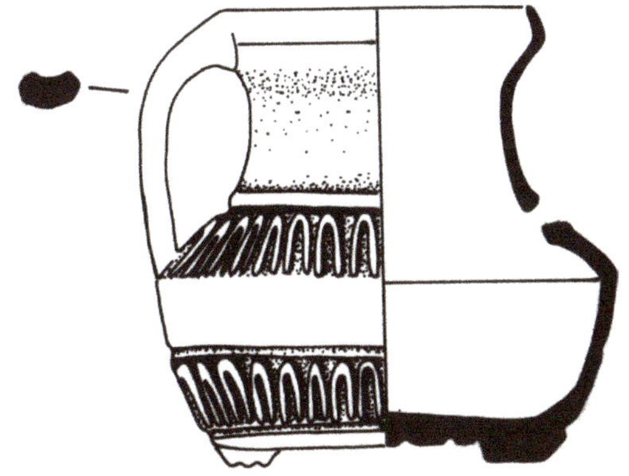

FW 159. CN 6836.
IIIB/C 6.1. Mixed Context.
Part of neck, rim, handle. PH 0.04; D rim (est.) 0.045. Grey clay 7.5YR 6/1. Dark grey slip.
Concave neck; gently in-turning rim. Strap handle attached to lip.

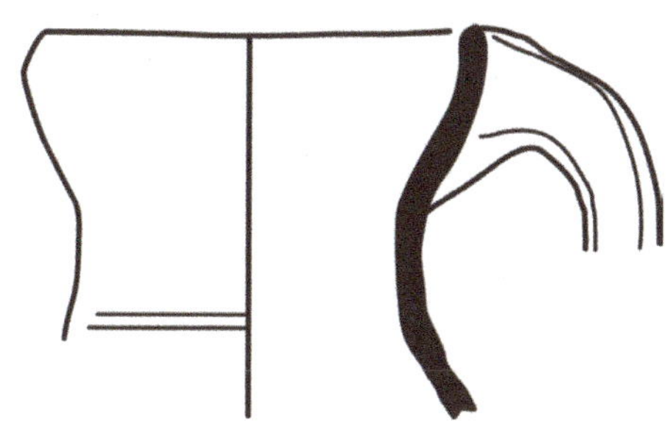

FW 160. CN 3493.
IIIQ 7.5. Mixed Context.
Part of neck. PH 0.03; PL 0.025; D rim (est.) 0.04. Grey clay 10YR 6/1. Dark grey slip.
Concave neck; everted simple rim.

FW 161. CN 7104.
XXIIIA 80.6. Mixed Context.
Part of rim, neck, shoulder, handle. PH 0.085; D rim
(est.) 0.045. White clay 10YR 8/1. Dull dark grey slip
over exterior of upper neck, rim.
Concave neck separated by horizontal groove from
shoulder. Horizontal row of raised globules above
and incised zigzag below. Vertical handle from rim
to shoulder.

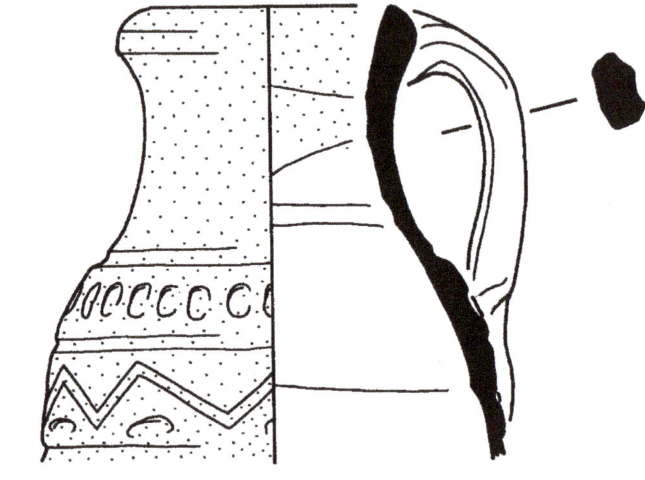

FW 162. CN 7771.
XXXIVB 12.5. Mixed Context.
Fragment of rim, neck. PH 0.07; PL 0.045; D rim
(est.) 0.04.
Grey clay 10YR 6/1. Dark grey slip.
Concave neck separated from shoulder by two
horizontal grooves; grooved lip.

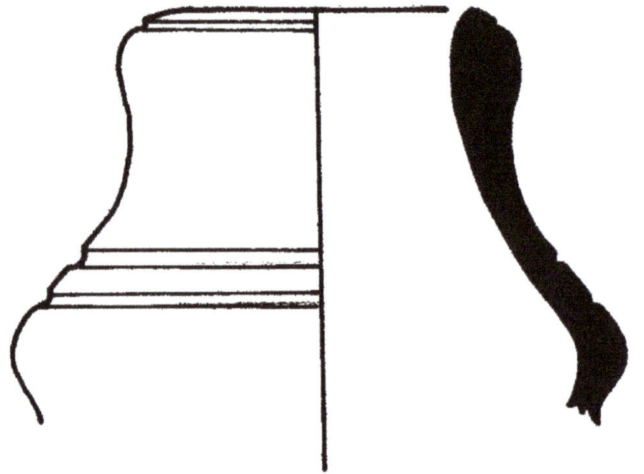

Bottles (FW 163–165)

FW 163. CN 7822.
XXIIID 44.2. Hellenistic 3C.
Part of rim, neck, shoulder. PH 0.075; D rim 0.04.
Light grey clay 7/1. Dark grey slip.
Vertical moulding around neck. Root of vertical
handle on lip.
Parallel: Hippos-Sussita (Mlynarczyk 2011:
pl. 245.51, very late 2nd–1st c. BC).

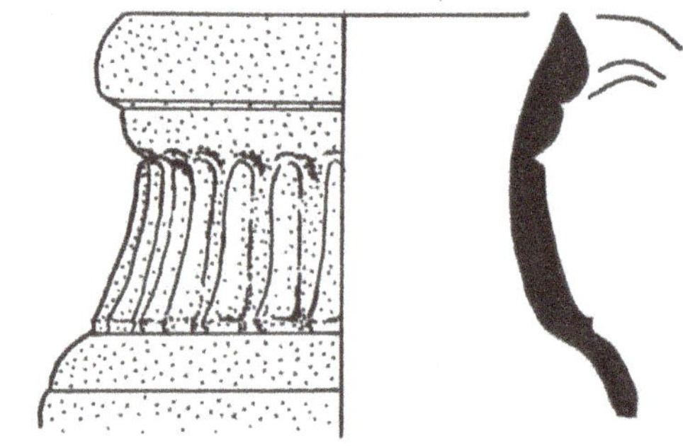

FW 164. CN 6565b.
XXIIIA 10.7. Hellenistic 3C.
Missing base, rim. PH 0.11; PL 0.06. Grey clay 10YR
6/1. Dark grey slip.
Tall body ending in sloping shoulder. Moulded
vertical herringbone.

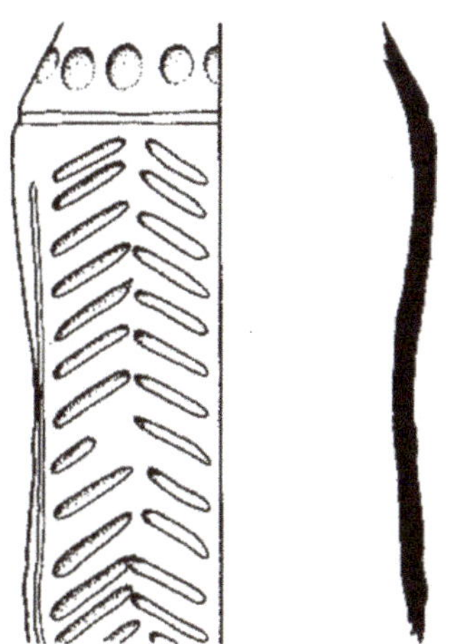

FW 165. CN 7827. (No line drawing) (Plate 44)
XXIIID 64.2. Mixed Context.
Part of base, lower wall. PH 0.025. D base (est.) 0.06;
Light grey clay 2.5Y 7/1. Grey slip.
Flat resting surface. Two rows of vertical moulding
on lower wall.

PAINTED WARES

With the exception of West Slope ware, vessels with painted decoration are rare at Pella, limited to the white-ground lagynos **FW 166** – recovered from a pit on the lower western slope of Jebel Sartaba (Area XIV) – as well as a crudely made jar and a further jar fragment (both with simple dark-on-light motifs) unearthed by the Wooster team (McNicoll et al. 1982: pls 14, 15c).

White-ground lagynos (FW 166)

The production of white-ground lagynoi decorated with dark paint commenced around the beginning of the second century BC, or perhaps earlier (Guz-Zilberstein 1995: 310; Rosenthal-Heginbottom 2015b: 677–8; Rotroff 1997b: 227; *contra* Hayes 1991b: 189 who suggests a starting date some fifty years later).[33] They became especially popular during the latter half of that century and lasted well into the first century BC (Pedley 2002: 383–5). The class may well have originated in Asia Minor, possibly near Pergamon – from which city a large number of fragments have been recovered (Schäfer 1968: 101ff, pls 42–8) – although other centres of manufacture sprang up in the Aegean, North Africa and the Levant (Rotroff 1997b: 225).

Lagynoi of this type are commonly decorated with garlands, wreaths and musical instruments; vessels used in feasting, including lagynoi themselves, are also depicted (for example, Schäfer 1968: pl. 43, F12–13; pl. 45, F 11). The "tambourine"[34] on **FW 166** – recovered out of context on the slopes of Jebel Sartaba (Area XIV) – finds parallels on the white-ground lagynos of more angular shape from the National Archaeological

---

33 Undecorated lagynoi with a thick creamy-white slip seem to have been turned out, at least in Cyprus, even earlier (Mitford 1980: 32–42). But see Lejeune 2009 (especially footnote 4) who argues for a date in the first quarter of the second century BC (rather than the late third century) for the Kafizin vases with their inscriptions and portraits. Also, Lund 2015: 74.

34 Hellström (1965: 18) also suggests that this motif is a musical instrument although he does not hazard a guess as to what type. Mertens (2019) (see **FW 166**) describes it as a basket.

Museum of Athens and another from the British Museum (Pedley 2002: 383, fig. 10.60)[35] as well as a fragment from Knidos (another centre of manufacture: Mandel 2000: pl. 94, a). The "gazebo" further to the left owes its inspiration to the Alexandrian genre of landscape painting, popular in the late third and early second century BC and reflected most convincingly in the great Nile Mosaic from Palestrina.[36]

The shape of **FW 166** is close to that of a white-ground lagynos from Aegina (Smetana-Scherrer 1982: pl. 51.667), recovered from a burial of the second half of the second century BC. The decoration on the Aegina example, however, is restricted to ribbons and garlands.

FW 166. CN 3276. (Plate 45)
XIV J 1.2, 2.2. Mixed Context.
Complete. H 0.18; D rim 0.05. Pink clay 7.5YR 7/4.
Well levigated; fine mica.
Thick white slip over exterior except for reserved base and lower body. Yellowish-red painted decoration 5YR 6/6–7/6–5/8. Five horizontal lines at belly. Shoulder decoration of wreaths, volute krater, "gazebo", "tambourine".
Ring base. Markedly globular body; tall concave neck; angular rim. Strap handle from upper neck to shoulder.
Parallels: for shape, Aegina (Smetana-Scherrer 1982: pl. 51.667); for decoration, Pergamon (Schäfer 1968: pl. 43, F12–13; pl. 45, F11); British Museum GR 1867.5–12.52 [vase F513] (= Pedley 2002: 383, fig.10.60); National Archaeological Museum of Athens, RN 26176; Metropolitan Museum of Art New York, Accession no. 47.11.1 (Mertens 2019: 153, fig. 10).

---

35 White ground lagynoi: National Museum of Athens: RN 26176 (I thank Monica Jackson for her help in obtaining the Registration Number); British Museum: GR 1867.5-12.52, vase F 513.

36 The mosaic was found in an apsidal nymphaeum in the lower town adjacent to the Sanctuary of Fortuna Primigenia (Meyboom 2016). Its date essentially depends on that of the nymphaeum, variously put at either the later second century BC (Ling 1998: 31; Meyboom 2016; R.R.R. Smith 1993: 180) or c. 80 BC (Pollitt 1986: 205).

West Slope ware

So-called "West Slope ware" was first systematically studied by Watzinger (1901). Although the technique – for despite its name it is not really a "ware" (Rotroff 1991: 60) – can be traced back to the ceramics of Archaic and Classical Greece, it seems to have originated in late fourth-century Athens as a result of the influence both of contemporary gilded black-gloss wares (Hayes 1991b: 191; Kopcke 1964) and, possibly, of the Gnathia pottery of southern Italy (Rotroff 1997b: 41).

Although widely encountered – even as far afield as southern Russia (Minns 1913: 351; Rotroff 1991: 69, 71) – West Slope pottery is relatively uncommon in the southern Levant. In Palestine it is restricted to sites such as 'Akko-Ptolemais, Ashdod, Beth-Zur, Gezer, Samaria, Scythopolis/Beth-Shean, Straton's Tower/

Table 2.7. Frequency of West Slope ware by areas, phases, shapes.

		PLATES	BOWLS	KANTHAROI	KRATERS	AMPHORAE	JARS
Area	III, IV (main mound)	1	3	2	1	1	0
	XXIII (main mound)	0	1	0	0	0	1
	XXVIII (main mound)	2	0	0	0	0	0
	XXXII (main mound)	3	0	0	0	0	2
Phase	3A (c. 200 –c. 140 BC)	4	0	0	0	0	2
	3B (c. 140 –c. 100 (?) BC)	0	0	1	0	0	0
	3C (c. 100 (?) –c. 80/79 BC)	0	1	0	0	0	1
	Mixed Context	2	3	1	1	1	0
Ware	Ware 1	0	0	0	0	1	0
	Ware 2 (BSP)/"Ivy Platter"	5	1	1	0	0	0
	Ware 3 (BSP)	0	1 ("Ivy Platter")	0	0	0	0
	Miscellaneous	1 ("Ivy Platter")	2	1 ("Ivy Platter")	1	0	3

Caesarea, Tel Anafa, Tel Dor and Tel Zahara.[37] It is infrequent east of the Jordan River although seen at Amman/Philadelphia and Gadara/Umm Qais.[38]

West Slope ware is not common at Pella with only seventeen catalogued pieces (**FW 167–83**) recovered. Most (including a further seven very small uncatalogued fragments) came from mixed deposits on the main mound and Tell Husn, with only seven fragments coming from stratified (mainly Hellenistic 3A) contexts on the main mound. The amphora fragment **FW 180** – from a pre-construction (Mixed Context) fill in IIIB/C – is the only import from Athens where the combination of diminishing rectangles on the shoulder and moulded mask at the handle base is seen on West Slope amphorae (Rotroff 1997b: pl. 45.446; Thompson 1934: figs 59, 60).

In both shape and decoration **FW 171** finds parallels with two "plates with flaring overhanging rim" from Tel Dor (Rosenthal-Heginbottom 1995: 227–8, fig. 5.10:13–14). Five other plates with grooved overhanging rim (**FW 167–70, FW 172**) should also be considered here. **FW 167–8** have a horizontal band of rudimentary ivy leaves in dark paint on the interior wall, and **FW 169** and **FW 172** a band of laurel. A faint rosette can just be discerned on the interior of the very fragmentary **FW 170**. **FW 167** also has two bands of rouletting on the interior. These plates, along with the bowl **FW 175** and krater **FW 179**, would appear to be products of the so-called "Ivy Platter" workshop, in operation by at least the second half of the third century, the location of which has been suggested by Rotroff (2002) to lie somewhere along the coast of southern Asia Minor or in coastal Syria or Lebanon.[39] On visual inspection, the ware of plates **FW 167–70** seems identical to "Ware 2" and that of **FW 175** identical to "Ware 3", raising the possibility that at least these five vessels may have been produced in the region of Antioch or its environs. To date, the products of this workshop have mainly been recovered from coastal sites along the eastern Mediterranean with relatively few from sites further inland (Rotroff 2002: 103–4; Tidmarsh 2011: 378–9). Rotroff has suggested that the workshop was no longer functioning by the later second century BC and the recovery of all the Pella examples from a Pre-Jannaeus Destruction – Hellenistic 3B – or unstratified "Mixed Context" does not challenge this.

None of the specimens from Pella is readily identifiable as a product of Pergamon or Ephesus which, along with the "Ivy Platter" workshop, were major production centres for West Slope ware in the Hellenistic East (Rotroff 2002).

---

37 Regev 2009/10: figs 7.35–6; 24.138–40; 33.209, 214, 219–20; 35:226–9 ('Akko-Ptolemais); Dothan 1971: 62–3, figs 8.20; 24.12; Dothan 1976: 31, fig. 32 (Ashdod); P.W. Lapp 1961: 220, no. 353.1.A (Beth-Zur); Macalister 1912: pl. CLXXXIV (Gezer); Crowfoot et al. 1957: 238, figs 44; 45.1–4; 47 (Samaria); Fitzgerald 1931: pl. XXXIV.5; Johnson 2006: 527, nos 20–4; 535, no. 98? (Scythopolis/Beth-Shean); Roller 1980: 36, fig. 2.1 (Straton's Tower/Caesarea); Slane 1997: 280, FW 32–4 (Tel Anafa); Rosenthal-Heginbottom 1995: 222–33; Stern 1995a: 436, pl. 2 (Tel Dor); Bar-Nathan and Gärtner 2013: fig. 3.15.134 (Tel Zahara).

38 Zayadine 1977–78: fig. 14.401 (Amman/Philadelphia); Kerner and Hoffman 1993: 368; Kenrick 2000: nos 116, 212 (Gadara/Umm Qais).

39 See also Berlin and Pilacinski (2003) and Mlynarczyk (2002) for the likelihood that products of this "workshop" may have been produced in more than one location, a suggestion perhaps supported by **FW 177** whose clay differs from the other "Ivy Platter" specimens in this catalogue.

Plates (FW 167–172)

FW 167. CN 7541.
XXXIIY 4.3. Hellenistic 3A.
Two joining fragments of wall, rim, base. Base fragment: PH 0.025. PL 0.13; Rim fragment: PH 0.02; PL 0.085; D rim (est.) 0.24. Reddish-yellow clay 7.5YR 7/6. Ware 2. Ivy Platter Group.
Thick mottled black-brown gloss on interior, exterior. Horizontal band of faded black ivy leaves on interior. Broad central depression with two rows of rouletting. Flaring wall separated on interior by two grooves from sharply down-turned rim. Part of ring base preserved.

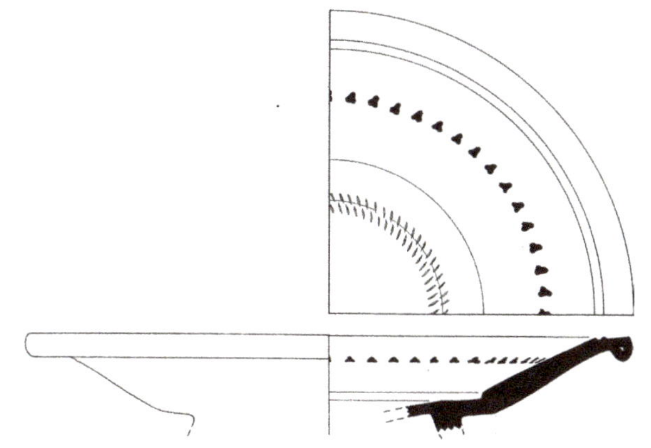

FW 168. CN 7531.
XXXIIY 2.2. Hellenistic 3A.
Five joining fragments forming part of wall, rim. PL 0.175; D rim (est.) 0.27. Reddish-yellow clay 7.5 YR 6/6. Ware 2. Ivy Platter Group.
Dark brown-black gloss on interior, exterior. Faint trace of horizontal band of ivy leaves on interior. Flaring wall separated by prominent ridge and scraped grooves from sharply down-turned rim on interior.

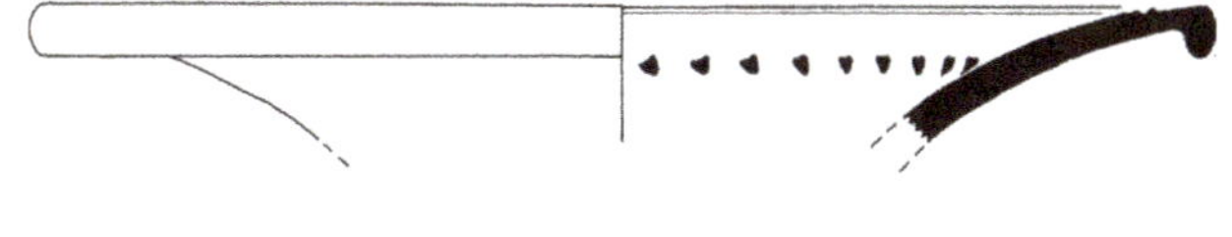

FW 169. CN 7190.
XXVIIIB 13.7/13/17. Hellenistic 3A.
Multiple fragments forming two non-joining pieces. (a) PH 0.045; PL 0.21; (b) PH 0.05, PL 0.26. D rim (est.) 0.33. Reddish-yellow clay 7.5 YR 6/6. Ware 2. Ivy Platter Group.
Good black-brown gloss. Incised central rib with painted white laurel leaves on each side. Central depression with two grooves and two bands of rouletting on interior floor. Wall flares slightly, separated by two grooves on each side of low ridge from sharply down-turned rim.

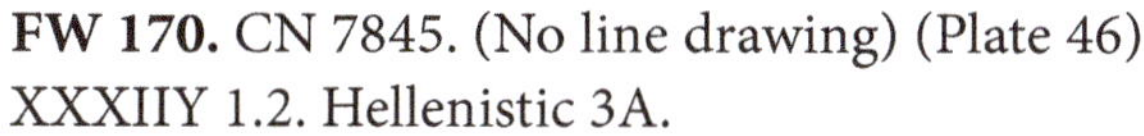

FW 170. CN 7845. (No line drawing) (Plate 46)
XXXIIY 1.2. Hellenistic 3A.
Two non-joining fragments of base, floor, rim. (a) PH 0.02; PL 0.12; (b) PL 0.085. D rim (est.) 0.10. Reddish-yellow clay 7.5YR 7/6. Ware 2. Ivy Platter Group.
Good brown gloss on interior, exterior, fired red in patches. Fugitive central rosette (eight petals). Two rows of rouletting. Tall ring base.

FW 171. CN 0485.
IIIB/C 1.25. Mixed Context.
Part of upper wall and rim. PH 0.075; PL 0.105;
D rim (est.) 0.30. Light grey clay 2.5Y 7/2.
Black gloss on interior, rim; unglazed exterior. Interior
decoration of white painted garland and ribbon bow
with group of three dots. Thickened vertical rim set
off on exterior by two grooves from flaring upper wall.
Parallels: Samaria (Crowfoot et al. 1957: fig. 47.7);
Tel Dor (Rosenthal-Heginbottom 1995: fig. 5.10:13,
14, 250–125 BC).

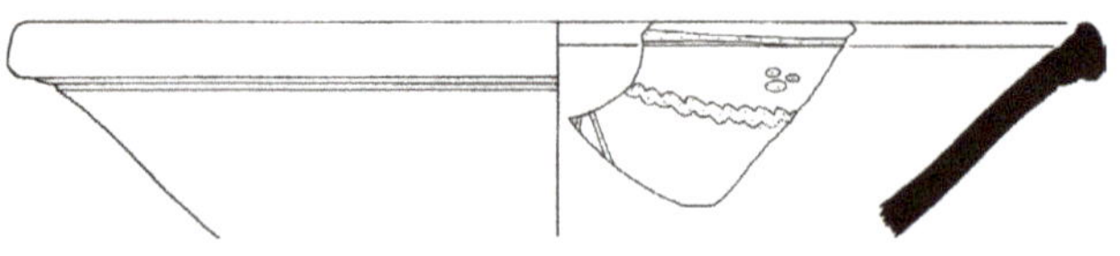

FW 172. CN 7181.
XXVIIIB 4.1. Mixed Context.
Part of wall, rim. PH 0.03; D rim (est.) 0.30. Reddish-
yellow clay 7.5YR 8/6. Ware 2. Ivy Platter Group.
Black gloss on interior, exterior. Faint trace of
horizontal band of laurel (?) on interior surface.
Flaring upper wall separated from vertical down-
sloping rim by two grooves and ridge.

Bowls (FW 173–176)

FW 173. CN 0216. (Plate 47)
IIIB/C 2.8. Hellenistic 3C.
Part of wall, rim. PH 0.06; PL 0.045. Reddish-yellow
clay 5YR 6/6.
Black gloss on interior, exterior. Alternating vertical
and horizontal white painted bands on interior of
rim. Out-turned upper wall; simple rim.
Parallel: Athens (Rotroff 1991: fig. 17; pl. 35.84;
pl. 55.585; pl. 134.1684 decoration; 1997b: fig. 21.349,
pl. 34.349 upper profile and decoration, before 125
BC; also, Thompson 1934: fig. 62.D 28).

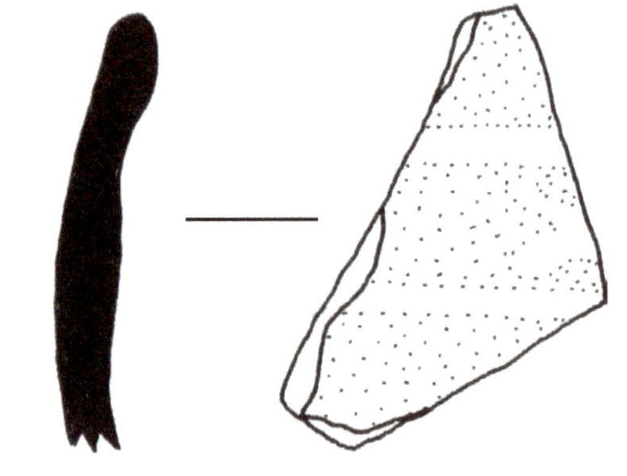

FW 174. CN 0444.
IIIB/C 1.22. Mixed Context.
Part of wall, rim. PH 0.09; PL 0.075; D rim (est.) 0.13.
Pink clay 7.5YR 8/4. Fine white inclusions.
Lustrous red gloss on interior; dull black gloss on
lower exterior. Black and white chequerboard and
incised cross-hatching on upper exterior. Convex wall
with two broad horizontal grooves midway. Narrow
out-turned lip separated by exterior groove from wall.
Parallel: Athens (Watzinger 1901: 79, no. 2; Rotroff
1991: fig. 30.117, fig. 31.118, pl. 45 for decoration);
Tarsus (F.F. Jones 1950: fig. 124.105).

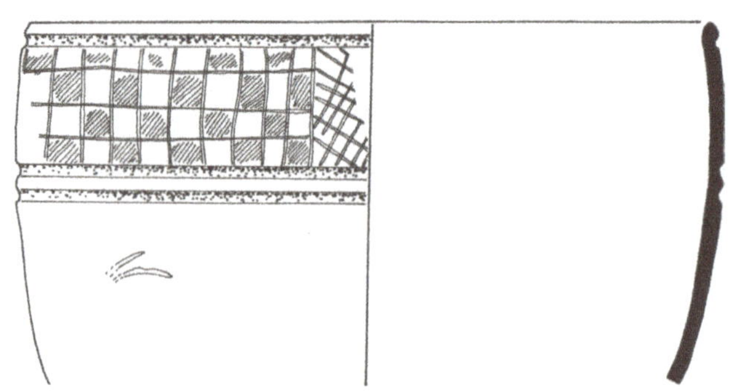

FW 175. CN 6968.
IIIQ. 11.22. Mixed Context.
Part of wall, rim. PH 0.025; PL 0.08; D rim (est.) 0.32.
Pale yellow clay 2.5Y 7/3. Ware 3? Ivy Platter Group.
Black gloss on interior; unglazed exterior. Fugitive
white cable (?) pattern on interior. Flaring upper wall;
thickened rim convex on exterior.

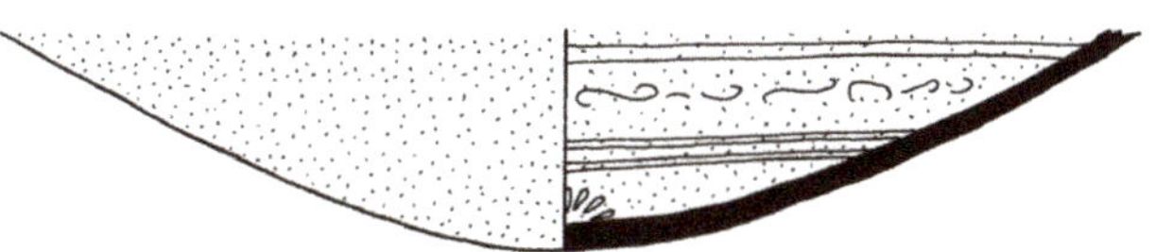

FW 176. CN 7521.
XXIIIA 111.1. Mixed Context.
Four joining fragments of wall, resting surface.
PH 0.05; PL 0.20. Reddish-brown clay 7.5YR 7/6.
Ware 2.
Black gloss on exterior; lustrous brown on interior.
Worn white painted rosette at base of interior
surrounded by two reserved parallel bands. Incised
tendrils with a further two parallel bands above.
Parallel: Athens (recalls Thompson 1934: fig. 31, C12,
second quarter of 2nd c. BC. See Rotroff 1982: 109 for
revised dates of Thompson's Group C.).

Kantharoi (FW 177–178)

FW 177. CN 6571.
IIIP 25.10. Hellenistic 3B.
Part of rim and shoulder. PH 0.04; PL 0.07; D rim
(est.) 0.13. Light red clay 10R 7/6. Ivy Platter Group.
Lustrous black gloss on exterior; red-black gloss on
interior. Two horizontal incised lines between neck
and shoulder. Faint band of white painted vertical
drops on shoulder. Slightly flaring rim.
Parallel: 'Akko-Ptolemais (Regev 2009/10:
fig. 33.209; Berlin and Stone 2016: fig. 9.20.1,
mid–late 2nd c. BC).

FW 178. CN 6646.
IVE 17.19. Mixed Context.
Part of shoulder, rim. PH 0.045; PL 0.05; D rim (est.)
0.14. Pink clay 7.5YR 7/4. Ware 2.
Dull black clay on interior, exterior. Incised horizontal
grooves on exterior above and below incised tendrils.
Slightly concave neck separated by external groove
from thickened rim. Traces of vertical fluting on
shoulder.
Parallels: 'Akko-Ptolemais (Berlin and Stone 2016:
fig. 9.27.9, unstratified); Pergamon (Behr 1988: pl. 17.6
for decoration; Schäfer 1968: pl. 16, D63 but unfluted);
Samaria (Reisner et al. 1924: fig. 173.20); Tarsus
(F.F. Jones 1950: fig. 124.96).

Krater (FW 179)

FW 179. CN 6751.
IVD 13.21. Mixed Context.
Part of neck, rim. PH 0.055; D rim (est.) 0.22. Light
brown clay 7.5YR 6/4.
Dull black-brown gloss on exterior, upper interior.
Olive wreath in thick pale pink paint on exterior.
Upright neck ending in thickened horizontal rim.
Parallels: Samaria (Crowfoot et al. 1957: fig. 45.1);
Tel Dor (close to Rosenthal-Heginbottom 1995:
fig. 5.11:7 upper profile, 275–150 BC).

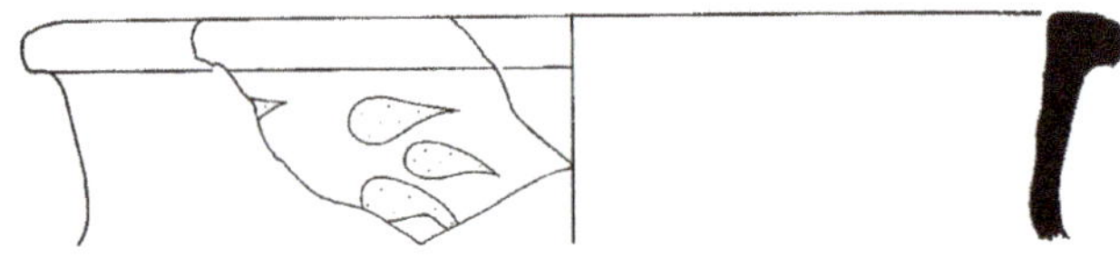

Amphora (FW 180)

FW 180. CN 0324.
IIIB/C 1.14. Mixed Context.
Part of shoulder, root of handle. PH 0.045; PL 0.09.
Pink clay 7.5YR 7/4. Ware 1.
Moulded head of Pan at base of twisted handle; on
either side, garland and diminishing rectangles of
fugitive white paint. Lustrous black gloss on interior,
exterior.
Parallel: Athens (Cook 1997: pl. 56A; Rotroff 1997b:
pl. 45.446, disturbed context; Thompson 1934: figs 59,
60); Samaria (Crowfoot et al. 1957: fig. 44.1).

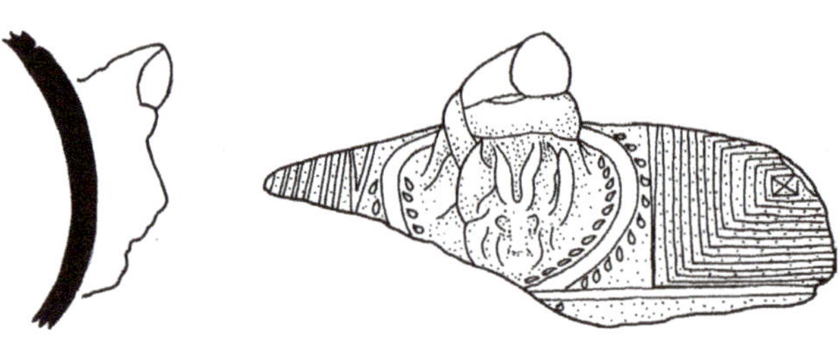

Jars (FW 181–183)

FW 181. CN 7854.
XXXIIY 1.2. Hellenistic 3A.
Part of rim, neck. PH 0.03; D rim (est.) 0.18. Reddish-
yellow clay 5YR 6/6.
Brown gloss on exterior neck above band of red gloss
between two horizontal incised grooves. Red gloss
on interior. Tall slightly concave neck; narrow collar
on lip.

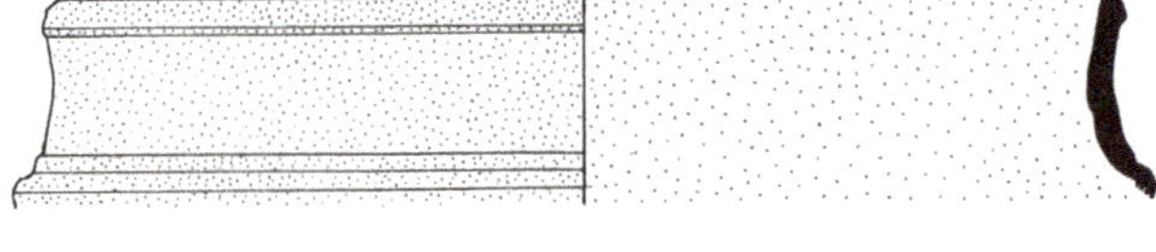

FW 182. CN 7860. (No line drawing) (Plate 48)
XXXIIY 1.3 Hellenistic 3A.
Part of rim, neck, shoulder. PH 0.03; PL 0.08; D rim
(est.) 0.12. Reddish-yellow clay 5YR 6/6.
Good brown gloss on exterior. Fugitive white ivy
leaf band on rim. Incised groove between neck and
shoulder. Thin wall. Upright neck; simple rim. Convex
shoulder.

Table 2.8. Frequency of thin-walled ware by areas, phases, shapes.

		BEAKERS	BOWL
Area	XXIII (main mound)	1	0
	XI (Tell Husn)	1	1
	XXXIV (Tell Husn)	1	0
Phase	Early Roman I (63 BC–late first century AD)	1	1
	Mixed	2	0

FW 183. CN 7833. (Plate 49)
XXIIID 59.3. Hellenistic 3C.
Missing fragments of body. H 0.20; D rim 0.09. Light brownish-grey clay 10YR 6/2.
Black-grey slip. Rudimentary "garland" on upper body represented by diagonal white strokes below a horizontal white band. Low ring base. Globular body. Tall neck with narrow collar. Vertical strap handles from shoulder to body.
Parallel: A similar "garland" is seen on a jar recovered from Pella by the Wooster team (McNicoll et al. 1982: pl. 15c).

THIN-WALLED WARES

Four fragments of so-called thin-walled pottery, one from an unstratified context in plot XXIIIA (main mound) and the other three from Tell Husn, of which two are from Early Roman strata (**FW 184, FW 187**), have been recovered. None of these fragments appears Nabatean, although it must be admitted that, in the case of small sherds, the distinction between Nabatean and non-Nabatean thin-walled wares can often be impossible to make with certainty.[40] **FW 184** and **FW 186**, body sherds of exquisite thinness embellished with horizontal rows of fine rouletting, are beaker fragments that can be compared to beakers of the second half of the first century BC from 'Akko-Ptolemais (Berlin and Stone 2016: fig. 9.23.1) and from the South Stoa at Corinth in a context dated c. 54–68 AD (Hayes 1973: 416, pl. 89.182). The equally delicate base **FW 187** most likely belongs to a bowl similar in shape to one from Belo of Claudian or Neronian date (Mayet 1975: 69, pl. XXXV.276).

Ceramic vessels in a very lightweight ware, often appearing to copy vessels in silver or glass but owing little to contemporary Hellenistic ceramic traditions, were first produced in Etruria and northern Italy in the early second century BC (Hayes 1997: 67; Moevs 1973: 35–45; Montana et al. 2003: 375–6). The extreme thinness (frequently less than 2 millimetres) of the walls of such vessels, which could be either thrown on the wheel or made in a mould, has led to the adoption of the general term "thin-walled wares" although it is clear that many regional production centres must have existed.[41] Although by the end of the second

---

40 No definite examples of Nabatean ceramics have been identified at Pella. At Jerash it is represented "en faible quantité", beginning in the first century BC and slowly increasing in numbers over the first three centuries AD (Rasson-Seigne and Seigne 2020a: 131–2).

41 Even amongst the relatively small number of thin-walled sherds at Sidi Khrebish (ancient Berenice), Kenrick was able to distinguish at least seven fabrics (Kenrick 1985: 307).

century BC, these ceramics were exported to Spain and the eastern Mediterranean, western "thin-walled" wares are not seen with any frequency in the East before the first century AD (Hayes 2008: 95–104; Lund 2004: 7–8; Slane 1997: 349; Stone 2014: 291). During the first century AD, workshops were also established in the eastern Mediterranean (Frangié-Joly 2014: 97), in north-west Asia Minor (Adamsheck 1979: 69) and, possibly, Palestine (Berlin 2005a: 49, 2006: 14–15). However, with the exception of Tel Anafa where some 240 sherds were recovered from the second campaign alone (Slane 1997: 349), relatively few examples imported from the west have been recovered from sites in modern Israel.[42] East of the Jordan River, thin-walled ceramics from the western Mediterranean appear to be especially rare.[43]

A variety of shapes and surface ornament is seen amongst the thin-walled pottery (Moevs 1973; Mayet 1975: 5–7, pls LXXVIII–LXXX), but drinking vessels – usually beakers, goblets, bowls and cups – comprise by far the largest class of shapes with rouletting or "dot-decoration" (**FW 184**, **FW 186**) and barbotine, the latter often represented by "thorn ware" (as seen on **FW 185**) and characteristic of the Late Republican and Augustan periods (Hayes 2008: 97, especially footnote 16 for references), the most popular form of decoration.

FW 184, **FW 187** and the unstratified **FW 186** were recovered from Tell Husn where Early Roman levels are well demonstrated; on the other hand, the unstratified nature of the context in which **FW 185** was found makes it uncertain whether the fragment was part of the Jannaeus Destruction debris or one of the few Early Roman sherds present on the main mound itself.

Beakers (FW 184–186)

FW 184. CN 3061.
XIA/B 2.3. Early Roman 1.
Part of upper wall. PH 0.03; PL 0.03. Reddish-yellow clay 5YR 6/6–5/8.
Three horizontal lines of faint rouletting. Outward-flaring wall.
Parallels: ʿAkko-Ptolemais (Berlin and Stone 2016: fig. 9.23.1, second half of 1st c. BC); Corinth, South Stoa (close to Hayes 1973: pl. 89.182).

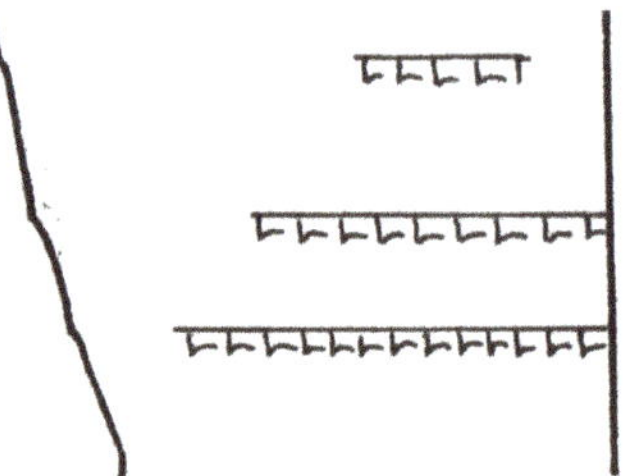

42 Examples are known from ʿAkko-Ptolemais (Berlin and Stone 2016: 185, fig. 9.23.1); Ashkelon (Carmi et al. 1994: fig. 4.11); Gamla (Berlin 2006: 14–15); Jaffa (Tsuf 2018: fig. 9.54.893–6); Jerusalem (Hayes 1985b: fig. 58.13–14; Rahmani 1967: fig. 12.5; Rosenthal-Heginbottom 2003: 209–10, 2014: 393–5, pls 2.4.55 beaker, 2.4.56 cup, table 23.5 listing thin-walled ware from the Jewish Quarter excavations); Qumran (Eshel and Broshi 2003: figs 8.3, 8.8); Straton's Tower/Caesarea (Berlin 1992: figs 51.1–3; 55.11–13; Roller 1980: fig. 2.37–8). It is also possible that some of the thin-walled beakers from Oboda (Negev 1986: 81–2) may be western imports rather than Nabatean (Slane 1997: 349, n. 318).

43 One "thorn ware" sherd was published from the Roman Forum at Amman/Philadelphia (Hadidi 1970: pl. III.12) with another thin-walled juglet (?) neck from the environs of that city (Sami' et al. 1991: fig. 6.17). A further example comes from Petra (Horsfield and Horsfield 1941: no. 388).

FW 185. CN 7690.

XXIIIA 10.9. Mixed Context.

Part of rim, wall. PL 0.065; PH 0.045; D base (est.) 0.10. Red clay 2.5YR 5/8. "Thorn ware".

Thin brown slip over exterior. Thickened convex rim; curving wall. Vertical "thorns" on exterior.

Parallel: Morgantina (Stone 2014: pl. 63.695).

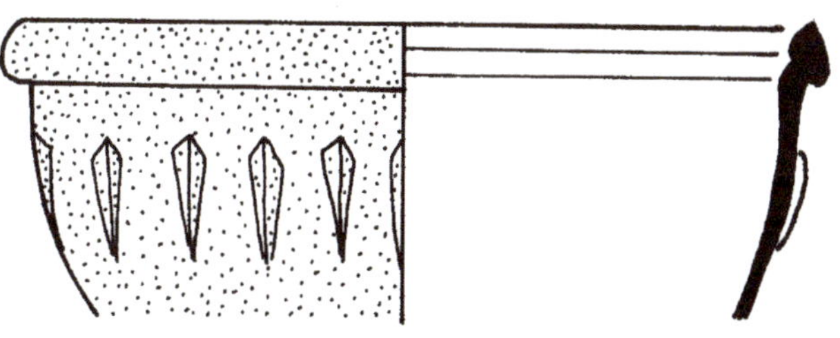

FW 186. CN 10829.

XXXIVN 1.14. Mixed Context.

Part of wall, rim. PH 0.045; PL 0.025; D rim (est.) 0.10. Weak red clay 10R 5/2.

Thin grey slip over exterior, interior. Vertical wall ending in thickened rim. Two horizontal bands of rouletting preserved on exterior.

Parallel: ʿAkko-Ptolemais (Berlin and Stone 2016: fig. 9.23.1, second half of 1st c. BC).

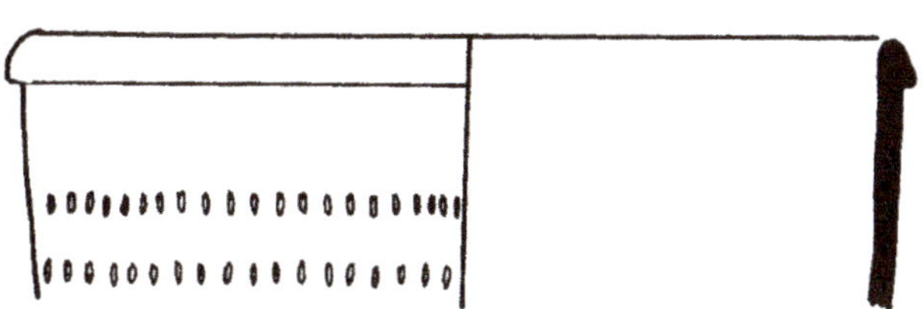

Bowl (FW 187)

FW 187. CN 3060.

XIA/B 2.3. Early Roman 1.

Complete base, part of lower wall. PH 0.09; PL 0.045. Pink clay 5YR 8/4.

Ring base; convex under-surface. Flaring lower wall.

Parallel: Belo necropolis (Mayet 1975: pl. XXXV.276).

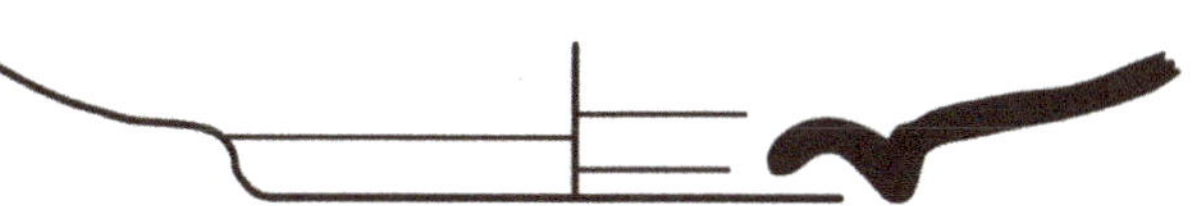

EASTERN SIGILLATA A WARES

Eastern Sigillata A (ESA) ware is characterised by a pale clay varying in colour from pink to creamish-white (Hellström 1965: 28; Slane 1997: 269), equivalent to a Munsell range of 10YR 8/4 to 7.5YR 7/6–8/6 (Hayes 1985a: 9).[44] As noted by Cox (1949: 7) at Dura-Europos, Kenyon (1957: 284) at Samaria and Vanderhoeven (1989: 23–7) at Apamea, variations of clay colour outside this range certainly occur and it would seem that much the same situation exists at Pella. The frequently shiny dark red gloss of ESA (Munsell 2.5YR 4/6–4/8) may, in later Hellenistic times, take on a slightly browner hue when a double-dipping streak is also frequently seen on plates and dishes (Hayes 1985a: 9, 1991a: 33).

Just as the ware itself is now well characterised, there is now little divergence of opinion as to the date of its initial appearance in the Levant. Currently, a date for the appearance of ESA – or at least its "black-slipped predecessor" – in the northern Levant around (or just after) the middle of the second century BC is generally favoured (Gitin 1996: 91; Hayes 1991a: 32, 2008: 19; Slane 1997: 269–74), although ESA may have only reached the southern Levant at a somewhat later date – most likely in the 130s – consistent with its rarity in Hellenistic 3B levels at Pella (Tables 2.9, 3.6; Berlin 2006: 13–14; Berlin et al. 2014).[45] Production of ESA continued until the end of the second century AD or beginning of the third (Hayes 1985a: 12–13). Worth noting is the appearance, towards the end of the first century BC and during the first century AD, of new forms that are generally more angular than the "Hellenistic" bowl and cup shapes (Hayes 1985a, forms 1–27) dominant for most of the previous two centuries BC. These "Early Roman" forms (Hayes Forms 28–51) seem to frequently resemble Arretine-derived shapes (Hayes 1985a: 27–37, 1991a: 35), although the actual degree of influence of these western Mediterranean wares on ESA is still open to debate (Gunneweg et al. 1983: 109; Slane 1997: 273–4).

Somewhat more controversial is the location of the centre (or centres) of production. Earlier studies (Crowfoot et al. 1957: 281ff.; Waagé 1948: 1, 20) had clearly shown that ESA was distributed throughout much of the eastern Mediterranean, with the greatest concentration being in Syria, Palestine and Lower Egypt. Thus, a production centre (or centres) within the Levant appeared likely (Hellström 1965: 31). In 1983 Gunneweg and colleagues published the results of a careful Neutron Activation Analysis of 157 pieces of Eastern Terra Sigillata I ware from sites both within and outside Israel: surprisingly, the study pointed to eastern Cyprus as the source of this material (Gunneweg et al. 1983: 11–14). Further work by Elam, Slane and others has, however, once again pointed to somewhere within the Levant as the production centre (Elam et al. 1989; Slane et al. 1993), with the Gulf of Iskenderun (Bes and Stone 2020; Hayes 2008: 13; Lund et al. 2006; Rosenthal-Heginbottom 2015b: 680–1; Zimmerman 2020b: 86) or the north Syrian littoral (possibly within the environs of Antioch) currently most favoured (G. Schneider 1995: 416, 2000: 532; Slane 1997: 272; Tidmarsh 2011: 326). A Phoenician origin (with a number of production centres) has also been proposed (Berlin 2005b: 442–4; Regev 2007, 2009/10: 170). Nevertheless, the above-mentioned variations in biscuit

---

44   The other Eastern Sigillata wares, viz. Eastern Sigillata B ("Samian" ware), Eastern Sigillata C ("Candarli" ware), and Eastern Sigillata D ("Cypriot" ware) have not been found at Pella.

45   Berlin and colleagues (2014) raise the possibility that BSP originated in different production centres (central or southern Phoenician cities?) from those producing ESA. Production of this former ware ceased towards the end of the second century BC (Slane 1997: 271). See also Élaigne (2007: 113–14) for the appearance of a "red slip predecessor" (RSP) in the ceramic corpus at Beirut (Site Bey 002) from the first half of the second century BC.

of ESA are more likely the result of different firing temperatures within the kilns of a single centre rather than of different clay sources (Garnett 2011; Slane 1997: 270).[46]

At Pella, ESA vessels, while common (**FW 188–258**), are found in nowhere near the large quantities seen at Antioch, Jebel Khalid in Syria, Tel Anafa or even the more modest numbers from Samaria.[47] "Early" and "Middle" Roman forms (Hayes Forms 28–61), along with Forms 4B (**FW 202–3, FW 208**), 9 (**FW 213**), 12 (**FW 214**) and 22B (**FW 225**) of Early Roman date, have been retrieved from Tell Husn, seemingly the main area of Early Roman settlement, together with a small number of Early Roman 2 (c. 100–c. 150 AD) fragments (**FW 243, FW 246–9**), from Plots IIIP, IIIQ and IVL on the main mound, which was largely uninhabited during the Early Roman period. However, most of the vessels in this catalogue can be classed within the Hellenistic-inspired shapes of Hayes Forms 1–27, which are found in the domestic deposits on the main mound and Tell Husn.

The most comprehensive typologies of ESA are those of Waagé (1948: 22–5) and Hayes (1985a: 13–48) but, as Slane (1997: 271) has pointed out, their usefulness is less for fragments. In the catalogue, therefore, the Hayes typology is supplemented by that from Tel Anafa (Slane 1997: 283–334) with this latter typology also modifying some of the dates supplied by Hayes (Rosenthal-Heginbottom 2015b: 680).[48]

"Hellenistic" forms

Fishplates (Hayes Form 1; Tel Anafa Type 11)

One of the earliest shapes in the ESA corpus, fishplates are uncommon in this ware throughout the eastern Mediterranean (Hayes 1985a: 13–14; Tidmarsh 2011: 328–9). At Tel Anafa, where some fifteen fishplate fragments in ESA were recovered (the largest number at any eastern Mediterranean site), Slane (1997: 275) has suggested that they were no longer being produced by the time construction of the Late Hellenistic Stuccoed Building commenced (c. 125 BC).

At Pella, **FW 189** was recovered from a Jannaeus Destruction deposit in IVD (main mound). This may suggest that the production of ESA fishplates lasted longer than suggested by Slane or, perhaps more likely, that **FW 189** is a residual fragment.

---

46 The alleged occurrence of several unfired vessels of ESA at Oboda (in use between 20 BC and 50 AD) suggested to Negev (1974: 35) that, from time to time, minor local production centres may have existed elsewhere. More recently, Goren and Fabian (2008) have demonstrated that the "potter's workshop" at Oboda was in fact a Roman mill-bakery with no link to pottery production. However, the presence, at Anemurium in Cilicia, of large quantities of gold mica in one of the three ESA clays at the site – an occurrence not seen in assemblages of ESA elsewhere – remains of interest (C. Williams 1989: 9, 117). It is worth noting that at various cities in northern Syria, such as Seleucia-on-Tigris and Dura-Europos, there occurs so-called "red-burnished ware" – a readily distinguishable imitation of ESA (Cox 1949: 22; Valtz 1991: 47); whilst during the first centuries BC and AD, potters at Jerash produced ceramics clearly influenced by ESA as regards shape and external slip (Braemer 1989; Rasson-Seigne and Seigne 2020b: 121–2).

47 While certainly not as common as it is in Syria, ESA still remains the predominant Terra Sigillata ware in the southern Levant (Malfitana 2002: 149–51). In Jerusalem, although ESA "is the predominant imported tableware", it is present in relatively modest quantities, seemingly not appearing until the mid-first century BC (Rosenthal-Heginbottom 2014: 387–9, see also Table 23.2 listing ESA from the Jewish Quarter excavations).

48 In his report on ESA recovered from the Athenian Agora, Hayes (2008: 13–30) has also modified a number of dates he had proposed in Hayes 1985a.

Table 2.9. Eastern Sigillata A forms, phases.

FORM	HELLENISTIC 3B c. 140–c. 100 (?) BC	HELLENISTIC 3C c. 100 (?)– c. 80/79 BC	EARLY ROMAN 63 BC–c. 135 AD	MIXED CONTEXT
Hayes 1	0	1	0	1
Hayes 3, 4	1	9	3	6
Hayes 5A	0	2	1	0
Hayes 6	0	0	0	1
Hayes 9	0	0	0	1
Hayes 12	0	0	0	1
Hayes 17B	0	1	0	1
Hayes 20	0	0	0	1
Hayes 22	0	4	1	3
Hayes 23	0	0	1	2
Hayes 24	0	0	1	0
Hayes "rare form c"	0	1	0	1
Hayes 28	0	0	1	2
Hayes 33	0	0	0	1
Hayes 34	0	0	0	1
Hayes 37A	0	0	0	1
Hayes 44	0	0	0	1
Hayes 47	0	0	1	0
Hayes 48	0	0	0	1
Hayes 54	0	0	0	2
Hayes 57	0	0	0	1
Hayes 59	0	0	1 (ER 2)	0
Hayes 60	0	0	1 (ER 2)	4
Hayes 101–102	0	1	1	7

Table 2.10. Eastern Sigillata A forms, areas (uncatalogued in brackets).

FORM	III, IV MAIN MOUND	XXIII MAIN MOUND	XI TELL HUSN	XXXIV TELL HUSN
Hayes 1	2	0	0	0
Hayes 3, 4	8 (15)	6	4	1 (18)
Hayes 5A	0	2	1	0
Hayes 6	1 (1)	0	0	0
Hayes 9	0	0	0	1
Hayes 12	0	0	0	1
Hayes 17B	2	0	0	0
Hayes 20	1	0	0	0
Hayes 22	4 (5)	3	1	(1)
Hayes 23	1	1	1	0
Hayes 24	0	0	0	1
Hayes "rare c"	1	1	0	0
Hayes 28	0	0	0	3
Hayes 33	0	0	0	1
Hayes 34	0	0	0	1
Hayes 37A	0	0	0	1
Hayes 44	0	0	0	1
Hayes 47	0	0	0	1
Hayes 48	0	0	0	1
Hayes 54	0	0	2	0
Hayes 57	1	0	0	0
Hayes 59	0	0	1	0
Hayes 60	4	0	1	0
Hayes 101–102	7 (1)	1	1	0

FW 188. CN 6991.
IIIP 7.1. Mixed Context.
Part of wall, rim. PH 0.02; PL 0.08; D rim (est.) 0.34.
Reddish-yellow clay 7.5YR 6/6.
Red gloss on interior, exterior. Flaring upper wall;
convex down-turned rim.

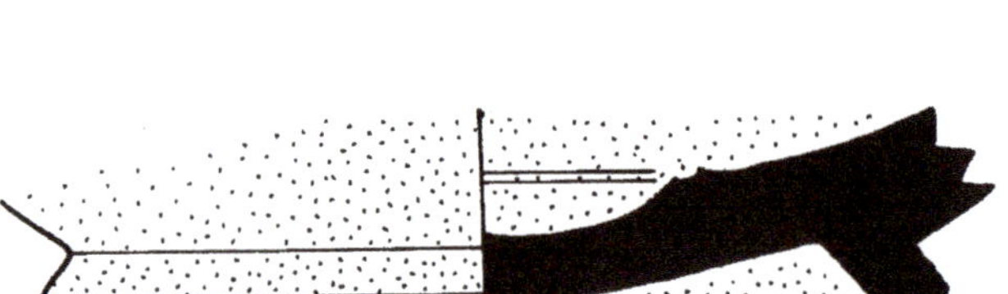

FW 189. CN 4295.
IVD 10.12. Hellenistic 3C.
Part of base, floor. PH 0.025; PL 0.10; D base (est.)
0.10. Very pale brown clay 10YR 7/4.
Red gloss on interior, exterior. Ring base. Central
depression surrounded by groove.

Broad flat plates with in-turned rim (Hayes Forms 3 and 4; Tel Anafa Type 13)

The most common ESA shape from Pella (**FW 190–208**) is the broad plate with ring base and relatively low,
upright or in-turned rim (Hayes Forms 3 and 4). Plates of this form are abundant at Tel Anafa where they
are included within Slane's Type 13 (variants a–e).

Most of the examples from Pella are fragmentary, consisting only of base or rim sherds; not surprisingly,
this makes any attempt at accurate subdivision difficult or impossible. The broad channel seen on the resting
surface of the base fragment **FW 190** recalls those plates of Type 13a from Tel Anafa (for example, Slane 1997:
FW 57), although the Tel Anafa examples have a sloping floor rather than the horizontal floor seen on this
fragment. Although lacking their base, the absence of an angular junction between floor and rim suggests
that **FW 191–2** may also belong here. This form "was no longer in use after 100/95 BCE" (Slane 1997: 286),
consistent with the Pre-Jannaeus Destruction (Hellenistic 3B) context of **FW 190**.

Plates **FW 193–9** and **FW 204** have enough of their profile preserved to demonstrate that floor and rim
joined at about a 90-degree angle. It is reasonable, therefore, to include them within Tel Anafa Type 13b.
At Pella, all the stratified examples of this type come from Jannaeus Destruction levels; none was recovered
from an Early Roman context, consistent with the evidence from Tel Anafa where plates of Type 13b were
largely confined to Hellenistic 3B–3C levels (c. 125–75 BC).

Although Tel Anafa Type 13c (Hayes Form 4A) – with its horizontal floor, rim upturned at about
60 degrees and slightly in-turned lip – is the most common form of plate at Tel Anafa (produced from the
late second century until the end of the first century BC), the type is only represented at Pella by **FW 200–1**.
The Jannaeus Destruction (Hellenistic 3C) and Early Roman contexts respectively of these two fragments
are consistent with the Tel Anafa chronology.

Amongst the large number of plates with up-curved rim at Tel Anafa, Slane was able to distinguish a late
variant of the shape (Type 13e = Hayes Form 4B) on the basis of its relatively small dimensions and open
form. The relatively few stratified examples from Anafa were recovered from Roman 1B–1C (that is, early to
mid-first century AD) contexts, broadly consistent with the Augustan date suggested by Hayes (1985a: 16).
Fragments **FW 202–3** and **FW 208** should be included within this type, with **FW 202** and **FW 208** from
Early Roman levels in plot XIA/B and **FW 203** unstratified but also from Tell Husn in plot XXXIVB from
which much Early Roman material was recovered.

FW 190. CN 7785.
XXIIID 11.18. Hellenistic 3B.
Fragment of base, floor. PH 0.02; PL 0.205; D base
0.09. Reddish-yellow clay 5YR 6/8.
Red gloss on interior, exterior. Low ring base with
broad channel on resting surface. Slightly rising floor.
Concentric grooves and ridges (but no rouletting)
on interior.

FW 191. CN 1090.
IVR 7.1. Mixed Context.
Part of wall, rim. PH 0.015; D rim (est.) 0.24. Reddish-
yellow clay 5YR 7/6.
Red gloss on interior, exterior. Sloping floor; upright
rim.

FW 192. CN 1482.
IIIB 17.1. Mixed Context.
Part of wall, rim. PH 0.02; D rim (est.) 0.30. Reddish-
yellow clay 7.5YR 7/6.
Red gloss on interior, exterior. Horizontal floor;
slightly thickened rim.
Parallel: Petra (Ch. Schneider 1996: 143, no. 539).

FW 193. CN 0036.
IIIB/C 1.1. Hellenistic 3C.
Part of base, wall, rim. H 0.035; D rim (est.) 0.23.
Pink clay 5YR 8/4.
Shiny red gloss on interior, exterior. Broad ring base.
Gently sloping floor; upright rim.
Parallels: Ashdod (Dothan and Freedman 1967:
fig. 6.1 [but lacking inscription], first half of 2nd c.
BC–mid-1st c. BC; Dothan 1971: fig. 15.12); Beirut
(Élaigne 2007: fig. 15.402–380, first half 1st c. BC); Jaffa
(Tsuf 2018: fig. 9.55.904); Oboda (Negev 1986: 22,
no. 138); Tel Yoqne'am (Ben-Tor et al. 1983: fig. 7.1).

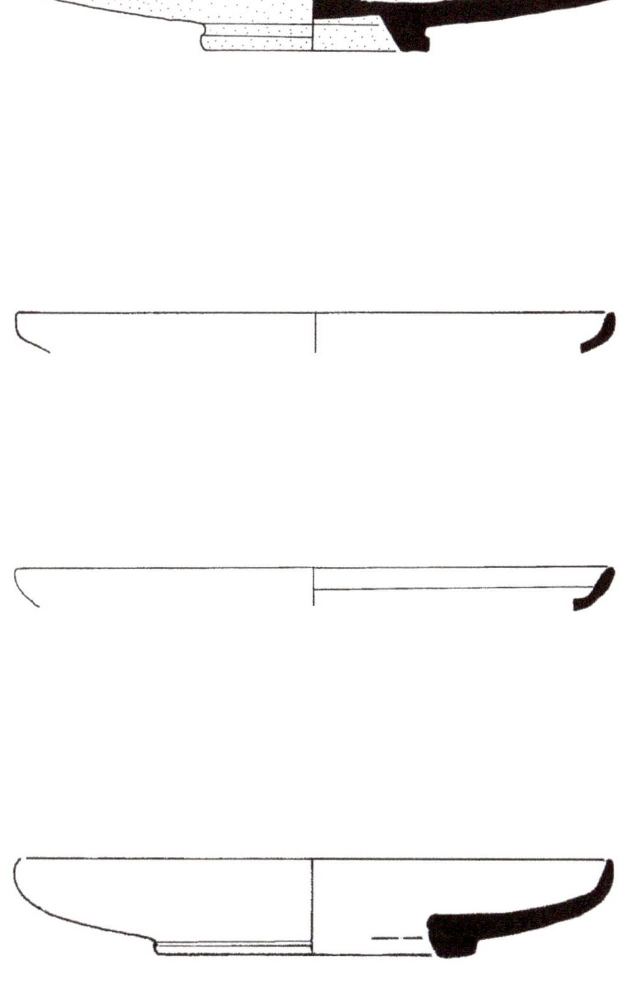

FW 194. CN 7164.

XXIIIA 10.17. Mixed Context.

Six joining fragments. Missing part of rim, wall, floor.
H 0.03; D rim 0.21. Reddish-yellow clay 5YR 7/6.
Slightly dull red gloss on interior, exterior. Broad ring
base. Horizontal floor; upright wall. Interior rosette
stamp surrounded by three shallow grooves outside of
which are four irregularly placed stamped palmettes
within another shallow groove.

Parallels: 'Akko-Ptolemais (Regev 2009/10: fig.
39.260); Ashdod (close to Dothan 1971: fig. 10.19,
2nd c. BC); Beirut (Élaigne 2007: fig. 15.402-374, first
half 1st c. BC).

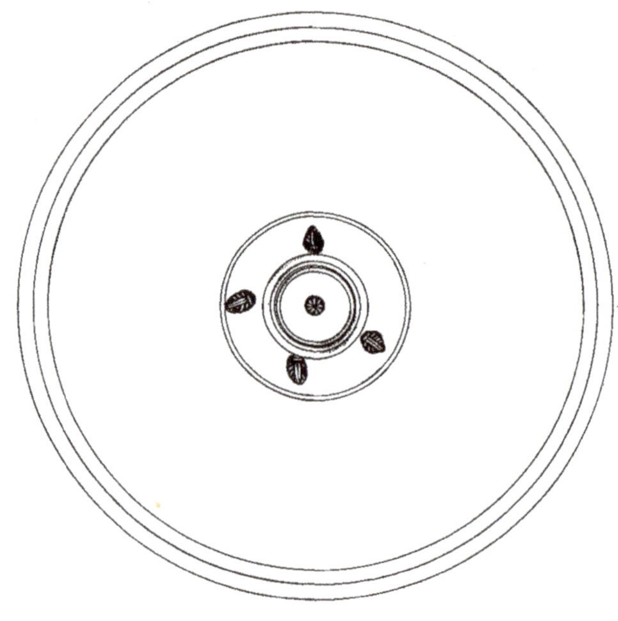

FW 195. CN 7522.

XXIIIA 11.2. Hellenistic 3C.

Part of base, wall, rim (three joining fragments).
PH 0.04; D rim (est.) 0.31. Pale yellow clay 2.5Y 7/3.
Lustrous red gloss on interior, exterior. Broad ring
base, convex on exterior. Horizontal floor; upright
wall, slightly convex on exterior.

FW 196. CN 0068.

IIIB/C 1.3. Hellenistic 3C.

Part of wall, rim. PH 0.025; D rim (est.) 0.22. Very
pale brown clay 10YR 8/4.

Red gloss 2.5YR 4/6 on interior, exterior.

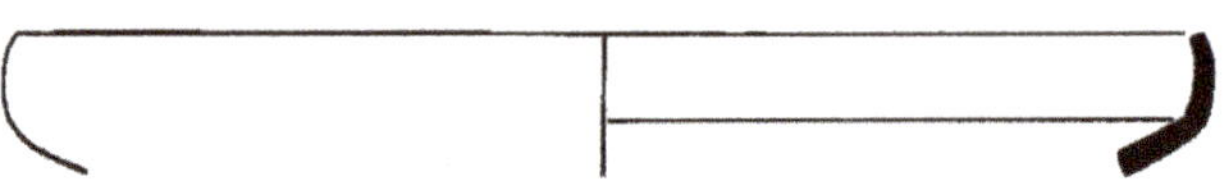

FW 197. CN 6850.
IIIB/C 1.4. Hellenistic 3C.
Part of wall, rim. PH 0.025; D rim (est.) 0.25. Very
pale brown clay 10YR 8/4. Tiny air holes.
Lustrous dark red gloss on interior, exterior. Sloping
floor; upright thickened rim.
Parallels: Oboda (Negev 1974: pl. 24.130); Tel Zahara
(Bar-Nathan 2013: fig. 3.7.63).

FW 198. CN 0918.
IIIB 14.3. Hellenistic 3C.
Part of wall, rim. PH 0.025; D rim (est.) 0.24. Reddish-
yellow clay 7.5YR 6/6.
Thin red gloss on interior, exterior.

FW 199. CN 6822.
IVD 13.10. Hellenistic 3C.
Upper wall, rim. PH 0.035; D rim (est.) 0.26. Reddish-
yellow clay 7.5YR 7/6.
Dark red gloss on interior, exterior.
Parallel: ʿAkko-Ptolemais (Berlin and Stone 2016: fig.
9.21.2, first half of 1st c. BC).

FW 200. CN 7728. (No line drawing) (Plate 50)
XXIIIA. 71.2. Hellenistic 3C.
Base, part of floor. PL 0.215; PH 0.015; D base 0.135.
Very pale brown clay 10YR 8/4.
Red gloss over interior, exterior. Broad ring base.
Horizontal floor with concentric bands of rouletting
on interior.

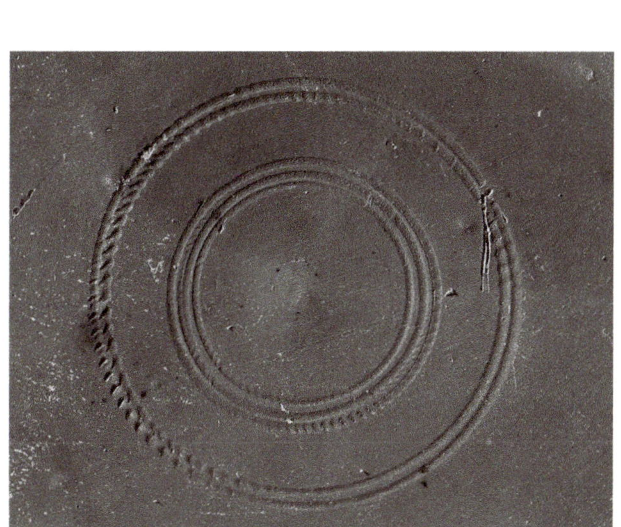

FW 201. CN 2642.
XIA/B 1.1/2. Early Roman 1.
Part of wall, rim. PH 0.045; D rim (est.) 0.24. Pink
clay 7.5YR 8/4.
Thick shiny reddish-brown gloss on interior, exterior.
Low ring base. Shallow plate with slightly in-curving
wall. Faint traces of rouletting and palmette decoration
on interior.
Parallels: Herodium (Bar-Nathan 1981: pl. 1.22);
Marisa (Kloner and Hess 1985: fig. 1.12); Samaria
(Crowfoot et al. 1957: fig. 73.3); Scythopolis/Beth-
Shean (Fitzgerald 1931: pl. XXXIV.31); Tel Anafa
(Slane 1997: pl. 12. FW 120, early–mid 1st c. AD).

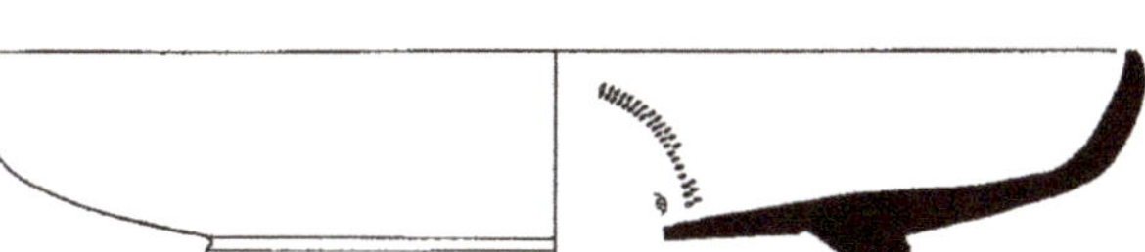

FW 202. CN 6800.
XIA/B 20.6. Early Roman 1.
Part of base, wall, rim. H 0.035; D rim (est.) 0.17.
Very pale brown clay 10YR 8/4.
Red gloss on interior, exterior. Broad ring base;
horizontal floor. Slightly everted wall.
Parallels: Ashkelon (Johnson 2008: fig. 2); Hama
(Christensen and Johansen 1971: fig. 26, no. 1.18);
Hippos-Sussita (Osband and Eisenberg 2018:
pl. 4.6.11, end 1st c. BC/beginning 1st c. AD).

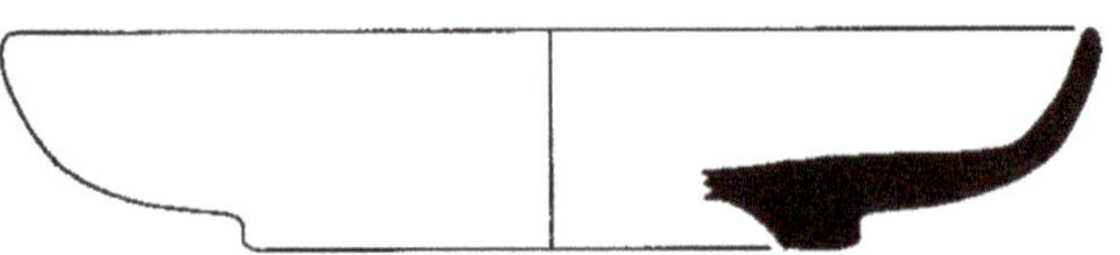

FW 203. CN 7524.
XXXIVB 5.10. Mixed Context.
Part of base, wall, rim. PH 0.035; D rim (est.) 0.20.
Reddish-yellow clay 5YR 6/6.
Worn red gloss on interior, exterior.
Parallels: ʿAkko-Ptolemais (Berlin and Stone 2016:
fig. 9.26.1, early 1st c. AD); Tel Anafa (Slane 1997:
pl. 12. FW 122, modern level).

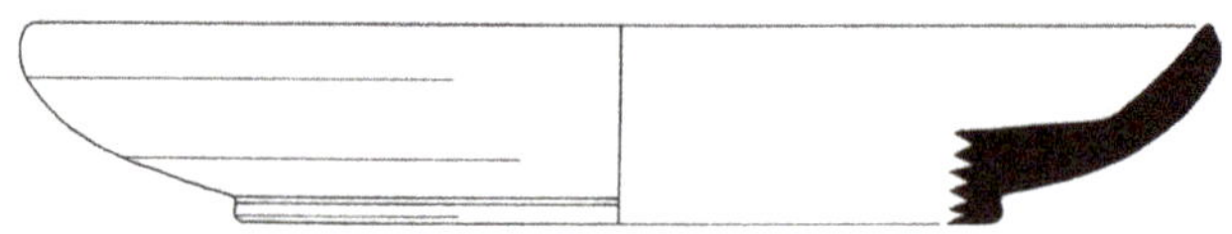

FW 204. CN 7779. (No line drawing). (Plate 51)
XXIIID 11.5. Hellenistic 3C.
Multiple fragments forming almost complete plate;
small parts of rim and floor missing. H 0.045; D rim
0.31; D base 0.195. Very pale brown clay 10YR 8/4.
Red gloss on interior, exterior. Low, broad ring
base. Horizontal floor with upright rim. One band
of rouletting on interior. Graffito (incised κ inside
π?) on base.

FW 205. CN 6823.
XXIIIA 11.1. Hellenistic 3C.
Base and lower wall. PH 0.015; D base 0.16. Very pale
brown clay 10YR 7/3. Well levigated.
Dark red gloss on interior, exterior. Discoloured due
to severe burning. Ring base. Broad horizontal floor.
Palmettes between two outer and two inner concentric
circles of rouletting.
Parallel: Straton's Tower/Caesarea (Berlin 1992:
fig. 52.8).

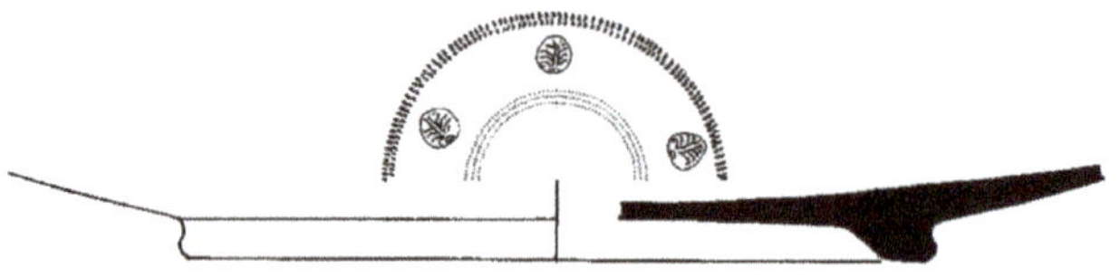

FW 206. CN 6691.
IIIP 25.7. Mixed Context.
Part of wall, rim. PH 002; D rim (est.) 0.22. Pink
clay 7.5YR 8/4.
Red gloss on interior, exterior.

FW 207. CN 0249.
XIA/B 2.5. Mixed Context.
Part of wall, rim. PH 0.025; D rim (est.) 0.24. Reddish-
yellow clay 7.5YR 6/6.
Red gloss on interior, exterior.

FW 208. CN 2644.
XIA/B 1.1/2. Early Roman 1.
Part of wall, rim. PH 0.04; D rim (est.) 0.24. Reddish-
yellow clay 7.5YR 6/6 clay.
Thick dark-red gloss on interior, exterior.
Parallels: Gezer (Gitin 1990: pl. 33.17, late 3rd–
early 2nd c. BC intrusive?); Tel Dor (Rosenthal-
Heginbottom 1995: fig. 5.7: 1, 275–150 BC).

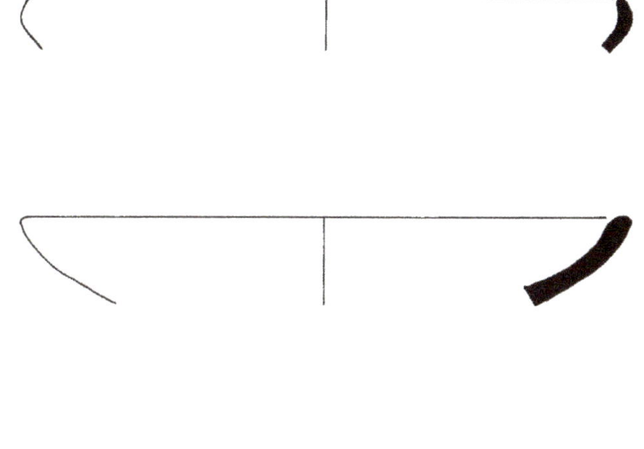

Deep plates with high wall (Hayes "rare form a" and Form 5A; Tel Anafa Types 14, 15)

Plates **FW 209–10** have a well-defined ring base with a tall, somewhat oblique wall, decorated on their exteriors with a horizontal ridge bounded by grooves, and beaded rim. This decorated form is relatively uncommon – Hayes classified it as "rare form a" – although seen at Tel Anafa (Type 15) where it was "current in the first quarter of the first century BCE, and perhaps earlier" (Slane 1997: 299). The occurrence of both examples within a Jannaeus Destruction level is consistent with the evidence from Anafa as regards chronology.

FW 211, from an Early Roman horizon, may belong to the same type although, without the upper wall to guide us, it may equally belong to Hayes Form 5A (Tel Anafa Type 14), produced throughout the first century BC.

FW 209. CN 6718.
XXIIIA 10.7. Hellenistic 3C.
Complete. H 0.05; D rim 0.21. Pink clay 5YR 7/4.
Dull red gloss interior, exterior. Deep bowl with broad
ring base; horizontal floor. Upright wall with simple
rim. Two concentric grooves below rim. Palmettes
within rouletting on floor.
Parallels: Ashdod (Dothan and Freedman 1967:
fig. 10.7, first half of 2nd c. BC–c. 70 AD); Tel Anafa
(Slane 1997: pl. 14. FW 142, no information).

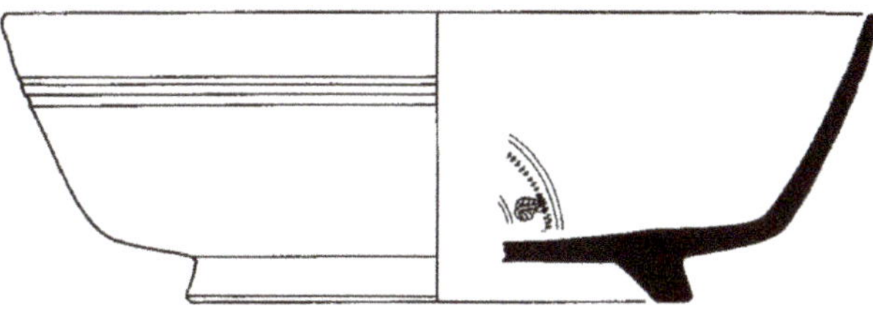

FW 210. CN 7823. (Plate 52)
XXIIID 31.3. Hellenistic 3C.
Part of rim, body, foot. H 0.06; D rim (est.) 0.15. Very pale brown clay 10YR 8/3.
Red gloss on interior, exterior. Tall ring foot. Flaring wall; simple rim. Horizontal grooves on exterior.
Parallel: Ashkelon (Johnson 2008: fig. 5).

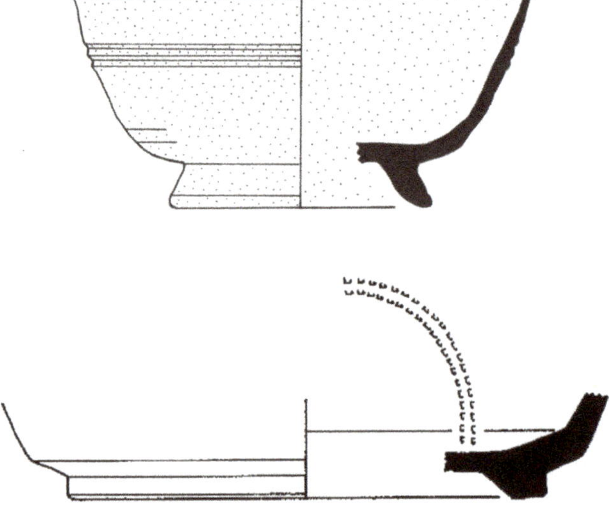

FW 211. CN 3056.
XIA/B 2.3. Early Roman 1.
Base, part of lower wall. PH 0.03; PL 0.105; D base 0.11. Very pale brown clay 10YR 8/4.
Red gloss on interior, exterior. Rouletting on interior.

Broad flat plate with grooved, offset rim (Hayes Form 6; Tel Anafa Type 12)

FW 212 is a rim sherd from an unstratified context. The groove on its lip suggests that it belongs to those broad plates with offset rim made in both black-gloss and ESA wares (Slane 1997: 283). Black-gloss examples are found quite frequently on Hellenistic sites and thus it is not surprising that their ESA counterparts were one of the earliest shapes turned out in that ware. At Samaria the ESA form ("Form 4") first appears in Roman I contexts, whereas at Tel Anafa it turns up (as Tel Anafa Type 12) in late second-century (Hellenistic 2A) deposits. Hayes (1985a: 17) suggests that manufacture of the ESA shape lasted until the middle years of the first century BC; the evidence from Tel Anafa, however, suggests that production may have ceased at the end of the second century BC or soon after (Slane 1997: 284).

FW 212. CN 1380.
IVU 1.1. Mixed Context.
Part of wall, rim. PH 0.015; D rim (est.) 0.22. Reddish-yellow clay 7.5YR 6/6.
Red gloss on interior, exterior.
Parallels: Alexandria (Élaigne 2000: fig. 2.12); Hippos-Sussita (Osband and Eisenberg 2018: pl. 3.2.12, 1st c. BC); Tarsus (F.F. Jones 1950: fig. 188.253); Tel 'Ira (Fischer and Tal 1999b: fig. 6.133.3).

Plate with hanging rim (Hayes Form 9; Tel Anafa Type 17)

In most plates of this form the hanging rim is decorated – usually with impressed patterns such as ovolo, guilloche or interlinked spirals – on either its superior aspect or exterior surface. Examples with undecorated rims (such as **FW 213**) also occur, albeit in limited numbers. **FW 213** is the only specimen from Pella of a form that "was probably not very common and probably short-lived" (Slane 1997: 301). Such plates occur in small numbers at the important Syrian centres of Antioch, Apamea and Hama as well as at lesser Levantine sites such as 'Ain Dara, Dura-Europos, Jebel Khalid in Syria, Samaria and Tel Anafa.[49]

---

49 Waagé 1934: 70, pl. XIV: 5; 1948: 22 fig. 4: 5–15 (Antioch); Vanderhoeven 1989: 31, 136, nos 261–2 (Apamea); Christensen and Johansen 1971: 84–8, figs 33–4, 36–7 (Form 8) (Hama); McClellan 1999: 21, no. F 90.3 ('Ain Dara); Cox 1949: pl. III: 56–7 (Dura-Europos); Tidmarsh 2011: fig. 118. FW 286–7 (Jebel Khalid in Syria); Reisner et al. 1924: fig. 185: 6a–b; Crowfoot et al. 1957: fig. 78: 1–7 (Samaria); Slane 1997: pl. 15. FW 145–6 (Tel Anafa).

Hayes suggests that plates of this form were produced between c. 50 and 25 BC, with Slane in broad agreement.[50] This is consistent with the findspot of **FW 213** on Tell Husn with its evidence of Early Roman occupation.

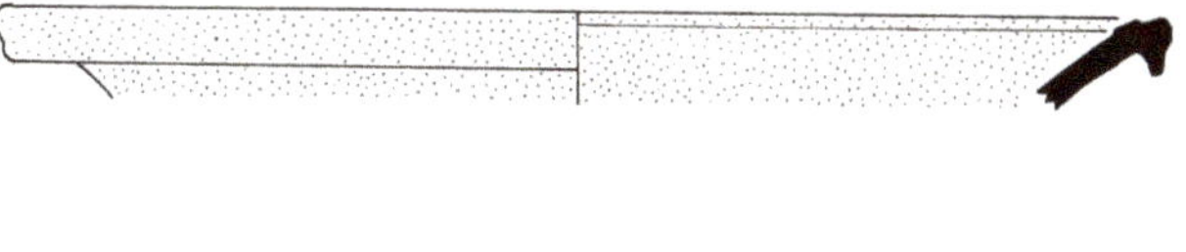

FW 213. CN 7707.
XXXIVG 5.2. Mixed Context.
Part of wall, rim. PH 0.02; PL 0.05; D rim (est.) 0.21.
Reddish-yellow clay 7.5YR 6/6.
Red gloss on interior, exterior. Flaring wall separated by horizontal moulding and groove from vertical, overhanging, undecorated rim.
Parallels: Hama (Christensen and Johansen 1971: fig. 33, no. 8.8); Tel Anafa (Slane 1997: pl. 15. FW 146, late 1st c. BC–early 1st c. AD).

Plate with beaded rim (Hayes Form 12; Tel Anafa Type 1)

Plate **FW 214** was recovered from a small pit on Tell Husn also containing the juglet **PW 227**. With its recessed base, in-curving wall and beaded rim, it belongs to Hayes Form 12, which he dates from 40 BC to c. 10 AD (Hayes 1985a: 20).

At Samaria, the occurrence of this form (Samaria Form 10) in both Vault Cistern 2 and the D deposits led Crowfoot to suggest a first century BC date (Crowfoot et al. 1957: 329); the evidence from other sites is broadly in agreement with a Herodian or Augustan date likely (Slane 1997: 303). At Tel Anafa this form (Type 19) first appears in Roman 1A levels and continues to turn up in Roman 1B and 1C contexts (late first century BC to mid-first century AD).

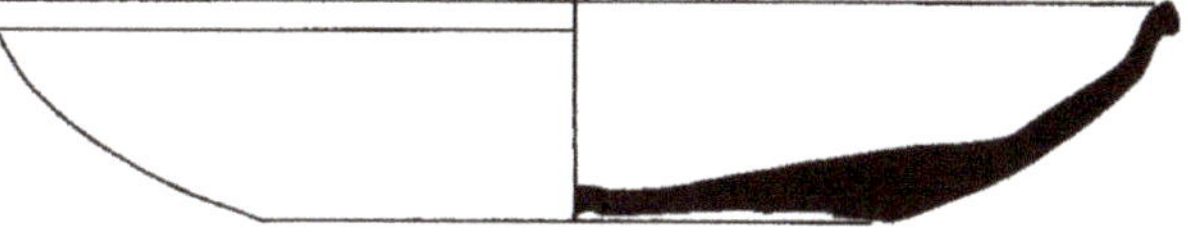

FW 214. CN 7157.
XXXIVB 8.34. Mixed Context.
Complete. H 0.04; D rim 0.19. Reddish-yellow clay 5YR 6/6.
Patchy red gloss on interior, exterior.
Parallels: Berenice (Kenrick 1985: fig. 41.319); Hama (Christensen and Johansen 1971: fig. 10.9); Jerusalem (Hayes 1985b: fig. 51.15); Oboda (Negev 1986: 23, no. 158 upper profile).

Bowl with interior moulding (Hayes Form 17B; Tel Anafa Type 26)

The distinctive moulding on the interior of the rims of **FW 215–16** groups them among those bowls of Hayes Form 17B. Hayes (1985a: 21) suggests a date in the second half of the second century, possibly extending into the first century BC, with much the same timespan (150–80 BC) in Gunneweg and colleagues (1983: 96). These dates are certainly consistent with the Jannaeus Destruction level from which **FW 216** was recovered. **FW 215** comes from an unstratified context.

---

50   Hayes 1985a: 18; Slane 1997: 301.

FW 215. CN 1660.

IIIN 7.1. Mixed Context.

Part of wall, rim. PH 0.02; D rim (est.) 0.15. Pink clay 7.5YR 8/4.

Red gloss on interior, exterior. In-turned rim, moulded on interior of rim and just below.

Parallels: 'Akko-Ptolemais (Regev 2009/10: fig. 40.266); Ashdod (Dothan 1971: fig. 16.15–16); Gezer (Gitin 1990: pls 38.16, mid-2nd c. BC; 40.5, late 2nd c. BC; 42.12, early 1st c. BC); Hippos-Sussita (Mlynarczyk 2011: pl. 247.103, late 2nd c. BC–mid-1st c. BC); Jaffa (Tsuf 2018: fig. 9.56.920); Petra (Ch. Schneider 1996: 144, no. 545); Samaria (Reisner et al. 1924: fig. 185.9a); Straton's Tower/Caesarea (Berlin 1992: fig. 52.4); Tel Dor (Rosenthal-Heginbottom 1995: fig. 5.6: 6, 250–125 BC); Tel Yoqne'am (Ben-Tor and Rosenthal 1978: fig. 8.19; Ben-Tor et al. 1983: fig. 7.4).

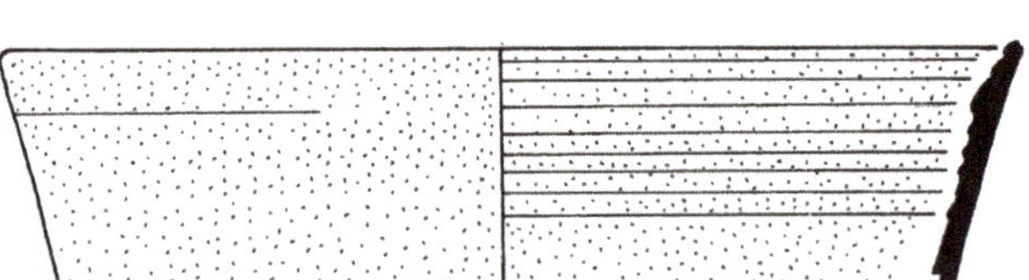

FW 216. CN 4332.

IVD 10.10. Hellenistic 3C.

Part of wall, rim. PH 0.03; PL 0.055; D rim (est.) 0.15. Reddish-yellow clay 5YR 6/8.

Dull red gloss on interior (worn) and exterior. Straight-sided bowl; moulded rim on interior and just below.

Bowl with in-turned rim (Hayes Form 20; Tel Anafa Type 24)

FW 217 belongs within those bowls of Hayes Form 20 and Tel Anafa Type 24. Hayes (1985a: 23) dates the form to the second half of the second century BC; at Tel Anafa the type is uncommon, with the three examples (FW176–8) coming from Hellenistic 2A–2B/C strata (c. 125–98/75 BC).

FW 217. CN 6702.

IIIP 25.20. Mixed Context.

Part of wall, rim. PH 0.04; D rim (est.) 0.12. Reddish-yellow clay 5YR 7/8. Fine mica.

Streaky red gloss on interior, upper exterior.

Parallels: Apollonia (Fischer and Tal 1999a: fig. 5.11.1); Gezer (Gitin 1990: pl. 44.7, mid-1st c. BC).

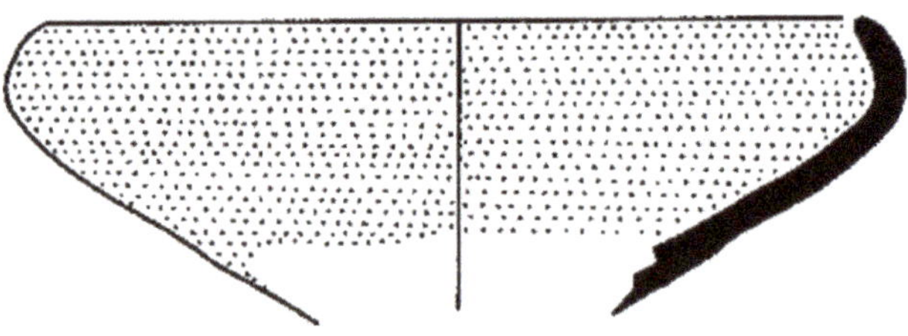

Hemispherical bowls (Hayes Forms 22A, 22B; Tel Anafa Types 25a, 25c)

FW 218 belongs with those footed hemispherical bowls of Hayes Form 22A dating from late in the second century BC into the early years of the first century AD (Hayes 1985a: 23). Although incomplete, bowls **FW 219–24** should be of similar form. **FW 218–20**, from Jannaeus Destruction (Hellenistic 3C) levels, have plain rims in contrast to the slightly thickened rims of **FW 221–2** from mixed deposits. Whereas at Samaria this feature formed the basis for differentiating bowls of forms 16 and 17 (Crowfoot et al. 1957: 332–6), at Tel Anafa, Slane (1997: 309) found it to be of no useful significance. At this latter site, cups of this type (Type 25a) were in use from before 128/125 BC until c. 75 BC.

Bowl **FW 225**, from an Early Roman deposit on Tell Husn, is of more open and shallower form and belongs to Hayes Form 22B (= Tel Anafa Type 25c), produced during Augustan/early first century AD (Roman 1B at Tel Anafa) times.

FW 218. CN 7855.
XXIIID 77.2. Hellenistic 3C.
Part of rim, wall, base. D rim (est.) 0.15; H.11; D base 0.07. Reddish-yellow clay 5YR 6/8.
Red gloss on interior, exterior. Pedestal base; simple rim.
Parallel: Jaffa (Tsuf 2018: fig. 9.56.924); Marisa (Levine 2003: fig. 6.1.8).

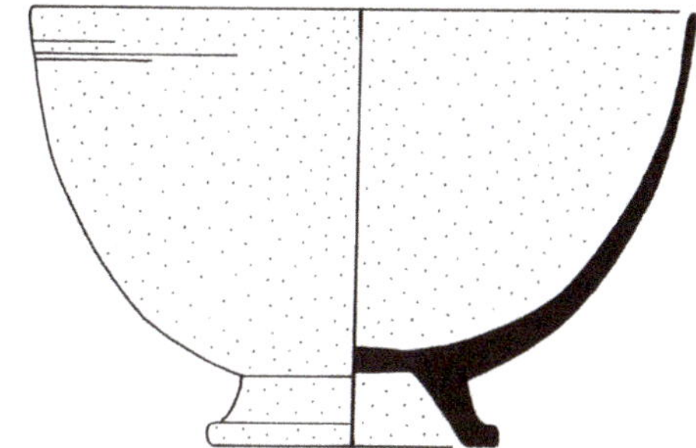

FW 219. CN 0904.
IIIB/C 15.2. Hellenistic 3C.
Part of wall, rim. PH 0.04; D rim (est.) 0.16. Reddish-yellow clay 7.5YR 8/6.
Dark red gloss on interior, exterior.
Parallels: 'Akko-Ptolemais (Berlin and Stone 2016: fig. 9.21.12, first half of 1st c. BC); Gezer (Gitin 1990: pl. 42.11, early 1st c. BC).

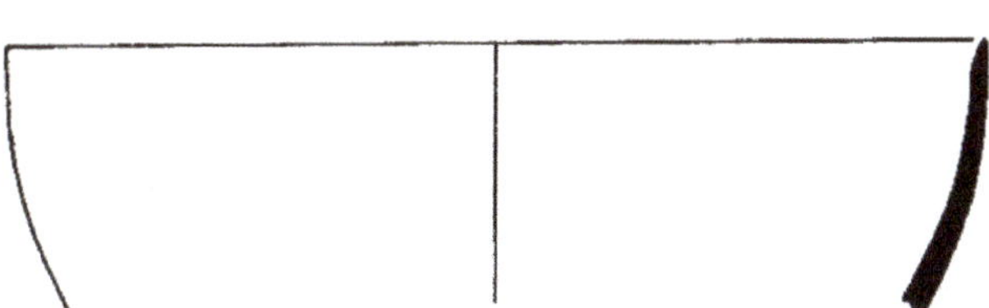

FW 220. CN 4293.
IVD 10.12. Hellenistic 3C.
Part of wall, rim. PH 0.035; D rim (est.) 0.15. Very pale brown clay 10YR 7/4.
Dark red gloss interior, exterior.
Parallels: 'Akko-Ptolemais (Berlin and Stone 2016: fig. 9.23.3, 2nd half of 1st c. BC; Beirut (Élaigne 2007: fig. 16.98–398, second half of 2nd and first half of 1st c. BC); Gadara/Umm Qais (Kenrick 2000: fig. 10.231); Gezer (Gitin 1990: pl. 38.14, mid-2nd c. BC); Oboda (Negev 1974: pl. 27.155); Paphos (Giudice et al. 1996: fig. 16.3); Regev 2009/10: fig. 41. 274); Samaria (Kenyon 1957: fig. 65.1); Tel Yoqne'am (Ben-Tor et al. 1983: fig. 7.2).

FW 221. CN 1254.
IVH 5.1. Mixed Deposit.
Part of wall, rim. PH 0.03; PL 0.03; D rim (est.) 0.15. Pinkish-white clay 7.5YR 8/2.
Red gloss on interior, exterior. Shallow groove separates wall from thickened rim.

FW 222. CN 1600.
IVR 7.8 Mixed Deposit.
Part of wall, rim. PH.05; D rim (est.).15. Reddish-yellow clay 7.5YR 7/6.
Red gloss on interior, exterior. Shallow groove separates wall from thickened rim.
Parallels: Gadara/Umm Qais (Kenrick 2000: fig. 10.215); Hesban (Gerber 2012: 223, fig. 3.11.26); Petra (Ch. Schneider 1996: 144, no. 549); Hippos-Sussita (Osband and Eisenberg 2018: pl. 3.2.5, 1st c. BC); Tel Yoqne'am (Avissar 1996: fig. X.1.19); Jebel Khalid in Syria (Tidmarsh 2016: fig. 9.57).

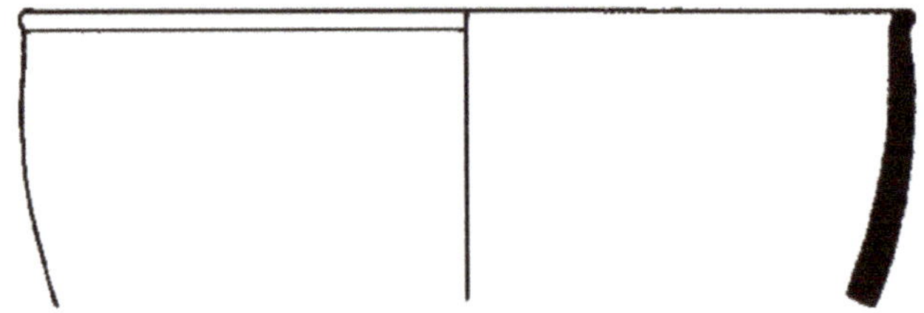

FW 223. CN 7765.
XXIIID 19.2. Hellenistic 3C.
Part of rim, wall. PH 0.06; PL 0.115; D base 0.06. Very pale brown clay 10YR 7/4.
Lustrous red gloss on interior, exterior.
Parallels: 'Akko-Ptolemais (Berlin and Stone 2016: fig. 9.25.9, 1st c. BC); Hippos-Sussita (Osband and Eisenberg 2018: pl. 2.5.7, 2nd c. BC).

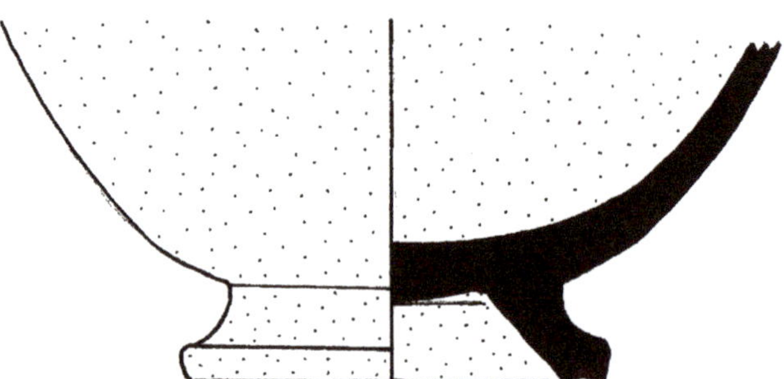

FW 224. CN 7839. (No line drawing)
XXIIID Clearing Wall 35. Mixed Deposit.
Whole base, part of wall. PH 0.06; PL 0.09; D base 0.07. Reddish-yellow clay 5YR 7/8.
Red gloss on interior, exterior. Ring base; flaring lower wall.

FW 225. CN 6535.
XIA/B 20.7. Early Roman 1.
Part of wall, rim, base. PH 0.035; PL 0.06; D rim (est.) 0.10. Reddish-yellow clay 7.5YR 8/6.
Red gloss on interior, exterior.
Parallels: Jerusalem (Hayes 1985b: fig. 52.3); Oboda (Negev 1974: pl. 27.152).

Deep bowl with out-turned rim (Hayes Form 23; Tel Anafa Type 29)

Although lacking their lower wall and base, **FW 226–8** should belong within this type. **FW 227** is from an Early Roman horizon on Tell Husn while **FW 226** and **FW 228** are unstratified.

The black-gloss bowl with out-turned rim is commonly seen on most Hellenistic sites throughout the Levant and elsewhere. At Tel Anafa numerous examples in ESA have been recovered, though the shape is much less frequently encountered in that ware on other sites (Slane 1997: 318).

Hayes (1985a: 24) suggests a *floruit* of 100–50 BC; at Tel Anafa the shape appears in Hellenistic 2A (c. 125 BC) contexts and may still have been in use at the end of the first century BC, consistent with the context of **FW 227**.

FW 226. CN 2683.
IVE 10.1. Mixed Deposit.
Part of wall, rim. PH 0.02; D rim (est.) 0.12. Reddish-yellow clay 7.5YR 8/6.
Red gloss on interior, exterior. Flaring wall; everted rim.

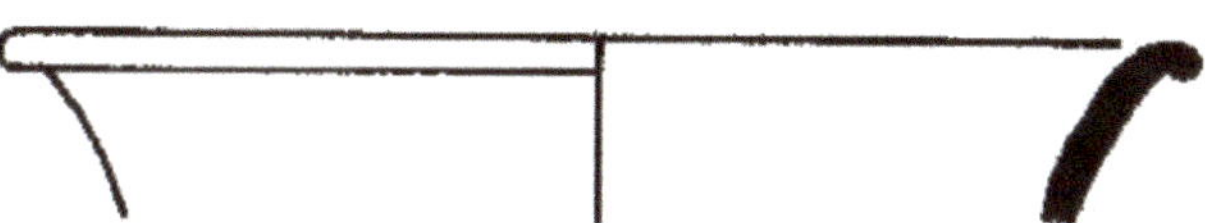

FW 227. CN 6573.
XIA/B 4.4. Early Roman 1.
Part of wall, rim. PH 0.035; PL 0.045; D rim (est.) 0.14. Reddish-yellow clay 5YR 6/6–7/6.
Slightly mottled red gloss on interior, exterior.
Parallels: Beirut (Élaigne 2007: fig. 16.98–394, second half of 2nd and first half of 1st c. BC); Hama (Christensen and Johansen 1971: fig. 64, no. 21.6).

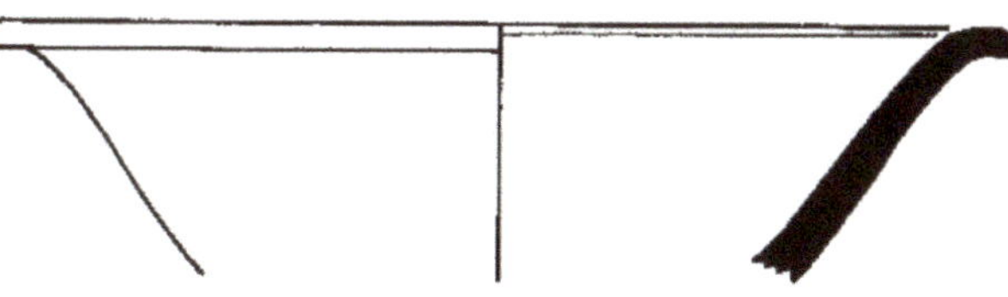

FW 228. CN 7523.
XXIIIA 73.3. Mixed Deposit.
Part of wall, rim. PH 0.055; D rim (est.) 0.17. Reddish-yellow clay 7.5YR 7/6.
Dull red gloss on interior, exterior.

Mould-made bowl (Hayes Form 24)

FW 229 is the only mould-made bowl in ESA from Pella. At Tel Anafa such bowls constitute 73 per cent of the approximately 1120 mould-made bowls recovered from the excavations (Cornell 1997) and are also numerous at Antioch, Hama and Tarsus but they are rare at Samaria (Form 20), while only thirteen fragments were recovered from Tel Dor, all in chronologically insignificant loci.[51] The gloss on ESA mould-made bowls becomes increasingly thin and dull during the later Hellenistic and Early Roman periods and is accompanied by a decline in the range and quality of the decorative motifs both on the rim (which may be plain) and on the body where they also become more widely spaced.

Hayes suggests that mould-made bowls in ESA were made throughout the first centuries BC and AD; the evidence from Tel Anafa, however, would suggest a starting date before 125 BC.[52] The thin matt gloss of **FW 229**, together with its simple ivy leaf and tendril decoration in low relief, points to a date late in the first century BC or even later; its recovery from an Early Roman floor deposit (27.7) in plot XXXIVB (Tell Husn) is consistent with such a date.

FW 229. CN 7617. (Plate 53)
XXXIVB 27.7. Early Roman 1.
Wall fragment. PH 0.055; PL 0.05. Reddish-yellow clay 7.5YR 7/6.
Thin red gloss on interior, exterior. Alternating upright and inverted linked ivy leaves.

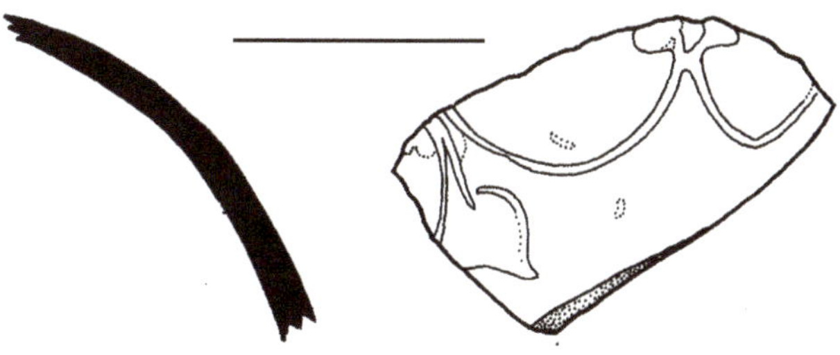

---

51 Waagé 1948: 29–31 (Antioch); Christensen and Johansen 1971: 124–59 (Hama); F.F. Jones 1950: 177–8, figs 138–42 (Tarsus); Cornell 1997: 407–12 (Tel Anafa); Crowfoot et al. 1957: 280, fig. 63: 22 (Samaria); Rosenthal-Heginbottom 1995: 212–15 (Tel Dor).
52 Hayes 1985a: 25. For the beginning of production c. 150 BC see also Rosenthal-Heginbottom (1995: 214–15) who also suggests that such bowls were only produced in large numbers following the decline of the "Ionian" workshops in the mid-first century BC.

Shallow bowl (saucer) with out-turned rim (Hayes "rare form c"; Tel Anafa Type 16)

More prevalent in black gloss, its ESA equivalent is rare at Tel Anafa (Type 16) and "missing at Tarsus, Antioch, Ashdod, and most other sites" (Slane 1997: 300). There were no examples recovered from the British campaigns at Samaria and only one was found during the previous Harvard excavations, although small numbers were present at Hama.[53] Hayes (1985a: 47) includes it as "rare form c" and suggests that it may be one of the earliest forms of ESA. At Tel Anafa, only two catalogued examples (FW 143, FW 144) were recovered, both probably in Hellenistic 2C+/Roman 1A (c. 75 BC–early first century AD) contexts. Slane (1997) tentatively dates the form to the early first century BC, which is consistent with the findspot of **FW 230**, the only stratified example from Pella.

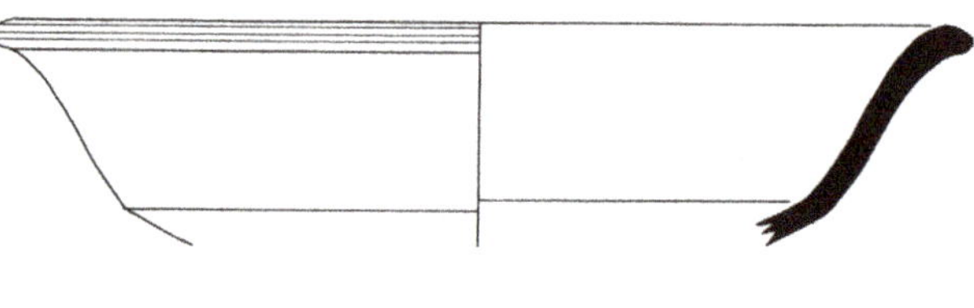

FW 230. CN 7526.
XXIIIA 10.7. Hellenistic 3C.
Part of wall, rim. PH 0.045; D rim (est.) 0.16. Reddish-
yellow clay 7.5YR 6/6.
Worn red gloss on interior, exterior. Out-turned upper
wall and rim.
Parallel: Jaffa (Tsuf 2018: fig. 9.57.944).

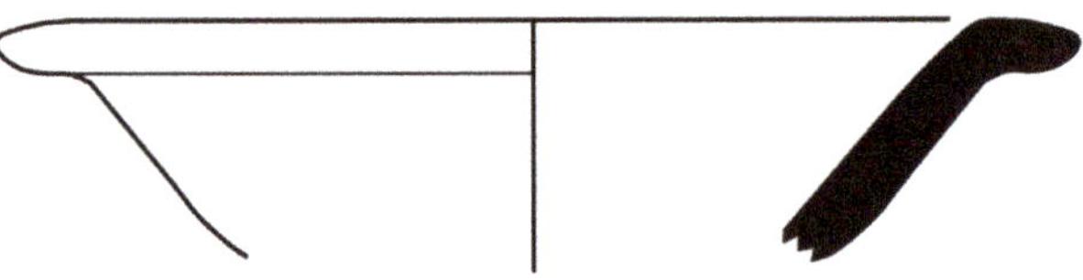

FW 231. CN 1154.
IIIB/C Walls 72/73. Mixed Context.
Part of wall, rim. PH 0.015; D rim (est.) 0.08. Reddish-
yellow clay 5YR 7/6.
Red gloss on interior, exterior. Straight flaring wall;
horizontal rim.

"Roman" forms

FW 232–49 are clearly based on shapes seen in Italian Sigillata, although the small size of many of the Pella fragments makes an accurate classification of forms somewhat tentative.[54] The majority of these specimens were recovered from Tell Husn (Areas XI, XXXIV), which, as already seen, has evidence of Early Roman occupation. A small number was found on the main mound in Plots IIIQ (**FW 243, FW 246–7, FW 249**) and IVL (**FW 248**) where, as noted previously, there may have existed an Early Roman structure later completely destroyed by extensive Byzantine and Ummayad building.

Small plates with grooved everted wall (Hayes Form 28; Tel Anafa Type 22)

Although only its upper wall and rim are preserved, **FW 232** with its rounded overhanging rim and interior moulding should belong to Hayes Form 28. Hayes (1985a: 27–28) has suggested that the form was influenced by the Italian Sigillata form Haltern 1 (Ettlinger et al. [1990] Forms 10–12) although the ESA examples often lack the sharply angled rim of their western counterparts. Plates of similar shape were also recovered from Antioch (Waagé 1948: 27–8, forms 110–13) and Hama (Christensen and Johansen 1971: 95–9, fig. 39, form 13) where, again, the connection with western forms was recognised. The western examples are all of Augustan date.

The Early Roman occupation level on Tell Husn for **FW 232** is consistent with Hayes' dates for the form ranging from very late in the first century BC (10/1 BC) to early in the following century (15/30 AD). At Tel Anafa, where 86 specimens came to light in the second campaign, Slane (1997: 306) regards it as a

---

53 Reisner et al. 1924: fig. 185: 17 (Samaria); Christensen and Johansen 1971: 88, fig. 36, Form 9 (Hama).

54 For a comprehensive typology of Italian Sigillatas see Ettlinger et al. (1990). For previous typologies of Italian Sigillatas see, for example, Dragendorff (1895); Hayes (1973); Loeschcke (1909); Pucci (1985). See also Slane's review (1993) of Ettlinger et al. (1990), outlining some of the problems in attempting a comprehensive typology.

"typically ROM 1B form", which is also consistent with Hayes' chronology. **FW 233–4** are further examples of the form, both of which are from unstratified deposits, also on Tell Husn.

FW 232. CN 7572.
XXXIVB 27.2. Early Roman 1.
Part of rim. PL 0.025; D rim (est.) 0.19. Reddish-yellow clay 5YR 6/8.
Red gloss on interior, exterior. Everted rim; grooved interior lip. Horizontal ridge on interior.

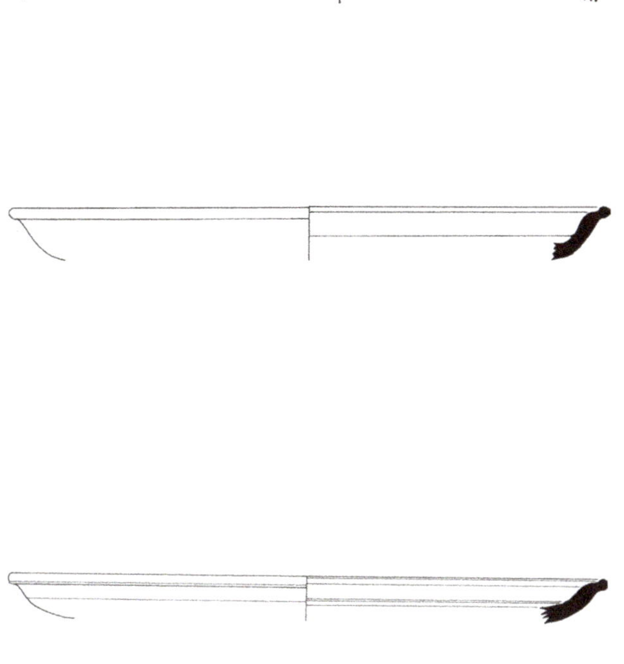

FW 233. CN 7546.
XXXIVB 2.7. Mixed Context.
Part of wall, rim. PH 0.035; PL 0.045; D rim (est.) 0.24. Very pale brown clay 10YR 7/4.
Red gloss over interior, exterior. Everted upper wall ending in thickened grooved rim. Narrow moulding on interior wall.
Parallels: Jerusalem (Hayes 1985b: fig. 52.9); Panayia Ematousa, Cyprus (Lund 1998: fig. 35.35).

FW 234. CN 7525.
XXXIVN 1.3. Mixed Context.
Part of wall, rim. PH 0.02; D rim (est.) 0.25. Very pale yellow clay 10YR 8/4.
Worn red gloss on interior, exterior. Floor separated from everted wall by horizontal ridge. Grooved rim.

Small cup with everted grooved rim (Hayes Form 33)

FW 235 is from an unstratified level on Tell Husn and, as suggested by Hayes (1985a: 29), is of a similar date (c. 1–30/50 AD) to **FW 232–4**.

FW 235. CN 7703.
XXXIVB 54.6. Mixed Context.
Part of wall, rim. PH 0.015; PL 0.015; D rim (est.) 0.14. Very pale brown clay 10YR 8/4.
Red gloss on interior, exterior. Narrow rim with horizontal groove and faint rouletting on exterior. Moulded interior.
Parallel: Antioch (Waagé 1948: pl. IV, form 412k).

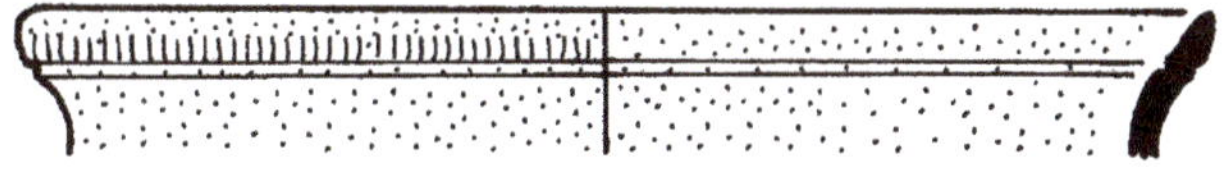

Plate with upright rim and sharp carination (Hayes Form 34)

FW 236, from a Mixed Context on Tell Husn, is perhaps slightly later in date than **FW 235** (Hayes' dates c. 25–50 AD).

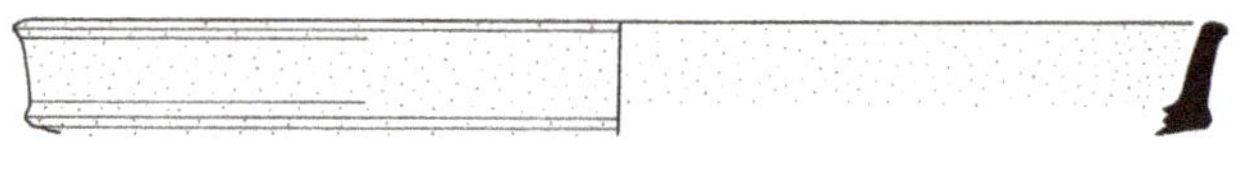

FW 236. CN 7361.
XXXIVB 8.22. Mixed Context.
Part of rim. PH 0.015; PL 0.04; D rim (est.) 0.16. Very pale brown clay 10YR 8/4.
Dark yellowish-brown gloss (10YR 4/6) on interior, exterior. Upright rim; bevelled out-sloping lip. Prominent exterior ridge at carination. Faint rouletting on exterior.
Parallels: Antioch (Waagé 1948: pl. IV, form 422); Ashkelon (Johnson 2008: fig. 12); Samaria (Crowfoot et al. 1957: fig. 79.15).

Large plate with sharp carination and upright rim (Hayes Form 37A; Tel Anafa Type 23)

FW 237, influenced by, but not imitating, Ettlinger et al. (1990) Form 18.2, is from an unstratified level in XXXIVB (Tell Husn). As Slane (1997: 307–8) points out, the chronology of this form has been uncertain: Kenyon and Paul Lapp (Kenyon 1957: 289–90, 295–98; P.W. Lapp 1961: 218) had suggested a Roman Ia date (20 BC–20 AD) whereas Hayes (1985a: 60) favoured a date within the second half of the first century AD. The evidence from Tel Anafa, however, where more than forty examples were recovered in the second campaign, shows it to be "essentially a Claudian–Neronian form" (Slane 1997: 308).

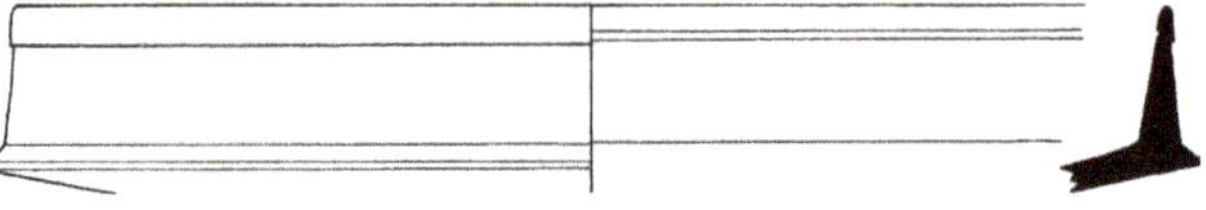

FW 237. CN 7612.
XXXIVB 100.1. Mixed Context.
Part of floor, wall, rim. PL 0.09; D rim (est.) 0.18. Reddish-yellow clay 6/6.
Red gloss on interior, exterior. Horizontal floor. Exterior ridge at base of vertical wall; narrow thickened rim.
Parallels: Corinth (Hayes 1973: pl. 85.127); Hesban (Gerber 2012: 228, fig. 3.12.16); Jerash (Braemer 1986: fig. 16.7); Samaria (Crowfoot et al. 1957: figs 68.6, 79.16); Tel Zahara (Bar-Nathan 2013: fig. 3.7.65).

Small cup with convex upper wall (Hayes Form 44)

FW 238, close to Ettlinger et al. (1990) Form 31, lacks much of its lower profile but should be grouped within Hayes Form 44 dated by him (2008: 28) to the first quarter of the first century AD.

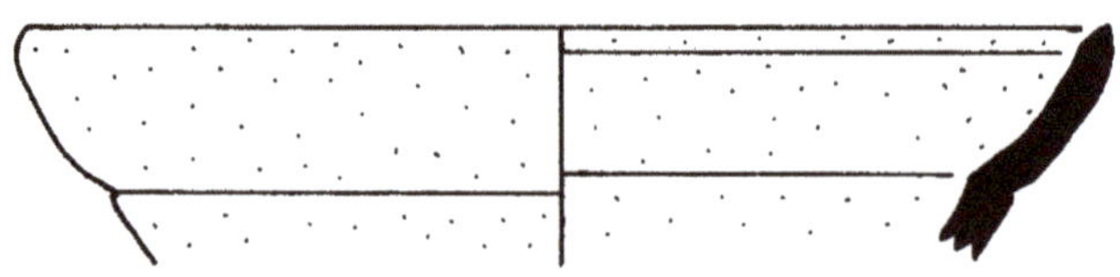

FW 238. CN 7814.
XXXIVG 5.2. Mixed Context.
Part of wall, rim. PH 0.015; D rim (est.) 0.09. Very pale brown clay 10YR 8.3.
Red gloss on interior, exterior. Flaring lower wall; upper section concave on interior.
Parallels: Sepphoris (Balouka 2013: pl. 41.4); Tel Anafa (Slane 1997: pl. 26. FW 312, Arab levels residual).

Cup with moulded rim (Hayes Form 47; Tel Anafa Type 34a)

FW 239, close to Ettlinger et al. (1990) Form 22.2, belongs to those cups of Hayes Form 47, of the first century (c. 10–60/70 AD).[55] Slane (1997: 324–8) has postulated similar dates for the type at Tel Anafa where it is most commonly seen in Roman 1B (early first century AD) levels, consistent with the Early Roman occupation level on Tell Husn from which **FW 239** was unearthed.

FW 239. CN 7595.
XXXIVB 27.2. Early Roman 1.
Part of rim. PL 0.025; D rim (est.) 0.15. Reddish-yellow clay 5YR 7/6.
Red gloss on interior, exterior. Rim convex-concave on exterior; low horizontal moulding on interior, exterior. Rouletted upper exterior.
Parallels: Antioch (Waagé 1948: pl. V.460k); Ashkelon (Johnson 2008: fig. 24); Corinth (Hayes 1973: pl. 86.147).

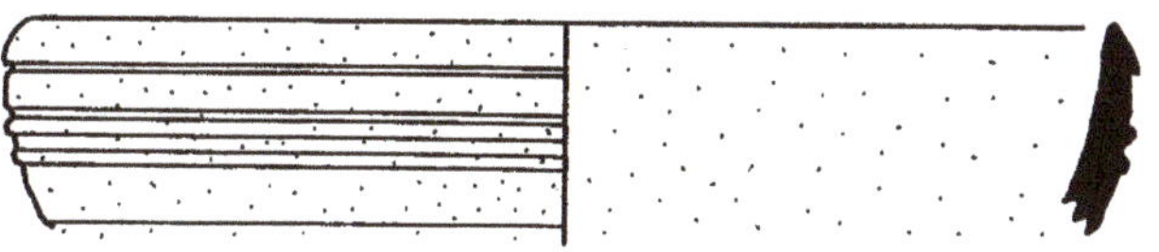

Hemispherical cup (Hayes Form 48)

The small fragment **FW 240** of a hemispherical cup with moulded exterior rim presents a profile consistent with that of Hayes Form 48 turned out c. 1–50 AD (Hayes 2008: 28).

FW 240. CN 7815.
XXXIVG 8.2. Mixed Context.
Part of wall, rim. PH 0.035; PL 0.025; D rim (est.) 0.125. Very pale brown clay 10YR 8.3.
Slightly thickened lip; horizontally ridged and grooved upper exterior. Red gloss on interior, exterior.
Parallels: Ashkelon (Johnson 2008: fig. 26); Scythopolis/Beth-Shean (Fitzgerald 1931: pl. XXXIV.18).

Plates with everted wall and offset rim (Hayes Form 54)

Although only a small fragment, **FW 241** – from a mixed deposit in Plot XIA/B (Tell Husn) – is the upper part of an offset rim, as is **FW 242**. As such, the plain lip on both fragments suggests that they should be grouped with those broad plates with everted wall and offset rim classified by Hayes as Form 54 and by Crowfoot at Samaria as Form 4 (Crowfoot et al. 1957: 326). At Samaria the form appears in first and second century AD contexts whilst Hayes (1985a: 38) would date it from c. 75–c. 150 AD. It is not seen at Tel Anafa.

FW 241. CN 3237.
XIA/B 5.4, 5.9. Mixed Context.
Part of wall, rim (two non-joining fragments).
PH 0.03; PL 0.065; D rim (est.) 0.20. Reddish-yellow clay 7.5YR 6/6.
Red gloss on interior, exterior. Flaring wall, offset rim with plain lip.

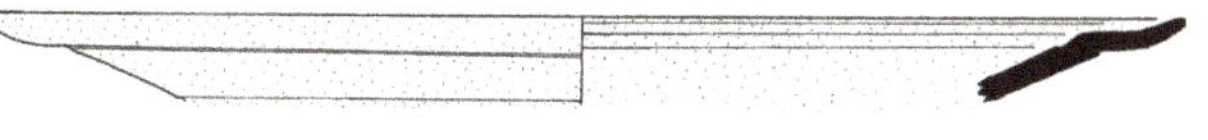

---

55   Hayes 1985a: 35.

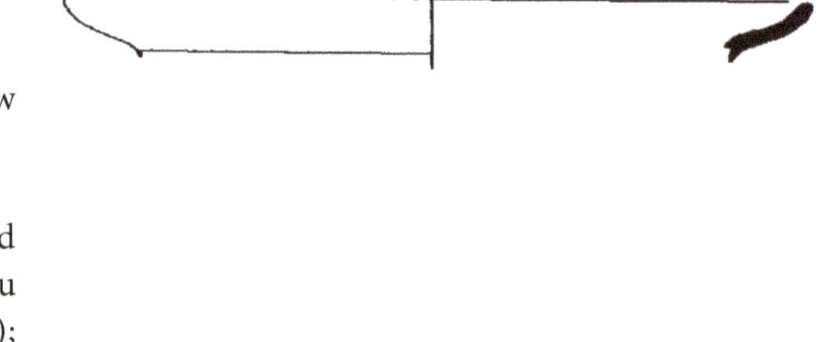

FW 242. CN 10006.
XIA/B 5.4. Mixed Context.
Part of rim. PH 0.02; D rim (est.) 0.19. Reddish-yellow clay 5YR 7/6.
Red gloss on interior, exterior.
Parallels: Amman/Philadelphia (Koutsokou and Najjar 1997: 106, no. 138 upper profile); Kerak Plateau Survey (Brown 1991: pl. 6.332 lacks rouletting); Oboda (Negev 1986: 23, no. 152).

Shallow plate with broad out-turned rim (Hayes Form 57)

FW 243, a shallow plate with flattened, out-turned almost horizontal rim and low ring base, belongs to the commonly seen Hayes Form 57, produced during the first half of the second century AD (Hayes 1985a: 39).

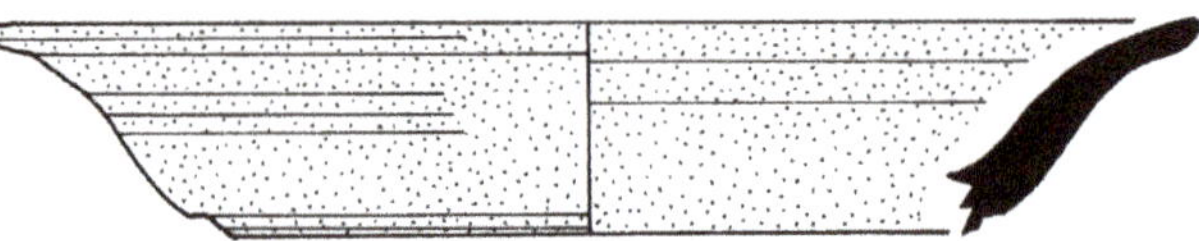

FW 243. CN 6925.
IIIQ 11.19. Mixed Context.
Part of base, wall, rim. PH 0.045; PL 0.51; D rim (est.) 0.14. Pink clay 7.5YR 7/4.
Red gloss on exterior; dull red-brown gloss on interior.
Parallel: Samaria (Crowfoot et al. 1957: fig. 77.10).

Shallow plate with grooved horizontal rim (Hayes Form 59)

Similar in date to the previous fragment, **FW 244** is a variant of Hayes Form 59 with its lightly grooved, rather than plain, lip.

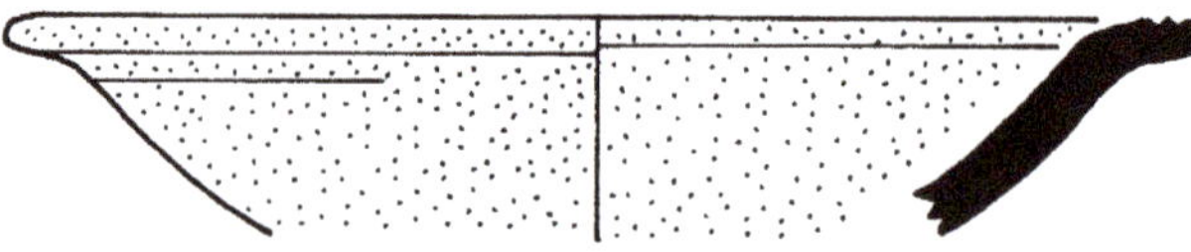

FW 244. CN 6781.
XIA/B 20.5. Early Roman 2.
Part of wall, rim. PH 0.03; PL 0.045; D rim (est.) 0.16.
Very pale brown clay 10YR 7/4.
Thin dull red gloss on interior, exterior.

Deep plate with flaring wall (Hayes Form 60; Tel Anafa Type 33)

The deep plates with flaring walls **FW 245** (Early Roman 2) and **FW 246–9** (all from non-stratified contexts) can be included within Hayes Form 60 dated within the second century AD (Hayes 1985a: 40). The presence of ridges and grooves on the interior rims of **FW 246–8** indicates that these bowls fall within Hayes Form 60A (first half of the second century AD); those without grooved rims (**FW 245, FW 249**) date more generally to the second century (Hayes Form 60B). A similar bowl, however, was found in a Herodian context at Machaerus (Loffreda 1996: fig. 48.27), perhaps indicating that bowls of this form were first produced earlier than generally proposed.

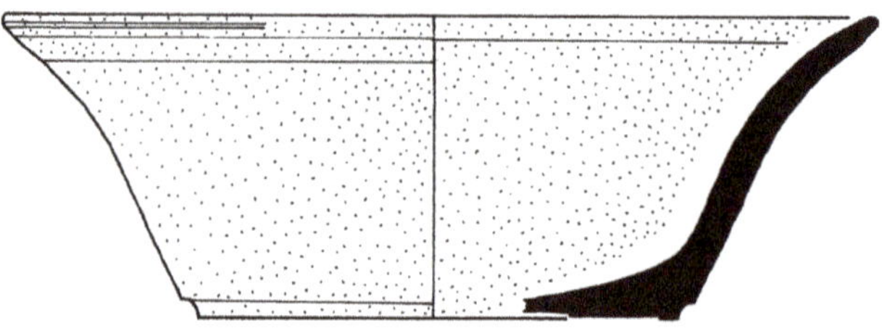

FW 245. CN 6780.
XIA/B. 20.5. Early Roman 2.
Part of base, wall, rim. H 0.055; PL 0.075; D rim (est.) 0.13. Very pale brown clay 10YR 7/4.
Worn red gloss on interior, exterior. Very low raised base. Flaring wall and plain rim.
Parallel: Scythopolis/Beth-Shean (Fitzgerald 1931: pl. XXXIV.24).

FW 246. CN 3848.
IIIQ 11.2, 11.3, 11.16. Mixed Context.
Part of wall, rim (three non-joining fragments).
PH 0.06; PL 0.075; D rim (est.) 0.15. Reddish-yellow
clay 7.5YR 7/6.
Worn red gloss on interior, exterior. Low raised base
separated on exterior by deep groove from flaring
lower wall. Everted rim with two interior grooves.
Parallels: Berenice (Kenrick 1985: fig. 43.339.1);
Hesban (Gerber 2012: 223, fig. 3.12.2); Jerash (Rasson-
Seigne and Seigne 2020a: 137, fig. 5).

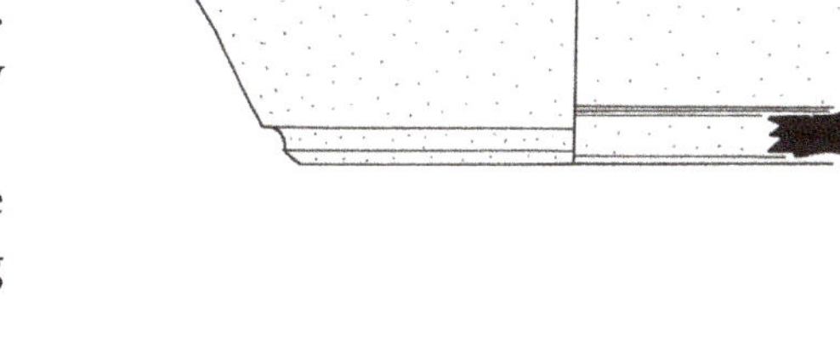

FW 247. CN 7706.
IIIQ 2.1. Mixed Context.
Part of wall, rim. PH 0.015; PL 0.055; D rim
(est.) 0.155. Reddish-yellow clay 7.5YR 7/6.
Red gloss on interior, exterior. Flaring wall. Grooved
exterior and interior rim.
Parallel: Athens (Hayes 2008: fig. 7.166, early 2nd
c. AD).

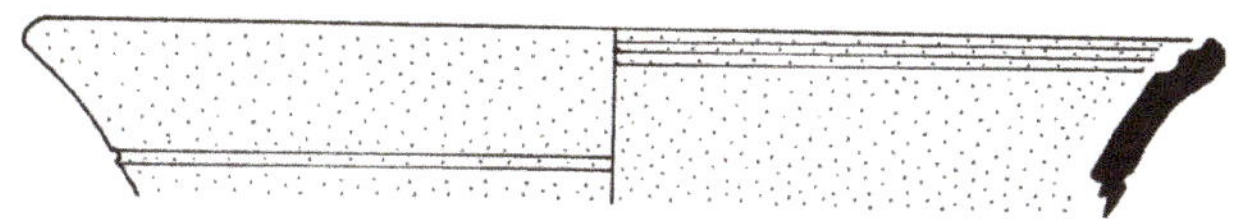

FW 248. CN 1496.
IVL 1.1. Mixed Context.
Part of wall, rim. PH 0.04; D rim (est.) 0.15. Reddish-
yellow clay 7.5YR 6/6.
Red gloss on interior, exterior. Grooved interior rim.
Parallels: Machaerus (Loffreda 1996: fig. 48.27); Petra
(Ch. Schneider 1996: 146, no. 564); Tell al-Birah
(Palumbo et al. 1996: fig. 37.67); Berenice (Kenrick
1985: fig. 43.339.1); Oboda (Negev 1986: 23, no. 154);
Tarsus (F.F. Jones 1950: fig. 193.410); Tel Dor (Rosenthal-
Heginbottom 1995: fig. 5.7: 10 upper profile).

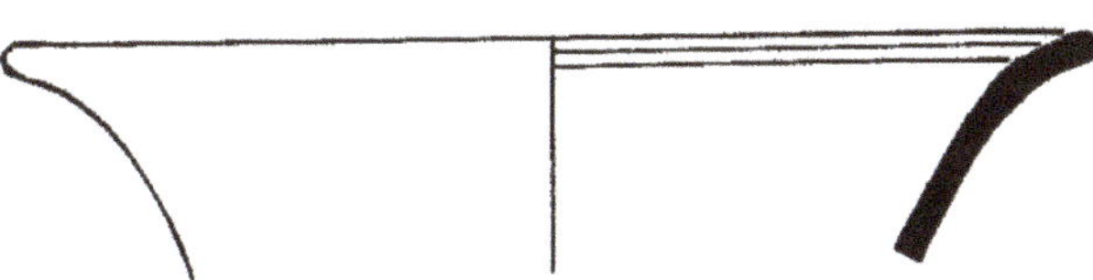

FW 249. CN 6935.
IIIQ 11.18. Mixed Context.
Part of base, wall, rim. H 0.055; D rim (est.) 0.15.
Very pale brown clay 10YR 8/4.
Dull orange gloss on interior, exterior. Low raised
base with slightly concave under-surface. Flaring wall;
everted plain rim.
Parallels: Oboda (Negev 1986: 23, no. 155); Samaria
(Crowfoot et al. 1957: fig. 77.7); Umm el-Tlel
(Majcherek and Taha 2004: 235.2).

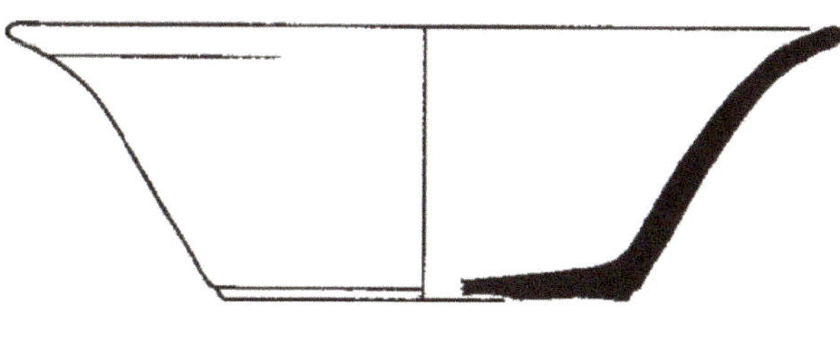

Closed shapes (Hayes Forms 101–112)

Nine fragments (**FW 250–8**) of closed shapes in ESA have been found at Pella. All appear to be jugs or lagynoi. With the exception of **FW 250**, the specimens consist only of bases. With its globular (rather than angular) body and characteristic pedestal foot, **FW 250** is of Hellenistic date as shown by its findspot in a Jannaeus Destruction (Hellenistic 3C) level, with the profile of its foot finding a parallel with that of a very fragmentary lagynos from Tel Anafa tentatively dated c. 128/125–100/95 BC (Slane 1997: 329–30, FW 289).

Due to the very fragmentary condition of the other eight pieces, exact classification is impossible for the remainder although the low ring base and flaring lower wall on fragments **FW 251–7** are seen in forms of the first century BC (Hayes Forms 101–112), with the exterior rouletting on **FW 258** perhaps pointing to a slightly later, first century AD, date (Hayes Form 111?).[56] Of these specimens, **FW 251** was found in an Early Roman context on Tell Husn in Area XI and the remaining seven were unearthed on the main mound from unstratified levels in plot IIIP where, as we have seen, a small structure of Early Roman date may have existed before its obliteration by later Byzantine or Ummayad building.

FW 250. CN 7165.
XXIIIA 10.11. Hellenistic 3C.
Missing handle and top of neck and rim. PH 0.18;
D body 0.15. Reddish-yellow clay 5YR 7/6.
Dull red gloss on exterior; unglazed interior. Tall
ring base. Globular wall; tall neck. Root of handle
preserved on shoulder.
Parallel: Samaria (Crowfoot et al. 1957: fig. 82.1).

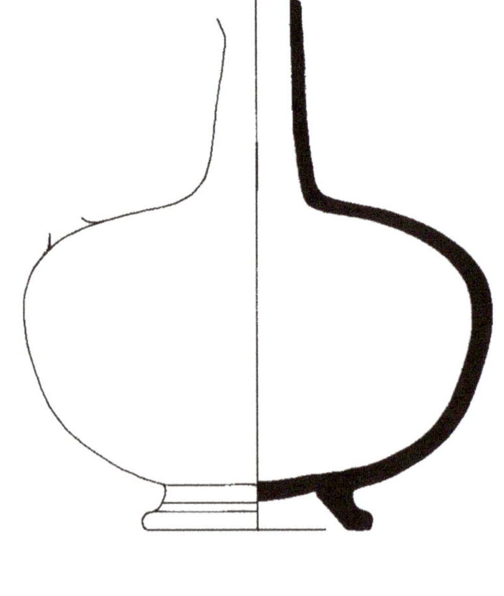

FW 251. CN 2643.
XIA/B 1.1/2. Early Roman 1.
Part of base and lower wall. PH 0.025; D base (est.) 0.09. Reddish-yellow clay 7.5YR 5/6.
Thick reddish-brown gloss on exterior; unglazed interior.
Parallel: Oboda (Negev 1986: 26, no. 181).

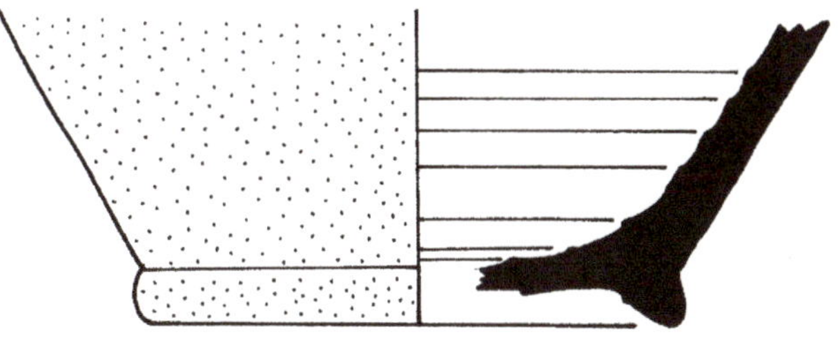

FW 252. CN 7689.
IIIQ 9.3. Mixed Context.
Part of base, lower wall. PH 0.045; PL 0.08; D base (est.) 0.09. Reddish-yellow clay 7.5YR 6/6.
Red gloss on exterior; unglazed interior.
Parallel: Esdraela (Grey 2014: fig. 7.4).

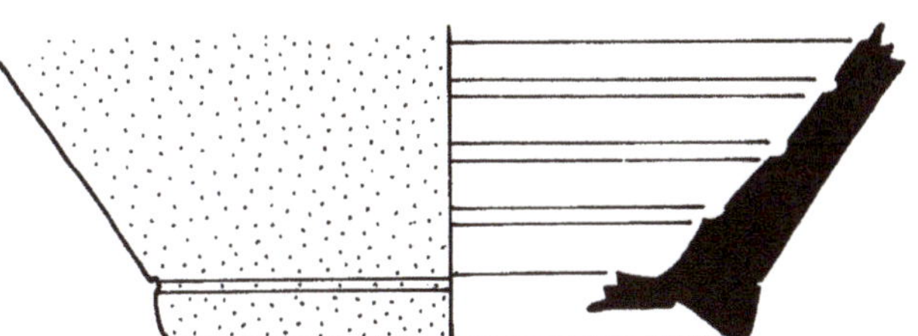

FW 253. CN 7704.
IIIQ 11.18. Mixed Context.
Two joining fragments forming part of base, lower wall. PH 0.04; PL 0.08; D base (est.) 0.07. Reddish-yellow clay 5YR 6/6.
Red gloss on exterior, unglazed interior.
Parallel: Hesban (Gerber 2012: 229, fig. 3.12.25).

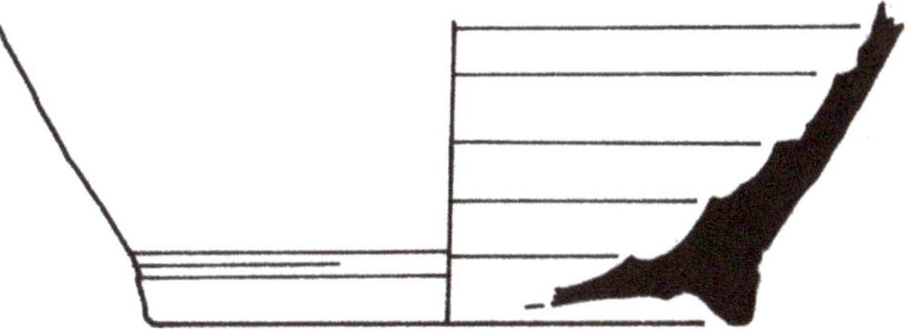

FW 254. CN 6924.
IIIQ 11.19. Mixed Context.
Part of base, lower wall. PH 0.035; PL 0.065; D base (est.) 0.09. Reddish-yellow clay 7.5YR 6/6.
Reddish-orange gloss on exterior; unglazed interior.
Parallel: Arqūb Rūmi (Berger 2020: fig. 9.4.1).

FW 255. CN 6915.
IIIQ 11.22. Mixed Context.
Part of base, lower wall. PH 0.045; PL 0.095; D base (est.) 0.11. Reddish-yellow clay 7.5YR 7/6.
Red gloss on exterior, unglazed exterior.

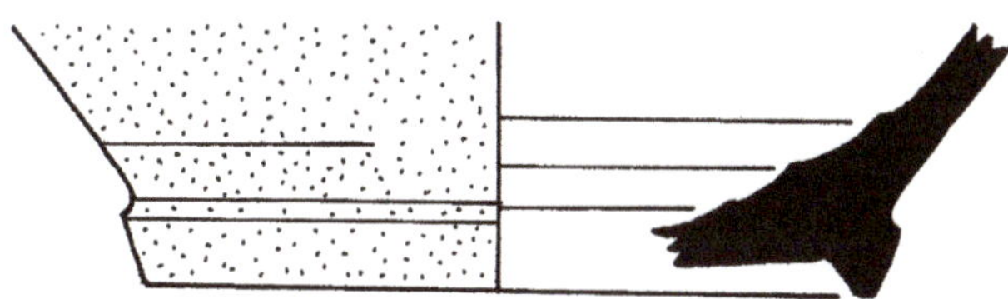

FW 256. CN 7687.
IIIQ 11.18. Mixed Context.
Part of base, lower wall. PH 0.03; PL 0.07; D base (est.) 0.08. Very pale brown clay 10YR 7/4.
Red gloss on exterior; unglazed interior.

FW 257. CN 7688.
IIIQ 11.18. Mixed Context.
Part of base, lower wall. PH 0.035; PL 0.065; D base
(est.) 0.07. Very pale brown clay 10YR 7/4.
Red gloss on exterior; unglazed interior.

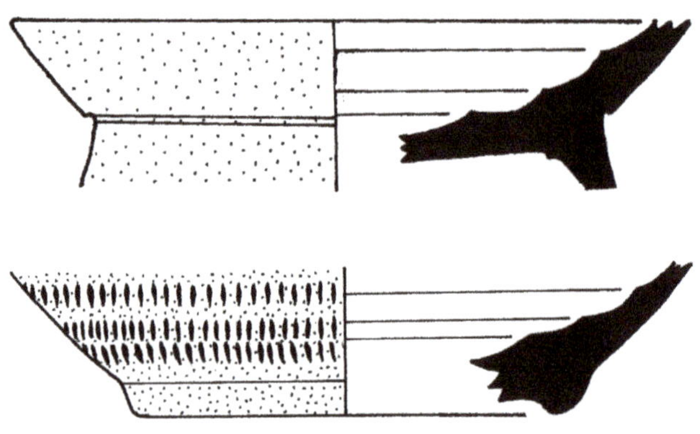

FW 258. CN 3870. (Plate 54)
IIIQ 11.2. Mixed Context.
Part of base, lower wall. PH 0.025; PL 0.15; D base
(est.) 0.07. Yellow clay 10YR 7/6.
Dull red gloss on exterior; unglazed interior. Low
ring base; flaring lower wall. Three horizontal rows
of rouletting preserved on exterior.

ITALIAN SIGILLATA WARES

Whilst ESA is commonly encountered at Pella, other sigillata wares are exceedingly rare. The only catalogued
example of Italian Sigillata (**FW 259**) is from an unstratified deposit in plot XXXIVN with two very small
sherds (uncatalogued) recovered from Early Roman contexts in plot XIA/B. Not surprisingly, these three
specimens are all from Tell Husn.[57]

The lustrous red-gloss Roman fine ware commonly known as "Terra Sigillata" was first produced at
Arretium (modern Arezzo) in northern Italy in the mid-first century BC or slightly later (Fülle 1997; Hayes
1997: 41; Kenrick 1993; Stone 2014: 207–28). The ware was remarkably popular throughout the western
Mediterranean from Augustan times onwards with numerous workshops, still little studied, springing up in
Italy as well as in Gaul and southern Spain.[58] It was the migration of Arretine potters such as Caius Sentius
and Quintus Pompeius Serenus to the western coast of Asia Minor during Augustan times that led to the
beginnings of Eastern Sigillata B in the eastern Mediterranean (Rotroff et al. 2018: 133–4; Zabehlicky-
Scheffeneger 1995).[59]

Italian Sigillata is frequently encountered in excavations at North African sites (Comfort 1982; Dore and
Schinke 1992: 117; Fulford 1989; Hayes 1976, 1978; Kenrick 1985: 125–222, 1987: 6–8, 1993, 1996) and has
also turned up as far afield as the east coast of India (Begley 1993: 102–3; Comfort 1991) and north-west
Sri Lanka (Silva and Bouzek 1985). In the eastern Mediterranean its distribution seems patchier. Although
not in the same quantities as Cypriot Sigillata, "Arretine" ware and other Italian sigillatas are present in
Cyprus (Hayes 1991a: 51–8) with significant numbers also recovered from centres such as Ephesus, Antioch
and Jerusalem (Comfort 1948; Hayes 1985b: 184; Zabehlicky-Scheffenegger 1995: 221). At Tarsus, although
more frequent than "Samian" ware, it was "never common" (F.F. Jones 1950: 187). Italian Sigillata is also
well represented at Oboda (Negev 1974: 29–34, 1986: 9–12); most Palestinian sites, however, have reported
very few specimens or none at all, possibly reflecting "a complex network of exchange mechanisms" and
a "variety of political, social and economic issues that varied from region to region, city to city, and even

---

57   A further "Arretine" bowl, dated to the late first century BC or early first century AD, was reported from Tomb 40
     in Area VI (McNicoll et al. 1982: 87). No further details were given as to its form.

58   The Italian workshops continued in production well into the second century AD (Slane 1987). For the
     considerable difficulties faced in identifying individual centres of manufacture see Fülle 1997; Kenrick 1985:
     126–9; Sackett and Branigan 1992: 153–6.

59   See also Rotroff et al. 2018 for "Sardian Sigillata", which the authors regard as "an offshoot" and local version of
     Italian Sigillata and Eastern Sigillata B, no doubt consistent with the establishment elsewhere of other "multiple,
     much smaller enterprises operating on a local or regional level".

within a city itself" (Papaioannou 2010: 59). It is worth noting that Italian Sigillata appears at the Decapolis city of Scythopolis/Beth-Shean, just across the Jordan River from Pella (Fitzgerald 1931: 47–8).[60]

East of the Jordan River, Italian Sigillata is relatively rare (Malfitana 2002: 149–51) although reported from Amman/Philadelphia, Gadara/Umm Qais, Hesban (?), Jerash, Petra, Tell al-Birah and Tell Zira'a as well as Pella.[61] **FW 259**, from an unstratified context, should be included within Ettlinger et al. (1990) Form 7.1, produced from the mid-to-late Augustan period with its Gaulish derivative (Dragendorff 1895: 33) lasting until at least well into the second century. The form appears rare in the eastern Mediterranean although present at Corinth (Slane 2004: 31, fig. 1.3; 33, fig. 4.8) and Alexandria (Élaigne 2004: 134, fig. 2.5).

Bowl (cup?)

FW 259. CN 7527.
XXXIVN 1.10. Mixed Context.
Bowl (cup?). Ettlinger et al. (1990) Form 7.1.
Part of wall, rim. PH 0.035; D rim (est.) 0.09. Reddish-yellow clay 5YR 7/6.
Lustrous, smooth red gloss of excellent quality on interior, exterior. Everted wall, concave and grooved on upper interior. Horizontal ridges and grooves on upper exterior; shallow groove further down. Simple rim.

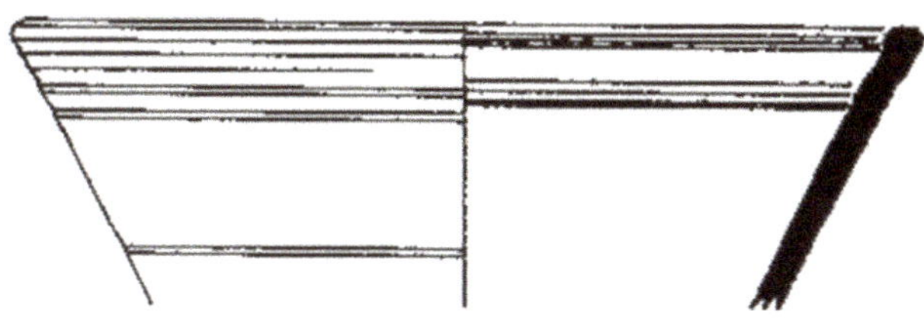

MOULD-MADE BOWLS (FW 260–305)

Although it is clear that the shape has no special connection with Megara, and in spite of various subsequent attempts to rename it, the term "Megarian bowl" is still frequently used to describe those hemispherical mould-made ceramic bowls with relief decoration serving as common drinking vessels from the late third century to the end of the Hellenistic period (Rotroff 1982: 2–3, 2005, 2006a).[62] In this study, however, the term "mould-made bowl" is preferred.

While mould-made bowls are regularly found in excavations in Palestine, they appear to be much less frequent east of the Jordan River. In Transjordan, besides Pella, examples have been published from Abila, Amman/Philadelphia, Gadara/Umm Qais, Khirbet Umm ad-Dananir, Petra, Tell es-Sa'idiyeh and Tell Zira'a. A further example, of probable Syrian origin, was identified by Brown in Miller's survey of the Kerak Plateau.[63] The origin of most of these bowls is unclear. Guldager Bilde (1993: 203) raised the possibility of a "profuse local production" of such bowls in Palestine and, if she is correct, as increasingly appears to be

---

60 Potters' stamps from Scythopolis/Beth-Shean include those of C. Amurius, a prolific potter found widely within and outside Italy (Comfort 1982: 503–4; Iliffe 1936: 27, 1939: 38–9) as well as the Arretine potters Sex. Annius and P. Cornelius, both of whom seem to have established branch factories outside Arezzo itself (Comfort 1982: 492–5). For the presence of "branch workshops" outside Arretium see Fülle 1997: 141–4.

61 Koutsoukou and Najjar 1997: 106, no. 131 (Amman/Philadelphia); Kerner 1997: 291 (Gadara/Umm Qais); Gerber 2012: 230, fig. 3.13.8? (Hesban); Braemer 1986: fig. 16.2, 3 (Jerash); Horsfield and Horsfield 1941: 191–4; Ch. Schneider 1996: 136–7; Zeitler 1990: fig. 9.1 (Petra); Palumbo et al. 1996: fig. 37.69 (Tell al-Birah); Kenkel 2020: 26, 128–9, pl. 1.6.TS1 (Tell Zira'a).

62 As Rotroff (2006a: 376) so succinctly points out, "the moulded bowl is mainly a marker of the 2nd (and 1st) century". For a brief summary of the manufacture and origin of these bowls see Rotroff 2003: 91–2.

63 Mare et al. 1982: 48 (Abila); Koutsoukou and Najjar 1997: 105, no. 114 (Amman/Philadelphia); Kenrick 2000: 235–6 passim; Kerner 1992: fig. 9.3, 1997: fig. 12.5; Weber 1989: 604–7 (Gadara/Umm Qais); McGovern 1989: 128, fig. 3 (Khirbet Umm ad-Dananir); Hadidi 1970: pls II.7 and IV.12, in ESA; Horsfield and Horsfield 1941: pl. XLVIII. 465–6; Ch. Schneider 1996: 145, nos 550–2 (Petra); Pritchard 1985: figs 19:14–16, 18 (Tell es-Sa'idiyeh); Kenkel 2020: 18–19, 118–119, pl. 1.1.Rb1–7 (Tell Zira'a); Brown 1991: 276, no. 310 (Kerak Plateau).

the case (Rosenthal-Heginbottom 2016b), it is likely that a small number of workshops also existed east of the Jordan River.[64]

A total of sixty-two mould-made bowl fragments have been recovered from Pella. Of these, forty-six have been catalogued. With few exceptions, those found at Pella consist of small rim and wall sherds. They are present in significant numbers in early second century BC levels (Hellenistic 3A) from XXVIIIB (main mound), with many fewer from the later second century and Jannaeus Destruction phases. **FW 265**, with its thick glossy brown-black gloss and slightly micaceous reddish-yellow clay, can be considered an Attic import. Below a plain, slightly out-turned rim, its upper border consists of well-defined egg-and-dart above a horizontal row of beading. Though little remains of the body decoration, what exists consists solely of bosses in high relief making it certain that the vessel belongs to Rotroff's class of "pine-cone bowls" (Rotroff 1982: 16).[65] This type was the least common of the Athenian mould-made bowls and may not have been produced after the end of the third century BC, consistent with its Hellenistic 3A context. Although imported Athenian pine-cone bowls are rare in the Levant, locally made examples are known from sites such as Antioch, Hama and Samaria.[66] **FW 283** is probably one such example. **FW 278**, with its pink clay and decorative patterns of guilloche (rim) and boar hunt (wall), is the only other Athenian imported mould-made bowl. Both Attic bowls were recovered from the Hellenistic 3A levels of XXVIIIB, a period during which the quantity of Athenian ceramic imports started to diminish.

The largest group of mould-made bowls from Pella has the same gloss and reddish-yellow clay – that is, Ware 2 – as seen in many of the black-gloss fine wares already discussed (Table 2.3). The locally made bowls from Antioch (Waagé 1948: 29) in this ware were exported in large numbers to Jebel Khalid in Syria (Tidmarsh 2011: 359–78) and also to Samaria and other cities in the southern Levant (Cornell 1997; Crowfoot et al. 1957: 272–81) as well as further to the east (Cox 1949: pl. 1.22–4).[67] The out-turned rim of the Pella bowls is also similar to that on the Antioch products, as is the egg-and-dart upper border of **FW 261**, **FW 274** and **FW 279**, while the cordate leaf ("floret") pattern of, for example, **FW 269** and **FW 280**, although seen elsewhere,[68] seems characteristic of the Orontes Valley (Christensen and Johansen 1971: 152–3; Waagé 1948: 29). On several of these bowls (for example, **FW 267**, **FW 274**, **FW 288**) horizontal beading is used to frame or demarcate the rim pattern from the decorative zone below; on **FW 273** and **FW 280** it is used to separate an upper and lower decorative wall register. Horizontal beading used in such a fashion is a standard device on mould-made bowls from Antioch (Callaghan 1996: 372).

Bowls **FW 263**, **FW 294**, **FW 297**, **FW 300** and **FW 302** have a clay that, while still well refined, is appreciably paler than that of the previous group. The gloss, however, is of better quality and varies from dull black to red-brown. The rim, as can be determined from **FW 263**, is out-turned. At Jebel Khalid mould-made ("moulded") bowls in this ware (Pella Ware 3 = Jebel Khalid "Fabric 3") were well represented and were probably also produced in Antioch or its environs (Tidmarsh 2011: 359).

---

64 At Jebel Khalid, in northern Syria, the recovery of a rosette mould stamp in local clay attests to a minor local production (Tidmarsh 2016: 237); for a similar mould stamp see Rotroff (2003: 92, pl. 79.422) who also comments on how few stamps have been found. There is certainly no reason for a similar production on a small scale not to have taken place further to the south.

65 While the rims on Athenian pine-cone bowls are usually plain with a straight or in-turned profile, decorated out-turning rims similar to **FW 265** are also seen (Rotroff 1982: pl. 2.8; also, Thompson 1934: fig. 49.C53 for plain but out-turned rim).

66 Waagé 1948: figs 14.12, 13 (Antioch); Christensen and Johansen 1971: figs 57.110, 112, 113 (Hama); Crowfoot et al. 1957: fig. 62.1 (Samaria).

67 With the exception of Tarsus, bowls of presumed Antiochene manufacture are much less common to the north of the capital, in Asia Minor, although isolated examples have been recovered from sites such as Labraunda (Hellström 1965: 23, no. 123). Generally speaking, Antiochene mould-made bowls circulated within the confines of the Seleucid kingdom (Lund 2014).

68 For example, on a small number of "Ionian" bowls (Kenrick 1985: pl. 21.151; Laumonier 1977: pl. 24, nos 2140, 2252). See also Rosenthal-Heginbottom 2016b: 128, footnote 67.

Table 2.11. Frequency of mould-made bowls by wares, areas.

	III, IV MAIN MOUND	XXIII MAIN MOUND	XXVIII MAIN MOUND	XXXII MAIN MOUND	XI TELL HUSN	XXXIV TELL HUSN
Ware 1	0	0	2	0	0	0
Ware 2 (BSP)	5	2	8	1	0	3
Ware 3 (BSP)	1	1	2	0	1	0
"Ionian"	1	2	1	0	0	3
Miscellaneous	7	0	2	0	0	4
Not recorded	0	(1)	(5)	0	0	(10)

Table 2.12. Frequency of mould-made bowls by wares, phases.

	3A c. 200– c. 140 BC	3B c. 140– c. 100 (?) BC	3C c. 140– c. 100 (?) BC	3B/3C c. 140– c. 80/79 bc	EARLY ROMAN 63 BC– c. 135 AD	MIXED
Ware 1	2	0	0	0	0	0
Ware 2 (BSP)	8	0	4	0	0	7
Ware 3 (BSP)	2	0	1	0	1	1
"Ionian"	1	1	1	0	0	4
Miscellaneous	1	0	0	0	1	11
Not recorded	(5)	0	(1)	(5)	0	(5)

A small number of "Ionian" mould-made bowls is also included amongst the Pella corpus. This class of bowls has been exhaustively studied by Laumonier (1973, 1977);[69] although clay and gloss can vary quite widely (Kenrick 1985: 105; Laumonier 1977: 14), the straight or in-turned rim remains characteristic (Laumonier 1977: pls 131–4). Bowls **FW 264** and **FW 275** – both from Pre-Jannaeus Destruction levels (Hellenistic 3A–3B) – along with **FW 272** (from a Jannaeus Destruction: Hellenistic 3C context), **FW 271**, **FW 277**, **FW 291** and **FW 305** (Mixed Contexts) can be classed within this "Ionian" group. Where the rim is preserved, it is either vertical (**FW 264, FW 275, FW 277**) or slightly in-turned (**FW 272**).

"Ionian" mould-made bowls make up the largest group at Tel Dor (Rosenthal-Heginbottom 1995: 209–12) and are encountered at most other coastal sites in the eastern Mediterranean (Guldager Bilde 1993: 197) as well as Cyprus (Neuru 1991). They are, however, less frequently seen at inland sites in the Levant, with only a few examples from Antioch, Hama, Jebel Khalid and, west of the Jordan River, Samaria, Shechem and Scythopolis/Beth-Shean. On the other hand, numerous examples of this class have been recovered from Tel Anafa, a site with strong links to the Phoenician cities on the coast (Cornell 1997: 408, 412).[70]

---

69 Laumonier's careful study has, amongst other things, demonstrated beyond doubt that the "Delian" bowls of Courby (1922) were not made on that island but, rather, were the products of a number of centres – in particular Ephesus – on the west coast of Asia Minor (Guldager Bilde 1993: 197–201; Laumonier 1977: 3; Rogl 1996, 2014). See also Mitsopoulos-Leon (1991).

70 Waagé 1948: figs 17.15, 20 (Antioch); Christensen and Johansen 1971: 24–5 (Hama); Tidmarsh 2011: 359 (Jebel Khalid in Syria); Crowfoot et al. 1957: 272–3 (Samaria); N.L. Lapp 2008: 60 (Shechem); Johnson 2006: 528 (Scythopolis/Beth-Shean).

In Amman/Philadelphia, one "Ionian" bowl was recovered from the Great Temple excavations on the Citadel (Koutsoukou and Najjar 1997: 105, no. 114) and, somewhat surprisingly, "Ionian" bowls were the only imported mould-made bowls identified by Kenrick at Gadara/Umm Qais (Kenrick 2000: 235).

Only one mould-made bowl of Eastern Sigillata A ware (**FW 229**) has been recovered from Pella (in an Early Roman context) and this is discussed above in the section on ESA (Hayes Form 24). It must be stated, however, that the origin of about one-third of the mould-made bowls within this catalogue cannot be identified.

Amongst the bowls, the range of decorative motifs is restricted and predictable. Egg-and-dart and ovolo (that is, without the dart) are the most commonly encountered rim patterns. The aforementioned cordate leaf ("floret") is also represented on a number of examples (such as **FW 269, FW 273, FW 280, FW 288**), as is guilloche (for example, **FW 270, FW 278**). Other rim patterns including the bead-and-reel (**FW 277**), enriched meander with diagonals in square – frequently seen on "Ionian" bowls (**FW 272**) – and pendant drops (**FW 279**) are rare.

The range of decorative motifs employed on the wall is also fairly standard.[71] As regards floral motifs we see (either singly or in combination) acanthus, tendrils, imbricate leaves, ferns, palmettes and nymphaea as well as the pine-cone decoration on **FW 283** and the previously discussed Attic import **FW 265**. The figured motifs consist mainly of a variety of animals – including horses (as part of a biga, a two-horse chariot, **FW 300**), leaping goats (**FW 299**), boars fleeing hunters (**FW 278**), felines (**FW 298**), dolphins (**FW 297**) as well as Erotes (**FW 295**), Nikai (**FW 280, FW 292**) and draped females (**FW 293**).

The few medallion fragments that have been recovered consist of rosettes within concentric ridges (**FW 301–5**).

FW 260. CN 7098.
XXIIIA 101.1. Hellenistic 3C.
Rim fragment. PH 0.045; PL 0.06; D rim (est.) 0.14.
Reddish-yellow clay 7.5YR 7/6. Ware 2.
Dull black gloss fired red in patches. Out-turned rim. Ovolo rim pattern between horizontal ridges and grooves.
Parallels: Ashdod (Dothan 1971: fig. 78.13, first half of 2nd c. BC–mid-1st c. BC); Tell es-Sa'idiyeh (Pritchard 1985: fig. 19.14).

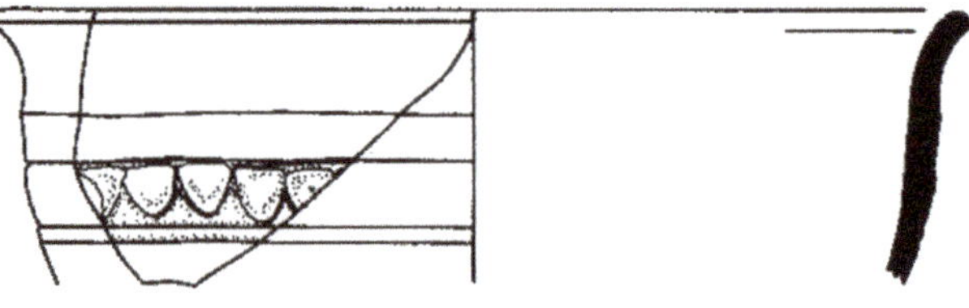

FW 261. CN 7219.
XXVIIIB 10.2. Hellenistic 3A.
Part of wall, rim. PH 0.035; D rim (est.) 0.16. Reddish-yellow clay 7.5YR 7/8. Ware 2.
Brown gloss exterior. Black gloss on upper interior; red gloss on lower interior. Out-turned rim. Horizontal beading above egg-and-dart.

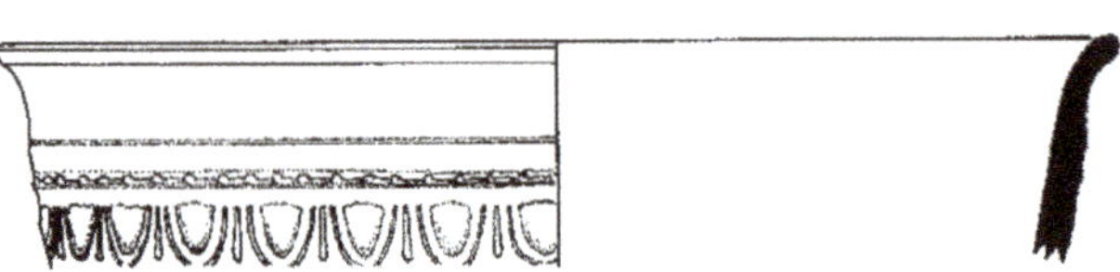

71　Broadly categorised by Rotroff (2003: 91) as "pinecone, imbricate, floral, figured, and simplified linear schemes".

FW 262. CN 0340.
IVD 1.3. Mixed Context.
Rim fragment. PH 0.055; D rim (est.) 0.14. Light brown clay 7.5YR 6/4.
Black gloss on interior, exterior. Flaring upper wall; concave rim. Egg-and-dart above horizontal beading. Parallels: Kedesh (Levantine Ceramics Project: n.d. K09P240, early–mid-2nd c. BC); Straton's Tower/ Caesarea (Rosenthal-Heginbottom 2016b: 141, 142.50).

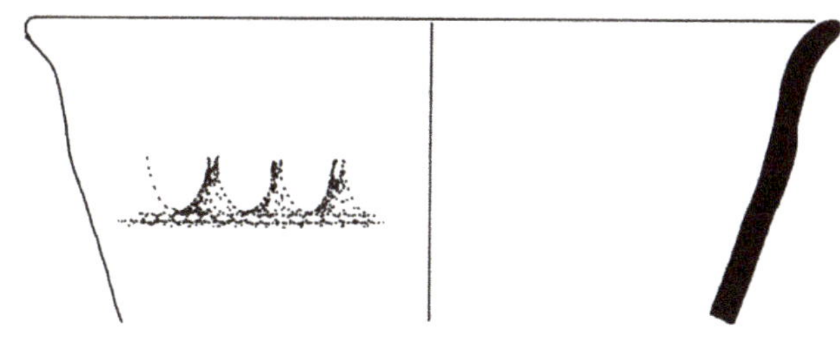

FW 263. CN 2974.
XIA/B 1.4/5. Early Roman (residual).
Rim fragment. PH 0.035; D rim (est.) 0.15. Very pale brown clay 10YR 7/4. Ware 3.
Dark black gloss, fired red in patches, on interior, exterior. Everted rim; egg-and-dart below horizontal groove.
Parallels: Ashdod (Dothan 1971: fig. 78.13, first half of 2nd c. BC–mid-1st c. BC); Oboda (Negev 1986: 5, no. 4); Tell es-Sa'idiyeh (Pritchard 1985: fig. 19.14).

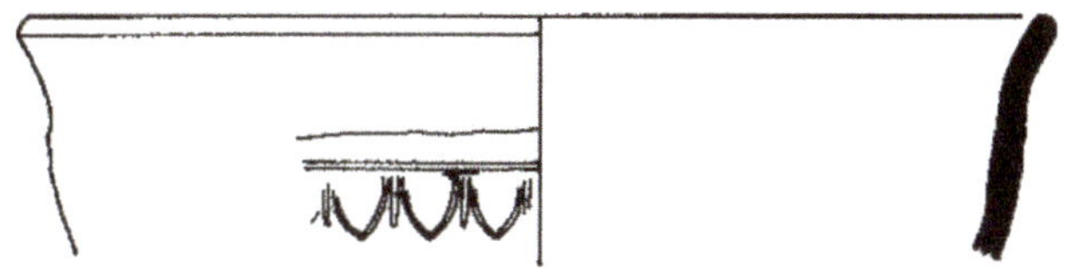

FW 264. CN 7325.
XXVIIIB 13.2. Hellenistic 3A.
Rim fragment. PH 0.025; D rim (est.) 0.11. Dense yellowish-red clay 5YR 5/6. "Ionian".
Red-brown gloss on interior, exterior. Almost vertical rim. Narrow ovolo pattern between two horizontal ridges.

FW 265. CN 7227.
XXVIIIB 10.4. Hellenistic 3A.
Part of wall, rim. PH 0.05; D rim (est.) 0.15. Reddish-yellow clay 5YR 6/6. Ware 1.
Thick, slightly lustrous black-brown gloss on exterior; fired patchy red on interior. Slightly out-turned rim. Egg-and-dart above horizontal beading. Pine-cone decoration on wall.

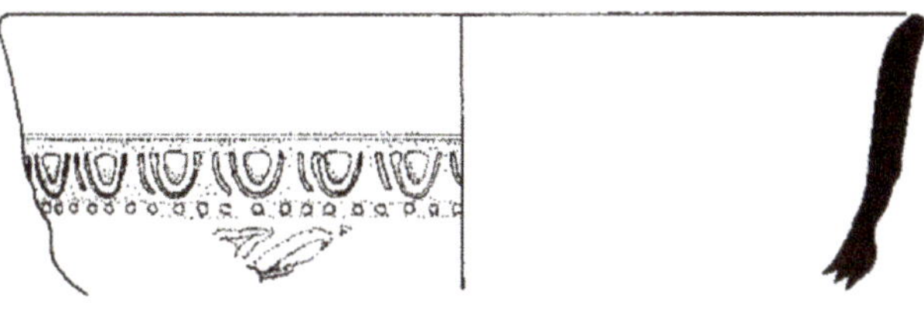

FW 266. CN 7734.
XXXIIM 56.1. Mixed Context.
Part of wall, rim. PH 0.04; PL 0.06; D rim (est.) 0.18. Reddish-yellow clay 7.5YR 6/6. Ware 2.
Reddish-brown gloss on exterior; mottled red-black on interior. Out-turned rim. Atypical egg-and-dart rim pattern.

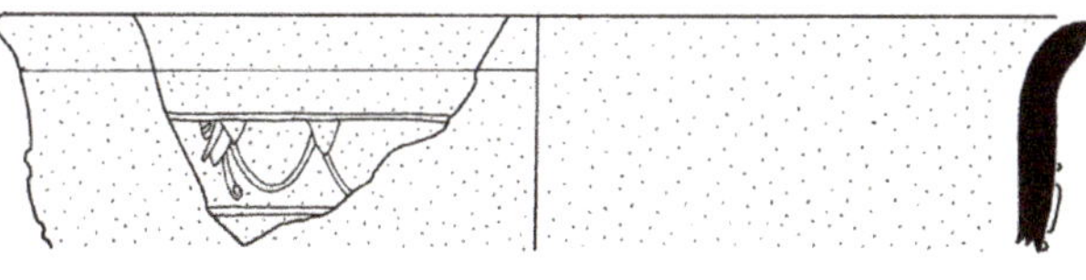

FW 267. CN 7132.

IIIP 113.5. Mixed Context.

Part of wall, rim. PH 0.05; D rim (est.) 0.12. Well levigated reddish-yellow clay 7.5YR 7/6. Fine mica. Good black gloss on interior, exterior. Slightly concave. Egg-and-dart between horizontal beading. Tip of acanthus leaf below.

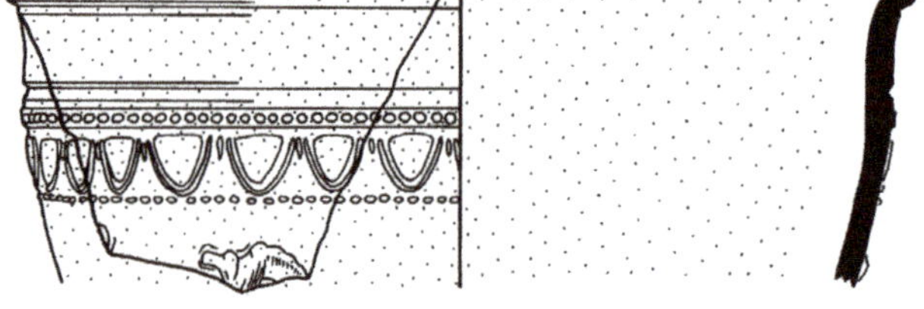

FW 268. CN 1377.

IVU 3.1. Mixed Context.

Part of wall, rim. PH 0.04; D rim (est.) 0.14. Reddish-yellow clay 7.5YR 6/6. Ware 2.

Purple-brown gloss on exterior; dull red gloss on interior. Concave everted rim with egg-and-dart. Pendant drops below.

Parallels: Ashdod (Dothan 1971: fig. 9.2, first half of 2nd c. BC–second half of 2nd c. BC); Hama (Christensen and Johansen 1971: fig. 10.102); Jaffa (Tsuf 2018: fig. 9.53.869); Paphos (Neuru 1991: fig. VII.16); Straton's Tower/Caesarea (Rosenthal-Heginbottom 2016b: 144, 145.61).

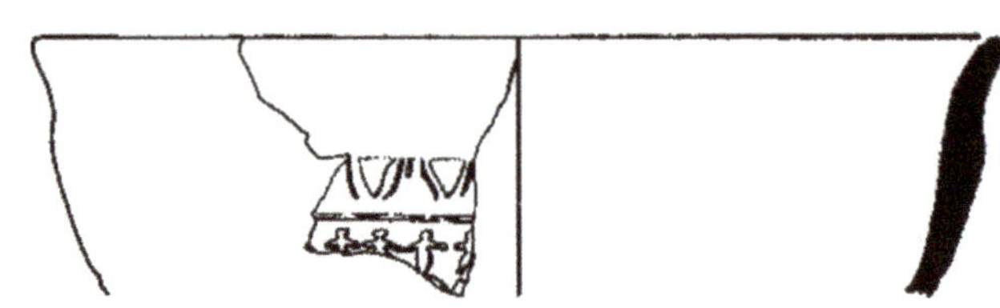

FW 269. CN 6605.

IVM 52.5. Mixed Context.

Rim fragment. PH 0.04; D rim (est.) 0.13. Reddish-yellow clay 7.5YR 6/6. Ware 2.

Concave everted rim. Cordate leaves between horizontal ridges and grooves.

Parallels: Apamea (Balty 2003: fig. 13.5); Ashdod (Dothan 1971: fig. 99.6); Beirut (Élaigne 2007: fig. 14.386–168, second half of 2nd and first half of 1st c. BC); Straton's Tower/Caesarea (Rosenthal-Heginbottom 2016b: 147.68); Tel Mevorakh (Rosenthal 1978: fig. 3.8).

FW 270. CN 3394.

IVE 13.4. Mixed Context.

Rim fragment. PH 0.035; D rim (est.) 0.14. Reddish-yellow clay 7.5YR 6/6. Well levigated with occasional air holes.

Red gloss on interior; reddish-brown gloss on exterior. Concave everted rim. Horizontal band of guilloche.

FW 271. CN 7366.

XXXIVB 10.8. Mixed Context.

Part of wall, rim. PH 0.025; PL 0.02; D rim (est.) 0.12. Yellowish-red clay 5YR 5/6. "Ionian".

Good black gloss on interior, exterior. Upright rim. Ovolo rim pattern; traces of floral below.

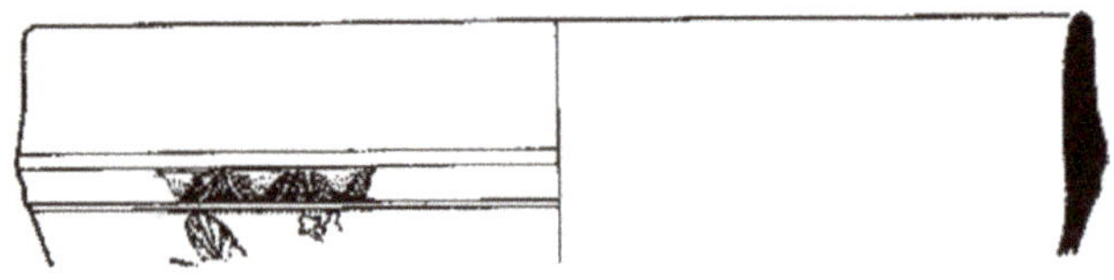

FW 272. CN 6788.

XXIIIA 10.5. Hellenistic 3C.

Part of wall, rim. PH 0.03; D rim (est.) 0.13. Reddish-yellow clay 5YR 6/8. Small white inclusions. "Ionian". Lustrous black gloss on rim. Red gloss on wall. Slightly in-turned rim. Enriched meander with diagonals in square on rim; indistinct floral pattern on wall. Parallels: ʿAkko-Ptolemais (Berlin and Stone 2016: fig. 9.18.1, mid–late 2nd c. BC); Straton's Tower/Caesarea (Rosenthal-Heginbottom 2016b: 152.84; 153.86). The rim pattern of enriched meander with diagonals in a square is frequently seen among "Ionian" bowls: for example, Laumonier 1977: pl. 2.428–477; pl. 10.5085; pl. 12.1798, 807e7, 9316 *passim*; Rogl 2014: 128, fig. 13.8. See also Shechem (N.L. Lapp 2008: pl. 3.30.11, 225–190 BC).

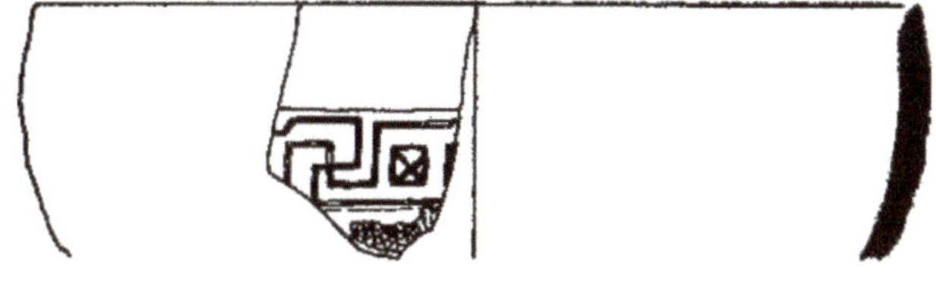

FW 273. CN 7206.

XXVIIIB 13.17. Hellenistic 3A.

Part of wall, rim. PH 0.11; D rim (est.) 0.17. Reddish-yellow clay 7.5YR 7/8. Ware 2.

Patchy red-brown gloss on interior, exterior. Concave rim. Cordate leaf decoration between horizontal beading. Wall decoration of palmettes above, separated by horizontal beading from tall ferns below. Calyx of short nymphaea leaves just visible.

FW 274. CN 7228.

XXVIIIB 10.4. Hellenistic 3A.

Part of wall, rim. PH 0.045; D rim (est.) 0.14. Reddish-yellow clay 7.5YR 7/6. Ware 2.

Dull, evenly applied red gloss on interior, exterior. Out-turned rim. Egg-and-dart between horizontal rows of beading. Upper part of acanthus leaf preserved. Parallels: ʿAkko-Ptolemais (Regev 2009/10: fig. 36.232); Tarsus (F.F. Jones 1950: fig.129.B).

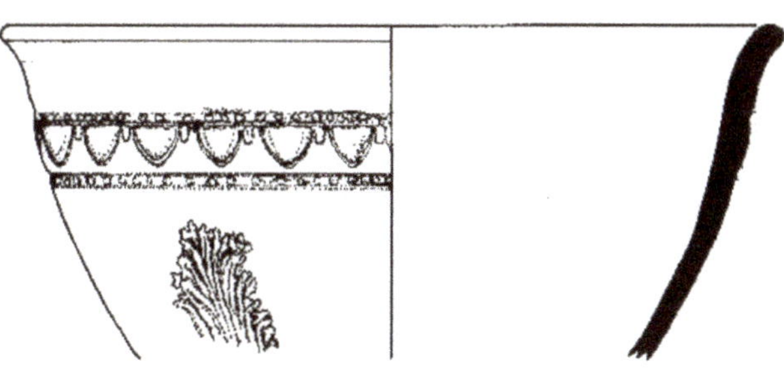

FW 275. CN 7079.

XXIIIA 109.4. Hellenistic 3B.

Rim fragment. PH 0.02; D rim (est.) 0.16. Yellowish-red clay 5YR 5/6. Slight mica. "Ionian".

Black gloss on interior; dull red gloss on exterior. Upright rim. Horizontal beading between ridges.

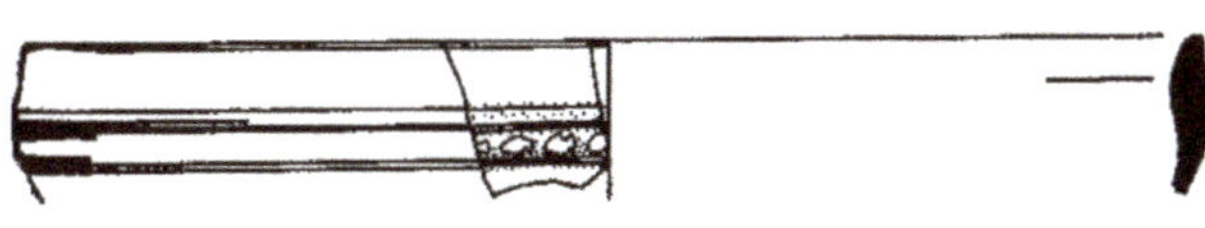

FW 276. CN 7220.
XXVIIIB 10.2. Hellenistic 3A.
Part of wall, rim. PH 0.06; D rim (est.) 0.14. Reddish-yellow clay 7.5YR 6/8. Ware 2.
Patchy brown-black gloss on interior, exterior. Rim curves outwards. Ovolo with horizontal beading below. Tip of an acanthus leaf on wall.

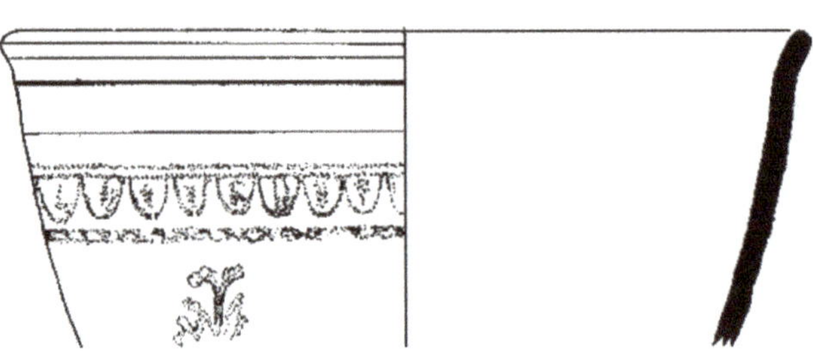

FW 277. CN 6708. (Plate 55)
IIIP 25.20. Mixed Context.
Two non-joining fragments of wall, rim. (a) PH 0.05; PL 0.05; (b) PH 0.045; PL 0.035; D rim (est.) 0.10. Yellowish-red clay 5YR 5/8. "Ionian".
Thin metallic black gloss on interior, exterior. Bead-and-reel on rim. Running spiral on upper wall separated by row of globules between ridges from draped female moving to right below.
Parallel: Ephesus (Rogl 2014: 128, fig. 13.11 for similar bead-and-reel).

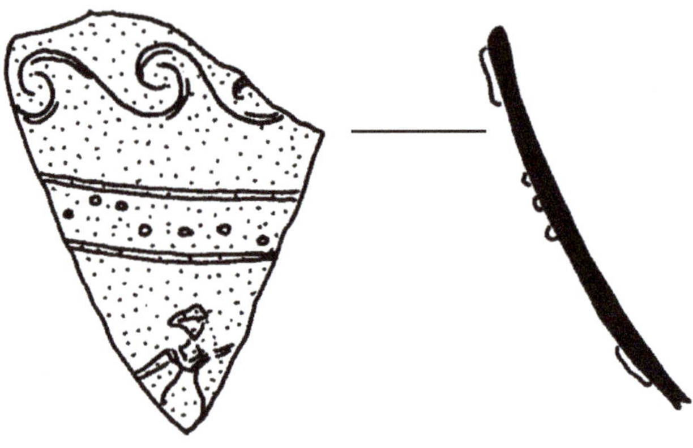

FW 278. CN 7194.
XXVIIIB 13.9/11.Hellenistic 3A.
Part of wall, rim. PH 0.07; D rim (est.) 0.15. Pink clay 7.5YR 8/3. Ware 1.
Red gloss on interior; thin black gloss on exterior. Out-turned rim. Horizontal band of guilloche on shoulder. Wall pattern (very worn) on each fragment, of boars, separated by schematic trees, fleeing to left.
Parallels: Athens (Rotroff 1982: pl. 50.252, late 3rd–early 2nd c. BC). Similar scenes also occur at Olympia (Hausmann 1996: table 22.92); see also Courby 1922: fig. 71.e.

FW 279. CN 4294.
IVD 10.12. Hellenistic 3C.
Part of wall, rim. PH 0.065; D rim (est.) 0.14. Reddish-yellow clay 7.5YR 7/6. Ware 2.
Dull black gloss on interior, exterior, except for rim which is red. Out-turned rim. Egg-and-dart between horizontal grooves; pendant drops below. Acanthus and palmette on wall.
Parallels: Antioch (Waagé 1948: fig. 9.26); Gezer (Gitin 1990: pl. 44.16, in ESA, mid-1st c. BC; Rosenthal-Heginbottom 2016b: 162, 163.11); Hama (Christensen and Johansen 1971: fig. 14.116); Marisa (close to Levine 2003: fig. 6.2.20); Tel Anafa (Cornell 1997: pl. 1.MB6, in ESA); Tel Yoqne'am (Ben-Tor et al. 1983: fig. 7.8).

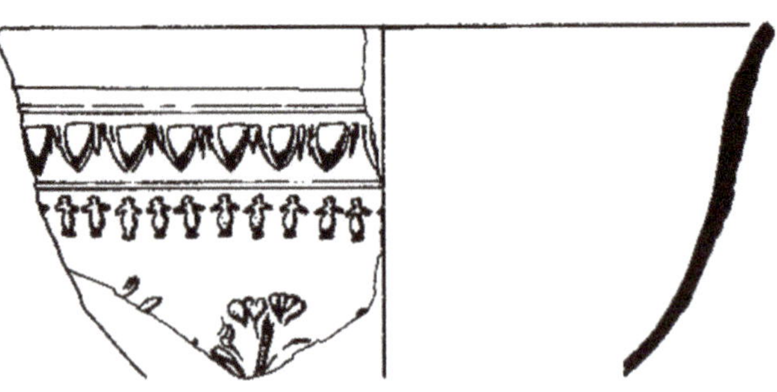

FW 280. CN 7193.

XXVIIIB 13.9. Hellenistic 3A.

Part of wall, rim. PH (largest fragment) 0.07; D rim (est.) 0.18. Reddish-yellow clay 5YR 7/6. Ware 2. Patchy red-black-dark brown gloss on interior, exterior. Out-turned rim. Cordate leaves above horizontal beading. On wall a figured zone of Nikai with trophies, alternating with rampant goats with shepherd's crook (?) and draped females. Tendrils and palmettes below horizontal beading.

FW 281. CN 7150.

XXXIVB 5.37; 5.39; 6.35; 6.40. Mixed Context. Three non-joining fragments of wall. PH 0.06 (largest fragment); D rim (est.) 0.13. Reddish-yellow clay 5YR 6/6. Good black gloss, fired red-brown in patches, on interior, exterior. Wave pattern on upper wall. Below, tendrils and palmettes bearing palm flowers and rosettes, with birds above flying to right.

FW 282 CN 7147. (Plate 56)

XXXIVB 5.37. Mixed Context. Two non-joining fragments of rim, wall, medallion. (a) PL 0.045; (b) PH 0.04; PL 0.075; D rim (est.) 0.15. Weak red clay 2.5YR 5/4. Ware 2. Rich brown gloss on interior, exterior. Upright rim. Ovolo below. Palmettes and tendrils on upper wall. Medallion of eight-petalled rosette surrounded by grooves; alternating palmettes and acanthus on calyx.

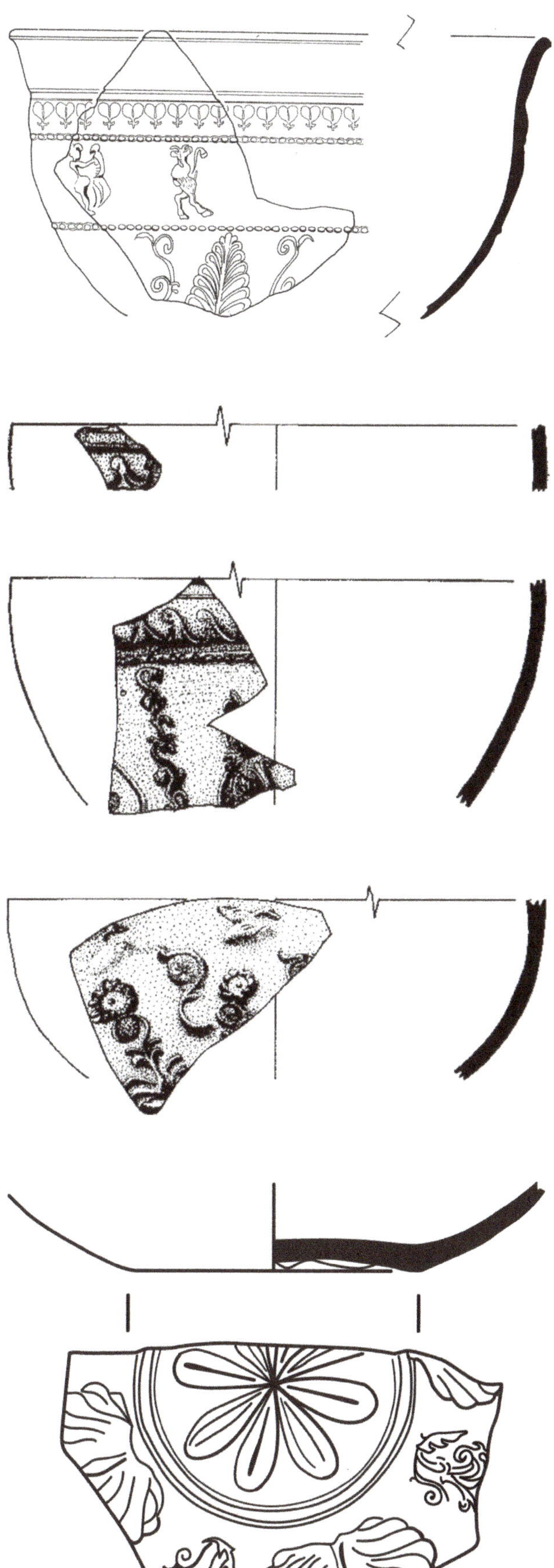

FW 283. CN 7788.
XXIIID 20.9. Hellenistic 3C.
Wall fragment. PH 0.045; PL 0.025. Reddish-yellow
clay 7.5YR 6/6. Ware 2.
Black-brown gloss on interior, exterior. Pine-cone
below horizontal row of globules.

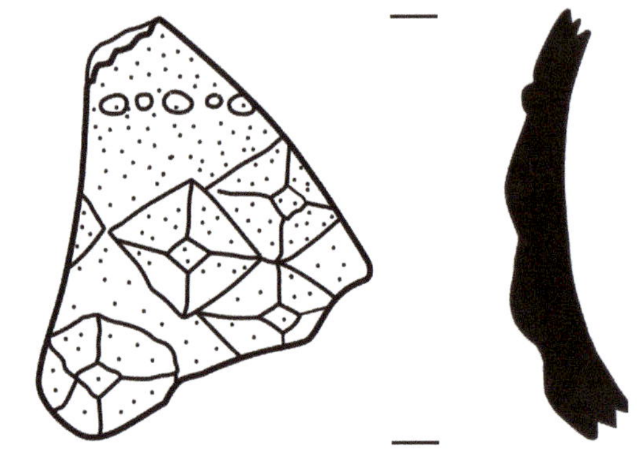

FW 284. CN 7233.
XXVIIIB 9.4. Mixed Context.
Wall fragment. PH 0.04; PL 0.045. Reddish-yellow
clay 5YR 6/6.
Reddish-brown gloss on interior, exterior. Acanthus,
long-ribbed petal (*Nymphaea caerulea*), rosette on wall.

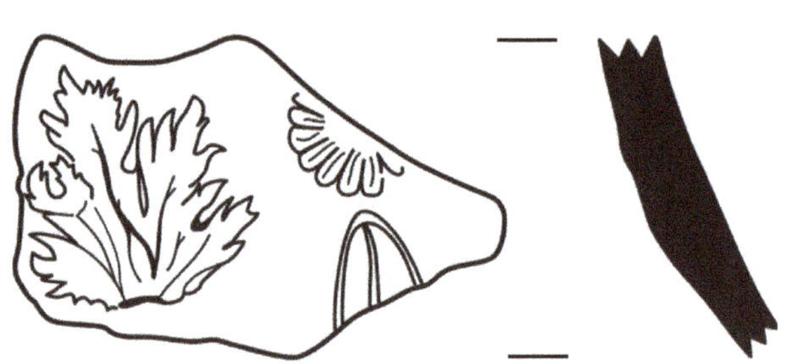

FW 285. CN 0162.
IIIB/C 2.6. Hellenistic 3C.
Two non-joining fragments of wall, rim. (a) PH 0.035;
PL 0.07; (b) PH 0.03; PL 0.045. Yellowish-red clay
5YR 5/6. Ware 2.
Mottled lustrous to dull brown gloss on interior, exterior.
Egg-and-dart on upper wall; imbricate leaves below.

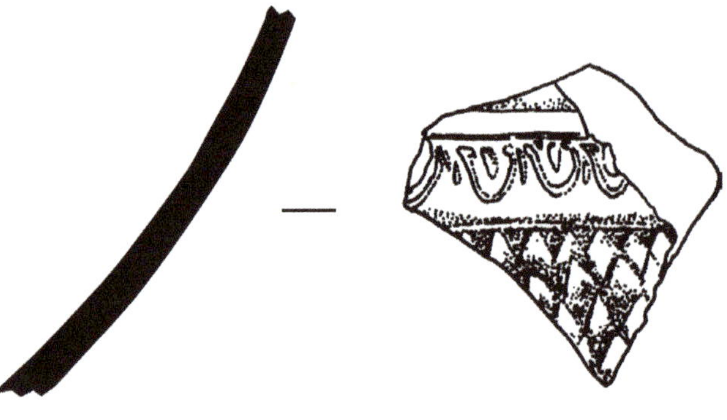

FW 286. CN 7152.
XXXIVB 5.39. Mixed Context.
Wall fragment. PH 0.03; PL 0.03. Yellowish-red clay
5YR 5/6.
Dark brown gloss, slightly worn in patches, on interior,
exterior. Palmette, tendril and acanthus on wall.
Parallel: Straton's Tower/Caesarea (Rosenthal-
Heginbottom 2016b: 134, 135.29).

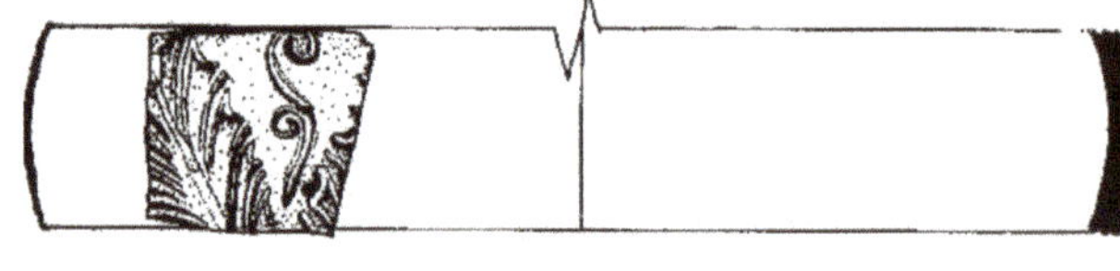

FW 287. CN 7160.
XXXIVB 6.40. Mixed Context.
Wall fragment. PH 0.035; PL 0.03. Reddish-yellow
clay 5YR 7/6.
Dark brown gloss on interior, exterior. Double row of
ovolo on upper zone above traces of floral decoration.

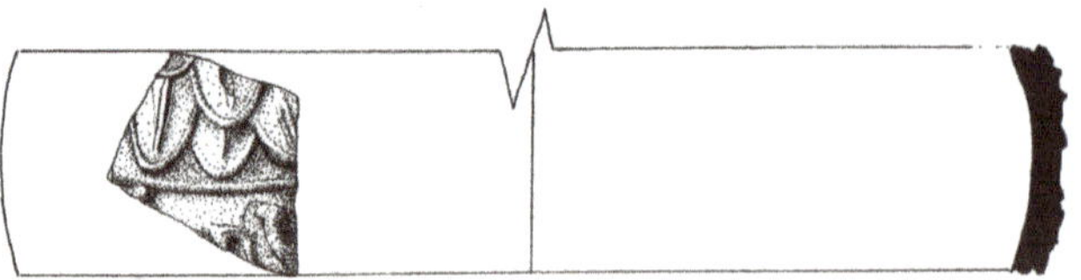

FW 288. CN 7239.
XXVIIIB. Hellenistic 3A.
Wall fragment. PH 0.045; PL 0.02. Reddish-yellow clay 7.5YR 7/6. Ware 2.
Thin, evenly applied gloss on interior, exterior. Palmette tendril scroll between horizontal rows of globules; florets above.
Parallel: Jebel Khalid in Syria (Tidmarsh 2011: fig. 127. FW 459).

FW 289. CN 6642.
IVE 20.5. Mixed Context.
Part of wall. PH 0.035; PL 0.04. Reddish-yellow clay 7.5YR 7/6. Ware 2.
Mottled orange-black gloss on exterior; red gloss on interior. Cordate leaves above horizontal beading; acanthus and tendril below.
Parallel: Straton's Tower/Caesarea (Rosenthal-Heginbottom 2016b: 129.11).

FW 290. CN 7717.
XXXIVB 6.46. Mixed Context.
Wall fragment. PL 0.045; PH 0.03. Reddish-yellow clay 7.5YR 6/8. Ware 2.
Good red-brown gloss on exterior. Thinner red gloss on interior. Pendant drops below horizontal row of globules. Tip of tendril below.

FW 291. CN 7141.
XXXIVA 2.9. Mixed Context.
Wall fragment. PH 0.045; PL 0.045. Dark grey clay 5Y 4/1. "Ionian".
Metallic black gloss on interior, exterior. Wreath of olive leaves above bead-and-reel between ridges. Trace of floral spray below.

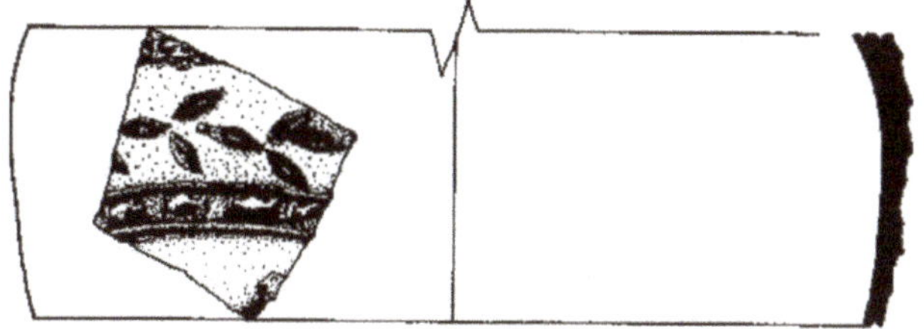

FW 292. CN 7344.
XXXIVB 6.27. Early Roman (residual).
Wall fragment. PH 0.035; PL 0.03. Yellowish-red clay 5YR 5/6.
Dark red-brown gloss on interior, exterior. Worn pattern of tendril on left of Nike (?) holding kantharos.

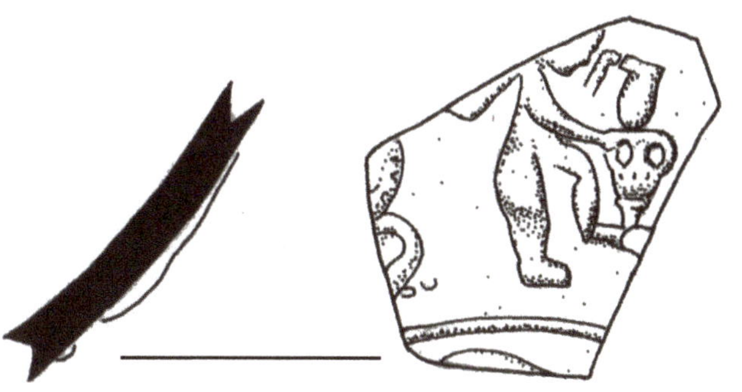

FW 293. CN 7191.
XXVIIIB 13.8. Hellenistic 3A.
Wall fragment. PH 0.06; PL 0.03. Reddish-yellow clay
5YR 7/8. Ware 2.
Red gloss on interior, exterior. Draped female
(missing part of right shoulder and head) with left
arm extended.
Possible parallels: holding spear, as Courby 1922:
fig. 69.2(?); dancing, as Edwards 1975: pls 37.829,
70.829(?); linking hands, as Reisner et al. 1924:
pl. 73.i(?). Also Antioch (Waagé 1948: fig. 9.49–50);
Olympia (Hausmann 1996: table 25.109).

FW 294. CN 6742.
IIIP 25.21. Mixed Context.
Wall fragment. PH 0.045; PL 0.03. Very pale brown
clay 10YR 7/4. Ware 3.
Mottled brown-black gloss on interior, exterior. Legs
of figure with shield above beaded border. Stylised
lotus petals below.

FW 295. CN 6733.
IIIP 24.19. Mixed Context.
Wall fragment. PH 0.045; PL 0.06. Very pale brown
clay 10YR 7/4.
Metallic black gloss on interior, exterior. Eros with
shield and spear in right hand facing rampant goat
to right. Draped figure to left.

FW 296. CN 7716.
XXVIIIB 13.10. Hellenistic 3A.
Part of wall. PL.03; PH.045. Reddish-yellow clay
5YR 6/8.
Thin mottled red-black gloss on exterior. Thin red slip
over interior. Narrow pattern of globules and vertical
ridges above. Below, Eros (?) carrying tambourine
and moving to right. Lower leg of further figure to
right. Horizontal ridge below.

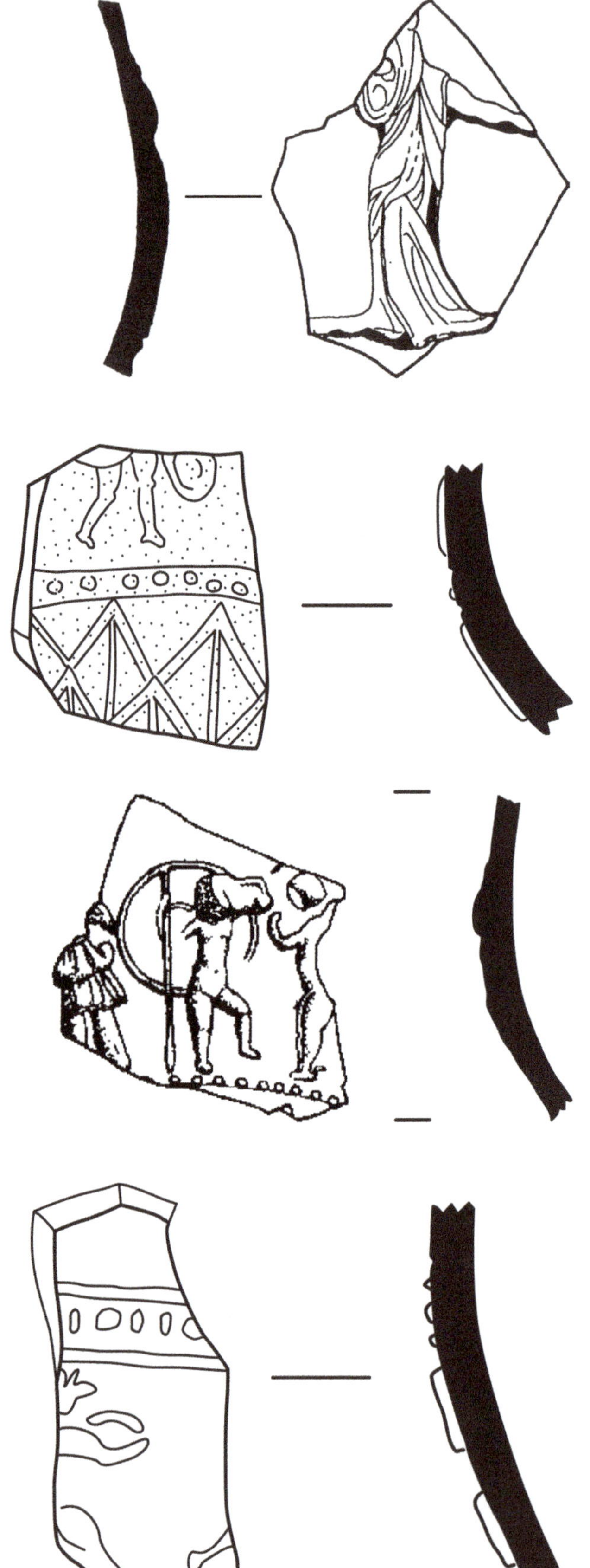

FW 297. CN 7196.

XXVIIIB 13.10. Hellenistic 3A.

Wall fragment. PL 0.05; PH 0.045. Very pale brown clay 10YR 8/3. Ware 3.

Red-brown gloss on interior, exterior. Dolphin to left; floral to right below horizontal ridge.

Parallels: Samaria (Reisner et al. 1924: pl. 72.d); Tel Zahara (Bar-Nathan and Gärtner 2013: fig. 3.15.134).

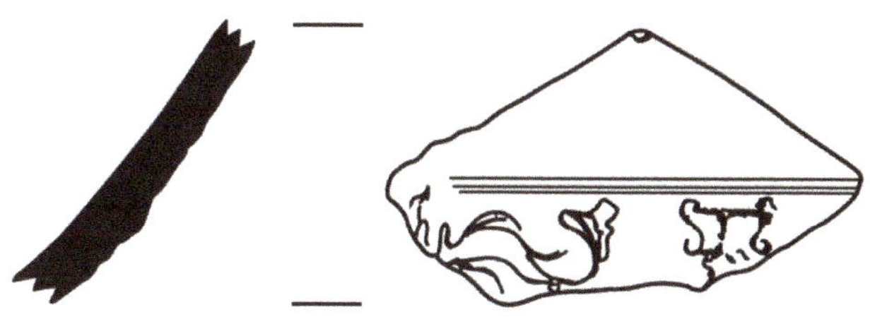

FW 298. CN 1335.

IVD 2.1. Mixed Context.

Wall fragment. PH 0.03; PL 0.045. Reddish-yellow clay 7.5YR 7/6.

Mottled brown gloss on exterior; red gloss on interior. Head and upraised paw of lion to right; hindquarters of hoofed animal to left.

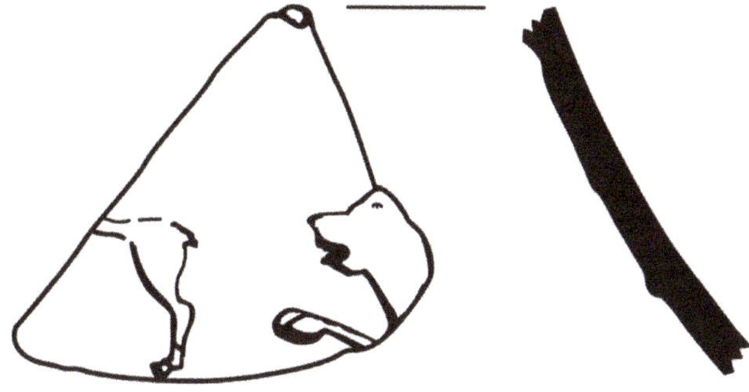

FW 299. CN 7713.

XXXIVG. 1.2. Mixed Context.

Part of wall. PL 0.025; PH 0.02. Reddish-yellow clay 7.5YR 7/6. Ware 2.

Red gloss on interior, exterior. Above, goat leaping to right. Below, indistinct figure with upraised arms. Further right, upper torso of a further figure?

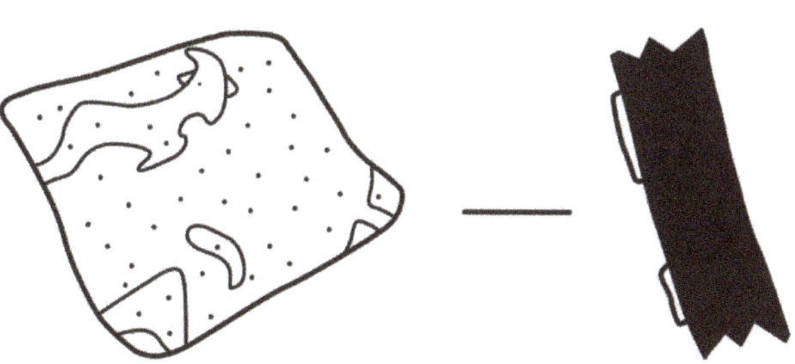

FW 300. CN 7230.

XXVIIIB 10.6. Hellenistic 3A.

Wall fragment. PH 0.02; PL 0.045. Very pale brown clay 10YR 7/4. Ware 3.

Dull black gloss on interior, exterior. Part of two-horse chariot (biga); horizontal beading below.

Parallels: Antioch (Waagé 1948: fig. 10.30); Athens (Rotroff 1982: pl. 28.150, second half of 3rd c.–first quarter 2nd c. BC; pl. 28.151–3; pl. 54.275, second half of 3rd c.–first quarter 2nd c. BC, pl. 54.276–7; pl. 67.384); Delos (Courby 1922: pl. XI.c); Tarsus (F.F. Jones 1950: fig. 131.F).

FW 301. CN 7198.
XXVIIIB 13.13/17. Hellenistic 3A.
Two joining fragments of lower wall, medallion.
PH 0.015; PL 0.035. Reddish-yellow clay 7.5YR 6/6.
Ware 2.
Dull black gloss on exterior; shiny dark brown gloss
on interior. Tendrils with buds and flowers alternating
with tall nymphaea petals. Ten-petalled rosette within
medallion.

FW 302. CN 6974.
XXIIIA 22.4. Hellenistic 3C.
Fragment of lower wall, medallion. PH 0.025;
PL 0.025. Very pale brown clay 10YR 7/3. Ware 3.
Rich brown gloss on interior, exterior. Acanthus
leaf corolla.

FW 303. CN 6645.
IVE 17.9. Mixed Context.
Part of lower wall, medallion. PH 0.015; PL 0.03; Pink clay 7.5YR 7/4.
Dull red gloss on interior, exterior. Medallion of eight-petalled palmette within beading. Lower half of acanthus leaf in calyx.

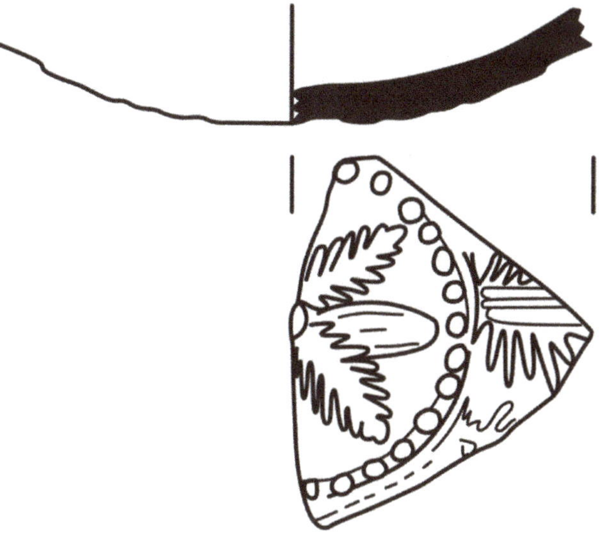

FW 304. CN 6604.
IIIP 24.8. Mixed Context.
Part of lower wall, medallion. PH 0.01; PL 0.055. Yellowish-red clay 5YR 5/8.
Lustrous metallic black gloss on interior, exterior. Medallion of eight-petalled rosette within beading. Calyx decoration of imbricated leaves.

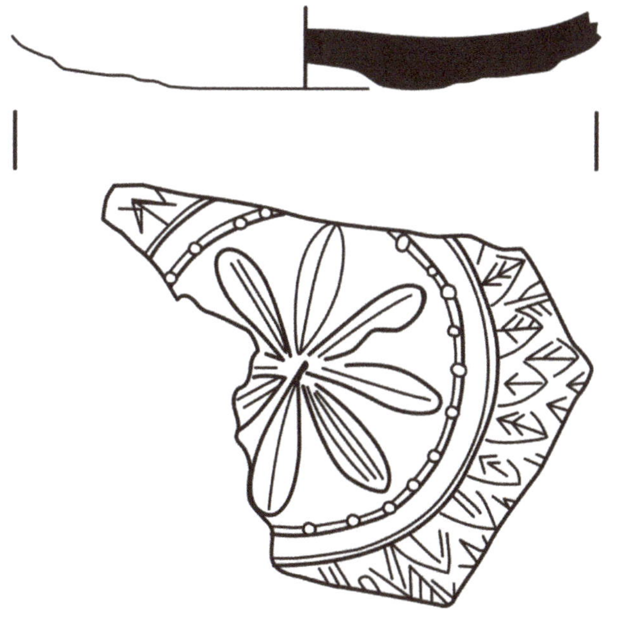

FW 305. CN 7278.
XXXIVG 3.13. Mixed Context.
Part of lower wall, medallion. PH 0.02; PL 0.10. Reddish-yellow clay 5YR 7/6. "Ionian".
Dull red gloss on interior, exterior. Curving lower wall. Faint rosette in medallion surrounded by two grooves and raised ridge. Calyx pattern of palmettes.

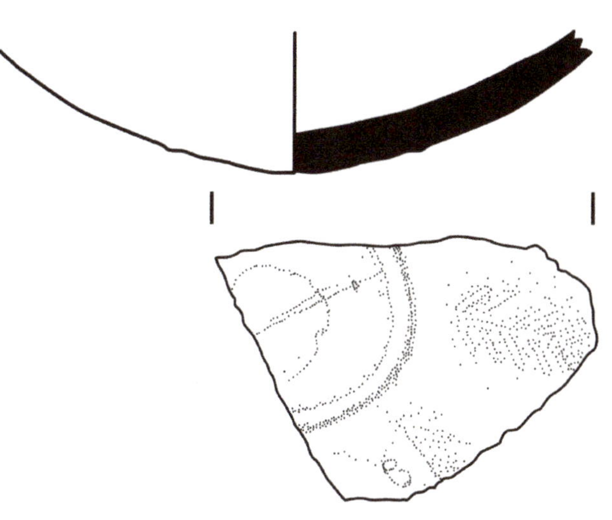

THE PLAIN WARES

Fragments of common household ceramics (designated here as "plain wares") constitute by far the great bulk of pottery collected at Pella from Hellenistic and Early Roman levels, with a similar situation occurring on most Near Eastern sites. With the environs of Pella possessing clays suitable for pottery manufacture (Bes et al. 2020: 70), it is to be expected that most of the plain wares are of local production; however, the workshops are yet to be located.[1] The majority of plain ware forms (fishplates, jars, cooking pots, etc.) can be further classified into types, which are listed in Table 2.15.

WARES

In earlier reports (for example, McNicoll et al. 1992: 114–15), most of the plain ware vessels were assigned to one of four main wares: Coarse Light Brown, Hard Pale, Metallic Buff, Metallic Coarse Terracotta. This classification remains essentially valid, although it is now clear that there are three other relatively uncommon wares (Yellow-slipped Coarse ware, Pink-slipped Coarse ware, "Galilean" ware) to be discussed below. It should be emphasised that, at Pella, these plain ware categories are currently separated by visual appearance rather than by chemical analysis.

With the exception of Coarse Light Brown ware – seen mainly in imitations of fine ware shapes, especially small bowls and the ubiquitous fishplate – the other wares are restricted largely to utilitarian vessels such as jars, jugs and cooking vessels. Included in Tables 2.13–2.46 is the number of shapes appearing in the different fabrics (for example, Tables 2.16, 2.17).

Coarse Light Brown ware

The clay is generally light brown (Munsell 7.5YR 6/6, 7/4, 7/6 to 10YR 8/3) and, while usually evenly fired throughout, a thin grey core is sometimes present. Despite its name, the ware is generally quite well levigated – although not to the same degree as most of the fine wares, for small white inclusions are frequently apparent. A thin, patchy slip – sometimes dull black but more commonly reddish-brown – is frequently seen, especially on the fishplates.[2] Rarely (for example, **PW 119**, **PW 123**), a crude attempt seems to have been made to imitate the deliberate black-red firing seen on black-gloss vessels such as **FW 71** or **FW 122**. Ring bases are commonly seen on vessels of this ware imitating imported fine ware shapes but, "whereas the bases of the imported vessels were applied, those of the local vessels were an integral part of the clay matrix from which the vessel was formed" (McNicoll et al. 1992: 115).

---

1   "Chaque cité de la région semble bien avoir eu ses propres centres de production, mais le commerce de cet artisanat apparaît limité à leur territoire respectif" (Rasson-Seigne and Seigne 2020b: 123). It is also worth noting that a very small sample ("Shuster 2": two sherds in fact) from 'Iraq al-Amir indicates clay sources from the Pella region (Zimmerman 2020b: 86).

2   These – usually Greek-inspired – plain ware ceramic forms with "a matt or sway slip of variable colour" are sometimes termed "Colour-Coated Wares" (Hayes 1991a: 23–5).

Table 2.13. Distribution of plain wares by wares, areas.

WARE	TOTAL	III, IV MAIN MOUND	XXIII MAIN MOUND	XXVIII MAIN MOUND	XXXII MAIN MOUND	XI TELL HUSN	XXXIV TELL HUSN
Coarse Light Brown	150	61	39	19	2	15	14
Hard Pale	125	14	33	37	2	3	36
Metallic Buff	104	11	17	3	0	48	25
Yellow-slipped	15	4	5	5	0	1	0
Pink-slipped	10	0	2	1	0	6	1
Metallic Coarse Terracotta	155	15	25	17	0	46	52
"Galilean"	8	1	0	0	0	4	3
Rhodian	14	0	3	5	0	1	5
Phoenician?	1	0	1	0	0	0	0
Miscellaneous	112	16	20	20	3	17	36

The origin of this ware is still to be determined – petrographic and chemical studies are yet to be carried out – but it may not be restricted to the Pella region: imitations of imported fine ware bowls and fishplates in a light brown fabric, often with a poor slip, are seen at Samaria and Tel Michal (Fischer 1989: 177–8). At Samaria, its equivalent is known as "household ware" (Crowfoot et al. 1957: 265) whilst at Tel Michal it goes by the appellation "Late Hellenistic homemade ware". It would also seem to have a number of similarities with the "Central Coastal Fine" ware from Kedesh described by Berlin and colleagues (2014), in which case it may have reached Pella via the Jezreel Valley.

Hard Pale ware

Hard Pale ware is mainly restricted to jugs and jars. The clay is relatively coarse, often with black or white inclusions, and shows some similarities to several of the better levigated Iron Age wares seen at Pella. The Munsell reading of the fired clay ranges from 5YR 6/6 to 10YR 7/4; frequently the firing is incomplete, leaving a dark grey core. The slip ranges from very pale brown (10YR 7/4) to a mottled pink (5YR 7/4). Hard Pale ware is especially common in the second century BC whereas, during the early first century BC, as shown by the Jannaeus Destruction (Hellenistic 3C) and Early Roman deposits, it largely gives way to Metallic Buff ware (Table 2.14).

Yellow-slipped Coarse ware

The clay is moderately well levigated with occasional coarse inclusions present. It fires a yellowish-brown (10YR 5/4–5/8) although, as with Hard Pale ware, the firing is often incomplete and a thick grey core is often present. The slip (5Y 8/3, 8/4) is usually thick and well applied. The ware is most commonly seen in Pre-Jannaeus Destruction levels but persists into the early first century BC.

Table 2.14. Distribution of plain wares by wares, phases.

WARE	2B c. 220– c. 200 BC	3A c. 200– c. 140 BC	3B c. 140– c. 100 (?) BC	3B/3C c. 140– c. 80/79 BC	3C c. 100 (?)– c. 80/79 BC	EARLY ROMAN 63 BC– c. 135 AD	MIXED
Coarse Light Brown	1	18	16	4	56	16	39
Hard Pale	7	48	10	14	21	6	17
Metallic Buff	1	3	4	3	17	56	18
Yellow-slipped	0	5	0	0	9	1	0
Pink-slipped	0	1	0	0	2	6	1
"Galilean"	0	0	0	0	1	6	1
Metallic Coarse Terracotta	3	13	8	4	28	58	36
Rhodian	2	5	0	3	2	1	1
Phoenician?	0	0	0	0	1	0	0

Pink-slipped Coarse ware

Pink-slipped Coarse ware is a relatively minor ware in second-century BC levels, becoming more common in Jannaeus Destruction and Early Roman deposits. It has a distinctive pink slip 5YR 7/4–7.5YR 7/4 that is patchily applied. The clay itself is relatively coarse – often with large white inclusions – and fires reddish-yellow (7.5YR 6/6). The ware is largely restricted to bowls.

Metallic Buff ware

Metallic Buff ware is also generally restricted to storage jars and jugs and, as mentioned above, is the predominant ware for these shapes at Pella by the later first century BC. The fired clay is somewhat coarse with a chalky pale brown or yellowish appearance and its Munsell readings range around 10YR 6/3–7/6. The thin slip is usually the same colour as the clay.

Metallic Coarse Terracotta ware

Metallic Coarse Terracotta ware would appear to have many of the same characteristics as the cooking-pot wares in much of the southern Levant during the Hellenistic period with similar wares used for cooking pots well into Byzantine times at Pella (McNicoll et al. 1982: 148, 154–7; Watson 1992: 235–7) and elsewhere (Kerner 1997: 293; Magness 1992, 1993: 216; Peleg 1989: 61ff.). At a number of Hellenistic sites, there is a noticeable tendency for the cooking-pot wares to become thinner and better levigated with time (Crowfoot et al. 1957: 228; Gitin 1990: 255–60) but at Pella it remains remarkably consistent throughout the Hellenistic and Early Roman levels. The ware is hard-fired (Mohs 4–4.5) with small- to medium-sized particles of quartz and other grit. The colour of the fired clay is a dark red-brown (Munsell 2.5YR 5/6–5YR 6/8), often with a grey core. At Pella, the ware is seen exclusively in cooking pots, casseroles and cooking bowls.

"Galilean" ware

A small number of cooking ware vessels from Pella, namely cooking pots (Type 7) and cooking bowls (Type 3), were manufactured west of the Jordan River in the Galilee as well as possibly to the north-east in the Golan. Adan-Bayewitz (1993, 2003) has nominated two important centres of production for kitchen ware used in the Galilee during the Roman and early Byzantine periods: Kfar Hananya (cooking wares) and Kfar Shikhin for non-cooking shapes such as storage jars, kraters, bell-shaped bowls, jugs and juglets.

For the Early Roman era Kfar Hananya (modern Kafr 'Inan), to the north-west of Lake Tiberias, seems to have been the chief source of this strictly utilitarian kitchen ware, though it is now clear that other centres in the Galilee and Golan were also involved in the production of similar forms (Adan-Bayewitz 2003; Adan-Bayewitz and Wieder 1992; Adan-Bayewitz et al. 1999; Aviam 2014; Vitto 1983–84).

Kfar Hananya ware is well described (Adan-Bayewitz 1993: 150–4) with the colour of the fired clay giving a Munsell reading of 2.5YR 5/8 or thereabouts. The vessels are usually well fired with very few having a grey core and, as is common for cooking wares, relatively hard (Mohs 4–6). However, at least macroscopically, these characteristics may appear indistinguishable from those cooking wares turned out at Yodefat (Aviam 2014) and, possibly, elsewhere. Thus, as things stand at present, "Galilean ware" rather than "Kfar Hananya ware" seems a more apt description and this term will be used here.[3]

Distribution of these "Galilean" kitchen wares is, understandably, largely restricted to the Galilee, Golan and surrounding areas (Adan-Bayewitz 1993: 211–19, fig. 11); of the Decapolis cities, Abila, Gadara/Umm Qais, Hippos-Sussita (modern Qal'at al-Husn on the east shore of Lake Tiberias), Scythopolis/Beth-Shean and Pella have yielded examples, with chemical analysis and thin section studies (Daszkiewicz et al. 2014) showing that Gadara served as a ready market for ceramic imports from the Galilee (and to a lesser degree the Golan) from the turn of the first century BC until the fifth century AD.[4] As yet, "Galilean" ware has been infrequently reported from elsewhere in modern Jordan.[5]

Table 2.15 Plain ware pottery forms (including sub-types) encountered at Pella in Hellenistic and Early Roman levels.

SHAPE/FORM	TYPE	FEATURE
Fishplates	Type 1	Broad, angled rim
	Type 2	Broad, drooping rim
	Type 3	Narrow, angled rim
	Type 4	Narrow, drooping rim
		Bases
Plates	Type 1	Thickened simple rim
	Type 2	Thickened undercut rim
	Upright rim	
Saucers		
Bowls	Type 1	Out-turned rim
	Type 2	In-turned rim
	Type 3	Angled rim

3   For concise summaries of the archaeological record in Kfar Hananya, Kfar Shikhin and Yodefat, see the relevant chapters in Fiensy and Strange 2015.

4   Mare et al. 1987: fig. 13.5 (Abila); Daszkiewicz et al. 2014 (Gadara/Umm Qais); Osband and Eisenberg 2018: 213–15 (Hippos-Sussita); Johnson 2006: 539, fig. 15.6.127–12 (Scythopolis/Beth-Shean). For the ceramic connections of Gadara/Umm Qais with the Galilee and Golan rather than with the southern Decapolis cities, see also Berger 2020: 320–1.

5   The "Galilean" bowl rim (Hanbury-Tenison 1984: 408) from the Wadi Arab may be an import from the Galilee, although the description of the ware is non-specific.

SHAPE/FORM	TYPE	FEATURE
	Type 4	Simple rim
	Type 5	Bevelled rim
	Type 6	Hemispherical
Skyphoi/kantharoi		
Cups		Narrow band rim; pinched handles
Kraters	Type 1	Flaring rim; vertical lip
	Type 2	Horizontal rim
	Type 3	Down-turned rim
	Type 4	Fluted
Table amphorae	Type 1	Projecting rim
	Type 2	Stepped interior
Jugs	Type 1	Thickened rim
	Type 2	Short-collared rim
	Type 3	Grooved rim
	Type 4	Flaring rim
	Type 5	Flanged rim
Juglets	Type 1	Simple rim
	Type 2	Collared rim
	Type 3	Flanged rim
	Type 4	Flaring rim
	Type 5	Cup-shaped rim
	Type 6	Wide mouth; grooved rim
Lagynoi	Type 1	Rounded body
	Type 2	Angular body
	Miscellaneous	
Flasks		Southern Palestinian type
Amphoriskoi		
Transport amphorae		
Mortaria		
Jars	Type 1A	Neckless; prominent shoulder
	Type 1B	Neckless; square rim
	Type 1C	Neckless; everted rim
	Type 2A	Short neck; everted simple rim
	Type 2B	Short neck; everted thickened rim
	Type 2C	Short neck; angular rim

SHAPE/FORM	TYPE	FEATURE
	Type 3	Thickened everted rim
	Type 4A	Short neck; short-collared square rim
	Type 4B	Short neck; short-collared triangular rim
	Type 4C	Short neck; short-collared rim, prominent edge
	Type 5A	Tall neck; short-collared square rim
	Type 5B	Tall neck; short-collared triangular rim
	Type 6A	Long-collared rim: uniform thickness
	Type 6B	Long-collared rim; prominent lower edge
	Type 7A	Neck ridge; simple lip
	Type 7B	Neck ridge; overhanging lip
Pithoi		
Cooking pots	Type 1	Simple rim
	Type 2	Flared rim
	Type 3	Ledge rim
	Type 4	Concave rim
	Type 5	Bevelled rim
	Type 6	Grooved rim
	Type 7	"Galilean"
	Type 8	Thickened lip
Casseroles	Type 1	Constricted neck; overhanging rim
	Type 2	Upright wall; overhanging rim
	Type 3	Interior flange; overhanging rim
	Type 4	Wide mouth; prominent shoulder
Cooking bowls	Type 1	Narrow ledge rim
	Type 2	Angled broad rim
	Type 3	"Galilean" bowl
Frying pans		
Lids		
Unguentaria	Type 1	Squat; rounded body
	Type 2	Slender; angular body
	Fragments	
Ointment pot		

PLATES AND BOWLS
Fishplates (PW 1–39)

As with the black-gloss form, fishplates in plain ware are commonly encountered at Pella with the great majority (Type 1 and, apart from **PW 15**, Type 2) from Jannaeus Destruction (Hellenistic 3C) levels. The one exception is those fishplates with narrow rims – angled or drooping (Types 3 and 4: **PW 30–5**) – that are largely confined to the Early Roman levels on Tell Husn.

Many of the plain ware fishplates have a raised ring around the central depression – a feature seen at Tel Dor and elsewhere and regarded as "typical of the 2nd century BCE" (Guz-Zilberstein 1995: 291). At Pella this characteristic certainly carries into the early first century BC as demonstrated by fishplates such as **PW 2–3**, **PW 5** and **PW 10** from Jannaeus Destruction (Hellenistic 3C) contexts.

With relatively few exceptions, the vessels are in the very common Coarse Light Brown ware that remains the dominant ware for fishplates (and other small shapes) throughout the Pre-Jannaeus Destruction, Jannaeus Destruction and Early Roman phases.

Table 2.16. Distribution of fishplates by types, wares, phases.

		BROAD ANGLED RIM (TYPE 1)	BROAD DROOPING RIM (TYPE 2)	NARROW ANGLED RIM (TYPE 3)	NARROW DROOPING RIM (TYPE 4)	BASES
Ware	Coarse Light Brown	13	15	2	4	3
	Hard Pale	0	1	0	0	0
	Miscellaneous	0	0	0	0	1
Phase	3A c. 200–c. 140 BC	0	1	0	0	0
	3B c. 140–c. 100 (?) BC	0	0	0	0	1
	3C c. 100 (?)–c. 80/79 BC	10 (7)	12 (3)	0 (2)	0 (1)	3
	Early Roman 63 BC–c. 135 AD	1 (residual)	0	2	4	0
	Mixed	2 (3)	3	0 (1)	0	0

Broad angled rim (Type 1)

PW 1. CN 3451.
IVD 10.10. Hellenistic 3C.
Part of base, wall, rim. H 0.045; D rim (est.) 0.20.
Reddish-yellow clay 7.5YR 8/6. Coarse Light Brown.
Mottled red-black slip over interior, exterior.
Parallels: Gadara/Umm Qais (Kerner 1997: fig. 12.3);
Tel Michal (Fischer 1989: fig. 13.2.16, 2nd c. BC).

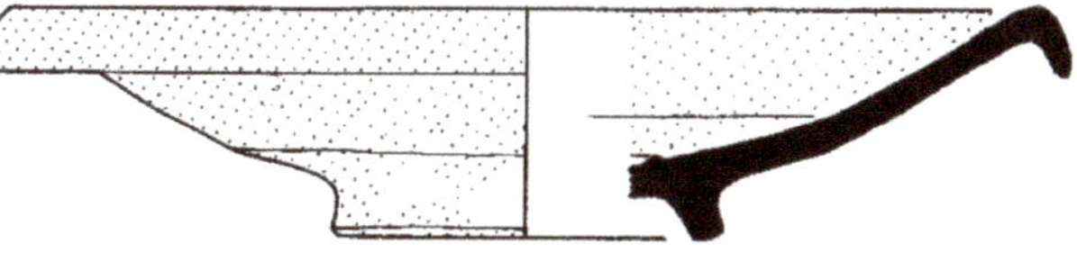

PW 2. CN 3448.
IVD 10.10. Hellenistic 3C.
Complete. H 0.045; D rim 0.20. Very pale brown clay
10YR 8/4; grey core. Coarse Light Brown.
Red slip over interior; mottled red-black slip over exterior.

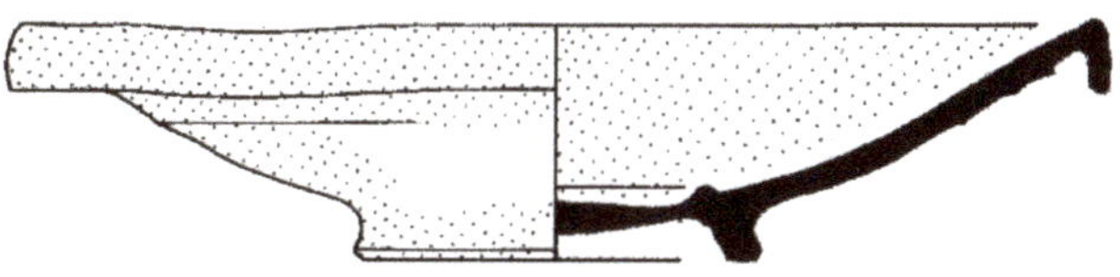

PW 3. CN 6528.
IVD 13.10. Hellenistic 3C.
Part of wall, rim. PH 0.025; PL 0.075; D rim (est.)
0.21. Yellowish-brown 10YR 5/4. Coarse Light Brown.
Thin patchy red slip over interior, exterior.
Parallel: Jerusalem (Geva 2003: pl. 5.1.34, 2nd c. BC).

PW 4. CN 4298.
IVD 10.10. Hellenistic 3C.
Missing base. PH 0.36; D rim (est.) 0.20. Reddish-
yellow clay 7.5YR 6/6. Coarse Light Brown.
Yellow-brown slip 5YR 5/8 over interior.

PW 5. CN 6979.
XXIIIA 11.1. Hellenistic 3C.
Part of wall, rim. H 0.055; PL 0.165; D rim (est.)
0.20. Light yellowish-brown clay 10YR 6/4. Coarse
Light Brown.

PW 6. CN 7797.
XXIIIA 71.1. Mixed Context.
Multiple joining fragments of rim, wall, base. H.055;
W.19; D rim (est.).24; D base.08. Light yellowish-
brown clay 10YR 6/4. Coarse Light Brown.

PW 7. CN 6541.
XXIIIA 11.1. Hellenistic 3C.
Complete. H 0.05; D rim 0.195. Very pale brown clay
10YR 7/3. Coarse Light Brown.

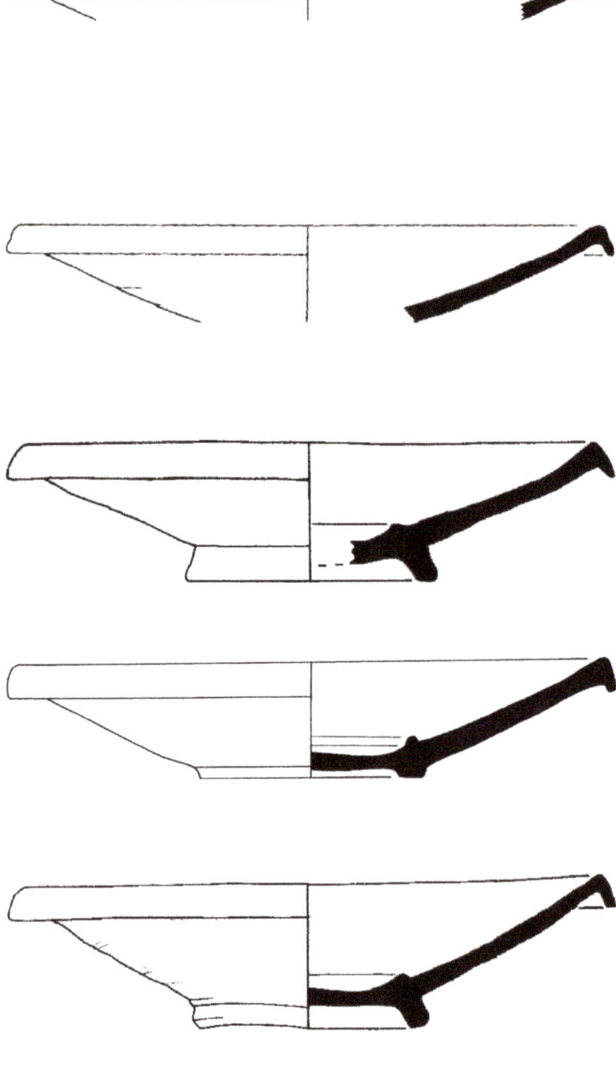

PW 8. CN 6954.
XXIIIA 11.1. Hellenistic 3C.
Multiple joining fragments missing part of wall and
rim. H 0.05; D rim (est.) 0.19. Very pale brown clay
10YR 7/4. Coarse Light Brown.
Orange-brown slip over interior.

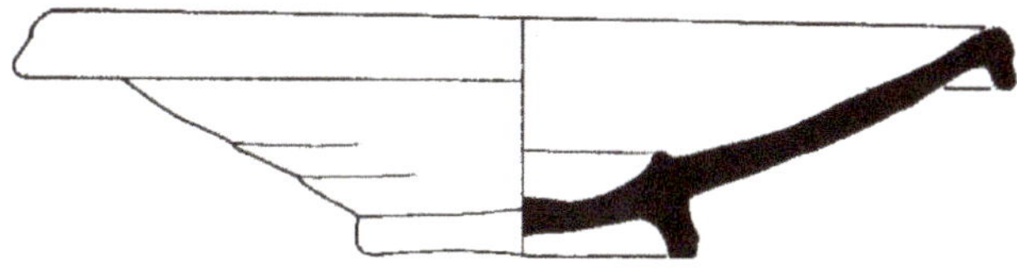

PW 9. CN 0058.
IIIB/C 1.3. Hellenistic 3C.
Part of base, wall, rim. H 0.04; PL 0.11; D rim
(est.) 0.21. Reddish-yellow clay 5YR 7/8. Coarse Light
Brown.
Red slip over exterior.

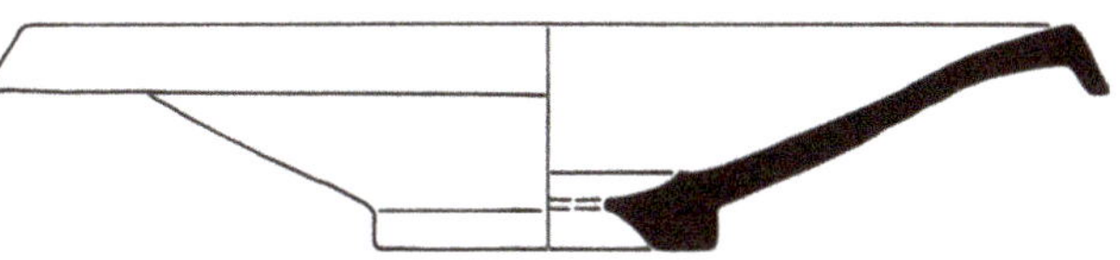

PW 10. CN 6980.
XXIIIA 11.1. Hellenistic 3C.
Part of wall, rim. H 0.05; PL 0.195; D rim (est.)
0.23. Light yellowish-brown clay 10YR 6/4. Coarse
Light Brown.
Thin brown slip over rim and interior.

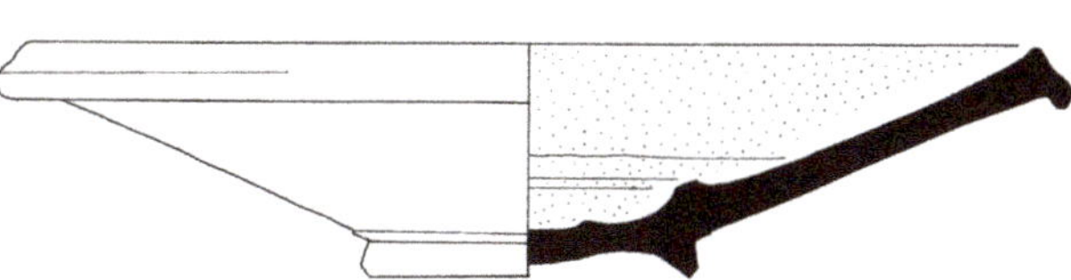

PW 11. CN 6955.
XXIIIA 11.1. Hellenistic 3C.
Multiple joining fragments forming complete vessel.
H 0.05; D rim 0.19. Brown clay 10YR 5/3. Coarse
Light Brown.
Orange-brown slip over interior.

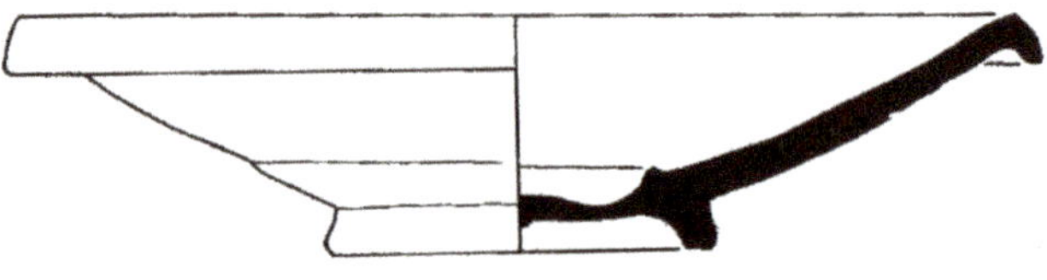

PW 12. CN 3064.
XIA/B1.5. Early Roman (residual).
Part of wall, rim. PH 0.015; D rim (est.) 0.18. Light
yellowish-brown clay 10YR 6/4. Coarse Light Brown.
Patchy red-brown slip over interior, exterior. Shallow
interior groove separates wall from markedly down-
turned rim.

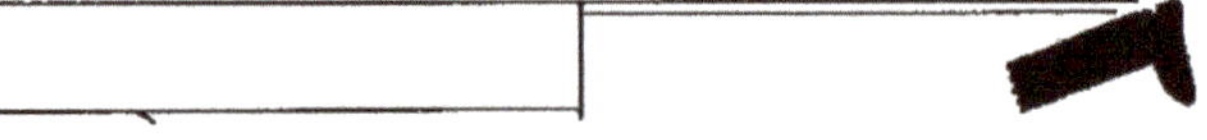

PW 13. CN 0401.
IIIB/C 1.14. Mixed Context.
Part of base, wall, rim. PH 0.03; D rim (est.) 0.18.
Very pale brown clay 10YR 8/4. Coarse Light Brown.
Flattened string-cut base; shallow internal depression.
Parallels: Marisa (Levine 2003: fig. 6.2.29); Shechem
(N.L. Lapp 2008: pl. 3.28.26, unstratified).

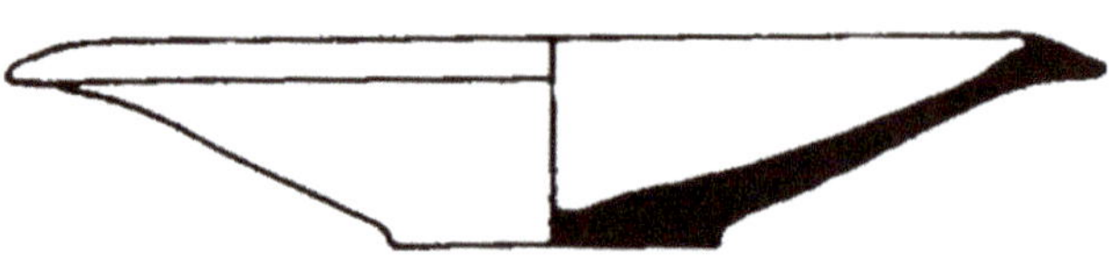

Broad drooping rim (Type 2)

PW 14. CN 7371.
XXXIVF 3.2. Mixed Context.
Two joining fragments of base, wall, rim. PL 0.01;
D rim (est.) 0.21. Reddish-yellow clay 5YR 6/8. Large
white inclusions. Hard Pale.

PW 15. CN 7218.
XXVIIIB 10.1. Hellenistic 3A.
Part of base, wall, rim. H 0.04; D rim (est.) 0.18.
Reddish-yellow clay 5YR 6/6. Coarse Light Brown.

PW 16. CN 0993.
IIIB/C 1.13. Mixed Context.
Part of wall, rim. PH 0.025; D rim (est.) 0.14. Reddish-
yellow clay 7.5YR 7/6. Coarse Light Brown.

PW 17. CN 4302.
IVD 10.10. Hellenistic 3C.
Part of wall, rim. PH 0.03; D rim (est.) 0.18. Reddish-
yellow clay 5YR 7/6. Coarse Light Brown.
Red brown slip over interior, exterior.

PW 18. CN 6568.
XXIIIA 10.5. Hellenistic 3C.
Complete. H 0.06; D rim 0.21. Reddish-yellow clay
5YR 6/8. Coarse Light Brown.

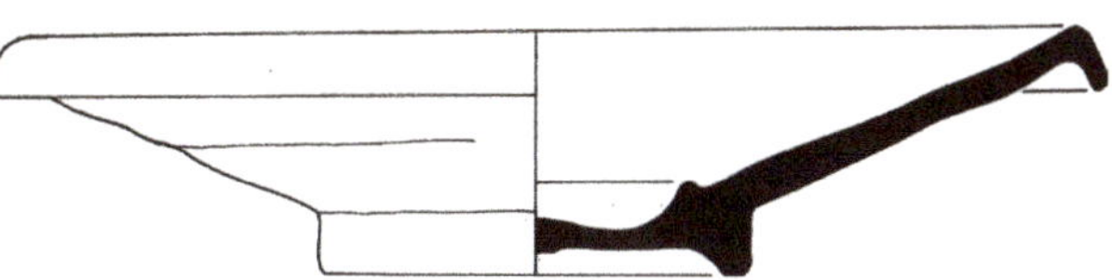

PW 19. CN 6969.
XXIIIA 11.2. Hellenistic 3C.
Multiple joining fragments forming complete vessel.
H 0.045; D rim 0.19. Very pale brown clay 10YR 7/4.
Coarse Light Brown.
Parallel: Kedesh (Levantine Ceramics Project: n.d.
K00P157, 200–140 BC).

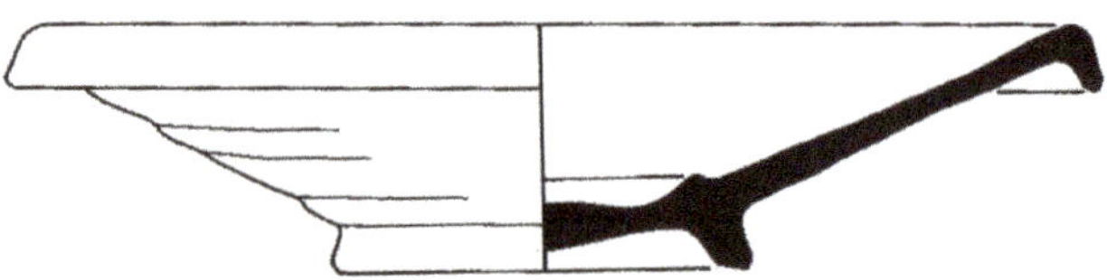

PW 20. CN 4303.
IVD 10.10. Hellenistic 3C.
Part of wall, rim. H 0.025; D rim (est.) 0.19. Light
grey clay 10YR 7/2. Coarse Light Brown.
Red slip over interior, exterior.

PW 21. CN 3450.
IVD 10.10. Hellenistic 3C.
Complete. H 0.06; D rim 0.21. Reddish-yellow clay
5YR 7/6. Coarse Light Brown.
Red slip over interior; mottled red-black slip over
exterior.
Parallel: Samaria (Crowfoot et al. 1957: fig. 54.9).

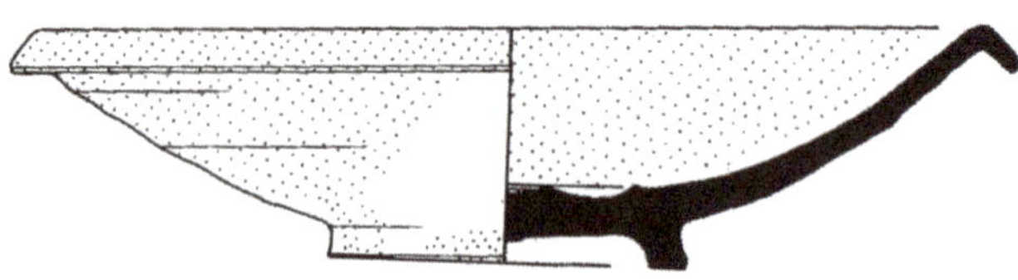

PW 22. CN 6639.
XXIIIA 10.7. Hellenistic 3C.
Part of wall, rim. PH 0.035; PL 0.10; D rim (est.) 0.21.
Reddish-yellow clay 5YR 6/8. Coarse Light Brown.
Thin patchy red slip over interior, exterior.

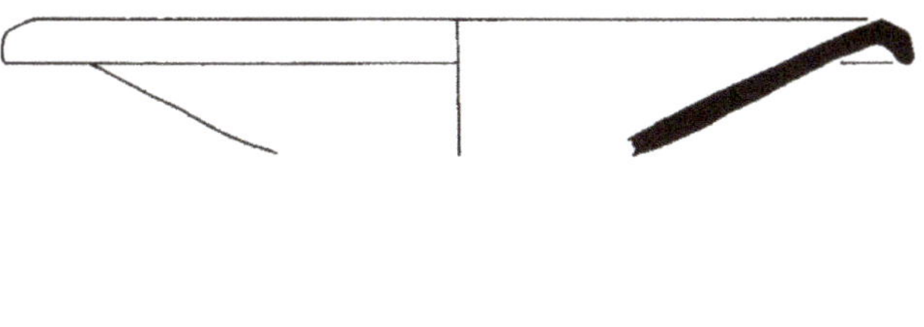

PW 23. CN 7045.
XXIIIA 105.1. Hellenistic 3C.
Part of wall, rim. PH 0.025; PL 0.055; D rim (est.) 0.21.
Reddish-yellow clay 7.5YR 7/6. Coarse Light Brown.
Streaky reddish-brown wash on exterior.
Parallel: Gezer (Gitin 1990: pl. 40.7, late 2nd c. BC).

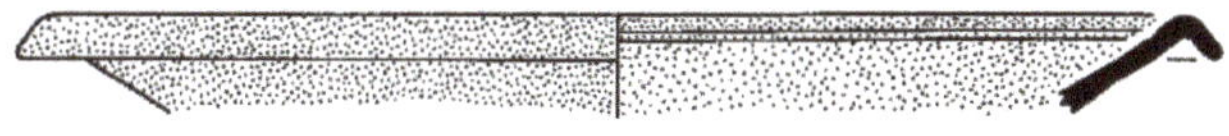

PW 24. CN 7025.
XXIIIA 100.3. Hellenistic 3C.
Part of wall, rim. PH 0.03; D rim (est.) 0.18. Very pale
brown clay 10YR 8/3. Coarse Light Brown.
Thin orange-red slip over interior, exterior; dull black
on exterior rim.
Parallel: Machaerus (Corbo and Loffreda 1981:
fig. 36.3).

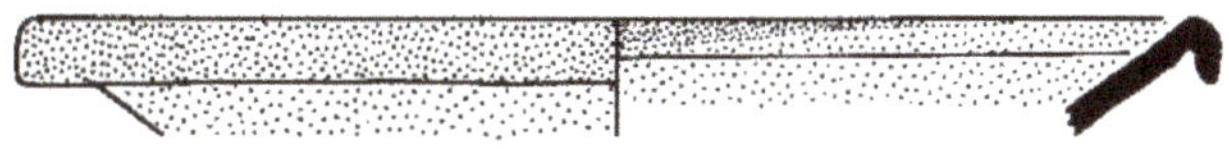

PW 25. CN 4304.
IVD 10.10. Hellenistic 3C.
Part of wall, rim. PH 0.03; D rim (est.) 0.20. Light
brownish-grey clay 10YR 6/2. Coarse Light Brown.
Purple-brown slip over interior, exterior.
Parallels: Kedesh (Levantine Ceramics Project: n.d.
K08P069, 200–140 BC); Machaerus (Corbo and
Loffreda 1981: fig. 36.2).

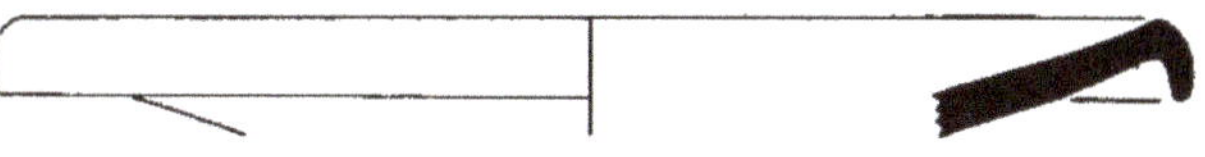

PW 26. CN 6982.
XXIIIA 11.1. Hellenistic 3C.
Base, part of wall, rim. H 0.05; PL 0.02; D rim
(est.) 0.20. Light yellowish-brown clay 10YR 6/4.
Coarse Light Brown.
Thin brown slip over interior, exterior.
Parallels: Marisa (Levine 2003: fig. 6.3.49); Philoteria/
Bet Yerah (Tal and Reshef 2017: fig. 3.42.4); Tell
es-Sa'idiyeh (Pritchard 1985: fig. 19.7).

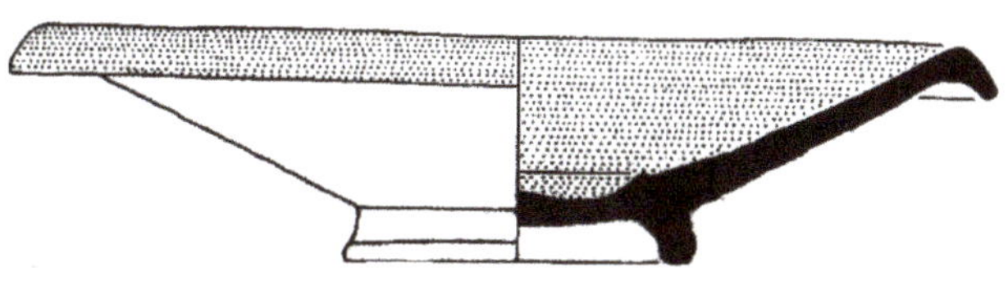

PW 27. CN 6967.
XXIIIA 11.1. Hellenistic 3C.
Complete. H 0.045; D rim 0.19. Reddish-yellow clay
7.5YR 6/6. Coarse Light Brown.
Orange-brown slip over interior, rim.

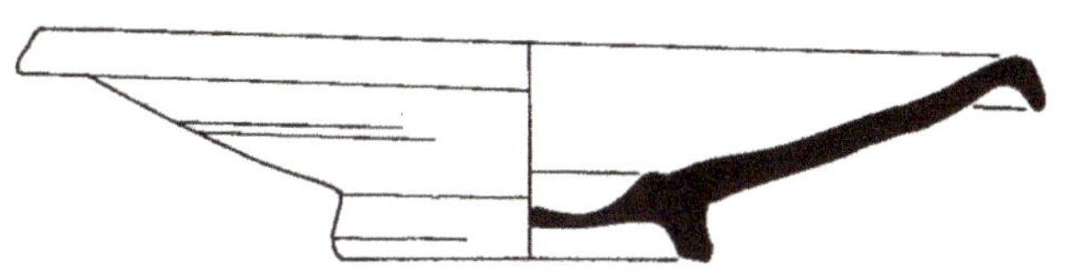

PW 28. CN 6653.
IIIP 24.18. Mixed Context.
Part of base, wall, rim. H 0.035; PL 0.08; D rim (est.)
0.18. Yellowish-brown 10YR 5/4. Coarse Light Brown.
Mottled brown-black slip over interior, exterior.

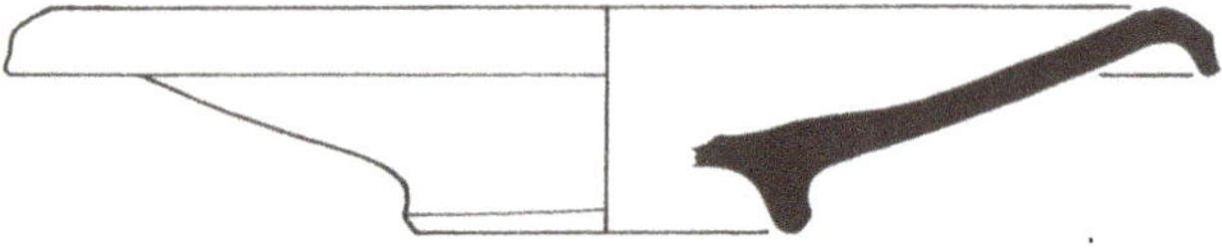

PW 29. CN 7834. (Plates 57 and 58)
XXIIID 63.2. Hellenistic 3C.
Missing two body fragments. H 0.07; D rim 0.21.
Reddish-yellow clay 7.5YR 7/6. Coarse Light Brown.
Carelessly made.

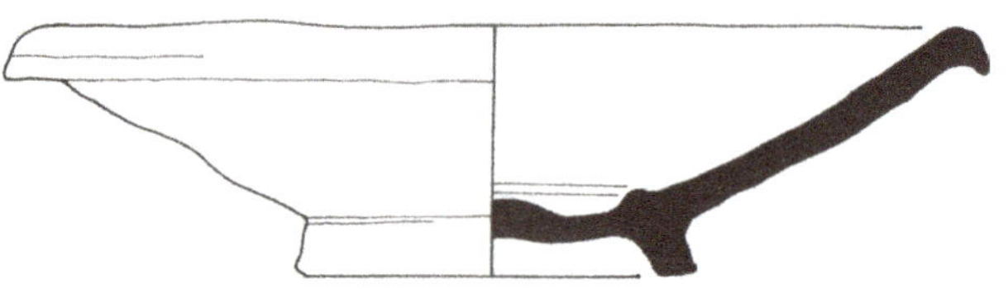

Narrow angled rim (Type 3)

The two catalogued fishplates of this type were recovered from Early Roman deposits although non-catalogued
sherds are present in very small numbers in Jannaeus Destruction layers. They are of smaller dimension than
those of Types 1 and 2, whilst the rim, sharply angled, is much narrower and may project on the interior.
This latter feature is made more noticeable by the presence of an interior groove between rim and upper
wall – a feature more characteristic of Attic fishplates.

PW 30. CN 2618.
XIA/B 1.5. Early Roman 1.
Part of wall, rim. PH 0.04; D rim (est.) 0.15. Reddish-
yellow clay 5YR 6/8. Coarse Light Brown.
Thin matt red-brown slip over interior, exterior.

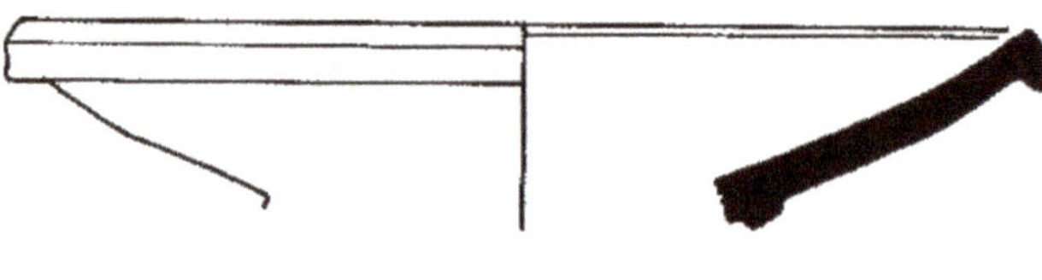

PW 31. CN 2953.
XIA/B 1.5. Early Roman 1.
Part of wall, rim. PH 0.035; D rim (est.) 0.155.
Reddish-yellow clay 7.5YR 6/6. Coarse Light Brown.

Narrow drooping rim (Type 4)

Like the previous type, the rim, although drooping rather than angular, is exceedingly narrow and the
dimensions small with a faint interior groove between upper wall and rim. The four catalogued specimens,
along with the majority of non-catalogued examples, come from Early Roman contexts.

A similar tendency towards a marked narrowing of the rim and smaller dimensions, as seen on this
type and Type 3, is not observed amongst fishplates from Tel Anafa, Tel Dor, Samaria, Gezer or elsewhere
in Palestine, though an isolated example was recovered from Stratum I at Tell es-Sa'idiyeh (Pritchard 1985:
fig. 19.3).

PW 32. CN 2993.
XIA/B 1.2/5. Early Roman 1.
Part of wall, rim. PH 0.025; D rim (est.) 0.18. Reddish-
yellow clay 7.5YR 6/8. Coarse Light Brown.
Thin black-brown slip over interior, exterior.

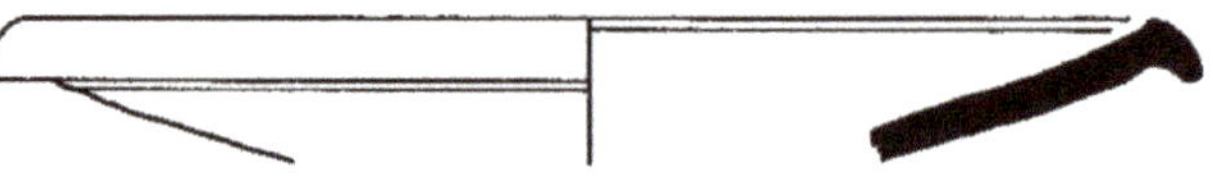

PW 33. CN 2941.
XIA/B 1.5. Early Roman 1.
Part of wall, rim. PH 0.03; D rim (est.) 0.16. Very pale brown clay 10YR 8/3. Coarse Light Brown.
Thin black slip over interior.

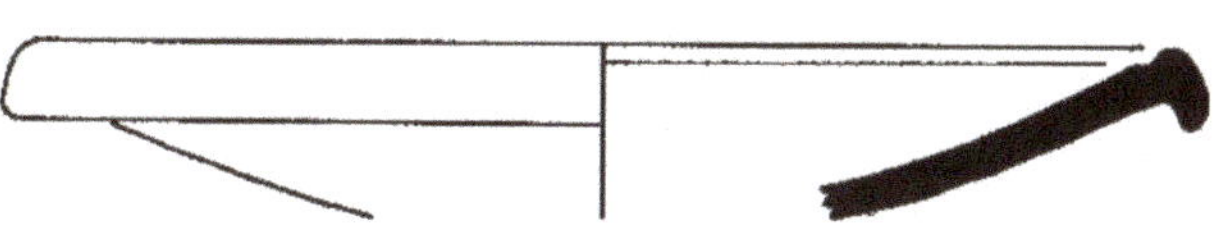

PW 34. CN 2962.
XIA/B 1.5. Early Roman 1.
Part of wall, rim. PH 0.03; D rim (est.) 0.16. Very pale brown clay 10YR 8/4. Coarse Light Brown.

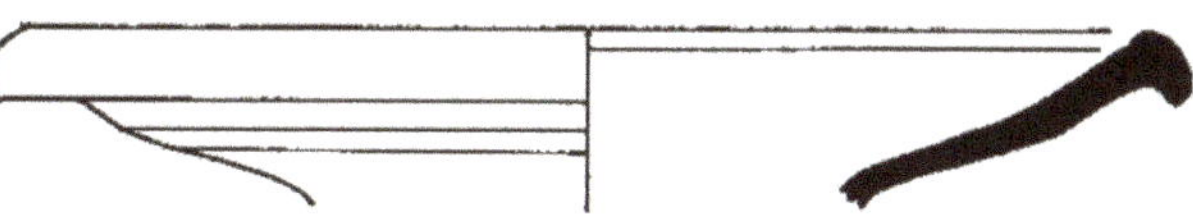

PW 35. CN 2952.
XIA/B 1.5. Early Roman 1.
Part of wall, rim. PH 0.03; D rim (est.) 0.16. Reddish-yellow clay 7.5YR 6/6. Coarse Light Brown. Black slip over interior.
Parallel: Tell es-Sa'idiyeh (Pritchard 1985: fig. 19.3).

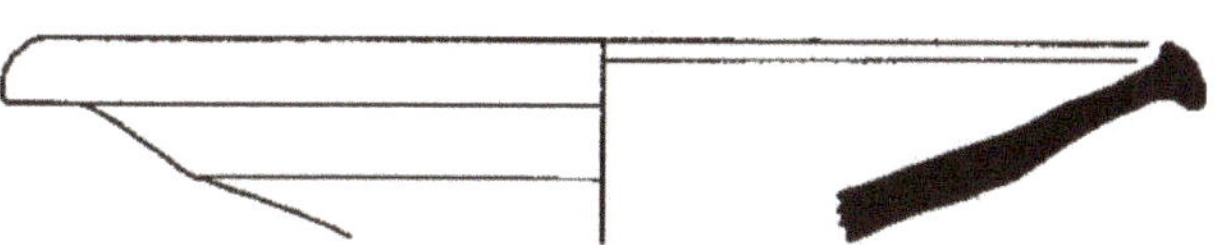

Bases

PW 36. CN 4322.
IVD 10.12. Hellenistic 3C.
Base. PH 9.04; D 0.075. Pink clay 7.5YR 7/4; light brownish grey core. Coarse Light Brown.
Patchy red slip over interior, exterior. Wide ring base. Ridged central depression.

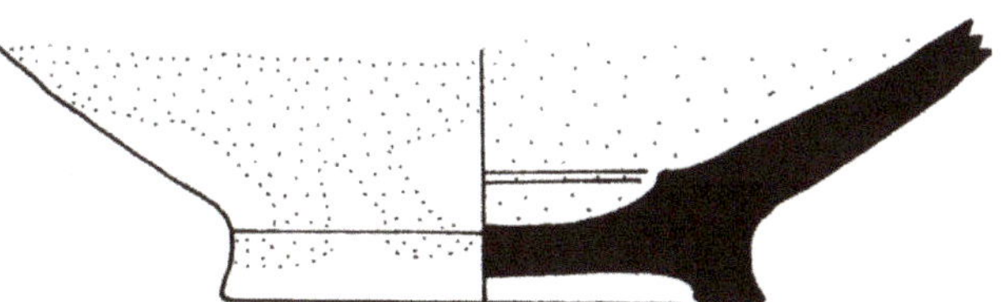

PW 37. CN 7042.
XXIIIA 104.1. Hellenistic 3C.
Base, part of wall. PH 0.04; PL 0.125. D base 0.07. Very pale brown clay 10YR 8/3. Coarse Light Brown.
Dull orange-brown slip over interior, patchily applied to exterior. Ring base. Ridged central depression.

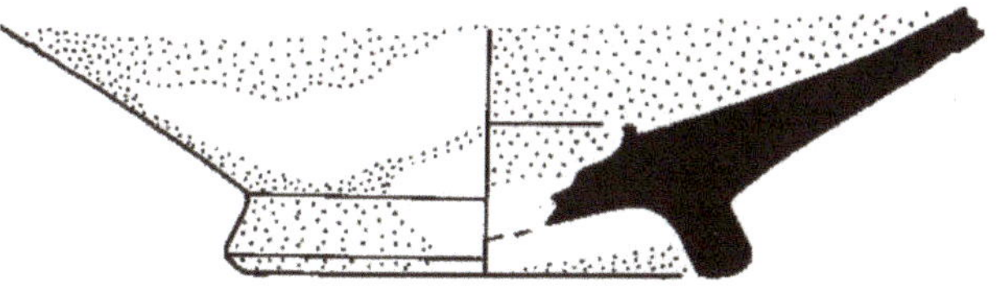

PW 38. CN 4323.
IVD 10.12. Hellenistic 3C.
Base, part of wall. PH 0.045; PL 0.18. Pink clay 7.5YR 7/4; light brownish grey core 2.5Y 6/2.
Black-brown slip over interior. Ring base. Ridged central depression.

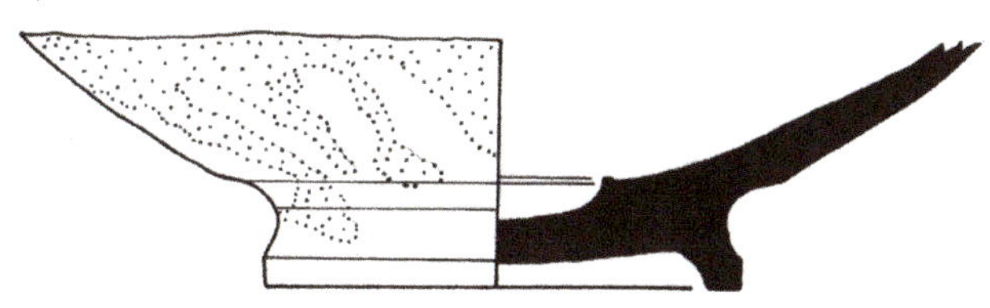

PW 39. CN 6533.
IIIP 24.2. Hellenistic 3B.
Base, part of wall. PH 0.035; D base 0.03. Very pale
brown clay 10YR 8/2. Coarse Light Brown.
Raised flat base; interior depression.

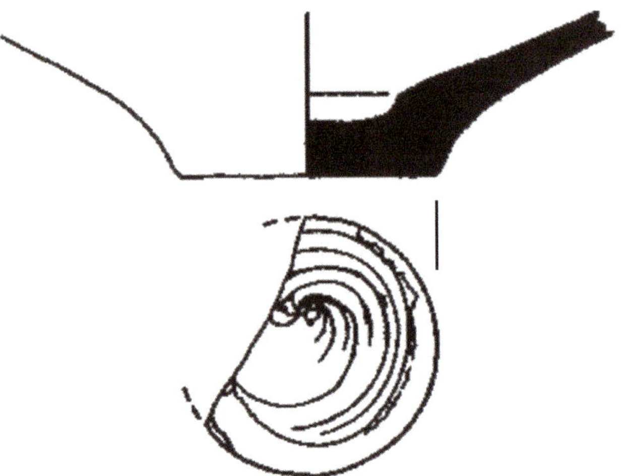

Plates: thickened rim (PW 40–86)

Plates with thickened rims are relatively uncommon at Pella amongst the fine wares; the shape is well represented in plain wares, particularly in Coarse Light Brown in the Hellenistic 3C and Early Roman levels. The thickened rim may either be "simple" – that is, without a noticeable undercutting – or markedly, and deliberately, undercut on the interior.

Table 2.17. Distribution of plates by types, wares, phases.

		THICKENED SIMPLE RIM (TYPE 1)	THICKENED UNDERCUT RIM (TYPE 2)	UPRIGHT RIM
Ware	Coarse Light Brown	16	18	2
	Hard Pale	2	4	0
	Metallic Buff	1	0	0
	Miscellaneous	2	2	0
Phase	2B c. 220–c. 200 BC	0 (4)	0	0
	3A c. 200–c. 140 BC	6	4	0
	3B c. 140–c. 100 (?) BC	0	3	0
	3C c. 100 (?)–c. 80/79 BC	2	8	2
	Early Roman 63 BC–c. 135 AD	5	0 (16)	0
	Mixed	8 (4)	9	0

Thickened simple rim (Type 1)

Plain ware plates of the thickened simple rim form, seen at Pella in **PW 40–60**, do not appear at Gezer nor are they seen at Samaria, although there is some similarity with the "spatter grooved rim" saucers from the Hellenistic 2A–2C deposits at Tel Anafa (Berlin 1997a: 78–9). At Tel Dor they are represented by those plates with flat-rolled grooved rims of Type BL 5c (Guz-Zilberstein 1995: 293) with the Dor specimens from earlier contexts and more carefully made than the Pella examples.

PW 40. CN 7372.
XXXIVF 3.2. Mixed Context.
Four joining fragments missing part of rim, wall. D base 0.08; D rim 9.21. Reddish-yellow clay 7.5YR 6/6. Coarse Light Brown.
Ring base.
Parallel: ʿAkko-Ptolemais (Berlin and Stone 2016: fig. 9.25.8, 1st c. BC).

PW 41. CN 7382.
XXXIVF 5.1. Mixed Context.
Part of base, wall, rim. PL 0.09; D rim (est.) 0.25. Brown clay 7.5YR 5/4. Occasional white inclusions. Hard Pale.
Ring base.

PW 42. CN 7455.
XXVIIIB 13.9. Hellenistic 3A.
Part of wall, rim. PH 0.03; D rim (est.) 0.15. Pink clay 7.5YR 8/3. Coarse Light Brown.
Parallel: ʿAkko-Ptolemais (Berlin and Stone 2016: fig. 9.9.3, late 3rd–mid-2nd c. BC).

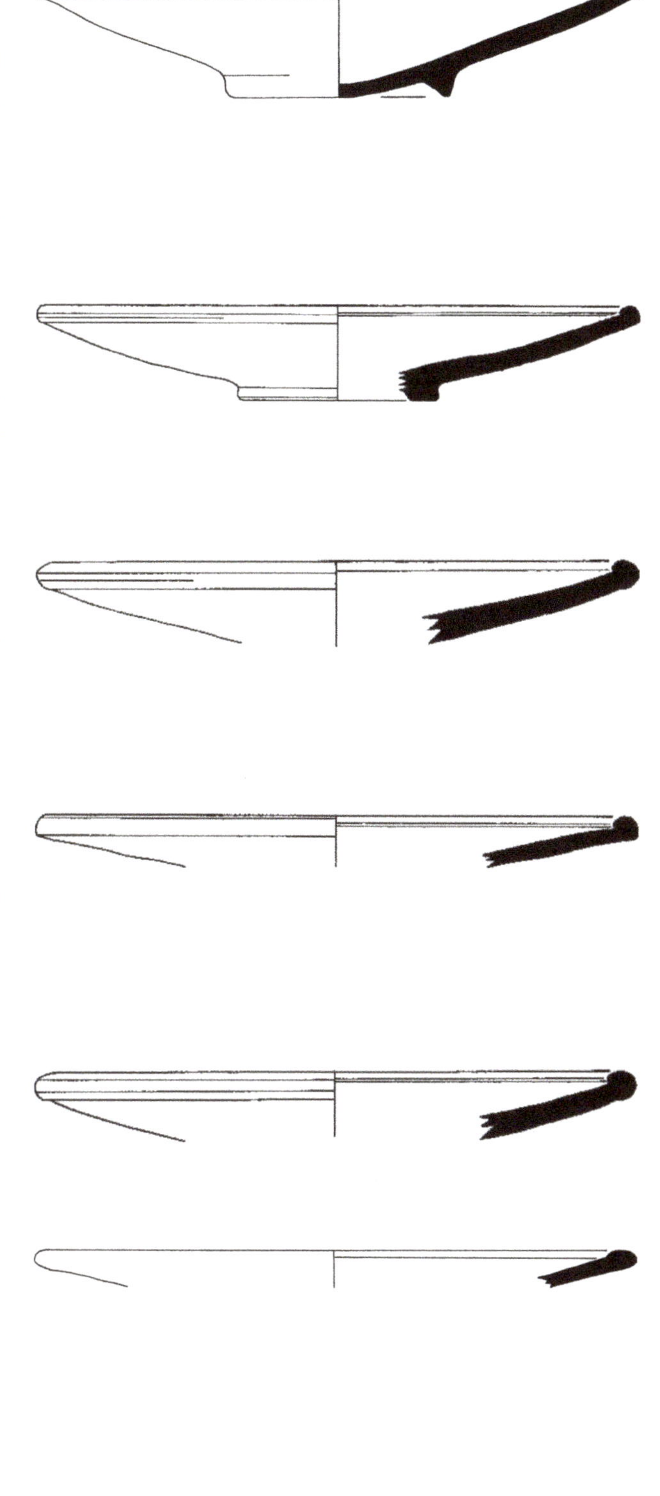

PW 43. CN 7212.
XXVIIIB 13.17. Hellenistic 3A.
Part of wall, rim. PH 0.01; D rim (est.) 0.15. Very pale brown clay 10YR 7/3. Coarse Light Brown.
Dull, thin, patchy brown slip over interior, exterior.
Parallel: Shechem (N.L. Lapp 1985: fig. 1b.37).

PW 44. CN 7434.
XXVIIIB 13.3. Hellenistic 3A.
Part of wall, rim. PH 0.025; D rim (est.) 0.15. Pale red clay 2.5YR 7/3. Coarse Light Brown.

PW 45. CN 1622.
IIIB/C. 1.21. Mixed Context.
Part of wall, rim. PH 0.02; PL 0.04; D rim (est.) 0.18. Very pale brown clay 10YR 8/4. Metallic Buff.
Parallels: Hesban (Gerber 2012: 206, fig. 3.7.19); Shechem (N.L. Lapp 2008: pl. 3.28.24, 190–150 BC).

PW 46. CN 7430.
XXVIIIB 13.2. Hellenistic 3A.
Part of wall, rim. PH 0.02; D rim (est.) 0.165. Very pale brown clay 10YR 8/3.
Parallels: Shechem (N.L. Lapp 2008: pl. 3.28.27, 190–150 BC); Tel Dor (Guz-Zilberstein 1995: fig. 6.69:6, 375–300 BC).

PW 47. CN 7429.
XXVIIIB 13.2. Hellenistic 3A.
Part of wall, rim. PH 0.02; D rim (est.) 0.21. Yellowish-red clay 5YR 5/6. Coarse Light Brown.
Patchy thin red slip over exterior.
Parallels: Jerusalem (Geva 2003: pl. 5.3.23, late 2nd–1st c. BC); Tel Dor (Guz-Zilberstein 1995: fig. 6.52:6, 275–150 BC).

PW 48. CN 7849.
XXXIIY 1.2. Hellenistic 3A.
Part of wall, rim. PH 0.02; PL 0.09; D rim (est.) 0.19. Reddish-yellow clay 5YR 7/6. Coarse Light Brown.

PW 49. CN 0535.
IIIB/C 1.22. Mixed Context.
Part of base, wall, rim. PH 0.05; D rim (est.) 0.17. Very pale brown clay 10YR 7/4. Coarse Light Brown
Thin brown slip over exterior.
Parallel: Samaria (Crowfoot et al. 1957: figs 37.9; 51.5).

PW 50. CN 6865.
IIIB/C 1.14. Mixed Context.
Part of wall, rim. PH 0.04; D rim (est.) 0.18. Light brown clay 7.5YR 6/4. Coarse Light Brown.

PW 51. CN 0171.
IIIB/C 1.11/1.19. Mixed Context.
Part of wall, rim. PH 0.04; D rim (est.) 0.17. Reddish-yellow clay 5YR 7/6. Coarse Light Brown.
Thin red slip over upper interior, exterior.
Parallel: Jerusalem (Sandhaus 2013: fig. 4.1:10, second half of 2nd c. BC).

PW 52. CN 0656.
IIIB/C 1.14. Mixed Context.
Part of wall, rim. PH 0.035; D rim (est.) 0.19. Very pale brown clay 10YR 7/4. Coarse Light Brown.
Thin red slip over rim, upper interior.

PW 53. CN 4320.
IVD 10.12. Hellenistic 3C.
Part of wall, rim. PH 0.04; D rim (est.) 0.18. Very pale brown clay 10YR 7/3. Coarse Light Brown.
Worn yellow-brown slip over interior, rim.

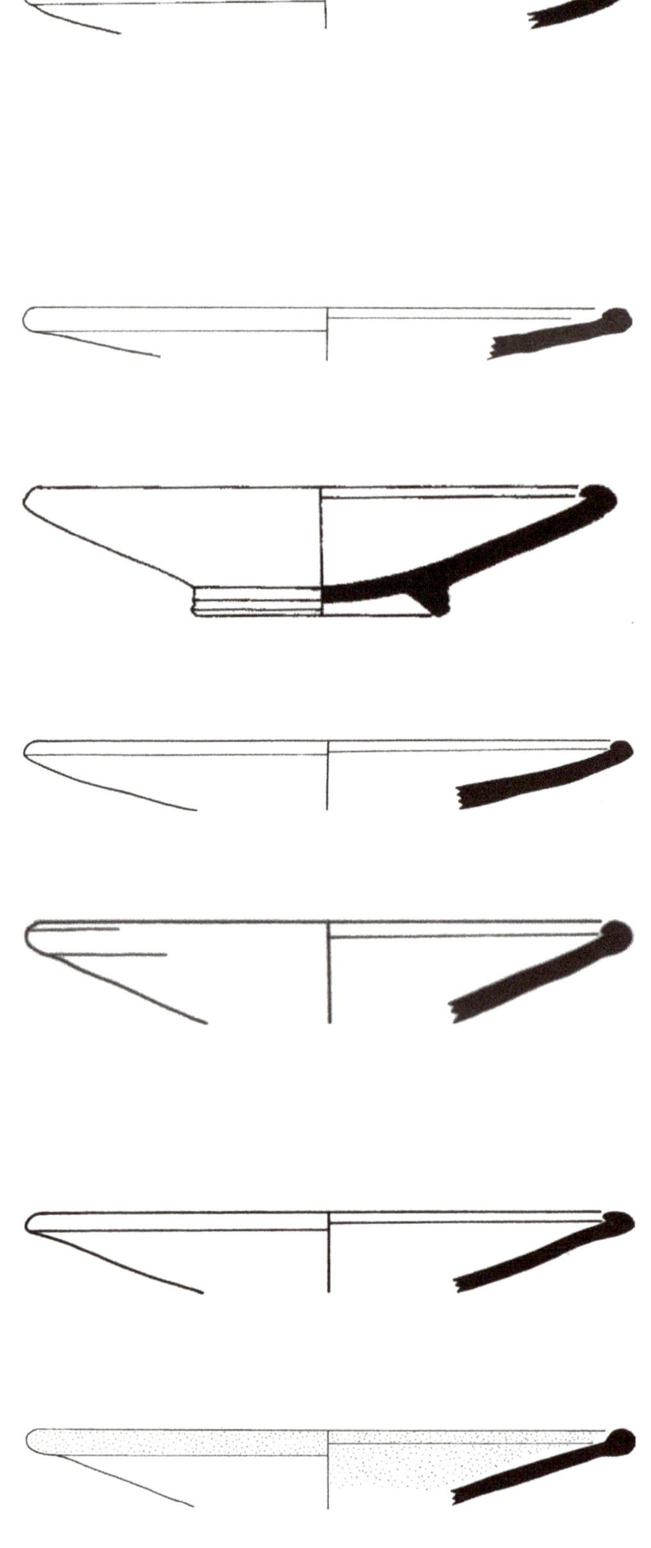

PW 54. CN 7041.
XXIIIA 104.1. Hellenistic 3C.
Part of wall, rim. PH 0.04; PL 0.045; D rim (est.) 0.19.
Very pale brown clay 10YR 7/4. Coarse Light Brown.
Parallels: Jericho (Netzer and Meyers 1977: fig. 6.1);
Kedesh (Levantine Ceramics Project: n.d. K06P075,
332–167 BC).

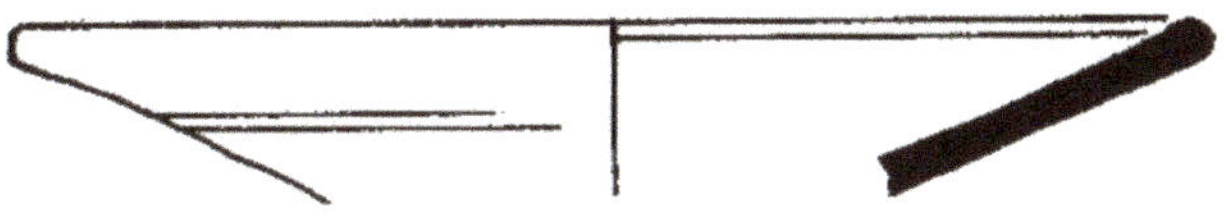

PW 55. CN 2617.
XIA/B 1.5. Early Roman 1.
Part of wall, rim. PH 0.025; PL 0.035; D rim (est.) 0.12.
Reddish-yellow clay 7.5YR 6/6. Coarse Light Brown.
Thin matt red-brown slip over interior, exterior.
Parallel: Jerusalem (Rahmani 1967: fig. 10.4).

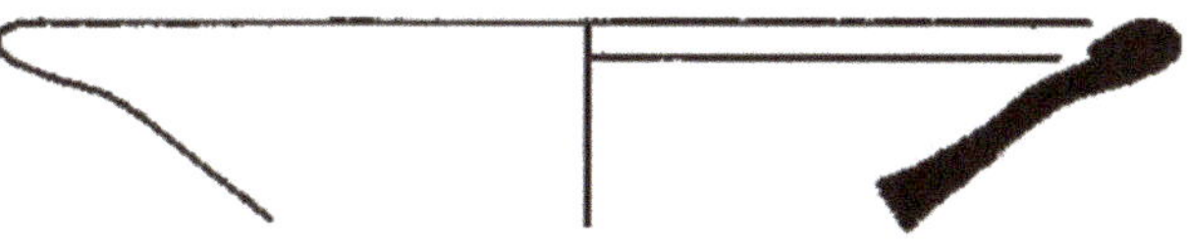

PW 56. CN 3074.
XIA/B 1.5. Early Roman 1.
Part of wall, rim. PH 0.035; PL 0.085; D rim (est.) 0.16.
Light brown clay 7.5YR 6/4. White inclusions.
Parallels: Jericho (Netzer and Meyers 1977: fig. 6.1); Tel
Michal (Derfler 1989: fig. 14.3.2, early 1st c. AD–68 AD).

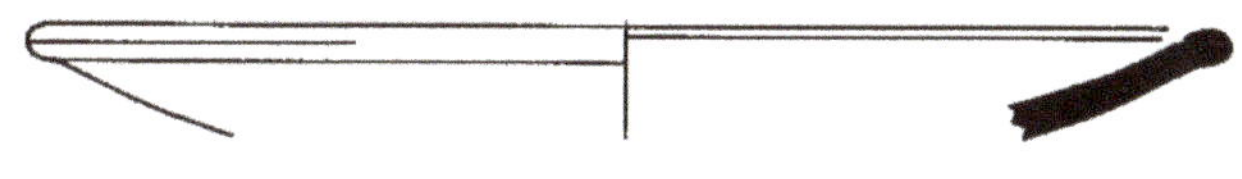

PW 57. CN 2955.
XIA/B 1.5. Early Roman 1.
Part of wall, rim. PH 0.03; PL 0.07; D rim (est.) 0.15.
Light brown clay 7.5YR 6/4. Coarse Light Brown.
Patchy red slip over interior, upper exterior.
Parallel: Tel Dor (Guz-Zilberstein 1995: fig. 6.69:6,
375–300 BC).

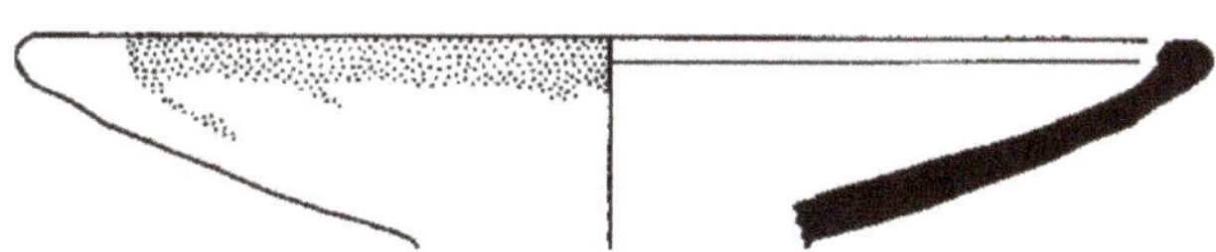

PW 58. CN 2948.
XIA/B 1.5. Early Roman 1.
Part of wall, rim. PH 0.04; D rim (est.) 0.22. Pink clay
7.5YR 7/4. Coarse Light Brown.
Red slip over interior.

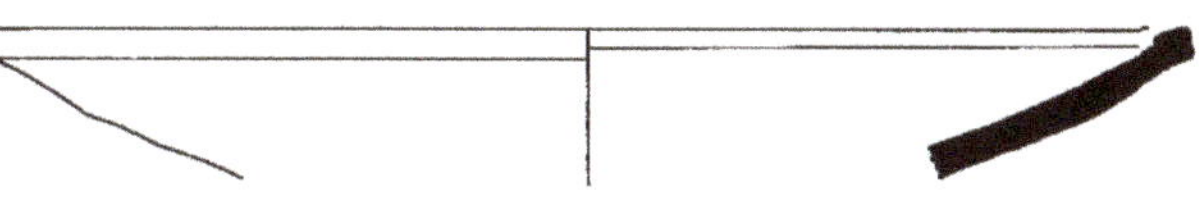

PW 59. CN 6705.
IIIP 25.20. Mixed Context.
Part of base, wall, rim. PH 0.045; D rim (est.) 0.15.
Reddish-yellow clay 7.5YR 6/6. Hard Pale.
Pale yellow slip over interior, exterior. Ring base.

PW 60. CN 7177.
XXXIVG 12.3. Early Roman 1.
Part of base, wall, rim. H 0.03; PL 0.11; D rim
(est.) 0.13. Pink clay 5YR 7/4. Coarse Light Brown.
Ring base.
Parallel: Samaria (Crowfoot et al. 1957: fig. 51.6
profile).

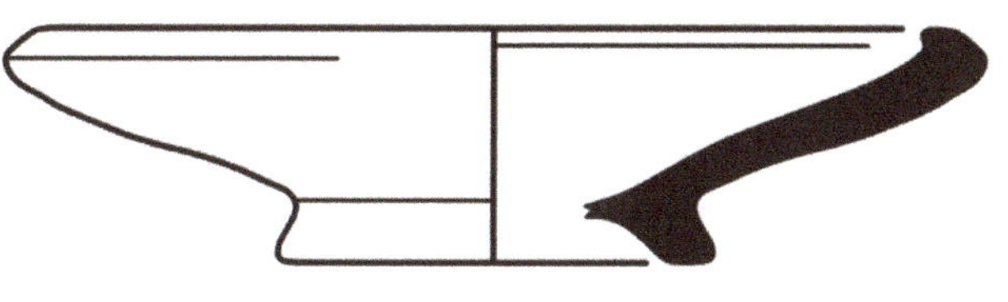

Thickened undercut rim (Type 2)

Plates of this type (**PW 61–84**) are encountered in early second-century BC (Stratum IV)[6] deposits at 'Iraq al-Amir (Zimmerman 2020b, Type 20.1) and in third-century as well as second-century BC horizons at Tel Dor (Guz-Zilberstein 1995: 292, Type 5BL 5a). At Samaria they are associated with the Hellenistic Fort Wall (c. 200–150 BC) and other structures (Crowfoot et al. 1957: figs 37:9–10; 51:5–6). They are infrequent at Gezer (Type 217) and do not appear at Tel Anafa.

There is, however, a certain variation within the type as regards the degree of undercutting on the interior of the rim. On plates such as **PW 80–1** this characteristic is only slight whereas on, for example, **PW 68–9** it is much deeper and thus clearly separates the rim from the interior wall. This latter feature is largely confined to plates of Coarse Light Brown ware. Marked undercutting of the rim is frequently seen in plain ware plates from Samaria, Tarsus and Antioch although in the latter city it tends to die out during the third century BC.[7]

PW 61. CN 7409.
XXVIIIB 10.6. Hellenistic 3A.
Part of wall, rim. PH 0.035; D rim (est.) 0.17. Very pale brown clay 10YR 7/3. Hard Pale.
Parallel: Tell es-Sa'idiyeh (Pritchard 1985: fig. 19.6).

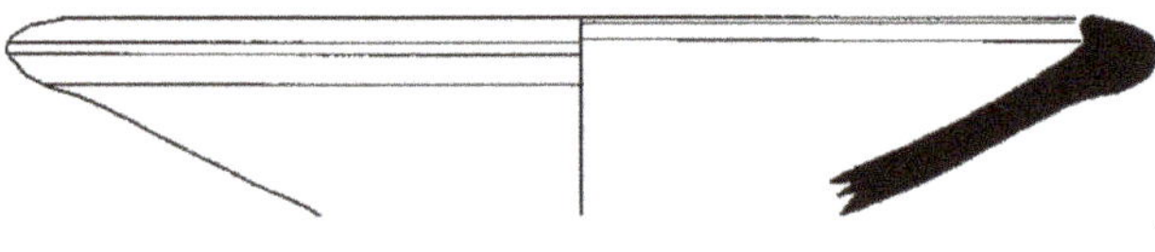

PW 62. CN 7480.
XXVIIIB 13.14. Hellenistic 3A.
Part of wall, rim. PH 0.02; D rim (est.) 0.11. Reddish-yellow clay 7.5YR 7/6.
Parallel: Sepphoris (Balouka 2013: pl. 3.8, 0–70 AD).

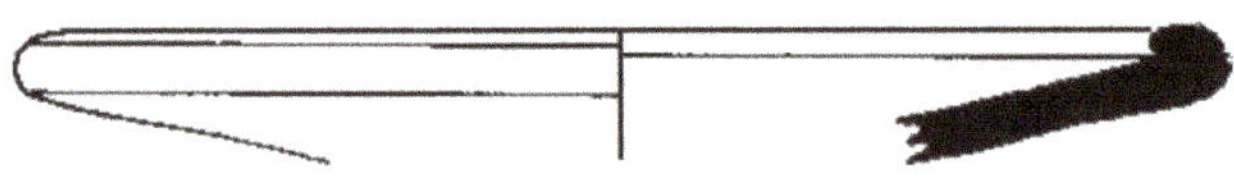

PW 63. CN 7415.
XXVIIIB 10.10. Hellenistic 3A.
Part of wall, rim. PH 0.025; D rim (est.) 0.13. Pink clay 7.5YR 7/3.
Parallels: Tell es-Sa'idiyeh (Pritchard 1985: fig. 19.6); Tel Zahara (Bar-Nathan and Gärtner 2013: fig. 3.12.105).

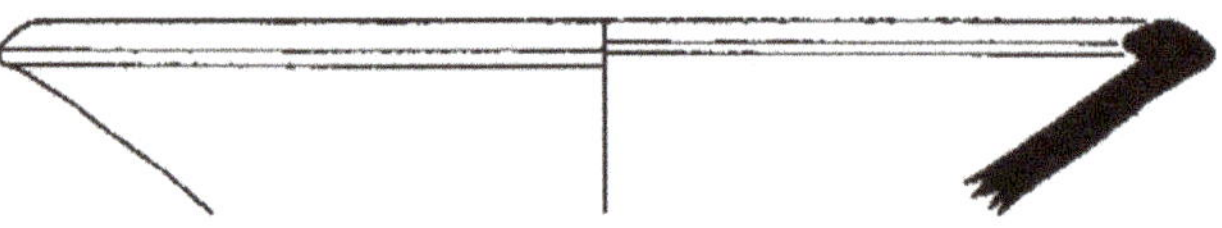

PW 64. CN 0369.
IIIB/C 1.14. Mixed Context.
Part of wall, rim. PH 0.03; D rim (est.) 0.15. Reddish-yellow clay 7.5YR 6/6. Hard Pale.
Rim projecting on interior and exterior.
Parallel: Tell Zira'a (Kenkel 2020: 37,134–5, pl.1.9: Sa3.1 upper profile).

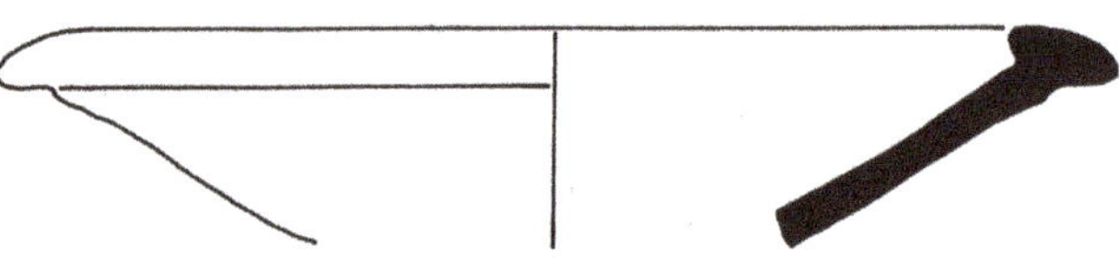

PW 65. CN 6864.
IIIB/C 1.14. Mixed Context.
Part of wall, rim. PH 0.04; PL 0.09; D rim (est.) 0.155. Reddish-yellow clay 7.5YR 6/6. Coarse Light Brown.
Parallel: Hesban (Gerber 2012: 207, fig. 3.7.21).

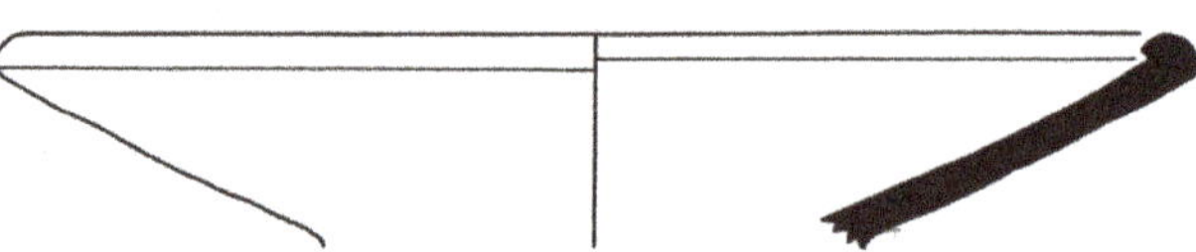

6   For Paul Lapp's chronology of Strata IV and IIIb of the Village site (Field 1) at 'Iraq al-Amir and the need for its re-evaluation, see Zimmerman 2020a, b.

7   Crowfoot et al. 1957: figs 37.9; 51.5 (Samaria); F.F. Jones 1950: figs 179.34, 36, 38 (Tarsus); Waagé 1948: 14–5, pl. I:1u, 2f, 2k (Antioch).

PW 66. CN 6863.
IIIB/C 1.19. Mixed Context.
Part of wall, rim. PH.03; PL 0.09; D rim (est.) 0.16. Light yellowish-brown clay 10YR 6/4. Coarse Light Brown.

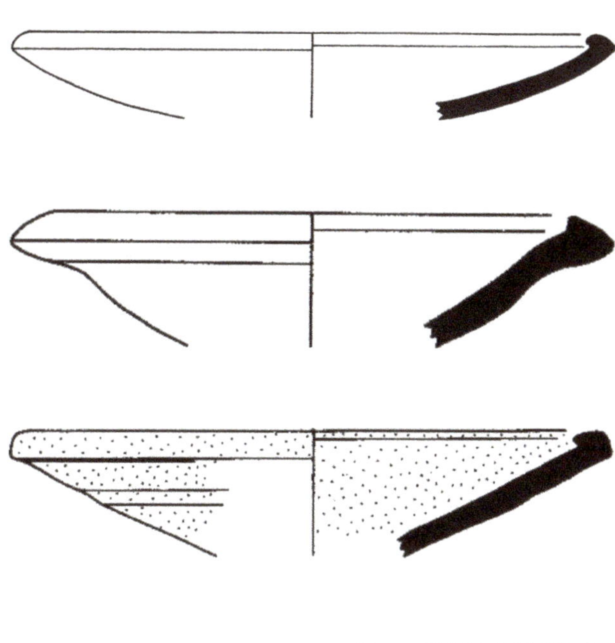

PW 67. CN 7081.
XXIIIA 109.4. Hellenistic 3B.
Part of wall, rim. PH 0.04; D rim (est.) 0.13. Strong brown clay 7.5YR 5/6. Hard Pale.
Crudely made.

PW 68. CN 7074.
XXIIIA 109.4. Hellenistic 3B.
Part of wall, rim. PH 0.04; PL 0.06; D rim (est.) 0.135. Pink clay 7.5YR 7/4. Coarse Light Brown.
Patchy thin red slip over interior, exterior.

PW 69. CN 7073.
XXIIIA 109.4. Hellenistic 3B.
Part of base, wall, rim. H 0.03; PL 0.08; D rim (est.) 0.15. Reddish-yellow clay 7.5YR 6/6. Coarse Light Brown.
Patchy red slip over interior, exterior. Low ring base.
Parallel: Shechem (N.L. Lapp 1985: fig. 1b.37).

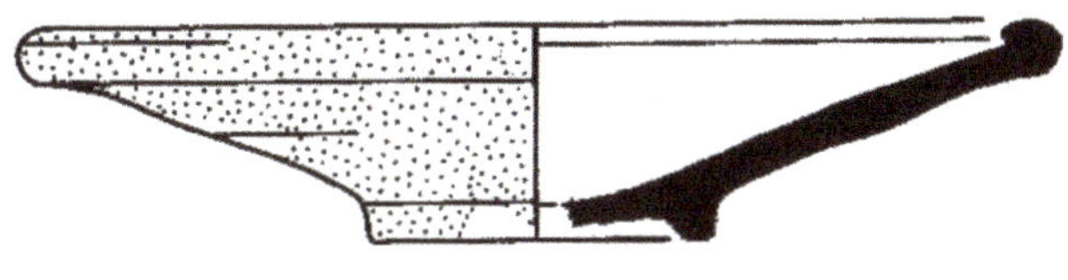

PW 70. CN 7240.
XXVIIIB 11.2. Hellenistic 3A.
Five fragments (three joining) of base, wall, rim. H 0.045; D rim (est.) 0.15. Brown clay 7.5YR 5/2. Large white inclusions. Hard Pale.
Flat base.
Parallel: 'Iraq al-Amir (Zimmerman 2020b: pl. 2.3.1, str. IV, early 2nd c. BC).

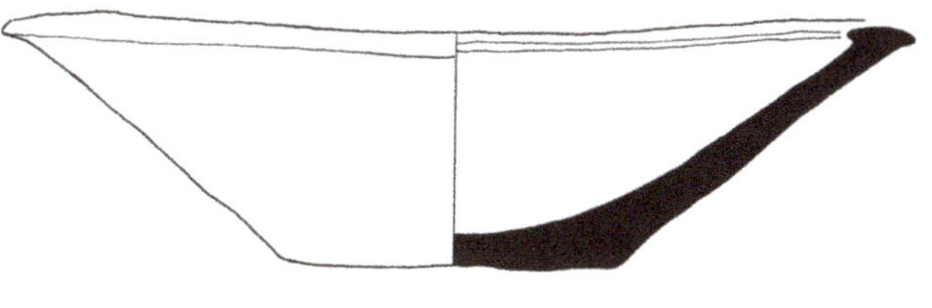

PW 71. CN 0463.
IIIB/C 1.19. Mixed Context.
Part of base, wall, and rim. PH 0.03; PL 0.09; D rim (est.) 0.12. Reddish-yellow clay 5YR 6/8. Coarse Light Brown.
Thin red slip over interior, exterior. Ring base.
Parallels: Marisa (Oren and Rappaport 1984: fig. 12.11); Tel Michal (Fischer 1989: fig. 13.1.6, 3rd c. BC).

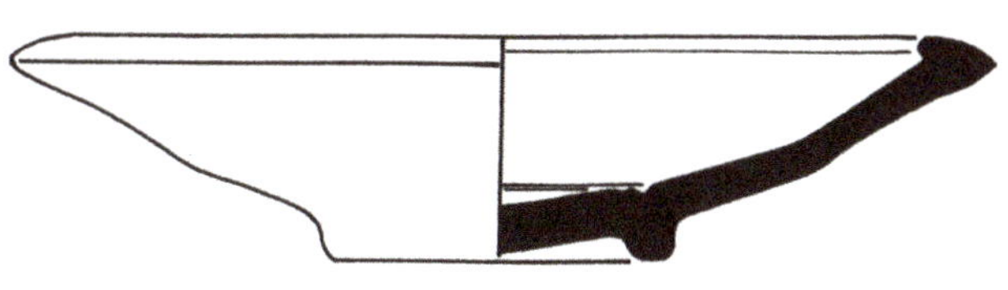

PW 72. CN 4308.
IVD 10.12. Hellenistic 3C.
Part of wall, rim. PH 0.02; PL 0.055; D rim (est.) 0.18. Very pale brown clay 10YR 7/4. Coarse Light Brown.
Red slip over interior, exterior.
Parallels: 'Iraq al-Amir (Zimmerman 2020b: pl. 2.3.4, str. II, c. 100 AD); Tel Dor (Guz-Zilberstein 1995: fig. 6.55:24).

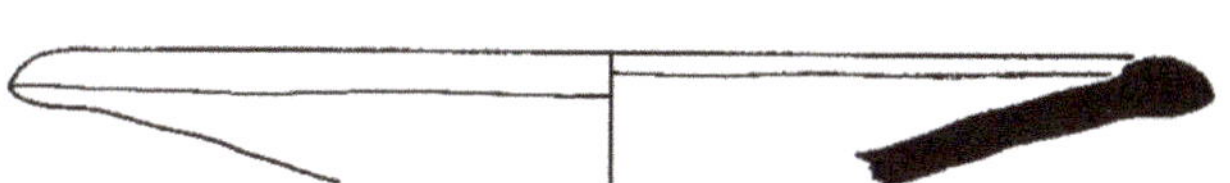

PW 73. CN 6930.
IVD 10.12. Hellenistic 3C.
Part of wall, rim. PH 0.04; PL 0.095; D rim (est.) 0.19.
Very pale brown clay 10YR 7/4. Coarse Light Brown.
Worn brown-black slip over interior, exterior. Uneven
wall.

PW 74. CN 4319.
IVD 10.12. Hellenistic 3C.
Complete. H 0.045; PL 0.18; D rim 0.18. Very pale
brown clay 10YR 7/3. Coarse Light Brown.
Brown matt slip over interior, rim. Ring base.

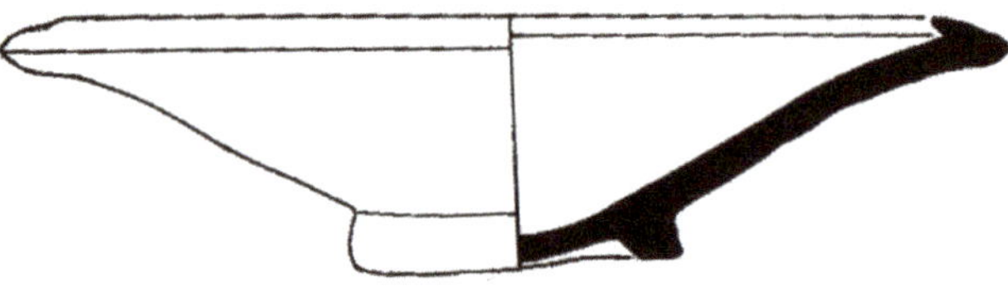

PW 75. CN 4318.
IVD 10.12. Hellenistic 3C.
Part of base, wall, rim. H 0.05; PL 0.20; D rim
(est.) 0.21. Very pale brown clay 10YR 7/4. Coarse
Light Brown.
Worn mottled black-brown-orange slip. Ring base.
Parallel: Shechem (N.L. Lapp 1985: fig. 1b.37).

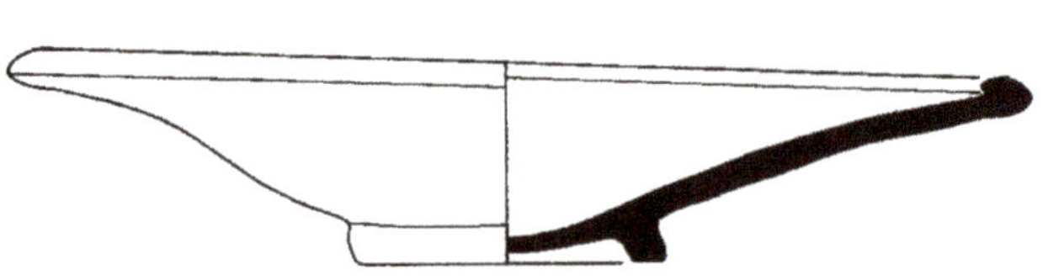

PW 76. CN 3925.
IVD 10.12. Hellenistic 3C.
Part of wall, rim. PH 0.035; D rim (est.) 0.19. Light
brown clay 7.5YR 6/4. Coarse Light Brown.

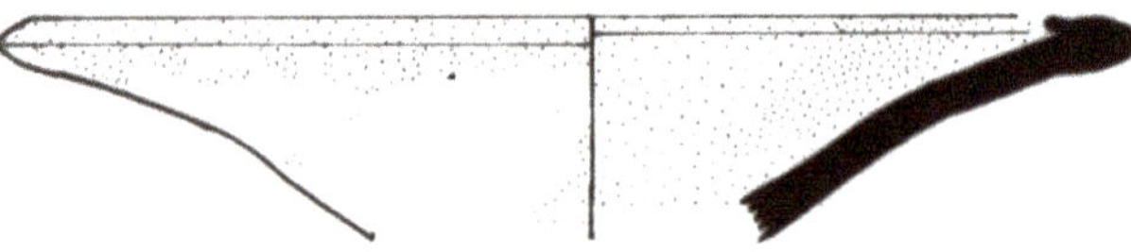

PW 77. CN 4306.
IVD 10.10. Hellenistic 3C.
Part of wall, rim. PH 0.04; D rim 0.18. Very
pale brown clay 10YR 7/4. Coarse Light Brown.
Patchy red slip over interior, exterior.

PW 78. CN 7047. (Plate 59)
XXIIIA 105.1. Hellenistic 3C.
Part of wall, rim, base. H 0.05; D rim (est.) 0.18. Very
pale brown clay 10YR 8/3. Coarse Light Brown.
Worn patchy brown slip over interior, rim. Ring base;
uneven wall.
Parallels: Machaerus (Loffreda 1980: pl. 97.46); Marisa
(Oren and Rappaport 1984: fig. 12.11); Samaria
(Crowfoot et al. 1957: fig. 51.5).

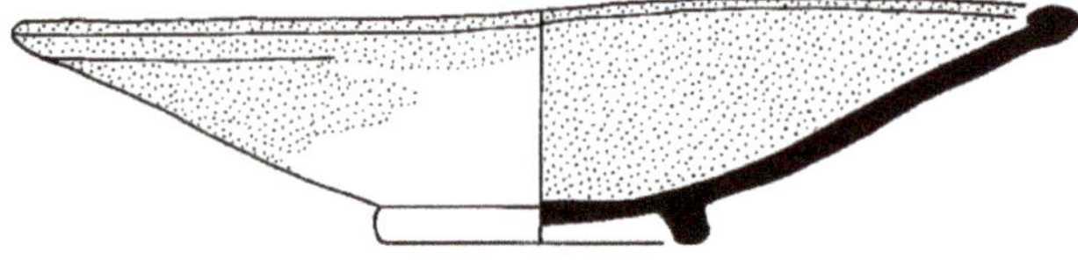

PW 79. CN 7048.
XXIIIA 105.1. Hellenistic 3C.
Missing part of base. H 0.05; D rim 0.20. Pink clay
7.5YR 8/3. Coarse Light Brown.
Thin worn greyish-brown slip over interior, exterior.
Ring base; uneven wall. Thickened undercut rim.

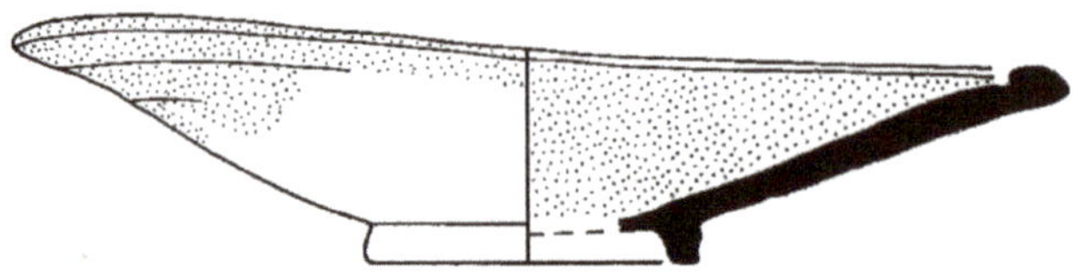

PW 80. CN 6710.
IIIP 24.11. Mixed Context.
Part of base, wall, rim. H 0.045; PL 0.085; D rim (est.)
0.18. Light brown clay 7.5YR 6/4. Coarse Light Brown.
Thin red slip over interior, rim. Ring base.

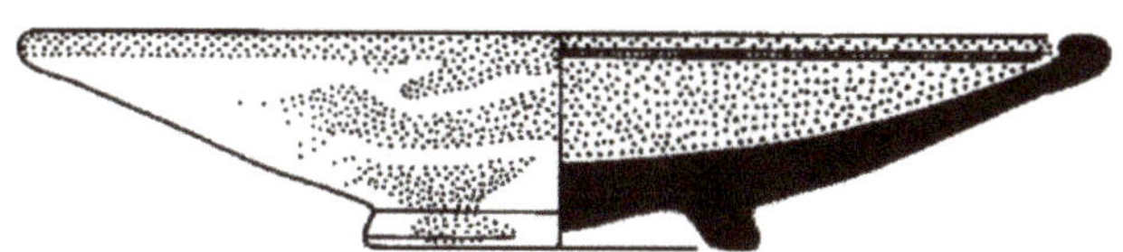

PW 81. CN 6698.
IIIP 24.17. Mixed Context.
Part of wall, rim. PL 0.45; D rim (est.) 0.20. Light
yellowish-brown clay 10YR 6/4. Coarse Light Brown.

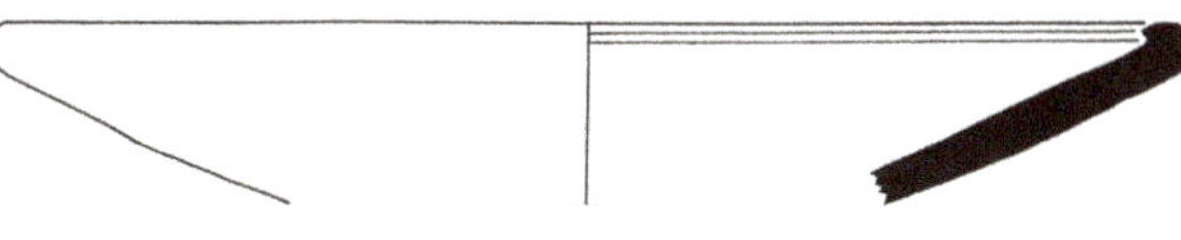

PW 82. CN 6651.
IIIP 24.17. Mixed Context.
Part of wall, rim. PH 0.025; PL 0.085; D rim (est.)
0.15. Brown clay 10YR 5/3. Coarse Light Brown.

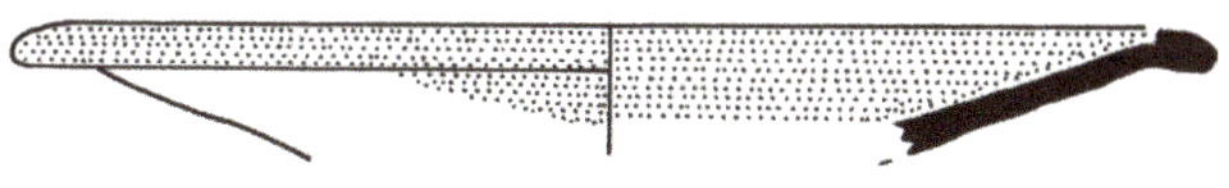

PW 83. CN 6697.
IIIP 24.17. Mixed Context.
Part of base, wall, rim (two non-joining fragments).
H 0.05; PL (a) 0.125 (b) 0.09; D rim (est.) 0.18. Light
yellowish-brown clay 10YR 6/4. Coarse Light Brown.
Ring base.

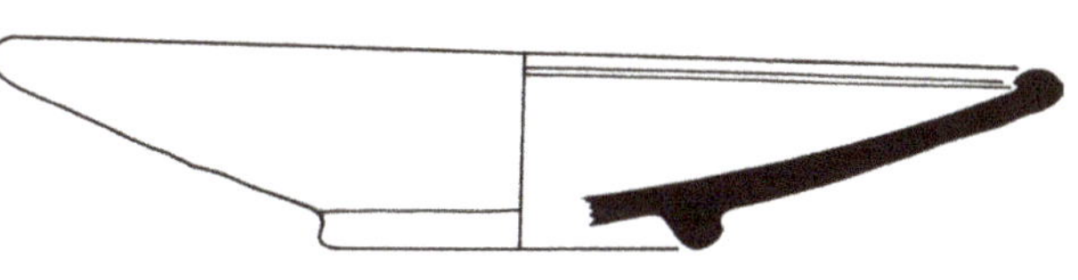

PW 84. CN 6690.
IIIP 25.21. Mixed Context.
Part of wall, rim. PH 0.03; D rim (est.) 0.18. Pink clay
5YR 7/4. Coarse Light Brown.
Matt red slip over interior, exterior.
Parallel: Hippos-Sussita (Osband and Eisenberg 2018:
pl. 2.2.18, 2nd c. BC).

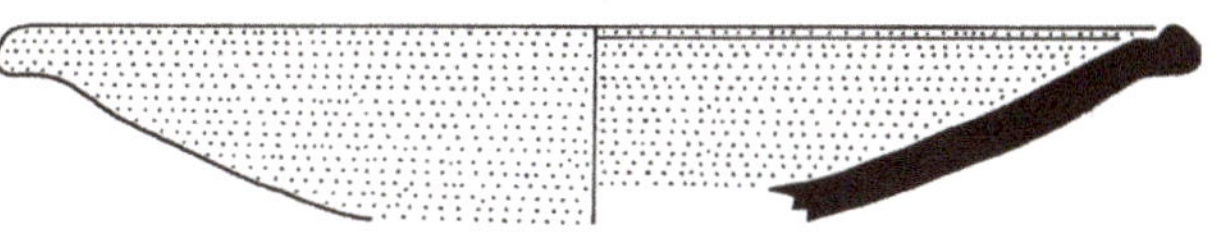

Upright rim

Three black-gloss examples – **FW 42–3** (Campana B) and **FW 44** (Ware 3) – of this form have already been
discussed. Two further examples, both in Coarse Light Brown ware, have been unearthed from Jannaeus
Destruction (Hellenistic 3C) deposits.

PW 85. CN 6570.
XXIIIA 10.5. Hellenistic 3C.
Part of wall, rim. PH 0.045; D rim (est.) 0.21. Reddish-
yellow clay 7.5YR 6/6. Coarse Light Brown.
Patchy thin brown slip over interior, rim.
Parallels: Amman/Philadelphia (Greene and 'Amr
1992: fig. 6.12); 'Iraq al-Amir (Zimmerman 2020b:
pl. 2.3.17, str. IIIB–II, c. 100 BC–c. 100 AD); Khirbet
al-Mukhayyat (Dolan and Foran 2016: fig. 7.k).

PW 86. CN 3449.
IVD 10.10. Hellenistic 3C.
Complete. H 0.065; D base 0.085; D rim 0.24. Light
brown clay 7.5YR 6/4. Coarse Light Brown.
Worn red slip over interior; red-brown slip over exterior.
Tall ring base. Two concentric grooves on floor.
Parallels: Amman/Philadelphia (Greene and ʿAmr 1992:
fig. 5.1); Marisa (Kloner and Hess 1985: fig. 1.10).

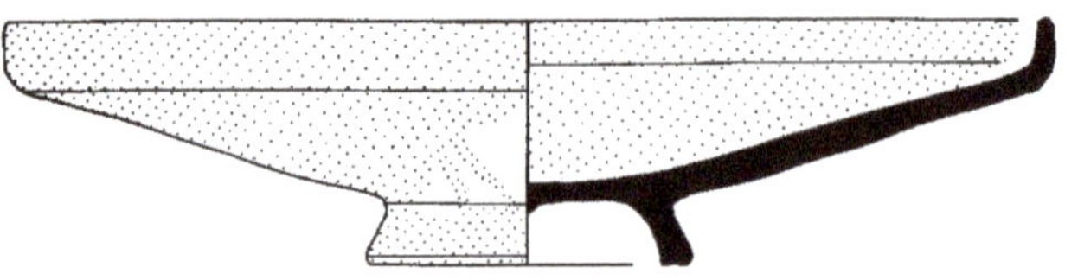

Saucers (PW 87–100)

The form is seen at Pella in both fine and plain wares. The small number of black-gloss examples is mainly
restricted to the second century BC with the plain ware forms (**PW 87, 98**) first seen in the "Antiochus
Destruction" level (Hellenistic 2B) and persisting into Early Roman deposits (**PW 96–7, 100**) where there
is a definite tendency for the junction between rim and wall to become more angular. There are no black-
gloss equivalents amongst these latter examples.

Table 2.18. Distribution of saucers by wares, phases.

Ware	Coarse Light Brown	11
	Hard Pale	3
Phase	2B c. 220–c. 200 BC	2
	3A c. 200–c. 140 BC	1
	3B/3C c. 140–c. 80/79 BC	4
	3C c. 100 (?)–c. 80/79 BC	1
	Early Roman 63 BC–c. 135 AD	3
	Mixed	3

PW 87. CN 7631.
XXXIVB 27.16. Hellenistic 2B.
Part of rim, wall. PH 0.03; PL 0.06; D rim (est.) 0.20.
Strong brown clay 7.5YR 5/6. Coarse Light Brown.
Thin yellowish-red wash on interior, exterior.

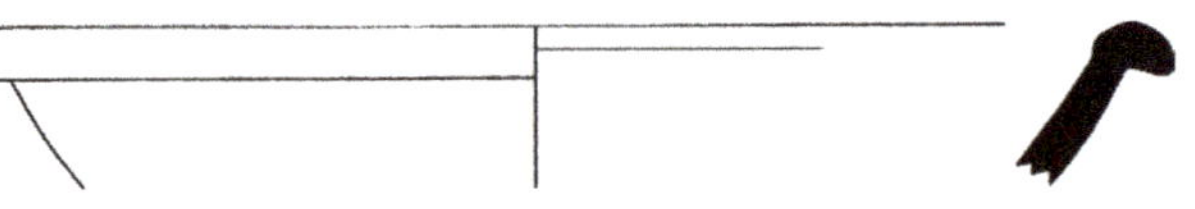

PW 88. CN 0219.
IIIB/C 1.10. Mixed Context.
Part of wall, rim. PH 0.025; D rim (est.) 0.155.
Reddish-yellow clay 7.5YR 7/6. Coarse Light Brown.
Thin reddish-black slip over interior, exterior.
Parallel: Tel Dor (Guz-Zilberstein 1995: fig. 6.40:2).

PW 89. CN 7238.
XXVIIIB 11.1. Hellenistic 3A.
Part of wall, rim. PH 0.03; D rim (est.) 0.15. Reddish-
yellow clay 7.5YR 7/6. Coarse Light Brown.

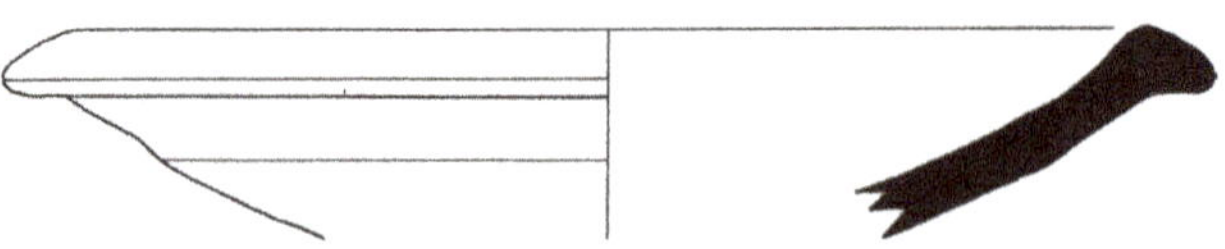

PW 90. CN 6919.
XXIIIA 10.7. Hellenistic 3C.
Part of wall, rim. PH 0.025; D rim (est.) 0.125. Very
pale brown clay 10YR 8/3. Coarse Light Brown.
Parallel: ʿAkko-Ptolemais (Berlin and Stone 2016: fig.
9.12.14, mid–late 2nd c. BC).

PW 91. CN 7577.
XXXIVB 28.2. Hellenistic 3B/3C.
Part of rim, wall. PL 0.12; D rim (est.) 0.18. Reddish-
yellow clay 7.5YR 6/8. Hard Pale.

PW 92. CN 7578.
XXXIVB 28.2. Hellenistic 3B/3C.
Part of rim, wall. PL 0.05; D rim (est.) 0.16. Brownish
yellow clay 10YR 6/6. Coarse Light Brown.
Thin reddish-brown slip over interior, exterior. Broad
rim overhanging interior, exterior.

PW 93. CN 7581.
XXXIVB 29.1. Hellenistic 3B/3C.
Part of rim, wall. PL 0.06; D rim (est.) 0.20. Yellowish-
red clay 5YR 5/6. Coarse Light Brown.
Patchy thin brown slip over interior, exterior.

PW 94. CN 7645.
XXXIVB 30.5. Hellenistic 3B/3C.
Part of rim, wall. PL 0.12; D rim (est.) 0.19. Yellowish-
brown clay 10YR 5/4. Coarse Light Brown.
Patchy thin dull black slip over interior, exterior.

PW 95. CN 6932.
IIIQ 11.19. Mixed Context.
Part of wall, rim. PH 0.025; D rim (est.) 0.15. Reddish-
yellow clay 7.5YR 6/6. Coarse Light Brown.
Worn brown slip over interior, exterior.
Parallels: Gadara/Umm Qais (Kerner 1997: fig. 12.4);
Hippos-Sussita (Osband and Eisenberg 2018: pl. 2.4.5,
2nd c. BC); Samaria (Hennessy 1970: fig. 9.19).

PW 96. CN 2949.
XIA/B 1.5. Early Roman 1.
Part of wall, rim. PH 0.025; D rim (est.) 0.16. Light
yellowish-brown clay 10YR 6/4. Coarse Light Brown.
Red slip over interior, exterior.
Parallel: Tel Dor (Guz-Zilberstein 1995: fig. 6.39:1).

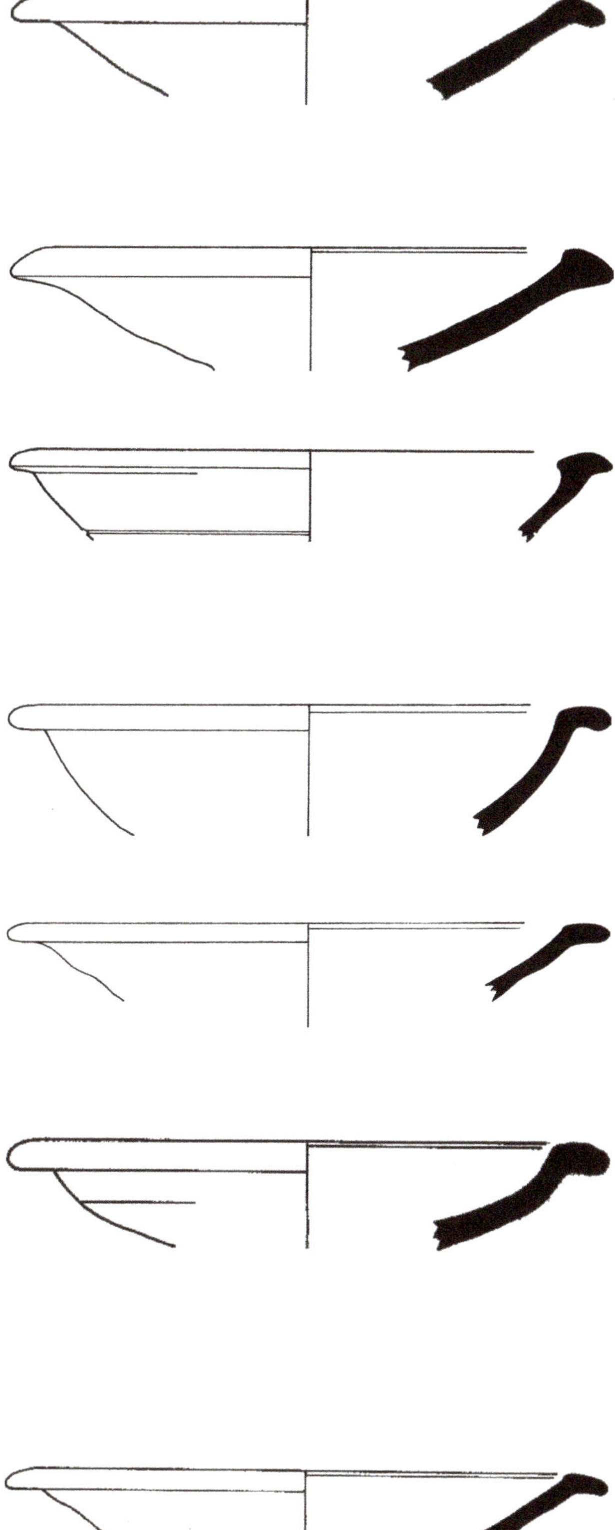

PW 97. CN 2995.
XIA/B 1.2/5. Early Roman 1.
Part of wall, rim. PH 0.025; D rim (est.) 0.15. Light
brown clay 7.5YR 6/4. Coarse Light Brown.
Red slip over interior, exterior.
Parallel: Tel Dor (Guz-Zilberstein 1995: fig. 6.4:17,
125 BC–105 AD).

PW 98. CN 7666.
XXXIVB 27.20. Hellenistic 2B.
Part of rim, wall and base. PL 0.07; D rim (est.) 0.20.
Reddish-yellow clay 7.5YR 6/6. Hard Pale.
Ring base.

PW 99. CN 7334.
XXXIVG 12.20. Mixed Context.
Part of wall, rim. PH 0.03; PL 0.045; D rim (est.) 0.16.
Reddish-yellow clay 5YR 6/6. Hard Pale.

PW 100. CN 3047.
XIA/B 2.1/2. Early Roman 1.
Part of wall, rim. PH 0.03; D rim (est.) 0.24. Very pale
brown clay 10YR 8/3. Coarse Light Brown.
Parallels: Gezer (Gitin 1990: pl. 34.8, early–mid-2nd c.
BC); Sha'ar ha-Amakim (Mlynarczyk 2000: pl. 117.4);
Straton's Tower/Caesarea (Berlin 1992: fig. 52.1).

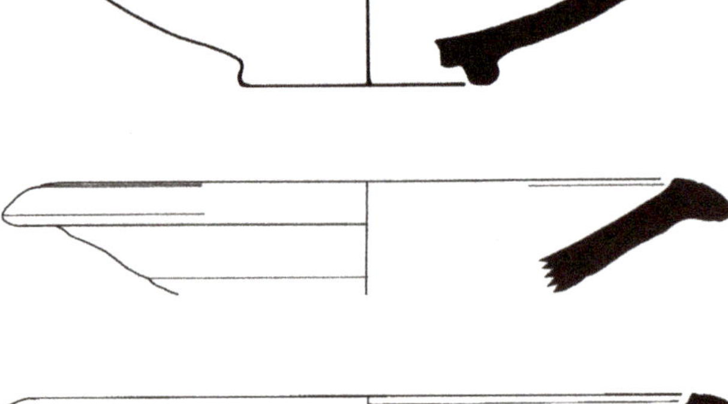

Bowls (PW 101–49)

As with their fine ware counterparts, bowls in plain wares (**PW 101–49**) are one of the major ceramic forms
from the Hellenistic and early Roman levels.

Table 2.19. Distribution of bowls by types, wares, phases.

		OUT-TURNED RIM (TYPE 1)	IN-TURNED RIM (TYPE 2)	FLAT BASE, ANGLED RIM (TYPE 3)	FLAT BASE, SIMPLE RIM (TYPE 4)	BEVELLED RIM (TYPE 5)	HEMI-SPHERICAL (TYPE 6)
Ware	Coarse Light Brown	5	28	3	2	1	4
	Miscellaneous	1	5	0	0	0	0
Phase	2B c. 220–c. 200 BC	0 (3)	1	0	0	0	0
	3A c. 200–c. 140 BC	0 (12)	3 (27)	0	0	0	0 (5)
	3B c. 140–c. 100 (?) BC	1	4	0	0	0	1
	3B/3C c. 140–c. 80/79 BC	0	2	0	0	0	0
	3C c. 100 (?)–c. 80/79 BC	4 (5)	8 (19)	3	2	1	2
	Early Roman 1 63 BC–late first century AD (c. 100 AD)	0 (7)	3 (28)	0	0	0	0 (2)
	Mixed	1	12 (12)	0	0	0	1

Out-turned rim (Type 1)

As well as black-gloss bowls, a small number of plain ware (mainly Coarse Light Brown) examples (**PW 101–6**) has also been recovered from deposits of the second and early first centuries BC (that is, Pre-Jannaeus Destruction and Jannaeus Destruction levels) as well as Early Roman strata.

PW 101. CN 0649.
IIIB/C 1.14. Mixed Context.
Part of base, wall, rim. H 0.045; D base 0.06; D rim (est.) 0.12. Reddish-yellow clay 5YR 6/6. Coarse Light Brown.
Thin reddish-brown slip over interior, upper half of exterior. Ring base.

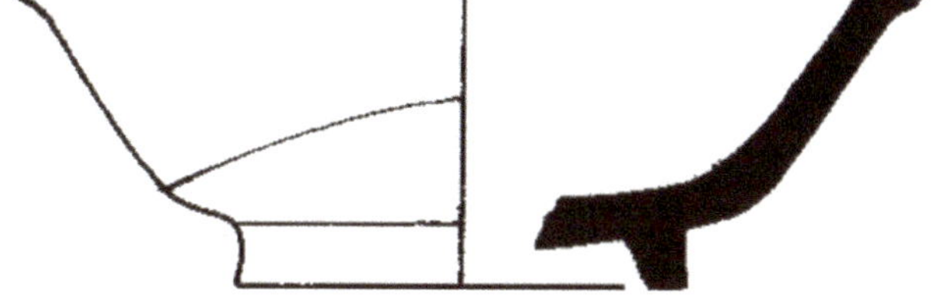

PW 102. CN 7077.
XXIIIA 109.4. Hellenistic 3B.
Part of wall, rim. PH 0.03; D rim (est.) 0.135. Very pale brown clay 10YR 8/3. Coarse Light Brown.
Parallel: Marisa (Kloner and Hess 1985: fig. 2.11 profile).

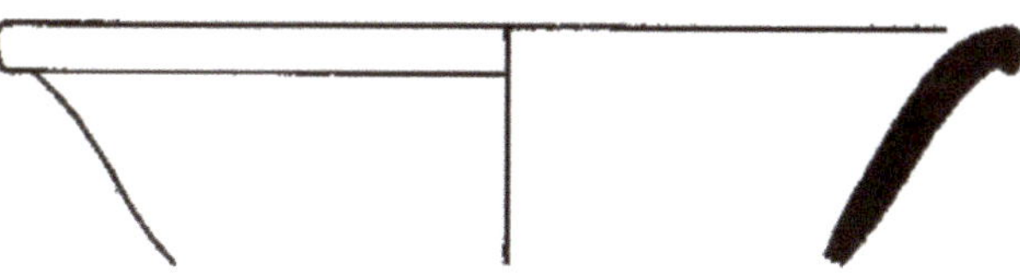

PW 103. CN 1429.
IIB/C 14.4. Hellenistic 3C.
Part of wall, rim. PH 0.03; D rim (est.) 0.20. Pink clay 5YR 7/3.
Parallel: Tel Dor (Guz-Zilberstein 1995: fig. 6.2:2, 400–275 BC).

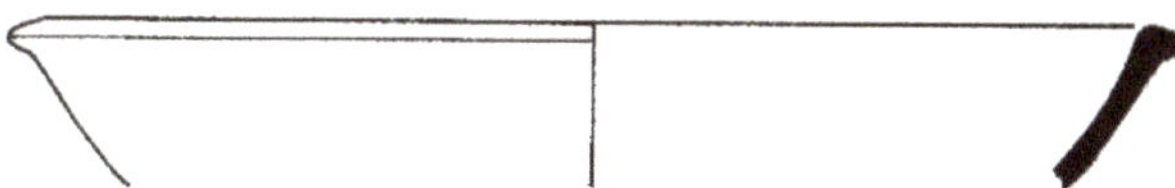

PW 104. CN 0908.
IIIB/C 15.2. Hellenistic 3C.
Part of wall, rim. PH 0.02; D rim (est.) 0.12. Very pale brown clay 10YR 7/3. Coarse Light Brown.

PW 105. CN 7026.
XXIIIA 100.3. Hellenistic 3C.
Part of wall, rim. PH 0.025; D rim (est.) 0.135. Reddish-yellow clay 7.5YR 6/6. Coarse Light Brown.
Thin orange slip over interior; patchy orange-brown slip over exterior.
Parallel: Apollonia (Fischer and Tal 1996: fig. 6.5); Tell es-Sa'idiyeh (Pritchard 1985: fig. 19.8);

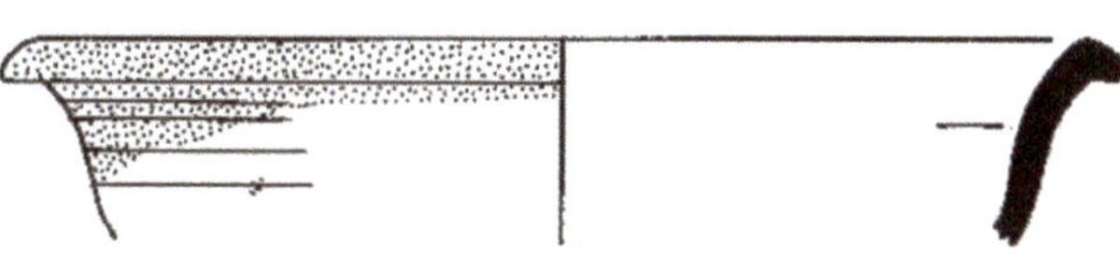

PW 106. CN 7039.
XXIIIA 103.2. Hellenistic 3C.
Part of wall, rim. PH 0.015; D rim (est.) 0.10. Pink clay 5YR 7/3. Coarse Light Brown.

In-turned rim (Type 2)

PW 107–39 are small deep bowls making up the largest bowl type (in both fine and plain wares) at Pella and seen in all chronological phases. In some examples, the wall gently curves in, in others it is straighter. At Pella there appears to be no chronological significance in this variation and so the two forms have been included within the one type. Well over half of the plain ware examples are of Coarse Light Brown ware although a variety of other fabrics, whose origin is unclear, are encountered.

PW 107. CN 7672.
XXXIVB 27.26. Hellenistic 2B.
Part of wall, rim. PL 0.075; D rim (est.) 0.17. Light yellowish-brown clay 10YR 6/4. Coarse Light Brown. Patchy brown slip over exterior.

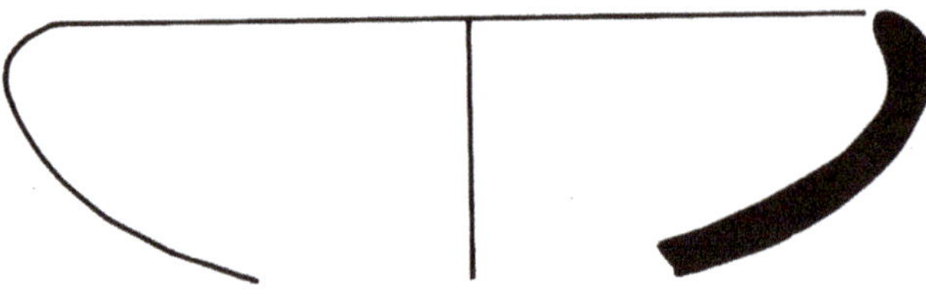

PW 108. CN 7648.
XXXIVB 27.18. Hellenistic 3B/3C.
Part of base, wall, rim. PL 0.12; D rim (est.) 0.15. Red clay 2.5YR 5/8.
Low ring base.

PW 109. CN 7584.
XXXIVB 29.1. Hellenistic 3B/3C.
Part of wall, rim. PL 0.08; D rim (est.) 0.13. Reddish-yellow clay 5YR 6/8. Coarse white inclusions.

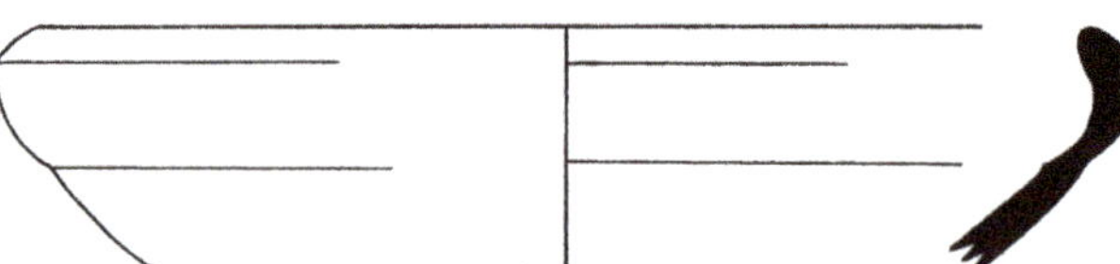

PW 110. CN 0288.
IIIB/C 1.10. Mixed Context.
Part of wall, rim. PH 0.035; D rim (est.) 0.19. Yellowish-red clay 5YR 5/6. Coarse Light Brown. Worn grey-brown slip over interior, exterior.
Parallels: ʿAkko-Ptolemais (Berlin and Stone 2016: fig. 9.10.14, late 3rd–mid-2nd c. BC); Hesban (Gerber 2012: 209, fig. 3.8.3); Hippos-Sussita (Osband and Eisenberg 2018: pl. 1.7, 3rd–first half of 2nd c. BC); ʿIraq al-Amir (Zimmerman 2020b: pl. 2.1.15, str. II, c. 100 AD).

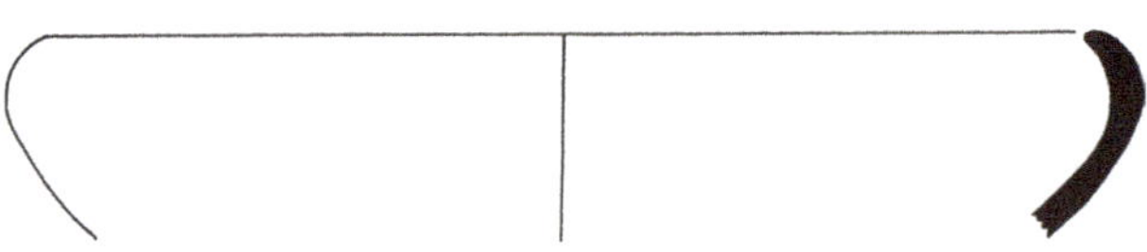

PW 111. CN 7405.
XXVIIIB 10.6. Hellenistic 3A.
Part of wall, rim. PH 0.025; D rim (est.) 0.13. Reddish-yellow clay 5YR 6/6. Coarse Light Brown. Worn red slip over interior, exterior.
Parallels: ʿAkko-Ptolemais (Berlin and Stone 2016: fig. 9.12.5, mid–late 2nd c. BC); Apollonia (Fischer and Tal 1996: fig. 9.5).

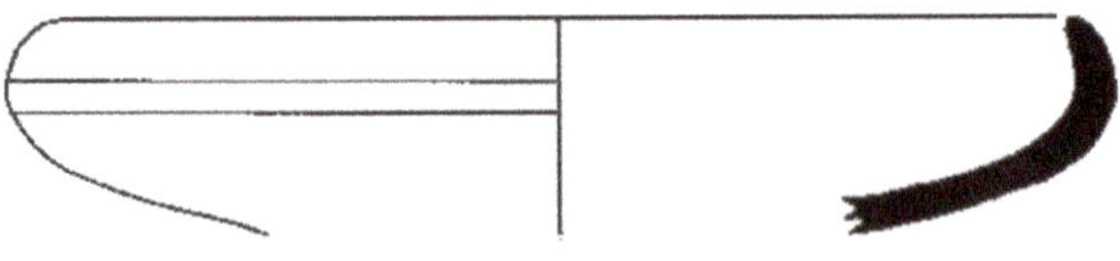

PW 112. CN 7475.
XXVIIIB 13.10. Hellenistic 3A.
Part of wall, rim. PH 0.03; D rim (est.) 0.18. Reddish-yellow clay 7.5YR 6/6. Coarse Light Brown.
Thin patchy red slip over interior, exterior.
Parallel: ʿAkko-Ptolemais (Dothan 1976: fig. 30.5).

PW 113. CN 0322.
IIIB/C 1.10. Mixed Context.
Part of base, wall, rim. PH 0.05; PL 0.06. Light grey clay 10YR 7/2. Coarse Light Brown.
Thin brown slip over interior, exterior. Low ring base.
Parallel: Gezer (Gitin 1990: pl. 42.4, early 1st c. BC).

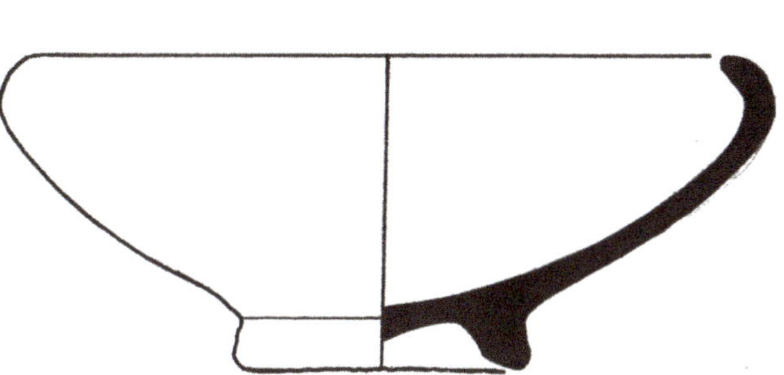

PW 114. CN 0452.
IIIB/C 1.19. Mixed Context.
Part of base, wall, rim. H 004; PL 0.10; D rim (est.) 0.11. Very pale brown clay 10YR 7/4. Coarse Light Brown.
Dull brown slip over interior, exterior. Ring base; grooved resting surface.
Parallels: Gezer (Gitin 1990: pl. 38.3, mid-2nd c. BC); Jerusalem (Geva 2003: pl. 5.3.27, late 2nd –1st c. BC); Marisa (Oren and Rappaport 1984: fig. 12.8); Tel Dor (Guz-Zilberstein 1995: fig. 6.1:13, 275–250 BC).

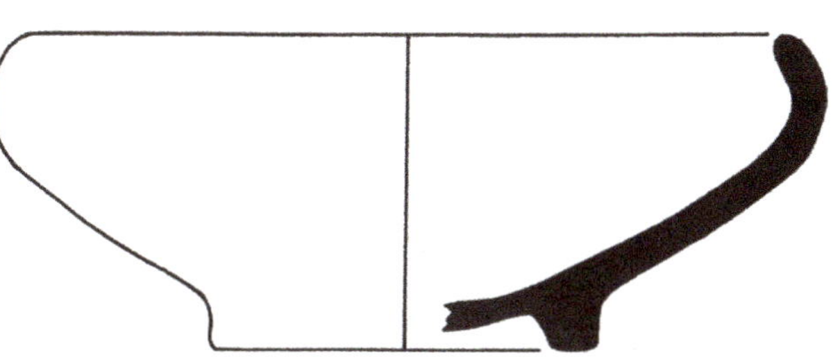

PW 115. CN 0368.
IIIB/C 1.14. Mixed Context.
Part of base, wall, rim. H 0.045; PL 0.10; D rim (est.) 0.11. Light grey clay 10YR 7/2. Coarse Light Brown.
Low ring base.
Parallels: ʿAkko-Ptolemais (Berlin and Stone 2016: fig. 9.26.2, early 1st c. AD); Ashdod (Dothan 1971: fig. 60.24); Philoteria/Bet Yerah (Tal and Reshef 2017: fig. 3.42.7); Tel Dor (Guz-Zilberstein 1995: fig. 6.1:14, 275–150 BC).

PW 116. CN 0032.
IIIB/C 1.1. Hellenistic 3C.
Part of wall, rim. PH 0.025; PL 0.09; D rim (est.) 0.10. Reddish-yellow clay 7.5YR 6/6. Coarse Light Brown.
Parallels: ʿAkko-Ptolemais (Berlin and Stone 2016: fig. 9.4.5, 3rd c. BC); ʿIraq al-Amir (Zimmerman 2020b: pl. 2.1.5, str. IV–IIIB, early 2nd c.–c. 100 BC); Tell es-Saʾidiyeh (Pritchard 1985: fig. 19.10); Samaria (Hennessy 1970: fig. 9.18); Straton's Tower/Caesarea (Berlin 1992: fig. 51.7).

PW 117. CN 0220.
IIIB/C 1.10. Mixed Context.
Part of wall, rim. PH 0.035; PL 0.095; D rim (est.)
0.125. Light grey clay 10YR 7/2. Coarse Light Brown.
Dull black slip over interior, exterior.

PW 118. CN 7075.
XXIIIA 109.4. Hellenistic 3B.
Part of wall, rim. PH 0.035; PL 0.06; D rim (est.) 0.18.
Reddish-yellow clay 5YR 7/6. Coarse Light Brown.
Thin patchy orange-red slip over interior, exterior.

PW 119. CN 7846.
XXXIIY 1.2. Hellenistic 3A.
Part of base, wall, rim. H 0.06; PL 0.055; D rim (est.)
0.14. Reddish-yellow clay 5YR 7/6. Coarse Light Brown.
Thin red-brown slip over interior, upper exterior.
Ring base.

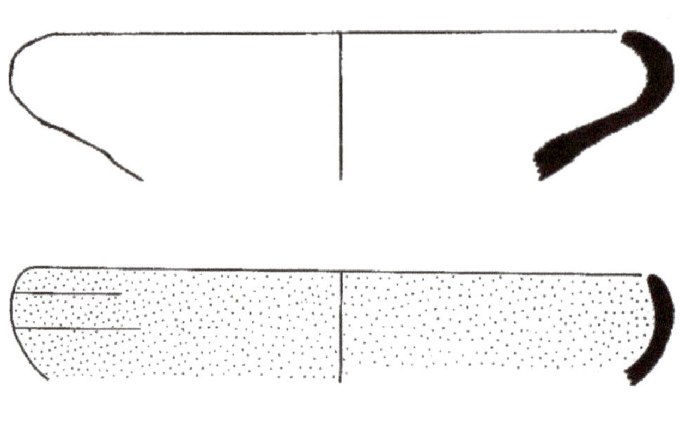

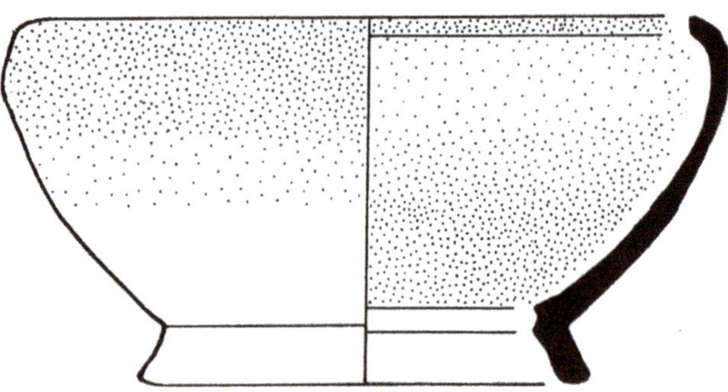

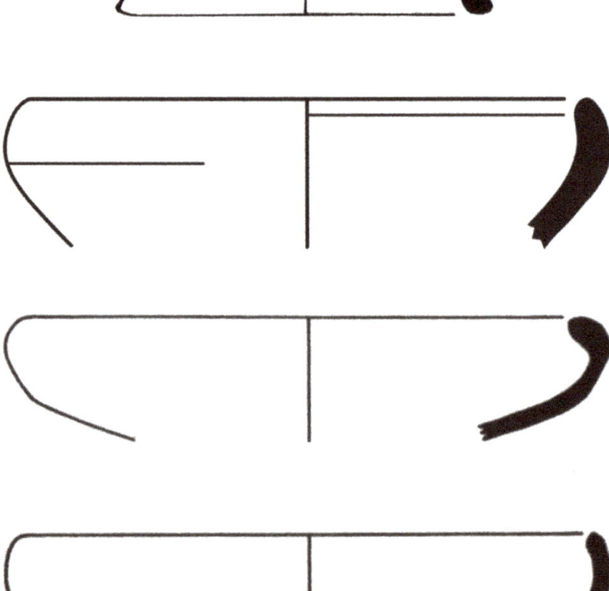

PW 120. CN 7069.
XXIIIA 109.3. Hellenistic 3B.
Part of wall, rim. PH 0.03; PL 0.035; D rim (est.) 0.11.
Light brown clay 7.5YR 6/4. Coarse Light Brown.
Parallel: Gezer (Gitin 1990: pl. 40.4, late 2nd c. BC).

PW 121. CN 0289.
IIIB/C 1.10. Mixed Context.
Part of wall, rim. PH 0.03; D rim (est.) 0.12. Greyish-
brown clay 10YR 5/2. Coarse Light Brown.
Thin black slip over interior, exterior.

PW 122. CN 0395.
IIIB/C 1.14. Mixed Context.
Part of wall, rim. PH 0.025; D rim (est.) 0.12. Reddish-
yellow clay 7.5YR 6/6. Coarse Light Brown.
Matt red slip over interior.

PW 123. CN 4301.
IVD 10.10. Hellenistic 3C.
Part of wall, rim. PH 0.06; PL 0.125; D rim (est.) 0.15.
Reddish-yellow clay 5YR 7/8. Coarse Light Brown.
Red slip over interior, exterior. Black slip over rim.

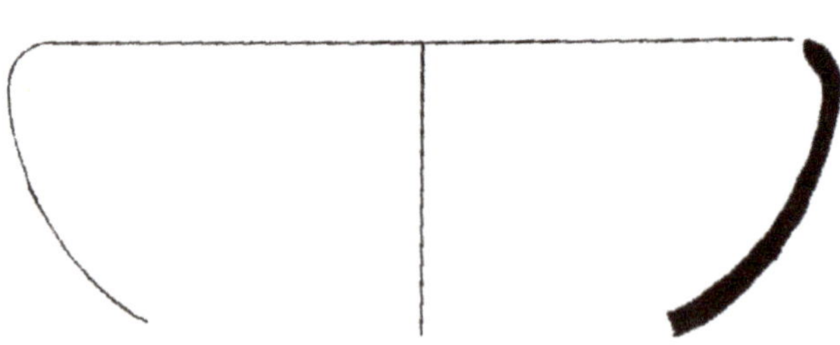

PW 124. CN 4300.
IVD 10.10. Hellenistic 3C.
Part of wall, rim. PH 0.03; PL 0.05; D rim (est.) 0.14.
Very pale brown clay 10YR 8/2. Coarse Light Brown.
Worn black-brown slip over interior, exterior.
Parallels: 'Iraq al-Amir (Zimmerman 2020b: pl. 2.1.6,
str. IIIB–II, c. 100 BC–c. 100 AD); Jerusalem (Hayes
1985b: fig. 48.6); Wadi Hasa Survey (MacDonald 1988:
pl. 13.13).

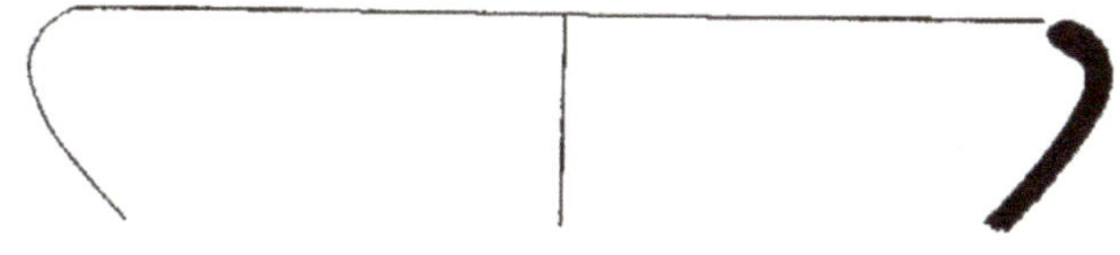

PW 125. CN 4313.
IVD 10.10. Hellenistic 3C.
Part of wall, rim. PH 0.03; PL 0.035; D rim (est.) 0.12.
Pink clay 5YR 8/3. Coarse Light Brown.
Worn red slip over interior, exterior.
Parallel: Tell Zira'a (Kenkel 2020: 34, 132–3, pl. 1.8: Sa1.16).

PW 126. CN 6790.
IVD 10.12. Hellenistic 3C.
Part of wall, rim. PH 0.04; PL 0.06; D rim (est.) 0.105.
Dusky red clay 2.5YR 4/2.
Matt orange-brown slip.
Parallels: Madaba (Ferguson 2014: 186, fig. 7.39,
c. 100–63 BC); Tell Zira'a (Kenkel 2020: 33–4, 132–3,
pl. 1.8: Sa1.15).

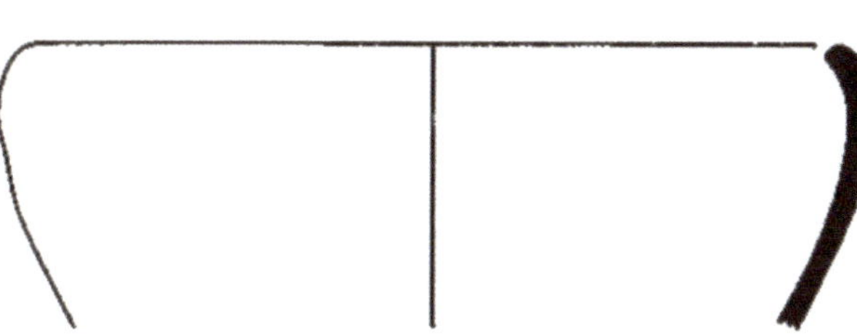

PW 127. CN 6791.
IVD 10.12. Hellenistic 3C.
Part of wall, rim. PH 0.045; D rim (est.) 0.105. Pink
clay 5YR 8/4. Coarse Light Brown.
Matt orange slip over interior; brown slip over rim,
exterior.
Parallel: Hippos-Sussita (Osband and Eisenberg 2018:
pl. 2.1.13, 2nd c. BC).

PW 128. CN 6918.
XXIIIA 10.7. Hellenistic 3C.
Part of wall, rim. PH 0.035; PL 0.04; D rim (est.)
0.105. Light brownish-grey clay 10YR 6/2. Coarse
Light Brown.
Grey-brown slip over interior, exterior.
Parallels: Gezer (Gitin 1990: pl. 38.1, mid-2nd c. BC);
Hesban (Gerber 2012: 209, fig. 3.8.21); Machaerus
(Corbo and Loffreda 1981: fig. 36.8); Tel Dor (Guz-
Zilberstein 1995: fig. 6.1:26, 275–175 BC?).

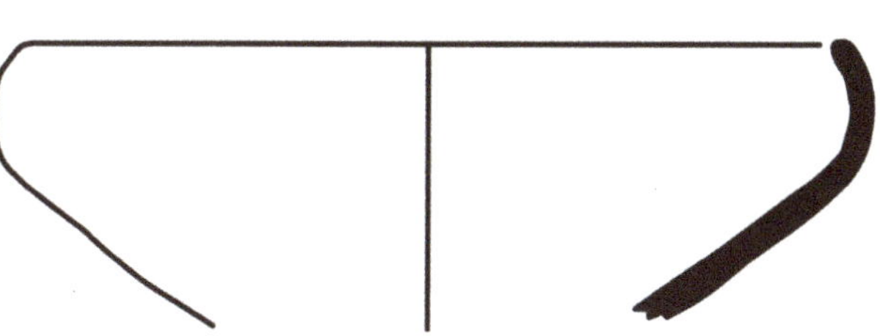

PW 129. CN 6985.
XXIIIA 22.9. Hellenistic 3C.
Part of wall, rim. PH 0.03; PL 0.05; D rim (est.) 0.08. Very
dark grey clay 10YR 3/1 (burnt). Coarse Light Brown.
Parallel: Gezer (Gitin 1990: pl. 40.4, late 2nd c. BC).

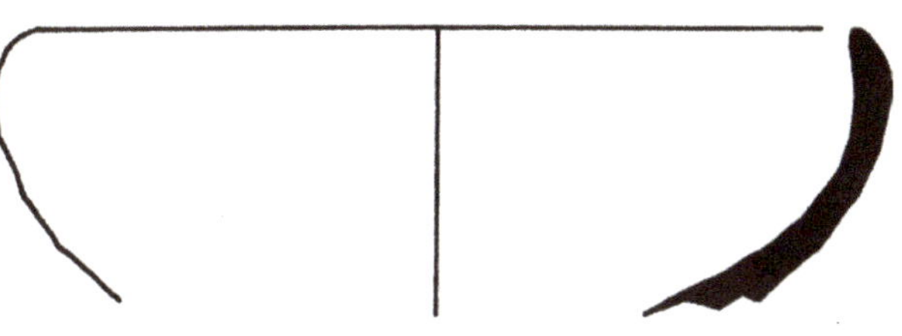

PW 130. CN 6557.

IIIP 25.10. Hellenistic 3B.

Complete. H 0.04; L 0.095; D rim 0.10. Reddish-yellow clay 7.5YR 6/6. Coarse Light Brown.

Brown slip over upper interior, exterior. Ring base. Crudely made.

Parallels: Marisa (Oren and Rappaport 1984: fig. 12.4); Philoteria/Bet Yerah (Tal and Reshef 2017: fig. 3.43.4).

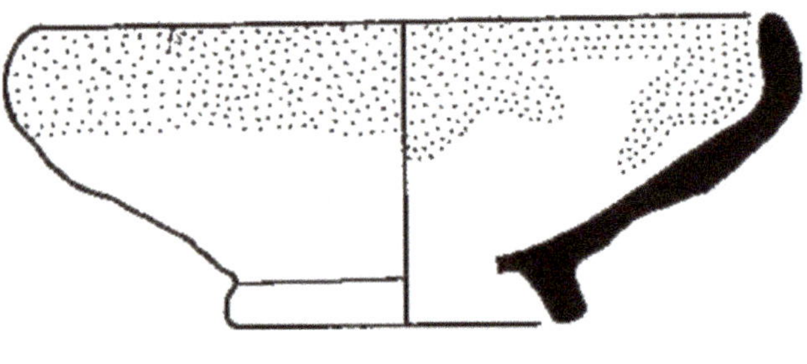

PW 131. CN 6671.

IIIP 25.11. Hellenistic 3B.

Part of wall, rim. PH 0.04; PL 0.05; D rim (est.) 0.125. Reddish-yellow clay 7.5YR 6/6. Coarse Light Brown.

Red slip over interior, exterior.

Parallels: ʿAkko-Ptolemais (Berlin and Stone 2016: fig. 9.17.3, mid–late 2nd c. BC); Gezer (Gitin 1990: pl. 35.5, early–mid-2nd c. BC); Jericho (Netzer and Meyers 1977: fig. 9.3); Khirbet al-Mukhayyat (Dolan and Foran 2016: fig. 7.b).

PW 132. CN 6743.

IIIP 25.21. Mixed Context.

Part of base, wall, rim. H 0.05; PL 0.11; D rim (est.) 0.12. Reddish-brown clay 7.5YR 6/8. Coarse Light Brown.

Patchy red slip over exterior. Ring base. Uneven wall.

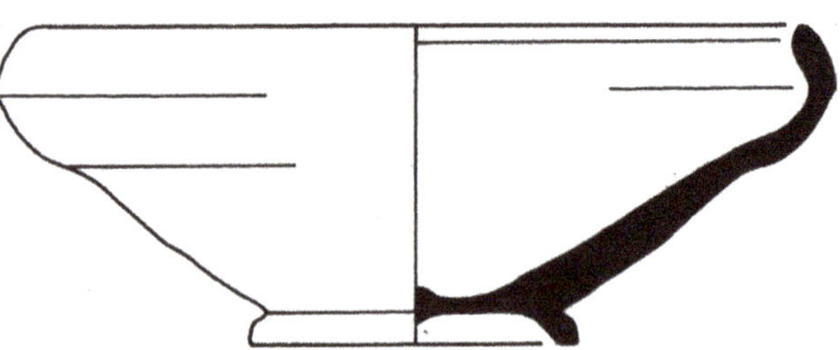

PW 133. CN 7280.

XXXIVG 3.11. Mixed Context.

Two joining fragments of base, wall, rim. H 0.08; D rim (est.) 0.12. Very pale brown clay 10YR 8/3. Coarse Light Brown.

Patchy dull brown-black slip over interior, exterior. Ring base.

Parallels: Madaba (Ferguson 2014: 186, fig. 7.42, c. 129–100 BC); Scythopolis/Beth-Shean (Fitzgerald 1931: pl. XXXIV.8).

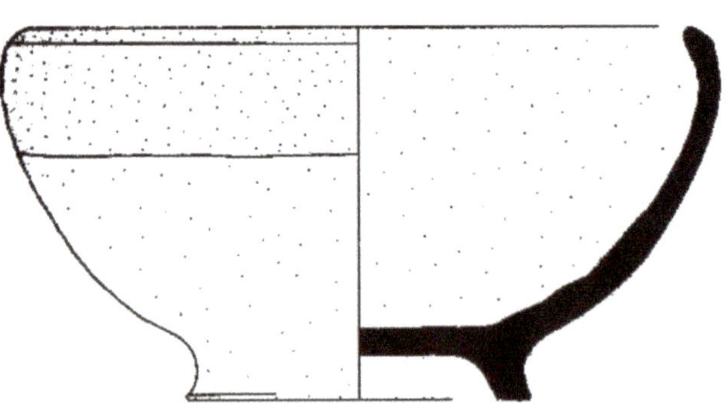

PW 134. CN 7176.

XXXIVG 11.4. Early Roman 1.

Part of base, wall, rim. H .045; PL 0.08; D rim (est.) 0.12. Very pale brown clay 10YR 7/4. Coarse Light Brown. Ring base.

Parallels: Apollonia (Fischer and Tal 1996: fig. 9.8); Ashdod (Dothan 1971: fig. 60. 24); Gezer (Gitin 1990: pl. 42.1 upper profile, early 1st c. BC); Machaerus (Loffreda 1980: pl. 97.50); Marisa (Levine 2003: fig. 6.2.38); Tel Dor (Guz-Zilberstein 1995: fig. 6.1:14, 275–150 BC).

PW 135. CN 6871.
IIIB/C 1.19. Mixed Context.
Part of base, wall, rim. H 0.05; PL 0.06; D rim (est.) 0.13.
Reddish-yellow clay 7.5YR 6/6. Coarse Light Brown.
Ring base.
Parallels: 'Akko-Ptolemais (Berlin and Stone 2016:
fig. 9.27.2, unstratified); Kedesh (Levantine Ceramics
Project: n.d. K08P263, 3rd –2nd c. BC); Marisa (Levine
2003: fig. 6.2.36).

PW 136. CN 6821.
IIIP 24.19. Mixed Context.
Part of base, rim, wall. H 0.045; PL 0.065; D rim
(est.) 0.11. Yellowish-red clay 5YR 5/6. Multiple coarse
white inclusions.
Brown slip over upper interior, exterior. Ring base;
uneven wall.
Parallels: 'Akko-Ptolemais (Berlin and Stone 2016: fig.
9.6.7, 3rd c. BC); Apollonia (Fischer and Tal 1996: fig.
6.7); Marisa (Oren and Rappaport 1984: fig. 12.8);
Samaria (Crowfoot et al. 1957: fig. 56.8).

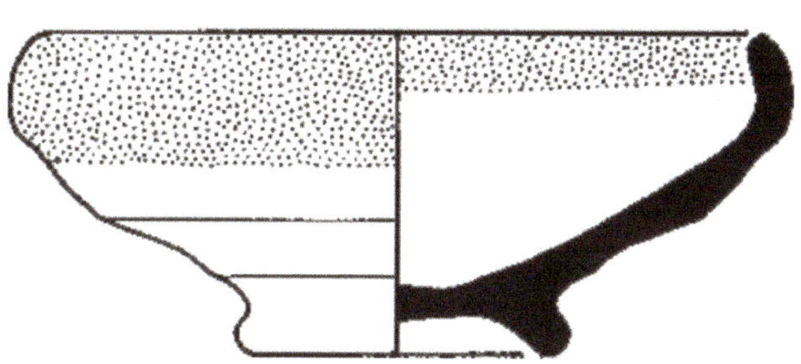

PW 137. CN 6851.
IIIB/C 1.10. Mixed Context.
Part of base, wall, rim. H 0.035; PL 0.06; D rim (est.) 0.105.
Yellowish-brown 10YR 5/4. Coarse white inclusions.
Low ring base.

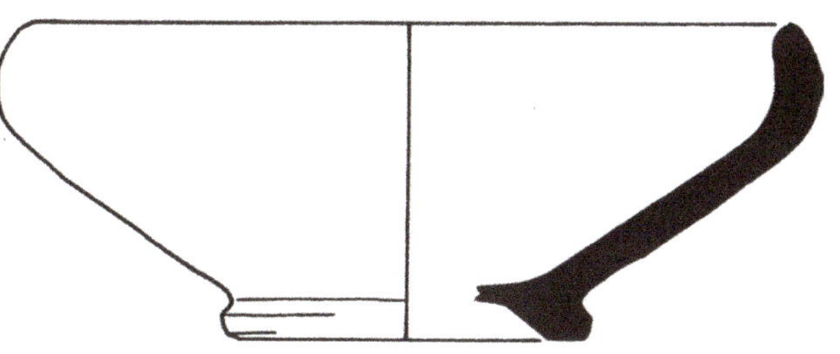

PW 138. CN 2956.
XIA/B 1.5. Early Roman 1.
Part of wall, rim. PH 0.03; PL 0.045; D rim
(est.) 0.12. Light yellowish-brown clay 10YR 6/4.
Coarse Light Brown.
Patchy black slip over upper interior, exterior.
Parallels: Jerusalem (Hayes 1985b: fig. 48.4); Tel Dor
(Guz-Zilberstein 1995: fig. 6.47:9, 250–200 BC); Tell
es-Sa'idiyeh (Pritchard 1985: fig. 19.11).

PW 139. CN 2944.
XIA/B 1.5. Early Roman 1.
Part of wall, rim. PH 0.025; PL 0.07; D rim (est.)
0.135. Light grey clay 10YR 7/2. Coarse Light Brown.
Patchy black slip over interior, exterior.
Parallels: Amman/Philadelphia (Zayadine 1977–78:
fig. 13.343); Betar (Singer 1993: fig. 1.4); Gezer
(Gitin 1990: pl. 35.5, early–mid-2nd c. BC); Tel Dor
(Guz-Zilberstein 1995: fig. 6.1:26, 275–175 BC?); Tell
es-Sa'idiyeh (Pritchard 1985: fig. 19.11).

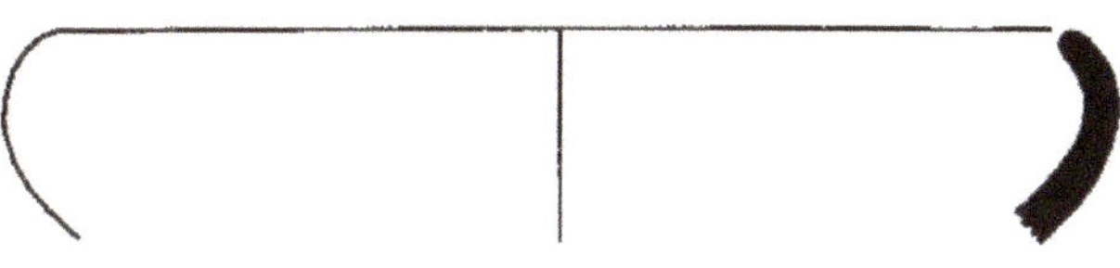

Flat base, angled rim (Type 3)

Bowls **PW 140–2** differ from those of the previous type in having a narrow, angled rim rather than one which is gently in-turned. The form is uncommon at Pella, where the three examples were recovered from an early first-century (Hellenistic 3C) deposit on the main mound. It has some similarities with a red-slipped bowl at Tel Dor (Guz-Zilberstein 1995: 290, fig. 6.1:33) dating to the second century BC and, along with the following type, recalls those simple bowls with flat string-cut bases (as with the Pella examples) seen at sites such as Tel Dor (Guz-Zilberstein 1995: figs 6.1:34–8) and Samaria (Crowfoot et al. 1957: fig. 56.9–11). The bowls from Pella are of Coarse Light Brown ware and, along with the following type, reflect a simplification of form (often poorly potted) that occurs in the later second century BC.

PW 140. CN 0033.
IIIB/C 1.1. Hellenistic 3C.
Complete. H 0.03; D rim 0.10. Very pale brown clay
10YR 7/4. Coarse Light Brown.
Crudely made.
Parallels: 'Aïn Feshka (de Vaux 1959: fig. 3.4); Ashdod
(Dothan 1971: fig. 59.8, 2nd c. BC?); Jericho (Kelso
and Baramki 1955 pl. 23.A80); Machaerus (Loffreda
1996: fig. 39.29); Khirbet al-Mukhayyat (Dolan and
Foran 2016: fig. 7.m upper profile).

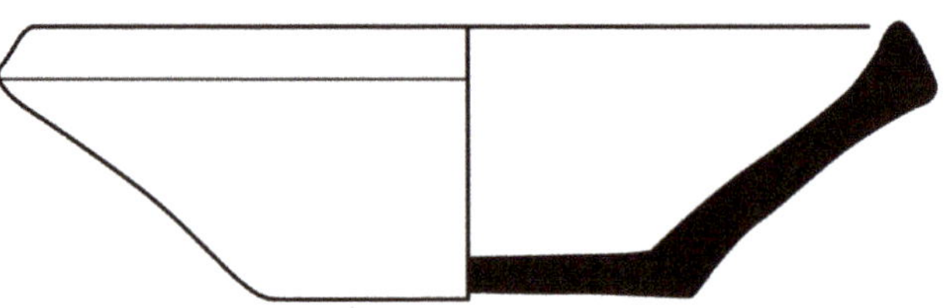

PW 141. CN 0046.
IIIB/C 1.3. Hellenistic 3C.
Complete. H 0.035; D rim 0.80; Pinkish-grey clay
7.5YR 7/2. Coarse Light Brown.
Thick flat base.
Parallels: Apollonia (Fischer and Tal 1996: fig. 9.11);
Ashdod (Dothan 1971: figs 10.11, 15.24, 16.3–4, 6,
60.32, 78.11; Dothan and Freedman 1967: fig. 10.1,
mid-1st c. BC–c. 70 AD); Jaffa (Tsuf 2018: fig. 9.1.8);
Jericho (Pritchard 1958: pl. 59.37); Jerusalem (Geva
and Rosenthal-Heginbottom 2003: pl. 6.2.39, 1st
c. BC; Sandhaus 2013: fig. 4.8:10, second half of 2nd
c. BC); Marisa (Kloner and Hess 1985: fig. 1.18; Levine
2003: fig. 6.2.39); Samaria (Crowfoot et al. 1957:
fig. 56.11); Tel Michal (Fischer 1989: fig. 13.2.1, 2, 2nd
c. BC); Wadi al-Kharrar (Abu Shmeis and Waheeb
2002: fig. 8.6).

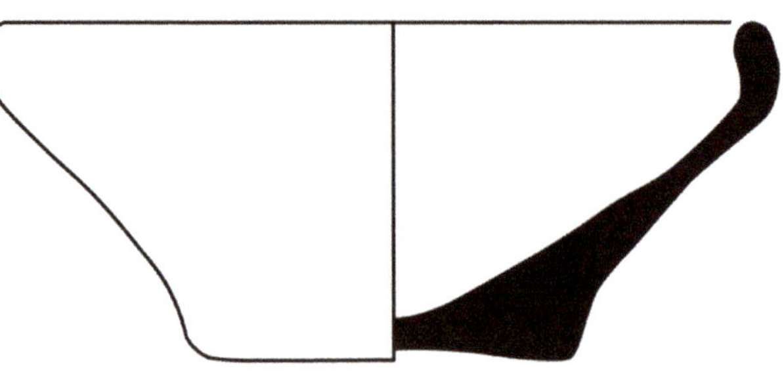

PW 142. CN 0047.
IIIB/C 1.3. Hellenistic 3C.
Complete. H 0.03; D 0.09; D rim 0.11. Pinkish-grey
clay 7.5YR 7/2. Coarse Light Brown.
Parallels: Ashdod (Dothan 1971: fig. 16.8; Dothan
and Freedman 1967: fig. 10.3, mid-1st c. BC–c. 70
AD); Jericho (Kelso and Baramki 1955: pl. 23.A79);
Jerusalem (Geva 2003: pl. 5.9.27, later 2nd–1st c. BC;
Rahmani 1967: fig. 10.2); Machaerus (Loffreda 1980:
pl. 97.48); Tell es-Sa'idiyeh (Pritchard 1985: fig. 19.13).

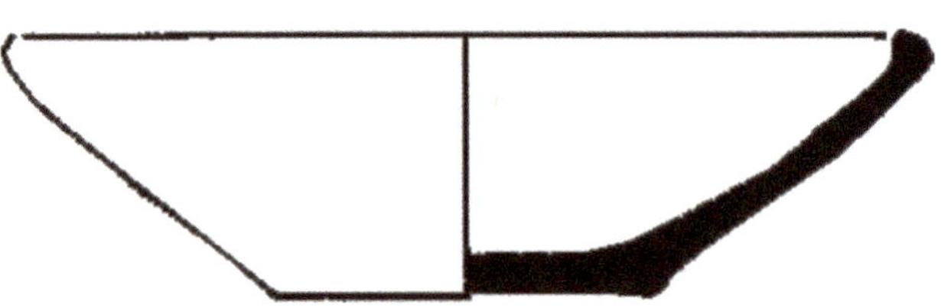

Flat base, simple rim (Type 4)

Both **PW 143** and **144** have a flat disc base and flaring wall ending in a simple rim. Apart from the difference in rims, their angular form is close to that of the preceding type and, like it, they only appear in an early first century BC context (main mound). The type is close to Gitin's Type 218 at Gezer (Gitin 1990: 253), although at this latter site the shape is first found in the mid-second century BC.

PW 143. CN 0035.
IIIB/C 1.1. Hellenistic 3C.
Complete. H 0.025; D rim 0.11. Pink clay 7.5YR 7/2.
Coarse Light Brown.
Thick flat base.
Parallel: Ashdod (Dothan 1971: fig. 61.5).

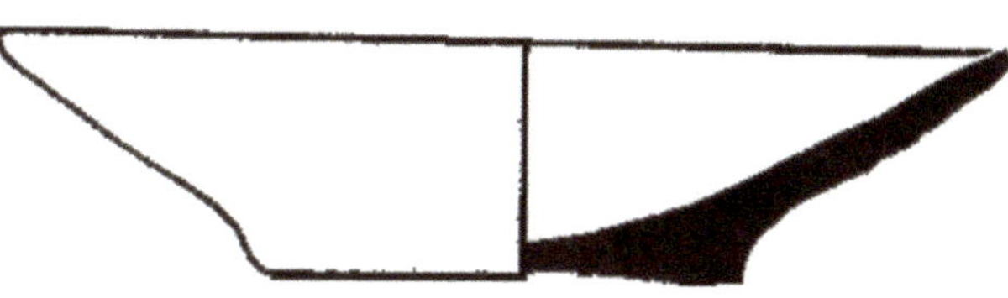

PW 144. CN 0038.
IIIB/C 1.2. Hellenistic 3C.
Complete. H 0.025; D rim 0.09. Very pale brown clay
10YR 8/2. Coarse Light Brown.
Flat string-cut base. Flaring wall; indistinct rim.
Parallel: Machaerus (Corbo and Loffreda 1981: fig.
36.4).

Bevelled rim (Type 5)

PW 145, of Coarse Light Brown ware and from a Jannaeus Destruction deposit on the main mound, has a flaring upper wall with a bevelled, inward-sloping rim; no other similar examples have been recovered at Pella. This simple form seems rare on both sides of the Jordan River: at Gezer, where it is classified as Type 198, only one example has been recovered (from a mid–second-century BC horizon) with a similar vessel found at Apollonia in an assemblage dating from the late fourth to the mid-second centuries BC (Fischer and Tal 1996: fig. 6.6). It does not appear at Samaria nor is it represented at Tel Dor or Tel Anafa.

PW 145. CN 7046.
XXIIIA 105.1. Hellenistic 3C.
Part of wall, rim. PH 0.015; D rim (est.) 0.225.
Reddish-yellow clay 7.5YR 6/6. Coarse Light Brown.
Streaky light brown slip over exterior.
Parallels: Apollonia (Fischer and Tal 1996: fig. 6.6);
Gadara/Umm Qais (Kenrick 2000: fig. 8.187); Gezer
(Gitin 1990: pl. 35.12, early-mid 2nd c. BC).

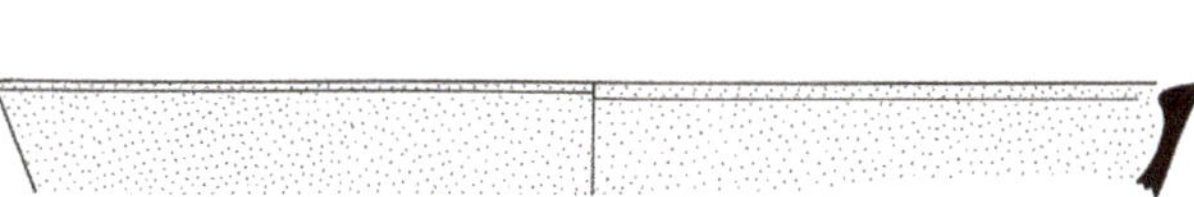

Hemispherical (Type 6)

PW 146–9 are of hemispherical shape. The rim on each is simple with only **PW 148** retaining its base. The shape is seen at Gezer only in ESA (Gitin 1990: Type 210A). At Samaria it appears both in ESA (Crowfoot et al. 1957: Form 16) and as a black-gloss form (Crowfoot et al. 1957: fig 53.2, 3) with a similar situation seen at Tel Anafa (TA Types 5 and 25). At Pella it is seen in ESA (Hayes Form 22A) as well as Coarse Light Brown ware (in second century BC and Early Roman strata); no black-gloss examples have been recovered.

PW 146. CN 7067.
XXIIIA 108.3. Hellenistic 3B.
Part of wall, rim. PH 0.03; PL 0.035; D rim (est.) 0.21.
Very pale brown clay 10YR 7/3. Coarse Light Brown.
Thin reddish-brown slip over interior, exterior.
Parallel: Gezer (Gitin 1990: pl. 42.10, early 1st c. BC).

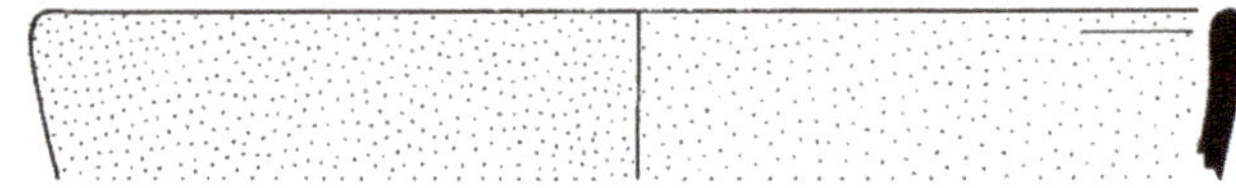

PW 147. CN 4329.
IVD 10.10. Hellenistic 3C.
Part of wall, rim. PH 0.055; D rim (est.) 0.12. Reddish-
yellow clay 7.5YR 6/6. Coarse Light Brown.
Orange-brown slip over interior, exterior. Wall separated
from slightly thickened rim by interior groove.
Parallel: Marisa (Kloner and Hess 1985: fig. 2.14).

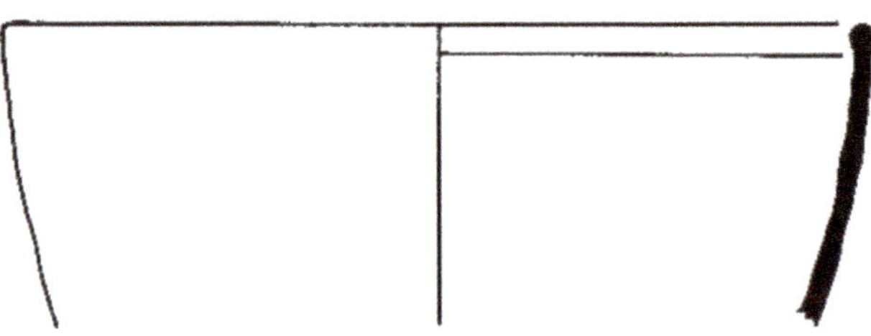

PW 148. CN 7163.
XXIIIB 1.1. Hellenistic 3C.
Part of wall, rim. PH 0.07; D rim 0.11. Greyish-yellow-
brown clay 10YR 6/2. Coarse Light Brown.
Dull black-brown slip over exterior. Ring base; lightly
ridged wall.

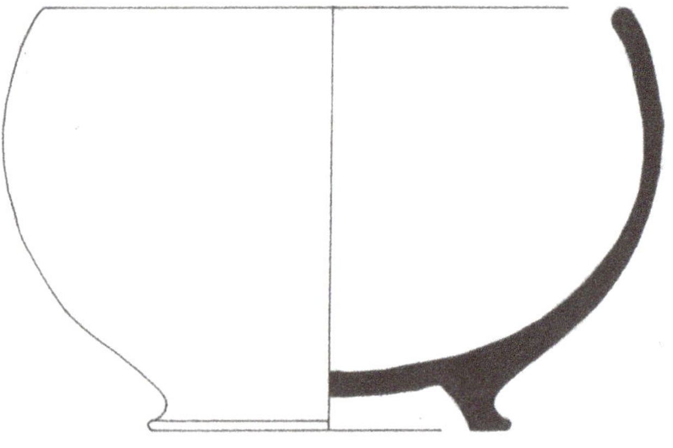

PW 149. CN 7241.
XXVIIIB 12.3. Mixed Context.
Part of wall, rim. PH 0.065; D rim (est.) 0.17. Red
clay 2.5YR 6/6. Coarse Light Brown.
Dull thin red-brown slip over interior, exterior. Rim
bevelled on interior.

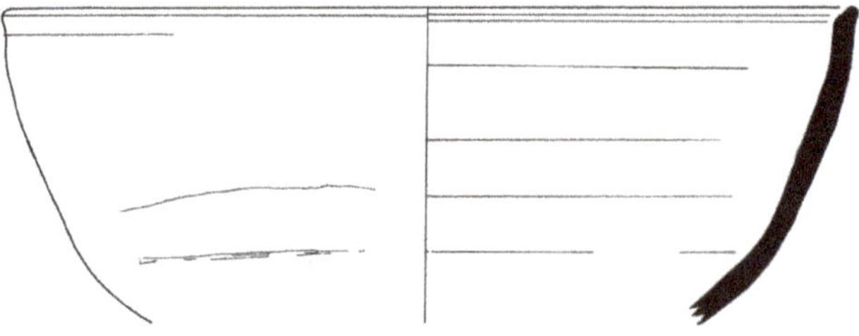

DRINKING VESSELS (PW 150-3)

The majority of Hellenistic drinking vessels recovered from second- and first-century BC levels comprise fine ware footless black-gloss or ESA bowls as well as small cups with narrow rims and pinched handles. The Greek-influenced skyphoi or kantharoi are rare at Pella in both fine wares (with the exception of West Slope kantharoi) and plain wares.

Table 2.20. Distribution of skyphoi/kantharoi and cups by wares, phases.

		SKYPHOS/KANTHAROS	CUPS
Ware	Coarse Light Brown	0	1
	Miscellaneous	1	2
Phase	3A c. 200–c. 140 BC	0	1
	3B c. 140–c. 100 (?) BC	0	2
	Mixed	1	0

Skyphos/kantharos

PW 150. CN 7722.
XXXIVB 57.8. Mixed Context.
Handle, part of rim, wall. PH 0.03; PL 0.03; D rim (est.) 0.12. Red clay 2.5YR 6/8.
Thin red slip over interior, exterior. Vertical spur handle. Simple rim; vertical upper wall.

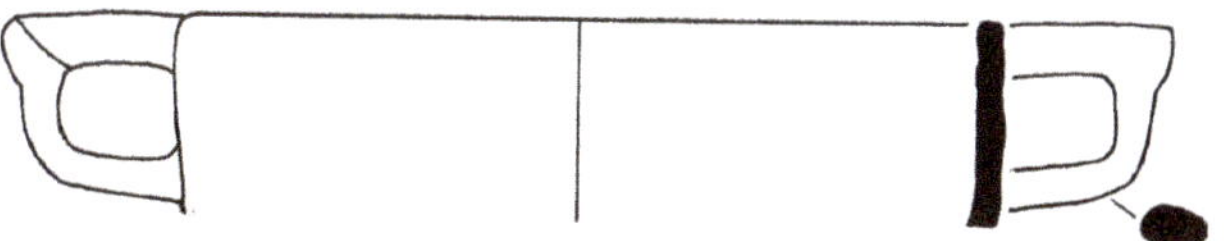

Cups: narrow band rim, pinched handles

At Pella three examples of this small cup (**PW 151–3**), more frequently seen amongst the fine wares, have been recovered from Pre-Jannaeus Destruction deposits.

PW 151. CN 7320.
XXVIIIB 13.2. Hellenistic 3A.
Part of wall, rim. PH 0.045; D rim (est.) 0.12. Brown clay 7.5YR 5/4. Small white inclusions.
Globular wall separated by groove from short flaring straight rim.
Parallel: ʿAkko-Ptolemais (Berlin and Stone 2016: fig. 9.12.15, mid–late 2nd c. BC).

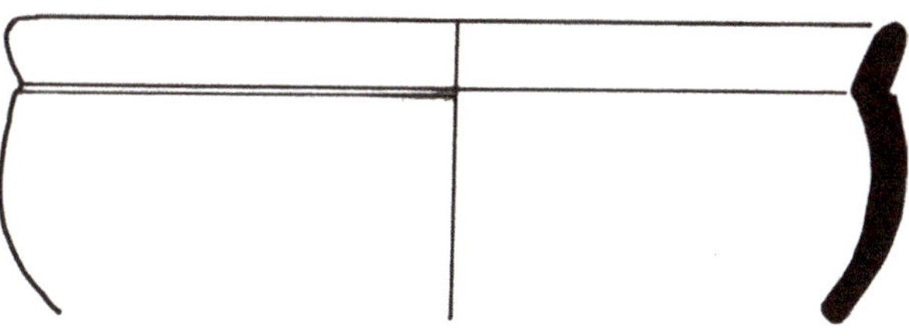

PW 152. CN 7782.
XXIIID 11.16. Hellenistic 3B.
Fragment of wall, rim, handle. PH 0.05; PL 0.07; D rim (est.) 0.15. Reddish-yellow clay 7.5YR 6/6.
Broad pinched handle.
Parallel: ʿAkko-Ptolemais (Berlin and Stone 2016: fig. 9.15.2, mid–late 2nd c. BC).

PW 153. CN 7297.
XXIIIB 2.3. Hellenistic 3B.
Part of wall, rim. PH 0.03; D rim (est.) 0.135. Pink
clay 7.5YR 7/4. Coarse Light Brown.
Patchy red-brown slip over interior, exterior.

KRATERS (PW 154–75)

Plain ware kraters appear in a wider variety of forms than in black-gloss and are also more numerous. Four distinct forms can be identified. Whereas at Pella kraters are seen in Hellenistic 3A levels, with the fluted krater **PW 174** even earlier, at 'Iraq al-Amir no krater fragments were found in levels before c. 100 BC (Zimmerman 2020b: 45).

Table 2.21. Distribution of kraters by types, wares, phases.

		FLARING RIM, VERTICAL LIP (TYPE 1)	HORIZONTAL RIM (TYPE 2)	DOWN-TURNED RIM (TYPE 3)	FLUTED (TYPE 4)
Ware	Coarse Light Brown	1	0	2	0
	Hard Pale	5	1	0	0
	Metallic Buff	2	1	0	0
	Miscellaneous	4	2	0	4
Phase	2B c. 220–c. 200 BC	0	0	0	1
	3A c. 200–c. 140 BC	4	2	2	0
	3B c. 140–c. 100 (?) BC	1	0	0	0
	3C c. 100 (?)–c. 80/79 BC	0	1	0	2 (1)
	Early Roman 63 BC–c. 135 AD	3	0	0	0
	Mixed	4 (2)	1	0	1 (3)

Flaring rim, vertical lip (Type 1)

Kraters of this type (**PW 154–65**) have been found at Pella mainly in early second-century BC contexts on the main mound (XXVIIIB) and Early Roman deposits on Tell Husn in plots XXXIVG and XIA/B where they constitute the sole variety of krater. The fragmentary nature of the Pella examples makes any attempt to recognise a chronological progression in shape meaningless. Despite its more rounded lip and ridged rim, **PW 163** (from an Early Roman horizon) has been included here; at Machaerus kraters of this form have been assigned to a separate group (Loffreda 1996: Group 59: figs 43.21–36), most examples of which are from Herodian deposits.

The form can be equated with the "coarse overhanging rim" kraters that make up the most common type at Tel Anafa (Berlin 1997a: 135, PW 393–9), first appearing in Hellenistic 2C (c. 98–75 BC) deposits there. At Tel Dor the type is also popular (Guz-Zilberstein 1995: 296, fig. 6.11:1–11, Type KR5). At this latter site, although the shape is first seen in third-century assemblages, most examples come from phases dated to 175–125 BC consistent with the Pre-Jannaeus Destruction finds from Pella. Both at Anafa and Dor, as well as Gamla (Berlin 2006: 29–30, figs 2.8.7–11), the form remains common well into Early Roman times as it does elsewhere in Palestine; east of the Jordan River it is seen at Hesban in contexts that have been designated "Early Roman II–III (37 BC–73 AD)", at 'Iraq al-Amir in ill-defined contexts (Zimmerman 2020b: pl. 2.6.1–3), and at Machaerus only in Herodian deposits (Gerber 2012: 246–9; Loffreda 1996: fig. 42, nos 11–24).

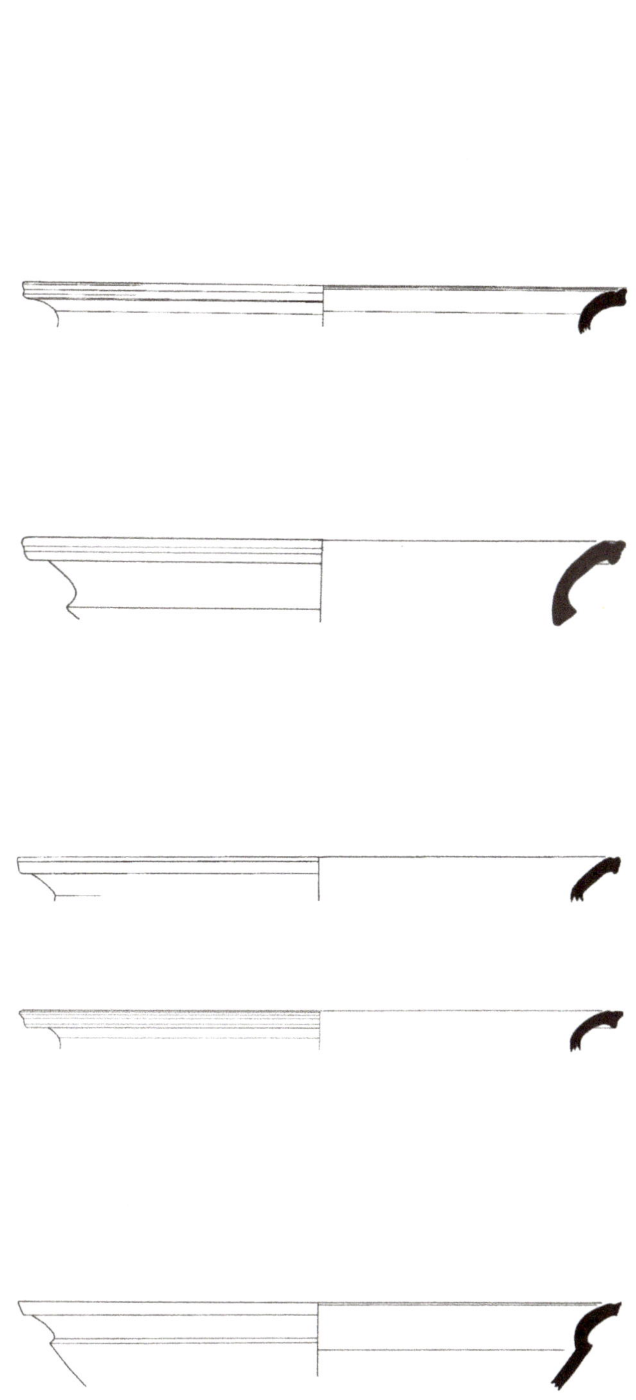

PW 154. CN 7259.
XXVIIIB 13.17. Hellenistic 3A.
Part of wall, rim. PH 0.015; D rim (est.) 0.36. Pink clay 7.5YR 7/4. Hard Pale.
Rim separated on interior by two ridges and a broad groove from lip.
Parallel: Tel Anafa (Berlin 1997a: pl.42. PW 398, ?–75 BC).

PW 155. CN 7436.
XXVIIIB 13.3. Hellenistic 3A.
Part of wall, rim. PH 0.03; D rim (est.) 0.36. Strong brown clay 7.5YR 5/6.
Rim separated on interior by groove from lip.
Parallel: Jericho (Pritchard 1958: pl. 58.12).

PW 156. CN 7266.
XXVIIIB 10.7. Hellenistic 3A.
Part of wall, rim. PH 0.03; D rim (est.) 0.27. Light yellowish-brown clay 10YR 6/4. Hard Pale.
Carination at base of fragment. Rim separated by deep groove on interior from lip.

PW 157. CN 7427.
XXVIIIB 13.2. Hellenistic 3A.
Part of wall, rim. PH 0.03; D rim (est.) 0.35. Pink clay 7.5YR 7/4. Grey core.
Rim separated by groove on interior from lip.

PW 158. CN 7265.
XXVIIIB 15.2. Mixed Context.
Part of wall, rim. PH 0.025; D rim (est.) 0.33. Reddish-yellow clay 7.5YR 6/6. Grey core. Hard Pale.
Broad groove on interior just below lip.
Parallels: Marisa (Kloner and Hess 1985: fig. 3.7); Tel Keisan (Briend 1980: pl. 10.3, late 4th–mid-2nd c. BC).

PW 159. CN 7790.
XXIIID 24.1. Hellenistic 3B.
Fragment of wall, rim. PH 0.06; PL 0.09; D rim (est.) 0.28. Red clay 2.5YR 6/8. Hard Pale.
Flaring upper wall; markedly out-turned rim. Vertical lip.
Parallel: Hesban (close to Gerber 2012: 249, fig. 3.19.1).

PW 160. CN 6703.

IIIP 25.20. Mixed Context.

Two joining fragments of wall, rim. PL 0.105; D rim (est.) 0.30. Reddish-yellow clay 7.5YR 7/6. Metallic Buff.

Everted wall. Flaring rim; vertical concave lip.

Parallels: Jerusalem (Geva and Rosenthal-Heginbottom 2003: pl. 6.6.12, early 1st c. AD; Tushingham 1985: fig. 23.10, 42/43–70 AD); Tel Dor (Guz-Zilberstein 1995: fig. 6.41:19, 125 BC–105 AD).

PW 161. CN 6740.

IIIP 25.21. Mixed Context.

Two joining fragments of wall, rim. PH 0.055; PL 0.09; D rim (est.) 0.26. Light yellowish-brown clay 10YR 6/4. Metallic Buff.

Everted wall sharply set off from flaring rim with vertical concave lip.

Parallel: Jerusalem (Geva and Rosenthal-Heginbottom 2003: pl. 6.6.13, early 1st c. AD).

PW 162. CN 7256.

XXXIVG 11.4. Early Roman 1.

Part of wall, rim. PH 0.015; D rim (est.) 0.32. Light reddish-brown clay 5YR 6/4. Hard Pale.

Flaring rim separated by narrow groove on interior from vertical lip.

Parallel: Ashdod (Dothan 1971: fig. 61.9 upper profile; southern Ghors and north-east 'Araba Survey (MacDonald 1992: pl. 21.1).

PW 163. CN 3063.

XIA/B 1.1/2. Early Roman 1.

Part of wall, rim. PH 0.045; D rim (est.) 0.32. Pale yellow clay 2.5Y 7/3.

Flaring upper wall. Concave neck; horizontal ridged rim.

Parallels: Hesban (Gerber 2012: 246, fig. 3.18.4); Kallirhoe (Clamer 1997: pl. 7.5); Machaerus (Loffreda 1996: fig. 43.32).

PW 164. CN 2937.

XIA/B 1.5. Early Roman 1.

Part of wall, rim. PH 0.035; D rim (est.) 0.32. Yellowish-red clay 5YR 5/6. Large lime inclusions.

Flaring upper wall; concave flaring rim. Vertical lip.

Parallels: Herodium (Bar-Nathan 1981: pl. 6.2); Jerusalem (Tushingham 1985: fig. 23.8); Tel Anafa (Berlin 1997a: pl. 42. PW 396, 75 BC–early 1st c. AD).

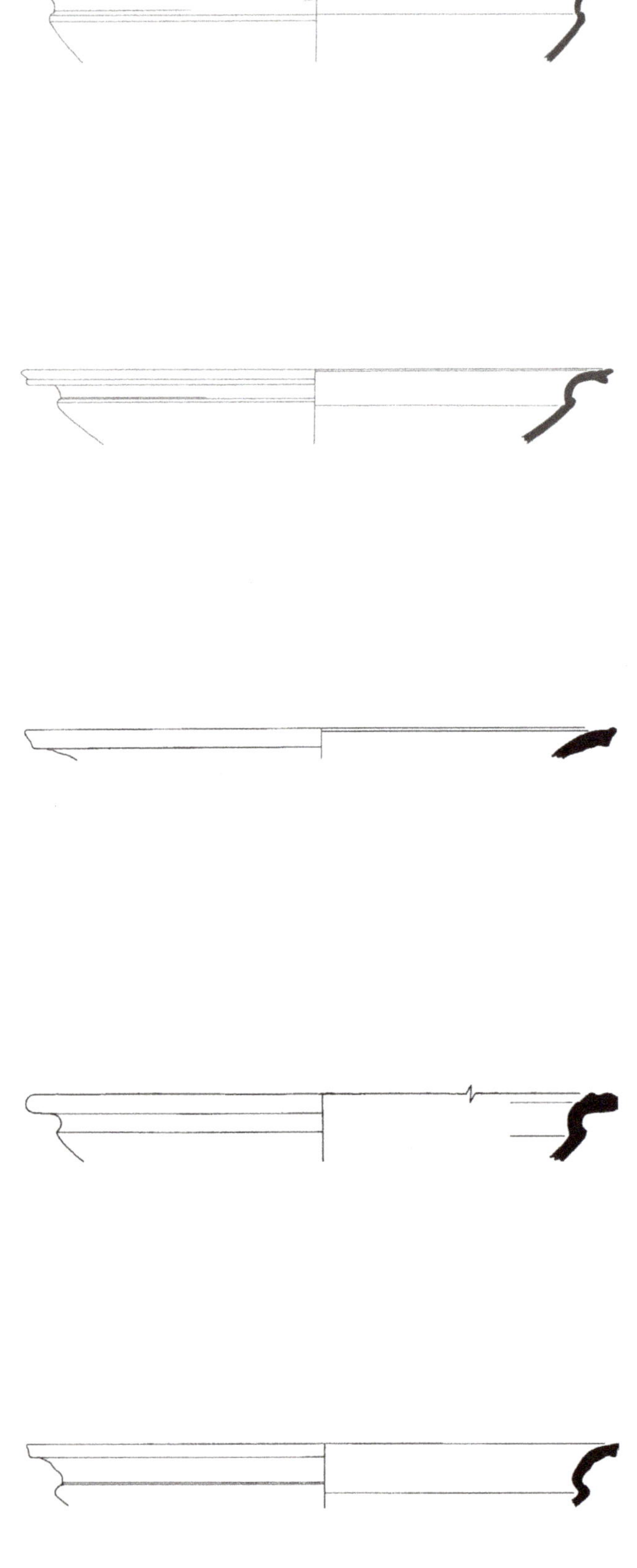

PW 165. CN 7337.
XXXIVB 14.4. Mixed Context.
Part of wall, rim. PH 0.06; PL 0.07; D rim (est.) 0.15.
Reddish-yellow clay 7.5YR 6/6. Coarse Light Brown.
Thin patchy red-brown slip over upper exterior, rim.
Gently in-curving wall; everted rim. Vertical lip with
"pie crust" decoration on lower edge.
Parallels: Herodium (Bar-Nathan 1981: pl. 6.2);
Hippos-Sussita (Osband and Eisenberg 2018: pl.
2.1.8, 2nd c. BC); Jericho (Kelso and Baramki 1955:
pl. 22.X93; Pritchard 1958: pl. 58.15); Machaerus
(Loffreda 1996: fig. 43.14); Shiqmona (Elgavish 1976:
fig. 2.3); Tel Dor (Guz-Zilberstein 1995: fig. 6.11:9,
200–125 BC).

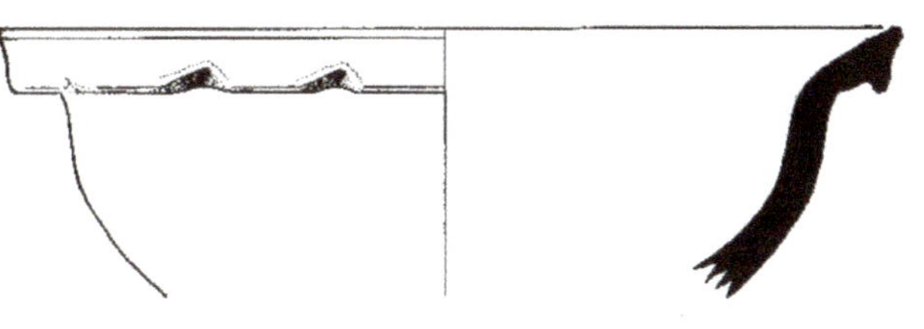

Horizontal rim (Type 2)

PW 166–9 are the only plain ware examples of this type in the corpus. They are of the same form as the
"small deep kraters" from Tel Dor (Guz-Zilberstein 1995: 296, fig. 6.12:1–6. Type KR10) recovered from
third- and second-century BC levels, with **PW 167** and **PW 169** from a similar horizon (Hellenistic 3A) on
the main mound. The form is also seen for example at Samaria, Scythopolis/Beth-Shean and sites further
to the north.[8]

PW 166. CN 7324.
XXVIIIB 9.7. Mixed Context.
Part of wall, rim. PH 0.06; D rim (est.) 0.14. Reddish-
yellow clay 5YR 6/6.
Concave upper body; flaring slightly convex neck.
Horizontal rim.
Parallel: Tel Keisan (Briend 1980: pl. 12.4, late 4th–
mid-2nd c. BC).

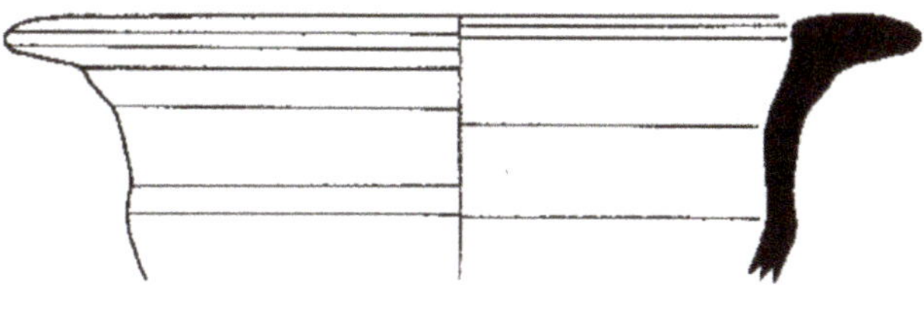

PW 167. CN 7264.
XXVIIIB 13.4. Hellenistic 3A.
Part of wall, rim. PH 0.03; D rim (est.) 0.20. Very
pale brown clay 10YR 7/4. Metallic Buff.
Upright wall. Broad horizontal slightly ridged rim.
Parallels: Hippos-Sussita (Osband and Eisenberg
2018: pl. 3.2.11, 1st c. BC); Tel Anafa (Berlin 1997a:
pl. 46. PW 418, 75 BC–early 1st c. AD); Tel Dor (Guz-
Zilberstein 1995: fig. 6.14:10, 250–125 BC).

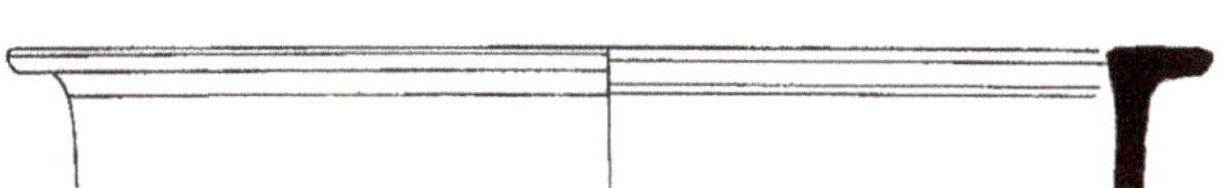

---

8   Jackson 2011a: 42–3, figs 29–31, pl. 5 (Jebel Khalid in Syria); Crowfoot et al. 1957: figs 57.5–7 (Samaria);
     Johnson 2006: fig. 15.2.39 (Scythopolis/Beth-Shean).

PW 168. CN 7766.
XXIIID 19.2. Hellenistic 3C.
Fragment of wall, rim. PH 0.035; PL 0.075; D rim
(est.) 0.22. Reddish-yellow clay 5YR 7/8.
Thin brown-red slip over interior, exterior. Flaring
upper wall. Narrow rim overhanging exterior.

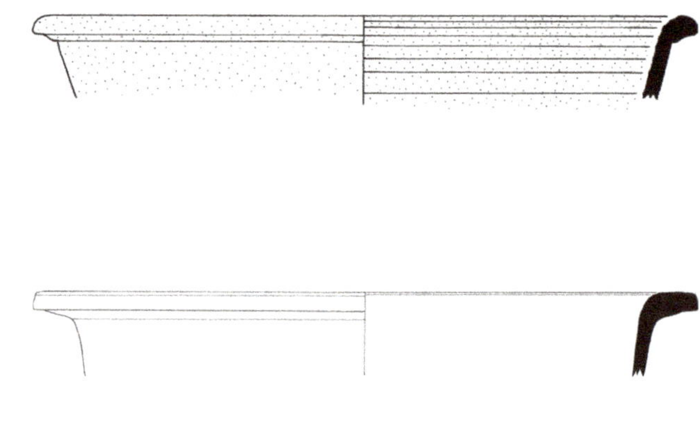

PW 169. CN 7221.
XXVIIIB 10.2. Hellenistic 3A.
Part of wall, rim. PH 0.055; D rim (est.) 0.24. Reddish-
yellow clay 7.5YR 7/6. Thin white slip. Hard Pale.
Upright wall. Thick horizontal rim.

Down-turned rim (Type 3)

The distinguishing characteristics of **PW 170–1** are the upper walls, which flare outwards, especially in the case of the latter specimen, and the downward sloping rims. Both examples come from Pre-Jannaeus Destruction (Hellenistic 3A) deposits on the main mound of the early second century BC. Although the form, in a "Second Temple period" context, is seen at Qumran (Eshel and Broshi 2003: 63, fig. 4.4), there are no close parallels from Kallirhoe, Machaerus or Palestinian sites.

PW 170. CN 7216.
XXVIIIB 13.17. Hellenistic 3A.
Part of wall, rim. PH 0.04; D rim (est.) 0.24. Reddish-
yellow clay 7.5YR 7/6. Coarse Light Brown.
Patchy thin brown slip over exterior. Flaring upper
wall. Angled down-turned rim.

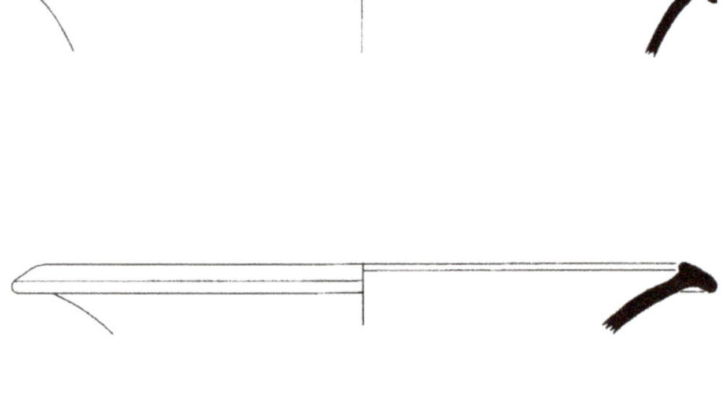

PW 171. CN 7457.
XXVIIIB 13.9. Hellenistic 3A.
Part of wall, rim. PH 0.04; D rim (est.) 0.30. Yellow
clay 2.5YR 7/6. Coarse Light Brown.
Flaring upper wall. Down-turned rim projecting on
interior, exterior.
Parallel: Qumran (Eshel and Broshi 2003: fig.4.4).

Fluted (Type 4)

Smith's "gouge-fluted ware" (McNicoll et al. 1982: 75) is represented by kraters **PW 172–5** along with four body sherds (uncatalogued), of which one is from a Jannaeus Destruction deposit in plot XXIIIA and three from unstratified levels. The "fluting" on the kraters of this type was achieved by means of a sculptor's burin rather than a mould; this technique was also employed, although rarely, in Athens itself (Townsend 1995: 148). These vessels, with their thin black or red slip, are clearly imitating the fine ware ribbed kraters (usually black- or red-gloss or true ESA) recovered from sites such as Antioch, Hama, Jebel Khalid, Marisa, Samaria, Tarsus and Tel Anafa.[9] A further similar specimen was uncovered by the Wooster team in area VIII (McNicoll et al. 1982: pl. 130.1).

---

9   Waagé 1948: 24, Form 160 (Antioch); Christensen and Johansen 1971: fig. 72, Form 27 (Hama); Tidmarsh 2011: fig. 108. FW137 (Jebel Khalid in Syria); Levine 2003: fig. 6.4.60 (Marisa); Reisner et al. 1924: fig. 185: 11a, 11b (Samaria); F.F. Jones 1950: 219 fig. 126, nos 120–2 (Tarsus); Slane 1997: 320–1, pls 22–3, Type 30 (Tel Anafa).

PW 172. CN 7166.
XXIIIA 10.11. Hellenistic 3C.
Multiple fragments. Missing part of wall, rim, neck,
handle. H 0.16; D rim (est.) 0.11. Red clay 2.5YR6/8.
Coarse white inclusions.
Patchy thin red slip over exterior. Broad raised base;
narrow foot; globular wall. Short neck with markedly
everted rim. Gouged fluting on body; three horizontal
grooves on shoulder. Part of one double handle
preserved.

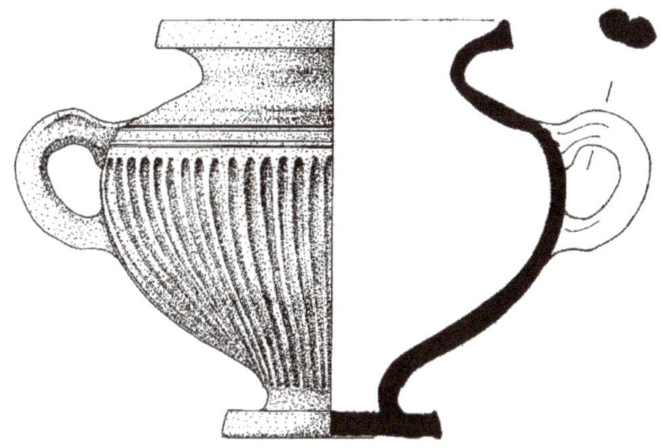

PW 173. CN 7102.
XXIIIA 80.6. Mixed Context.
Part of rim, neck, shoulder, handle (five fragments).
PH 0.08; D rim (est.) 0.14. Red clay 2.5YR 6/8. Grey
core. Coarse white inclusions.
Dull black-brown slip over upper interior, exterior.
Short concave neck; flaring rim. Part of double handle
preserved. Trace of fluting on upper body.

PW 174. CN 7654.
XXXIVB 27.19. Hellenistic 2B.
Part of wall, handle. PH 0.075; PL 0.07. Light
yellowish-brown clay 10YR 6/4.
Worn red-brown slip over exterior; dark brown on
interior. Curved wall. Vertical gouging below two
horizontal grooves. Stub of handle above.

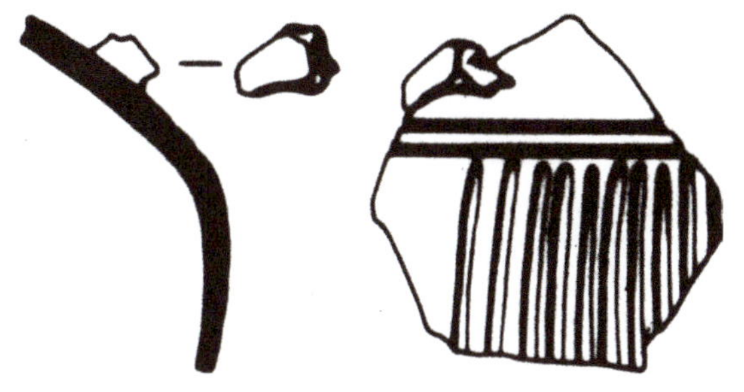

PW 175. CN 7809.
XXIIID 32.1. Hellenistic 3C.
Wall fragment. PH 0.045; PL 0.06. Yellowish-red clay
5YR 5/6.
Worn dull red slip over interior, exterior. Sloping
shoulder separated from body by two horizontal
grooves. Vertical gouging on body.

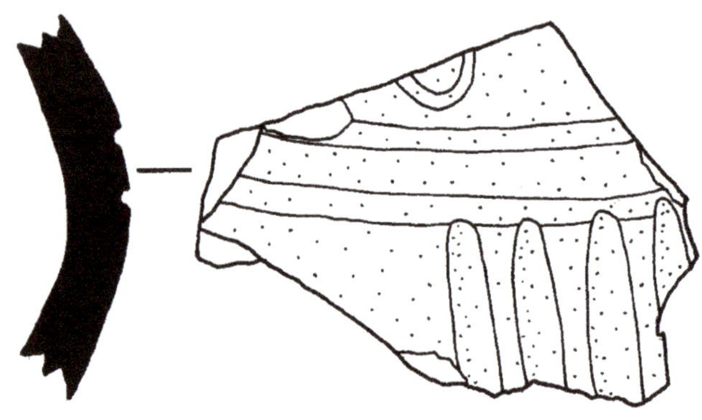

TABLE AMPHORAE (PW 176-85)

Of the Pella table amphorae, used for serving liquids at the table rather than their long-term storage,
PW 184 is the earliest, from within the "Antiochus Destruction" deposit on Tell Husn (Hellenistic 2B) of
the late third century BC. Further catalogued (**PW 176–80**) and two uncatalogued specimens have been
found on the main mound in Pre-Jannaeus Destruction (Hellenistic 3A–B) deposits from plot XXVIIIB with
PW 182–3 from a Jannaeus Destruction (Hellenistic 3C) context, **PW 181** from the pre-construction fill
(Mixed Context) in plot IIIB/C, and **PW 185** from an unstratified context in plot IIIP.

Although ceramic examples are known from the third century, they only appear in regular use from
the second century BC (Berlin 2015: 635). Table amphorae are by no means common in Israel and even
less common east of the Jordan River though seen at Pella, Hesban, Madaba and Tell Zira'a.[10] On the other
hand, large numbers occur at Tel Anafa with the great majority (the "semi-fine angled rim" variety) being of
Phoenician manufacture, thus emphasising the close ties between Hellenistic Tel Anafa and southern Phoenicia
(Berlin 1997a: 38; c). Similar examples, but in a variety of wares, are seen at Tel Dor (Guz-Zilberstein 1995:
309, Type JG 7b); given the strength of Phoenician involvement with Dor during the Persian and earlier
Hellenistic periods (Stern 1995a; 1995b: 2–3), it is clear that while some are Phoenician products (Berlin
1997c), others are merely imitations of the Phoenician shape, as also seems to be the case at Pella.

As regards the Pella table amphorae, none has its full profile. On **PW 176**, **PW 180** and **PW 185**, the
handle is attached to the neck but none of the Pella examples preserves its lower handle attachment or base.
Most have a rim projecting on the exterior, either horizontally or slightly downwards, and a concave neck that

---

10   Gerber 2012: 199–200, fig. 3.6.21–2 (Hesban); Ferguson 2014: 180, fig. 5.9 (Madaba); Kenkel 2020: 42–3, 140–1,
     pl. 1.12.Tg 3.1–8 (Tell Zira'a).

(on the basis of **PW 183**) runs smoothly into the body. On **PW 184–5** the rim also projects to the exterior but the stepped interior (possibly to fit a lid) results in a markedly different upper profile.

The ware of only **PW 183** seems close to the Phoenician semi-fine ware, described by Berlin (1997a: 9) as "fairly soft, well-levigated, and pale buff to pink in colour". Its chalky texture and "fine, dusty film" – adhering to the fingers on handling – are also characteristic. Vessels in this ware (juglets, table jugs, amphorae, amphoriskoi, unguentaria, funnels, lagynoi, ointment pots, saucer lids, jars) have been recovered from Cyprus, coastal Palestine and the Hula Valley. Only one example of this ware – an amphoriskos from Tell es-Shuna (Philip and Baird 1993: fig. 11.1) – has been reported from Transjordan; it seems likely, however, that a "jug" from Tell es-Sa'idiyeh (Pritchard 1985: fig. 20.13) also fits into this category in which case, like the Tell es-Shuna amphoriskos and (possibly) the Tell es-Sa'idiyeh "jug", **PW 178** may have reached its destination either via the Hula Valley in the north (Berlin 1997c: 84) or from coastal sites such as 'Akko-Ptolemais through the Jezreel Valley and across the Jordan River (Berlin and Stone 2016: 140–1).

The presence of **PW 183** in a Jannaeus Destruction deposit is consistent with Berlin's suggestion (1997c: 79–80) that the production (or at least the distribution) of Phoenician semi-fine wares commenced during the second half of the second century BC. Berlin (1997c) has pointed out that those semi-fine vessels found in Early Roman levels from sites such as Tel Anafa are residual and this should also apply to a further fragment (non-catalogued) from an Early Roman level in plot XXXIVG.

Table 2.22. Distribution of table amphorae by wares, phases.

Ware		
	Coarse Light Brown	2
	Phoenician?	1
	Miscellaneous	7
Phase	2B c. 220–c. 200 BC	1
	3A c. 200–c. 140 BC	5
	3B c. 140–c. 100 (?) BC	0 (2)
	3C c. 100 (?)–c. 80/79 BC	2
	Mixed	2

Projecting rim (Type 1)

PW 176. CN 7262.
XXVIIIB 13.2/7. Hellenistic 3A.
Two joining fragments of neck, rim, handle. PH 0.055;
D rim (est.) 0.12. Reddish-yellow clay 7.5YR 6/6.
Parallels: 'Akko-Ptolemais (Berlin and Stone 2016:
fig. 9.12.20, mid–late 2nd c. BC); Tell es-Sa'idiyeh
(Pritchard 1985: fig. 20.13 upper profile).

PW 177. CN 7263.
XXVIIIB 13.1. Hellenistic 3A.
Two joining fragments of neck, rim. PH 0.03; D rim
(est.) 0.12. Reddish-yellow clay 5YR 6/8. Pale yellow
slip over interior, exterior.

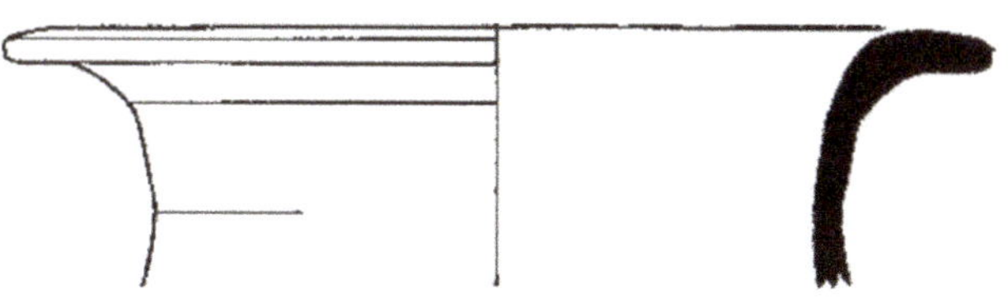

PW 178. CN 7410.
XXVIIIB 10.6. Hellenistic 3A.
Part of neck and rim. PH 0.04; D rim (est.) 0.12.
Reddish-yellow clay 7.5YR 7/6. Pale yellow slip over interior, exterior.
Parallels: 'Akko-Ptolemais (Berlin and Stone 2016: fig. 9.11.3, late 3rd–mid-2nd c. BC); Tel Yoqne'am (Ben-Tor et al. 1983: fig. 7.15 upper profile).

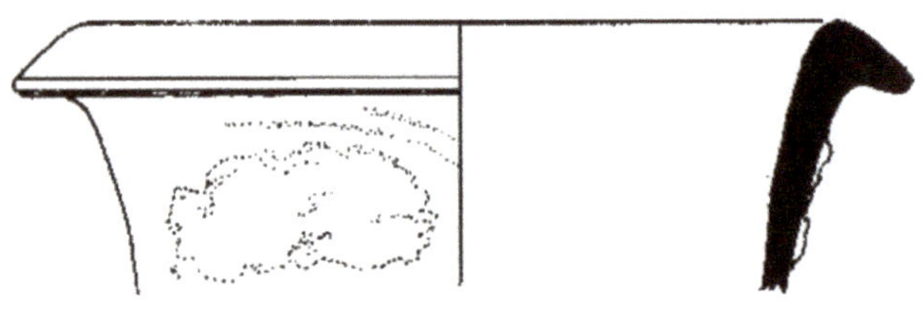

PW 179. CN 7450.
XXVIIIB 13.8. Hellenistic 3A.
Part of wall, rim. PH 0.03; D rim (est.) 0.12. Strong brown clay 7.5YR 5/8.

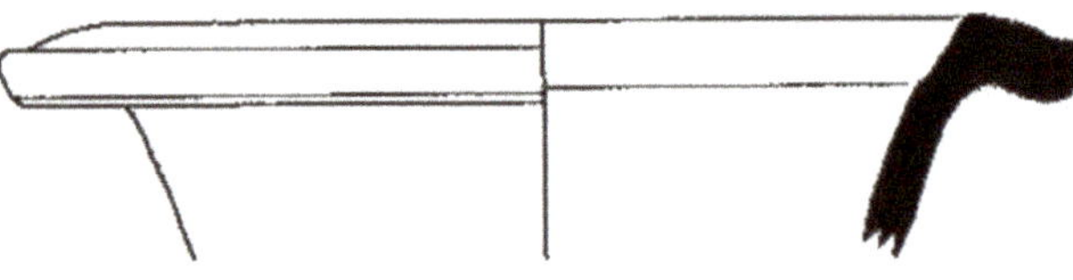

PW 180. CN 7453.
XXVIIIB 13.8. Hellenistic 3A.
Part of wall, rim, handle. PH 0.055; D rim (est.) 0.11.
Reddish-yellow clay 5YR 7/6. Coarse Light Brown.
Thin patchy dull red slip over upper interior, exterior.
Strap handle joined to neck.

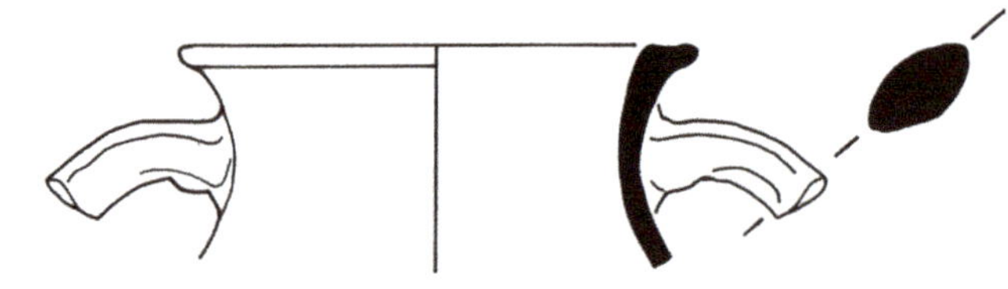

PW 181. CN 0486.
IIIB/C 1.25. Mixed Context.
Part of wall, rim. PH 0.04; D rim (est.) 0.165. Reddish-yellow clay 5YR 7/6. Coarse Light Brown.
Thin red slip over rim, upper interior.

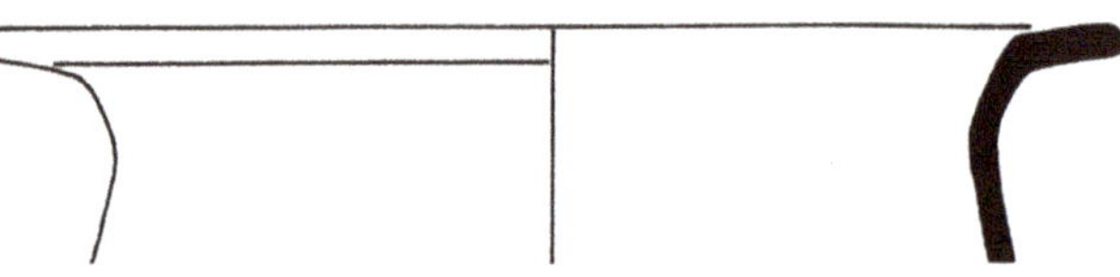

PW 182. CN 7744.
XXIIID 19.1. Hellenistic 3C.
Fragment of neck, rim. PH 0.05; D rim (est.) 0.13.
Light brown clay 7.5YR 6/4.
Worn brown slip over interior.
Parallel: 'Akko-Ptolemais (Berlin and Stone 2016: fig. 9.21.16, 1st half of 1st c. BC).

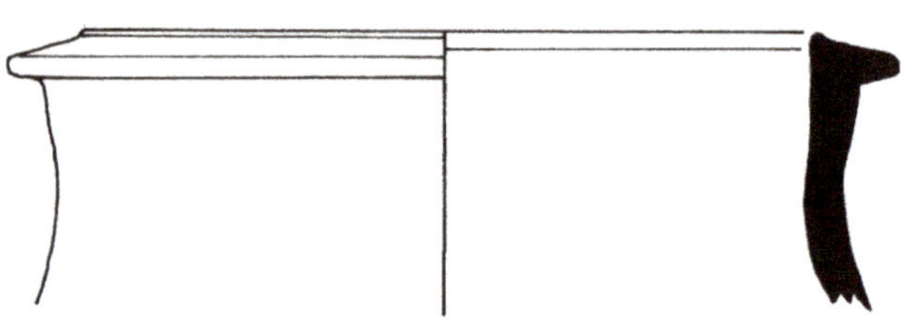

PW 183. CN 7544.
XXIIIA 71.2. Hellenistic 3C.
Part of neck and rim. PH 0.075; D rim (est.) 0.15.
Light yellowish-brown clay 10YR 6/4. Moderately well levigated; occasional white inclusions. Phoenician semi-fine ware?
Wall separated by horizontal groove and ridge on exterior from upright neck.

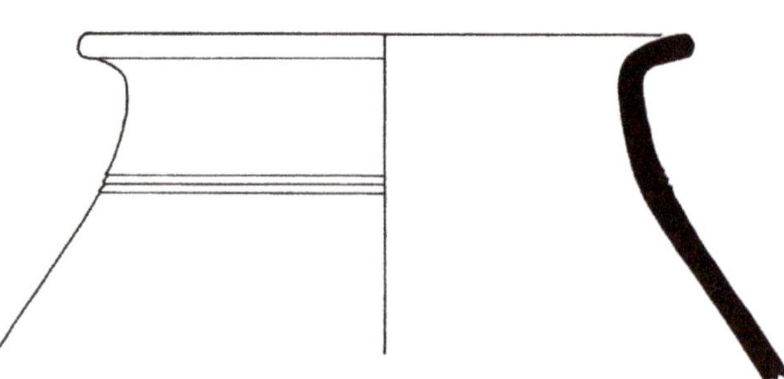

Stepped interior (Type 2)

PW 184. CN 7695.
XXXIVB 41.2. Hellenistic 2B.
Part of wall, rim. PH 0.045; PL 0.065; D rim
(est.) 0.16. Reddish-yellow clay 7.5YR 6/6.
Patchy brown slip over interior, exterior. Concave
upper body; upright neck. Horizontal rim overhanging
exterior.
Parallels: 'Akko-Ptolemais (Berlin and Stone 2016:
fig. 9.9.4, late 3rd–mid-2nd c. BC); Gadara/Umm
Qais (Kenrick 2000: fig. 5.55); Jerusalem (Geva 2003:
pl. 5.2.33, late 2nd–1st c. BC).

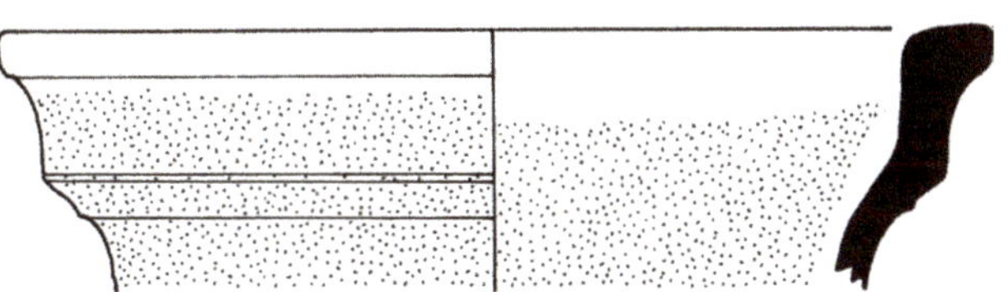

PW 185. CN 6706.
IIIP 25.20. Mixed Context.
Part of neck, rim, handle. PH 0.085; PL 0.09; D rim
(est.) 0.13. Reddish-yellow clay 7.5YR 6/6. Thin dull
black slip over interior, exterior rim.
Horizontal rim with broad groove. Concave neck
widening below rim. Vertical strap handle.
Parallel: Jebel Khalid in Syria (Jackson 2011a:
fig. 55.11, 225–70 BC).

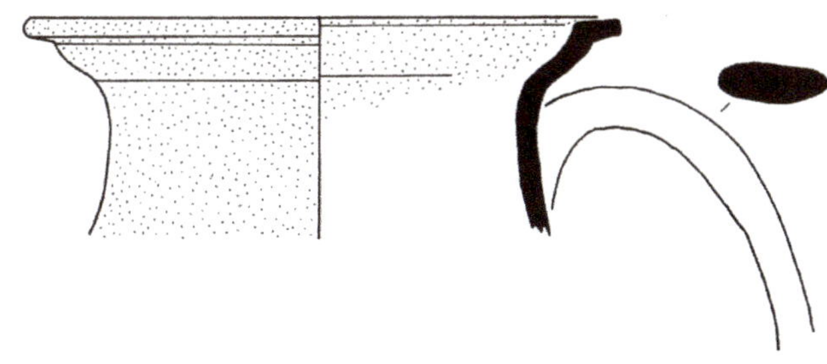

JUGS (PW 186–211)

Jugs are single-handled vessels used to pour liquids: as such, the neck is usually relatively narrow in order to regulate the flow. Unless the rim is substantially intact, they are often hard to differentiate from small jars; possibly for this reason, both jugs and juglets are relatively few in number in the corpus. As very few have their full profile preserved, both jugs and juglets are classified here on the basis of rim form.

Thickened rim (Type 1)

Jugs of this form (**PW 186–91**), with elongated gently concave neck and slightly thickened rim, are seen at Pella from "Antiochus Destruction" to Jannaeus Destruction levels on Tell Husn and the main mound (Hellenistic 2B, 3A, 3C). Only **PW 188** preserves its underside, which is markedly concave, possibly for ease of transport on the head when the vessel is filled (Berlin 2015: 637).

Jugs with rim forms similar to our Type 1 were recovered from 'Iraq al-Amir, Hippos-Sussita and Jerusalem in second-century BC to first-century AD horizons.[11]

---

11   Mlynarczyk 2011: pl. 243.15, 17, later 2nd–1st c. AD; pl. 247.99, 2nd c.–mid-1st c. AD; Osband and Eisenberg 2018: pl. 2.2.4, 2nd c. AD (Hippos-Sussita,); Zimmerman 2020b: pl. 2.15.2–7, early 2nd c. BC–1st c. AD ('Iraq al-Amir); Geva 2003: pl. 5.2.35 (Jerusalem).

Table 2.23. Distribution of jugs by types, wares, phases.

		THICKENED RIM (TYPE 1)	SHORT-COLLARED RIM (TYPE 2)	GROOVED RIM (TYPE 3)	FLARING RIM (TYPE 4)	FLANGED RIM (TYPE 5)
Ware	Hard Pale	1	0	1	0	2
	Metallic Buff	1	0	0	1	4
	Coarse Light Brown	3	1	2	0	2
	Miscellaneous	1	2	2	1	2
Phase	2B c. 220–c. 200 BC	1	0	0	0	0
	3A c. 200–c. 140 BC	1	0	4	0	1 (intrusive)
	3B/3C c. 140–c. 80/79 BC	0	0	0	0	1
	3C c. 100 (?)–c. 80/79 BC	3	3	0	1	2
	Early Roman 63 BC–c. 135 AD	0	0	1 (residual)	1	4
	Mixed	1	0	0	0	2

PW 186. CN 7663.
XXXIVB 27.22. Hellenistic 2B.
Part of wall, rim. PH 0.08; D rim (est.) 0.09. Very pale brown clay 10YR 7/4. Metallic Buff.
Parallel: ʿIraq al-Amir (N.L. Lapp 1979: fig. 2.11).

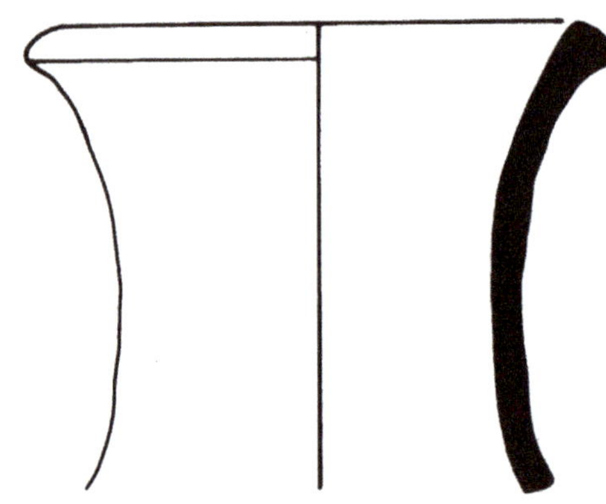

PW 187. CN 7187.
XXVIIIB 13.5. Hellenistic 3A.
Two non-joining fragments of wall, rim. PH 0.045; D rim .07. Reddish-yellow clay 5YR 6/8. Coarse Light Brown.
Parallels: ʿIraq al-Amir (Zimmerman 2020b: pl. 2.15.4, Str. IIIb–IIIa, c. 100 BC–50 AD); Jerusalem (Geva 2003: pl. 5.2.35, late 2nd–1st c. BC).

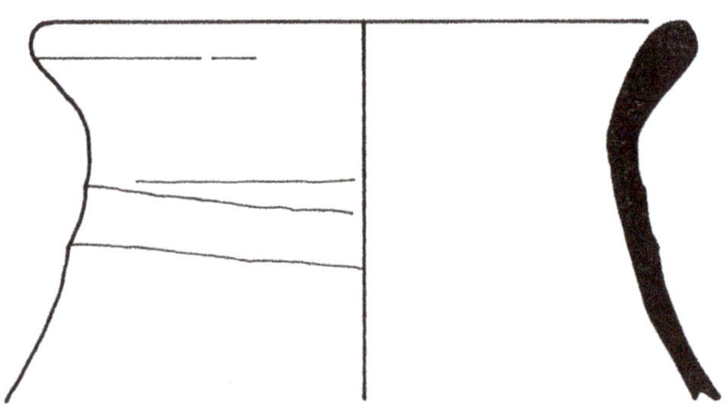

PW 188. CN 6893.
XXIIIA 12.8. Mixed Context.
Part of base, wall, rim. H 0.21; D rim (est.) 0.08.
Reddish-yellow clay 5YR 7/6. Coarse Light Brown.
Raised concave base; ovoid body.
Parallels: ʿAkko-Ptolemais (Berlin and Stone 2016:
fig. 9.15.10 upper profile, mid–late 2nd c. BC); Ashdod
(close to Dothan 1971: fig. 60.1, first half of 2nd
c. BC–mid-1st c. BC).

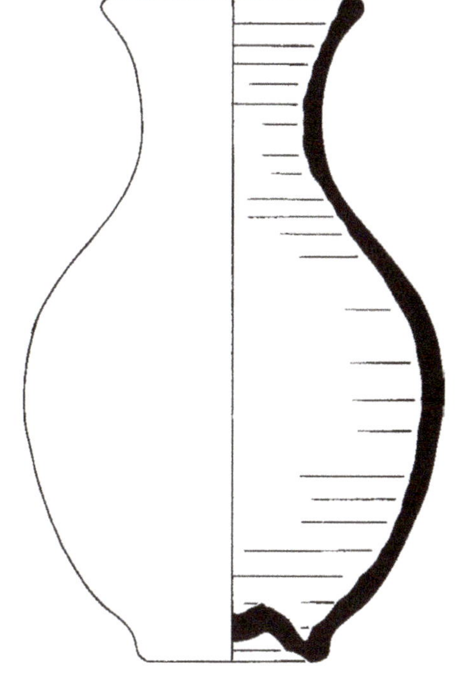

PW 189. CN 7043.
XXIIIA 105.1. Hellenistic 3C.
Part of rim, handle. PH 0.03; D rim (est.) 0.09. Light
brown clay 7.5YR 6/4. Occasional small white inclusions.
Thin patchy reddish-brown slip over interior, exterior.
Root of strap handle on mid-neck.
Parallels: Gezer (Gitin 1990: pl. 39.17, late 2nd c.
BC); Hippos-Sussita (Osband and Eisenberg 2018:
pl. 2.2.4, 2nd c. BC).

PW 190. CN 1417.
IIIB/C 14.3. Hellenistic 3C.
Part of wall, rim. PH 0.04; D rim (est.) 0.10. Reddish-
yellow clay 7.5YR 6/6. Hard Pale.

PW 191. CN 7752.
XXIIID 18.6. Hellenistic 3C.
Part of wall, rim. PH 0.035; PL 0.045; D rim (est.) 0.10.
Very pale brown clay 10YR 7/4. Coarse Light Brown.

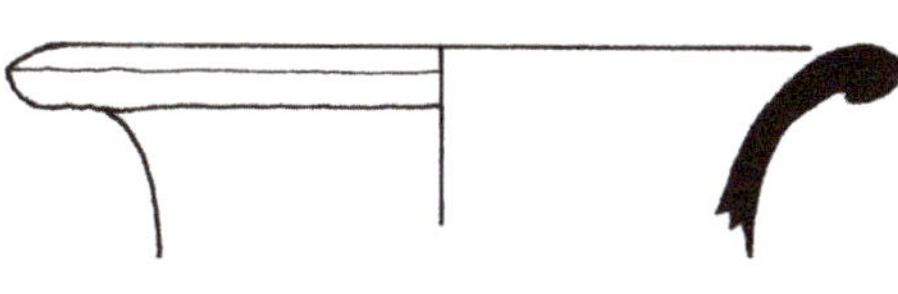

Short-collared rim (Type 2)

All three examples (**PW 192–4**), from Jannaeus Destruction levels (main mound), possess a concave neck and narrow collared rim also seen at Pella on jars of Type 4, although the globular profile of **PW 192** clearly differs from the more sack-like form of **PW 194**. Jugs of this form were recovered from second-century BC levels at Tel Dor (Guz-Zilberstein 1995: 308–9, fig. 6.30) with similar jug rim fragments seen in a first-century BC context at Hippos-Sussita (Osband and Eisenberg 2018: pl.3.1.1, 1st c. BC).

PW 192. CN 7009.
XXIIIA 71.5. Hellenistic 3C.
Whole vessel. H 0.21; D rim 0.05. Red clay 2.5YR 5/8. Coarse white inclusions.
Globular body with faint ridging. Strap handle from shoulder to rim.
Parallels: Amman/Philadelphia (Hadidi 1970: pl. III.7); Kedesh (Levantine Ceramics Project: n.d. K08P265, 3rd–2nd c. BC).

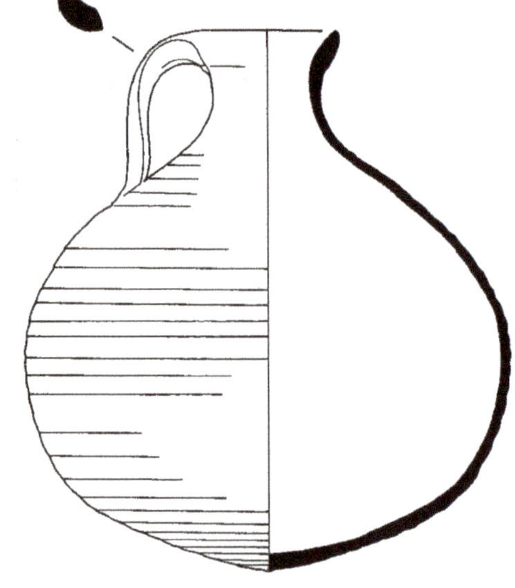

PW 193. CN 7795.
XXIIIA 71.2,5. Hellenistic 3C.
Complete rim, handle. Multiple body fragments. Rim fragment: PH 0.115; PL 0.13; D rim 0.095. Very pale brown clay 10YR 7/4.
Collared rim. Single strap handle from lip to shoulder. Carelessly made.

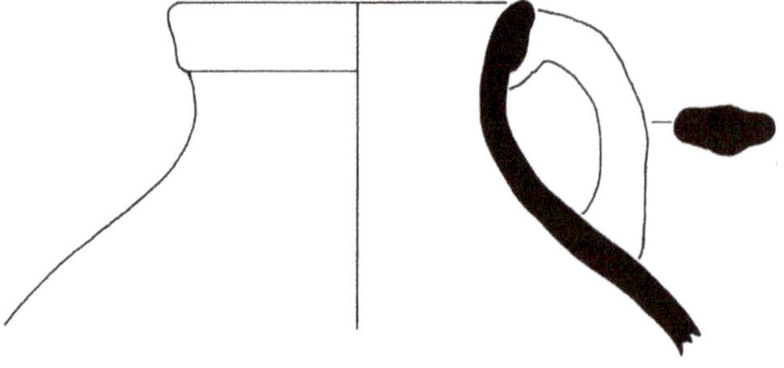

PW 194. CN 7158.
XXIIIA 74.2. Hellenistic 3C.
Missing part of rim, resting surface and several body fragments. PH 0.26; D rim 0.10. Very pale brown clay 10YR 7/4. Coarse Light Brown.
Patchy greyish-brown slip over exterior. Rounded resting surface; bag-shaped body. Collared rim. Strap handle from rim to shoulder.
Parallel: Tel Zahara (Bar-Nathan and Gärtner 2013: fig. 3.10.92 upper profile).

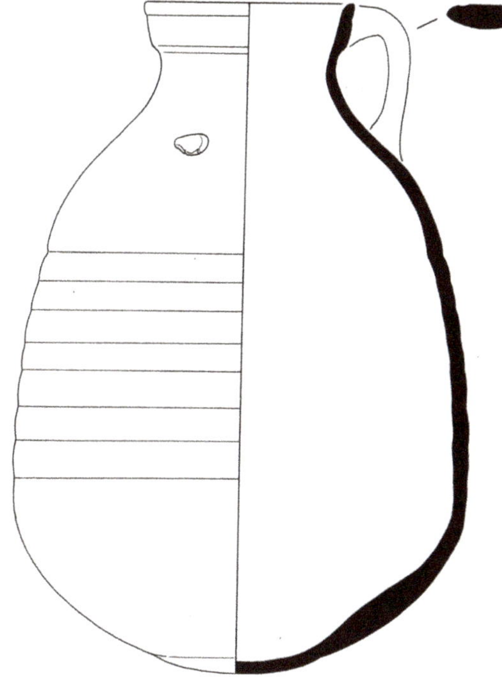

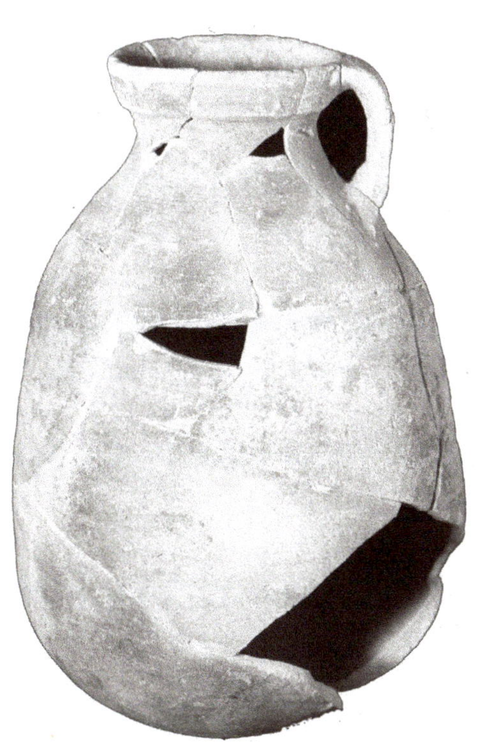

Grooved overhanging rim (Type 3)

Jugs of similar type to those from the main mound and Tell Husn (**PW 195–9**), with short concave neck, grooved rim overhanging the exterior and a low ring base (only preserved on **PW 195),** are seen at 'Iraq al-Amir (Zimmerman 2020b, Type 90.3, pl. 2.15.8–9) as well as Tel Dor amongst Guz-Zilberstein's Type JG 4 (Guz-Zilberstein 1995: 309, fig. 6.31:2) where the type is most common during the second century BC, as is the case with the Pella examples (**PW 195–9**).

PW 195. CN 7539.
XXXIIY 4.3. Hellenistic 3A.
Two non-joining fragments preserving base, part of wall, rim. (a) PH 0.11; (b) PH 0.04; D rim (est.) 0.09; D base 0.075. Reddish-yellow clay 5YR 6/6. Hard Pale. Globular body; low ring base. Concave neck; grooved overhanging rim.

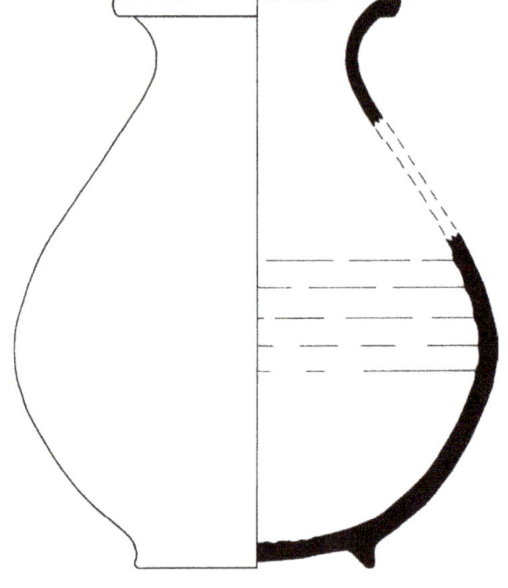

PW 196. CN 7853.
XXXIIY 1.2. Hellenistic 3A.
Part of wall, rim. PH 0.04; D rim (est.) 0.07. Red clay 2.5YR 5/8. Occasional white inclusions.

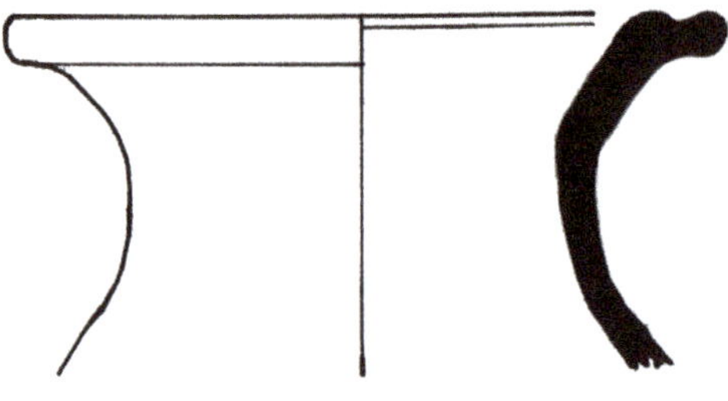

PW 197. CN 7261.
XXVIIIB 13.7. Hellenistic 3A.
Part of wall, rim. PH 0.03; D rim (est.) 0.08. Pale red clay 2.5YR 7/3. Coarse Light Brown.
Parallels: Apollonia (Fischer and Tal 1996: fig. 7.6); Marisa (Oren and Rappaport 1984: fig. 13.7); Shechem (N.L. Lapp 2008: pl. 3.19.1, 225–190 BC); Tel Dor (Guz-Zilberstein 1995: fig. 6.31:1, 500–375 BC).

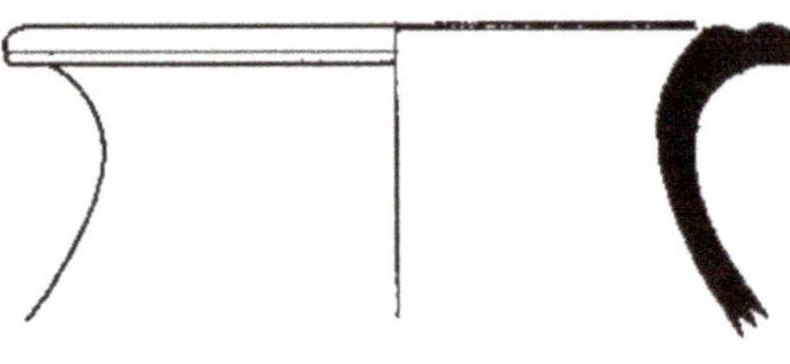

PW 198. CN 7406.
XXVIIIB 10.6. Hellenistic 3A.
Part of wall, rim. PH 0.03; D rim (est.) 0.09. Reddish-yellow clay 7.5YR 6/6. Coarse Light Brown.

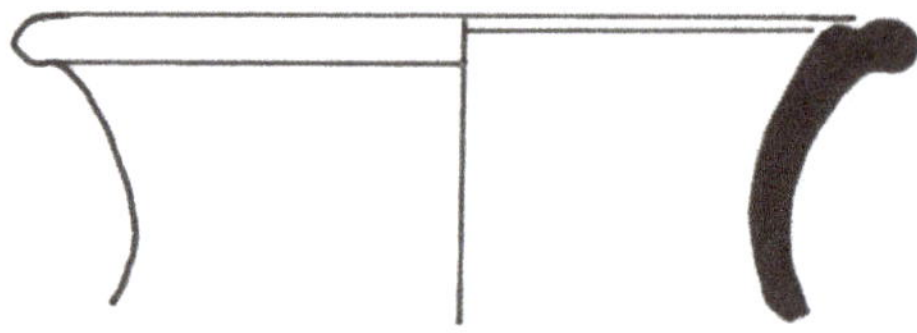

PW 199. CN 7738.
XIA/B 4.6. Early Roman 1 (residual?).
Two joining fragments of part of wall, rim. PH 0.04;
PL 0.055; D rim (est.) 0.07. Strong brown clay 7.5YR
5/6. Reddish-yellow slip 7.5YR 7/6.

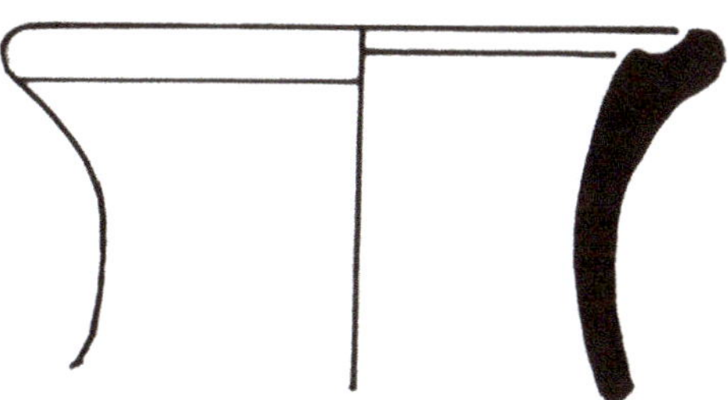

Flaring rim (Type 4)

The concave rim of **PW 200** (Jannaeus Destruction level) is sharply set off from its concave upper neck, as is that of **PW 201** (Early Roman horizon on Tell Husn). Jugs of similar type were recovered only from Herodian levels (c. 30 BC–72 AD) at Machaerus (Loffreda 1996: Group 31: fig. 25).

PW 200. CN 7033.
XXIIIA 100.5. Hellenistic 3C.
Part of wall, rim. PH 0.035; D rim (est.) 0.07. Pink
clay 7.5YR 7/4. Metallic Buff.
Lip bevelled to exterior.

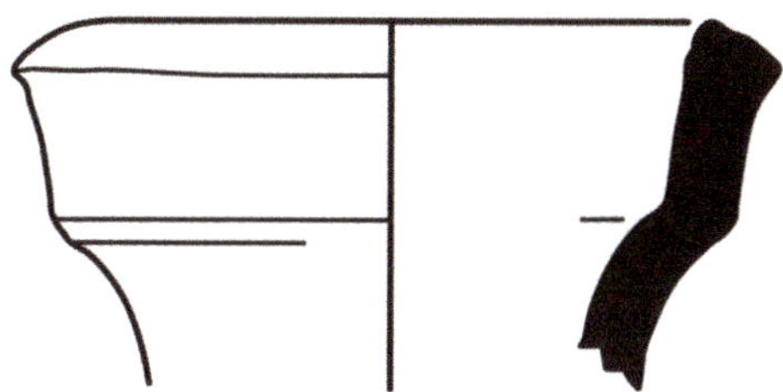

PW 201. CN 2986.
XIA/B 1.2/3. Early Roman 1.
Part of wall, rim. PH 0.045; D rim (est.) 0.07. Reddish-
yellow clay 5YR 6/8.
Parallels: Amman/Philadelphia (Hadidi 1970:
pl. III.8); Capernaeum (Loffreda 1974: fig. 4.8);
Herodium (Bar-Nathan 1981: pls 1.13; 4.17); ʿIraq
al-Amir (Dentzer et al. 1983: fig. 64.20); Jericho
(Kelso and Baramki 1955: pl. 24.X77); Jerusalem
(Tushingham 1985: fig. 18.8); Kallirhoe (Clamer
1997: pl. 5.5); Kedesh (Levantine Ceramics Project:
n.d. K09P188 upper profile, mid–late 2nd c. BC); Tel
Anafa (Berlin 1997a: pl. 49. PW 440 upper profile,
Arab levels residual); Tel Dor (Guz-Zilberstein 1995:
fig. 6.29:11, 250–200 BC).

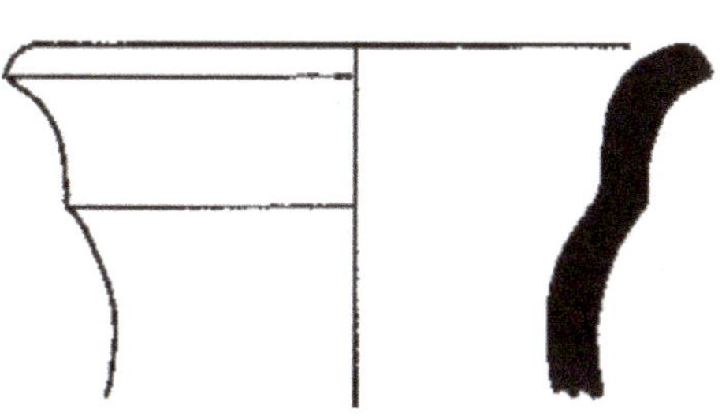

Flanged rim (Type 5)

With the exception of **PW 202**, the flanged rims of this type (**PW 202–11**) are most common at Pella in Late Hellenistic or Early Roman contexts (first century BC or first century AD) from the main mound and Tell Husn. Similar jugs were recovered from Early Roman deposits at Hippos-Sussita (Osband and Eisenberg 2018: pls 4.6.10) and Madaba (Ferguson 2014: fig. 5.4) although appearing earlier at ʿAkko-Ptolemais (Berlin and Stone 2016: figs 9.6.12, 9.8.7) and Marisa (Levine 2003: figs 6.11.106–7, 109, 110).

PW 202. CN 7260.
XXVIIIB 10.2. Hellenistic 3A.
Part of wall, rim. PH 0.045; D rim (est.) 0.09. Weak
red clay 2.5YR 6/4. Coarse Light Brown.

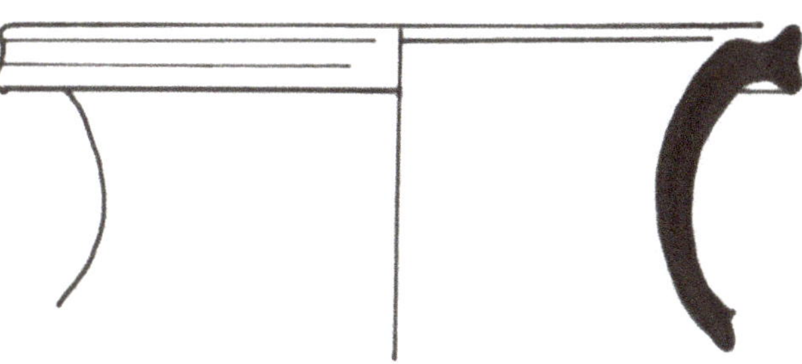

PW 203. CN 7336.
XXXIVB 6.48. Hellenistic 3B/3C.
Part of wall, rim. PH 0.05; PL 0.065; D rim (est.) 0.075.
Light yellowish-brown clay 10YR 6/4. Metallic Buff.
Parallels: Jerusalem (Geva 2003: pl. 5.6.18, 2nd c. BC;
Geva and Rosenthal-Heginbottom 2003: pl. 6.5.13,
early 1st c. AD); Kallirhoe (Clamer 1997: pl. 1.22);
Samaria (Hennessy 1970: fig. 7.25); Tel Yoqne'am
(Avissar 1996: fig. X.7.7); Ziqim (Zissu and Rokach
1999: fig. 5.17).

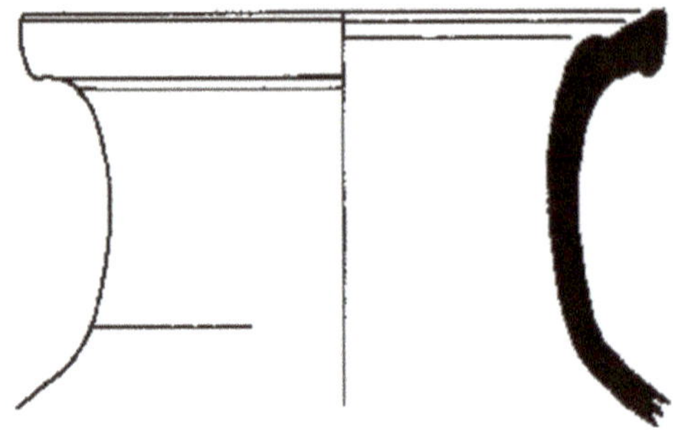

PW 204. CN 6976.
XXIIIA 10.7. Hellenistic 3C.
Part of rim. PH 0.06; D rim (est.) 0.105. Very pale
brown clay 10YR 8/3. Metallic Buff.
Parallels: Jaffa (Tsuf 2018: fig. 9.6.140); Jerusalem
(Machline and Gadot 2017: fig. 8.2; Tchekhanovets
2013: fig. 5.18:9, 1st c. BC–70 AD).

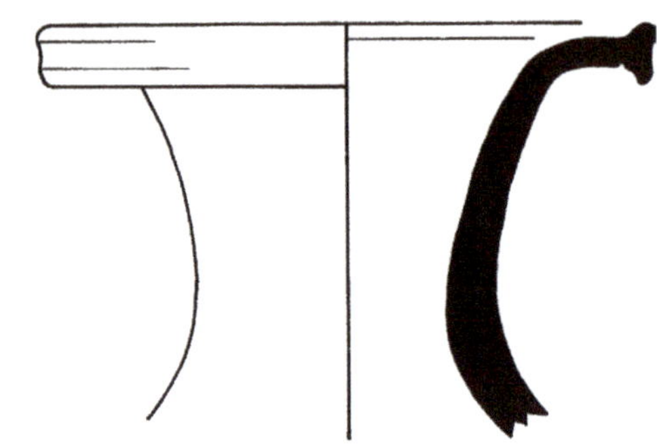

PW 205. CN 0919.
IIIB/C 14.3. Hellenistic 3C.
Part of wall, rim. PH 0.03; D rim (est.) 0.105. Reddish-
yellow clay 7.5YR 6/6. Hard Pale. Thick creamy-buff
slip over exterior.
Parallel: Hippos-Sussita (Osband and Eisenberg 2018:
pl. 4.5.10, end 1st c. BC/beginning 1st c. AD).

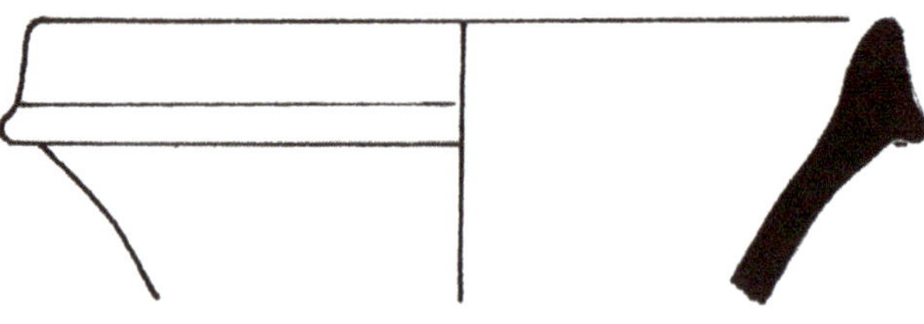

PW 206. CN 2663.
XIA/B 1.1/2. Early Roman 1.
Part of wall, rim. PH 0.05; D rim (est.) 0.21. Reddish-
yellow clay 5YR 7/6. Metallic Buff.
Parallel: Shechem (N.L. Lapp 1985: fig. 4.2).

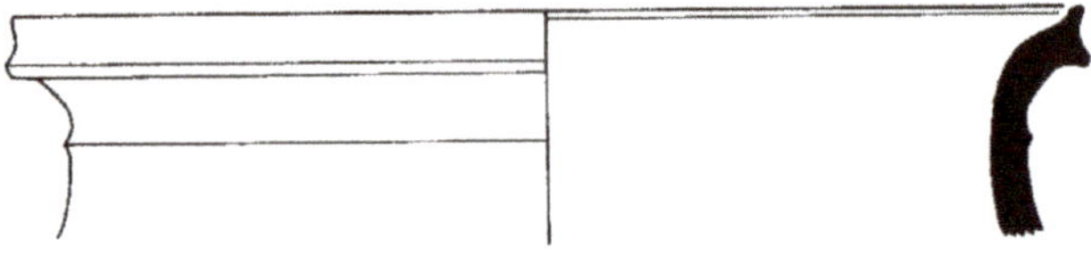

PW 207. CN 2667.
XIA/B 1.1/2. Early Roman 1.
Part of rim. PH 0.03; D rim (est.) 0.23. Reddish-yellow
clay 5YR 7/6. Metallic Buff.
Parallels: Marisa (Kloner and Hess 1985: fig. 4.4);
Tel Zahara (Bar-Nathan 2013: fig. 3.4.26).

PW 208. CN 7741.
XIA/B 20.6. Early Roman 1.
Part of wall, rim. PH 0.025; PL 0.065; D rim (est.) 0.16. Reddish-yellow clay 7.5YR 6/6.
Parallels: Hesban (Gerber 2012: 205, fig. 3.7.14); Jerusalem (Geva 2003: pl. 5.8.17, later 2nd–1st c. BC; Tchekhanovets 2013: fig. 5.3:8, 1st c. BC–70 AD); Nahal Hever (Aharoni 1961: fig. 7.13).

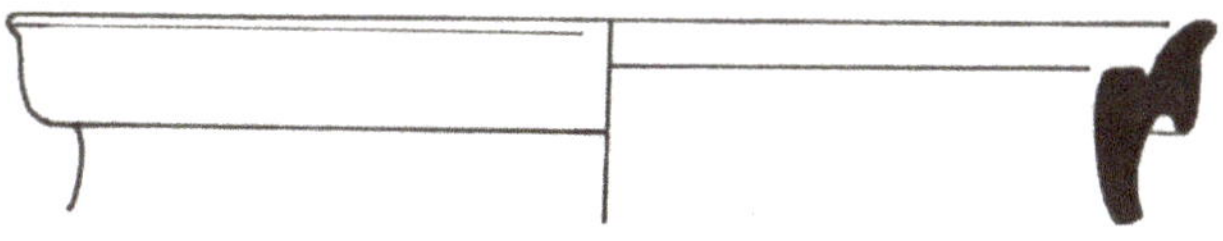

PW 209. CN 7151.
XXXIVB 5.37. Mixed Context.
Part of wall, rim. PH 0.025; D rim (est.) 0.13. Reddish-yellow clay 5YR 7/6. Coarse Light Brown.
Patchy thin brown slip.
Parallel: ʿAkko-Ptolemais (Berlin and Stone 2016: fig. 9.6.12, 3rd c. BC).

PW 210. CN 7686.
XXXIVB 55.12. Mixed Context.
Part of wall, rim. PH 0.03; PL 0.04; D rim (est.) 0.17. Strong brown clay 7.5YR 5/6. Hard Pale.

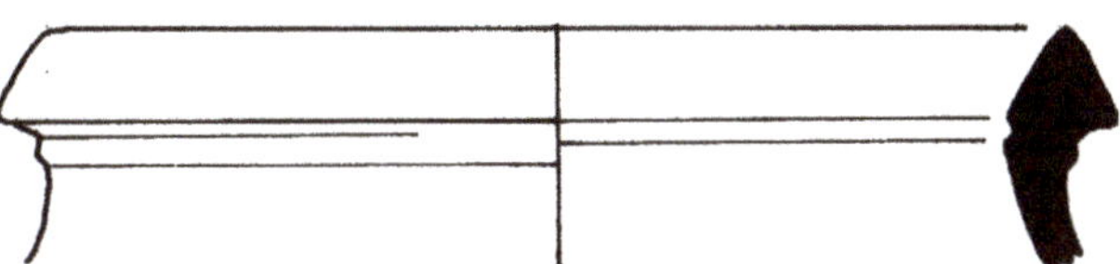

PW 211. CN 7740.
XIA/B 20.6. Early Roman 1.
Part of rim, neck. PH 0.025; PL 0.055; D rim (est.) 0.12. Light yellowish-brown clay 10YR 6/4.
Parallels: ʿAkko-Ptolemais (Berlin and Stone 2016: fig. 9.8.7, 3rd c. BC); Jerusalem (Tchekhanovets 2013: fig. 5.7:19, 1st c. BC–70 AD); Madaba (Ferguson 2014: 180, fig. 5.4, c. 15 BC–106 AD); Scythopolis/Beth-Shean (Johnson 2006: fig. 15.5.94).

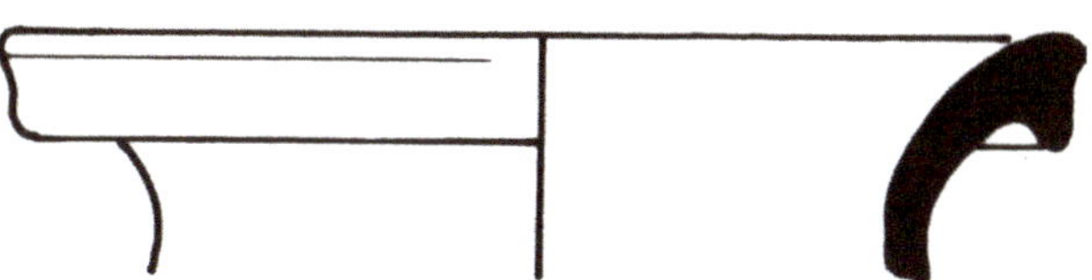

JUGLETS (PW 212–27)

Juglets are small single-handled pouring vessels, differing from jugs only in their dimensions. There are no strict criteria, as regards size, in making the distinction between the two, and so, in this catalogue, as in many others, the separation between jugs and juglets is somewhat arbitrary.[12]

Simple rim (Type 1)

Similar juglets or small jugs, with elongated narrow neck and simple, slightly everted rim, are seen as early as the third century at Tel Dor (Guz-Zilberstein 1995: fig. 6.55:14) with the form lasting into the first century AD (P.W. Lapp 1961: 164, Type 32). At Pella similar jugs (**PW 212–8**) are seen on the main mound from the early second century BC (**PW 212**) and Jannaeus Destruction deposits (Hellenistic 3C, **PW 213–4**) as well as Early Roman deposits on Tell Husn (**PW 215–6**, **PW 218**).

---

12 At Tel Anafa, Berlin (1997a: 142) chose a size "under about 15 cm" in height. While the very fragmentary nature of the Pella juglets makes an estimation of height difficult, the two more-or-less complete specimens (**PW 225**, **PW 227**) are 10 cm and 15 cm in height respectively.

Table 2.24. Distribution of juglets by types, wares, phases.

		SIMPLE RIM (TYPE 1)	COLLARED RIM (TYPE 2)	FLANGED RIM (TYPE 3)	FLARING RIM (TYPE 4)	CUP-SHAPED RIM (TYPE 5)	WIDE MOUTH, GROOVED RIM (TYPE 6)
Wares	Hard Pale	2	0	0	0	0	0
	Metallic Buff	1	1	0	0	3	0
	Coarse Light Brown	2	0	0	0	0	1
	Miscellaneous	2	0	2	1	1	0
Phase	3A c. 200–c. 140 BC	1 (6)	0	0	0	0	0
	3B c. 140–c. 100 (?) BC	0	0	0 (1)	0	0	0
	3C c. 100 (?)–c. 80/79 BC	2	0	0	0	3	0
	Early Roman 63 BC –c. 135 AD	3	0 (2)	2	1 (ER 2)	1	0
	Mixed	1	1	0 (2)	0	1 (1)	1

PW 212. CN 7189.

XXVIIIB 13.7. Hellenistic 3A.

Part of wall, rim. PH 0.045; D rim (est.) 0.06. Reddish-yellow clay 7.5YR 7/6. Coarse Light Brown.

Parallels: Ashdod (Dothan 1971: fig. 61.19); 'Iraq al-Amir (N.L. Lapp 1979: fig. 2.11); Kerak Plateau Survey (Brown 1991: pl. 5.303); Samaria (Zayadine 1966: pl. XXVIII.31); Tel Dor (Guz-Zilberstein 1995: fig. 6.55:14, 275–175 BC); Tell Nimrin (Dornemann 1990: fig. 2.38).

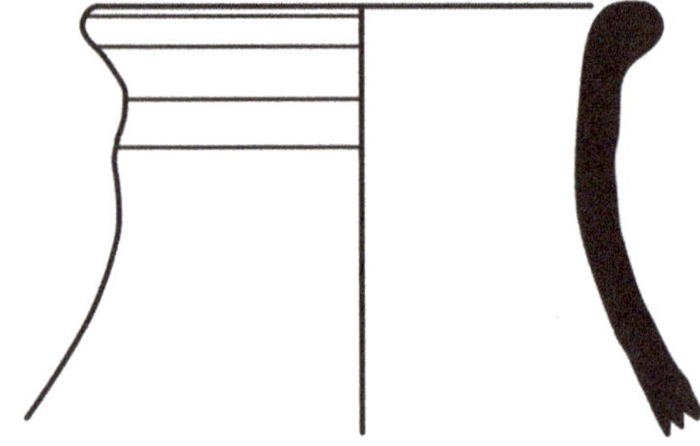

PW 213. CN 6988.

XXIIIA 22.5. Hellenistic 3C.

Part of wall, rim. PH 0.035; PL 0.055; D rim (est.) 0.06. Reddish-yellow clay 7.5YR 6/6. Hard Pale.

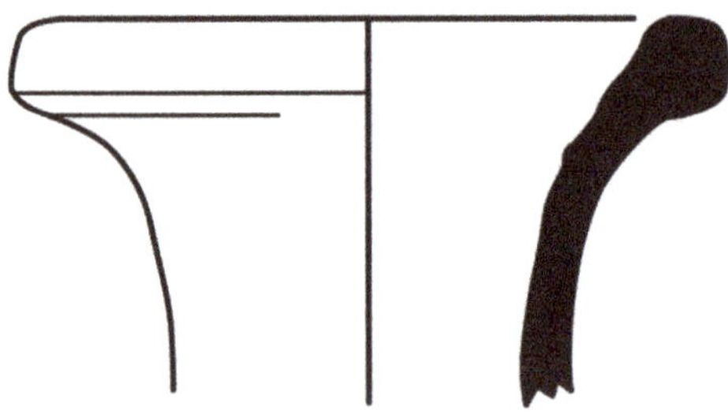

PW 214. CN 7023.

XXIIIA 100.2. Hellenistic 3C.

Part of wall, neck, rim. PH 0.02; D rim (est.) 0.06. Reddish-yellow clay 7.5YR 7/6. Coarse Light Brown.

Parallel: Samaria (Crowfoot et al. 1957: fig. 58.1).

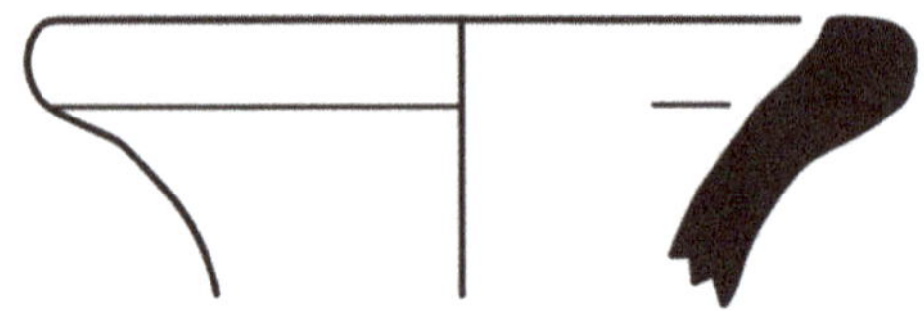

PW 215. CN 2632.
XIA/B 1.5. Early Roman 1.
Part of wall, rim. PH 0.04; D rim (est.) 0.06. Reddish-yellow clay 5YR 6/8. Pale brown slip over exterior.
Parallels: Herodium (Bar-Nathan 1981: pl. 1.5); Machaerus (Loffreda 1996: fig. 26.4); Meiron (Meyers et al. 1981: pl. 8.16.5); Samaria (Hennessy 1970: fig. 10.22); Tel Dor (Guz-Zilberstein 1995: fig. 6.49:21).

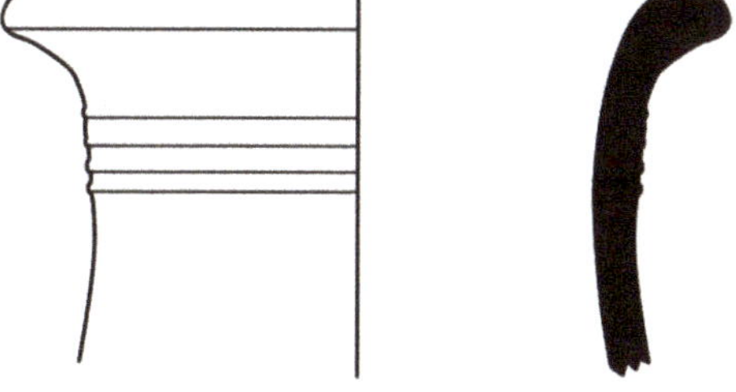

PW 216. CN 2979.
XIA/B 1.1/3. Early Roman 1.
Part of wall, rim. PH 0.04; PL 0.065; D rim (est.) 0.08. Yellowish-red clay 5YR 5/6. Hard Pale.
Parallels: Gezer (Gitin 1990: pl. 37.7, mid-2nd c. BC); Herodium (Bar-Nathan 1981: pl. 4.7 upper profile); Jerusalem (Tushingham 1985: fig. 20.3); Marisa (Oren and Rappaport 1984: fig. 13.16); Samaria (Hennessy 1970: fig. 6.14).

PW 217. CN 7341.
XXXIVB 5.42. Mixed Context.
Part of wall, rim. PH 0.04; PL 0.055; D rim (est.) 0.06. Weak red clay 2.5YR 6/4. Metallic Buff.
Concave neck; everted rim.

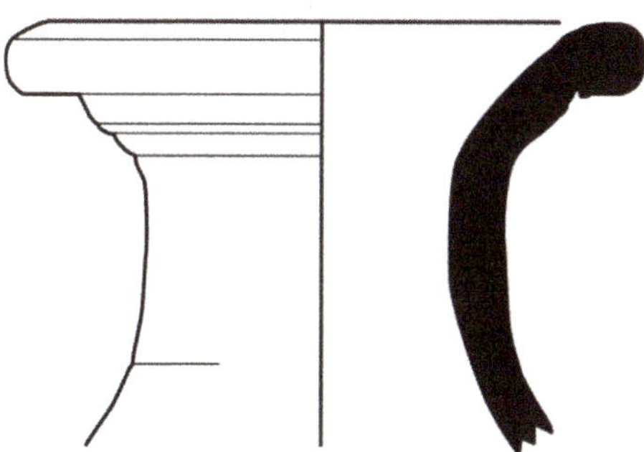

PW 218. CN 7739.
XIA/B 4.6. Early Roman 1.
Part of wall, neck, rim. PH 0.04; PL 0.04; D rim (est.) 0.06. Yellowish-red clay 5YR 5/6.
Parallel: Hippos-Sussita (Osband and Eisenberg 2018: pl. 4.2.15, end 1st c. BC/beginning 1st c. AD).

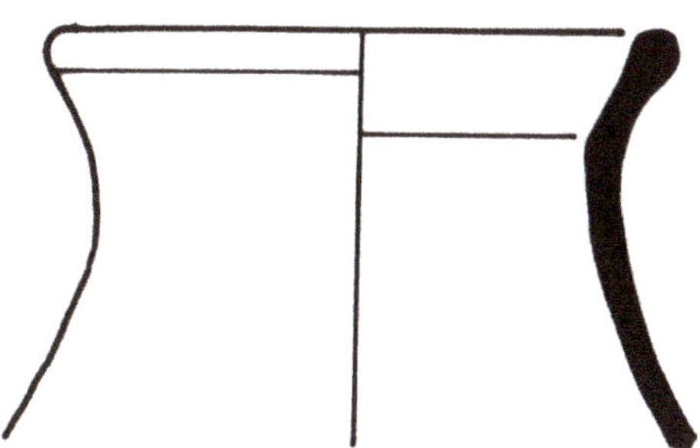

Collared rim (Type 2)

The one catalogued (Mixed Context) and two uncatalogued (Early Roman from Tell Husn) examples from Pella have a similar rim form to the collared rim jugs (Type 2) discussed above.

PW 219. CN 7101.
XXIIIA 80.3. Mixed Context.
Part of wall, rim. PH 0.03; D rim (est.) 0.045. Very pale brown clay 10YR 8/2. Metallic Buff.
Dull black slip over interior, exterior.

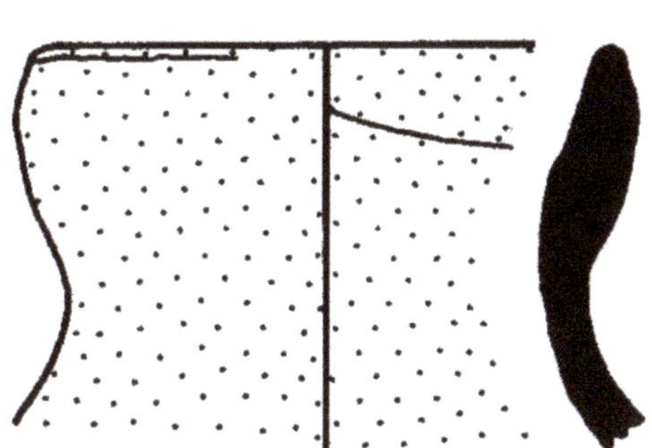

Flanged rim (Type 3)

The rim form is similar to that of the Type 5 jugs. Both catalogued juglets (**PW 220–1**), with tall concave neck flaring to a flanged vertical rim, are from Tell Husn in Early Roman strata, consistent with the Early Roman contexts of similar juglets from Jericho (Kelso and Baramki 1955: pl. 22.X21; Netzer and Meyers 1977: fig. 6.8) and Jerusalem (Tushingham 1985: fig. 21.17).

PW 220. CN 6621.
XIA/B 20.6. Early Roman 1.
Part of neck, rim, handle. PH 0.035; D rim (est.) 0.04.
Red clay 2.5YR 5/8.
Narrow, faintly ribbed neck. Base of handle at mid-neck.
Parallels: Jericho (Kelso and Baramki 1955: pl. 22.X21; Netzer and Meyers 1977: fig. 6.8); Jerusalem (Tushingham 1985: fig. 21.17).

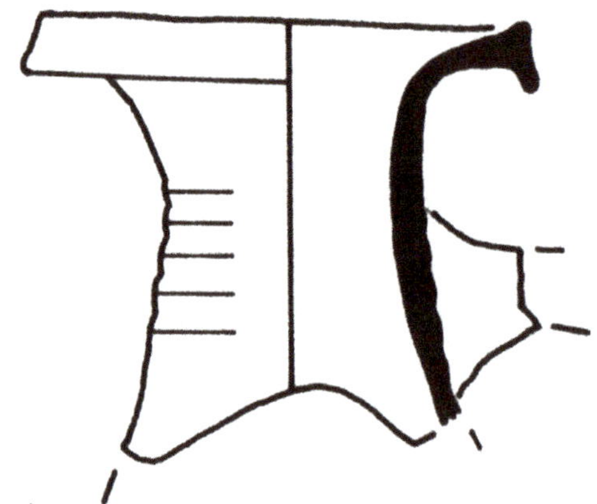

PW 221. CN 2957.
XIA/B 1.5. Early Roman 1.
Part of neck, rim, handle. PH 0.07; D rim (est.) 0.05.
Yellowish-red clay 5YR 5/6. Sparse large lime inclusions.
Base of strap handle at mid-neck.
Parallel: Jericho (Kelso and Baramki 1955: pl. 25.X36 – twisted handles).

Flaring rim (Type 4)

From Tell Husn, **PW 222**, most likely a product of Kfar Shikhin, one of the two most important Galilean centres for kitchen ware during the Roman period (Adan-Bayewitz 1993, 2003), is a juglet form (narrow neck, flaring plain rim) commonly seen in the Galilee and encountered elsewhere in Palestine (Adan-Bayewitz and Wieder 1992: 196). Diez Fernandez has suggested that these juglets (Diez Fernandez 1983: 115, 229, Type 8.2) were produced between the mid-first century BC until the mid-first century AD but at Sepphoris they appear to continue throughout the later first century AD into the third century (Balouka 2013: 45–6), consistent with the Early Roman 2 context of **PW 222**.

PW 222. CN 6786.
XIA/B 20.5. Early Roman 2.
Part of wall, rim, handle. PH 0.05; D rim (est.) 0.03.
Very pale brown clay 10YR 7/4.
Narrow neck separated by horizontal ridge from tall
concave rim. Base of strap handle on neck ridge.
Parallels: Capernaeum (Loffreda 1974: fig. 4.3);
Hippos-Sussita (Osband and Eisenberg 2018:
pl. 4.2.14, end 1st c. BC/beginning 1st c. AD); Iotapata
(Adan-Bayewitz and Aviam 1997: fig. 12.19); Karm
er-Ras (Alexandre and Shapiro 2016: fig. 6.9);
Sepphoris (Balouka 2013: pl. 11.7, 70–135 AD);
Tel Yoqne'am (Avissar 1996: fig. X.7.25).

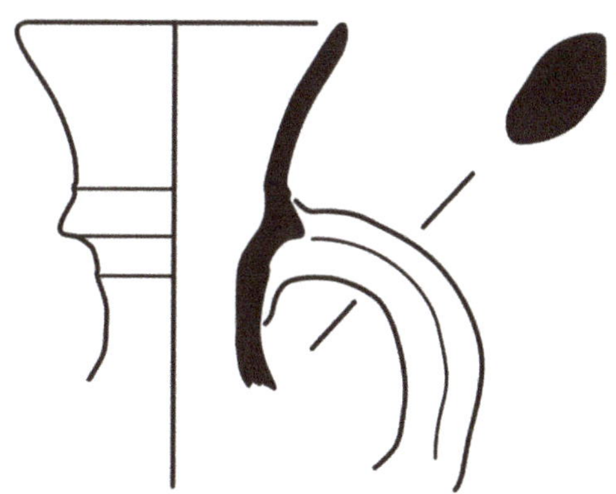

Cup-shaped rim (Type 5)

The distinguishing feature of the type (**PW 223–6**) is the distinct angle between rim and neck, a characteristic
that starts to appear elsewhere during the second century BC. The type corresponds to Lapp's Type 31.1D–F
(P.W. Lapp 1961: 162), spanning the first centuries BC and AD respectively, and to juglet Type 187B at Gezer,
associated with a mid-first-century BC horizon. Of the 57 registered examples (Loffreda 1996: Group 26:
fig. 22) from Machaerus, the great majority were from Early Roman levels (Loffreda 1996: 61). A further
example, found in a cave near Qumran and wrapped in palm fibres (Patrich and Arubas 1989: fig. 4, pls.
6A–B), is of interest in that residual analysis of its contents indicated a viscous plant oil whose chemical
composition resembles no modern plant oil. The authors thus raise the possibility that this juglet may have
contained "the famous balsam … one of the most precious products of the Jericho Valley and the 'En Gedi
region" (Patrich and Arubas 1989).[13]

Juglets of this form appear in the southern Levant during the second century BC (Berlin 2015: 638),
becoming more popular on both sides of the Jordan River during the first centuries BC and AD. The form first
appears at Pella in Jannaeus Destruction levels (**PW 223–5**) on the main mound and continues into Early
Roman levels on Tell Husn (**PW 226**), a chronological range that is mirrored at 'Iraq al-Amir (Zimmerman
2020b, Type 100, pl. 2.17.1–8).

PW 223. CN 7757.
XXIIID 18.1. Hellenistic 3C.
Fragment of wall, rim, handle. PH 0.045; PL 0.04;
D rim 0.018. Reddish-yellow clay 5YR 6/6.
Vertical strap handle from top of lip.

---

13 For a more complete discussion as to the nature and production of ancient balsam, see Hadas 2007.

PW 224. CN 7122.

XXIIIA 71.2. Hellenistic 3C.

Part of rim, handle. PH 0.045; D rim (est.) 0.03. Very pale brown clay 10YR 7/3. Metallic Buff.

Base of handle preserved at top of rim.

Parallels: Hesban (Gerber 2012: 204, fig. 3.7.8); 'Iraq al-Amir (Zimmerman 2020b: pl. 2.17.2, str. IIIb, c. 100 BC); Madaba (Ferguson 2014: 182, fig. 5.14, c. 129–100 BC); Tell Zira'a (Kenkel 2020: 97, 192–3, pl. 1.38, Pk3.1).

PW 225. CN 3490.

IVD 10.10. Hellenistic 3C.

Complete. H 0.10; D rim 0.03. Pale brown clay 10YR 6/3. Metallic Buff.

Rounded resting surface; globular body. Thin strap handle from rim to shoulder.

Parallels: Ashdod (Dothan and Freedman 1967: fig. 6.9, second half of 2nd c. BC–mid-1st c. BC); 'Iraq al-Amir (Zimmerman 2020b: pl. 2.17.7, str. II–I, c. 100–200 AD); Jaffa (Tsuf 2018: fig. 9.11.258); Jericho (Netzer and Meyers 1977: fig. 9.7); Jerusalem (Sandhaus 2013: fig. 4.2:11, second half of 2nd c. BC; Tushingham 1985: fig. 23.16), Machaerus (Corbo and Loffreda 1981: fig. 36.11; Loffreda 1980: pl. 97.56); Tell es-Sa'idiyeh (Pritchard 1985: fig. 19.31); Tell Zira'a (Kenkel 2013: fig. 1.6); Wadi al-Kharrar (Abu Shmeis and Waheeb 2002: fig. 5.1).

PW 226. CN 2965.

XIA/B 1.5. Early Roman 1.

Part of wall, rim. PH 0.035; D rim (est.) 0.03. Pale brown clay 10YR 6/3. Metallic Buff.

Base of handle on rim.

Parallels: Amman/Philadelphia (Sami' et al. 1991: fig. 6.17); Ashdod (Dothan 1971: fig. 17.14); Herodium (Bar-Nathan 1981: pl. 4.24); Hesban (Gerber 2012: 204, fig. 3.7.7); Jericho (Netzer and Meyers 1977: fig. 9.7; Pritchard 1958: pl. 59.39); Jerusalem (Geva and Rosenthal-Heginbottom 2003: pl. 6.2.3, 1st c. BC; Strange 1975: fig. 15.28; Tchekhanovets 2013: fig. 5.8:6, 1st c. BC–70 AD; Tushingham 1985: figs 19.27, 21.27); Kerak Plateau Survey (Brown 1991: pl. 6.342); Madaba (Ferguson 2014: 179, fig. 5.2, c. 15 BC–106 AD); Nahal Hever (Aharoni 1961: fig. 7.10); Ras Abu Ma'aruf (Rapuano 1999: fig. 2.26); Tel Anafa (Berlin 1997a: pl. 49. PW 439, early 1st c. AD); Tel Michal (Derfler 1989: fig. 14.3.10, early 1st c. AD–68 AD; Fischer 1989: fig. 13.2.17, 2nd c. BC); Tell Zira'a (Kenkel 2020: 192–3, pl. 1.38: Pk2); Wadi al-Kharrar (Abu Shmeis and Waheeb 2002: fig. 5.3).

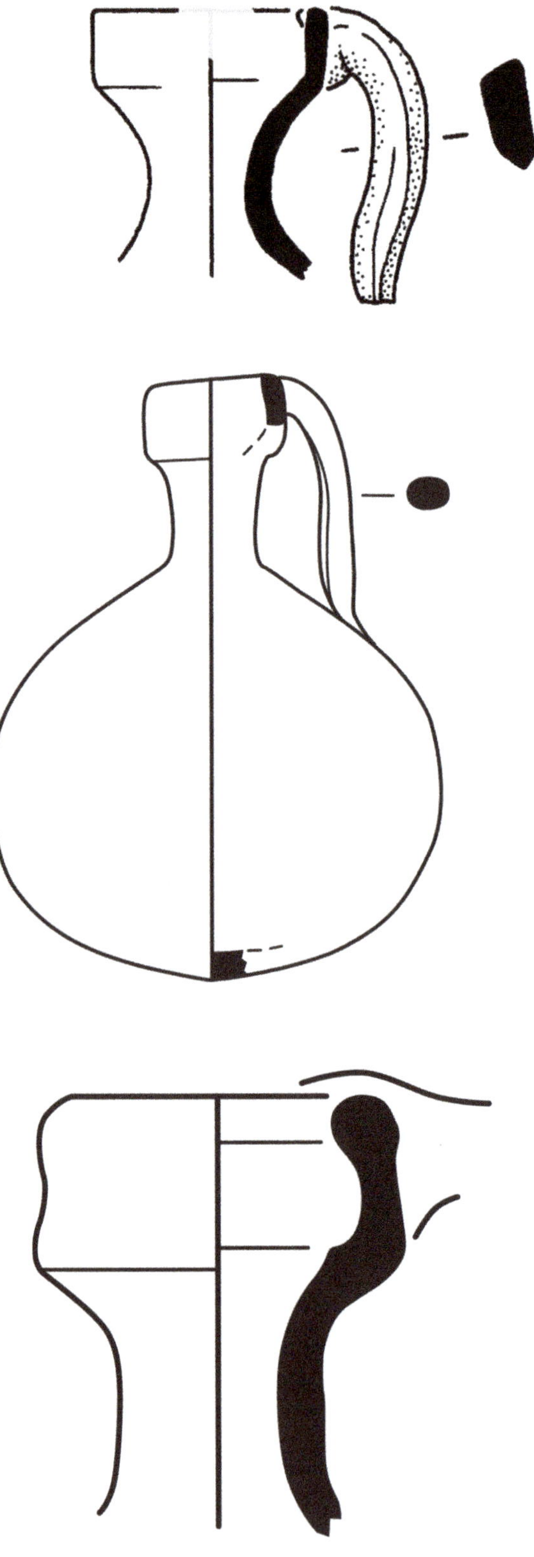

Wide mouth, grooved rim (Type 6)

The vertical rim is grooved on the exterior below the lip, the neck of which ends in a wide mouth. From an unstratified context, found in a pit on Tell Husn (XXXIVB) along with the Herodian or Augustan ESA plate **FW 214**, **PW 227** is substantially intact and can be seen to rest on a low ring base. Parallels to this shape are uncommon although somewhat similar juglets were recovered from Late Jewish contexts in Jerusalem (Tushingham 1985: 56–7, fig. 23.23) and Masada (Bar-Nathan 2006: 102–3, pl. 18.16).

PW 227. CN 7161.
XXXIVB 8.34. Mixed Context.
Missing part of rim. H 0.15; D rim (est.) 0.05. Light brown clay 7.5YR 6/4. Coarse Light Brown.
Dull brown slip over inside of rim, upper exterior. Low ring base. Globular body. Narrow neck; wide mouth. Vertical rim separated on exterior by groove from flattened lip.
Parallels: Jerusalem (Tchekhanovets 2013: fig. 5.3:7, 1st c. BC–70 AD; close to Tushingham 1985: fig. 23.23); Masada (close to Bar-Nathan 2006: pl. 18.16).

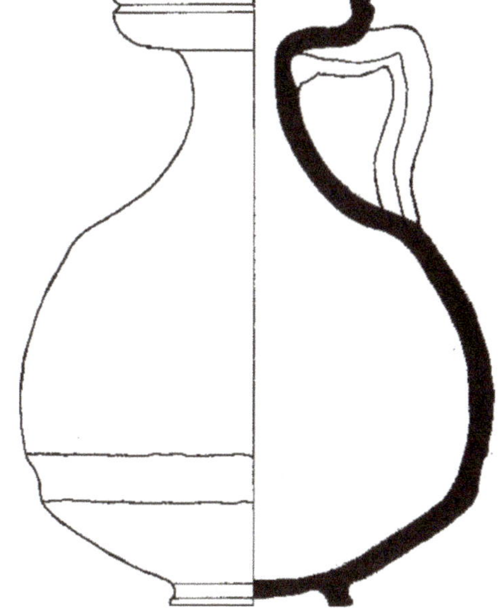

LAGYNOI (PW 228–32)

The lagynos is a specialised form of wine jug, or oinochoe, used for festive occasions and peculiar to the Hellenistic Period (Thompson 1934: 450). Its characteristics are a long narrow neck, vertical strap – or twisted – handle, and squat body that may be carinated or globular; it usually rests on a low ring base. Throughout its history it is seen in a great variety of forms and wares (Berlin 1997a: 42) including black-gloss, ESA, white-ground, West Slope and moulded relief wares as well as various plain wares.

Although its origin is unclear, the lagynos is most strongly associated with those areas of the east Mediterranean under Ptolemaic control – Cyprus, south-west Asia Minor and Egypt itself – and thus may well have been an Alexandrian innovation (Berlin 1997a: 42–3; Kehrberg 2004b). As yet, the earliest known example, in plain ware, is not from those areas but from Koroni in Attica (Vanderpool et al. 1962: 39, no. 50), used as a base for the forces of Ptolemy II during the Chremonidean war of 265–261 BC (Vanderpool et al. 1964).

The pioneering work of Leroux (1913) concluded that, at least for white-ground specimens, the wide variations seen in form and ware were of no chronological significance, and so this diversity was more likely explained on regional rather than temporal grounds. While many scholars have accepted these conclusions for lagynoi in general, others such as Westholm (1956: 75, 78) have claimed that a chronological progression does indeed exist as the carinated type of lagynos did not occur, at least in Cyprus, until towards the end of the Hellenistic I period (c. 150 BC).

The great variation in ware amongst the lagynoi has yet to be investigated in any detail. Athens produced only a small number of black-gloss specimens (Rotroff 1997b: 127) with Edwards and James finding no evidence of the local manufacture of fine ware examples at Corinth (Edwards 1975: 49–50; James 2018); lagynoi were produced at Pergamon and other centres in Asia Minor (Schäfer 1968: 101–15) as well as Cyprus (Hayes 1991a: 18–21; Lund 2015: 66–96). The source of other such vessels can be recognised through their stamped handles suggesting workshops in Chios, Rhodes and (perhaps) Knidos (Hayes 1991a: 18).

Lagynoi have been recovered in small numbers from various sites in Palestine including Ashdod, Marisa, Samaria, Straton's Tower/Caesarea, Tel Anafa, Tel Michal, Tel Yoqne'am and, further north, from Antioch, Hama and Tarsus; east of the Jordan River they are less common, with examples coming from Amman/Philadelphia, Jerash and Pella.[14] Berlin (1988: 151–2, 1997a: 43) has pointed out the absence of these vessels from excavations carried out within the territory of the Hasmonean kingdom – a fact that is further emphasised by the lack of examples from Gitin's ceramic corpus from Gezer although, it should be noted, one was recovered from Macalister's earlier excavations (Macalister 1912: vol. III, pl. CLXXX.10). On the other hand, at least 65 fragmentary lagynoi were recovered, mainly from the Late Hellenistic levels, from Tel Anafa, which lay to the north of Jewish kingdom and which, by the end of the second century BC, was oriented towards Phoenicia and the Mediterranean world (Berlin 1997a: 43–4).

Only a small number of lagynoi have been found at Pella.[15] Apart from **PW 228**, **PW 230**, and the fine white-ground specimen **FW 166**, they are in very fragmentary condition, making any attempt at a typological classification difficult. On the basis of a much larger sample, Westholm (1956: 59) was able to divide the Cypriot lagynoi into two broad groups: the first (and slightly earlier) was characterised by an almost horizontal shoulder and gently curving body and the second (seemingly more prevalent) by a

---

14 Bennett 1979: 168, pl. 74. 2, incorrectly called a "squat lekythos"; Harding 1944: 72, fig. 39, pl. XVII.39 (Amman/Philadelphia); Waagé 1948: 28 (Antioch); Dothan 1971: figs 11:3, 14:1, 4, 61:21, 79:6, 7; Dothan and Freedman 1967: fig. 2:12 (Ashdod); Christensen and Johansen 1971: 21–4 (Hama); Kehrberg 2004b: 303 (Jerash); Bliss and Macalister 1902: pl. 59.2 (Marisa); Reisner et al. 1924: fig. 185:14a; Crowfoot et al. 1957: 340 (Samaria); Roller 1980: fig. 2.32 (Straton's Tower/Caesarea); F.F. Jones 1950: figs 132.189, 145.512 (Tarsus); Berlin 1997a: 42–7 (Tel Anafa); Fischer 1989: fig. 13.3:26 (Tel Michal); Ben-Tor et al. 1983: fig. 7.13 (Tel Yoqne'am).

15 A further specimen was recovered during the Wooster excavations in Area VIII (McNicoll et al. 1982: pl. 130.3).

sharply carinated body.[16] The imported lagynoi from the Athenian agora can be divided in similar fashion (Rotroff 1997b: 228) with the angular form seemingly more popular by the early first century BC. Both forms occur amongst the Jannaeus Destruction levels (Hellenistic 3C) on the main mound from where, with the exception of **FW 166**, all the lagynoi have been recovered. Thus **PW 228–9**, as well as the white-ground **FW 166**, are more gently rounded in comparison to the carinated vessel **PW 230**. Lagynoi **PW 231–2** are too fragmentary for any conclusions to be drawn.

The wares of the various lagynoi are diverse with **FW 166** being the only white-ground example. The clay of **PW 230** and **PW 232** is well levigated, with fine mica particles and an orange-pink colour (Munsell 2.5 YR7/6–7.5YR 7/6). All three have a somewhat patchy red-brown slip but no other trace of surface decoration. The origin of these lagynoi is unclear although the similarity of the ware to Hayes' Series 6 lagynoi from the House of Dionysus at Paphos (Hayes 1991a: 20) may suggest Cypriot manufacture. **FW 166**, on the other hand, was probably produced by a workshop in the neighbourhood of Pergamon; the origin of the remaining examples is not known.

Table 2.25. Distribution of lagynoi by types, wares, phases.

		ROUNDED BODY (TYPE 1)	ANGULAR BODY (TYPE 2)	MISCELLANEOUS
Ware	Miscellaneous	2	1	2
Phase	3C c. 100 (?)–c. 80/79 BC	2	1	2

---

16 It is likely that multiple production centres for lagynoi existed on Cyprus (Hayes 1991a: 18; Kehrberg 2004b; Lund 2015: 66–95).

Rounded body (Type 1)

PW 228, with its globular body, belongs here. With the exception of **FW 166**, it is the only lagynos in this corpus to exhibit surface decoration. Its decorative scheme of five groups of vertical flutes and a single horizontal ovolo band may well be inspired by the vertical ribbing seen on contemporary ceramic or metalware kraters and jugs. Although only the upper part of **PW 229** survives, its gently rounded almost horizontal shoulder suggests that it should be included within this type.

PW 228. CN 3457.
IVD 10.10. Hellenistic 3C.
Complete. H 0.19; D rim 0.05. Pink clay 2.5YR 7/4–7/6. Very well levigated.
Mottled red slip over exterior. Tall upright neck; everted rim. Globular body. Five groups of gouged vertical fluting on lower body below horizontal grooves and incised ovolo pattern. Twisted band handle from neck to shoulder.
Parallel: Ashdod (Dothan 1971: fig. 79.6 profile, mid-1st c. BC–c. 70 AD).

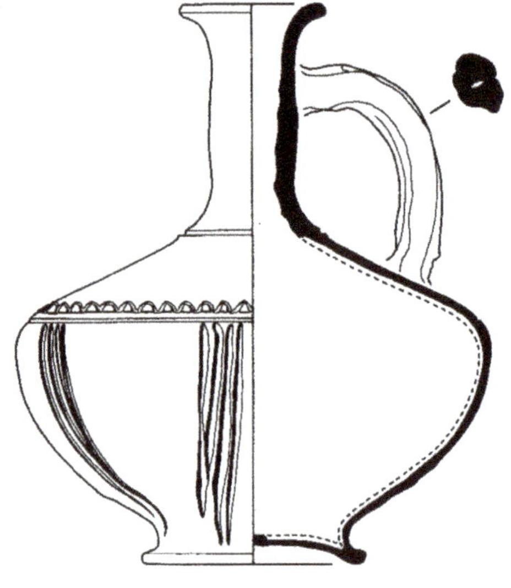

PW 229. CN 0049.
IIIB/C 1.3. Hellenistic 3C.
Part of wall, neck, rim. PH 0.12; D rim (est.) 0.03.
Reddish-yellow clay 5YR 7/6. Hard fired.
Streaky worn reddish-yellow slip over exterior. Tall
vertical neck; bevelled rim projecting on exterior.
Slightly convex shoulder. Base of strap handle mid-
way up neck.

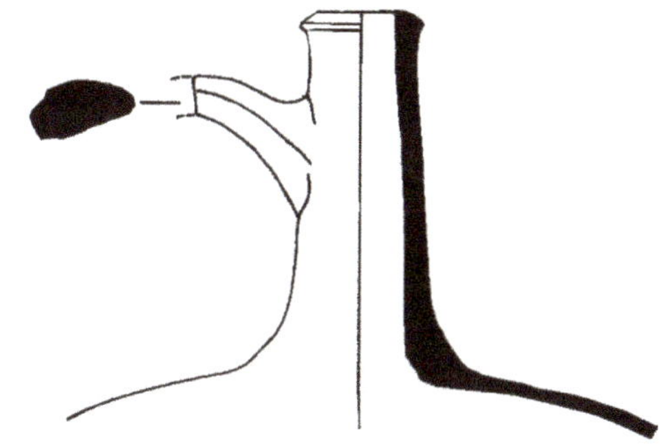

Angular body (Type 2)

PW 230 is the only example from Pella of a lagynos with carinated body. While close to the local lagynos
recovered from subterranean complex 70 at Marisa (Levine 2003: 106, fig. 6.12.118), it is much less angular
than similar lagynoi in Cyprus (for example, Vessberg and Westholm 1956: figs 28.10–11, 29.1–4) or the
almost contemporary lagynoi of Rotroff Shape 2 from Sullan destruction debris (c. 86 BC) at Athens (Rotroff
1997b: figs 89.1512, 90.1529, 91.1530, 1532, all 115–86 BC.

PW 230. CN 6562.
XXIIIA 10.7. Hellenistic 3C.
Missing base, lower wall, rim. PH 0.17. Reddish-
yellow clay 5YR 7/6. Matt reddish-yellow slip 5YR 6/6.
Burnished. Tall narrow neck. Strap handle from
shoulder to neck.
Parallels: Tel Dor (Guz-Zilberstein 1995: fig. 6.33:7,
200–125 BC); Tel Yoqne'am (Ben-Tor et al. 1983: fig.
7.13 lower profile).

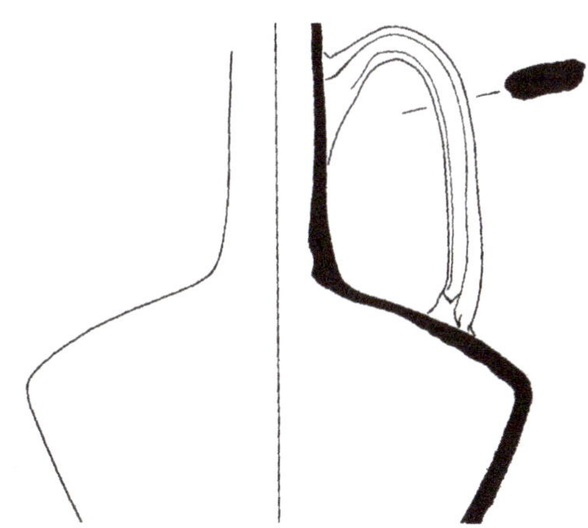

Miscellaneous

As they are too fragmentary for meaningful typological classification, **PW 231–2** are included here. The
ware of both is visually similar to that of **PW 230**, suggesting a possible Cypriot origin.

PW 231. CN 6592.
XXIIIA 10.7. Hellenistic 3C.
Part of neck, rim, handle. PH 0.12; D rim 0.02. Pale
brown clay 10YR 6/3. Many small white inclusions.
Streaky red slip over exterior. Vertical burnishing on
neck. Tall narrow neck; bevelled rim projecting on
exterior. Part of strap handle attached to neck.

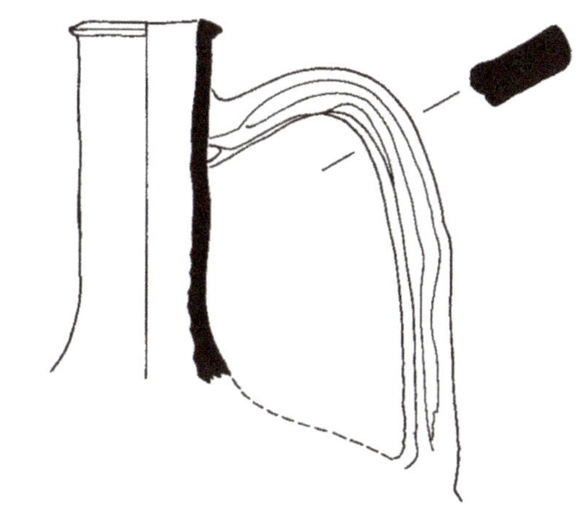

PW 232. CN 6941.
IVD 10.12. Hellenistic 3C.
Part of neck, rim, handle. PH 0.06; D rim (est.) 0.03.
Reddish-yellow clay 5YR 6/6. Small lime inclusions.
Tall narrow neck; thickened everted rim. Part of strap
handle attached to neck.
Parallels: Apollonia (Fischer and Tal 1996: fig. 7.4);
Marisa (Levine 2003: fig. 6.12.116).

TRANSPORT VESSELS (PW 233–54)

Flasks: southern Palestinian type

The lentoid flask, with its tall narrow neck, two opposed handles and round-bottomed body is "particularly suited to land transport, tied to the sides of people or their mounts" (Berlin 1997a: 140). The shape itself originated in the Late Bronze Age in Palestine (Amiran 1969: 166–7, pl. 51; Mullins and Yannai 2019: 166–7, pl. 3.41) and continued in use in the southern Levant into Islamic times (McNicoll et al. 1982: pls 141.1, 144.1).

At Pella only three flasks (**PW 233–5**) have been recovered, all from Tell Husn. With their long necks and relatively small dimensions, they are typical of those found in the southern Levant (Guz-Zilberstein 1995: 310–11). **PW 233–5** can be distinguished from those stouter, shorter-necked flasks seen at Tel Anafa (Berlin 1997a: 141–2) and elsewhere in northern Palestine. Flasks of this type are seen at 'Iraq al-Amir, Gezer, Machaerus and Tel Dor.[17] Both at Gezer and in P.W. Lapp's assemblage of flasks (P.W. Lapp 1961: Type 29) there is a progression from the wider neck of the second century to a narrow neck seen in the first centuries BC and AD: this progression may be reflected in the Pella flasks (admittedly a very small sample), with the wider necked **PW 233** and **PW 234** from third-century BC deposits and the narrower **PW 235** from an Early Roman context.

PW 233. CN 7670.
XXXIVB 27.26. Hellenistic 2B.
Part of neck, rim, handles. PH 0.06; D rim (est.) 0.032.
Greyish brown clay 10YR 5/2.
Roots of strap handles on neck.

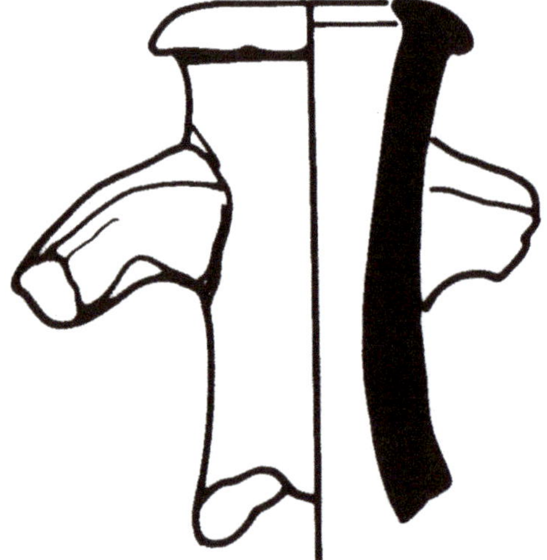

---

17 Gitin 1990: Type 183B (Gezer); Zimmerman 2020b: Type 70, pl. 2.14.1–4 ('Iraq al-Amir); Loffreda 1996: Group 25: fig. 21 (Machaerus); Guz-Zilberstein 1995: 310–11, fig. 6.34 (Tel Dor).

PW 234. CN 7669.

XXXIVB 27.26. Hellenistic 2B.

Part of neck, rim, handles. PH 0.075; D rim (est.) 0.05. Red clay 2.5YR 6/8.

Roots of strap handles on neck.

Parallels: Hesban (Gerber 2012: 203, fig. 3.7.4); 'Iraq al-Amir (Zimmerman 2020b: pl. 2.14.4, str. IIIb, c. 100 BC); Jerusalem (Geva 2003: pl. 5.6.24, 2nd c. BC; Tchekhanovets 2013: fig. 5.18:3, 1st c. BC–70 AD); Marisa (Levine 2003: fig. 6.9.90); Tel Dor (Guz-Zilberstein 1995: fig. 6.34:2, 225–200 BC).

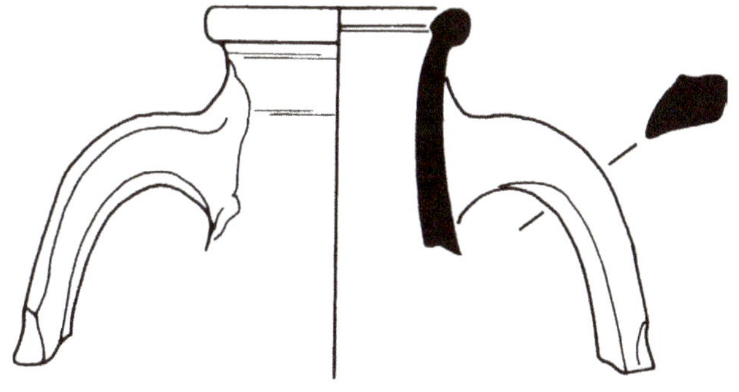

PW 235 CN 2980.

XIA/B 1.1/3. Early Roman 1.

Part of neck, rim, handles. PH 0.06; D rim (est.) 0.03. Pale brown neck, clay 10YR 6/3. Metallic Buff.

Roots of strap handles on neck.

Parallels: Ashdod (Dothan 1971: fig. 9.18, 1st half of 2nd c. BC–2nd half of 2nd c. BC); 'En el-Ghuweir (Bar-Adon 1977: fig. 15.3, 6); Gezer (Gitin 1990: pl. 41.24, early 1st c. BC); Jericho (Kelso and Baramki 1955: pl. 25.A208; Pritchard 1958: pl. 59.35); Jerusalem (Geva 2003: pl. 5.4.24, late 2nd–1st c. BC; Geva and Rosenthal-Heginbottom 2003: pl. 6.1.44, 1st c. BC; Machline and Gadot 2017: fig. 8.12; Strange 1975: fig. 15.35; Tchekhanovets 2013: fig. 5.3:5, 1st c. BC –70 AD); Machaerus (Loffreda 1996: fig. 21.9); Ras Abu Ma'aruf (Rapuano 1999: fig. 2.28).

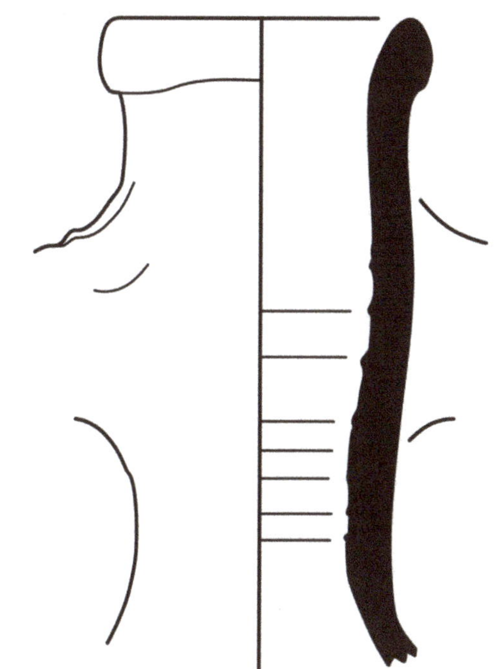

Amphoriskos

A similar amphoriskos to **PW 236** was recovered from beneath Shop 2 in the Civic Centre at Pella by the Wooster team (Smith and Day 1989: 77, pl. 15.15) where it was dated to the third century AD. Amphoriskoi of this type (AMP3) are common at Sepphoris in strata from the end of the first (?) or second to the third centuries AD (Balouka 2013: 42). The recovery of **PW 236** from plot XIA/B, in an Early Roman level on Tell Husn, is consistent with a late first- or earlier second-century AD context for this vessel.

Table 2.26. Distribution of flasks, amphoriskos, by wares, phases.

		FLASK	AMPHORISKOS
Ware	Metallic Buff	1	1
	Miscellaneous	2	0
Phase	2B c. 220–c. 200 BC	2	0
	Early Roman 1 63 BC–late 1st century AD	1	1

PW 236. CN 2670. (Plate 60)
XIA/B 2.2. Early Roman 1.
Two non-joining fragments of complete profile.
PH 0.27; D rim (est.) 0.08. Pale brown clay 10YR
6/3. Metallic Buff.
Tall neck set off sharply from vertical rim; lip projects
on interior. Low ring base. Ovoid wall with prominent
ridging. Vertical handles from shoulder to neck.
Parallels: Pella (Smith and Day 1989: pl. 15.15);
Sepphoris (Balouka 2013: pl. 11.3: but missing rim,
70–135 AD).

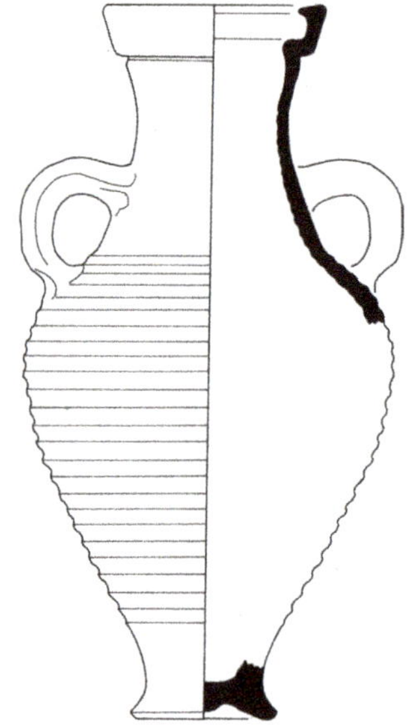

Transport amphorae

At Pella, as is commonly seen in the Levant, Rhodian amphorae make up the great bulk of recovered transport amphorae (Rosenthal-Heginbottom 2015b: 683–4). Amongst the approximately fifty stamped amphora handles to be presented in a separate study, some eighty-five per cent are of Rhodian origin with single examples from Knidos, Sinope and Kos. Along with the stamped handle CN 7768, there are several other small fragments (uncatalogued) of double-reeded handles characteristic of Coan amphorae, although "it is notoriously difficult to distinguish between Coan and Pseudo-Coan" (Jackson 2011a: 79).

Of the unstamped amphora fragments presented here (**PW 237–54**), there are only four (**PW 239, PW 241, PW 253–4**) whose ware appears not to be Rhodian with **PW 239** and **PW 241** of Hard Pale ware – one of the most common plain wares encountered at Pella, especially during the second century BC. The clay of **PW 254** is non-Rhodian though its upper profile with rolled thickened rim and long cylindrical neck certainly seems typical. It may well be that this "Rhodian" amphora was manufactured in a workshop in the Rhodian Peraea rather than on the island itself (Şenol et al. 2004).

Table 2.27. Distribution of unstamped transport amphorae by wares, areas, phases.

Ware	Rhodian	14
	Hard Pale	2
	Miscellaneous	2
Phase	2B c. 220–c. 200 BC	2
	3A c. 200–c. 140 BC	5
	3B c. 140–c. 100 (?) BC	0
	3B/3C c. 140–c. 80/79 BC	7
	3C c. 100 (?)–c. 80/79 BC	2
	Early Roman 63 BC–c. 135 AD	1
	Mixed	1
Areas	XXIII (main mound)	3
	XXVIII (main mound)	5
	XXXIV (Tell Husn)	9
	XI (Tell Husn)	1

PW 237. CN 7662.
XXXIVB 27.22. Hellenistic 2B.
Part of wall, rim. PH 0.04; PL 0.12; D rim (est.) 0.12.
Reddish-yellow clay 7.5YR 6/6. Rhodian.

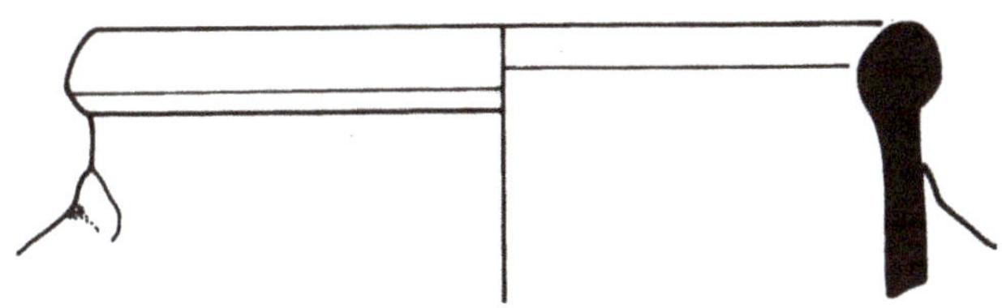

PW 238. CN 7659.
XXXIVB 27.22. Hellenistic 2B.
Part of wall, rim. PH 0.08; PL 0.05; D rim (est.) 0.12.
Reddish-yellow clay 5YR 6/8. Rhodian.

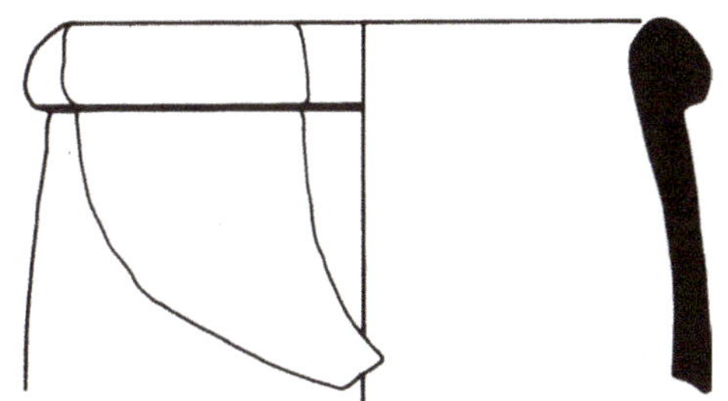

PW 239. CN 7601.
XXXIVB 29.10. Hellenistic 3B/3C.
Part of wall, rim. PH 0.07; PL 0.06; D rim (est.) 0.13.
Strong brown clay 7.5YR 5/6. Hard Pale.
Tall neck; thickened square rim.

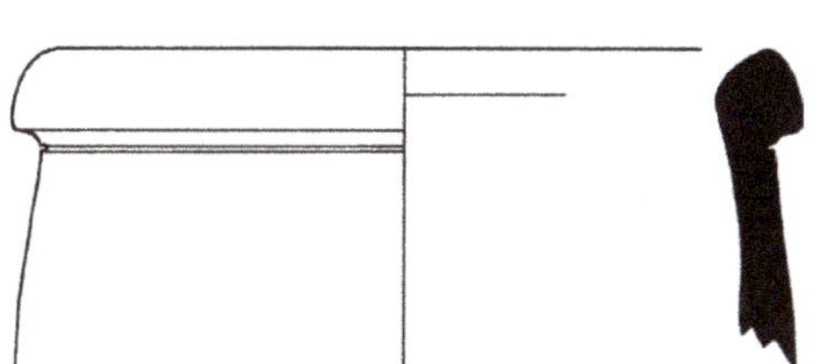

PW 240. CN 7574.
XXXIVB 28.2. Hellenistic 3B/3C.
Part of wall, rim. PH 0.06; PL 0.055; D rim (est.) 0.14.
Reddish-yellow clay 5YR 7/8. Rhodian.

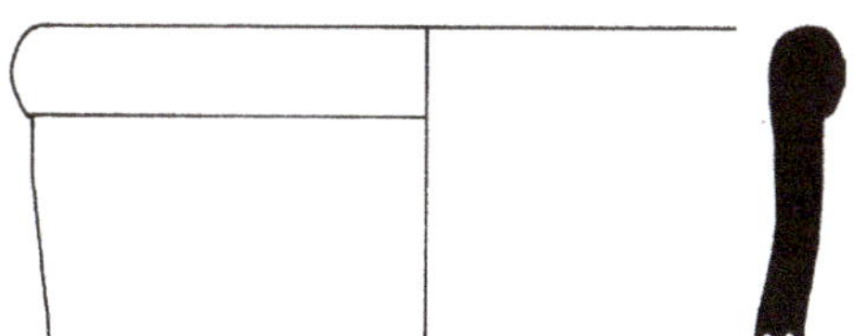

PW 241. CN 7589.
XXXIVB 29.5. Hellenistic 3B/3C.
Part of wall, rim. PH 0.05; PL 0.05; D rim (est.) 0.14.
Yellowish-red clay 5YR 5/8. Hard Pale.
Upright neck. Thickened rim.

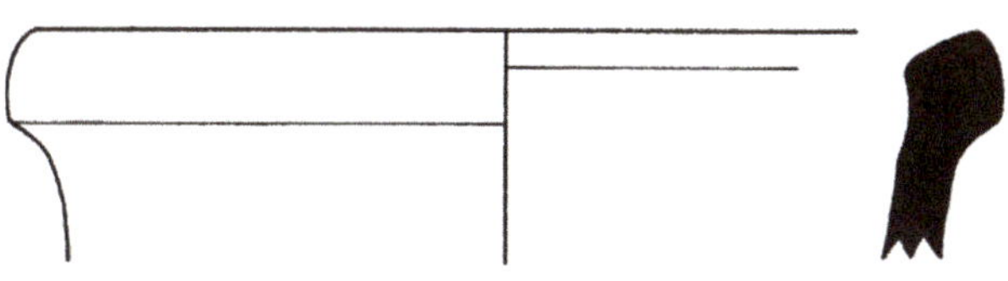

PW 242. CN 7613.
XXXIVB 29.10. Hellenistic 3B/3C.
Part of wall, rim. PL 0.05; D rim (est.) 0.12. Reddish-
yellow clay 5YR 7/8. Rhodian.

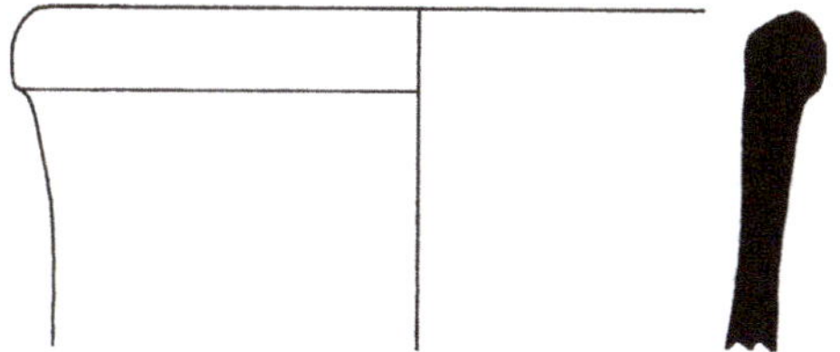

PW 243. CN 7575.
XXXIVB 28.2. Hellenistic 3B/3C.
Part of wall, rim. PH 0.05; PL 0.07; D rim (est.) 0.12.
Reddish-yellow clay 7.5YR 7/6. Rhodian.

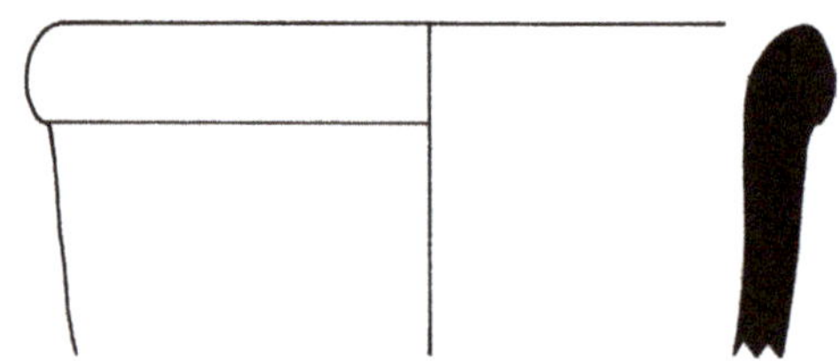

PW 244. CN 7426.
XXVIIIB 13.2. Hellenistic 3A.
Part of wall, rim. PH 0.035; D rim (est.) 0.12. Pink
clay 7.5YR 8/4. Rhodian.
Parallel: Qumran (Eshel and Broshi 2003: fig. 5.1).

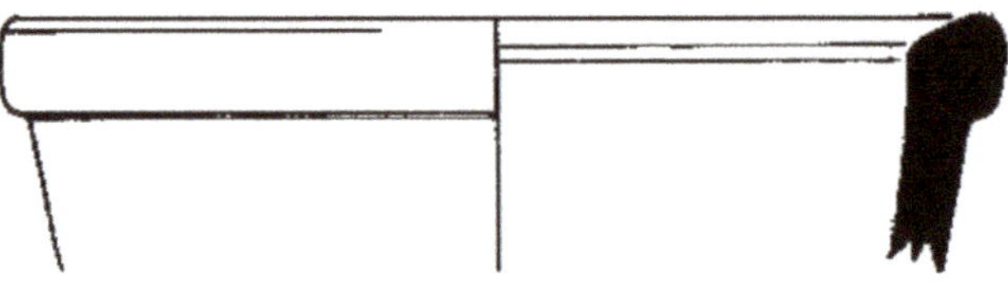

PW 245. CN 7413.
XXVIIIB 10.7. Hellenistic 3A.
Part of wall, rim. PH 0.04; D rim (est.) 0.12. Pink clay
7.5YR 8/3. Rhodian.

PW 246. CN 7505.
XXVIIIB 13.17. Hellenistic 3A.
Part of wall, rim. PH 0.075; D rim (est.) 0.12. Reddish-
yellow clay 5YR 6/6. Rhodian.

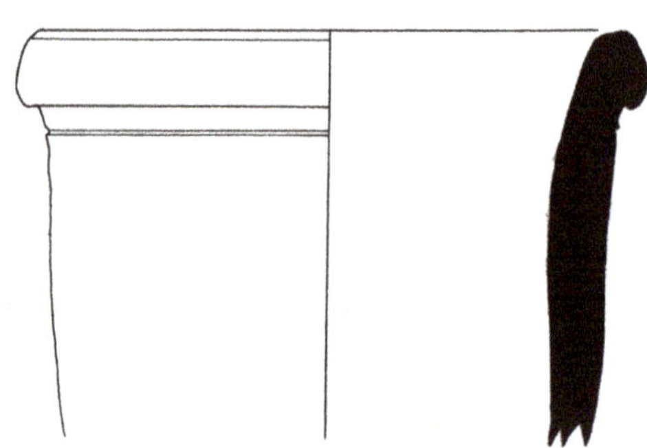

PW 247. CN 7312.
XXVIIIB 10.6. Hellenistic 3A.
Part of wall, rim. PH 0.06; D rim (est.) 0.135. Pink
clay 7.5YR 7/3. Rhodian.

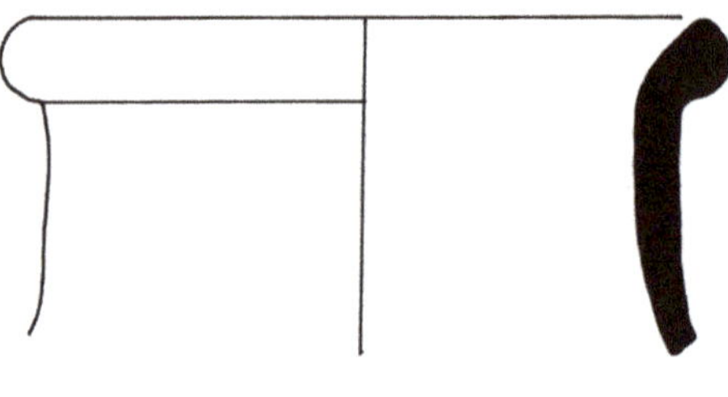

PW 248. CN 7329.
XXVIIIB 13.8. Hellenistic 3A.
Part of wall, rim. PH 0.06; D rim (est.) 0.135. Reddish-
yellow clay 7.5YR 6/6. Rhodian
Tall upright neck; thickened convex rim.

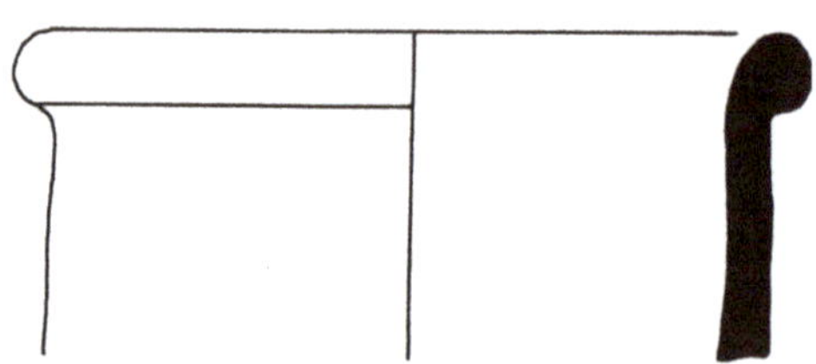

PW 249. CN 7088.
XXIIIA 103.1. Hellenistic 3C.
Part of wall, rim. PH 0.03; PL 0.044; D rim (est.) 0.12.
Reddish-yellow clay 5YR 6/6. Rhodian.

PW 250. CN 7777.
XXIIID 19.5. Hellenistic 3C.
Part of wall, rim. PH 0.045; PL 0.08; D rim (est.) 0.10.
Reddish-yellow clay 5YR 6/6. Rhodian.

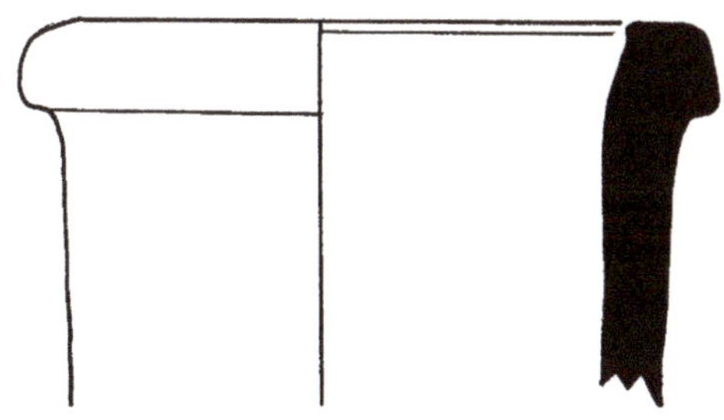

PW 251. CN 2964.
XIA/B 1.5. Early Roman 1.
Part of wall, rim. PH 0.04; D rim (est.) 0.13. Light
yellowish-brown clay 10YR 6/4. Rhodian.

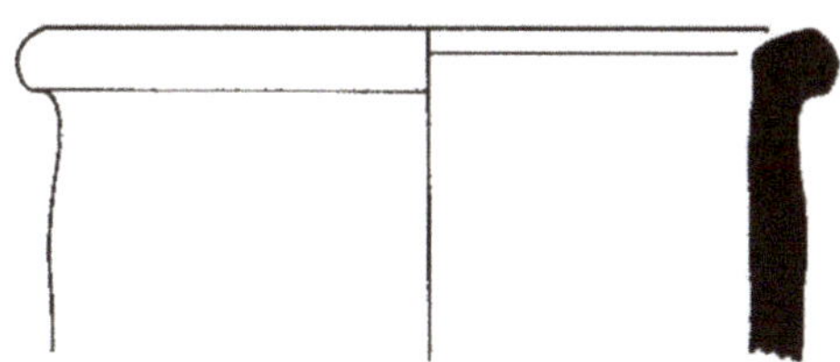

PW 252. CN 7118.
XXIIIA 77.4. Mixed Context.
Part of neck, rim, handle. D rim (est.) 0.12; PH 0.06.
Reddish-yellow clay 5YR 7/6. Rhodian.
Tall upright neck; convex rim. Upper section of each
handle on neck.

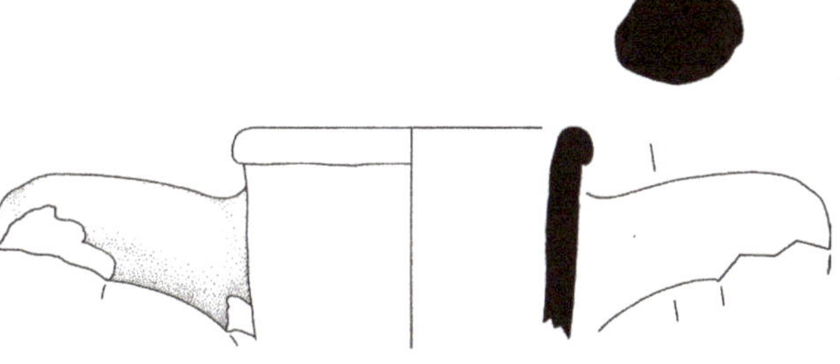

PW 253. CN 7586.
XXXIVB 29.2. Hellenistic 3B/3C.
Part of toe, lower wall. PH 0.11. Reddish-yellow clay
5YR 6/6.
Simple peg toe.

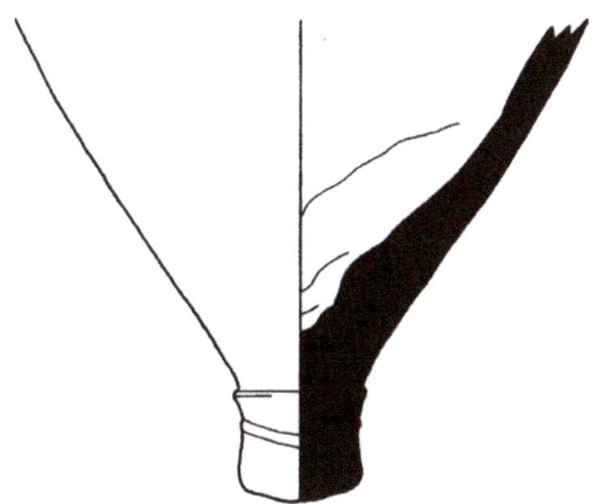

PW 254. CN 7600.
XXXIVB 29.8. Hellenistic 3B/3C.
Part of rim, neck. PL 0.07; D rim (est.) 0.14. Brown
clay 10YR 5/3.
Tall upright neck. Convex thickened rim overhanging
exterior.

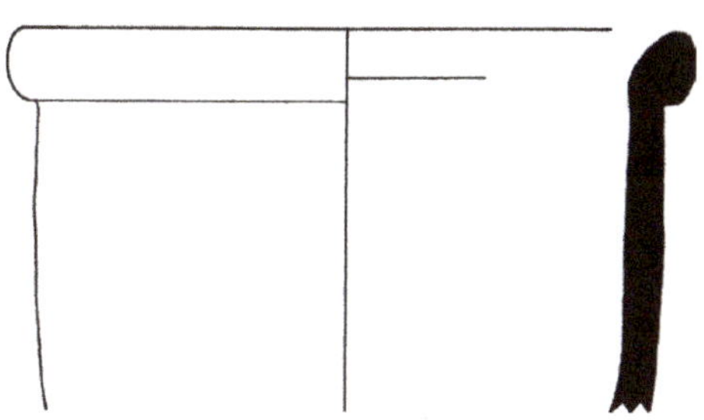

FOOD PREPARATION AND STORAGE VESSELS

Food transport and storage vessels are one of the largest categories of pottery items, with nearly 250 catalogued items (**PW255–487**) or similar. Mortaria, pithoi and, in particular, jars are the shapes that are found in this category.

Mortaria (PW 255–259)

Mortaria are broad open bowls, either in terracotta or stone, used mainly for the grinding and, in the case of stone vessels, for the pounding of foodstuffs (Berlin 1997a: 123–4; Villing and Pemberton 2010: 557–9). They are, therefore, one of the most ancient forms of kitchen ware (Sparkes and Talcott 1970: 221).[18]

With relatively little divergence in form and generally found in small numbers, mortaria continue in use at numerous Palestinian sites during Hellenistic and Roman times. An exception is the large number of such vessels recovered from Tel Anafa, enabling Berlin (1997a: 123–32) to construct a convincing typology based mainly on changes in both rim size and form. These changes, developed over time, must have made it easier to grip the vessel during food preparation. Mortaria were recovered from all levels at Tel Anafa; most were found in Late Hellenistic (c. 125–80 BC) strata with a significant drop in numbers during Early Roman times.

At Pella, the five mortarium fragments (**PW 255–9**), all recovered from stratigraphically significant levels in plot XXVIIIB on Tell Husn, were from early second-century BC (Hellenistic 3A) deposits, with one uncatalogued example from later in the same century (Hellenistic 3B). With their curving lower wall and thickened rim projecting on both exterior and interior, exact parallels are lacking but they are close in form to those "thickened rim" mortaria first appearing in Palestine in the late fourth century BC and remaining common throughout the Hellenistic period (Berlin (1997a: 125–8, PW 348–56). They also find parallels amongst the Hellenistic mortaria from ʿAkko-Ptolemais (Berlin and Stone 2016: fig. 9.2.15) and Tel Dor (Guz-Zilberstein 1995: 295, Type BL 14a, fig. 6.9:10–13), both from similar Early Hellenistic contexts.

Table 2.28. Distribution of mortaria by wares, phases.

Ware	Hard Pale	4
	Miscellaneous	1
Phase	3A c. 200–c. 140 BC	5 (2)
	3B c. 140–c. 100 (?) BC	0 (1)

PW 255. CN 7458.
XXVIIIB 13.9. Hellenistic 3A.
Part of wall, rim. PH 0.04; D rim (est.) 0.27. Pink clay 7.5YR 7/3. Coarse. Hard Pale.
Parallel: Tel Dor (Guz-Zilberstein 1995: fig. 6.9:11, 275–175 BC?).

PW 256. CN 7490.
XXVIIIB 13.16. Hellenistic 3A.
Part of wall, rim. PH 0.045; D rim (est.) 0.23. Light grey clay 10YR 7/2. Hard Pale.

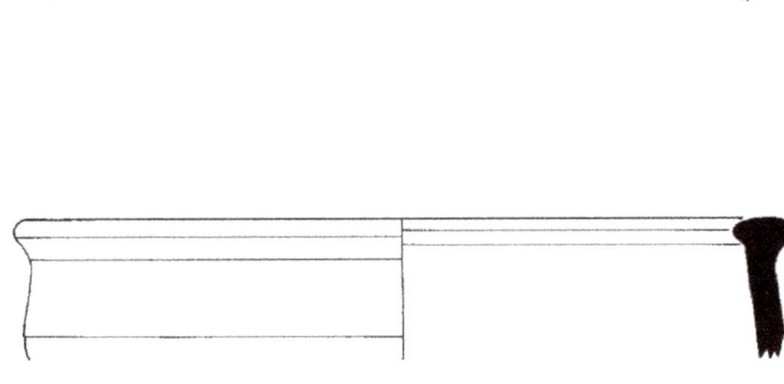

---

18 However, Guz-Zilberstein (1995: 295) and Jackson (2011a: 41), amongst others, point out that the name is sometimes used in more recent Near Eastern pottery studies to denote a large thick-walled bowl of uncertain function.

PW 257. CN 7471.
XXVIIIB 13.10. Hellenistic 3A.
Part of wall, rim. PH 0.045; D rim (est.) 0.37.
Brownish-yellow clay 10YR 6/6.
Thin red slip over interior, exterior of rim.

PW 258. CN 7308.
XXVIIIB 10.4. Hellenistic 3A.
Part of wall, rim. PH 0.06; D rim (est.) 0.24. Pink
7.5YR 7/3. Hard Pale.
Red-brown slip over interior, rim.
Parallel: ʿAkko-Ptolemais (Berlin and Stone 2016: fig.
9.2.15, 3rd c. BC).

PW 259. CN 7512.
XXVIIIB 13.17. Hellenistic 3A.
Part of wall, rim. PH 0.03; D rim (est.) 0.36. Reddish-
yellow clay 7.5YR 6/6. Hard Pale.
Thin red slip over rim.

Jars (PW 260–483)

The basic functions of a jar are those of storage and transport of solids (usually foodstuffs, especially grain) or liquids (oil, wine). Accordingly, the shapes of these vessels are simple and utilitarian, although the size of the container itself may vary significantly; the larger the jar, the more likely it is to have been used for storage rather than for transport, although this is not invariable. When present, handles are usually in pairs (for ease of moving when full) rather than singly as is the case for jugs or juglets. Unfortunately, few jars in this corpus preserve their complete profile but it would seem that the great majority of jars from Pella (excluding Type 1) were cylindrical or bag-shaped with typical round base.

Due to the lack of whole vessels in this corpus, the jars have been classified according to the shape of neck and rim. It can be seen that the rim form of Types 1–3 harks back to the Persian era with the collared rims seen in Types 4–7 representing a new development in the Hellenistic period.

Neckless (Type 1)

The four jars of Type 1 can be further divided into three sub-types, according to rim and shoulder profile.

Table 2.29. Distribution of jars Type 1 by sub-types, wares.

	NECKLESS – PROMINENT SHOULDER (TYPE 1A)	NECKLESS – SQUARE RIM (TYPE 1B)	NECKLESS – EVERTED RIM (TYPE 1C)
Metallic Buff	0	1	0
Miscellaneous	2	0	1

Neckless – prominent shoulder (Type 1A)

PW 260–1 are examples from Pella of a type of jar or amphora that was extremely common in the eastern Mediterranean during the sixth to the fourth centuries BC but, in the Hellenistic period, its distribution was markedly reduced.[19] Often referred to as a Phoenician amphora, it appears in Israel in large numbers along the coastal plain at most Persian-period sites and is also encountered further inland (Gitin 1990: 229–30). Similar vessels have been found in the Persian strata at Tel Keisan in the Galilee, and in the Jezreel Valley at Tel Qiri. East of the Jordan River they are rare, although encountered at Tell Deir 'Alla, with a further example reported from the Kerak Plateau Survey.[20]

At coastal Tel Dor, predictably, many such vessels have been recovered from Persian levels; here the type continues into the third century BC and even later as it does at 'Akko-Ptolemais, Tel Dor, Tel Anafa and Tel Yoqne'am.[21]

The form and context (Hellenistic 3A) of **PW 260**, from the main mound, suggest a date in the late third century or early second century for its manufacture. The findspot (Tell Husn) and narrower shoulder of **PW 261** point to a somewhat later second century date, consistent with its Hellenistic 3B/3C context.

PW 260. CN 7543.
XXXIIY 4.3. Hellenistic 3A.
Part of wall, rim, handle. PH 0.10; D rim (est.) 0.10.
Reddish-yellow clay 7.5YR 6/6. Moderately coarse.
Thickened convex rim. Sloping shoulder; inward-sloping ridged upper wall. Root of band handle preserved.
Parallels: 'Akko–Ptolemais (Regev 2009/10: fig. 1.1); Iotapata (Avshalom-Gorni and Getzov 2002: 78, fig. 5.2.1); Jaffa (Tsuf 2018: fig. 9.33.578); Marisa (Stern 2019: fig. 2.4.7); Tel Dor (Guz-Zilberstein 1995: fig. 6.38:8, 250–200 BC); Tel Yoqne'am (Avissar 1996: fig. X.5.5).

PW 261. CN 7640.
XXIVB 30.6. Hellenistic 3B/3C.
Part of wall, rim. PH 0.035; PL 0.07; D rim (est.) 0.11.
Reddish-yellow clay 7.5YR 6/6.
Thickened convex rim. Sloping shoulder; almost vertical upper wall.

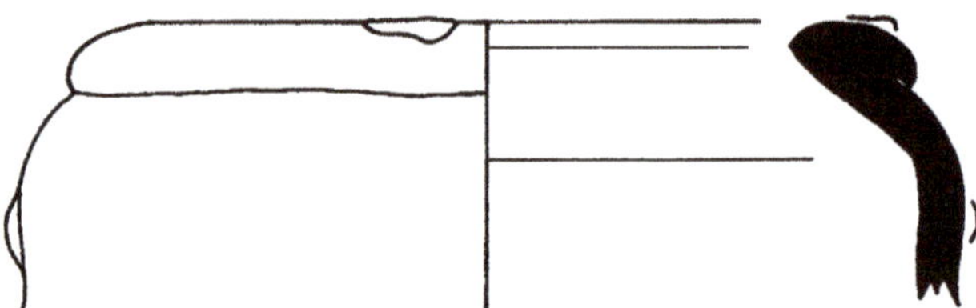

---

19   The type has been thoroughly discussed by a number of scholars including Berlin 1997a: 151–2, 155–6; Regev 2004: 344–5, 2009/10: 120–4 with further references; Stern 1982: 107–10; 1995c: 58–62; Tal 1999: 103–4.

20   Brown 1991: pl. 5.297 (Kerak Plateau); Groot 2009: 172, fig. 5.2-l (Tell Deir 'Alla); Nodet 1980: pls 18.1–1, 25.1–8, 26.1–9, 27.1–9b (Tel Keisan); Avissar 1987: 19, fig.4.10–14 (Tel Qiri).

21   Regev 2009/10: 122 ('Akko-Ptolemais); Avshalom-Gorni and Getzov 2002: 78; Guz-Zilberstein 1995: 312, fig. 6.38; Stern 1995c: 58–62, figs 2.7, 2.8 (Tel Dor); Berlin 1997a: 152, pl. 57, PW 480–3 (Tel Anafa); Avissar 1996: fig. X.5.5 (Tel Yoqne'am).

Neckless – square rim (Type 1B)

PW 262 is from an Early Roman deposit on Tell Husn, with its Metallic Buff fabric consistent with a Late Hellenistic or Early Roman date. Jars of similar profile have been recovered from a Herodian context at Machaerus (Loffreda 1996: Group 6: figs 8.1, 2, 8) and Early Roman Sepphoris (Balouka 2013: pl. 1.20).

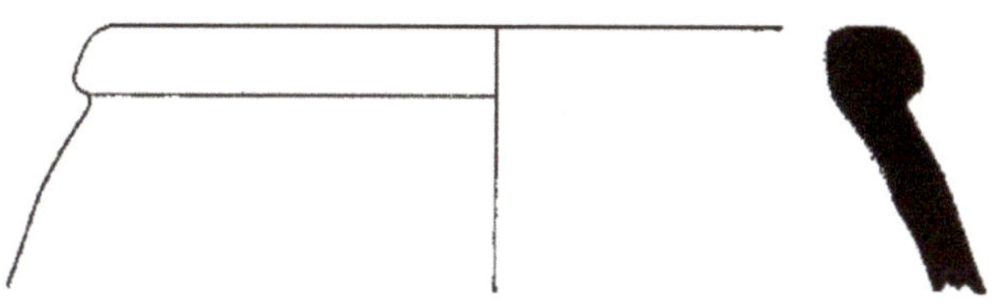

PW 262. CN 7178.
XXXIVG 9.5. Early Roman 1.
Part of neck, rim. PH 0.035; D rim (est.) 0.11.
Reddish-yellow clay 7.5YR 7/6. Metallic Buff.
Convex rim. Slightly convex upper wall.
Parallels: ʿAkko-Ptolemais (Berlin and Stone 2016:
fig. 9.22.3, first half of 1st c. BC); Gezer (Gitin 1990:
pl. 36.23, mid-2nd c. BC); Qumran (Eshel and Broshi
2003 fig. 8.6); Samaria (Hennessy 1970: fig. 12.33);
Sepphoris (Balouka 2013: pl. 1.20, 2nd–1st c. BC); Tel
Dor (Guz-Zilberstein 1995: fig. 6.42:4, 250–125 BC);
Ziqim (Zissu and Rokach 1999: fig. 5.20).

Neckless – everted rim (Type 1C)

PW 263 is from an Early Roman stratum on Tell Husn with its rim and shoulder profile matching that of P.W. Lapp's Jar Type 19A (P.W. Lapp 1961: 156) recovered from a Qumran context of 50–68 AD (de Vaux 1954: fig. 5.5).

PW 263. CN 7564.
XXXIVB 27.2. Early Roman 1.
Fragment of wall, rim. PH 0.02; PL 0.07; D rim (est.)
0.18. Pink clay 7.5YR 7/4. Thick white inclusions.
Broad triangular rim. Sloping shoulder.
Parallel: Straton's Tower/Caesarea (Berlin 1992:
fig. 54.6).

Short concave neck; everted rim (Type 2)

This form (**PW 264–74**), occurring on both the main mound and Tell Husn throughout the Hellenistic (2B–3C) levels, can be subdivided according to rim type. A similar diversity of rim form and chronological span amongst the short-necked storage jars is also seen at ʿIraq al-Amir (Zimmerman 2020b: 47–8, Types 50.1–3, pl. 2.8).

Table 2.30. Distribution of jars Type 2 by sub-types, wares, phases.

		SHORT NECK – EVERTED SIMPLE RIM (TYPE 2A)	SHORT NECK – EVERTED THICKENED RIM (TYPE 2B)	SHORT NECK – ANGULAR RIM (TYPE 2C)
Ware	Hard Pale	2	5	3
	Metallic Buff	0	1	0

Table 2.30. Distribution of jars Type 2 by sub-types, wares, phases (continued).

Phase				
	2B c. 220–c. 200 BC	0	1 (2)	1 (5)
	3A c.200–c. 140 BC	0	2	0 (2)
	3B c. 140–c. 100 (?) BC	0	0	0 (1)
	3B/3C c. 140–c. 80/79 BC	0	2	0
	3C c. 100 (?)–c. 80/79 BC	2	1	1
	Mixed	0	0 (2)	1

Short neck – everted simple rim (Type 2A)

At Jerusalem and Hippos-Sussita similar jars are seen in second and first century BC strata, consistent with the context (Hellenistic 3C) of both examples of a type uncommon at Pella.

PW 264. CN 7292.
XXIIIB 1.4. Hellenistic 3C.
Part of wall, rim. PH 0.04; PL 0.045; D rim (est.) 0.14.
Pink clay 7.5YR 7/4. Hard Pale.

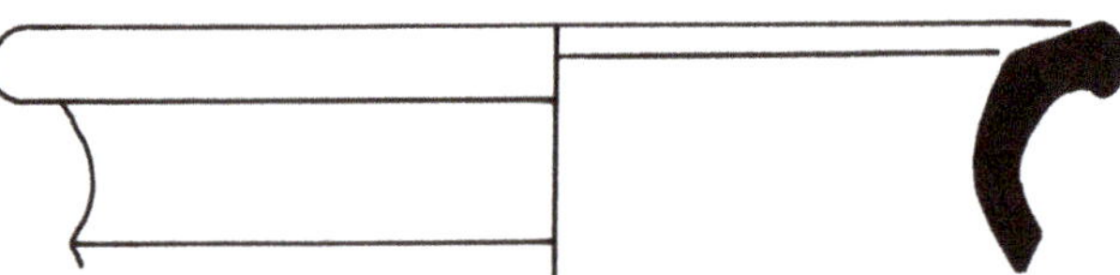

PW 265. CN 7061.
XXIIIA 106.1. Hellenistic 3C.
Part of wall, rim. PH 0.02; D rim (est.) 0.10. Strong brown clay 7.5YR.
Parallels: Gezer (Gitin 1990: pl. 39.2); Hippos-Sussita (Osband and Eisenberg 2018: pl. 2.1.4, 2nd c. BC); Jerusalem (Geva 2003: pl. 5.6.14, 2nd c. BC; Geva and Rosenthal-Heginbottom 2003: pl. 6.1.34, 1st c. BC); Khirbet as-Suwwan (Ji and Lee 1999: 530, no.1); Tell Nimrin (Dornemann 1990: fig. 3.9).

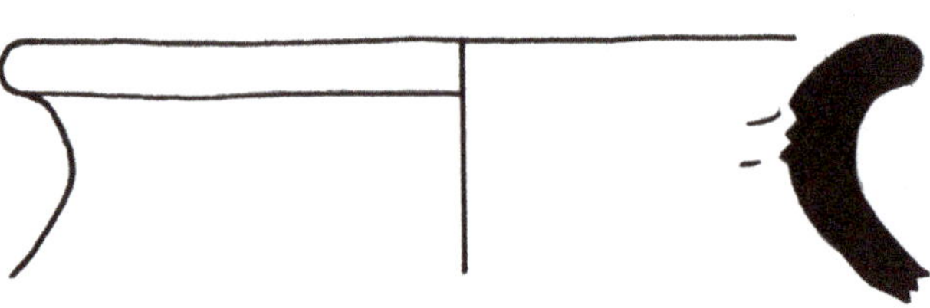

Short neck – everted thickened rim (Type 2B)

PW 266–71 have short, poorly defined necks, with thickened, slightly everted rims. They are from all Hellenistic (2B, 3A–3C) horizons. The form becomes widespread in the southern Levant during the Persian period (Guz-Zilberstein 1995: 311). Similar examples were recovered from Early Hellenistic contexts at Gezer, Samaria, Shechem and Tel Dor with a rim of similar profile from a First Revolt (that is, c. 70 AD) stratum at Machaerus.[22]

PW 266. CN 7583.
XXXIVF 6.5. Hellenistic 2B.
Rim, part of shoulder. PH 0.07; D rim 0.11. Reddish-yellow clay 5YR 6/6. Hard Pale.
Parallels: Gadara/Umm Qais (Kerner 1997: fig. 12.12); Samaria (Zayadine 1966: pl. XXVII.3); Shechem (N.L. Lapp 1964: fig. 1a.3, 2008: pl. 3.2.14,

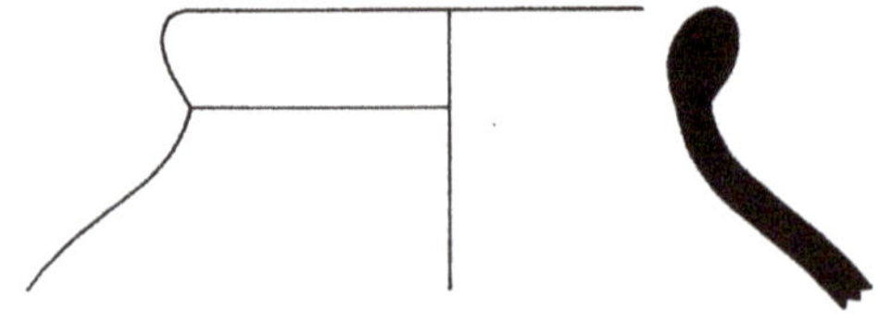

---

22 Gitin 1990: pl. 32.4 (Gezer); Loffreda 1980: pl. 93.7 (Machaerus); Zayadine 1966: pl. XXVIII.3 (Samaria); N.L. Lapp 2008: 42, 230–3, pl. 3.3 (Shechem); Guz-Zilberstein 1995: fig. 6.35:1, Type JR1a (Tel Dor).

250–190 BC); Straton's Tower/Caesarea (Berlin 1992: fig. 54.3); Tel Dor (Guz-Zilberstein 1995: fig. 6.35:4, c.275/250–200 BC).

PW 267. CN 7383.
XXXIVB 29.1. Hellenistic 3B/3C.
Part of wall, rim. PH 0.055; PL 0.07; D rim (est.) 0.10.
Reddish-yellow clay 5YR 6/6. Hard Pale.
Parallels: Kedesh (Levantine Ceramics Project: n.d. K12P027, 5th–3rd c. BC); Scythopolis/Beth-Shean (Johnson 2006: fig. 15.3.64); Shechem (N.L. Lapp 2008: pl. 3.3.7, 325–250 BC).

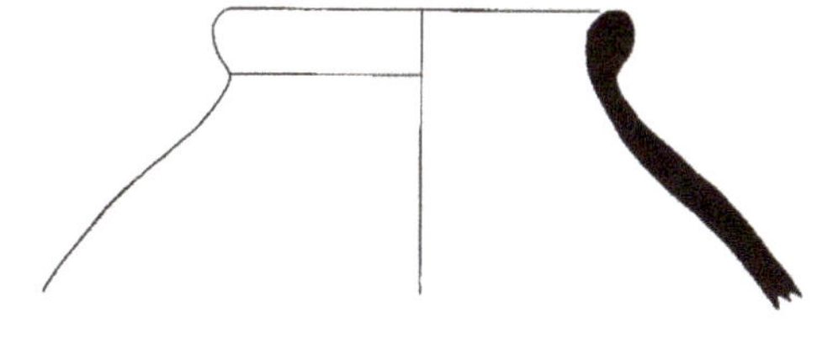

PW 268. CN 7408.
XXVIIIB 10.6. Hellenistic 3A.
Part of wall, rim. PH 0.055; D rim (est.) 0.10. Very pale brown clay 10YR 8/3. Hard Pale.
Parallels: 'Akko-Ptolemais (Berlin and Stone 2016: fig. 9.7.2, 3rd c. BC); Hippos-Sussita (Osband and Eisenberg 2018: pl. 1.1, 3rd–first half 2nd c. BC); 'Iraq al-Amir (Brown 1983: fig. 54.1); Jerusalem (Geva 2003: pl. 5.2.18, late 2nd–1st c. BC).

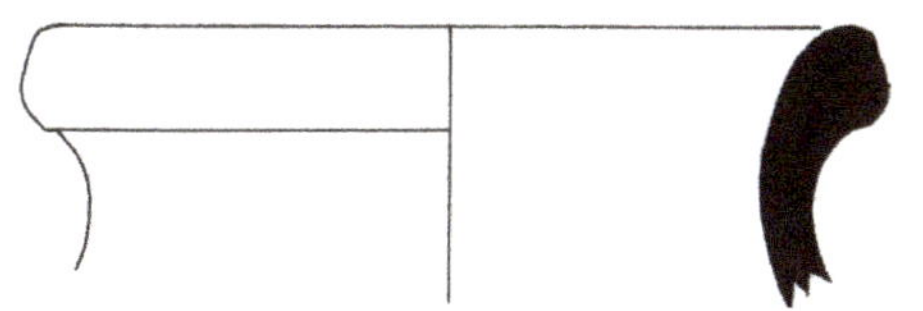

PW 269. CN 7258.
XXVIIIB 13.17. Hellenistic 3A.
Part of wall, rim. PH 0.035; D rim (est.) 0.10. Pink clay 7.5YR 7/4. Metallic Buff.
Parallel: Samaria (Crowfoot et al. 1957: fig. 42.10, c. 200–150 BC).

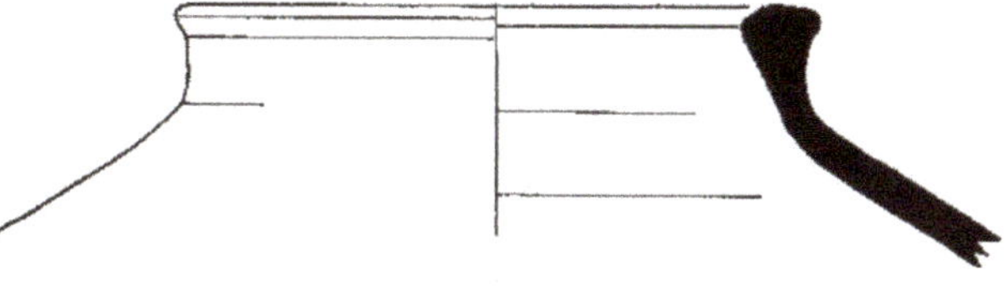

PW 270. CN 7636.
XXXIVB 30.1. Hellenistic 3B/3C.
Part of neck, rim. PH 0.045; PL 0.045; D rim (est.) 0.08. Reddish-yellow clay 7.5YR 6/6. Hard Pale.
Parallels: 'Iraq al-Amir (Zimmerman 2020b: pl. 2.8.9, str. IIIb, c. 100 BC); Ziqim (Zissu and Rokach 1999: fig. 5.21).

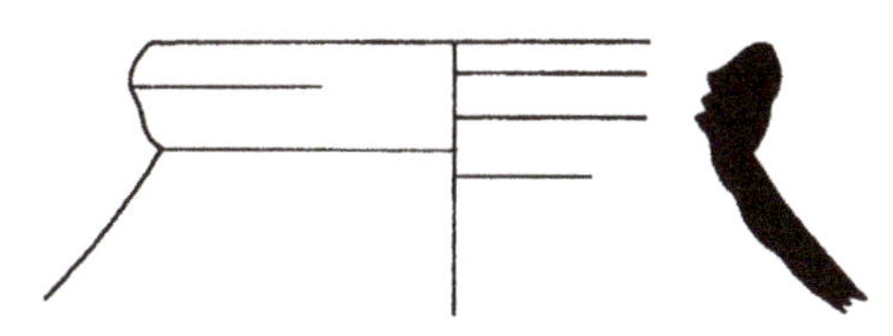

PW 271. CN 7035.
XXIIIA 100.5. Hellenistic 3C.
Part of wall, rim. PH 0.03; PL 0.065; D rim (est.) 0.10. Very pale brown clay 10YR 7/3. Hard Pale.
Parallels: 'Akko-Ptolemais (Berlin and Stone 2016: fig. 9.22.4, first half of 1st c. BC); Jaffa (Tsuf 2018: fig. 9.34.589); Jerusalem (Geva 2003: pl. 5.4.13, late 2nd–1st c. BC); Tel Zahara (Bar-Nathan and Gärtner 2013: fig. 3.8.75).

Short neck – angular rim (Type 2C)

In contrast to the following sub-types, jars of Type 2C have a short, indistinct neck and thickened everted rim, triangular in section. Eleven examples from the main mound and Tell Husn (**PW 272–4**), along with eight non-catalogued specimens, were recovered, occurring in all Hellenistic levels. Jars of this type are similar in form to those of Type JR 1b at Tel Dor (Guz-Zilberstein 1995: 311, fig. 6.36), a type that appears in Early Hellenistic horizons at sites west of the Jordan River including Samaria, Sha'ar ha-Amakim, Shechem and Tel Keisan.[23] At Gezer, however, similar jars (Gitin 1990: Type 166), although rare, are seen in mid-second-century contexts and last into the first century BC.

PW 272. CN 7381.
XXXIVF 6.1. Hellenistic 2B.
Multiple fragments making up part of wall, rim, handles. PH 0.09; PL 0.49; D rim (est.) 0.12. Strong brown clay 7.5YR 5/6. Hard Pale.
Parallels: 'Akko-Ptolemais (Berlin and Stone 2016: fig. 9.3.4, 3rd c. BC); 'Iraq al-Amir (Dentzer et al. 1983: fig. 64.13; Zimmerman 2020b: fig. 2.8.2, str. IV, early 2nd c. BC); Jerusalem (Geva 2003: pl. 5.1.8, 2nd c. BC); Machaerus (Corbo and Loffreda 1981: fig. 35.7); Samaria (Crowfoot et al. 1957: fig. 42.10; Hennessy 1970: figs 6.13, 9.11, 10.11); Sha'ar ha-Amakim (Mlynarczyk 2000: pl. 115.4); Shechem (N.L. Lapp 2008: pl. 3.1.2); Tel Dor (Guz-Zilberstein 1995: fig. 6.55:16, 275–250 BC?); Tel Keisan (Briend 1980: pl. 8.1b, late 4th–mid-2nd c. BC); Tell Nimrin (Dornemann 1990: fig. 3.8).

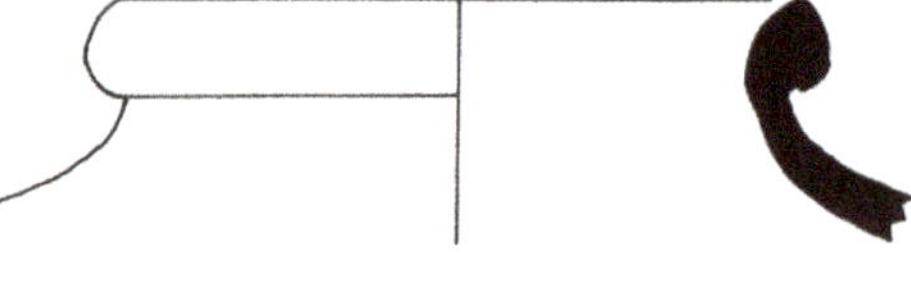

PW 273. CN 6977.
XXIIIA 10.7. Hellenistic 3C.
Part of wall, rim. PH 0.045; PL 0.075; D rim (est.) 0.12. Light brown clay 7.5YR 6/4. Hard Pale.
Parallel: Kedesh (Levantine Ceramics Project: n.d. K00P050, 5th–3rd c. BC).

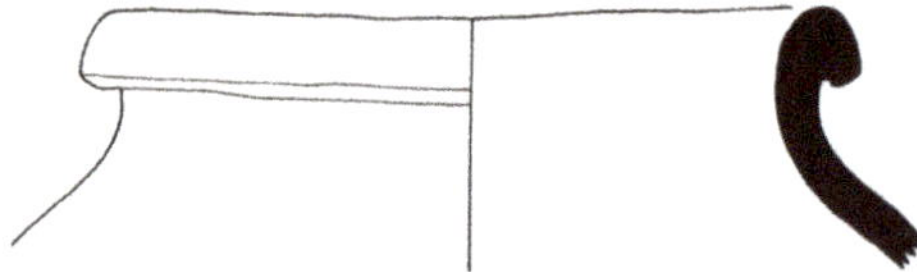

PW 274. CN 7332.
XXXIVG 12.17. Mixed Context.
Part of wall, rim. PH 0.055; PL 0.08; D rim (est.) 0.15. Reddish brown clay 5YR 5/4. Hard Pale.

Thickened everted rim (Type 3)

Jars **PW 275–303** have a thickened everted rim set off from a tall, well-defined neck, concave on the exterior. At Pella jars of this type are seen on both the main mound and Tell Husn in deposits of the later third and second centuries (Hellenistic 2B, 3A–3B) as well as from Jannaeus Destruction (Hellenistic 3C) and Early Roman horizons. At Gezer the shape "is one of the two major jar forms of the first half of the Hellenistic horizon" and first appears in the mid-third century BC (Gitin 1990: 238, Type 159), consistent with the Pella

23 Crowfoot et al. 1957: fig. 42.8–10; Zayadine 1966: pl. XXVII.1–10 (Samaria); Mlynarczyk 2000: 226–8, pl. 115 (Sha'ar ha-Amakim); N.L. Lapp 2008: 41–2, 220–9, pls 3.1–2 (Shechem); Briend 1980: 105, pl. 8.3–7 (Tel Keisan).

evidence, although by the late second century – in contrast to Pella – it has largely disappeared. Similar jars are also common in Stratum IIIb levels (c. 100 BC) at 'Iraq al-Amir (Zimmerman 2020b, Type 51.5, pl. 2.10.5–80, as well as at Tel Dor (Type JR 1a) in all phases of the Hellenistic period (Guz-Zilberstein 1995: 311, fig. 6.35).

Table 2.31. Distribution of jars Type 3 by wares, phases.

Ware	Hard Pale	17
	Metallic Buff	5
	Yellow-slipped	1
	Miscellaneous	6
Phase	2B c. 220–c. 200 BC	3
	3A c. 200–c. 140 BC	4 (4)
	3B c. 140–c. 100 (?) BC	3 (1)
	3B/3C c. 140–c. 80/79 BC	3
	3C c. 100 (?)–c. 80/79 BC	7 (4)
	Early Roman 63 BC–c. 135 AD	1 (3)
	Mixed	8

PW 275. CN 7384.
XXXIVF 6.5. Hellenistic 2B.
Part of rim. PH 0.03; D rim (est.) 0.135. Yellowish-red clay 5YR 5/6. Hard Pale.
Parallels: Amman/Philadelphia (Zayadine 1977–78: fig. 12.416); Gezer (Gitin 1990: pl. 32.3, mid-3rd c. BC); Jerusalem (Tushingham 1985: fig. 18.1); Samaria (Hennessy 1970: fig. 6.7).

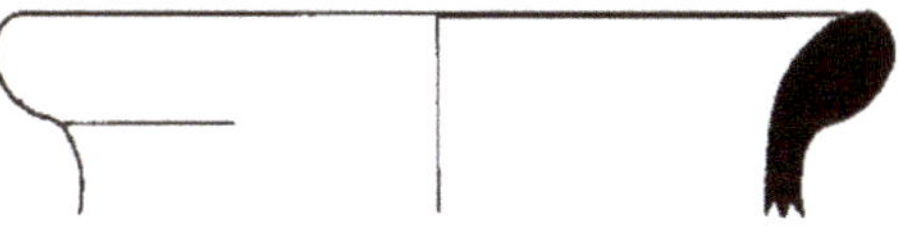

PW 276. CN 7378.
XXXIVF 4.1. Mixed Context.
Part of wall, rim. PH 0.035; PL 0.065; D rim (est.) 0.12. Yellowish-red clay 5YR 5/6. Hard Pale.
Parallel: 'Iraq al-Amir (Zimmerman 2020b: pl. 2.8.7, str. IV, early 2nd c. BC).

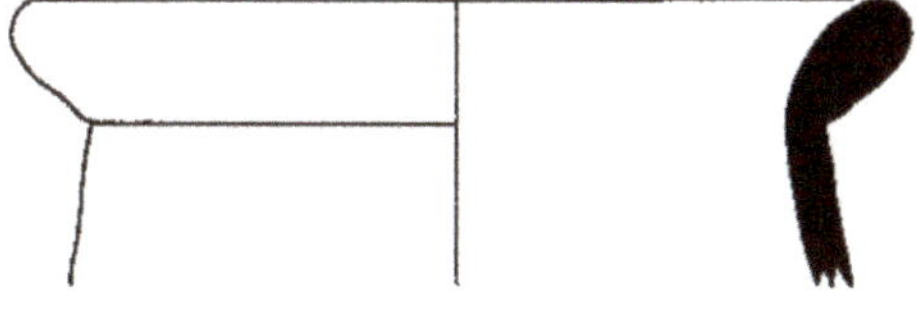

PW 277. CN 7376.
XXXIVF 4.1. Mixed Context.
Part of upper wall, neck, rim. PH 0.065; D rim (est.) 0.10. Brown 7.5YR 5/4. Hard Pale.
Parallel: Samaria (Zayadine 1966: pl. XXVIII.20).

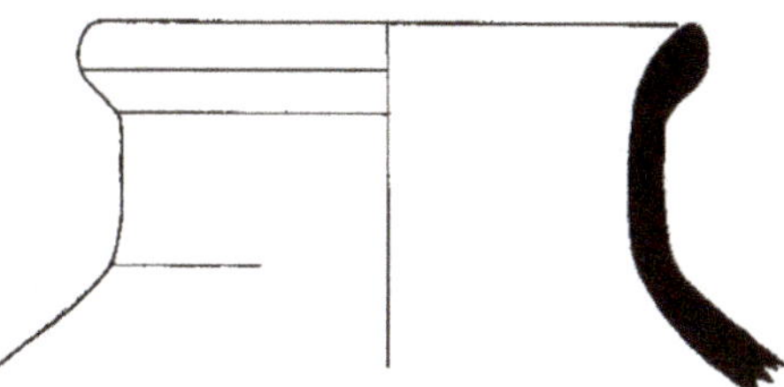

PW 278. CN 7671.
XXXIVB 27.26. Hellenistic 2B.
Part of wall, rim. PL 0.085; D rim (est.) 0.12. Reddish-yellow clay 7.5YR 6/6.
Undercut rim.
Parallel: 'Iraq al-Amir (N.L. Lapp 1983: fig. 30.1).

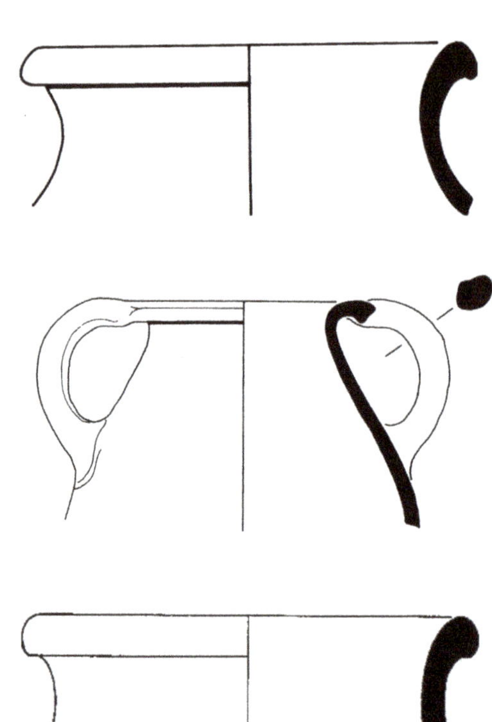

PW 279. CN 7667.
XXXIVB 27.20. Hellenistic 2B.
Part of rim, neck, shoulder, handle. PH 0.09; PL 0.05; D rim (est.) 0.12. Light brown clay 7.5YR 6/4. Hard Pale.
Narrow strap handle from lip to shoulder.

PW 280. CN 7377.
XXXIVF 4.1. Mixed Context.
Part of wall, rim. PH 0.04; PL 0.08; D rim (est.) 0.12. Reddish-yellow clay 7.5YR 6/6. Hard Pale.
Parallels: Iotapata (Adan-Bayewitz and Aviam 1997: fig. 12.9); Samaria (Crowfoot et al. 1957: fig. 42.5); Scythopolis/Beth-Shean (Johnson 2006: fig. 15.4.70).

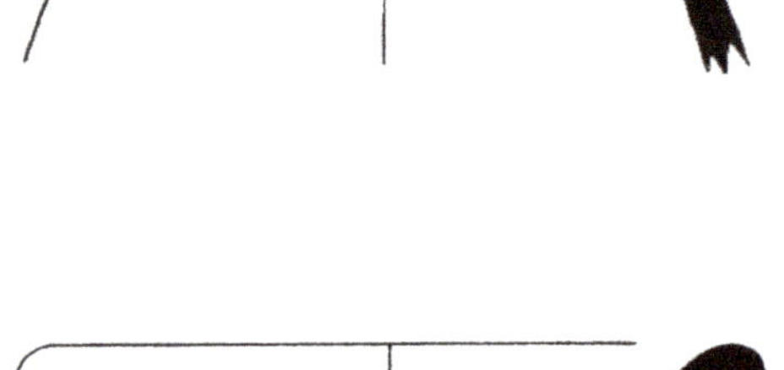

PW 281. CN 7643.
XXXIVB 30.7. Hellenistic 3B/3C.
Part of wall, rim. PH 0.06; PL 0.09; D rim (est.) 0.12. Reddish-yellow clay 7.5YR 6/6. Hard Pale.

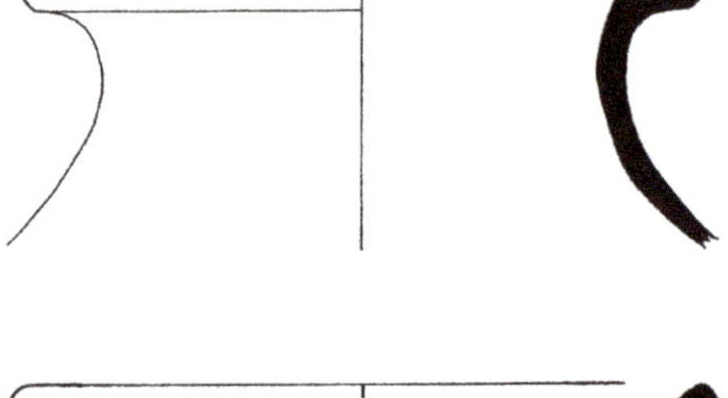

PW 282. CN 7650.
XXXIVB 30.10. Hellenistic 3B/3C.
Part of wall, rim. PH 0.06; PL 0.08; D rim (est.) 0.12. Brown clay 7.5YR 5/4.
Parallels: 'Iraq al-Amir (Zimmerman 2020b: pl. 2.10.7, str. IIIa, c. 50 AD); Jerusalem (Geva 2003: pl. 5.9.10, later 2nd–1st c. BC).

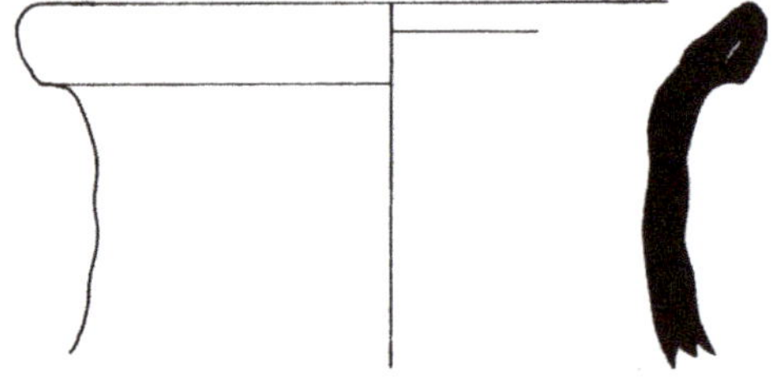

PW 283. CN 7432.
XXVIIIB 13.3. Hellenistic 3A.
Part of wall, rim. PH 0.065; D rim (est.) 0.11. Pale yellow clay 2.5YR 8/2. Hard Pale.
Strap handle from rim to shoulder.
Parallel: Ras Abu Ma'aruf (Rapuano 1999: fig. 1.10).

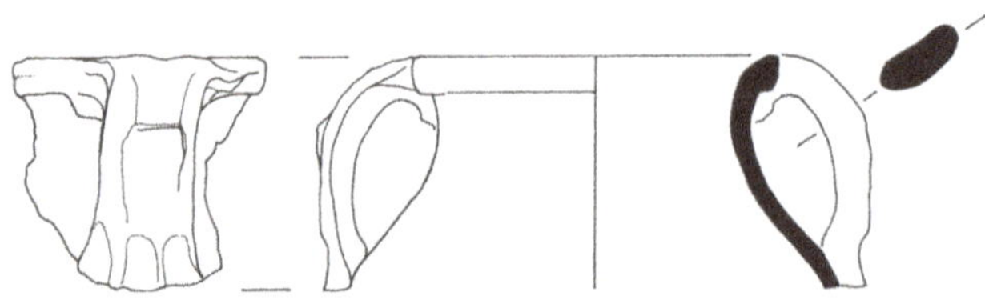

PW 284. CN 7294.
XXIIIB 2.1. Hellenistic 3B.
Part of wall, rim. PH 0.04; PL 0.06; D rim (est.) 0.135.
Very pale brown clay 10YR 7/4. Hard Pale.

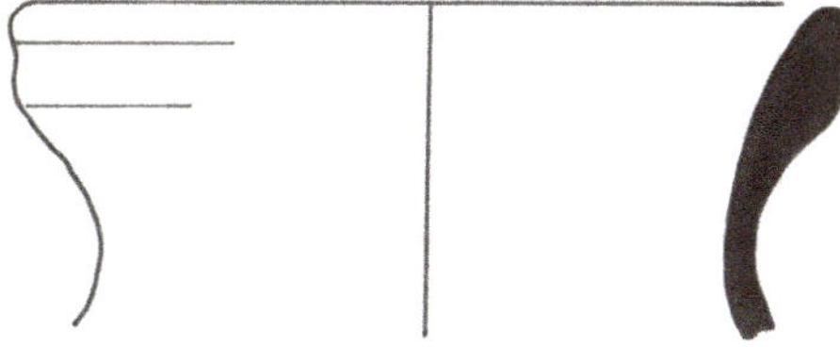

PW 285. CN 7225.
XXVIIIB 10.3. Hellenistic 3A.
Part of wall, neck, rim. PH 0.06; D rim (est.) 0.095.
Light yellowish-brown clay 10YR 6/4. Hard Pale.
Parallels: Gezer (Gitin 1990: pl. 34.14, mid-2nd
c. BC); Samaria (Zayadine 1966: pl. XXVII.9).

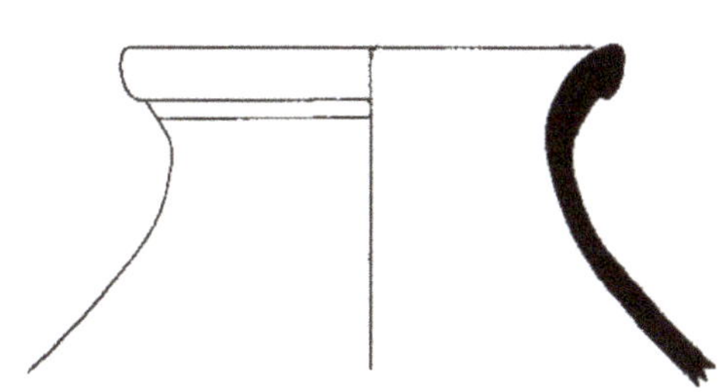

PW 286. CN 7326.
XXVIIIB 13.3. Hellenistic 3A.
Part of wall, neck, rim, handle. PH 0.18; D rim
(est.) 0.11. Pink clay 5YR 7/3. Hard Pale.
Strap handle from shoulder to rim.

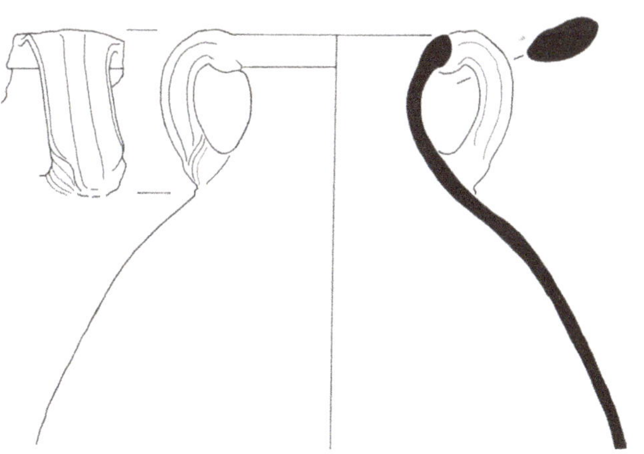

PW 287. CN 7398.
XXVIIIB 10.4. Hellenistic 3A.
Part of wall, rim. PH 0.03; D rim (est.) 0.09. Very
pale brown clay 10YR 8/3. Metallic Buff.
Parallels: Apollonia (Fischer and Tal 1999a:
fig. 5.15.6); Gezer (Gitin 1990: pl. 32.3, mid-3rd
c. BC); 'Iraq al-Amir (N.L. Lapp 1979: fig. 2.2, 1983:
fig. 30.10a); Samaria (Crowfoot et al. 1957: fig.
42.5); Tel Dor (Guz-Zilberstein 1995: fig. 6.35:6,
275–150 BC).

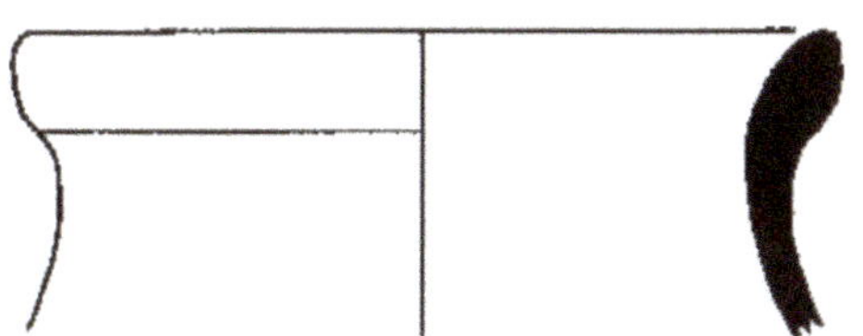

PW 288. CN 7299.
XXIIIB 3.8. Hellenistic 3B.
Three joining fragments of neck, rim. PH 0.06; D rim
(est.) 0.11. Red clay 2.5YR 5/6.
Parallels: 'Akko-Ptolemais (Berlin and Stone 2016:
fig. 9.13.4, mid–late 2nd c. BC); 'Iraq al-Amir
(Zimmerman 2020b: pl. 2.10.8, str. IV–IIIb, early
2nd c.–c. 100 BC).

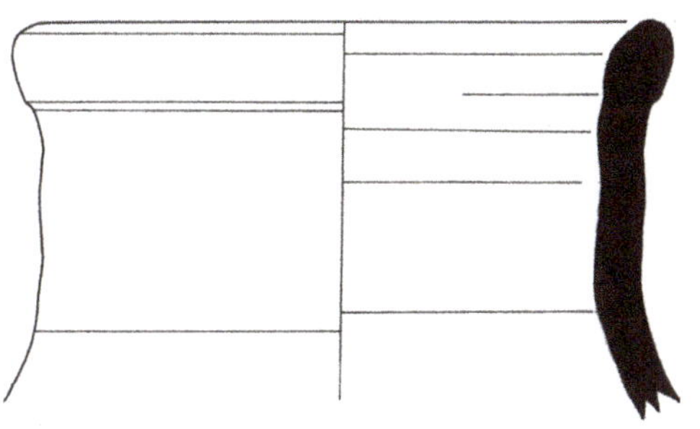

PW 289. CN 0982.
IIIB/C.1.13 Mixed Context.
Part of wall, rim. PH 0.06; PL 0.08; D rim (est.) 0.12.
Light yellowish-brown clay 10YR 6/5. Coarse white inclusions.

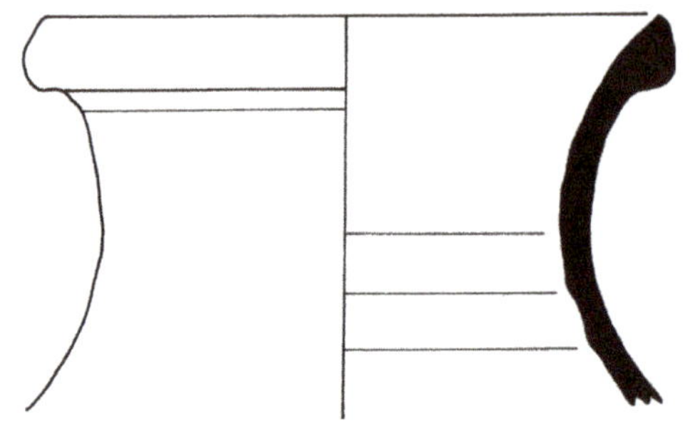

PW 290. CN 0476.
IIIB/C.1.19. Mixed Context.
Part of wall, rim, handle. PH 0.07; D rim (est.) 0.105.
Reddish-yellow clay 7.5YR 7/6. Hard Pale.
Strap handle from rim to shoulder.

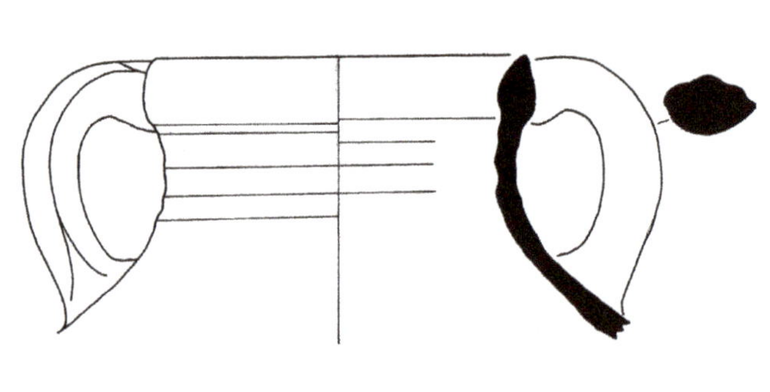

PW 291. CN 7084.
XXIIIA 109.4. Hellenistic 3B.
Part of wall, rim. PH 0.03; PL 0.05; D rim (est.) 0.13.
Light brown clay 7.5YR 6/4. Hard Pale.
Parallels: Amman/Philadelphia (Greene and 'Amr
1992: figs 5.7, 9); Jerusalem (Tushingham 1985:
fig. 18.4); Tell Nimrin (Dornemann 1990, fig. 2.48).

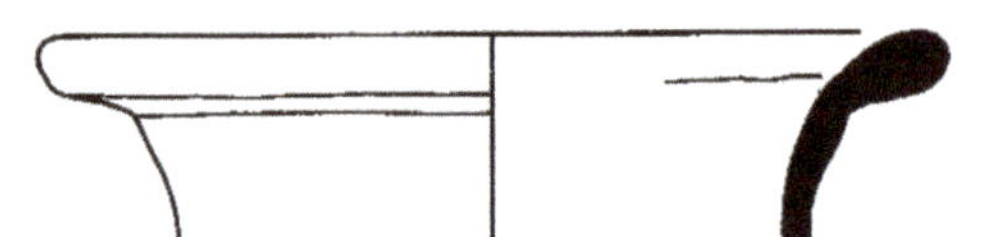

PW 292. CN 6892.
XXIIIA 10.7. Hellenistic 3C.
Part of wall, rim, handle. PH 0.22; D rim (est.) 0.13.
Light brown clay 7YR 6/3.
Strap handle from shoulder to upper body.

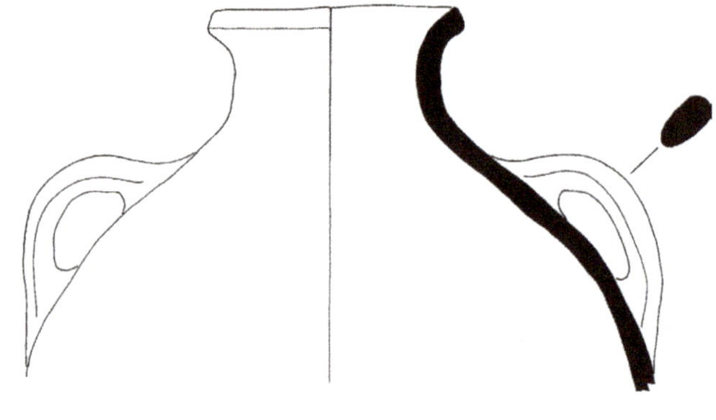

PW 293. CN 6883.
XXIIIA 10.5. Hellenistic 3C.
Part of wall, neck, rim. PH 0.04; PL 0.065; D rim
(est.) 0.13. Reddish-brown clay 5YR 5/4. Hard Pale.
Parallels: Hesban (Gerber 2012: 181, fig. 3.1.10); Tel
'Ira (Fischer and Tal 1999b: fig. 6.128.18); Tell Nimrin
(Dornemann 1990: fig. 2.49); Wadi al-Kharrar (Abu
Shmeis and Waheeb 2002: fig. 2.5).

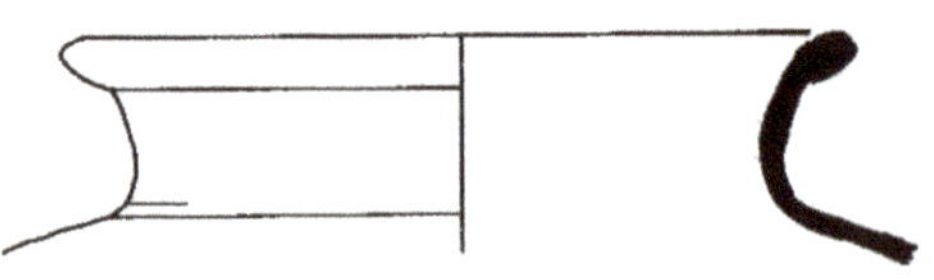

PW 294. CN 6975.
XXIIIA 20.4. Hellenistic 3C.
Part of wall, rim. PH 0.07; D rim (est.) 0.105. Very
pale brown clay 10YR 7/3. Metallic Buff.

PW 295. CN 7087.
XXIIIA 103.1. Hellenistic 3C.
Part of wall, rim. PH 0.05; PL 0.05; D rim (est.) 0.09.
Reddish-yellow clay 7.5YR 6/6. Hard Pale.
Parallels: Hesban (Gerber 2012: 181, fig. 3.2.1);
Hippos-Sussita (Osband and Eisenberg 2018: pl.
2.1.3, 2nd c. BC); Samaria (Crowfoot et al. 1957:
fig. 42.5; Hennessy 1970: fig. 11.15).

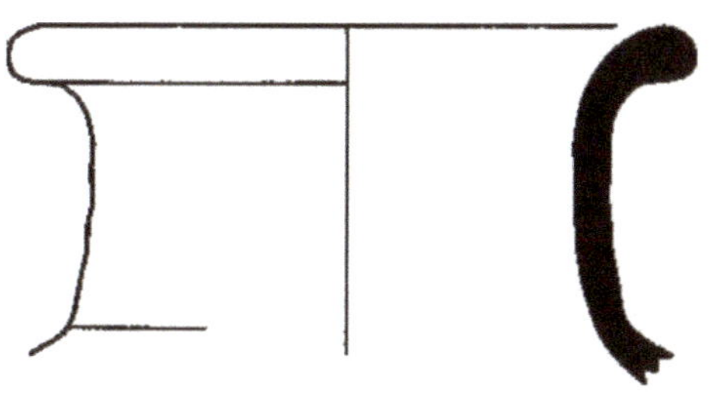

PW 296. CN 7058.
XXIIIA 103.3. Hellenistic 3C.
Part of rim. PH 0.025; PL 0.06; D rim (est.) 0.11. Very
pale brown clay 10YR 8/3. Metallic Buff.
Parallels: Amman/Philadelphia (Greene and ʿAmr
1992: fig. 5.9; Zayadine 1977–78: fig. 15.420).

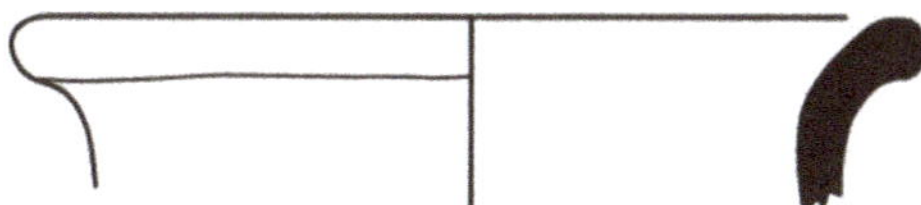

PW 297. CN 0528.
IIIB/C 1.1. Hellenistic 3C.
Part of wall, rim. PH 0.055; D rim (est.) 0.11. Light
brown clay 7.5YR 6/4. Yellow-slipped Coarse Ware.

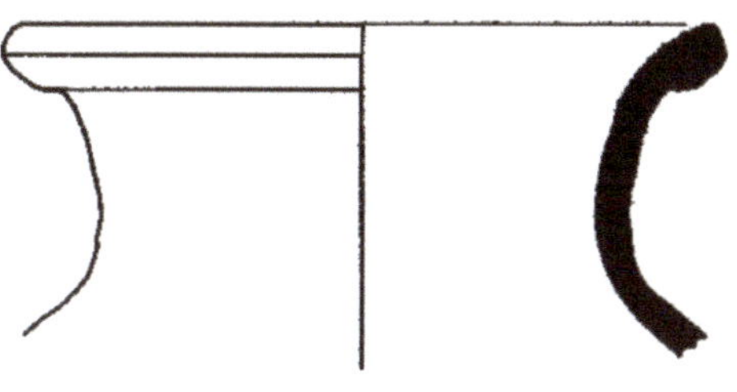

PW 298. CN 7066.
XXIIIA 103.3. Hellenistic 3C.
Part of wall, rim. PH 0.04; PL 0.075; D rim (est.) 0.12.
Pink clay 7.5YR 7/4. Hard Pale.
Parallels: ʿAkko-Ptolemais (Berlin and Stone 2016:
fig. 9.24.2, second half of 1st c. BC); Jerusalem
(Tushingham 1985: fig. 17.30).

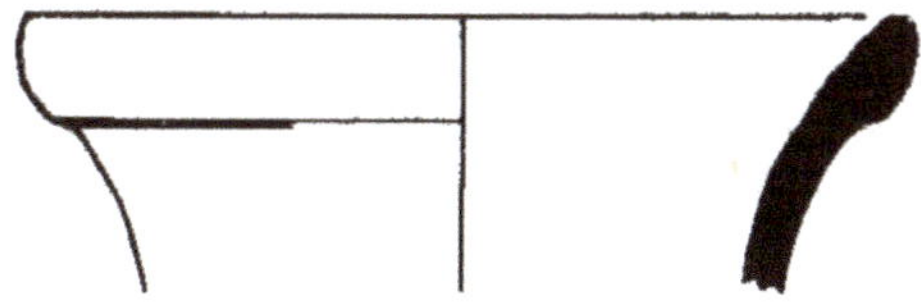

PW 299. CN 7175.
XXXIVG 11.4. Early Roman 1.
Part of wall, rim. PH 0.05; D rim (est.) 0.105. Reddish-
yellow clay 7.5YR 6/6. Metallic Buff.
Parallels: Hippos-Sussita (Osband and Eisenberg
2018: pl. 2.2.7, 2nd c. BC); Jerusalem (Geva 2003: pl.
5.6.6, 2nd c. BC; Tushingham 1985: fig. 18.6); Tel Dor
(Guz-Zilberstein 1995: figs 6.30:2, 6.52:16, 400–275
BC); Tell Nimrin (Dornemann 1990: fig. 3.5).

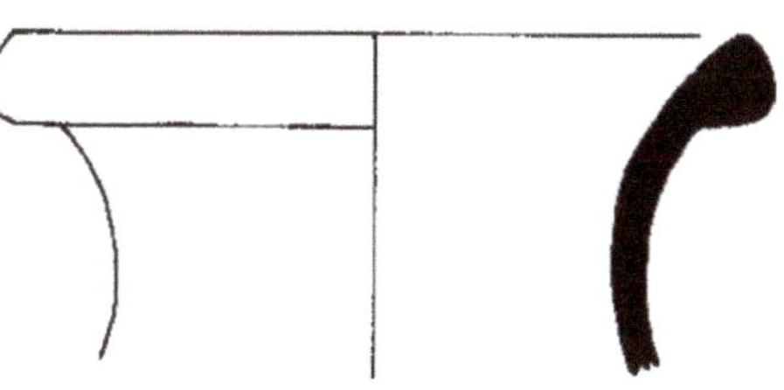

PW 300. CN 6713.
IIIP 25.19. Mixed Context.
Part of wall, rim. PH 0.045; D rim (est.) 0.08. Very
pale brown clay 10YR 7/3. Metallic Buff.

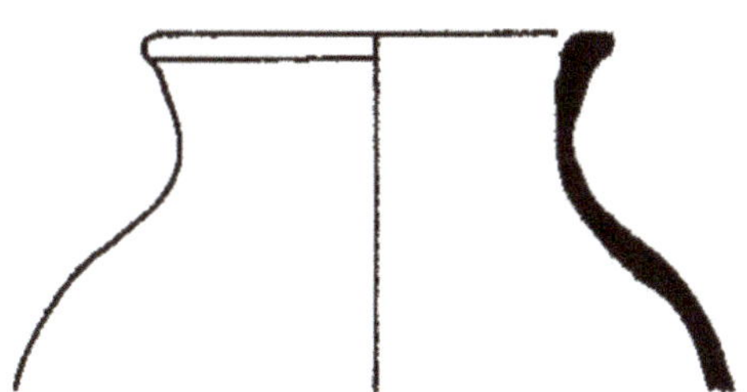

PW 301. CN 6665.
IIIP 25.18. Mixed Context.
Part of wall, rim. PH 0.05; PL 0.075; D rim (est.) 0.10.
Strong brown clay 7.5YR 5/6. Hard Pale.
Parallel: 'Iraq al-Amir (N.L. Lapp 1983: fig. 31.19).

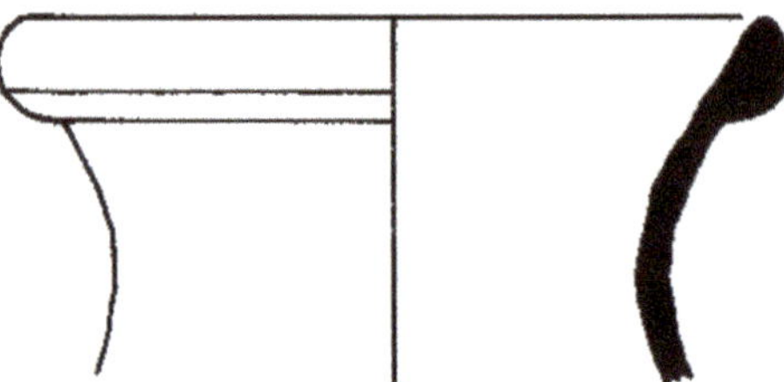

PW 302. CN 7106.
XXIIIA 81.3. Mixed Context.
Part of wall, rim. PH 0.08; D rim (est.) 0.10. White
clay 10YR 8/1. Dull black slip over interior, exterior.
Pie-crust decoration on rim.

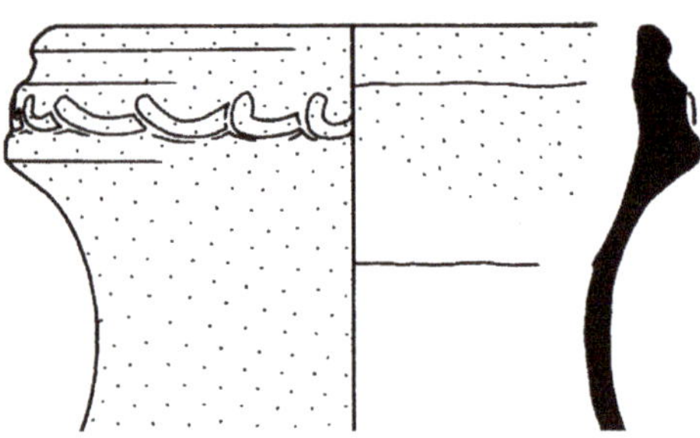

PW 303. CN 7579.
XXXIVB 28.2. Hellenistic 3B/3C.
Part of wall, rim. PL 0.075; D rim (est.) 0.10. Reddish-
yellow clay 5YR 7/6. Hard Pale.
Pie crust decoration on rim.

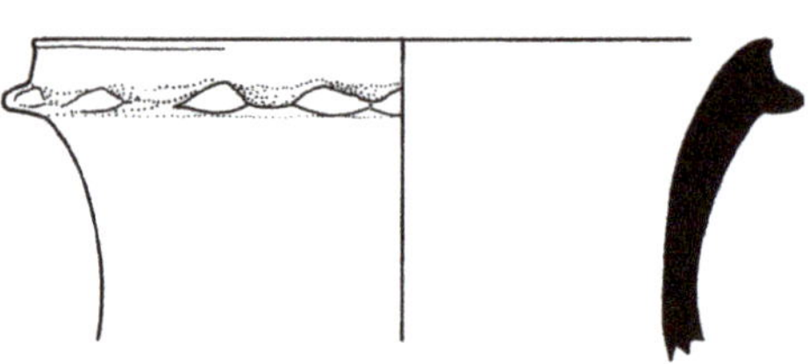

Short neck; short-collared rim (Type 4)

On the rims of **PW 304–81** we see the beginnings of the definite straight-sided thickening, conventionally referred to as a "collar".[24] Jars of Type 4 have a relatively short and ill-defined neck whereas those of the following Type 5 have a longer and more well-defined neck.

In Type 4A the collar is well set off from the neck and generally square or slightly rectangular (**PW 304–55**) whereas in Type 4B it adopts a more triangular profile in section (**PW 356–73**). In Type 4C (**PW 374–81**) it is slightly longer and concave with a prominent lower edge. The nearly complete jars **PW 333** and **PW 342** show that the vertical handles are usually placed high on the shoulder.

Jars with short-collared triangular rims (Type 4B) are already present in Hellenistic 2B levels on Tell Husn, with both Types 4A and 4B recovered from the Hellenistic 3A, 3B and 3B/3C deposits of the main mound and Tell Husn. Type 4A jars are also numerous in Jannaeus Destruction (Hellenistic 3C) strata whereas there are no examples of Type 4B jars from these levels on the main mound. Type 4C jars are all from Early Roman levels on Husn or, in the case of **PW 381**, from a Mixed Context containing pottery from the later second century BC through to Early Roman times. Type 4A jars remain popular throughout the later Hellenistic period at Pella with a similar timespan also the case at Hesban (Gerber 2012: 189–90, figs 3.3.11–21, 3.4.1–16); on the other hand, collared rims (short-collared or long) are not a feature of those jars recovered from the Village site (Field 1) at 'Iraq al-Amir, a situation indicating that a re-evaluation of Paul Lapp's chronology for Field 1 is necessary (Zimmerman 2020b: 79–80).

---

24 "Collared rim jars" are present in Late Bronze and Early Iron Age contexts in the southern Levant on coastal sites and also in the interior on both sides of the Jordan River (Amiran 1969: 232–3; Artzy 1994; Chang-Ho 1997: 405–13; Ibrahim 1978; A. Mazar 1990: 345–8; Mullins and Yannai 2019: 161).

Table 2.32. Distribution of jars Type 4 by sub-types, wares, phases.

		SHORT NECK – SHORT-COLLARED SQUARE RIM (TYPE 4A)	SHORT NECK – SHORT-COLLARED TRIANGULAR RIM (TYPE 4B)	SHORT NECK – SHORT-COLLARED RIM, PROMINENT EDGE (TYPE 4C)
Ware	Hard Pale	34	14	2
	Metallic Buff	8	2	4
	Yellow-slipped	5	0	0
	Pink-slipped	3	0	2
	Miscellaneous	2	2	0
Phase	2B c. 220–c. 200 BC	0	3 (3)	0
	3A c. 200–c. 140 BC	22 (56)	2	0
	3B c. 140–c. 100 (?) BC	1	3 (4)	0
	3B/3C c. 140–c. 80/79 BC	4 (1)	8	0
	3C c. 100 (?)–c. 80/79 BC	20	0	0
	Early Roman 63 BC–c. 135 AD	1 (3)	0	7
	Mixed	4	2	1

Short neck – short-collared square rim (Type 4A)

PW 304. CN 7602.
XXXIVB 29.10. Hellenistic 3B/3C.
Part of body, neck, rim. PH 0.10; PL 0.12; D rim (est.) 0.10. Brown clay 7.5YR 4/2. Coarse black inclusions.

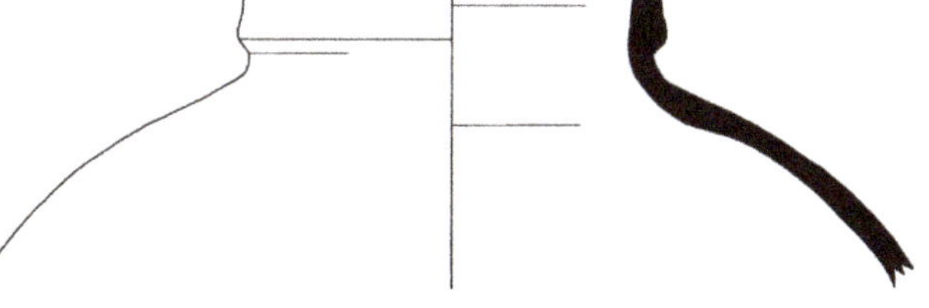

PW 305. CN 7585.
XXXIVB 29.1. Hellenistic 3B/3C.
Part of wall, rim. PL 0.04; D rim (est.) 0.015. Reddish-yellow clay 5YR 6/8. Hard Pale.

PW 306. CN 7646.
XXXIVB 30.5. Hellenistic 3B/3C.
Part of neck, rim. PH 0.05; PL 0.055; D rim (est.) 0.12. Reddish-yellow clay 7.5YR 6/6. Hard Pale.
Parallel: Tel Zahara (Bar-Nathan and Gärtner 2013: fig. 3.9.82).

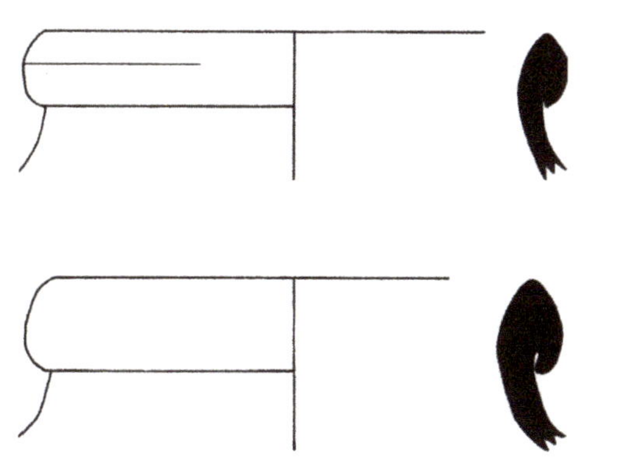

PW 307. CN 7597.
XXXIVB 29.6. Hellenistic 3B/3C.
Part of wall, rim. PL 0.04; D rim (est.) 0.12. Very pale
brown clay 10YR 7/4. Metallic Buff.

PW 308. CN 7370.
XXXIVF 1.3. Mixed Context.
Part of wall, neck, rim. PH 0.06; PL 0.095; D rim
(est.) 0.09. Pale yellow clay 2.5YR 8/2. Metallic Buff
Parallel: Jericho (Pritchard 1958: pl. 58.3).

PW 309. CN 7322.
XXVIIIB 13.2. Hellenistic 3A.
Part of wall, rim. PH 0.055; D rim (est.) 0.10. Light
brownish grey clay 10YR 6/2. Hard Pale.
Parallels: Apollonia (Fischer and Tal 1996: fig.10.14);
'Iraq al-Amir (N.L. Lapp 1979: fig. 2.43); Jericho
(Pritchard 1958: pl. 58.3); Jerusalem (Geva 2003: pl. 5.6.8,
2nd c. BC); Tel Zahara (Bar-Nathan and Gärtner 2013:
fig. 3.9.81). Tell es-Sa'idiyeh (Pritchard 1985: fig. 20.10).

PW 310. CN 7328.
XXVIIIB 13.7. Hellenistic 3A.
Part of wall, rim. PH 0.05; D rim (est.) 0.10. Light
grey clay 10YR 7/2. Hard Pale.

PW 311. CN 7315.
XXVIIIB 10.10. Hellenistic 3A.
Part of body, neck, rim. PH 0.05; D rim (est.) 0.10.
Pale brown clay 10YR 6/3. Hard Pale.
Parallel: Shechem (N.L. Lapp 1985: fig. 2.1).

PW 312. CN 7489.
XXVIIIB 13.16. Hellenistic 3A.
Part of wall, rim. PH 0.06; D rim (est.) 0.08. Very
pale brown clay 10YR 7/3. Hard Pale.

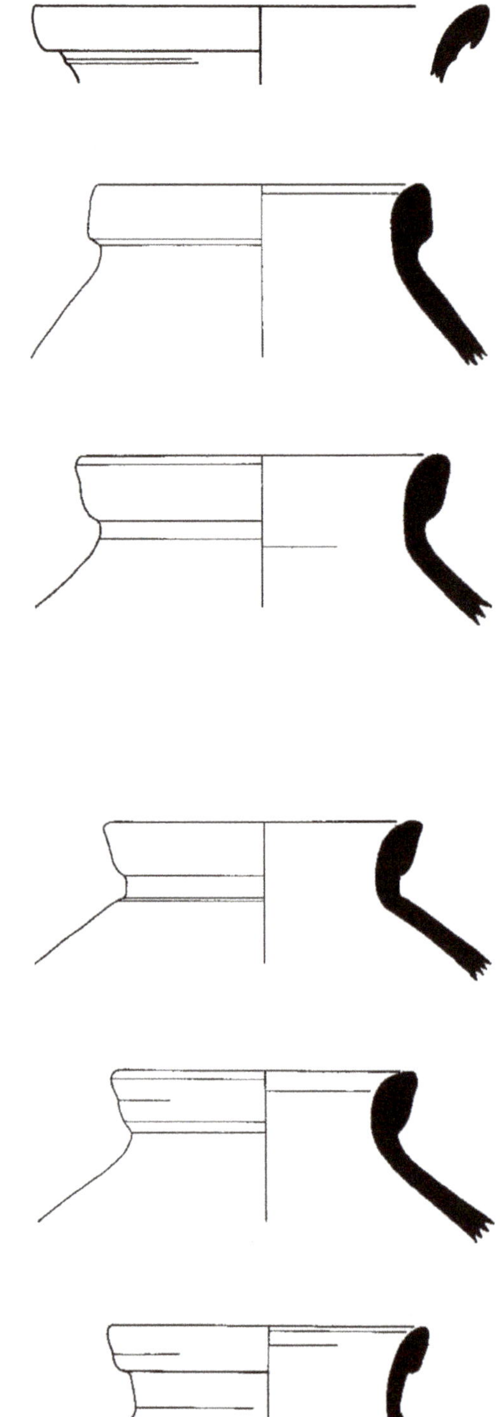

PW 313. CN 7435.
XXVIIIB 13.3. Hellenistic 3A.
Part of wall, rim. PH 0.04; D rim (est.) 0.10. Pale red clay 2.5YR 7/3. Yellow-slipped Coarse Ware.
Parallels: Hippos-Sussita (Osband and Eisenberg 2018: pl. 2.1.6, 2nd c. BC); Iotapata (Adan-Bayewitz and Aviam 1997: fig. 12.6); Shechem (N.L. Lapp 1964: fig. 2.1); Ziqim (Zissu and Rokach 1999: fig. 5.22).

PW 314. CN 7504.
XXVIIIB 13.17. Hellenistic 3A.
Part of wall, rim. PH 0.03; D rim (est.) 0.11.
Light grey clay 10YR 7/2. Hard Pale.
Parallel: Shechem (N.L. Lapp 2008: pl. 3.8.3, 225–190 BC).

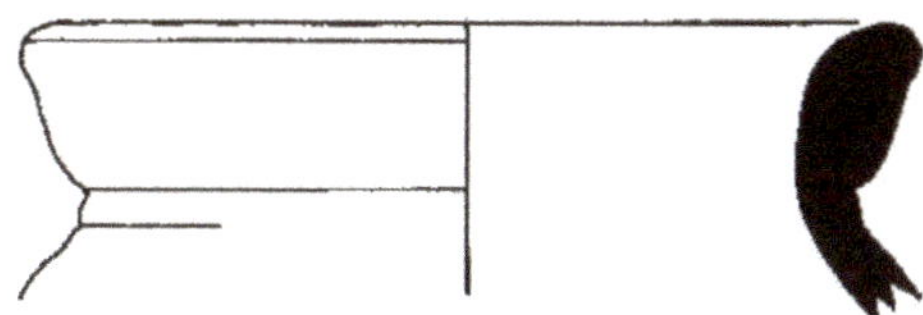

PW 315. CN 7424.
XXVIIIB 13.2. Hellenistic 3A.
Part of wall, rim. PH 0.035; D rim (est.) 0.09. Light grey clay 2.5Y 7/2. Hard Pale.

PW 316. CN 7439.
XXVIIIB 13.4. Hellenistic 3A.
Part of wall, rim. PH 0.045; D rim (est.) 0.10. Pale yellow clay 2.5YR 8/2. Hard Pale.

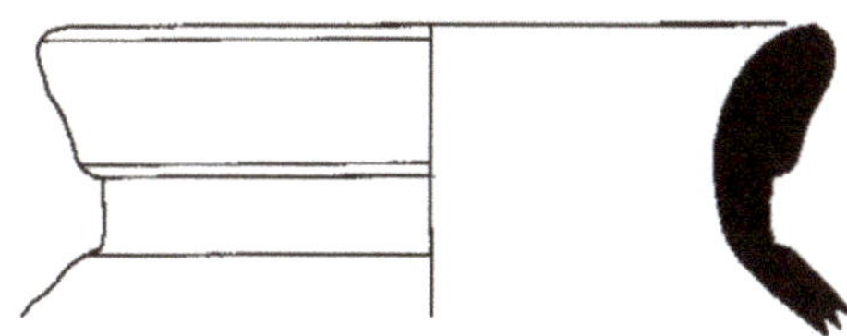

PW 317. CN 7226.
XXVIIIB 10.3. Hellenistic 3A.
Part of wall, rim. PH 0.05; D rim (est.) 0.10. Reddish-yellow clay 5YR 6/8. Hard Pale.

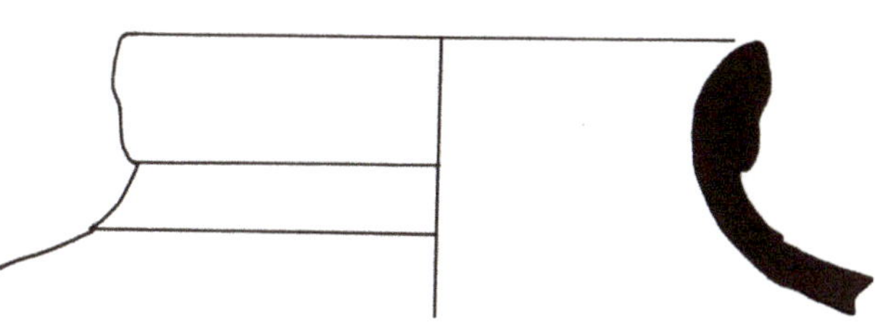

PW 318. CN 7508.
XXVIIIB 13.17. Hellenistic 3A.
Part of wall, rim. PH 0.035; D rim (est.) 0.105. Pink clay 5YR 7/4. Hard Pale.

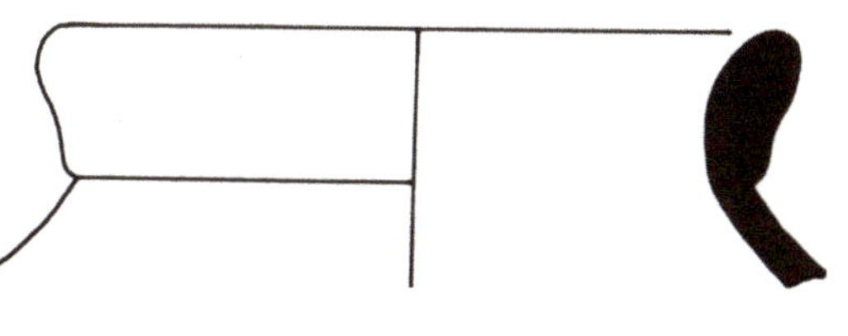

PW 319. CN 7433.
XXVIIIB 13.3. Hellenistic 3A.
Part of wall, rim. PH 0.05; D rim (est.) 0.10. Pink clay 5YR 8/3. Hard Pale.
Parallels: Hippos-Sussita (Osband and Eisenberg 2018: pl. 3.1.2, 1st c. BC); Jerusalem (Tchekhanovets 2013: fig. 5.2:2, 1st c. BC–70 AD); Tell Zira'a (Kenkel 2020: 74, 172–3, pl. 1.28: Am2.3).

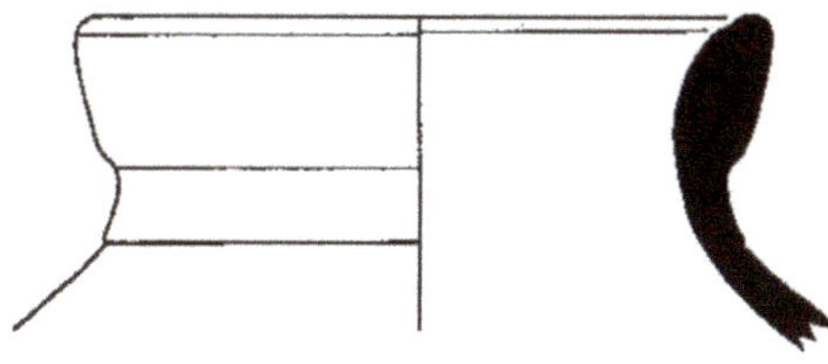

PW 320. CN 7425.
XXVIIIB 13.2. Hellenistic 3A.
Part of wall, rim. PH 0.035; D rim (est.) 0.10. Reddish-yellow clay 7.5YR 7/6. Hard Pale.

PW 321. CN 7506.
XXVIIIB 13.17. Hellenistic 3A.
Part of wall, rim. PH 0.055; D rim (est.) 0.11. Very pale brown clay 10YR 8/3. Hard Pale.

PW 322. CN 7477.
XXVIIIB 13.11. Hellenistic 3A.
Part of wall, rim. PH 0.055; D rim (est.) 0.10. Reddish-yellow clay 5YR 6/6. Yellow-slipped Coarse Ware.
Parallel: 'Akko-Ptolemais (Berlin and Stone 2016: fig. 9.19.2, mid–late 2nd c. BC).

PW 323. CN 7459.
XXVIIIB 13.9. Hellenistic 3A.
Part of wall, rim. PH 0.055; D rim (est.) 0.105. Very pale brown clay 10YR 8/2. Hard Pale.
Parallels: Hippos-Sussita (Osband and Eisenberg 2018: pl. 3.2.1, 1st c. BC); Kedesh (Levantine Ceramics Project: n.d. K00P305 upper profile, mid–late 2nd c. BC); Sepphoris (Balouka 2013: pl. 1.22, 2nd–1st c. BC).

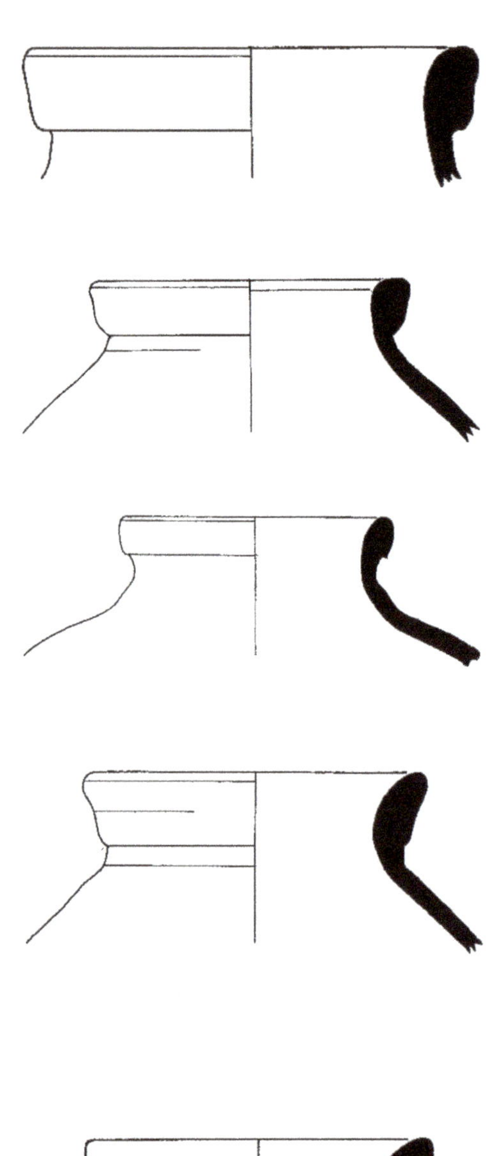

PW 324. CN 7507.
XXVIIIB 13.17. Hellenistic 3A.
Part of wall, rim. PH 0.045; D rim (est.) 0.10. Pink clay 7.5YR 8/3. Mottled slip. Pink-slipped Coarse Ware.
Parallels: Hippos-Sussita (Osband and Eisenberg 2018: pl. 2.3.2, 2nd c. BC); Shechem (N.L. Lapp 2008: pl. 3.8.2, 325–190 BC).

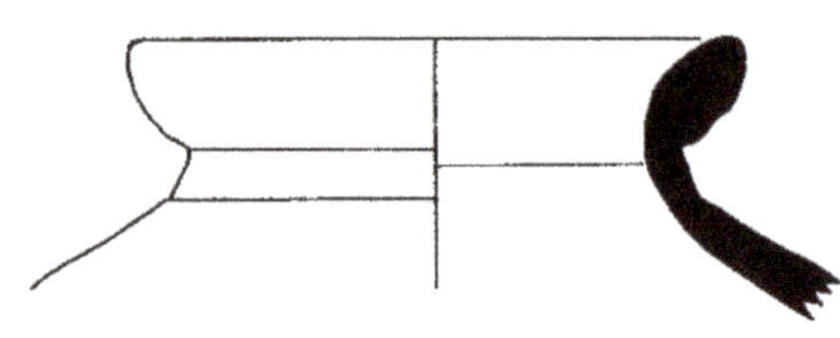

PW 325. CN 7399.
XXVIIIB 10.4. Hellenistic 3A.
Part of wall, rim. PH 0.03; D rim (est.) 0.11. Very pale brown clay 10YR 7/3. Hard Pale.
Parallels: Shechem (N.L. Lapp 2008: pl. 3.8.3, 225–190 BC); southern Ghors and north-east Arabah survey (MacDonald 1992: pl. 21.14); Straton's Tower/Caesarea (Berlin 1992: fig. 54.4).

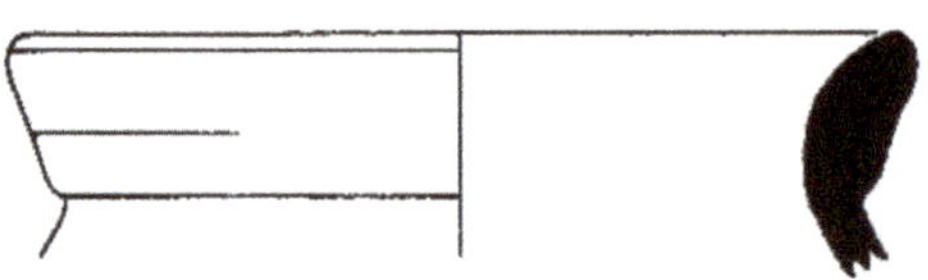

PW 326. CN 7451.
XXVIIIB 13.8. Hellenistic 3A.
Part of wall, rim. PH 0.045; D rim (est.) 0.10. Pale yellow clay 2.5Y 8/3. Yellow-slipped Coarse Ware.

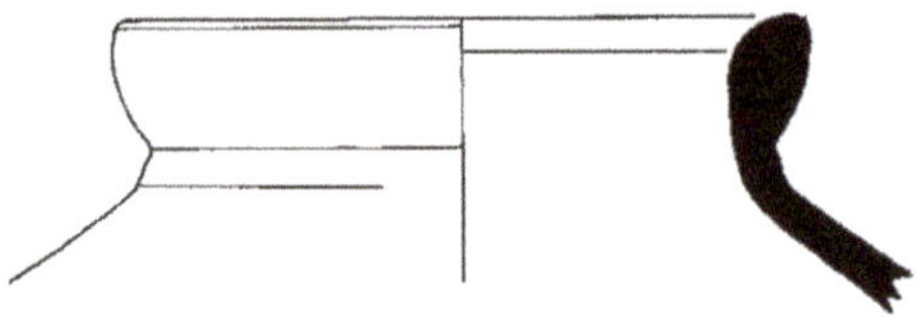

PW 327. CN 7420.
XXVIIIB 13.1. Hellenistic 3A.
Part of wall, rim. PH 0.07; D rim (est.) 0.09. Pink clay
7.5YR 7/4. Hard Pale.

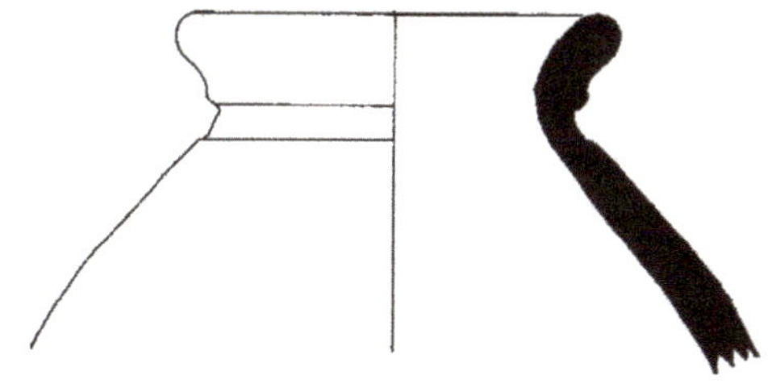

PW 328. CN 7311.
XXVIIIB 10.4. Hellenistic 3A.
Part of shoulder, neck, rim. PH 0.05; D rim
(est.) 0.11. Light grey clay10YR 7/2. Hard Pale.
Parallels: Apollonia (Fischer and Tal 1996: fig.
10.10); Gezer (Gitin 1990: pl. 33.5, late 3rd–early 2nd
c. BC); Shechem (N.L. Lapp 2008: pl. 3.9.13, 150–110
BC); southern Ghors and north-east Arabah survey
(MacDonald 1992: pl. 21.12).

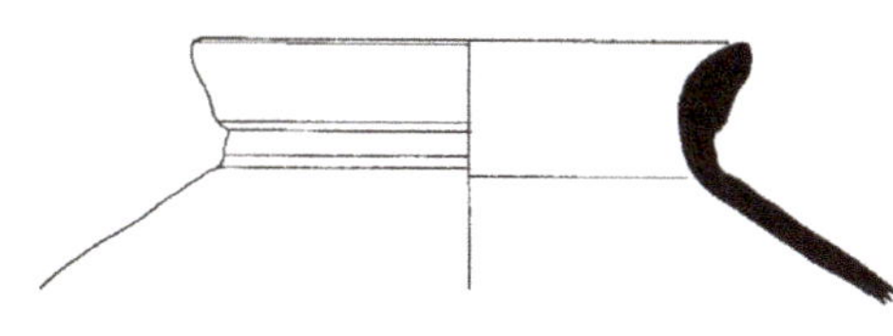

PW 329. CN 7463.
XXVIIIB 13.9. Hellenistic 3A.
Part of neck, rim. PH 0.03; D rim (est.) 0.09. Very
pale brown clay 10YR 8/2. Hard Pale.

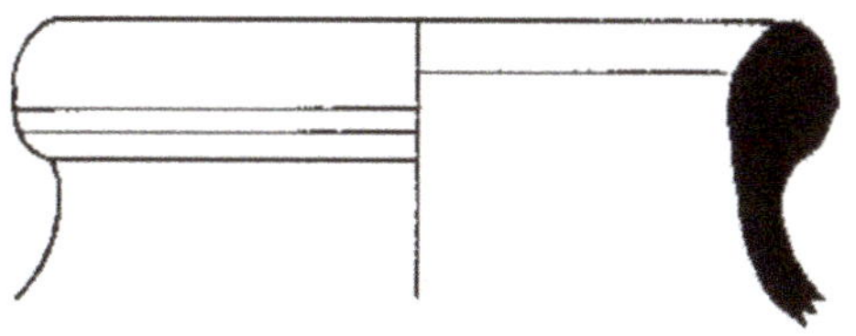

PW 330. CN 7304.
XXVIIIB 10.2. Hellenistic 3A.
Part of wall, neck, rim. PH 0.055; D rim (est.) 0.12.
Light grey 10YR 7/2. Hard Pale.

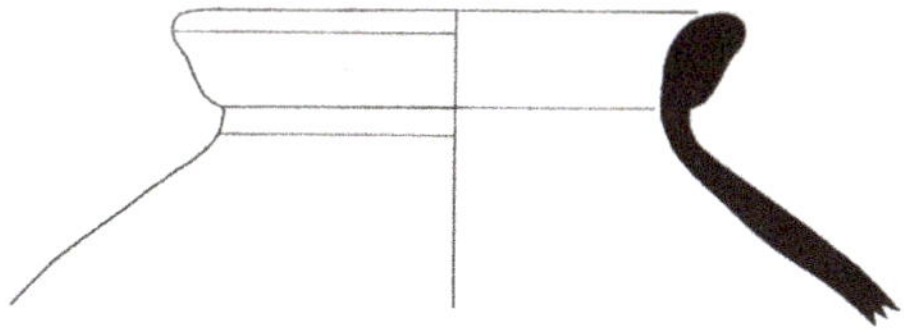

PW 331. CN 6868.
IIIB/C 1.19. Mixed Context.
Part of wall, neck, rim. PH 0.06; PL 0.095; D rim
(est.) 0.11. Red clay 2.5YR 6/6. Hard Pale.
Parallel: Gezer (Gitin 1990: pl. 34.17, early–mid-
2nd c. BC).

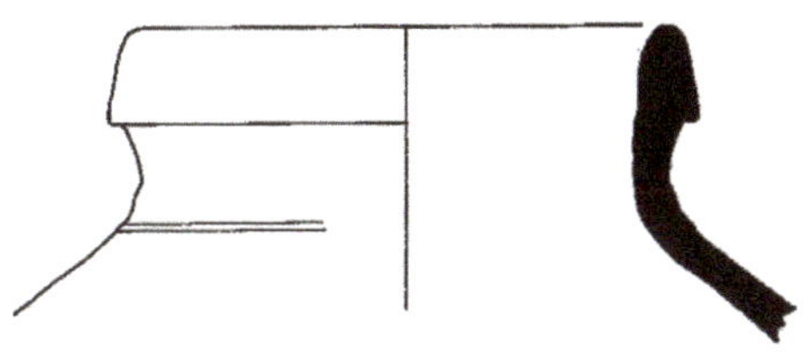

PW 332. CN 7793.
XXIIID 24.1. Hellenistic 3B.
Fragment of wall, rim. PH 0.06; PL 0.09; D rim
(est.) 0.12. Red clay 2.5YR 6/6. Hard Pale.

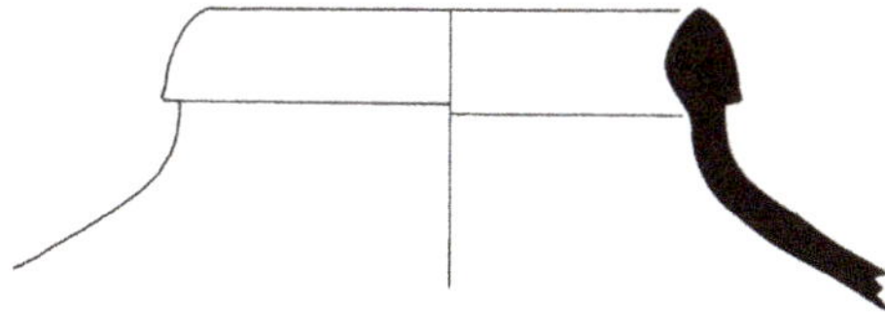

PW 333. CN 3931.
IVD 10.12. Hellenistic 3C.
Missing part of base. PH 0.34; D rim 0.09. Yellow
clay 10YR 7/6. Metallic Buff.
Two vertical strap handles on shoulder.
Parallels: Ashdod (Dothan 1971: fig. 22.4); Shechem
(N.L. Lapp 1985: figs 1a.14; 2.3).

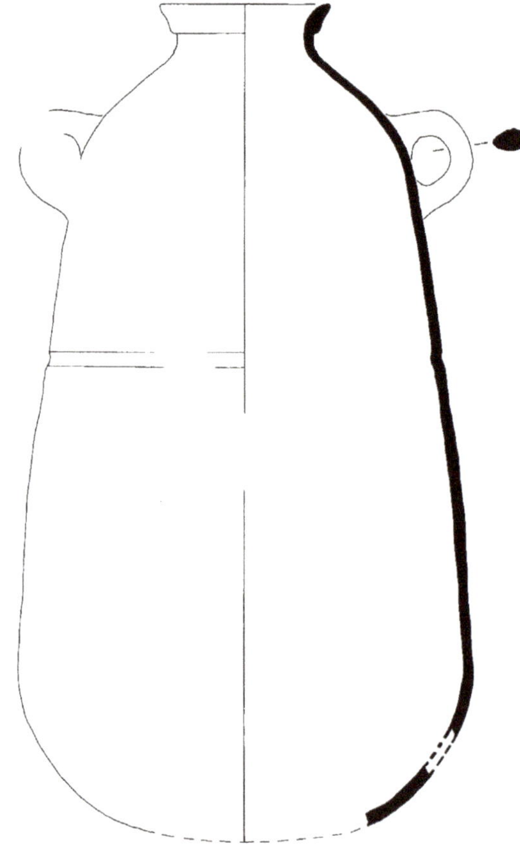

PW 334. CN 0184.
IIIB/C 4.1. Hellenistic 3C.
Part of wall, rim. PH 0.03; D rim (est.) 0.09. Very
pale brown clay 10YR 8/3. Hard Pale.
Parallel: Gezer (Gitin 1990: pl. 43.22, mid-1st c. BC).

PW 335. CN 6677.
IVD 10.14. Hellenistic 3C.
Part of wall, rim. PH 0.05; PL 0.09; D rim (est.) 0.10.
Reddish-yellow clay 5YR 7/6. Coarse with many
inclusions.

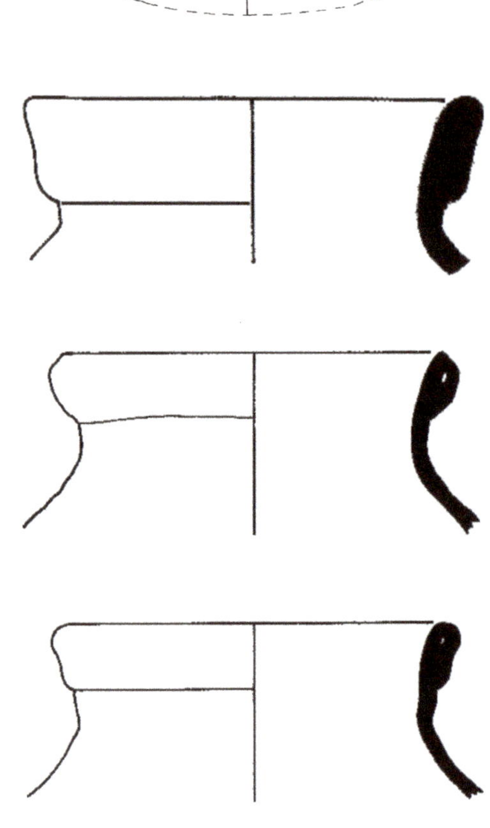

PW 336. CN 6580.
IVD 10.12. Hellenistic 3C.
Part of wall, rim. PH 0.045; D rim (est.) 0.10. Very
pale brown clay 10YR 7/4. Metallic Buff.
Parallel: Gezer (Gitin 1990: pl. 41.10, early 1st c. BC).

PW 337. CN 6679.
IVD 10.14. Hellenistic 3C.
Part of rim. PH 0.03; PL 0.05; D rim (est.) 0.10. Brown clay 7.5YR 5/4. Hard Pale.
Parallel: Amman/Philadelphia (Greene and 'Amr 1992: fig. 5.10).

PW 338. CN 6678.
IVD 10.14. Hellenistic 3C.
Part of rim. PH 0.03; D rim (est.) 0.09. Yellowish-brown 10YR 5/4. Yellow-slipped Coarse Ware.

PW 339. CN 6906.
IIIQ 11.47. Mixed Context.
Part of shoulder, neck, rim. PH 0.045; PL 0.06; D rim (est.) 0.12. Very pale brown clay 10YR 7/3. Metallic Buff.

PW 340. CN 6926.
IIIQ 11.19. Mixed Context.
Part of wall, rim. PH 0.02; PL 0.06; D rim (est.) 0.10. Reddish-yellow clay 7.5YR 6/6. Hard Pale.
Parallel: Iotapata (Adan-Bayewitz and Aviam 1997: fig. 12.7).

PW 341. CN 7021.
XXIIIA 100.2. Hellenistic 3C.
Part of wall, rim. PH 0.02; PL 0.035; D rim (est.) 0.10. Reddish-yellow clay 5YR 6/8. Hard Pale.
Parallels: 'Akko-Ptolemais (Berlin and Stone 2016: fig. 9.24.2, second half 1st c. BC); Gezer (Gitin 1990: pl. 43.17, mid-1st c. BC); 'Iraq al-Amir (N.L. Lapp 1983: fig. 32.48).

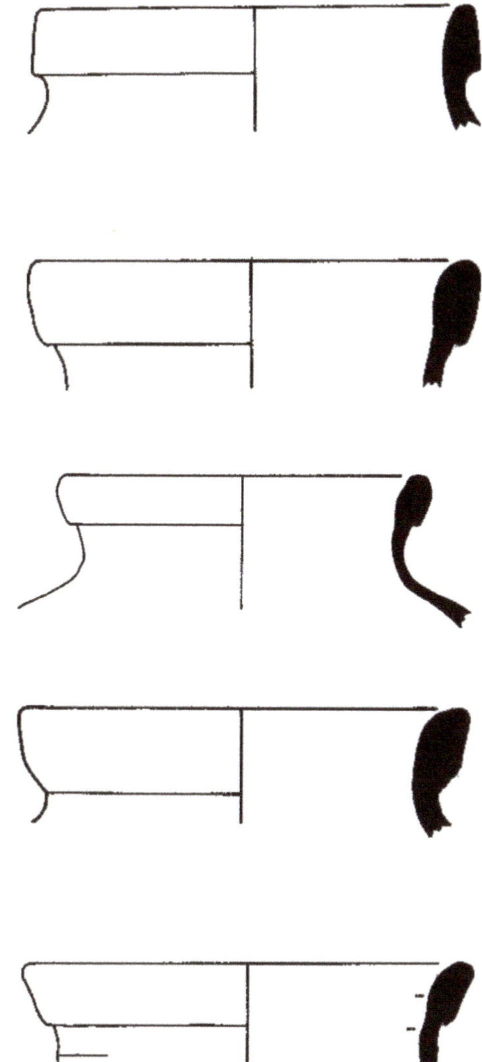

PW 342. CN 7159.
XXIIIA 75.2. Hellenistic 3C.
Almost complete, several body fragments missing.
H 0.40; D rim 0.10. Very pale brown clay 10YR 7/3.
Metallic Buff.
Rounded under-surface; sack-like body. Thin but
definite collared rim. Vertical handle on each shoulder.
Parallels: Jericho (Bar-Nathan 2002: pl. 3.18 = Berlin
2015: pl. 6.1.15. no. 1, 2nd–1st c. BC); Shiqmona
(Elgavish 1976: pl. 15E).

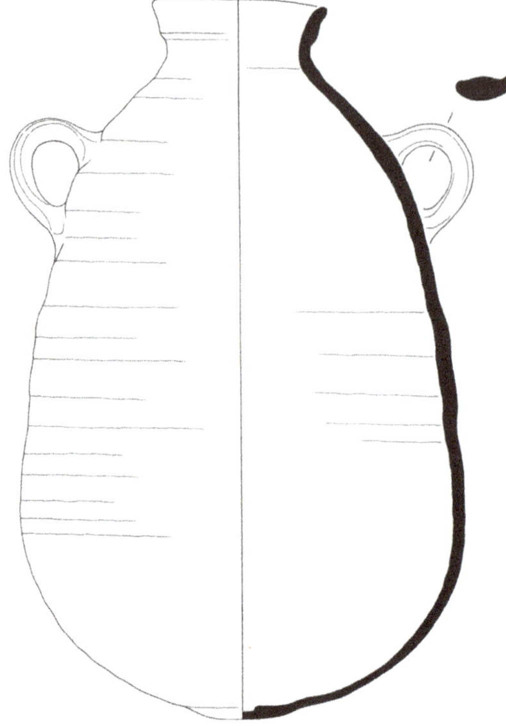

PW 343. CN 7288.
XXIIIB 1.1. Hellenistic 3C.
Part of wall, rim. PH 0.05; D rim (est.) 0.105. Brown
clay 7.5YR 5/4. Hard Pale.
Parallels: Jerusalem (Machline and Gadot 2017:
fig. 10.3); Sepphoris (Balouka 2013: pl. 3.19, 0–70
AD); Wadi al-Kharrar (Abu Shmeis and Waheeb 2002:
fig. 2.11).

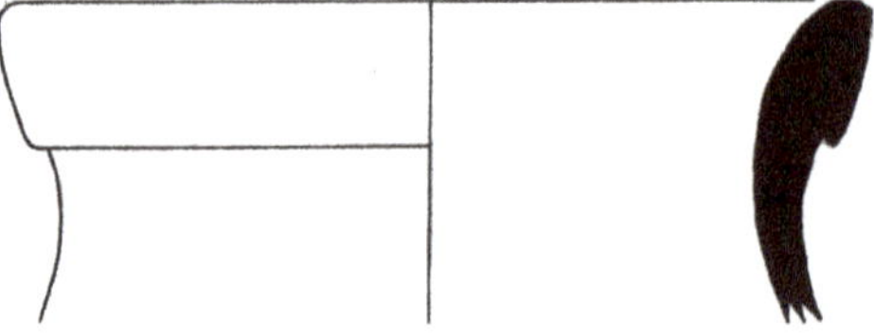

PW 344. CN 7747.
XXIIID 18.2. Hellenistic 3C.
Fragment of neck, rim. PH 0.045; PL 0.06; D rim (est.) 0.12. Reddish-yellow clay 7.5YR 7/6. Hard Pale. Parallels: Rujm Umm Haddar (Ji and Lee 1999: 529, no. 3); Tell Zira'a (Kenkel 2020: 75, 172–3, pl. 1.28: Am3.2).

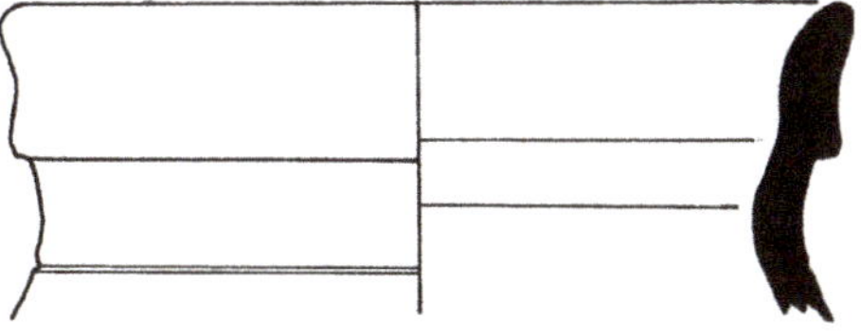

PW 345. CN 6987.
XXIIIA 22.9. Hellenistic 3C.
Part of wall, neck, rim. PH 0.055; PL 0.09; D rim (est.) 0.10. Greyish-brown clay 10YR 5/2. Pink-slipped Coarse Ware.
Markedly undercut rim.
Parallel: Gezer (Gitin 1990: pl. 36.13, mid-2nd c. BC).

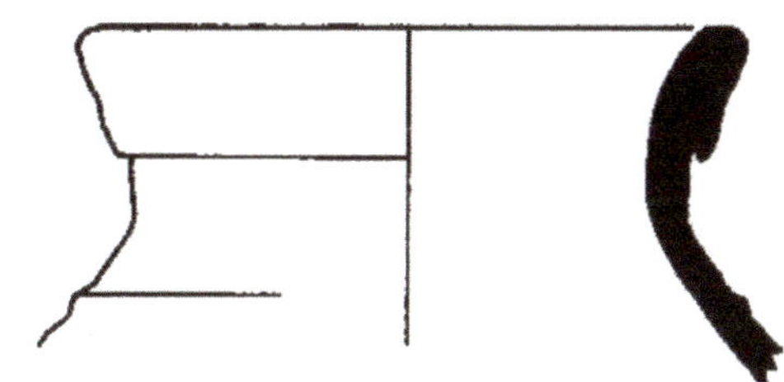

PW 346. CN 7769.
XXIIIA 85.1. Hellenistic 3C.
Fragment of wall, rim. PH 0.135; PL 0.11; D rim (est.) 0.11. Reddish-yellow clay 5YR 6/6. Hard Pale.
Parallel: 'Akko-Ptolemais (Berlin and Stone 2016: fig. 9.16.7, mid–late 2nd c. BC).

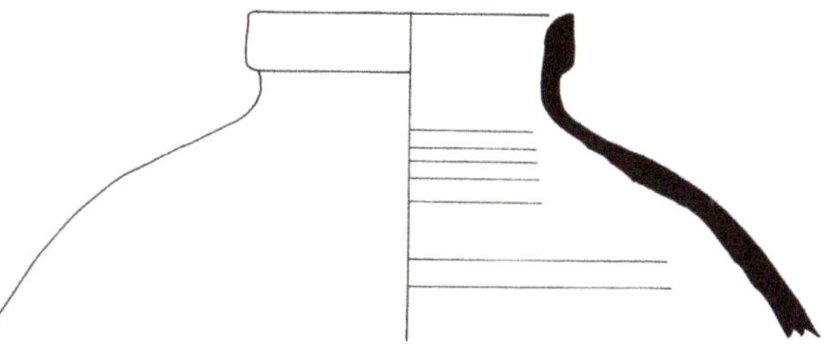

PW 347. CN 7289.
XXIIIB 1.3. Hellenistic 3C.
Part of rim, upper neck. PH 0.03; D rim (est.) 0.11. Light grey 10YR 7/2. Metallic Buff.
Parallel: Hesban (Gerber 2012: 185, fig. 3.2.17).

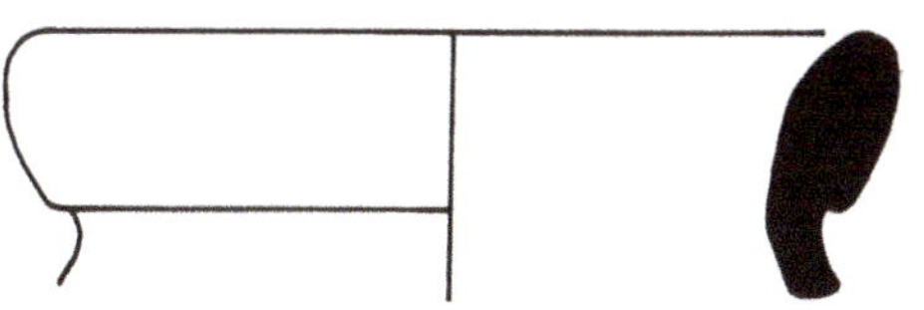

PW 348. CN 7840.
XXIIID 30.2. Hellenistic 3C.
Part of wall, neck, rim. PH 0.05; PL 0.07; D rim (est.) 0.10. Red clay 2.5YR 6/6. Hard Pale.

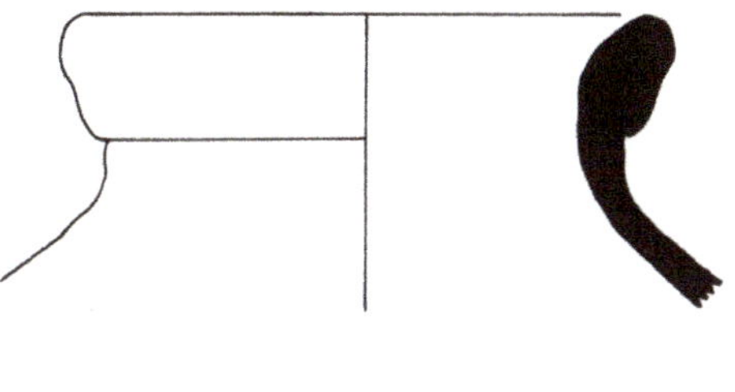

PW 349. CN 7028.
XXIIIA 100.5. Hellenistic 3C.
Part of rim. PH 0.015; D rim (est.) 0.10. Light yellowish-brown clay 10YR 6/4. Yellow-slipped Coarse Ware.

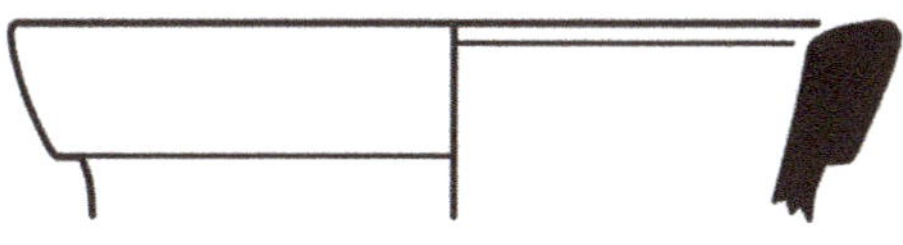

PW 350. CN 7044.
XXIIIA 105.1. Hellenistic 3C.
Part of wall, neck, rim. PH 0.045; D rim (est.) 0.10. Light brown clay 7.5YR 6/4. Hard Pale.
Parallel: Gezer (Gitin 1990: pl. 36.17, mid-2nd c. BC).

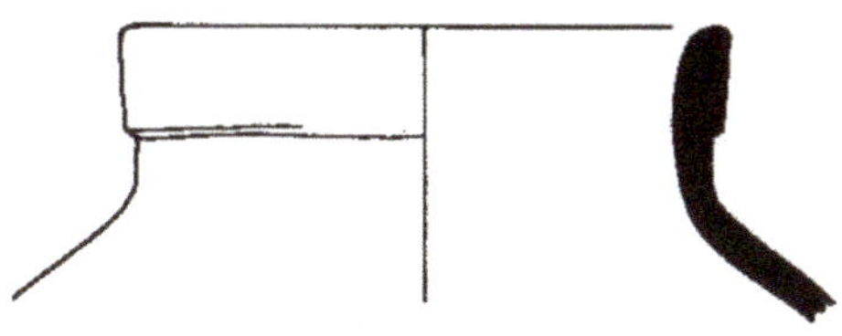

PW 351. CN 7843.
XXIIID 63.3. Hellenistic 3C.
Part of wall, neck, rim. PH 0.045; PL 0.08; D rim
(est.) 0.115. Light brown clay 7.5YR 6/4. Hard Pale.

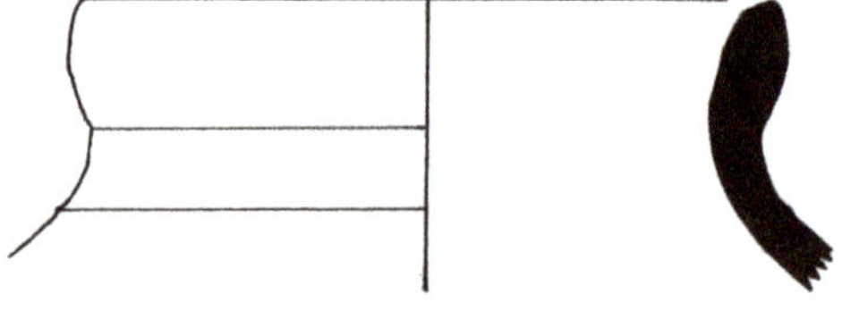

PW 352. CN 7762.
XXIIID 20.5. Hellenistic 3C.
Two joining fragments of rim. PH 0.045; PL 0.105;
D rim (est.) 0.10. Red clay 2.5YR 6/8. Hard Pale.
Parallels: Jerusalem (Geva 2003: pl. 5.2.26, late
2nd–1st c. BC; Geva and Rosenthal-Heginbottom
2003: pl. 6.1.4, 1st c. BC).

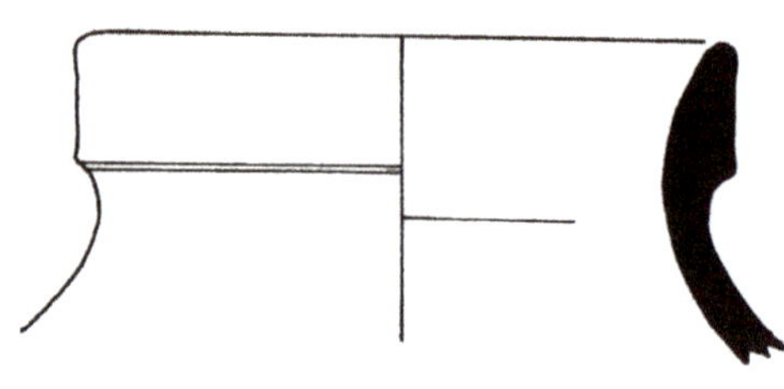

PW 353. CN 7060.
XXIIIA 104.2. Hellenistic 3C.
Part of wall, rim. PH 0.045; D rim (est.) 0.105.
Reddish-yellow clay 5YR 6/6. Pink-slipped Coarse
Ware.
Parallel: Jerusalem (Geva 2003: pl. 5.10.8, later
2nd–1st c. BC).

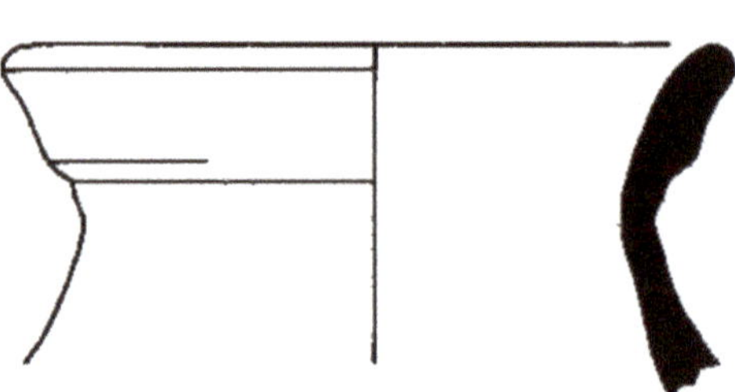

PW 354. CN 7095.
XXIIIA 100.1. Hellenistic 3C.
Part of wall, rim. PH 0.03; PL 0.045; D rim (est.) 0.10.
Reddish-yellow clay 5YR 6/8. Hard Pale.
Parallel: Jerusalem (Tchekhanovets 2013: fig. 5.2:2,
1st c. BC–70 AD).

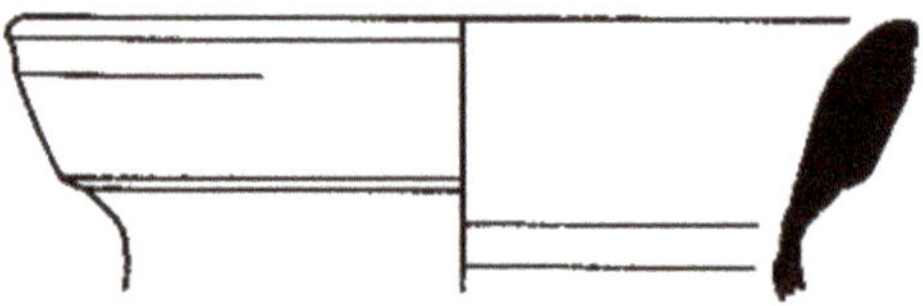

PW 355. CN 7820.
XXXIVG 6.8. Early Roman 1.
Part of wall, rim. PH 0.04; D rim (est.) 0.10. Reddish-
yellow clay 7.5YR 6/6. Metallic Buff.

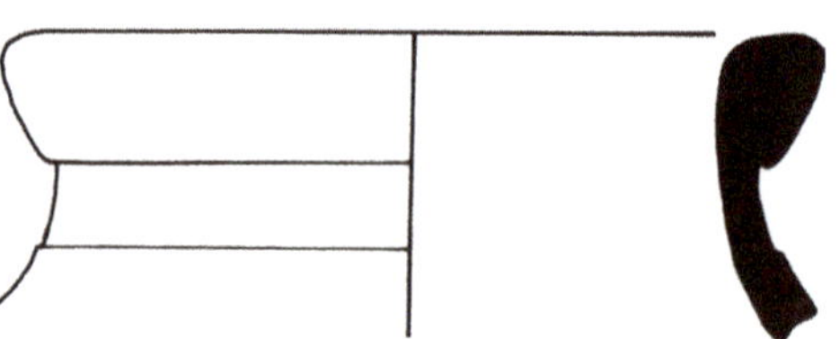

Short neck – short-collared triangular rim (Type 4B)

PW 356. CN 7664.
XXXIVB 27.22. Hellenistic 2B.
Part of wall, rim. PH 0.05; D rim 0.10. Yellowish-
brown clay 10YR 5/4. Hard Pale.
Parallel: Jerusalem (Geva 2003: pl. 5.2.24, late 2nd–1st
c. BC).

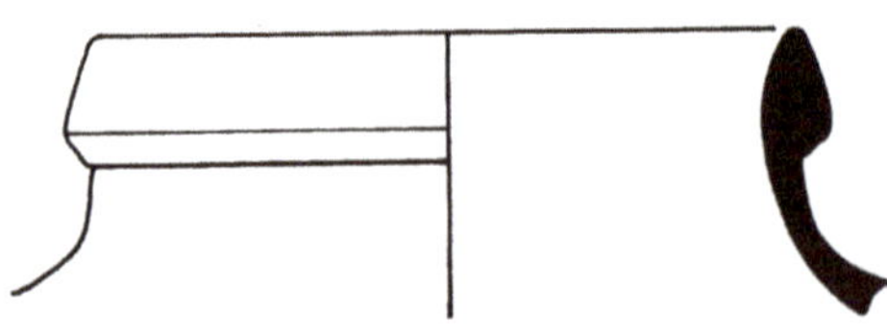

PW 357. CN 7268.
XXVIIIB 10.1. Hellenistic 3A.
Part of wall, rim. PH 0.05; D rim (est.) 0.10. Brown
clay 7.5YR 5/4. Hard Pale.

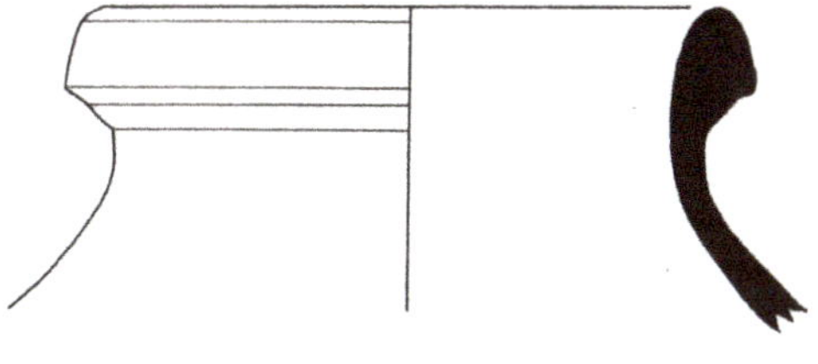

PW 358. CN 7323.
XXVIIIB 13.2. Hellenistic 3A.
Part of wall, neck, rim. PH 0.05; D rim (est.) 0.10.
Light yellowish-brown clay 10YR 6/4. Hard Pale.
Parallels: Amman/Philadelphia (Zayadine 1977–78:
fig. 12.140); Gezer (Gitin 1990: pl. 36.10, mid-
2nd c. BC); 'Iraq al-Amir (N.L. Lapp 1979: fig. 2.56);
Samaria (Crowfoot et al. 1957: fig. 42.8, c. 150–100 BC;
Hennessy 1970: fig. 9.11; Zayadine 1966: pl. XXVII.8);
Shechem (N.L. Lapp 1985: fig. 2.2); Tell es-Sa'idiyeh
(Pritchard 1985: fig. 20.9).

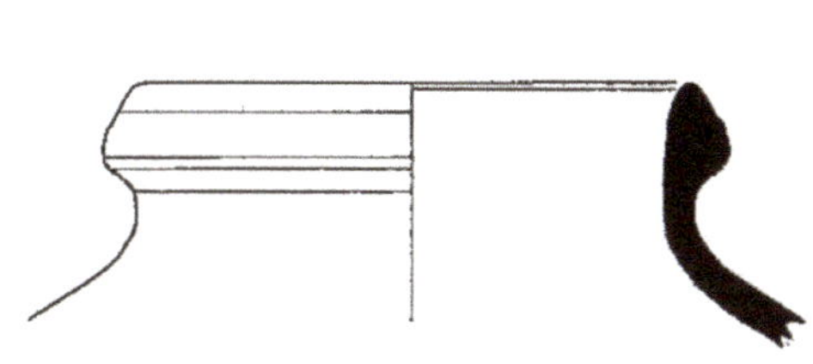

PW 359. CN 7668.
XXXIVB 27.26. Hellenistic 2B.
Part of wall, rim. PH 0.05; PL 0.09; D rim (est.) 0.10.
Reddish-yellow clay 7.5YR 7/6. Hard Pale.
Parallel: Shechem (N.L. Lapp 2008: pl. 3.9.3,
225–190 BC).

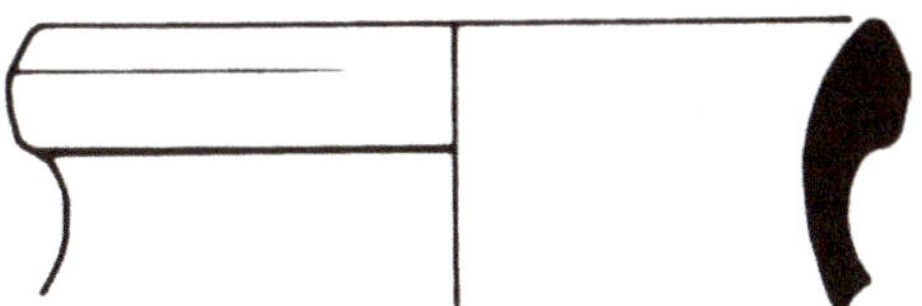

PW 360. CN 7698.
XXXIVB 41.2. Hellenistic 2B.
Part of wall, rim. PH 0.04; PL 0.08; D rim (est.) 0.105.
Reddish-yellow clay 7.5YR 6/6. Hard Pale.

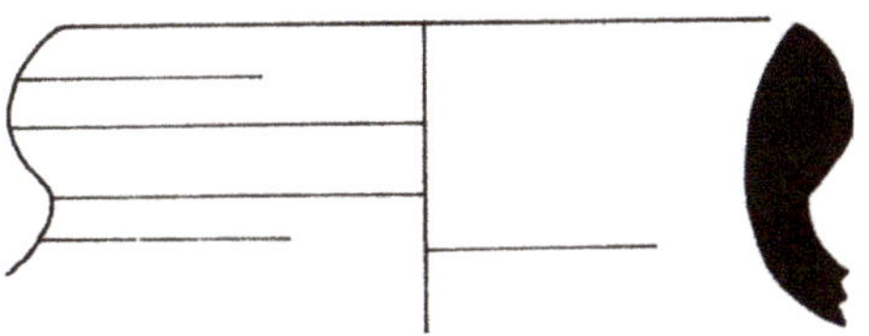

PW 361. CN 7699.
XXXIVB 41.2. Hellenistic 3B/3C.
Part of wall, rim. PH 0.04; PL 0.05; D rim (est.) 0.10.
Reddish-yellow clay 7.5YR 6/6. Hard Pale.

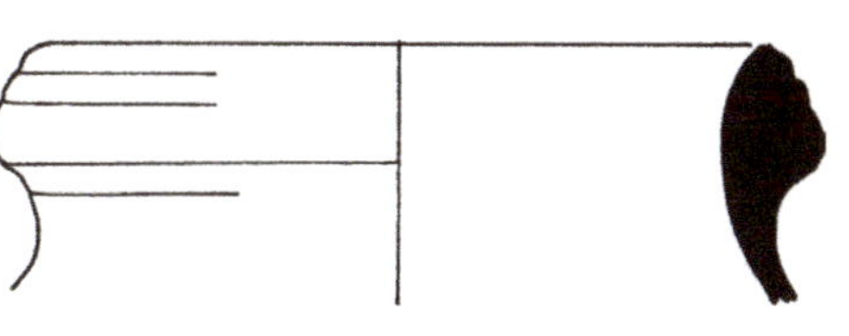

PW 362. CN 7629.
XXXIVB 27.14. Mixed Context.
Part of wall, rim. PH 0.03; PL 0.09; D rim (est.) 0.105.
Reddish-yellow clay 5YR 6/8. Hard Pale.
Parallel: Rujm Umm Haddar (Ji and Lee 1999: 529,
no. 4).

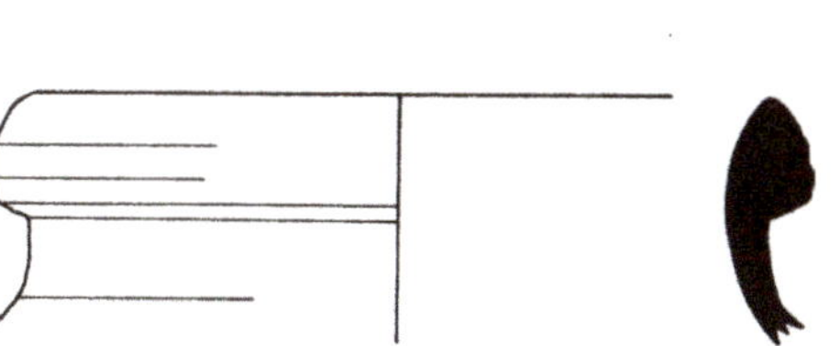

PW 363. CN 7647.
XXXIVB 30.5. Hellenistic 3B/3C.
Part of wall, rim. PH 0.03; PL 0.085; D rim (est.) 0.10.
Reddish-yellow clay 7.5YR 6/6. Hard Pale.
Parallel: Tel Keisan (Briend 1980: pl. 8.1a, late 4th–
mid-2nd c. BC).

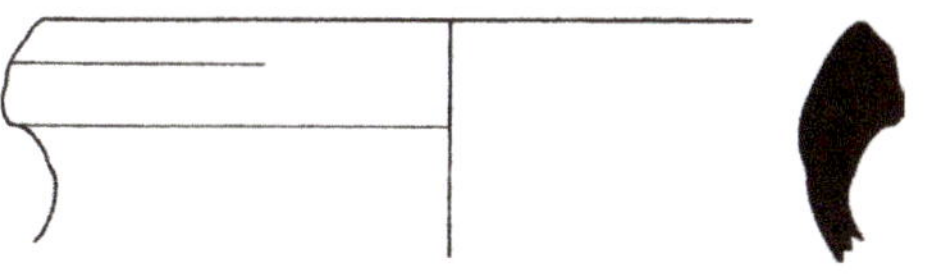

PW 364. CN 7582.
XXXIVB 29.1. Hellenistic 3B/3C.
Part of wall, rim. PH 0.03; PL 0.045; D rim (est.) 0.12.
Reddish-yellow clay 5YR 7/6. Hard Pale.

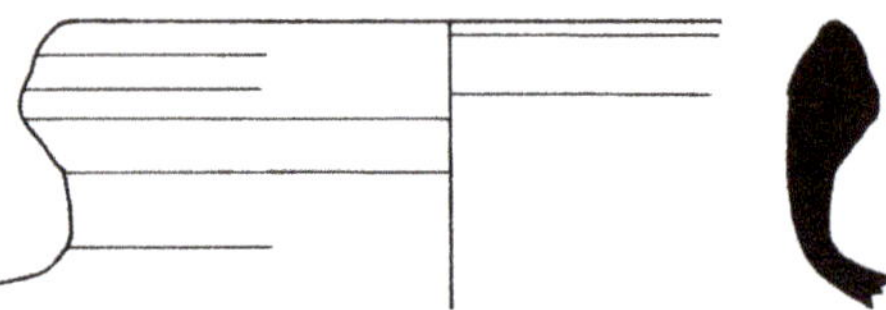

PW 365. CN 7622.
XXXIVB 30.1. Hellenistic 3B/3C.
Part of wall, rim, handle. PH 0.03; PL 0.11; D rim (est.)
0.09. Yellowish-brown clay 10YR 5/4. Metallic Buff.

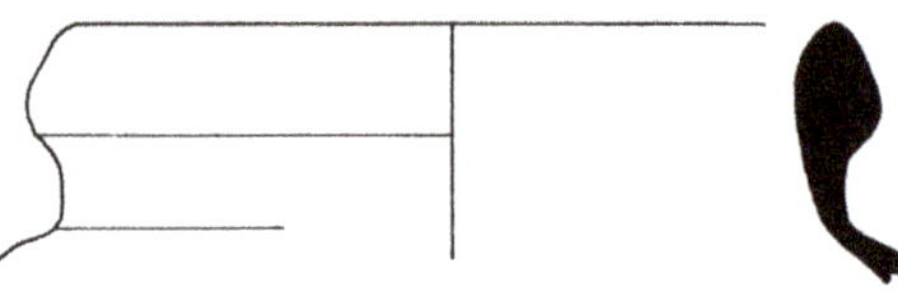

PW 366. CN 7599.
XXXIVB 29.8. Hellenistic 3B/3C.
Part of wall, neck, rim, neck. PH 0.03; PL 0.09;
D rim (est.) 0.09. Light yellowish-brown clay 10YR
6/4. Hard Pale.

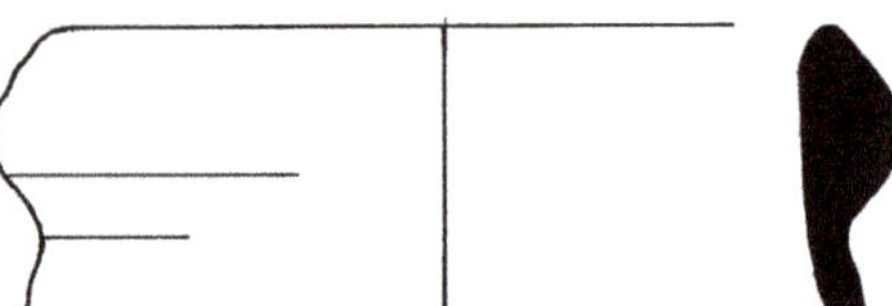

PW 367. CN 7576.
XXXIVB 28.2. Hellenistic 3B/3C.
Part of wall, rim. PH 0.035; PL 0.065; D rim
(est.) 0.12. Brown clay 7.5YR 5/2.

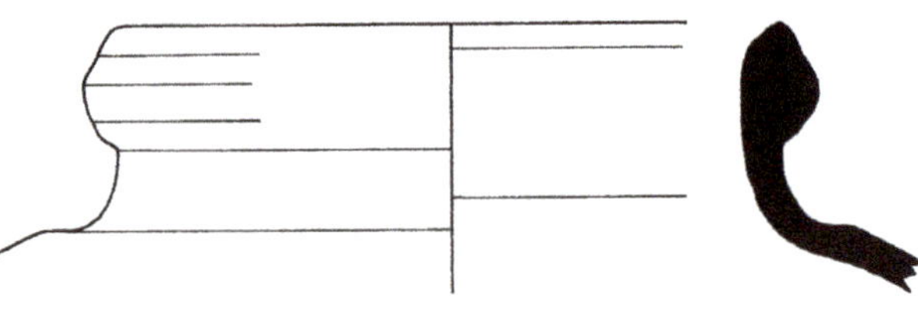

PW 368. CN 7633.
XXXIVB 30.3. Hellenistic 3B/3C.
Part of wall, rim. PH 0.04; PL 0.085; D rim (est.) 0.12.
Reddish-yellow clay 5YR 6/6. Hard Pale.

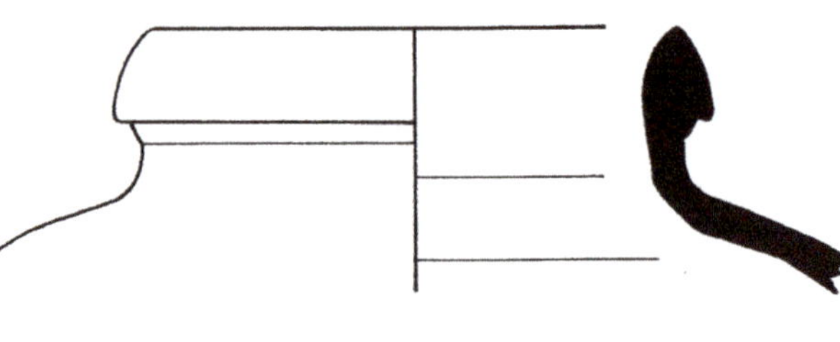

PW 369. CN 7598.
XXXIVB 29.7. Hellenistic 3B/3C.
Part of wall, neck, rim. PH 0.045; PL 0.085; D rim
(est.) 0.10. Brown clay 10YR 5/3.

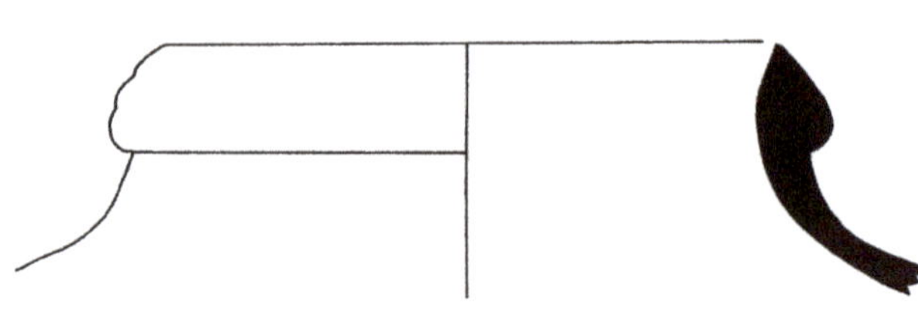

PW 370. CN 7792.
XXIIID 24.1. Hellenistic 3B.
Part of wall, rim. PH 0.05; PL 0.055; D rim (est.) 0.12.
Reddish-yellow clay 7.5YR 6/6. Hard Pale.
Parallel: Jerusalem (Geva 2003: pl. 5.2.24, late 2nd–1st
c. BC).

PW 371. CN 7293.
XXIIIB 2.1. Hellenistic 3B.
Two joining fragments of wall, rim. PH 0.045; D rim
(est.) 0.10. Reddish-brown clay 5YR 5/4. Hard Pale.
Parallel: Jerusalem (Geva and Rosenthal-Heginbottom
2003: pl. 6.1.20, 1st c. BC).

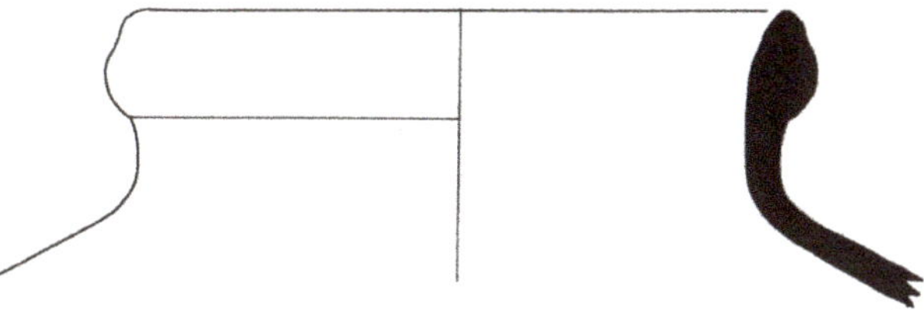

PW 372. CN 6905.
IIIQ 11.47. Mixed Context.
Part of wall, rim. PH 0.04; PL 0.095; D rim (est.) 0.10.
Reddish-yellow clay 5YR 7/6. Hard Pale.

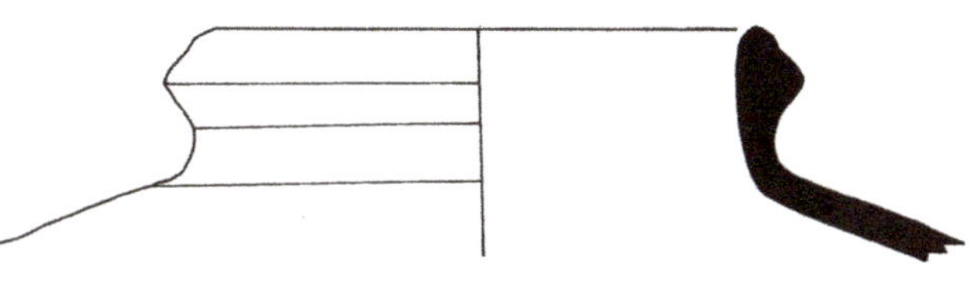

PW 373. CN 7068.
XXIIIA 109.3. Hellenistic 3B.
Part of wall, rim. PH 0.03; PL 0.07; D rim (est.) 0.105.
Very pale brown clay 10YR 7/4. Metallic Buff.
Parallel: Apollonia (Fischer and Tal 1996: fig. 7.10).

Short neck – short-collared rim, prominent edge (Type 4C)

PW 374. CN 2938a.
XIA/B 1.4. Early Roman 1.
Part of wall, rim. PH 0.11; D rim (est.) 0.10. Reddish-
yellow clay 7.5YR 6/6. Pink-slipped Coarse Ware.
Parallels: 'En el-Ghuweir (Bar-Adon 1977: fig. 10.8);
Jerusalem (Geva 2003: pl. 5.9.8, later 2nd–1st c. BC;
Rahmani 1967: fig. 17.7; Tushingham 1985: fig. 19.20);
Samaria (Hennessy 1970: fig. 9.2). Tell Zira'a (Kenkel
2020: 75–6, 172–3, pl. 1.28: Am4.2).

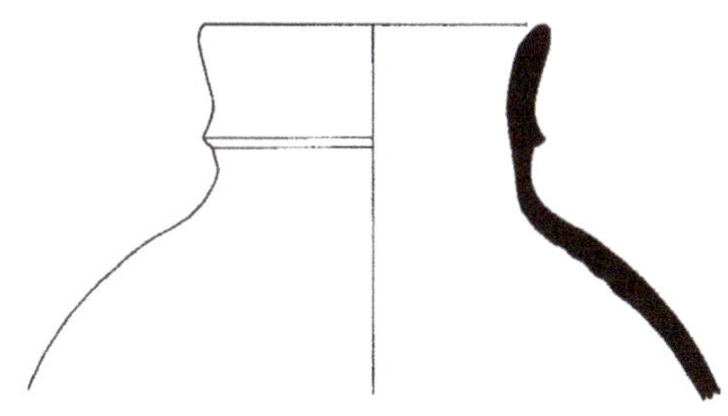

PW 375. CN 2550.
XIA/B 1.1. Early Roman 1.
Part of wall, neck, rim. PH 0.045; PL 0.075; D rim
(est.) 0.10. Yellowish-brown clay 10YR 5/4. Hard Pale.
Parallels: Herodium (Bar-Nathan 1981: pl. 10.7);
Samaria (Hennessy 1970: fig. 6.5).

PW 376. CN 2976.
XIA/B 1.1/3. Early Roman 1.
Part of rim. PH 0.03; D rim (est.) 0.10. Brown clay
10YR 5/4. Metallic Buff.
Parallel: Amman/Philadelphia (Hadidi 1970:
pl. III.7).

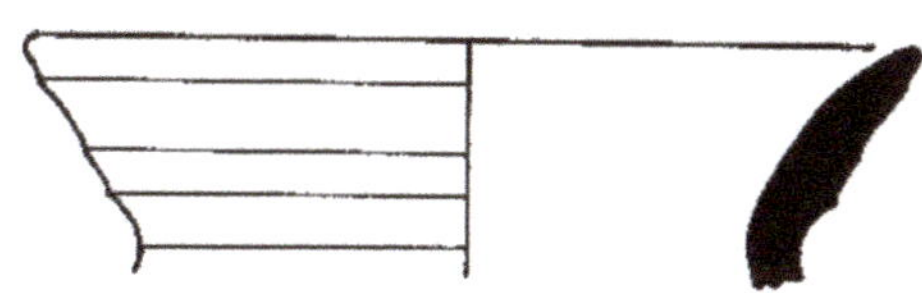

PW 377. CN 2998.

XIA/B 1.3/5. Early Roman 1.

Part of wall, neck, rim. PH 0.065; PL 0.085; D rim (est.) 0.10. Very pale brown clay 10YR 7/3. Metallic Buff.

Parallels: Herodium (Bar-Nathan 1981: fig. 1.2); Tel Jezreel (Grey 1994: fig. 1.2).

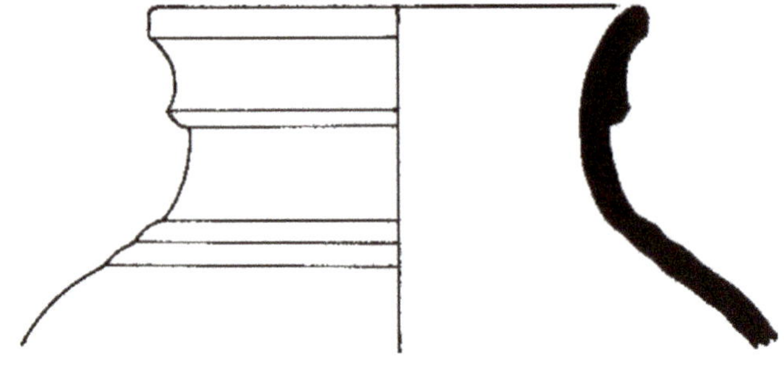

PW 378. CN 2966.

XIA/B 1.5. Early Roman 1.

Part of wall, rim. PH 0.06; PL 0.08; D rim (est.) 0.11. Light yellowish-brown clay 10YR 6/4. Metallic Buff.

Parallels: Amman/Philadelphia (Hadidi 1970: pl. III.11); Betar (Singer 1993: fig. 2.10); Jaffa (Tsuf 2018: fig. 9.35.604); Hippos-Sussita (Osband and Eisenberg 2018: pl. 4.2.3, end 1st c. BC/beginning 1st c. AD); Qumran (Eshel and Broshi 2003: fig. 5.3).

PW 379. CN 2938b.

XIA/B 1.5. Early Roman 1.

Part of wall, rim. PH 0.045; PL 0.045; D rim (est.) 0.10. Reddish-yellow clay 7.5YR 6/6. Pink-slipped Coarse Ware.

Parallel: Kallirhoe (Clamer 1997: pl. 2.15).

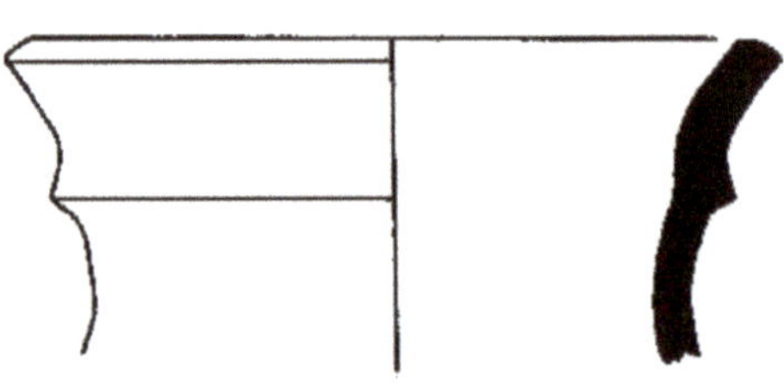

PW 380. CN 2546.

XIA/B 1.1. Early Roman 1.

Part of wall, rim. PH 0.055; D rim (est.) 0.10. Pale brown clay 10YR 6/3. Metallic Buff.

Parallels: Amman/Philadelphia (Greene and 'Amr 1992: fig. 6.9); Hippos-Sussita (Osband and Eisenberg 2018: pl. 3.2.3, 1st c. BC); Jerusalem (Geva 2003: pl. 5.7.22, later 2nd–1st c. BC).

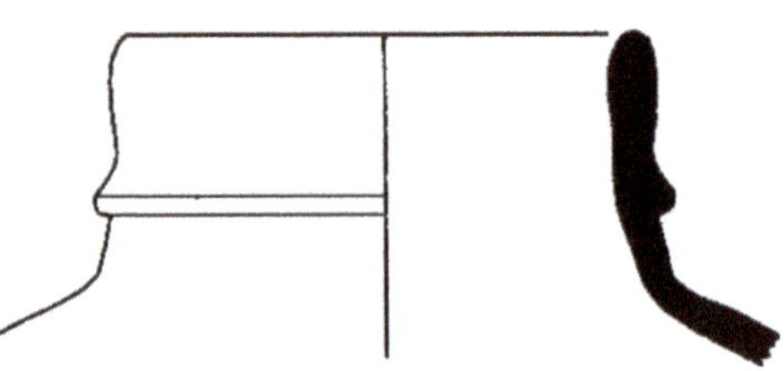

PW 381. CN 7363.

XXXIVB 5.40. Mixed Context.

Part of wall, rim. PH 0.055; PL 0.08; D rim (est.) 0.09. Yellowish-red clay 5YR 5/6. Hard Pale.

Parallels: 'En el-Ghuweir (Bar-Adon 1977: fig. 10.8); Ras Abu Ma'aruf (Rapuano 1999: fig. 1.11).

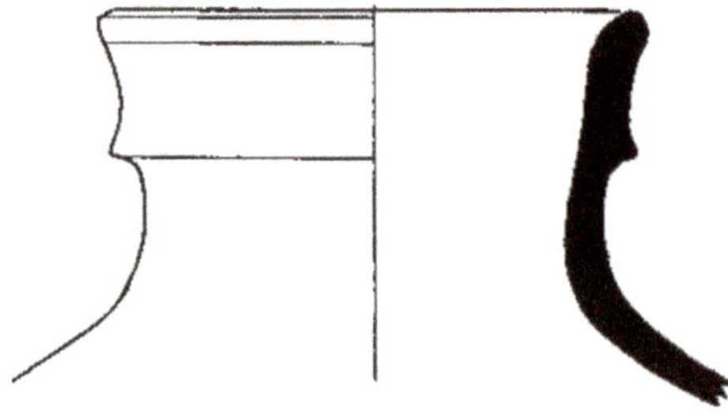

Table 2.33. Distribution of jars Type 5 by sub-types, wares, phases.

		TALL NECK; SHORT-COLLARED SQUARE RIM (TYPE 5A)	TALL NECK; SHORT-COLLARED TRIANGULAR RIM (TYPE 5B)
Ware	Hard Pale	5	1
	Metallic Buff	5	2
	Yellow-slipped	5	0
	Miscellaneous	1	0
Phase	3A c. 200–c. 140 BC	4	0
	3B c. 140–c. 100 (?) BC	2	1
	3C c. 100 (?)–c. 80/79 BC	9 (31)	2
	Mixed	1	0

Tall neck; short-collared rim (Type 5)

The tall-necked jars of Type 5 (**PW 382–400**) possess a short collar with either a square, rectangular (Type 5A, **PW 382–97**) or triangular (Type 5B, **PW 398–400**) rim. Jars of the former type are seen in both Pre-Jannaeus and Jannaeus Destruction (Hellenistic 3A–C) strata with those of Type 5B from Hellenistic 3B or 3C horizons. All were recovered from the main mound.

Tall neck – short-collared square rim (Type 5A)

PW 382. CN 7419.
XXVIIIB 13.1. Hellenistic 3A.
Part of wall, neck, rim. PH 0.07; D rim (est.) 0.10. Pale yellow clay 2.5Y 7/3. Yellow-slipped Coarse Ware.

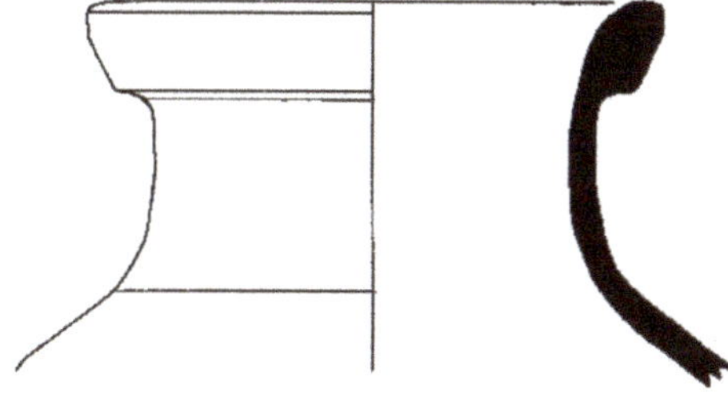

PW 383. CN 7460.
XXVIIIB 13.9. Hellenistic 3A.
Part of wall, rim. PH 0.055; D rim (est.) 0.10. Very pale brown clay 10YR 7/3. Yellow-slipped Coarse Ware.

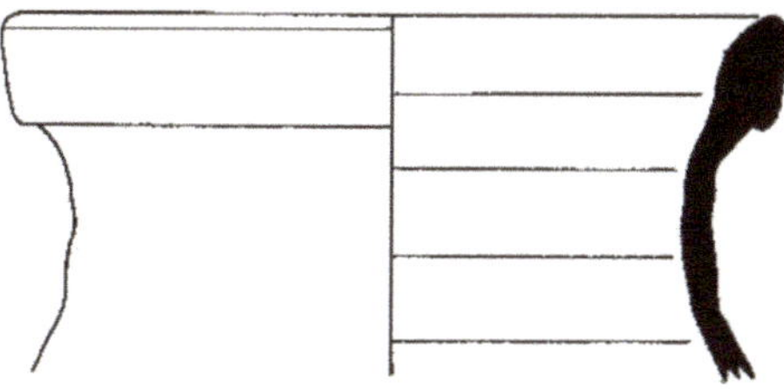

PW 384. CN 7444.
XXVIIIB 13.7. Hellenistic 3A.
Part of wall, rim. PH 0.05; D rim (est.) 0.09. Reddish-yellow clay 5YR 6/6 (core); very pale brown clay 10YR 8/3 (surface). Hard Pale.

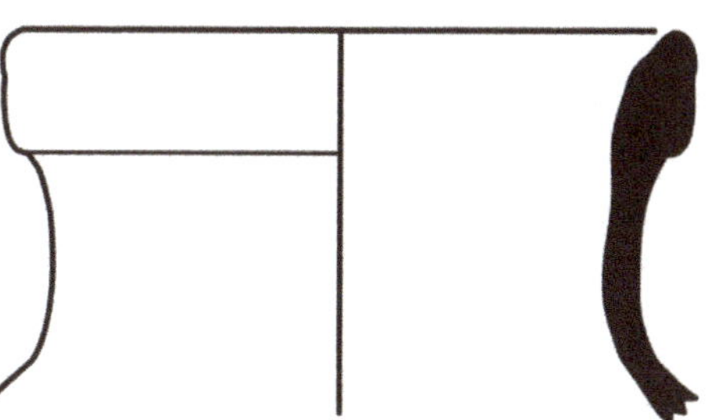

PW 385. CN 7316.
XXVIIIB 10.10. Hellenistic 3A.
Part of wall, rim. PH 0.05; D rim (est.) 0.10. Grey clay 10YR 6/1. Hard Pale.

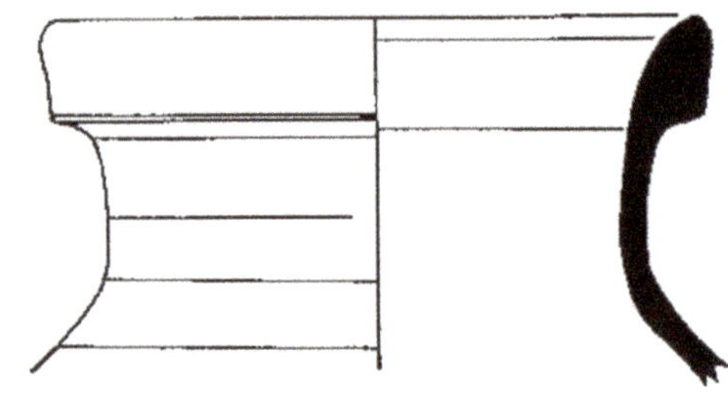

PW 386. CN 7784.
XXIIID 23.1. Hellenistic 3B.
Part of wall, rim. PH 0.09; PL 0.15; D 0.09. Reddish-yellow clay 5YR 6/8.
Parallel: Esdraela (Grey 2014: fig. 2.2).

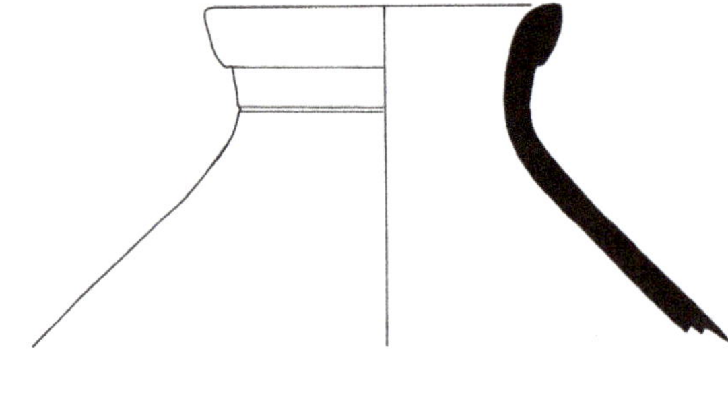

PW 387. CN 7082.
XXIIIA 109.2. Hellenistic 3B.
Part of wall, rim. PH 0.03; PL 0.045; D rim (est.) 0.095.
Light brown clay 7.5YR 6/4. Metallic Buff.
Parallels: Amman/Philadelphia (Zayadine 1977–78: fig. 15.410); Gezer (Gitin 1990: pls 36.15, mid-2nd c. BC, 43.16, mid-1st c. BC).

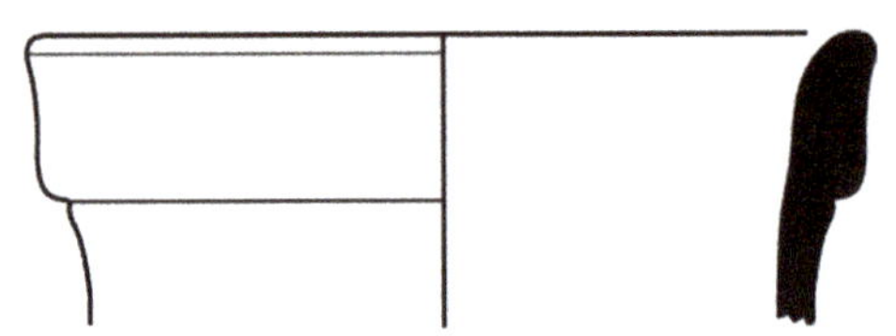

PW 388. CN 6940.
IVD 10.10. Hellenistic 3C.
Part of wall, rim. PH 0.055; PL 0.06; D rim (est.) 0.11.
Strong brown clay 7.5YR 5/6. Hard Pale.

PW 389. CN 6942.
IVD 10.10. Hellenistic 3C.
Part of wall, rim, handle. PH 0.11; D rim (est.) 0.11.
Brown clay 10YR 4/3. Yellow-slipped Coarse Ware.
Strap handle from rim to shoulder.
Parallel: Ashdod (Dothan 1971: fig. 100.4).

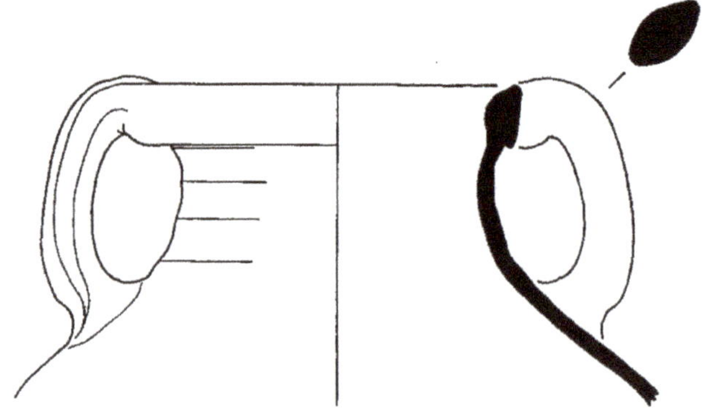

PW 390. CN 6961.
XXIIIA 10.7. Hellenistic 3C.
Part of wall, rim. PH 0.05; PL 0.065; D rim (est.) 0.12.
Pale yellow clay 2.5Y 7/3. Metallic Buff.
Parallel: Amman/Philadelphia (Zayadine 1977–78:
fig. 15.410).

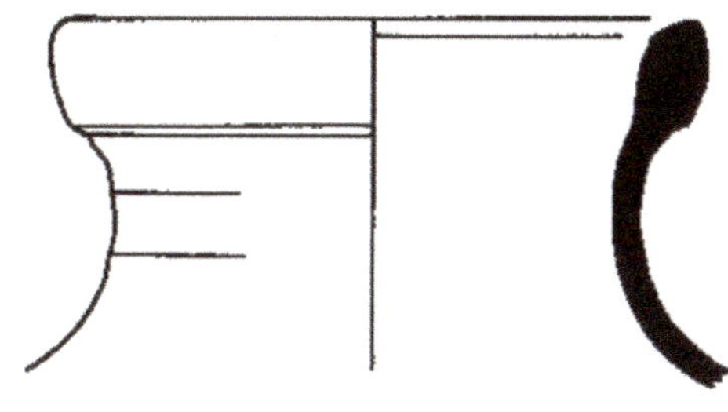

PW 391. CN 7040.
XXIIIA 104.1. Hellenistic 3C.
Part of wall, rim. PH 0.05; PL 0.065; D rim (est.) 0.09.
White clay 10YR 8/2. Metallic Buff.

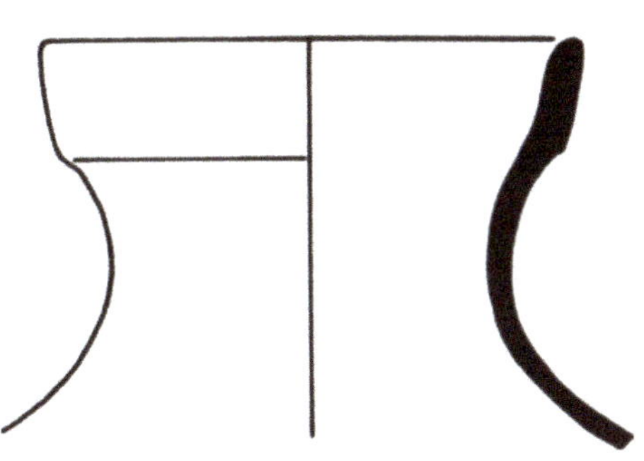

PW 392. CN 0069.
IIIB/C 1.3. Hellenistic 3C.
Part of wall, rim. PH 0.065; D rim (est.) 0.09. Very pale
brown clay 10YR 7/3. Yellow-slipped Coarse Ware.

PW 393. CN 0112.
IIIB/C 2.2. Hellenistic 3C.
Complete. H 0.24; D rim 0.10. Red clay 2.5YR 5/6.
Metallic Buff.
Ring base. Tall swelling body. Two vertical strap
handles on shoulder.

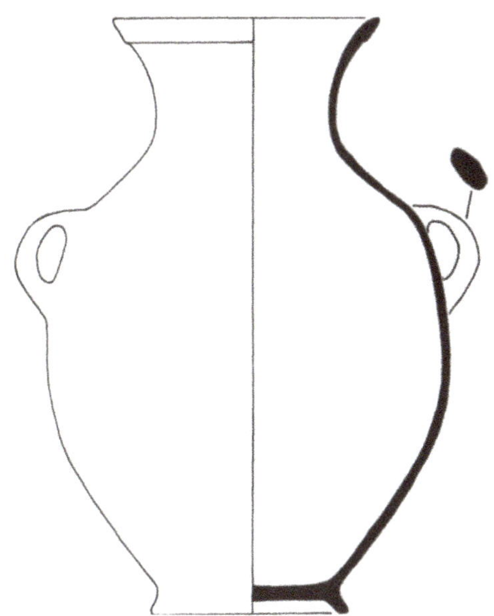

PW 394. CN 6960.
XXIIIA 10.7. Hellenistic 3C.
Part of wall, rim. PH 0.045; D rim (est.) 0.10. Very pale
brown clay 10YR 7/4. Yellow-slipped Coarse Ware.
Parallel: Hesban (Gerber 2012: 189, fig. 3.3.13).

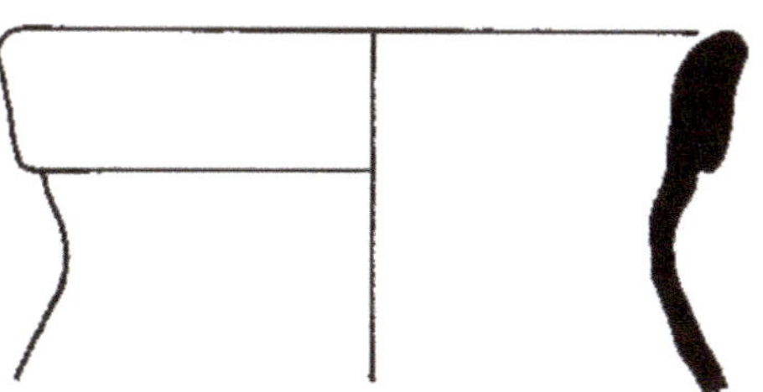

PW 395. CN 6886.
XXIIIA 10.5. Hellenistic 3C.
Part of wall, rim. PH 0.055; PL 0.10; D rim (est.) 0.10.
Reddish-yellow clay 7.5YR 6/6. Hard Pale.

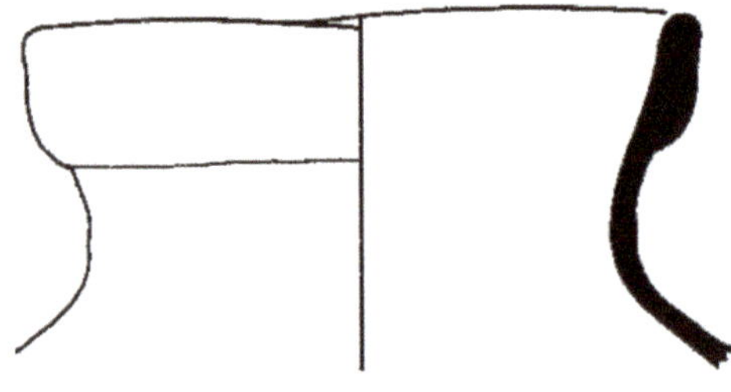

PW 396. CN 7857.
XXIIID 77.2. Hellenistic 3C.
Part of neck, rim. PH 0.07; D rim (est.) 0.10. Very
pale brown clay 7.5YR 10/4. Metallic Buff.

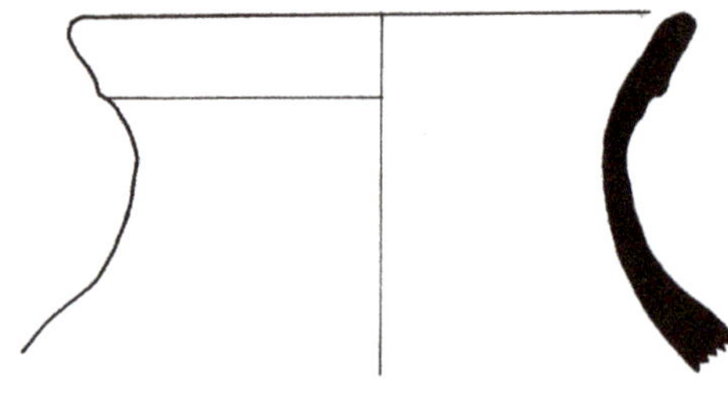

PW 397. CN 7483.
XXVIIIB 13.18. Mixed Context.
Part of wall, rim. PH 0.05; D rim (est.) 0.09. Very
pale brown clay 10YR 8/2. Hard Pale.

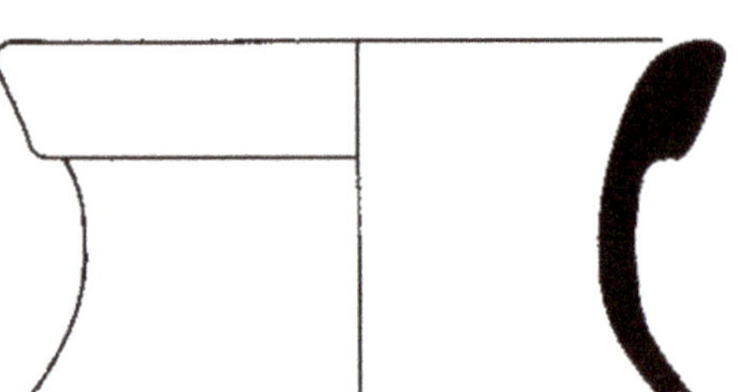

Tall neck – short-collared triangular rim (Type 5B)

PW 398. CN 7036.
XXIIIA 103.2. Hellenistic 3C.
Part of wall, rim. PH 0.05; PL 0.085; D rim (est.) 0.11.
White clay 10YR 8/2. Metallic Buff.
Parallels: Amman/Philadelphia (Zayadine 1977–78:
fig. 15.405); Shechem (N.L. Lapp 1985: fig. 1a.5); Tel
Zahara (Bar-Nathan and Gärtner 2013: fig. 3.9.84);
Tell Nimrin (Dornemann 1990: fig. 3.5).

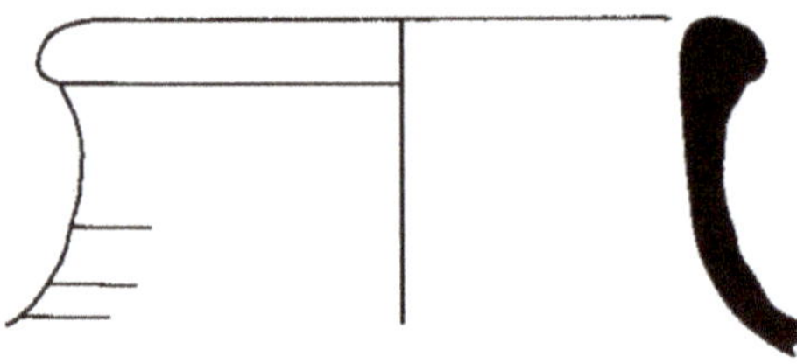

PW 399. CN 7296.
XXIIIB 2.3. Hellenistic 3B.
Part of wall, rim. PH 0.055; PL 0.075; D rim (est.) 0.12.
Light yellowish-brown clay 10YR 6/4. Metallic Buff.
Parallels: Gezer (Gitin 1990: pl. 36.10, mid-2nd c. BC);
Jerusalem (Geva 2003: pl. 5.8.1, later 2nd–1st c. BC).

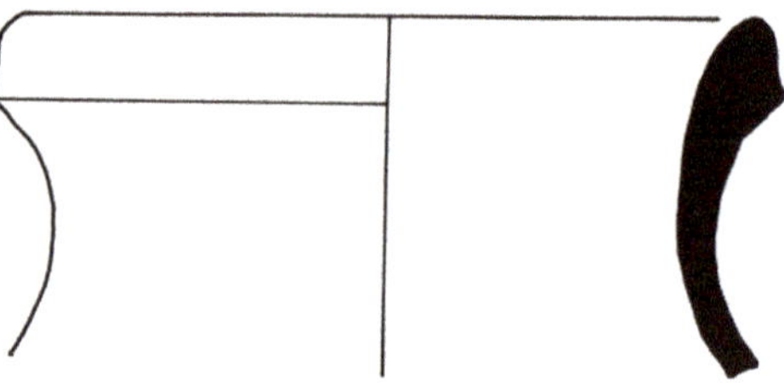

PW 400. CN 6937.
IVD 10.10. Hellenistic 3C.
Part of wall, rim, handle. PH 0.045; PL 0.085; D rim
(est.) 0.10. Very pale brown clay 10YR 7/4. Hard Pale.
Single handle from rim to shoulder.

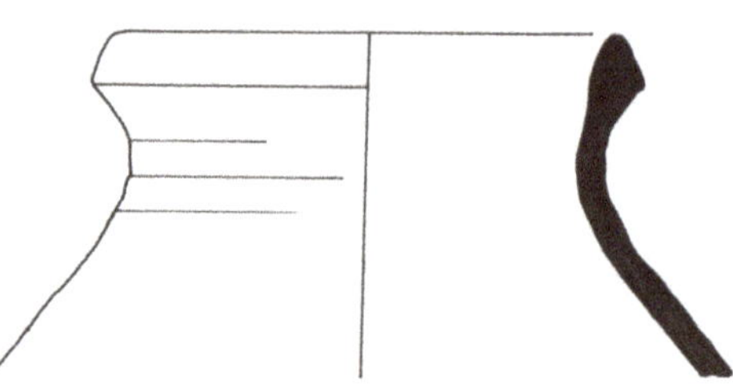

Long-collared rim (Type 6)

The collared rims of this type (**PW 401–35**) are clearly longer and more pronounced than those of Types 4–5. The rims on Type 6A (**PW 401–10**) – all from Jannaeus Destruction (main mound) and Early Roman (Tell Husn) levels – are not as elongated and lack the prominent lower edge seen in Type 6B (**PW 411–35**), most of which are from Early Roman contexts on Tell Husn. On these latter specimens, the increase in rim length is accompanied by a shortening of the neck.

Table 2.34. Distribution of jars Type 6 by sub-types, wares, phases.

		LONG-COLLARED RIM: UNIFORM THICKNESS (TYPE 6A)	LONG-COLLARED RIM: PROMINENT LOWER EDGE (TYPE 6B)
Ware	Hard Pale	7	0
	Metallic Buff	1	21
	Yellow-slipped	2	0
	Pink-slipped	0	3
	Miscellaneous	0	1
Phase	3C c. 100 (?)–c. 80/79 BC	10	0 (3)
	Early Roman 63 BC–c. 135 AD	0 (7)	21 (8)
	Mixed	0	4 (2)

Long-collared rim – uniform thickness (Type 6A)

PW 401. CN 4330.
XXIIIA 10.7. Hellenistic 3C.
Part of wall, rim. PH 0.065; PL 0.11; D rim (est.) 0.11.
Dark yellowish-brown clay 10YR 4/4. Hard Pale.

PW 402. CN 6887.
XXIIIA 10.7. Hellenistic 3C.
Part of wall, rim, handle. PH 0.19; D rim (est.) 0.10.
Light yellowish-brown clay 10YR 6/4. Hard Pale.
Vertical strap handles on shoulder.

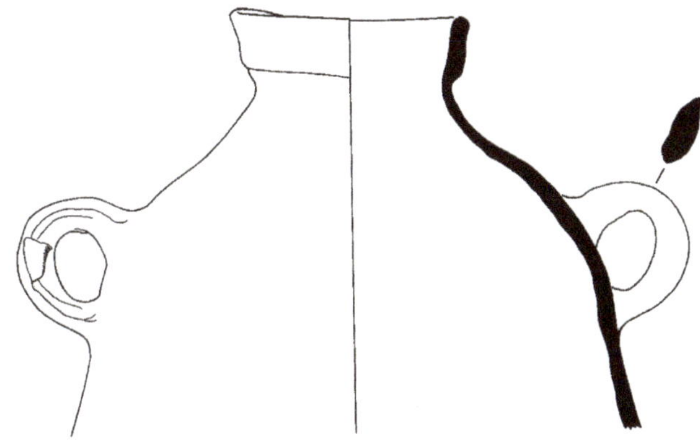

PW 403. CN 6888.
XXIIIA 10.7. Hellenistic 3C.
Part of wall, rim. PH 0.055; PL 0.05; D rim (est.) 0.09.
Light yellowish-brown clay 10YR 6/4. Hard Pale.
Parallels: 'Aïn Feshka (de Vaux 1959: fig. 3.11);
Jerusalem (Geva 2003: pl. 5.4.17, late 2nd–1st c. BC).

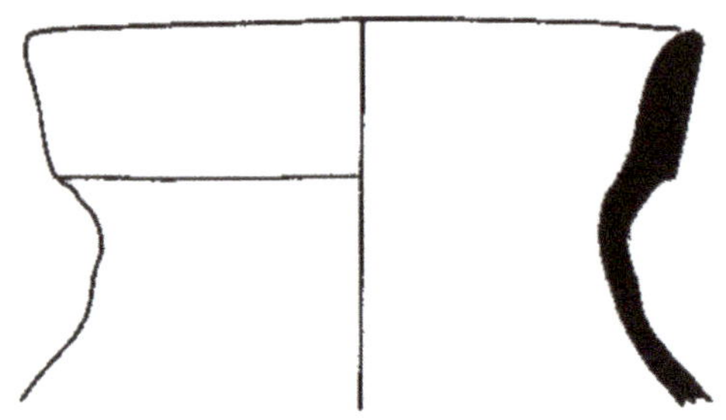

PW 404. CN 6569.
XXIIIA 10.7. Hellenistic 3C.
Part of wall, rim. PH 0.09; PL 0.115; D rim (est.)
0.10. Light brownish-grey clay 10YR 6/2. Hard Pale.
Parallel: 'En el-Ghuweir (Bar-Adon 1977: fig. 10.8).

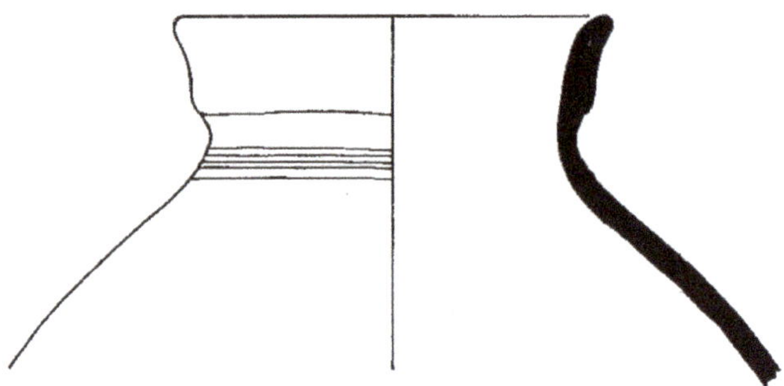

PW 405. CN 4325.
XXIIIA 10.7. Hellenistic 3C.
Part of wall, rim. PH 0.055; D rim (est.) 0.09. Light
brown clay 7.5YR 6/4. Yellow-slipped Coarse Ware.
Parallels: Gezer (Gitin 1990: pl. 43.20, mid-1st c. BC);
Samaria (Hennessy 1970: fig. 6.3).

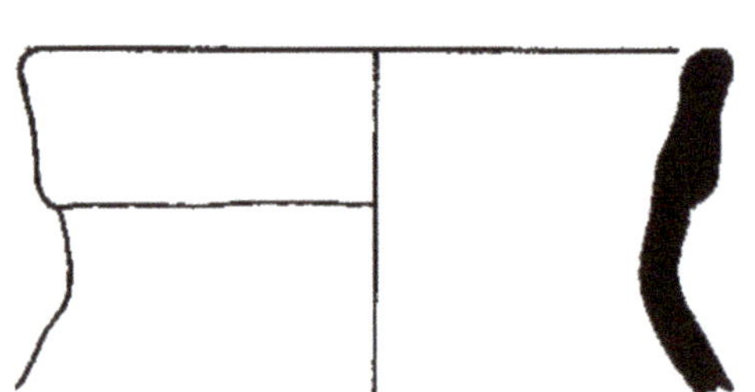

PW 406. CN 6581.
XXIIIA 10.7. Hellenistic 3C.
Part of wall, rim. PH 0.09; D rim 0.11. Reddish-yellow
clay 7.5YR 6/6. Hard Pale.

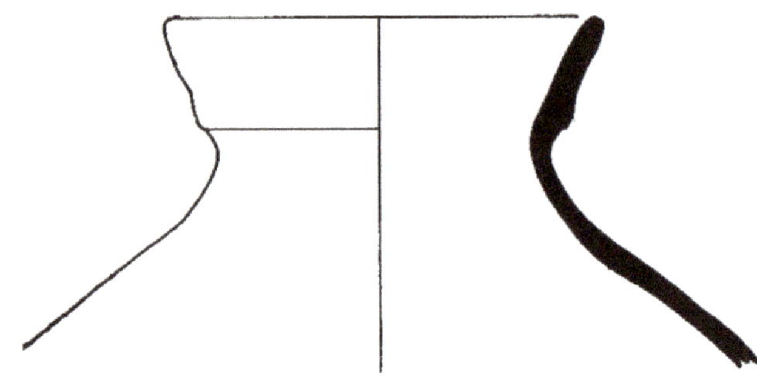

PW 407. CN 7091.
XXIIIA 100.1. Hellenistic 3C.
Part of wall, rim. PH 0.055; PL 0.06; D rim (est.) 0.09.
White clay 10YR 8/2. Metallic Buff.

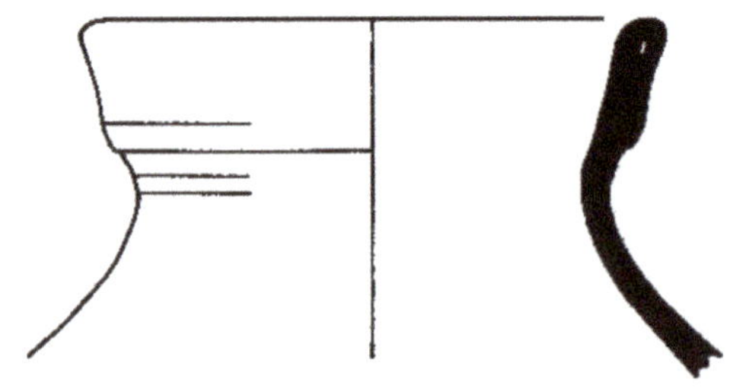

PW 408. CN 7090.
XXIIIA 100.1. Hellenistic 3C.
Two non-joining fragments of wall, rim. PH 0.04;
PL 0.095; D rim (est.) 0.12. Yellowish-red clay 5YR
5/8. Hard Pale.
Parallel: Jerusalem (Tchekhanovets 2013: fig. 5.16:6,
1st c. BC–70 AD).

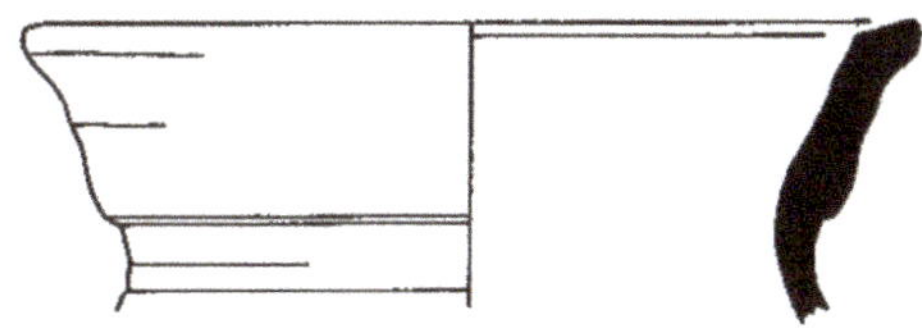

PW 409. CN 7826.
XXIIID 44.2. Hellenistic 3C.
Part of wall, rim. PH 0.08; D rim (est.) 0.11. Reddish-
yellow clay 5YR 6/8. Yellow-slipped Coarse Ware.

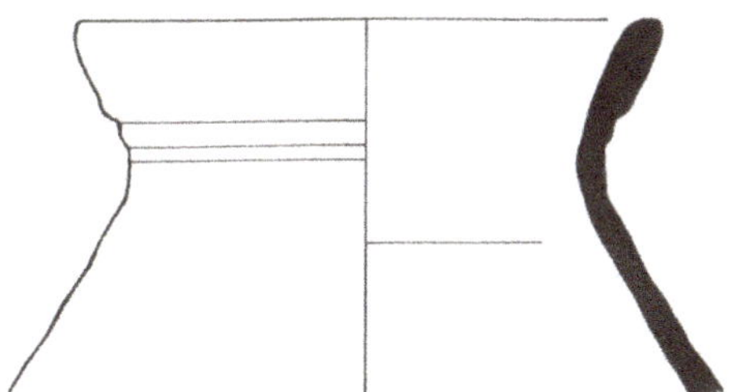

PW 410. CN 7109.
XXIIIA 83.4. Hellenistic 3C.
Part of wall, rim. PH 0.045; D rim (est.) 0.12. Pale
brown clay 10YR 5/4. Hard Pale.

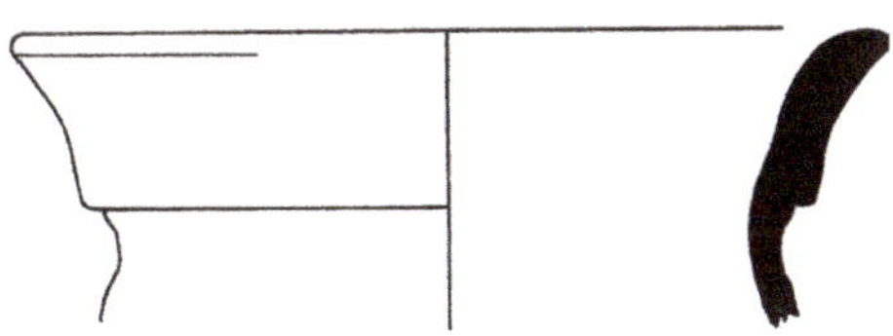

Long-collared rim – prominent lower edge (Type 6B)

PW 411. CN 7562.
XXXIVB 27.3. Early Roman 1.
Part of wall, rim. PH 0.04; PL 0.04; D rim (est.) 0.105.
Pale yellow clay 2.5Y 2/3. Metallic Buff.

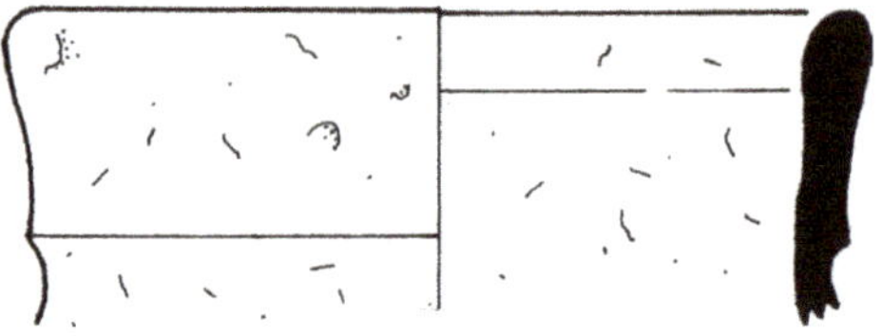

PW 412. CN 7560.
XXXIVB 25.6. Early Roman 1.
Part of wall, rim. PH 0.04; PL 0.08; D rim (est.) 0.10.
Brown clay 10YR 5/3. White inclusions.

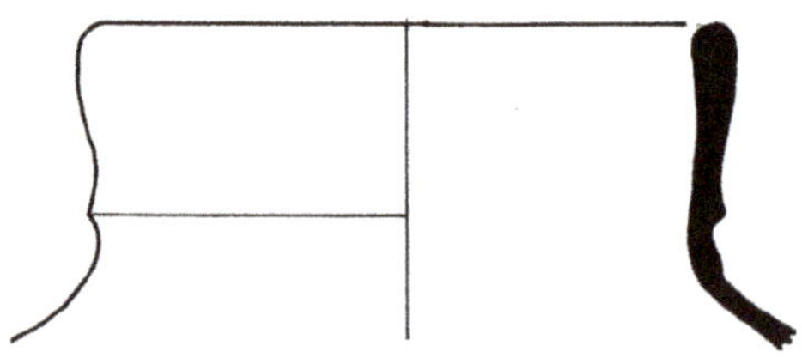

PW 413. CN 7627.
XXXIVB 27.10. Mixed Context.
Part of wall, rim. PH 0.05; PL 0.06; D rim (est.) 0.10.
Pale yellow clay 2.5Y 7/4. Metallic Buff.
Parallel: Tell Zira'a (Kenkel 2020: 76–7, 172–3,
pl. 1.28: Am4.6).

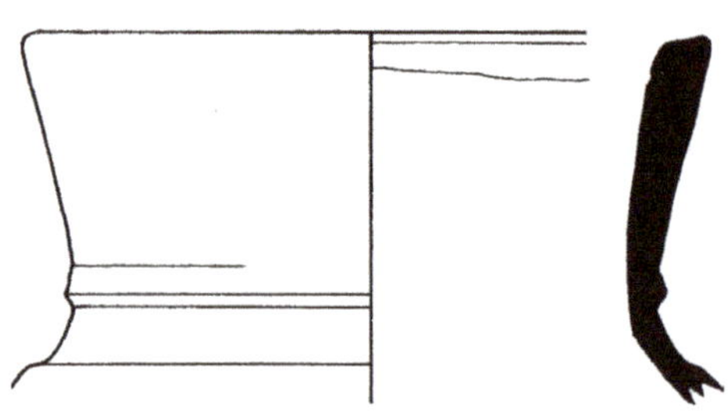

PW 414. CN 7628.
XXXIVB 27.10. Mixed Context.
Part of wall, rim. PH 0.045; PL 0.045; D rim
(est.) 0.105. Pale yellow clay 2.5Y 7/4. Metallic Buff.

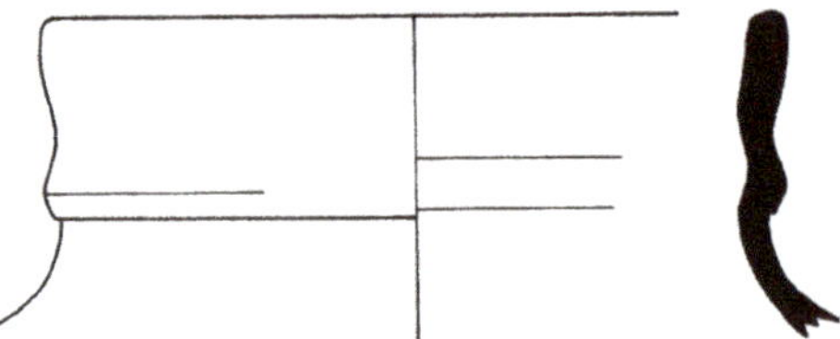

PW 415. CN 7620.
XXXIVB 27.9. Mixed Context.
Part of wall, rim. PH 0.045; PL 0.05; D rim (est.) 0.12.
Reddish-yellow clay 7.5YR 7/6. Metallic Buff.
Parallels: Hippos-Sussita (Osband and Eisenberg
2018: pl. 4.4.12, end 1st c. BC/beginning 1st c. AD);
Jaffa (Tsuf 2018: fig. 9.35.612).

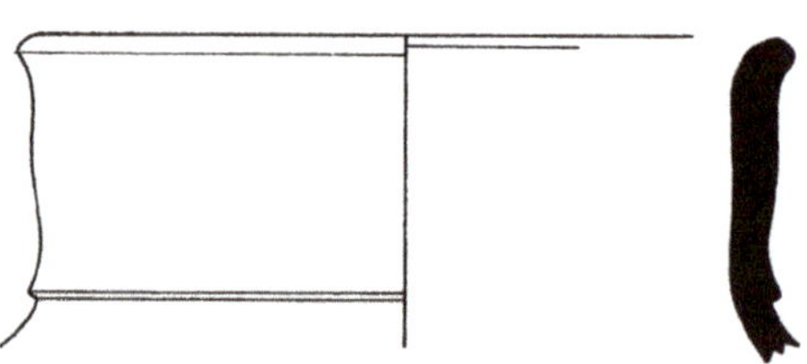

PW 416. CN 7349.
XXXIVB 6.27. Early Roman 1.
Part of wall, rim. PH 0.045; D rim (est.) 0.10. Light
brown clay 7.5YR 6/4. Metallic Buff.
Parallels: 'En el-Ghuweir (Bar-Adon 1977: fig. 10.2);
Jericho (Netzer and Meyers 1977: fig. 6.21); Jerusalem
(Tchekhanovets 2013: fig. 5.6:19, 1st c. BC–70 AD).

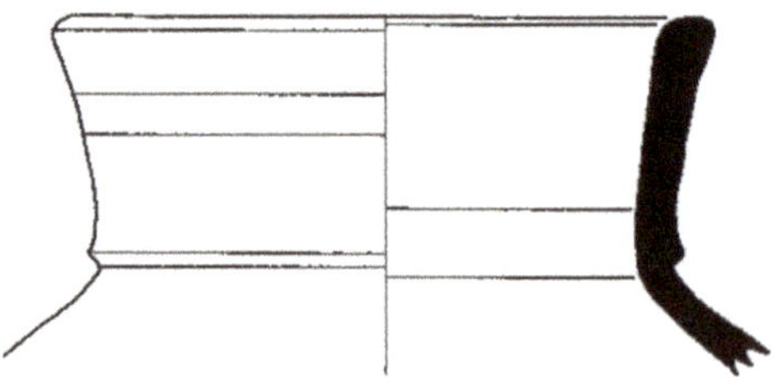

PW 417. CN 7346.
XXXIVB 6.27. Early Roman 1.
Part of rim. PH 0.045; PL 0.055; D rim (est.) 0.09.
Weak red clay 2.5YR 6/3. Metallic Buff.

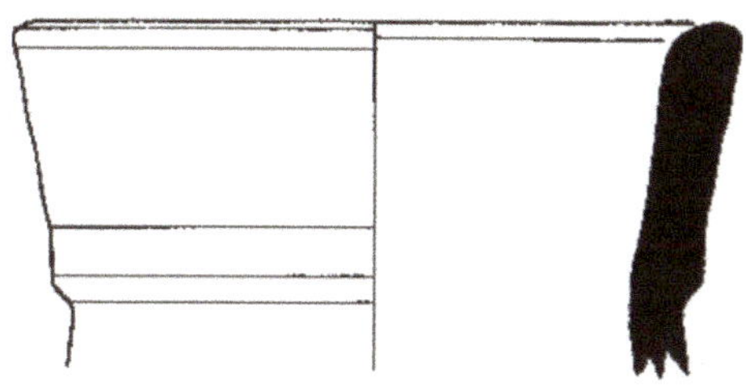

PW 418. CN 7350.
XXXIVB 6.27. Early Roman 1.
Part of wall, rim. PL 0.055; PH 0.04; D rim (est.) 0.10.
Light yellowish-brown clay 10YR 6/4. Metallic Buff.
Parallels: Hesban (Gerber 2012: 233, fig. 3.15.1);
Jerusalem (Tushingham 1985: fig. 19.29).

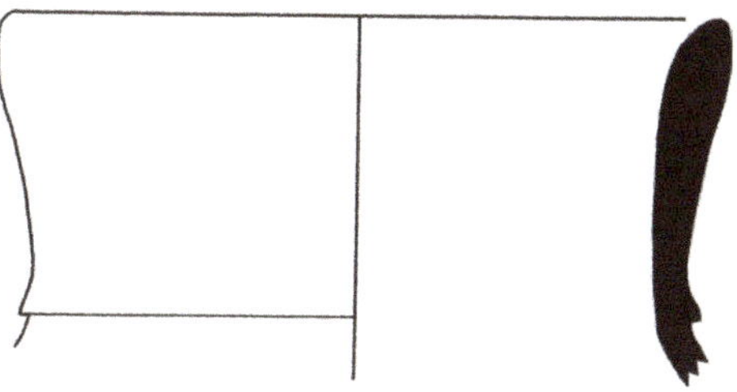

PW 419. CN 7684.
XXXIVB 55.5. Mixed Context.
Part of wall, rim. PH 0.045; PL 0.05; D rim (est.) 0.11.
Light yellowish-brown clay 10YR 6/4. Metallic Buff.
Parallels: 'Aïn Feshka (de Vaux 1959: fig. 3.16);
Jerusalem (Rahmani 1967: fig. 17.6; Tchekhanovets
2013: fig. 5.16:15, 1st c. BC–70 AD).

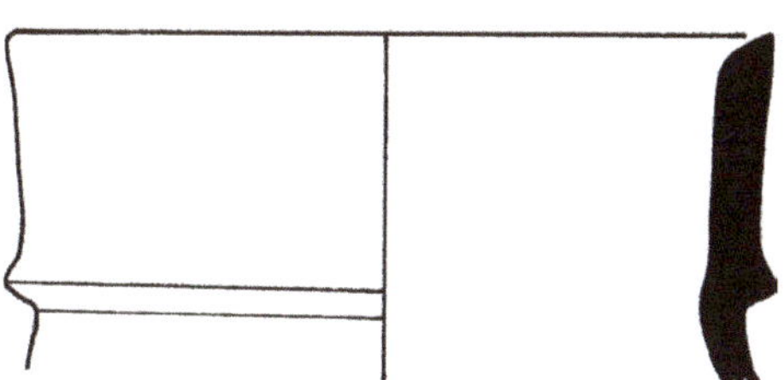

PW 420. CN 7174.
XXXIVG 6.10. Early Roman 1.
Part of wall, rim. PH 0.04; D rim (est.) 0.10. Reddish-
yellow clay 5YR 6/8. Metallic Buff.
Parallel: Machaerus (Loffreda 1996: fig. 2.7).

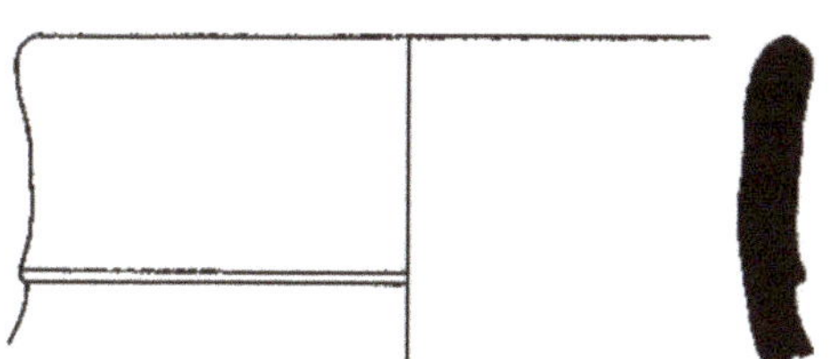

PW 421. CN 7173.
XXXIVG 6.10. Early Roman 1.
Part of rim. PH 0.45; D rim (est.) 0.10. Reddish-yellow
clay 7.5YR 7/6. Metallic Buff.
Parallels: Ashdod (Dothan and Freedman 1967:
fig. 7.6, first half of 2nd c. BC–mid-1st c. BC);
Jerusalem (Strange 1975: fig. 15.15; Tushingham 1985:
fig. 21.40); Machaerus (Loffreda 1996: fig. 1.11).

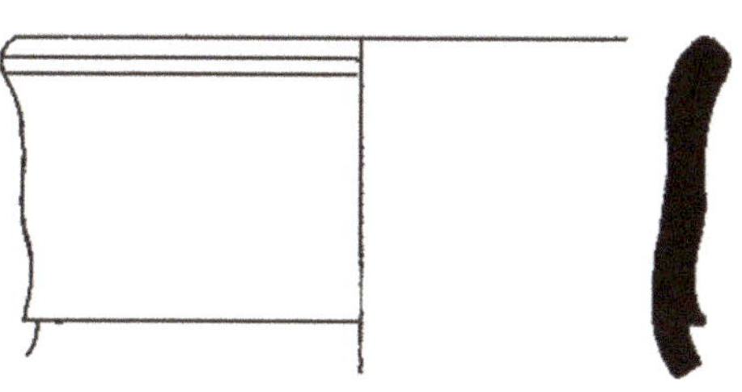

PW 422. CN 7172.
XXXIVG 6.10. Early Roman 1.
Part of wall, rim. PH 0.045; D rim (est.) 0.095. Very
pale brown clay 10YR 7/4. Metallic Buff.
Parallel: 'En el-Ghuweir (Bar-Adon 1977: fig. 10.2).

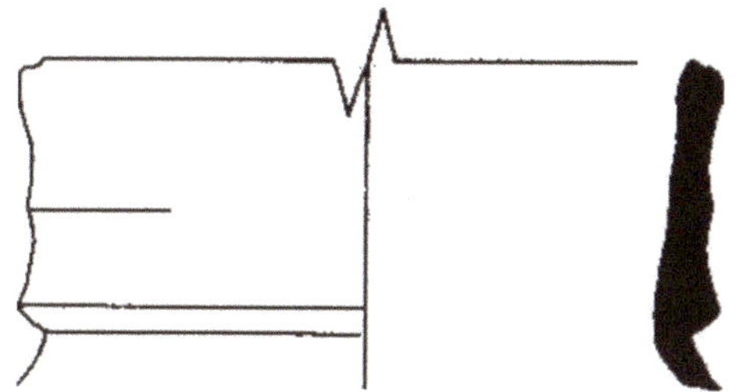

PW 423. CN 7168.
XXXIVG 6.7. Early Roman 1.
Part of wall, rim. PH 0.06; D rim 0.105. Reddish-yellow clay 5YR 7/6. Thin slip. Pink-slipped Coarse Ware.

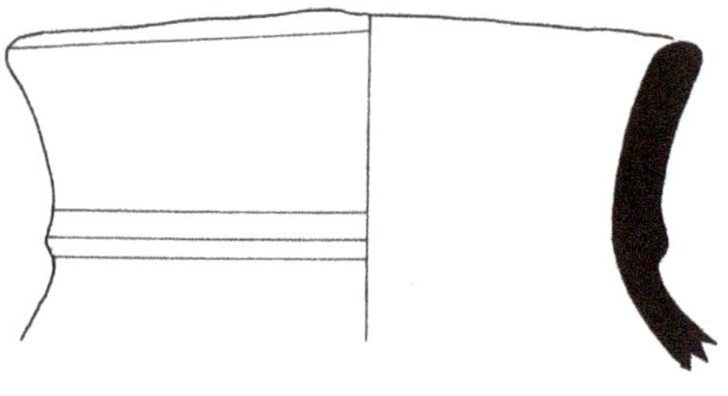

PW 424. CN 7286.
XXXIVG 6.2. Early Roman 1.
Part of wall, rim. PH 0.03; D rim (est.) 0.09. Pinkish-white clay 7.5YR 8/2. Metallic Buff.
Parallel: Jerusalem (Tchekhanovets 2013: fig. 5.6:18, 1st c. BC–70 AD).

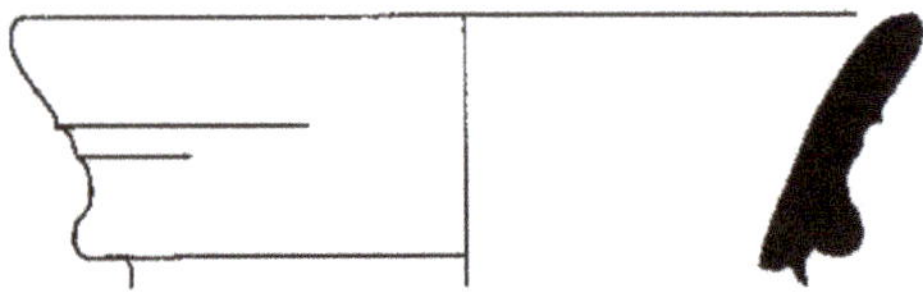

PW 425. CN 2967.
XIA/B 1.5. Early Roman 1.
Part of wall, rim. PH 0.05; PL 0.055; D rim (est.) 0.09. Very pale brown clay 10YR 7/4. Metallic Buff.
Parallel: 'En el-Ghuweir (Bar-Adon 1977: fig. 21.3).

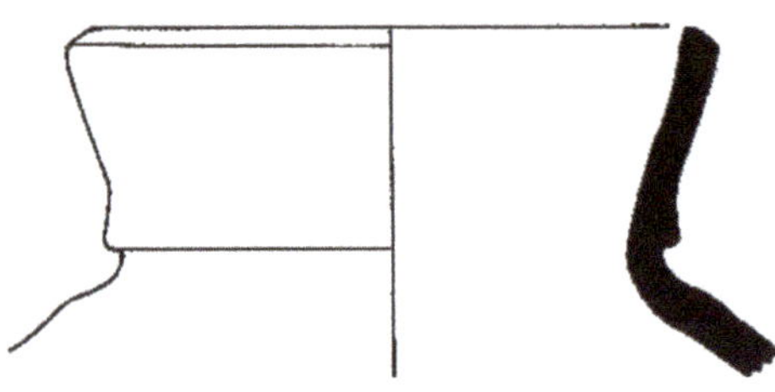

PW 426. CN 3048.
XIA/B 2.1/2. Early Roman 1.
Part of wall, rim. PH 0.055; D rim (est.) 0.095. Yellowish-red clay 5YR 5/6. Thin slip. Pink-slipped Coarse Ware.

PW 427. CN 2544.
XIA/B 1.1. Early Roman 1.
Part of rim. PH 0.05; D rim (est.) 0.09. Very pale brown clay 10YR 8/2. Metallic Buff.

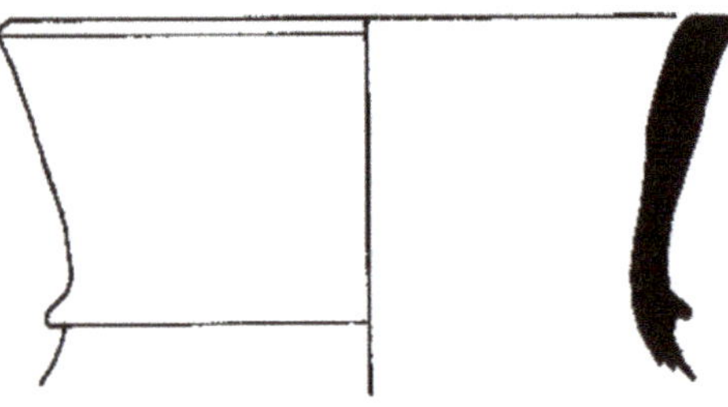

PW 428. CN 2655.
XIA/B 1.2. Early Roman 1.
Part of wall, rim. PH 0.07; PL 0.07; D rim (est.) 0.09. Reddish-yellow clay 5YR 6/6. Metallic Buff.

PW 429. CN 2545.
XIA/B 1.1. Early Roman 1.
Part of rim. PH 0.05; D rim (est.) 0.09. Very pale
brown clay 10YR 8/3. Metallic Buff.
Parallel: Hesban (Gerber 2012: 238, fig. 3.16.11).

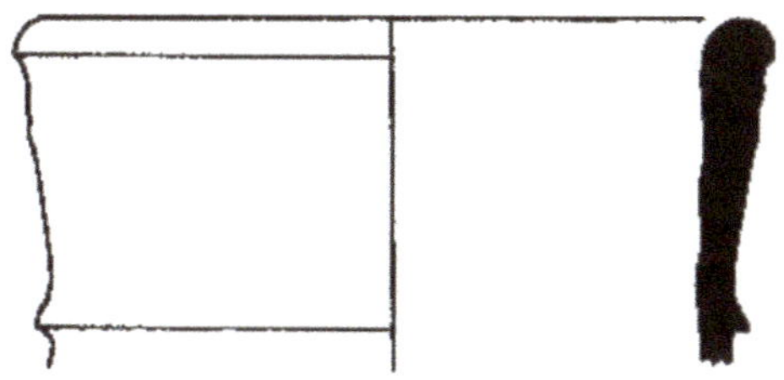

PW 430. CN 2631.
XIA/B 1.5. Early Roman 1.
Part of wall, rim. PH 0.06; PL 0.06; D rim (est.) 0.10.
Yellowish-brown clay 10YR 5/4. Metallic Buff.
Parallels: 'Aïn Feshka (de Vaux 1959: fig. 3.14);
Hesban (Gerber 2012: 233, fig. 3.15.2); Jericho (Netzer
and Meyers 1977: fig. 6.21); Jerusalem (Geva and
Rosenthal-Heginbottom 2003: pl. 6.1.27, 1st c. BC;
Tchekhanovets 2013: fig. 5.2:5, 1st c. BC–70 AD);
Machaerus (Loffreda 1996: fig. 3.56); Ras Abu Ma'aruf
(Rapuano 1999: fig.1.12).

PW 431. CN 2981.
XIA/B 1.1. Early Roman 1.
Part of wall, rim. PH 0.045; D rim (est.) 0.09. Pale
yellow clay 2.5Y 8/2. Metallic Buff.
Parallels: Jaffa (Tsuf 2018: fig. 9.35.617); Jerusalem
(Tushingham 1985: fig. 22.43); Machaerus (Corbo
and Loffreda 1981: fig. 35.15).

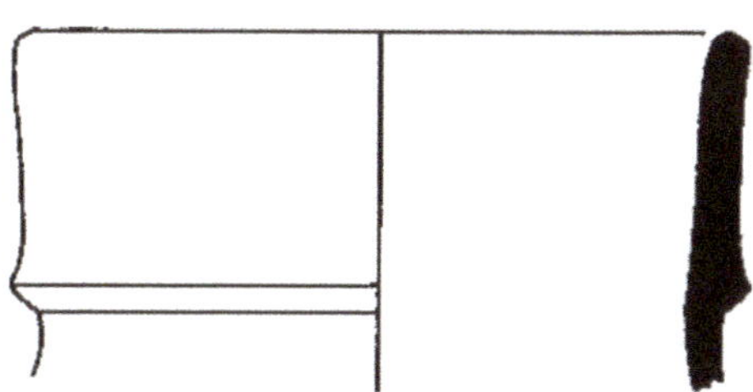

PW 432. CN 3101.
XIA/B 1.3. Early Roman 1.
Part of wall, rim. PH 0.06; D rim (est.) 0.10. Pale
yellow clay 2.5Y 8/3. Metallic Buff.

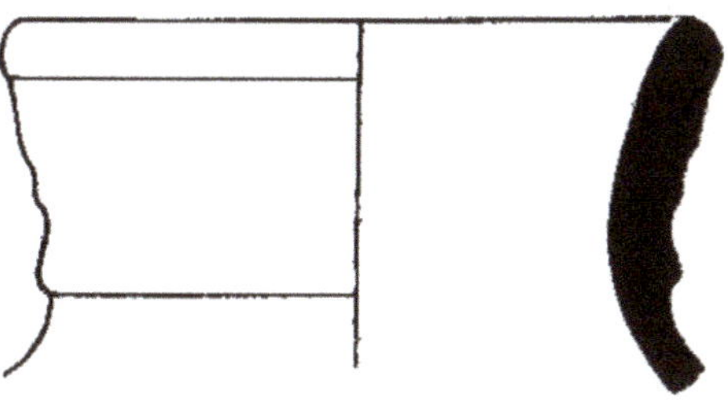

PW 433. CN 2990.
XIA/B 1.2/3. Early Roman 1.
Part of wall, rim. PH 0.055; D rim (est.) 0.09. Pale
yellow clay 2.5Y 7/4. Metallic Buff.
Parallel: Tell Zira'a (Kenkel 2020: 77, 172–3,
pl. 1.28: Am4.7).

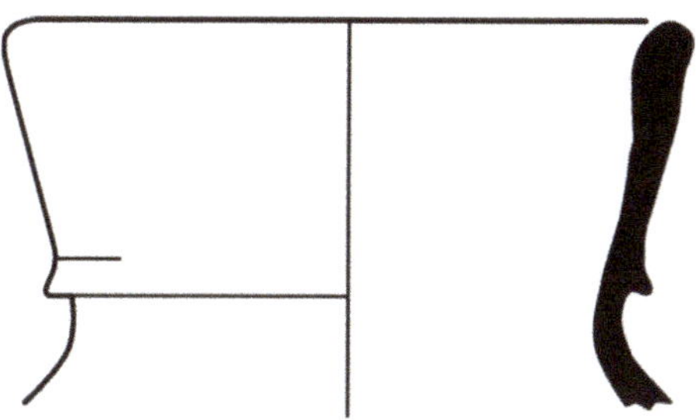

PW 434. CN 2629.
XIA/B 1.5. Early Roman 1.
Part of wall, rim. PH 0.06; D rim (est.) 0.095.
Yellowish-red clay 5YR 5/6. Mottled slip. Pink-slipped
Coarse Ware.

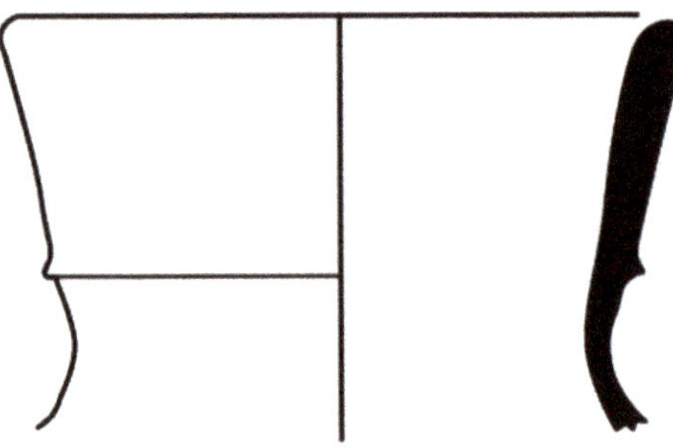

PW 435. CN 6754.
XIA/B 20.4. Early Roman 1.
Part of wall, rim. PH 0.04; PL 0.055; D rim (est.) 0.09.
Reddish-yellow clay 5YR 6/6. Metallic Buff.

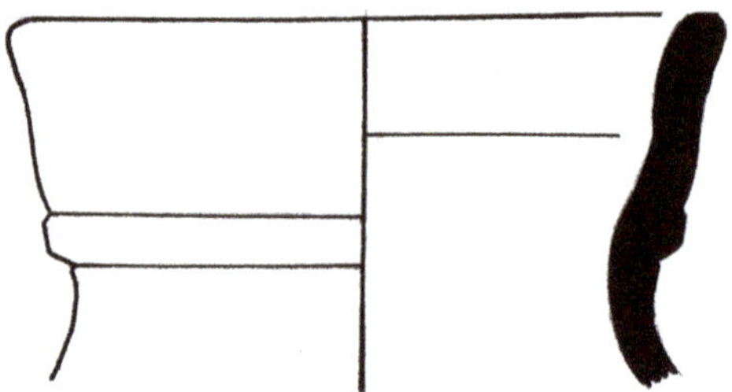

Neck ridge (Type 7)

A definite ridge at the junction of neck and shoulder is seen on jars from the beginning of the first century AD, or slightly earlier, in southern Palestine at sites such as Betar, Herodium, Samaria and Jerusalem itself.[25] At sites further to the north lying within an area of continued Phoenician influence (Berlin 1997c), including Tel Anafa and Tel Dor, this feature is not present. In Transjordan the neck ridge is seen on storage jars from Early Roman contexts at 'Iraq al-Amir (examples of which are seen in Zimmerman 2020b: pls 2.9–2.12) and Early Roman II–IV (that is, 37–135 AD) jars from Hesban, as well as those from Herodian levels at Kallirhoe and Machaerus and on jar fragments recovered from the Kerak Plateau.[26] This characteristic persists well into Byzantine times on both sides of the Jordan River (Bar-Nathan 1981, pl. 12, nos 1, 6; Clamer 1997: pl. 21, nos 7–9; McNicoll et al. 1982, pl. 139, nos 6, 8).

At Pella the neck ridge is already seen on a small number of fragmentary jars from Jannaeus Destruction (Hellenistic 3C) contexts in plots IVD and XXIIID on the main mound (**PW 436, PW 460–1**); in Early Roman levels on Tell Husn it has become common. Present on jars with plain lips (Type 7A: **PW 436–59**), it also occurs on jars whose lip projects on the exterior (Type 7B: **PW 460–83**); this latter type has the same chronological range as Type 7A.

---

25   Singer 1993: fig. 2, nos 1–8 (Betar); Bar-Nathan 1981: pls 2, 3, 10 (Herodium); Rahmani 1967: fig. 17 (Jerusalem); Crowfoot et al. 1957: fig. 71.2, 3 (Samaria). A similar neck ridge is also the characteristic feature of those "collared rim jars" seen on both sides of the Jordan River in Late Bronze and Iron I contexts.
26   Gerber 2012: figs 3.16, 3.17, 3.20, *passim* (Hesban); Clamer 1997: 71, Type 3.8.1b (Kallirhoe); Brown 1991: pl. 6.339–41(Kerak Plateau); Loffreda 1996: Groups 6–16 (Machaerus).

Table 2.35. Distribution of jars Type 7 by sub-types, wares, phases.

		NECK RIDGE; SIMPLE LIP (TYPE 7A)	NECK RIDGE; OVERHANGING LIP (TYPE 7B)
Ware	Hard Pale	4	1
	Metallic Buff	17	19
	Yellow-slipped	1	1
	Pink-slipped	0	2
	Miscellaneous	2	1
Phase	3C c. 100 (?)–c. 80/79 BC	1	2
	Early Roman 63 BC–c. 135 AD	ER 1=15 (3) ER 2=3	21 (21)
	Mixed	5	1

Neck ridge – simple lip (Type 7A)

PW 436. CN 6809.
IVD 13.10. Hellenistic 3C.
Part of wall, rim. PH 0.055; PL 0.085; D rim (est.) 0.12. Reddish-yellow clay 5YR 6/8. Hard Pale. Parallels: Jerusalem (Geva 2014: pl. 19.1.9); Nahal Hever (Aharoni 1961: fig. 10.5); Tel Zahara (Bar-Nathan 2013: fig. 3.2.9).

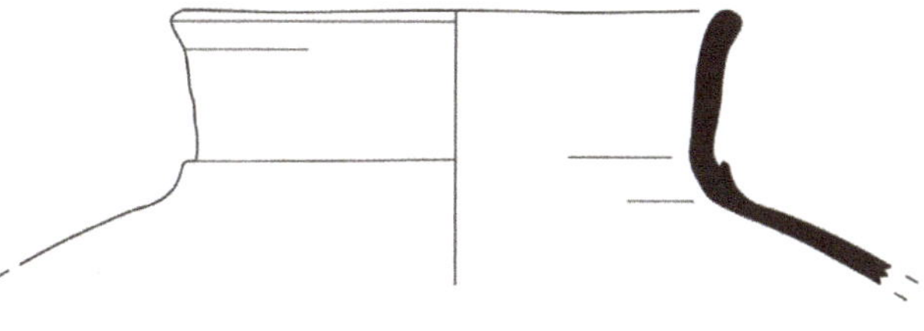

PW 437. CN 3932.
IVE 17.13. Mixed Context.
Part of wall, rim. PH 0.07; PL 0.135; D rim (est.) 0.10. Pale brown clay 10YR 6/3. Metallic Buff.
Parallels: Herodium (Bar-Nathan 1981: pl. 1.4); Jerusalem (Strange 1975: fig. 15.6).

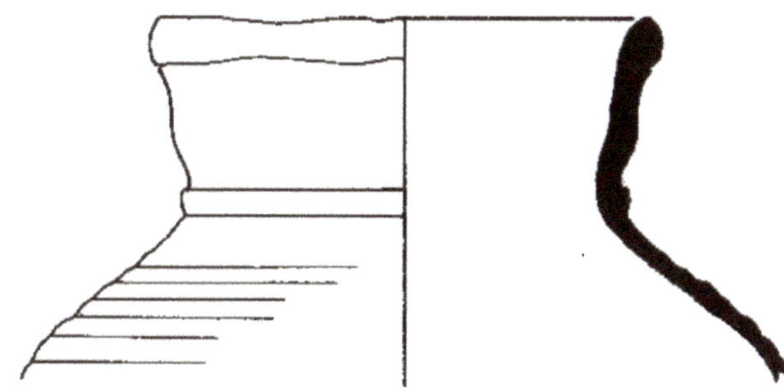

PW 438. CN 7616.
XXXIVB 27.7. Early Roman 1.
Part of wall, rim. PH 0.045; PL 0.07; D rim (est.) 0.095. Yellowish-red clay 5YR 5/8.
Parallel: Jerusalem (Geva and Rosenthal-Heginbottom 2003: pl. 6.1.31, 1st c. BC; Rahmani 1967: fig. 17.3).

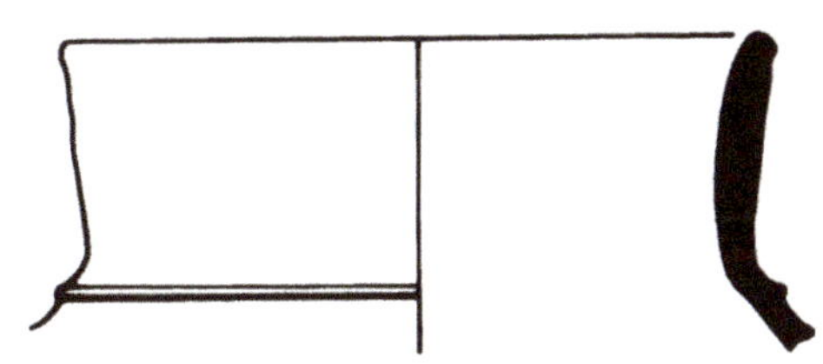

PW 439. CN 7610.
XXXIVB 27.6. Early Roman 1.
Part of wall, rim. PH 0.04; PL 0.08; D rim (est.) 0.10.
Reddish-yellow clay 5YR 6/6. White inclusions. Pale
orange slip over exterior.

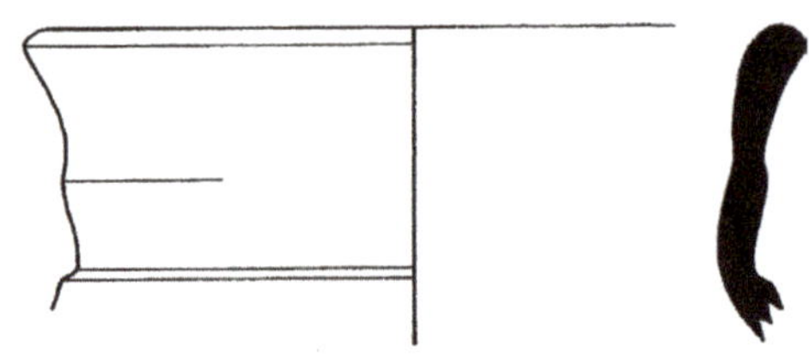

PW 440. CN 7559.
XXXIVB 25.6. Early Roman 1.
Three joining fragments of rim, wall. PH 0.16; D rim
0.085. Very pale brown clay 10YR 7.3. Metallic Buff.
Parallel: Jerusalem (Rahmani 1967: fig. 17.1).

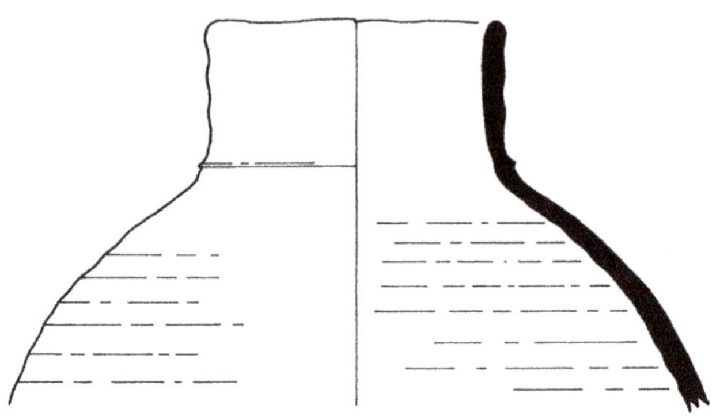

PW 441. CN 7343.
XXXIVB 7.17. Early Roman 1.
Part of rim. PH 0.045; PL 0.04; D rim (est.) 0.12. Very
pale brown clay 10YR 7/3. Metallic Buff.
Parallel: Jerusalem (Geva and Rosenthal-Heginbottom
2003: pl. 6.10.4, c. 30–70 AD).

PW 442. CN 7287.
XXXIVG 6.7. Early Roman 1.
Part of wall, rim. PH 0.045; D rim 0.10. Red clay
2.5YR 6/6. Hard Pale.

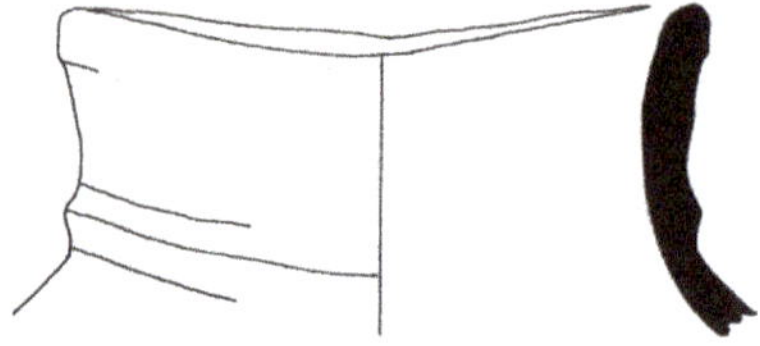

PW 443. CN 7277.
XXXIVG 3.1. Mixed Context.
Part of wall, rim. PH 0.06; D rim (est.) 0.11. Reddish-
yellow clay 5YR 6/6. Hard Pale.
Parallels: Herodium (Bar-Nathan 1981: pl. 1.4);
Jerusalem (Tushingham 1985: fig. 21.40).

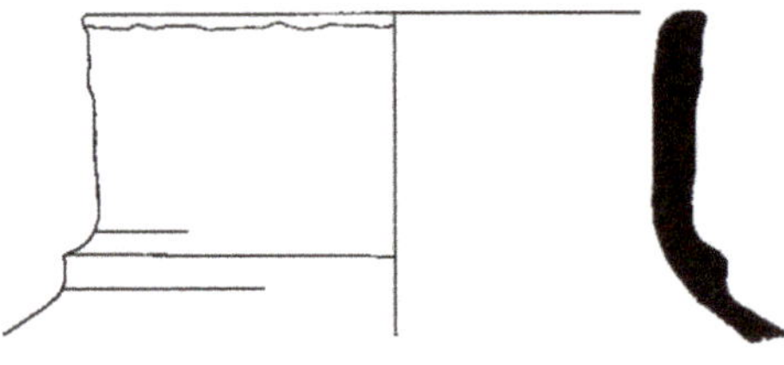

PW 444. CN 7276.
XXXIVG 3.13. Mixed Context.
Part of wall, rim. PH 0.05; D rim (est.) 0.10. Very
pale brown clay 10YR 7/3. Metallic Buff.
Parallels: Jerusalem (Geva and Rosenthal-
Heginbottom 2003: pl. 6.10.4, c. 30–70 AD; Strange
1975: fig. 15.6). Machaerus (Loffreda 1996: fig. 10.13);
Wadi al-Kharrar (Abu Shmeis and Waheeb 2002: fig.
2.8).

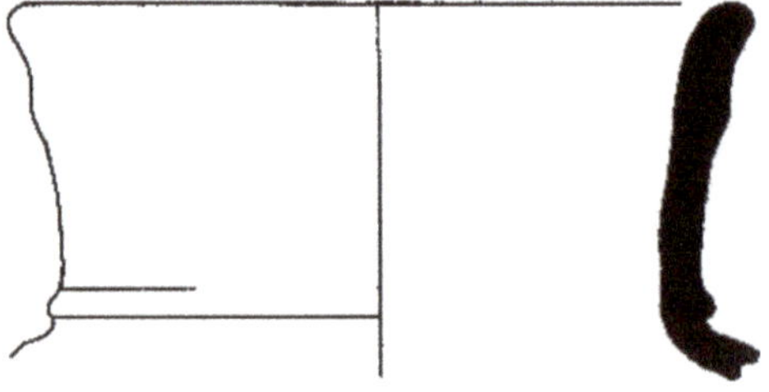

PW 445. CN 2654.
XIA/B 1.1/2. Early Roman 1.
Part of wall, rim. PH 0.05; PL 0.055; D rim (est.) 0.095. Very pale brown clay 10YR 7/4. Metallic Buff.

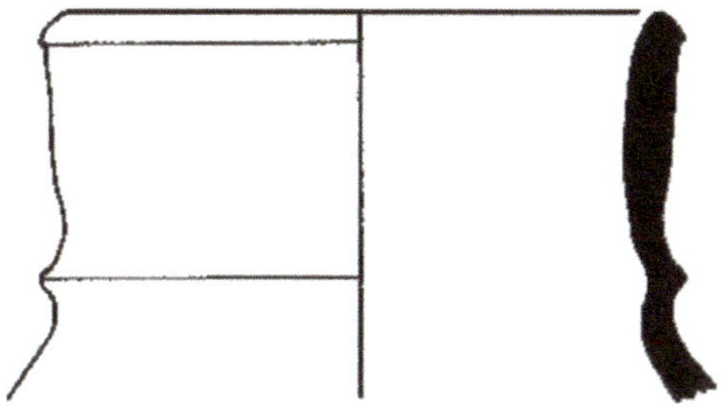

PW 446. CN 6796.
XIA/B 20.5. Early Roman 2.
Part of wall, rim. PH 0.05; PL 0.055; D rim (est.) 0.095. Very pale brown clay 10YR 7/4. Metallic Buff. Parallels: 'En el-Ghuweir (Bar-Adon 1977: fig. 10.4); Hesban (Gerber 2012: 261, fig. 3.21.12); Kerak Plateau Survey (Brown 1991: pl. 6.340); Tell Nimrin (Dornemann 1990: fig. 3.3).

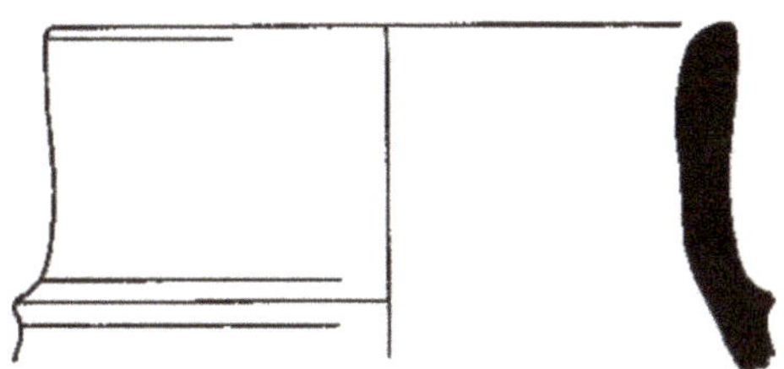

PW 447. CN 2989.
XIA/B 1.2/3. Early Roman 1.
Part of wall, rim. PH 0.045; PL 0.05; D rim (est.) 0.09. Yellowish-red clay 5YR 5/6. Metallic Buff.

PW 448. CN 2557.
XIA/B 1.1. Early Roman 1.
Part of wall, rim. PH 0.045; PL 0.05; D rim (est.) 0.09. Very pale brown clay 10YR 7/4. Metallic Buff.

PW 449. CN 3099.
XIA/B 3.1. Mixed Context.
Part of wall, rim. PH 0.04; D rim (est.) 0.10. Very pale brown clay 10YR 7/4. Metallic Buff.

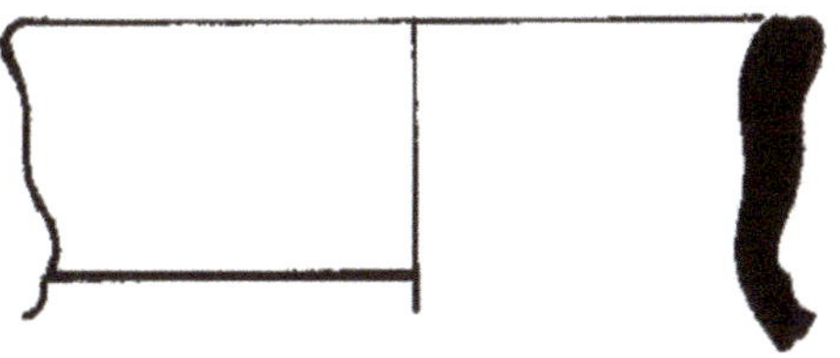

PW 450. CN 3053.
XIA/B 2.2. Early Roman 1.
Part of wall, rim. PH 0.05; PL 0.09; D rim (est.) 0.095. Yellowish-brown clay 10YR 5/4. Metallic Buff. Parallel: Tel Zahara (Bar-Nathan 2013: fig. 3.3.16).

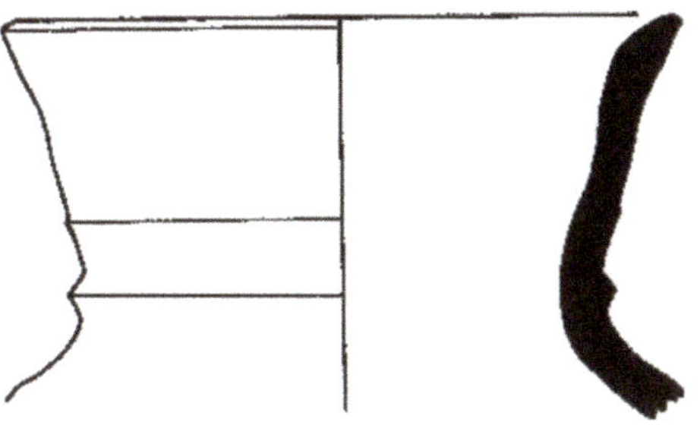

PW 451. CN 2977.
XIA/B 1.1/3. Early Roman 1.
Part of wall, rim. PH 0.055; D rim (est.) 0.095.
Reddish-yellow clay 7.5YR 8/6. Metallic Buff.
Parallels: Betar (Singer 1993: fig. 1.8); Hippos-Sussita
(Osband and Eisenberg 2018: pl. 4.2.29, end 1st
c. BC/beginning 1st c. AD); Masada Camp F (Magness
2009: fig. 4.3, 72/73 or 73/74 AD); Meiron (Meyers et
al. 1981: pl. 8.15.14).

PW 452. CN 6798.
XIA/B 20.5. Early Roman 2.
Part of wall, rim. PH 0.05; D rim (est.) 0.10. Very
pale brown clay 10YR 7/3. Metallic Buff.
Parallel: Tell Zira'a (Kenkel 2020: 77, 172–3,
pl. 1.28: Am4.7).

PW 453. CN 6801.
XIA/B 20.6. Early Roman 1.
Part of wall, rim. PH 0.055; D rim (est.) 0.09. Very
pale brown clay 10YR 8/3. Metallic Buff.
Parallels: Hippos-Sussita (Osband and Eisenberg
2018: pl. 4.4.10, end 1st c. BC/beginning 1st c. AD);
Jerusalem (Geva 1983: fig. 5.2; Machline and Gadot
2017: fig. 10.12); Kallirhoe (Clamer 1997: pl. 3.21).

PW 454. CN 6775.
XIA/B 20.5. Early Roman 2.
Part of wall, rim. PH 0.07; D rim (est.) 0.115. Very
pale brown clay 10YR 8/3. Metallic Buff.

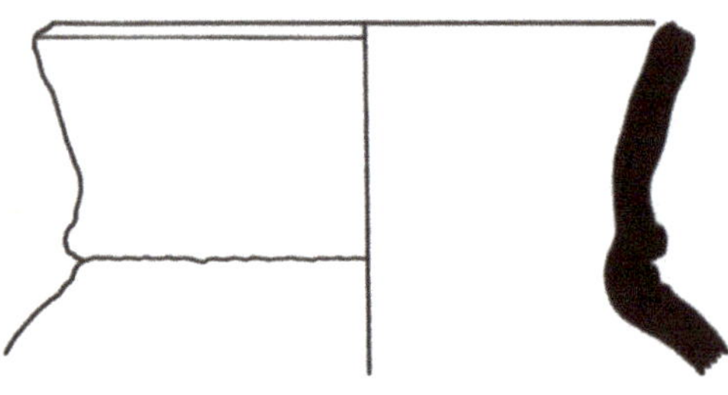

PW 455. CN 2988.
XIA/B 1.2/3. Early Roman 1.
Part of wall, rim. PH 0.06; PL 0.05; D rim (est.) 0.11.
Reddish-yellow clay 7.5YR 6/6. Yellow-slipped Coarse
Ware.
Parallel: Hippos-Sussita (Osband and Eisenberg 2018:
pl. 4.5.5, end 1st c. BC/beginning 1st c. AD).

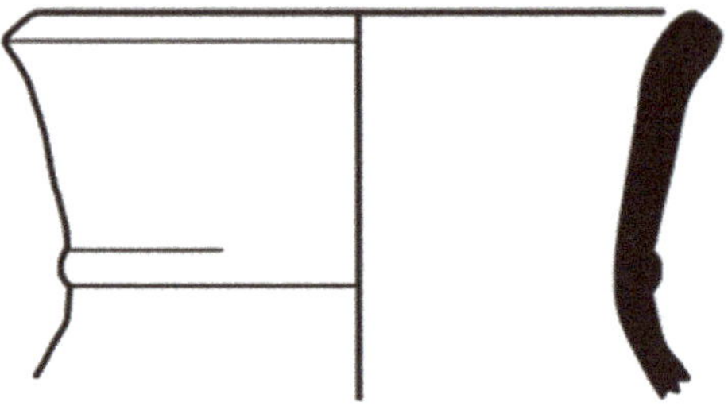

PW 456. CN 2553.
XIA/B 1.1. Early Roman 1.
Part of wall, rim. PH 0.075; PL 0.08; D rim (est.) 0.10.
Red clay 2.5YR 6/8. Metallic Buff.

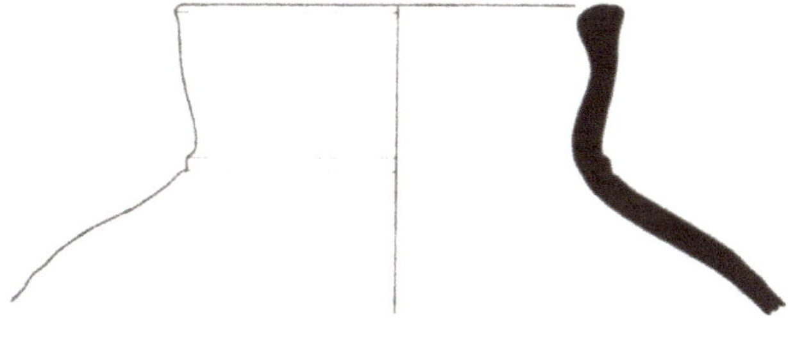

PW 457. CN 6547.
XIA/B 21.2. Mixed Context.
Part of wall, rim. PH 0.06; D rim (est.) 0.105. Very
pale brown clay 10YR 8/3. Metallic Buff.

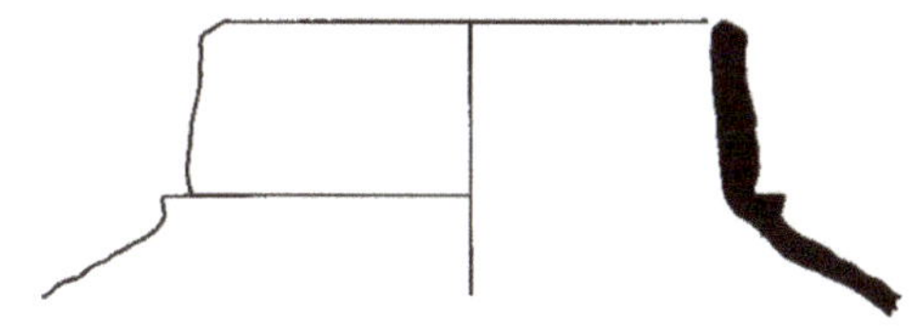

PW 458. CN 2548.
XIA/B 1.1. Early Roman 1.
Part of wall, rim. PH 0.05; PL 0.06; D rim (est.) 0.10.
Reddish-yellow clay 5YR 6/6. Hard Pale.

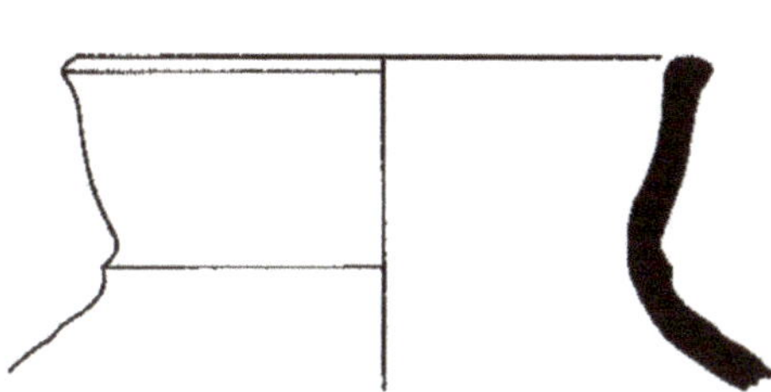

PW 459. CN 2555.
XIA/B 1.1. Early Roman 1.
Part of wall, rim. PH 0.05; PL 0.085; D rim (est.) 0.095.
Pale yellow clay 2.5Y 7/4. Metallic Buff.
Parallels: Jericho (Pritchard 1958: pl. 58.31); Tell
Nimrin (Dornemann 1990: fig. 3.3).

Neck ridge – overhanging lip (Type 7B)

PW 460. CN 6582.
IVD 10.12. Hellenistic 3C.
Part of wall, rim. PH 0.06; PL 0.09; D rim (est.) 0.10.
Light yellowish-brown clay 10YR 6/4. Metallic Buff.
Parallels: 'Iraq al-Amir (Zimmerman 2020b: pl. 2.9.5,
str. IIIa–I, c. 50–c. 200 AD); Jerusalem (Geva and
Rosenthal-Heginbottom 2003: pls 6.5.7, early 1st
c. AD, 6.10.7, c. 30–70 AD).

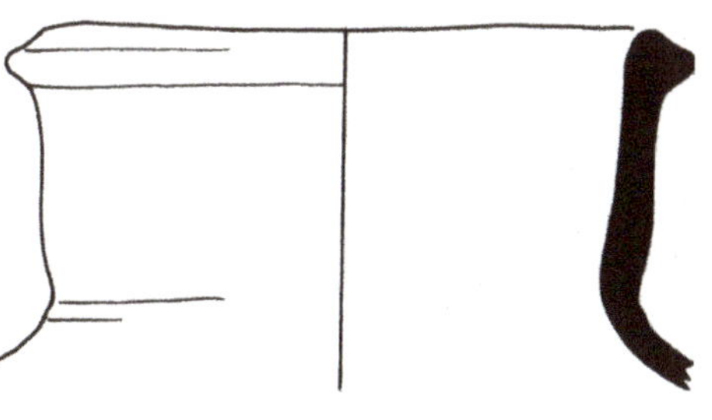

PW 461. CN 7749.
XXIIID 18.2. Hellenistic 3C.
Part of wall, rim. PH 0.05; PL 0.045; D rim (est.) 0.12.
Red clay 2.5YR 6/8. Yellow-slipped Coarse Ware.
Parallel: Hesban (Gerber 2012: 261, fig. 3.21.8).

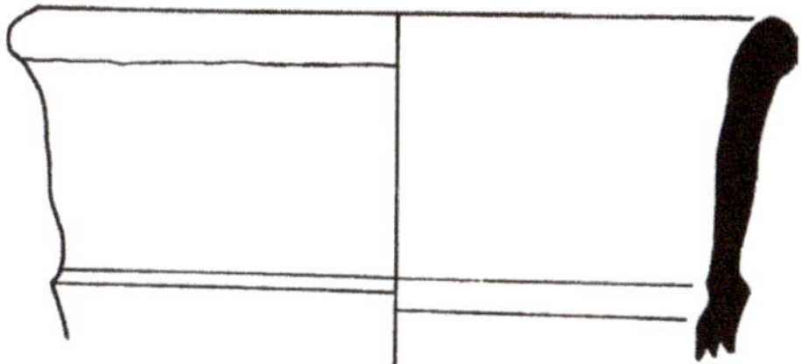

PW 462. CN 7549.
XXXIVB 27.1 Early Roman 1.
Two joining fragments of wall, rim. PH 0.045; PL 0.095; D rim (est.) 0.10. Pale yellow clay 2.5Y 7/3. Parallels: Jerusalem (Tchekhanovets 2013: fig. 5.12:12, 1st c. BC–70 AD); Masada Camp F (Magness 2009: fig. 9.10, late 1st/early 2nd century AD); Tel Zahara (Bar-Nathan 2013: fig. 3.2.10).

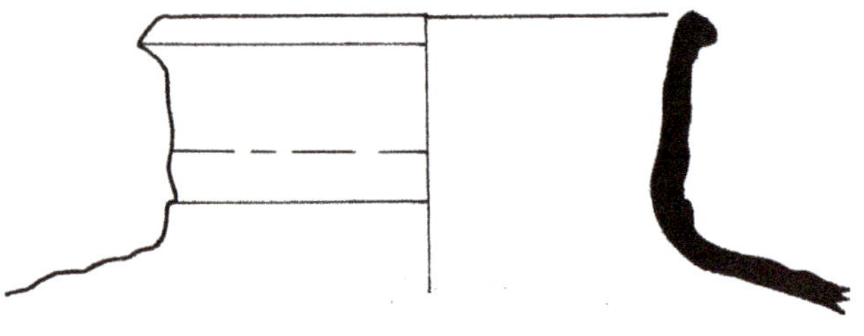

PW 463. CN 7338.
XXXIVB 16.2. Early Roman 1.
Part of wall, rim. PH 0.045; PL 0.07; D rim (est.) 0.10. Brown clay 10YR 5/3. Hard Pale.

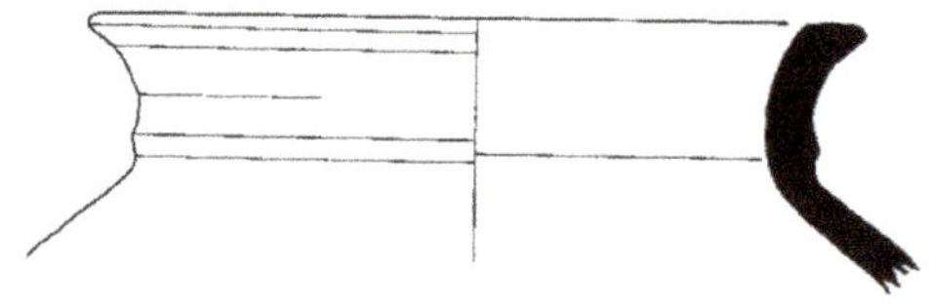

PW 464. CN 7179.
XXXIVG 9.6. Early Roman 1.
Part of wall, rim. PH 0.035; D rim (est.) 0.09. Light brownish-grey clay 10YR 6/2. Metallic Buff. Parallels: Betar (Singer 1993: fig. 2.4); 'Iraq al-Amir (Brown 1983: fig. 54.6); Kerak Plateau Survey (Brown 1991: pl. 6.341); Samaria (Hennessy 1970: fig. 6.6).

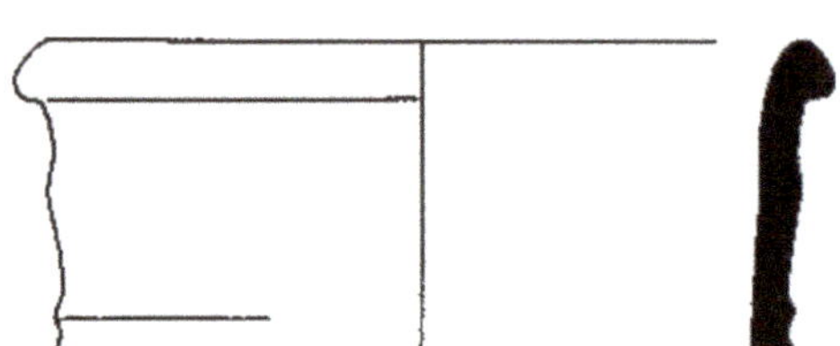

PW 465. CN 2865. (Plate 61)
XIA/B 2.2. Early Roman 1.
Complete. H 0.50; D rim 0.07. Pale brown clay 10YR 6/3. Metallic Buff.
Rounded resting surface. Tall bag-shaped jar with prominent ridging on upper part. Handles extend from upper wall to shoulder.
Parallels: 'En el-Ghuweir (Bar-Adon 1977: fig. 10.6); 'En Gedi (Hirschfeld 2000: fig. 24.2); Straton's Tower/ Caesarea (Berlin 1992: fig. 54.5 rim profile).

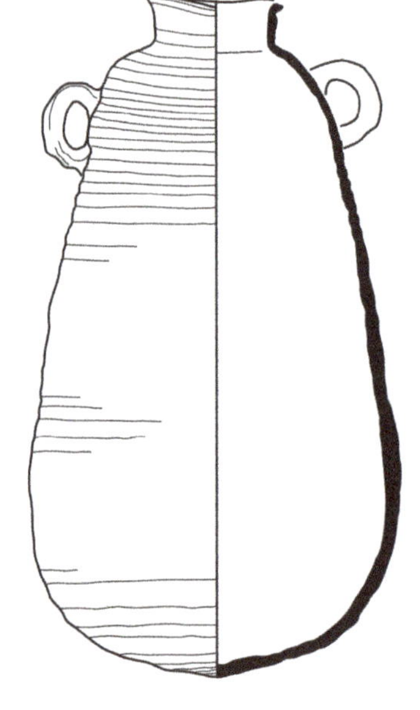

PW 466. CN 6753.
XIA/B 20.4. Early Roman 1.
Part of wall, rim. PH 0.06; D rim (est.) 0.12. Pale brown clay 10YR 6/3. Metallic Buff.

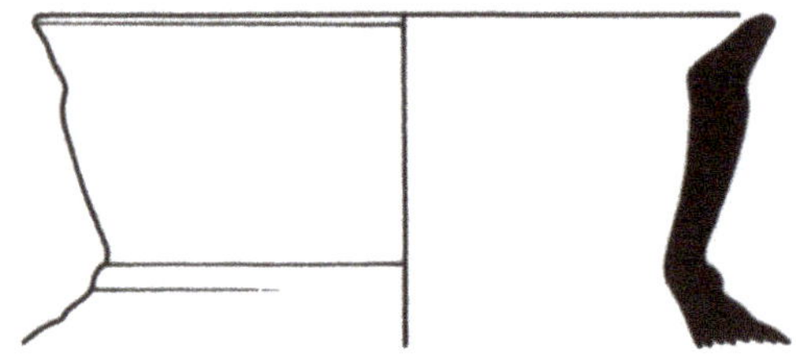

PW 467. CN 2572.
XIA/B 1.1. Early Roman 1.
Part of wall, rim. PH 0.04; PL 0.065; D rim (est.) 0.09.
White clay 10YR 8/1. Metallic Buff.
Parallels: Herodium (Bar-Nathan 1981: fig. 10.5);
Jerusalem (Geva 1983: fig. 5.4; Machline and
Gadot 2017: fig. 10.18); Machaerus (Loffreda 1996:
fig. 12.30); Samaria (Hennessy 1970: fig. 7.32); Tel
Zahara (Bar-Nathan 2013: fig. 3.3.17).

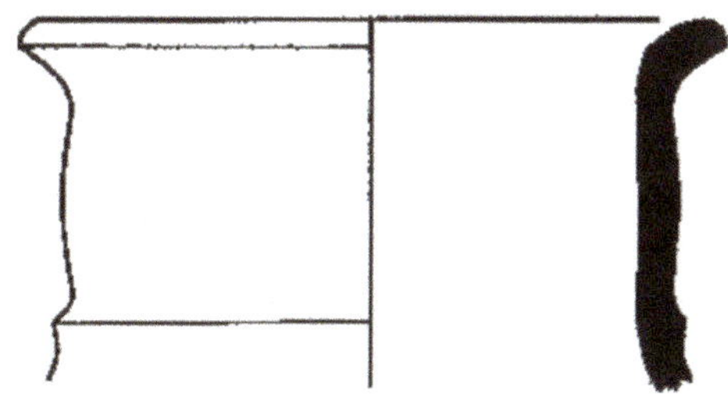

PW 468. CN 2658.
XIA/B 1.2. Early Roman 1.
Part of wall, rim. PH 0.04; D rim (est.) 0.09. Pale
brown clay 10YR 6/3. Metallic Buff.
Parallel: Jerusalem (Geva 1983: fig. 4.2).

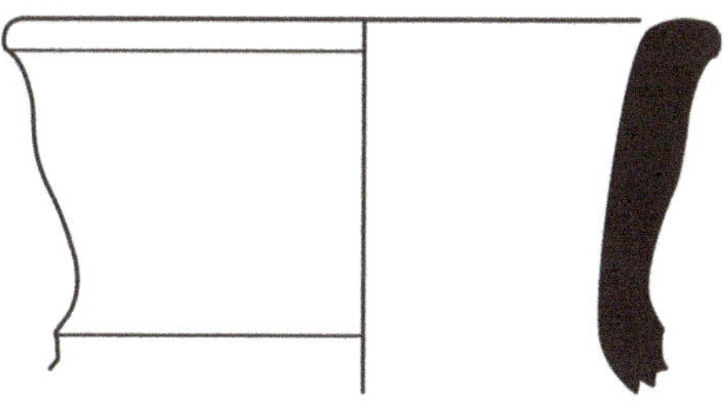

PW 469. CN 2554.
XIA/B 1.1. Early Roman 1.
Part of wall, rim. PH 0.05; PL 0.07; D rim (est.) 0.09.
Pink clay 5YR 7/4. Metallic Buff.
Parallels: Betar (Singer 1993: fig. 2.7); 'En el-Ghuweir
(Bar-Adon 1977: fig. 21.1); Jericho (Pritchard 1958: pl.
58.30); Jerusalem (Geva and Rosenthal-Heginbottom
2003: pls 6.5.10, early 1st c. AD, 6.10.6, c. 30–70
AD); Machaerus (Corbo and Loffreda 1981: fig.
34.5; Loffreda 1996: fig. 13.19); Marisa (Oren and
Rappaport 1984: fig. 13.3); Ras Abu Ma'aruf (Rapuano
1999: fig. 1.14); Wadi al-Kharrar (Abu Shmeis and
Waheeb 2002: fig. 2.9).

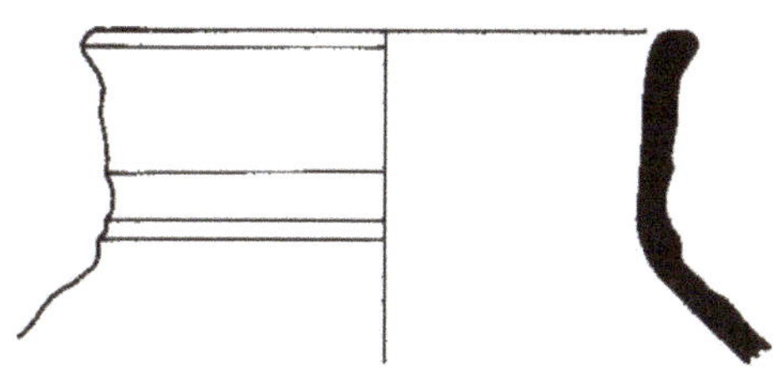

PW 470. CN 2571.
XIA/B 1.1. Early Roman 1.
Part of wall, rim. PH 0.055; PL 0.075; D rim (est.)
0.08. Yellowish-brown clay 10YR 5/4. Metallic Buff.
Parallels: Betar (Singer 1993: fig. 2.7); 'Iraq al-Amir
(Zimmerman 2020b: pl. 2.11.7, str.1V–II, early
2nd c.–c. 100 AD); Jerusalem (Tchekhanovets 2013:
fig. 5.7:5, 1st c. BC–70 AD); Tell Nimrin (Dornemann
1990: fig. 3.4); Wadi al-Kharrar (Abu Shmeis and
Waheeb 2002: fig. 2.6).

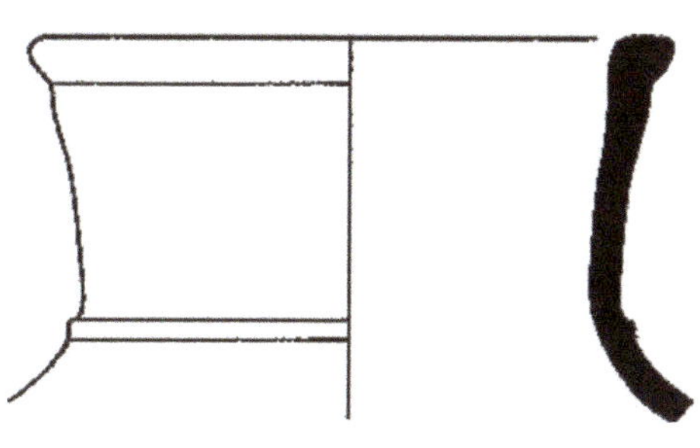

PW 471. CN 2573.
XIA/B 1.1. Early Roman 1.
Part of wall, rim. PH 0.045; PL 0.065; D rim
(est.) 0.095. Very pale brown clay 10YR 8/2.
Metallic Buff.
Parallels: Betar (Singer 1993: fig. 2.4); Scythopolis/
Beth-Shean (Johnson 2006: fig. 15.4.75).

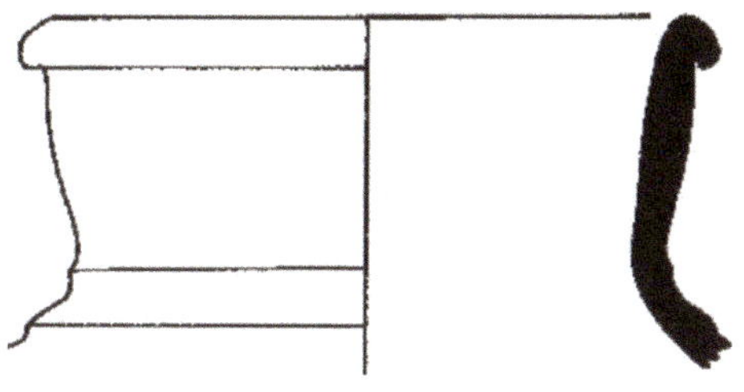

PW 472. CN 2556.
XIA/B 1.1. Early Roman 1.
Part of rim. PH 0.035; PL 0.06; D rim (est.) 0.085.
Very pale brown clay 10YR 8/2. Metallic Buff.

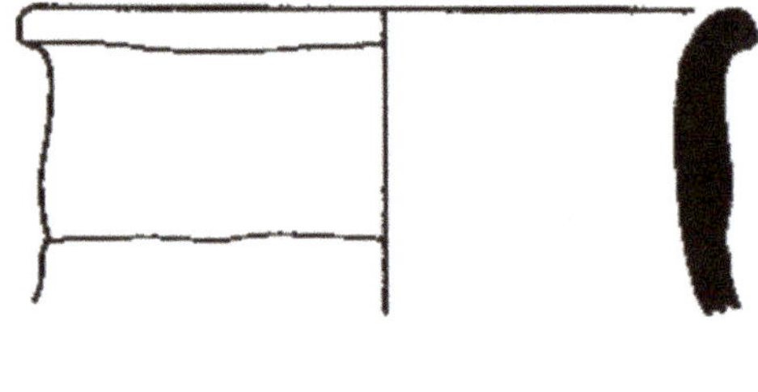

PW 473. CN 2650.
XIA/B 1.1/2. Early Roman 1.
Part of wall, rim. PH 0.04; PL 0.055; D rim
(est.) 0.095. Very pale brown clay 10YR 7/4.
Metallic Buff.

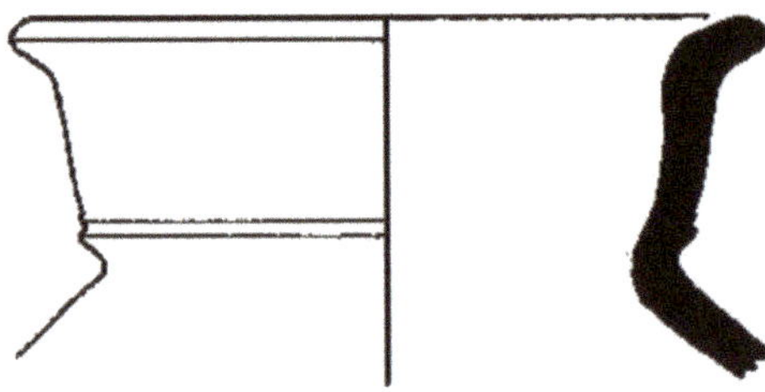

PW 474. CN 2547.
XIA/B 1.1. Early Roman 1.
Part of rim. PH 0.035; PL 0.05; D rim (est.) 0.095.
Yellowish-red clay 5YR 7/6. Metallic Buff.

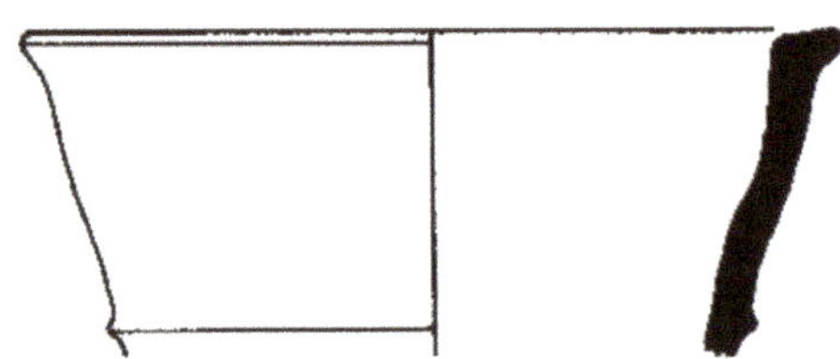

PW 475. CN 6537.
XIA/B 20.7. Early Roman 1.
Part of wall, rim. PH 0.04; PL 0.08; D rim (est.) 0.10.
Pinkish-white clay 7.5YR 8/2. Metallic Buff.
Parallels: Hippos-Sussita (Osband and Eisenberg
2018: pl. 5.1, 1st c. AD/beginning 2nd c.); Machaerus
(Loffreda 1996: fig. 16.8); Tel Michal (Derfler 1989:
fig. 14.3.6, early 1st c. AD–68 AD).

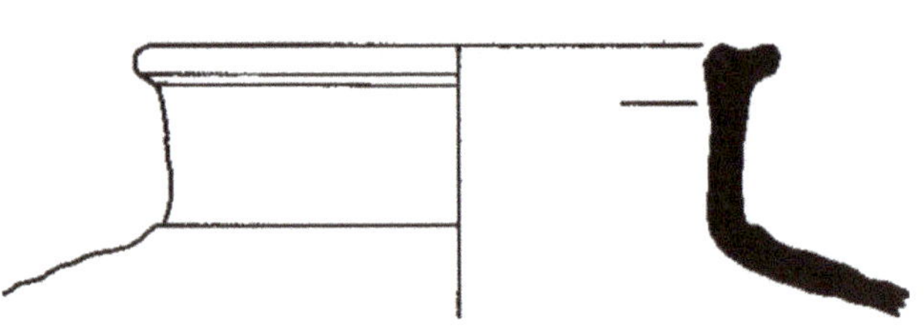

PW 476. CN 6552.
XIA/B 20.6. Early Roman 1.
Part of wall, rim. PH 0.035; D rim (est.) 0.10. Pink
clay 10YR 7/3-8/3. Metallic Buff.
Parallel: Jerusalem (Tushingham 1985: fig. 22.40).

PW 477. CN 2959.
XIA/B 1.4. Early Roman 1.
Part of wall, rim. PH 0.045; PL 0.085; D rim
(est.) 0.09. Brown clay 7.5YR 5/4. Mottled slip. Pink-
slipped Coarse Ware.
Parallel: Gezer (Gitin 1990: pl. 36.25, mid-2nd c. BC).

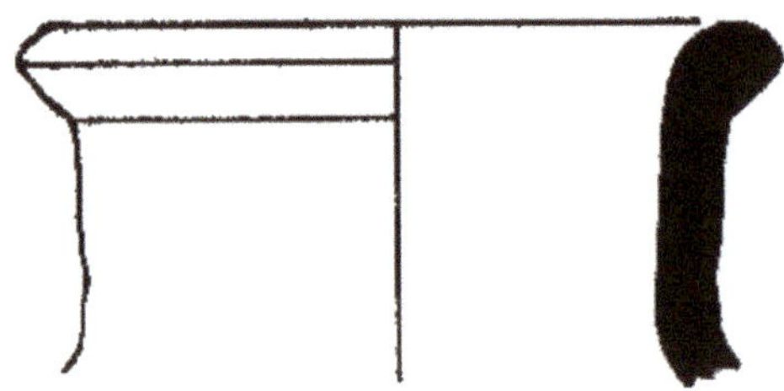

PW 478. CN 2570.
XIA/B 1.1. Early Roman 1.
Part of rim. PH 0.035; PL 0.085; D rim (est.) 0.10.
Very pale brown clay 10YR 7/4. Metallic Buff.
Parallel: Nahal David (Avigad 1962: fig. 5.3).

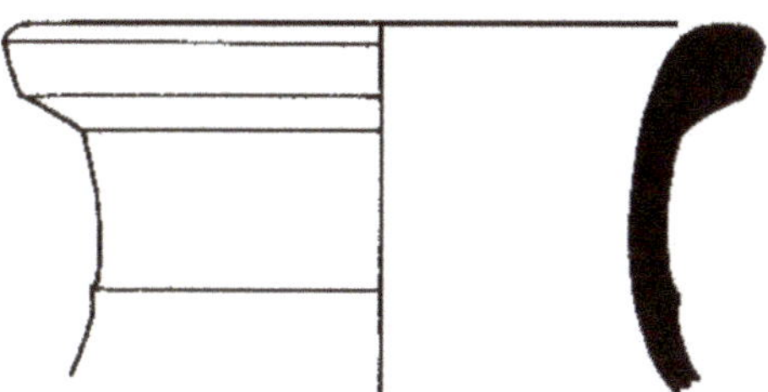

PW 479. CN 2630.
XIA/B 1.5. Early Roman 1.
Part of wall, rim. PH 0.05; D rim (est.) 0.10. Brown
clay 7.5YR 5/4. Pink-slipped Coarse Ware.

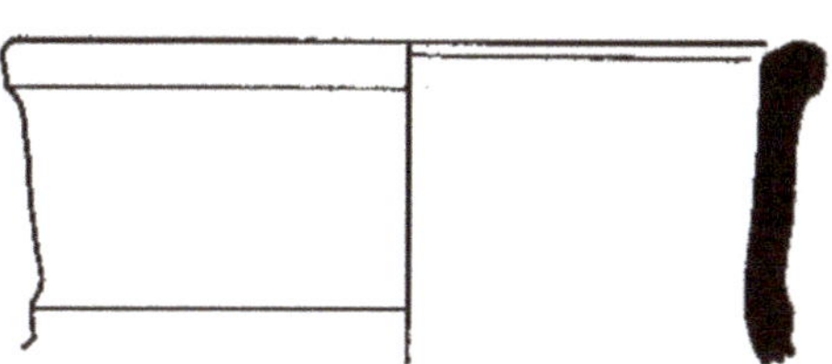

PW 480. CN 2657.
XIA/B 1.1/2. Early Roman 1.
Part of wall, rim. PH 0.035; PL 0.04; D rim
(est.) 0.095. Yellowish-brown clay 10YR 5/4. Pale
brown slip over exterior. Metallic Buff.

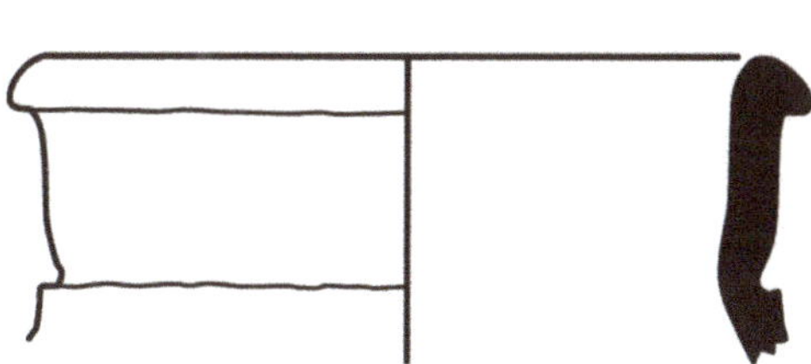

PW 481. CN 6618.
XIA/B 4.6. Early Roman 1.
Part of rim. PH 0.045; PL 0.075; D rim (est.) 0.10.
Yellowish-red clay 5YR 5/8. Pale brown slip over
exterior. Metallic Buff.
Parallels: Jerusalem (Geva and Rosenthal-Heginbottom
2003: pl. 6.10.8, c. 30–70 AD); Madaba (Ferguson 2014:
179–80, fig. 5.3, c. 15 BC–106 AD); Tell Zira'a (Kenkel
2020: 85, 180–1, pl. 1.32, Am23.3d).

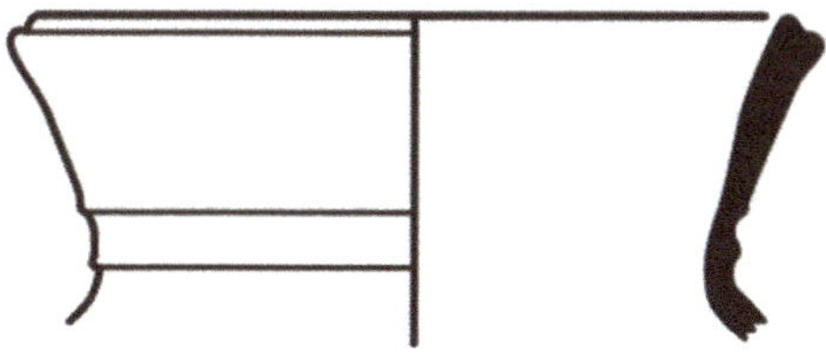

PW 482. CN 3055.
XIA/B 2.3. Early Roman 1.
Part of wall, rim. PH 0.06; D rim (est.) 0.10. Reddish-
yellow clay 5YR 6/6. Pale brown slip over exterior.
Metallic Buff.

PW 483. CN 6759.
XIA/B 10.3. Mixed Context.
Part of rim. PH 0.05; D rim (est.) 0.09. Yellowish-red
clay 5YR 5/8. Metallic Buff.
Parallels: 'En Gedi (Hirschfeld 2000: fig. 24.4);
Hesban (Gerber 2012: 256, fig. 3.20.11); Jerusalem
(Tchekhanovets 2013: fig. 5.7:5, 1st c. BC–70 AD).

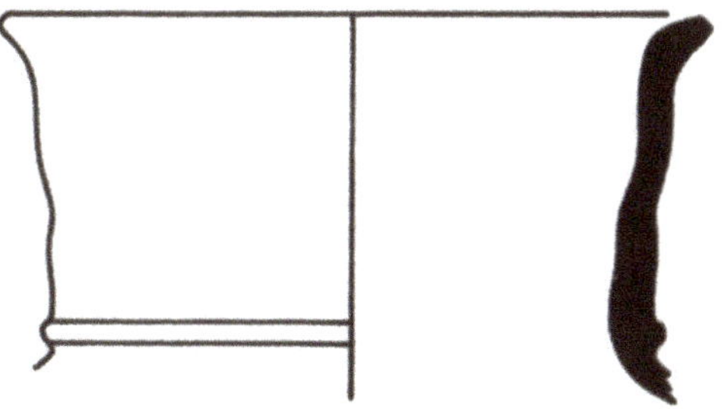

Pithoi (PW 484–487)

The rims of three large storage jars – pithoi – have been recovered from third-century BC levels on Tell Husn (**PW 484–6**) with a fourth from a Hellenistic 3B/3C occupation deposit, also on Husn (**PW 487**), and a further uncatalogued example from a Jannaeus Destruction level on the main mound. All have a very short neck and thickened convex rim. Interestingly, they are of diverse coarse fabrics, suggesting that a variety of clay sources (presumably local) were used.

Table 2.36. Distribution of pithoi by phases, wares.

PHASE		2B c. 220–c. 200 BC	3B/3C c. 140–c. 80/79 BC	3C c. 100 (?)–c. 80/79 BC
		3	1	(1)
Ware	Miscellaneous	3	1	0

PW 484. CN 7679.
XXXIVB 27.30. Hellenistic 2B.
Part of wall, rim. PH 0.06; PL 0.165; D rim (est.) 0.27.
Yellowish-brown clay 10YR 5/6.

PW 485. CN 7680.
XXXIVB 27.21. Hellenistic 2B.
Part of shoulder, rim. PH 0.075; PL 0.09; D rim (est.) 0.32. Very pale brown clay 10YR 7/4.

PW 486. CN 7661.
XXXIVB 27.22. Hellenistic 2B.
Part of shoulder, rim. PH 0.09; PL 0.185; D rim (est.) 0.26. Reddish-brown clay 7.5YR 6/6.

PW 487. CN 7573.
XXXIVB 28.2. Hellenistic 3B/3C.
Part of wall, rim. PH 0.06; PL 0.095; D rim (est.) 0.26.
Reddish-yellow clay 5YR 4/6.

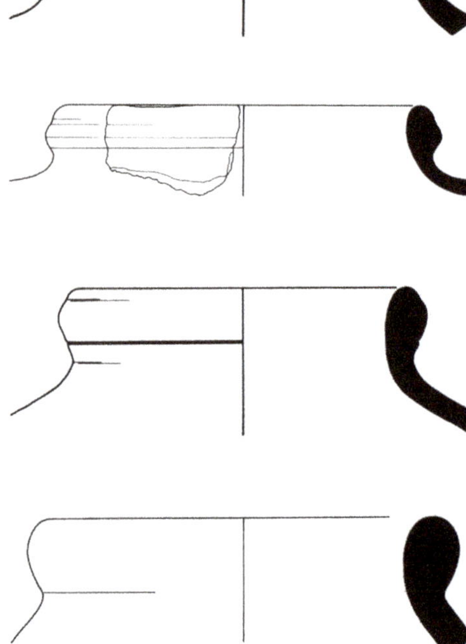

COOKING VESSELS

Most of the almost two hundred cooking vessels (**PW 488–671**) recovered from the Hellenistic and Early Roman levels at Pella represent two distinct ceramic traditions: those of the Levant (cooking pots with globular or sack-like bodies); and of mainland Greece (casseroles or open cooking bowls). With the notable exception of the "Galilean" (Type 7) vessels, the great majority of the globular/sack-like cooking pots are of Metallic Coarse Terracotta ware; the casseroles and cooking bowls, on the other hand, show much more variety in their fabrics.

Cooking pots (PW 488–619)

Cooking pot Types 1–8 comprise the most common form of Hellenistic cooking vessel – a deep, closed vessel of globular shape, generally rounded resting surface and two handles that run from shoulder to the upper part of the short vertical or everted rim. The shape derives from the common form of cooking vessel seen in the Persian period in Palestine (Stern 1982: 100–2, 199) and is particularly suitable for slow cooking where water loss needs to be kept to a minimum (Berlin 1993: 41). Although these latter cookpots are clearly related to an earlier Iron IIC form encountered throughout the southern Levant (for example, Amiran 1969: pl. 76, nos 15–17; Bienkowski 2015: pl. 3.6.2, nos 5–6; Gilboa 2015: pl. 3.1.3, nos 4, 7–8), it is worth noting that a somewhat similar shape – the *chytra* – is seen in Athenian cooking ware of the sixth century BC onwards (Hannestad 1983: 63; Sparkes and Talcott 1970: 224–6). The *chytra*, however, more commonly has one handle rather than two.

Not surprisingly, the Early Hellenistic (that is, third-century BC) cooking pots from sites such as Tel Anafa (Berlin 1997a: 85, the two "neckless" varieties PW 178–83, 184–6), Tel Dor (Guz-Zilberstein 1995: 298, fig. 6.17:1–7, Type CP 1) and Gezer (Gitin 1990: Type 154) are close to their Persian-period ancestors, but by the second century BC a wide variety of rim forms is seen throughout the southern Levant. It is these relatively minor variations in rim form that often constitute the basis for the separation of the cooking vessels into various types.

During Late Hellenistic and Early Roman times more open cook-ware shapes, such as the casserole (suitable for braised meals or stews) and the pan (less common), take a more prominent place in the ceramic assemblage of the Levant indicating "an expansion in local cooking practices" (Berlin 2015: 636) and implying a "widening palate of the local inhabitants to new tastes and foods" (Sandhaus 2020: 115). Nevertheless, the closed cooking pot remains a major form in the Roman and Byzantine East. In these later periods, the cooking pot's walls are often appreciably thinner than they are in Hellenistic times.

Table 2.37. Distribution of cooking pots by types, wares, phases.

		SIMPLE RIM (TYPE 1)	FLARED RIM (TYPE 2)	LEDGE RIM (TYPE 3)	CONCAVE RIM (TYPE 4)	BEVELLED RIM (TYPE 5)	GROOVED RIM (TYPE 6)	"GALILEAN" (TYPE 7)	THICKENED LIP (TYPE 8)
Ware	Metallic Coarse Terracotta	31	3	25	24	25	5	0	9
	"Galilean"	0	0	0	0	0	0	3	0
	Miscellaneous	0	0	2	0	2	1	2	0
Phase	2B c. 220–c. 200 BC	0 (3)	0	0	1 (1)	0	0	0	0
	3A c. 200–c. 140 BC	8 (18)	0	6	2	0	0	0	0
	3B c. 140–c. 100 (?) BC	1	0	1 (3)	0	0 (1)	1	0	0
	3B/3C c. 140–c. 80/79 BC	1	0	1	1	2	0	0	0
	3C c. 100 (?)–c. 80/79 BC	4 (7)	0	13 (8)	5 (1)	2	0	1	1
	Early Roman 63 BC–c. 135 AD	10 (8) 1 (ER2)	1	1	11	19 (10)	4 (2)	4	8
	Mixed	6 (7)	2	5 (1)	4 (6)	4 (5)	1	0	0

Globular; tall everted neck; simple rim (Type 1)

This type (**PW 488–518**) has a tall, slightly everted, neck. The shape is seen in the Persian period in Palestine (Gitin 1990: 79, pl. 31.14–15, Type 154B) and is also one of the major Hellenistic cooking pot forms at Hesban (Gerber 2012: 190–6, figs 3.4.17–29; 3.5) and at Gezer (Gitin 1990: Type 235), where it is present in an "early mid-second century BC horizon" (Gitin 1990: 256). At Pella the type is seen in early second-century BC levels (Hellenistic 3A) on the main mound and continues throughout later Hellenistic and Early Roman phases on both the main mound and Husn.

In the second-century examples from Pella, the lip is usually slightly flattened with a tendency to become more rounded or pointed, and the neck more upright, on those vessels from the Jannaeus Destruction (Hellenistic 3C) and Early Roman levels; a similar progression is seen at Tel Anafa where cooking pots of the "necked pointed rim form" are especially common in Roman 1A and 1B horizons (Berlin 1997a: 87–9, PW 187–90). These later examples can be compared with Loffreda's Group 36 from Machaerus, examples of which were found in both Hasmonean and Herodian contexts (Loffreda 1996: 71–2, figs 27.10–14, 18–32).

The fragmentary nature of the Pella vessels makes any comment about body shape tentative but **PW 488, PW 498–9** demonstrate a strongly globular profile, with **PW 516–7** suggesting that this feature continues on at least some cooking pots into the Early Roman phase.

PW 488. CN 7492.

XXVIIIB 13.16. Hellenistic 3A.

Part of wall, rim, handle. PH 0.01; D rim (est.) 0.15.
Red clay 2.5YR 6/6. Metallic Coarse Terracotta.
Globular upper wall. Strap handle from rim to shoulder.
Parallels: Amman/Philadelphia (Zayadine 1977–78:
fig. 15.403); Gezer (Gitin 1990: pl. 44.4, mid-1st
c. BC); Jaffa (Tsuf 2018: fig. 9.20.372); Marisa (Kloner
and Hess 1985: fig. 2.23); Shechem (N.L. Lapp 1964:
fig. 3.17); Tel Dor (Guz-Zilberstein 1995: fig. 6.17:2,
375–250 BC); Tel Yoqne'am (Avissar 1996: fig. X.3.3),
Tell Nimrin (Dornemann 1990: fig. 3.23).

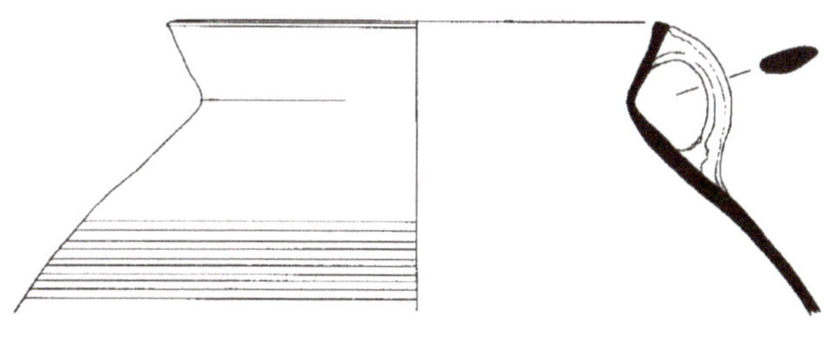

PW 489. CN 7317.

XXVIIIB 13.2. Hellenistic 3A.

Part of wall, rim, handle. PH 0.06; D rim (est.) 0.115.
Weak red clay 2.5YR 5/4. Metallic Coarse Terracotta.
Strap handle from shoulder to rim.
Parallels: Jerusalem (Tchekhanovets 2013: fig. 5.1:10,
1st c. BC–70 AD); Marisa (Kloner and Hess 1985: fig.
3.1); Tel 'Ira (Fischer and Tal 1999b: fig. 6.128.12);
Tell Zira'a (Kenkel 2020: 53, 152–3, pl. 1.18; Kt2.1).

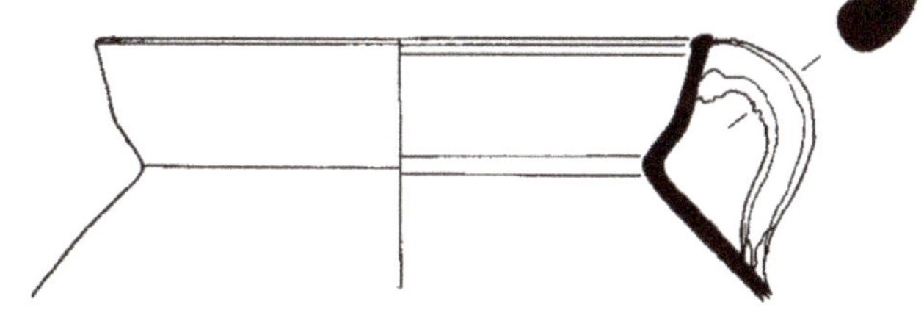

PW 490. CN 7491.

XXVIIIB 13.16. Hellenistic 3A.

Part of wall, rim. PH 0.04; D rim (est.) 0.10. Red clay
2.5YR 5/6. Metallic Coarse Terracotta.
Parallels: 'Akko–Ptolemais (Dothan 1976: fig. 30.14;
Regev 2009/10: fig. 28.152); Madaba (Ferguson 2014:
184, fig. 6.29, c. 129–100 BC); Sepphoris (Balouka 2013:
pl. 1.3, 2nd–1st c. BC); Shechem (N.L. Lapp 1964: fig.
3.6); Tel Dor (Guz-Zilberstein 1995: fig. 6.60:26, 275–200
BC?).

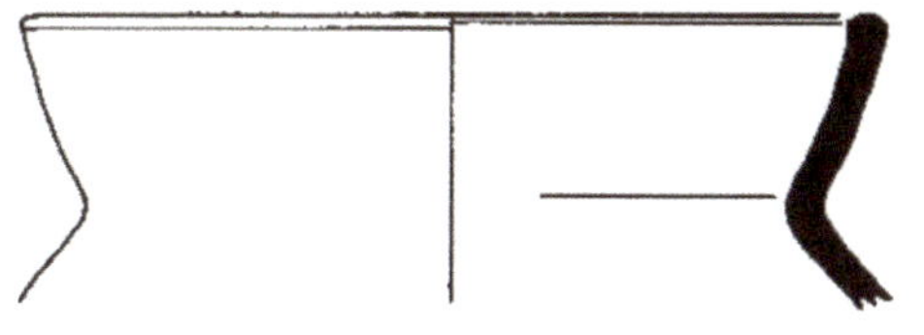

PW 491. CN 7464.

XXVIIIB 13.9. Hellenistic 3A.

Part of wall, rim, handle. PH 0.055; D rim
(est.) 0.135. Reddish-yellow clay 5YR 6/6. Metallic
Coarse Terracotta.
Strap handle from lip to shoulder.

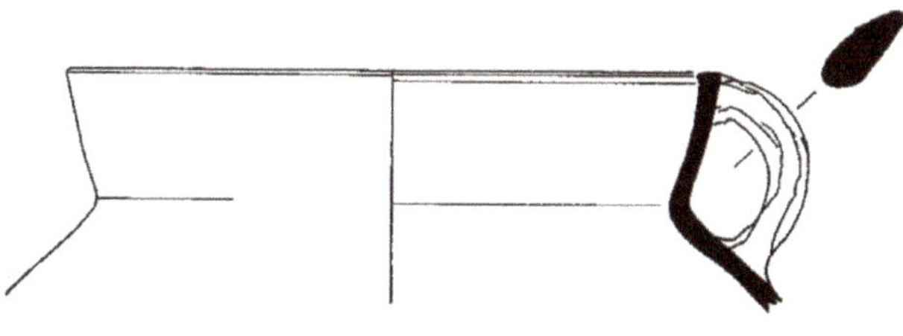

PW 492. CN 7438.

XXVIIIB 13.3. Hellenistic 3A.

Part of wall, rim. PH 0.05; D rim (est.) 0.105. Red
clay 2.5YR 6/6. Metallic Coarse Terracotta.
Parallel: Madaba (Ferguson 2014: 184, fig. 6.26,
c. 100–63 BC).

PW 493. CN 7502.
XXVIIIB 13.17. Hellenistic 3A.
Part of wall, rim, handle. PH 0.05; D rim (est.) 0.15. Reddish-yellow clay 5YR 6/6. Metallic Coarse Terracotta.
Strap handle from rim to shoulder.

PW 494. CN 7222.
XXVIIIB 10.2. Hellenistic 3A.
Part of wall, rim, handle. PH 0.065; D rim (est.) 0.15. Red clay 2.5YR 5/8. Metallic Coarse Terracotta.
Parallels: Kedesh (Levantine Ceramics Project: n.d. RN K08P267, 2nd c. BC); Madaba (Ferguson 2014: 184, fig. 6.27, c. 100–63 BC).

PW 495. CN 7437.
XXVIIIB 13.3. Hellenistic 3A.
Part of wall, rim. PH 0.045; D rim (est.) 0.105. Red clay 2.5YR 5/8. Metallic Coarse Terracotta.
Parallels: Tel Keisan (Briend 1980: pl. 11.3); Tel Michal (Fischer 1989: fig. 13.3.13, 1st c. BC: Alexander Jannaeus).

PW 496. CN 7083.
XXIIIA 109.4. Hellenistic 3B.
Part of rim. PH 0.025; D rim (est.) 0.12. Dark red clay 2.5YR 4/8. Metallic Coarse Terracotta.

PW 497. CN 7780.
XXIIID 22.1. Hellenistic 3C.
Part of wall, rim. PH 0.05; PL 0.06; D rim (est.) 0.11. Red clay 2.5YR 6/8. Metallic Coarse Terracotta.

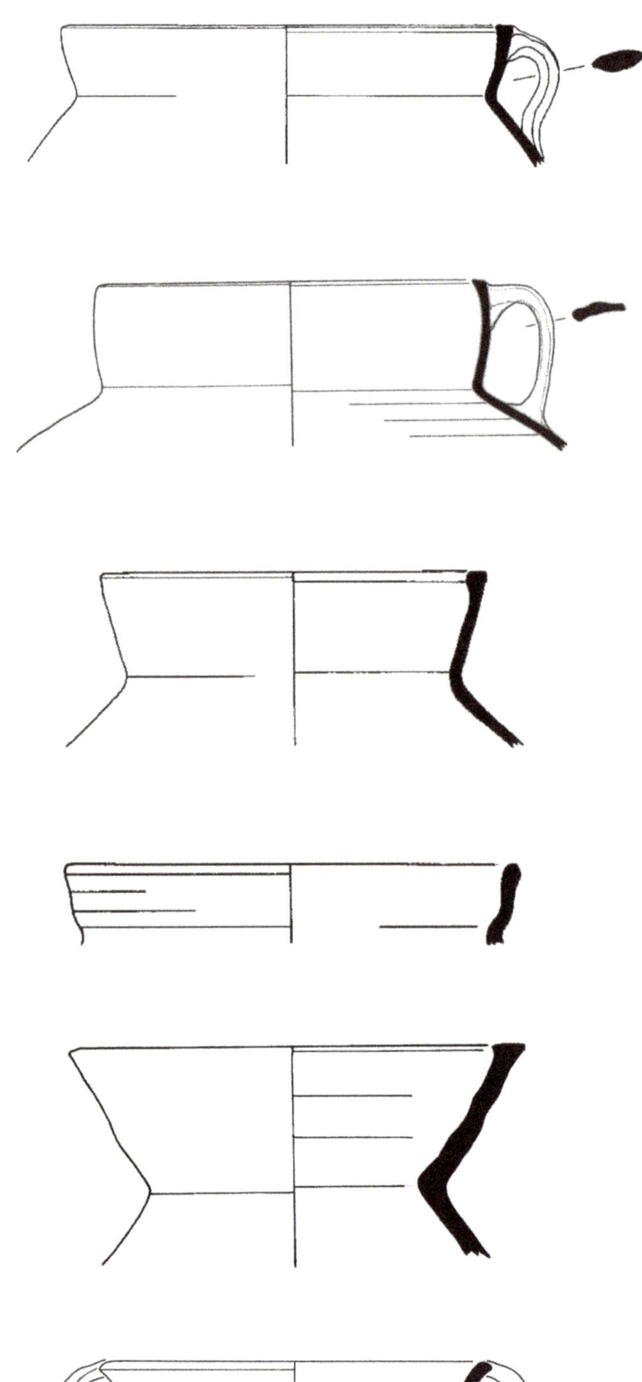

PW 498. CN 7139.
IVD 10.12. Hellenistic 3C.
Part of wall, rim, handle. PH 0.12; D rim (est.) 0.18. Red clay 2.5YR 5/6. Metallic Coarse Terracotta.
Globular body with faint ribbing. Centrally ribbed strap handle from rim to shoulder.
Parallels: Esdraela (Grey 2014: fig. 2.5, labelled as "bowl"); Hippos-Sussita (Osband and Eisenberg 2018: pl. 3.2.7, 1st c. BC); Marisa (Levine 2003: fig. 6.6.74); Shechem (N.L. Lapp 2008: pl. 3.38.15, 250–190 BC).

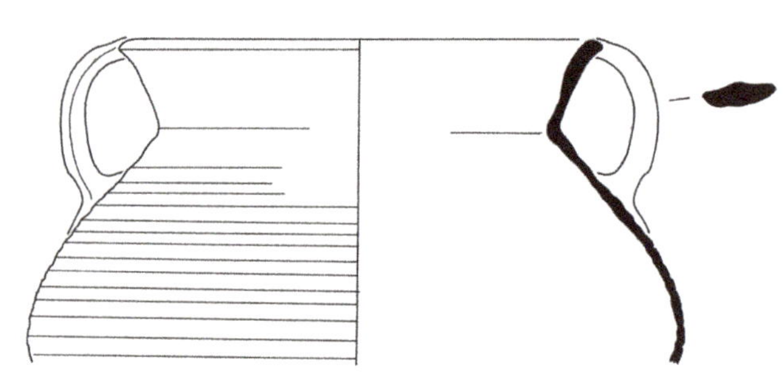

PW 499. CN 0089.
IIIB/C 1.3. Hellenistic 3C.
Missing part of wall. H 0.17; D rim 0.095. Red clay
2.5YR 5/6. Metallic Coarse Terracotta.
Globular body. Flat resting surface. Two strap handles
from shoulder to rim.
Parallels: Machaerus (Loffreda 1980: pl. 95.19); Tell
Nimrin (Dornemann 1990: fig. 3.22).

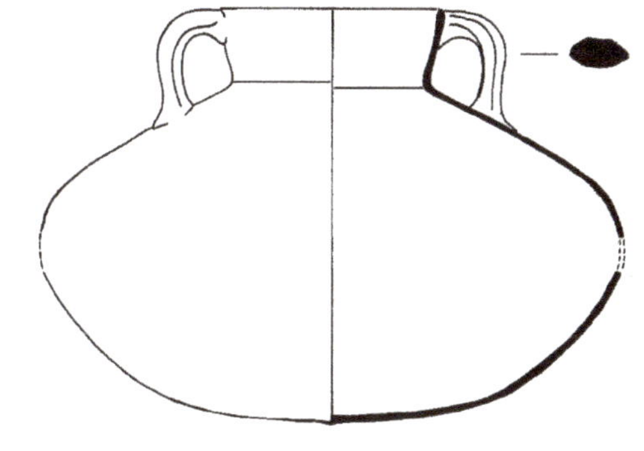

PW 500. CN 6579.
IVD 10.12. Hellenistic 3C.
Part of wall, rim, handle. PH 0.07; D rim (est.) 0.13.
Red clay 2.5YR 5/8. Metallic Coarse Terracotta.
Strap handle from shoulder to rim.
Parallels: ʿAkko-Ptolemais (Dothan 1976: fig. 30.13);
Ashdod (Dothan 1971: fig. 24.1).

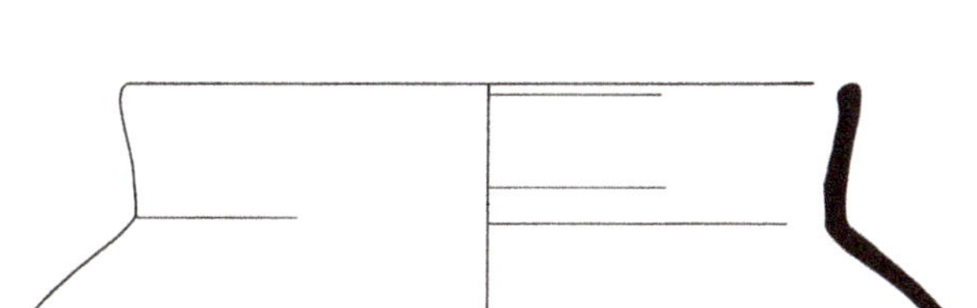

PW 501. CN 7590.
XXXIVB 29.5. Hellenistic 3B/3C.
Part of wall, rim. PH 0.06; PL 0.065; D rim (est.)
0.125. Red clay 2.5YR 5/8. Metallic Coarse Terracotta.
Parallels: ʿIraq al-Amir (Zimmerman 2020b: pl.
2.19.5, str. IV, early 2nd c. BC); Jerusalem (Geva
2003: pl. 5.3.2, late 2nd–1st c. BC); Shaʿar ha-Amakim
(Mlynarczyk 2000: pl. 120b.4).

PW 502. CN 7154.
XXXIVB 5.40. Mixed Context.
Part of wall, rim. PH 0.075; D rim (est.) 0.105.
Reddish-yellow clay 5YR 6/8. Metallic Coarse
Terracotta.
Parallels: Ashdod (Dothan 1971: fig. 61.13); Gadara/
Umm Qais (Kerner 1997: fig. 12.15); Jerusalem
(Strange 1975: fig. 14.12 upper profile; Tchekhanovets
2013: fig. 5.1:10, 1st c. BC–70 AD); Tel Yoqneʿam (Ben-
Tor et al. 1983: fig. 7.10).

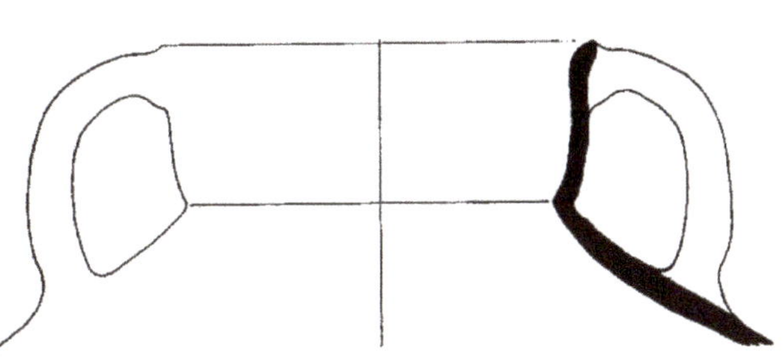

PW 503. CN 7353.
XXXIVB 6.27. Early Roman 1.
Part of wall, rim, handle. PL 0.015; PH 0.075; D rim
(est.) 0.095. Yellowish-red 5YR 5/8. Metallic Coarse
Terracotta.
Strap handle from shoulder to rim.

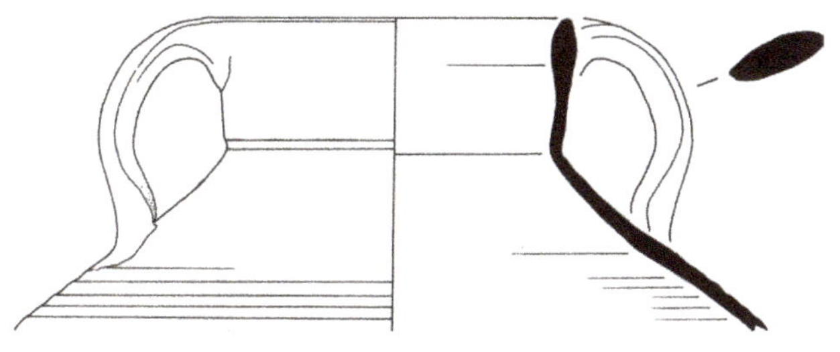

PW 504. CN 7641.

XXXIVB 150.3. Mixed Context.

Part of rim, wall, handle. PH 0.045; PL 0.08; D rim (est.) 0.12. Red clay 2.5YR 5/8. Metallic Coarse Terracotta.

Strap handle from rim to shoulder.

Parallels: 'Akko-Ptolemais (Berlin and Stone 2016: fig. 9.5.1, 3rd c. BC); Gamla (Berlin 2006: fig. 2.10.6, upper profile, 1st c. BC/early 1st c. AD); Hesban (Gerber 2012: 193, fig. 3.5.9); Jerusalem (Sandhaus 2013: fig. 4.9:6, second half of 2nd c. BC); Sepphoris (Balouka 2013: pl. 1.1, 2nd–1st c. BC); Tel Zahara (Bar-Nathan and Gärtner 2013: fig. 3.13.111).

PW 505. CN 6693.

IIIP 25.13. Mixed Context.

Part of wall, rim, handle. PH 0.05; D rim (est.) 0.10. Very dark grey clay 5YR 3/1. Metallic Coarse Terracotta.

Strap handle from rim to shoulder.

Parallels: Gezer (Gitin 1990: pl. 32.21, mid-3rd c. BC); Marisa (Kloner and Hess 1985: fig. 3.1).

PW 506. CN 7275.

XXIIIA 21.3. Mixed Context.

Part of wall, rim. PH 0.055; D rim (est.) 0.17. Reddish-yellow clay 5YR 6/8. Metallic Coarse Terracotta.

Parallels: Gezer (Gitin 1990: pl. 35.15, early–mid-2nd c. BC); Kedesh (Levantine Ceramics Project: n.d. K08P108, mid–late 2nd c. BC); Marisa (Oren and Rappaport 1984: fig. 13.18); Shechem (N.L. Lapp 1964: fig. 3.6); Tel Keisan (Briend 1980: pl. 11.3a).

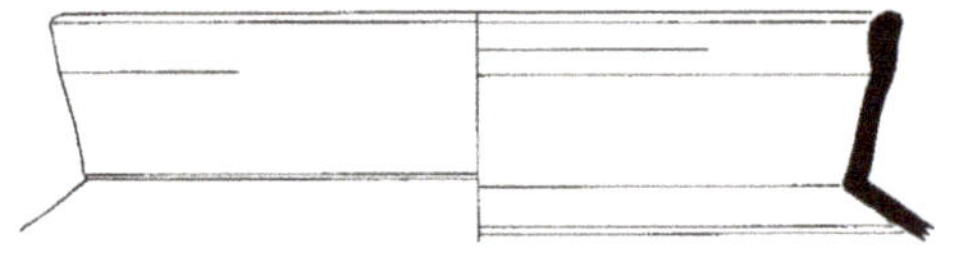

PW 507. CN 7051.

XXIIIA 110.1. Mixed Context.

Part of rim, body, handle. PH 0.045; D rim (est.) 0.15. Red clay 2.5YR 5/6. Metallic Coarse Terracotta.

Strap handle from rim to shoulder.

Parallels: Jerusalem (Geva 2003: pl. 5.6.36, 2nd c. BC); Kallirhoe (Clamer 1997: pl. 4.11); Tel Keisan (Briend 1980: pl. 11.3b, late 4th–mid-2nd c. BC); Tel Michal (Fischer 1989: fig. 13.3.19, 1st c. BC: Alexander Jannaeus).

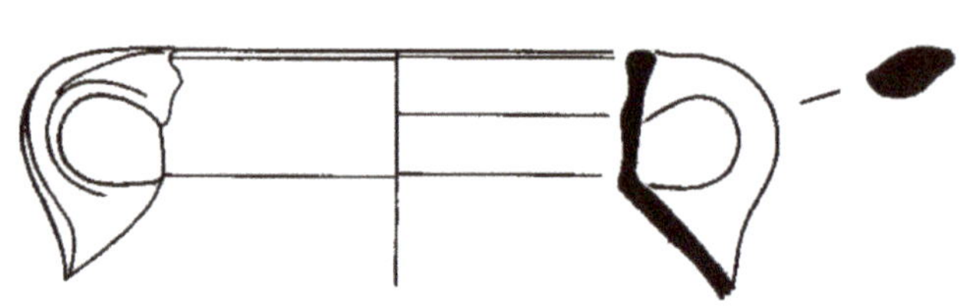

PW 508. CN 7153.
XXXIVB 5.40. Mixed Context.
Part of shoulder, rim. PH 0.035; D rim (est.) 0.165.
Yellow clay 10YR 7/8. Metallic Coarse Terracotta.
Parallels: Amman/Philadelphia (Zayadine 1977–78:
fig. 15.403); Jerusalem (Tushingham 1985: fig. 19.3);
Shechem (N.L. Lapp 2008: pl. 3.40.11, 190–150 BC).

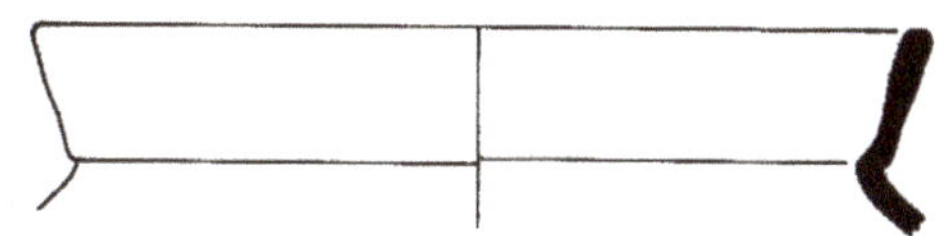

PW 509. CN 2968.
XIA/B 1.5. Early Roman 1.
Part of wall, rim, handle. PH 0.07; D rim (est.) 0.16.
Red clay 2.5YR 5/8. Metallic Coarse Terracotta.
Strap handle from rim to shoulder.
Parallels: Jericho (Netzer and Meyers 1977: fig. 6.6);
Jerusalem (Tushingham 1985: fig. 24.5); Samaria
(Crowfoot et al. 1957: fig. 41.1, c. 200–150 BC);
Tel Anafa (Berlin 1997a: pl. 21.PW 186, 125–? BC
residual).

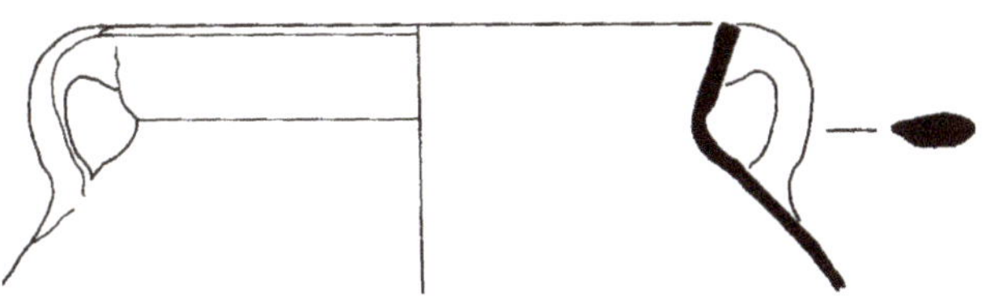

PW 510. CN 2626.
XIA/B 1.5. Early Roman 1.
Part of wall, rim. PH 0.05; D rim (est.) 0.085. Red
clay 2.5YR 5/8. Metallic Coarse Terracotta.
Parallels: Jerusalem (Strange 1975: fig. 14.12);
Machaerus (Loffreda 1996: fig. 27.29).

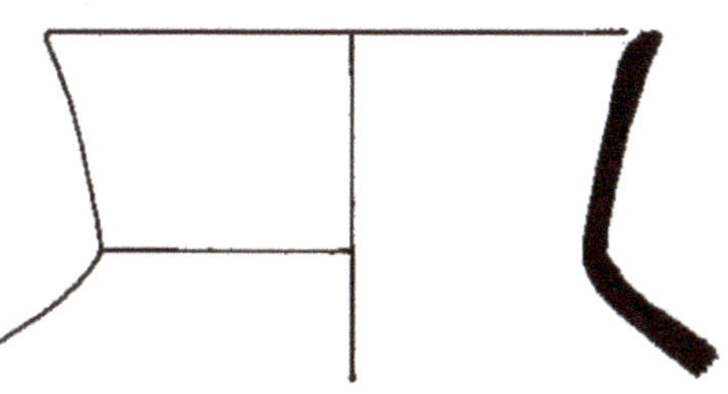

PW 511. CN 2653.
XIA/B 1.1/2. Early Roman 1.
Part of body, rim. PH 0.36; D rim (est.) 0.09. Red clay
2.5YR 5/6. Metallic Coarse Terracotta.
Parallels: Amman/Philadelphia (Zayadine 1977–78:
fig. 15.403); Gezer (Gitin 1990: pl. 44.4, mid-1st
c. BC); Jericho (Netzer and Meyers 1977: fig. 6.7);
Marisa (Oren and Rappaport 1984: fig. 13.18); Samaria
(Crowfoot et al. 1957: fig. 43.13, c. 150–108 BC); Tel
Dor (Guz-Zilberstein 1995: fig. 6.17:2, 375–250 BC);
Tell Nimrin (Dornemann 1990: fig. 3.27).

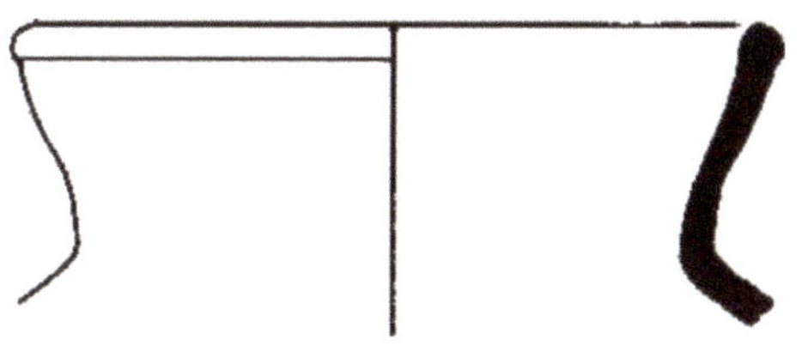

PW 512. CN 2969.
XIA/B 1.5. Early Roman 1.
Part of wall, rim, handle. PH 0.045; PL 0.075; D rim
(est.) 0.09. Yellowish-red clay 5YR 4/6–5/6. Metallic
Coarse Terracotta.
Strap handle from rim to shoulder.
Parallels: Beth-Zur (P.W. Lapp and N.L. Lapp 1958: fig.
2.1); Jerusalem (Geva 2003: pl. 5.8.36, later 2nd–1st
c. BC; Strange 1975: fig. 14.3; Tushingham 1985: fig.
19.3); Wadi Hasa survey (MacDonald 1988: pl. 13.5).

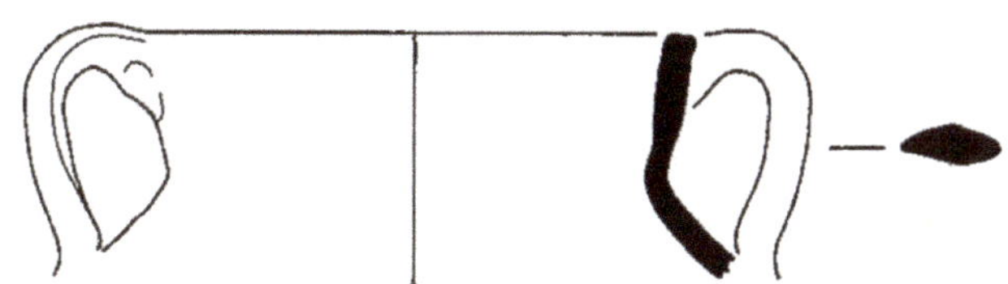

PW 513. CN 3052.
XIA/B 2.2. Early Roman 1.
Part of wall, rim, handle. PH 0.06; D rim (est.) 0.10.
Red clay 2.5YR 5/8. Metallic Coarse Terracotta.
Strap handle from rim to shoulder.
Parallels: Kerak Plateau Survey (Brown 1991:
pl. 6.337); Samaria (Crowfoot et al. 1957: fig. 41.2,
c. 200–150 BC); Tel Keisan (Briend 1980: pl. 11.3a).

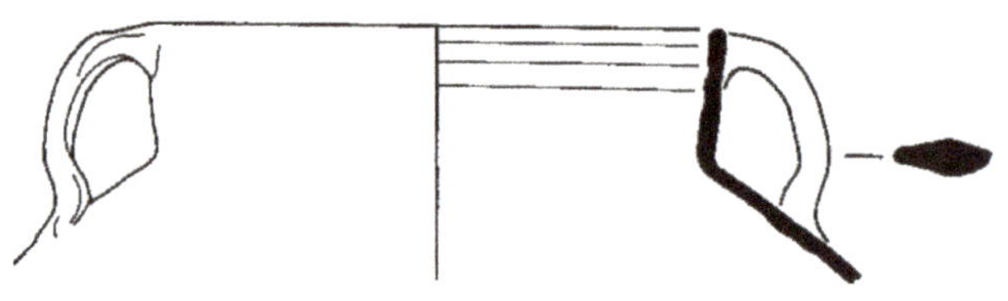

PW 514. CN 2621.
XIA/B 1.1. Early Roman 1.
Part of wall, rim, handle. PH 0.07; D rim (est.)
0.095. Reddish-yellow clay 5YR 7/6. Metallic Coarse
Terracotta.
Strap handle from rim to shoulder.
Parallels: 'Iraq al-Amir (N.L. Lapp 1983: fig. 32.58);
Jerusalem (Strange 1975: fig. 14.21); Tel Anafa
(Berlin 1997a: pl. 21. PW 190, 332–125 BC); Tel Dor
(Guz-Zilberstein 1995: fig. 6.17:3, 200–125 BC); Tel
Yoqne'am (Ben-Tor et al. 1983: fig. 7.10).

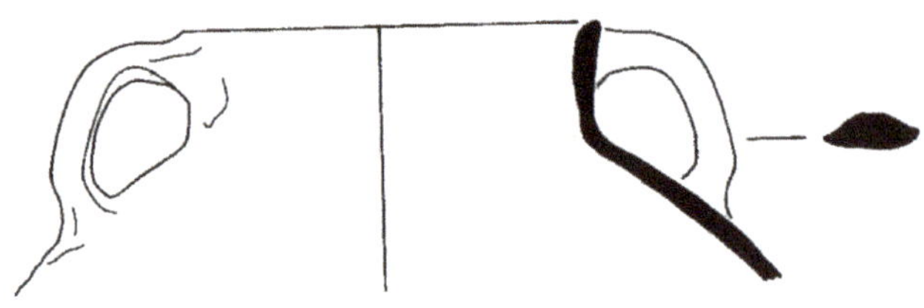

PW 515. CN 3071.
XIA/B 1.5. Early Roman 1.
Part of wall, rim, handle. PH 0.06; D rim (est.) 0.085.
Weak red clay 2.5YR 5/4. Metallic Coarse Terracotta.
Strap handle from rim to shoulder.
Parallels: Gezer (Gitin 1990: pl. 35.15, early–mid-
2nd c. BC); Jerusalem (Machline and Gadot 2017:
fig. 11.1); Kerak Plateau Survey (Brown 1991:
pl. 6.337); Machaerus (Loffreda 1996: fig. 27.26); Tel
Anafa (Berlin 1997a: pl. 21. PW 190, 332–125 BC);
Tell Nimrin (Dornemann 1990: fig. 3.22).

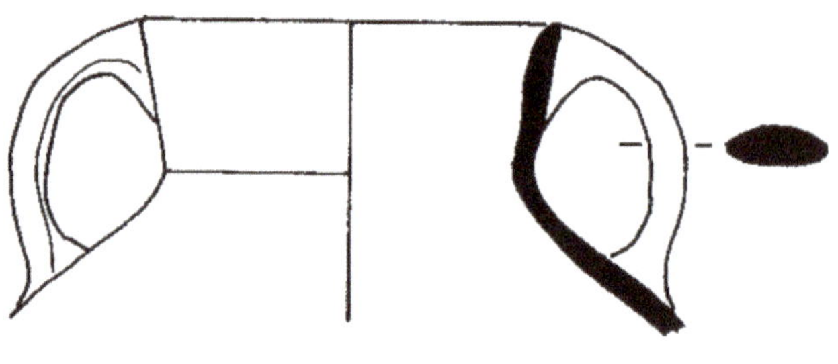

PW 516. CN 2984.
XIA/B 1.2/3. Early Roman 1.
Part of rim, wall, handle. PH 0.04; D rim (est.) 0.09.
Red clay 2.5YR 5/8. Metallic Coarse Terracotta.
Prominent ridges on exterior. Strap handle from rim
to shoulder.
Parallels: Hippos-Sussita (Osband and Eisenberg 2018:
4.1.3, end 1st c. BC/beginning 1st c. AD); Jerusalem
(Geva 2003: pl. 5.10.24, later 2nd–1st c. BC); Meiron
(Meyers et al. 1981: pl. 8.16.7).

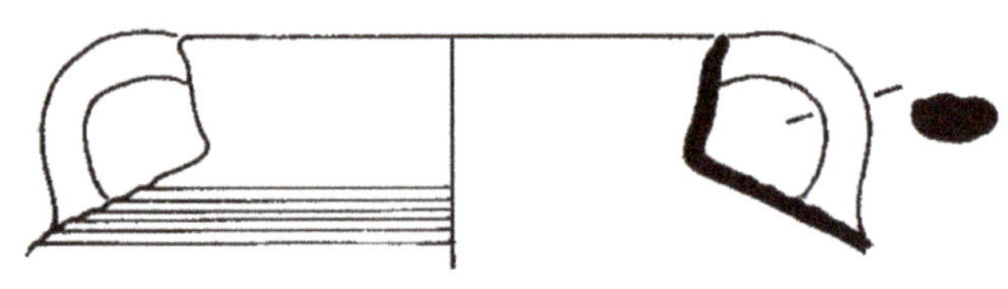

PW 517. CN 2565.
XIA/B 1.1. Early Roman 1.
Part of wall, rim, handle. PH 0.045; D rim (est.) 0.12.
Weak red clay 2,5YR 6/4. Metallic Coarse Terracotta.
Strap handle from rim to shoulder.

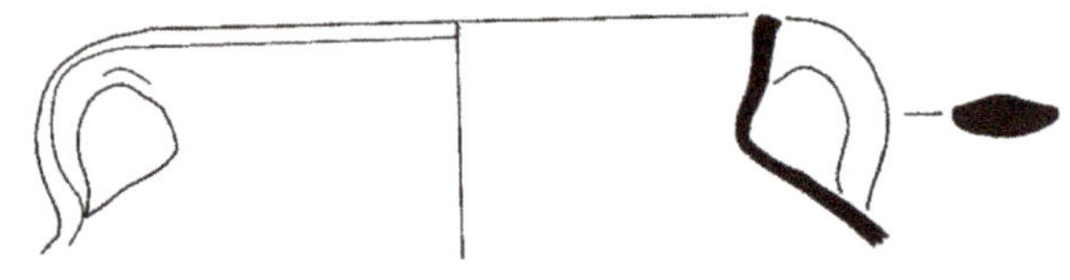

PW 518. CN 6538.
XIA/B 20.5. Early Roman 2.
Part of wall, rim. PH 0.03; PL 0.09; D rim (est.) 0.14.
Dark red clay 2.5YR 4/8. Metallic Coarse Terracotta.
Parallel: ʿAkko-Ptolemais (Berlin and Stone 2016: fig.
9.16.5, mid–late 2nd c. BC).

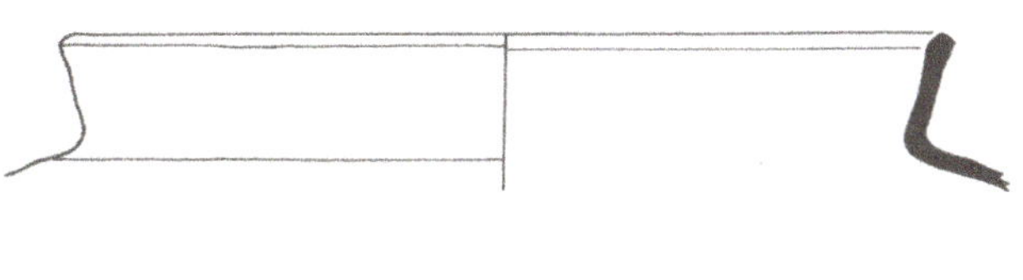

Globular; short flared rim (Type 2)

This form is rare at Pella with only three examples (**PW 519–21**) recovered from the University of Sydney
excavations (all catalogued), of which **PW 520** is from an Early Roman level on Tell Husn with the other two
examples (**PW 519, PW 521**) from unstratified deposits. From Area IX the Wooster team recovered another
specimen from the lower levels of Sounding 9, which Smith and Day dated to "about the first century AD"
(Smith and Day 1989: 98, pl. 45.2).

At Gezer, cooking pots of this form are classified within Gitin's Type 239 (Gitin 1990: 257–8), one of the
major cooking pot forms in the Hellenistic corpus. The type as a whole is seen at Gezer from the mid-second
until the early first century BC; however, the short, flared necks of the Pella vessels find their closest parallels
with Gezer Type 239E, occurring there only in early first-century BC contexts. Other examples were recovered
from Jerusalem in a Late Hellenistic context (Strange 1975: fig. 13.5) and from Late Hasmonean (earlier
first-century BC) levels at Machaerus (Loffreda 1996: Group 35: figs 27.1–9, 15–17). In general, cooking pots
of this form are not common, with none published from Tel Anafa, Gamla or Tel Dor.

PW 519. CN 0493.
IIIB/C 1.22. Mixed Context.
Part of wall, rim. PH 0.02; D rim (est.) 0.19. Yellowish-
red clay 5YR 4/6. Metallic Coarse Terracotta.

PW 520. CN 7351.
XXXIVB 6.27. Early Roman 1.
Part of wall, rim. PH 0.03; D (est.) 0.18. Yellowish-red
clay 5YR 5/6. Metallic Coarse Terracotta.
Parallels: Betar (Singer 1993: fig. 1.10); Hippos-Sussita
(Osband and Eisenberg 2018: pl. 4.2.10, end 1st c.
BC/beginning 1st c. AD); Jerusalem (Geva 2014: pl.
19.2.17; Tushingham 1985: fig. 22.32); Machaerus
(Loffreda 1996: fig. 27.6); southern Ghors and north-
east ʿArabah survey (MacDonald 1992: pl. 21.11);
Ziqim (Zissu and Rokach 1999: fig. 5.14).

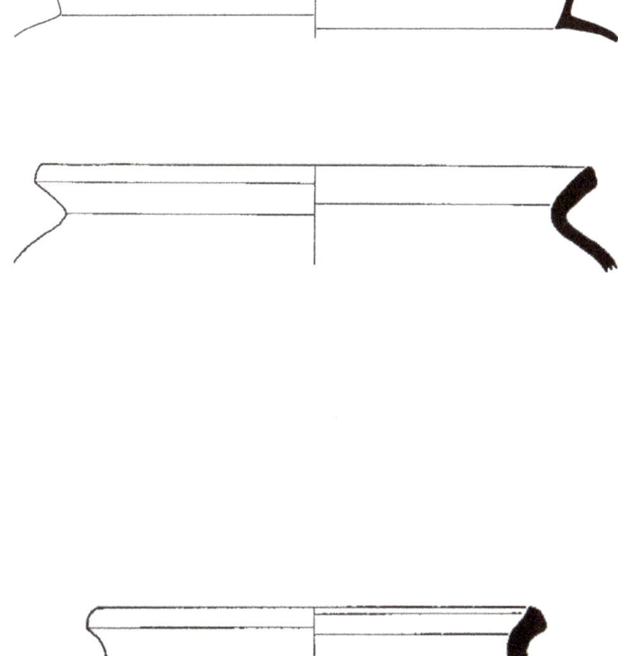

PW 521. CN 7358.
XXXIVB 8.22. Mixed Context.
Part of wall, rim. PH 0.02; PL 0.05; D rim (est.) 0.12.
Dark red clay 2.5YR 4/8. Metallic Coarse Terracotta.
Parallels: Hippos-Sussita (Osband and Eisenberg
2018: pl. 4.2.34, end 1st c. BC/beginning 1st c. AD);
Jerusalem (Geva 2003: pl. 5.3.14, late 2nd–1st c. BC;
Strange 1975: fig. 13.5); Ras Abu Maʿaruf (Rapuano
1999: fig. 1.7).

Globular; ledge rim (Type 3)

Characteristic of the type, **PW 522–48**, is the small but definite ledge arising from the rim and projecting on the interior and/or exterior of the lip. The neck is usually everted and may be slightly concave on the interior (for example, **PW 522, PW 527, PW 543, PW 546**); in later vessels there is a tendency for the rim to become triangular in section and the neck may become more upright, a progression that is mirrored at Machaerus (Loffreda 1996: fig. 28) among the cooking pots of Groups 37 (Hasmonean/Herodian) and 38 (Herodian). This later development also recalls those "necked triangular rim cooking pots" from Tel Anafa first appearing in Hellenistic 2C deposits, and becoming most numerous in Roman 1A and 1B horizons (Berlin 1997a: 87, 90–1, PW 207–10).

The type as a whole is first seen on the main mound in an early second-century (Hellenistic 3A) context at Pella and becomes increasingly popular in the Jannaeus Destruction (Hellenistic 3C) horizon. Fewer examples were recovered from Tell Husn (Area XXXIV), with most being from mixed contexts. At Gezer (Gitin 1990: Type 233A) it becomes the dominant cooking-pot form in the second half of the third century and, with minor variations, remains so during the second century BC; large numbers are also seen in second century loci at Tel Dor (Guz-Zilberstein 1995: 298, fig. 6.17: 8–2 Type CP2). At Tel Anafa the "necked ledge rim" form (Berlin 1997a: 90, PW 201–6) is seen in Hellenistic 2A deposits (c. 125 BC) and runs at least into the first century BC; at Gamla the type is included within Berlin's "cooking pots with high neck and flattened/bevelled rim" (for example, Berlin 2006: fig. 2.12.3) seen in both the first centuries BC and AD (Berlin 2006: 32–40).

PW 522. CN 7330.
XXVIIIB 13.13. Hellenistic 3A.
Part of wall, rim. PH 0.05; D rim (est.) 0.12. Dark red clay 2.5YR 4/6. Metallic Coarse Terracotta.
Parallels: Amman/Philadelphia (Zayadine 1977–78: fig. 15.418); Gezer (Gitin 1990: pl. 32.21, mid-3rd c. BC).

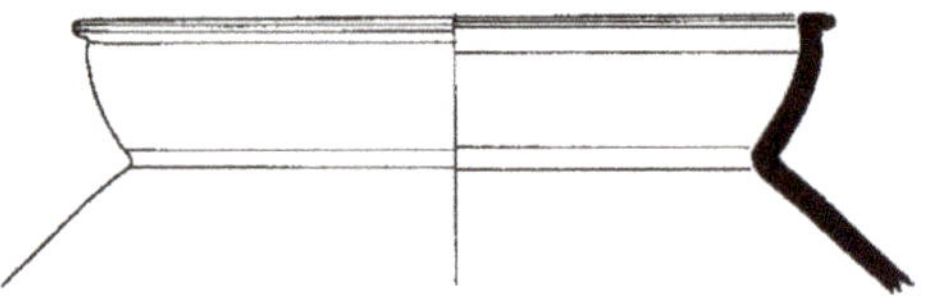

PW 523. CN 7318.
XXVIIIB 13.2. Hellenistic 3A.
Part of wall, rim, handle. PH 0.06; D rim (est.) 0.075. Red clay 2.5YR 6/8. Metallic Coarse Terracotta. Strap handle from rim to shoulder.
Parallels: Hippos-Sussita (Osband and Eisenberg 2018: pl. 2.2.8); Samaria (Crowfoot et al. 1957: fig. 43.12, c. 150–108 BC).

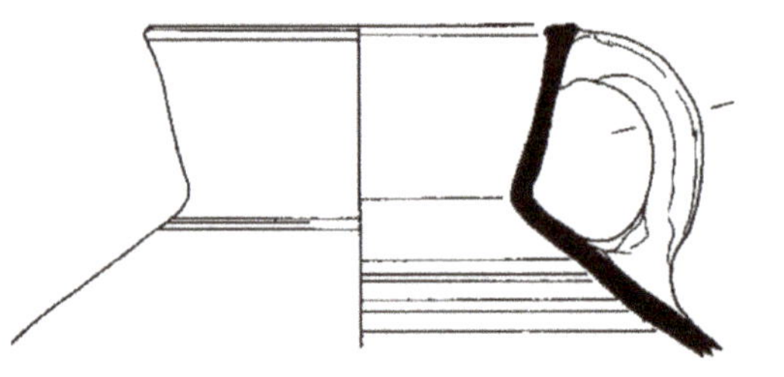

PW 524. CN 7417.
XXVIIIB 13.1. Hellenistic 3A.
Part of wall, rim. PH 0.05; D rim (est.) 0.10. Reddish-yellow clay 5YR 6/8. Metallic Coarse Terracotta.
Parallel: Amman/Philadelphia (Greene and 'Amr 1992: fig. 5.6).

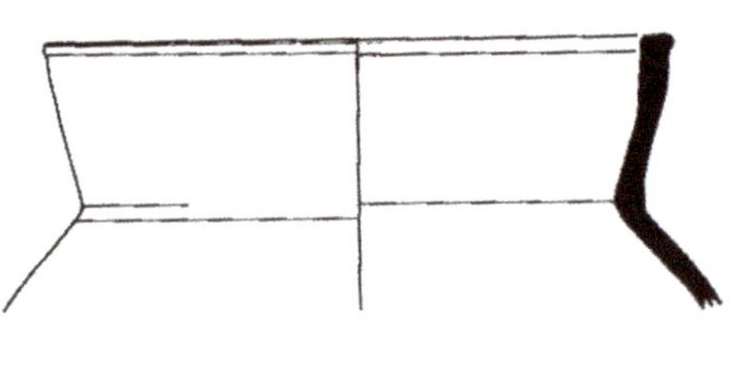

PW 525. CN 7414.
XXVIIIB 10.7. Hellenistic 3A.
Part of wall, rim. PH 0.04; D rim (est.) 0.095. Reddish-yellow clay 5YR 6/6. Metallic Coarse Terracotta.
Parallel: Gezer (Gitin 1990: pl. 37.14, mid-2nd c. BC).

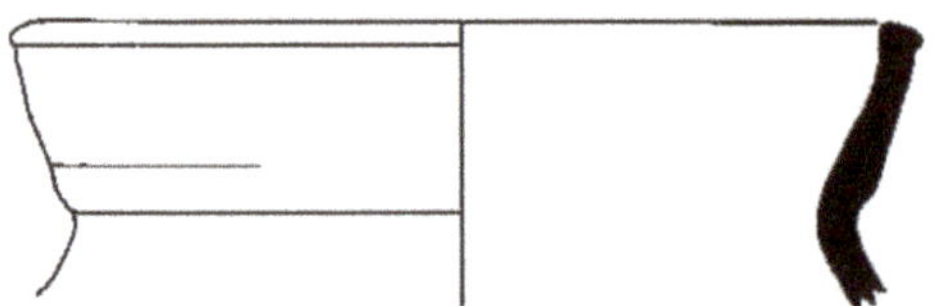

PW 526. CN 7418.
XXVIIIB 13.1. Hellenistic 3A.
Part of wall, rim. PH 0.035; D rim (est.) 0.11. Red clay 2.5YR 6/6. Metallic Coarse Terracotta.

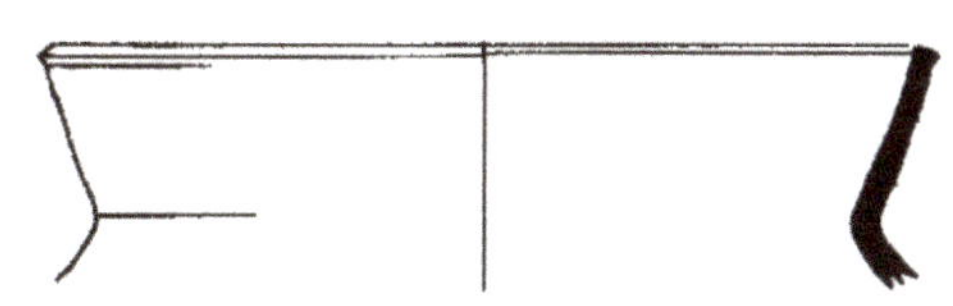

PW 527. CN 7503.
XXVIIIB 13.17. Hellenistic 3A.
Part of wall, rim, handle. PH 0.055; D rim (est.) 0.13. Red clay 2.5YR 6/6. Metallic Coarse Terracotta. Strap handle from rim to shoulder.
Parallel: Marisa (Levine 2003: fig. 6.6.73).

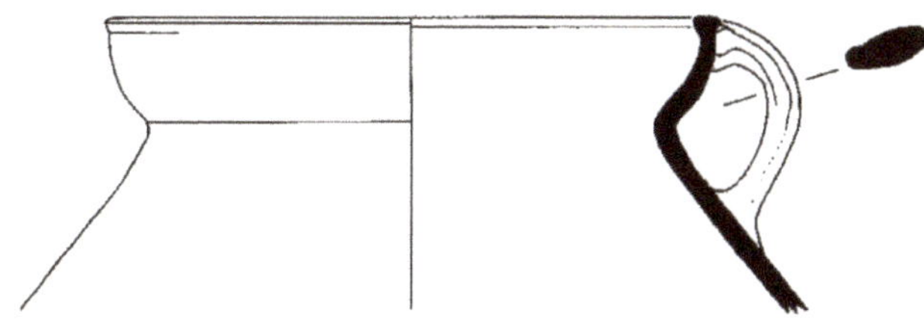

PW 528. CN 7789.
XXIIID 24.1. Hellenistic 3B.
Part of rim, wall, handle. PH 0.04; PL 0.09; D rim (est.) 0.14. Red clay 2.5YR 5/8. Metallic Coarse Terracotta. Root of strap handle on rim.

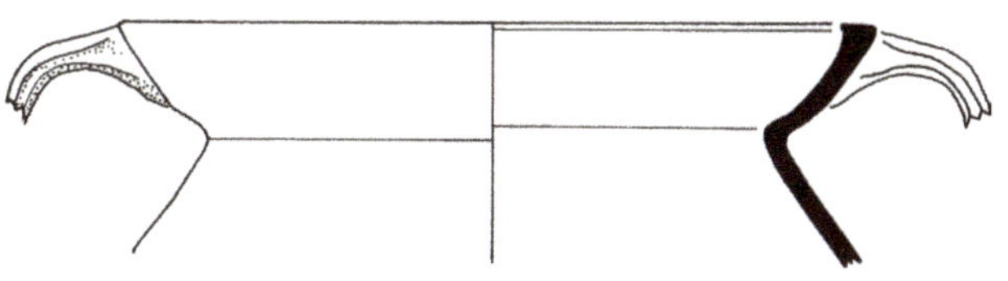

PW 529. CN 0083.
IIIB/C 1.3. Hellenistic 3C.
Part of wall, rim. PH 0.05; D rim (est.) 0.115. Reddish-yellow clay 7.5YR 6/6. Metallic Coarse Terracotta.
Parallels: Hippos-Sussita (Osband and Eisenberg 2018: pl. 2.3.3, 2nd c. BC); Marisa (Kloner and Hess 1985: fig. 3.2); Tel 'Ira (Fischer and Tal 1999b: fig. 6.127.5); Tell Zira'a (Kenkel 2020: 56, 154–5, pl. 1.19: Kt16.2).

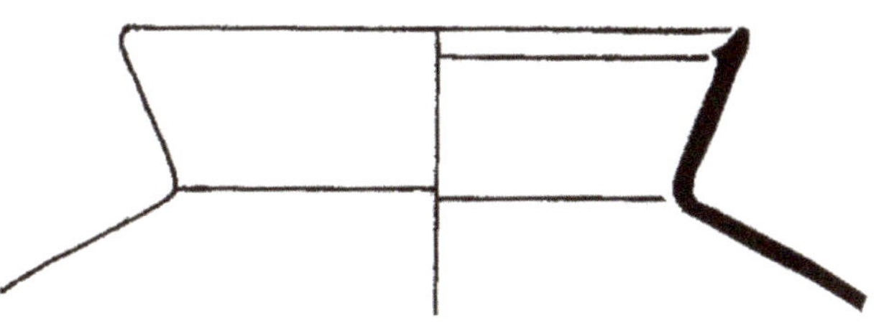

PW 530. CN 6684.
IVD 12.1. Hellenistic 3C.
Part of rim. PH 0.04; D rim (est.) 0.09. Red clay 2.5YR 5/8. Metallic Coarse Terracotta.

PW 531. CN 6943.
IVD 10.12. Hellenistic 3C.
Part of rim. PH 0.04; D rim (est.) 0.13. Reddish-yellow clay 5YR 6/8. Metallic Coarse Terracotta.
Parallels: Samaria (Crowfoot et al. 1957: fig. 43.12, c. 150–108 BC); Tel Dor (Guz-Zilberstein 1995: fig. 6.65:41, 400–275 BC).

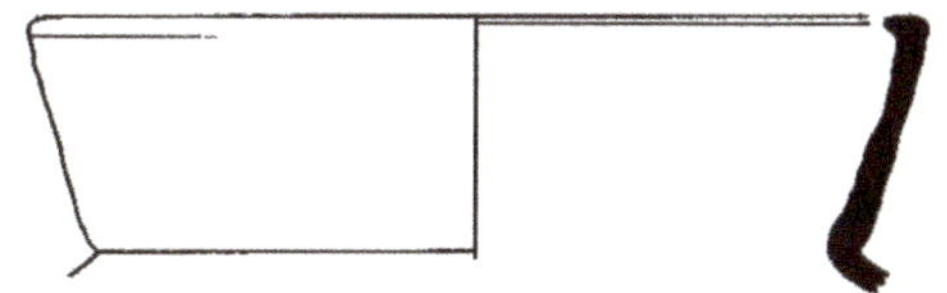

PW 532. CN 6962.
XXIIIA 10.7. Hellenistic 3C.
Two non-joining fragments of wall, rim. PH 0.035; (a) PL 0.115; (b) PL 0.095; D rim (est.) 0.105. Reddish-yellow clay 5YR 6/8. Metallic Coarse Terracotta. Roots of strap handles preserved on rim.

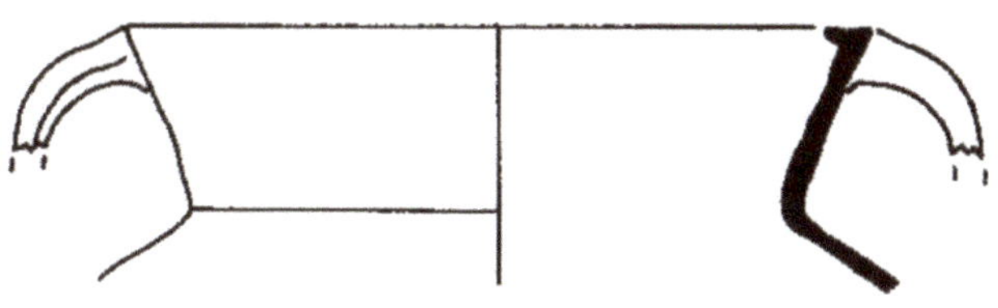

PW 533. CN 7859.
XXIIID 77.2. Hellenistic 3C.
Part of wall, rim. PH 0.06; PL 0.09; D rim (est.) 0.12.
Red clay 10R 4/6.

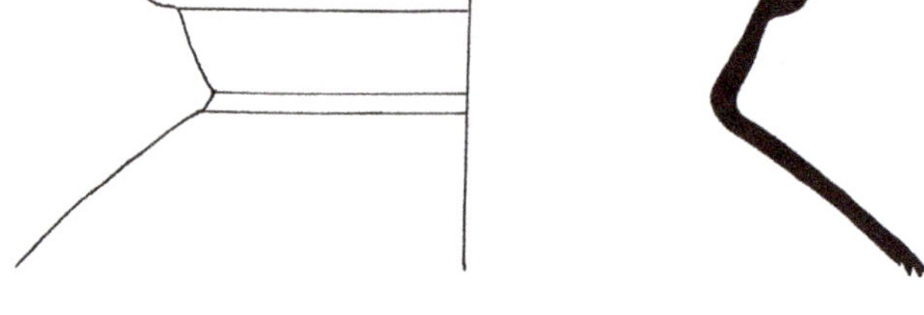

PW 534. CN 7008.
XXIIIA 75.2. Hellenistic 3C.
Missing handle and part of rim. H 0.18;
D rim 0.11. Reddish-yellow clay 5YR 6/8. Metallic
Coarse Terracotta.
Slightly convex resting surface. Globular lower body
with fairly straight upper wall. Faint ribbing. Strap
handle from rim to shoulder.
Parallels: Jerusalem (Tushingham 1985: figs 18.31,
32 upper profile); Samaria (Crowfoot et al. 1957:
fig. 41.6, c. 200–150 BC); Sha'ar ha-Amakim
(Mlynarczyk 2000: pl. 121.4 upper profile); Tel Anafa
(Berlin 1997a: pls 23, PW 202, early 1st c. AD residual,
24, PW 208, 98–75 BC); Tel Dor (Guz-Zilberstein
1995: fig. 6.59:10 upper profile).

PW 535. CN 7120.
XXIIIA 71.2/5. Hellenistic 3C.
Part of rim, handles. PH 0.07; D rim 0.10. Yellow clay
2.5YR 7/6. Metallic Coarse Terracotta.
Strap handles from rim to shoulder with central rib.

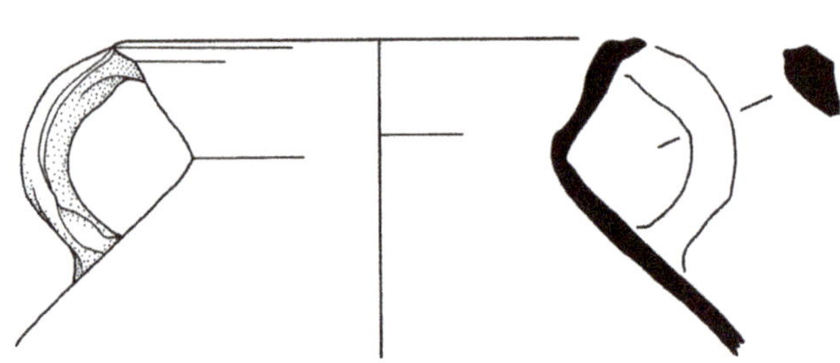

PW 536. CN 6885.
XXIIIA 10.5. Hellenistic 3C.
Part of wall, rim, handle. PH 0.065; PL 0.085; D rim
(est.) 0.11. Greyish-brown clay 10YR 5/2 with many
small inclusions.
Strap handle from shoulder to rim.
Parallel: ʿIraq al-Amir (Zimmerman 2020b: pl. 2.20.5,
str.1, c. 200 AD).

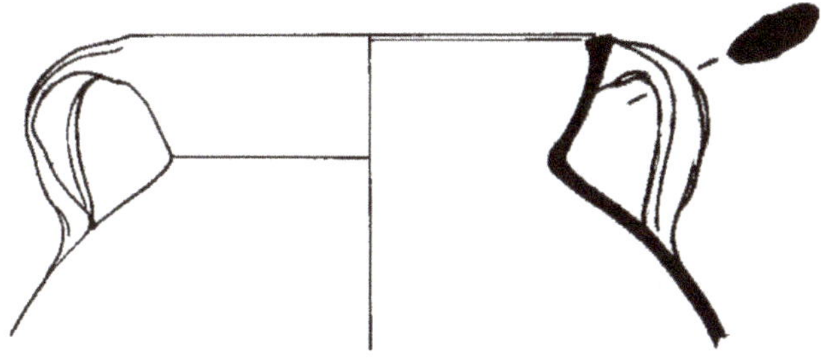

PW 537. CN 6889.
XXIIIA 10.7. Hellenistic 3C.
Part of wall, rim, handle. Multiple joining and
non-joining fragments. PH 0.075; PL 0.11 (largest
fragment); D rim (est.) 0.115. Reddish-yellow clay
5YR 6/8. Metallic Coarse Terracotta.
Strap handle from rim to shoulder.
Parallels: ʿAkko-Ptolemais (Berlin and Stone 2016:
fig. 9.19.7, mid–late 2nd c. BC); Gezer (Gitin 1990:
pl. 32.21, mid-3rd c. BC).

PW 538. CN 7092.
XXIIIA 100.1. Hellenistic 3C.
Part of wall, rim, handle. PH 0.06; PL 0.105; D rim
(est.) 0.095. Reddish-yellow clay 5YR 6/8. Metallic
Coarse Terracotta.
Strap handle with central rib from rim to shoulder.
Parallels: Jerusalem (Geva 2003: pl. 5.6.32, 2nd
c. BC); Tel Zahara (Bar-Nathan and Gärtner 2013:
fig. 3.13.116).

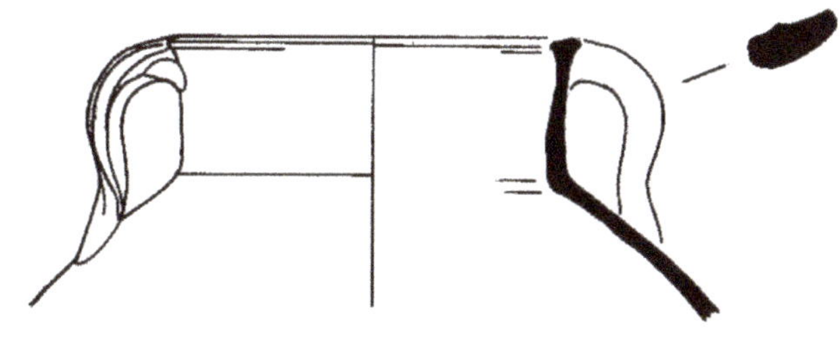

PW 539. CN 7755.
XXIIID 20.1. Hellenistic 3C.
Part of rim. PH 0.04; PL 0.07; D rim (est.) 0.16. Red
clay 2.5YR 5/8. Metallic Coarse Terracotta.

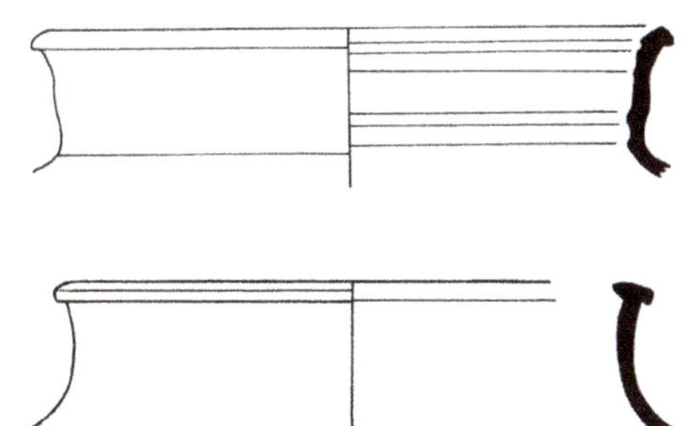

PW 540. CN 7591.
XXXIVB 29.5. Hellenistic 3B/3C.
Part of wall, rim. PH 0.03; PL 0.04; D rim (est.) 0.14.
Dark red clay 2.5YR 4/8. Metallic Coarse Terracotta.

PW 541. CN 7865.

XXXIVE Surface. Mixed Context.

Multiple joining and non-joining fragments forming part of rim, neck, shoulder, handle. PH 0.18; D rim (est.) 0.11. Red clay 10R 6/8. Metallic Coarse Terracotta. Globular body. Two vertical strap handles from lip to shoulder.

Parallels: Amman/Philadelphia (Koutsoukou and Najjar 1997: 75–6, no. 197); Madaba (Ferguson 2014: 184, fig. 6.27, c. 100–63 BC); Shechem (N.L. Lapp 2008: pl. 3.39.7, 190–150 BC).

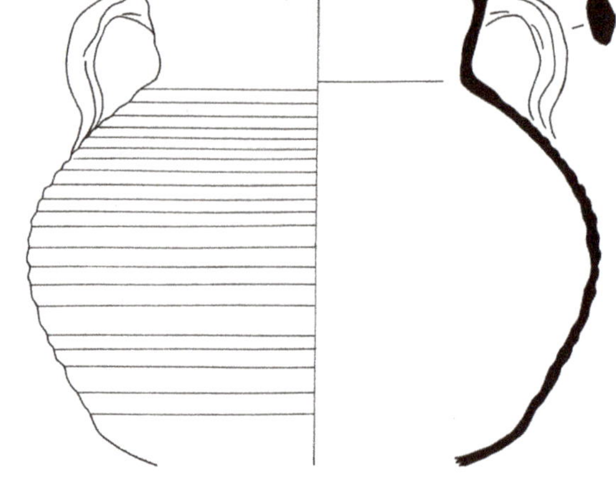

PW 542. CN 7333.

XXXIVG 12.19. Mixed Context.

Part of wall. PH 0.03; PL 0.055; D rim (est.) 0.135. Yellowish-red clay 5YR5/6. Metallic Coarse Terracotta. Parallel: Hippos-Sussita (Osband and Eisenberg 2018: pl. 4.3.14, end 1st c. BC/beginning 1st c. AD).

PW 543. CN 7169.

XXIVG 6.8. Early Roman 1.

Part of wall, rim. PH 0.04; D rim (est.) 0.12. Red clay 2.5YR 6/8. Metallic Coarse Terracotta.

Parallel: Wadi Hasa survey (MacDonald 1988: pl. 13.4).

PW 544. CN 7858.

XXIIID 77.2. Hellenistic 3C.

Two non-joining fragments of wall, rim, handle. PH (a) 0.075, (b) 0.085; PL (a) 0.095, (b) 0.13; D rim (est.) 0.12. Red clay 2.5YR 5/8. Metallic Coarse Terracotta.

Vertical strap handle from rim to shoulder.

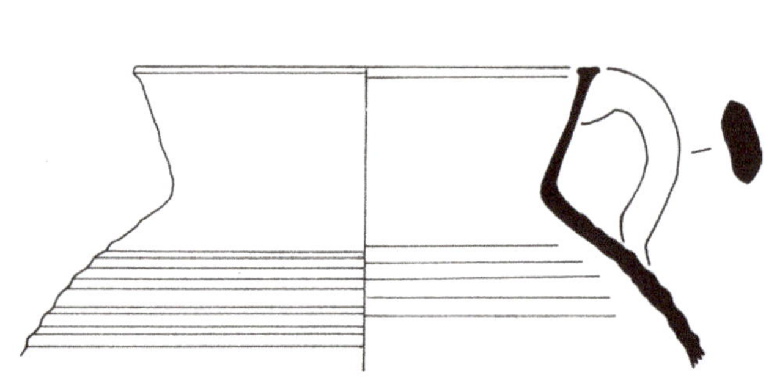

PW 545. CN 7272.

XXIIIA 10.11. Hellenistic 3C.

Multiple fragments. Missing part of lower wall, rim. PH 0.20; D rim (est.) 0.14. Reddish-yellow clay 5YR 6/6. Metallic Coarse Terracotta.

Parallels: ʿAkko-Ptolemais (Berlin and Stone 2016: fig. 9.26.11, early 1st c. AD); Gamla (Berlin 2006: fig. 2.12.3, 1st c. BC/early 1st c. AD).

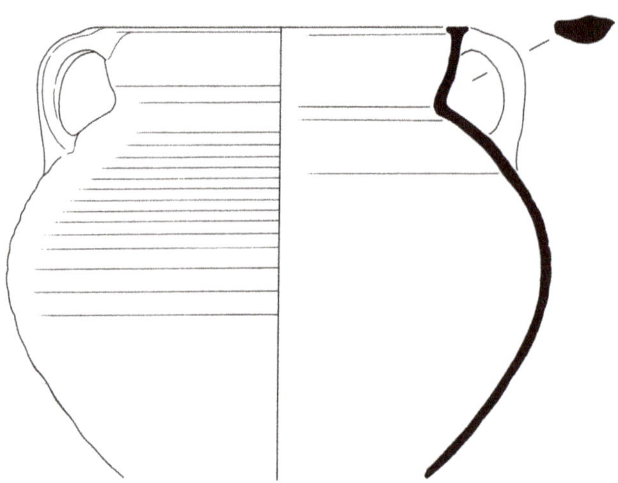

PW 546. CN 7156.
XXXIVB 5.39. Mixed Context.
Part of wall, rim. PH 0.085; D rim (est.) 0.15. Red clay 2.5YR 5/8. Metallic Coarse Terracotta.

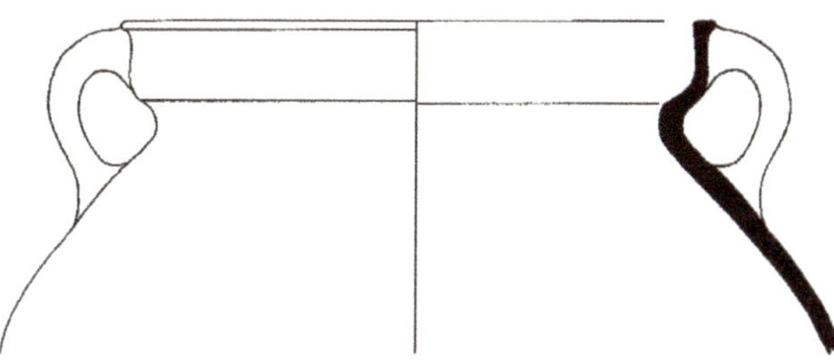

PW 547. CN 7107.
XXIIIA 81.4. Mixed Context.
Part of wall, rim, handle. PH 0.075; D rim (est.) 0.15. Red clay 2.5YR 6/8. Metallic Coarse Terracotta.
Strap handle from shoulder to rim.
Parallel: Shechem (N.L. Lapp 2008: pl. 3.39.7, 190–150 BC).

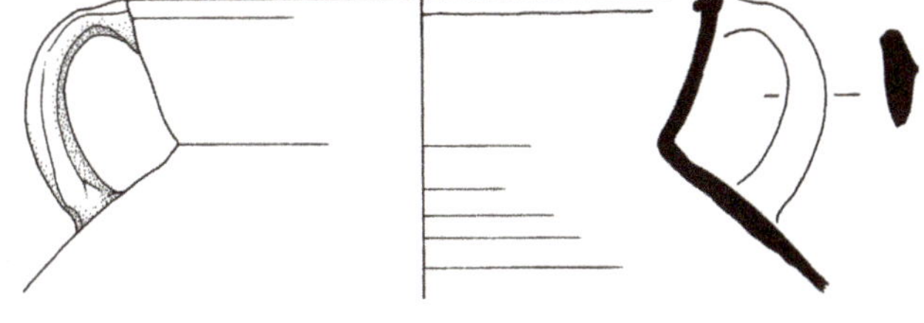

PW 548. CN 6709.
IIIP 25.20. Mixed Context.
Part of wall, rim, handle. PH 0.13; D rim 0.12. Yellowish-red clay 5YR 5/8. Metallic Coarse Terracotta.
Strap handle from rim to shoulder.

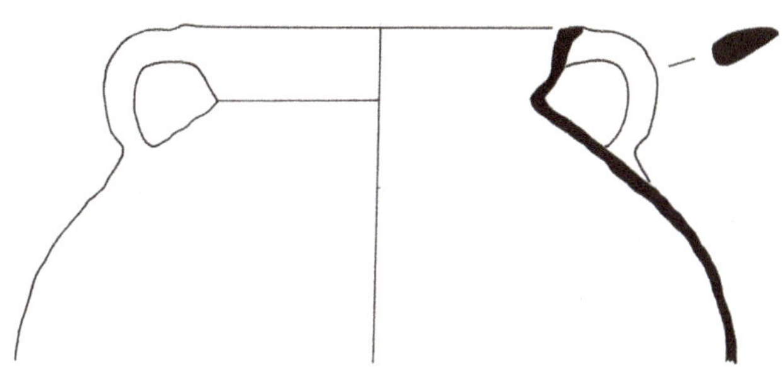

Globular; concave rim (Type 4)

Cooking pots **PW 549–72** differ from those of the preceding type in the shape of the rim, which shows a marked concavity on the interior. The shape is more commonly seen at Pella in Hellenistic 3C (main mound) and Early Roman (Tell Husn) horizons with two examples (**PW 549** and one uncatalogued) recovered from an earlier Hellenistic 2B context, also on Husn. The necks on those vessels found in Early Roman levels tend to be shorter and more everted, and the bodies increasingly globular. The profiles of these latter vessels recall those of the casseroles recovered from Early Roman levels at Pella.

While these pots appear in levels as early as the third century BC at Tel Dor (Guz-Zilberstein 1995: 299, Type CP 4) and in early second-century contexts at ʿIraq al-Amir (Zimmerman 2020b: Type 112.1, pl. 2.20.1–3), at Gamla they are included amongst those cooking pots "with splayed/convex neck" (for example, Berlin 2006: fig. 2.10.10) in use from early in the first century BC to the city's destruction in 67 AD (Berlin 2006: 32–40).

The globular short-necked form seen in Early Roman levels at Pella finds parallels in the "angled neck" cooking pots from chronologically similar horizons at Tel Anafa (Berlin 1997a: 92, PW 219–21). In contrast, at Kallirhoe and Machaerus cooking pots of this type (Clamer 1997: 68, Type 3.4.1c; Loffreda 1996: Group 43: fig. 32) are restricted to Herodian contexts; most, however, are of the later form encountered in the Early Roman levels at Pella.

PW 549. CN 7660.
XXXIVB 27.22. Hellenistic 2B.
Part of wall, rim. PH 0.03; PL 0.045; D rim (est.)
0.14. Red clay 2.5YR 5/8. Metallic Coarse Terracotta.
Parallels: 'Akko-Ptolemais (Berlin and Stone 2016:
fig. 9.5.3, 3rd c. BC); Hesban (Gerber 2012: 245,
fig. 3.17.21).

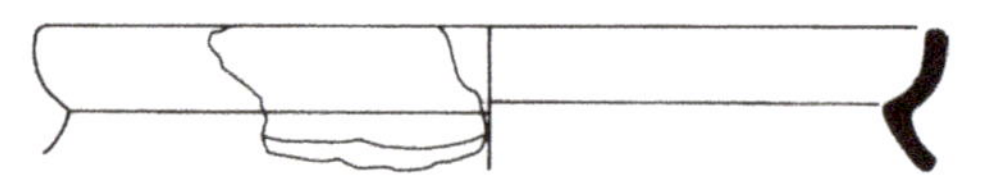

PW 550. CN 7213.
XXVIIIB 13.17. Hellenistic 3A.
Part of wall, rim, handle. PH 0.045; D rim
(est.) 0.095. Reddish-yellow clay 5YR 6/8. Metallic
Coarse Terracotta.
Strap handle from rim to shoulder.

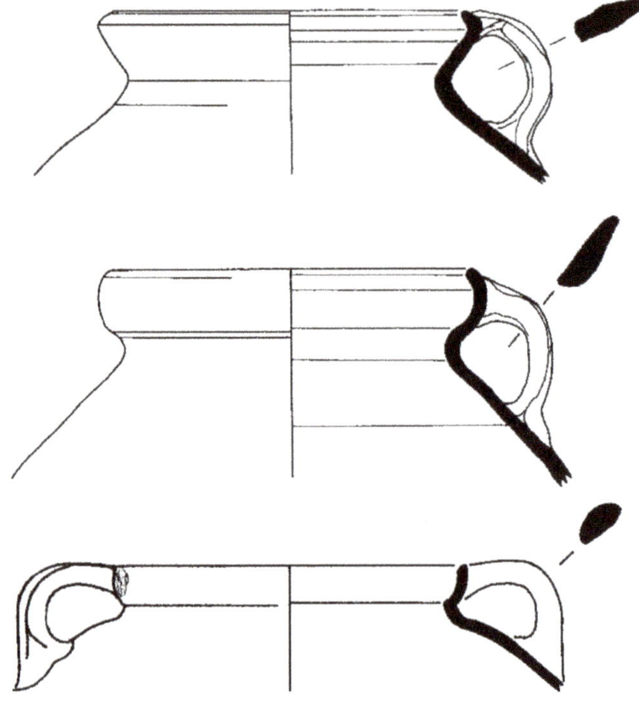

PW 551. CN 7186.
XXVIIIB 13.2. Hellenistic 3A.
Part of wall, rim, handle. PH 0.065; D rim (est.) 0.11.
Red clay 2.5YR 6/8. Metallic Coarse Terracotta.
Parallels: Samaria (Crowfoot et al. 1957: fig. 41.16,
c. 200–150 BC); Tel Keisan (Briend 1980: pl. 11.5, late
4th–mid-2nd c. BC).

PW 552. CN 6869.
IIIB/C 1.19. Mixed Context.
Part of wall, rim, handle. PH 0.045; D rim (est.) 0.11.
Red clay 10R 5/6. Metallic Coarse Terracotta.
Strap handle from rim to shoulder.
Parallels: 'Akko-Ptolemais (Berlin and Stone 2016:
fig. 9.2.3, 3rd c. BC); Jaffa (Tsuf 2018: fig. 9.20.375);
Jerusalem (Sandhaus 2013: fig. 4.6:1, second half
of 2nd c. BC); Samaria (Hennessy 1970: fig. 9.14);
Sha'ar ha-Amakim (Mlynarczyk 2000: pl. 120b.3);
Straton's Tower/Caesarea (Berlin 1992: fig. 53.12); Tel
Dor (Guz-Zilberstein 1995: fig. 6.19:14, 275–200 BC).

PW 553. CN 0335.
IIIB/C 1.14. Mixed Context.
Part of wall, rim, handle. PH 0.06; D rim (est.) 0.12.
Red clay 2.5YR 5/8. Metallic Coarse Terracotta.
Strap handles from rim to shoulder.

PW 554. CN 7125.
XXIIIA 71.2/5. Hellenistic 3C.
Part of wall, rim. PH 0.03; D rim (est.) 0.12. Yellow
clay 2.5YR 7/6. Metallic Coarse Terracotta.

PW 555. CN 7754.

XXIIID 20.1. Hellenistic 3C.

Part of wall, rim, handle. PH 0.045; PL 0.07; D rim (est.) 0.12. Red clay 2.5YR 5/8. Metallic Coarse Terracotta.

Strap handle from rim to shoulder.

Parallels: Ashdod (Dothan 1971: fig. 61.13); Gamla (Berlin 2006: fig. 2.10.12, 1st c. BC/early 1st c. AD); 'Iraq al-Amir (Zimmerman 2020b: pl. 2.20.3, str. IIIa, c. 50 AD); Madaba (Ferguson 2014: 184, fig. 6.25, c. 63–15 BC); Scythopolis/Beth-Shean (Johnson 2006: fig. 15.3.44).

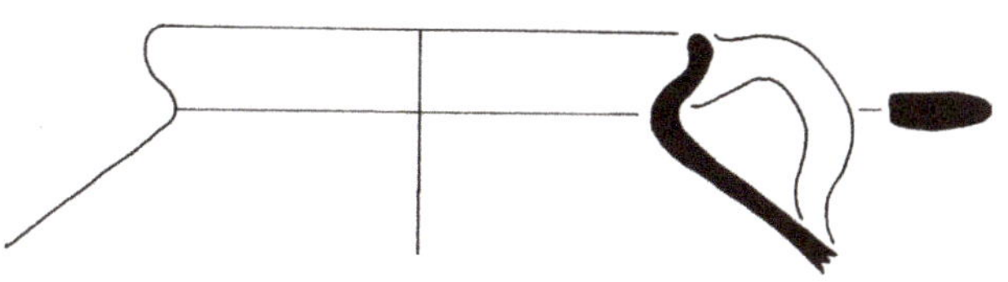

PW 556. CN 7761.

XXIIID 20.4. Hellenistic 3C.

Multiple joining and non-joining fragments of rim, wall, handle. PH 0.075; PL 0.19; D rim (est.) 0.11. Reddish-yellow clay 7.5YR 6/6. Metallic Coarse Terracotta.

Strap handle from rim to shoulder.

Parallel: Nahal Hever (Aharoni 1961: fig. 7.8).

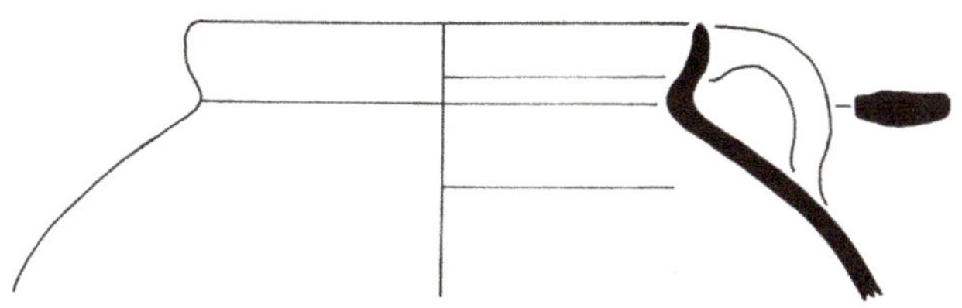

PW 557. CN 7776.

XXIIID 11.10. Hellenistic 3C.

Part of rim, wall, handle. PH 0.055; PL 0.055; D rim (est.) 0.11. Red clay 2.5YR 5/6. Metallic Coarse Terracotta.

Strap handle from rim to shoulder.

Parallels: 'Akko-Ptolemais (Berlin and Stone 2016: fig. 9.5.3, 3rd c. BC); Jerusalem (Geva 2003: pl. 5.6.35, 2nd c. BC); Sha'ar ha-Amakim (Mlynarczyk 2000: pl. 120b.3).

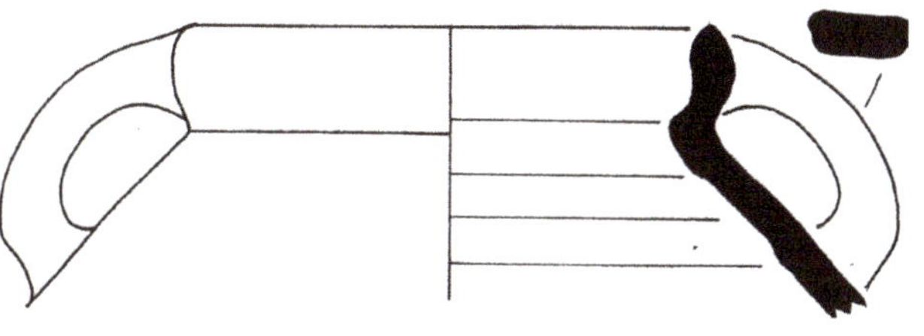

PW 558. CN 7624.

XXXIVB 27.13. Mixed Context.

Part of rim, wall. PH 0.03; PL 0.055; D rim (est.) 0.12. Yellowish-red clay 5YR 5/8. Metallic Coarse Terracotta.

Parallel: Khirbet al-Mukhayyat (Dolan and Foran 2016: fig. 7.u).

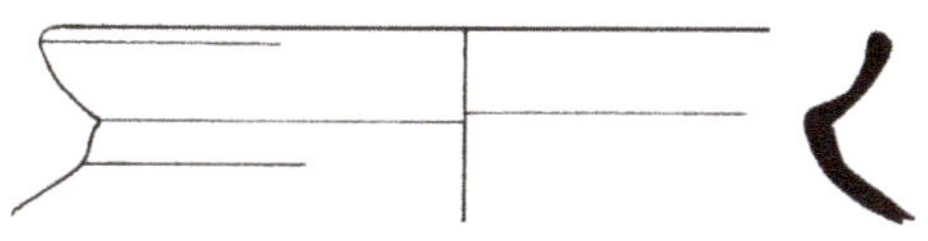

PW 559. CN 7649.

XXXIVB 30.10. Hellenistic 3B/3C.

Part of rim. PH 0.025; PL 0.04; D rim (est.) 0.13. Red clay 2.5YR 5/8. Metallic Coarse Terracotta.

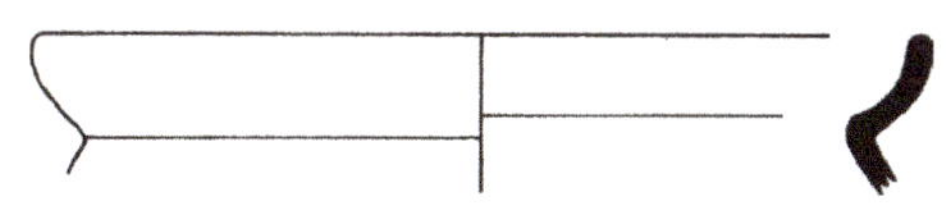

PW 560. CN 7748.
XXIIID 18.2. Hellenistic 3C.
Part of rim, wall, handle. PH 0.055; PL 0.09; D rim
(est.) 0.13. Red clay 2.5YR 5/8. Metallic Coarse
Terracotta.

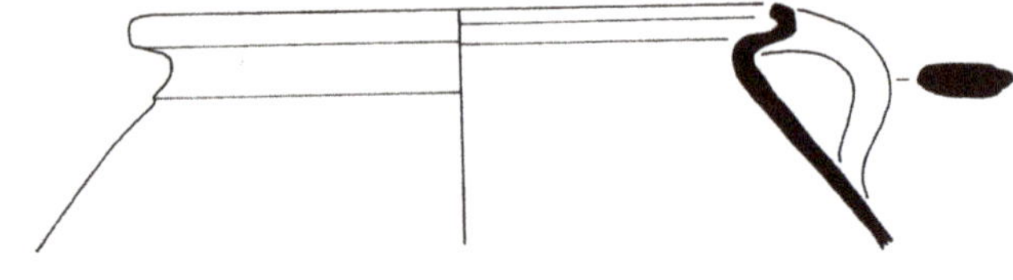

PW 561. CN 7606.
XXXIVB 27.5. Early Roman 1.
Part of wall, rim, handle. PH 0.03; PL 0.09; D rim
(est.) 0.11. Dark red clay 2.5YR 4/8. Metallic Coarse
Terracotta.
Parallel: Jerusalem (Tchekhanovets 2013: fig. 5.1:17,
1st c. BC–70 AD).

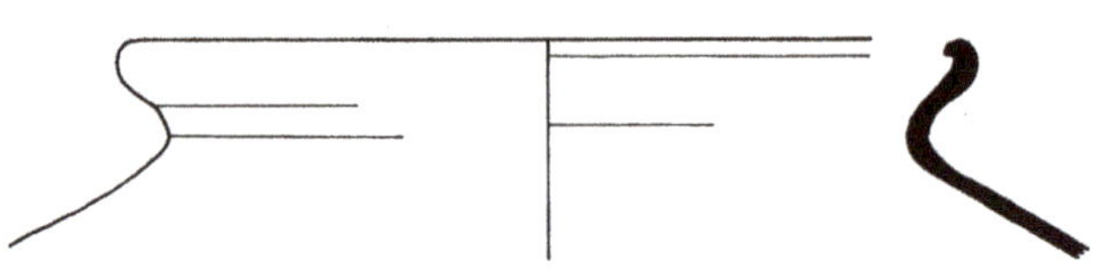

PW 562. CN 7607.
XXXIVB 27.5. Early Roman 1.
Part of wall, rim. PH 0.03; PL 0.08; D rim (est.) 0.11.
Dark red clay 2.5YR 4/8. Metallic Coarse Terracotta.

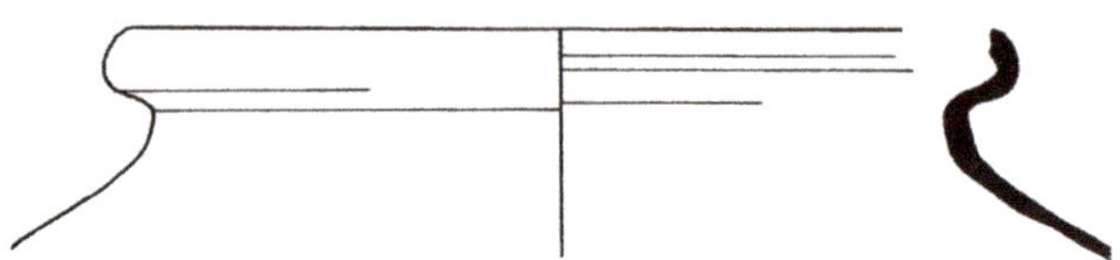

PW 563. CN 7552.
XXXIVB 26.1/2. Early Roman 1.
Part of wall, rim, handle. PH 0.045; PL 0.115; D rim
(est.) 0.13. Dark red clay 2.5YR 4/8. Metallic Coarse
Terracotta.
Strap handle from rim to shoulder.
Parallel: Iotapata (Adan-Bayewitz and Aviam 1997:
fig. 12.11).

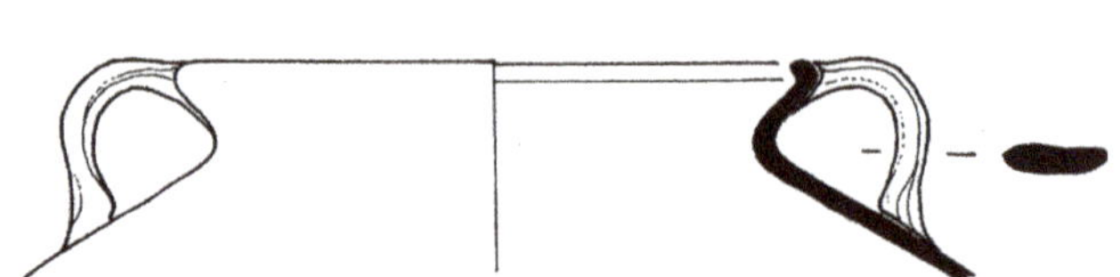

PW 564. CN 7553.
XXXIVB 26.1/2. Early Roman 1.
Part of wall, rim, handle. PH 0.045; PL 0.11; D rim
(est.) 0.12. Dark red clay 2.5YR 4/8. Metallic Coarse
Terracotta.
Faint ribbing. Strap handle from rim to shoulder.

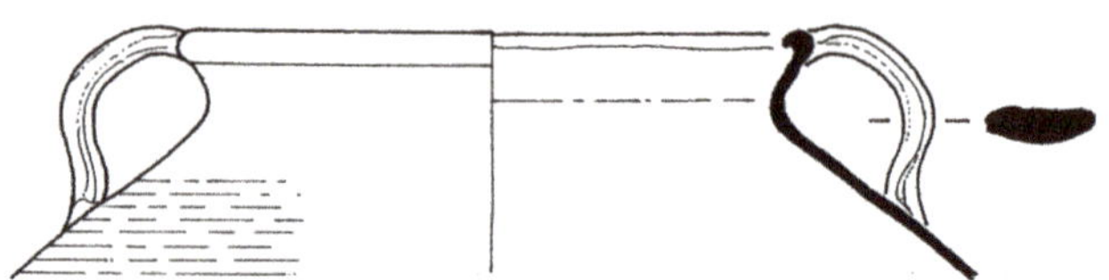

PW 565. CN 7567.
XXXIVB 27.2. Early Roman 1.
Part of wall, rim, handle. PH 0.04; PL 0.105; D rim
(est.) 0.11. Red clay 2.5YR 5/8. Metallic Coarse
Terracotta.
Strap handle from rim to shoulder. Lightly ribbed.
Parallel: Machaerus (Loffreda 1996: fig. 32.5).

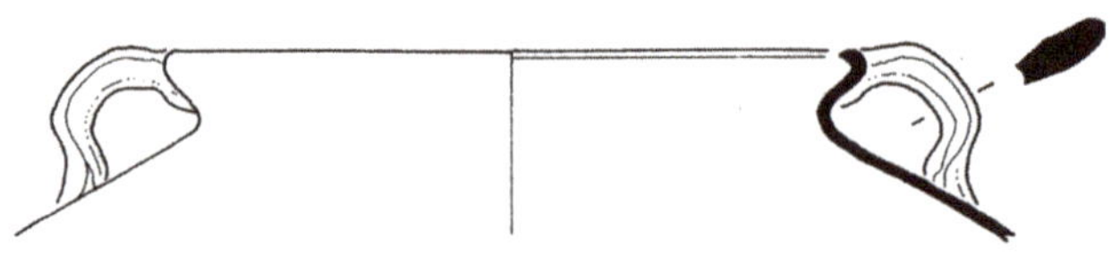

PW 566. CN 7568.
XXXIVB 27.2. Early Roman 1.
Fragment of wall, rim. PH 0.045; PL 0.065; D rim (est.)
0.13. Red clay 2.5YR 5/8. Metallic Coarse Terracotta.
Strap handle from rim to rounded shoulder. Lightly
ribbed.
Parallels: Kallirhoe (Clamer 1997: pl. 13.16);
Machaerus (Loffreda 1996: fig. 32.11).

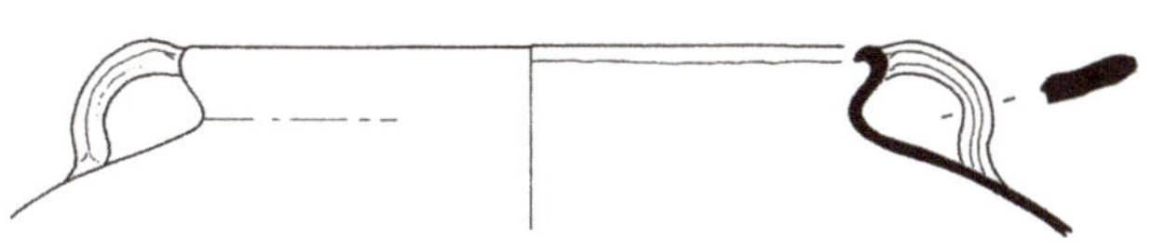

PW 567. CN 7571.
XXXIVB 27.2. Early Roman 1.
Part of wall, rim. PH 0.06; PL 0.08; D rim (est.) 0.12.
Red clay 2.5YR 5/8. Metallic Coarse Terracotta.

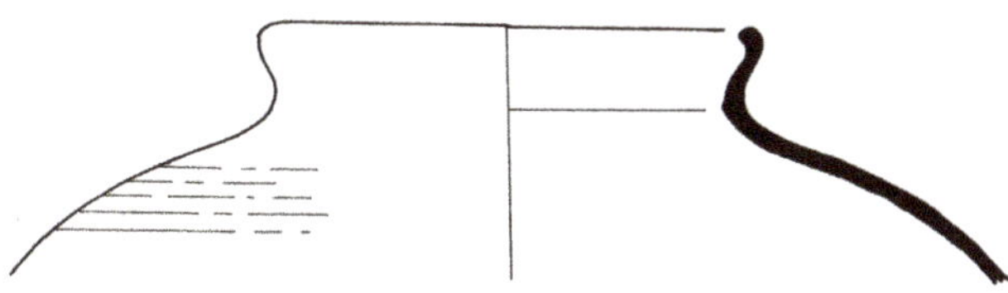

PW 568. CN 2620.
XIA/B 1.5. Early Roman 1.
Part of rim, wall, handle. PH 0.06; PL 0.125; D rim
(est.) 0.12. Red clay 2.5YR 5/6. Metallic Coarse
Terracotta.
Strap handle from rim to shoulder.
Parallels: Apollonia (Fischer and Tal 1996:
fig. 7.3); Jericho (Kelso and Baramki 1955: pl. 23.X76);
Straton's Tower/Caesarea (Berlin 1992: fig. 53.12); Tel
Michal (Fischer 1989: fig. 13.3.17, 1st c. BC: Alexander
Jannaeus).

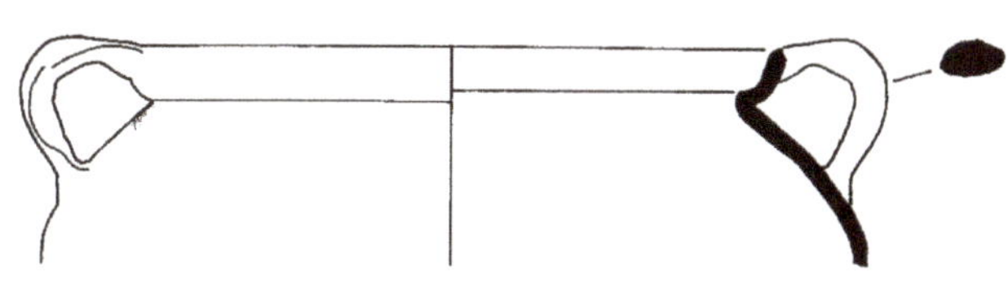

PW 569. CN 2563.
XIA/B 1.1. Early Roman 1.
Part of wall, rim. PH 0.04; PL 0.07; D rim (est.) 0.12.
Red clay 2.5YR 5/8. Metallic Coarse Terracotta.
Parallels: Ashdod (Dothan 1971: fig. 24.8); Madaba
(Ferguson 2014: 182, fig. 6.20, c. 15 BC–106 AD).

PW 570. CN 2564.
XIA/B 1.1. Early Roman 1.
Part of wall, rim. PH 0.02; PL 0.045; D rim (est.)
0.09. Red clay 2.5YR 5/8. Metallic Coarse Terracotta.
Parallels: Kallirhoe (Clamer 1997: pl. 2.13); Machaerus
(Loffreda 1980: pl. 95.22); Tel Anafa (Berlin 1997a:
pl. 26, PW 221, late 1st c. BC–early 1st c. AD).

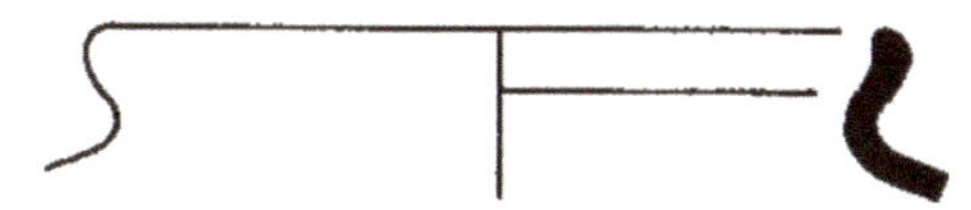

PW 571. CN 2652.
XIA/B 1.1/2. Early Roman 1.
Part of wall, rim. PH 0.03; PL 0.09; D rim (est.) 0.14.
Red clay 2.5YR 5/6. Metallic Coarse Terracotta.
Parallels: Samaria (Hennessy 1970: fig. 9.14);
Tel Keisan (Briend 1980: pl. 11.5b, late 4th–mid-
2nd c. BC).

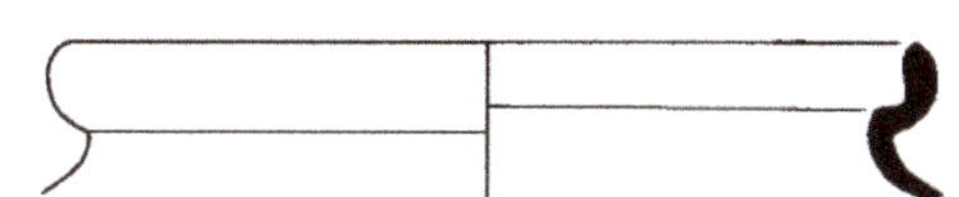

PW 572. CN 7359.
XXXIVB 8.22. Mixed Context.
Part of wall, rim. PL 0.045; PH 0.02; D rim
(est.) 0.12. Yellowish-red clay 5YR 4/6. Metallic
Coarse Terracotta.
Parallel: Machaerus (Loffreda 1996: fig. 32.18).

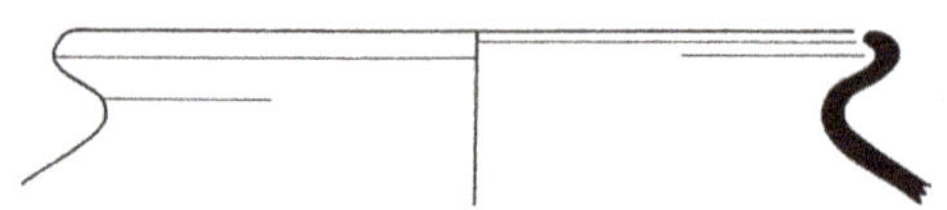

Globular; bevelled rim (Type 5)

With a few exceptions (**PW 573–4**, **PW 581**, **PW 586**), cooking pots of this type – **PW 573–99** – are
encountered in Early Roman horizons on Tell Husn where they make up the most popular form. The neck is
short and upright or slightly everted with the rim bevelled to the exterior, often forming a distinctly triangular
outline. The rim may be very lightly grooved but without the definite groove of the following Type 6. This
type corresponds to P.W. Lapp (1961) Type 71.1, form N1, appearing in Palestine in deposits of the second
half of the first century BC and first half of the first century AD (P.W. Lapp 1961: 187–8). Cooking pots of
similar form and date have been recovered from many sites west of the Jordan River where they constitute one
of the most common forms of cooking pot from the Second Temple period (Berlin 2005a: 36–8); at Gamla
the form is included within Berlin's "cooking pots with high neck and flattened/bevelled rim" (Berlin 2006:
32–40, for example, fig. 2.12.4). East of the Jordan this type is well represented within the Herodian and Early
Roman phases at Hesban (Gerber 2012: figs 3.17.15–16, 3.22.1–5) and Kallirhoe (Clamer 1997: pls 2.11–12,
4.13) while at 'Iraq al-Amir it is seen in all four strata from the Village site (Zimmerman 2020b: Type 110).
Although included within our Type 5, the Early Roman cooking pot **PW 590** is noteworthy for the distinct
broad shoulder (but much less angled than those of the Pella Type 5 casseroles) that it possesses. The feature
is seen at Herodium, Kallirhoe, Machaerus and Ramat Rahel but the shape is generally uncommon in the
southern Levant.[27]

PW 573. CN 7362.
XXIIIA 10.7. Hellenistic 3C.
Part of rim. PH 0.035; PL 0.065; D (est.) 0.12. Red
clay 2.5YR 5/8. Metallic Coarse Terracotta.

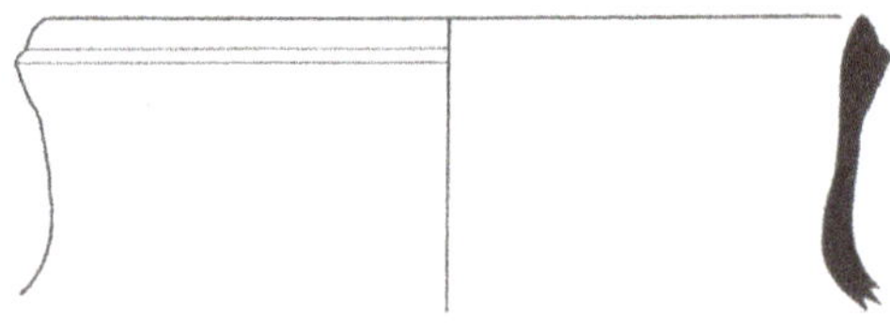

PW 574. CN 0845.
IIIB/C 14.2. Hellenistic 3C.
Part of rim. PH 0.025; D rim (est.) 0.14. Burnt dark
grey clay 5YR 4/1. Metallic Coarse Terracotta.
Parallel: 'Iraq al-Amir (Zimmerman 2020b: pl. 2.18.9,
str. II–I, c. 100–200 AD).

PW 575. CN 7357.
XXXIVB 5.10. Mixed Context.
Part of wall, rim, handle. PH 0.04; PL 0.065; D rim
(est) 0.14. Yellowish-red clay 5YR 5/8. Metallic Coarse
Terracotta.
Parallel: Samaria (Crowfoot et al. 1957: fig. 67.4; Abu
Shmeis and Waheeb 2002: fig. 2.16).

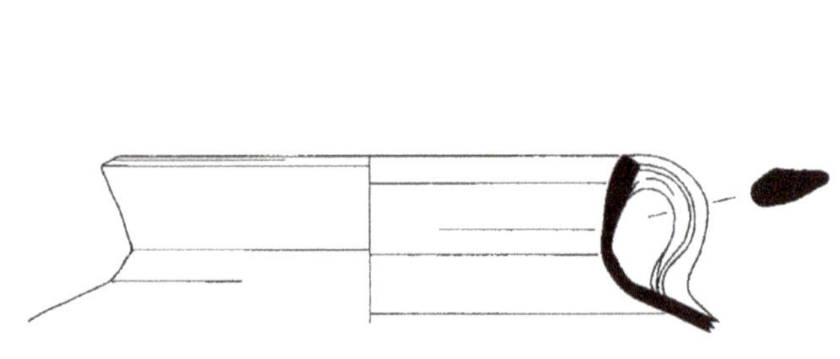

27 Bar-Nathan 1981: pl. 5.17 (Herodium); Clamer 1997: pl. 3.7 (Kallirhoe); Loffreda 1996: Group 41: fig. 30
   (Machaerus); Aharoni 1962: fig. 28, nos 5, 11, 12 (Ramat Rahel).

PW 576. CN 7354.
XXXIVB 6.27. Early Roman 1.
Part of wall, rim, handle. PH 0.035; PL 0.075;
D rim (est.) 0.10. Red clay 2.5YR 5/6. Metallic Coarse
Terracotta.
Strap handle from rim to shoulder.
Parallels: Jerusalem (Geva 2003: pl. 5.3.12, late 2nd–1st
c. BC; Sandhaus 2013: fig. 4.1:15, second half of 2nd
c. BC; Tushingham 1985: fig. 19.1); Ras Abu Ma'aruf
(Rapuano 1999: fig. 1.5); Samaria (Crowfoot et al.
1957: fig. 41.1); Shechem (N.L. Lapp 1964: fig. 3.17).

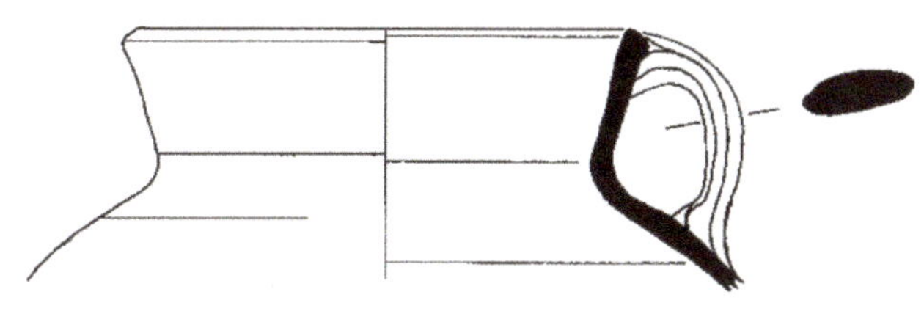

PW 577. CN 7550.
XXXIVB 27.1. Early Roman 1.
Part of rim. PH 0.03; PL 0.025; D rim (est.) 0.09.
Reddish-brown clay 5YR 5/4. Metallic Coarse
Terracotta.

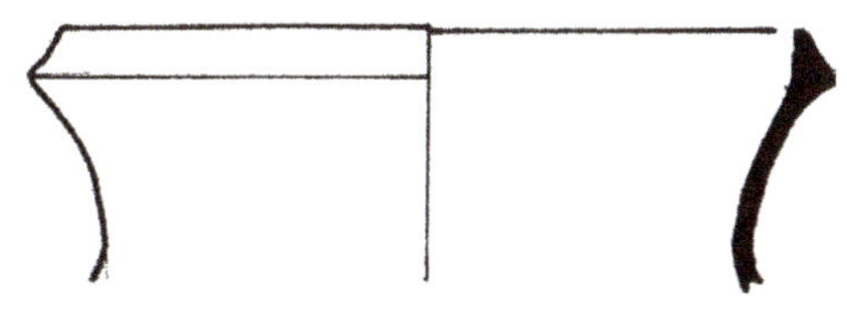

PW 578. CN 7561.
XXXIVB 27.3. Early Roman 1.
Part of wall, rim, handle. PH 0.05; PL 0.09; D rim
(est.) 0.14. Yellowish-red clay 5YR 5/8. Metallic
Coarse Terracotta.
Parallels: Hesban (Gerber 2012: fig. 3.22.1); Jerusalem
(Geva 1983: fig. 5.7); Masada Camp F (Magness 2009:
fig. 463, 72/73 or 73/74 AD).

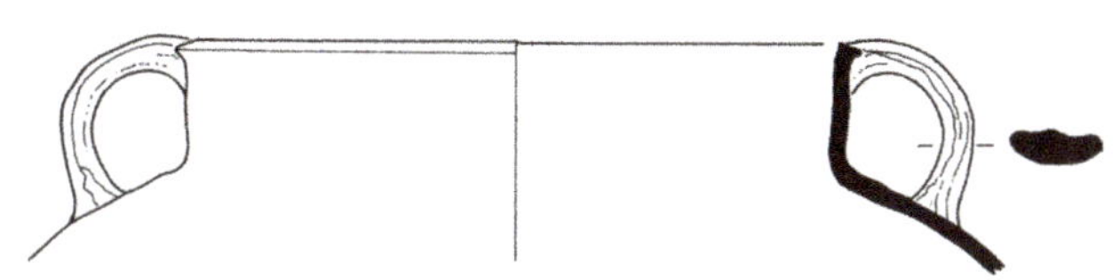

PW 579. CN 7614.
XXXIVB 27.7. Early Roman 1.
Part of wall, rim, handle. PH 0.06; PL 0.09; D rim (est.)
0.11. Dark yellowish-brown clay 10YR 4/6. Metallic
Coarse Terracotta.

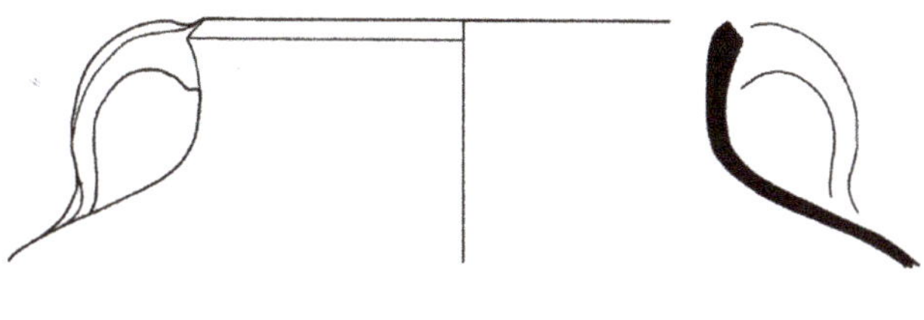

PW 580. CN 7623.
XXXIVB 27.11. Mixed Context.
Part of rim, shoulder, handle. PH 0.045; PL 0.065; D
rim (est.) 0.11. Reddish-brown clay 5YR 5/4. Metallic
Coarse Terracotta.
Strap handle from rim to shoulder.
Parallels: Betar (Singer 1993: fig. 1.6); Hesban (Gerber
2012: 263, fig. 3.22.2).

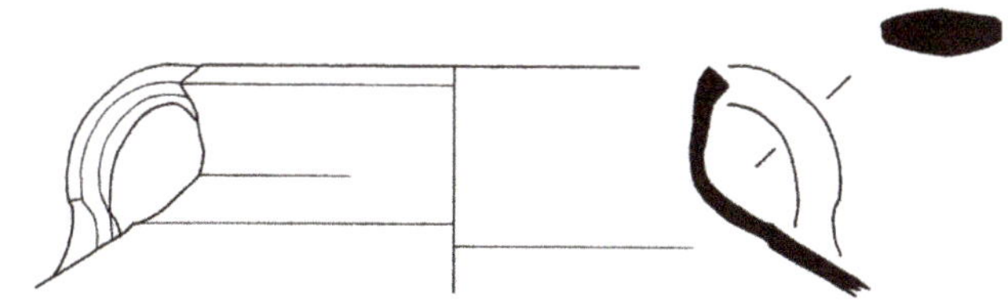

PW 581. CN 7644.
XXXIVB 30.5. Hellenistic 3B/3C.
Part of wall, rim, handle. PH 0.06; PL 0.06 D rim
(est.) 0.11. Reddish-yellow clay 5YR 6/8.
Strap handle from rim to shoulder.
Parallels: Hippos-Sussita (Osband and Eisenberg
2018: pl. 4.2.7, end 1st c. BC/beginning 1st c. AD); 'Iraq
al-Amir (Zimmerman 2020b: pl. 2.18.4, str. IIIb–II,
c. 100 BC–c. 100 AD); Kallirhoe (Clamer 1997: pl.
13.26); Masada Camp F (Magness 2009: fig. 7.4, late
1st/early 2nd century AD).

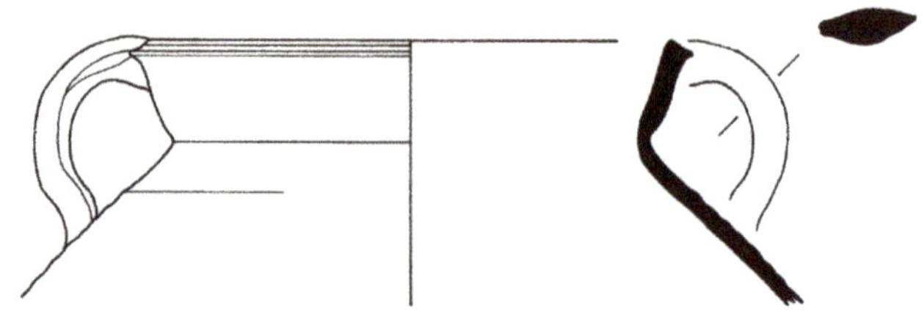

PW 582. CN 7723.
XXXIVB 43.1. Mixed Context.
Part of wall, rim, handle. PH 0.04; PL 0.085; D rim
(est.) 0.11. Reddish-brown clay 5YR 5/4. Metallic
Coarse Terracotta.
Strap handle from rim to upper body.
Parallel: Kallirhoe (Clamer 1997: pl. 12.6).

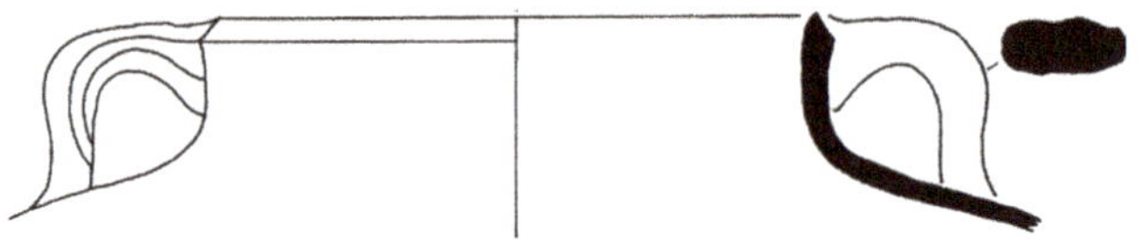

PW 583. CN 7731.
XXXIVB 43.2. Mixed Context.
Part of rim, wall. PH 0.035; PL 0.085; D rim (est.)
0.10. Red clay 2.5YR 5/8. Metallic Coarse Terracotta.

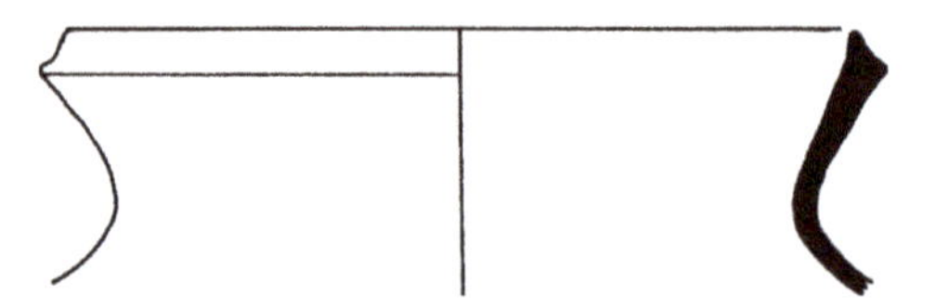

PW 584. CN 7548.
XXXIVB 25.5. Early Roman 1.
Part of wall, rim, handle. PH 0.03; PL 0.06; D rim
(est.) 0.14. Dark red clay 2.5YR 4/6.
Parallel: Hippos-Sussita (Osband and Eisenberg 2018:
pl. 4.6.6, end 1st c. BC/beginning 1st c. AD).

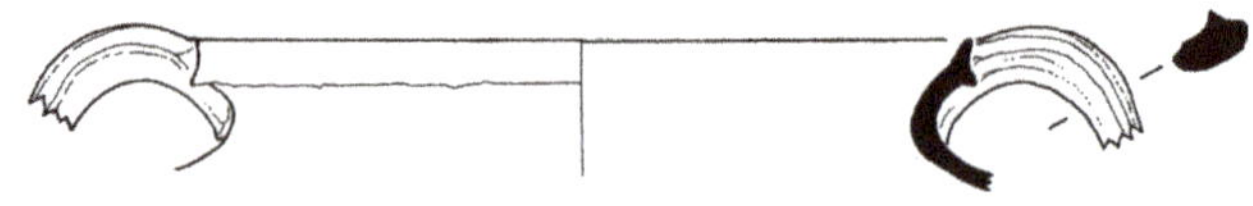

PW 585. CN 7570.
XXXIVB 27.2. Early Roman 1.
Part of wall, rim. PH 0.035; PL 0.06; D rim (est.)
0.11. Red clay 2.5YR 5/8. Metallic Coarse Terracotta.
Parallels: Hippos-Sussita (Osband and Eisenberg 2018:
pl. 3.2.4, 1st c. BC); Jaffa (Tsuf 2018: fig. 9.20.382).

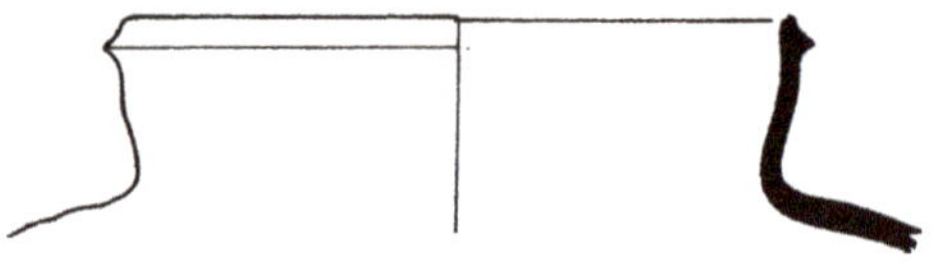

PW 586. CN 7637.
XXXIVB 30.2. Hellenistic 3B/3C.
Part of wall, rim. PH 0.03; PL 0.06; D rim (est.) 0.10.
Dark red clay 2.5YR 4/8. Metallic Coarse Terracotta.

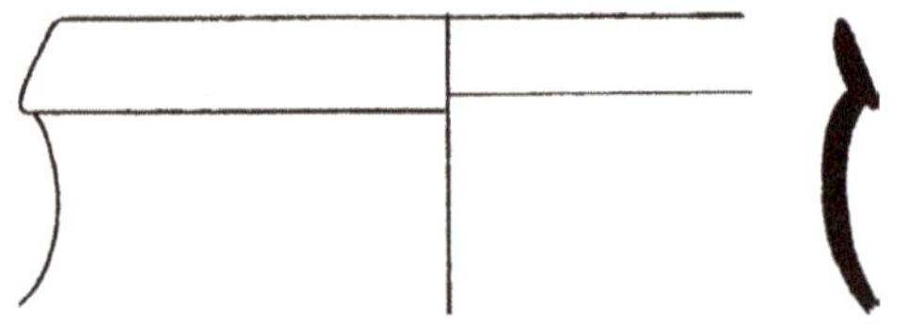

PW 587. CN 7254.

XXXIVG 6.2. Early Roman 1.

Part of wall, rim. PH 0.025; D rim (est.) 0.10. Strong brown clay 7.5YR 5/6. Metallic Coarse Terracotta. Parallels: Arqūb Rūmi (Berger 2020: fig. 9.5.6); Jerusalem (Geva 2003: pl. 5.3.14, late 2nd–1st c. BC; Strange 1975: fig. 14.17); Machaerus (Corbo and Loffreda 1981: fig. 36.15 upper profile); Nahal Hever (Aharoni 1961: fig. 10.9).

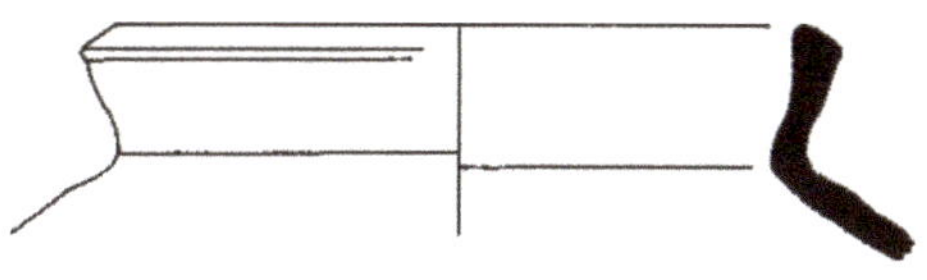

PW 588. CN 7253.

XXXIVG 6.11. Early Roman 1.

Part of wall, rim. PH 0.02; D rim (est.) 0.14. Red clay 2.5YR 5/8. Metallic Coarse Terracotta.

Parallels: Gezer (close to Gitin 1990: pl. 37.21, mid-2nd c. BC); Herodium (Bar-Nathan 1981: pl. 5.18); Jerusalem (Bagatti and Alliata 1981: fig. 3.29; Tushingham 1985: fig. 23.25).

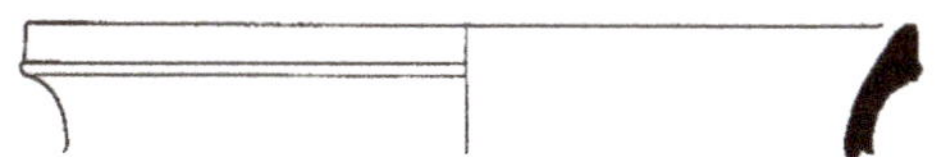

PW 589. CN 3051.

XIA/B 2.1. Early Roman 1.

Almost complete. H 0.17; D rim 0.10. Red clay 2.5YR 5/8. Metallic Coarse Terracotta.

Two strap handles from rim to shoulder.

Parallels: Abila (Mare 1994: fig. 10.4); ʿAkko-Ptolemais (Dothan 1976: fig. 45.10); Beth-Zur (P.W. Lapp and N.L. Lapp 1958: fig. 4.2); Herodium (Bar-Nathan 1981: pl. 9.7); ʿIraq al-Amir (Zimmerman 2020b: pl. 2.18.8, str. II, c. 100 AD); Kallirhoe (Clamer 1997: pl. 4.16); Machaerus (Corbo and Loffreda 1981: fig. 36.16; Loffreda 1980: pl. 95.23); Jericho (Pritchard 1958: pl. 59.1); Jerusalem (Geva 1983: fig. 5.6; Strange 1975: fig. 13.18).

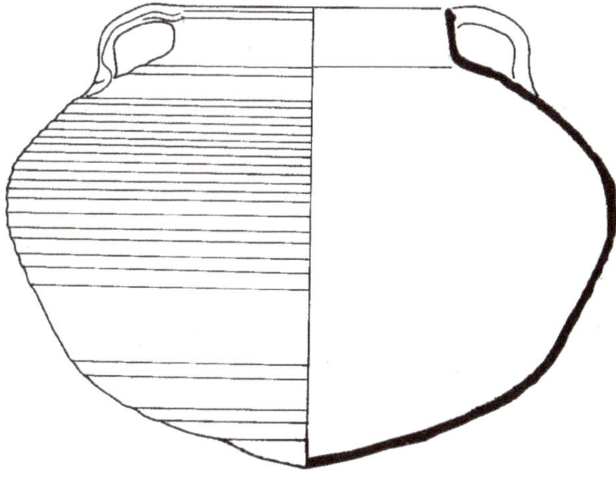

PW 590. CN 6616.

XIA/B 4.6. Early Roman 1.

Part of wall, rim. PH 0.035; D rim (est.) 0.11. Very dark grey clay 5YR 3/1. Metallic Coarse Terracotta. Parallel: Herodium (Bar-Nathan 1981: pl. 1.9).

PW 591. CN 2651.

XIA/B 1.1/2. Early Roman 1.

Part of wall, rim, handle. PH 0.45; D rim (est.) 0.12. Weak red clay 2.5YR 5/4. Metallic Coarse Terracotta. Strap handle from rim to shoulder.

Parallels: Herodium (Bar-Nathan 1981: pl. 5.9); Samaria (Crowfoot et al. 1957: fig. 67.4, Herodian).

PW 592. CN 2567.
XIA/B 1.1. Early Roman 1.
Part of rim. PH 0.025; D rim (est.) 0.12. Weak red clay 2.5YR 5/4. Metallic Coarse Terracotta.
Parallels: 'En el-Ghuweir (Bar-Adon 1977: fig. 14.4); Gezer (Gitin 1990: pl. 35.17, mid-2nd c. BC); Jerusalem (Strange 1975: fig. 13.2); Tell es-Sa'idiyeh (Pritchard 1985: fig. 20.7).

PW 593. CN 3069.
XIA/B 1.5. Early Roman 1.
Part of wall, rim. PH 0.065; PL 0.10; D rim (est.) 0.160. Red clay 2.5YR 6/8. Metallic Coarse Terracotta.
Parallels: Gezer (Gitin 1990: pl. 40.25, late 2nd c. BC); Hesban (Gerber 2012: 243, fig. 3.17.16); Machaerus (Loffreda 1996: fig. 27.7).

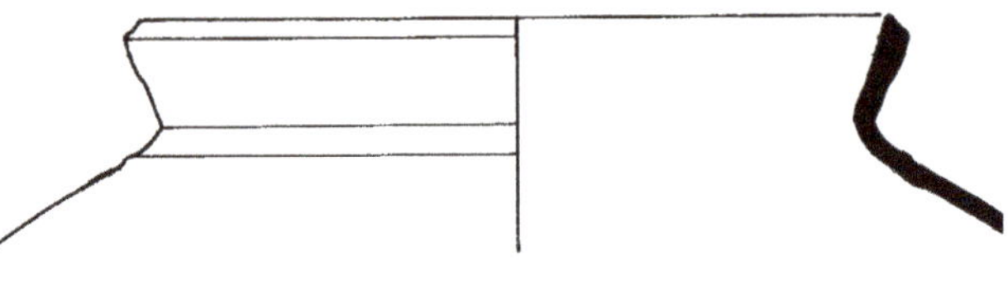

PW 594. CN 2622.
XIA/B 1.1. Early Roman 1.
Part of rim. PH 0.03; D rim (est.) 0.09. Red clay 2.5YR 6/8. Metallic Coarse Terracotta.
Parallels: Gezer (Gitin 1990: pl. 42.26, early 1st c. BC); Qumran (Eshel and Broshi 2003: fig. 4.13).

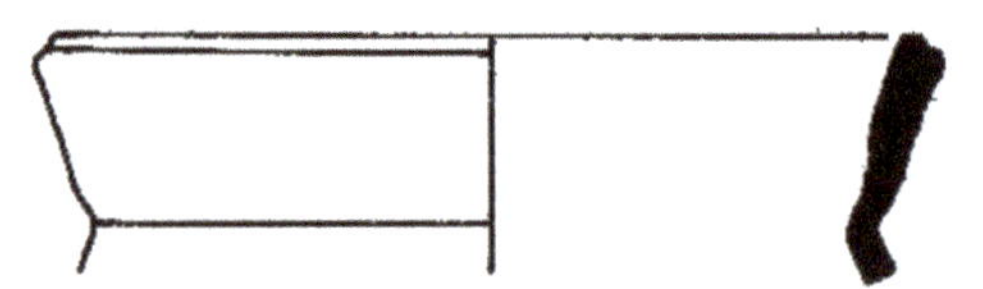

PW 595. CN 2623.
XIA/B 1.5. Early Roman 1.
Part of wall, rim, handle. PH 0.045; PL 0.08; D rim (est.) 0.10. Red clay 2.5YR 5/6. Metallic Coarse Terracotta.
Strap handle from rim to shoulder.
Parallels: Betar (Singer 1993: fig. 1.8); 'Iraq al-Amir (Brown 1983: fig. 54.4); Madaba (Ferguson 2014: 182, fig. 6.24, c. 63–15 BC).

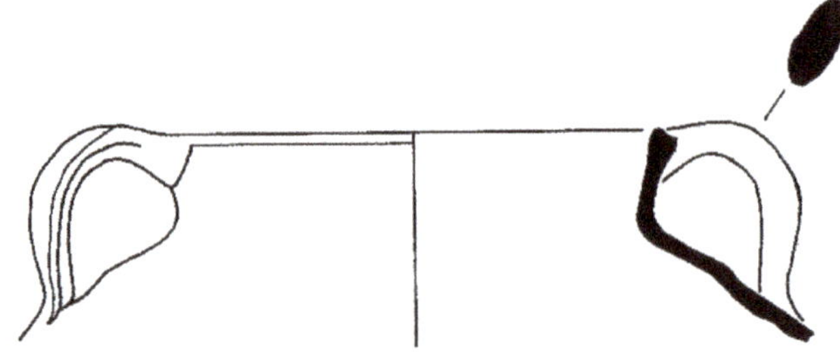

PW 596. CN 2961.
XIA/B 1.4. Early Roman 1.
Part of wall, rim, handle. PH 0.06; D rim (est.) 0.15. Red clay 2.5YR 5/6. Metallic Coarse Terracotta.
Strap handle from rim to shoulder. Lightly ridged body.
Parallels: Gezer (Gitin 1990: pl. 33.21, mid-3rd c. BC); Jericho (Netzer and Meyers 1977: fig. 6.5); Jerusalem (Geva and Rosenthal-Heginbottom 2003: pl. 6.9.17, c. 30–70 AD; Strange 1975: fig. 13.13); Madaba (Ferguson 2014: 182, fig. 6.19, c. 15 BC–100 AD); Tel Anafa (Berlin 1997a: pl. 21. PW 185); Tel Jezreel (Grey 1994: fig. 2.4).

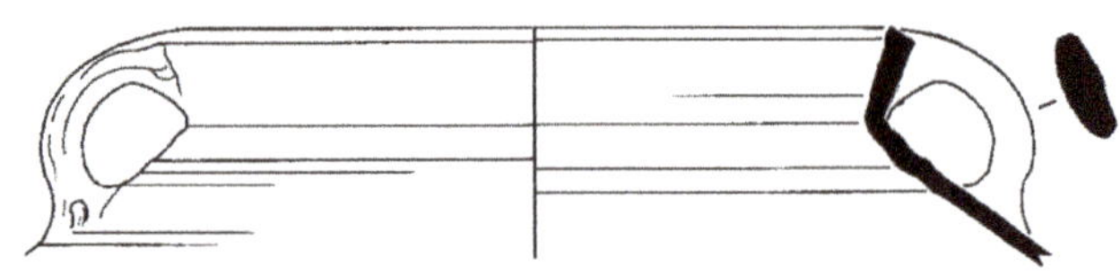

PW 597. CN 2970.

XIA/B 1.5. Early Roman 1.

Part of wall, rim, handle. PH 0.06; D rim (est.) 0.115. Reddish-brown clay 5YR 5/4. Metallic Coarse Terracotta.

Strap handle from rim to shoulder.

Parallels: 'Iraq al-Amir (Zimmerman 2020b: pl. 2.18.7, str. II, c. 100 AD); Jerusalem (Strange 1975: fig. 13.18).

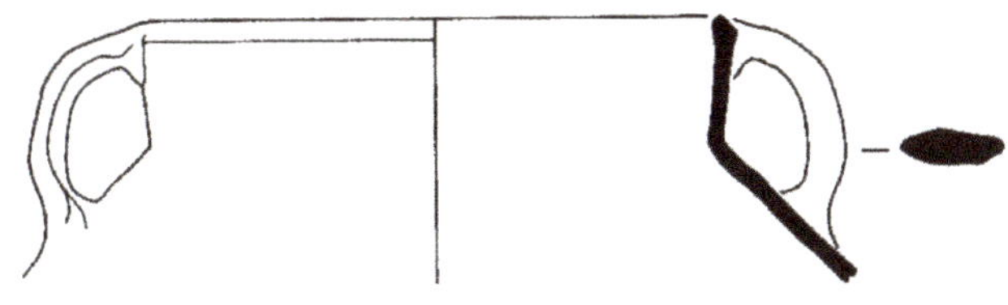

PW 598. CN 2933.

XIA/B 1.5. Early Roman 1.

Part of wall, rim, handle. PH 0.05; PL 0.07; D rim (est.) 0.10. Red clay 10R 5/6. Metallic Coarse Terracotta.

Strap handle from rim to shoulder.

Parallels: Apollonia (Fischer and Tal 1996: fig. 7.2); Gezer (Gitin 1990: pl. 40.23, late 2nd c. BC); Jerusalem (Bagatti and Alliata 1981: fig. 3.33a); Samaria (Crowfoot et al. 1957: fig. 41.4, c. 200–150 BC; Hennessy 1970: fig. 9.13); Tel Dor (Guz-Zilberstein 1995: fig. 6.18:10, 225–200 BC); Tel Keisan (Briend 1980: pl. 11.1j, late 4th–mid-2nd c. BC).

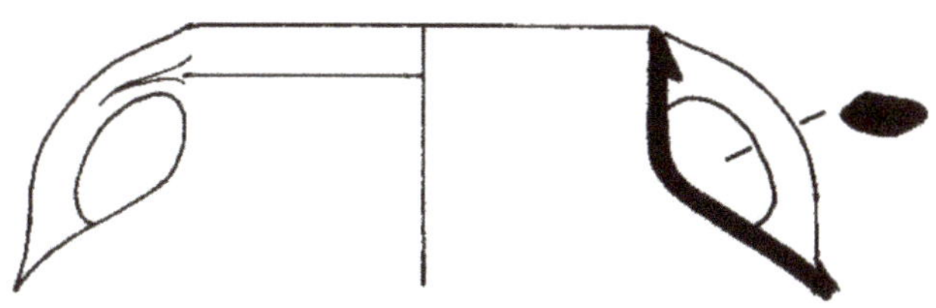

PW 599. CN 2983.

XIA/B 1.2/3. Early Roman 1.

Part of wall, rim, handle. PH 0.045; D rim (est.) 0.10. Yellowish-red clay 5YR 5/6. Metallic Coarse Terracotta.

Strap handle from rim to shoulder.

Parallels: Jerusalem (Geva and Rosenthal-Heginbottom 2003: pl. 6.5.39, early 1st c. AD; Strange 1975: fig. 13.8); Tel Anafa (Berlin 1997a: pl. 21, PW 185, 125–? BC residual); Tell Zira'a (Kenkel 2020: 54, 152–3, pl. 1.18: Kt5.2).

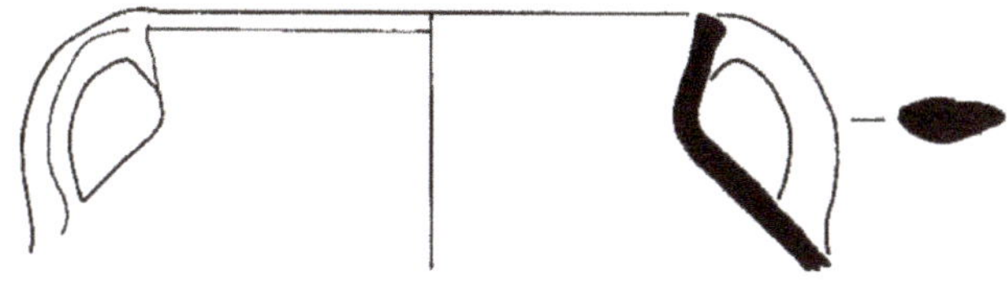

Globular; grooved rim (Type 6)

PW 600–5 are the only examples from Pella of the globular cooking pot with grooved rim seen at Gamla in second and first century BC contexts, where it is the earliest form of cooking pot (Berlin 2006: 32, figs 2.10.1–2), and also at Tel Anafa from much the same time span (Berlin 1997a: 89–90, PW 197–200). Four of the six stratified specimens were from Early Roman contexts on Husn with the fourth (**PW 605**) from an earlier, Hellenistic 3B, stratum on the main mound.

PW 600. CN 6613.

XIA/B 4.6. Early Roman 1.

Part of wall, rim, handle. PH 0.03; PL 0.075; D rim (est.) 0.12. Red clay 2.5YR 5/8. Metallic Coarse Terracotta.

Strap handle from rim to prominent shoulder.

Parallels: Jerusalem (Tchekhanovets 2013: fig. 5.1:13, 1st c. BC–70 AD); Tell Zira'a (Kenkel 2020: 57, 154–5, pl. 1.19: Kt16.5).

PW 601. CN 6594.
XIA/B 4.5. Early Roman 1.
Part of wall, rim. PH 0.03; PL 0.09; D rim
(est.) 0.11. Yellowish-red clay 5YR 5/8. Metallic
Coarse Terracotta.
Ridged body.
Parallels: Jaffa (Tsuf 2018: fig. 9.21.401); Kedesh
(Levantine Ceramics Project: n.d. K08P120,
3rd –2nd c. BC).

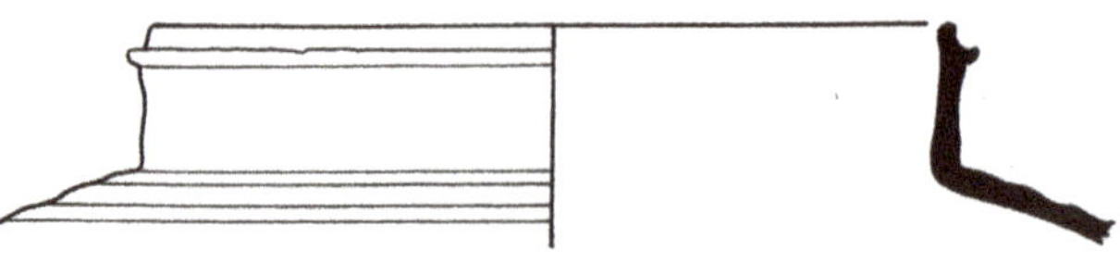

PW 602. CN 6601.
XIA/B 4.6. Early Roman 1.
Part of wall, rim. PH 0.03; PL 0.11; D rim (est.) 0.21.
Dark red clay 2.5YR 4/8. Metallic Coarse Terracotta.

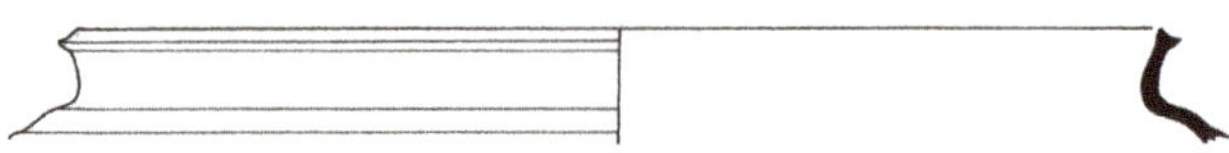

PW 603. CN 2566.
XIA/B 1.1. Early Roman 1.
Part of rim, handle. PH 0.015; D rim (est.) 0.09. Red
clay 2.5YR 6/6. Metallic Coarse Terracotta.
Strap handle from rim to shoulder.
Parallels: Straton's Tower/Caesarea (Berlin 1992:
fig. 55.15 rim profile); 'En el-Ghuweir (Bar-Adon
1977: fig. 14.7); Tel Anafa (Berlin 1997a: pl. 24. PW
210, 75–20 BC).

PW 604. CN 7360.
XXXIVB 5.1. Mixed Context.
Part of rim. PL 0.045; PH 0.03; D rim (est.) 0.095.
Yellowish-red clay 5YR 5/8. Metallic Coarse
Terracotta.
Parallels: Hesban (Gerber 2012: 262, fig. 3.21.20); Tel
Zahara (Bar-Nathan 2013: fig. 3.5.34).

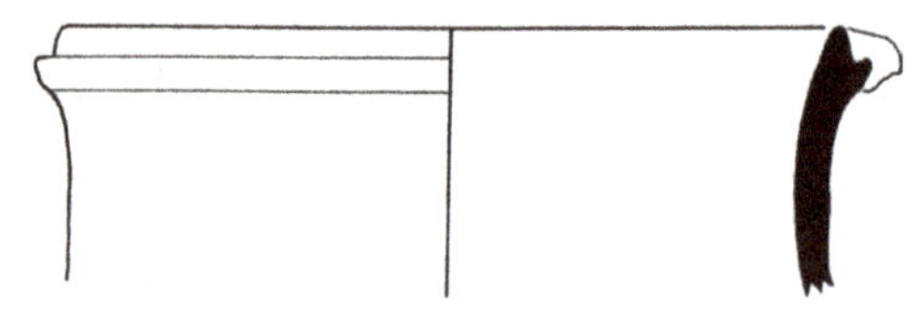

PW 605. CN 6674.
IIIP25.11. Hellenistic 3B.
Part of wall, rim. PH 0.02; D rim (est.) 0.14. Red clay
2.5YR 5/8.
Parallels: 'En el-Ghuweir (Bar-Adon 1977: fig.
14.4); Hippos-Sussita (Osband and Eisenberg 2018:
pl. 4.5.4, end 1st c. BC/beginning 1st c. AD); Jerusalem
(Tchekhanovets 2013: fig. 5.1:13, 1st c. AD–70 AD); Tel
'Ira (Fischer and Tal 1999b: fig. 6.127.3); Tel Zahara
(Bar-Nathan and Gärtner 2013: fig. 3.13.115).

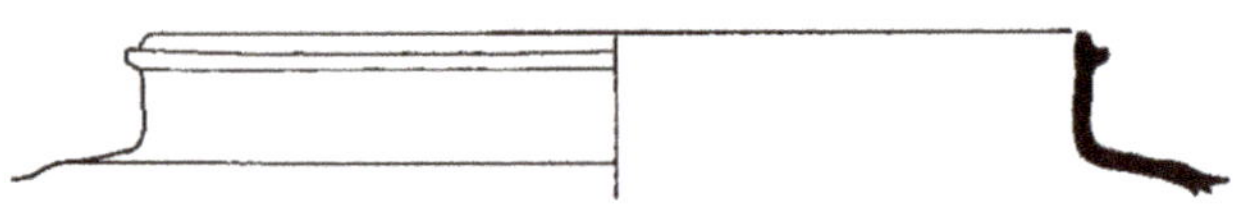

"Galilean" type: globular; grooved interior rim (Type 7)

PW 606–10 have an upright or slightly everted neck, with an obvious groove just inside the lip. Adan-Bayewitz (1993: 124–5) suggested that this form, corresponding to Kfar Hananya Form 4A, was introduced into the Galilee region during the latter half of the first century BC and continued to be made – at least at Kfar Hananya – for the following two centuries. He recognised that, due to the extreme paucity of well-dated Late Hellenistic sites in the Galilee and Golan, the initial date of production of this form (and of Form 3A) may need to be revised by "several decades" (Adan-Bayewitz 1993: 117). Berlin (2006: 40) has suggested that Gamla potters produced a similar form "sometime in the second quarter of the first century BC" with Kfar Hananya workshops turning out their own versions soon after. The recovery of **PW 606**, from well within a Jannaeus Destruction (Hellenistic 3C) deposit on the main mound with no potentially contaminating overlying Early Roman level, suggests that by c. 80 BC Galilean settlements at Kfar Hananya or elsewhere may have been turning out cooking pots of this type, though no doubt in small numbers.

Cooking pots of similar form have been recovered in significant numbers from Gamla (Berlin 2006: 32–40), Sepphoris (CP2: Balouka 2013: 21) and Tel Anafa where they are especially common in Roman 1A and 1B (late first-century BC and early first-century AD) contexts (Berlin 1997a: 87, pl. 25, PW 211–15). Along with other Kfar Hananya forms, these pots became widespread throughout the Galilee during this period, possibly as a result of the campaigns there of Alexander Jannaeus in the early years of the first century BC (Adan-Bayewitz 1993: 200–23; Berlin 2006: 40, 143–4). Outside the Galilee, these forms are rare and are seen neither at Tel Dor nor Gezer.

The fabric of **PW 606–8** is visually close or identical to those products of Kfar Hananya but, for the reasons discussed above, the more general term "Galilean" ware is preferred.

PW 606. CN 1134.
IIIB/C 14.2. Hellenistic 3C.
Part of rim. PH 0.05; D rim (est.) 0.135. Red clay 2.5YR 5/8. "Galilean" ware.
Parallels: Hippos-Sussita (Osband and Eisenberg 2018: pl. 4.1.2 upper profile, end 1st c. BC/beginning 1st c. AD); Jerusalem (Machline and Gadot 2017: fig. 11.7); Tell Zira'a (Kenkel 2020: 57, 154–5, pl. 1.19 Kt16.5).

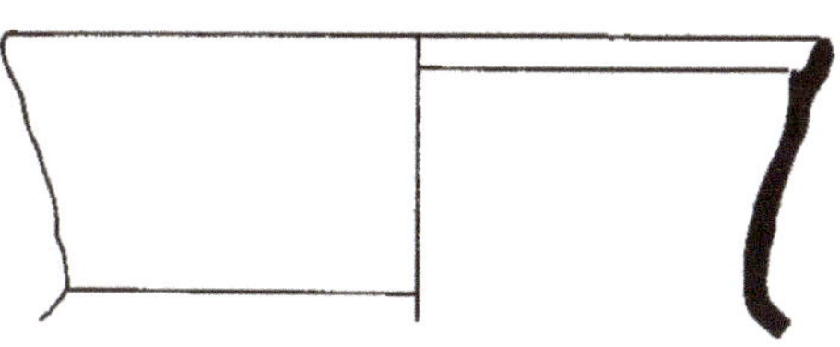

PW 607. CN 7569.
XXXIVB 27.2. Early Roman 1.
Part of wall, rim, handle. PH 0.045; PL 0.06; D rim (est.) 0.14. Red clay 2.5YR 5/8. "Galilean" ware.
Strap handle from rim to shoulder.
Parallels: Hippos-Sussita (Osband and Eisenberg 2018: pls 4.1.2, end 1st c. BC/beginning 1st c. AD, 4.2.37 of Galileean fabric, end 1st c. BC/beginning 1st c. AD); Sepphoris (Balouka 2013: pl. 8.1, 70–135 AD).

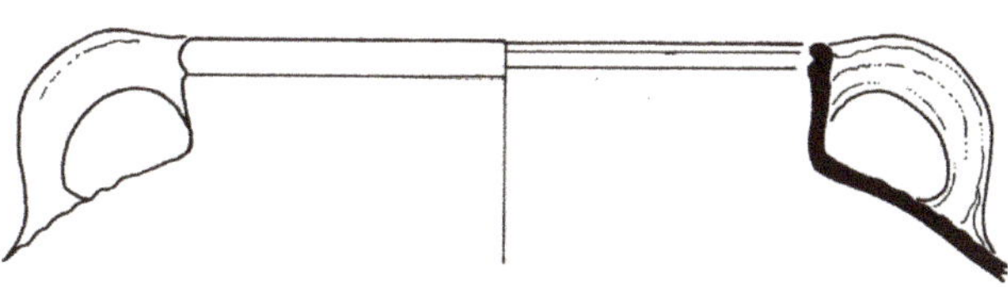

PW 608. CN 2978.
XIA/B 1.1/3. Early Roman 1.
Part of rim. PH 0.035; PL 0.04; D rim (est.) 0.10. Red clay 2.5YR 4/6–5/6. "Galilean" ware.
Parallels: Capernaeum (Loffreda 1974: fig. 2.12); Hippos-Sussita (Mlynarczyk 2011: pl. 245.60, very late 2nd–1st c. BC).

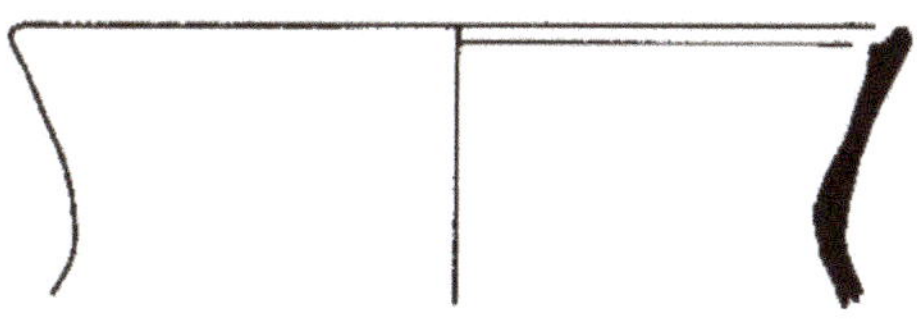

PW 609. CN 2985.
XIA/B 1.2/3. Early Roman 1.
Part of rim, wall. PH 0.035; PL 0.08; D rim (est.) 0.10.
Yellowish-red clay 5YR 5/8.

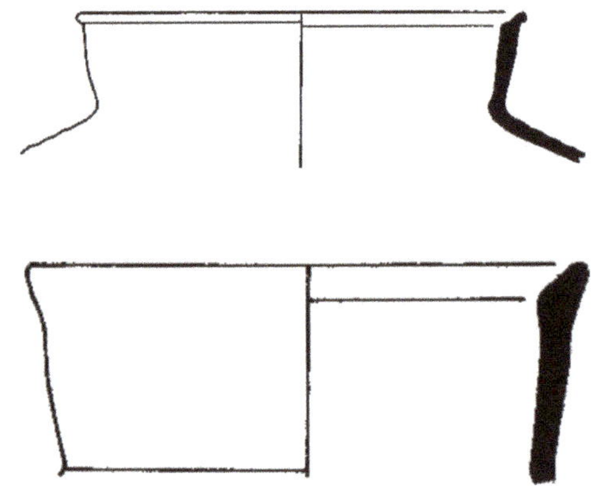

PW 610. CN 2560.
XIA/B 1.1. Early Roman 1.
Part of wall, rim. PH 0.025; D rim (est.) 0.095. Red
clay 2.5YR 5/6. Pink slip 5YR 8/4 on exterior.
Parallels: Jerusalem (Sandhaus 2013: fig. 4.9:1,
second half of 2nd c. BC); Meiron (Meyers et al. 1981:
pl. 8.16.6); Tel Anafa (Berlin 1997a: pl. 59, PW 494,
198–c. 125 BC).

Globular; thickened lip (Type 8)

PW 611–9 constitute a series of cooking pots of thin ware with tall necks ending in a narrow, thickened
collar. With the exception of **PW 611** (Hellenistic 3C), all are from Early Roman contexts on Tell Husn. The
rim of a similar vessel was recovered from an Early Roman stratum in the Civic Complex by the Wooster
Team (Smith and Day 1989: 99, pl. 44.34, close to **PW 616**).

PW 611. CN 7830.
XXIIID 68.4. Hellenistic 3C.
Part of rim, shoulder. PH 0.06; PL 0.08; D rim (est.)
0.115. Red clay 10R 5/6. Metallic Coarse Terracotta.
Faint ribbing on shoulder. Thin wall.

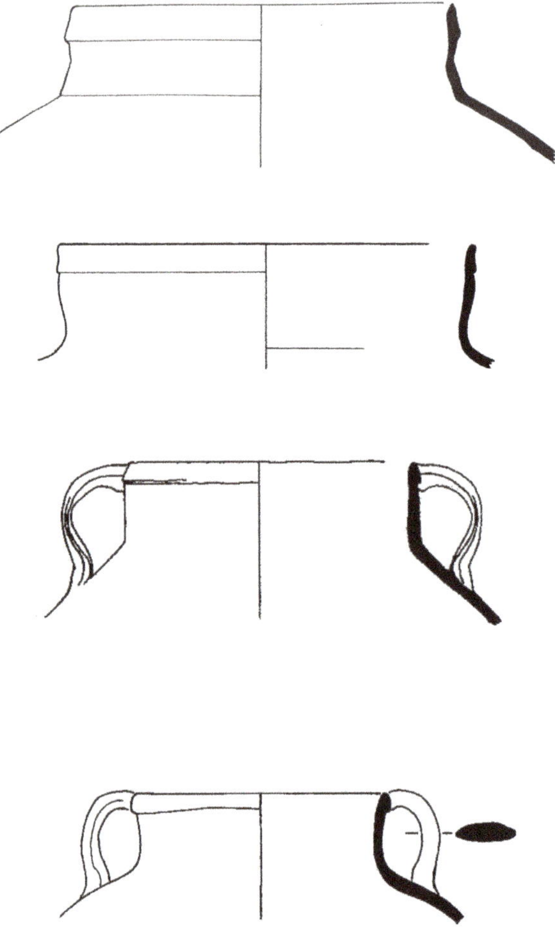

PW 612. CN 7611.
XXXIVB 27.6. Early Roman 1.
Two joining fragments of neck. PH 0.035; PL 0.08;
D rim (est.) 0.125. Red clay 2.5YR 5/6. Metallic Coarse
Terracotta.

PW 613. CN 7285.
XXXIVG 8.11. Early Roman 1.
Part of wall, neck, rim, handle. PH 0.045; D rim (est.)
0.095. Red clay 2.5YR 6/8. Metallic Coarse Terracotta.
Strap handle from rim to shoulder.
Parallels: Ashdod (Dothan and Freedman 1967: fig.
11.4, mid-1st c. BC–c. 70 AD); Herodium (Bar-Nathan
1981: pl. 5.10); Machaerus (Loffreda 1980: pl. 95.25).

PW 614. CN 2934.
XIA/B 1.5. Early Roman 1.
Part of rim, shoulder, handle. PH 0.05; D rim
(est.) 0.10. Brownish-yellow clay 10YR 6/8. Metallic
Coarse Terracotta.
Strap handle from rim to shoulder.
Parallel: Machaerus (Loffreda 1996: fig. 28.6a).

PW 615. CN 3058.
XIA/B 2.3. Early Roman 1.
Part of wall, rim. PH 0.085; D rim (est.) 0.125. Red clay 2.5YR 6/8. Metallic Coarse Terracotta.

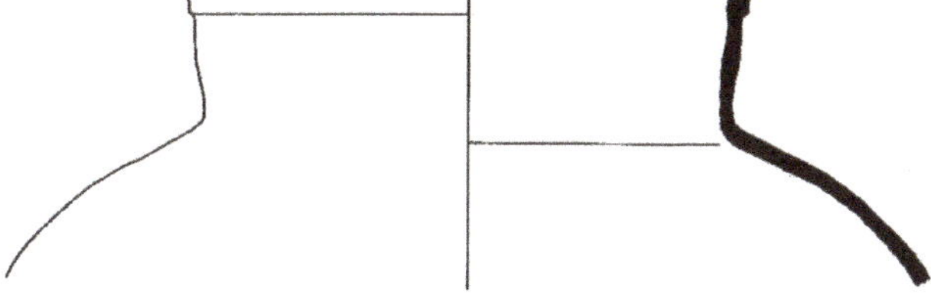

PW 616. CN 6596.
XIA/B 4.5. Early Roman 1.
Part of rim, neck, wall. PH 0.05; PL 0.085; D rim (est.) 0.95. Red clay 2.5YR 5/8. Metallic Coarse Terracotta. Thin wall.

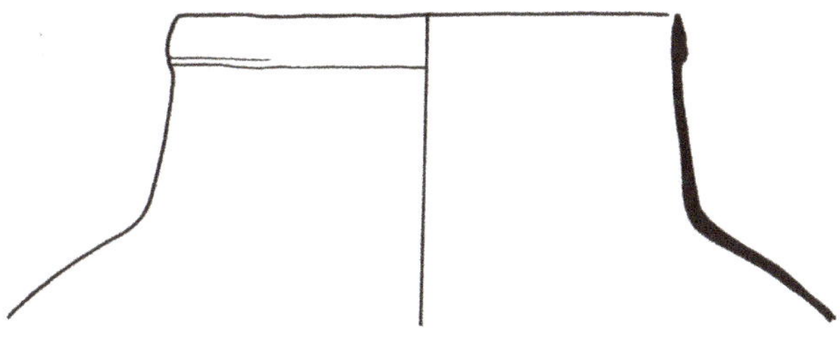

PW 617. CN 7367.
XXXIVB 12.3. Early Roman 1.
Part of wall, rim. PH 0.035; PL 0.10; D rim (est.) 0.11. Reddish-yellow clay 5YR 6/8. Metallic Coarse Terracotta.

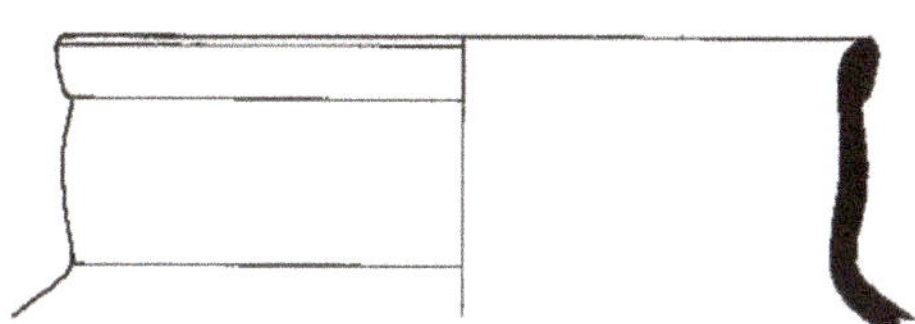

PW 618. CN 7355.
XXXIVB 6.27. Early Roman 1.
Part of rim. PH 0.035; PL 0.02; D rim (est.) 0.095. Red clay 2.5YR 5/8. Metallic Coarse Terracotta.

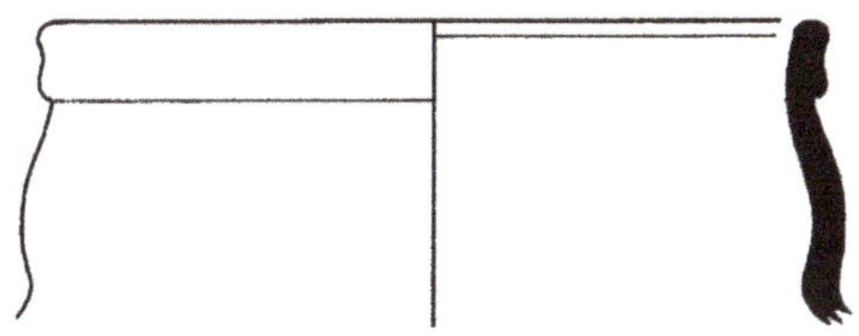

PW 619. CN 3046.
XIA/B 2.1/2. Early Roman.
Part of rim. PH 0.045; D rim (est.) 0.105. Light reddish-brown clay 5YR 6/4. Metallic Coarse Terracotta.

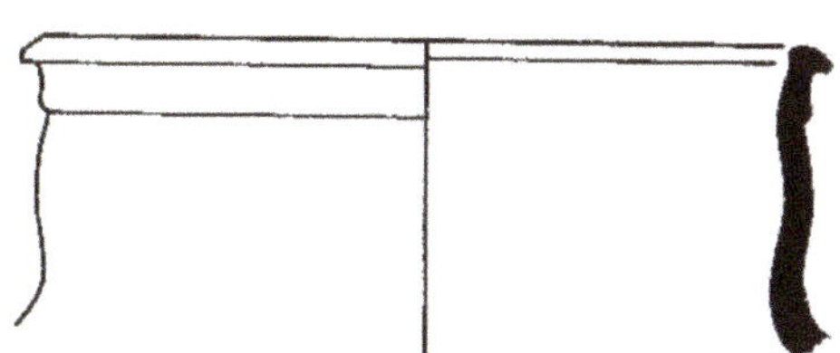

Casseroles (PW 620–46)

The other main form of cooking vessel – the casserole – is derived from the *lopas*, an open, shallow, lidded cooking vessel that became very popular in Athens and elsewhere in Greece from the third quarter of the fifth century onwards (Edwards 1975: 124–8; Rotroff 2006b: 178–86; Sparkes and Talcott 1970: 227; Thompson 1934: 466–8).[28] Its earliest appearance in the southern Levant now seems to be in the mid-fourth century at Tel Dor (Guz-Zilberstein 1995: 299) whilst by the third century it is seen in Jerusalem (Berlin 2012: fig. 2.1.7) and in the Central Shephelah (Sandhaus 2020: fig. 1.9). However, it only becomes common in the

---

28 The Athenian *lopas* of the fifth and fourth centuries BC is a relatively shallow vessel with a tall, almost vertical rim (Sparkes and Talcott 1970: figs 18.1962–1968). During the Hellenistic period it becomes deeper with the rim more horizontal and the underside flat or slightly concave (Rotroff 2006b: figs 82–5; Thompson 1934: fig. 121). However, as far as can be ascertained from their fragmentary condition, the Pella examples do not follow the same progression.

later Hellenistic period though mainly confined to sites that either contain Greek settlers or are receptive to Greek influence (Berlin 1988: 68, 1997a: 95, 2015: 636; Sandhaus 2020: 113). As Berlin (1993: 42) has suggested, in many instances the casseroles must have been supported over the fire by braziers such as those Late Hellenistic examples with interior lug supports described by Rahmani (1984).

At Tel Anafa, the casserole is seen in impressive numbers from Hellenistic 2A (c. 125 BC) onwards (Berlin 1997a: 94–103). By the second century BC it was also common at Tel Dor (Guz-Zilberstein 1995: 299–300). At Gamla it appears during the first century BC (Berlin 2006: 41) and during the following century at Kallirhoe (Clamer 1997: pl. 7.1–6). Though common throughout the Galilee and Golan (Balouka 2013: 27), the casserole was never popular at Gezer where few examples have been recovered (Gitin 1990: Types 243–5) – a situation that may be consistent with the relatively conservative Hasmonean population of that city. At Machaerus the shape is also uncommon (Loffreda 1996: Group 46: fig. 34), although limited numbers have been recovered from levels belonging to the end of the Hasmonean occupation right up to the destruction of the Herodian fortress in 72 AD. At 'Iraq al-Amir casseroles make their appearance in Stratum IV (early second century BC) and, in a variety of forms, remain in use until the third century AD (Zimmerman 2020b: 61–3). Casseroles are not recorded at Hesban.

At Pella casseroles appear as early as the later third century BC on Tell Husn (**PW 620–2**), in a similar chronological horizon to that seen in Jerusalem (Berlin 2012: 10, fig. 2.1.7); more frequently, however, they are encountered within the Early Roman phase on that *tell*. The majority belong to Type 1 which, in profile, recalls Kfar Hananya Form 3A, produced at that settlement during the years between the first century BC and the mid-second century AD (Adan-Bayewitz 1993: 111–19).

Table 2.38. Distribution of casseroles by types, wares, phases.

		ROUNDED BODY; CONSTRICTED NECK; OVERHANGING RIM (TYPE 1)	UPRIGHT WALL; OVERHANGING RIM (TYPE 2)	CARINATED; INTERIOR FLANGE; OVERHANGING RIM (TYPE 3)	WIDE MOUTH; GROOVED RIM; PROMINENT SHOULDER (TYPE 4)
Ware	Metallic Coarse Terracotta	7	5	2	4
	"Galilean"	2?	0	0	0
	Miscellaneous	5	1	1	0
Phase	2B c. 220–c. 200 BC	3	0	0	0
	3A c. 200–c. 140 BC	0	0	2	0
	3B c. 140–c. 100 (?) BC	0 (2)	0	1	0
	3B/3C c. 140–c. 80/79 BC	1	0	0	0
	3C c. 100 (?)–c. 80/79 BC	1	1	0	0
	Early Roman 63 BC–c. 135 AD	8 (4)	5	0	3
	Mixed	1	0	0	1

Rounded body; constricted neck; overhanging rim (Type 1)

The distinguishing characteristics of this form, **PW 620–33**, the earliest casserole type at Pella, are its broad rim, overhanging the exterior to a marked degree, and a constriction at the neck that then progresses to a convex body. The rim may be more or less horizontal (for example, **PW 622**, **PW 624**, **PW 627**) or angled upwards (for example, **PW 623**, **PW 628**) and usually ends in a rounded tip, although in **PW 632–3** it is squared off. Several examples (**PW 620**, **PW 629–31**) have a prominent interior flange as a lid device which clearly sets off the rim from the interior wall.

Casseroles of this form (Zimmerman 2020b: Type 120.1 at 'Iraq al-Amir) are similar in shape to those open cooking pots (OCP 1a) from Sepphoris (Balouka 2013: 27) as well as those with angled rim from Gamla (Berlin 2006: 41–4) and the Jerusalem International Convention Centre (Binyane Ha 'Umma) site in Jerusalem (Berlin 2005a: 50–1, figs 19.1–4). The casseroles from this latter site date to ceramic phase 4 (mid-first century AD to 70 AD). While **PW 624–5** are possibly Galilean products, the variety of fabrics points to other centres of manufacture as well.

PW 620. CN 7675.
XXXIVB 27.26. Hellenistic 2B.
Part of wall, rim. PH 0.03; PL 0.075; D rim (est.) 0.19. Red clay 2.5YR 5/8. Metallic Coarse Terracotta.

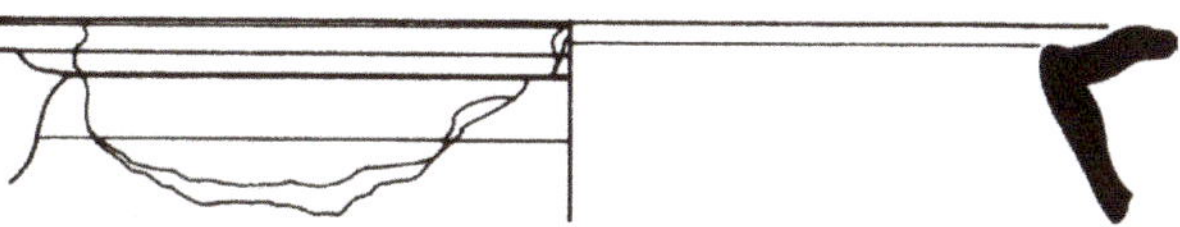

PW 621. CN 7385.
XXXIVF 6.5. Hellenistic 2B.
Part of wall, rim. PH 0.03; D rim (est.) 0.19. Yellowish-red clay 5YR 4/6.
Parallels: 'Akko-Ptolemais (Berlin and Stone 2016: fig. 9.2.6, 3rd c. BC); Capernaeum (Loffreda 1974: fig. 6.8); Central Shephelah (Sandhaus 2020: fig. 1.9); Jerusalem (Tchekhanovets 2013: fig. 5.1:15, 1st c. BC–70 AD); Meiron (Meyers et al. 1981: pl. 8.11.22); Sha'ar ha-Amakim (Mlynarczyk 2004: pl. 310.2); Tel Dor (Guz-Zilberstein 1995: fig. 6.47:19, 275–200 BC); Tell Zira'a (Kenkel 2020: 48, 146–17, pl. 1.15 Kas2.1).

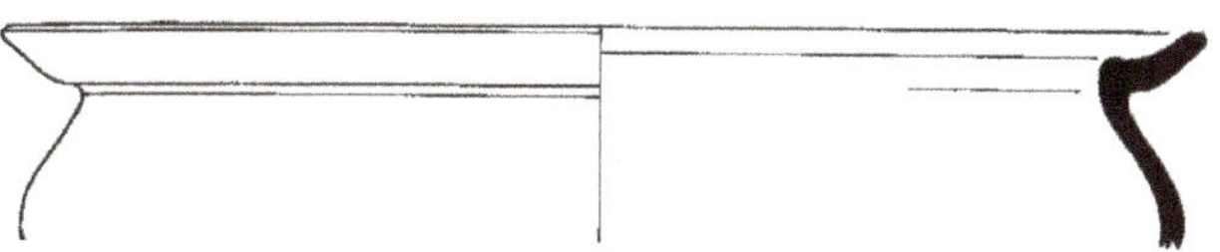

PW 622. CN 7387.
XXXIVF 6.5. Hellenistic 2B.
Part of wall, rim, handle. PH 0.03; D rim (est.) 0.16. Dark red clay 2.5YR 4/6.
Vertical strap handle from rim to mid-body.
Parallels: Capernaeum (Loffreda 1974: fig. 6.10); Jaffa (Tsuf 2018: fig. 9.23.422); Jerusalem (Tchekhanovets 2013: fig. 5.1:15, 1st c. BC–70 AD); Machaerus (Loffreda 1996: fig. 34.10); Meiron (Meyers et al. 1981: pl. 8.11.29); Tel Dor (Guz-Zilberstein 1995: fig. 6.53:12, 275–150 BC); Tel Keisan (Briend 1980: pl. 11.9, late 4th–mid-2nd c. BC).

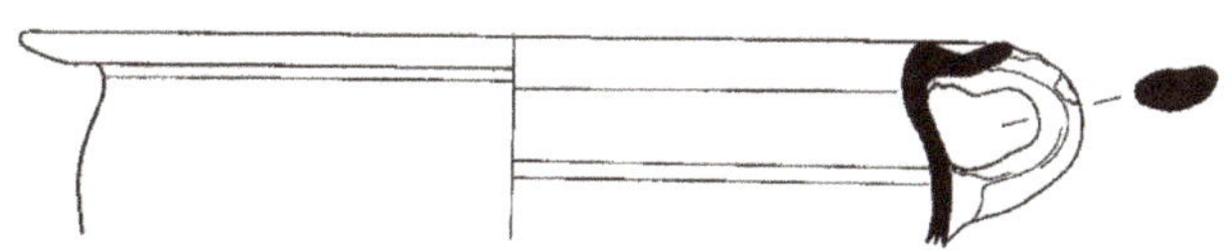

PW 623. CN 7767.

XXIIID 19.2. Hellenistic 3C.

Multiple fragments of wall, rim, handles. Largest fragment: PH 0.085; PL 0.20; D rim (est.) 0.15. Red clay 2.5YR 5/8. Metallic Coarse Terracotta.

Two strap handles from rim to shoulder.

Parallels: Jerusalem (Berlin 2012: fig. 2.1.7, late 3rd c. BC; Rahmani 1967: fig. 16.6); Sepphoris (Balouka 2013: pl. 2.14, 0–70 AD).

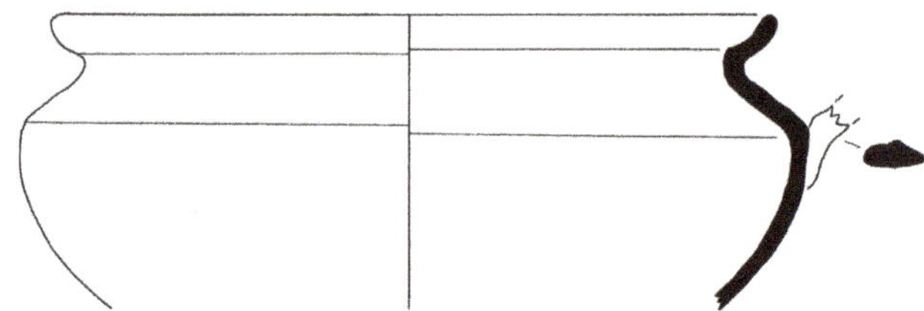

PW 624. CN 2552.

XIA/B 1.1. Early Roman 1.

Part of wall, rim, handle. PH 0.04; D rim (est.) 0.18. Red clay 2.5YR 5/6. "Galilean" ware?

Parallels: Ashdod (Dothan and Freedman 1967: fig. 11.1, mid-1st c. BC–c. 70 AD); Dothan 1971: fig. 24.3); Capernaeum (Loffreda 1974: fig. 6.14); Herodium (Bar-Nathan 1981: pl. 5.19); 'Iraq al-Amir (Zimmerman 2020b: pl. 2.21.2, str. IIIb–II, c. 100 BC–c. 100 AD); Sepphoris (Balouka 2013: pl. 9.1, 70–135 AD).

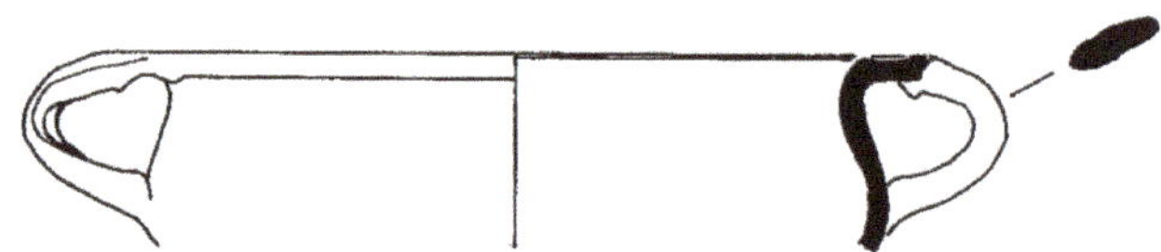

PW 625. CN 2975.

XIA/B 1.1/3. Early Roman 1.

Part of wall, rim. PH 0.04; D rim (est.) 0.24. Red clay 2.5YR 5/8. "Galilean" ware?

Parallels: Apollonia (Fischer and Tal 1996: fig. 9.16); Capernaeum (Loffreda 1974: fig. 6.12); Central Shephelah (Sandhaus 2020: fig. 2.8); Gezer (Gitin 1990: pl. 44.3, mid-1st c. BC); Hesban (Gerber 2012: 281, fig. 3.26.3); Jerusalem (Geva 2003: pl. 5.7.2, 2nd c. BC; Geva and Rosenthal-Heginbottom 2003: pl. 6.2.29, 1st c. BC); Sepphoris (Balouka 2013: pl. 2.15, 0–70 AD); Tel Dor (Guz-Zilberstein 1995: fig. 6.21:1, 350–275 BC); Tel Zahara (Bar-Nathan 2013: fig. 3.2.12).

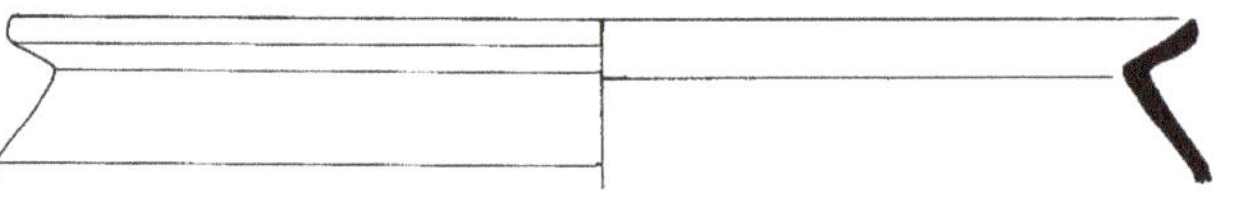

PW 626. CN 2996.

XIA/B 1.3/5. Early Roman 1.

Part of wall, rim. PH 0.085; D rim (est.) 0.185. Light reddish-brown clay 5YR 6/4.

Parallels: Capernaeum (Loffreda 1974: fig. 6.13); Jerusalem (Bagatti and Alliata 1981: fig. 3.38); Tel Dor (Guz-Zilberstein 1995: fig. 6.20:10, 125 BC–75 AD).

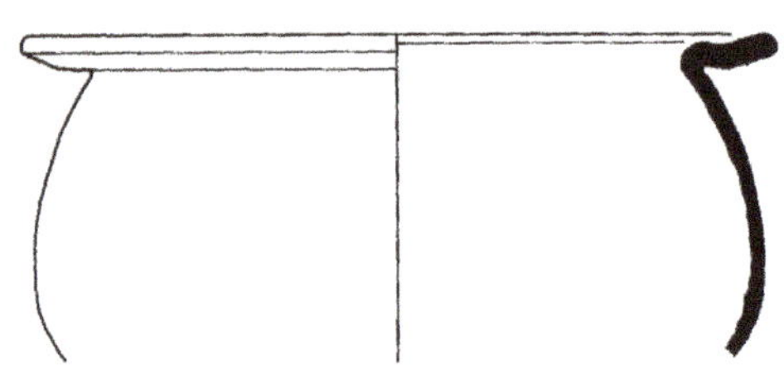

PW 627. CN 7335.
XXXIVB 6.48. Hellenistic 3B/3C.
Part of wall, rim, handle. PH 0.08; PL 0.13; D rim
(est.) 0.17. Yellowish-red clay 5YR 5/8.
Strap handle from rim to mid-body.
Parallels: 'Akko-Ptolemais (Dothan 1976: fig. 30.12);
Ashdod (Dothan 1971: fig. 24.3); Hippos-Sussita
(Osband and Eisenberg 2018: pl. 2.5.2, 2nd c. BC);
Machaerus (Loffreda 1996: fig. 34.14); Madaba
(Ferguson 2014: 182, fig. 6.22, c. 63–15 BC).

PW 628. CN 7345.
XXXIVB 7.17. Early Roman 1.
Part of wall, rim. PL 0.065 PH 0.025; D rim (est.)
0.20. Red clay 2.5YR 5/8. Metallic Coarse Terracotta.
Parallels: Jaffa (Tsuf 2018: fig. 9.24.435); Marisa
(Kloner and Hess 1985: fig. 2.20).

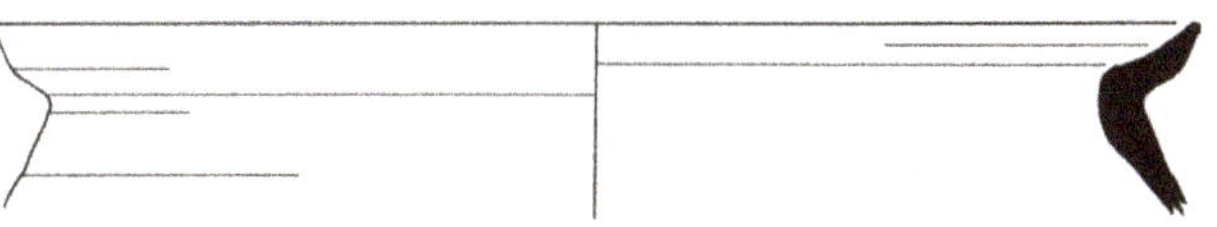

PW 629. CN 7257.
XXXIVG 11.1. Early Roman 1.
Part of wall, rim. PH 0.06; D rim (est.) 0.22. Dark
red clay 2.5YR 4/6.
Parallels: 'Akko-Ptolemais (Berlin and Stone 2016: figs
9.19.10, mid–late 2nd c. BC; 9.22.9, first half of 1st c.
BC); Ashdod (Dothan 1971: fig. 24.7); Hippos-Sussita
(Osband and Eisenberg 2018: pl. 2.4.4, 2nd c. BC);
Jaffa (Tsuf 2018: fig. 9.23.418); Jerusalem (Geva 2003:
pl. 5.8.37, later 2nd–1st c. BC); Kedesh (Levantine
Ceramics Project: n.d. K08P058, 3rd – 2nd c. BC);
Marisa (Levine 2003: fig. 6.6.77); Straton's Tower/
Caesarea (Berlin 1992: fig. 53.13); Tel Anafa (Berlin
1997a: pl. 30. PW 261, 98 BC–early 1st c. AD residual);
Tel Dor (Guz-Zilberstein 1995: fig. 6.20:7, 275–125
BC); Tel Yoqne'am (Ben-Tor et al. 1983: fig. 7.12).

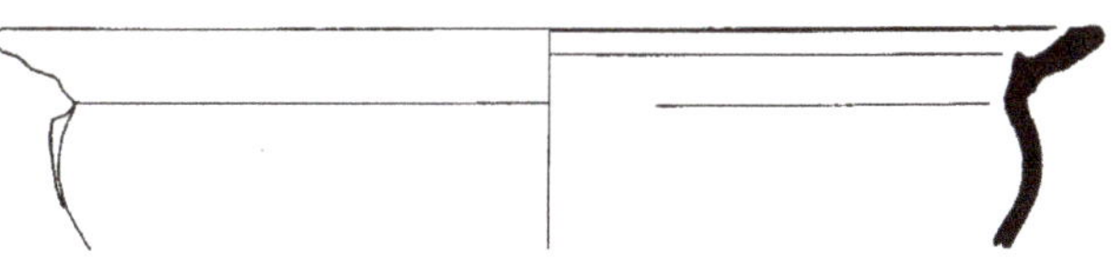

PW 630. CN 3070.
XIA/B 1.5. Early Roman 1.
Part of wall, rim. PH 0.035; D rim (est.) 0.22. Red clay
2.5YR 4/8–5/8. Metallic Coarse Terracotta.
Parallels: Gezer (close to Gitin 1990: pl. 40.27, late
2nd c. BC); Tel Keisan (Briend 1980: pl. 11.6 upper
profile).

PW 631. CN 7632.
XXXIVB 100.9. Mixed Context.
Part of wall, rim. PH 0.03; PL 0.08; D rim (est.) 0.19.
Red clay 2.5YR 5/6. Heavy burning on exterior.
Metallic Coarse Terracotta.
Parallels: Jerusalem (Sandhaus 2013: fig. 4.6:6, second
half of 2nd c. BC); Philoteria/Bet Yerah (Tal and
Reshef 2017: fig. 3.43.4); Shechem (N.L. Lapp 2008:
pl. 3.41.15, unstratified).

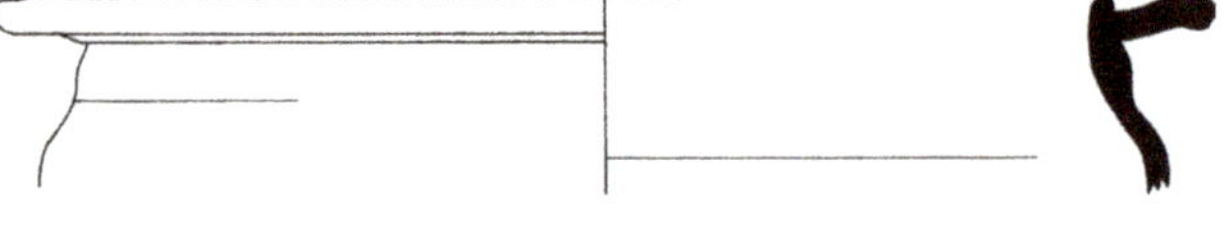

PW 632. CN 7255.
XXXIVG 6.10. Early Roman 1.
Part of wall, rim, handle. PH 0.035; D rim (est.)
0.15. Yellowish-red clay 5YR 4/6. Metallic Coarse
Terracotta.
Strap handle from rim to shoulder.
Parallel: Jerusalem (Tushingham 1985: fig. 22.27).

PW 633. CN 2935.
XIA/B 1.5. Early Roman 1.
Part of rim. PH 0.025; D rim (est.) 0.14. Red clay
2.5YR 6/6. Metallic Coarse Terracotta.

Upright wall; overhanging rim (Type 2)

PW 634–9 have the overhanging rim of the previous type but the upper wall is essentially vertical rather than convex. None of the specimens, however, preserves its complete profile, making it uncertain whether the carination in the lower wall is sharply angled or more gently shaped.

The squared-off rims of **PW 634** and **PW 639** are similar to those seen on **PW 632–3** of the previous form as well as the predominantly Early Roman (but appearing first towards the end of the second century) "bevelled lip" casseroles from Tel Anafa (Berlin 1997a: 98–9, PW 241–7). At Pella casseroles of this form first appear on the main mound in a Jannaeus Destruction (Hellenistic 3C) deposit (**PW 634**), although they are more frequent in Early Roman levels on Husn.

PW 634. CN 7127.
XXIIIA 71.2. Hellenistic 3C.
Part of wall, rim. PH 0.035; D rim (est.) 0.20. Red
clay 2.5YR 5/8. Metallic Coarse Terracotta.
Parallel: Jerusalem (Geva and Rosenthal-Heginbottom
2003: pl. 6.2.27, 1st c. BC).

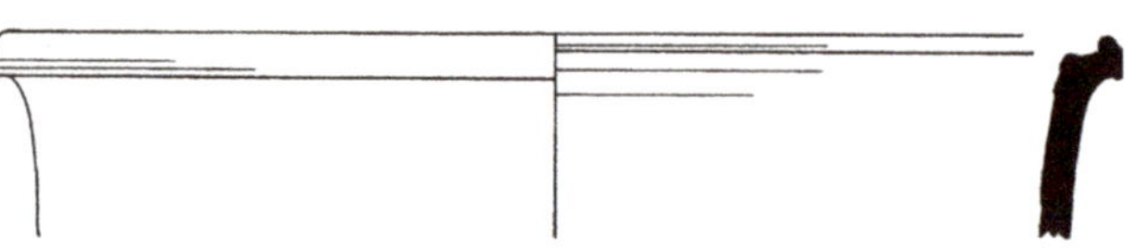

PW 635. CN 7565.
XXXIVB 27.2. Early Roman 1.
Part of wall, rim. PH 0.045; PL 0.075; D rim (est.)
0.20. Red clay 10R 4/8. Metallic Coarse Terracotta.
Parallels: Hippos-Sussita (Osband and Eisenberg 2018:
pl. 4.3.16, end 1st c. BC/beginning 1st c. AD); Madaba
(Ferguson 2014: 182, fig. 6.17, c. 15 BC–100 AD).

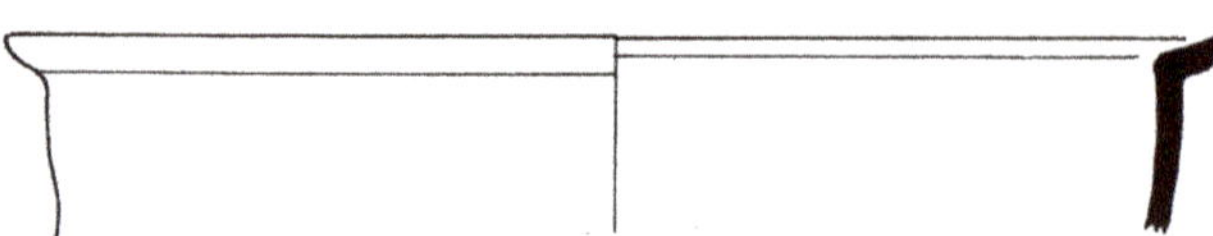

PW 636. CN 2628.
XIA/B 1.5. Early Roman 1.
Part of wall, rim, handle. PH 0.06; D rim (est.) 0.22.
Red clay 2.5YR 5/6.
Strap handle from rim to mid-wall.
Parallels: Jerusalem (Geva 2003: pl. 5.9.26, later
2nd–1st c. BC; Tushingham 1985: fig. 23.4); Machaerus
(Loffreda 1980: pl. 96.36); Meiron (Meyers et al. 1981:
pl. 8.11.25).

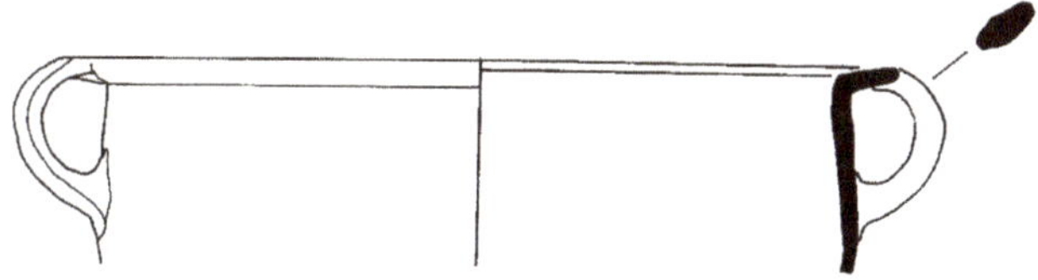

PW 637. CN 2936.
XIA/B 1.5. Early Roman 1.
Part of wall, rim. PH 0.03; D rim (est.) 0.19. Red clay
10R 4/8. Metallic Coarse Terracotta.
Parallels: Hippos-Sussita (Osband and Eisenberg
2018: pl. 4.1.4, end 1st c. BC/beginning 1st c. AD).

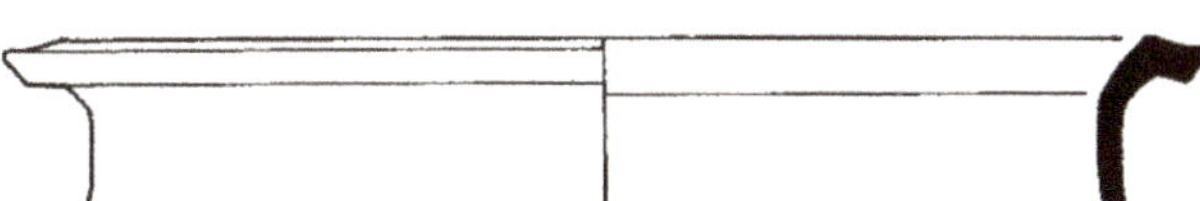

PW 638. CN 7352.
XXXIVB 6.27. Early Roman 1.
Part of wall, rim. PH 0.03; PL 0.04; D rim (est.) 0.19.
Reddish-brown 5YR 5/4. Metallic Coarse Terracotta.

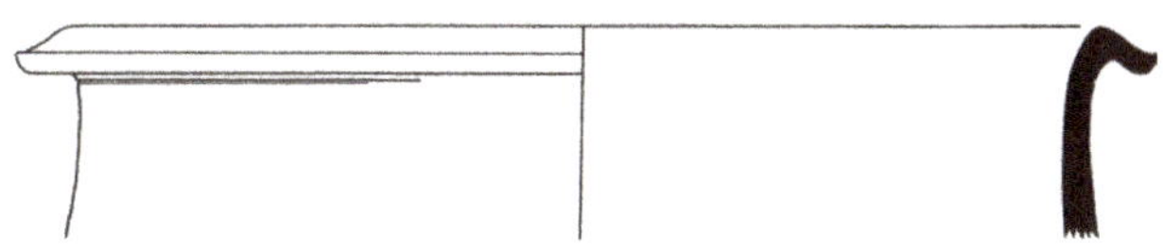

PW 639. CN 2973.
XIA/B 1.4/5. Early Roman 1.
Part of wall, rim. PH 0.05; D rim (est.) 0.195. Red
clay 10YR 5/6. Metallic Coarse Terracotta.

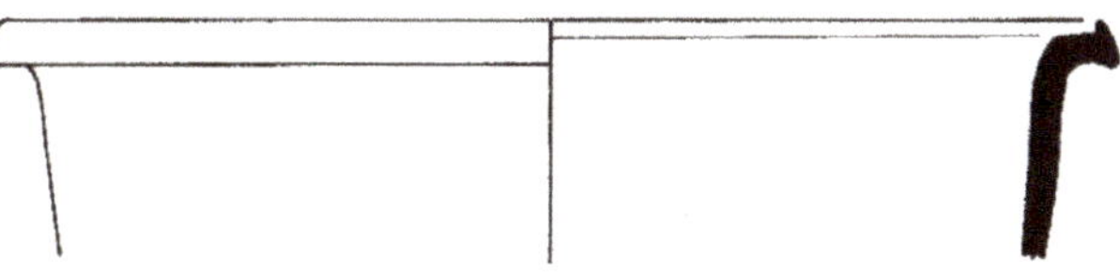

Carinated; interior flange; overhanging rim (Type 3)

Similar casseroles to **PW 640–2** have been recovered, albeit in small numbers, from third- and second-century
BC contexts at Tel Dor (Guz-Zilberstein 1995: 300, fig. 6.21, CP 7). Whereas the everted upper wall and
lid device (interior flange) are seen in both the Tel Dor and Pella examples, the rim form on most (but not
all, for example Guz-Zilberstein 1995: fig. 6.21.13) of those casseroles from the former site tends to curve
upwards or horizontally rather than downwards as seen at Pella. A similar profile to the Pella examples is
also seen on a casserole from Samaria (Crowfoot et al. 1957: fig. 43.15; P.W. Lapp 1961: 189, Type 72.1.G).
Like the Tel Dor and Samaria casseroles, all three Pella examples are from essentially second-century BC
(Hellenistic 3A–3B) contexts on the main mound.

PW 640. CN 7224.
XXVIIIB 10.3. Hellenistic 3A.
Two joining fragments of wall, rim. PH 0.04; D rim
0.18. Red clay 2.5YR 5/6. Metallic Coarse Terracotta.
Parallels: 'Akko-Ptolemais (Berlin and Stone 2016:
fig. 9.5.5, 3rd c. BC; Regev 2009/10: fig. 30.181);
Samaria (Crowfoot et al. 1957: fig. 43.15).

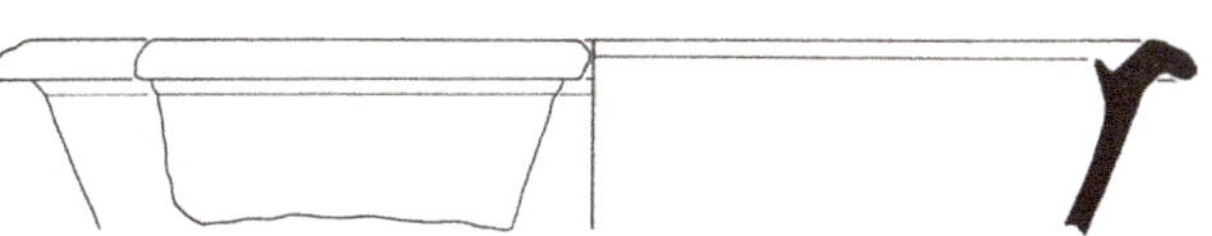

PW 641. CN 7182.
XXVIIIB 13.1. Hellenistic 3A.
Part of wall, rim. PH 0.03; PL 0.91; D rim (est.) 0.20.
Red clay 2.5YR 5/8.
Parallels: Ashdod (Dothan 1971: fig. 24.2); Samaria
(Crowfoot et al. 1957: fig. 43.15, c. 150–108 BC);
Scythopolis/Beth-Shean (Johnson 2006: fig. 15.3.53);
Tel Dor (Guz-Zilberstein 1995: fig. 6.21:13, 125 BC–75
AD); Tel Keisan (Briend 1980: pl. 17.6).

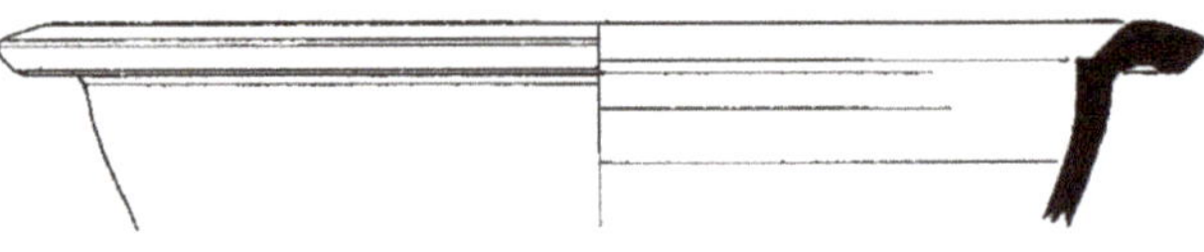

PW 642. CN 7787.
XXIIID 11.18. Hellenistic 3B.
Fragment of wall, rim. PH 0.055; PL 0.065; D rim (est.)
0.21. Red clay 10R 4/6. Metallic Coarse Terracotta.
Parallel: ʿAkko-Ptolemais (Berlin and Stone 2016: fig.
9.13.13, mid–late 2nd c. BC).

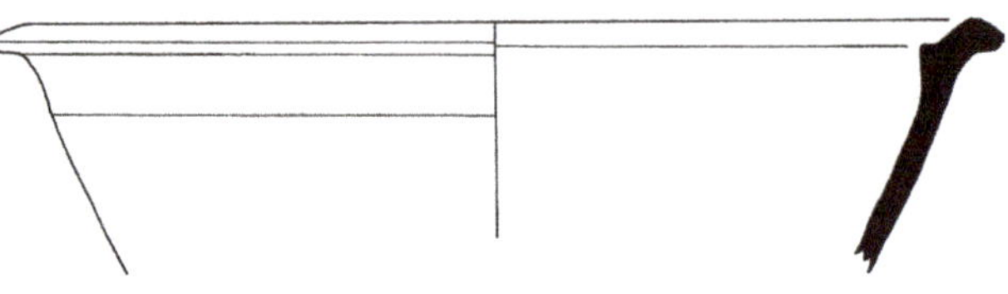

Wide mouth; grooved rim; prominent shoulder (Type 4)

Four examples (**PW 643–6**), three from Early Roman contexts of plots XIA/B and XXXIVB on Tell Husn, and the other, **PW 646**, from a Mixed Context on the main mound in IIIP), have been found at Pella. As stated previously, evidence suggests that IIIP (along with IIIQ, IVL) was the site of an Early Roman structure completely destroyed by later Byzantine and Ummayad construction.

West of the Jordan River, in Judea, the cooking vessel with prominent shoulder (Kahane Type B), in all probability inspired by a Roman shape in bronze (Berlin 2005a: 41–2), first appears late in the first century BC (Kahane 1952: 130–1). Although not a major form, it persists well into the following century (Bar-Nathan 1981: 61; P.W. Lapp 1961: 190) and, in the environs of Jerusalem, perhaps into the early second century AD (Strange 1975: 52–3). Excavations at the Jerusalem International Convention Centre (Binyane Ha ʿUmma) site have identified a workshop active from the third quarter of the first century BC through to 70 AD for the manufacture of cooking wares including the Type 4 casseroles produced there in ceramic phases 3 and 4 – from early in the first century AD to 70 (Berlin 2005a: especially 39–42) – consistent with the context of the Pella examples.[29] Outside Judaea, the shape is less common with only one example ("in form … actually a casserole") from Tel Anafa (Berlin 1997a: 93–4, PW 227) with six vessels from Gamla (Berlin 2006: 41, fig. 2.16.15–17) and none from Tel Dor.

In Transjordan, cooking vessels of this type are present at ʿIraq al-Amir (Zimmerman 2020b, Type 121) and common at Machaerus where Loffreda (1996: 79–81) has divided them into two distinct groups. His Group 44 (Loffreda 1996: figs 33.1–17), a deeper form with more rounded profile, is similar to Pella numbers **PW 643–4**, and could be considered as a cooking pot, while the shallower and more carinated vessels of Group 45 (Loffreda 1996: figs 33.18–37) – nearer to the form of a casserole – are close to **PW 645–6**. With the possible exception of two members of Group 44, all the Machaerus specimens were found in Early Roman levels.

---

29 Although still using the same clay ("Motza") as the workshop located at the Jerusalem International Convention Centre (Binyane Ha ʿUmma) site, it seems likely that other ceramic workshops existed within its vicinity or further afield within the Jerusalem area (Berlin 2005a: 45–55).

PW 643. CN 2999.

XIA/B 1.1. Early Roman 1.

Part of wall, rim. PH 0.045; D rim (est.) 0.16. Reddish-yellow clay 5YR 7/6. Metallic Coarse Terracotta.
Parallels: Herodium (Bar-Nathan 1981: pl. 5.15); Jericho (Kelso and Baramki 1955: pl. 23.A172); Jerusalem (Geva and Rosenthal-Heginbottom 2003: pl. 6.5.43, early 1st c. AD; Machline and Gadot 2017: fig. 11.9; Strange 1975: fig. 13.10; Tchekhanovets 2013: fig. 5.11:3, 1st c. BC–70 AD; Tushingham 1985: fig. 23.5); Machaerus (Loffreda 1980: pl. 96.27); Madaba (Ferguson 2014: 182, fig. 6.18, c. 15 BC–100 AD); Samaria (Crowfoot et al. 1957: fig. 72.14; Hennessy 1970: fig. 7.27).

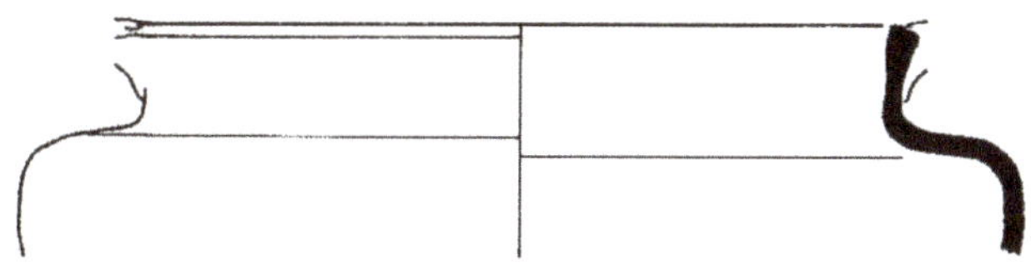

PW 644. CN 3059.

XIA/B 2.3. Early Roman 1.

Part of wall, rim. PH 0.045; D rim (est.) 0.17. Red clay 2.5YR 5/8. Metallic Coarse Terracotta.
Parallels: Gamla (Berlin 2006: fig. 2.16.16, later 1st c. BC/early 1st c. AD–67 AD); Herodium (Bar-Nathan 1981: pl. 1.8); ʿIraq al-Amir (Dentzer et al. 1983: fig. 64.10; Zimmerman 2020b: pl. 2.22.6, unstrat.); Machaerus (Loffreda 1996: fig. 33.11); Jericho (Kelso and Baramki 1955: pl. 23 X1); Jerusalem (Geva 1983: fig. 5.8; Geva and Rosenthal-Heginbottom 2003: pl. 6.5.43, early 1st c. AD; Rahmani 1967: fig. 16.7; Tushingham 1985: fig. 22.28); Samaria (Crowfoot et al. 1957: fig. 72.12); Tel Anafa (Berlin 1997a: pl. 27. PW 227, Arab levels residual).

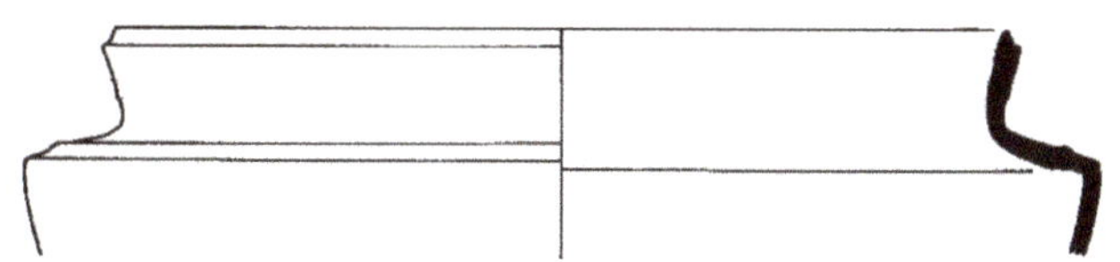

PW 645. CN 7615.

XXXIVB 27.7. Early Roman 1.

Part of wall, rim. PH 0.045; PL 0.075; D rim (est.) 0.16. Dark red clay 2.5YR 4/8. Metallic Coarse Terracotta.
Parallel: Jerusalem (Berlin 2005a: fig. 7.6, c. 50 BC –70 AD; Geva and Rosenthal-Heginbottom 2003: pl. 6.2.30, 1st c. BC).

PW 646. CN 6563.

IIIP23.1. Mixed Context.

Part of wall, rim, handle. PH 0.07; D rim (est.) 0.195. Yellowish-red clay 5YR 5/8. Metallic Coarse Terracotta.

Strap handle from rim to upper wall.

Parallels: ʿIraq al-Amir (Zimmerman 2020b: pl. 2.22.5, str. II, c. 100 AD); Wadi al-Kharrar (Abu Shmeis and Waheeb 2002: fig. 2.14).

Cooking bowls/pans (PW 647–661)

With their upright or slightly everted walls, these vessels can be classed as cooking bowls (or pans), a shape that had its origin in Italy in the third century BC but did not appear in the eastern Mediterranean until the late second/early first century BC (Berlin 1993, 1997a: 104). As opposed to the frying pan, which seems to have been used purely for cooking, the Italian-inspired cooking bowl was preferred for pies, quiches, and other such foodstuffs where a certain shape was required. Both imported and locally produced examples appear in appreciable numbers at Tel Anafa, comprising some 13 per cent of the site's Early Roman period cooking vessels (Berlin 1997a: 104–9, 2002); they are, however, much less commonly seen elsewhere in the Levant (Loffreda 1996: 84). At Pella, the only stratified examples are from Early Roman deposits on Tell Husn (Areas XI, XXXIV); those from unstratified contexts also from Tell Husn or from the main mound in Plot IIIP are the source of much Early Roman material.

Table 2.39. Distribution of cooking bowls/pans and frying pan by types, wares, phases.

		UPRIGHT WALL; NARROW LEDGE RIM (TYPE 1)	UPRIGHT WALL; ANGLED BROAD RIM (TYPE 2)	GROOVED RIM; "GALILEAN" BOWL (TYPE 3)	FRYING PAN
Ware	Metallic Coarse Terracotta	2	4	2	1
	"Galilean"	0	0	3	0
	Miscellaneous	1	1	2	0
Phase	Early Roman 63 BC–c. 135 AD	3	4 (1)	4 (2)	0
	Mixed	0	1	3	1

Upright wall; narrow ledge rim (Type 1)

The upright walls of **PW 647–9** end in a flattened horizontal rim with the resting surface slightly convex or horizontal. Similar vessels, from Roman 1A and 1B levels (late first century BC to early first century AD), were recovered from Tel Anafa and Gamla (Berlin 1997a: 108, PW 291–4; 2006: 45, figs 2.19.1–6).

PW 647. CN 7554.
XXXIVB 26.1/2. Early Roman 1.
Fragment of wall, rim, floor. PH 0.03; PL 0.09; D rim (est.) 0.17. Dark red clay 2.5YR 4/8. Metallic Coarse Terracotta.
Narrow rim overhanging exterior.
Parallel: Hippos-Sussita (Osband and Eisenberg 2018: pl. 4.4.9, end 1st c. BC/beginning 1st c. AD).

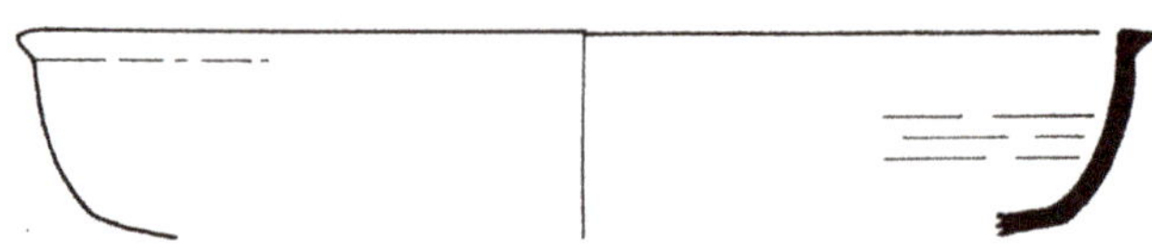

PW 648. CN 2665.
XIA/B 1.1/2. Early Roman 1.
Part of wall, rim. PH 0.07; D rim (est.) 0.20. Reddish-yellow clay 5YR 6/8.
Parallels: Samaria (Hennessy 1970: fig. 10.16); Tel Anafa (Berlin 1997a: pl. 33, PW 291, early 1st c. AD).

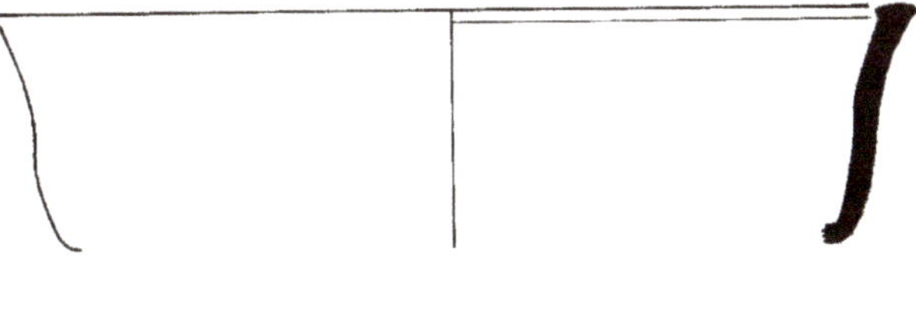

PW 649. CN 6612.
XIA/B 4.6. Early Roman 1.
Part of wall, rim. PH 0.035; PL 0.06; D rim (est.) 0.20.
Dark red clay 2.5YR 4/8. Metallic Coarse Terracotta.

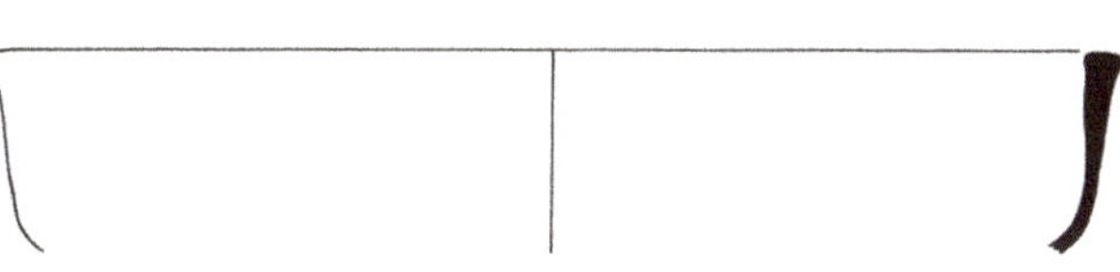

Upright wall; angled broad rim (Type 2)

PW 650–4 can be included with those "ledge rim" pans from Gamla (Berlin 2006: 45, fig.2 .19.1–6) recovered from Early Roman levels (late first century BC to mid-first century AD) and, with the exception of **PW 654**, are consistent with the Early Roman (Tell Husn) context of the Pella examples. It should be noted, however, that **PW 654** was recovered from the main mound in plot IIIP – the apparent site, as previously stated, of a later-destroyed Early Roman structure. Similar cooking bowls of much the same date are seen at Machaerus within Loffreda's Group 47 (Loffreda 1996: 83–4, fig. 35.1–5) and at 'Iraq al-Amir (Zimmerman 2020b, Type 132).

PW 650. CN 3054.
XIA/B 2.3. Early Roman 1.
Part of wall, rim. PH 0.04; D rim (est.) 0.19. Reddish-brown clay 2.5YR 4/4–5/4. Metallic Coarse Terracotta.
Rim overhanging exterior.

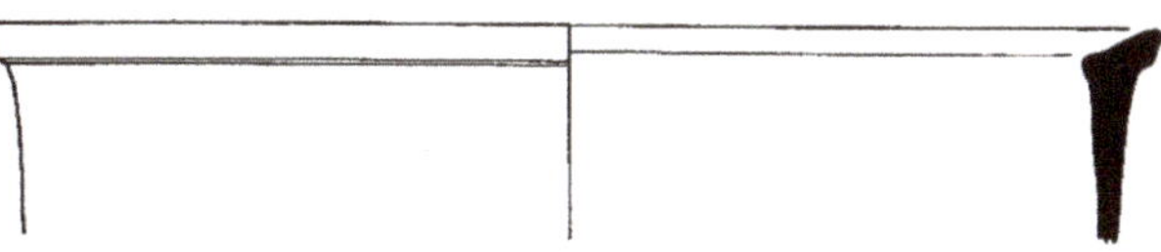

PW 651. CN 7566.
XXXIVB 27.2. Early Roman 1.
Fragment of rim, wall. PH 0.04; PL 0.03; D rim (est.) 0.16. Red clay 2.5YR 5/8. Metallic Coarse Terracotta.
Rim overhanging interior, exterior.

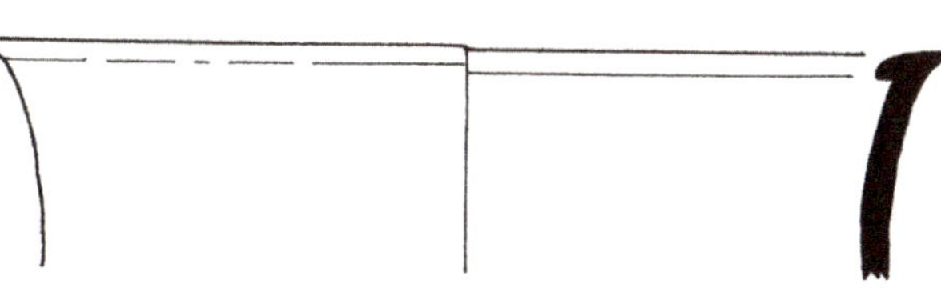

PW 652. CN 7593.
XXXIVB 27.4. Early Roman 1.
Part of wall, rim. PH 0.03; PL 0.06; D rim (est.) 0.22. Dark red clay 2.5YR 4/8. Metallic Coarse Terracotta.
Rim overhanging interior, exterior.

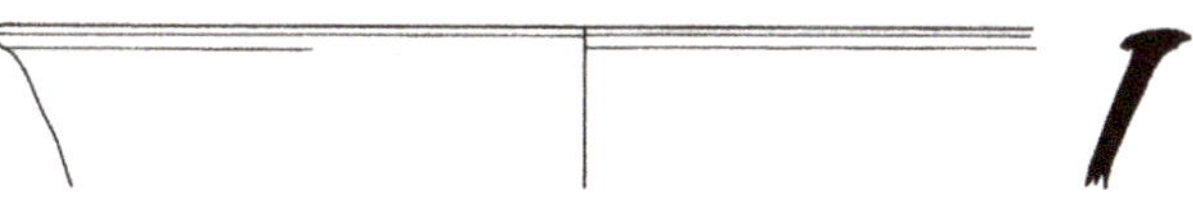

PW 653. CN 7551.
XXXIVB 27.1. Early Roman 1.
Fragment of rim, wall. PH 0.04; PL 0.045; D rim (est.) 0.20. Reddish-brown clay 5YR 4/4. White inclusions. Coarse.

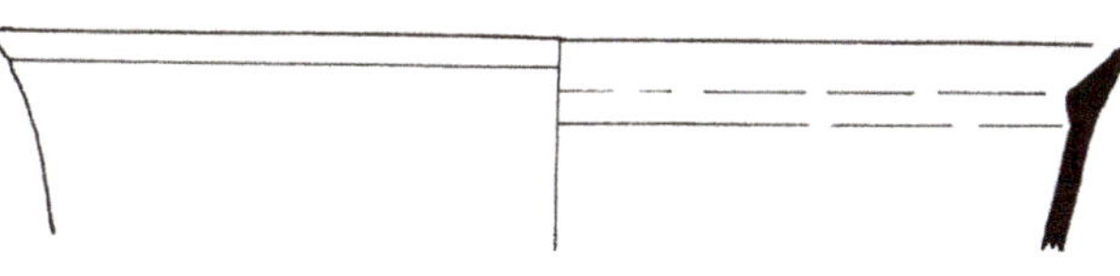

PW 654. CN 6623.
IIIP24.2. Mixed Context.
Part of wall, rim. PH 0.045; D (est.) 0.195. Red clay
2.5YR 5/6. Metallic Coarse Terracotta.
Parallels: ʿIraq al-Amir (Zimmerman 2020b: pl. 2.23.6,
str. IIIa–II, c. 50–c. 100 AD); Jerusalem (Sandhaus
2013: fig. 4.1:17, second half of 2nd c. BC); Machaerus
(Loffreda 1996: fig. 35.3).

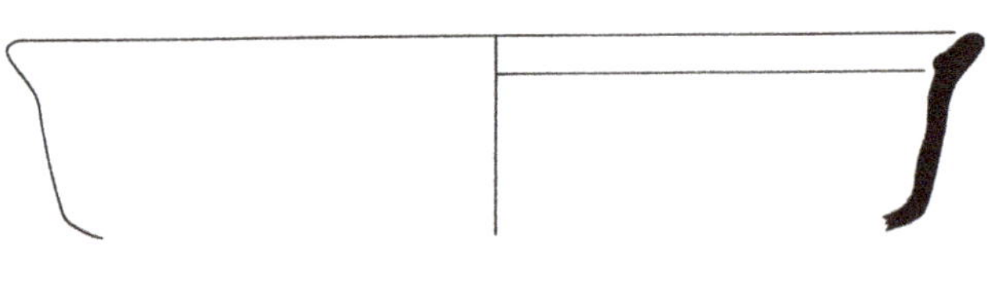

Grooved rim; "Galilean" bowl (Type 3)

PW 655–61 can be classed under the broad heading of "Galilean" bowls. The ware of bowls **PW 655–6**, **PW 659** would seem, at least macroscopically, typical of "Galilean" cooking ware while those others of this type are of similar form but different wares, including Metallic Coarse Terracotta. All the Pella examples are from Tell Husn, with the exception of **PW 657** found on the main mound in plot IIIP, previously noted as the findspot of Early Roman ceramics, although no structure of this date remains. With their single grooved rim, **PW 655–6** belong within Adan-Bayewitz's Form 1A, produced in Kfar Hananya and elsewhere from the later first century AD through to the second half of the third century and distributed throughout the Upper and Lower Galilee as well as the Golan (Adan-Bayewitz 1993: 88–91). The Wooster expedition uncovered four more "Galilean" bowls (Smith and Day 1989: 99–100, pls 44.4, 7, 8, 45.7) in their excavations in the Civic Complex (Area IX).

PW 660–1, with two grooves on the exterior rim, should be included within Adan-Bayewitz's Form 1B. Bowls of this common form were first produced in the late first or early second century AD; the latest date of manufacture is uncertain although they may continue to have been turned out as late as the mid-fourth century (Adan-Bayewitz 1993: 91–7).

The "Galilean" bowl has been discussed by, amongst others, Loffreda (1974), Meyers et al. (1976: 170–80) and Adan-Bayewitz (1982: 14–15). More recently, Adan-Bayewitz (1993: 87–109) has subdivided these bowls into five distinct forms, all of which were produced in Kfar Hananya and elsewhere, and widely distributed throughout the Galilee and Golan during the Roman era (Berlin 1997a: 112–13, 2006: 45–7).[30] The charring on many of the examples recovered throughout the Galilee indicates that they were used for cooking as well as for tableware.

PW 655. CN 7555.
XXXIVB 26.1/2. Early Roman 1.
Part of wall, rim. PH 0.03; PL 0.045; D rim (est.) 0.19.
Red clay 2.5YR 5/8. "Galilean" ware.
Single groove on narrow rim.

PW 656. CN 7691.
XXXIVB 54.4. Mixed Context.
Part of wall, rim. PH 0.035; PL 0.035; D rim
(est.) 0.24. Red clay 2.5YR 5/8. "Galilean" ware.
Single groove on narrow rim.
Parallel: ʿAkko-Ptolemais (Berlin and Stone 2016: fig.
9.26.10, early 1st c. AD).

---

30 Cooking ware bowls seem to have been absent during the Hellenistic period. At Tel Anafa, where it first appears in Roman IA levels, a further type of "Galilean" bowl – the "Galilean ledge rim cooking ware bowl" – has been identified. It is also present at Kfar Hananya, being the earliest in the series there (Berlin 1997a: 112–13).

PW 657. CN 6597.
IIIP25.5. Mixed Context.
Part of wall, rim. PH 0.045; PL 0.05; D rim (est.) 0.22.
Dark red clay 2.5YR 4/8.
Upright wall; single groove on narrow rim.

PW 658. CN 6611.
XIA/B 4.6. Early Roman 1.
Part of wall, rim. PH 0.045; PL 0.08; D rim (est.) 0.18.
Dark red clay 2.5YR 4/8. Metallic Coarse Terracotta.
Single groove on narrow rim.
Parallels: Pella (Smith and Day 1989: pl. 44.8); Tell
Zira'a (Kenkel 2020: 52, 150–1, pl. 1.17, Gb2).

PW 659. CN 3095.
XIA/B 3.1. Mixed Context.
Part of wall, rim. PH 0.045; D rim (est.) 0.20. Red
clay 2.5YR 5/6. "Galilean" ware.
Single groove on rim.
Parallels: Capernaeum (Loffreda 1974: fig. 5.5); Tel
Zahara (Bar-Nathan 2013: fig. 3.6.48).

PW 660. CN 6614.
XIA/B 4.6. Early Roman 1.
Part of wall, rim. PH 0.03; D rim (est.) 0.21. Yellowish-
red clay 5YR 6/6.
Two grooves on rim.
Parallel: Galilee (Adan-Bayewitz 1993: pl. 1B.1).

PW 661. CN 6600.
XIA/B 4.6. Early Roman 1.
Part of wall, rim. PH 0.045; PL 0.065; D rim (est.) 0.20.
Dark red clay 2.5YR 4/8. Metallic Coarse Terracotta.
Two grooves on rim.
Parallel: Sepphoris (Balouka 2013: pl. 9.25,
70–135 AD).

Frying pan (PW 662)

From a Mixed Context, **PW 662**, with its flat resting surface, short upright rim and tubular handle, is the sole example of a frying pan from the University of Sydney's excavations, although a further specimen, missing its handle, was recovered from the Early Roman levels in the Civic Complex (Area IX) by the Wooster team (Smith and Day 1989: pl. 45.1). Frying pans have been recovered from Hellenistic levels at sites such as Gezer, Samaria, Sha'ar ha-Amakim, Tel Dor, Tel Keisan and Tel Michal as well as Early Roman horizons as far afield as Tell Asmar near Aswan.[31]

---

31 Dever et al. 1970: pl. 23.2 (Gezer); Crowfoot et al. 1957: figs 40.1, 41.23 (Samaria); Mlynarczyk 2004: pl. 312.1–4 (Sha'ar ha-Amakim); Guz-Zilberstein 1995: 300, fig. 6.23a: 1–10 (Tel Dor); Briend 1980: pl. 11.4 (Tel Keisan); Fischer 1989: fig. 13.3.27 (Tel Michal); Jaritz and Rodziewicz 1993: 126 (Tell Asmar).

PW 662. CN 0477.

IIIB/C 1.25. Mixed Context.

Part of base, wall, handle. H 0.035; PL 0.17; D rim (est.) 0.23. Yellowish-red clay 5YR 5/6. Metallic Coarse Terracotta.

Flat base; low upright wall. Elongated tubular handle. Parallels: Kedesh (Levantine Ceramics Project: n.d. K09P059, missing handle, 2nd c. BC); Samaria (Crowfoot et al. 1957: fig. 41.23); Tel Dor (Guz-Zilberstein 1995: figs 6.23a:2, 125 BC–75 AD, 6.48:6); Tel Keisan (Briend 1980: pl. 11.4, first half of 2nd c. BC); Tel Michal (Fischer 1989: fig. 13.3.27).

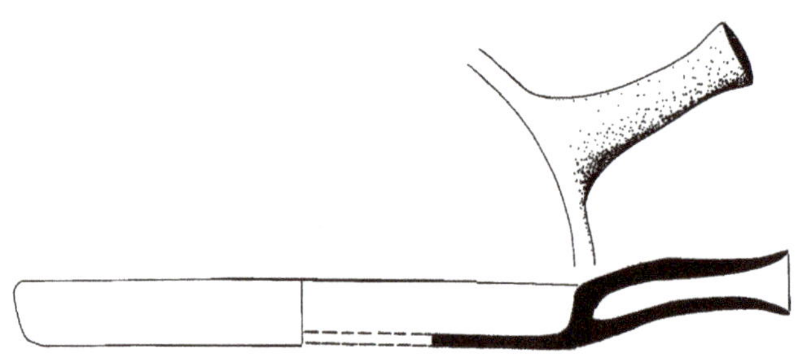

Lids (PW 663–71)

Nine lid fragments have been catalogued from the Hellenistic and Early Roman levels at Pella. Lids tend to be uncommon even in large ceramic assemblages for, unless substantially intact, they are hard to distinguish from small bowls or plates that may themselves, on occasions, serve this function.[32] The exception here is Tel Anafa where some eighty-nine cooking-ware lid fragments were identified: all seem to have been used to cover casseroles rather than globular cooking pots (Berlin 1997a: 115).[33] Even at Tel Anafa the range of lid forms and decoration is narrow when compared to Hellenistic Athens, where lids were used on a wide variety of vessels including fine wares (Rotroff 1997b: 192–7, 200–1).

As regards wares, most of the lids here are of Metallic Terracotta and thus associated with cooking. **PW 665**, **PW 667** and **PW 669**, on the other hand, are not of cooking-ware fabrics and so more likely to be employed as lids on jars or other storage vessels.

PW 663–4, with their splaying walls and well-defined solid knob handles, were recovered from Hellenistic 2B contexts on Tell Husn. Similar lids are found in phase 3 levels (c. 275–125 BC) at Tel Dor where they are presumed to have covered casseroles (Guz-Zilberstein 1995: 302, fig. 6.24, nos 4–10). **PW 666** appears of similar form, in which case it would be a residual fragment from the Early Roman foundation trench (1.5) of Wall 1 in Area XI on Tell Husn. Of those lids with vertical sides (**PW 667–9**), all are from Mixed Contexts. The fragmentary nature of the Pella specimens makes firm parallels tenuous, but somewhat similar lids are present in later Hellenistic and Early Roman contexts (P.W. Lapp 1961: 181, Types 61C, 62).

The large dimensions and globular shape of **PW 670–1** suggest that they served as lids for casseroles with similar lids being recovered from mid–second-century BC contexts at Gezer (Gitin 1990: Type 251).

---

32 Thus, lids are "not well attested" at Gezer (Gitin 1990: 260) and are rare at Samaria (Crowfoot et al. 1957: fig. 41.22; Zayadine 1966: pl. XXXI.93). They do not appear at all in the Hellenistic corpora from Tel Michal (Fischer 1989) or Tel ʿIra although at this latter site they are present in later deposits (Fischer and Tal 1999b; Hershkovitz 1999). Their periodic use as bowls or plates explains why it is not uncommon to see examples published upside down (for example, Avissar 1996: fig. X.2.2; Fischer and Tal 1999a: fig. 5.12.6).

33 A further group of small saucer-like vessels in Phoenician semi-fine ware was also recovered from Tel Anafa (Berlin 1997a: 79–83, PW 162–77). These may well have been used as lids although, as Berlin points out, "no semi fine shape has been found at Anafa for which these vessels would be suitable covers".

Table 2.40. Distribution of lids by wares, phases.

Ware	Metallic Coarse Terracotta	6
	Hard Pale	1
	Miscellaneous	2
Phase	2B c. 220–c. 200 BC	2
	3A c. 200–c. 140 BC	1
	3C c. 100 (?)–c. 80/79 BC	1
	Early Roman 63 BC–c. 135 AD	2
	Mixed Context	3

PW 663. CN 7665.
XXXIVB 27.22. Hellenistic 2B.
Part of handle, wall. PH 0.025; PL 0.14. Reddish-yellow clay 5YR 5/8. Metallic Coarse Terracotta.
Knob handle; broad sloping wall.
Parallels: 'Akko-Ptolemais (Berlin and Stone 2016: fig. 9.5.4, lower profile, 3rd c. BC); Jerusalem (Geva 2003: pl. 5.1.31, 2nd c. BC); Kedesh (Levantine Ceramics Project: n.d. K00P205, 3rd–2nd c. BC); Sha'ar ha-Amakim (Mlynarczyk 2000: pl. 121.6); Shechem (N.L. Lapp 2008: pl. 3.41.18, unstratified).

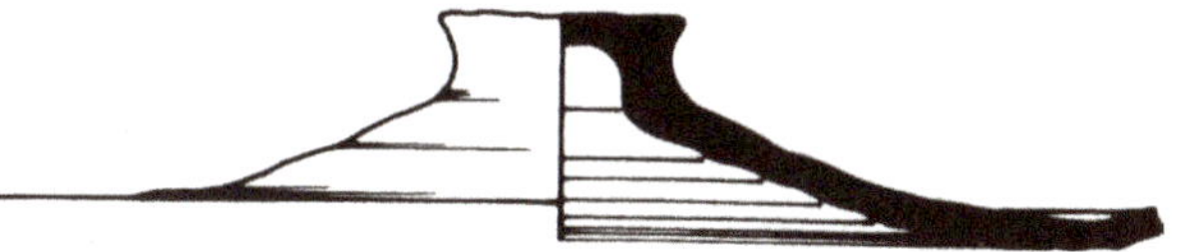

PW 664. CN 7700.
XXXIVB. 41.2. Hellenistic 2B.
Part of handle, wall. PH 0.03; PL 0.095. Red clay 10R 4/8. Metallic Coarse Terracotta.
Knob handle; sloping wall.
Parallel: Jerusalem (Geva 2003: pl. 5.1.32).

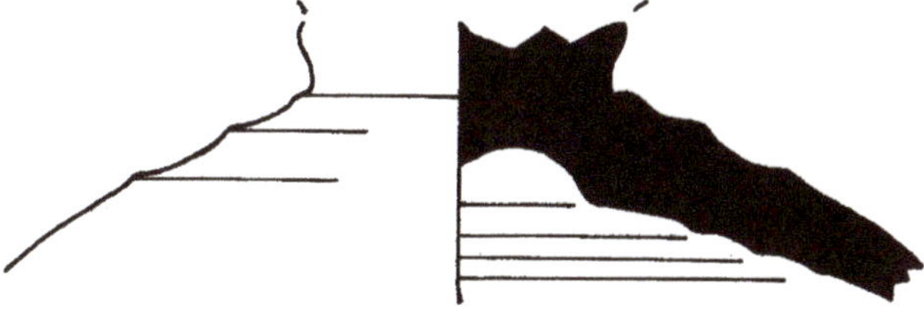

PW 665. CN 7537.
XXXIIY 4.3. Hellenistic 3A.
Part of handle, wall. PH 0.03; D rim (est.) 0.16. Light brown clay 7.5 YR 6/4. Hard Pale.
Knob handle; convex wall.
Parallels: 'Akko-Ptolemais (Berlin and Stone 2016: fig. 9.13.17, mid–late 2nd c. BC); Jerusalem (Geva 2003: pl. 5.8.39, later 2nd–1st c. BC; Geva and Rosenthal-Heginbottom 2003: pl. 6.2.31, 1st c. BC); Kedesh (Levantine Ceramics Project: n.d. K08P021, mid–late 2nd c. BC); Shechem (N.L. Lapp 2008: pl. 3.41.19, unstratified).

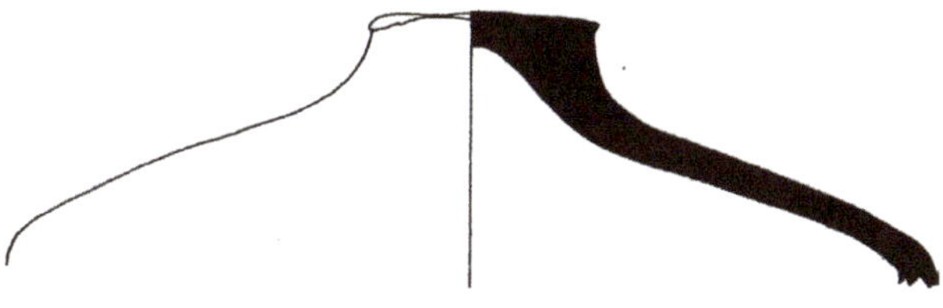

PW 666. CN 2951.
XIA/B 1.5. Early Roman 1.
Part of wall, rim. PH 0.015; D rim (est.) 0.15. Reddish-yellow clay 5YR 6/8. Metallic Coarse Terracotta.
Flattened lip; splaying lower wall.
Parallels: Ashdod (Dothan 1971: fig. 24.11); Jerusalem (Tushingham 1985: fig. 23.42); Tel Dor (Guz-Zilberstein 1995: fig. 6.62:24, 275–225 BC); Tel Keisan (Briend 1980: pl.11.10, 3rd c. BC).

PW 667. CN 7625.
XXXIVB 27.13. Mixed Context.
Part of wall, rim. PH 0.025; PL 0.065; D rim (est.) 0.20. Reddish-yellow clay 7.5YR 6/6.
Short vertical rim, sloping wall.

PW 668. CN 7103.
XXIIIA 80.8. Mixed Context.
Two joining fragments of rim, wall. PH 0.055; D rim (est.) 0.22. Red clay 2.5YR 5/6. Metallic Coarse Terracotta.
Short vertical rim, sloping wall.
Parallel: 'Akko-Ptolemais (Regev 2009/10: fig. 31.199 lower profile).

PW 669. CN 7681.
XXXIVB 55.2. Mixed Context.
Part of wall, rim. PH 0.03; PL 0.07; D rim (est.) 0.17. Yellow clay 10YR 7/6. Dull red brown slip over exterior.
Short vertical rim, sloping wall.

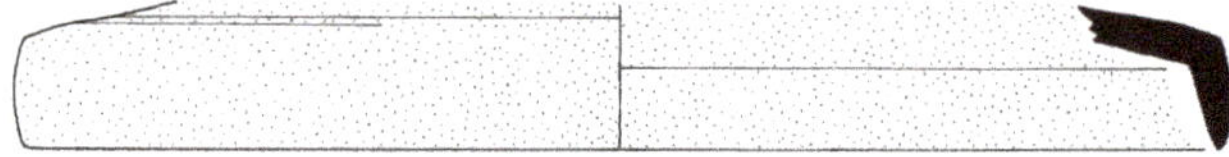

PW 670. CN 6884.
XXIIIA 10.5. Hellenistic 3C.
Part of wall, rim. PH 0.03; D rim (est.) 0.18. Reddish-yellow clay 5YR 6/8. Metallic Coarse Terracotta.
Slightly everted narrow rim; convex wall.
Parallels: Kallirhoe (Clamer 1997: pl. 13.13); Machaerus (Loffreda 1996: fig. 36.10); Tel Dor (Guz-Zilberstein 1995: fig. 6.62:25, 275–225 BC); Tell Nimrin (Dornemann 1990: fig. 3.20).

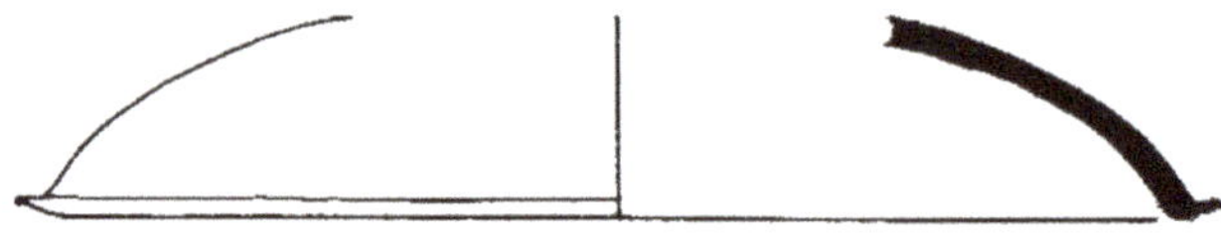

PW 671. CN 6617.
XIA/B 4.6. Early Roman 1.
Part of rim, wall. PH 0.03; PL 0.05; D rim (est.) 0.18. Red clay 10R 5/8. Metallic Coarse Terracotta.
Narrow horizontal rim; convex wall.
Parallels: Gezer (Gitin 1990: pl. 35.9, early–mid-2nd c. BC); 'Iraq al-Amir (Zimmerman 2020b: pl. 2.24.4, str. II, c. 100 AD).

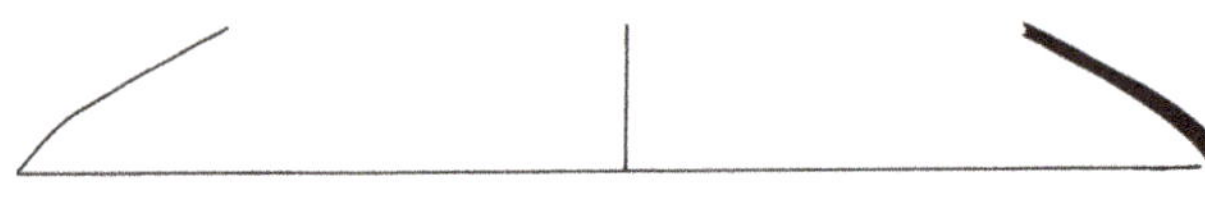

VESSELS FOR OTHER PURPOSES

Unguentaria (PW 672–93)

The unguentaria recovered so far from Pella are all examples of the "fusiform" (spindle-shaped) type, "one of the most ubiquitous and characteristic of Hellenistic vases" (Thompson 1934: 472).[34] The unguentarium, in its earlier globular form, first appears in the western Mediterranean in the fifth century BC (Anderson-Stojanovic 1987: 108) with a similar shape – but generally referred to as a "bottle" – seen in Persian-period assemblages along the Levantine coast and somewhat inland (Guz-Zilberstein 1995: 304; Stern 1982: 125). Although examples of the slender fusiform unguentarium have been recovered from fourth-century contexts in Palestine (Berlin 1997a: 59, n. 143; Guz-Zilberstein 1995: 305), it was not until the second century BC that the form became widespread throughout the region.

As regards function, the unguentarium was the successor to the small lekythos that in turn succeeded the sixth-century aryballos (Pemberton 1985: 285); as such, it became extremely common in Hellenistic domestic and, especially, burial contexts as a small container of perfume or oil or other precious liquids, a function that in earlier times had often been performed by glass or stone vessels (Anderson-Stojanovic 1987: 114–22; Berlin 2015: 639, 1997a: 5, 8; Pemberton 1985: 284; Rotroff 2006b). By Late Hellenistic times in Rhodes and elsewhere, the unguentarium was virtually the only ceramic shape used as a grave offering (Filimonos and Giannikouri 1999: 206, 216). All the examples in this corpus, however, come from occupation deposits, as the Hellenistic cemetery has not yet been explored.

The wide distribution of these vessels and the great variety amongst them as regards shape, decoration and ware hinder any attempt at an overall typology (Anderson-Stojanovic 1987: 109), although one has been put forward by Camilli (1999).[35] Nevertheless, typologies have been proposed for a number of centres outside the Levant including Athens (Rotroff 1984: 258; Thompson 1934: 472–4), Ampurias (Almagro 1953: 396–7), Cyprus (Westholm 1956: 60–1, 73–4), Corinth (Pemberton 1985: 284–6) and Stobi (Anderson-Stojanovic 1987: 106–14).[36] However, the development of the Hellenistic shape in the Levant is far from clear, though a general progression from a short bulbous shape to one that was more elongated and slender seems definite (Berlin 1997a: 58–60).

Despite being recovered from numerous sites within Palestine (Berlin 1988: 217–35; Kahane 1952: 132; P.W. Lapp 1961: 197–8, Type 91), fusiform unguentaria seem less common in Transjordan, where examples have been published from Abila, Hesban, Petra, Tell es-Sa'idiyeh, Tell esh-Shuna North and Tell Zira'a.[37] This scarcity probably suggests the more restricted trade in perfumed oils and other valuable commodities to the east of the Jordan River when compared with the Levantine coast, while also reflecting the relatively limited number of Hellenistic tombs that have, as yet, been excavated in Transjordan.

By the late first century BC, the fusiform unguentarium had largely been replaced by the piriform type, with its bulbous body and flattened resting surface. Most scholars have assumed that this latter shape was based on those pear-shaped glass prototypes that, as a result of the introduction of glass-blowing into the region in the mid-first century BC (Avigad 1984: 186–91; Harden 1969: 47), began to be turned out by Levantine centres during the latter half of that century. Although this assumption is most likely correct, it is worth noting that isolated examples of the piriform unguentarium have been recorded in contexts from the second century BC (Anderson-Stojanovic 1987: 113, n. 41; Valtz 1993: 176) and even earlier (Berlin 1997a: 60, n. 146; Kahane 1952: 179).

---

34   See the thorough discussion (with ample references) of this vessel in Rotroff 2006b: 137–60.

35   See also Berlin (1997a: 58) for the inadvisability of attempting to classify unguentaria of different wares according to shape alone.

36   For Athens, see Rotroff 1982: 107–10 for a revision of Thompson's chronology.

37   Mare 1991: fig. 9, 1994: fig. 9.2 (Abila); Gerber 2012: 206, figs 3.7.15–16 (Hesban); Horsfield and Horsfield 1939: 119, 127, 1941: 190 (Petra); Pritchard 1985: fig. 18, no. 17, fig. 19, nos 32, 33 (Tell-es-Sa'idiyeh); Philip and Baird 1993: fig. 11, nos 1–2 (Tell esh-Shuna North); Kenkel 2020: 96–7, 192–3, pl. 1.38.U1–U7.2 (Tell Zira'a).

So far, no terracotta (as opposed to glass) examples of piriform unguentara have been recovered from Pella, despite being found at other Transjordanian sites including Abila, Amman/Philadelphia, Beit Zar'a, Dhat-Ras, Jerash and Petra.[38] Their abundance at Petra is not surprising as they are "one of the most prevalent artifacts in Nabatean sites in the Hellenistic and Roman periods" (D.J. Johnson 1990: 235), no doubt due to the central role of the Nabateans in the incense trade (Graf and Sidebotham 2003).

Only a small number of fusiform unguentaria – the majority from Pre-Jannaeus Destruction (Hellenistic 2B, 3A–3B) levels – have been found at Pella, at least in part reflecting, as we have seen, the fact that the Hellenistic cemetery is yet to be located. The clays vary, suggesting numerous (as yet identified) manufacturing centres, with the largest number of examples of the same Coarse Light Brown ware encountered more commonly amongst the bowls and fishplates. **PW 683**, **PW 685** and **PW 687** share a clay that seems similar to the naked eye while a similar situation is seen with **PW 690** and **PW 692**. The origin of both these clays is unclear. Only two unguentaria (**PW 682**, **PW 684**) are of the grey fabric that makes up the "overwhelming majority" of unguentaria seen at Athens (Rotroff 2006b: 140–57) and in smaller numbers on many sites in the eastern Mediterranean where they may have originated.[39] Among the Pella unguentaria, only **PW 675** and an unguentarium recovered by the Wooster team from Area VIII (McNicoll et al. 1982: pl. 130.11) have the painted horizontal bands sometimes seen on the exterior; along with **PW 673–4** (of similar fabric and shape but no obvious banding), they should be included within those Phoenician fusiform unguentaria seen "only at northern Palestinian sites or those with Greek, or Graeco-Phoenician, populations" (Berlin 1997a: 59, 61, 2015: 639, pl. 6.1.20: 8–9, 11–15).

The small number of unguentaria as well as their largely fragmentary nature (only **PW 675** and **PW 677** are substantially complete) and variety of fabrics makes any attempt at classification unsatisfactory, although, broadly speaking, they can be divided into two types according to their more rounded (**PW 672–8**) or elongated (**PW 679–81**) profile.[40] Both types – catalogued and non-catalogued examples – first appear in third-century (Hellenistic 2B) contexts.

---

38 Mare 1984: fig. 9.14; Mare et al. 1987: 213 (Abila); Harding 1946: 60–1, pl. XX (Amman/Philadelphia); Khadija 1974: 160–2 (Beit Zar'a); Zayadine 1970: 135 (Dhat-Ras); Abu-Dalu 1995: 170 (Jerash); D.J. Johnson 1990; Khairy 1980 (Petra).

39 Jackson 2011a: 94–5, figs 84–8 (Jebel Khalid in Syria). See also Berlin and Stone 2016: figs 9.15.19, 9.20.9; Regev 2009/10: 143, figs 124–6 ('Akko-Ptolemais); Dothan 1971: figs 9.6, 79.15, 99.22 (Ashdod); Johnson 2006: fig. 15.5.109 (?) (Scythopolis/Beth-Shean); Guz-Zilberstein 1995: 306 (Tel Dor); Kenkel 2020: 96, 192–3, pl. 1.38.U1 (Tell Zira'a).

40 In this catalogue, these are the terms used to describe the sections making up the unguentarium: stem with its rim, body with its shoulder, foot with its base.

Table 2.41. Distribution of unguentaria and ointment pot by types, wares, phases.

		SQUAT; ROUNDED BODY (TYPE 1)	SLENDER; ANGULAR BODY (TYPE 2)	FRAGMENTS	OINTMENT POT
Ware	Hard Pale	0	0	0	
	Coarse Light Brown	3	2	1	
	Miscellaneous	4	1	11	1
Phase	2B c. 220–c. 200 BC	3	0 (2)	0	
	3A c. 200–c. 140 BC	0	2	8 (4)	
	3B c. 140 –c. 100 (?) BC	1	1	0	
	3B/3C c. 140 –c. 80/79 BC	0	0	1	
	3C c. 100 (?) –c. 80/79 BC	2	0	1 (2)	
	Early Roman 63 BC–c. 135 AD	0	0	1	
	Mixed	1	0	1	1

Squat; rounded body (Type 1)

PW 672. CN 7389.

XXXIVF 6.5. Hellenistic 2B.

Part of base, foot, body. PH 0.055; D base (est.) 0.02.
Light brown clay 7.5YR 6/4. Very pale brown slip over exterior. Coarse Light Brown.

Parallel: Samaria (Zayadine 1966: pl. XXXI.94 lower profile); Tel Yoqne'am (Avissar 1996: fig. X.7.15–17).

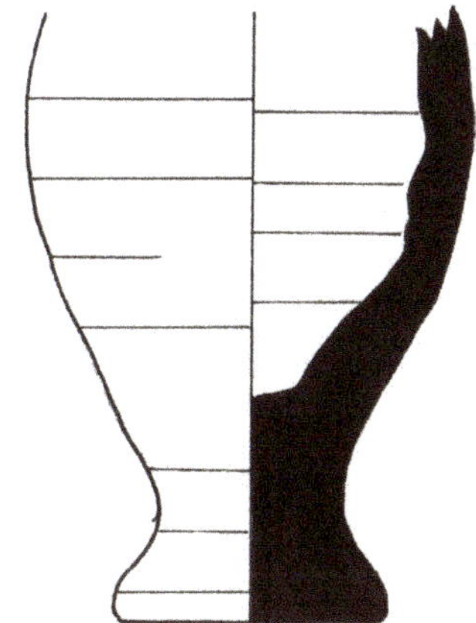

PW 673. CN 7708.
XXXIVB 41.2. Hellenistic 2B.
Two joining fragments of base, foot, body. PH 0.085;
D body 0.045. Reddish-yellow clay 7.5YR 6/6. Red
slip over upper exterior.
Parallel: Philoteria /Bet Yerah (Tal and Reshef 2017:
fig. 3.41.9).

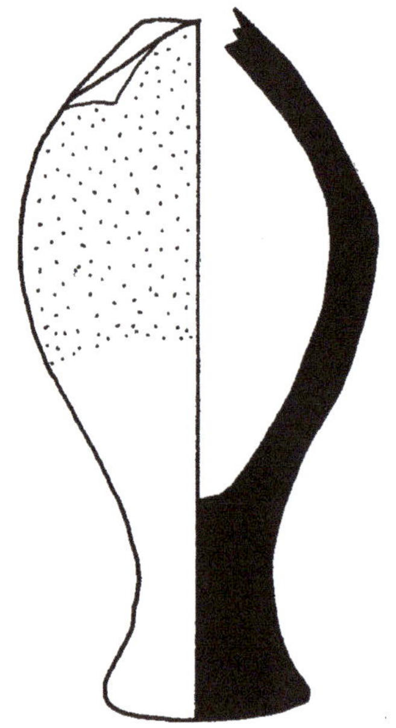

PW 674. CN 7697.
XXXIVB 41.2. Hellenistic 2B.
Part of body, foot. PH 0.065; PL 0.045. Reddish-yellow
clay 5YR 6/6.

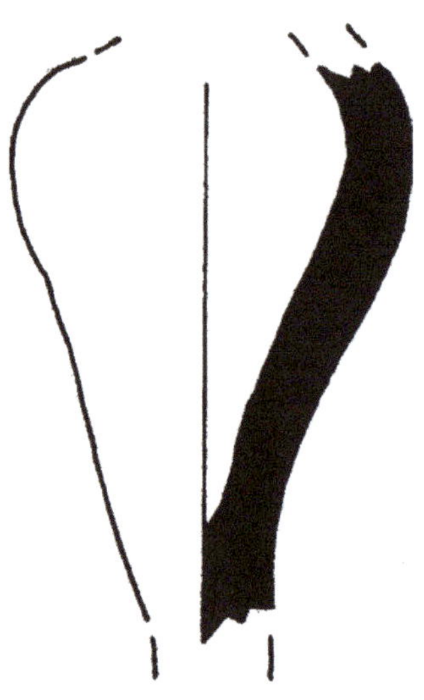

PW 675. CN 7778. (Plate 62)
XXIIID 11.18. Hellenistic 3B.
Complete except for small chips on rim. H 0.17;
D rim 0.03; D base 0.025. Reddish-yellow clay 5YR
7/8. Hard Pale.
Five horizontal red bands (four narrow and one
broad) on upper body and neck.
Parallels: Pella (Area VIII, McNicoll et al. 1982:
pl. 130.11); Tel Anafa (Berlin 1997a: pl. 13. PW 85–89,
pl. 75).

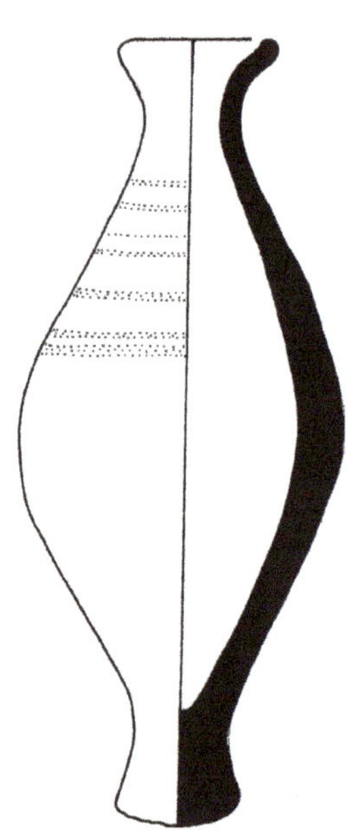

PW 676. CN 7011.
XXIIIA 71.5. Hellenistic 3C.
Part of body, foot. PH 0.11. Very pale brown clay
10YR 7/4. Coarse Light Brown.
Parallels: Ashdod (Dothan 1971: fig. 18.9); Jerusalem
(Geva 2003: pl. 5.9.19, later 2nd–1st c. BC); Marisa
(Levine 2003: 6.14.147); Tel Zahara (Bar-Nathan and
Gärtner 2013: fig. 3.14.118).

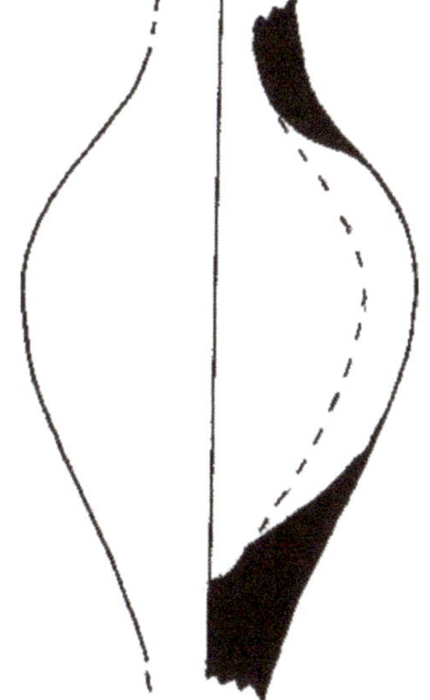

PW 677. CN 7798.
XXIIID 30.1. Hellenistic 3C.
Missing part of rim, foot. PH 0.17; D rim 0.03. Light
yellowish-brown clay 10YR 6/4. Coarse Light Brown.

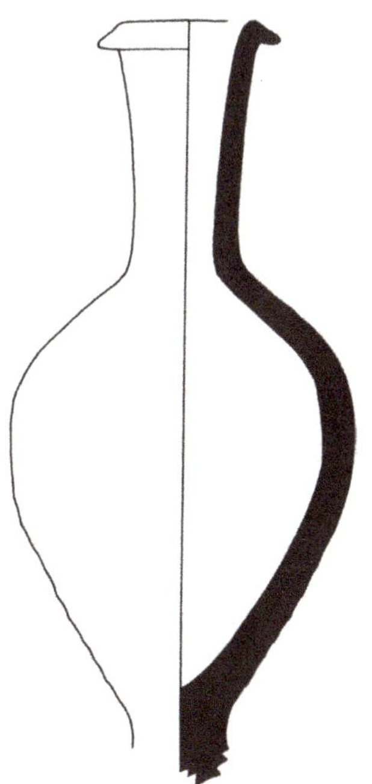

PW 678. CN 7730.
XXXIVB 201.1. Mixed Context.
Part of lower body, foot. PH 0.05; PL 0.05. Light reddish-brown clay 5YR 6/4.
Low broad foot.
Parallel: Scythopolis/Beth-Shean (Johnson 2006: fig. 15.5.107).

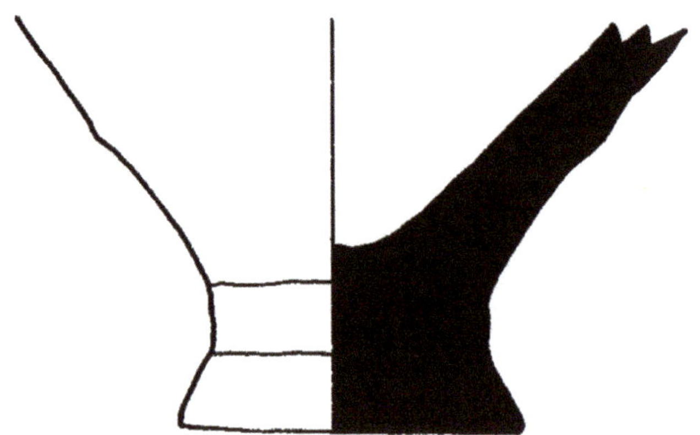

Slender; angular body (Type 2)

PW 679. CN 7202.
XXVIIIB 13.14. Hellenistic 3A.
Part of neck, body. PH 0.09. Pink clay 7.5YR 7/4. Patchy thin faint brown slip over exterior. Coarse Light Brown.
Parallels: 'Akko-Ptolemais (Dothan 1976: fig. 30.16); Ashdod (Dothan 1971: figs 10.8, first half of 2nd c. BC–second half 2nd c. BC, 99.25, first half of 2nd c. BC–mid-1st c. BC); Jerusalem (Geva 2003: pl. 5.10.16, later 2nd–1st c. BC; Tushingham 1985: fig. 22.13); Tel Yoqne'am (Avissar 1996: fig. X.7.13).

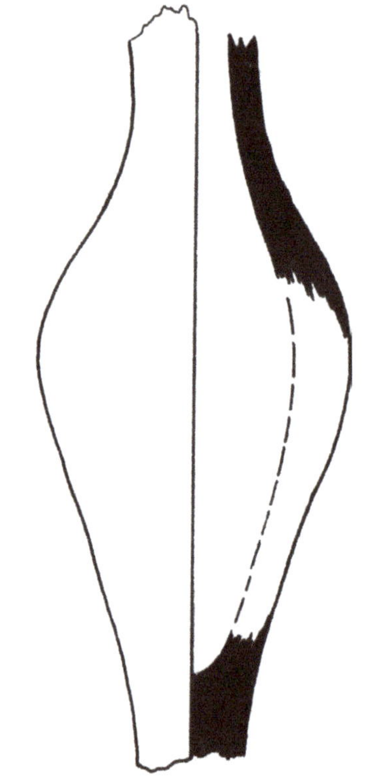

PW 680. CN 7208.
XXVIIIB 13.17. Hellenistic 3A.
Missing lower body, foot. PH 0.14; D rim 0.03.
Reddish-yellow clay 7.5YR 7/6. Coarse Light Brown.
Down-turned rim overhanging exterior.
Parallel: Marisa (Levine 2003: 6.14.148).

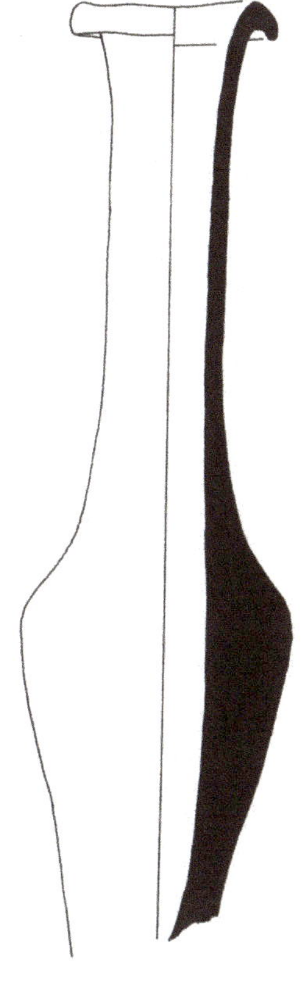

PW 681. CN 7072.
XXIIIA 109.4. Hellenistic 3B.
Part of neck, body, foot. PH 0.10. Light yellowish-brown clay 10YR 6/4. Patchy thin red slip over upper exterior.
Parallels: Abila (Mare 1991: fig. 9, left example); Jaffa (Tsuf 2018: fig. 9.9.203); Tel Anafa (Berlin 1997a: pl. 13. PW 98, 125–98 BC).

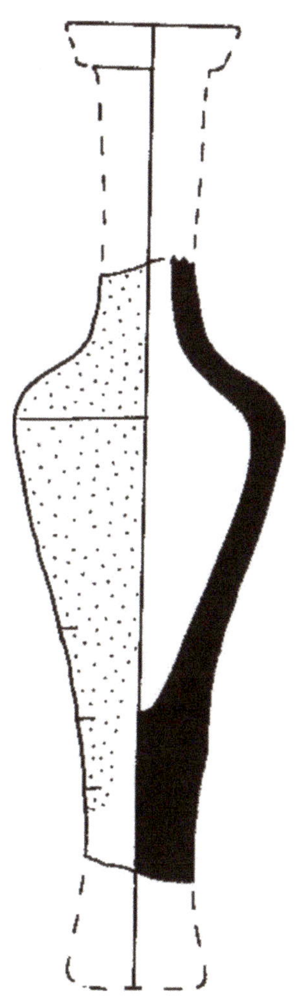

Necks, rims, bases

PW 682. CN 6828.
IIIP25.13. Mixed Context.
Part of body, rim. PH 0.065; D rim (est.) 0.03. Grey
clay 5YR 6/1. Thin brownish-grey slip over exterior.
Tall neck. Down-turned rim overhanging exterior.
Parallel: 'Akko-Ptolemais (Berlin and Stone 2016: fig.
9.20.7, mid–late 2nd c. BC).

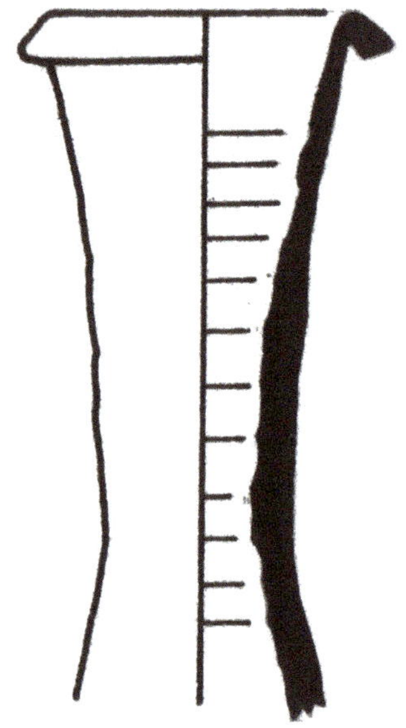

PW 683. CN 7519.
XXVIIIB 13.17. Hellenistic 3A.
Part of body, rim. PH 0.065; D rim (est.) 0.03. Pale
brown clay 10YR 6/3.
Tall neck. Down-turned rim overhanging exterior.
Upper profile as **PW 680**.
Parallels: Jerusalem (Geva 2003: pl. 5.4.27, late
2nd–1st c. BC; Geva and Rosenthal-Heginbottom
2003: pl. 6.2.14); Tel Dor (Guz-Zilberstein 1995:
fig. 6.26:26, 375 BC–75 AD).

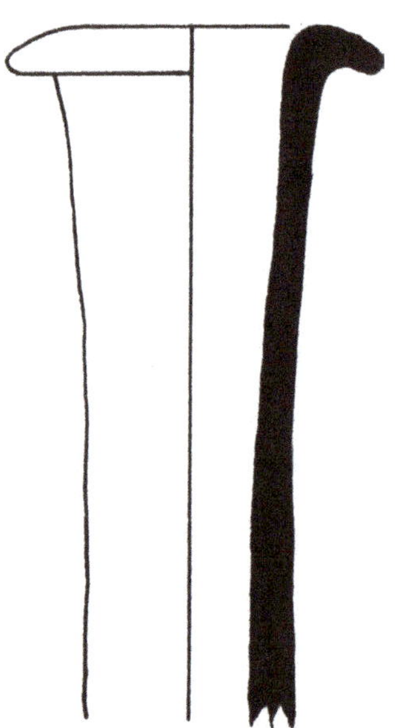

PW 684. CN 7850.
XXXIIY 1.2. Hellenistic 3A.
Complete neck, rim. PH 0.06; D rim 0.025. Greenish-
grey clay 10R 5/1.
Tall neck; bevelled down-sloping rim.
Parallel: Hesban (Gerber 2012: 206, fig. 3.7.15).

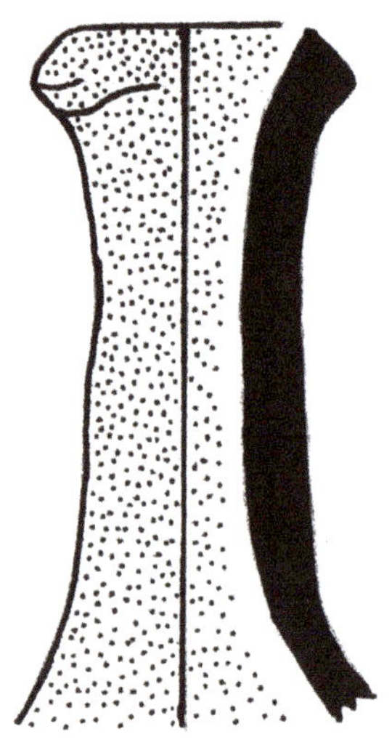

PW 685. CN 7411.
XXVIIIB 10.6. Hellenistic 3A.
Part of body, rim. PH 0.035; D rim (est.) 0.04. Pale
brown clay 10YR 6/3.
Parallel: Tell es-Sa'idiyeh (Pritchard 1985: fig. 19.32).

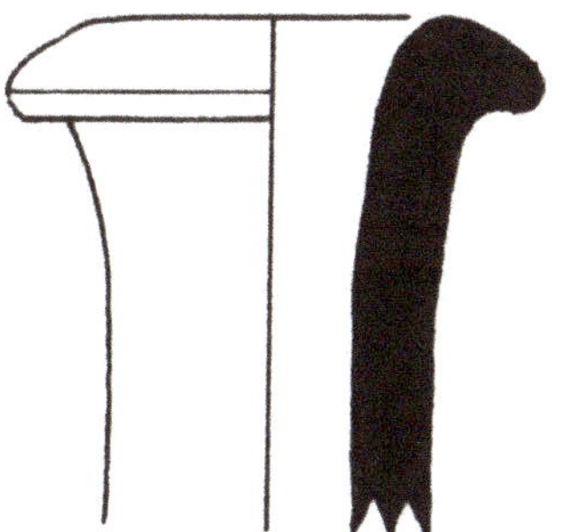

PW 686. CN 7520.
XXVIIIB 13.17. Hellenistic 3A.
Part of body, rim. PH 0.03; D rim (est.) 0.02. Very
pale brown clay 10YR 7/4.
Slightly everted ill-defined rim.

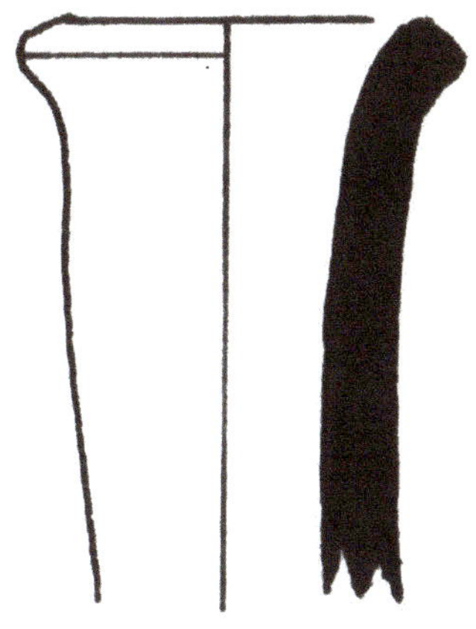

PW 687. CN 7467.
XXVIIIB 13.9. Hellenistic 3A.
Part of body, rim. PH 0.04; D rim (est.) 0.03. Very
pale brown clay 10YR 7/3.
Tall upright neck; down-turned rim.

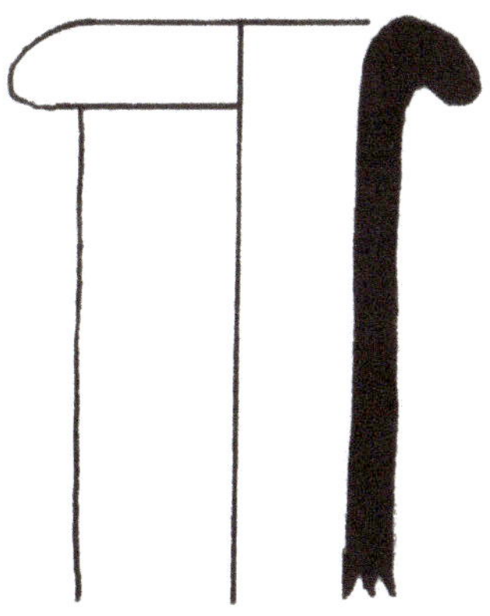

PW 688. CN 7851.
XXXIIY 1.2. Hellenistic 3A.
Part of body, rim. PH 0.05; D rim 0.03. Reddish-
yellow clay 5YR 6/6. Thin worn red slip over exterior.
Tall neck. Down-turned rim overhanging exterior.

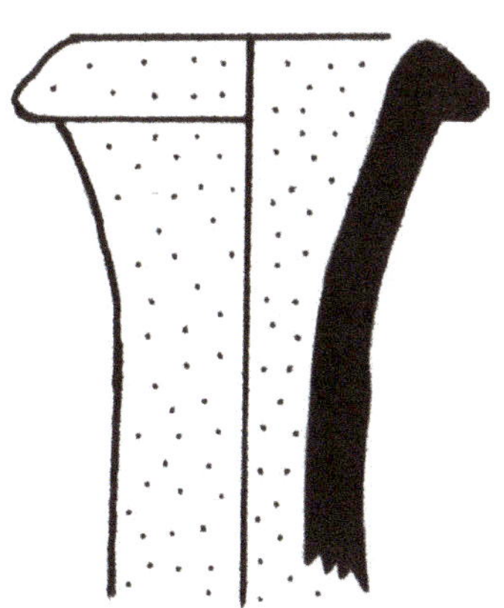

PW 689. CN 2666.
XIA/B 1.1/2. Early Roman 1.
Part of body, rim. PH 0.04; D rim 0.03. Yellowish-red clay 5YR 5/6.
Broad rim projecting on exterior.
Parallel: Hesban (Gerber 2012: 206, fig. 3.7.16).

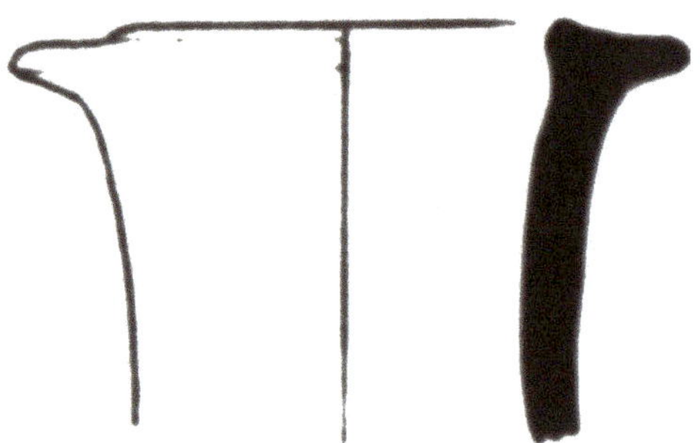

PW 690. CN 7431.
XXVIIIB 13.2. Hellenistic 3A.
Part of foot, base. PH 0.045; D base 0.04. Reddish-yellow clay 5YR 6/6. Several streaks of thin red slip over exterior.

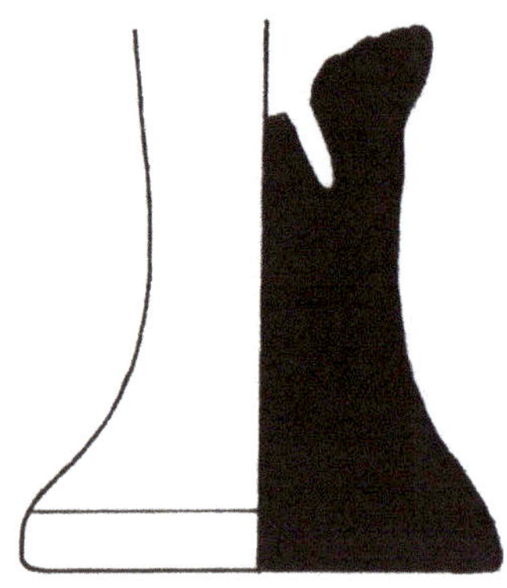

PW 691. CN 7588.
XXXIVB 28.2. Hellenistic 3B/3C.
Part of foot, base. PH 0.04; D base 0.025. Yellowish-brown clay 10YR 5/4. Coarse Light Brown.

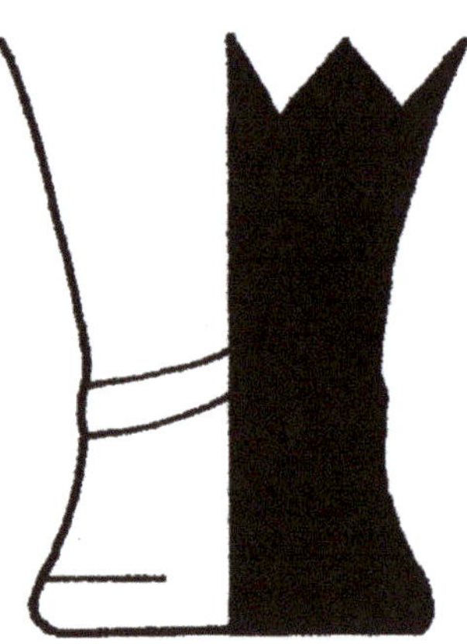

PW 692. CN 7518.
XXVIIIB 13.17. Hellenistic 3A.
Part of foot, base. PH 0.045; D base 0.03. Reddish-yellow clay 5YR 7/6.
Parallels: Gezer (Gitin 1990: pl. 48.27, Late Hellenistic); Tel Dor (Guz-Zilberstein 1995: fig. 6.26:28, 275 BC –75 AD); Wadi al-Kharrar (Abu Shmeis and Waheeb 2002: fig. 8.1).

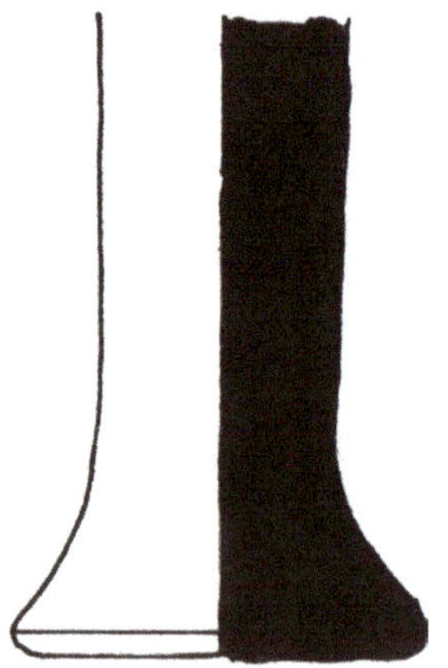

PW 693. CN 0070.
IIIB/C 1.3. Hellenistic 3C.
Part of foot, base. PH 0.05; D base 0.04. Reddish-
yellow clay 5YR 7/6.
Parallels: Hesban (Gerber 2012: 216, 218, fig. 3.10.27);
Jerusalem (Geva 2003: pl. 5.8.26, later 2nd–1st c. BC);
Tel Dor (Guz-Zilberstein 1995: fig. 6.26:27, 250–125 BC).

Ointment pot (PW 694)

"Ointment pots" are rare at Pella.[41] One specimen (*PIJ* 1:pl. 130, no.7), of biconical form, was recovered by the College of Wooster team from the Hellenistic levels in Area VIII (the West Cut) whilst the small piriform ointment pot **PW 694** is from an Early Roman deposit in plot XXXIVB.[42] Although these vessels may carry a stamped inscription denoting either the contents (commonly lykion) and/or the dispenser of the unguent, this is not the case with the Pella specimens.

Ointment jars in a limited variety of forms are widespread in the eastern Mediterranean during the Hellenistic period, where they are found in funerary and settlement contexts as well as – less frequently – religious sanctuaries. Interestingly, both green-gloss and coarse ware examples commonly turn up in Parthian levels from centres further to the east.[43] It is clear, therefore, that during Hellenistic and Early Roman times an appreciable trade in lykion and other therapeutic and cosmetic ointments was being conducted throughout these regions.[44]

Some sixty specimens were recovered from Morgantina, particularly in third-century BC levels (Sjöquist 1960; Stone 2014: 111–13); in Palestine they appear at ʿAkko-Ptolemais, Jaffa, Jerusalem, Samaria, Tel Anafa, Tel Dor and elsewhere.[45] At Tel Dor, ointment pots of this form are seen in Hellenistic levels as early as the third century BC (Guz-Zilberstein 1995: 320–37 *passim*), although at Tel Anafa the type (in Phoenician semi-fine ware) first appears only in Hellenistic 2B (c. 110–100 BC) strata.

Common in Palestine and elsewhere in the eastern Mediterranean, the ointment pot seems rare east of the Jordan River although this may be due more to the relative dearth of published Hellenistic ceramic material from Transjordan. Thus, with the exception of Pella, the only other published specimen may be from Petra (Horsfield and Horsfield 1941: pl. XXVI.199).[46]

---

41   For a discussion of these vessels as regards shape, contents, inscriptions and distribution, see, amongst others, Calvet (1982); Hershkovitz (1986); Sjöquist (1960).

42   See Berlin 2015: 639 for the two main body profiles: piriform and biconical.

43   Debevoise 1934: 51–3, nos 38–59; 109, no. 321 (Seleucia-on-the-Tigris); Dyson 1968: fig. 3, nos 48–9, fig. 11, nos 65, 278, 280; Toll 1943: Type X-A, fig. 27 (Dura-Europos).

44   Sjöquist (1960). Also, Smith (1992) who discusses an example that, from its inscription, may have contained some type of beauty cream rather than a medicinal ointment.

45   Regev 2009/10: 143 (ʿAkko-Ptolemais); Tsuf 2018: figs 9.10.222–38 (Jaffa); Hershkovitz 1986 (Jerusalem); Reisner et al. 1924: figs 181.17a, 17b, 17g (Samaria); Berlin 1997a: 68–72 (Tel Anafa); Guz-Zilberstein 1995: 302–4, fig. 6.25:3–15 (Tel Dor). Other Palestinian sites include Beth Yerah, Masada, Ramat Rahel, Tel el-Ful (see Hershkovitz 1986 for references) as well as Kedesh (Berlin 2015: pl. 6.1.21, no. 2) and Tel Yoqneʿam (Avissar 1996: fig. X.7.26), although this last example is described as a "basket-vessel".

46   Berlin (1997a: 71) has suggested the pot is an ointment jar although it is described as a "small pot with a deposit of food inside" and of "red clay blackened with fire".

As regards form, **PW 694** can be compared with the small group of vessels seen at Tel Anafa and classified by Berlin (Berlin 1997a: 70–1, PW 123–6) as "semi-fine squat ointment pots". The ware of the Pella pot, however, does not correspond to the Phoenician semi-fine ware seen in the table amphora **PW 183** and shown by Berlin to have been produced in, or very close to, Tyre (Berlin 1997c: 77–8).

PW 694. CN 7339.
XXXIVB 16.1. Mixed Context.
Part of wall, rim. H 0.06; D rim 0.025; Reddish-yellow clay 7.5YR 6/6. Finely levigated.
Low raised base. Bulbous central body. Slightly concave neck.
Parallels: Jaffa (Tsuf 2018: close to fig. 9.10.225); Samaria (Reisner et al. 1924: fig. 181.17a).

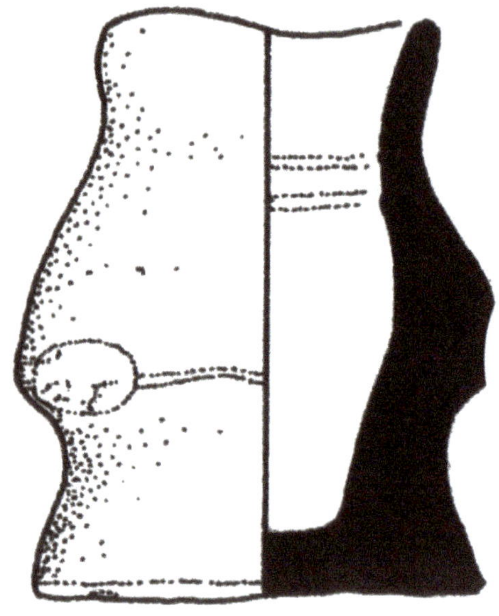

Table 2.42. Distribution of catalogued plain wares (plates, bowls, drinking vessels) by areas.

	III, IV MAIN MOUND	XXIII MAIN MOUND	XXVIII MAIN MOUND	XXXII MAIN MOUND	XI TELL HUSN	XXXIV TELL HUSN
Fishplates Type 1: broad angled rim	6	6	0	0	1	0
Fishplates Type 2: broad drooping rim	6	8	1	0	0	1
Fishplates Type 3: narrow angled rim	0	0	0	0	2	0
Fishplates Type 4: narrow drooping rim	0	0	0	0	4	0
Fishplate bases	3	1	0	0	0	0
Plates Type 1: thickened simple rim	7	1	5	1	4	3
Plates Type 2: thickened undercut rim	15	5	4	0	0	0
Plates with upright rim	1	1	0	0	0	0
Saucers	2	1	1	0	3	7
Bowls Type 1: out-turned rim	3	3	0	0	0	0
Bowls Type 2: in-turned rim	19	4	2	1	2	5
Bowls Type 3: flat base, angled rim	3	0	0	0	0	0
Bowls Type 4: flat base, simple rim	2	0	0	0	0	0
Bowls Type 5: bevelled rim	0	1	0	0	0	0
Bowls Type 6: hemispherical	1	2	1	0	0	0
Skyphoi/kantharoi	0	0	0	0	0	1
Cups	0	2	1	0	0	0

Table 2.43. Distribution of catalogued plain wares (vessels for transporting and serving liquids) by areas.

	III, IV MAIN MOUND	XXIII MAIN MOUND	XXVIII MAIN MOUND	XXXII MAIN MOUND	XI TELL HUSN	XXXIV TELL HUSN
Kraters Type 1: flaring rim, vertical lip	2	1	5	0	2	2
Kraters Type 2: horizontal rim	0	1	3	0	0	0
Kraters Type 3: down-turned rim	0	0	2	0	0	0
Kraters Type 4: fluted	0	3	0	0	0	1
Table amphorae	2	2	5	0	0	1
Jugs Type 1: thickened rim	1	3	1	0	0	1
Jugs Type 2: short-collared rim	0	3	0	0	0	0
Jugs Type 3: grooved rim	0	0	2	2	1	0
Jugs Type 4: flaring rim	0	1	0	0	1	0
Jugs Type 5: flanged rim	1	1	1	0	4	3
Juglets Type 1: simple rim	0	2	1	0	3	1
Juglets Type 2: collared rim	0	1	0	0	(2)	0
Juglets Type 3: flanged rim	0	0	0	0	2	0
Juglets Type 4: flaring rim	0	0	0	0	1	0
Juglets Type 5: cup-shaped rim	1	2	0	0	1	1
Juglets Type 6: wide mouth, grooved rim	0	0	0	0	0	1
Lagynoi Type 1: rounded body	2	0	0	0	0	0
Lagynoi Type 2: angular body	0	1	0	0	0	0
Lagynoi: miscellaneous	1	1	0	0	0	0
Flasks	0	0	0	0	1	2
Amphoriskoi	0	0	0	0	1	0
Transport amphorae	0	3	5	0	1	9

Table 2.44. Distribution of catalogued plain wares (mortaria, storage vessels) by areas.

	III, IV MAIN MOUND	XXIII MAIN MOUND	XXVIII MAIN MOUND	XXXII MAIN MOUND	XI TELL HUSN	XXXIV TELL HUSN
Mortaria	0	0	5	0	0	0
Jars Type 1A: neckless; prominent shoulder	0	0	0	1	0	1
Jars Type 1B: neckless; square rim	0	0	0	0	0	1
Jars Type 1C: neckless; everted rim	0	0	0	0	0	1
Jars Type 2A: short neck; everted simple rim	0	2	0	0	0	0
Jars Type 2B: short neck; everted thickened rim	0	1	2	0	0	3
Jars Type 2C: short neck; angular rim	0	1	0	0	0	2
Jars Type 3: thickened everted rim	5	10	4	0	0	10
Jars Type 4A: short neck; short-collared square rim	9	15	22	0	0	6
Jars Type 4B: short neck; short-collared triangular rim	1	3	2	0	0	12
Jars Type 4C: short neck; short-collared rim with prominent edge	0	0	0	0	7	1
Jars Type 5A: tall neck; short-collared square rim	4	7	5	0	0	0
Jars Type 5B: tall neck; short-collared triangular rim	1	2	0	0	0	0
Jars Type 6A: long-collared rim: uniform thickness	0	10	0	0	0	0
Jars Type 6B: long-collared rim; prominent edge	0	0	0	0	11	14
Jars Type 7A: neck ridge; simple lip	2	0	0	0	15	7
Jars Type 7B: neck ridge; overhanging lip	1	1	0	0	19	3
Pithoi	0	0	0	0	0	4

Table 2.45. Distribution of catalogued plain wares (cooking vessels) by areas.

	III, IV MAIN MOUND	XXIII MAIN MOUND	XXVIII MAIN MOUND	XXXII MAIN MOUND	XI TELL HUSN	XXXIV TELL HUSN
Cooking pots Type 1: simple rim	4	4	8	0	10	5
Cooking pots Type 2: flared rim	1	0	0	0	0	2
Cooking pots Type 3: ledge rim	4	12	6	0	0	5
Cooking pots Type 4: concave rim	2	5	2	0	4	11
Cooking pots Type 5: bevelled rim	1	1	0	0	11	14
Cooking pots Type 6: grooved rim	1	0	0	0	4	1
Cooking pots Type 7: "Galilean"	1	0	0	0	3	1
Cooking pots Type 8: thickened lip	0	1	0	0	4	4
Casseroles Type 1: constricted neck; overhanging rim	0	1	0	0	5	8
Casseroles Type 2: upright wall; overhanging rim	0	1	0	0	3	2
Casseroles Type 3: interior flange; overhanging rim	0	1	2	0	0	0
Casseroles Type 4: wide mouth; prominent shoulder	1	0	0	0	2	1
Cooking bowls (pans) Type 1: narrow ledge rim	0	0	0	0	2	1
Cooking bowls (pans) Type 2: angled broad rim	1	0	0	0	1	3
Cooking bowls (pans) Type 3: grooved rim; "Galilean" bowl	1	0	0	0	4	2
Frying pans	1	0	0	0	0	0
Lids	0	2	0	1	2	4

Table 2.46. Distribution of catalogued plain wares (lids, unguentaria, ointment pot) by areas.

	III, IV MAIN MOUND	XXIII MAIN MOUND	XXVIII MAIN MOUND	XXXII MAIN MOUND	XI TELL HUSN	XXXIV TELL HUSN
Unguentaria Type 1	0	3	0	0	0	4
Unguentaria Type 2	0	1	2	0	0	0
Unguentaria: miscellaneous	2	0	6	2	1	1
Ointment pot	0	0	0	0	0	1

Part 3
OVERVIEW

Table 3.1. Pella: Summary of Hellenistic and Early Roman occupation sequence. College of Wooster and University of Sydney excavations. Note: This is a repeat of Table 1.1 for ease of reference.

OCCUPATION	STRATUM	DATE	REMAINS	DATABLE MATERIAL
Alexander/ *Diadochi* 334–301 BC	Hellenistic 1	334–301 BC	None	Stray lamp CN 7129 (Tell Husn, Hellenistic 1 or 2A) Feline sculpture? (north-west of main mound)
Ptolemaic 301–c. 200 BC	Hellenistic 2A	301–c. 220 BC	None	Lamp CN 7129 (Hellenistic 1 or 2A)
	Hellenistic 2B	c. 220–c. 200 BC	XXXIVF (Tell Husn) Rubbish fill (?)	Lamps CN 7143, 7390 Coin RN 16036 (?)
	Hellenistic 2B	c. 220–c. 200 BC	XXXIVB (Tell Husn) "Antiochus Destruction" level (c. 217 BC? 200 BC?)	Stamped Rhodian amphora handles (SAHs): CN 7655, 7656, 7657, 7658, 7678 Coin: RN 090279 Lamp: CN 7674
Seleucid c. 200–63 BC	Hellenistic 3A	c. 200–c. 140 BC	XXVIIIB (Main mound) Dwelling	Mould-made bowls Lamp CN 7391
	Hellenistic 3A	c. 200–c. 140 BC	XXXIIY (Main mound) Wash	SAH CN 7868
	Hellenistic 3B	c.140–c. 100 (?) BC	XXIII A–D (Main mound) Earlier walls	Lamp: CN 7392 Coins: Sheedy et al. (2001) CN 1.015; RN 110982, 111554 Eastern Sigillata A (ESA)
	Hellenistic 3B/3C (Tell Husn)	c. 140–c. 80/79 BC	XXXIVB, XXXIVG (Tell Husn) Earlier walls	ESA

OCCUPATION	STRATUM	DATE	REMAINS	DATABLE MATERIAL
	Hellenistic 3C	c. 100 (?)–c. 80/79 BC	III, IV, XXIII A–D VIII (Wooster) (Main mound) Latest walls, Jannaeus Destruction Level	Coins: Sheedy et al. (2001) CN 1.019, 1.020, 1.023, 2.002, 2.006, 2.007; RN 110973, 110668, 110889 ESA "Galilean" cooking pot
	Hellenistic 3D	c. 80/79–63 BC		No firmly dated material
Early Roman 63 BC–c. 135 AD	Early Roman 1	63 BC–late first century (c. 100) AD	XIA/B, XXXIVB, XXXIVG XXXIVT (Tell Husn) Fortification wall (XIA/B, XXXIVT) Domestic walls (XXXIVB, XXXIVG) Paved stylobate (XXXIVB) VIII, IX (Wooster) (VIII: Main mound; IX: Wadi Jirm al-Moz)	ESA Hayes Forms: 4B, 9, 12, 22B, 24, 28, 33, 34, 37A, 44, 47, 48, 111 Long-collared and ridged neck jars (Types 6B, 7A, 7B)[1] "Galilean" cooking pot (Type 7) "Herodian" lamps Chalkstone vessels Coins: Sheedy et al. (2001), CN 2.014, 2.018; RN 16040.
	Early Roman 2	Late first century (c. 100–c. 135 AD)	IIIP, IIIQ, IVL (Main mound) XIA/B, XXXIVT (Tell Husn) No architectural remains in Areas III, IV; Fortification wall in XIA/B, XXXIVT	ESA Hayes Forms: 54, 57, 59, 60, 111(?) Coins: Sheedy et al. (2001) CN 3.002

1   See under "Abbreviations in text", for the explanation of "type".

THE HELLENISTIC LEVELS

RE-FOUNDATION

Alexander's conquests heralded the climax of Greek expansion into the Levant that had started to gather pace over the preceding centuries.[2] After his death in 323 BC, further expansion was mainly carried out by military conquest as the *Diadochi* struggled to carve out their own empires. Thus Antigonus, Demetrius, Ptolemy and their generals crossed and recrossed Palestine in a series of continual wars in which "the cities suffered through their struggles and lost many of their inhabitants" (Josephus *Ant. Jud.* XII.3). The general upheaval during 323–301 BC and the hardships the inhabitants of the southern Levant had to endure are well illustrated by the fact that Jerusalem itself changed hands some seven times during this period of little more than twenty years (Bickerman 1988: 22). Undoubtedly many Syro-Palestinian cities would have harboured garrisons during these years of chaos, although whether those with Macedonian names, such as Beroea, Dion, Arethusa, Pella and Hippos, were founded or renamed in this period or earlier, during Alexander's march through the southern Levant, cannot at present be determined with certainty (Frézouls 1990; Grainger 1990: 31–66; Hengel 1974: 14; Tcherikover 1959: 97–105). When

and by whom Pella was refounded as a Macedonian city – at least initially for the purpose of "providing a permanent alien garrison force in an unquiet territory" (Bosworth 1988: 245–50) – remains a matter for debate. What seems certain is that it followed a period of either abandonment or, at least, minor occupation under Achaemenid rule (a picture seen throughout Transjordan) for, with the exception of a blue-greenish translucent glass conical stamp seal from a late Byzantine context, no unequivocally Persian-period material has been recovered from the city.[3]

During his return from Egypt, Alexander was forced to act against the Samaritans who had rebelled against their governor, Andromachus, and burnt him alive (Curtius IV, 8–9; Hammond 1989: 131). As a result, the city was destroyed by Alexander's troops, the rebels mercilessly hunted down and the site resettled with Macedonian veterans (Bickerman 1988: 8–12). It is doubtful that Alexander was personally involved in these events for at this stage of his expedition he seems to have kept firmly to the coast. Accordingly, Eusebius (*Chronikon* ii. 114) nominates Perdiccas as the founder of the city of Samaria suggesting that this man, one of Alexander's most trusted generals and later *chiliarch*, was charged

---

2   The literature on Greek expansion (along with its influence) in the Levant before Alexander is abundant. Thus, for general outlines (with references) see the relevant chapters in Boardman 1999; Chrubasik and King (eds.) 2017; Killebrew and Steiner 2013; Kuhrt 1995; Tsetskhladze 2006. Amongst many others, see also Akurgal and Kerschner 2002; Niemeier 1995, 2001, 2002; Nunn 2014; E. Stern 1989; Waldbaum 1994, 1997.

3   For the paucity of settlements in Transjordan during the Achaemenid period, see Bienkowski 2008; Mueller 2006: 50–3; Tidmarsh 2000: 82–96. For a ceramic aspect, N.C.F. Groot 2009. I thank Margaret O'Hea for the information and the following comments on the seal (pers. com.): "It is remarkable that such an object, used for either mercantile or official records, could have found its way to Pella in a period with scant evidence of any occupation on site. It is more likely that it was brought in to the city as an antique stamp-seal used in the Hellenistic period, if not simply kept as a curiosity by some inhabitant of the Romano-Byzantine city."

with both suppressing the revolt and transforming the city into a Macedonian colony (Cohen 2006: 274–5).[4] During this campaign it is likely that some of Alexander's troops crossed the Jordan River under the command of Perdiccas who may have also settled Macedonian veterans at Jerash and at several other locations nearby (Cohen 2006: 248; Hengel 1974: 14; A.H.M. Jones 1983: 237; Lane Fox 1973: 222; Seyrig 1965: 25–8; Tcherikover 1959: 105). At Jerash a cult of Perdiccas existed in later (third-century) Roman times, as shown by an inscription noted by Kraeling (1938: 28–9, 423). As to when the cult was established is not clear (Lichtenberger 2022: 215) but the fact that Perdiccas who was, after all, a much less charismatic figure than Alexander, was associated in later times with both Jerash and Samaria suggests that he may well have been in charge of affairs within the interior of Syria-Palestine. As Perdiccas seems to have been involved with the establishment of a Macedonian settlement at Jerash, it is quite possible that he undertook much the same thing elsewhere in the area.[5] With its strongly Macedonian name – being the birthplace of Alexander – Pella must be high on the list of possibilities, especially as its Macedonian name is close to the earlier Semitic appellation – *Pihil* or *Pahil* – for the city.

Although we have at Pella nothing comparable to the aforementioned Perdiccas inscription from Jerash, there exist several literary references to its "foundation". Chief amongst these is that of Stephanus Byzantinus (*Ethnika* s.v. Dion) that should be read as stating both Pella and Dion – the latter also a member of the Decapolis as listed by both Pliny (*Nat. Hist.* V.16, 74) and Ptolemy (*Geog.* V.14.18) – were founded by Alexander himself. As we have seen, however, it is probable that Alexander confined himself to the coast, leaving Perdiccas to campaign within the interior.

On the other hand, both Appian (*Syr.* 57) and Eusebius (*Chronikon.* See Smith 1973: 34–5: probably 119th Olympiad, not 118th as Smith) list Pella as a foundation of Seleucus Nicator. Early in its history,

the great Seleucid city of Apamea in the Orontes valley was settled by Macedonians, most likely on the orders of Antigonus (Strabo *Geog.* XVI.752; Billows 1990: 299), and was also known as Pella – a name it "retained in parallel with Apamea for some time" (Grainger 1990: 39). Appian mentions Apamea as a foundation of Seleucus in the same passage as he mentions Pella, but both these names could still refer to the same city (that is, Apamea) bearing in mind that the Seleucid kingdom did not extend as far south as the area of the later Decapolis until the second century BC (Josephus *Ant. Jud.* XII.130–7). Much the same observation can be made in the case of Eusebius who, anyhow, may well have relied on Appian or a source common to both.

Another possible candidate must be the veteran general Antigonus Monophthalmus, the most energetic of all the *Diadochi* (Billows 1990: 292–305) for he (or at least his son Demetrius Poliorcetes) is known to have campaigned in Coele-Syria (alternatively, Koile Syria) as far south as the region of Petra (Diod. XIX.94–100; Billows 1990: 130–1; Romm 2022: 33–44; Wheatley and Dunn 2020: 49–83) before his final defeat at Ipsus in 301 BC.[6] Hengel (1974: 14) has suggested that both Pella and Dion may have been settled by Antigonus in order to serve as a defence against the Arab tribes but, in reality, their purpose must remain conjectural.

In summary, the strongly Macedonian name of Pella (which, as well as the birthplace of Alexander was also the capital of the Macedonian kingdom during the fourth century BC) points to a foundation at some time during Alexander's conquests or early in the *Diadochenzeit* with Perdiccas or (perhaps) Antigonus Monophthalmus being the most likely candidates. Seleucus Nicator also furnished Syrian cities with Macedonian and Greek names but we have seen that the Seleucid kingdom did not extend as far south as Pella before the second century BC. On the other hand, although the southern Levant fell under the control of Ptolemy I Soter at the end of

---

4   For Perdiccas, see P. Green 1990: 3–15; Heckel 2009: 197–202; Hughes 2022.

5   It should be noted, however, that current archaeological investigations (including analysis of the stamped Rhodian amphora handles) point to Jerash (originally a small village existing at least as early as the Iron Age) being refounded no earlier than the reign of Antiochus III or Antiochus IV when it was named "Antioch on the Chrysorrhoas" (Duplessis et al. 2020; Lichtenberger 2003: 316; Lichtenberger and Raja 2015: 483–6; Schmid 2008: 355).

6   Eusebius (*Chronikon* 2.118) tells us that Demetrius was once again campaigning in southern Coele-Syria in 296/295 BC (or, possibly, 298 BC) when he sacked Samaria (Wheatley and Dunn 2020: 293).

the fourth century, this monarch seems to have had little interest in using place names from Macedon, the land of his birth.

It should be stressed that despite the late fourth-/early third-century BC Attic lamp (CN 7129) of Howland Type 25 A or B Prime recovered from an unstratified context in plot XXXIVB on Tell Husn, we have no definite archaeological evidence of occupation (let alone of a foundation date) prior to the later third century BC. Relevant here is the statue of a feline (most likely a panther) recovered by a local farmer from the fields north-west of Khirbet Fahl (Figures 3.1–2; McNicoll et al. 1992: 117–18). The statue, somewhat worse for wear and most likely serving as a funerary monument, has been attributed to the late fourth century BC (McNicoll et al. 1992; Weber 1993: 54–60) and certainly appears close in style and proportions to the well-known panther of similar date from the hunt scene on the Alexander Sarcophagus and to the leopard depicted on a fourth-century mosaic from Pella in Macedon (Pollitt 1986: 37–46; Robertson 1975: 481–2, 579, pls 151c, 153b).[7] On the other hand, it shares a number of characteristics, as regards treatment of the eyes and forequarters, with the somewhat later (earlier second-century BC) sculpted panther fountain panels[8] from the *Qasr al-ʿAbd* at ʿIraq al-Amir, works that also betray Greek influence (Hill 1963; Magness 2013: 74–5; Queyrel 1991; Rosenberg 2012) and so a later date for this provincial piece – Ptolemaic or Seleucid (more consistent with the archaeological findings at Pella up until now) – is certainly not out of the question.

PTOLEMAIC PELLA

In 301 BC the forces of Seleucus and Lysimachus combined to crush the Antigonids at Ipsus in Phrygia, with Antigonus Monophthalmus himself being killed (Diod. XIX–XX). Although Ptolemy was also nominally part of the anti-Antigonid coalition, he took no part in the decisive battle but, rather, occupied Coele-Syria, which he kept for himself at the subsequent division of the spoils among the victors. Seleucus, in part due to his friendship with Ptolemy who had earlier given him refuge from Antigonus, did not press his claim to this territory despite making it clear that he did not renounce it altogether (Diod. XXI.1.5; Bosworth 2002: 261). Although this claim was the cause of lengthy hostilities between the Ptolemies and Seleucids, the southern half of Syria (to the south of the River Eleutherus, modern Nahr al-Kabir) remained in Ptolemaic hands until the end of the third century BC (Tcherikover 1937: 24–8).

In occupying Coele-Syria Ptolemy I was adhering to the time-honoured stratagem for defending Egypt (Polybius *Hist.* V.34; Heinen 1984: 442–5; Turner 1984: 133–4), an approach that went back to at least the time of Ramesses II (Tubb and Chapman 1990: 72–5).[9] Not only did this stratagem provide a buffer for Egypt against Seleucid attacks from the north and for Ptolemaic-held Palestine against Bedouin forays from Transjordan, it was also designed to include the harbours and ships of the Phoenicians as well as the forests of Lebanon that were the basis of Ptolemaic naval strength, just as they had previously been for the Achaemenid Great King (Bickerman 1988: 69–73; Hölbl 2001: 23). Furthermore, it provided a fertile ground for the recruitment of mercenaries amongst its Jews, Arabs and other inhabitants. Along with its military value, Coele-Syria also represented the meeting place of the great trade routes from Mesopotamia and the Persian Gulf in the north with those of the Arabian coast to the east for, as Tcherikover (1937: 53) so succinctly put it, "it is the historic fate of Palestine to be a crossroad". It stood to reason, therefore, that southern Syria must be kept at all costs and the long series of "Syrian" wars between Ptolemies and Seleucids demonstrates how tenaciously both sides stuck to this aim (Grainger 2010; Heinen 1984; Johannsen 2023: 191–280).

---

7   For the Pella (Macedon) mosaic see also the image on the front cover of Robertson 1981.

8   Initial excavations in 1962 uncovered the first (east) panel (Hill 1963) with the second (west) only being revealed in 1976. Water, stored in plastered reservoirs behind the fountains, flowed through copper pipes into the mouths of the panthers (Rosenberg 2006: 118–20, 2012: 49).

9   But see Meeus (2014) who argues that Ptolemy's occupation of Coele-Syria was actually the first step in acquiring all of Alexander's empire rather than "a monument to the rewards of carefully limited ambitions"; *contra* Anson (2018: 21): "Ptolemy was not simply in favour of partition, but in the ultimate dissolution of the empire and its attendant Argead monarchy."

Figure 3.1. Limestone statue of feline recovered from the fields north-west of Khirbet Fahl (the main mound).

While archaeological explorations west of the Jordan River over the last fifty or more years have done much to elucidate the social and economic conditions existing in Palestine during the fourth and third centuries BC (Berlin 1997b: 3–14; Honigman et al. 2021; E. Stern 1995b), the Zenon papyri remain an important source for the southern Levant under Ptolemaic rule (Pestmann 1981; Rostovtzeff 1922; Tcherikover 1937). This archive, numbering around four thousand documents and discovered in the Egyptian Fayum in the early twentieth century, represents the correspondence and business archives of Zenon, the superintendent of the estate at Philadelphia of Apollonius, *dioiketes* of Ptolemy II. In 259/8 BC Zenon made a journey on behalf of his master to Palestine and Transjordan lasting some twelve months; the correspondence concerned with this journey formed part of the great collection of Zenon's records. On this journey Zenon spent most of his time in Cisjordan but at one stage crossed to the east of the Jordan River, where he passed through

Abella and Sourabit. Zayadine (1991, 2004, 2011) has argued that Abella should be identified with Tell al-Hammam in the Wadi al-Kufrein (although Abila of the Decapolis is perhaps a stronger candidate), but his suggestion that Sourabit refers to the Citadel ("*birta*") of Amman/Philadelphia, rather than 'Iraq al-Amir/ Tyros (as Rosenberg 2006: 17) is less convincing.

It is clear from the accounts of Zenon's journey that the southern Levant played a great role in trade with Egypt during the third century BC (Austin 1981: 407–10). Among its own products, grain, oil, wine and slaves seem to have been the chief exports although small quantities of other products undoubtedly found their way to Egypt. The papyri also demonstrate clearly that southern Syria was the transit centre of an appreciable trade in imports (mainly foodstuffs) from mainland Greece, the Aegean islands and Asia Minor. No doubt many of these items would have reached Egypt by sea, the Palestinian coast being under Ptolemaic control (Bickerman 1988: 71), as would the homegrown Syrian products mentioned

Figure 3.2. Limestone statue of feline (close-up of head) recovered from the fields north-west of Khirbet Fahl (the main mound).

previously. The great incense trade route, stretching from southern Arabia to Egypt, also passed through southern Syria via the Nabatean centre of Petra and the coastal city of Gaza before arriving at the Egyptian town of Pelusium. The small quantity of goods emanating from Transjordan and bound for Egypt could either reach the coast of Palestine via the Jezreel Valley and 'Akko-Ptolemais, from where they could be transported by sea, or (perhaps more likely) travel south down the King's Highway to Petra and thus join the overland route to Gaza.

Also of importance in this context were the lands traditionally belonging to the rich native sheikhs such as Tobiah and Jeddus mentioned in the Zenon papyri.[10] Of particular interest is the former: not only does he appear to have governed the territory of Ammonitis in Transjordan, but he was clearly of some importance, as his correspondence with Apollonius and his leadership of the Ptolemaic cleruchy in Ammonitis demonstrate (B. Mazar 1957; Tcherikover 1937: 42; Will 1991b). It is perhaps more likely that the Tobiad capital and chief fortress (*birta*) – where a document for the sale of a Sidonian slave-girl was drawn up by Zenon's party (Tcherikover and Fuks 1957: 120–1) – was located at Amman/Philadelphia rather than at 'Iraq al-Amir, which must "have served Tobias and his entourage as a *baris* and Persian-style *paradeisos*, a place where royal officials

10   For Tobiah: P. Cair. Zen. 59003, 59005, 59075, 59076; P. Lond. inv. 2358A; for Jeddus: P. Cair. Zen. 59018.

Table 3.2. Phase Hellenistic 2B: stratified deposits.

AREA/PLOT	PHASE	DEPOSIT
XXXIVB (Tell Husn)	Hellenistic 2B c. 220–c. 200 BC	27.16–30, 41.2
XXXIVF (Tell Husn)	Hellenistic 2B c. 220–c. 200 BC	6.1–5

such as Zenon could be entertained and impressed" (MacAdam 1992: 29; *contra* Berlin 1997b: 11).[11] From the Ptolemies' point of view, the advantage of this fiefdom across the Jordan was, primarily, that it served as a defence against the desert Bedouin to the east and, less importantly, as a means of policing the southern part of the great trade route leading from southern Arabia north to Damascus. This route, the old King's Highway, had already fallen into decline in Achaemenid times due, at least in part, to the decrease in settlement that occurred in much of Transjordan during this period. During the third century, as only the southern sector was safely in Ptolemaic hands, it is likely that the highway north of Amman/Philadelphia remained of little importance. Nonetheless it is certainly clear that the Tobiads held great sway over the native population, and thus Ptolemy would have regarded cordial relations with them as an important means of controlling those lands east of the Jordan River (Johannsen 2023: 395–442). Although literary and archaeological evidence does not help us on this point, it is likely that other Ptolemaic cleruchies existed in Transjordan – possibly also under the command of influential native sheikhs (Tcherikover 1937: 43, 1959: 64–6). As we can ascertain from the list of the names of the cleruchs under the command of Tobias (Tcherikover 1937: 44, 1959: 70–1), these cleruchies would also have been a focal point for the intermingling of people from many different lands.

It is worth emphasising that the overwhelming impression gained from the Zenon papyri is that almost all of the commercial activity and trade undertaken in Ptolemaic Syria during the third century was confined to the coast and hinterland west of the Jordan River where Egyptian governmental bureaucracy seems to have been established early on (Berlin and Herbert 2021). Transjordan appears to have played only a minor role in this activity although it was undoubtedly a source of slaves, along with mules, horses and other such animals (MacAdam 1992: 30; Rosenberg 2006: 19; Rostovtzeff 1922: 25–6) with Amman/Philadelphia also involved in the transhipment of exotic animals from further east. All in all, though, it is hard not to gain an impression from the papyri that the territory east of the Jordan River was just as much a backwater as it had been in Achaemenid times, with its prime function being to serve the Ptolemies as a defensive buffer against the Seleucids to the north (Bienkowski 2008; Mueller 2006: 50–3; Tidmarsh 2001).

Hellenistic 2B (c. 220–c. 200 BC): Area XXXIV (Tell Husn)

As previously discussed, the Hellenistic remains on the main mound (Khirbet Fahl), while abundant, are almost completely confined to the period of Seleucid rule (c. 200–c. 80/79 BC). A coin of Ptolemy II (Sheedy et al. 2001: no. 1.001) and two stamped Rhodian amphora handles (RN 20310, RN 20338) from the pre-construction fill of the small dwelling in IIIB/C, along with two stray coins of the same Ptolemy (Sheedy et al. 2001: nos 1.002–1.003), constitute all the third-century material recovered from the mound. On Tell Husn, however, the picture is different, for archaeological evidence confirms that there was indeed a Ptolemaic-period presence at Pella, at least by the last quarter of the third century, consistent with our information that it was seized (temporarily) from the Ptolemies by Antiochus III in 218/217 and again (permanently) in 200/199 BC (Josephus *Ant. Jud.* XII.130–137; Polybius *Hist.* V.60–71).

---

11 For a discussion of the terms *baris* and *birta* see Lemaire and Lozachmeur 1987, 1995; Will 1987, 1991a. Tuplin (1996: 112) suggests that under Hyrcanus, 'Iraq al-Amir served as a working estate rather than purely as a *paradeisos* or hunting park, in which the *Qasr al-Abd* functioned as a (seemingly) "floating palace" (Netzer 2000). For a comprehensive treatment of the site see Rosenberg 2006, 2012 (in which it is suggested that the *Qasr al-Abd* was a mausoleum of the Tobiad family); Will and Larché 1991; Zimmerman 2020a. See also Dušek 2012: 134; Rosenberg 2006:17; Zayadine 2004: 276–7; 2011.

As well as the previously mentioned late fourth/ early third-century BC Attic lamp (CN 7129), early excavations on Tell Husn had brought to light (out of context) a bronze coin of Ptolemy IV (221–204 BC) minted at Alexandria (Sheedy et al. 2001: no. 1.004) from Plot XIA/B. Further work in plot XXXIVF in 1988 and 1993 isolated a rubbish fill that, on the evidence of lamp fragments (CN 7143, CN 7390) and a worn Ptolemaic coin (RN 16063), was laid down in the second half of the third century – in all likelihood discarded from the Ptolemaic garrison discussed below.

In 2007, below Hellenistic wash levels in XXXIVB, was uncovered a thick destruction deposit of ash, charcoal and burnt mudbrick, seemingly washed down from higher ground to the north-east. The recovery of five stamped Rhodian amphora handles dating to the years c. 240–200 BC along with a black-gloss Attic lamp fragment manufactured between the years c. 400–c. 270 and a bronze coin, most probably of Ptolemy IV (221–204 BC), date this destruction level to the last quarter of the third century BC, raising the possibility that it may have been related to the campaigns undertaken by Antiochus III in 218/217 or 200/199 BC to gain control of the southern Levant.[12] As yet, no architectural remains from the third century have been unearthed, largely due to the necessity of preserving the important Byzantine barracks covering much of Husn (Watson and Tidmarsh 1996).

The later third-century ceramic corpus recovered from the Ptolemaic-period levels in XXXIVB and XXXIVF on Tell Husn is small and not linked to any architectural remains, although both deposits should relate to the Ptolemaic fortress or garrison that must have existed at this strategic location by at least the second half of the third century (Errington 2008: 158). This is reflected in the ceramic assemblage with the fine wares (catalogued, uncatalogued and body fragments) few in number. Only five black-gloss specimens – plates, bowls, saucer, those "sophisticated Hellenistic vessels for food service … from classical Greek prototypes" (Rosenthal-Heginbottom 2015: 680) – were catalogued, when compared with the much larger quantities of utilitarian plain ware eating, cooking and (in particular) storage vessels. These latter vessels comprise Types 2–4 jars and three out of the four catalogued pithoi recovered at Pella. It is worth noting, however, that only one example of the globular cooking pot (**PW 549**) was unearthed, whereas the presence of three examples of the casserole Type 1 (**PW 620–2**) is consistent with at least some of the garrison having adopted different cooking practices (Berlin 2015: 636). Taken as a whole, the ceramic assemblage points to some diversity within the dietary practices of the garrison's personnel but, currently, the absence of architectural remains and the small size of the assemblage itself prevent any firm conclusions as to whether this may have been based on cultural or ethnic differences.[13]

Like Scythopolis/Beth-Shean, seven kilometres to the north-west and clearly visible from Pella on the western side of the Jordan River (A. Mazar 2006), it is probable that Pella would have served as a garrison during the Ptolemaic era (and possibly during the period of the *Diadochoi* and before) when, located on Tell Husn, it functioned along with Hippos-Sussita, Gadara/Umm Qais and Itabyrium – the last also mentioned by Polybius (*Hist.* V.70) – as a link in a long chain of fortresses running north–south, designed to command the whole of the Jordan Valley while serving to control the important river crossing between Pella and Scythopolis/Beth-Shean.[14] With a clear view of the Jordan Valley, the garrison on Tell Husn would also have controlled access to that

---

12 Stamped Rhodian amphora handles CN 7655–7658, 7678; Attic lamp fragment CN 7674; bronze coin RN 090279.

13 Valuable here are the comprehensive studies of the integration of multi-ethnic groups into the Ptolemaic army (both within and outside Egypt) by Fischer-Bovet (2014, 2015). See also Hauben (2016).

14 Mueller 2006: 50–3. For Gadara/Umm Qais and Hippos-Sussita as Ptolemaic fortresses that fell to Antiochus III see Polybius *Hist.* V.71. See also Bührig 2011: 286–7; Hoffman 2001: 391, 2002: 101 (Gadara/Umm Qais); Eisenberg 2017; Segal 2004: 26–27 (Hippos-Sussita). As yet there is no trace of a Ptolemaic fortification wall at Gadara/ Umm Qais (although one must have existed) with the visible impressive wall probably completed before the mid-second century BC (Jansen 2021). I thank Brita Jansen of the German Archaeological Institute for her generosity in discussing this information with me. However, in an earlier article, Hoffman (2000) had suggested that traces of the Ptolemaic wall could be discerned. See also Bührig (2009, 2011); also, Jansen (2021: 73) for the possibility that Tell Zira'a to the south served as a Ptolemaic fortress for Gadara/Umm Qais.

Table 3.3. Phase Hellenistic 2B: ceramic assemblage.

		XXXIVB (TELL HUSN)	XXXIVF (TELL HUSN)
Fine ware shapes	Black gloss		
	Fishplates		FW 3
	Plates Type 1: simple thickened rim	FW 31	
	Saucers		FW 45
	Bowls Type 2: in-turned rim		FW 100
	Bowls Type 3: ovoid, plain/ grooved rim		FW 114
Plain ware shapes	Saucers	PW 87, 98	
	Bowls Type 2: in-turned rim	PW 107	
	Kraters Type 4: fluted	PW 174	
	Table amphorae	PW 184	
	Jugs Type 1: thickened rim	PW 186	
	Flasks: southern Palestinian type	PW 233–4	
	Transport amphorae	PW 237–8	
	Jars Type 2B: short neck; everted; thickened rim		PW 266
	Jars Type 2C: short neck; angular rim		PW 272
	Jars Type 3: thickened everted rim	PW 278–9	PW 275
	Jars Type 4B: short neck; short-collared triangular rim	PW 356, 359–60	
	Pithoi	PW 484–6	
	Cooking pots Type 4: concave rim	PW 549	
	Casseroles Type 1: constricted neck; overhanging rim	PW 620	PW 621–2
	Lids	PW 663–4	
	Unguentaria Type 1: squat; rounded body	PW 673–4	PW 672

valley from the hinterland via the strategic Wadi Malawi. This would be consistent with the statement of Stephanos Byzantinos (*Ethnika*, s.v. "Berenikai poleis") that "There is also another Berenike, in Syria, which they call Pella". As Smith (1973: 35) has pointed out, Pella in Jordan is really the only candidate and, while Stephanos is the only authority to make this claim, there is no strong reason to question it. The city could only have been given this name during the third century BC – at the time of Ptolemaic control of the southern Levant – leaving us with two strong candidates (Cohen 2006: 265–8; Hölbl 2001): namely, Berenike I, the wife of Ptolemy I (332–282 BC) and mother of Ptolemy II (282–246 BC), and Berenike II, the wife of Ptolemy III (246–222 BC). A third Berenike (Syra), daughter of Ptolemy II and Arsinoe I but never a Ptolemaic queen, although the second wife of the Seleucid ruler Antiochos II (Coşkun 2016; P. Green 1990: 148–50), is less likely. As things stand, the lack of archaeological material definitely earlier than the mid-third century BC tends to favour the city being (re-)named after the wife of Ptolemy III (Clayman 2014; Tcherikover 1959: 99); however, this could change with further excavation, bearing in mind that Beth-Shean was seemingly refounded as Scythopolis by Ptolemy II c. 260 BC (A. Mazar 2006: 37–40; Mazor and Atrash 2017).[15] Under Ptolemaic control, the newly named Scythopolis functioned as a garrison controlling access to the Palestinian coast from the Jordan Valley via the Valley of Jezreel and as such was confined to Tel Beth-Shean itself. Early in the second century (c. 175 BC), most of its population was transferred from the ancient Tel Beth-Shean to the lower hill of Tel Istaba on the other side of the Jalud River ravine where it underwent extensive settlement,

seemingly culminating in being granted the status as a *polis* by Antiochus IV who also renamed it "Nysa" (Νύσα) after his daughter (Ariel 2004, 2006; Mazor and Atrash 2017; Tsafrir 2011).[16] Much the same situation seems to have occurred at Pella, where, from the early second century, increasing signs of settlement appear on the less-defensible main mound (Khirbet Fahl).[17] It was only during this period – of Seleucid rule (when it presumably regained its pre-Ptolemaic name of Pella) – that a prosperous town (if not a *polis*) covering much of the main mound itself replaced the earlier Ptolemaic garrison on Husn.[18]

SELEUCID PELLA

After the battle of Panium, Coele-Syria passed from Ptolemaic control into the hands of the Seleucids, with the forces of Antiochus now greatly reinforced by men from the upper satrapies (Josephus *Ant. Jud.* XII. 130–137; Grabbe 2021: 24–7; Grainger 2015b: 98–114; Johstono 2017; Strootman 2021: 23–4).[19] Unlike the Ptolemies, whose foreign policy was focused firmly on the eastern Mediterranean littoral (Berlin 1997b: 4–14; Cohen 1983: 68–74), leaving the territory east of the Jordan River relatively neglected, the Seleucid monarchs had always pursued an energetic policy of urbanising those lands subject to them (Musti 1984: 197). This policy seems to have begun with Seleucus Nicator (Appian *Syr* 57) and continued with his son Antiochus: between them they may have founded more than 90 "cities" (*poleis*), although many were no doubt refounded or served purely as military garrisons (Cohen 1978: 11; Davis and Kraay 1973: 185). Regardless of the true number of foundations, there is no doubt that this settlement

---

15 It is also worth noting that Amman/Philadelphia – "sans doute vers 250, s'appela Philadelphie par la grâce du deuxième Lagide" (Will 1985: 239) – and nearby pre-Classical Beth Yerah, on the south-western shore of the Sea of Galilee, were renamed Philoteria in the mid-third century BC apparently after the sister of Ptolemy II (Cohen 2006: 273–4; Greenberg et al. 2017: 4). For an overview of the foreign policy of Ptolemy II, see Marquaille 2008.

16 However, the origins of the toponyms "Scythopolis" and "Nysa" are still debatable. For an outline of the general arguments see Cohen (2006: 290–3).

17 As yet, excavations have uncovered no sign of the wall that presumably defended Seleucid Khirbet Fahl or, indeed, the presumed Ptolemaic wall that must have defended Tell Husn.

18 While, in general, cities that had received Ptolemaic eponyms during the third century reverted to their old names under Seleucid rule, 'Akko-Ptolemais – apart from a short period when it was known as Antiocheia – kept its Ptolemaic name (Mueller 2006: 76–84; Regev 2009/10: 191).

19 The year of the battle of Panium has been much debated. For a recent discussion based on the numismatic evidence see Lorber (2021) who states: "198 is the only possible date for the battle of Panium, followed by a rapid conquest of the entire province of Syria and Phoenicia in the summer of that year" (Lorber 2021: 37).

program was carried out on a vast scale (Cohen 1978: 2–5; Sherwin-White and Kuhrt 1993: 20).

The nucleus of the Seleucid state consisted of Mesopotamia, northern Syria and Cilicia (Musti 1984: 181) and it is within this area that the Seleucid cities were concentrated. After Panium, the southern Levant also experienced an increase in urbanisation during the second century BC, with both the foundation of new cities and the expansion and/or renaming of pre-existing ones (Barghouti 1982; Smith 1990: 125–6).[20] In particular, the region east of the Jordan River was now entering a new sedentary phase of the nomadic-sedentary continuum that continued to exist in Transjordan until well into the twentieth century (LaBianca 1985, 1990: 237–9; LaBianca et al. 1995: 117).

In Palestine, the increase in settled population, along with the marked acceleration in trade that accompanied it, is reflected in the numerous sites yielding second-century BC remains and artefacts (Smith 1990). Much has already been published, and so a reasonably full picture of the material culture of second-century Palestine – both before and after the outbreak of the Hasmonean Revolt – can be gleaned (for example, Berlin 1997b: 14–36; Magness 2013: 63–107). East of the Jordan River, an increase in settled life can also be observed during the second century BC, although the data from surveys, including that from the Pella hinterland (Hannestad 2011: 266–70; Tidmarsh 2000: 108–51; Watson and O'Hea 1996) and reports from sites such as Abila, Amman/Philadelphia, Gadara/Umm Qais, Hippos-Sussita and Jerash (to name but a few) suggest that this took place more in existing settlements than in the general countryside.[21]

Seleucid phases at Pella

In contrast to the small garrison existing on Tell Husn from at least the last third of the third century BC, the Hellenistic remains from Areas III, IV, VIII, XXIII, XXVIII and XXXII make it clear that, by at least the later second century, settlement had spread over much of the main mound. Settlement had also expanded on Tell Husn itself with second- and first-century BC remains and artefacts, found in plots XXXIVB and XXXIVG, lying directly above Bronze Age strata. However, the absence of Hellenistic levels in most of the trenches sunk so far on Husn demonstrates that it was not as densely occupied as the main mound to the north, with limited soundings by the Wooster team in the Wadi Jirm al-Moz (Area IX) suggesting that some degree of Late Hellenistic building had also taken place there (Smith and Day 1989: 2–3, 97).

Hellenistic 3A (c. 200–c. 140 BC): Areas XXVIII, XXXIIY (main mound)

The earliest of the Seleucid phases is seen in Plot XXVIIIB in the south-west sector of the main mound where rich stratified deposits were encountered. The structure associated with these deposits, only incompletely revealed, would appear to be part of a substantial multi-roomed domestic residence partially destroyed by later Byzantine building. From two of these rooms was uncovered an undisturbed series of floors, occupation levels and subfloor fills from which most of the ceramic material was recovered, including black-gloss wares, West Slope bowls and mould-made bowls, most of high quality. The presence in the earliest occupation levels of the latter bowls, first produced around 220 BC but not in common use for another thirty or forty years (Rotroff 2006a), and the Athenian lamp CN 7391 (Figure 1.52) belonging with Howland's Type 29B produced in that city during the second and third quarters of the third century BC, along with the absence of ESA throughout its Hellenistic strata – a ware first introduced to the southern Levant in the mid-second century BC (or slightly later) and commonly encountered in all the later Hellenistic levels at Pella – indicate that the dwelling was constructed at the very end of the third century BC or, more likely, in the early years of the second century BC.

Worth noting also is Plot XXXIIY, on the crest of the southern slope of the mound. Fragments of

---

20 In Palestine at least, this increase in urbanisation seems to have been accompanied by a somewhat slower rate of change in administrative practices (Ecker et al. 2017).

21 Wineland 2001: 103 (Abila); for example, Greene and 'Amr 1992: 127–8; Humbert and Zayadine 1991: 504–5; Zayadine 1977–78: 27–8 *passim* (Amman/Philadelphia); Hoffman 2001, 2002: 103–12 (Gadara/Umm Qais); Eisenberg 2017 (Hippos-Sussita); Barghouti 1982: 220; Braemer 1986: 63, 1987: 527–9; Lichtenberger and Raja 2015: 483–6; Seigne 1997: 76; Uscatescu and Martín-Bueno 1997: 67 (Jerash).

Table 3.4. Phases Hellenistic 3A–3B/3C: stratified deposits.

AREA	PHASE	DEPOSIT
XXVIIIB (main mound)	Hellenistic 3A c. 200–c. 140 BC	10.1–7, 10.9–10, 11.1–5, 13.1–17
XXXIIY (main mound)	Hellenistic 3A	1.2, 1.6, 2.1–2, 2.5, 4.3
IIIP (main mound)	Hellenistic 3B c. 140–c. 100 (?) BC	24.2–6; 25.10–11
IIIQ (main mound)	Hellenistic 3B	11.35
IVE (main mound)	Hellenistic 3B	15.5, 15.9, 16.8–9, 17.10, 17.12–3
XXIIIA (main mound)	Hellenistic 3B	108.2–6, 109.1–4
XXIIIB (main mound)	Hellenistic 3B	2.1–14, 3.1–2, 3.6–7, 3.9–16
XXIIID (main mound)	Hellenistic 3B	11.7, 11.9, 11.11–13, 11.16, 11.18, 23.1, 24.1–3, 32.2, 33.1, 35.1, 36.1
XXXIVB (Tell Husn)	Hellenistic 3B/3C c. 140–c. 80/79 BC	13.5–7, 13.9, 13.11, 15.1–2, 18.1–3, 18.5, 18.7–11, 16.2, 16.4, 17.1–2, 28.1–2, 29.1–10, 30.1–10

black-gloss bowls, fishplates and other fine wares (but not ESA) along with table amphorae, jars and cooking pots were found within a discrete and easily identifiable yellow layer that, though associated with no architectural remains, appears to have originated from unexcavated areas further to the north either as a wash level or as a result of later, deliberate, clearance. From within this layer was recovered the Rhodian amphora handle CN 7868 (belonging to Period Va c. 145–c. 133) indicating, when combined with the absence of ESA, a probable date for the deposit of very early in the second half of the second century BC.

It is worth observing that, of all the plots sunk on the main mound reaching in situ Hellenistic levels, only XXVIIIB (along with the wash/clearance stratum XXXIIY) has revealed no trace of the thick destruction levels associated with the sack of Alexander Jannaeus, suggesting that the dwelling uncovered here had gone out of use well before the Jannaeus sack.

Hellenistic 3B (c. 140–c. 100 (?) BC): Areas XXIII, XXXII (main mound), XXXIV (Tell Husn)

In Area XXIII, beneath the latest phase of an impressive structure (probably a large house or "villa"), as yet only partially revealed, was an earlier Hellenistic phase as demonstrated by a series of walls orientated north–south and east–west. From an occupation deposit (108.2) in XXIIIA came a bronze coin of Antiochus VIII Grypus (126/5–96 BC) while in XXIIID these walls were associated with the thin, tamped-earth surface on which lay a bronze of Antiochus VII/Demetrius II (138–125 BC).[22] Also relevant is lamp CN 7392 from XXIIIB, a local copy (most likely of the second century) of a third-century Athenian lamp (Howland Type 29 A or B; Scheibler's Form FSL 1 or 2). Thus, the numismatic and ceramic evidence, including the presence of ESA fragments, is consistent with a date in the second half of the second century BC for this earlier phase.

On Tell Husn, below the Early Roman levels in Plots XXXIVB and XXXIVG, limited excavations have partially revealed the upper courses of earlier walls, along with abundant ceramic material (including ESA) from XXXIVB, furnishing evidence for occupation from approximately the mid-second century (or slightly later) down to the Jannaeus conquest c. 80/79 BC (Hellenistic 3B/3C).

Within the Pre-Jannaeus Destruction phases (Hellenistic 3A–3B) the proportion of fine wares is high, with almost half the black-gloss pottery from Pella recovered from these levels. Most of the fine wares were retrieved from plot XXVIIIB rather than those from the earlier phases in Area XXIII, the mixed

---

22 Coin of Antiochus VIII Grypus, Sheedy et al. 2001: no. 1.015; coin of Antiochus VII/Demetrius II RN 111554.

pre-destruction levels of plot IIIB/C, or the wash/clearance level of plot XXXIIY. A similar pattern was seen for the stratified Attic black-gloss (Ware 1) vessels, found mainly in XXVIIIB rather than in later deposits, consistent with the evidence from most Hellenistic sites in Asia Minor and the Levant that the later third century onwards witnessed a progressive decline in the arrival of Athenian pottery (Hannestad 1983: 85, 1990: 179). Fine-ware plates are almost exclusively fishplates in black-gloss whereas, in this period but not Hellenistic 3C, the shape is uncommon in plain wares, replaced, it would seem, by the thickened rim plates Types 1–2. The fine-ware bowl forms are restricted to those with out-turned or in-turned rim in Hellenistic 3A as also seen in the plain wares, with two black-gloss ovoid bowls seen in Hellenistic 3B strata. These bowl forms, along with the fishplate, were widely imitated in the Syro-Palestinian area (Hannestad 1983: 85) with the marked predominance of black-gloss wares 2 and 3 in these Greek-inspired shapes, consistent with the beginnings of production of black-slipped predecessor.

Almost half of the mould-made ("Megarian") bowls were found in unstratified levels; amongst the stratified examples the majority were from plot XXVIIIB (Hellenistic 3A) with two of this latter group (**FW 265**, **FW 278**) produced in Athens and ten from Antioch or its environs (Wares 2, 3). The small number of West Slope–ware vessels was also found mainly in levels of the first half of the second century (Hellenistic 3A). ESA is not represented in XXVIIIB – hardly surprising, given the fact that

Table 3.5. Phase Hellenistic 3A: pottery.

		XXVIIIB (MAIN MOUND)	XXXIIY (MAIN MOUND)
Fine ware	Fishplates	FW 1, 9–14, 16–7, 27–8, 30 (green-glazed)	
	Plates Type 3: grooved thickened rim	FW 36–7	FW 39
	Saucers	FW 48	
	Bowls Type 1: out-turned rim	FW 59, 61–7, 73	FW 57–8
	Bowls Type 2: in-turned rim	FW 80–94, 101,	
	Kraters Type 2: everted rim	FW 126	FW 127
	Cups: "Palestinian form"		FW 143
	Moulded grey ware juglets	FW 145	
	West Slope ware	FW 169 (plate)	FW 167–8, 170 (plates); 181–2 (jars)
	Mould-made bowls	FW 261, 264–5, 273–4, 276, 278, 280, 288, 293, 296–7, 300–1	
Plain ware	Fishplates Type 1: broad angled rim	PW 15	
	Plates Type 1: thickened simple rim	PW 42–4, 46–7	PW 48
	Plates Type 2: thickened undercut rim	PW 61–3, 70	
	Saucers	PW 89	
	Bowls Type 2: in-turned rim	PW 111–12	PW 119
	Cups: narrow band, pinched handles	PW 151	

	XXVIIIB (MAIN MOUND)	XXXIIY (MAIN MOUND)
Kraters Type 1: flaring rim, vertical lip	PW 154–7	
Kraters Type 2: horizontal rim	PW 167, 169	
Kraters Type 3: down-turned rim	PW 170–1	
Table amphorae	PW 176–80	
Jugs Type 1: elongated neck; thickened rim	PW 187	
Jugs Type 3: grooved rim	PW 197–8	PW 195–6
Jugs Type 5: flanged rim	PW 202	
Juglets Type 1: simple rim	PW 212	
Transport amphorae	PW 244–8	
Mortaria	PW 255–9	
Jars Type 1A: neckless; prominent shoulder		PW 260
Jars Type 2B: short neck; everted thickened rim	PW 267–8	
Jars Type 3: thickened everted rim	PW 283, 285–7	
Jars Type 4A: short neck; short-collared square rim	PW 309–30	
Jars Type 4B: short neck; short-collared triangular rim	PW 357–8	
Jars Type 5A: tall neck; short collared square rim	PW 382–5	
Cooking pots Type 1: simple rim	PW 488–95	
Cooking pots Type 3: ledge rim	PW 522–7	
Cooking pots Type 4: concave rim	PW 550–1	
Casseroles Type 3: interior flange; overhanging rim	PW 640–1	
Lids		PW 665
Unguentaria Type 2: slender; angular body	PW 679–80, 683, 685–7, 690, 692	PW 684, 688

Table 3.6. Phase Hellenistic 3B: pottery.

		IIIP (MAIN MOUND)	XXIII A, B, D (MAIN MOUND)
Fine ware	Fishplates	FW 19–20	FW 2, 15
	Plates Type 3: grooved thickened rim	FW 38	
	Saucers	FW 50	FW 51
	Bowls Type 1: out-turned rim		FW 75
	Bowls Type 2: in-turned rim	FW 96, 98	
	Bowls Type 3: ovoid; plain/grooved rim	FW 110	FW 112
	Cups: band rim, pinched handles		FW 135–6
	West Slope ware	FW 177	
	ESA Hayes 3		FW 190
	Mould-made bowls		FW 275
Plain ware	Fishplates: base	PW 39	
	Plates Type 2: thickened undercut rim		PW 67–9
	Bowls Type 1: out-turned rim		PW 102
	Bowls Type 2: in-turned rim	PW 130–1	PW 118, 120
	Bowls Type 6: hemispherical		PW 146
	Cups: narrow band; pinched handles		PW 152–3
	Kraters Type 1: flaring rim, vertical lip		PW 159
	Jars Type 3: thickened everted rim		PW 284, 288, 291
	Jars Type 4A: short neck; short-collared square rim		PW 332
	Jars Type 4B: short neck; short-collared triangular rim		PW 370–1, 373
	Jars Type 5A: tall neck; short-collared square rim		PW 386–7
	Jars Type 5B: tall neck; short-collared triangular rim		PW 399
	Cooking pots Type 1: simple rim		PW 496
	Cooking pots Type 3: ledge rim		PW 528
	Cooking pots Type 6: grooved rim	PW 605	
	Casseroles Type 3: interior flange; overhanging rim		PW 642
	Unguentaria Type 1: squat; rounded body		PW 675
	Unguentaria Type 2: slender; angular body		PW 681

the ware was first produced around the mid-second century BC – but small numbers of catalogued and non-catalogued specimens (mainly Hayes Form 3 bowls) appear in the Hellenistic 3B levels.

As regards the plain wares, mortaria (with one non-catalogued exception) are restricted to the Hellenistic 3A levels of XXVIIIB and would thus appear to be the latest examples of a type widely distributed throughout Palestine in the Achaemenid era and present in Iron II levels at Pella where, at this latter site, with their thickened rims they may have functioned both as bowls and vessels for grinding and mixing foodstuffs (for example, McNicoll et al. 1982: pl. 126, nos 8, 9). In fact, the paucity of ceramic mortaria, along with the virtual absence of stone implements used in food preparation from the Hellenistic and Early Roman levels may indicate that excavations are yet to uncover those areas of intensive food preparation. Cooking-pot forms also continue earlier Iron Age and Persian traditions, being almost wholly restricted to those globular types with either everted, ledge or concave rims (Types 1, 3, 4); only three Greek-inspired casserole fragments were recovered from the Hellenistic 3A and 3B levels.

On the other hand, the Hellenistic 3A and 3B storage jars largely represent a significant change in ceramic form with the great majority comprising examples with short collar and square rim or undercut rims (Type 4) along with a smaller number with the longer collars seen on Type 5 in both phases. Earlier jar types (Types 2 and 3) are now much less frequent in Hellenistic 3B.

Hellenistic 3C (c. 100 (?)–c. 80/79 BC): Areas III, IV, XXIII (main mound), XXXIV (Tell Husn)

Josephus (*Ant. Jud.* XIII.395) tells us that under the Hasmonean ruler Alexander Jannaeus "the Jews held the following cities of Syria, Idumaea and Phoenicia …

and Pella – this last city Alexander's men demolished because the inhabitants would not agree to adopt the national customs of the Jews". And so, it would seem that the destruction levels seen across the main mound in Areas III, IV, VIII and XXIII, putting an end to the Hellenistic occupation, must have been the work of the Hasmonean king with the presence of the previously mentioned Alexander Jannaeus "Year 25" (Meshorer 2001: Group L) bronze coin (RN 110889) well within the Jannaeus Destruction level pointing to a date for the destruction of 80/79 BC (or soon after) rather than the more generally accepted 83/82 BC. In this regard it needs to be emphasised that, while the coinage of Alexander Jannaeus is presumed to have continued in circulation after his death, nowhere at Pella have first-century BC post-Jannaeus ceramics or coinage (or, in fact, any other artefact) been recovered from this destruction level.[23]

Due to the depth at which the Hellenistic levels lie on Khirbet Fahl and Tell Husn and because of the damage inflicted by later rebuilding, along with the necessity to preserve important later structures (problems all too familiar for those working on large *tell* sites), a wide exposure of the remains cannot be carried out (Table 3.7): accordingly, little can be said about the overall town plan of the Seleucid settlement during its latest, most explored, phase. The existence of laneways or small streets has been shown on the main mound in areas III, IV and VIII, and on Tell Husn in XXXIV but as to whether these were laid out as part of a Hippodamian (orthogonal) plan – as seems to be the case at Gadara/Umm Qais (Hoffman 2001: 394) – cannot be ascertained.

The Hellenistic structures uncovered so far (with the exception of those forts on Jebel Hammeh and Jebel Sartaba whose exact purpose remains uncertain until they are more fully investigated)[24] are domestic in nature with no fortification wall – rarely preserved in the Hellenistic phase of the Decapolis cities (R.W. Smith 2011) – or religious or civic buildings

---

23   It has been suggested (for example, Hirschfeld and Ariel 2005: 86; Meshorer 2001: 42) that during the reign of Alexandra, widow of Jannaeus, Group L coins may have continued to be produced. In the case of the Pella destruction, however, the re-assigning of coin RN 110889 (and hence the destruction) to Alexandra would mean completely discounting the evidence of Josephus, which I am loath to do.

24   Sabar (2022) suggests that both forts were constructed by Alexander Jannaeus to defend his newly won eastern territory, although, clearly, that on Sartaba never fulfilled this function.

Table 3.7. Phase Hellenistic 3C: stratified deposits.

AREA: MAIN MOUND	DEPOSIT
IIIB/C	1.1–5, 2.1–9, 3.1–3, 4.1–2, 9.1, 14.1–6, 15.2–3
IVD	10.10, 10.12, 10.14, 11.1, 12.1, 13.10, 13.13–4, 13.17–8, 14.1–2
IVE	13.6, 13.11, 15.3–4, 15.6, 16.2–3, 17.6–7, 19.10
XXIIIA	10.5, 10.7–8, 10.11, 11.1–3, 13.3, 19.23, 20.4, 22.2–11, 71.2, 71.4–5, 72.5, 72.9, 74.2, 75.2, 77.2, 78.1, 83.4–5, 84.1–2, 84.4, 85.1–3, 87.2–4, 100.1–6, 101.1–2, 102.1, 103.1–4, 104.1–3, 105.1–3, 106.1, 107.1, 108.1, 110.1
XXIIIB	1.1–5
XXIIID	11.4–6, 11.10, 16.3, 17.1, 18.1–9, 19.1–6, 20.1–10, 21.1, 22.1, 29.15–25, 30.1–2, 31.1–3, 32.1, 43.1–2, 44.1–2, 45.2–4, 59.3, 63.2, 67.1, 68.1–5, 69.1, 70.2, 71.2, 74.2–3, 75.1, 76.1, 77.2, 80.1, 82.1–2, 83.1–2

located.[25] The Hellenistic cemetery also remains to be located, although the recovery of the previously discussed statue of a feline (panther?), most likely a funerary monument, from the fields north-west of the main mound indicates a possible location.

The architecture of the mainly modest houses uncovered on Khirbet Fahl and Tell Husn is very uniform: the interior floors were of tamped earth, thin plaster or unbaked clay tiles with courtyard surfaces of much thicker plaster on a base of small stones. The walls are for the most part constructed of rubble masonry in their lower courses with the stones set into a mud mortar. Rectangular "headers" – no doubt to strengthen (rather than embellish) the wall – are sometimes employed as is also the case with "stretchers". These stone walls generally served a simple utilitarian function with many supporting upper courses of pisé or mudbrick that, at least as seen in IIIB/C, could be of several different sizes. Though the masonry of Pella's Seleucid-period walls is generally unimpressive, the archaeological evidence shows that several of them were plastered. In some cases, the plaster was white with no trace of painted decoration, as in XXXIVG where it was still in situ on several of the walls. Small fragments of red- and green-painted plaster were also noted in the remains of a further house in IVD/IVE (McNicoll et al. 1992: 111).[26] On current evidence the techniques and materials used in constructing these walls seem little changed (apart from a more frequent use of "headers" and "stretchers" in the Hellenistic walls) from those of the preceding Iron Age at Pella, with the plan of the structures themselves also similar (McNicoll et al. 1982: 55–63, 1992: 83–101).

Not all the houses of Seleucid Pella could be called "modest" as is demonstrated by the large "villa" being revealed in Area XXIII on the main mound. This dwelling combined domestic use with textile weaving and metalworking, as well as the preparation of food and storage of wine on an impressive scale. It possessed numerous clay ovens, resting either on tamped earth floors or the cobbled surfaces of multiple courtyards within the complex. The "fine stone floor" uncovered by Funk and Richardson (1958: 89) was most probably the surface of a further courtyard; as yet this is the only Hellenistic stone-paved floor of high quality unearthed at Pella. Close

25 For Hellenistic/Early Roman temples in the Decapolis and beyond, see Peleg-Barkat 2013, 2017. Also, Bührig 2011: 287; Hoffman 2002: 103–8; Shiyab et al. 2017 (Gadara/Umm Qais); Schmid 2008: 355; Seigne 2002: 12–15 (Jerash); Segal et al. 2003: 11–18, 2004: 20–30 (Hippos-Sussita). See also Bührig (2016) for religious sanctuaries within the Gadara/Umm Qais hinterland survey area.

26 In this regard it is worth noting that decorative painted plaster of a similar nature to that encountered in IVD/IVE and XXIIIA has been revealed in Late Hellenistic/Early Roman houses from Gadara/Umm Qais (Kerner 1997: 294–5). I also express my sincere thanks to Brita Jansen for sharing with me her as yet unpublished chapter on the late third- or early second-century BC painted wall plaster from Tell Zira'a.

to 100 clay loom weights have so far been recovered from the dwelling and equally noteworthy is the large quantity of Rhodian wine amphora fragments also found. While similar Rhodian amphora handles and fragments turn up elsewhere on the site they do so in much smaller numbers. With the exception of the possible metal recycling area in Plot XXIIID, these disparate functions seem not to have been confined to discrete areas within the "villa", consistent with the multi-functional role of many rooms within ancient houses (Berlin 2005b: 448). However, this observation should be treated with caution due to the disruption caused by the Funk and Richardson sounding, along with the as yet incomplete excavation of the "villa".

From the Jannaeus Destruction levels of this "villa" were recovered numerous fragments of plaster – both moulded and painted in red, green and white – adorning the upper walls or, more likely, decorating an upper storey, part of which may still be preserved in the unexcavated sector in the east of the plot. If only in a modest way, these fragments of moulded and painted panels with their egg-and-dart motifs reflect the art of Alexandria and other great Ptolemaic and Seleucid centres (McKenzie 1990: 61–83, 2007: 71–118; Venit 2002) and recall the Greek-inspired interior decoration of well-to-do houses elsewhere in the Hellenistic world. Though the impressive "House A" and "Plaster House", from the village mound at 'Iraq al-Amir, are similar as regards date, plaster decoration and paved courtyard (J. Groot 1983: 75–7), examples of these grand houses are rare in Jordan during Seleucid times with nothing to compare, so far, with the "Late Hellenistic Stuccoed Building" at Tel Anafa (Herbert 1994: 31–100 *passim*) or, further to the north, "The House of the Painted Frieze" or "Acropolis

Palace" at Jebel Khalid on the Euphrates (Jackson 2009, 2014: 26–9, 45–166, 2016). From his examination of the painted wall plaster from the "Late Hellenistic Stuccoed Building" at Tel Anafa (Gordon 1979) and the Hellenistic "villa" at Pella, Robert Gordon (pers. com.) has suggested that both decoration projects may have been "by the same workshop".[27]

The presence of the Rhodian wine amphorae demonstrates a taste for imported Greek wines while the use of the ornate painted and moulded plaster further suggests the Hellenic tastes of the owner. Perhaps not surprising, therefore, is the recovery here of part of a bronze torso draped very much in Greek style as well as a life-size bronze finger (seemingly from a separate statue) and the flexed arm of an imported marble statuette (Figures 1.18–19; Plates 5, 8). The archaeological context from which these sculptural fragments were recovered suggests a later Hellenistic (Seleucid) date for each of them. In particular, whilst the location of the workshops in which the statuette arm (the marble of which awaits analysis) and bronze fragments were produced may be open to debate, the treatment of each, in particular the bronze drapery with its well-modelled oblique folds of varying thickness (Weber 1993: 71–3, table 7.1), is undoubtedly Greek in inspiration.[28]

Along with the painted plaster, the pottery recovered both from the main mound and from Tell Husn demonstrates that at least some of Pella's inhabitants were receptive to Greek cultural influence during the second and early first centuries BC (Tidmarsh 2004)– an influence consistent with Pella's inclusion by both Pliny (*Nat. Hist.* V.16.74) and Ptolemy (*Geog.* V.14.18) amongst the cities of the Decapolis. Greek-inspired (both in their black-gloss

---

27   At Jerash, the Late Hellenistic "Naos" on the lower terrace, below the later Temple of Zeus, shows ample traces of both painted and moulded plaster (Seigne 2002: 12–15); at Petra decorative stucco was widely used on tombs, temples and domestic dwellings from at least the late first century BC (Zayadine 1987). Noteworthy in the present context are the traces of architectural stucco decoration in the remains of two houses on the eastern face of el-Habis (Zayadine 1987: 133–5). In a much better state of preservation, but of Early Roman date (*terminus post quem* of c. 20 AD), is the impressive painted plaster mural decoration of Second Pompeian Style from room 1 of the wealthy private dwelling uncovered by the Swiss Liechtenstein team in the area of az-Zantur at Petra (Kolb 1997: 234–40). Small fragments of decorative stucco have also been recovered from late Herodian contexts at Machaerus (Corbo 1979: pl. 48) and Kallirhoe (Clamer 1997: 80, fig. 91b). For a review of decorative wall painting and stucco in Transjordan from Hellenistic to Roman times and later see Vibert-Guige 2016, 2018. Also, Vibert-Guige and Barbet (1982) for painted Roman tombs in north Jordan.

28   See Martens 2021 (with references) for the increasingly recognised role played by the eastern Mediterranean basin (as opposed to the Roman west) as a market for "copies" or adaptations (especially marble statuettes) of classical-looking or Hellenistic sculpture produce in centres such as Delos, Athens and Rhodes.

and shape) fishplates and bowls are numerous as are mould-made bowls. The large number of Rhodian amphora fragments (handles and body sherds) shows that the wine of that island was also appreciated, although undoubtedly some of these vessels would have been reused as containers of other liquids, including local Syrian wine, and foodstuffs (Grace 1979; Smith 1990: 128). Also of Greek inspiration is the lagynos, with the fine imported white-ground specimen **FW 166** found out of context on the slopes of Jebel Sartaba; locally made undecorated lagynoi are known to have been manufactured at Jerash (Kehrberg 2004a: 195, 2004b: 303), whilst moulded lamps of closed Greek form have completely supplanted the earlier, eastern "open saucer" type.[29]

By the early first century BC, the number of black-gloss bowls and plates is much reduced (most notably Wares 2 and 3) with many more of these small shapes now of Coarse Light Brown ware. The vessels in this local ware, however, exhibit a progressive deterioration in quality and care of manufacture, readily detected in those examples recovered from the Jannaeus Destruction levels (for example, **PW 74–6**). This decline is especially apparent amongst the multiple fishplates (Figure 1.9) and bowls that, from the evidence at Pella and elsewhere, were still being turned out by at least some southern Levantine potters. The sharp metallic lines seen in many of the black-gloss examples degenerate into a much less certain profile amongst the plain wares (for example **PW 11, PW 27**), with the crisp ring-base, always applied on imported black-gloss examples, often replaced by an uneven concave disc (**PW 140–4**). Also, in Hellenistic 3C levels, the numerous examples of moulded grey ware vessels (mainly bottles and juglets), probably produced at Jerash or (less likely) the environs of Pella itself, are a further sign of the increasing popularity of local wares. Whereas some centres in the Levant continue to turn out pottery of a high standard, as the numerous diagnostic and non-diagnostic fragments of ESA show,[30] the overall decline in ceramic quality probably reflects the unsettled conditions accompanying the disintegration of the

Seleucid empire during this period (Bellinger 1949; Coşkun 2019; Erikson and Ramsey 2011; Grainger 2015a; Kosmin 2014: 242–51; Sherwin-White and Kuhrt 1993: 217–29).

Not surprisingly, in view of their purely utilitarian function, the Hellenistic 3C cooking pots still have their antecedents largely in the Iron Age shapes of the Levant: very few "casseroles", a shape first made in Classical Greece and inspired by Greek dietary tastes (Berlin 1993: 42, 2015: 636), and no cooking bowls (pans) have been recovered from these levels whereas they become relatively common in Early Roman contexts. This provides an interesting contrast with Samaria-Sebaste, for here the casserole is common in second-century BC deposits (Crowfoot et al. 1957: fig. 41, nos 8–20) but appears not to continue into the Roman period (Crowfoot et al. 1957: 230). Likewise, several of the storage jars follow Iron Age traditions, although the prominent collar seen on many examples (Types 4–6) is uncommon before the early second century BC; there is, however, nothing to suggest that this feature was borrowed from Greek prototypes.

From the time it entered the Seleucid realm until its destruction by Jannaeus in c. 80/79 BC, Pella remained a city relatively open to the wider Mediterranean world with at least some of its inhabitants eating and drinking Rhodian wine from vessels of Greek shape and served from Alexandrian-inspired lagynoi, decorating their houses in the Hellenistic *koine* and importing Greek statuary.[31] There is, however, nothing to suggest that the great increase in population during the second century BC, which saw the main mound densely settled for the first time since the early Iron Age, was achieved by a further influx of settlers from the Greek world, for following the Seleucid defeat at the battle of Magnesia (189 BC) the flow of Greek settlers into the Levant had virtually dried up (Cohen 1978: 29; A.H.M. Jones 1983: 247). Rather, the plain wares would suggest that the new inhabitants belonged very much to the world of the southern Levant, consistent with Cohen (1978: 38) that "the normal sequence in uniting the Greeks or Macedonians with the natives was to first establish

---

29 Relevant here is the discovery at Jerash of a Late Hellenistic hypogeum tomb of a child of a well-to-do merchant containing, amongst other objects, a lagynos and three ceramic models of camels conveying Rhodian amphorae (Kehrberg 2004b; Kehrberg-Ostrasz 2018; Kehrberg and Manley 2002).

30 Many, if not most, of these ESA vessels would have arrived at Pella from the coast via the Jezreel Valley and Scythopolis/Beth-Shean with this city possessing significant quantities of ESA (Malfitana 2002: 149).

31 "Hellenised" Pella would be too emphatic a description. See Strootman 2020: 201–5.

Table 3.8. Phase Hellenistic 3C: pottery.

		III B, C; IV D, E (MAIN MOUND)	XXIII A, B, D (MAIN MOUND)
Fine ware	Fishplates	FW 21–3	FW 24
	Plates Type 1: simple thickened rim	FW 33	
	Plates with upright rim	FW 42–3	FW 44
	Saucers	FW 53–4	
	Bowls Type 1: out-turned rim	FW 77–9	
	Bowls Type 2: in-turned rim	FW 102, 105–6	FW 95, 97, 103–4
	Bowls Type 4: ovoid, decorated rim	FW 116	
	Applied relief bowls		FW 119
	Skyphoi/kantharoi	FW 129, 132	
	Cups: band rim, pinched handles	FW 138, 140	FW 137
	Moulded grey ware juglets	FW146–8	FW 149–57
	Moulded grey ware bottles		FW 163–4
	West Slope ware	FW 173 (bowl)	FW 183 (jar)
	ESA Hayes 1	FW 189	
	ESA Hayes 3	FW 193, 196–9	FW 195, 200, 204
	ESA Hayes 4A		FW 205
	ESA "rare form a"		FW 209–10
	ESA "rare form c"		FW 230
	ESA Hayes 17B	FW 216	
	ESA Hayes 22A	FW 219–20	FW 218, 223
	ESA Closed form		FW 250
	Mould-made bowls	FW 279, 285	FW 260, 272, 283, 302
Plain ware	Fishplates Type 1: broad angled rim	PW 1–4, 9	PW: 5, 7, 8, 10, 11
	Fishplates Type 2: broad drooping rim	PW 17, 20, 21, 25	PW 18–19, 22–4, 26–7, 29
	Fishplate bases	PW 36, 38	PW 37
	Plates Type 1: thickened simple rim	PW 53	PW 54
	Plates Type 2: thickened undercut rim	PW 72–7	PW 78–9
	Plates with upright rim	PW 86	PW 85
	Saucers		PW 90
	Bowls Type 1: out-turned rim	PW 103–4	PW 105–6
	Bowls Type 2: in-turned rim	PW 116, 123–7	PW 128–9
	Bowls Type 3: flat base, angled rim	PW 140–2	
	Bowls Type 4: flat base, simple rim	PW 143–4	
	Bowls Type 5: bevelled rim		PW 145
	Bowls Type 6: hemispherical	PW 147	PW 148
	Kraters Type 2: horizontal rim		PW 168

	III B, C; IV D, E (MAIN MOUND)	XXIII A, B, D (MAIN MOUND)
Kraters Type 4: fluted		PW 172, 175
Table amphorae		PW 182–3
Jugs Type 1: thickened rim	PW 190	PW 189, 191
Jugs Type 2: short-collared rim		PW 192–4
Jugs Type 4: flaring rim		PW 200
Jugs Type 5: flanged rim	PW 205	PW 204
Juglets Type 1: simple rim		PW 213–4
Juglets Type 5: cup-shaped rim	PW 225	PW 223–4
Lagynoi Type 1: rounded body	PW 228–9	
Lagynoi Type 2: angular body		PW 230
Lagynoi: miscellaneous	PW 232	PW 231
Transport amphorae		PW 249–50
Jars Type 2A: short neck; everted simple rim		PW 264–5
Jars Type 2B: short neck; everted thickened rim		PW 271
Jars Type 2C: short neck; angular rim		PW 273
Jars Type 3: thickened everted rim	PW 297	PW 292–6, 298
Jars Type 4A: short neck; short-collared square rim	PW 333–8	PW 341–54
Jars Type 5A: tall neck; short-collared square rim	PW 388–9, 392–3	PW 390–1, 394–6
Jars Type 5B: tall neck; short collared triangular rim	PW 400	PW 398
Jars Type 6A: long-collared rim: uniform thickness		PW 401–10
Jars Type 7A: neck ridge; simple lip	PW 436	
Jars Type 7B: neck ridge; overhanging lip	PW 460	PW 461
Cooking pots Type 1: simple rim	PW 498–500	PW 497
Cooking pots Type 3: ledge rim	PW: 529–31	PW 532–9, 544–5
Cooking pots Type 4: concave rim		PW 554–7, 560
Cooking pots Type 5: bevelled rim	PW 574	PW 573
Cooking pots Type 7: "Galilean"	PW 606	
Cooking pots Type 8: thickened lip		PW 611
Casseroles Type 1: constricted neck; overhanging rim		PW 623
Casseroles Type 2: upright wall; overhanging rim		PW 634
Lids		PW 670
Unguentaria Type 1: squat; rounded body		PW 676–7
Unguentaria: fragment	PW 693	

Table 3.9. Phase Hellenistic 3B/3C: pottery.

		XXXIVB (TELL HUSN)
Fine ware	Saucers	FW 52
	Bowls Type 1: out-turned rim	FW 60
Plain ware	Saucers	PW 91–4
	Bowls Type 2: in-turned rim	PW 108–9
	Jugs Type 5: flanged rim	PW 203
	Transport amphorae	PW 239–43, 253–4
	Jars Type 1A: neckless; prominent shoulder	PW 261
	Jars Type 2B: short neck; everted thickened rim	PW 269–70
	Jars Type 3: thickened everted rim	PW 281–2, 303
	Jars Type 4A: short neck; short-collared square rim	PW 304–7
	Jars Type 4B: short neck; short-collared triangular rim	PW 361, 363–9
	Pithoi	PW 487
	Cooking pots Type 1: simple rim	PW 501
	Cooking pots Type 3: ledge rim	PW 540
	Cooking pots Type 4: concave rim	PW 559
	Cooking pots Type 5: bevelled rim	PW 581, 586
	Casseroles Type 1: constricted neck; overhanging rim	PW 627
	Unguentaria: fragments	PW 691

the colony and then transfer the natives". The ethnic and tribal affiliations of these new settlers still remain unclear to us; nevertheless, it is tempting to argue that with the re-institution during the earlier second century of a strong, central Seleucid authority – albeit temporary – many must have been descendants of those same tribes ruled by Tobiah, Jeddus and other influential native sheikhs when the lands east of the Jordan River were still part of the Ptolemaic realm.

EARLY ROMAN PELLA

After the death in 67 BC of Salome Alexandra, the widow of Alexander Jannaeus, civil war broke out between her sons Aristobolus II and Hyrcanus II – a conflict that continued until Pompey sided with Hyrcanus in 63 BC (Josephus *BJ* I.122–55). The subsequent defeat of Aristobolus effectively signalled the end of the Hasmonean dynasty. Its territories, with the exception of Judea, eastern Idumea, Galilee,

and the Peraea were dismantled. And so, with the exception of the Peraea, those cities east of the Jordan that had been under Hasmonean control, were "liberated" (or, in the case of Gadara, which Jannaeus had destroyed, "re-founded") and handed over to their inhabitants (Josephus *BJ* I.155–7; *Ant. Jud.* XIV.74–6). It was at this time, therefore, that the southern Levant first came under Roman control. During the first century AD most of the territory east of the Jordan River – with the exception of the Peraea in which lay the palace/fortress of Machaerus (Vörös 2013, 2019a, b) and thermal springs of Kallirhoe (Josephus *Ant. Jud.* 17.171; *BJ* I.657; Clamer 1997; Wimmer 2019a, 2019b) – remained outside the boundaries of the kingdoms of Herod and his successors, lying within either the province of Syria or the Nabatean realm. As a result, Transjordan remained largely removed from the vicissitudes that affected Roman Palestine although, with the onset of the First Jewish Revolt in 66 AD, Josephus (*BJ* II.457–65) tells us that Pella, Jerash, Amman/Philadelphia, Hesban and other cities east of the Jordan River were pillaged by bands of Jews enraged at the slaughter of many of their number by the inhabitants of Caesarea. Furthermore, Eusebius (*Ecclesiastical History* 3, 5) and Epiphanius of Salamis (*Panarion* 29, 7–8; 30, 2) recount the tradition, still the source of much controversy (for example, Balabanski 1997: 107–34; Bourke 2013), that during this period Pella served as a refuge for Christians fleeing across the Jordan River from Jerusalem to Pella before the destruction of their city in 70 AD).[32]

In effect, therefore, Transjordan was divided between those cities to the north – some of which (including Jerash, Amman/Philadelphia, Gadara/Umm Qais and Pella) went to make up the Decapolis (possibly a creation of Pompey himself in, or soon after, 63 BC) – and the Nabatean kingdom whose border lay not far to the south of Amman/Philadelphia (Millar 1993: 397).[33] It is worth noting here that during the later first century AD and well into the second century, many Syrian cities, among which were those of the Decapolis (including Pella and Scythopolis/Beth-Shean), undertook energetic and substantial building programs with the construction of plazas, colonnaded streets, and civic and religious structures such as baths, theatres, nymphaea and temples (Bührig 2011: 290–3; Cimadomo 2019: 172, table 3; Foerster 1993; Foerster and Tsafrir 1992; Freeman 2008: 421–5; Lichtenberger 2022: 217–19; Sartre 2005: 151–205; Segal 1997; Tsafrir 2011: 5).[34] To the south, a similar picture of grandiose building projects, commencing at much the same time and lasting at least until Trajan's annexation in 106 AD, is seen in

the Nabatean kingdom – in particular at its capital of Petra (Markoe 2003; McKenzie 1990; Schmid 2008).[35] Despite the territorial reorganisation that accompanied Trajan's annexation, with the formation of Provincia Arabia and the effective breaking-up of the Decapolis (resulting in some of its cities being transferred to the new province and others – including Gadara/Umm Qais and Pella – probably remaining within the province of Syria), the overall impression during the remainder of the second century is one of continuing prosperity in both the major cities and surrounding countryside (Freeman 2008).

Early Roman 1–2 (63 BC–c. 135 AD): Areas XI A/B, XXXIVB, XXXIVG (Tell Husn)

Apart from the few fragments of "Roman" forms of ESA in plots IIIP, IIIQ, IVL (**FW 243**, **FW 246–9**) and late cooking vessels **PW 646**, **PW 654**, **PW 657** in IIIP, along with a coin of Trajan (Sheedy et al. 2001: no. 3.002) from IIIP, a knife-pared "Herodian" lamp nozzle (CN 3872) in the same Mixed Context as **FW 246**, and the possibility of a thin and disturbed Early Roman level isolated in Area VIII, no post-Jannaeus/"Early Roman" (c. 80/79 BC–c. 150 AD) levels, pottery or other artefacts have been uncovered on the main mound, with Roman material from the third century AD immediately overlying the Jannaeus Destruction level.[36] And yet, even if we question Josephus' account of the pillaging of Pella and neighbouring towns by bands of Jews at the beginning of the Jewish War and disregard the tradition that the Jerusalem Christians fled across the

---

32 See Smith 1973: 42–3 for a discussion of this episode.

33 From at least the 1st century BC there was also a Nabatean presence in the marginal zone to the east of the Decapolis, between the Transjordanian plateau and the desert, and extending northwards into the southern Hauran (Millar 1993: 392). Parker's *Limes Arabicus* survey (Parker 1987) has shown Nabatean/Early Roman settlement on the edge of the steppe to the east of the Decapolis; whilst the Hauran may have been more densely settled (Millar 1993: 392), the southern Hauran survey of Kennedy and Freeman leaves this open to question (Kennedy and Freeman 1995: 60).

34 For the vexed question as to whether the "Decapolis" was constituted as a political and administrative unit or a *koinon* of ten (and later more) cities preserving their Greek heritage see, for example, Bietenhard 1977; Bowersock 1983: 30–1 *passim*; Graf 1992, 2002; Isaac 1981; Parker 1975: 440; Tsafrir 2011; Tsafrir and Foerster 1986–87. Also, more recently, Cimadomo 2019: 88–180; Lichtenberger 2022.

35 As to whether Trajan's annexation of the Nabatean kingdom was peaceful remains controversial. See, for example, Cimadomo 2018.

36 While the "Roman" forms of ESA, Trajan coin and "Herodian" lamp nozzle from the contiguous areas III and IV suggest the presence of an Early Roman structure, later Byzantine and Ummayad construction has resulted in its total obliteration.

Table 3.10. Phases Early Roman 1–2: stratified deposits.

AREA: TELL HUSN	DEPOSIT
XIA/B	1.1–5, 2.1–3, 2.5, 4.3–6, 20.4–7
XXXIVB	6.27, 6.42, 6.48, 7.17, 12.2–3, 25.4–7, 26.1–2, 27.1–7
XXXIVG	6.1–4, 6.7–11, 7.12, 8.11–2, 9.5–6, 11.1–5, 12.1, 12.3, 13.2

Jordan River to Pella before the destruction of their city in 70 AD, Early Roman occupation should exist somewhere at Pella for the city sporadically minted coins as early as the reign of Domitian (Carson 2001; Smith 1973: 45–6; Spijkerman 1978: 210–17) while the Jerash–Pella road seems to have been delineated by milestones at least as early as the first half of the second century AD (Kennedy 2007: 88–91; McNicoll et al. 1992: 122–4). Furthermore, to the south-west of Tell Husn (Area VI) several Roman tombs containing material as early as the late first century AD have been opened (McNicoll et al. 1992: 124–33) and in the Civic Complex, located in the Wadi Jirm al-Moz (Area IX) and mainly of Late Roman and Byzantine construction, the Wooster expedition partially uncovered substantial structures (odeum, baths, parvis) that were, with some caution, dated to Early Roman times (Smith and Day 1989: 3–7, 97–100 *passim*).

Work on Tell Husn has helped to clarify this situation. As well as the abundant remains of impressive Bronze Age occupation (Bourke 1997, 2015/2016) and a Byzantine military and cavalry complex of the fifth and sixth centuries AD (Watson and Tidmarsh 1996: 294–305), excavations in Plots XXXIVB and XXXIVG have partially revealed dwellings from the Early Roman period overlying, in both plots, Hellenistic structures, still to be fully revealed. Both these latter structures contain ceramic material identical to the Late Hellenistic (c. 150–c. 80/79 BC: Hellenistic 3B and 3C) ceramics on the main mound; however, in neither of these structures is there evidence of a Jannaeus Destruction level (as seen on the main mound) but, rather, directly above the Hellenistic levels in both plots are walls associated with Early Roman occupation surfaces and, in XXXIVB, a paved stylobate, part of which has been destroyed by later Byzantine construction.

The pottery from the Early Roman levels on Tell Husn spans almost two centuries: from shortly after the Jannaeus Destruction until the mid-second century AD or slightly later. It is not surprising, therefore, that the assemblage shows both a continuation of older Hellenistic shapes and the appearance of new ceramic forms. Like the small stratified deposits of Early Roman pottery retrieved by the Wooster expedition from Area IX (Smith and Day 1989: 4, 97–100), much of the assemblage consists of functional types that must have been produced in centres not far from Pella; on the other hand, more distant imports such as the Italian Sigillata fragment **FW 259** and the thin-walled ware fragments **FW 184–7**, along with the ESA mould-made bowl fragment **FW 229** (from an Early Roman horizon), are decidedly rare, a situation seemingly mirrored at nearby Jerash (Kehrberg 2004a).

Seen in larger numbers in plain wares in the Jannaeus Destruction levels, fishplates are less common in the Early Roman assemblage; most are now of the narrow, angled rim forms uncommon in earlier Hellenistic 3C levels but not seen before that. Plain ware bowls are less varied in form with only the small bowls with in-turned rim common. With the exception of the ESA bowl **FW 229** and the residual fragment **FW 263**, mould-made bowls are no longer encountered. "Hellenistic" forms of ESA are in much smaller numbers with ESA mainly represented by plates of Early Roman date (though sometimes from Mixed Contexts) **FW 201–2**, **FW 208**, **FW 213–4** and **FW 225**, as well as the more angular "Roman" forms (**FW 232–49**) based on shapes seen in Italian Sigillatas and encountered with increasing frequency on many sites from the later first century BC onwards.

Of note is the presence of the "Galilean" cooking pots **PW 607–10** and cooking bowls (pans) of "Galilean" form **PW 655–61**. The presence of "Galilean" ware is not surprising when one considers the constant traffic between the Galilee and the region of the Decapolis during Roman times (Freyne 1980: 134);[37] it is tempting to think that these vessels arrived via Scythopolis/Beth-Shean which, from Hellenistic times on, served as a commercial and military centre linking the towns and villages in Lower Galilee with the territory further east (Freyne 1980: 108–13, 1997; Horsley 1996: 160–1). They may equally have arrived from other Decapolis cities with Jewish populations (see below).

Amongst the jars, the basic shapes – those with simple or thickened rims (Types 1–3) – have largely gone out of favour, whereas jars with well-defined short- or long-collared rims with prominent lower edge (Types 4C, 6B) are numerous. Seen in small numbers in the Jannaeus Destruction levels (Hellenistic 3C) are jars of Type 7, which become the dominant jar form in this Early Roman assemblage. The major characteristic of this type is a well-defined ridge setting off shoulder from neck. This characteristic occurs in P.W. Lapp's Type 12, dated by him from 75 BC to 70 AD (P.W. Lapp 1961: 152). East of the Jordan it is seen at 'Iraq al-Amir, at Machaerus on jars in Herodian and First Revolt (c. 66–73 AD) levels and at the Herodian complex of Kallirhoe.[38] On both sides of the Jordan River, therefore, the neck ridge virtually heralds the onset of the Early Roman period.

Amongst the kitchen wares, cooking pots of Hellenistic globular shape are still dominant. Cooking pots with both tall everted and concave rims (Types 1, 4) and with bevelled rim (Type 5) are forms encountered in much larger numbers. Although Hellenistic-inspired cooking pot forms continue, the Early Roman phase sees the introduction of the shouldered cooking pot (Type 7), an increase in the use of the casserole (a vessel rare in the earlier phases at Pella), and the arrival of the cooking bowl (pan). This latter vessel points to a change – or more likely a broadening – of dietary habits for at least some of the inhabitants of Pella, perhaps not surprising after the conquest of the Roman general Pompey (Berlin 1993: 43–4, 2005b: 437–42). In Palestine the shouldered cooking pot (= Lapp Type 72.2) is seen in Early Roman deposits (P.W. Lapp 1961: 190) in similar contexts at Machaerus (Loffreda 1980: pl. 96.27–8); thus, it would appear that at many sites on both sides of the Jordan River – in much the same way as do the ridged neck jars of Type 6 – their presence, along with that of the cooking bowls (pans), serves to distinguish between Late Hellenistic and Early Roman contexts. Absent from the Early Roman assemblage are recognisable fragments of lagynoi or unguentaria – either fusiform or (surprisingly) piriform – whilst, with the exception of several mould-made lamp fragments along with the fluted bowl recovered by the Wooster team (Smith et al. 1980: 38, pl. XXXVIII), there is also no trace of the moulded grey ware vessels seen especially in the earlier Jannaeus Destruction (Hellenistic 3C) levels.

Not present at Pella before the Early Roman phase on Tell Husn are wheelmade knife-pared ("Herodian") lamps (Figure 1.56; Plate 19), first appearing in Palestine in well-dated contexts of the late first century BC and continuing until the mid-second century AD (Avigad 1984: 88; Barag and Hershkovitz 1994: 24–58, *passim*; Magness 2011: 64–6; Rosenthal and Sivan 1978: 80–1; Smith 1961: 54–7, 1966: 3–4).[39] Lamps of this type, along with chalkstone vessels, serve as indicators of an Early Roman horizon at Palestinian sites (Berlin 2005b: 429–36; Magen 1994: 256) although in some areas of the Galilee, such as Sepphoris, manufacture and use of the latter vessels may have continued longer (Sherman et al. 2020). Because of their ritual purity in Jewish religious practice,[40] soft chalkstone vessels in a variety of forms (for example, bowls, mugs, goblets, jars, lids, "inkwells") were produced (by hand or on the lathe or using both techniques on the same

---

37 Thus Matthew 4:23–5 where, whilst Jesus "went round the whole of Galilee … Great crowds followed him, from Galilee and the Decapolis, from Jerusalem and Judaea, and from Transjordan". See also Mark 5:20; 7:31.

38 For example, Singer 1993: fig. 2, nos 1–8 (Betar); Bar-Nathan 1981: pls. 1–3 (Herodium); Zimmerman 2020b: pls 2.9–2.12 ('Iraq al-Amir); Geva 1983: fig. 4, 2010: pl. 4.2.1–9, 2014: pl. 19.1.9; Strange 1975: fig. 15, nos 6–11; Tchekhanovets 2013: fig. 5.12 *passim* (Jerusalem); Clamer 1997: 71, Type 3.8.1b (Kallirhoe); Loffreda 1996: groups 6–17 (Machaerus).

39 A further "Herodian" lamp, associated with two discus lamps, was recovered from the Early Roman tomb 54 (McNicoll et al. 1992: 124–33, pl. 87.2–4).

40 But note Wassen 2019. Also, Sherman et al. 2020: 81, "it is impossible to determine if the widespread use of stone vessels in the 1st century C.E. was for religious, national, or personal motives". But, *contra*, Adler 2021.

Table 3.11. Phases Early Roman 1–2: pottery.

		XI A/B (TELL HUSN)	XXXIV B, G (TELL HUSN)
Fine ware	Fishplates	FW 6–7 (both residual)	FW 5 (residual)
	Saucers		FW 55 (residual)
	Spouted bowls	FW 118 (residual?)	
	Skyphos/kantharoi	FW 130 (residual?)	
	Thin-walled wares	FW 184, 187	
	ESA Hayes 4A	FW 201–2, 208	
	ESA "rare form a"	FW 211	
	ESA Hayes 22B	FW 225	
	ESA Hayes 23	FW 227	
	ESA Hayes 24		FW 229
	ESA Hayes 28		FW 232
	ESA Hayes 47		FW 239
	Hayes 59	FW 244	
	ESA Hayes 60	FW 245	
	ESA Closed form	FW 251	
	Mould-made bowls	FW 263 (residual), 292 (residual?)	
Plain ware	Fishplates Type 1: broad angled rim	PW 12 (residual?)	
	Fishplates Type 3: narrow angled rim	PW 30–1	
	Fishplates Type 4: narrow drooping rim	PW 32–5	
	Plates Type 1: thickened simple rim	PW 55–8	PW 60
	Saucers	PW 96–7, 100	
	Bowls Type 2: in-turned rim	PW 138–9	PW 134
	Kraters Type 1: flaring rim, vertical lip	PW 163–4	PW 162
	Jugs Type 3: grooved rim	PW 199 (residual?)	
	Jugs Type 4: flaring rim	PW 201	
	Jugs Type 5: flanged rim	PW 206–8, 211	
	Juglets Type 1: simple rim	PW 215–6, 218	
	Juglets Type 3: flanged rim	PW 220–1	
	Juglets Type 4: flaring rim	PW 222 (ER 2)	
	Juglets Type 5: cup-shaped rim	PW 226	
	Flasks: southern Palestinian type	PW 235	

	XI A/B (TELL HUSN)	XXXIV B, G (TELL HUSN)
Amphoriskois	PW 236	
Transport amphorae	PW 251	
Jars Type 1B: neckless; square rim		PW 262
Jars Type 1C: neckless; everted rim		PW 263
Jars Type 3: thickened everted rim		PW 299
Jars Type 4A: short neck; short-collared square rim		PW 355
Jars Type 4C: short neck; short-collared rim with prominent edge	PW 374–80	
Jars Type 6B: long-collared rim; prominent edge	PW 425–35	PW 411–2, 416–8, 420–4
Jars Type 7A: neck ridge; simple lip	PW 445–8, 450–6, 458–9	PW 438–42
Jars Type 7B: neck ridge; overhanging lip	PW 465–82	PW 462–4
Cooking pots Type 1: simple rim	PW 509–18	PW 503
Cooking pots Type 2: flared rim		PW 520
Cooking pots Type 3: ledge rim		PW 543
Cooking pots Type 4: concave rim	PW 568–71	PW 561–7
Cooking pots Type 5: bevelled rim	PW 589–99	PW 576–9, 584–5, 587–8
Cooking pots Type 6: grooved rim	PW 600–3	
Cooking pots Type 7: "Galilean"	PW 608–10	PW 607
Cooking pots Type 8: thickened lip	PW 614–6, 619	PW 612–3, 617–8
Casseroles Type 1: constricted neck; overhanging rim	PW 624–6, 630, 633	PW 628–9, 632
Casseroles Type 2: upright wall; overhanging rim	PW 636–7, 639	PW 635, 638
Casseroles: Type 3 interior flange; overhanging rim	PW 643–4	PW 645
Cooking bowls (pans) Type 1: narrow ledge rim	PW 648–9	PW 647
Cooking bowls (pans) Type 2: angled broad rim	PW 650	PW 651–3
Cooking bowls (pans) Type 3: "Galilean" bowl	PW 658, 660–1	PW 655
Lids	PW 666, 671	
Unguentaria: miscellaneous	PW 689	

vessel) in large numbers in Jerusalem and elsewhere, including the lower Galilee and Golan during the Second Temple period (Avigad 1984: 174–83; Ben-Dov 1985: 157–60; Berlin 2005b: 429–34; Cahill 1992; Gibson 2003; Magen 1994) and as such their occurrence in archaeological excavations has been used by some scholars to indicate a Jewish presence at those sites (Gibson 2003: 300–3; Hirschfeld 1997: 74). At Pella fragments of such vessels, restricted to Tell Husn but unstratified (CN 2668, CN 2987 – Figure 1.58 – CN 7137, CN 7281), may merely indicate the arrival of Jewish forces during Jannaeus' campaign.[41] More likely, however, is a Jewish presence after his sack of the city, in which case the vessels, along with "Herodian" lamps, may have travelled across the Jordan from Scythopolis/Beth-Shean – both a production centre for "Herodian" lamps (Adan-Bayewitz et al. 2008) and home to a relatively large number of Jews during Hellenistic and Roman times (Ben David 2011: 309–11; Freyne 1980: 110–11) – or from some of the other nearby Decapolis cities, also with Jewish inhabitants, such as Jerash or Gadara (including the nearby site of Tel Zira'a).[42] The presence of "Roman" forms of Eastern Sigillata A and Early Roman style discus lamps, the latter possibly avoided by some Jews because of their figured images (Magness 2011: 65), along with chalkstone vessels, cooking bowls (pans), wheelmade knife-pared ("Herodian")

lamps – "definitely favoured by Jews and pagans alike" (Rosenthal-Heginbottom 2016a: 431–2) – and faunal remains of both ovicaprid and pig (Wesselingh pers. com.) would suggest that this resettlement, as at other Decapolis cities, included both Jewish and non-Jewish inhabitants (Adan-Bayewitz et al. 2008: 46–7; Berlin 2002, 2005b).[43]

Nevertheless, it remains likely that Pella was abandoned for a period soon after the Jannaeus conquest – as suggested by the absence of Shachar's Jannaeus Type 7 coins (Meshorer 2001: Group L, subgroups L7–17) struck, according to Shachar, in the last three years of Jannaeus' reign and after his death, along with the absence of autonomous "City" editions usually seen in settlements where occupation under later Hasmonean rule continued (Shachar 2004: 10, 20–3). In this case it may have been only resettled after the arrival of Pompey in 63 **FW 259** when he "liberated from their rule all the towns in the interior which they [the Jews] had not already razed to the ground, namely Hippos, Scythopolis, Pella, Samaria" (Josephus *BJ* I.156). It is probable that with Pompey's arrival, or soon after, the aforementioned well-made ashlar wall partially uncovered on both the north and south slopes of Tell Husn in Plots XIA/B and XXXIVT was erected.

And so, current evidence indicates that although much of the city was destroyed by Alexander

---

41 See also Smith and Day 1989: 100, pl. 44.9 for a chalkstone vessel unearthed by the Wooster Expedition from an Early Roman context in the Civic Complex (Area IX). A further chalkstone bowl (CN 7137), of similar form to CN 2987 (Figure 1.57) from plot XIA/B was recovered (out of context) from Tell Husn in XXXIVC. The Pella lamps and chalkstone vessels are not included in this volume but will be dealt with in a further publication planned to include both typological and chemical studies.

42 In this regard it is worth noting that during the 1st century AD Josephus refers to Jews (either ethnic or converts/descended from converts) living in Gadara (*BJ* 2.478) and Jerash (*BJ* 2.480) as well as other Decapolis cities (Goodman 1992). For chalkstone vessels from the region of Gadara, Tel Zira'a and Jerash see Adler et al. 2021; Lichtenberger and Raja 2015: 494–5; Uscatescu 2021; Vieweger 2003: 214. The stone vessels from Machaerus (Loffreda 1996: 116–17, fig. 53) and Kallirhoe (Clamer 1997: 79–80) are also consistent with the Jewish occupation of these "palaces" during Herodian times, while those from Khirbat al-Mukhayyat, along with ceramic and numismatic evidence and the presence of a *miqveh*, indicate Hasmonean control of the Peraea during the late second/earlier first century BC (Dolan and Foran 2016). The presence of a further *miqveh* at Tell el-'Umayri, some 20 kilometres to the north-east of Khirbat al-Mukhayyat, also points to Hasmonean control of the region (Herr et al. 1997: 17, 96, 2002: 45, 105). For the presence of miqva'ot at Herodian Machaerus see Vörös 2016, 2017 and 2018, and, possibly, at Kallirhoe see Wimmer 2019a, b.

43 Mould-made discus lamps of Early Roman style are, in fact, relatively uncommon at Pella. Apart from those associated with Roman-period tombs (for example, tombs 54 and 64 – McNicoll et al. 1992: 124–41) a small number of these lamp fragments are found on Tell Husn and scattered across the main mound where they are not associated with Early Roman architectural remains. They are most numerous in Area III in the same vicinity from which the first and second centuries AD Eastern Sigillata A fragments were recovered. I thank Margaret O'Hea, Kate da Costa and Pamela Watson for this information.

Jannaeus, this was not the case on Tell Husn – perhaps accounting for the discrepancy between Josephus (*Ant. Jud.* XIII.395) where Pella was "demolished because the inhabitants would not agree to adopt the national customs of the Jews" and Josephus (*BJ* I.156) where Pella was not "already razed to the ground".[44] After a period of abandonment, Early Roman occupation – seemingly sparse and so far confined to XXXIVB and XXXIVG (both of which appear to be domestic in nature) along with XIA/B and XXXIVT (stretches of the probable Pompey-era fortification wall) – was resumed towards the end of the first century BC or early in the first century AD before spreading on to the main mound some two centuries later.[45] However, whereas the XIA/B–XXXIVT fortification wall appears to have remained in use until at least the second century AD – an impression based on an admittedly limited number of ESA fragments (**FW 241–2, 244–5**) from occupation and mixed wash levels in XIA/B[46] – there is so far no ceramic or other evidence that the domestic structures uncovered in XXXIVB and XXXIVG continued in use later than the end of the first century AD. However, it is quite possible that this *lacuna* along with the apparent absence or paucity of Early Roman occupation on Khirbet Fahl may be filled with further exploration on Tell Husn and on the main mound further to the west and north of the current excavations.

44　For further discussion on the vexed question of Pella's destruction by Jannaeus see Atkinson 2016: 130–2; Schwartz 2011. I thank Donald Ariel for these references.

45　This brief period of abandonment or minimal occupation following the Jannaeus sack may well account for the difficulty Scaurus had in supplying his troops, who were in the grip of famine, in the neighbourhood of Pella during his expedition into Arabia in 62 BC (Josephus *BJ* I.159) – a situation consistent with the apparent absence of Hellenistic and Early Roman farmsteads detected during the Pella hinterland survey (Watson and O'Hea 1996). But see Josephus (*Ant. Jud.* 14.80) where the famine seems to have occurred closer to Petra, possibly as a result of the earthquake of c. 31 BC (J.B. Williams et al. 2012). I thank Sandra Gordon for alerting me to these references in *Ant. Jud.*

46　In this regard it is of note that the well-known bronze coin of Pella, struck during the reign of Commodus in 183/184 AD and depicting a large hexastyle temple on Tell Husn (Smith 1973: 54; for an illustration see Meshorer 1985: 92, no.250), shows no trace of this wall. It would seem, therefore, that by the late second century AD the wall had largely been dismantled – a hypothesis that would fit the ceramic evidence.

ADDITIONAL TABLES

These tables summarise details of the pottery recovered from the Mixed Context deposits.

Table 3.12. Mixed Contexts: deposits.

AREA	DEPOSIT
IIIA (main mound)	9.5
IIIB/C (main mound)	1.6–11, 1.13–25, 5.1, 5.7, 6.1, 17.1
IIIF (main mound)	1.28
IIIN (main mound)	7.1
IIIP (main mound)	7.1, 22.7, 23.1, 24.8, 24.11, 24.14–15, 24.17–19, 25.5, 25.7, 25.13, 25.16, 25.18–21, 113.5
IIIQ (main mound)	2.1, 7.1, 7.5, 9.3, 11.2–3, 11.16, 11.18–19, 11.22, 11.47
IVD (main mound)	1.3, 2.1, 13.21, 14.6
IVE (main mound)	10.1, 13.4, 14.22, 17.9, 17.19, 20.5
IVG (main mound)	1.2
IVH (main mound)	5.1
IVJ (main mound)	19.3
IVL (main mound)	1.1
IVM (main mound)	52.5
IVR (main mound)	7.1, 7.8
IVU (main mound)	1.1, 3.1
XIA/B (Tell Husn)	2.4–5, 3.1, 5.4, 5.9, 10.3, 21.2
XIVJ (Jebel Sartaba)	1.2, 2.2
XXIIIA (main mound)	10.9, 10.17, 12.8, 21.3, 71.1, 72.7, 73.3, 77.4, 80.3, 80.6, 80.8, 81.3–4, 110.1, 111.1
XXIIID (main mound)	64.2
XXVIIIB (main mound)	4.1, 5.8, 9.4, 9.7, 12.3, 13.18, 15.2
XXXIIM (main mound)	8.1, 56.1
XXXIVA (Tell Husn)	2.9, 8.9
XXXIVB (Tell Husn)	2.7, 3.3, 4.1, 5.1, 5.10–48, 5.42, 6.35–6, 6.40, 6.46, 8.22, 8.34, 10.8, 12.5, 14.4, 16.1, 27.8–15, 43.1–2, 54.4–6, 55.2, 55.5, 55.12, 57.8, 58.1, 100.1, 100.9, 150.3–4, 201.1
XXXIVF (Tell Husn)	1.3, 3.2, 4.1, 5.1
XXXIVG (Tell Husn)	1.2, 2.3, 3.1, 3.11, 3.13, 5.2, 8.2, 8.14–20, 12.2, 12.17, 12.19–20, 13.3–6, 13.9
XXXIVN (Tell Husn)	1.3, 1.10, 1.14

Table 3.13. Stratified and Mixed Contexts: fine wares

	SHAPE	STRATIFIED	MIXED CONTEXT
Black-gloss	Fishplates	24	6
	Plates Type 1: simple thickened rim	2	2
	Plates Type 2: undercut thickened rim	0	1
	Plates Type 3: grooved thickened rim	4	2
	Plates with upright rim	3	0
	Saucers	8	4
	Bowls Type 1: out-turned rim	16	7
	Bowls Type 2: in-turned rim	25	4
	Bowls Type 3: ovoid; plain/grooved rim	3	4
	Bowls Type 4: ovoid; decorated rim	1	1
	Spouted bowls	1	0
	Applied relief bowls	1	0
	Bowls: uncertain shape	3	2
	Kraters Type 1: horizontal rim	0	1
	Kraters Type 2: everted rim	2	1
	Skyphos/kantharoi	3	1
	Cups: band rim, pinched handles	5	5
	Cups: "Palestinian form"	1	1
Moulded grey ware	Juglets	13	5
	Bottles	2	1
Painted	White-ground lagynos	0	1
	Plates	4	2
	Bowls	1	3
	Kantharoi	1	1
	Kraters	0	1
	Amphorae	0	1

	SHAPE	STRATIFIED	MIXED CONTEXT
	Jars	3	0
Thin-walled	Beakers	1	2
	Bowls	1	0
ESA form	Hayes 1	1	1
	Hayes 3, 4	13	6
	Hayes 5A	3	0
	Hayes 6	0	1
	Hayes 9	0	1
	Hayes 12	0	1
	Hayes 17B	1	1
	Hayes 20	0	1
	Hayes 22	5	3
	Hayes 23	1	2
	Hayes 24	1	0
	Hayes "rare form c"	1	1
	Hayes 28	1	2
	Hayes 33	0	1
	Hayes 34	0	1
	Hayes 37A	0	1
	Hayes 44	0	1
	Hayes 47	1	0
	Hayes 48	0	1
	Hayes 54	0	2
	Hayes 57	0	1
	Hayes 59	1	0
	Hayes 60	1	4
	Hayes 101–2	2	7
Italian Sigillata		0	1
Mould-made		23	23
Total fine wares		**183**	**122**

Table 3.14. Stratified and Mixed Contexts: plain wares.

SHAPE	STRATIFIED	MIXED CONTEXT
Fishplates Type 1: broad angled rim	11	2
Fishplates Type 2: broad drooping rim	13	3
Fishplates Type 3: narrow angled rim	2	0
Fishplates Type 4: narrow drooping rim	4	0
Fishplate bases	4	0
Plates Type 1: thickened simple rim	13	8
Plates Type 2: thickened undercut rim	15	9
Plates with upright rim	2	0
Saucers	11	3
Bowls Type 1: out-turned rim	5	1
Bowls Type 2: in-turned rim	21	12
Bowls Type 3: flat base, angled rim	3	0
Bowls Type 4: flat base, simple rim	2	0
Bowls Type 5: bevelled rim	1	0
Bowls Type 6: hemispherical	3	1
Skyphos/kantharos	0	1
Cups: narrow band, pinched handles	3	0
Kraters Type 1: flaring rim, vertical lip	8	4
Kraters Type 2: horizontal rim	3	1
Kraters Type 3: down-turned rim	2	0
Krater Type 4: fluted	3	1
Table amphorae Type 1: projecting rim	7	1
Table amphorae Type 2: stepped interior	1	1
Jugs Type 1: thickened rim	5	1
Jugs Type 2: short-collared rim	3	0
Jugs Type 3: grooved rim	5	0
Jugs Type 4: flaring rim	2	0
Jugs Type 5: flanged rim	8	2
Juglets Type 1: simple rim	6	1
Juglets Type 2: collared rim	0	1
Juglets Type 3: flanged rim	2	0
Juglets Type 4: flaring rim	1	0
Juglets Type 5: cup-shaped rim	4	0

SHAPE	STRATIFIED	MIXED CONTEXT
Juglets Type 6: wide mouth, grooved rim	0	1
Lagynoi Type 1: rounded body	2	0
Lagynoi Type 2: angular body	1	0
Lagynoi: miscellaneous	2	0
Flasks	3	0
Amphoriskoi	1	0
Transport amphorae	17	1
Mortaria	5	0
Jars Type 1A: neckless; prominent shoulder	2	0
Jars Type 1B: neckless; square rim	1	0
Jars Type 1C: neckless; everted rim	1	0
Jars Type 2A: short neck; everted simple rim	2	0
Jars Type 2B: short neck; everted thickened rim	6	0
Jars Type 2C: short neck; angular rim	2	1
Jars Type 3: thickened everted rim	21	8
Jars Type 4A: short neck; short-collared square rim	48	4
Jars Type 4B: short neck; short-collared triangular rim	16	2
Jars Type 4C: short neck; short-collared rim with prominent edge	7	1
Jars Type 5A: tall neck; short-collared square rim	15	1
Jars Type 5B: tall neck; short-collared triangular rim	3	0
Jars Type 6A: long-collared rim: uniform thickness	10	0
Jars Type 6B: long-collared rim; prominent edge	21	4
Jars Type 7A: neck ridge; simple lip	19	5
Jars Type 7B: neck ridge; overhanging lip	23	1
Pithoi	4	0
Cooking pots Type 1: simple rim	25	6
Cooking pots Type 2: flared rim	1	2
Cooking pots Type 3: ledge rim	22	5
Cooking pots Type 4: concave rim	20	4
Cooking pots Type 5: bevelled rim	23	4
Cooking pots Type 6: grooved rim	5	1
Cooking pots Type 7: "Galilean"	5	0
Cooking pots Type 8: thickened lip	9	0

SHAPE	STRATIFIED	MIXED CONTEXT
Casseroles Type 1: constricted neck; overhanging rim	13	1
Casseroles Type 2: upright wall; overhanging rim	6	0
Casseroles Type 3: interior flange; overhanging rim	3	0
Casseroles Type 4: wide mouth; prominent shoulder	3	1
Pans Type 1: narrow ledge rim	3	0
Pans Type 2: angled broad rim	4	1
Pans Type 3: "Galilean" bowl	4	3
Frying pans	0	1
Lids	6	3
Unguentaria Type 1: squat; rounded body	6	1
Unguentaria Type 2: slender; angular body	3	0
Unguentaria: fragments	11	1
Ointment pot	0	1
Total plain wares	**575**	**119**

POTTERY CONCORDANCE

INVENTORY NUMBER	CATALOGUE NUMBER	INVENTORY NUMBER	CATALOGUE NUMBER	INVENTORY NUMBER	CATALOGUE NUMBER
0032	PW 116	0234	FW 140	0486	PW 181
0033	PW 140	0235	FW 138	0493	PW 519
0035	PW 143	0244	FW 76	0528	PW 297
0036	FW 193	0249	FW 207	0535	PW 49
0038	PW 144	0288	PW 110	0572	FW 29
0046	PW 141	0289	PW 121	0649	PW 101
0047	PW 142	0322	PW 113	0656	PW 52
0049	PW 229	0324	FW 180	0845	PW 574
0058	PW 9	0325	FW 68	0904	FW 219
0064	FW 106	0335	PW 553	0905	FW 77
0068	FW 196	0336	FW 69	0908	PW 104
0069	PW 392	0340	FW 262	0918	FW 198
0070	PW 693	0344	FW 74	0919	PW 205
0083	PW 529	0368	PW 115	0970	FW 56
0089	PW 499	0369	PW 64	0982	PW 289
0112	PW 393	0385	FW 144	0993	PW 16
0116	FW 158	0395	PW 122	1090	FW 191
0162	FW 285	0401	PW 13	1134	PW 606
0171	PW 51	0416	FW 71	1154	FW 231
0174	FW 46	0444	FW 174	1254	FW 221
0184	PW 334	0447	FW 70	1335	FW 298
0216	FW 173	0452	PW 114	1377	FW 268
0219	PW 88	0463	PW 71	1380	FW 212
0220	PW 117	0476	PW 290	1417	PW 190
0228	FW 4	0477	PW 662	1429	PW 103
0229	FW 47	0485	FW 171	1482	FW 192

INVENTORY NUMBER	CATALOGUE NUMBER	INVENTORY NUMBER	CATALOGUE NUMBER	INVENTORY NUMBER	CATALOGUE NUMBER
1496	FW 248	2626	PW 510	2944	PW 139
1600	FW 222	2628	PW 636	2948	PW 58
1622	PW 45	2629	PW 434	2949	PW 96
1660	FW 215	2630	PW 479	2951	PW 666
2520	FW 107	2631	PW 430	2952	PW 35
2544	PW 427	2632	PW 215	2953	PW 31
2545	PW 429	2642	FW 201	2954	FW 7
2546	PW 380	2643	FW 251	2955	PW 57
2547	PW 474	2644	FW 208	2956	PW 138
2548	PW 458	2647	FW 130	2957	PW 221
2550	PW 375	2650	PW 473	2959	PW 477
2552	PW 624	2651	PW 591	2961	PW 596
2553	PW 456	2652	PW 571	2962	PW 34
2554	PW 469	2653	PW 511	2964	PW 251
2555	PW 459	2654	PW 445	2965	PW 226
2556	PW 472	2655	PW 428	2966	PW 378
2557	PW 448	2657	PW 480	2967	PW 425
2560	PW 610	2658	PW 468	2968	PW 509
2563	PW 569	2663	PW 206	2969	PW 512
2564	PW 570	2665	PW 648	2970	PW 597
2565	PW 517	2666	PW 689	2973	PW 639
2566	PW 603	2667	PW 207	2974	FW 263
2567	PW 592	2670	PW 236	2975	PW 625
2570	PW 478	2683	FW 226	2976	PW 376
2571	PW 470	2865	PW 465	2977	PW 451
2572	PW 467	2933	PW 598	2978	PW 608
2573	PW 471	2934	PW 614	2979	PW 216
2617	PW 55	2935	PW 633	2980	PW 235
2618	PW 30	2936	PW 637	2981	PW 431
2620	PW 568	2937	PW 164	2983	PW 599
2621	PW 514	2938a	PW 374	2984	PW 516
2622	PW 594	2938b	PW 379	2985	PW 609
2623	PW 595	2941	PW 33	2986	PW 201

INVENTORY NUMBER	CATALOGUE NUMBER	INVENTORY NUMBER	CATALOGUE NUMBER	INVENTORY NUMBER	CATALOGUE NUMBER
2988	PW 455	3276	FW 166	4312	FW 116
2989	PW 447	3394	FW 270	4313	PW 125
2990	PW 433	3448	PW 2	4316	FW 54
2993	PW 32	3449	PW 86	4318	PW 75
2995	PW 97	3450	PW 21	4319	PW 74
2996	PW 626	3451	PW 1	4320	PW 53
2998	PW 377	3457	PW 228	4322	PW 36
2999	PW 643	3487	FW 146	4323	PW 38
3002	FW 6	3490	PW 225	4325	PW 405
3046	PW 619	3492	FW 148	4327	FW 102
3047	PW 100	3493	PW 160	4329	PW 147
3048	PW 426	3848	FW 246	4330	PW 401
3051	PW 589	3870	FW 258	4332	FW 216
3052	PW 513	3925	PW 76	4396	FW 152
3053	PW 450	3926	FW 42	4397	FW 150
3054	PW 650	3927	FW 33	6528	PW 3
3055	PW 482	3928	FW 21	6533	PW 39
3056	FW 211	3929	FW 22	6535	FW 225
3058	PW 615	3930	FW 43	6537	PW 475
3059	PW 644	3931	PW 333	6538	PW 518
3060	FW 187	3932	PW 437	6541	PW 7
3061	FW 184	4293	FW 220	6547	PW 457
3063	PW 163	4294	FW 279	6552	PW 476
3064	PW 12	4295	FW 189	6557	PW 130
3069	PW 593	4298	PW 4	6561	FW 20
3070	PW 630	4300	PW 124	6562	PW 230
3071	PW 515	4301	PW 123	6563	PW 646
3072	FW 118	4302	PW 17	6565a	FW 124
3074	PW 56	4303	PW 20	6565b	FW 164
3095	PW 659	4304	PW 25	6568	PW 18
3099	PW 449	4306	PW 77	6569	PW 404
3101	PW 432	4308	PW 72	6570	PW 85
3237	FW 241	4311	FW 78	6571	FW 177

INVENTORY NUMBER	CATALOGUE NUMBER	INVENTORY NUMBER	CATALOGUE NUMBER	INVENTORY NUMBER	CATALOGUE NUMBER
6573	FW 227	6653	PW 28	6743	PW 132
6579	PW 500	6665	PW 301	6749	FW 111
6580	PW 336	6668	FW 123	6751	FW 179
6581	PW 406	6671	PW 131	6753	PW 466
6582	PW 460	6674	PW 605	6754	PW 435
6586	FW 110	6676	FW 147	6759	PW 483
6589	FW 25	6677	PW 335	6763	FW 72
6592	PW 231	6678	PW 338	6764	FW 49
6594	PW 601	6679	PW 337	6770	FW 109
6596	PW 616	6680	FW 53	6775	PW 454
6597	PW 657	6681	FW 79	6780	FW 245
6600	PW 661	6684	PW 530	6781	FW 244
6601	PW 602	6690	PW 84	6786	PW 222
6604	FW 304	6691	FW 206	6788	FW 272
6605	FW 269	6693	PW 505	6790	PW 126
6611	PW 658	6697	PW 83	6791	PW 127
6612	PW 649	6698	PW 81	6796	PW 446
6613	PW 600	6700	FW 141	6798	PW 452
6614	PW 660	6702	FW 217	6800	FW 202
6616	PW 590	6703	PW 160	6801	PW 453
6617	PW 671	6705	PW 59	6809	PW 436
6618	PW 481	6706	PW 185	6814	FW 23
6621	PW 220	6708	FW 277	6821	PW 136
6623	PW 654	6709	PW 548	6822	FW 199
6626	FW 98	6710	PW 80	6823	FW 205
6628	FW 50	6711	FW 96	6828	PW 682
6639	PW 22	6713	PW 300	6834	FW 142
6642	FW 289	6718	FW 209	6836	FW 159
6645	FW 303	6727	FW 41	6847	FW 105
6646	FW 178	6731	FW 26	6850	FW 197
6647	FW 19	6733	FW 295	6851	PW 137
6649	FW 38	6740	PW 161	6863	PW 66
6651	PW 82	6742	FW 294	6864	PW 65

INVENTORY NUMBER	CATALOGUE NUMBER	INVENTORY NUMBER	CATALOGUE NUMBER	INVENTORY NUMBER	CATALOGUE NUMBER
6865	PW 50	6943	PW 531	7033	PW 200
6868	PW 331	6954	PW 8	7034	FW 97
6869	PW 552	6955	PW 11	7035	PW 271
6871	PW 135	6958	FW 129	7036	PW 398
6878	FW 139	6960	PW 394	7039	PW 106
6879	FW 134	6961	PW 390	7040	PW 391
6880	FW 32	6962	PW 532	7041	PW 54
6883	PW 293	6963	FW 151	7042	PW 37
6884	PW 670	6967	PW 27	7043	PW 189
6885	PW 536	6968	FW 175	7044	PW 350
6886	PW 395	6969	PW 19	7045	PW 23
6887	PW 402	6974	FW 302	7046	PW 145
6888	PW 403	6975	PW 294	7047	PW 78
6889	PW 537	6976	PW 204	7051	PW 507
6892	PW 292	6977	PW 273	7057	FW 103
6893	PW 188	6979	PW 5	7058	PW 296
6895	FW 128	6980	PW 10	7060	PW 353
6905	PW 372	6982	PW 26	7061	PW 265
6906	PW 339	6985	PW 129	7065	FW 51
6915	FW 255	6987	PW 345	7066	PW 298
6916	FW 104	6988	PW 213	7067	PW 146
6918	PW 128	6991	FW 188	7068	PW 373
6919	PW 90	7008	PW 534	7069	PW 120
6924	FW 254	7009	PW 192	7070	FW 135
6925	FW 243	7011	PW 676	7072	PW 681
6926	PW 340	7012	FW 149	7073	PW 69
6930	PW 73	7013	FW 156	7074	PW 68
6932	PW 95	7019	FW 24	7075	PW 118
6935	FW 249	7021	PW 341	7077	PW 102
6937	PW 400	7023	PW 214	7078	PW 75
6940	PW 388	7025	PW 24	7079	FW 275
6941	PW 232	7026	PW 105	7081	PW 67
6942	PW 389	7028	PW 349	7082	PW 387

INVENTORY NUMBER	CATALOGUE NUMBER	INVENTORY NUMBER	CATALOGUE NUMBER	INVENTORY NUMBER	CATALOGUE NUMBER
7083	PW 496	7152	FW 286	7191	FW 293
7084	PW 291	7153	PW 508	7192	FW 64
7085	FW 112	7154	PW 502	7193	FW 280
7087	PW 295	7156	PW 546	7194	FW 278
7088	PW 249	7157	FW 214	7196	FW 297
7089	FW 44	7158	PW 194	7197	FW 80
7090	PW 408	7159	PW 342	7198	FW 301
7091	PW 407	7160	FW 287	7199	FW 16
7092	PW 538	7161	PW 227	7201	FW 30
7095	PW 354	7163	PW 148	7202	PW 679
7098	FW 260	7164	FW 194	7203	FW 37
7101	PW 219	7165	FW 250	7204	FW 81
7102	PW 173	7166	PW 172	7206	FW 273
7103	PW 668	7168	PW 423	7208	PW 680
7104	FW 161	7169	PW 543	7209	FW 65
7106	PW 302	7170	FW 5	7210	FW 66
7107	PW 547	7172	PW 422	7211	FW 48
7109	PW 410	7173	PW 421	7212	PW 43
7114	FW 117	7174	PW 420	7213	PW 550
7118	PW 252	7175	PW 299	7214	FW 91
7120	PW 535	7176	PW 134	7215	FW 83
7122	PW 224	7177	PW 60	7216	PW 170
7125	PW 554	7178	PW 262	7217	FW 90
7127	PW 634	7179	PW 464	7218	PW 15
7132	FW 267	7181	FW 172	7219	FW 261
7139	PW 498	7182	PW 641	7220	FW 276
7141	FW 291	7183	FW 10	7221	PW 169
7142	FW 3	7184	FW 126	7222	PW 494
7144	FW 100	7186	PW 551	7224	PW 640
7145	FW 45	7187	PW 187	7225	PW 285
7147	FW 282	7188	FW 12	7226	PW 317
7150	FW 281	7189	PW 212	7227	FW 265
7151	PW 209	7190	FW 169	7228	FW 274

INVENTORY NUMBER	CATALOGUE NUMBER	INVENTORY NUMBER	CATALOGUE NUMBER	INVENTORY NUMBER	CATALOGUE NUMBER
7229	FW 36	7287	PW 442	7335	PW 627
7230	FW 300	7288	PW 343	7336	PW 203
7232	FW 67	7289	PW 347	7337	PW 165
7233	FW 284	7290	FW 95	7338	PW 463
7235	FW 192	7292	PW 264	7339	PW 694
7236	FW 125	7293	PW 371	7341	PW 217
7238	PW 89	7294	PW 284	7343	PW 441
7240	PW 70	7296	PW 399	7344	FW 292
7241	PW 149	7297	PW 153	7345	PW 628
7253	PW 588	7299	PW 288	7346	PW 417
7254	PW 587	7304	PW 330	7349	PW 416
7255	PW 632	7308	PW 258	7350	PW 418
7256	PW 162	7309	FW 86	7351	PW 520
7257	PW 629	7311	PW 328	7352	PW 638
7258	PW 269	7312	PW 247	7353	PW 503
7259	PW 154	7313	FW 87	7354	PW 576
7260	PW 202	7315	PW 311	7355	PW 618
7261	PW 197	7316	PW 385	7356	FW 55
7262	PW 176	7317	PW 489	7357	PW 575
7263	PW 177	7318	PW 523	7358	PW 521
7264	PW 167	7319	FW 9	7359	PW 572
7265	PW 158	7320	PW 151	7360	PW 604
7266	PW 156	7322	PW 309	7361	FW 236
7268	PW 357	7323	PW 358	7362	PW 573
7272	PW 545	7324	PW 166	7363	PW 381
7275	PW 506	7325	FW 264	7366	FW 271
7276	PW 444	7326	PW 286	7367	PW 617
7277	PW 443	7328	PW 310	7370	PW 308
7278	FW 305	7329	PW 248	7371	PW 14
7280	PW 133	7330	PW 522	7372	PW 40
7282	FW 115	7332	PW 274	7373	FW 18
7285	PW 613	7333	PW 542	7376	PW 277
7286	PW 424	7334	PW 99	7377	PW 280

INVENTORY NUMBER	CATALOGUE NUMBER	INVENTORY NUMBER	CATALOGUE NUMBER	INVENTORY NUMBER	CATALOGUE NUMBER
7378	PW 276	7432	PW 283	7480	PW 62
7381	PW 272	7433	PW 319	7481	FW 34
7382	PW 41	7434	PW 44	7482	FW 99
7383	PW 267	7435	PW 313	7483	PW 397
7384	PW 275	7436	PW 155	7484	FW 94
7385	PW 621	7437	PW 495	7485	FW 11
7387	PW 622	7438	PW 492	7486	FW 62
7388	FW 114	7439	PW 316	7487	FW 59
7389	PW 672	7440	FW 14	7489	PW 312
7398	PW 287	7441	FW 88	7490	PW 256
7399	PW 325	7444	PW 384	7491	PW 490
7401	FW 28	7445	FW 101	7492	PW 488
7404	FW 84	7446	FW 1	7493	FW 27
7405	PW 111	7449	FW 92	7494	FW 121
7406	PW 198	7450	PW 179	7495	FW 120
7408	PW 268	7451	PW 326	7496	FW 89
7409	PW 61	7453	PW 180	7497	FW 93
7410	PW 178	7454	FW 13	7498	FW 61
7411	PW 685	7455	PW 42	7499	FW 63
7413	PW 245	7457	PW 171	7500	FW 82
7414	PW 525	7458	PW 255	7502	PW 493
7415	PW 63	7460	PW 383	7503	PW 527
7417	PW 524	7463	PW 329	7504	PW 314
7418	PW 526	7464	PW 491	7505	PW 246
7419	PW 382	7466	FW 145	7506	PW 321
7420	PW 327	7467	PW 687	7507	PW 324
7424	PW 315	7469	FW 73	7508	PW 318
7425	PW 320	7470	FW 17	7512	PW 259
7426	PW 244	7471	PW 257	7518	PW 692
7427	PW 157	7475	PW 112	7519	PW 683
7429	PW 47	7477	PW 322	7520	PW 686
7430	PW 46	7479	FW 85	7521	PW 176
7431	PW 690	7459	PW 323	7522	FW 195

INVENTORY NUMBER	CATALOGUE NUMBER	INVENTORY NUMBER	CATALOGUE NUMBER	INVENTORY NUMBER	CATALOGUE NUMBER
7523	FW 228	7569	PW 607	7611	PW 612
7524	FW 203	7570	PW 585	7612	FW 237
7525	FW 234	7571	PW 567	7613	PW 242
7526	FW 230	7572	FW 232	7614	PW 579
7527	FW 259	7573	PW 487	7615	PW 645
7528	FW 127	7574	PW 240	7616	PW 438
7529	FW 122	7575	PW 243	7617	FW 229
7531	FW 168	7576	PW 367	7620	PW 415
7535	FW 143	7577	PW 91	7622	PW 365
7537	PW 665	7578	PW 92	7623	PW 580
7539	PW 195	7579	PW 303	7624	PW 558
7540	FW 57	7580	FW 52	7625	PW 667
7541	FW 167	7581	PW 93	7627	PW 413
7543	PW 260	7582	PW 364	7628	PW 414
7544	PW 183	7583	PW 266	7629	PW 362
7546	FW 233	7584	PW 109	7631	PW 87
7548	PW 584	7585	PW 305	7632	PW 631
7549	PW 462	7586	PW 253	7633	PW 368
7550	PW 577	7588	PW 691	7636	PW 270
7551	PW 653	7589	PW 241	7637	PW 586
7552	PW 563	7590	PW 501	7640	PW 261
7553	PW 564	7591	PW 540	7641	PW 504
7554	PW 647	7593	PW 652	7642	FW 35
7555	PW 655	7595	FW 239	7643	PW 281
7559	PW 440	7597	PW 307	7644	PW 581
7560	PW 412	7598	PW 369	7645	PW 94
7561	PW 578	7599	PW 366	7646	PW 306
7562	PW 411	7600	PW 254	7647	PW 363
7564	PW 263	7601	PW 239	7648	PW 108
7565	PW 635	7602	PW 304	7649	PW 559
7566	PW 651	7606	PW 561	7650	PW 282
7567	PW 565	7607	PW 562	7652	FW 60
7568	PW 566	7610	PW 439	7654	PW 174

INVENTORY NUMBER	CATALOGUE NUMBER	INVENTORY NUMBER	CATALOGUE NUMBER	INVENTORY NUMBER	CATALOGUE NUMBER
7659	PW 238	7704	FW 253	7765	FW 223
7660	PW 549	7706	FW 247	7766	PW 168
7661	PW 486	7707	FW 213	7767	PW 623
7662	PW 237	7708	PW 673	7769	PW 346
7663	PW 186	7709	FW 113	7771	FW 162
7664	PW 356	7712	FW 133	7772	FW 155
7665	PW 663	7713	FW 299	7773	FW 157
7666	PW 98	7715	FW 132	7775	FW 131
7667	PW 279	7716	FW 296	7776	PW 557
7668	PW 359	7717	FW 290	7777	PW 250
7669	PW 234	7719	FW 40	7778	PW 675
7670	PW 233	7722	PW 150	7779	FW 204
7671	PW 278	7723	PW 582	7780	PW 497
7672	PW 107	7728	FW 200	7781	FW 2
7673	FW 31	7730	PW 678	7782	PW 152
7675	PW 620	7731	PW 583	7784	PW 386
7679	PW 484	7734	FW 266	7785	FW 190
7680	PW 485	7738	PW 199	7787	PW 642
7681	PW 669	7739	PW 218	7788	FW 283
7684	PW 419	7740	PW 211	7789	PW 528
7686	PW 210	7741	PW 208	7790	PW 159
7687	FW 256	7744	PW 182	7791	FW 15
7688	FW 257	7747	PW 344	7792	PW 370
7689	FW 252	7748	PW 560	7793	PW 332
7690	FW 185	7749	PW 461	7795	PW 193
7691	PW 656	7752	PW 191	7797	PW 6
7695	PW 184	7753	FW 137	7798	PW 677
7696	FW 8	7754	PW 555	7799	FW 153
7697	PW 674	7755	PW 539	7809	PW 175
7698	PW 360	7757	PW 223	7810	FW 136
7699	PW 361	7761	PW 556	7814	FW 238
7700	PW 664	7762	PW 352	7815	FW 240
7703	FW 235	7763	FW 154	7820	PW 355

INVENTORY NUMBER	CATALOGUE NUMBER
7822	FW 163
7823	FW 210
7826	PW 409
7827	FW 165
7829	FW 119
7830	PW 611
7833	FW 183
7834	PW 29
7835	FW 108
7839	FW 224
7840	PW 348
7843	PW 351
7845	FW 170
7846	PW 119
7847	FW 58
7848	FW 39
7849	PW 48
7850	PW 684
7851	PW 688
7853	PW 196
7854	FW 181
7855	FW 218
7857	PW 396
7858	PW 544
7859	PW 533
7860	FW 182
7865	PW 541
10006	FW 242
10829	FW 186

BIBLIOGRAPHY

BIBLIOGRAPHIC ABBREVIATIONS

ADAJ	*Annual of the Department of Antiquities of Jordan*
AJA	*American Journal of Archaeology*
Josephus *Ant. Jud.*	*Antiquitates Judaicae* Josephus, *Jewish Antiquities* (English translation by Ralph Marcus, Loeb Classical Library)
Appian *Mithridates*	Appian Alexandrinus, *The Mithradatic Wars*
Appian *Syr.*	Appian Alexandrinus, *The Syrian Wars*
ARAM	*Proceedings of the ARAM Society for Syro-Mesopotamian Studies*
Arr.	Flavius Arrianus, *Anabasis of Alexander*
BASOR	*Bulletin of the American Schools of Oriental Research*
Josephus *BJ*	*Bellum Judaicum,* Josephus, *The Jewish War* (English translation by H. St.J Thackeray, Loeb Classical Library)
Chronikon	Eusebius, *The Chronicle*
Curtius	Quintus Curtius Rufus, *The History of Alexander*
Diod.	Diodorus Siculus, *Bibliotheke historike*
Ecclesiastical History	Eusebius, *The Ecclesiastical History*
Ethnika	Stephanus of Byzantinus, *Ethnika*
IEJ	*Israel Exploration Journal*
LCP	*Levantine Ceramics Project* (http://www.levantineceramics.org/)
Panarion	*The Panarion of Epiphanius of Salamis*
Pliny *Nat. Hist.*	Gaius Plinius Secundus, *Natural History*
Plutarch *Sulla*	Lucius Mestrius Plutarchus, *Parallel Lives: Life of Sulla*
Polybius *Hist*	Polybius, *The Histories*
SHAJ	*Studies in the History and Archaeology of Jordan*
Geog.	Strabo, *Geography*

Abu-Dalu, R. 1995. Three tombs near the hippodrome at Jarash. A preliminary report. *ADAJ* 39: 169–73.

Abushmais, A. 2022. The Hellenistic period. In J. Haron and D.R. Clark (eds), *The pottery of Jordan. A manual*: 70–2. Alexandria, Virginia and Amman, Jordan: The American Center of Research.

Abu Shmeis, A., and M. Waheeb 2002. Recent discoveries in the baptism site. The pottery. *ADAJ* 46: 561–82.

Adams, R.B. 2008. Archaeology in Jordan: a brief history. In R.B. Adams (ed.), *Jordan. An archaeological reader*: 1–6. London: Equinox.

Adams, R.B. (ed.) 2008. *Jordan. An archaeological reader*. London: Equinox.

Adamsheck, B. 1979. *Kenchreai IV. The pottery*. Leiden: Brill.

Adan-Bayewitz, D. 1982. The ceramics from the Synagogue of Horvat 'Ammudim and their chronological implications. *IEJ* 32: 13–31.

Adan-Bayewitz, D. 1993. *Common pottery in Roman Galilee, a study of local trade*. Ramat Gan, Israel: Bar–Ilan University Press.

Adan-Bayewitz, D. 2003. On the chronology of the common pottery of northern Roman Judaea/Palestine. In G.C. Bottini et al. (eds), *One land – many cultures. Archaeological studies in honour of S. Loffreda*: 5–32. Jerusalem: Studium Biblicum Franciscanum.

Adan-Bayewitz, D., and M. Aviam 1997. Iotapata, Josephus, and the siege of 67: preliminary report on the 1992–94 seasons. *Journal of Roman Archaeology* 10: 131–65.

Adan-Bayewitz, D., and M. Wieder 1992. Ceramics from Roman Galilee: a comparison of several techniques for fabric characterization. *Journal of Field Archaeology* 19: 189–205.

Adan-Bayewitz, D., F. Asaro and R.D. Giauque 1999. Determining pottery provenance: application of a high-precision x-ray fluorescence method and comparison with instrumental neutron activation analysis. *Archaeometry* 41: 1–24.

Adan-Bayewitz, D., F. Asaro et al. 2008. Preferential distribution of lamps from the Jerusalem Area in the Late Second Temple Period (late first century B.C.E.–70 C.E.). *BASOR* 350: 37–85.

Adler, Y. 2021. Watertight and rock solid: stepped pools and chalk vessels as expressions of Jewish ritual purity. *Biblical Archaeology Review* 47(1): 44–51.

Adler, Y., A. Aryalon et al. 2021. Geochemical analyses of Jewish chalk vessel remains from Roman-era production and settlement sites in the southern Levant. *Archaeometry* 63: 266–83.

Aharoni, Y. 1961. The caves of Nahal Hever. *Atiqot* 3: 148–62 (English series).

Aharoni, Y. 1962. Expedition B – the cave of horror. *IEJ* 12: 186–99.

Akurgal, M., M. Kerschner et al. 2002. *Töpferzentren der Ostägäis: Archäometrische und archäologische Untersuchungen zur mykenischen, geometrischen und archaischen Keramik aus Fundorten in Westkleinasien*. Ergänzungshefte zu den Jahresheften des Österreichischen Achäologischen Instituts 3. Vienna.

Alexandre, Y., and A. Shapiro 2016. Karm er-Ras, Area AA: a pottery dump from the beginning of the Early Roman Period. *Hadashot Arkheologiyot – Excavations and Surveys in Israel* 128: 1–12.

Almagro, M. 1953. *Las necropolis de Ampurias* I. Barcelona: Seix y Barral.

Amiran, R. 1969. *Ancient Pottery of the Holy Land*. Jerusalem: Masada Press.

Anderson-Stojanovic, V.R. 1987. The chronology and function of ceramic unguentaria. *AJA* 91: 105–22.

Anson, E. 2018. Ptolemy and the destruction of the first regency. In T. Howe (ed.), *Ptolemy I Soter: a self-made man*: 19–35. Oxford: Oxbow.

Ariel, D. 2004. Stamped amphora handles from Bet-She'an: evidence for the urban development of the city in the Hellenistic period. In J. Eiring and J. Lund (eds), *Transport amphorae and trade in the Eastern Mediterranean. Acts of the International Colloquium at the Danish Institute at Athens, September 26–29, 2002*: 23–30. Monographs of the Danish Institute at Athens 5. Aarhus: Aarhus University Press.

Ariel, D. 2006. The stamped amphora handles. In A. Mazar, *Excavations at Tel Beth-Shean 1989–1996*, vol. I, *From the Late Bronze Age IIB to the Medieval Period*: 594–606. Jerusalem: The Hebrew University.

Artzy, M. 1994. Incense, camels and collared rim jars: desert trade routes and maritime outlets in the second millennium. *Oxford Journal of Archaeology* 13: 121–47.

Atkinson K. 2016: *A history of the Hasmonean state: Josephus and beyond*. Jewish and Christian Texts in Contexts and Related Studies 23. London: Bloomsbury.

Austin, M.M. 1981. *The Hellenistic world from Alexander to the Roman conquest: a selection of ancient sources in translation*. Cambridge, UK: Cambridge University Press.

Aviam, M. 2014: 'Kefar Hananya Ware' made in Yodefat. Pottery production at Yodefat in the first century AD. In B. Fischer-Genz, Y. Gerber and H. Hamel (eds), *Roman pottery in the Near East. Local production and regional trade. Proceedings of the round table held in Berlin, 19–20 February 2010*: 139–46. Oxford: Archaeopress.

Avigad, N. 1962. Expedition A-Nahal David. *IEJ* 12: 169–83.

Avigad, N. 1984. *Discovering Jerusalem*. Oxford: Basil Blackwell.

Avissar, M. 1987. The Medieval to Persian periods: architecture, stratigraphy and finds. In *Tell Qiri. A village in the Jezreel Valley. Report of the archaeological excavations 1975–1977*: 7–26. Qedem 24, Jerusalem.

Avissar, M. 1996. The Hellenistic and Roman pottery. In A. Ben-Tor, M. Avissar and Y. Portugali (eds), *Yoqne'am I. The Late Periods*: 48–59. Qedem 3. Jerusalem.

Avshalom-Gorni, D., and N. Getzov 2002. Phoenicians and Jews: a ceramic case-study. In A.M. Berlin and J.A. Overman (eds), *The First Jewish revolt. Archaeology, history, and ideology*: 74–83. London and New York: Routledge.

Bagatti, B., and E. Alliata 1981. Ritrovamento Archeologico Sul Sion. *Liber Annus* 31: 249–56.

Bagnall, R.S. 1976. *The administration of the Ptolemaic possessions outside Egypt*. Leiden: Brill.

Bailey, D.M. 1975. *A catalogue of the lamps in the British Museum I, Greek, Hellenistic and Early Roman pottery lamps*. London: British Museum Press.

Balabanski, V. 1997. *Eschatology in the making. Mark, Matthew and the didache*. Cambridge, UK: Cambridge University Press.

Balouka, M. 2013. Roman pottery. In E. Meyers and C. Meyers, *The pottery from ancient Sepphoris*: 13–129. University Park, PA: Eisenbrauns.

Balty, J.C. 2003. À la recherche de l'Apamée hellénistique: les témoinages archéologiques. *Topoi* Suppl. 4: 223–52.

Bar-Adon, P. 1977. Another settlement of the Judaean desert sect at 'En el-Ghuweir on the shores of the Dead Sea. *BASOR* 227(1977): 1–25.

Barag, D., and M. Hershkovitz 1994. Lamps from Masada. In A. Aviram, G. Foerster and E. Netzer (eds), *Masada IV. The Yigael Yadin Excavations 1963–1965. Final Reports*: 1–147. Jerusalem: Israel Exploration Society.

Barghouti, A.N. 1982. Urbanization of Palestine and Jordan in Hellenistic and Roman times. *SHAJ* I, 209–29.

Bar-Nathan, R. 1981. Pottery and stone vessels of the Herodian period. In E. Netzer, *Greater Herodium*: 54–70. Qedem 13. Jerusalem.

Bar-Nathan, R. 2002. *Hasmonean and Herodian palaces at Jericho: Final reports of the 1973–1987 excavations III: the pottery*. Jerusalem: Israel Exploration Society.

Bar-Nathan, R. 2006. *Masada VII. The Yigael Yadin excavations 1963–1965 final reports. The pottery of Masada*. Jerusalem: Israel Exploration Society.

Bar-Nathan, R. 2013. The Roman pottery. in S. Cohen (ed.), *Excavations at Tel Zahara (2006–2009): final report. The Hellenistic and Roman strata*: 31–48. Oxford: British Archaeological Reports International Series.

Bar-Nathan, R., and J. Gärtner 2013. The Hellenistic pottery. In S. Cohen (ed.), *Excavations at Tel Zahara (2006–2009): final report. The Hellenistic and Roman strata*: 48–73. Oxford: British Archaeological Reports International Series.

Begley, V. 1993. New investigations at the port of Arikamedu. *Journal of Roman Archaeology* 6: 93–107.

Behr, D. 1988. Neue Ergebnisse zur pergamenischen Westabhangkeramik. *Istanbuler Mitteilungen* 38: 97–178.

Bellinger, A.R. 1949. The end of the Seleucids. *Transactions of the Connecticut Academy of Arts and Sciences* 38: 51–102.

Ben David, C. 2011. The Jewish settlements in the district of Scythopolis, Hippos and Gadara. *ARAM* 23: 309–23.

Ben-Dov, M. 1985. *In the shadow of the Temple*. New York: Harper & Row.

Bennett, C.M. 1979. Excavations in the citadel (Al Qal'a), Amman, 1978. Fourth preliminary report. *ADAJ* 23: 161–71.

Ben-Tor, A., and R. Rosenthal 1978. The first season of excavations at Tel Yoqne'am, 1977. *IEJ* 28: 57–82.

Ben-Tor, A., Y. Portugali and M. Avissar 1979. The second season of excavations at Tel Yoqne'am, 1978. *IEJ* 29: 65–83.

Ben-Tor, A., Y. Portugali and M. Avissar 1983. The third and fourth season of excavations at Tel Yoqne'am, 1979 and 1981. *IEJ* 33: 30–54.

Berger, L.C. 2020. Pottery from sanctuaries in the hinterland of Gadara/Umm Qays (Jordan). In A. Lichtenberger and R. Raja (eds), *Hellenistic and Roman Gerasa. The archaeology and history of a Decapolis city*: 313–24. Turnhout, Belgium: Brepols.

Berlin, A.M. 1988. *The Hellenistic and Early Roman common-ware pottery from Tel Anafa*. PhD thesis, University of Michigan.

Berlin, A.M. 1992. Hellenistic and Roman pottery, preliminary report, 1990. In R.L. Vann (ed.), *Caesarea Papers*: 112–28. Ann Arbor, MI: University of Michigan.

Berlin, A.M. 1993. Italian cooking vessels and cuisine from Tel Anafa. *IEJ* 43: 35–44.

Berlin, A.M. 1997a. The plain wares. In S.C. Herbert (ed.), *Tel Anafa* II, i. *The Hellenistic and Roman pottery*: 1–246. Ann Arbor: University of Michigan.

Berlin, A.M. 1997b. Between large forces: Palestine in the Hellenistic period. *Biblical Archaeologist* 60: 2–51.

Berlin, A.M. 1997c. From monarchy to markets: the Phoenicians in Hellenistic Palestine. *BASOR* 306: 75–88.

Berlin, A.M. 2002. Romanization and anti-Romanization in pre-revolt Galilee. In A.M. Berlin and J.A. Overman (eds), *The first Jewish revolt. Archaeology, history, and ideology*: 57–73. London and New York: Routledge.

Berlin, A.M. 2005a. Pottery and pottery production in the Second Temple period. In B. Arubas and H. Goldfus (eds), *Excavations on the site of the Jerusalem International Convention Centre (Binyanei Ha'uma): a settlement of the Late First to Second Temple Period, the Tenth Legion's kilnworks, and a Byzantine monastic complex*: 29–60, Portsmouth, RI: Journal of Roman Archaeology Supplementary Series 60.

Berlin, A.M. 2005b. Jewish life before the revolt: the archaeological evidence. *Journal for the Study of Judaism* 36: 417–70.

Berlin, A.M. 2006. *Gamla I. The pottery of the Second Temple period*. Israel Antiquities Authority Reports 29. Jerusalem.

Berlin, A.M. 2012. The pottery of strata 8–7 (the Hellenistic period). In A. De Groot and H. Bernick-Greenberg (eds), *Excavations at the City of David 1978–1985 directed by Yigal Shiloh*. Vol. VIIB. *Area E: the finds*: 5–29. Qedem 54. Jerusalem.

Berlin, A.M. 2015. Hellenistic period. In S. Gitin (ed.), *The ancient pottery of Israel and its neighbors from the Iron Age through the Hellenistic period*. Vol. 2: 629–71. Jerusalem: Israel Exploration Society.

Berlin, A.M., and S.C. Herbert 2021. The Achaemenid–Ptolemaic transition. In S. Honigman, C. Nihan and O. Lipschits (eds), *Times of transition. Judea in the Early Hellenistic period*: 143–59. University Park, PA: Penn State University Press.

Berlin, A.M., and A. Pilacinski 2003. The pottery of the Early and Middle Hellenistic period. In D. Pilides (ed.), *Excavations at the Hill of Ayios Georgios (PA.S.D.Y.), Nicosia: 2002 season – preliminary report*: 201–36. Report of the Department of Antiquities, Cyprus.

Berlin, A.M., and P.J. Stone 2016. The Hellenistic and Early Roman pottery. In M. Hartal, D. Syon et al. (eds), *'Akko II. The 1991–1998 excavations. The early periods*: 133–202. Israel Antiquities Authority Reports 60. Jerusalem.

Berlin, A.M., S. Herbert and P. Stone 2014. Dining in state: the table wares from the Persian-Hellenistic administrative building at Kedesh. In P. Guldager Bilde and M. Lawall (eds), *Pottery, peoples and places. Study and interpretation of Late Hellenistic pottery*: 307–21. Aarhus: Aarhus University Press.

Bes, P. M., and P.J. Stone 2020. Eastern Sigillata at home. In I. Kamenjarin and M. Ugarcović (eds), *Exploring the neighborhood. The role of ceramics in understanding place in the Hellenistic world. Proceedings of the 3rd Conference of the International Association for Research on Pottery of the Hellenistic Period, Kastela, June 2017, 1st–4th*: 655–65. Vienna: Phoibos Verlag.

Bes, P.M., T. Brughmans et al. 2020. Ceramics in cities in context: an overview of published Roman Imperial to Umayyad pottery in the Southern Levant. In A. Lichtenberger and R. Raja (eds), *Hellenistic and Roman Gerasa. The archaeology and history of a Decapolis city*: 55–118. Turnhout, Belgium: Brepols.

Bickerman, E.J. 1988. *The Jews in the Greek age*. Cambridge, MA: Harvard University Press.

Bienkowski, P. 2008. The Persian period. In R.B. Adams (ed.), *Jordan. An archaeological reader*: 335–52. London: Equinox.

Bienkowski, P. 2015. Iron Age IIC: Transjordan. In S. Gitin (ed.), *The Ancient pottery of Israel and its neighbors from the Iron Age through the Hellenistic period*, vol. 1: 419–34. Jerusalem: Israel Exploration Society.

Bietenhard, H. 1977. Die Syrische Dekapolis von Pompeius bis Traian. *Aufstieg und Niedergang der Römischen Welt* II(8): 220–61.

Billows, R.A. 1990: *Antigonos the One-eyed and the creation of the Hellenistic state*. Berkeley: University of California Press.

Birney, K.J. 2022. *Ashkelon 9. The Hellenistic Period*. University Park, PA: Eisenbrauns.

Bliss, F.J., and R.A.S. Macalister 1902. *Excavations in Palestine during the years 1898–1900*. London.

Boardman, J. 1999. *The Greeks overseas*. 4th edn. London: Thames & Hudson.

Bosworth, A.B. 1988. *Conquest and empire. The reign of Alexander the Great*. Cambridge, UK: Cambridge University Press.

Bosworth, A.B. 2002. *The legacy of Alexander. Politics, warfare, and propaganda under the successors*. Oxford: Oxford University Press.

Bourke, S.J. 1997. Pre-Classical Pella in Jordan 1985–1995: a conspectus of ten years' work. *Palestine Exploration Quarterly* 129: 94–115.

Bourke, S.J. 2005. Excavating Pella's Bronze Age Temple precinct: the 1999 and 2001 field seasons. *Mediterranean Archaeology* 18: 109–18.

Bourke, S.J. 2008. Making history: forty years of excavations at Pella in Jordan (1967–2007). *Ancient History: Resources for Teachers* 37/1: 1–35.

Bourke, S.J. 2013. The Christian flight to Pella: true or tale? *Biblical Archaeology Review* 39: 30–9.

Bourke, S.J. 2014. Urban origins in the Early Bronze Age Jordan Valley: recent discoveries from Pella in Jordan. In F. Höflmayer and R. Eichmann (eds), *Egypt and the Southern Levant in the Early Bronze age*: 3–18. Berlin: DAI Orient Archäologie 31.

Bourke, S.J. 2015/2016. Pella in Jordan 2007–2009: prehistoric, Bronze, and Iron Age investigations on Khirbet Fahl, and renewed work across the Tell Husn summit. *Mediterranean Archaeology* 28/29: 125–40.

Bourke, S.J., R.T. Sparks and L.D. Mairs 1999. Bronze Age occupation on Tell Husn (Pella): report on the University of Sydney's 1994/95 field seasons. *Mediterranean Archaeology* 12: 51–66.

Bowersock, G.W. 1983. *Roman Arabia*. Cambridge, MA: Harvard University Press.

Braemer, F. 1986. Études stratigraphiques au N.E. de la facade du temple de Zeus. In F. Zayadine (ed.), *Jerash archaeological project 1981–1983* I: 61–5. Amman: Department of Antiquities of Jordan.

Braemer, F. 1987. Two campaigns of excavations on the ancient Tell of Jarash. *ADAJ* 31: 525–9.

Braemer, F. 1989. Une fabrique (locale?) de céramique fine à Jerash au tournant de l'ère. *Syria* 66: 153–67.

Briend, J. 1980. Vestiges hellénistiques. In J. Briend and J-B. Humbert (eds), *Tell Keisan (1971–1976)*: 101–16. Fribourg: Editions Universitaires.

Brizzi, M. 2022. Review of Lichtenberger, A. and R. Raja (eds) 2020, *Hellenistic and Roman Gerasa. The archaeology and history of a Decapolis city*. Turnhout, Belgium: Brepols. *American Journal of Archaeology* 126: 106–8.

Brown, R. 1983. The 1976 ASOR soundings. In N. Lapp (ed.), *The excavations at Araq el-Emir*: vol. I. *Annual of the American Schools of Oriental Research* 47: 105–32. Boston, MA.

Brown, R. 1991. The ceramics from the Kerak plateau. In J.M. Miller (ed.), *Archaeological survey of the Kerak plateau*: 169–280. Atlanta, GA: Scholars Press.

Bührig, C. 2009. Das Theater-Tempel-Areal von Gadara/Umm Qais. Struktureller Wandel eines urbanen Raums. *Zeitschrift für Orient-Archäologie* 2: 162–207.

Bührig, C. 2011. The development of urban structures in the Decapolis city of Gadara. *ARAM* 23: 285–307.

Bührig, C. 2016. Land-use and settlement activity around Gadara/Umm Qays. *SHAJ* XII: 101–16.

Byrd, J., and D.D. Owens 1997. A method for measuring relative abundance of fragmented archaeological ceramics. *Journal of Field Archaeology* 24: 315–20.

Cahill, J.M. 1992. Chalk vessel assemblages of the Persian/Hellenistic and Early Roman periods. In A. de Groot and D.T. Ariel (eds), *Excavations at the City of David 1978–1985 directed by Yigal Shiloh*, vol. III: 190–274. Qedem 33. Jerusalem.

Callaghan, P.J. 1996. An Antiochene bowl in Cambridge. *Annual of the British School at Athens* 91: 369–75.

Calvet, Y. 1982. Pharmacopée antique. Un pot à lykion de Beyrouth. *Archéologie au Levant, Receuil R. Saidah*: 281–86. CMO 12, Série Archéologique 9. Lyon: MOM Editions.

Camilli, A. 1999. *Ampullae. Balsamari ceramici di èta ellenistica e romana*. Rome: Fratelli Colombi.

Carmi, I., I. Eldar-Nir et al. 1994. The dating of ancient water-wells by archaeological and 14C methods: comparative study of ceramics and wood. *IEJ* 44: 184–200.

Carson, R. 2001. Roman coins. In K. Sheedy, R. Carson and A. Walmsley, *Pella in Jordan 1979–1990. The coins*: 31–7. Sydney: Adapa Monographs.

Chang-Ho, J. 1997. A note on the Iron Age four-room house in Palestine. *Orientalia* 66, 387–413.

Chapman, H.C., and Z. Rodgers 2016. *A companion to Josephus*. New Jersey: Wiley-Blackwell.

Christensen, A.P., and C.F. Johansen 1971. *Hama: fouilles et recherches 1931–1938. Vol. III, ii. Les poteries hellénistiques et les terres sigillées orientales*. Copenhagen: Copenhagen Foundation Carlsberg.

Chrubasik, B., and D. King (eds) 2017. *Hellenism and the local communities of the eastern Mediterranean: 400 BCE–250 CE*. Oxford: Oxford University Press.

Cimadomo, P. 2018. The controversial annexation of the Nabatean kingdom. *Levant* 50: 258–66.

Cimadomo, P. 2019. *The southern Levant during the first centuries of Roman rule (64 BCE–135 CE)*. Oxford: Oxbow.

Clamer, C. 1997. *Fouilles archéologiques de 'Ain ez-Zara/Callirhoe, villégiature herodienne*. Beirut: Institut français du Proche-Orient (IFPO).

Clayman, D. 2014. *Berenice II and the golden age of Ptolemaic Egypt*. Oxford: Oxford University Press.

Cohen, G.M. 1978. *The Seleucid colonies*. Wiesbaden: Steiner.

Cohen, G.M. 1983. Colonization and population transfer in the Hellenistic world. *Studia Hellenistica* 27: 63–74.

Cohen, G.M. 2006. *The Hellenistic settlements in Syria, the Red Sea Basin, and North Africa*. Oakland, CA: University of California Press.

Comfort, H. 1948. Imported Western Terra Sigillata. In F.O. Waagé (ed.), *Antioch-on-the-Orontes*, vol. IV, i: 61–77. Princeton, NJ: Princeton University.

Comfort, H. 1982. Signatures and decoration on Italian and Gaulish Sigillata at Sabratha. *AJA* 86: 483–507.

Comfort, H. 1991. Terra Sigillata at Arikamedu. In V. Begley and R.D. de Puma (eds), *Rome and India. The ancient sea trade:* 134–50. Madison, WI: University of Wisconsin Press.

Cook, R.M. 1997. *Greek painted pottery.* 3rd edn. London: Routledge.

Corbo, V. 1979. Macheronte. La Reggia-Fortezza Erodiana. *Liber Annus* 29, 315–26.

Corbo, V. and S. Loffreda 1981. Nuove scoperte alla Fortezza di Macheronte. *Liber Annus* 31: 257–86.

Cornell, L. 1997. A note on the molded bowls. In S.C. Herbert (ed.), *Tel Anafa II, i. The Hellenistic and Roman pottery:* 407–16. Ann Arbor, MI: Journal of Roman Archaeology.

Coşkun, A. 2016. Laodike I, Berenike Phernophoros, dynastic murder, and the outbreak of the Third Syrian War (253–246 BC). In A. Coşkun and A. McAuley (eds), *Seleukid royal women. Creation, representation and distortion of Hellenistic queenship in the Seleukid empire:* 107–34, Stuttgart: Franz Steiner Verlag.

Coşkun, A. 2019. Epilogue: Rome, the Seleukid East and the disintegration of the largest of the successor kingdoms in the 2nd century BC. In A. Coşkun and D. Engles (eds), *Rome and the Seleukid East: selected papers from Seleukid Study Day V, Brussels, 21–23 August 2015:* 457–79. Collection Latomus. Vol. 360, Leuven: Peeters.

Courby, F. 1922. *Les vases grecs à reliefs.* Paris: Editions de Boccard.

Cox, D.H. 1949. *The excavations at Dura-Europos.* Final Report IV. Part 1. Fascicle 2. *The Greek and Roman pottery.* New Haven, CT: Yale University Press.

Crewe, L. 2002. Spindle-whorls and loomweights. In G.W. Clarke et al., *Jebel Khalid on the Euphrates,* vol. 1: 217–43. Sydney: Meditarch.

Crowfoot, J.W., G.M. Crowfoot and K.M. Kenyon (eds), 1957. *Samaria-Sebaste: reports of the expedition in 1931–33 and of the British expedition in 1935.* Vol. III, *The objects.* London: Palestine Exploration Fund.

Daszkiewicz, M., B. Liesen and G. Schneider 2014. Provenance study of Hellenistic, Roman and Byzantine kitchen wares from the Theatre-Temple Area of Umm Qais/Gadara, Jordan. In B. Fischer-Genz, Y. Gerber and H. Hamel (eds), *Roman pottery in the Near East. Local production and regional trade. Proceedings of the round table held in Berlin, 19–20 February 2010:* 147–58. Oxford: Archaeopress.

Davis, N., and C.M. Kraay 1973. *The Hellenistic kingdoms.* London: Thames & Hudson.

Debevoise, N.C. 1934. *Parthian pottery from Seleucia on the Tigris.* Ann Arbor, MI: University of Michigan Press.

Dentzer, J.-M., F. Villeneuve and F. Larché 1983. The monumental gateway and the princely estate of Araq el-Emir. In N.L. Lapp, *The excavations at Araq el-Emir, vol. I:* 133–48. *Annual of the American Schools of Oriental Research* 47. Boston, MA.

Derfler, S. 1989. Roman Fortress (Stratum II). In Z. Herzog, O. Negbi and G.R. Jr. (eds), *Excavations at Tel Michal, Israel:* 188–94. Minneapolis: University of Minnesota Press.

Dever, W.G., H.D. Lance and G.E. Wright 1970. *Gezer I: preliminary report of the 1964–66 seasons. Vol. I.* Jerusalem: Keter Publishers.

Diez Fernandez, F. 1983. *Cerámica común Romana de la Galilea: aproximaciones y diferencias con la cerámica del resto de Palestina y regiones circundantes.* Madrid: Escuela Biblica.

Dobbins, J.J. 2012. The lamps. In A.M. Berlin and S.C. Herbert (eds), *Tel Anafa II, ii. The glass vessels, lamps, objects of metals, and groundstone and other stone tools and vessels:* 99–212. Ann Arbor, MI: Journal of Roman Archaeology.

Dolan, A.E., and D. Foran 2016. Immersion is the new ritual: the *miqveh* at Khirbat al-Mukhayat (Jordan) and Hasmonean agro-economic policies in the Late Hellenistic period. *Levant* 48: 284–99.

Dore, J.N., and R. Schinke 1992. First report on the pottery. In N.B Lazreg and D.J. Mattingly (eds), *Leptiminus (Lamta): a Roman port city in Tunisia:* 116–56. Report no. 1. Ann Arbor, MI: University of Michigan.

Dornemann, R.H. 1990. Preliminary comments of the pottery traditions at Tell Nimrin, illustrated from the 1989 season of excavations. *ADAJ* 34: 153–82.

Dothan, M. 1971. Ashdod II–III. The second and third seasons of excavations, 1963, 1965. Atiqot (English Series, Vol. IX–X).

Dothan, M. 1976. Akko: interim excavation report first season, 1973/4. *BASOR* 224: 1–48.

Dothan, M., and D.N. Freedman 1967. Ashdod I. The first season of excavations 1962. Atiqot (English Series, vol. VII)

Dragendorff, H. 1895. Terra Sigillata. Ein Beitrag zur Geschichte der griechischen und römischen Keramik. *Bonner Jahrbücher* 96: 18–155.

Duplessis, S., F. Di Napoli and J. Seigne 2020. Les timbres amphoriques trouvés á Jerash. In A. Lichtenberger and R. Raja (eds), *Hellenistic and Roman Gerasa. The archaeology and history of a Decapolis city:* 145–72. Turnhout, Belgium: Brepols.

Dušek, J. 2012. *Aramaic and Hebrew inscriptions from Mt. Gerizim and Samaria between Antiochus III and Antiochus IV Epiphanes*. Leiden: Brill.

Duyrat, F. 2016. *Wealth and warfare. The archaeology of money in ancient Syria*. New York: American Numismatic Society.

Dyson, S.L. 1968. *The excavations at Dura Europos*. Final Report 4. Part 1. Fascicle 3. *The commonware pottery. The brittle ware*. New Haven, CT: Yale University Press.

Ebeling, J., and M. Rogel 2015. The *tabun* and its misidentification in the archaeological record. *Levant* 47: 328–49.

Ecker, A., G. Finkielsztein et al. 2017. The southern Levant in Antiochos III's time: between continuity and immediate or delayed changes. In C. Feyel and L. Graslin-Thomé (eds), *Antiochos III et l'Orient*: 161–207. Paris: Editions de Boccard.

Edwards, G.R. 1975. *Corinth*. VII.iii. *Corinthian Hellenistic Pottery*. Princeton, NJ: American School of Classical Studies.

Edwards, P.C. 1992. The Epipalaeolithic period. In A. McNicoll, P.C. Edwards et al., *Pella in Jordan 2*: 1–16. Sydney.

Edwards, P.C. 2007. A 14000 year-old hunter-gatherer's toolkit. *Antiquity* 81: 865–76.

Edwards, P.C. (ed.) 2013. *Wadi Hammeh 27, an early Natufian settlement at Pella in Jordan*. Leiden: Brill.

Edwards, P.C., S.J. Bourke et al. 1990. Preliminary report on the University of Sydney's tenth season of excavations at Pella (Tabaqat Fahl) in 1988. *ADAJ* 34: 57–94.

Eisenberg, M. 2017. A military portrait of Hippos – from Ptolemaic fortress to Seleucid polis. *Michmanim* 27: 57–69 (Hebrew with an English abstract).

Élaigne, S. 2000. Fine ware from Late Hellenistic, Augustan and Tiberian deposits in Alexandria. *Rei Cretariae Romanae Fautorum Acta* 36: 19–30.

Élaigne, S. 2004. L'apport italique sigillées en Egypte au début du Haut-Empire: le cas d'Alexandrie et de Coptos. In J. Poblome, P. Talloen et al. (eds), *Early Italian Sigillata*: 133–44. Leuven: Peeters.

Élaigne, S. 2007. Les importations de céramiques fines hellénistiques á Beyrouth (Site Bey 002): aperçu du faciès nord levantin. *Syria* 84: 107–42.

Élaigne, S. 2012: *La vaisselle fine de l'habitat alexandrine*. Études Alexandrines 21. Cairo: IFAO.

Elam, J.M., M.D. Glascock and K.W. Slane 1989. A re-examination of the provenance of Eastern Sigillata A. In R.M. Farquhar et al. (eds), *Proceedings of the 26th International Archaeometry Symposium (Toronto 1988)*: 179–83. Toronto: University of Toronto.

Elgavish, J. 1976. Pottery from the Hellenistic stratum at Shiqmona. *IEJ* 26: 65–76.

Erikson, K., and G. Ramsay (eds) 2011. *Seleucid dissolution: the sinking of the anchor*. Wiesbaden: Harrassowitz.

Errington, R.M. 2008. *A history of the Hellenistic world 323–30 BC*. Malden, MA and Oxford: Blackwell.

Eshel, H., and M. Broshi 2003. Excavations at Qumran, summer of 2001. *IEJ* 53: 61–73.

Ettlinger, E., B. Hedinger and B. Hoffman 1990. *Conspectus formarum terrae sigillatae italico modo confectae. Materialien zur römisch-germanischen Keramik 10*. Bonn: R. Habelt.

Evridiki, L. 2002. Hellenistic relief pottery in Asia Minor. *Encyclopaedia of the Hellenic World, Asia Minor*. http://www.ehw.gr/l.aspx?id=8014

Ferguson, J. 2014. Late Hellenistic and Early Roman ceramic trends at Tall Mādabā, Jordan. In B. Fischer-Genz, Y. Gerber and H. Hamel (eds), *Roman pottery in the Near East. Local production and regional trade. Proceedings of the round table held in Berlin, 19–20 February 2010*: 171–88. Oxford: Archaeopress.

Fiensy, D.A., and J.R. Strange 2015. *Galilee in the Late Second Temple and Mishnaic periods*. Vol. 2. *The archaeological record from cities, towns, and villages*. Minneapolis, MN: Fortress Press.

Filimonos, M., and A. Giannikouri 1999. Grave offerings from Rhodes: pottery and jewellery. In V. Gabrielsen, P. Bilde et al. (eds), *Hellenistic Rhodes: politics, culture, and society*: 205–26. Aarhus: Aarhus University Press.

Finkielsztejn, G. 2001. *Chronologie détaillée et révisée des éponyms amphoriques rhodiens, de 270 à 108 av. J.-C. environ. Premier bilan*. British Archaeological Reports International Series 990. Oxford.

Fischer, M.B. 1989. Hellenistic pottery (strata V–III). In Z. Herzog, G. Rapp Jr. and O. Negbi (eds), *Excavations at Tel Michal, Israel*: 117–87. Minneapolis: University of Minneapolis Press.

Fischer, M.B., and O. Tal 1996. Two ceramic assemblages from Hellenistic Apollonia. *Tel Aviv* 23: 213–34.

Fischer, M.B., and O. Tal 1999a. The Hellenistic period. In I. Roll and O. Tal (eds), *Apollonia-Arsuf. Final report of the excavations*. Vol. I. *The Persian and Hellenistic Periods*: 223–61. Tel Aviv: Tel Aviv University.

Fischer, M.B., and O. Tal 1999b. Hellenistic and Early Roman periods. In I. Beit-Arieh (ed.), *Tel 'Ira. A stronghold in the biblical Negev*: 290–6. Tel Aviv: Tel Aviv University

Fischer-Bovet, C. 2014. *Army and society in Ptolemaic Egypt: from invasion to integration*. Cambridge, UK: Cambridge University Press.

Fischer-Bovet, C. 2015. Social unrest and ethnic coexistence in Ptolemaic Egypt and the Seleucid empire. *Past and Present* 229: 3–45.

Fitzgerald, G.M. 1931. *Beth-Shan excavations 1921–1923.* Vol. III. Philadelphia, PA: University of Pennsylvania Press.

Foerster, G. 1993. Beth-Shean at the foot of the mound. In E. Stern (ed.), *The new encyclopedia of archaeological excavations in the Holy Land*, vol. 1: 223–35. Jerusalem: Israel Exploration Society.

Foerster, G., and Y. Tsafrir 1992. Nysa-Scythopolis in the Roman period. A Greek city of Coele-Syria – evidence from the excavations at Bet-Shean. *ARAM* 4 (1 and 2): 117–39.

Frangié-Joly, D. 2014. Economy and cultural transfers: evidence of Hellenization and early Romanization in Beirut. In B. Fischer-Genz, Y. Gerber and H. Hamel (eds), *Roman pottery in the Near East. Local production and regional trade. Proceedings of the round table held in Berlin, 19–20 February 2010:* 89–101. Oxford: Archaeopress.

Freeman, P. 2008. The Roman period. In R.B. Adams (ed.), *Jordan. An archaeological reader:* 413–41. London: Equinox.

Freyne, S. 1980. *Galilee. From Alexander the Great to Hadrian 323 BCE to 135 CE.* Notre Dame, IN: University of Notre Dame Press.

Freyne, S. 1997. Galilee in the Hellenistic through Byzantine periods. In E.M. Meyers (ed. in chief), *The Oxford encyclopedia of archaeology in the Near East*, vol. 2: 370–6. Oxford: Oxford University Press.

Frézouls, E. 1990. Fondations et refondations dans l'Orient syrien – problémes d'identification et d'interprétation. In P.-L. Gatier, B. Helly and J-P Rey-Coquais, *Géographie Historique au Proche-Orient:* 111–31. Paris: Editions du Centre National de la Recherche Scientifique.

Fulford, M.G. 1989. To east and west: the Mediterranean trade of Cyrenaica and Tripolitania in antiquity. *Libyan Studies* 20: 160–91.

Fülle, G. 1997. The internal organisation of the Arretine *Terra Sigillata* industry: problems of evidence and interpretation. *Journal of Roman Studies* 87: 111–55.

Funk, R.W., and H.N. Richardson 1958. The 1958 sounding at Pella. *Biblical Archaeologist* 21: 82–96.

Gardin, J-C. 1973. Les céramiques. In P. Bernard, *Fouilles d'Ai Khanoum*, vol. I: 121–88. Paris: Memoires de la Delegation Archeologique Française.

Garnett, D. 2011. Geochemical characteristics of imported Hellenistic pottery from Jebel Khalid, Antioch, and Pella. In H. Jackson and J.C. Tidmarsh, *Jebel Khalid on the Euphrates*, vol. 3, *The pottery:* 527–43. Sydney: Meditarch.

Geraty, L.T., and L.G. Herr (eds) 1986. *The archaeology of Jordan and other studies.* Berrien Springs, MI: Andrews University Press.

Gerber, Y. 2012. Classical period pottery. In J.A. Sauer and L.G. Herr (eds), *Hesban 11. Typological and technological studies of the pottery remains from Tell Hesban and vicinity:* 175–503. Berrien Springs, MI.

Geva, H. 1983. Excavations in the Citadel of Jerusalem, 1979–1980. *IEJ* 33: 55–71.

Geva, H. 2003. Hellenistic pottery from areas W and X-2. In H. Geva (ed), *Jewish Quarter excavations in the Old City of Jerusalem conducted by Nahman Avigad, 1969–1982*, vol. II, *The finds from areas A, W and X-2. Final report:* 113–75. Jerusalem: Israel Exploration Society.

Geva, H. 2010a. Early Roman pottery. In H. Geva, *Jewish Quarter excavations in the Old City of Jerusalem conducted by Nahman Avigad, 1969–1982*, vol. IV, *The burnt house of Area B and other studies:* 118–53. Jerusalem: Israel Exploration Society.

Geva, H. 2010b. Stone Artifacts. In H. Geva, *Jewish Quarter excavations in the Old City of Jerusalem conducted by Nahman Avigad, 1969–1982*, vol. IV, *The burnt house of Area B and other studies:* 154–212. Jerusalem: Israel Exploration Society.

Geva, H. 2014. Hellenistic pottery from Area Z. In H. Geva, *Jewish Quarter excavations in the Old City of Jerusalem conducted by Nahman Avigad, 1969–1982*, vol. VI, *Areas J, N, Z and other studies. Final report:* 353–61. Jerusalem: Israel Exploration Society.

Geva, H., and R. Rosenthal-Heginbottom 2003. Local pottery from Area A. In H. Geva, *Jewish Quarter excavations in the Old City of Jerusalem conducted by Nahman Avigad, 1969–1982*, vol. II, *The finds from areas A, W and X-2. Final report:* 176–91. Jerusalem: Israel Exploration Society.

Gibson, S. 2003. Stone vessels of the Early Roman period from Jerusalem and Palestine. A reassessment. In G.C. Bottini et al. (eds), *One land – many cultures. Archaeological studies in honour of S. Loffreda:* 287–308. Jerusalem: Studium Biblicum Franciscanum.

Gilboa, A. 2015. Iron Age IIC: Northern Coast, Carmel Coast, Galilee, and Jezreel Valley. In S. Gitin (ed.), *The ancient pottery of Israel and its neighbors from the Iron Age through the Hellenistic period*, vol. 1: 301–26. Jerusalem.

Gitin, S. 1990: *Gezer III: a ceramic typology of the Late Iron II, Persian and Hellenistic periods at Tell Gezer.* Jerusalem: Nelson Glueck School of Biblical Archaeology.

Gitin, S. 1996. Formulating a ceramic corpus: the Late Iron II, Persian and Hellenistic pottery at Tell Gezer. In J. Seger (ed.), *Retrieving the past: essays on archaeological research and methodology in honor of Gus W. Van Beek*. Winona Lake, IN: Eisenbrauns.

Guidice, F., R.A. Oliveri et al. 1996. Paphos, Garrison's camp. Campagna 1991. *Report of the Department of Antiquities, Cyprus*: 171–267.

Goodman, M. 1992. Jews in the Decapolis. *ARAM* 4 (1 and 2): 49–56.

Gordon, R.L. 1979. *The stucco wall decoration from Tell Anafa*. PhD thesis, University of Missouri-Columbia.

Goren, Y., and P. Fabian 2008. The Oboda potter's workshop reconsidered. *Journal of Roman Archaeology* 21: 340–51.

Grabbe, L.L. 2021. The Ptolemaic period: a dark age in Jewish history? In S. Honigman, C. Nihan and O. Lipschits (eds), *Times of transition. Judea in the Early Hellenistic period*: 19–29. University Park, PA: Penn State University Press.

Grace, V.R. 1979. *Amphoras and the ancient wine trade*. Excavations of the Athenian Agora Picture Book 6. (Revised edn.) Princeton, NJ.

Graf, D.F. 1992. Hellenisation and the Decapolis. *ARAM* 4 (1 and 2): 1–48.

Graf, D.F. 2002. Die Dekapolis – ein Prolog. In A. Hoffman and S. Kerner (eds), *Gadara – Gerasa und die Dekapolis*: 4–5. Mainz am Rhein: Philipp von Zabern.

Graf, D.F., and S. Sidebotham 2003. Nabatean trade. In G. Markoe (ed.), *Petra rediscovered: lost city of the Nabateans*: 65–73. London: Thames & Hudson.

Grainger, J.D. 1990. *The cities of Seleukid Syria*. Oxford: Clarendon Press.

Grainger, J.D. 2010. *The Syrian wars*. Mnemosyne Supplements 320. Leiden: Brill.

Grainger, J.D. 2015a. *The fall of the Seleukid empire 187–75 BC*. Barnsley, UK: Pen and Sword Military.

Grainger, J.D. 2015b. *The Seleukid empire of Antiochus III 223–187 BC*. Barnsley, UK: Pen and Sword Military.

Green, J.D., B.A. Porter and G.P. Shelton 2018. *The Archaeology in Jordan Newsletter*. Amman: American Center for Oriental Research.

Green, P. 1990. *Alexander to Actium*. London: Thames & Hudson.

Greenberg, R., O. Tal and T. Da'adli 2017: *Bet Yerah*. Vol. III. *Hellenistic Philoteria and Islamic al-Sinnabra*. Israel Antiquities Authority Reports 61. Jerusalem.

Greene, J.A., and K. 'Amr 1992. Deep sounding on the lower terrace of the Amman Citadel: Final report. *ADAJ* 36: 113–44.

Grey, A.D. 1994. The pottery of the later periods from Tel Jezreel: an interim report. *Levant* 26: 51–62.

Grey, A.D. 2014. Esdraela: the ceramic record from a settlement of Hellenistic and Roman times to late antiquity in Palestine. *Palestine Exploration Quarterly* 146 (2): 105–34.

Groot, J. 1983. Wall decoration. In N. Lapp, *The excavations at Araq el-Emir*, vol. 1: 75–86. *Annual of the American Schools of Oriental Research* 47, Boston MA.

Groot, N.C.F. 2009. The early Persian period at Tell Deir 'Allā: a ceramic perspective. In E. Kaptijn and L.P. Petit (eds), *A timeless vale: archaeology and related studies of the Jordan Valley in honour of Gerrit van der Kooij on the occasion of his sixty-fifth birthday*: 167–80. Leiden: Leiden University Press.

Guldager Bilde, P. 1993. Mouldmade bowls, centres and peripheries in the Hellenistic world. In P. Bilde, T. Engberg-Pedersen et al., *Centre and periphery in the Hellenistic world*: 192–206. Aarhus: Aarhus University Press.

Gunneweg, J., I. Perlman and J. Yellin 1983. *The provenience, typology and chronology of Eastern Terra Sigillata*. Qedem 17. Jerusalem.

Guz-Zilberstein, B. 1995. The typology of the Hellenistic coarse ware and selected loci of the Hellenistic and Roman periods. In E. Stern, *Excavations at Dor, final report, vol. IB, Areas A and C: the finds*: 289–433. Qedem 2. Jerusalem.

Hadas, G. 2007. The Balsam *Afarsemon* and Ein Gedi during the Roman-Byzantine period. *Revue Biblique* 114: 161–73.

Hadidi, A. 1970. The pottery from the Roman Forum at Amman. *ADAJ* 15: 11–15.

Haerinck, E. 1983. *La céramique en Iran pendant la période Parthe*. Ghent: Universitaire Stichting van België.

Hammond, N.G.L. 1989. *Alexander the Great*. 3rd edn. London: Chatto & Windus.

Hanbury-Tenison, J.W. 1984. Wadi Arab Survey 1983. *ADAJ* 28: 385–416.

Handberg, S., J. Petersen and P.J. Stone 2013. Uncommon tastes: the consumption of Campana A pottery in the southern Levant and the Black Sea region. In H. Thomasen, A. Rathje and K.B. Johannsen (eds), *Vessels and variety. New aspects of ancient pottery*: 51–80. Chicago, IL: University of Chicago Press.

Hannestad, L. 1983. *Ikaros 2:1. The Hellenistic pottery*. Aarhus: Jutland Archaeological Society.

Hannestad, L. 1990. Change and conservatism. Hellenistic pottery in Mesopotamia and Iran. *Akten des XIII. Internationalen Kongresses für Klassische Archäologie Berlin 1988*: 179–86.

Hannestad, L. 2011. Koile-Syria: an archaeological contribution. In Z.H. Archibald, J.K. Davies and V. Gabrielsen (eds), *The economies of Hellenistic societies, third to first centuries BC*: 251–79. Oxford: Oxford University Press.

Harden, D.B. 1969. Ancient glass II: Roman. *The Archaeological Journal* 126: 44–77.

Harding, G.L. 1944. Two Iron Age tombs from 'Amman. *Quarterly of the Department of Antiquities of Palestine* 11: 67–74.

Harding, G.L. 1946. A Nabatean tomb at 'Amman. *Quarterly of the Department of Antiquities of Palestine* 12: 58–62.

Harding, G.L. 1967. *The antiquities of Jordan.* (Revised edn.) London: Lutterworth Press.

Hauben, H. 2016. Army and Society in Ptolemaic Egypt: from Invasion to Integration. *Bulletin of the American Society of Papyrologists* 53: 395–409.

Hausmann, U. 1996. *Hellenistische Keramik: eine Brunnenfüllung nördlich von Bau C und Reliefkeramik verschiedener Fundplätze in Olympia.* Berlin: De Gruyter.

Hayes, J.W. 1973. Roman pottery from the south stoa at Corinth. *Hesperia* 42: 416–70.

Hayes, J.W. 1976. Pottery: stratified groups. In J.H. Humphrey (ed.), *Excavations at Carthage 1975*: 47–123. Ann Arbor, MI: University of Michigan.

Hayes, J.W. 1978. Pottery report – 1976. In J.H. Humphrey (ed.) *Excavations at Carthage 1976*: 23–98. Ann Arbor, MI: University of Michigan.

Hayes, J.W. 1985a. Sigillate Orientali. In *Enciclopedia dell'arte antica. Atlante delle forme ceramiche* II: 1–96. Rome: Istituto dell'Enciclopedia Italiana.

Hayes, J.W. 1985b. Hellenistic to Byzantine fine wares and derivatives in the Jerusalem corpus. In A.D. Tushingham, *Excavations in Jerusalem 1961–1967*, vol. I: 183–94. Toronto: Royal Ontario Museum.

Hayes, J.W. 1991a: *Paphos III. The Hellenistic and Roman pottery.* Nicosia: Department of Antiquities Cyprus.

Hayes, J.W. 1991b. Fine wares in the Hellenistic world. In T. Rasmussen and N. Spivey (eds), *Looking at Greek vases*: 183–202. Cambridge, UK: Cambridge University Press.

Hayes, J.W. 1997. *Handbook of Mediterranean Roman pottery.* London: British Museum Press.

Hayes, J.W. 2008. *The Athenian Agora XXXII. Roman Pottery. Fine-Ware Imports.* Princeton, NJ: American School of Classical Studies at Athens.

Heckel, W. 2009. *Who's who in the age of Alexander the Great.* Malden, MA, and Oxford: Wiley-Blackwell.

Heinen, H. 1984. The Syrian-Egyptian wars and the new kingdoms of Asia Minor. *Cambridge Ancient History* II(i): 412–45. Cambridge, UK: Cambridge University Press.

Hellström, P. 1965. *Labraunda: Swedish excavations and researches,* II,i. *Pottery of Classical and later date, terracotta lamps and glass.* Lund, Sweden.

Hengel, M. 1974. *Judaism and Hellenism,* trs. J. Bowden. Philadelphia, PA: Fortress Press.

Hengel, M. 1980. *Jews, Greeks, and barbarians: aspects of the Hellenisation of Judaism in the pre-Christian period,* trs. J. Bowden. Philadelphia, PA: SCM Press. (Originally published Stuttgart 1976).

Hengel, M. 1989. *The 'Hellenization' of Judaea in the first century after Christ.* London: SCM Press.

Hennessy, J.B. 1970. Excavations at Samaria-Sebaste, 1968. *Levant* 2: 1–21.

Hennessy, J.B., A.W. McNicoll et al. 1983. Preliminary report on the fourth season of excavations at Pella, 1982. *ADAJ* 27: 325–61.

Herbert, S.C. 1994: *Tel Anafa. Final report on ten years of excavation at a Hellenistic and Roman settlement in northern Israel,* I,i and I,ii. Ann Arbor, MI: University of Michigan.

Herbert, S.C., and A.M. Berlin 2003. A new administrative center for Persian and Hellenistic Galilee: preliminary report of the University of Michigan/University of Minnesota excavations at Kedesh. *BASOR* 329: 15–59.

Herr, L.G., D.R. Clark et al. 1997. *Madaba Plains project: the 1989 season at Tell el-'Umeiri and vicinity and subsequent studies.* Berrien Springs, MI: Andrews University Press.

Herr, L.G., D.R. Clark et al. 2002. *Madaba Plains project: the 1994 season at Tall al 'Umayri and subsequent studies.* Berrien Springs, MI: Andrews University Press.

Hershkovitz, M. 1986. Miniature ointment vases from the Second Temple period. *IEJ* 36: 45–51.

Hershkovitz, M. 1999. The Second Temple period. In I. Beit-Arieh (ed.), *Tel 'Ira. A stronghold in the biblical Negev*: 297–345. Tel Aviv: Institute of Archaeology.

Hill, D.K. 1963. The animal fountain of 'Arâq El-Emîr. *BASOR* 1963: 45–55.

Hillard, T.W. 1992. A mid-1st c. BC date for the walls of Straton's Tower? In R.L. Vann (ed.), *Caesarea Papers*: 42–8. Ann Arbor, MI: University of Michigan.

Hirschfeld, Y. 1997. Jewish rural settlement in Judaea in the Early Roman period. In S.E. Alcock (ed.), *The Early Roman empire in the East*: 72–88. Oxford: Oxbow.

Hirschfeld, Y. 2000. A settlement of hermits above 'En Gedi. *Tel Aviv* 27: 103–55.

Hirschfeld, Y., and D. Ariel 2005. A coin assemblage from the reign of Alexander Jannaeus found on the shore of the Dead Sea. *IEJ* 55: 66–89.

Hoff, M.C. 1997. *Laceratae Athenae:* Sulla's siege of Athens in 87/6 B.C. and its aftermath. In M.C. Hoff and S.I. Rotroff (eds), *The Romanization of Athens:* 33–51. Oxford: Oxbow.

Hoffman, A. 2000. Die Stadtmauern der Hellenistisch-Römischen Dekapolisstadt Gadara. *Archäologischer Anzeiger*, 175–233.

Hoffman, A. 2001. Hellenistic Gadara. *SHAJ* 7: 391–7.

Hoffman, A. 2002. Topographie und Stadtgeschichte von Gadara/Umm Qais. In A. Hoffman and S. Kerner (eds), *Gadara – Gerasa und die Dekapolis*: 98–124. Mainz am Rhein: Philipp von Zabern.

Hölbl, G. 2001. *A history of the Ptolemaic empire.* London and New York: Routledge.

Homès-Fredericq, D., and J.B. Hennessy (eds) 1989. *Archaeology of Jordan*, vol. II. Leuven: Peeters.

Honigman, S., C. Nihan and O. Lipschits (eds) 2021. *Times of transition. Judea in the early Hellenistic period.* University Park, PA: Penn State University Press.

Horsfield, G., and A. Horsfield 1939. Sela-Petra. *Quarterly of the Department of Antiquities of Palestine* 8: 87–115.

Horsfield, G., and A. Horsfield 1941. Sela-Petra. *Quarterly of the Department of Antiquities of Palestine* 9: 105–204.

Horsley, R.A. 1996. *Archaeology, history and society in Galilee: the social context of Jesus and the rabbis.* Philadelphia, PA: Valley Forge.

Howland, R.H. 1958. *The Athenian Agora IV. Greek lamps and their survivals.* Princeton, NJ: American School of Classical Studies at Athens.

Hughes, T. 2022: *The Perdiccas years, 323–320 BC.* Barnsley, UK: Pen and Sword Military.

Humbert, J-B., and F. Zayadine 1991. Citadelle d'Amman 1991 – Troisième Terrasse. *Liber Annus* 41: 502–6.

Ibrahim, M. 1978. The collared-rim jar of the early Iron Age. In P.R.S. Moorey and P. Parr (eds), *Archaeology in the Levant: essays for Kathleen Kenyon*: 116–26. Warminster: Aris and Phillips.

Iliffe, J.H. 1936. Sigillata wares in the Near East. *Quarterly of the Department of Antiquities of Palestine* 6: 4–53.

Iliffe, J.H. 1939. Sigillata wares in the Near East II. More Potters' Stamps. *Quarterly of the Department of Antiquities of Palestine* 9: 31–76.

Irby, C.L, and J. Mangles 1823. *Travels in Egypt, and Nubia, Syria and the Holy Land.* London: T. White & Co.

Isaac, B. 1981. The Decapolis in Syria, a neglected inscription. *Zeitschrift für Papyrologie und Epigraphik* 44: 67–74.

Jackson, H. 2009. Erotes on the Euphrates – a figured frieze in a private house at Hellenistic Jebel Khalid on the Euphrates. *AJA* 113: 231–53.

Jackson, H. 2011a. The plain wares from the housing insula. In H. Jackson and J.C. Tidmarsh, *Jebel Khalid on the Euphrates*, vol. 3, *The pottery*: 1–261. Sydney: Meditarch.

Jackson, H. 2011b. The green-glazed wares from Jebel Khalid, 1986–2006. In H. Jackson and J.C. Tidmarsh, *Jebel Khalid on the Euphrates*, vol. 3, *The pottery*: 431–95. Sydney: Meditarch.

Jackson, H. 2014. *Jebel Khalid on the Euphrates.* Vol. 4. *The housing insula.* Sydney: Meditarch.

Jackson, H. 2016. Stucco fragments from the Acropolis palace. In G. Clarke, H. Jackson et al., *Jebel Khalid on the Euphrates.* Vol. 5. *Report on the excavations 2000–2010*: 259–67. Sydney: Meditarch.

Jacobson, D.M. 1999. Palestine and Israel. *BASOR* 313, 65–74.

James, S.A. 2018. *Corinth VII.7. Hellenistic pottery. The fine wares.* Princeton, NJ: American School of Classical Studies at Athens.

Jansen, B. 2021. The Hellenistic fortification of Seleukia Gadara (Umm Qays): form, function and origin of the military architecture at the southern edge of the Seleucid empire. In M. Eisenberg and R. Khamisy (eds), *The art of siege warfare and military architecture from the Classical World to the Middle Ages*: 73–9. Oxford: Oxbow.

Jaritz, H., and M. Rodziewicz 1993. The investigation of the ancient wall extending from Aswan to Philae. *Mitteilungen des Deutschen Archäologischen Instituts Abteilung Kairo* 49: 119–32.

Ji, C.C., and J-K. Lee 1999. The 1998 season of archaeological survey in the regions of 'Iraq al-'Amir and Wadi al-Kafrayn. A preliminary report. *ADAJ* 43: 521–39.

Johannsen, O. 2023. *Imperialer Wandel und ptolemäischer Imperialismus in Syrien: Konnektivität, Konkurrenz und Kooperation.* Antike Imperien, 3. Paderborn: Brill Schöningh.

Johnson, B.L. 2006. The Hellenistic to Early Islamic pottery. In A. Mazar, *Excavations at Tel Beth-Shean 1989–1996, vol. I, From the Late Bronze Age IIB to the Medieval Period*: 523–89. Jerusalem: Israel Exploration Society.

Johnson, B.L. 2008: *Ashkelon 2. Imported pottery of the Roman and Late Roman eriods*, University Park, PA: Eisenbrauns.

Johnson, D.J. 1990. Nabatean piriform unguentaria. *ARAM* 2(1 and 2): 235–48.

Johstono, P. 2017. 'No strength to stand': defeat at Panium, the Macedonian class, and Ptolemaic decline. In J.H. Clark and B. Turner (eds), *Brill's companion to military defeat in ancient Mediterranean society*: 162–87. Leiden: Brill.

Jones, A.H.M. 1983. *Cities of the eastern provinces*. 2nd edn. Oxford: Clarendon Press.

Jones, F.F. 1950. The pottery. In H. Goldman (ed.), *Excavations at Gozlu Kule, Tarsus*, vol. I, *The Hellenistic and Roman periods*: 149–296. Princeton, NJ: Princeton University Press.

Kahane, P. 1952. Pottery types from Jewish ossuary tombs around Jerusalem. *IEJ* 2: 125–39, 176–82.

Kehrberg, I. 2004a. Late Hellenistic and Early Roman pottery of Gerasa in view of international norms in the eastern Mediterranean. *SHAJ* 8: 189–96.

Kehrberg, I. 2004b. A Late Hellenistic link between Jordan and Cyprus: a view from Gerasa. *Mediterranean Archaeology 17. Festschrift in Honour of J. Richard Green*: 299–306. University of Sydney.

Kehrberg, I., and J. Manley 2002. The Earliest Hellenistic tomb find in Jerash or Antioch on the Chrysorhoas. The Jerash City Walls Project: excavations 2001. *Occident and Orient* 7(1): 7–8.

Kehrberg-Ostrasz, I. 2018. A caravan merchant family of 'Antioch on the Chrysorhoas'. A glimpse of Hellenistic Gerasa as a caravanserai. In L. Nehme and A. al-Jallad (eds), *'To the Madbar and back again' – studies dedicated to Michael C.A. Macdonald*: 439–48. Leiden: Brill.

Kelso, J.L., and D.C. Baramki 1955. *Excavations at New Testament Jericho and Khirbet en-Nitla. Annual of the American Schools of Oriental Research 29–30*. New Haven, CT: Yale University Press.

Kenkel, F. 2012. *Untersuchungen zur Hellenistischen, Römischen und Byzantinischen Keramik des Tall Zīrāʾa im Wādī al-ʾArab (Nordjordanien) – Handelsobjekte und Alltagsgegenstände einer ländlichen Siedlung im Einflussgebiet der Dekapolisstädte*. PhD thesis, University of Köln. (In a more concise form in English: Kenkel 2020.)

Kenkel, F. 2013. The Hellenistic pottery from Tall Zira'a in northern Jordan – material from a village within the spheres of influence of the Decapolis cities Gadara, Gerasa and Pella. In N. Fenn and C. Römer-Strehl (eds), *Networks in the Hellenistic World. According to the pottery in the Eastern Mediterranean and beyond*: 301–8. British Archaeological Reports, International Series 2539.

Kenkel, F. 2020. The Hellenistic, Roman and Byzantine pottery. In D. Vieweger and J. Häser (eds), *Tall Zira'a. The Gadara Region Project (2001–2011)*, vol. 6, *From Hellenistic to Ummayad Strata (8–3)*: 15–225. Open Access Monograph Series. Jerusalem/Amman/Wuppertal.

Kennedy, D. 2007. *Gerasa and the Decapolis. A virtual island in northwest Jordan*. London: Duckworth.

Kennedy, D.L., and P. Freeman 1995. Southern Hauran survey. *Levant* 27: 39–73.

Kenrick, P.M. 1985. *Excavations at Sidi Khrebish Benghazi (Berenice)*, III.1: *The fine pottery*. Tripoli, Libya: Department of Antiquities.

Kenrick, P.M. 1987. Hellenistic and Roman fine wares. In D. White (ed.), *The extramural sanctuary of Demeter and Persephone at Cyrene, Libya. Final reports*, Part III, 1–12. Philadelphia, PA: University of Pennsylvania.

Kenrick, P.M. 1993. Italian Terra Sigillata: a sophisticated Roman industry. *Oxford Journal of Archaeology* 12: 235–42.

Kenrick, P.M. 1996. The importation of Italian Sigillata to Algeria. *Antiquités africaines* 32: 37–44.

Kenrick, P.M. 2000. Fine wares from the City Wall section at Bait Nawashi (Area XLII). *Archäologischer Anzeiger*: 235–65.

Kenyon, K.M. 1957. In J.W. Crowfoot, G.M. Crowfoot and K.M. Kenyon (eds), *Samaria-Sebaste: reports of the expedition in 1931–33 and of the British expedition in 1935*. Vol. III, *The objects*: 281–306. London: Palestine Exploration Fund.

Kerner, S. 1992. Umm Qais-Gadara: recent excavations. *ARAM* 4 (1 and 2): 407–23.

Kerner, S. 1997. Umm Qays-Gadara: A preliminary report 1993–1995. *ADAJ* 41: 283–302.

Kerner, S., and A. Hoffman 1993. Gadara-Umm Qeis. Preliminary report on the 1991 and 1992 seasons. *ADAJ* 37: 359–84.

Khadija, M.M. 1974. Beit Zar'a tombs. *ADAJ* 19: 157–63.

Khairy, N.I. 1980. Nabatean piriform unguentaria. *BASOR* 240: 85–91.

Kidd, B., and R.L. Gordon, Jr, 2018. Decorative wall plaster. In A.M. Berlin and S.C. Herbert (eds), *Tel Anafa II, iii. Decorative wall plaster, objects of personal adornment and glass counters, tools for textile manufacture and miscellaneous bone, terracotta and stone figurines, pre-Persian pottery, Attic pottery, and Medieval pottery*: 1–78. Ann Arbor, MI: University of Michigan.

Killebrew, A.E., and M. Steiner 2013. *The Oxford handbook of the archaeology of the Levant: c. 8000–332 BCE*. Oxford: Oxford University Press.

Kloner, A., and O. Hess 1985. A columbarium in Complex 21 at Maresha. *Atiqot* 17: 122–33.

Knapp, A.B. 1993. *Society and polity at Bronze Age Pella*. Sheffield, UK: Sheffield Academic Press.

Kögler, L. 2014. Table ware from Knidos: the local production during the 2nd and 1st centuries BC. In P. Guldager Bilde and M. Lawall (eds), *Pottery, peoples and places. Study and interpretation of Late Hellenistic pottery*: 157–73. Aarhus, Aarhus University Press.

Kolb, B. 1997. Swiss-Lichtenstein excavations at Az-Zantur in Petra 1996. The seventh season. *ADAJ* 41, 231–54.

Kopcke, G. 1964. Golddekorierte attische Schwarzfirniskeramik des vierten Jahrh. v.Chr. *Mitteilungen des Deutschen Archäologischen Instituts, Athenische Abteilung* 79: 22–84.

Kosmin, P.J. 2014. *The land of the Elephant Kings: space, territory, and ideology in the Seleucid empire*. Cambridge, MA: Harvard University Press.

Kouky, F. 1992. The environs of Pella: roads, fords, and occupational sites. In A. McNicoll, P.C. Edwards et al., *Pella in Jordan 2*: 199–204. Sydney: Mediterranean Archaeology Supplement 2.

Koutsoukou, A. 1997. Ceramic lamps. In A. Koutsoukou et al., *The Great Temple of Amman. The excavations*. Amman: The American Center of Oriental Research.

Koutsoukou, A., and M. Najjar 1997. Pottery. In A. Koutsoukou et al., *The Great Temple of Amman. The excavations*: 55–118. Amman: The American Center of Oriental Research.

Kraeling, C.H. 1938. *Gerasa: City of the Decapolis*. New Haven, CT: American Schools of Oriental Research.

Kuhrt, A. 1995. *The ancient Near East c. 3000–330 BC*. London: Routledge.

LaBianca, O.S. 1985. The return of the nomad: an analysis of the process of nomadization in Jordan *ADAJ* 19: 251–4.

LaBianca, O.S. 1990. *Hesban 1. Sedentarization and nomadization*. Berrien Springs, MI: Andrews University Press.

LaBianca, O., L.G. Herr et al. 1995. Madaba Plains Project: a preliminary report on the 1989 season at Tell El-'Umeiri and Hinterland. *Annual of the American Schools of Oriental Research* 52: 93–119. Boston, MA.

Lamboglia, N. 1952. Per una classificazione preliminare della ceramica campana. *Atti del I. Congesso di Studi Liguri*: 139–206. Bordighera.

Lane Fox, R. 1973: *Alexander the Great*. London: Allen Lane.

Lapp, N.L. 1964. Pottery from some Hellenistic loci at Balatah (Shechem). *BASOR* 175: 14–26.

Lapp, N.L. 1979. The Hellenistic pottery from the 1961 and 1962 excavations at 'Iraq el-Emir. *ADAJ* 23: 5–15.

Lapp, N.L. 1983. Hellenistic pottery from the Qasr and square building. In N.L. Lapp, *The excavations at Araq el-Emir, vol. I*: 63–74. *Annual of the American Schools of Oriental Research* 47. Boston, MA.

Lapp, N.L. 1985. The stratum V pottery from Balâtah (Shechem). *BASOR* 257: 19–43.

Lapp, N.L. 2008. Shechem IV. The Persian-Hellenistic pottery of Shechem/Tell Balâtah. *American Schools of Oriental Research Archeological Reports 11*. Boston, MA.

Lapp, N.L. (ed.) 2020. *The excavations of 'Iraq Al-Amir. vol. II*. Annual of the American Schools of Oriental Research, 74. Boston, MA.

Lapp, P.W. 1961. *Palestinian ceramic chronology: 200 BC–AD 70*. New Haven, CT: American Schools of Oriental Research.

Lapp, P.W., and N.L. Lapp 1958. A comparative study of a Hellenistic pottery group from Beth-Zur. *BASOR* 151: 16–27.

Laumonier, A. 1973. Bols hellénistiques à reliefs. *Bulletin de correspondence hellénique* suppl. I: 253–62. Paris: Editions de Boccard.

Laumonier, A. 1977. *La céramique hellénistique à reliefs*. Vol. I. *Ateliers 'ioniens', Exploration archéologique de Délos* XXXI. Paris.

Lejeune, S. 2009. Kafizin, portraits d'un nymphaion. *Cahiers du Centre d'Études Chypriotes* 39: 309–24.

Lemaire, A., and H. Lozachmeur 1987. Birah/Birta en Araméen. *Syria* 64: 261–6.

Lemaire, A., and H. Lozachmeur 1995. La birta en Mediterranée Orientale. *Semitica* 43–4: 75–8.

Leroux, G. 1913. *Lagynos recherches sur la céramique et l'art ornemental hellénistiques*. Paris: Journal des Savants.

Levantine Ceramics Project n.d. levantineceramics.org.

Levine, T. 2003. Pottery and small finds from subterranean complexes 21 and 70. In A. Kloner, *Maresha Excavations Final Report I. Subterranean Complexes 21, 44, 40*: 73–130. Israel Antiquities Authority Reports 17. Jerusalem.

Lichtenberger, A. 2003. Kulte und Kultur der Dekapolis: untersuchungen zu numismatischen, archäologischen und epigraphischen Zeugnissen. *Abhandlungen des Deutschen Palästina-Vereins* 29. Wiesbaden: Harrassowitz.

Lichtenberger, A. 2022. The Decapolis. In T. Kaizer (ed.), *A companion to the Hellenistic and Roman Near East*: 213–22. Hoboken, NJ: Wiley Blackwell.

Lichtenberger, A., and R. Raja 2015. New Archaeological research in the northwest quarter of Jerash and its implications for the urban development of Roman Gerasa. *AJA* 119: 483–500.

Lichtenberger, A., and R. Raja (eds) 2020. *Hellenistic and Roman Gerasa. The archaeology and history of a Decapolis city*. Turnhout, Belgium: Brepols.

Ling, R. 1998. *Ancient mosaics*. Princeton, MA: Princeton University Press.

Loeschcke, S. 1909. Keramische Funde in Haltern. *Mitteilungen der Altertumskommission für Westfalen* 5: 101–322.

Loffreda, S. 1974. *Cafarnao II. La ceramica*. Jerusalem: Franciscan Press.

Loffreda, S. 1980. Alcuni vasi ben datati della Fortezza di Macheronte. *Liber Annuus* 30: 377–402.

Loffreda, S. 1996. *La Ceramica di Macheronte e dell'Herodion (90 a.C–135 d.C.)*. Jerusalem.

Lorber, C.L. 2021. Numismatic evidence and the chronology of the Fifth Syrian War. In S. Honigman, C. Nihan and O. Lipschits (eds), *Times of transition. Judea in the Early Hellenistic period*: 31–41. University Park, PA: Penn State University Press.

Lund, J. 1998. The ceramic finewares from the Late Classical to the Late Antique period found in 1995 and 1996. In L.W. Sorensen, A. Destrooper-Georgiades et al., *Third preliminary report of the Danish archaeological excavations at Panayia Ematousa, Aradippou, Cyprus. Proceedings of the Danish Institute at Athens II*: 319–82. Athens.

Lund, J. 2004. Italian-made fine wares and cooking wares in the Eastern Mediterranean before the time of Augustus. In J. Poblome et al. (eds), *Early Italian Sigillata. The chronological framework and trade patterns*: 3–15. Leuven: Peeters.

Lund, J. 2014. Pots and politics: reflections on the circulation of pottery in the Ptolemaic and Seleukid kingdoms. In P. Guldager Bilde and M. Lawall (eds), *Pottery, peoples and places. Study and interpretation of Late Hellenistic pottery*: 297–305. Aarhus: Aarhus University Press.

Lund, J. 2015. *A study of the circulation of ceramics in Cyprus from the 3rd century BC to the 3rd century* AD. Aarhus: Aarhus University Press.

Lund, J., J. Poblome and D. Malfitana 2006. Rhosica vasa mandavi (Cicero, *Att.* 6.1.13): towards the identification of a major tableware industry of the eastern Mediterranean: Eastern Sigillata A. *Archaeologia Classica* 57: 491–507.

Lyonnet, B. 2012. Questions on the date of the Hellenistic pottery from Central Asia (Ai Khanoum, Marakanda and Koktepe). *Ancient civilizations from Scythia to Siberia* 18: 143–73.

MacAdam, H.I. 1992. The history of Philadelphia in the Classical period. In A. Northedge (ed.), *Studies on Roman and Islamic 'Amman*: 27–46. Oxford: Council for British Research.

Macalister, R.A.S. 1912. *The excavation of Gezer 1902–1905 and 1907–1909*, vols I–III. London: J. Murray.

MacDonald, B. 1988. *The Wadi el Hasa Archaeological Survey 1979–1983, West-Central Jordan*. Waterloo, Ontario: Wilfrid Laurier University Press.

MacDonald, B. 1992. *The southern Ghors and northeast Arabah archaeological survey*. Sheffield: J.R. Collis Publications.

MacDonald, B., R. Adams and P. Bienkowski (eds) 2001. *The Archaeology of Jordan*. Sheffield: Sheffield Academic Press.

Machline, H., and Y. Gadot 2017. Wading through Jerusalem's garbage: chronology, function, and formation process of the pottery assemblages of the city's Early Roman landfill. *Journal of Hellenistic Pottery and Material Culture* 2: 102–39.

Macumber, P. 1992. The geology and geomorphology of the Wadi al-Hammah–Wadi Jirm el-Moz region, north-western Jordan. In A. McNicoll, P.C. Edwards et al., *Pella in Jordan 2*: 205–14. Sydney: Mediterranean Archaeology Supplement 2.

Magen, Y. 1994. Jerusalem as a centre of the stone vessel industry during the Second Temple period. In H. Geva (ed.), *Ancient Jerusalem revealed*: 244–56. Jerusalem: Israel Exploration Society.

Magness, J. 1992. Late Roman and Byzantine pottery, preliminary report 1990. In R.L. Vann (ed.), *Caesarea Papers*: 112–53. Ann Arbor, MI: University of Michigan.

Magness, J. 1993. *Jerusalem ceramic chronology c. 200–800 CE*. Sheffield: Sheffield Academic Press.

Magness, J. 2009. The pottery from the 1995 excavations in Camp F at Masada. *BASOR* 353: 75–107.

Magness, J. 2011. *Stone and dung, oil and spit. Jewish daily life in the time of Jesus*. Grand Rapids, MI: Eerdmanns.

Magness, J. 2013. *The archaeology of the Holy Land*. Cambridge, UK: Cambridge University Press.

Magness, J. 2021. *The archaeology of Qumran and the Dead Sea scrolls*. 2nd edn. Grand Rapids, MI: Eerdmanns.

Majcherek, G., and A. Taha 2004. Roman and Byzantine layers at Umm el-Tlel: ceramics and other finds. *Syria* 81: 229–48.

Malfitana, D. 2002. Eastern terra sigillata wares in the eastern Mediterranean. Notes on an initial quantitative analysis. In F. Blondé, P. Ballet and J.-F. Salles, *Céramiques hellénistiques et romaines. Production et diffusion en Méditerranée orientale (Chypre, Égypte et côte syro-palestinienne)*: 133–57. Besançon: Université de Franche-Comté.

Malfitana, D., and G. Giuseppe Cacciaguerra 2015. Archeologia della produzione ceramica nella sicilia ellenistica e romana. Primi dati dal quartiere artigianale di Siracusa. *Herom* 4(2): 223–75.

Mandel, U. 2000. Weißgrundige Lagynoi aus Knidos. In Ε' Επιστημονική Συνάντηση για την Ελληνιστική Κεραμική. Πρακτικά: 179–88. Athens.

Mare, H.W. 1984. The 1982 season at Abila of the Decapolis. *ADAJ* 28: 39–54.

Mare, H.W. 1991. The 1988 season of excavation at Abila of the Decapolis. *ADAJ* 35: 203–20.

Mare, H.W. 1994. The 1992 season of excavation at Abila of the Decapolis. *ADAJ* 38: 359–77.

Mare, H.W., C.J. Lenzen et al. 1982. The Decapolis Survey Project: Abila, 1980 background and analytical description of Abila of the Decapolis, and the methodology used in the 1980 survey. *ADAJ* 26: 37–65.

Mare, H.W., M.J. Fuller et al. 1987. The 1986 season at Abila of the Decapolis. *ADAJ* 31: 205–19.

Margane, A., A. Subah and Z. Hajali 2010: *Delineation of groundwater protection zones for the springs in Wadi Shuayb*. Amman, Jordan: German-Jordanian Technical Cooperation.

Markoe, G.E. (ed.) 2003: *Petra rediscovered: lost city of the Nabateans*. London: Thames & Hudson.

Marquaille, C. 2008. The foreign policy of Ptolemy II. In P. McKechnie and P. Guillaume (eds), *Ptolemy II Philadelphus and his world*: 39–64. Leiden: Brill.

Martens, B. 2021. Delos and the Late Hellenistic art trade: archaeological directions. *AJA* 125: 535–70.

Mayet, F. 1975. *Les céramiques à parois fines dans la Péninsule Ibérique*. Paris: Editions de Boccard.

Mazar, A. 1990. *Archaeology of the land of the Bible 10,000–586 B.C.E.* New York: Anchor Bible Reference Library.

Mazar, A. 2006: *Excavations at Tel Beth-Shean 1989–1996*. Vol. I. *From the Late Bronze Age IIB to the Medieval Period*. Jerusalem: Israel Exploration Society.

Mazar, B. 1957. The Tobiads. *IEJ* 7: 137–45, 229–38.

Mazor, G., and W. Atrash 2017. Nysa-Scythopolis: the Hellenistic Polis. *Journal of Hellenistic Pottery and Material Culture* 2: 82–101.

McClellan, M.C. 1999. Hellenistic and Roman pottery from 'Ain Dara. In E.C. Stone and P.E. Zimansky, *The Iron Age settlement at 'Ain Dara, Syria*. BAR International Series 786: 19–22.

McGovern, P.E. 1989. The Baq'ah Valley Project 1987, Khirbet Umm ad-Dananir and al-Qesir. *ADAJ* 33: 123–36.

McKenzie, J. 1990. *The architecture of Petra*. Oxford: Oxford University Press.

McNicoll, A.W. 1992. The Hellenistic period. In A. McNicoll, P.C. Edwards et al., *Pella in Jordan 2*: 103–18. Sydney.

McNicoll, A.W. 1997. *Hellenistic fortifications from the Aegean to the Euphrates*. Oxford: Clarendon Press.

McNicoll, A.W., and J.B. Hennessy 1980. The winter session. In R. Smith, Preliminary Report on the 1979 Season of the Sydney-Wooster Joint Expedition to Pella. *ADAJ* 24: 13–40.

McNicoll, A.W., R.H. Smith et al. 1980. The 1979 Season at Pella of the Decapolis. *BASOR* 240: 63–84.

McNicoll, A.W., R.H. Smith and J.B. Hennessy 1982. *Pella in Jordan* 1. Canberra: Australian National Gallery.

McNicoll, A.W., P.C. Edwards et al. 1986. Preliminary report on the University of Sydney's seventh season of excavations at Pella (Tabaqat Fahl) in 1985. *ADAJ* 30: 155–98.

McNicoll, A.W., P.C. Edwards et al. 1992. *Pella in Jordan 2*. Sydney: Mediterranean Archaeology Supplement 2.

Meeus, A. 2014. The territorial ambitions of Ptolemy I. *Studia Hellenistica* 53: 263–306.

Mertens, J.R. 2019. Innovation in Athenian pottery: the evolution from painted to relief wares. In S. Hemingway and N. Karoglou (eds), *Art of the Hellenistic kingdoms: from Pergamon to Rome*: 148–57. New York: Metropolitan Museum of Art.

Meshorer, Y. 1982. *Ancient Jewish coinage*. New York: Amphora Books.

Meshorer, Y. 1985. *City coins of Eretz-Israel and the Decapolis in the Roman period*. Jerusalem: The Israel Museum.

Meshorer, Y. 2001. *A treasury of Jewish coins*. Jerusalem: Yad Ben-Zvi Press.

Meyboom, P.G.P. 2016. *The Nile mosaic of Palestrina: early evidence of Egyptian religion in Italy*. Leiden: Brill.

Meyers, E.M., A.T. Kraabel et al. 1976. *Ancient synagogue excavations at Khirbet Shema, Upper Galilee, Israel 1970–1972*. Durham, NC: Duke University Press.

Meyers, E.M., J.F. Strange and C.L. Meyers 1981. *Excavations at Ancient Meiron, Upper Galilee, Israel 1971–72, 1974–75, 1977*. Cambridge, MA: American Schools of Oriental Research.

Meyers, E.M. (ed.). 1997. *The Oxford encyclopedia of archaeology in the Near East*. Oxford: Oxford University Press.

Millar, F. 1987. The problem of Hellenistic Syria. In A. Kuhrt and S. Sherwin-White (eds), *Hellenism in the East*: 110–33. London: Duckworth.

Millar, F. 1993. *The Roman Near East 31 BC–AD 337*. Cambridge, MA: Harvard University Press.

Minns, E.H. 1913. *Scythians and Greeks*. Cambridge, UK: Cambridge University Press.

Mitford, T.B. 1980. *The nymphaeum of Kafizin: the inscribed pottery*. Kadmos Supplement 2. Berlin and New York: De Gruyter.

Mitsopoulos-Leon, V. 1991. *Forschungen in Ephesos IX 2/2. Die Basilika am Staatsmarkt in Ephesos Kleinfunde. 1. Teil: Keramik hellenistischer und römischer Zeit*. Vienna: Schindler.

Mlynarczyk, J. 2000. Pottery from the Hellenistic cistern at Sha'ar ha-Amakim. In Ε' Επιστημονική Συνάντηση για την ελληνιστική κεραμική: 225–35. Athens.

Mlynarczyk, J. 2002. Hellenistic fine wares at Tell Keisan. A pattern of importations. In F. Blondé et al., *Céramiques hellénistiques et romaines. Productions et diffusion en Méditerranée orientale (Chypre, Égypte et côte syro-palestinienne)*: 117–32. Besançon: Université de Franche-Comté.

Mlynarczyk, J. 2004. Between Phoenicia and Galilee: kitchen pottery from Hellenistic Deposits at Sha'ar ha-Amakim. In Στ' επιστημονική συνάντηση για την Ελληνιστική κεραμική: 631–40. Athens.

Mlynarczyk, J. 2011. Hellenistic pottery deposits at Hippos of the Dekapolis. Contribution to the study of Hellenistic ceramics production and distribution on the Sea of Galilee. In Ζ' Επιστημονική συνάντηση για την ελληνιστική κεραμική: 577–90. Athens.

Moevs, M.T.M. 1973. The Roman thin walled pottery from Cosa (1948–1954), *Memoirs of the American Academy in Rome 32*.

Montana, G., H. Mommsen et al. 2003. The petrography and chemistry of thin-walled ware from a Hellenistic-Roman site at Segesta (Sicily). *Archaeometry 45*: 375–89.

Moorey, R. 1991. *A century of biblical archaeology*. Cambridge, UK: The Lutterworth Press.

Morel, J.-P. 1981. *Céramique Campanienne: les formes*. Rome Ecole Française.

Morel, J.-P. 1986. Céramiques à vernis noir d'Italie trouvées à Délos. *Bulletin De Correspondence Hellénique* 110: 461–93.

Morel, J.-P. 2014. Les campaniennes A et B, deux aspects d'une 'globalisation'. In P. Guldager and M. Lawall, *Pottery, peoples and places. Study and interpretation of Late Hellenistic pottery*: 323–35. Aarhus: Aarhus University Press.

Mueller, K. 2006. Settlements of the Ptolemies. City foundations and new settlement in the Hellenistic world. *Studia Hellenistica* 43. Leuven: Peeters.

Mullins, R.A., and E. Yannai 2019. Late Bronze Age I–II. In S. Gitin (ed.), *The ancient pottery of Israel and its neighbours*, vol. 3: 151–257. Jerusalem: Israel Exploration Society.

Musti, D. 1984. Syria and the East. In *Cambridge ancient history* VII.i, 2nd edn: 175–220. Cambridge, UK: Cambridge University Press.

Negev, A. 1974. *The Nabatean potter's workshop at Oboda*. Bonn: Habelt.

Negev, A. 1986. *The Late Hellenistic and Early Roman pottery of Nabatean Oboda*. Qedem 22. Jerusalem.

Netzer, E. 2000. Tyros, the 'floating palace'. In S.G. Wilson and M. Desjardins (eds), *Text and artifact in the religions of Mediterranean antiquity*: 340–53. Waterloo, Ontario: Wilfrid Laurier University Press.

Netzer, E., and E.M. Meyers 1977. Preliminary report on the joint Jericho Excavation Project. *BASOR* 228: 15–27.

Neuru, L.L. 1991. Megarian relief ware. In J.W. Hayes, *Paphos* III. *The Hellenistic and Roman pottery*: 13–17. Nicosia: Department of Antiquities, Cyprus.

Niemeier, W.-D. 1995. Greek mercenaries in Phoenicia: new evidence from Tel Kabri. *AJA* 99: 304–05.

Niemeier, W.-D. 2001. Archaic Greeks in the Levant: textual and archaeological evidence. *BASOR* 322: 11–32.

Niemeier, W.-D. 2002. Greek mercenaries at Tel Kabri and other sites in the Levant. *Tel Aviv* 29: 328–31.

Nodet, E. 1980. Niveaux perses. In J. Briend and J-B. Humbert (eds), *Tell Keisan (1971–1976)*: 117–29. Fribourg: University of Fribourg.

Nunn, A. 2014. Attic pottery imports and their impact on 'identity discourses': a reassessment. In C. Frevel K. Pyschny and I. Cornelius, *A 'religious revolution' in Yehûd? The material culture of the Persian period as a test case*: 391–429. Orbis Biblicus et Orientalis. Fribourg, Switzerland: Academic Press Fribourg.

Oates, D., and J. Oates 1958. Nimrud 1957: the Hellenistic settlement. *Iraq* 20: 114–57.

Oren, E.D., and U. Rappaport 1984. The necropolis of Maresha-Beth Govrin. *IEJ* 34: 14–153.

Orton, C., and M. Hughes 2013: *Pottery in archaeology*. Cambridge, UK: Cambridge University Press.

Osband, M., and M. Eisenberg 2018. Summary of the pottery finds. In M. Eisenberg, *Hippos-Sussita of the Decapolis. The first twelve seasons of excavations 2000–2011*, vol. II: 210–75. Haifa: University of Haifa.

Palumbo, G., M. Munzi et al. 1996. The Wadi az-Zarqa/Wadi ad-Dulayl excavations and survey project: report on the October–November 1993 fieldwork season. *ADAJ* 40: 375–428.

Papaioannou, M. 2010. East meets West: the pottery evidence from Abdera. *Bollettino di Archeologia on Line, Volume Speciale C/C9/5*: 53–65.

Parigi, C. 2019. *Atene e il sacco di Silla evidenze archeologiche e topografiche fra l'86 e il 27 a.C.* Kölner Schriften zur Archäologie, Band 2. Wiesbaden, Germany: Reichert.

Parker, S.T. 1975. The Decapolis reviewed. *Journal of Biblical Literature* 94: 437–41.

Parker, S.T. (ed.) 1987. *The Roman frontier in Central Jordan: interim report on the Limes Arabicus Project, 1980–1985*. British Archaeological Reports International Series. Oxford.

Parker, S.T. 2022. The Roman period. In J. Haron and D.R. Clark (eds), *The pottery of Jordan. A manual*: 78–83. Alexandria, VA, and Amman, Jordan: American Center of Research.

Patrich, J., and Arubas, B. 1989. A juglet containing balsam(?) oil from a cave near Qumran. *IEJ* 39: 43–59.

Pedley, J.G. 2002. *Greek art and archaeology*. 3rd edn. London: Laurence King Publishing.

Peleg, M. 1989. Domestic pottery. In V. Tzaferis, *Excavations at Capernaum I, 1978–1982*: 31–113. Winona Lake, IN: Eisenbrauns.

Peleg-Barkat, O. 2013. The introduction of Classical architectural decoration into cities of the Decapolis: Hippos, Gadara, Gerasa and Scythopolis. *ARAM* 23: 425–45.

Peleg-Barkat, O. 2017. Classical archaeology in the Holy Land: the case of Classical architectural decor in the Hellenistic period. In A. Lichtenberger and R. Raja (eds), *The diversity of Classical archaeology*: 141–60. Turnhout, Belgium: Brepols.

Pemberton, E.G. 1985. Ten Hellenistic graves in ancient Corinth. *Hesperia* 54: 271–307.

Pestmann, P.W. 1981. *A guide to the Zenon papyri*. Leiden: Brill.

Philip, G., and D. Baird 1993. Preliminary report on the second (1992) season of excavations at Tell esh-Shuna North. *Levant* 25: 13–36.

Pollitt, J.J. 1986. *Art in the Hellenistic age*. Cambridge, UK: Cambridge University Press.

Pritchard, J.B. 1958. *The excavation at Herodian Jericho, 1951, Annual of the American Schools of Oriental Research 32–3*. New Haven, CT.

Pritchard, J.B. 1985. *Tell es-Sa'idiyeh: excavations on the tell, 1964–1966*. Philadelphia, PA: University of Pennsylvania Museum.

Pucci, G. 1985. Terra Sigillata Italica. In *Enciclopedia dell'arte antica. Atlante delle Forme Ceramiche* II: 359–405. Rome: Istituto dell'Enciclopedia Italiana.

Queyrel, F. 1991. Le décor sculpté. In E. Will and F. Larché, *'Iraq al Amir. Le chateau du Tobiade Hyrcan*: 209–51. Paris: Librairie Orientaliste Paul Geuther.

Rahmani, L.Y. 1967. Jason's tomb. *IEJ* 17: 61–100.

Rahmani, L.Y. 1984. Hellenistic brazier fragments from Israel. *IEJ* 34: 224–31.

Rappaport, U. 1984. Numismatics. In W.D. Davies and L. Finkelstein, *Cambridge History of Judaism*, vol. I: 25–59. Cambridge, UK: Cambridge University Press.

Rapuano, Y. 1999. The Hellenistic through Early Islamic pottery from Ras Abu Ma'aruf (Pisgat Ze'ev East A). *Atiqot* 38: 171–203.

Rasson-Seigne, A.-M., and Seigne, J. 2020a. La céramique importée á Jerash pendant l'époque romaine (fin Ier siècle avant J.-C. – IIIe siècle après J.-C.): l'apport des fouilles du sanctuaire de Zeus. In A. Lichtenberger and R. Raja (eds), *Hellenistic and Roman Gerasa. The archaeology and history of a Decapolis city*: 129–44. Turnhout, Belgium: Brepols.

Rasson-Seigne, A.-M., and Seigne, J. 2020b. Les productions de céramiques locales de Jerash au début de la période romaine (Ier siècle avant J.-C. – IIe siècle après J.-C.): influences et diffusion. In A. Lichtenberger and R. Raja (eds), *Hellenistic and Roman Gerasa. The archaeology and history of a Decapolis city*, 119–28. Turnhout, Belgium: Brepols.

Regev, D. 2004. The Phoenician transport amphora. In J. Eiring and J. Lund, *Transport amphorae and trade in the eastern Mediterranean. Acts of the International Colloquium at the Danish Institute at Athens, September 26–29, 2002*: 337–52. Monographs of the Danish Institute at Athens 5. Aarhus: Aarhus University Press.

Regev, D. 2007. A new approach on the origin of Eastern Sigillata A. *Topoi. Orient-Occident* Suppl. 8: 189–200.

Regev, D. 2009/10. 'Akko–Ptolemais, a Phoenician city: the Hellenistic pottery. *Mediterranean Archaeology* 22/23: 115–91.

Reinders, H. R. 1988. *New Halos: a Hellenistic town in Thessalía, Greece*. Utrecht: HES Publishers.

Reisner, G.A., C.S. Fisher and D.G. Lyon 1924. *Harvard excavations at Samaria 1908–1910*. Cambridge, MA: Harvard University Press.

Robertson, M. 1975. *A history of Greek art*. Cambridge, UK: Cambridge University Press.

Robertson, M. 1981. *A shorter history of Greek art*. Cambridge, UK: Cambridge University Press.

Robinson, E. 1856. *Later biblical researches in Palestine, and in the adjacent regions*. Boston, MA: Crocker and Brewster.

Rogers, D.K. 2021. Sulla and the siege of Athens: Reconsidering crisis, survival, and recovery in the first century B.C. In S. Fachard and E.M. Harris (eds), *The destruction of cities in the ancient Greek world: integrating the archaeological and literary evidence*: 288–318. Cambridge, UK: Cambridge University Press.

Rogl, C. 1996. Hellenistische Reliefbecher aus der Stadt. *Jahreshefte des Österreichischen Archäologischen Institutes in Wien* 65: 114–58.

Rogl, C. 2014. Mouldmade relief bowls from Ephesos – the current state of research. In P. Guldager Bilde and M.L. Lawall (eds), *Pottery, peoples, and places. Study and interpretation of Late Hellenistic pottery*: 113–39. Aarhus: Aarhus University Press.

Roller, D.W. 1980. Hellenistic pottery from Caesarea Maritima: a preliminary study. *BASOR* 238: 35–42.

Romano, I.B. 1994. A Hellenistic deposit from Corinth. Evidence for Interim Period activity (146–44 BC). *Hesperia* 63: 60–104.

Romm, J. 2022: *Demetrius: sacker of cities*. New Haven, CT, and London: Yale University Press.

Rosenberg, S.G. 2006. *Airaq al-Amir. The architecture of the Tobiads*. British Archaeological Reports International Series 1544. Oxford.

Rosenberg, S.G. 2012. 'Castle of the slave' – mystery solved. *Biblical Archaeology Review* 38 (3): 45–53.

Rosenthal, R. 1978. The Hellenistic pottery. In E. Stern, *Excavations at Tel Mevorakh (1973–1976). Part one: from the Iron Age to the Roman period*: 23–5. Qedem 9. Jerusalem.

Rosenthal, R., and R. Sivan 1978. *Ancient lamps in the Schloessinger collection*. Qedem 8. Jerusalem.

Rosenthal-Heginbottom, R. 1995. Imported Hellenistic and Roman pottery. in E. Stern, *Excavations at Dor, final report*, vol. IB, *Areas A and C: the finds*: 183–288. Qedem 2. Jerusalem.

Rosenthal-Heginbottom, R. 2003. Hellenistic and Early Roman fine ware and lamps from Area A. In H. Geva, *Jewish Quarter excavations in the Old City of Jerusalem conducted by Nahman Avigad, 1969–1982*, vol. II, *The finds from Areas A, W and X-2. Final report*: 192–223. Jerusalem: Israel Exploration Society.

Rosenthal-Heginbottom, R. 2009. The sacred number seven – reflections on the Hellenistic seven-nozzled lamps from Tel Dor. *Eretz-Israel. Archaeological, historical and geographical studies*, vol. 29: 194–208. Jerusalem.

Rosenthal-Heginbottom, R. 2014. Imported Hellenistic and Early Roman pottery – an overview of the finds from the Jewish Quarter excavations. In H. Geva, *Jewish Quarter excavations in the Old City of Jerusalem conducted by Nahman Avigad 1969–1982*, vol. VI, *Areas J, N, Z and other studies. Final report*: 377–413. Jerusalem: Israel Exploration Society.

Rosenthal-Heginbottom, R. 2015a. Persian Period imports. In S. Gitin (ed.), *The ancient pottery of Israel and its neighbors from the Iron Age through the Hellenistic Period*, vol. 2: 619–28. Jerusalem: Israel Exploration Society.

Rosenthal-Heginbottom, R. 2015b. Hellenistic Period imported pottery. In S. Gitin (ed.), *The ancient pottery of Israel and its neighbors from the Iron Age through the Hellenistic Period*, vol. 2: 673–708. Jerusalem: Israel Exploration Society.

Rosenthal-Heginbottom, R. 2016a. Innovation and stagnation in the Judaean lamp production in the late Second Temple Period (150 BC–70 AD). In S. Japp and P. Kögler (eds), *Traditions and innovations. tracking the development of pottery from the Late Classical to the Early Imperial periods. Proceedings of the 1st Conference of IARPotHP Berlin, November 2013, 7th–10th*: 429–42. Vienna: Phoibos Verlag.

Rosenthal-Heginbottom, R. 2016b. Moldmade bowls from Straton's Tower (Caesarea Maritima). *Journal of Hellenistic Pottery and Material Culture* 1: 112–68.

Rosenthal-Heginbottom, R. 2019. Imported pottery and selected locally made vessels. in I. Stern, *Excavations at Maresha subterranean complex 169: final report. seasons 2000–2016*: 41–87. Jerusalem: Nelson Glueck School of Biblical Archaeology.

Rosenthal-Heginbottom, R. 2020/2021. Contextualizing the star-shaped lamps in the Levant. *Journal of Hellenistic Pottery and Material Culture* 5: 55–89.

Rostovtzeff, M.A. 1922. *A large estate in Egypt in the third century BC*. Madison, WI: Hardpress.

Roth, R. 2013. Before Sigillata: black-gloss pottery and its cultural dimensions. In J. DeRose Evans (ed.), *A companion to the archaeology of the Roman Republic*: 81–96. Chichester, UK: Blackwell Publishing.

Rotroff, S.I. 1982. *The Athenian Agora XXII. Hellenistic Pottery. Athenian and imported moldmade bowls*. Princeton, NJ: American School of Classical Studies at Athens.

Rotroff, S.I. 1983. Three cistern systems on the Kolonos Agoraios. *Hesperia* 52: 257–97.

Rotroff, S.I. 1984. The origins and chronology of Hellenistic gray unguentaria. *AJA* 88: 258.

Rotroff, S.I. 1991. Attic West Slope vase painting. *Hesperia* 60: 59–102.

Rotroff, S.I. 1997a. Coins and stratigraphy. In K.A. Sheedy and Ch. Papageorgiadou-Banis (eds), *Numismatic archaeology. Archaeological numismatics*: 8–16. Oxford: Oxbow.

Rotroff, S.I. 1997b: *The Athenian Agora* XXIX.1–2. *Hellenistic Pottery. Athenian and imported wheelmade table ware and related material*. Princeton, NJ: American School of Classical Studies at Athens.

Rotroff, S.I. 1997c. From Greek to Roman in Athenian ceramics. In M.C. Hoff and S.I. Rotroff (eds), *The Romanization of Athens*: 97–116. Oxford: Oxbow.

Rotroff, S.I. 2002. West Slope in the East. In F. Blondé et al., *Céramiques hellénistiques et romaines. Productions et diffusion en Méditerranée orientale (Chypre, Égypte et côte syro-palestinienne)*: 97–115. Lyon: Maison de l'Orient et de la Méditerranée Jean Pouilloux.

Rotroff, S.I. 2003. Relief wares. In S.I. Rotroff and A. Oliver, Jr, *The Hellenistic pottery from Sardis: the finds through 1994*: 91–178. Cambridge, MA: Harvard University Press.

Rotroff, S.I. 2005. Four centuries of Athenian pottery. In V. Stolba and L. Hannestad (eds), *Chronologies of the Black Sea area in the period c. 400–100 BC*: 11–30. Aarhus: Aarhus University Press.

Rotroff, S.I. 2006a. The introduction of the moldmade bowl revisited. Tracking a Hellenistic innovation. *Hesperia* 75: 357–78.

Rotroff, S.I. 2006b. *The Athenian Agora XXXIII. Hellenistic Pottery. The Plain Wares*. Princeton, NJ: American School of Classical Studies at Athens.

Rotroff, S.I., M. Daszkiewicz et al. 2018. Eastern Sigillata at Sardis: evidence for a local industry. *BASOR* 380: 133–204.

Sabar, R. 2022. Ḥorvat Tefen: a Hasmonean fortress in the hinterland of ʿAkko-Ptolemais. *BASOR* 387: 55–85.

Sackett, L.H., and K. Branigan 1992. *Knossos: from Greek city to Roman colony: excavations at the unexplored mansion II*. British School of Archaeology at Athens, supp. vol. 21. Athens.

Salles, J.-F. 1990. Questioning the BI–ware. In *Failaka, fouilles françaises 1986–1988. Sous la direction de Yves Calvet et Jacqueline Gachet*: 303–34. Lyon, France: Maison de l'Orient et de la Méditerranée Jean Pouilloux.

Samiʿ, A. (Abu Dayyah), A. Dayyah et al. 1991. Archaeological survey of Greater Amman, phase 1: final report. *ADAJ* 35: 361–95.

Sandhaus, D. 2013. The Hellenistic pottery. In D. Ben-Ami, *Excavations in the Tyropoeon Valley (Givʿati parking lot) I*: 83–108. Israel Antiquities Authority Reports 52. Jerusalem.

Sandhaus, D. 2020. Continuity, innovation and transformation in cooking habits. The Central and southern Shephelah between the late fourth and the first centuries BCE. In P. Altmann, A. Angelini and A. Spiciarich (eds), *Food taboos and biblical prohibitions: reassessing archaeological and literary perspectives*: 107–120. Tübingen: Mohr Siebeck.

Sartre, M. 2005: *The Middle East under Rome*. Cambridge, MA: Harvard University Press.

Sauer, J.A. 1979. Parthian glazed amphora found near Rajib. *Biblical Archaeologist* 42: 134.

Schäfer, J. 1968. *Hellenistische Keramik aus Pergamon*. Berlin: De Gruyter.

Scheibler, I. 1976. *Kerameikos: Ergebnisse der Ausgrabungen. XI. Griechische Lampen*. Berlin.

Schmid, S.G. 1997. Nabatean fine ware pottery and the destructions of Petra in the late first and early second century AD. *SHAJ* 6: 413–20.

Schmid, S.G. 2008. The Hellenistic Period and the Nabateans. In R.B. Adams (ed.), *Jordan. An archaeological reader*: 353–411. London: Equinox.

Schneider, Ch. 1996. Die Importkeramik. in A. Bignasca et al., *Petra. Ez-Zantur* I: 129–49. Mainz: Philipp von Zabern.

Schneider, G. 1995. Roman red and black slipped pottery from NE-Syria and Jordan. First results of chemical analysis. In H. Meyza and J. Mlynarczyk (eds), *Hellenistic and Roman pottery in the east Mediterranean – advances in scientific studies. Acts of the II Nieborów pottery workshop*: 415–22. Warsaw: Polish Academy of Sciences.

Schneider, G. 2000. Chemical and mineralogical studies of Late Hellenistic to Byzantine pottery production in the eastern Mediterranean. *Rei Cretariae Romanae Fautorum Acta* 36: 525–36.

Schumacher, G. 1888. *Pella of the Decapolis*. London: Palestine Exploration Fund.

Schürer, E. 1973–87: *History of the Jewish people in the age of Jesus Christ*. Vols I–III. London: Bloomsbury (G. Vermes et al. revised edn.)

Schwartz, D.R. 2011. Yannai and Pella, Josephus and circumcision. *Dead Sea Discoveries* 18: 339–59.

Segal, A. 1997. *From function to monument. Urban landscapes of Roman Palestine, Syria and Provincia Arabia*. Oxford: Oxbow.

Segal, A., J. Mlynarczyk et al. 2003. *Hippos-Sussita, fourth season of excavation (June–July 2003)*. Haifa: University of Haifa.

Segal, A., J. Mlynarczyk et al. 2004: *Hippos-Sussita, fifth season of excavation (September–October 2004) and summary of all five seasons (2000–2004)*. Haifa: University of Haifa.

Seigne, J. 1997. Habitat hellénistique et romain de Gerasa. In C. Castel, M. Al-Maqdissi and F. Villeneuve et al. (eds), *Les maisons dans la Syrie antique du IIIe millénaire aux débuts de l'islam. Pratiques et representations de l'espace domestique*: 73–82. Beirut: Institut français du Proche-Orient (IFPO).

Seigne, J. 2002. Gerasa-Jerasch–Stadt der 1000 Säulen. In A. Hoffman and S. Kerner (eds), *Gadara–Gerasa und die Dekapolis*: 6–22. Mainz: Philipp von Zabern.

Şenol, G., A.K. Şenol and E. Doğer 2004. Amphora production in the Rhodian Peraea in the Hellenistic Period. In J. Eiring and J. Lund (eds), *Transport amphorae and trade in the eastern Mediterranean. Acts of the International Colloquium at the Danish Institute at Athens, September 26–29, 2002*: 353–59. Monographs of the Danish Institute at Athens 5. Aarhus: Aarhus University Press.

Seyrig, H. 1965. Antiquités Syriennes. *Syria* 42: 25–34.

Shachar, I. 2004. The historical and numismatic significance of Alexander Jannaeus's later coinage as found in archaeological excavations. *Palestine Exploration Quarterly* 136: 5–33.

Sheedy, K. 2001. Hellenistic coins. In K. Sheedy, R. Carson and A. Walmsley, *Pella in Jordan 1979–1990. The coins*: 15–25. Sydney: Adapa Monographs.

Sheedy, K., R. Carson and A. Walmsley, *Pella in Jordan 1979–1990. The coins*. Sydney: Adapa Monographs.

Sherman, M., Z. Weiss et al. 2020. Chalkstone vessels from Sepphoris: Galilean production in Roman times. *BASOR* 383: 79–95.

Sherwin-White, S., and A. Kuhrt 1993. *From Samarkhand to Sardis*. Los Angeles: University of California Press.

Shiyab, A., et al. 2017. Discovery of Hellenistic temple at Umm Qeis site Gadara in northern Jordan: first results. *Mediterranean Archaeology and Archaeometry* 17: 137–48.

Silva, R., and J. Bouzek 1985. Mantai – a second Arikamedu? *Antiquity* 49: 46–7.

Singer, K. 1993. Pottery of the Early Roman Period from Betar. *Tel Aviv* 20: 98–103.

Sjöquist, E. 1960. Morgantina: Hellenistic medicine bottles. *AJA* 64: 78–83.

Slane, K.W. 1987. Italian Sigillata imported to Corinth. *Rei Cretariae Romanae Fautorum Acta* 25/26: 189–205.

Slane, K.W. 1997. The fine wares. In S. Herbert (ed.), *Tel Anafa* II,i. *The Hellenistic and Roman Pottery*: 247–405. Ann Arbor, MI: Journal of Roman Archaeology.

Slane, K.W. 2004. Corinth: Italian sigillata and other Italian imports to the early colony. In J. Poblome et al. (eds), *Early Italian Sigillata*: 31–42. Leuven: Peeters.

Slane, K.W., J.M Elam, et al. 1993. Compositional analysis (NAA) of Eastern Sigillata A and other wares from Tel Anafa. *AJA* 97(2): 325–6.

Smetana-Scherrer, R. 1982. Spätklassische und hellenistische Keramik. In H. Walter (ed.), *Alt-Ägina* II.1: 56–91. Mainz: Phillipp von Zahern.

Smith, R.H. 1961. The 'Herodian' lamp of Palestine: types and dates. *Berytus* 14(1): 53–65.

Smith, R.H. 1966. The household lamps of Palestine in New Testament times. *Biblical Archaeologist* 29: 2–27.

Smith, R.H. 1973: *Pella of the Decapolis. Vol. 1: The 1967 season of the College of Wooster Expedition to Pella*. Ohio: College of Wooster.

Smith, R.H. 1981. A preliminary report on a second season of excavation at Pella, Jordan. *ADAJ* 25: 311–26.

Smith, R.H. 1990. The southern Levant in the Hellenistic Period. *Levant* 22: 123–30.

Smith, R.H. 1992. 'Bloom of youth': a labelled Syro-Palestinian unguent jar. *Journal of Hellenic Studies* 112: 163–17.

Smith, R.H., and L.P. Day 1989. *Pella of the Decapolis: Vol. 2*. Ohio: College of Wooster.

Smith, R.H., and A.W. McNicoll 1992. The Roman Period. In A. McNicoll, P.C. Edwards et al., *Pella in Jordan 2*: 119–44, Sydney.

Smith, R.H., A.W. McNicoll et al. 1980. Preliminary report on the 1979 season of the Sydney-Wooster joint expedition to Pella. *ADAJ* 24: 13–40.

Smith, R.H., A.W. McNicoll et al. 1981. The 1980 season at Pella of the Decapolis. *BASOR* 243: 1–30.

Smith, R.H., A.W. McNicoll et al. 1982. The 1981 season at Pella of the Decapolis. *BASOR* 249: 45–78.

Smith, R.R.R. 1993. The Hellenistic Period. In J. Boardman (ed.), *The Oxford history of Classical art*: 151–216. Oxford: Oxford University Press.

Smith, R.W. 2011. Walls of the Decapolis. *ARAM* 23: 489–507.

Sparkes, B.A., and L. Talcott 1970. *The Athenian Agora XII. Black and Plain Pottery of the 6th, 5th, and 4th Centuries BC*. Princeton, NJ: American School of Classical Studies at Athens.

Spijkerman, A. 1978. *The coins of the Decapolis and Provincia Arabia*. Jerusalem: Studium Biblicum Franciscanum.

Stern, E. 1982. *Material culture of the land of the Bible in the Persian Period 538–332 BC.* Warminster, UK: Aris & Phillips.

Stern, E. 1989. The beginning of the Greek settlement in Palestine in the light of the excavations at Tel Dor. In S. Gitin and W. Dever (eds), *Recent excavations in Israel: studies in Iron Age archaeology*: 107–24. Warminster, UK: Aris and Phillips.

Stern, E. 1995a. Between Persia and Greece: trade, administration and warfare in the Persian and Hellenistic periods (539–63 BCE). In T.E. Levy (ed.), *The archaeology of society in the Holy Land*: 432–45. Leicester, UK: Leicester University Press.

Stern, E. 1995b. Introduction. In E. Stern, *Excavations at Dor, final report,* vol. IA. *Areas A and C: Introduction and Stratigraphy*: 1–12. Qedem 1. Jerusalem.

Stern, E. 1995c. Local pottery of the Persian Period. In E. Stern, *Excavations at Dor, final report,* vol. IB. *Areas A and C: The finds*: 51–92. Qedem 2. Jerusalem.

Stern, E. (ed.). 1993–2008. *The new encyclopedia of archaeological excavations in the Holy Land*, vol. 1–5. Jerusalem: Israel Exploration Society.

Stern, I. 2019. The local ceramic assemblage. In I. Stern, *Excavations at Maresha subterranean complex 169: final report. Seasons 2000–2016*: 13–40. Jerusalem: Nelson Glueck School of Biblical Archaeology.

Stone, S.C. 2014. *Morgantina studies.* vol. VI. *The Hellenistic and Roman fine pottery.* Princeton, NJ: Princeton University Press.

Strange, J.F. 1975. Late Hellenistic and Herodian ossuary tombs at French Hill, Jerusalem. *BASOR* 219: 39–67.

Strootman, R. 2020. Hellenism and Persianism in Iran: culture and empire after Alexander the Great. *Dabir* 7: 201–27.

Strootman, R. 2021. The Seleukid empire. In R. Mairs (ed.), *The Graeco-Bactrian and Indo-Greek world*: 11–37. London: Routledge.

Tal, O. 1999. The Persian Period. In I. Roll and O. Tal (eds), *Apollonia-Arsuf. Final report of the excavations,* vol. I, *The Persian and Hellenistic periods*: 83–222. Tel Aviv: Tel Aviv University.

Tal, O., and N. Reshef 2017. Hellenistic stratigraphy and architecture. In R. Greenberg, O. Tal and T. Da'adli, *Bet Yerah*, vol. III, *Hellenistic Philoteria and Islamic al-Sinnabra*: 13–58. Israel Antiquities Authority Reports 61. Jerusalem.

Tchekhanovets, Y. 2013. The Early Roman pottery. In D. Ben-Ami, *Excavations in the Tyropoeon Valley (Giv'ati parking lot)* I: 109–49. Israel Antiquities Authority Reports 52. Jerusalem.

Tcherikover, V. 1937. Palestine under the Ptolemies. *Mizraim* 4–5: 9–90.

Tcherikover, V. 1959. *Hellenistic civilization and the Jews,* trs. D. Applebaum. New York: Jewish Publication Society.

Tcherikover, V., and A. Fuks 1957: *Corpus Papyorum Judaicarum*, vol. 1. Cambridge, MA: Harvard University Press.

Thompson, H.A. 1934. Two centuries of Hellenistic pottery. *Hesperia* 3: 311–476.

Tidmarsh, J.C. 1989. Pella. The Hellenistic and Roman Periods. In D. Homès-Fredericq and J.B. Hennessy (eds), *Archaeology of Jordan,* II.2: 426–38. Leuven: Peeters.

Tidmarsh, J. C. 1990. Excavations in Area XXIII (The Hellenistic Period). In P. Edwards, S.J. Bourke et al., Preliminary report on the University of Sydney's tenth season of excavations at Pella (Tabaqat Fahl) in 1988. *ADAJ* 34: 71–6.

Tidmarsh, J.C. 1996. The Hellenistic/Early Roman lccupation. In P. Watson and J. Tidmarsh, Pella/Tall al-Husn excavations 1993. The University of Sydney – 15th season. *ADAJ* 40: 305–13.

Tidmarsh, J.C. 2000. *The Hellenistic and Early Roman pottery from Pella in Jordan.* PhD thesis, University of Sydney.

Tidmarsh, J.C. 2001. The problem of Early Hellenistic Jordan. In A. Walmsley (ed.), *Australians in Jordan: Fifty years of Middle Eastern archaeology*: 191–205. Sydney: University of Sydney.

Tidmarsh, J.C. 2004. How Hellenized was Pella in Jordan in the Hellenistic Period? *SHAJ* 8: 459–68.

Tidmarsh, J.C. 2011. The imported fine wares at Jebel Khalid. In H. Jackson and J.C. Tidmarsh, *Jebel Khalid on the Euphrates*, vol. 3, *The pottery*: 279–429. Sydney: Meditarch.

Tidmarsh, J.C. 2016. The fine wares. In G. Clarke, H. Jackson et al., *Jebel Khalid on the Euphrates*, vol. 5, *Report on excavations 2000–2010*: 213–58. Sydney: Meditarch.

Toll, N.P. 1943. *The excavations at Dura-Europos.* Final report IV. Part 1. Fascicle 1. *The green glazed pottery.* New Haven, CT: Yale University Press.

Townsend, R.F. 1995. *The Athenian Agora XXVII. The East Side of the Agora. The remains beneath the Stoa of Attalos.* Princeton, NJ: American School of Classical Studies at Athens.

Treister, M.Y. 2012. Silver phalerae with a depiction of Bellerophon and the chimaira from a Sarmatian burial in Volodarka (Western Kazakhkstan). A reappraisal of the question of the so-called Graeco-Bactrian Style in Hellenistic toreutics. *Ancient Civilizations from Scythia to Siberia* 18: 51–109.

Tsafrir, Y. 2011. The Decapolis again – further notes on the meaning of the term. *ARAM* 23: 1–10.

Tsafrir, Y., and G. Foerster 1986–7. Nysa-Scythopolis – a new inscription and the titles of the city on its coins. *Israel Numismatic Journal* 9: 53–8.

Tsetskhladze, G. (ed.) 2006. *Greek colonisation. An account of Greek colonies and other settlements overseas.* Mnemosyne Supplements vol: 193/1. Leiden: Brill.

Tsuf, O. 2018. The pottery. In O. Tsuf, *Ancient Jaffa from the Persian to the Byzantine Period. Kaplan excavations (1955–1981).* Studien zu Geschichte, Kultur und Religion Ägyptens und des Alten Testaments Band 89: 95–416. Munster: Zaphon.

Tubb, J.N., and R.L. Chapman 1990. *Archaeology and the Bible.* London: British Museum Press.

Tuplin, C. 1996. *Achaemenid Studies.* Stuttgart: Franz Steiner Verlag.

Turner, E. 1984. Ptolemaic Egypt. In F.W. Walbank, A.E. Astin et al. (eds), *The Hellenistic world. Cambridge ancient history* VII.i: 118–74. Cambridge, UK: Cambridge University Press.

Tushingham, A.D. 1985: *Excavations in Jerusalem 1961–1967.* Toronto: Royal Ontario Museum.

Uscatescu, A. 2021. Pottery oil lamps from the northwest quarter of Jerash. In A. Lichtenberger and R. Raja (eds), *Glass, lamps, and Jerash bowls. Final publications from the Danish-German Jerash Northwest Quarter Project III,* 53–226. Turnhout, Belgium: Brepols.

Uscatescu, A., and M. Martín-Bueno 1997. The *Macellum* of Gerasa (Jerash, Jordan): from a market place to an industrial area. *BASOR* 307: 67–88.

Valtz, E. 1991. New observations on the Hellenistic pottery from Seleucia-on-the-Tigris. In K. Schippmann, A. Herling and J.-F. Salles, *Golf-Archäologie*: 45–56. Buch am Erlbach: Marie L. Leidorf.

Valtz, E. 1993. Pottery and exchanges: imports and local production at Seleucia-Tigris. In A. Invernizzi and J-F Salles (eds), *Arabia Antiqua: Hellenistic centres around Arabia,* Serie Orientale Roma, 167–82. Rome: Istituto italiano per il Medio ed Estremo Oriente.

Vanderhoeven, M. 1989. *Fouilles d'Apamée de Syrie, IX.1. Les Terres Sigillées (1966–1972).* Brussels: belge de recherches archéologiques à Apamée de Syrie.

Vanderpool, E., J.R. McCredie and A. Steinberg 1962. Koroni: a Ptolemaic Camp on the east coast of Attica. *Hesperia* 31: 26–61.

Vanderpool, E., J.R. McCredie and A. Steinberg 1964. Koroni: the date of the camp and the pottery. *Hesperia* 33: 69–75.

de Vaux, R. 1954. Fouilles au Khirbet Qumrân. *Revue Biblique* 61: 206–36.

de Vaux, R. 1959. Fouilles de Feshka. *Revue Biblique* 66: 225–55.

Venit, M.S. 2002. *The monumental tombs of ancient Alexandria: the theater of the dead.* Cambridge, UK: Cambridge University Press.

Vessberg, O. and A. Westholm 1956. *The Swedish Cyprus Expedition,* vol. IV.3. *The Hellenistic and Roman Periods in Cyprus.* Stockholm: The Swedish Cyprus Expedition.

Vibert-Guige, Cl. 2016. Wall painting and stucco in Jordan: from miniature to megalography. *SHAJ* 12: 329–47.

Vibert-Guige, Cl. 2018. Les peintres de l'Antiquité en Jordanie, des royaumes d'époque hellénistique à l'empire romain. In Y. Dubois and U. Niffeler (eds), *Pictores per provincias II – status quaestionis. Actes du 13e Colloque de l'Association Internationale pur la Peinture Murale Antique (AIPMA), Lausanne 12–16 septembre 2016*: 121–34. Basel, Switzerland.

Vibert-Guige, Cl., and A. Barbet 1982. Tombeaux peints du nord de la Jordanie a l'Epoque Romaine. *ADAJ* 26: 67–83.

Vickers, M., and D. Gill 1994. *Artful crafts: ancient Greek silverware and pottery.* Oxford: Clarendon Press.

Vieweger, D. 2003. Der Tell Zera'a im Wadi el-'Arab: die Region südlich von Gadara. *Das Altertum* 48(3): 191–216.

Villing, A., and E.G. Pemberton 2010. Mortaria from ancient Corinth: form and function. *Hesperia* 79: 555–638.

Vitto, F. 1983–84. A look into the workshop of a Late Roman Galilean potter. *Bulletin of the Anglo-Israel Archaeological Society* 3: 19–22.

Vogeikoff, N. 1993. Italian black-glazed pottery in Hellenistic Athens. *AJA* 97: 340.

Vörös, G. 2013: *Machaerus I. History, archaeology and architecture of the fortified Herodian royal palace and city overlooking the Dead Sea in Transjordan. Final report of the excavations and surveys 1807–2012.* Collectio Maior 53. Jerusalem: Studium Biblicum Franciscanum.

Vörös, G. 2016. Bathing and immersing in Machaerus: the Herodian royal bathhouse and the four ritual purification baths (miqva'oth). *Liber Annuus* 66: 321–49.

Vörös, G. 2017. Machaerus. A palace-fortress with multiple miqva'ot. *Biblical Archaeological Review* 43: 30–9.

Vörös, G. 2018. Machaerus Project: preliminary report on the 2016–2017 archaeological excavation seasons that led to the discovery of the lost northern wing in the Herodian royal palace. *ADAJ* 59: 435–54.

Vörös, G. 2019a: *Machaerus III. The golden jubilee of the archaeological excavations. Final report on the Herodian Citadel 1968–2015*. Collectio Maior 56. Jerusalem: Studium Biblicum Franciscanum.

Vörös, G. 2019b. 50 years of excavations at the Herodian fortified royal palace and city overlooking the Dead Sea in Transjordan (1968–2018). In M. Peilstöcker and S. Wolfram (eds), *Life at the Dead Sea. Proceedings of the International Conference held at the State Museum of Archaeology Chemitz (smac), February 21–24, 2018, Chemnitz*: 235–50. Munster: Zaphon.

Waagé, F.O. 1934. Lamps, pottery, metal and glass ware. In G.W. Elderkin (ed.), *Antioch-on-the-Orontes* I, *The excavations of 1932*: 58–73. Princeton, NJ.

Waagé, F.O. 1948. Hellenistic and Roman tableware of North Syria. In F.O. Waagé (ed.), *Antioch-on-the-Orontes* IV, i, *Ceramics and Islamic coins*: 1–60. Princeton, NJ.

Waldbaum, J.C. 1994. Early Greek contacts with the southern Levant, ca.1000–600 BC: the Eastern perspective. *BASOR* 293: 53–66.

Waldbaum, J.C. 1997. Greeks *in* the East or Greeks *and* the East? Problems in the definition and recognition of presence. *BASOR* 305: 1–17.

Walker, A.S. 1997. Excavation coins: the use and misuse of numismatic evidence in archaeology. In K.A. Sheedy and Ch. Papageorgiadou-Banis (eds), *Numismatic archaeology. Archaeological numismatics*: 17–26. Oxford: Oxbow.

Wassen, C. 2019. Stepped pools and stone vessels. *Biblical Archaeological Review* 45(4–5): 52–8.

Watson, P.M. 1992. Change in foreign and regional economic links with Pella in the seventh century AD: the ceramic evidence. In P. Canivet and J.-P. Rey-Coquais (eds), *La Syrie de Byzance à l'Islam VIIe–VIIIe siècles*: 233–48. Damascus: Institut français de Damas.

Watson, P.M. 1993. Tell el-Husn (Area XXXIV). In A.G. Walmsley, P.G. Macumber et al., The eleventh and twelfth seasons of excavations at Pella (Tabaqat Fahl) 1989–1990. *ADAJ* 37: 198–210.

Watson, P.M., and M. O'Hea 1996. Pella hinterland survey 1994: preliminary report. *Levant* 28: 63–76.

Watson, P., and J. Tidmarsh 1996. Pella/Tall al-Husn excavations 1993 the University of Sydney – 15th season. *ADAJ* 40: 293–314.

Watzinger, C. 1901. Vasenfunde aus Athen. *Mitteilungen des Deutschen Archäologischen Instituts, Athenische Abteilung* 26: 50–102.

Weber, T. 1989. Um Qeis. In D. Homès-Fredericq and J.B. Hennessy, *Archaeology of Jordan*, II.1: 606–11. Leuven: Peeters.

Weber, T. 1993. *Pella Decapolitana*. Wiesbaden: Harrassowitz Verlag.

Westholm, A. 1956. Pottery. In O. Vessberg and A. Westholm, *The Swedish Cyprus Expedition*, vol. IV.3. *The Hellenistic and Roman Periods in Cyprus*: 53–81. Stockholm: Swedish Cyprus Expedition.

Wheatley, P. and C. Dunn 2020. *Demetrius the Besieger*. Oxford and New York: Oxford University Press.

Will, E. 1985. L'urbanisation de la Jordanie aux époques hellénistique et romaine: conditions géographiques et ethniques. *SHAJ* 2: 237–41.

Will, E. 1987. Qu'est-ce qu'une Baris? *Syria* 64: 253–9.

Will, E. 1991a. Qu'est-ce qu'une Baris? In E. Will and F. Larché, *'Iraq al Amir. Le chateau du Tobiade Hyrcan*: 31–5. Paris: Librairie Orientaliste Paul Geuther.

Will, E. 1991b. Les Tobiades en Transjordanie et à Jerusalem. In Will, E. and F. Larché, *'Iraq al Amir. Le château du Tobiad Hyrcan*. Paris: Librairie Orientaliste Paul Geuther.

Will, E. and F. Larché 1991. *'Iraq al Amir. Le château du Tobiad Hyrcan*. Paris: Librairie Orientaliste Paul Geuther.

Williams, C. 1989: *Anemurium. The Roman and Early Byzantine pottery*. Toronto, Canada: Pontifical Institute of Medieval Studies.

Williams, J.B., M.J. Schwab and A. Braver 2012. An early first century earthquake in the Dead Sea. *International Geology Review* 54(10): 1219–28.

Wimmer, S. 2019a. The port of Machaerus: Callirrhoe – a retrospection on the German excavations (1985–1989) after 30 years. In G. Vörös, Machaerus III. *The golden jubilee of the archaeological excavations. Final report on the Herodian Citadel 1968–2018*: 460–91. Collectio Maior 56. Jerusalem: Studium Biblicum Franciscanum.

Wimmer, S. 2019b. Kallirhoe – Herod's hot springs resort. The German excavations by August Strobel 1986–1989. In M. Peilstöcker and S. Wolfram (eds), *Life at the Dead Sea. Proceedings of the International Conference held at the State Museum of Archaeology Chemitz (smac), February 21–24, 2018, Chemnitz*: 251–61. Munster, Germany: Zaphon.

Wineland, J. D. 2001. *Ancient Abila. An archaeological history*. British Archaeological Reports International Series 989. Oxford.

Winter, F.E. 1971: *Greek fortifications*. London: Routledge.

Zabehlicky-Scheffenegger, S. 1995. Subsidiary factories of Italian Sigillata potters: the Ephesian evidence. In H. Koester (ed.), *Ephesos. Metropolis of Asia*: 217–28. Cambridge, MA: Harvard University Press.

Zayadine, F. 1966. Early Hellenistic pottery from the theater excavations at Samaria. *ADAJ* 11: 53–64.

Zayadine, F. 1970. Une tombe Nabatéenne près de Dhat-
Ras. *Syria* 47: 107–35.

Zayadine, F. 1977–78. Excavations on the Upper Citadel
of Amman-Area A (1975–77). *ADAJ* 22: 20–56.

Zayadine, F. 1987. Decorative stucco at Petra and other
Hellenistic sites. *SHAJ* 3: 131–42.

Zayadine, F. 1991. Les Tobiades en Transjordanie et à
Jerusalem. In E. Will and F. Larché, *'Iraq al Amir.
Le château du Tobiade Hyrcan*: 2–23. Paris: Librairie
Orientaliste Paul Geuther.

Zayadine, F. 2004. Le grand domaine des Tobiades et la
politique économique des Lagides et des Séleucides.
Topoi. Orient-Occident suppl. 6: 267–90.

Zayadine, F. 2011. Hellenistic pottery from the estate of
the Tobiads. In J.-F. Salles and D. Frangié, *Lampes
antiques du Bilad es Sham. Jordanie, Syrie, Liban,
Palestine. Ancient Lamps of Bilad es Sham. Actes du
Colloque de Pétra-Amman (6-13 novembre 2005*:
167–81. Paris: Editions de Boccard.

Zeitler, J.P. 1990. A private building from the first
century BC in Petra. *ARAM* 2(1 and 2): 385–420.

Zimmerman, M.S. 2020a. A brief history of the site of
'Iraq al-Amir. In N.L. Lapp (ed.), *The excavations of
'Iraq Al-Amir*, vol. II: 1–22. *Annual of the American
Schools of Oriental Research* 74. Boston, MA.

Zimmerman, M.S. 2020b. The Hellenistic and Roman
Pottery of the Village. In N.L. Lapp (ed.), *The
excavations of 'Iraq Al-Amir*, vol. II: 23–174. *Annual
of the American Schools of Oriental Research* 74.
Boston, MA.

Zissu, B., and S. Rokach 1999. A Hellenistic
columbarium at Ziqim. *Atiqot* 38: 65–73.